Includes Exercise Files an

MW01676049

Mac OS X Panther

Hands-On Training

lynda.com/books

Garrick Chow | with Lynda Weinman

Mac OS X Panther | H•O•T
Hands-On Training

By Garrick Chow
Developed with Lynda Weinman

lynda.com/books | Peachpit Press
800 East 96th Street • Indianapolis, IN • 46240
800.571.5840 • 317.428.3000
317.428.3280 (fax)
http://www.lynda.com/books
http://www.peachpit.com

lynda.com/books is published
in association with Peachpit Press,
a division of Pearson Education

ISBN: 0-321-24171-1

0 9 8 7 6 5 4 3

Printed and bound in the
United States of America

H•O•T | Credits

Original Design: Ali Karp, Alink Newmedia *(alink@earthlink.net)*

Editor: Jake McFarland

Copyeditor: Darren Meiss

Compositors: Rick Gordon, Deborah Roberti

Beta Testers: Marla Rebenschied, Crystal Waters

Cover Illustration: Bruce Heavin *(bruce@stink.com)*

Indexer: Larry Sweazy

Proofreader: Beth Trudell

H•O•T | Colophon

The original design for *Mac OS X Panther H•O•T* was sketched on paper. The layout was heavily influenced by online communication–merging a traditional book format with a modern Web aesthetic.

The text in *Mac OS X Panther H•O•T* was set in Akzidenz Grotesk from Adobe and Triplex from Emigré. The cover illustration was painted in Adobe Photoshop 7.0 and Adobe Illustrator 10.

This book was created using QuarkXPress 4.1, Adobe Photoshop 7.0, Microsoft Office 2003, and OS X Panther on a Macintosh G4, running Mac OS X (10.3). It was printed on 50 lb. Utopia Filmcoat at Phoenix Book Tech.

Dedication

To Jon. Now get a Mac already.

Mac OS X Panther | H•O•T — Table of Contents

Introduction

| A Note from Lynda | About the Author |
| Acknowledgments | How to Use This Book |
| Mac OS X 10.3 System Requirements |
| H•O•T CD-ROM Contents |

H•O•T

Mac OS X Panther

A Note from Lynda Weinman

I developed the *Hands-On Training* book series because it's my experience that people buy computer books to educate themselves. Most books and manuals are reference-based, and although there is nothing wrong with reference books in general, it seemed that a book with hands-on tutorials would be of great value. I am personally the type of learner who learns by doing. I enjoy a reference manual or book after I know my way around a program, but those types of materials don't help me get up to speed as quickly as I need to. I created this series of books with my own learning style in mind.

The H•O•T series of books is written by top educators who understand the teaching and learning process. We do not simply hire writers who know how to write these books. We hire teachers who know how to teach. I know I'm not alone in my impatience to get productive in a tool as soon as humanly possible. I also know the difference between lesson plans developed by an experienced teacher versus someone who knows the technicalities of product features.

In this book, you will find carefully developed lessons and exercises that have been thoroughly tested by a diverse group of testers to help you learn OS X Panther. If you are new to OS X Panther or even if you've owned a previous version of OS X, this book will teach you many new things. That's mostly because there are so many new features in the latest version that even experienced users will be on new ground.

This book is targeted toward beginning- to intermediate-level users who are looking for a great tool to manage Internet services, documents, images, movies, and audio. The premise of the hands-on exercise approach is to get you up to speed quickly in these programs, while actively working through the book's lessons. It's one thing to read about an operating system, but an entirely different one to try the program and get measurable results.

Many exercise-based books take a paint-by-numbers approach to teaching, by offering instructions that tell you what to do but not why or when the instruction will apply to your work later. Although this approach sometimes works, it's often difficult to figure out how to apply those lessons to a real-world situation, or understand why or when you would use the technique again. What sets this book apart is that the lessons contain lots of background information for each given subject, which is designed to help you understand the process as well as the particular exercise.

At times, pictures are worth a lot more than words. When necessary, we have also included short QuickTime movies to show any process that's difficult to explain in writing. These files are located on the **H•O•T CD-ROM** inside a folder called **movies**. We approach teaching from many different angles because we know that some people are visual learners, whereas others like to read, and still others like to get out there and try things. This book combines a lot of teaching approaches so you can learn OS X as thoroughly as you want to.

What we saw missing from the bookshelves was a process-oriented book that taught readers core principles, techniques, and tips in a hands-on training format. The latest version of OS X is remarkable in its feature set and wide range of functionality–from storing files, searching the Internet, making movies, storing pictures, or listening to your favorite music. Garrick Chow is a gifted teacher who shares his knowledge with sensitivity and a dry humor that kept me laughing out loud throughout most of the book. I think you will all recognize Garrick's gift for teaching once you dig in and start completing exercises.

It's our hope that this book will raise your skills in working with this robust operating system. If it does, we have accomplished the job we set out to do!

- We welcome your comments at **pantherhot@lynda.com**.
- Please visit our Web site as well at **http://www.lynda.com**.
- The URL for support for this book is **http://www.lynda.com/books/HOT/OSX103**.

–Lynda Weinman

NOTE | About lynda.com/books and lynda.com

lynda.com/books is dedicated to helping Web designers and developers understand tools and design principles. lynda.com offers hands-on workshops, training seminars, conferences, on-site training, training videos, training CDs, and "expert tips" for Web design and development. To learn more about our training programs, books, and products, be sure to give our site a visit: **www.lynda.com**.

About the Author

Garrick Chow has been using Apple computers since sixth grade, when he was introduced to the Apple IIe. He is a freelance computer instructor who has traveled the country providing on-site training for private corporations as well as state and federal agencies. In addition to being a Mac devotee, Garrick is also an Adobe Certified Expert of Acrobat, and he teaches a wide selection of programs ranging from Macromedia Dreamweaver and Fireworks to Adobe Photoshop and QuarkXPress. In an effort to never hold down a regular day job, he plays bass and writes songs as a member of the pop-rock band The Jellybricks (**www.thejellybricks.com**). He can often be found playing music when he should be writing, and writing when he should be playing music.

Acknowledgments

My deepest thanks and appreciation to:

Lynda Weinman, for your guidance, faith, and expert insight.

Garo Green, for keeping everything on and ahead of schedule.

Bruce Heavin, for your fantastic cover art and for many late-night discussions of OS X via iChat AV.

Greg Chow, for your invaluable assistance throughout the writing of this book.

My beta testers, **Marla Rebenschied** and **Crystal Waters**. You both did a great job of finding the little (okay, sometimes big) mistakes I made throughout the book. Your input was essential in making this book useful in the real world.

Dan Schimpf, for generously allowing me (again) to use the installer for your excellent MacJournal application.

John Faye and **Cliff Hillis**, for your contributions of music to the iTunes chapter.

My bandmates: **Bryce Connor**, **Larry Kennedy**, and **Tom Kristich**.

Everyone at **lynda.com**, **Peachpit Press**, and **New Riders**.

And **Leigh Ann Berry**, for being the first person to read every word I wrote and editing my awkward-at-times structures of sentences. You vastly strengthened the foundation of this project–as usual, I couldn't have done it without you.

How to Use This Book

Please read this section–it contains important information that's going to help you as you use this book. The chart below outlines the information we cover:

Mac OS X H•O•T
Information in This Section:
The Formatting in This Book
Mac OS X 10.3 System Requirements
What's on the CD-ROM

The Formatting in This Book

This book has several components, including step-by-step exercises, commentary, notes, tips, warnings, and movies. Step-by-step exercises are numbered, and file names and command keys are shown in bold so they pop out more easily. Captions and commentary are in italicized text: *This is a caption.* File names/folders, command keys, and menu commands are bolded: **images** folder, **Ctrl+click**, and **File > Open**. URLs are also in bold: **www.lynda.com**.

A string of menu commands is represented by the > symbol. For example, **File > Open Recent > example.jpg** means to click the **File** menu item, then select **Open Recent**, and then select the file **example.jpg**.

Mac OS X 10.3 System Requirements

This book requires that you use an Apple computer (PowerMac G3, G4, or G5; iMac; eMac; Cube; PowerBook G3 or G4; or iBook) running at least Mac OS X version 10.3.1. We suggest that you have at least 128 MB of RAM in your system, but you'll find that the more RAM installed in your Mac, the better OS X runs.

If you're not sure which version of OS X you're running, click the **Apple** icon in the upper left-hand corner of your screen and select **About this Mac**. The resulting window informs you of your version number as well as how much RAM is installed in your Mac.

What's on the CD-ROM?

The course files used in this book are located inside a folder called **exercise files** on the **H•O•T CD-ROM**. These files are divided into chapter folders, and you will be instructed to copy the chapter folders to your hard drive during several of the exercises. In most cases, you can delete the chapter exercise folders from your hard drive upon completing a chapter, with the only exception being Chapter 17, "*iDVD*," which uses files you create in Chapter 16, "*iMovie*."

Some chapters have accompanying movies that demonstrate the exercises as well as additional features. The movies are mentioned in the book at appropriate times and can be found in the **movies** folder on the **H•O•T CD-ROM**.

Section I

Basics

| Chapter 1 – Background |

| Chapter 2 – Working with Files and Folders |

| Chapter 3 – Using the Dock |

| Chapter 4 – System Preferences |

| Chapter 5 – Universal Access and Speech |

| Chapter 6 – Printing, Fonts, and Faxing |

| Chapter 7 – Installing Applications |

Chapters 1 through 7 are designed to get you up and running with Mac OS X. You'll start by learning how to use the Desktop interface to manage files and folders. Once you're comfortable with finding your way around the Desktop, you'll learn how to customize your Mac to suit your needs. You'll then move on to more involved activities, such as printing documents, installing fonts, and installing applications.

I. Background

no exercise files

Mac OS X Panther H•O•T CD-ROM

Recently, Apple Computer released the newest version of its ultra-modern, breakthrough operating system, Mac OS X (pronounced "mack oh ess ten"). Even though its predecessor, version 10.2 ("Jaguar"), was no slowpoke, version 10.3, also known as "Panther," greatly improves upon the speed and performance of the previous system. Sporting a redesigned interface, new applications, and tons of new features, Panther vastly improves the way you work with your Mac.

When it first appeared on the scene, Mac OS X marked a radical departure from previous Macintosh operating systems. Even at a glance, you could see how different it looked on the surface; more significant changes became apparent as you explored further. In the wider scope, OS X stood as a revolutionary milestone in the overall evolution of computer operating systems. With OS X, Apple dispensed with the original code for the Mac operating system it created back in 1984 and introduced a highly stable, easy-to-use operating system based on the solid foundation of another operating system known as Unix.

This brief chapter will give you the background you need to understand where OS X came from and where it stands today. It also tells you about the structure and general layout of this book. If you're already familiar with an earlier version of OS X, be sure to check out the "What's New" section at the end of the chapter for a listing of Panther's new features and where they're covered in the book.

Do I Have to Learn Unix?

If you've heard of Unix, an image of computer geeks typing line after line of indecipherable code into a terminal may spring to mind. But you can put these thoughts out of your head. Fortunately for most users, Apple has wrapped the underlying Unix code of OS X in a beautiful graphical user interface they've dubbed "Aqua." Although Aqua does bear some resemblance to the classic Mac OS (at least to users who are familiar with the original operating system), beneath its shiny surface, Mac OS X is pure Unix and has little in common with previous incarnations of the Mac OS. Unix itself is more than 30 years old, and after three decades of refinement by tens of thousands of users, it has become one of the most stable and reliable operating systems available. But for the general public, the downside of Unix is that it's a text-based operating system, meaning that using it requires knowing how to type command lines. This makes it pretty inaccessible to the average user who just wants to use a computer to check email, edit movies, or play games. The beauty of OS X's Aqua interface is that it doesn't require you to know a single thing about Unix; you can appreciate all of Unix's advantages while remaining oblivious to its complexities.

A Brief History of OS X

The road to OS X hasn't been an easy one for Apple. For nearly 15 years, Apple attempted to produce a successor to the original Mac operating system. While developing this new OS, Apple continued to update the existing operating system, improving speed and addressing compatibility issues. But though it continued to improve over the years, by the mid-90s, many users agreed that the Mac OS had become bloated and stale. Finally, in May 1998, Apple officially announced that they were developing a brand-new operating system to be called "Mac OS X." This announcement was followed several months later by the release of the Mac OS X Public Beta. For a mere $29, the general public could try out the not-quite-complete version of the new OS. Apple was able to gather valuable feedback from software developers and Mac users, and incorporate their suggestions into the official release of the operating system.

When Apple first released Mac OS X in March 2001, many users were hesitant to adopt it right away, and with good reason. Even after the public beta testing, the initial release of OS X (version 10.0) was slow and buggy, and very few applications were available for it. But Apple continued to release periodic updates and improve on the system. When Mac OS 10.1 was released in September 2001, many people felt that OS X had finally reached a usable level–bugs had been fixed, interface elements had been tweaked, and the system had gained some appreciable speed. Word of mouth and favorable reviews in Mac magazines and Web sites convinced many people to switch to OS X. But several major software applications such as Adobe Photoshop and Macromedia Dreamweaver were not yet available for OS X, so many users opted to stay with their current operating systems.

After the release of 10.1, many software developers finally began to catch up with Apple and started releasing titles for OS X. Dozens of titles appeared each week over the next several months. Still, there were those who played it safe and waited (somewhat impatiently) for the next major release of OS X. In August 2002, Apple released Mac OS 10.2 (code name "Jaguar"), and elevated the Mac OS far above being merely "usable." Jaguar was fast, looked great, and–finally–had thousands of applications available for it. With its speed, elegance, and ease of use, Jaguar was arguably the best operating system ever released for a personal computer, Mac or otherwise.

And now, Apple has released the next major update of OS X–version 10.3 or "Panther." Panther not only improves upon Jaguar's already sleek design, but it also introduces some brand new features. A revamped Desktop interface, features such as Exposé for managing multiple open windows, and programs like Font Book for managing your font collections (just to mention a few), make OS X even easier to use. If you've waited until now to transition into the world of OS X, you couldn't have picked a better time.

NOTE | Code Names and Version Numbers

It's a common practice among software and hardware developers to give their projects code names. At Apple, Mac OS 8 was known internally as "Tempo," and Mac OS 9 was called "Sonata." But to the public, they were known simply (and somewhat mundanely) as OS 8 and OS 9. But with OS X, Apple made the "Jaguar" code name a major part of the promotion and marketing of the new operating system. Although OS X releases 10.0 and 10.1 carried the code names of "Cheetah" and "Puma," OS 10.2 was the first operating system to be publicly marketed under its code name. Apple has continued this strategy by marketing OS 10.3 under the name "Panther." Therefore, you may find that when talking about Mac OS 10.3, many people refer to it as "Panther." This book will refer to OS 10.3 by both its version number and its code name.

iLife and the Digital Hub

Apple has stated that one of the primary goals of Mac OS X is to make the Macintosh the "digital hub" of your life. To that end, Apple created a suite of four applications, collectively known as "iLife," that allows you to manage the wide array of electronic gadgets you may use. Whether you own a video camera, an MP3 player, or a digital camera, iLife can act as the command center for all of these devices. The iLife applications that help make your (digital) life easier to manage are as follows:

- **iTunes 4**–Helps you edit and manage your music collection. (You'll learn about this in Chapter 14, "*iTunes.*")
- **iPhoto 2**–Helps you edit and manage your digital photos (Chapter 15, "*iPhoto 2*").
- **iMovie 3**–Helps you edit your home movies or videos (Chapter 16, "*iMovie 3*").
- **iDVD 3**–Copies your edited movies onto DVD discs that can be played in home DVD players (Chapter 17, "*iDVD 3*").

Although these four applications work fine as stand-alone products, the real power of iLife is that all of the programs are integrated into one another. For instance, you can access your iTunes music library from iPhoto to place music behind a photo slideshow; or you can access your iPhoto pictures from iMovie to place still images into a video project.

So how do you get iLife? If you purchased your Mac after January 2003, iLife is already on your computer. For Panther users with slightly older Macs, iTunes, iMovie, and iPhoto can each be downloaded for free from Apple's Web site. iDVD, on the other hand is much too large a file to download and must be purchased for $49, which gets you the entire iLife suite on CD-ROM.

In addition to iLife, there are other "i-applications" available in OS X for managing other aspects of your digital life.

- **iChat AV**–Enables you to chat with people over the Internet or over your network (Chapter 10, "*Address Book, Mail, and iChat AV*").
- **iCal**–Helps you to manage your various schedules and calendars (Chapter 13, "*iCal and iSync*").
- **iSync**–Allows you to synchronize digital devices such as PDAs and cellular phones with your calendar and address book (Chapter 13, "*iCal and iSync*").

These are the primary applications Apple has included with Panther. This book will also cover applications such as Mail, Address Book, and many others that will help to simplify your interaction with your digital devices. No other operating system offers such a wide array of free, quality software right out of the box. In most cases, OS X lets you start working with your digital devices right away, without having to install extra applications or drivers.

About This Book

Of course, before you can jump in and start using the digital hub applications, you first need to know how to get around your Mac using Panther. This book is divided into several sections. The first covers the basics of using the Mac OS X graphical user interface. In this section, you'll learn how to open files, folders, and applications. You'll learn how to copy and save files, and how to find them again once they've been saved. And because you don't want to be just okay at getting around Panther, you'll also find lots of tips on using Panther quickly and efficiently. After all, this is the fastest Mac OS ever created. You want to be able to take advantage of its speed, right?

Section II of the book will get you onto the Internet. You'll not only find out how to get online, but you'll also learn how to do a lot of cool things once you get there. You'll start with basic skills such as browsing the World Wide Web, and then you'll move on to tasks such as setting up an email account, organizing your address book and schedule, and performing searches with Panther's Sherlock application.

Section III of the book is devoted to the digital hub applications. Each chapter focuses on a different application. Exercise files are provided on the **H•O•T CD-ROM** (found inside the back cover of the book) so you'll be able to get hands-on experience with making movies, organizing and exporting photos, and importing and playing MP3 music files. If your Mac has a built in SuperDrive, you'll be able to put everything together with iDVD and make your own DVD video.

Finally, Section IV will cover the most important aspects of creating and maintaining a network with your Macs. You'll learn how to communicate with both other Macs and PCs on your network.

Note: Although Mac OS X is based upon the Unix operating system, OS X has been designed so that most users will never have to interact with Unix at all. Therefore, this book does not cover working directly with Unix. If you feel like jumping into Unix after you've made it through this book, check out *UNIX for Mac OS X* by Matisse Enzer (Peachpit Press).

What's New?

If you're already familiar with Jaguar and just want to quickly get up to speed with Panther, here's a list of the chapters you'll definitely want to read.

Chapter 2, "*Working with Files and Folders*." Even if you already know how to use the Finder in Jaguar, you've never seen a Finder like this. This chapter covers new features such as the Places sidebar and the revamped toolbar. Be sure to read this chapter to establish a solid foundation in working with your files and folders.

Chapter 4, "*System Preferences*." The System Preferences panel has been reorganized: some preference panes have been combined, some moved elsewhere, and some have been completely removed. In this chapter, you'll also get the lowdown on brand-new features such as Exposé and FileVault.

Chapter 6, "*Printing, Faxing, and Fonts*." This chapter covers Panther's new direct faxing capability. It also shows you how to use Font Book, the new font management program, which lets you install, preview, search, activate, and deactivate fonts in OS X.

Chapter 8, "*Getting Online*." The layout and organization of OS X's Network settings have changed. This chapter shows you where everything went, while teaching you how to get your Mac on the Internet.

Chapter 9, "*Safari*." The previous version of this book covered the beta release version of Apple's own Web browser; this chapter covers Safari's official release and its multitudes of advanced capabilities such as tabbed browsing and managing cookies.

Chapter 10, "*Address Book, Mail, and iChat AV*." Apple's email program, Mail, runs faster than ever and also includes new features such as message thread tracking and draggable email addresses. And the former iChat has now become iChat AV, featuring audio and video chatting capabilities.

Chapter 11, "*Sherlock and Searching*." Panther vastly improves upon the process of searching your Mac for files and folders. You can search from any Finder window, and Panther searches and narrows down the results list as you type.

Chapter 14, "*iTunes*." Covering the latest version of Apple's breakthrough music playing and management software, this chapter also shows you how to purchase and download music from the iTunes Music Store.

Whether you're new to the Mac or just new to Panther, after completing the lessons in this book, you'll have learned everything you need to know to be the master of all your digital devices, including your Mac. Turn the page and get started!

2. Working with Files and Folders

| Working with Windows in the Finder
| The Places Sidebar | Folder Views |
| Opening Applications | Creating New Folders | Saving Files |
| Moving, Copying, and Deleting Files |

no exercise files

Mac OS X Panther
H•O•T CD-ROM

In this chapter, you'll learn how to work with files and folders in OS X. This is one of the longest chapters in the book, but if you're new to the Mac operating system, it's also one of the most important. This chapter will acquaint you with the Aqua interface and teach you how to get around your Mac. If you're already familiar with the classic Mac OS, but this is your first foray into OS X, be prepared for a few changes. Although in many ways OS X looks and behaves like Mac OS 9, you'll find that Panther includes many new features, and moves or even eliminates some of the old ones. Spend plenty of time familiarizing yourself with the ins and outs of Panther so you can take full advantage of what it has to offer.

The first section of this chapter will introduce you to the basic elements of the OS X Desktop. Once you're comfortable with these features and the terminology used to describe them, you'll next run through several exercises to gain some hands-on experience with the operating system. The exercises in this chapter use items already found on your Mac, so you don't need to copy any files from the **H•O•T CD-ROM**.

A Quick Tour of the Desktop

Before you start learning about the specifics of working with OS 10.3, it's a good idea to get acquainted with the Desktop. The Desktop refers to what you see on your screen after your Mac boots up. Rather than seeing a command line prompting you to start typing a bunch of Unix code, you instead see Aqua, the graphical interface wrapped around the Unix core. Apple created Aqua so that Mac users won't have to worry about OS X's Unix underpinnings. Running the Aqua interface is the Finder, the program that allows you to see and access files by clicking on them rather than typing lines of code. Many people use the terms "Finder" and "Desktop" interchangeably. For practical purposes this is fine, although technically the Finder is an application, and the Desktop is part of the Finder.

If you're accustomed to working with earlier versions of the Mac Desktop, the one in OS X should look familiar. But don't be fooled by its appearance–Apple has made many changes to the layout of the items in the Desktop.

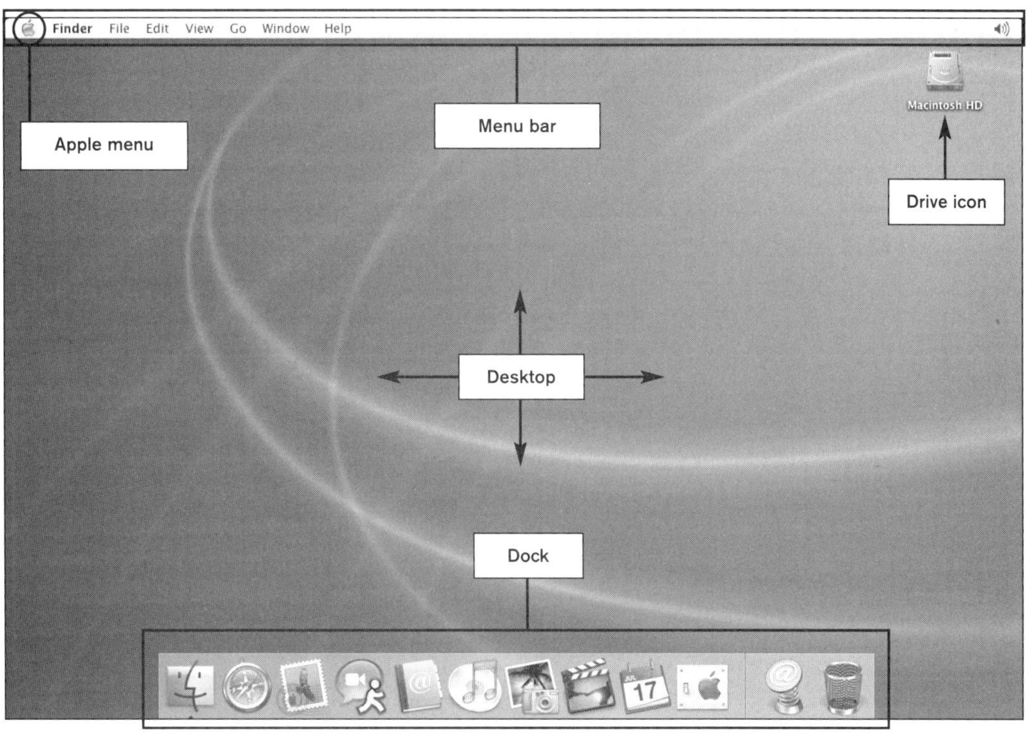

You'll be working with each section of the Desktop throughout this book. The following chart provides brief descriptions of each of these elements.

Finder Elements	
Item	**Description**
Menu bar	The menu bar contains commands specific to the application in which you're working. Many of the commands from previous versions of the Mac OS appear in the OS X menu bar, but some commands have moved from previous Mac operating systems, or have been eliminated altogether.
Apple menu	In OS X, the Apple menu no longer acts as a tool for switching between active applications. Instead, the Apple menu now contains commands for setting certain preferences, accessing recent files, and for shutting down the computer.
Drive icon	Any drives connected to your Mac will be represented by an icon on the Desktop. Double-clicking the drive icon will display the contents of the drive in a window. If you don't see your hard drive icon on the Desktop, you can make it appear by choosing **Finder > Preferences** from the menu bar and then, under the **General** section, checking **Hard Disks**. See the charts at the end of this chapter for a description of Finder preferences.
Dock	The Dock debuted in OS X and has been the subject of many heated discussions between Mac users. When OS X was first released, many users felt that the Dock took up too much real estate on the screen, but it has been refined over the different versions of OS X, and, as you'll soon see, it's quite customizable. The Dock contains icons for accessing often-used applications, as well as any additional applications that are presently "open," and it can be customized to suit your needs.

I. Working with Windows in the Finder

In this short exercise, you'll view the contents of your hard drive to familiarize yourself with the elements found in the Desktop windows. In Panther, Apple has significantly redesigned the way you access items on your Mac, so even if you're a former Jaguar user, you'll want to read through this chapter to acquaint yourself with OS 10.3's new Finder features.

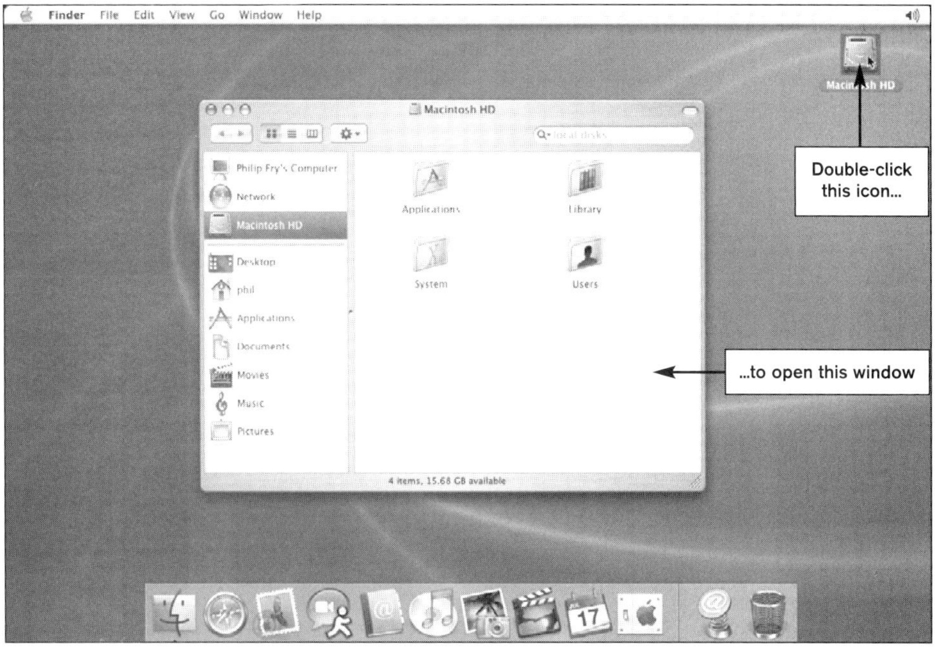

1. Double-click your **hard drive** icon. This will open a window displaying the contents of your hard drive. Any window that appears on the **Desktop** and is not part of an application can be referred to as a **Finder** window, which simply means that this window appears in the Finder. If you're familiar with earlier versions of OS X, the first thing you might notice is that the Finder window now sports the "brushed metal" look common to many other Apple application windows.

Before you look any further into your hard drive's contents, you'll take a look at the elements of a Finder window.

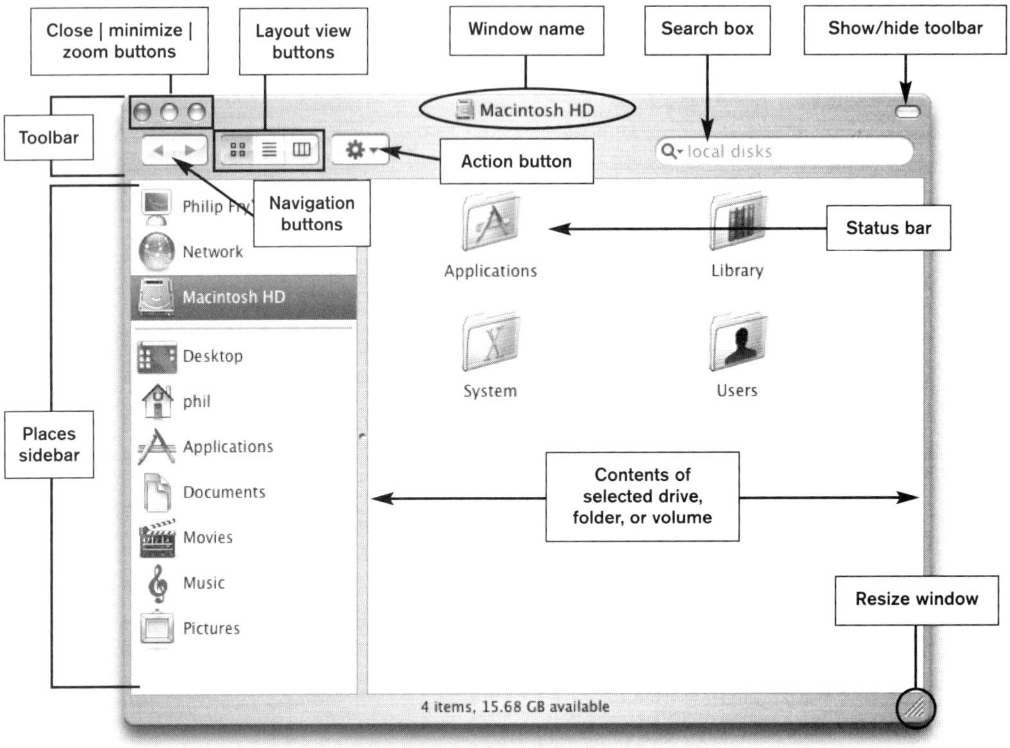

This screen shot lists the names of the items found in a typical Finder window. Refer back to this figure if you come across an unfamiliar term in this chapter.

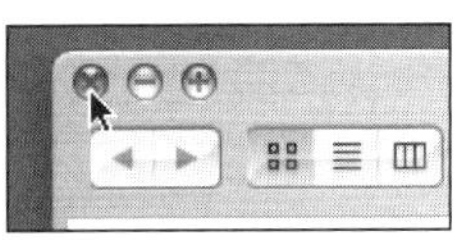

2. Place the mouse cursor over the area in the upper-left corner of the window where the **close**, **minimize**, and **zoom** buttons are located. Notice that the X, –, and + symbols appear in them, respectively. This is just a visual indicator telling you that the window knows you've placed the mouse there and that the window will react appropriately when you click one of these three buttons.

Now you'll click each button to see its effect on the window.

---

3. Click the red **close** button (the one on the far left). The window closes and you see the visual effect of it "shrinking" and returning to the hard drive icon. Double-click the **hard drive** icon to open its window again.

When you're done working with a window, clicking the close button removes it from the Desktop, freeing up valuable screen space. But there may be times when you'll simply want to momentarily hide a window from view. In this case, minimizing the window would be preferable to closing it.

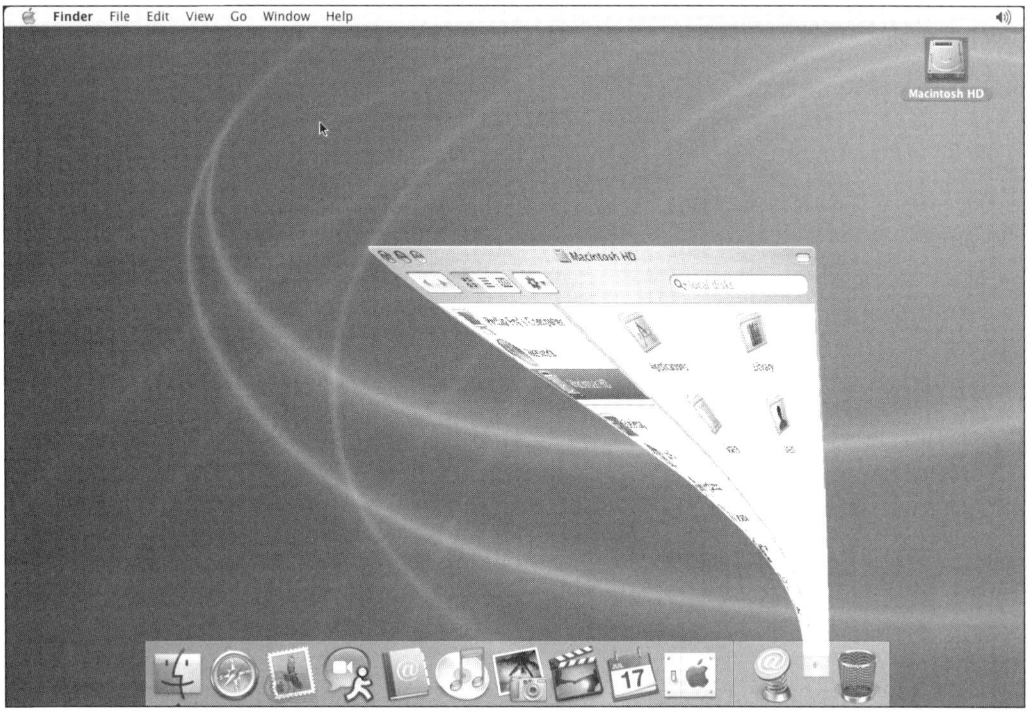

4. Click the yellow **minimize** button (the one in the center) and prepare for a visual treat. Unless you've previously changed your preferences, you'll see the window getting sucked into the Dock at the bottom of the screen. This is referred to as the Genie effect. (In the next chapter, you'll learn how to change this effect.)

Tip: *You can also minimize a window by double-clicking its toolbar.*

When you minimize any window, it is placed into the Dock where it remains, just a click away, until you need it again. Notice that the docked window has a little smiley-face icon indicating that it belongs to the Finder. Any time you minimize a window, an icon appears with it, indicating which application it belongs to.

---

5. Click the docked window to bring it back onto the **Desktop**. You'll see the Genie effect again–this time in reverse.

Useless Tip: *Hold the* ***Shift*** *key on your keyboard while minimizing a window to see the Genie effect in slow motion. This serves no practical purpose other than killing some time, showing off for your friends, or taking up a few lines in this chapter.*

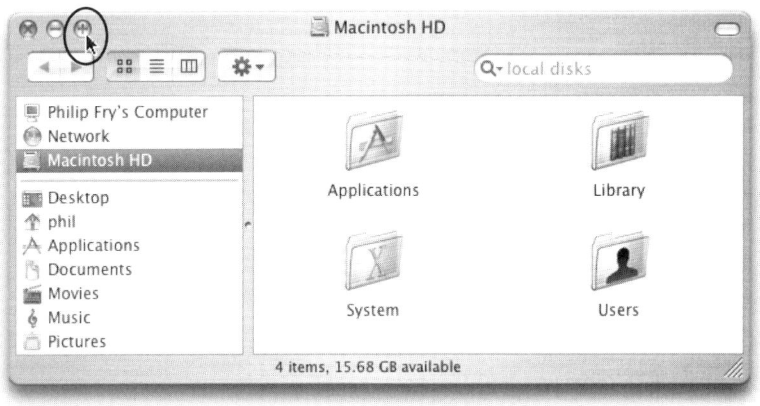

6. Now click the green **zoom** button (the one on the right) in the window. In the **Finder**, the **zoom** button can be used to resize a window to fit its contents. Now click it again to return the window back to its original size.

In some applications, such as Apple's Web browser, Safari (which you'll learn about in Chapter 9, "Safari"), the zoom button can be used to expand the window to fit the height of your screen. In this case, however, clicking the zoom button resized the window and eliminated a lot of the empty space it occupied. This is a very useful tactic when you have a lot of windows open and want to make sure that you're using screen space efficiently.

Now that you've been introduced to the close, minimize, and zoom buttons, you'll spend some time exploring the contents of your hard drive while learning how to use the toolbar and status bar.

You can think of your hard drive as a filing cabinet. When you double-click its icon, you're displaying its contents within a window on the Desktop. And, just like a real filing cabinet, you can organize the contents of your hard drive by category to make it easier to find things when you need them. Your hard drive already contains thousands of items. Fortunately, they've been organized into folders to help you find specific files or programs more easily.

7. Double-click the **Applications** folder to reveal its contents.

Notice that three things have happened: The same window in which you just clicked now displays the contents of the Applications folder; the Back button in the toolbar has become active; and Applications has been highlighted in the Places sidebar, indicating that you're viewing this folder's contents. (You'll learn more about the Places sidebar later.) This is a major change from pre–OS X versions of the Mac OS, in which double-clicking on a new folder would display its contents in a separate window. Opening subsequent folders would then open new windows for each folder clicked, sometimes resulting in a multitude of windows open at once.

In OS X, only one window is needed to navigate through a series of folders nested within one another. If you need to return to a previous folder, you simply click the Back button in the toolbar.

Scroll Bars

When a window contains more items than can be displayed at once, a scroll bar appears on the right side of the window (and along the bottom if necessary), allowing you to scroll through the contents of the window to find the items you're looking for. You can use the scroll bar in one of three ways to navigate the contents of the window.

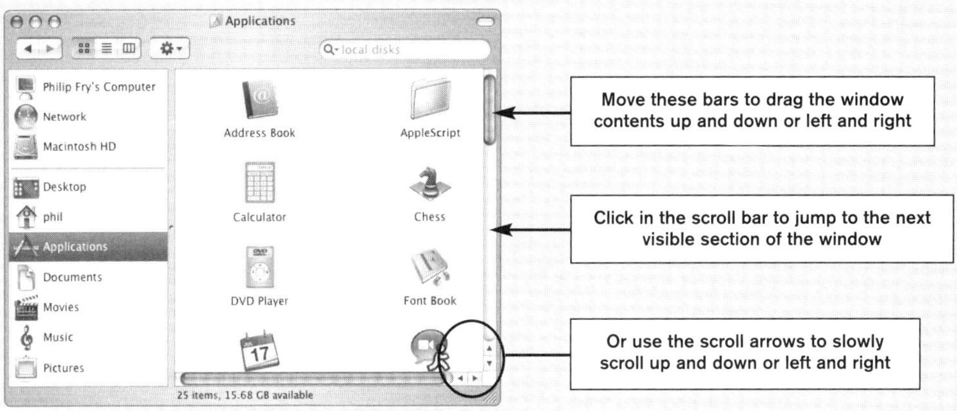

Drag the scroll bar to see the content scroll as you drag.

Click in the scroll bar area on either side of blue scroll button to jump to a specific section of the window.

Use the arrows to slowly scroll through the window. (Your scroll arrows may appear differently depending on your setup. You'll learn how to customize their placement in Chapter 4, "*System Preferences*.")

8. Scroll down until you see the **Utilities** folder. Double-click it to view its contents.

Again, notice that the same window you clicked in has now changed to display the contents of the Utilities folder.

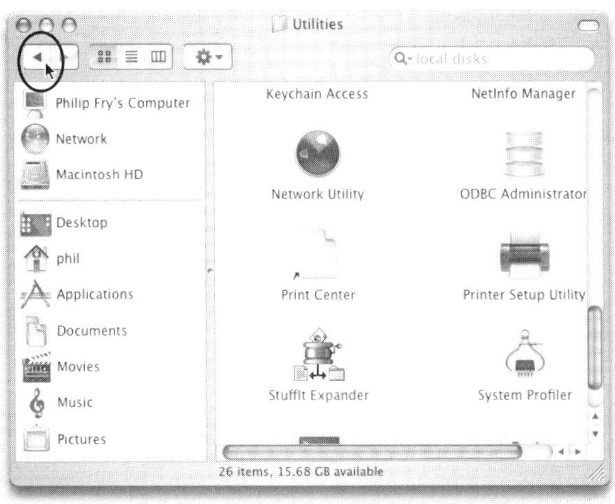

9. Click the **Back** button two times. Each time will take you back one folder until you reach the first folder displaying the contents of the hard drive. You can control your navigation path both backward and forward this way.

As you can see, working with only one window can be much more convenient than working with multiple windows. But if you're an old-fashioned Mac user, and you really like working with multiple windows, there's an easy solution available to you: Buy an old Mac. Just kidding–do this instead:

10. Click the **Show/hide toolbar** button. This will hide the **toolbar** and the **Places** sidebar, effectively mimicking the appearance of pre–OS X Finders.

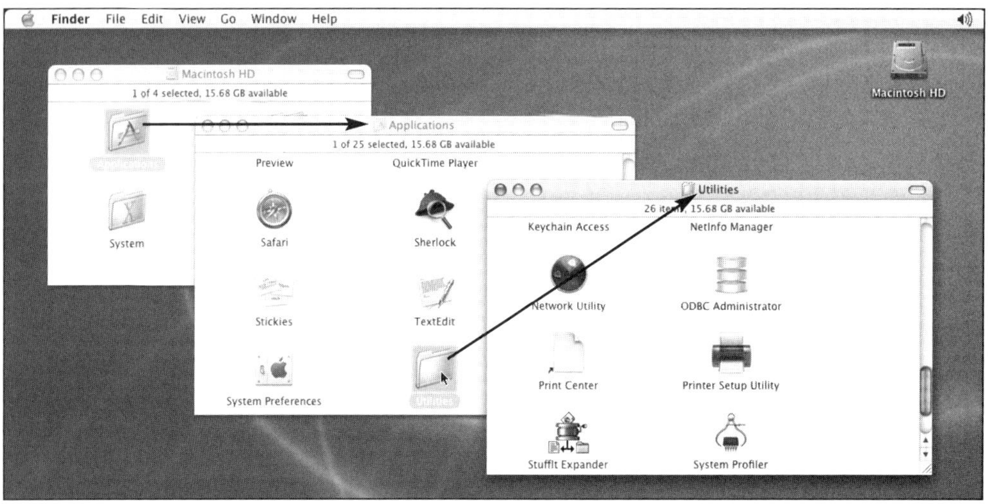

11. Double-click the **Applications** folder to view its contents again. Notice now that a new window has opened on top of the **hard drive** folder. In the **Applications** folder, find and double-click the **Utilities** folder. Its contents also appear in a new window.

This is just how things used to work in the Mac OS before OS X. Something that was introduced in OS X, however, is the capability to close windows in the background without making them active first.

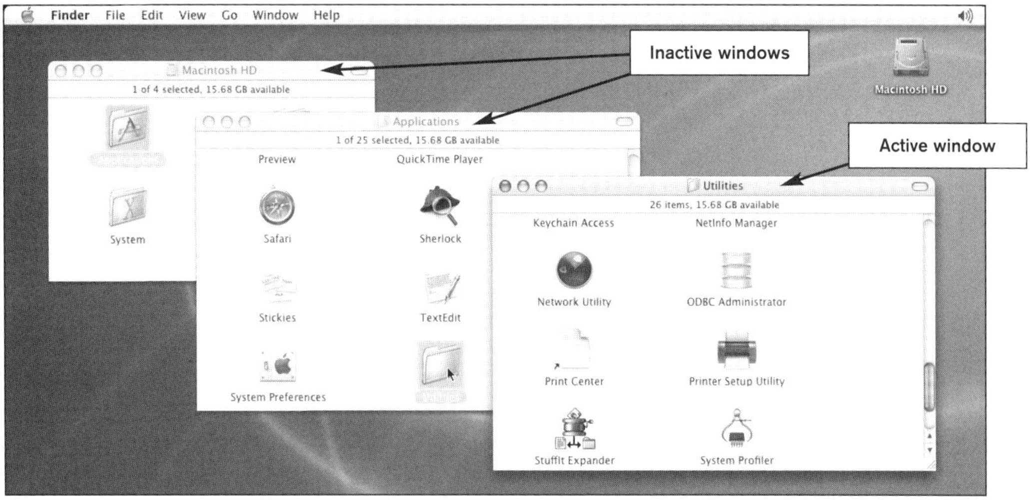

Currently, the Utilities window is the active window. You can tell this not only because it's the front-most window, but also because its close, minimize, and zoom buttons are in color; and its title bar is a light shade of gray. The two windows in the background, however, have nearly white title bars containing extremely subtle horizontal lines (look closely), and the buttons are uncolored.

In previous versions of the Mac OS, to close the Applications window you would first have to click it to bring it to the front as the active window, and then click its close button. But why activate a window that you simply want to close? In OS X, if you can see a window's close button, you can close it at any time.

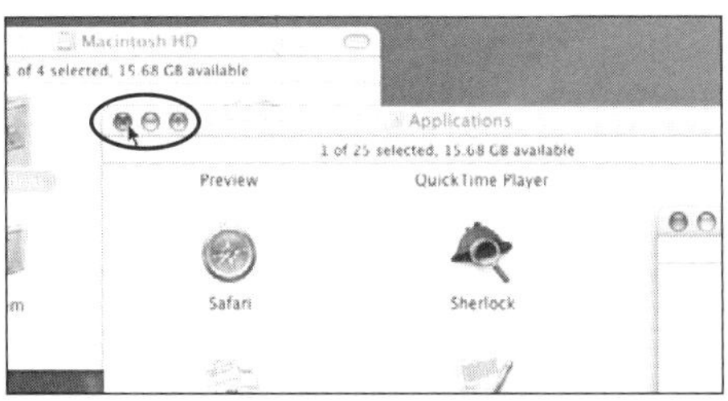

12. Place the mouse over the **Applications** window's **close** button. Notice that all three buttons light up with color, while the title bar remains unchanged, indicating that the window is still inactive. Click the **close** button to close the **Applications** window. The **Utilities** window remains the active window. Close the two remaining windows to clear the **Desktop**.

Tip: *If you have multiple windows open, you can* ***Option+click*** *(hold down the* ***Option*** *key on the keyboard while clicking) any window's close button to close all open windows. Similarly, you can* ***Option+click*** *any* ***minimize*** *button to send all open windows to the* ***Dock****. Unfortunately, there's no command to bring all the windows back from the Dock at once.*

Moving and Resizing Windows

Often, when managing multiple windows, you'll need to resize or reposition them in order to work with them more efficiently.

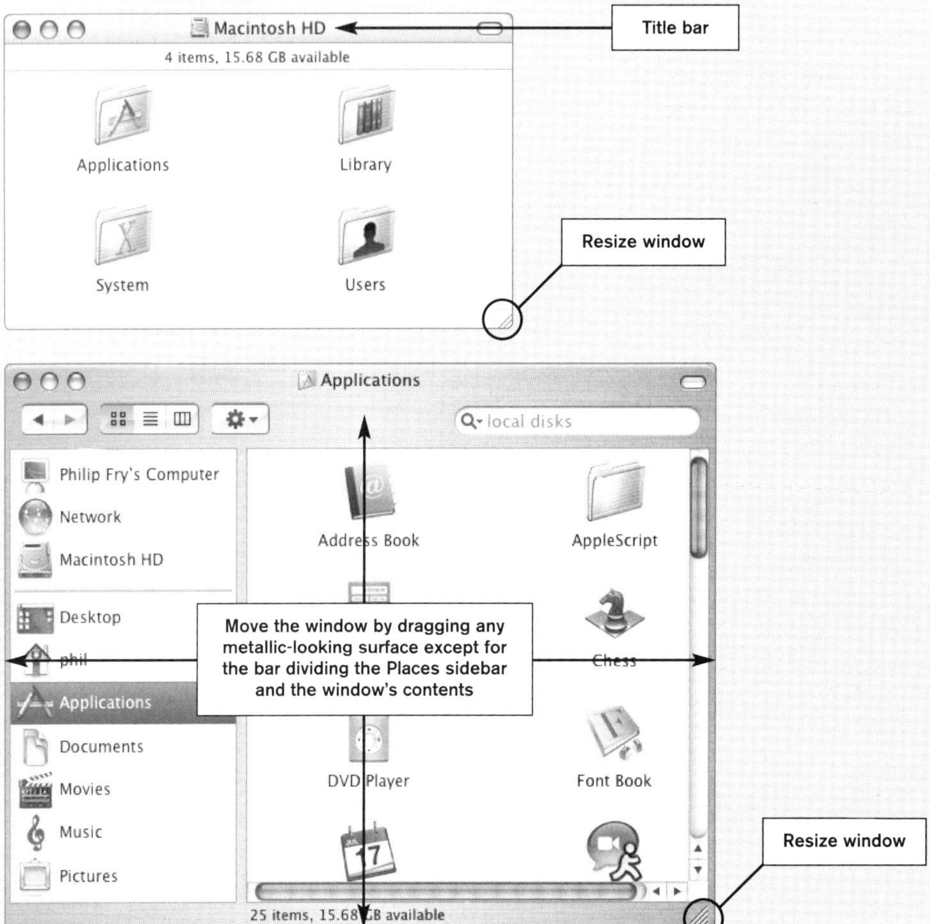

To move a window, simply drag it by its title bar. If the toolbar and Places sidebar are visible (and they should be if you've truly extricated yourself from the pre–OS X mindset), you can drag any portion of the window's outside border that's not occupied by a button to move it. To resize a window, drag the **resize window** button.

2. The Places Sidebar

The look of the Finder's windows is probably the most immediately noticeable change in Panther. Apple based the appearance of these windows on the windows found in some of their other applications such as Safari, iPhoto, and iTunes. The biggest change to the Finder windows is the addition of the **Places sidebar**. Prior to Panther, it sometimes took as many as five double-clicks to get to an item in your own User folder. But with the Places sidebar, you now have quick access to the drives, folders, and files that you use the most. Apple calls this a "user-centric" interface (as opposed to the "computer-centric" interface of pre-Panther systems). This exercise shows you how to make the most of the Places sidebar.

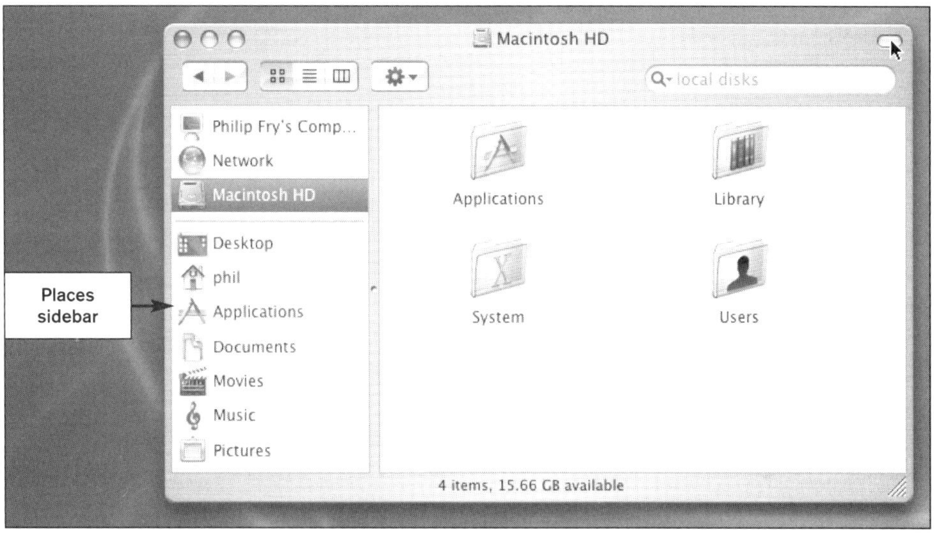

1. Double-click your **hard drive** icon to view its contents in a **Finder** window. Click the **Show/hide toolbar** button if you don't see the **Places** sidebar.

Note: *Depending on how your preferences are set, you may find more or fewer items in your Places sidebar than you see in the screen shot here. You'll learn how to set your preferences shortly.*

The Places sidebar is divided into two sections. The top section contains icons for your computer, your hard drive(s), the network (if you're on a network), any CDs or DVDs you've inserted, and your iDisk (if you have a .Mac account–covered in Chapter 12, ".Mac"). The lower part of the sidebar contains icons for the most common folders you'll access while working with your Mac–your Home folder (covered later in this chapter), Desktop, Applications, Documents, Movies, Music, and Pictures.

To view the contents of a folder listed in the sidebar, simply single-click it.

2. Click **Applications** in the **Places** sidebar. The items within your Applications folder are immediately displayed. Click some of the other items in the sidebar to view their contents. You may or may not see items in each folder, depending on whether items have been saved within them.

But who is Apple to claim which items on your computer you'll need to access the most? Fortunately, the lower portion of the Places sidebar can be customized, allowing you to drag items in and out of it as needed.

3. Click the **Applications** icon again to display that folder's contents. Use the scroll bar to locate the **Calculator** program. Let's assume that you use the calculator all the time and would like to have quick access to it.

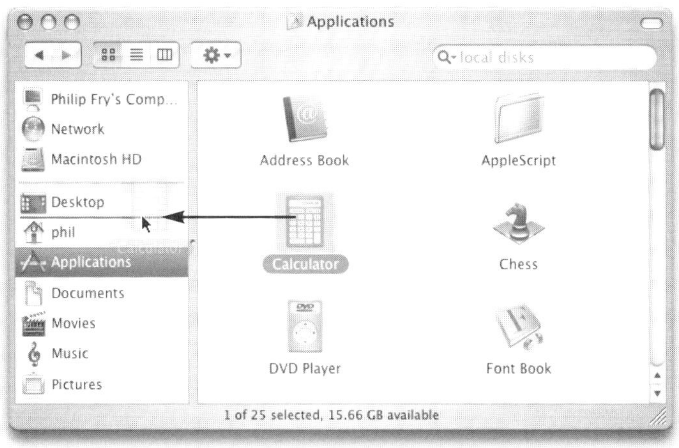

4. Click and drag (dragging means to hold down the mouse button as you move the mouse) the **Calculator** icon into the lower portion of the **Places** sidebar. Observe that a line appears between the icons already located there. Wherever the line is when you release the mouse is where the icon will be dropped. For this step, make sure the line appears between **Desktop** and your **Home** folder and release the mouse.

Note: *Be careful not to drop the Calculator icon on top of one of the existing folders, otherwise you'll move the calculator into that folder. If you do this by accident, choose* ***Edit > Undo Move of "Calculator"*** *from the menu bar (or press* ***Cmd+Z****) to return the Calculator to its original location and try again. Moving files and folders is covered later in this chapter.*

A shortcut to the Calculator now appears in the Places sidebar. If you wanted, you could change its location by dragging its icon up and down in the lower portion of the sidebar.

5. Click the **Macintosh HD** icon (or whatever your **hard drive** icon is named). Notice that the **Calculator** icon stays in the **Places** sidebar. No matter which folder or drive's contents you're currently looking at, the items in the sidebar remain in place, ensuring you quick access to your favorite folders and applications.

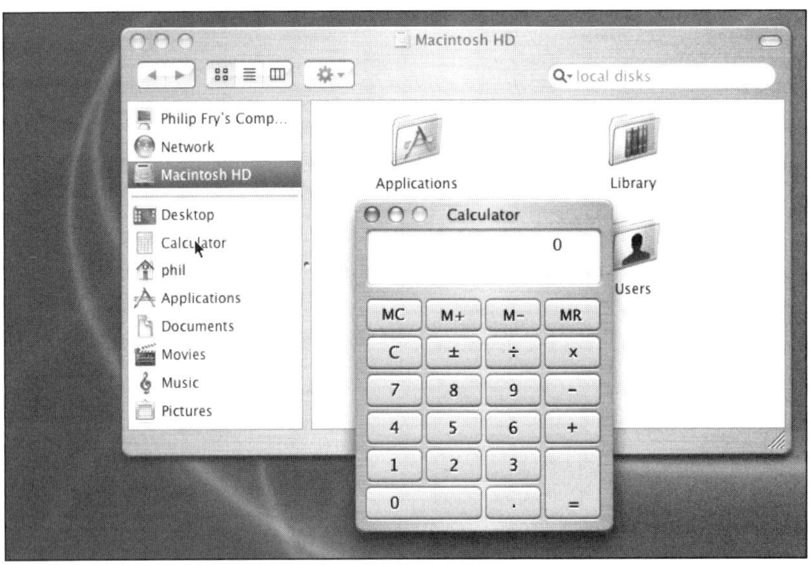

6. Click the **Calculator** icon to launch Calculator. The program immediately opens. Choose **Calculator > Quit Calculator** from the menu bar to close it.

Now you'll remove its icon from the Places sidebar. Removing an icon from the sidebar is as easy as adding one. All you have to do is drag the icon off the sidebar.

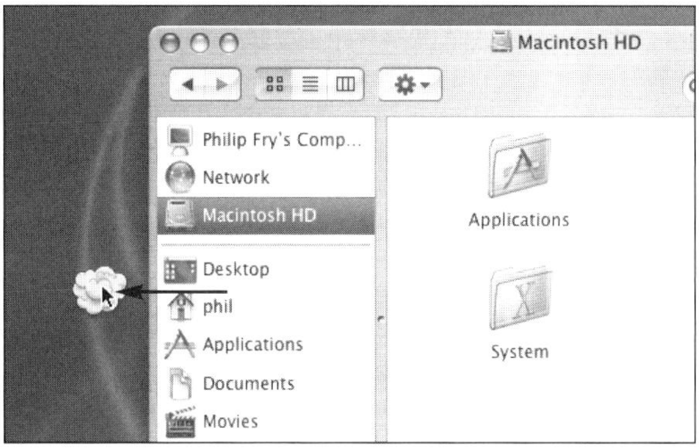

7. Click and hold down on the Calculator icon. Drag it to the left, out of the sidebar, and release the mouse. The icon disappears in a puff of smoke, and the remaining icons resize and shift around to fill in the empty space. It's important to note here that you didn't remove the Calculator program itself from your computer–it's still sitting safely in your Applications folder. All you did was remove its shortcut.

Note: *Only items in the lower section of the sidebar can be removed.*

As you can see, it's easy to customize the Places sidebar. But it doesn't stop there. The next few steps show you how to further tailor its appearance. For instance, you may be thinking the Places sidebar is a nice feature, but that it takes up too much window space.

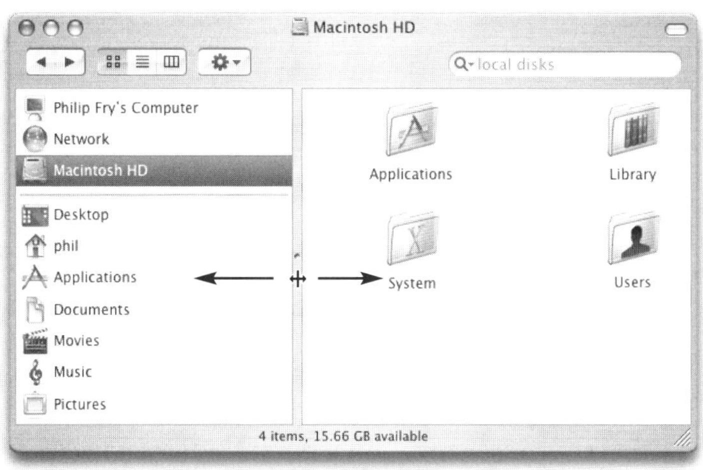

8. Place your mouse cursor over the border between the **Places** sidebar and the window's contents. Drag the border back and forth to the left and right. Notice how you can resize the sidebar and how the icons and text within it automatically resize to fit the available space.

If you drag the border to the left, it will snap into place when only the icons themselves are showing. This can be a convenient, space-saving view once you've learned which item each icon represents.

If you drag the border to the extreme left, you can hide the Places sidebar completely. This is different than clicking the Show/hide toolbar button, as you learned to do at the end of Exercise 1, because double-clicking folders still opens them in the current window instead of a new window. ***Tip:*** *You can quickly hide or show the Places sidebar by double-clicking the border.*

9. Return the **Places** sidebar to its original size (or a size you prefer).

As mentioned earlier, you can't drag items in or out of the top section of the Places sidebar. You can, however, exercise some control over which items appear in this section.

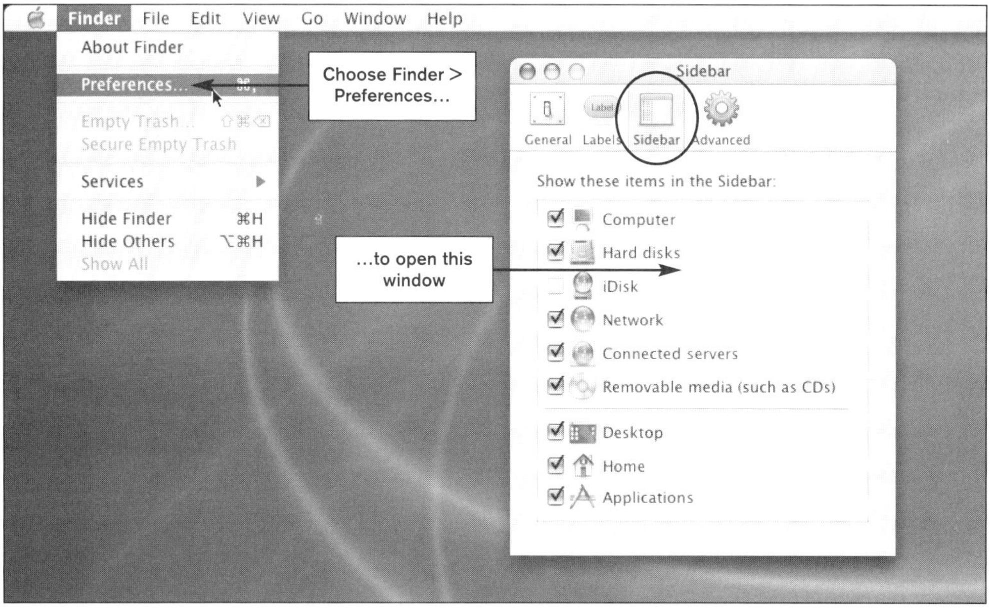

10. From the menu bar, choose **Finder > Preferences.** In the window that opens, click the **Sidebar** button at the top. From here, you can determine which items you want to appear in the **Places** sidebar. Notice that this window is separated much like the sidebar itself, with drives, discs, and servers appearing in the top section and folders appearing in the lower portion.

11. Uncheck the **Hard disks** icon and notice how it immediately disappears from the sidebar. If you prefer to access your hard drive by double-clicking its icon on the Desktop, you might want to leave this unchecked to save space in the sidebar. For now, however, recheck the **Hard disks** icon to return it to the sidebar. Close the **Sidebar** window when you're done.

12. Close the open **Finder** window.

What Happened to the Favorites Folder?

If you're a seasoned Mac veteran, you might be accustomed to using the Favorites folder to store shortcuts for the items you commonly use. In Panther, the Favorites folder has taken a backseat to the Places sidebar, which itself is convenient place to store your frequently used items. The Favorites folder still exists, however–you can find it in the Library folder located in your Home holder. The downside is that a shortcut to this folder is not automatically included in the Finder windows. If you'd like to have quick access to this folder, drag it into the Places sidebar.

3. Folder Views

So far, you've been working with windows in Icon view, meaning that the files and folders you've been viewing have been represented by little pictures. Icons are useful when viewing a few items at a time, but when you're working with many files and folders, icons can slow you down by reducing the number of items you can view at once. In this exercise, you'll examine the different window views that OS X offers.

1. Double-click the **hard drive** icon to display its contents in a window.

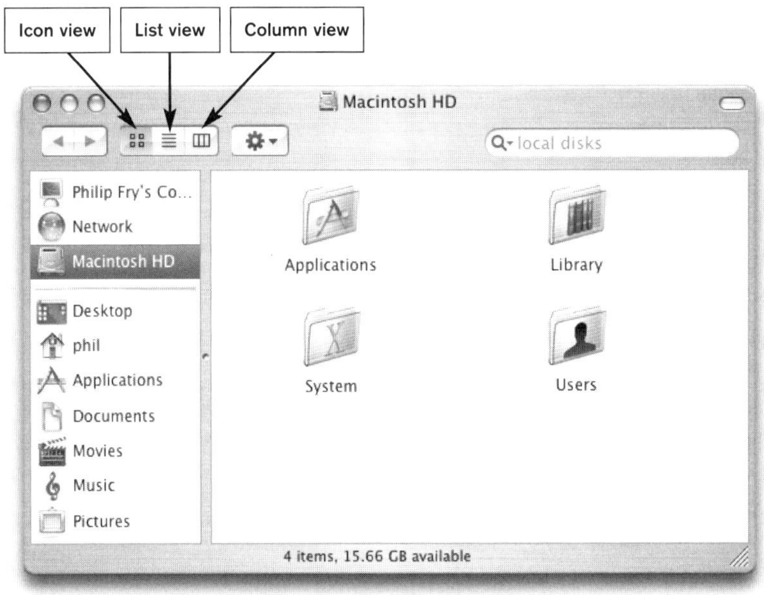

*The three available views–**Icon view**, **List view**, and **Column view**–appear as buttons in the toolbar. These three buttons provide very different ways of viewing and navigating files on your Mac. Each can be customized to your own personal tastes. In the following steps, you'll learn how to set preferences for these three views.*

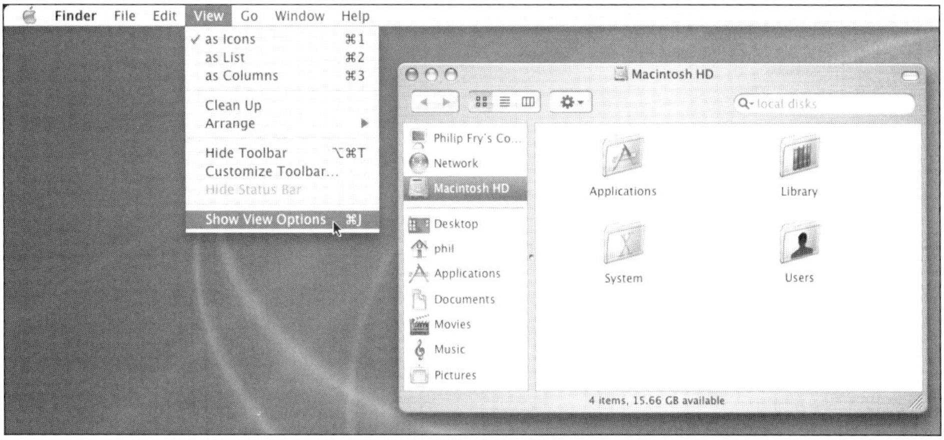

2. With the hard drive window active (meaning its buttons are colored instead of grayed-out), click **View > Show View Options** from the menu bar. This will open a floating window containing options for customizing the appearance of your Finder windows.

Note: *The term "floating window" refers to a type of window that remains above all other windows no matter where you position it. The floating window is often used in applications to change settings. It is distinguished by its narrower title bar containing only a close button.*

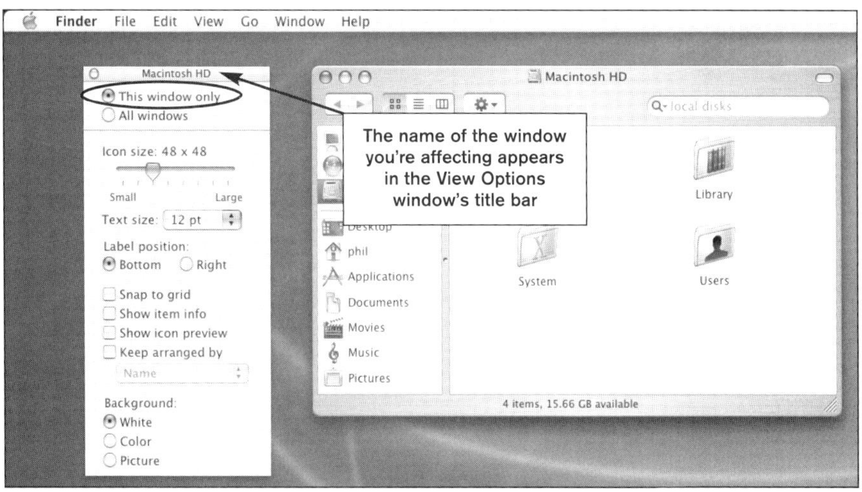

3. Position the two windows as shown here. This way, you'll be able to see the changes you make right away. Click the **This window only** radio button to ensure that the selections you make here will apply only to the hard drive window. You may want to note the current settings, just in case you want to revert to them after completing this exercise.

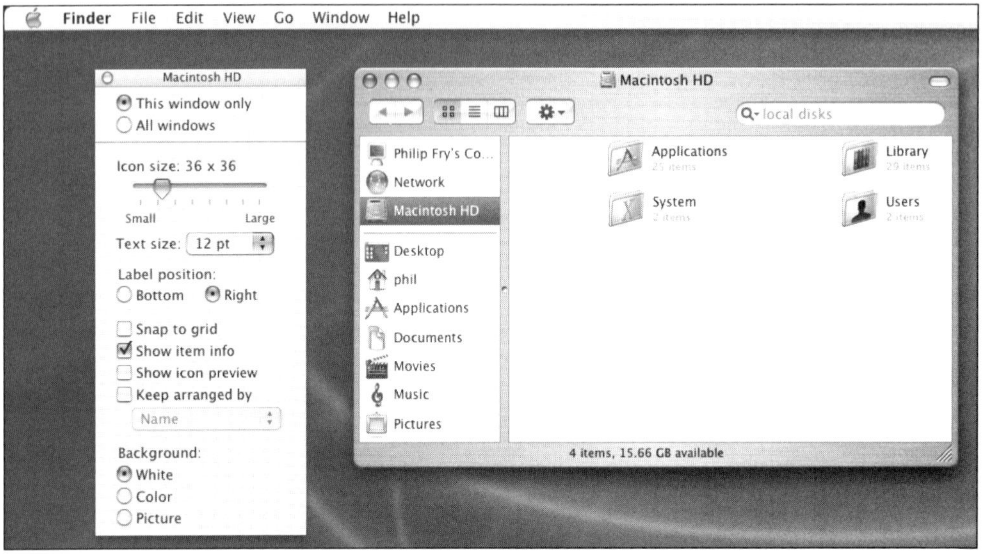

4. Take a moment to play around with the settings in the floating window and observe their effects on the active window. The following chart details the options available. When you're done examining these options, take a moment to revert the window's settings back to their original state, and then close the **View Options** floating window.

View Options: Icon View

Item	Description
This window only/ All windows	Your selection here determines whether the changes you make will affect only the active window or all the windows you view in the Finder.
Icon size	By dragging the slider, you can change the size of the icons from "really teensy" to "humongous" (to put things technically). Notice that one of the advantages of working with icons in OS X is that they remain crisp and sharp no matter what their size.
Text size	In addition to changing the icon size, you can also change the size of the icon's accompanying text by using this menu. Click the menu and choose a text size that you feel works best with your icon size.
Label position	This option allows you to determine whether the text accompanying the icon appears underneath or to the right of it. Click either **Bottom** or **Right** to see the results.

continues on next page

View Options: Icon View *continued*

Item	Description
Snap to grid	Although OS X allows you to drag icons anywhere you want within a window, sometimes you want the icons to look tidy in nice rows and columns. Checking this item ensures that all the icons in the window will line up with one another.
Show item info	Checking this item will reveal text underneath a folder's name that indicates how many items it contains.
Show icon preview	For image files, checking this option will display a thumbnail-sized version of the actual image as the file's icon rather than a generic icon.
Keep arranged by	You can choose to have the icons arrange themselves by **Name**, **Date Modified** (the last time the file was saved), **Date Created**, **Size**, **Kind**, and **Label**.
Background	If you just don't like that window's plain white background, you can click **Color** to select a different color, or click **Picture** to place an image in the background. (If you choose **Picture**, but you're not sure how to select an image, hang tight—you'll learn how to select files shortly.)

Next, you'll examine the options available in List view.

5. Click the **List view** button in the toolbar of the hard drive window.

List view is an incredibly useful way of examining a folder's contents. Not only can you see more items at once, but you can also see more information about each item than either Icon or Column view can provide.

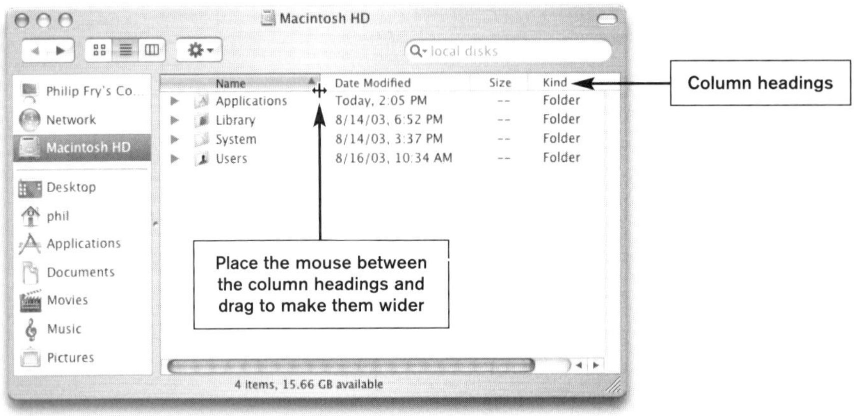

In List view, the window is divided into a series of columns. The column headings you see at the top of the list depend on how you have set your view options. If you're not seeing multiple columns in the window, either expand the width of the window by dragging the resize window button or resize the width of the columns by placing your cursor between the column headings and dragging left or right.

You can quickly choose how you'd like to sort the window items by clicking on the column headings in List view.

6. Click the **Date Modified** heading to sort the items by the date they were last changed. This is a very helpful way to sort your window if you're interested in finding the most recently altered documents in a folder.

List view is the only view that allows you to sort the contents of a window by category. It's not possible to sort a window by Date Modified, Size, Kind, and so on in either Icon or Column view. A description of each of the List view headings appears in the chart coming up shortly.

7. Click the **Name** column heading to sort the list alphabetically by name.

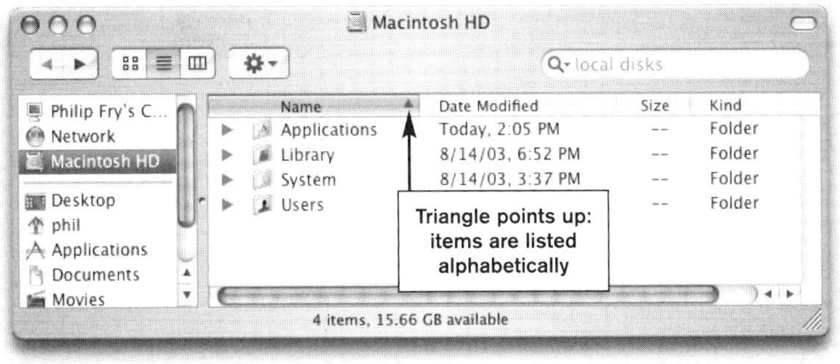

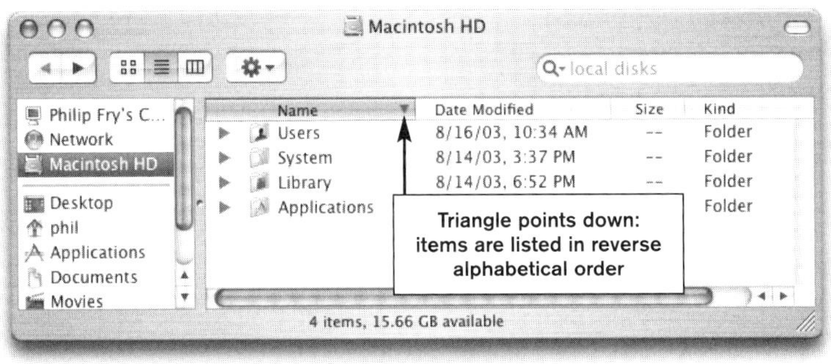

Note: *Clicking on a column heading that's already selected will reverse the current order of the list. For example, clicking on the Name heading while it's selected will list the items in reverse alphabetical order. This is quicker than scrolling to the bottom of the long list to find an item at the end of the alphabet.*

Another advantage of working in List view is that you can see the contents of folders without double-clicking on them. Notice that just to the left of each folder in the window is a small triangle pointing to the right. These triangles indicate that these folders contain additional items. To view a folder's contents, all you have to do is click the triangle.

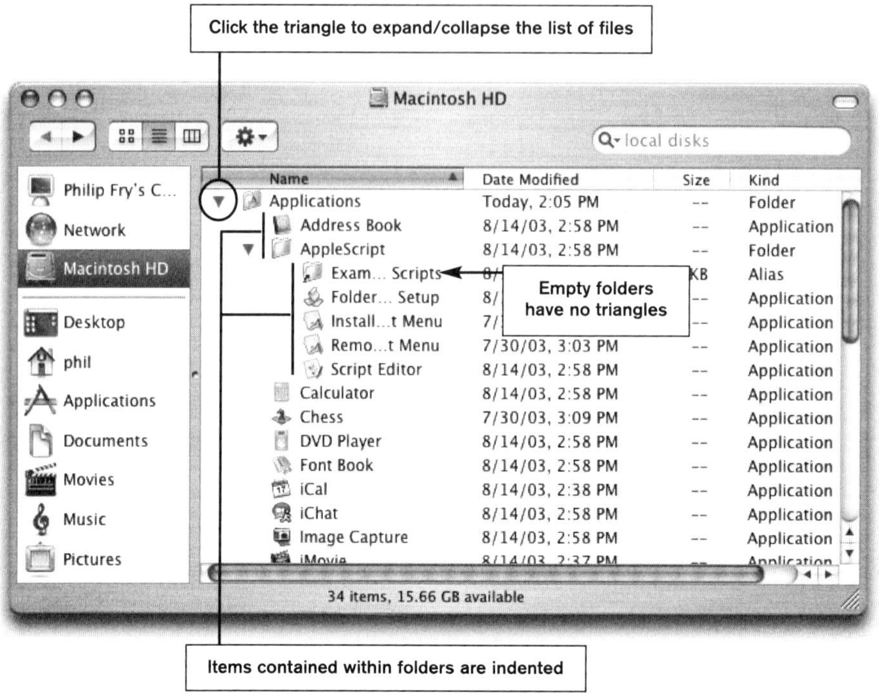

8. Click the triangle next to the **Applications** folder. The triangle flips down, revealing the contents of the folder. Notice that these items are indented to indicate that they are contained within the **Applications** folder. Click the triangle next to the **AppleScript** folder and notice that its items are further indented. In this simple way, you can easily view the contents of numerous folders within one Finder window. To close the expanded list, just click the triangle again.

*Tip: Holding the **Option** key while clicking a triangle in **List** view will display the contents of the folder and the contents of any folders within that folder.*

*If you prefer to navigate through your folders without clicking the triangles, you can do so by double-clicking on either the folder's **small icon** or its **name** to view its contents in the Finder window without an indented list. You can always return to a previous folder by clicking the **Back** button in the toolbar, or you can click the **Forward** button to move forward through the hierarchy once you have established a path.*

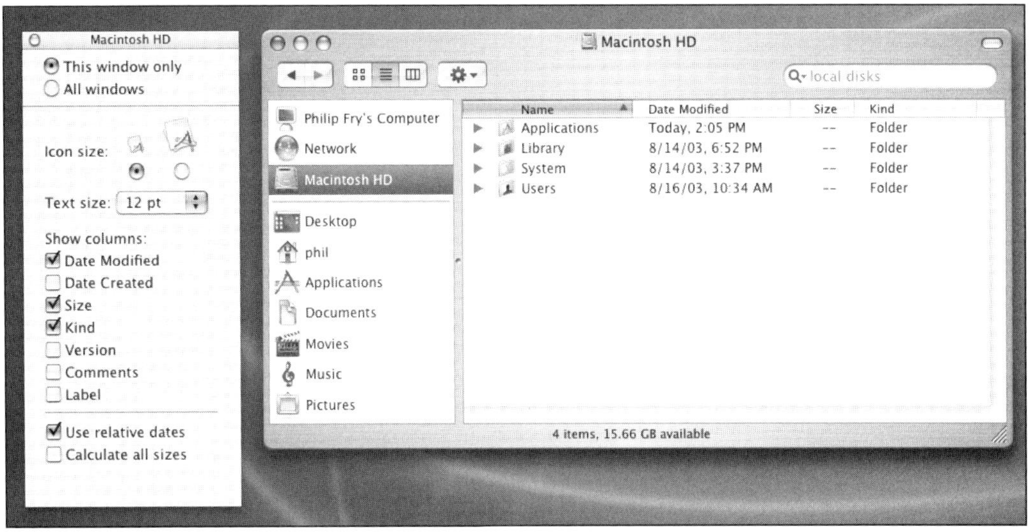

*Just like with **Icon** view, you can customize the appearance of a window in **List** view by making sure the window is active and then selecting **View > Show View Options** from the menu bar. The following chart describes the items found in the View Options floating window for List view.*

View Options: List View

Item	Description
This window only/ All windows	Your selection here determines whether the changes you make will affect only the active window or all the windows you view in the Finder.
Icon size	Unlike in Icon view, which allows you to choose from a wide range of icon sizes, you have only two size choices in List view. This is okay, though, because you're using List view to see information about your files, not to see their icons.
Text size	Click the menu to choose a size for the text within the window.
Show columns	You can check or uncheck the items under this heading to determine which columns you want to appear in the window.
Date Modified	When checked, this column provides the date and time when the file was last saved.

continues on next page

View Options: List View *continued*

Item	Description
Date Created	Displays the date and time when the file was saved for the first time
Size	Displays the amount of disk space that each item occupies. See **Calculate all sizes** at the end of the table.
Kind	Displays the item's file type. For example, application, folder, document, and so on.
Version	Displays the version number of applications. For items to which version numbers don't apply, a dash will appear in this column.
Comments	Displays any comments that have been entered about the item. See the "Comments" sidebar for more information.
Label	Displays the color of the label (if a color has been applied). See the "Adding Labels" sidebar at the end of this exercise.
Use relative dates	When this box is checked, the dates listed in the **Date Modified** and **Date Created** columns will display the dates of older items in standard format, but list the dates of recently created items as "Today" and "Yesterday," where applicable. This sometimes makes it easier to locate newer items.
Calculate all sizes	When this box is selected, the **Size** column will show the size of the files listed in the window. But unless you have the **Calculate all sizes** option selected, folders sizes are not calculated, but are instead represented by dashes. Just be aware that calculating the size of some folders will take several seconds or, in some cases, minutes.

Comments

As mentioned in the preceding chart, one of the categories you can display in List view is Comments. In OS X, you can add comments to a file or folder by single-clicking its icon and then choosing **File > Get Info**.

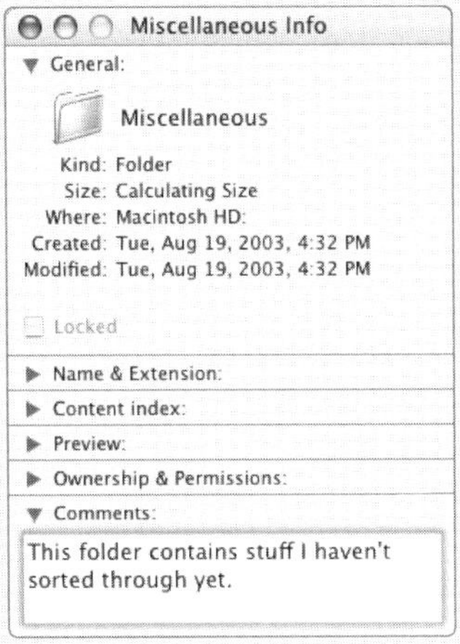

In the **Miscellaneous Info** window that appears, click the triangle next to **Comments**. You can use this text field to enter any relevant information about the file or folder.

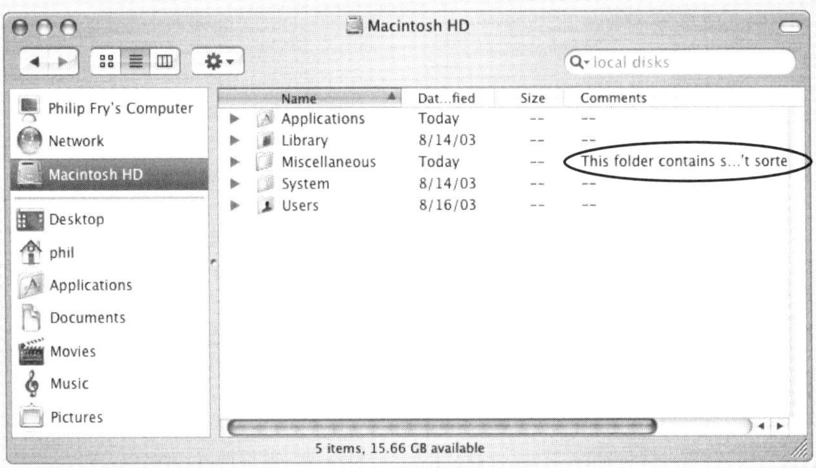

After you close the Info window, the comment you enter will appear in the item's **Comments** column (if you've chosen to display **Comments** in **List** view).

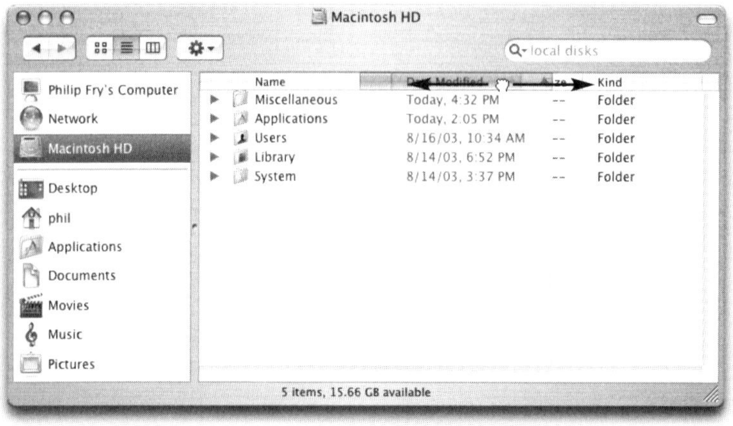

Tip: You can further customize the appearance of a window in List view by rearranging the order of the columns. Although the Name column must stay on the far left of the window, you can rearrange the other columns by dragging the column headings to the left or right.

9. Close any open windows on the **Desktop**.

*As you can see, both Icon view and List view have their advantages. The third and final available view for Finder windows is **Column** view. Icon and List views have been available in the Mac OS since its inception; Column view, however, is a feature that was introduced in OS X. In the following steps, you'll examine Column view and learn how to open an application.*

10. Double-click your **hard drive** icon to open a Finder window and then click the **Column view** button in the toolbar. Adjust the width of the window with the resize window button to match the picture shown here. For this exercise, you should only see the **Places** sidebar and two columns.

The idea behind Column view is pretty simple. You start by clicking on one of the disks or folders in either the Places sidebar or in the adjacent column, revealing its contents in the next column. You can then click one of the folders in this new column to see its contents in the next column. You continue in this fashion until you find the application or file that you're looking for. Depending on the width of your window, a horizontal scroll bar will appear after a few clicks, allowing you to scroll back to the left to see the path you've taken to arrive at your file. In a way, Column view is kind of like a horizontal List view, but much tidier. You still need to deal with only one window in Column view, but navigating through large folders requires much less scrolling. The following steps walk you through working in Column view.

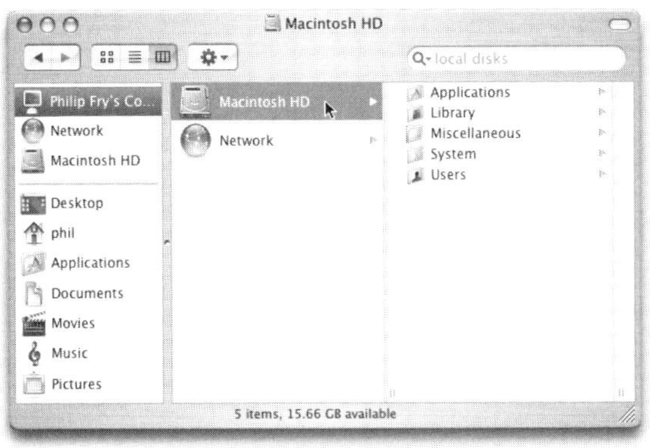

*Your hard drive icon should already be selected in the second column. In the screen shot shown here, the hard drive is named **Macintosh HD**; yours may be named otherwise.*

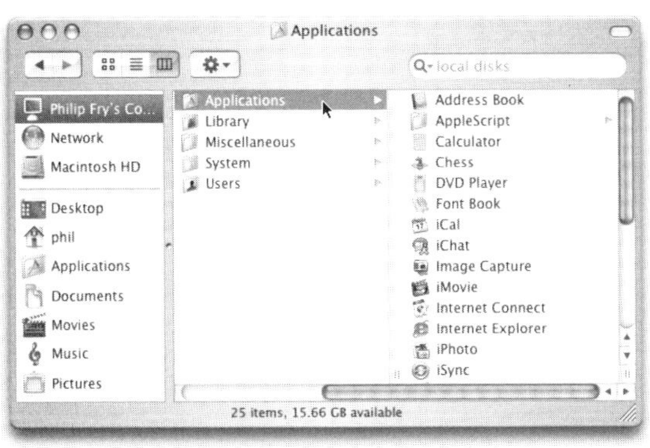

11. Click the **Applications** folder. Immediately, the column containing your hard drive icon slides to the left and the contents of the **Applications** folder slide in from the right. Notice that the **Places** sidebar didn't move. This is a great advantage of working in column view in Panther; no matter how far you go into a folder, you can always click your **hard drive** icon (or another folder) in the sidebar to return to the main folder, without having to scroll back to the beginning.

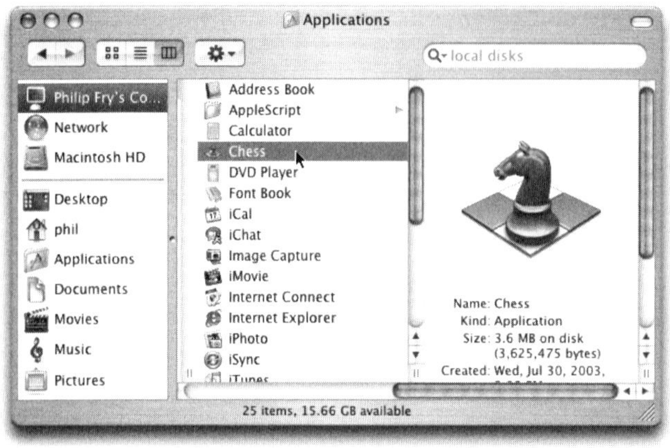

12. Click once on the **Chess** application in the far right column. You know this is an application because the adjacent column tells you. Clicking on any of the nonfolder items will display the item's icon and related information.

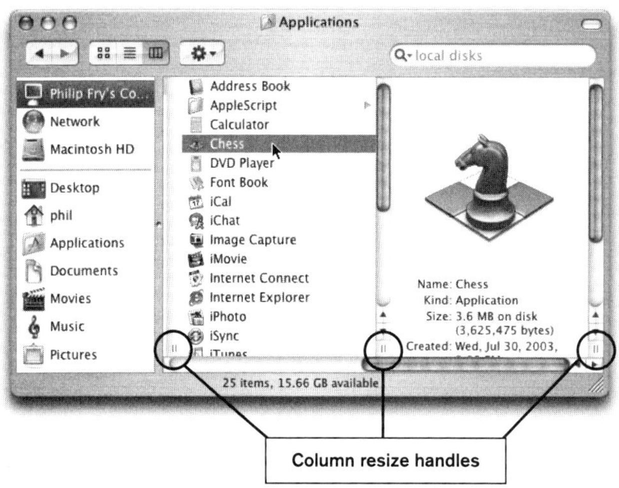

***Tip:** In Column view, each column has its own resize handle. Drag any column's handle to resize it. Press the **Option** key while dragging to resize all the columns simultaneously.*

In the next exercise, you'll learn to open and manage some of these applications, but first you'll take a look at the View options that are available for Column view.

---

13. Choose **View > Show View Options** from the menu bar.

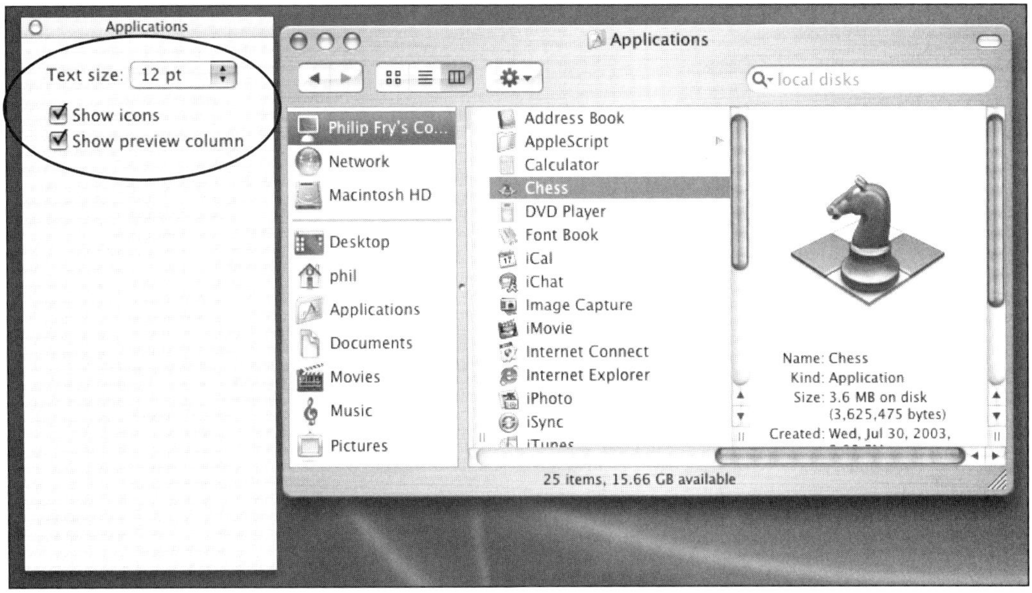

Unlike Icon and List views, which offer many different options for customizing your windows, Column view has just three available options.

View Options: Column View

Item	Description
Text size	Use the pop-up menu to select a size for the text in Column view.
Show icons	This is selected by default. If you uncheck this option, Column view will not display the icons for any of the items.
Show preview column	Also selected by default. If unchecked, you won't see the icon or information for applications or files in the final column.

14. After you're done examining these options, close the floating window and the hard drive window.

Adding Labels

To the great relief and delight of many veteran Mac users, labels, a staple of the classic Mac OS, have finally reappeared in OS X. For people who never used them, the lack of labels made no difference when they transitioned from OS 9 into OS X, but for many other users, it was a great loss.

In brief, labels allow you to color-code files and folders. By coloring your files, you can distinguish a file's type at a glance without necessarily having to read its name. Also, as you saw when working with List view, you can sort windows to display items by label. Therefore, adding labels allows you to apply a unifying attribute to files and folders that OS X wouldn't otherwise be able to group together. For example, you might add a red label to all the text files and images related to a project you're working on, or label all your personal correspondence green.

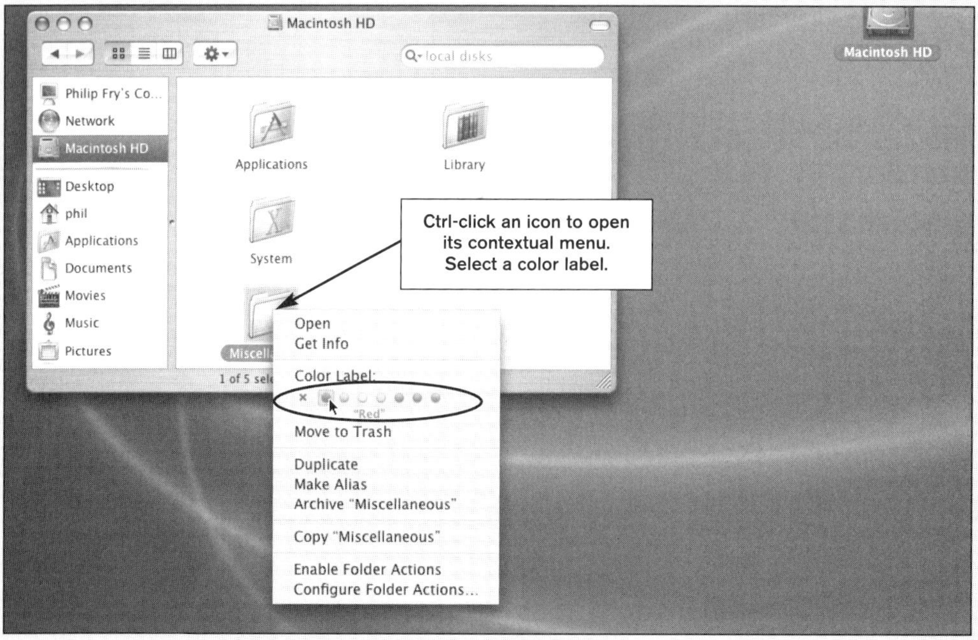

You can apply a label to an icon in several ways. **Ctrl+clicking** (holding down the **Ctrl** key on your keyboard while clicking) the icon opens a contextual menu from which you can select a color. If your mouse has more than one button, right-clicking the icon will open the same menu.

continues on next page

Adding Labels *continued*

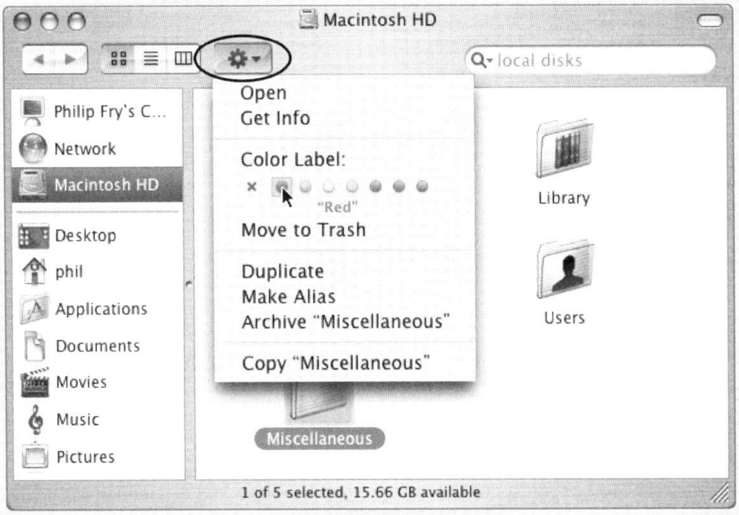

You can also select the icon and then click the **Action** button, which is new to Panther and is essentially the equivalent of a **Ctrl+click**. Depending on what file or folder you've selected, the Action button displays different options.

Lastly, you can select an icon and then click the **File** menu to choose a colored label from the bottom of the drop-down menu, but this method is probably the most time consuming.

Once you've labeled an item, the color you've chosen appears around its name in Icon, List, and Column views. To remove a label, simply **Ctrl+click** the item and choose the **x** icon next to the colors.

Customizing the Toolbar

One of the most convenient features of the Finder window is the toolbar running across the top of the window. In Panther, Apple has left the navigation, view, and search buttons in the toolbar but has moved the other buttons such as Home, Applications, and Computer (all three formerly found in the Jaguar toolbar) to the new Places sidebar. But even though the toolbar has been trimmed down both in size and content, you can still customize its appearance to fit your own needs.

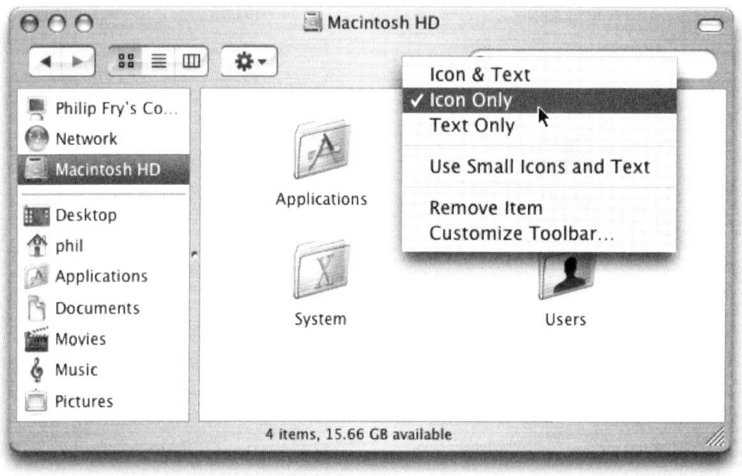

To customize the toolbar, **Ctrl+click** anywhere in the top portion of a **Finder** window to open a contextual menu. This menu is divided into three sections. In the uppermost section, you can determine how the buttons in the toolbar appear: as **Icon & Text** (pictures with names below them), **Icon Only** (just the pictures), or **Text Only**. The Icon & Text option takes up the most room; the Text Only option keeps the toolbar as slim and unobtrusive as possible. If you choose **Use Small Icons and Text**, the overall size of the text in the toolbar will be slightly reduced. (Remember, if you don't want to see the toolbar at all, click the **Show/hide toolbar** button.)

The bottom section of the toolbar's contextual menu deals with removing and adding items from the toolbar. If you want to add items or otherwise alter the configuration of the toolbar, select **Customize Toolbar**.

Tip: Anytime a menu command is followed by an ellipsis (...), this indicates that a window will open containing choices for you to make. For example, choosing **Go > Connect to Server...** opens a window asking you to choose which server you'd like to connect to, just as choosing **Customize Toolbar...** from the toolbar's contextual menu opens a window allowing you to, well, customize the toolbar.

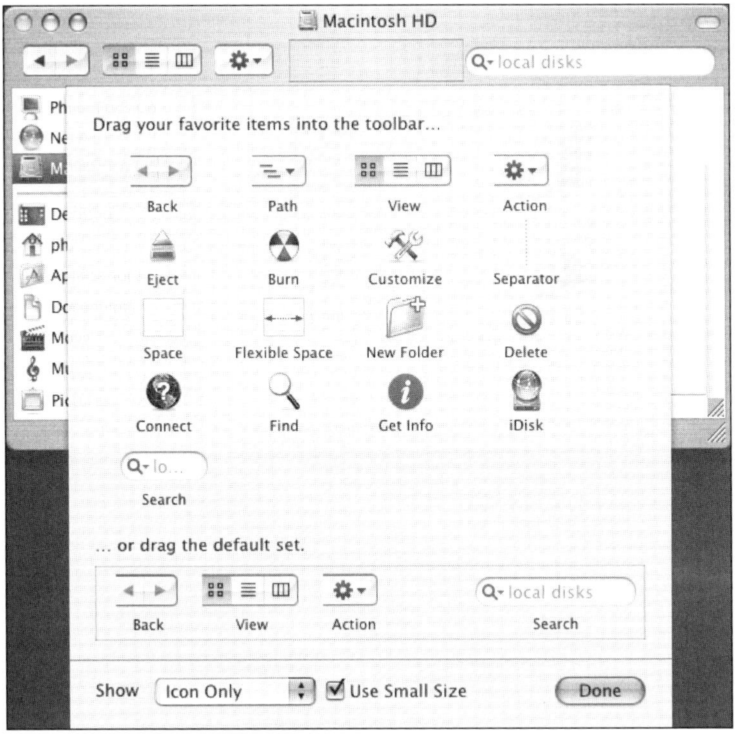

In this window, you're presented with a collection of different items that you can simply drag into the toolbar. For instance, if you always find yourself hunting for the Eject button on your keyboard, you can drag the Eject icon into the toolbar to give yourself an easy way to eject discs from your Mac. You can revert to the default set of toolbar items at anytime by dragging it to the toolbar as well.

4. Opening Applications

You should now be fairly comfortable with navigating the Finder windows. In this next exercise, you'll open a few applications and learn how to switch between active programs and the Finder.

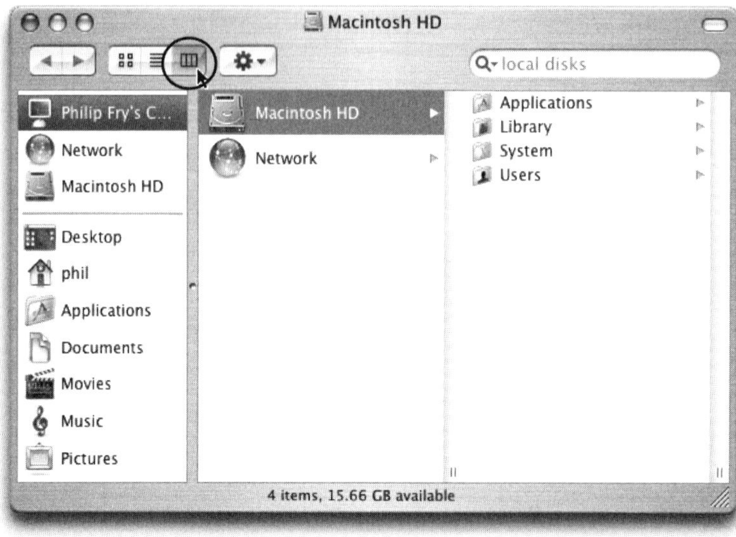

1. Double-click the **hard drive** icon to reveal its contents in a Finder window. Switch to **Column** view.

---

2. Click the **Applications** folder in either the **Places** sidebar or in the right column. (Remember, you don't have to double-click folders to open them in Column view).

As you've probably gathered by now, the Applications folder is where you'll find the programs that were installed with OS X. To open an application, all you have to do is double-click its icon or its name.

Keep the Applications in the Applications Folder

As a general rule, it's a good idea to keep the files and applications installed by OS X in their original locations. Before OS X, you could pretty much move applications to anywhere on your hard drive, but moving applications from the Applications folder can potentially cause problems in OS X. Although you're absolutely free to create folders and file structures for your personal files, it's best to leave the pre-installed items where they are.

3. Double-click the **Chess** application. Its icon will start bouncing in the **Dock** (unless this feature has been turned off), indicating that the application is starting up.

When you open an application, it immediately becomes the active application. Prior to opening Chess, the Finder was the active application. But notice now that the menu bar items have changed to reflect the commands available in Chess. The name of the front-most application always appears as the first item on the menu bar. Chess's icon has also been added to the Dock. The black triangle underneath this icon indicates that the program is running (you'll learn more about this in the next chapter).

Now you'll open another application. To do so, you'll return to the Finder and the Applications folder. You can always return to the Finder from within the current application by either clicking on the ***Desktop*** *or by clicking on the* ***Finder*** *icon in the* ***Dock*** *(more on the Dock in the following chapter).*

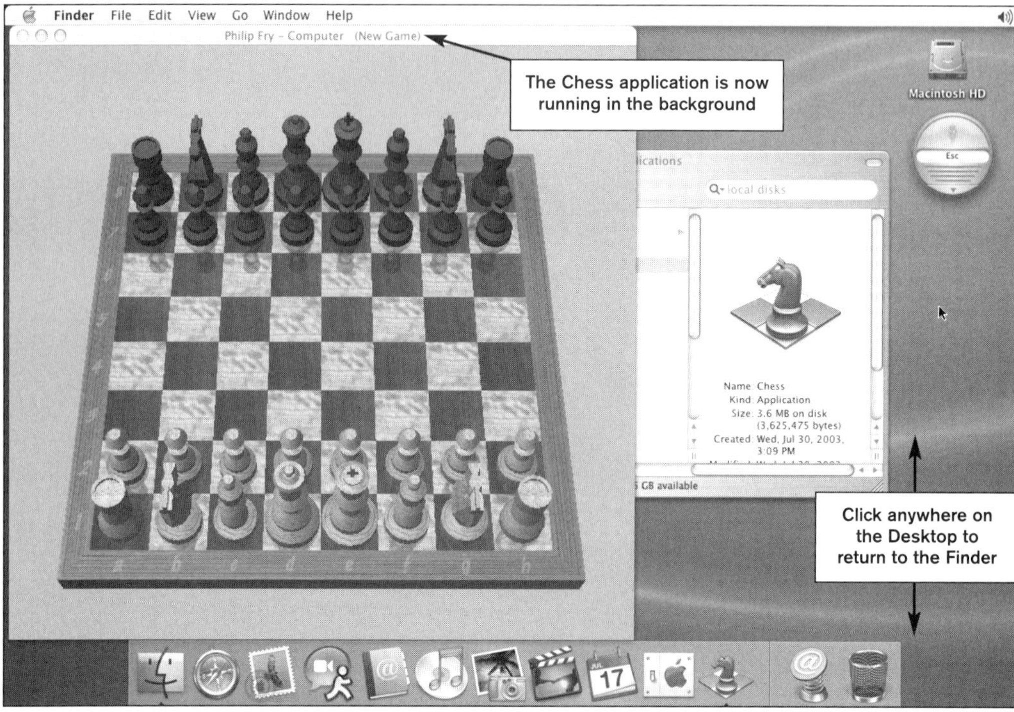

4. Click anywhere on the **Desktop** tomake the **Finder** active. Notice that the menu bar now displays the Finder's items, and that the title bar of the Chess program's window has changed from gray to a subtly-striped white, indicating that it is not currently the active application.

---

5. Click anywhere in the **Applications** window to bring it to the front.

Note: *If your Applications window is completely obscured by the Chess program's window, click the* ***Finder*** *icon in the* ***Dock****. Clicking the Finder icon will always bring all open Finder windows to the front.*

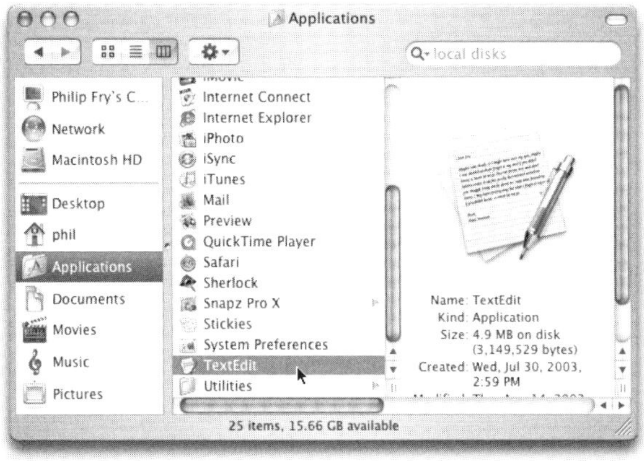

6. In the **Applications** window, locate and double-click **TextEdit**, which is a simple word processing program. Its icon will appear in the **Dock**, and after a moment, a blank word processing document will appear onscreen.

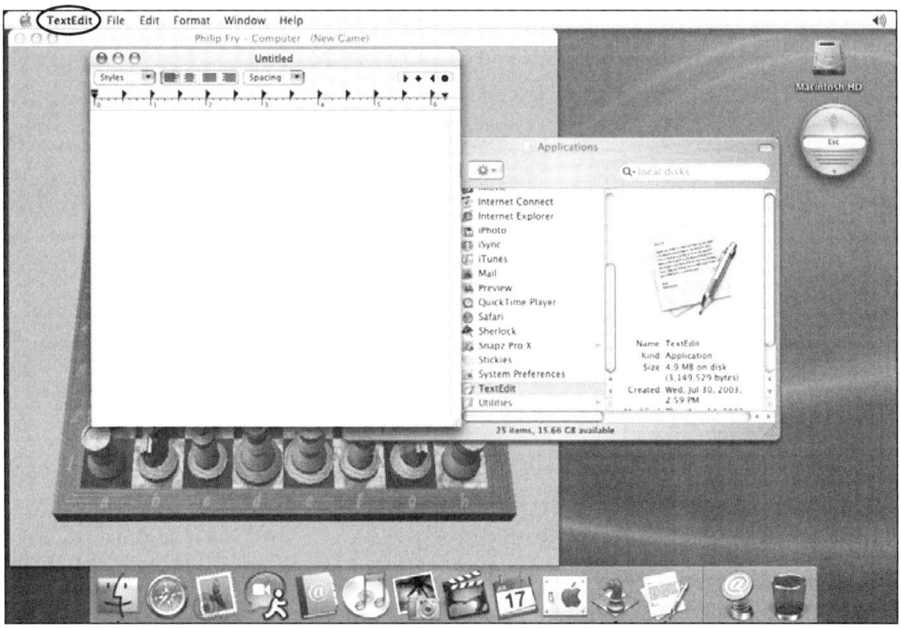

Notice now that because TextEdit is the front-most application, its name appears in the menu bar.

You can now easily switch back and forth between the three running applications (the Finder, Chess, and TextEdit) by clicking anywhere in their respective windows, or by clicking their icons in the ***Dock****.* *Now you'll quit the Chess and TextEdit programs.*

7. Click the **Chess** icon in the **Dock**. From the menu bar, choose **Chess > Quit Chess**. Its icon disappears from the **Dock**, indicating that it's no longer running. You can also press **Cmd+Q** to quit. (The **Cmd** key is the one labeled with the cloverleaf and/or Apple icon.) **Cmd+Q** is the keyboard command for quitting an active application.

8. Click the **TextEdit** icon in the **Dock** and press **Cmd+Q** on the keyboard to quit. Its icon also disappears from the **Dock** to indicate that it's no longer running. (In the next chapter, you'll learn how to keep items in the **Dock** whether they're running or not.)

9. Close any open **Finder** windows.

How Many Applications Can I Run at Once?

In the pre–OS X days, you really had to keep a limit on how many applications you ran at once. Whenever you opened an application, it would grab a portion of your Mac's memory (RAM) for itself and refuse to share it with any other applications. Like a greedy wedding guest at the reception buffet, it would stack its plate high with RAM, leaving little for those who came along later.

If you had only, say, 128 MB of RAM, you quickly found out that you couldn't run more than three or four applications at once–pretty annoying if you often had to jump from your word processing program to your photo-editing program to your page-layout program, and so on. Sometimes, applications wouldn't take enough memory for themselves, forcing you to manually allocate more memory to them in an attempt to make them run more efficiently. You did have the option of buying more RAM or running virtual memory (which essentially used your hard drive as RAM space), but RAM was pretty expensive, and virtual memory tended to make your Mac a bit sluggish, as if it had been drugged or had just eaten a large meal.

With Mac OS X, the days of manually allocating memory and quitting applications to free up RAM are gone. Although OS X's memory management scheme can still be called "virtual memory," it's light years ahead of the virtual memory scheme used in earlier systems. In OS X, the responsibility of memory allocation has been taken away from the applications and is now handled entirely by the operating system. Memory is dynamically allocated to each application, meaning that each application uses only the amount of RAM that it needs at any particular moment.

Therefore, you can now run many more programs at once than you ever could with pre–OS X systems. Even with 128 MB of memory, you can run more than a half-dozen applications simultaneously. The front-most program is always allotted the most memory to keep it running smoothly; the programs running in the background are given just what they need to keep running. When you switch to another application, memory allotments are immediately shifted again. You can run your Mac all day and never need to quit an application.

You may find, however, that your Mac runs sluggishly if you're performing memory-intensive tasks, such as video editing, with several other programs running in the background. But unlike in pre–OS X systems, you don't need to worry about the operating system crashing because of low memory situations. You'll just notice that things begin to run more slowly. If you sense that your Mac's slowing down, just quit some of the other open applications.

Finally, even though OS X can handle running many applications at once, you should still load up on RAM if you can afford to do so (RAM is cheaper than ever these days). Adding more RAM will only make OS X happier. You'll notice an improvement in speed as well. (A great place to check current RAM prices is **www.dealram.com**.)

5. Creating New Folders

In this exercise you'll learn how to create new folders on your hard drive and how to move them from one location to another. You'll also learn the preferred (at least by OS X) locations for creating and saving new folders and files.

Like in previous Mac operating systems, you can pretty much create and place folders and files anywhere on your hard drive. It's all a matter of preference. If you're the sole user of your Mac, you can stick files all over the place, and, as long as you know where you put them, you shouldn't run into many problems. However, OS X is a multiuser operating system, and its folder structure has been set up to allow several users to use a single Mac without interfering with each other's work and files. If you've ever let someone borrow your car, you probably know how annoying it is to get it back to find your seat, steering wheel, and mirrors all out of place. Before you can start driving, you first have to spend the time readjusting everything to just the way you like it (unless, of course, you have one of those fancy cars with programmable seats that remember your preferred positions, in which case you can ignore this analogy, and congratulations on your success). In Mac OS X, a file structure has been established that allows multiple users to create their own individual custom settings and preferences and to store their files in specific locations where they'll be inaccessible to other users. Even if you're the only one using your Mac, it's still not a bad idea to use the folders that OS X has created for you. As you're about to see, it's a nice way to keep yourself organized.

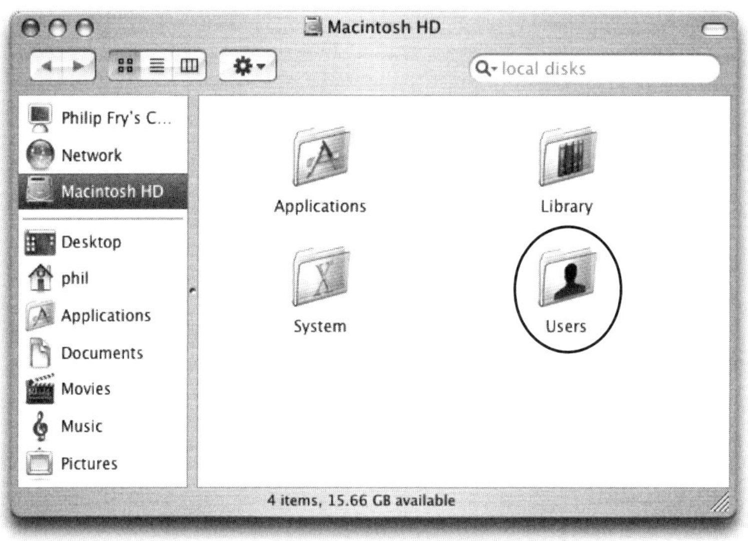

1. Double-click the **hard drive** icon on the **Desktop**. See that folder called **Users**? That's where OS X places the information about all of the authorized users of your Mac.

2. Double-click the **Users** folder to view its contents.

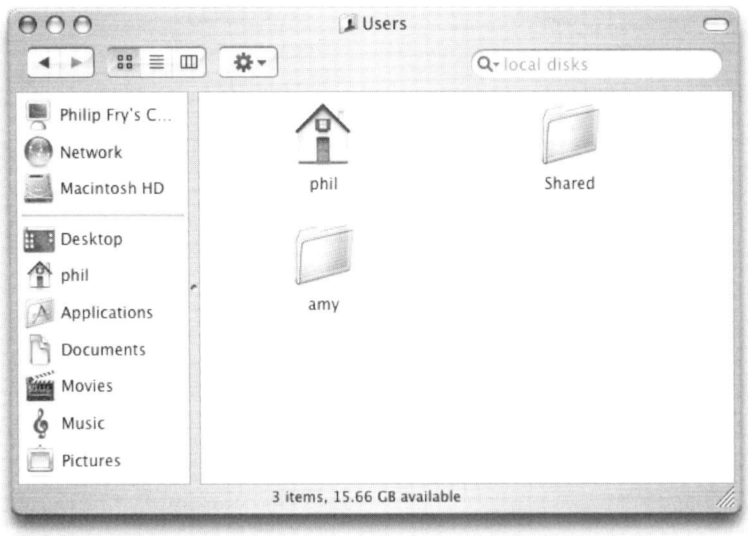

Within the Users folder, you'll find the names of every authorized user of this Mac. Each user is given a ***Home*** *folder in which to store his or her files and folders. Your own Home folder is identified by the short name you created when you set up your Mac, and by the Home icon. (Your Home folder also appears in the Places sidebar.) In the screen shot above, you can see that this computer is being shared by Phil and Amy, with Phil being the currently logged-in user. If Amy were logged in, the Home icon would appear next to her name, with Phil's Home folder represented by the generic folder icon. Of course, if you're the only user of your Mac, you'll see only your own name in this folder. (You'll learn how to add users to your Mac in Chapter 4,* "System Preferences."*) The Shared folder you see here in the Users folder is for storing items that you want to have available to all users. With the exception of the Public and Sites folders, the contents of each user's Home folder is inaccessible to other users.*

3. Double-click any user's folder but your own. (If you're the only user, just read through the next few steps and observe the screen shots.)

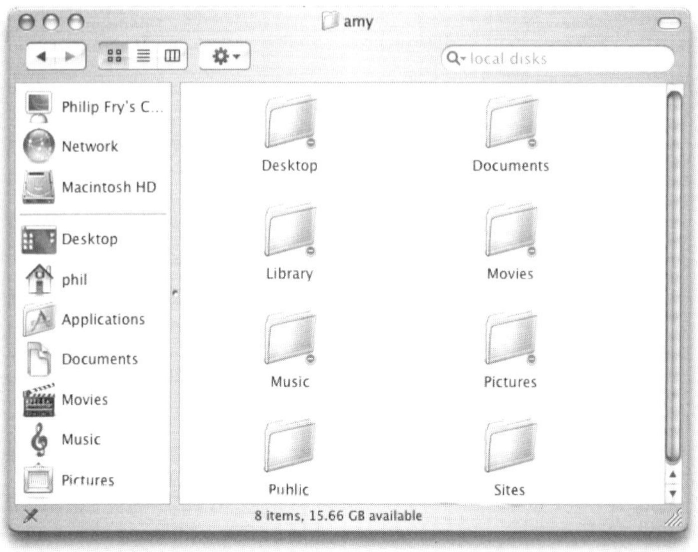

Notice that most of the folders have a little "Do Not Enter" icon on them. There's also a little pencil icon with a slash through it in the lower-left corner of the window, indicating that you can't alter the contents of this folder. The only folders you have access to are Public and Sites. The Public folder is for placing files that you want to give to this user. The Sites folder is where the user can set up a Web page for other users to view.

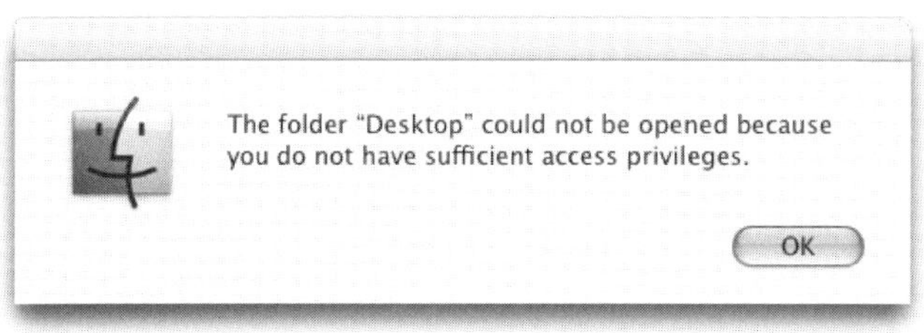

As for the rest of the folders, OS X is aware that you're not the owner of these files; if you double-click any of these folders, you'll be presented with a message similar to this one.

Now you'll take a look inside your own Home folder.

4. Click your **Home** icon in the **Places** sidebar.

As you can see, in your own Home folder, you have complete access to all the folders contained within. OS X has created folders for just about any type of file your may want to save. It's a good idea to use these folders, and to not save your files just anywhere on your hard drive, not only to keep yourself organized, but also to protect your files from other users. The following chart details the purpose of each folder found in your Home folder.

Home Folder Contents

Folder	Description
Desktop	Here's one of Mac OS X's little secrets: When you put a file on the Desktop, it's not really on the Desktop. It's placed into this folder in your Home folder. Anything placed into this folder shows up on the Desktop when you're logged in, but remains inaccessible to other users when they're logged into their own accounts. This way, each user can have his or her Desktop as cluttered with items as he or she likes without them showing up when someone else logs onto the Mac.
Documents	This is where OS X suggests you keep word processing documents, page-layout files, or any other documents you work with. In many applications, when you save a file, the Documents folder is the default save location. You'll be creating some subfolders in this folder later in this exercise.

continues on next page

Home Folder Contents *continued*	
Folder	**Description**
Library	You may have noticed a folder called Library in your main hard drive window. That folder is for storing the general preference files, fonts, and help files for the entire computer. The Library folder here in your Home folder also contains these items, but the items here are for your personal use and do not affect other users' preferences. For instance, your preferences for application settings, Desktop pictures, and email settings are all stored in this folder. Your interaction with this folder is, for the most part, indirect. Settings you choose in applications and system preferences affect the items found in this folder. You'll rarely open this folder to change items manually.
Movies, Music, Pictures	As you might imagine, these three folders are for storing various multimedia files on your system. Not only are these three folders a good way to keep your different files organized, but iMovie, iTunes, and iPhoto all make use of these folders. Respectively, iTunes and iPhoto use the Music and Pictures folders automatically when you copy music and photos onto your Mac, and iMovie defaults to the Movies folder when you save your movie projects. You'll learn more about these applications later in the book.
Public	This folder is here for other users who may want to pass files along to you from over a network or when they're logged onto your Mac. If you double-click the Public folder, you'll see that it contains a folder named **Drop Box**, which is the only folder other users can access within your Home folder. You can tell other users on your network to place files into the Drop Box, and you'll be able to access them immediately.
Sites	If your Mac is connected to the Internet at all times, you can use OS X's built-in Web server to host your own Web page in this folder. When you place a Web site into this folder and select the necessary settings in System Preferences, anyone on the Internet can view your site.

As you can see, the structure of your Home folder can keep you well organized if you use it properly. Now you'll create a few new folders within your Documents folder to further organize your files.

5. Double-click the **Documents** folder to open it (or click its icon in the **Places** sidebar). This folder may be empty, or it may already contain some files you've previously saved. It doesn't matter–you're just going to create some new folders.

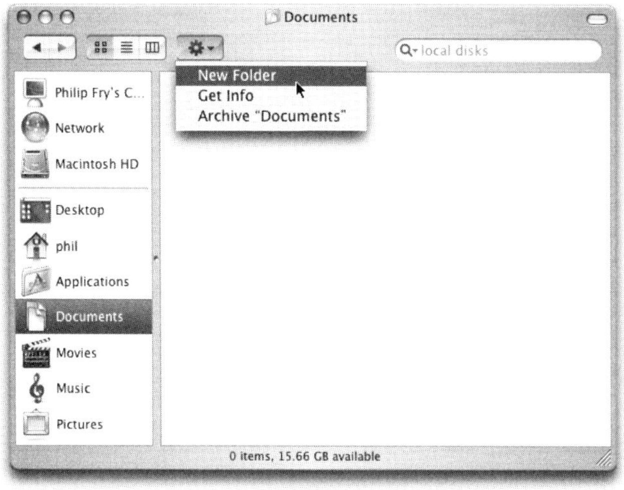

6. With the **Documents** window open and active, click the **Action** button and select **New Folder** from the menu that appears.

Note: *If you prefer to use the keyboard command to create a new folder, the command is* ***Shift+Cmd+N****. This is different from pre–OS X systems, where the command was just* ***Cmd+N****, which is now used to open a new Finder window. Additionally, you can* ***Ctrl+click*** *in the* ***Documents*** *window and select* ***New Folder*** *from the contextual menu that appears, or select* ***File > New Folder****.*

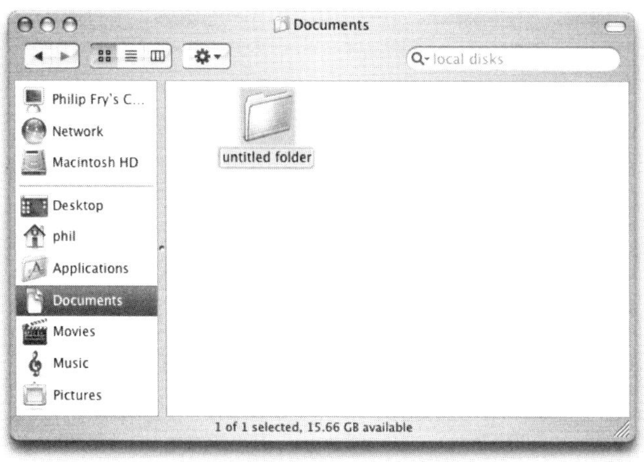

A new folder appears in the Documents folder. Anytime you create a new folder, it appears with the default name of ***untitled folder*** *highlighted, prompting you to give it a more descriptive name.*

Renaming Items in the Finder

At this point, it's important for you to be able to recognize the different states of an icon when its selected, deselected, or highlighted.

When you first view most files, they're not selected. They're just sitting there waiting for you to do something with them. When you click once on a file's icon, you've selected it. The icon of a selected file is surrounded by a dark square with rounded corners (in Icon view), and its name is also highlighted. To change the name of a file, click once on its name and wait. After a second, the file's name will be highlighted allowing you to change it. Once the name is highlighted, just type, and your new text will appear. When you're done renaming the file, press **Return**.

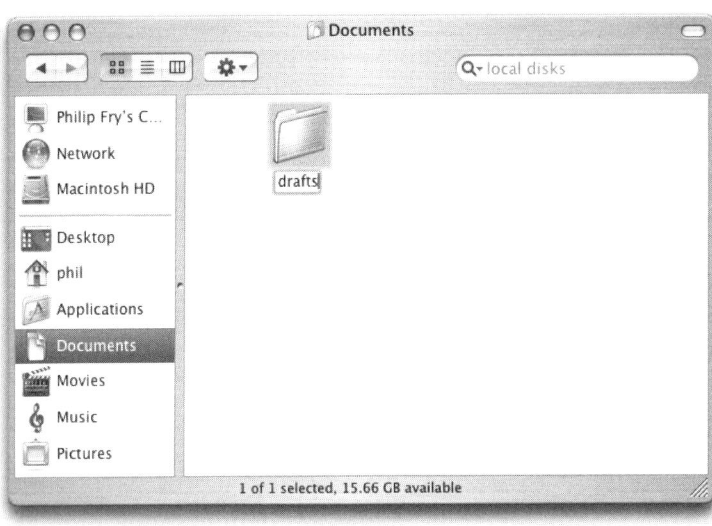

7. Making sure that the folder's name is highlighted, type **drafts** to rename this folder. Remember, anytime a folder or file's name is highlighted you can immediately rename it by just typing. If you accidentally clicked off the new folder, single-click its name and wait for it to highlight, then go ahead and name it.

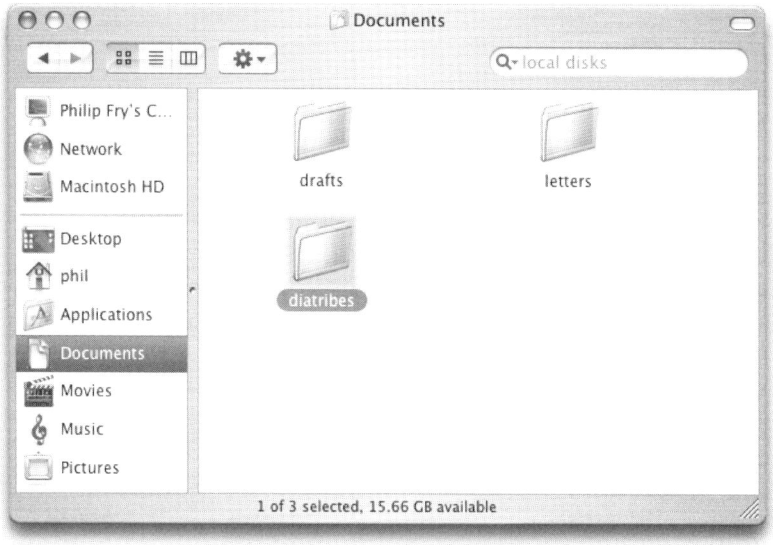

8. Create two more folders called **letters** and **diatribes**. You now have three subfolders within your **Documents** folder to store different types of documents. In the following exercise, you'll place some files into these folders.

9. Close any open windows.

6. Saving Files

In this exercise, you'll create some simple text documents and learn how to save them in different areas of your hard drive.

1. Double-click the **hard drive** icon to open a Finder window. You're going to open **TextEdit** again to create a small text file. **TextEdit** is found in your **Applications** folder. So far, you've opened your **Applications** folder by double-clicking its icon in the main hard drive contents and by clicking its icon in the **Places** sidebar. Another quick way to get to your **Applications** folder (especially when you have no Finder windows open) is to use the **Go** menu bar item.

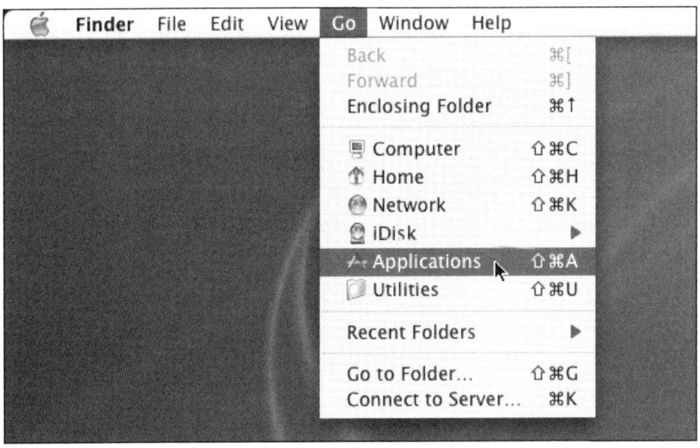

2. From the menu bar, click **Go** and notice that it lists several common destinations. Choose **Go > Applications**. This immediately opens a window displaying the contents of your Applications folder.

*Tip: You can also use the keyboard shortcut of **Shift+Cmd+A** to open **Applications**. Apple has made it super easy to open the items under the Go menu with keyboard shortcuts. Just remember to hold **Shift+Cmd**, and then press the first letter of the folder you want to open. For example, **Shift+Cmd+H** opens your **Home** folder, and **Shift+Cmd+U** opens your **Utilities** folder.*

3. In the **Applications** folder, locate and double-click **TextEdit** to run the program.

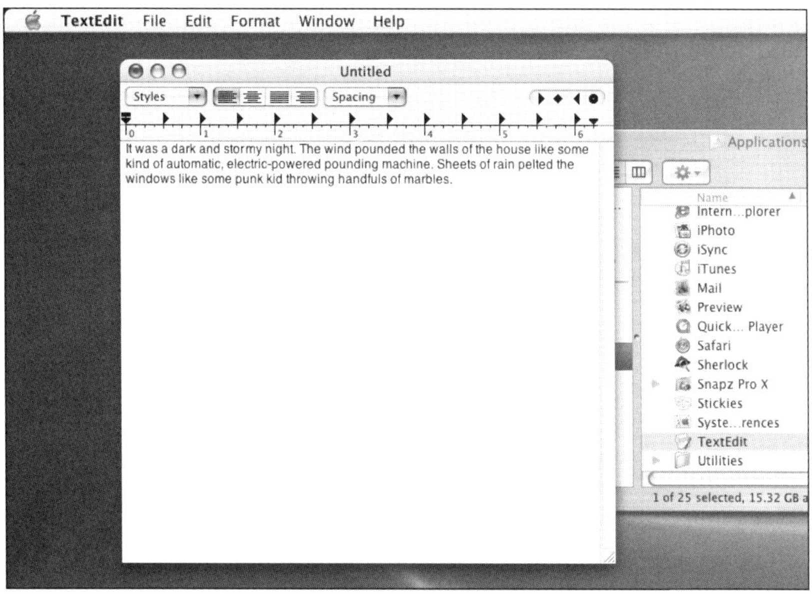

4. When TextEdit opens, you'll be presented with a blank word processing document. Type a few lines of text.

*Next, you'll save this file in one of the folders you created inside your **Documents** folder.*

5. Choose **File > Save** (or press **Cmd+S**). A dialog box will descend from the top of the document window. This is known as a "sheet." In OS X, many dialog boxes like this one remain attached to the document you're working with so it remains clear which window this sheet refers to. Notice that the default save location is **Documents**. Your Mac is trying to keep you organized by offering to save this file into the **Documents** folder in your **Home** folder. You'll leave **Documents** as the default location for now, but you should give this file a better name than **Untitled** before you save it.

Note: *New to TextEdit in Panther is the File Format menu, which allows you to save TextEdit documents as either RTF (**R**ich **T**ext **F**ormat) files, which can be read by nearly every word processor out there, or as Word Format, which saves the document in a form that can be read and edited by Microsoft Word. For this exercise, you'll leave the file format as RTF.*

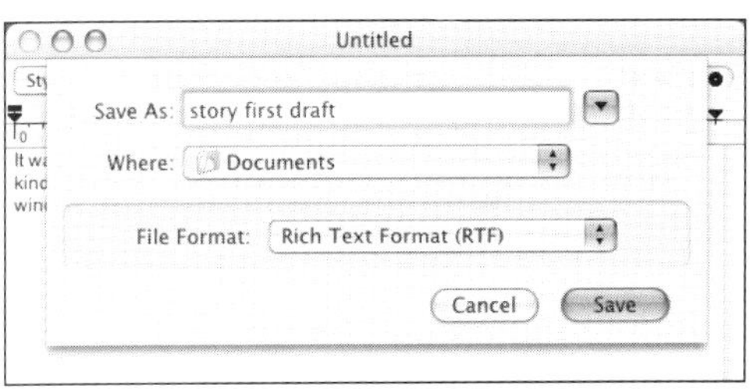

6. Type **story first draft** to name the file. Click **Save** or press **Return** on your keyboard.

Tip: *Whenever a dialog window presents a choice of buttons to click (in this example, you're presented with **Cancel** and **Save**), you can always select the blue, pulsing button by pressing **Return** on your keyboard. There's no need to type the file name, and then grab the mouse just to click the **Save** button. Additionally, you can invoke the **Cancel** button in nearly every application by pressing **Cmd+period**.*

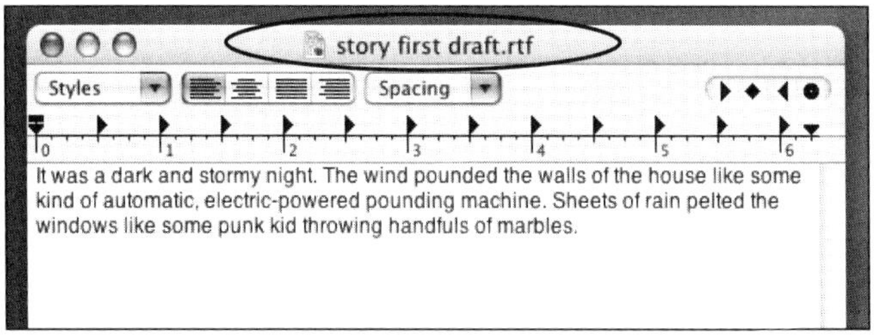

*Because you've saved and named the file, its name appears in the title bar of the document window. The file itself has been saved in your **Documents** folder.*

---

7. Click the **close** button to close the document window. **TextEdit** itself will continue running.

Now you'll make sure that your file was saved in the proper location.

---

8. Click the **Finder** window to make it active (it should still be displaying your **Applications** folder's contents), and then click **Documents** in the **Places** sidebar to quickly jump to the **Documents** folder in your **Home** folder.

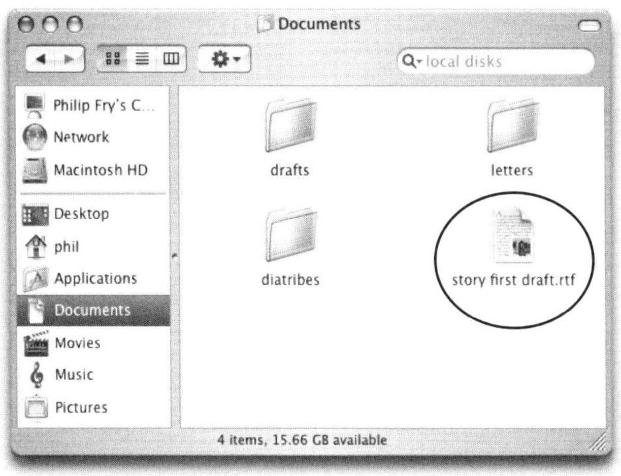

*Inside **Documents**, you'll find the three folders you created earlier, as well as your TextEdit document.*

Next, you'll create two more documents and save them in different locations.

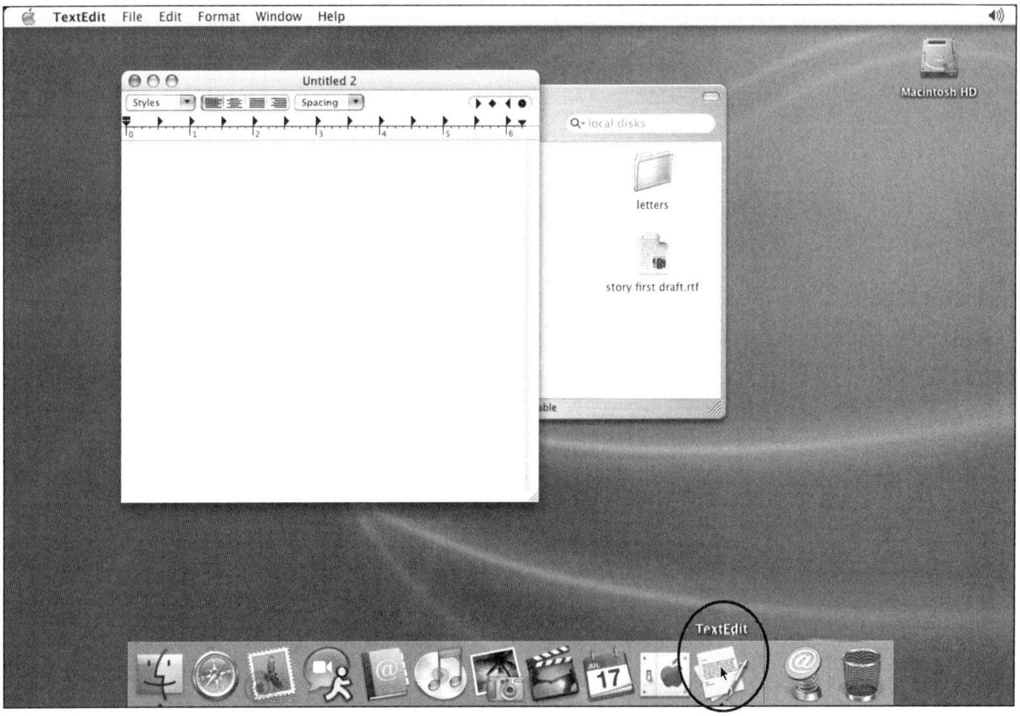

9. Keep the **Documents** window open. Click the **TextEdit** icon in the **Dock** to return to **TextEdit**. A new document window will open.

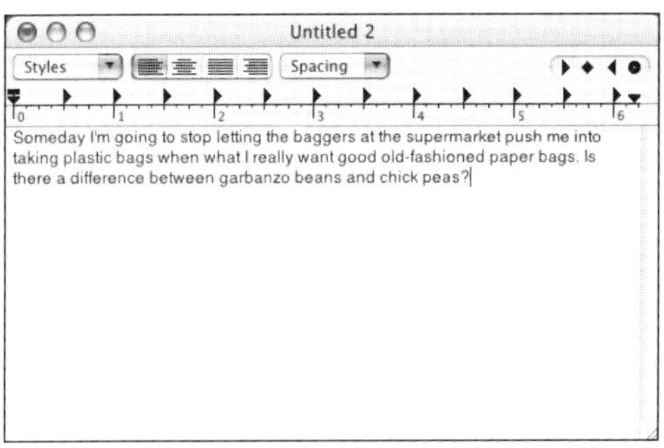

10. Type some text.

11. Choose **File > Save** to save this document. Name this file **ramblings**, but don't press **Return** or click **Save** yet. You're again prompted to save this file in your **Documents** folder. This time, however, you'll save this file to the **Desktop**.

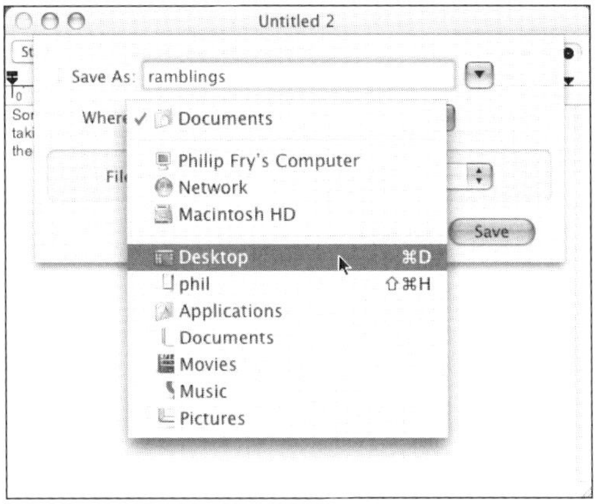

12. Click **Documents** to reveal a list of destinations for your file. But notice that the selection is limited. You can't choose just anywhere to save your file from this menu: You have to choose one of the locations listed here. Choose **Desktop** and then click **Save**.

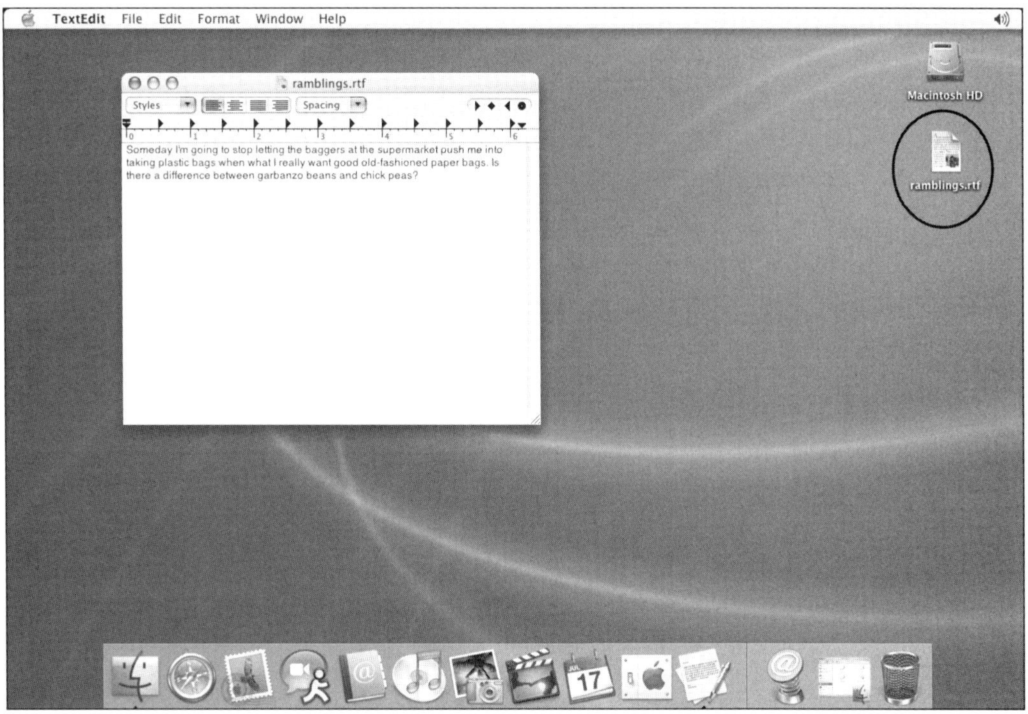

After clicking Save, you'll see the newly saved file appear on your Desktop.

13. Close **ramblings**. You'll create one more file now.

14. In **TextEdit**, choose **File > New** or press **Cmd+N** to create a new blank document, and type the following:

To the Editor:
I think Garrick Chow is an incredibly gifted writer with a keen eye for detail. He probably never misses deadlines as a result of playing video games instead of writing. He deserves a raise.
Sincerely,
[Your Name]

*Because this is a letter, you'll save it in the **letters** folder you created in the **Documents** folder.*

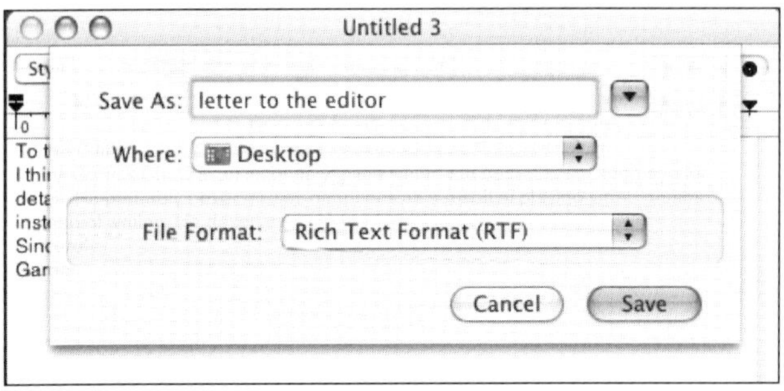

15. Choose **File > Save**, and name this file **letter to the editor**.

*As you saw when you saved the previous file, the **Where** menu offers a limited selection of destinations for your file. Nowhere in this menu will you find the **letters** folder you created. To save this file into the **letters** folder, you'll need to expand your choices.*

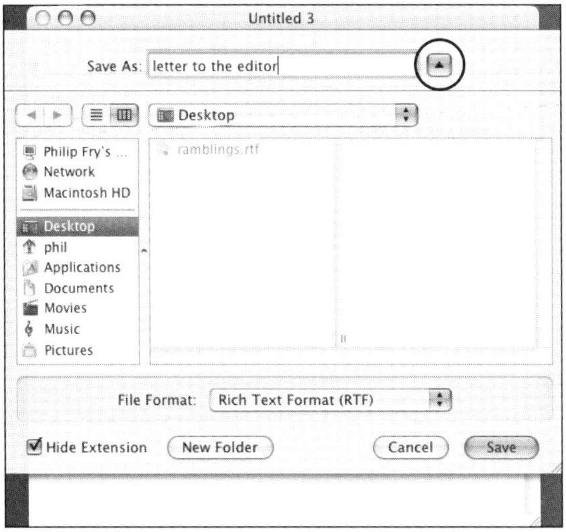

16. Click the little triangle to the right of the **Save As** field to expand this **Save** sheet into **Column** view. You now have complete access to your entire hard drive. New to Panther is the inclusion of the **Places** sidebar in the **Save** sheet, which gives you quick access to all the commonly used places on your Mac.

17. Click the **Documents** folder in the **Places** sidebar to reveal its contents.

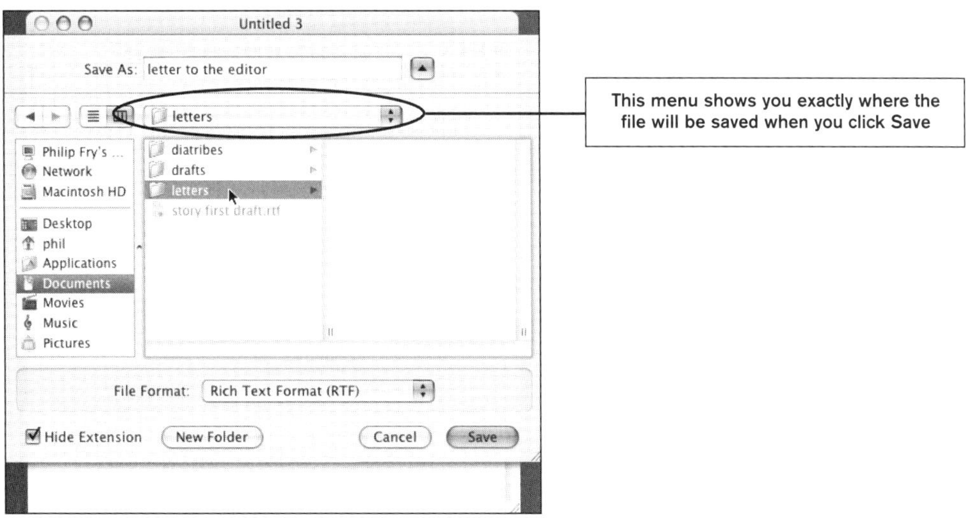

18. Click the **letters** folder to select it. Notice that the **Where** menu (even though it's not labeled as such in this view) indicates that you've selected this folder. Click **Save** to save your file in **letters**.

19. Quit **TextEdit** and close any open windows on the **Desktop**.

Congratulations! You've successfully saved three files in three locations. Next, you'll see what you can do if you change your mind about where you put your files.

List View in the Save and Open Sheets

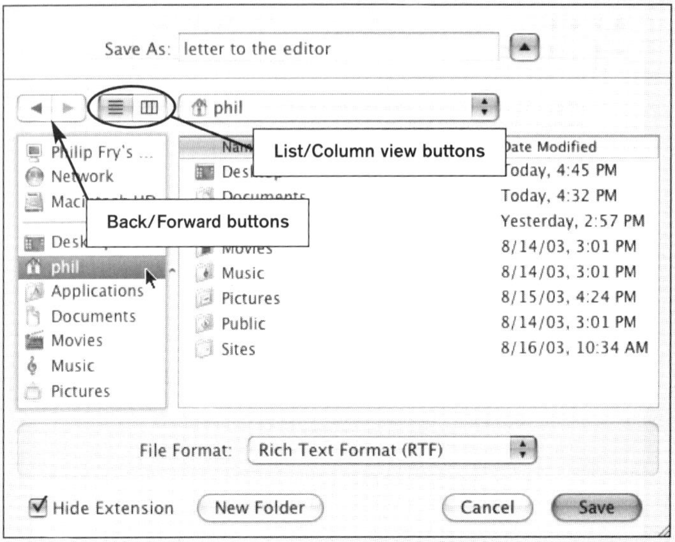

In addition to the Places sidebar, two other new additions to the **Save As** dialog box in Panther are the **List view** and **Column view** buttons and the **Back/Forward** navigation buttons. The inclusion of these buttons makes using the Save As dialog box more like using actual Finder windows. Perhaps more importantly for many users, the Places sidebar and the view buttons also appear in the Open dialog box when you choose **File > Open** in most applications. For the first time in OS X, you can switch to **List** view, click the **Date Modified** column heading, and find files based on the date they were last saved, rather than by their names.

7. Moving, Copying, and Deleting Files

In this exercise, you'll learn how to move files around, copy them, and delete them from your hard drive when you don't need them anymore.

1. From the **Finder** menu bar, choose **Go > Home**. This is a quick and easy way to open your **Home** folder without having to double-click your hard drive icon. (Remember, you can also press **Shift+Cmd+H** to open your **Home** folder.)

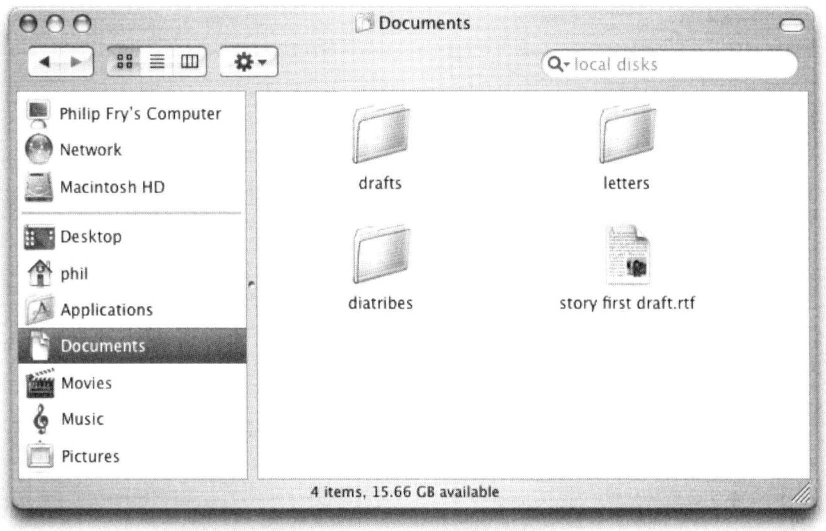

2. Double-click the **Documents** folder (or click **Documents** in the **Places** sidebar) to view its contents and make sure you're in Icon view.

*Here's where you saved your first document, **story first draft**. Although there's really nothing wrong with leaving this file where it is, wouldn't it be so much more organized to place it in the **drafts** folder? Of course it would. To move an item into a folder, all you have to do is (get ready for this) move it into the folder.*

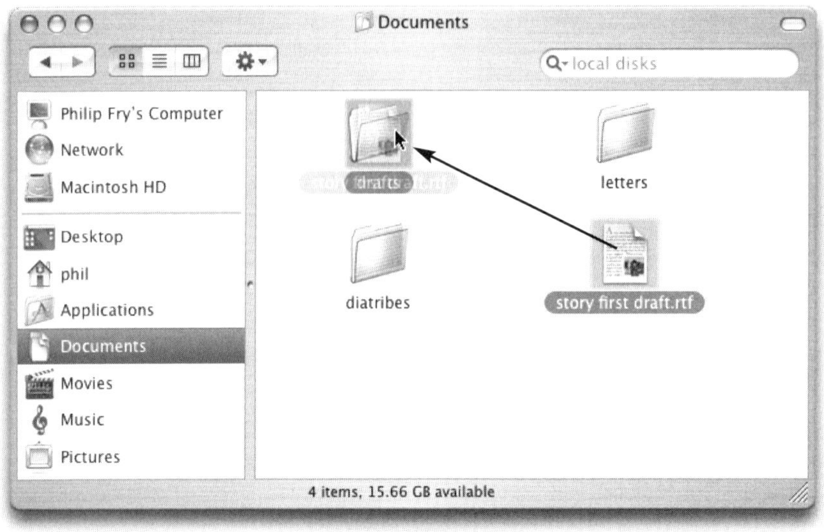

3. Drag **story first draft** onto the **drafts** folder. In a display of great detail-oriented design, not only is the folder highlighted, but the icon also appears to open up to accept your file. When you see this visual cue, release the mouse button. You've just placed the file into the folder. Hey, if only the rest of your life was this easy.

---

4. Close the **Documents** window.

Tip: *After you move a file, or if you accidentally place a file in an incorrect folder, you can easily put the file back where it started by choosing **File > Undo** from the **Finder** menu bar.*

Next, you'll learn how to move a file by using spring-loaded folders, a popular feature introduced back in 1997 with Mac OS 8, which was absent from the initial releases of OS X. After many users complained, spring-loaded folders made their return in Jaguar and remain part of the Panther's feature set.

*On your Desktop is the **ramblings** file that you saved. You'll move this into the **diatribes** folder you created in the **Documents** folder. Instead of navigating through your hard drive to find the **diatribes** folder and then dragging **ramblings** into this folder, you'll use Panther's spring-loaded folders feature to move this file.*

Note: *You might want to read through these steps first before you try them. It's important that after you click the mouse button down in Step 5, you don't release it until Step 7.*

5. Drag **ramblings** over your **hard drive** icon and hold it there. After a few seconds, the hard drive "springs" open to reveal its contents.

6. Continue holding the mouse button down and drag **ramblings** over **Documents** in the **Places** sidebar until it flashes and the window changes to show the contents of the **Documents** folder.

7. Drag **ramblings** into the **diatribes** folder and release the mouse. And that's all there is to spring-loaded folders. Whether you find it useful or not depends on the way you work. Some people find it extremely useful having to only click down once to move a file several levels deep into their hard drives. Others prefer to click several times to open the destination folder and then drag the file in.

***Tip:** If you don't feel like waiting the few seconds for a folder to spring open, press the **spacebar** as soon as you move your file over the folder, and it will immediately pop open. You can also adjust the time it takes for the folder to open. See "Setting Finder Preferences" at the end of the chapter.*

MOVIE | spring_loaded.mov

See the movie **spring_loaded.mov** on the **H•O•T CD-ROM** for a demonstration of spring-loaded folders.

Okay, now that you know how to move files around, you'll take a look at how to get rid of them. It's really quite simple.

8. The **Documents** folder should still be open. If it's not, click **Documents** in the **Places** sidebar.

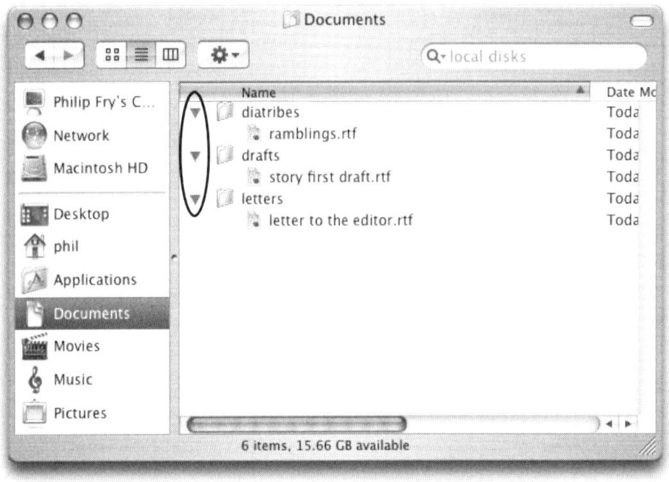

9. Switch to **List** view and toggle open all three folders by clicking on the triangles next to them. This will allow you to view the contents of each folder in one window.

Let's say you've decided to get rid of the ***ramblings*** *file. To remove a file from your hard drive, the first step is to place it in the* ***Trash****, which is located on the far-right side of the* ***Dock****.*

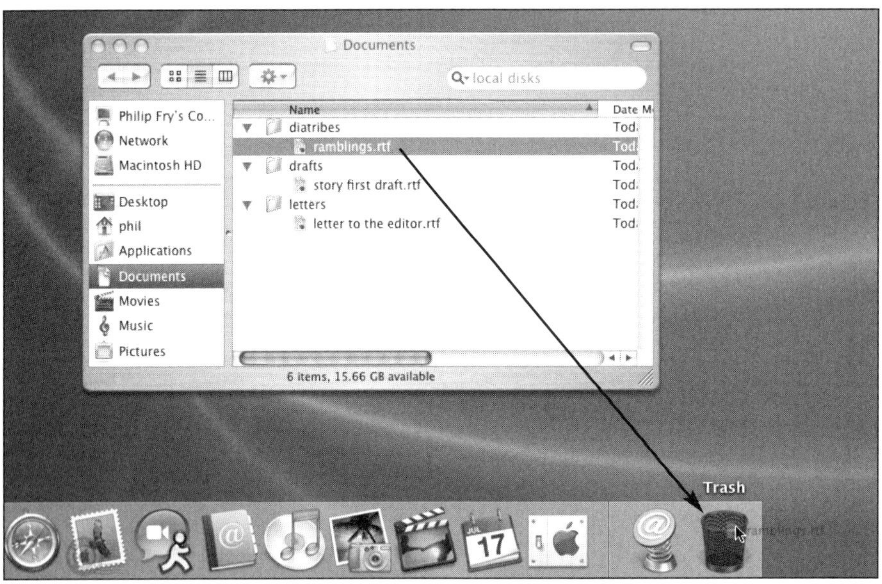

10. Drag **ramblings** from the **Documents** window to the **Trash**. When you see the **Trash** highlight, release the mouse button.

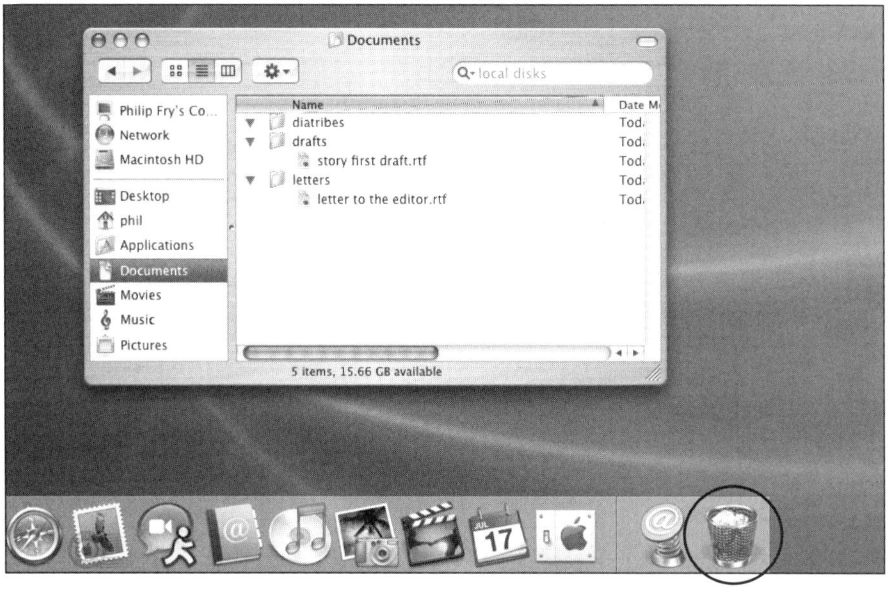

*The **ramblings** file has been moved from the **diatribes** folder into the **Trash**. Notice that the **Trash** icon has changed to indicate that it now contains an item. It's important to note here that you haven't yet deleted the **ramblings** file.*

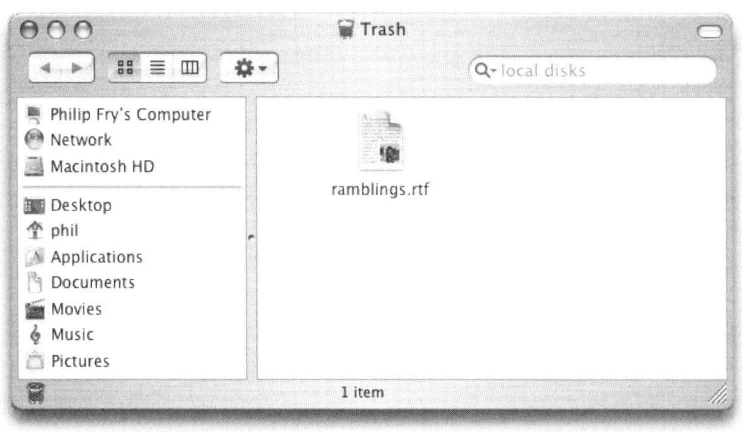

11. Click the **Trash** icon in the **Dock**. A window will open to display its contents. If you needed to, you could still rescue **ramblings** from the **Trash** right now by simply dragging it out of there and into another folder or onto the **Desktop**. Leaving the file in the **Trash** will ensure that it's deleted the next time you empty the **Trash**.

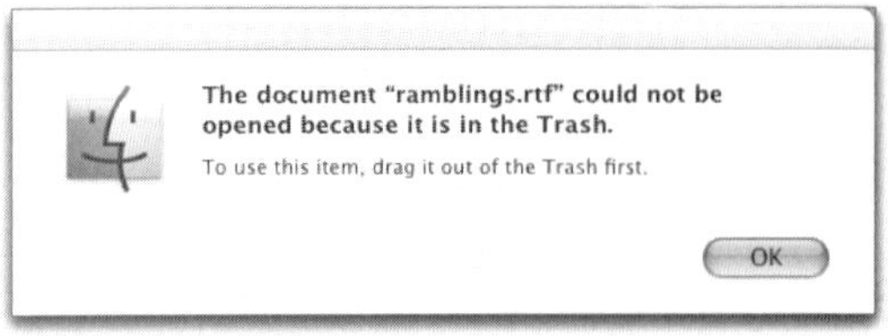

12. Double-click the **ramblings** file in the **Trash**. You're presented with a smiling dialog box informing you that items in the **Trash** cannot be opened. This is an important point: You cannot work with items while they reside in the **Trash** folder. Click **OK**, and close the **Trash** window.

*Before you permanently delete this file, you'll move some more items to the Trash. You no longer need the items in either the **diatribes** folder or the **drafts** folder. Instead of dragging them into the Trash one by one, you'll move them all at once.*

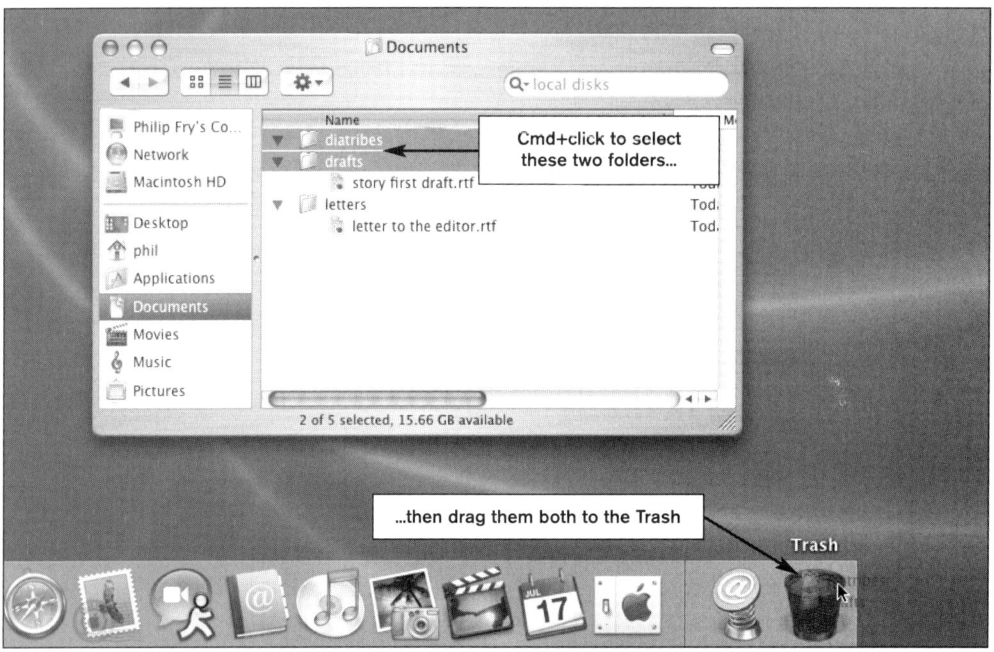

13. In the **Documents** window, click once on the **diatribes** folder to select it. Now hold the **Cmd** key and click the **drafts** folder. Holding the **Cmd** key allows you to select multiple items. With both folders selected, click either one and drag them to the **Trash**. (Because **story first draft** is contained in the **drafts** folder, it also ends up in the **Trash**.)

***Note:** In Panther, you can also move files to the **Trash** by selecting them, clicking the **Action** button in the toolbar and choosing **Move to Trash** from the menu.*

Selecting Multiple Items

As you just saw, holding the **Cmd** key allows you to select multiple items. In fact, there are several methods for selecting more than one item at a time:

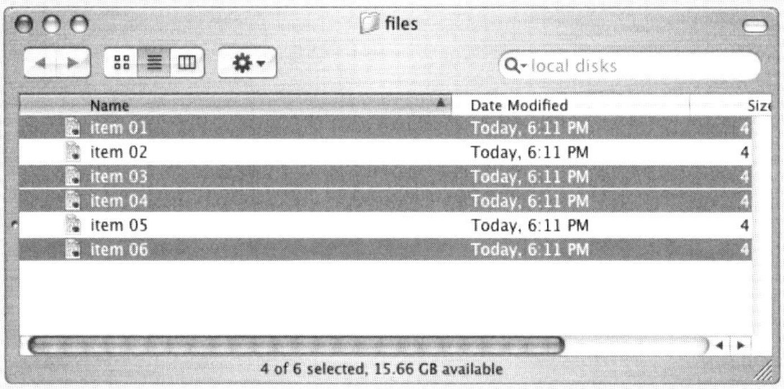

Cmd+click–Holding the **Cmd** key while clicking allows you select multiple items in **Icon**, **List**, and **Column** views.

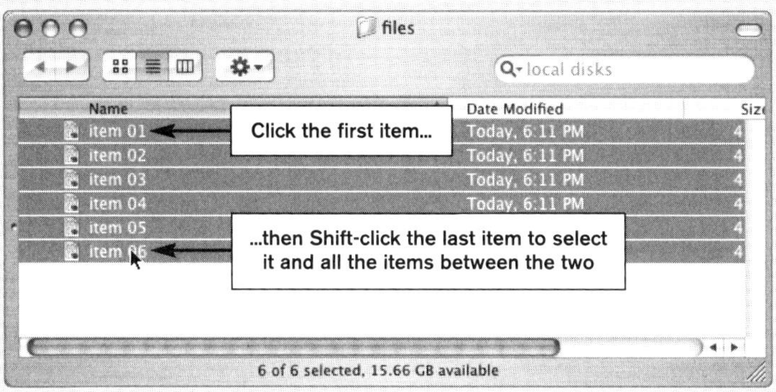

Shift+click–Holding **Shift** while clicking works the same as **Cmd+clicking** in **Icon** view, but in **List** and **Column** views, **Shift+clicking** selects contiguous items. In the previous example, item 01 was clicked first, and then item 06 was Shift+clicked, causing all the files between items 01 and 06 to be selected (as well as items 01 and 06 themselves).

continues on next page

Selecting Multiple Items *continued*

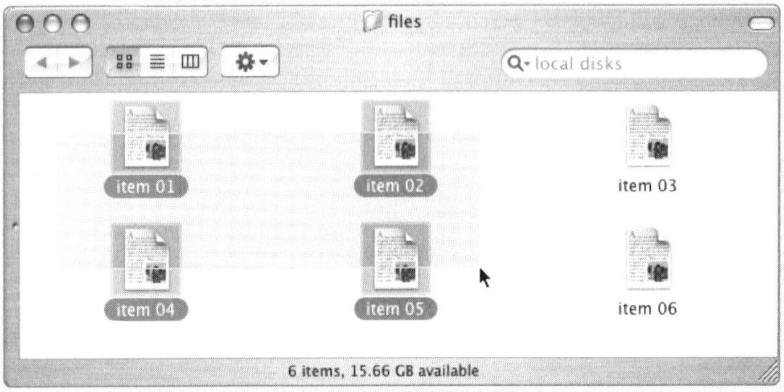

Use a marquee–Click and drag your mouse around a few files to create what's referred to as a marquee. Dragging a marquee around items in **Icon** view allows you to select multiple items. You can drag in **List** and **Column** views as well, but no marquee appears. Just be sure not to click directly on a file when you want to drag a marquee; otherwise, you'll end up dragging the file itself around.

Select All–If you need to select the entire contents of a folder, choose **Edit > Select All** from the menu bar, or press **Cmd+A** on your keyboard.

MOVIE | multiple_selections.mov

See the movie **multiple_selections.mov** on the **H•O•T CD-ROM** for a demonstration of these techniques.

*Before you delete the **letter to the editor** file, you'll first make a copy of it on your **Desktop**.*

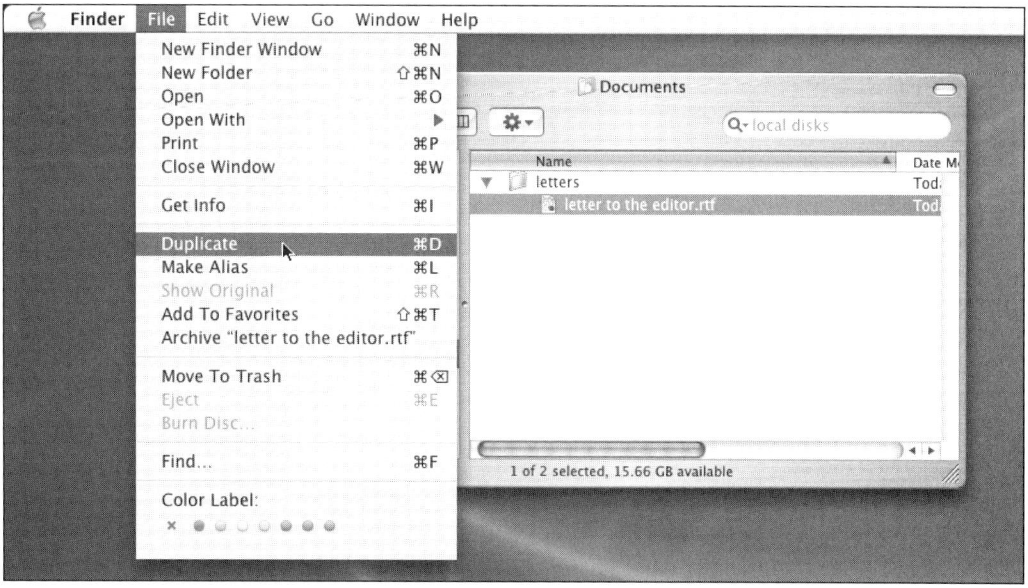

14. Click once on **letter to the editor** to select it. From the menu bar, choose **File > Duplicate**. This creates an exact copy of the file in the **letters** folder.

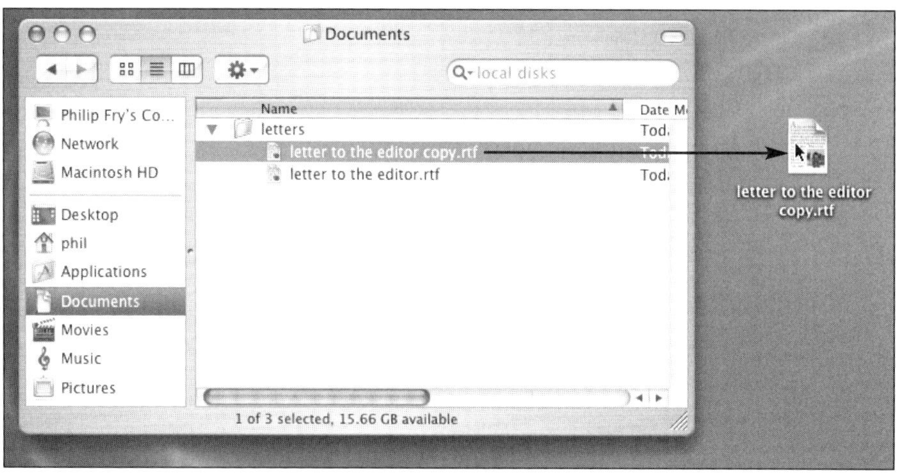

15. Drag **letter to the editor copy** to the **Desktop**. You now have a copy of this letter on your **Desktop** so you're free to delete the one in your **Documents** folder.

Copy by Dragging

Instead of selecting a file and choosing **File > Duplicate**, you can instantly copy a file by holding down the **Option** key and dragging the file to your preferred destination. The big green plus symbol indicates that you're copying the file. Be sure to release the mouse button before releasing the **Option** key. Otherwise, you'll just be moving the file instead of copying it.

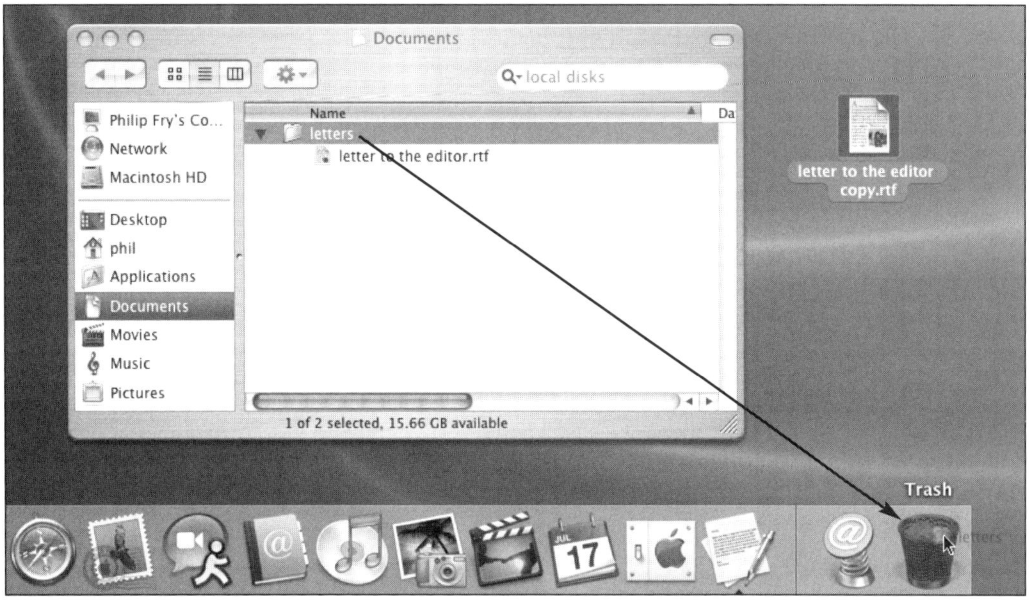

16. Drag the **letters** folder to the **Trash**. Your **Documents** folder is now back to the way it was before you started this chapter.

Now you're ready to empty the Trash. Remember, before emptying the Trash, you can always retrieve any of its contents by clicking the Trash icon and dragging out the files you want. After emptying the Trash, the files contained in it are gone for good (unlike say, emptying your kitchen trash, where there always seem to be some leftovers clinging to the bottom of the wastebasket).

---

17. From the menu bar, choose **Finder > Empty Trash**.

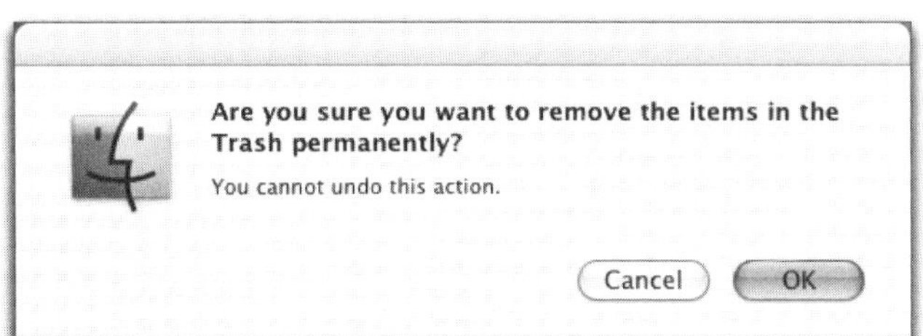

A dialog box appears asking if you're sure that you want to delete the items contained in the Trash. (If you don't see this dialog box, someone, possibly you, has turned off this feature. See "Setting Finder Preferences" at the end of this chapter to learn how to turn it back on.)

18. Click **OK**. The files are deleted and the **Trash** icon returns to its "empty" appearance. It's important to reiterate that once you empty the **Trash**, the files are really gone. Always make sure that you know what's in the **Trash** by clicking on the **Trash** icon before emptying it.

*Now you'll get rid of the **letter to the editor copy** on your **Desktop**.*

---

19. Click once on **letter to the editor copy** to select it. An alternative to dragging an item to the Trash is to press **Cmd+Delete** on your keyboard. Press **Cmd+Delete** to move this file to the **Trash**.

Now you'll empty the Trash again.

20. This time, hold the **Ctrl** key on your keyboard and click the **Trash** icon. This will open a contextual menu, allowing you empty the Trash from here, rather than choosing **Finder > Empty Trash**. Select **Empty Trash** to delete the file.

---

21. Close any open windows on the **Desktop**.

Really Emptying the Trash

Okay, I lied. When you empty the Trash, there's a slight possibility that the data you "deleted" can be recovered. Normally when you empty the Trash, the files there are just removed from your Mac's directory, meaning that they still exist, but you've given the system the okay to write over them with new information. If you don't save or move any other files after emptying the Trash, there's a good chance that the data can be brought back by data recovery software, such as Norton Utilities. This can be a good thing if you accidentally erased a vital file and need to get it back. Professional data recovery businesses charge big bucks for recovering deleted files. (You can find their ads at the back of most computer magazines.)

But this also means that other, more disreputable people could also get at your so-called "erased" data. Stories abound of credit card numbers and other personal information being harvested from junked computers that had supposedly been erased. Luckily, Panther comes with a new feature called **Secure Empty Trash**. If you want to ensure that your erased files can't be recovered, choose **File > Secure Empty Trash**. This command writes random bits of data over the old data, completely eradicating the file. Depending on how many files are in the Trash, this process might take a little longer than simply emptying the Trash, but it gives you the security of knowing that the files are really gone.

Contextual Menus

As you've seen in this chapter, contextual menus are often a convenient way of accessing common commands without having to use the menu bar. Sometimes it's much quicker to Ctrl+click the file you're working with than it is to first select the file, and then move the mouse to another part of the screen just to select a command. Try Ctrl+clicking some items around your Desktop. You'll find many of the commands that have been covered in this chapter are available as contextual menu commands.

If you like this feature, you may want to invest in a multibutton mouse. Many third-party mice are available today, and they allow you to program their buttons to act as a Ctrl+click so you can single-handedly access contextual menus.

Also remember that Panther's new Action button in the Finder window doubles as a Ctrl+click for a selected item most of the time.

Setting Finder Preferences

Now that you're accustomed to the Finder, and you're aware of how many of its features work, you can examine some ways of customizing its settings. Select **Finder > Preferences** to open the **Finder Preferences** window.

The Finder preferences are divided into four categories. Click one of the four buttons at the top of the window to display a different selection of options. The following chart describes the items found in each category's window.

Finder Preferences

General

Item	Description
Show these items on the Desktop	By checking or unchecking the three boxes found below this heading, you can choose whether you want to see the icons for hard drives, removable media (such as CDs, DVDs, and ZIP disks), and connected servers on the Desktop. Some users prefer to keep the Desktop as uncluttered as possible and choose not to have any of these items appear on the Desktop. Instead, they access them through Finder windows.
New Finder windows open	Click the menu below to determine what's displayed anytime you open a new window in the Finder (by selecting **File > New Window** or by pressing **Cmd+N**).
Always open folders in a new window	This is the favorite item for fans of the classic Mac OS. Checking this item will make new windows open for every folder you double-click.
Open new windows in column view	If this item is checked, choosing **File > New Window** from the menu bar will display the window in Column view.
Spring-loaded folders and windows	You can choose to activate or deactivate spring-loaded folders by checking or unchecking this item. When checked, the **Delay** slider determines how long you have to hold an item over a folder before it springs open.

Labels

Item	Description
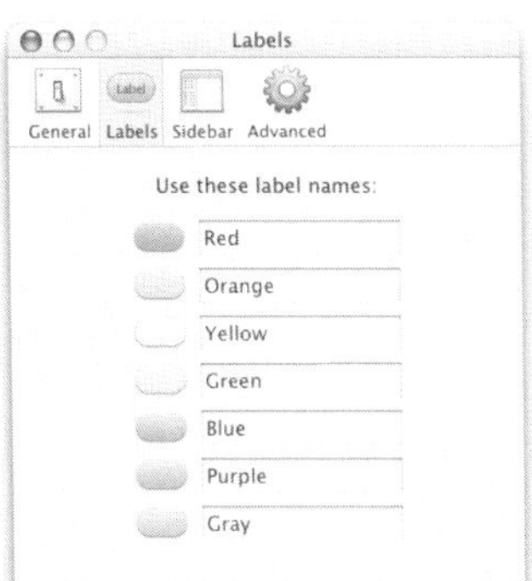	Under the Labels section of the Finder preferences, you can rename the colored labels with names that might be more useful to you. For instance, you could name the colors to associate them with certain projects you're working on. Or if you wanted to be retro, you could give them the names of labels from the pre–OS X days: Essential, Hot, In Progress, Cool, Personal, Project 1, and Project 2.

continues on next page

Finder Preferences *continued*

SIDEBAR

Item	Description
	Under the Sidebar section of Finder preferences, you can check or uncheck boxes to determine which items appear in the Places sidebar. This area can be especially useful as your sidebar begins to fill up with your personal items. By opening the Sidebar preferences, you can choose not to display the icons for items you rarely use, leaving more space for your own items.

ADVANCED

Item	Description
Show all file extensions 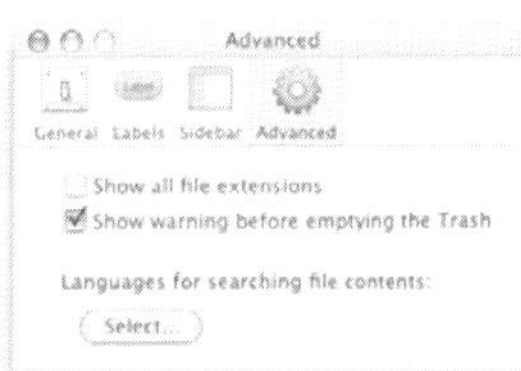	Check this if you prefer to see the file extensions for your files. Extensions are the three- or four-letter suffixes at the end of file names. For example, .gif, .jpg, .txt, and so on. OS X hides these from you by default.
Show warning before emptying the Trash	You can uncheck this item if you always want the Trash to immediately empty itself when you choose Empty Trash. When checked, you'll see the dialog box asking if you're sure that you want to empty the Trash. Be careful if this option is unchecked—you won't get another chance to view the Trash's contents before they're deleted.
Languages for searching file contents	Click the **Select** button to choose the languages you want to use when searching your hard drive for files. The fewer languages you choose, the faster the searches will be, and the more disk space you'll save. You may want to click the **Select** button and deselect some languages you're sure you'll never search for.

Working with External Media

Although this chapter covered working with files directly from your hard drive, you'll no doubt find yourself working with other types of media, such as CD-ROMs, ZIP disks, or external drives, quite often. Fortunately, working with these types of media and devices is not that much different than working with your hard drive. When you insert a CD-ROM or any type of disk, or when you attach an external hard drive, the item's icon will show up on your Desktop or in the Places sidebar (depending on how your Finder Preferences have been set) where you can then click it to view its contents, or drag files to and from it (unless it's a CD-ROM in which case you'll only be able to copy files from it). You'll learn more about copying and moving files between drives in later chapters.

In this chapter, you learned how to work with files, folders, and applications. The next chapter takes a close look at the Dock and shows you how to make the most out of this unique OS X feature.

3. Using the Dock

| Opening Applications from the Dock |

| Adding Items to the Dock | Setting Dock Preferences |

no exercise files

Mac OS X Panther
H•O•T CD-ROM

When Mac OS X debuted, one of the operating system's most prominent new features was the Dock. If you're familiar with pre–OS X versions of the Mac operating system, you'll notice that the Dock combines the features of both the old Apple menu and the old Application menu into the single strip of icons you see on your screen. Initially, some Mac users complained about the Dock: It takes up too much space on the Desktop, it looks clunky, it's new and different and I don't accept change very well, and so on. But after learning to use the Dock properly, most users can't believe that they ever got along without it.

In the previous chapter, you had some brief interaction with the Dock. You saw how application icons appeared in the Dock when the program was running and how they disappeared when you quit the application. You also learned to delete files by dragging them to the Trash icon in the Dock. This chapter takes a detailed look at the Dock. You'll not only learn how to use it, but you'll also find out how to customize it to best suit your purposes. As in the previous chapter, the exercises in this chapter use items already found on your Mac, so there are no files to copy from the **H•O•T CD-ROM**.

I. Opening Applications from the Dock

One of the primary purposes of the Dock is to provide you with a means of quickly opening applications and folders without having to double-click your hard drive icons and drill down through the various levels of folders until you find the item you're looking for. Although the addition of the Places sidebar in Panther makes it easier to get to many of your destinations quickly, you still have to open a Finder window to get to the sidebar. The Dock, however, is always on the Desktop, keeping your most important applications and files just one click away. In fact, once you get comfortable with the Dock and customize it to suit your needs, you may never need to double-click your hard drive icon again. In this exercise, you'll open some of the default items that Apple has placed in the Dock for your convenience.

1. Take a look at the Dock. As you saw in the last chapter, active applications are indicated by the small, black triangle found underneath the application's icon. (The one application that's always running in OS X is the Finder, which is why you always see the black triangle under the Finder's icon.)

When you roll your mouse over the icons in the Dock, the names of the Docked items immediately appear. To open any items in the Dock, all you need is a single click.

2. Click the icon for **Address Book**. Its icon begins to bounce, letting you know that the application is starting up. (If the icon doesn't bounce, this preference has been changed on your Mac. You'll learn how to change it back later.)

Tip: *Break (or try not to develop) the habit of double-clicking icons in the Dock. Although it's harmless, it's also completely unnecessary. Plus, it makes you look like an amateur to snooty Mac users.*

Once the application is open, the icon stops bouncing, and the black triangle appears beneath it.

Note: *If you haven't used your Address Book before, you'll probably see only your own name and Apple Computer's address listed here. You'll learn how to use this application and add more names in Chapter 10* "Address Book, Mail, and iChat AV."

Now you'll open a second application from the Dock.

3. Click the **iCal** icon. The icon bounces for a second and then the main **iCal** window appears. You won't be doing anything in iCal yet; you'll learn all about this great app in Chapter 13, "*iCal and iSync*."

You now have both Address Book and iCal running simultaneously, with iCal being the current application. Theoretically, you could continue opening applications from the Dock to your heart's (or your RAM's) content (whichever fills up first).

Now you'll quit these applications.

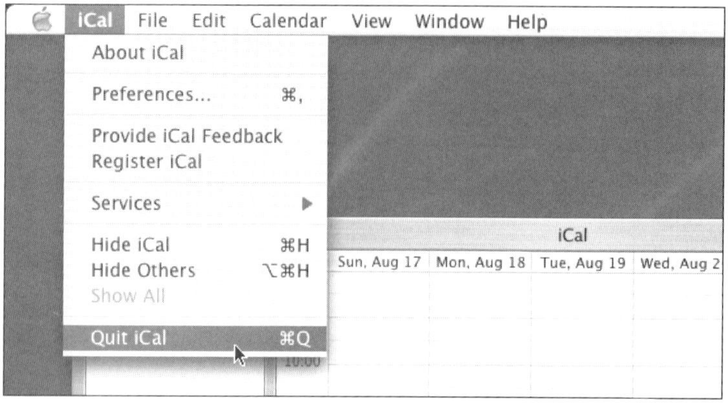

4. Choose **iCal > Quit iCal** from the menu bar to quit, you guessed it, iCal. The **iCal** window immediately closes and the triangle underneath its Dock icon disappears. For you pre–OS X Mac veterans, note that instead of the generic **File > Quit** command you're familiar with, the OS X menu commands are designed to let you know exactly which application you're quitting. The keyboard command, however, is still the same: **Cmd+Q**.

You're left with Address Book as the current application. Instead of using the menu bar command to quit this program, you'll use a contextual menu in the Dock.

5. Ctrl+click the **Address Book** icon in the **Dock** to view its contextual menu. Choose **Quit**.

As you learned in the last chapter, there is usually little need to quit an application in OS X unless you're sure that you won't need it again for a while. You can just leave all your open applications running and switch back and forth between them as needed. But for the purposes of this exercise, it was important for you to learn the methods for quitting applications.

"Show In Finder" and "Force Quit"

So now you know how to quit an application by **Ctrl+clicking** its icon in the **Dock** and choosing **Quit**, but what other commands are available in that contextual menu? This contextual menu also contains a useful command called **Show In Finder** that reveals the true location of the item you're clicking on. When you select **Show In Finder**, a **Finder** window opens to display the folder in which the item is located.

Additionally, you can hold the **Option** key after **Ctrl+clicking** an icon to change the **Quit** command into the **Force Quit** command. This is very useful if you're dealing with an application that, for one reason or another, has stopped responding. Although Mac OS X itself is rock solid in terms of stability, occasional application crashes and freezes still occur. Use **Force Quit** to completely shut down the offending application. You'll be happy to know that unlike with pre–OS X Force Quit situations, you can continue to use other applications after Force Quitting without having to reboot your Mac. Just be aware that if you Force Quit, you will lose any unsaved changes you may have made to documents in use.

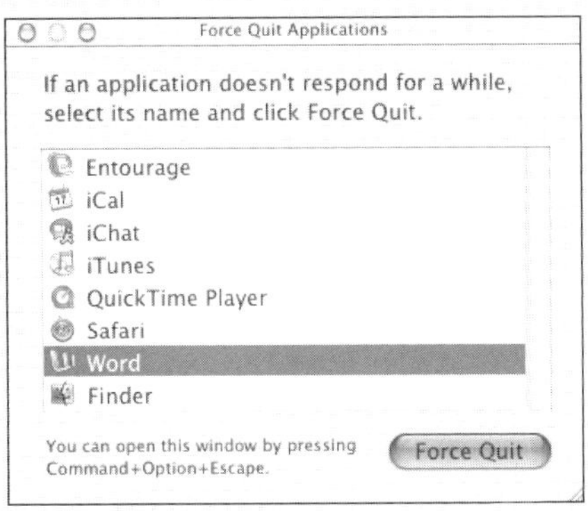

As with earlier versions of the operating system, you can still press **Option+Cmd+Esc** on your keyboard (the old three-finger salute) to Force Quit, but in OS X, this keyboard command opens a floating window that lists all applications presently running on the machine. Any unresponsive applications are highlighted in red.

2. Adding Items to the Dock

Apple's default selection of icons is a good introduction to using the Dock, but what good would the Dock be if you couldn't customize it to suit your needs? In this exercise, you'll learn how to add your own items to the Dock and how to remove the ones you no longer need.

1. Double-click your **hard drive** icon to open a **Finder** window. Open the **Applications** folder.

There are a couple of ways to add an item to the Dock. One way is to drag an application's icon directly to the Dock. It doesn't matter which view your window is in (Icon, List, or Column), but Icon view might make it easier for you to manipulate the icon.

Before you drag your first icon to the Dock, take a closer look at the Dock itself. Notice the thin dividing line near the right side? The Dock is actually separated into two sections: The left side of the Dock is for application icons; the right side of the Dock is for folders, files, and minimized windows. This an important point to remember: You can only drag application icons to the left of the dividing line.

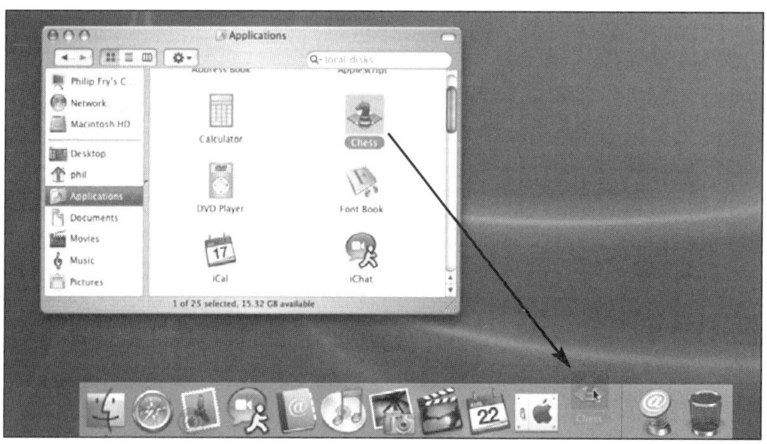

2. Locate the **Chess** application's icon and drag it to the **Dock**. Without letting go of the mouse button, first drag it to the right side of the divider line, and notice that the icons there don't move. The most that might happen is that the **Trash** icon is highlighted (but don't throw **Chess** away!). Now drag the **Chess** icon to the left of the divider line. All the other application icons move over and make room for it. You can place the **Chess** icon anywhere except to the left of the **Finder** icon. Place the **Chess** icon immediately to the left of the divider line.

Congratulations, you've successfully added your first item to the Dock. Now you can easily access the Chess game from the Dock without having to navigate through your hard drive.

3. Click the **Chess** icon in the **Dock** to start the **Chess** application. After you've seen the program open, choose **Chess > Quit Chess**.

Tip: *Once you've placed an icon in the Dock, you can always move it to another location in the Dock simply by dragging it between two other icons. You can continue to add as many items to the Dock as you like. Don't worry about running out of room; as you add more items, the rest of the icons simply shrink to make more space.*

Now you'll take a look at another method for adding items to the Dock.

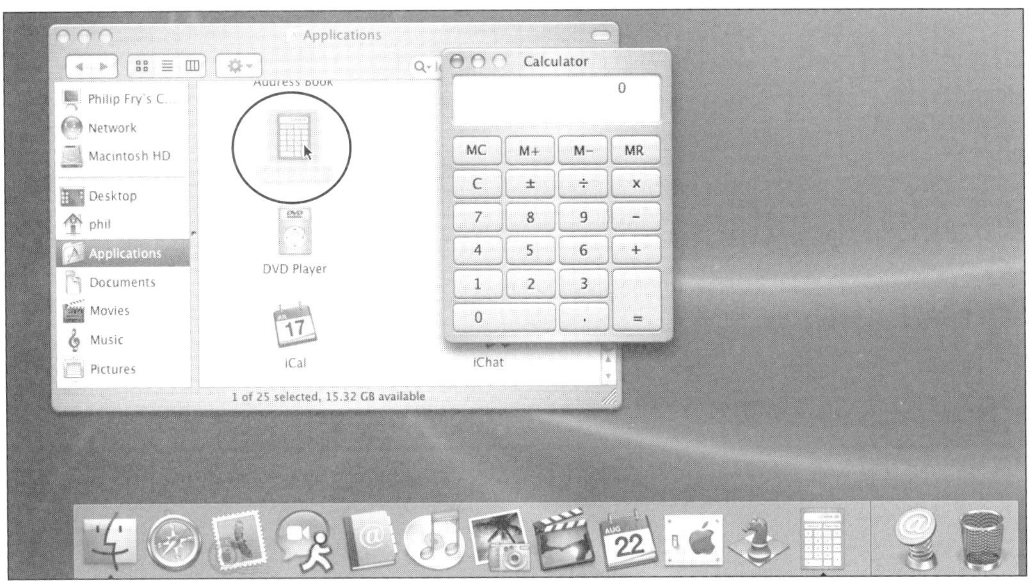

4. From the **Applications** window, double-click the **Calculator** application to open it.

There may be times when you're working with an application that you realize would be convenient to add to the Dock. For instance, you might find yourself frequently using the Calculator program. Since its icon is already in the Dock, you can choose to keep it there, rather than quitting the program and then dragging its icon to the Dock again.

5. Ctrl+click on the **Calculator** icon to open the contextual menu. In addition to the **Show in Finder**, **Hide**, and **Quit** commands, this menu also contains a command called **Keep in Dock**. This tells OS X that you want to keep this icon in the **Dock** even after you quit. Choose **Keep in Dock**.

6. Now quit **Calculator**. Notice that the black triangle underneath its icon disappears, yet the icon itself remains. You've now added your second item to the **Dock**.

Next, you'll add some folders to your Dock.

7. In the **Finder** window, click your **Home** button in the **Places** sidebar. If you closed the **Finder** window, remember that you can access the **Home** folder either by pressing **Cmd+Shift+H**, or by choosing **Go > Home** from the menu bar.

If you've decided to follow OS X's recommended structure for storing your personal files and documents, it might make sense to add some of the folders found in your Home folder to the Dock since you'll most likely be accessing them quite often. Because these are folders and not applications, they can only be placed to the right of the dividing line in the Dock.

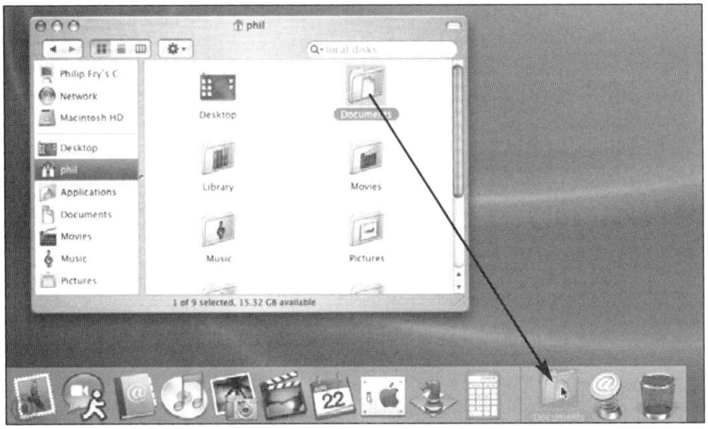

8. Drag the **Documents** folder to the right side of the dividing line. (If you want, try dragging it to the left of the dividing line and notice how none of the icons move out of the way. If you release the mouse with the icon to the left of the dividing line, the **Documents** icon just shoots back up to the **Finder** window.)

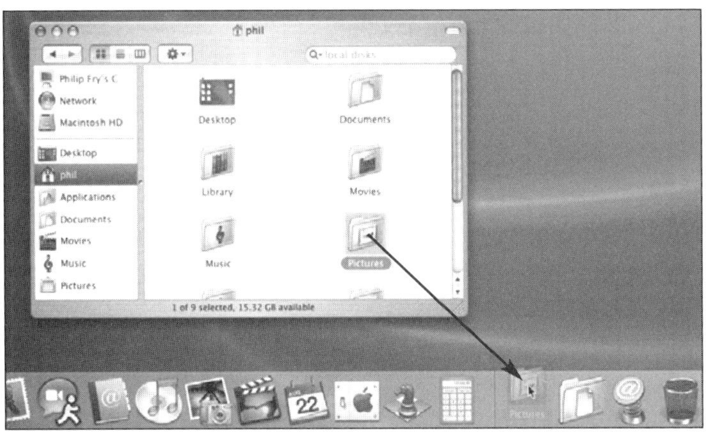

9. Next, drag the **Pictures** folder to the **Dock**. Notice that the icons in the **Dock** just keep making room every time you add another item.

As you can see, adding folders to the Dock isn't much different than adding applications; you just have to remember which items belong on which sides of the Dock.

Another important point to note is that when you add an item to the Dock, you aren't adding the actual application or the actual folder itself. You're merely adding a shortcut to the item into the Dock. For that reason, it's quick and painless to remove items from the Dock. To remove an item, all you have to do is drag it off the Dock. Next, you'll get rid of some of the icons you recently added to the Dock.

10. Drag the **Chess** icon up and off the **Dock**. As soon as you release the mouse, the icon disappears in a puff of smoke (cute, huh?). The remaining icons in the **Dock** resize and move to fill the empty space.

It's important to note here that by dragging the Chess icon off the Dock, you did absolutely nothing to the Chess application itself. You just removed its shortcut from the Dock; the application itself is still sitting safe and sound in the Applications folder. You can't undo the action of removing an icon from the Dock, but as you now know, it's a simple matter to add an icon to the Dock.

Next, you'll remove the two folders you added to the Dock and replace them with your Home folder.

---

11. Drag the icons for the **Documents** and **Pictures** folders off the **Dock**.

*At this point your Home folder should still be open on the Desktop. If it isn't, choose **Go > Home** from the menu bar.*

Because your Home folder contains so many of the folders you'll be accessing, you'll add it to the Dock. But how do you add an open window to the Dock? One way would be to double-click your hard drive, open your Users folder, and then drag the Home icon to the Dock. But as you've probably already guessed, there's an easier way.

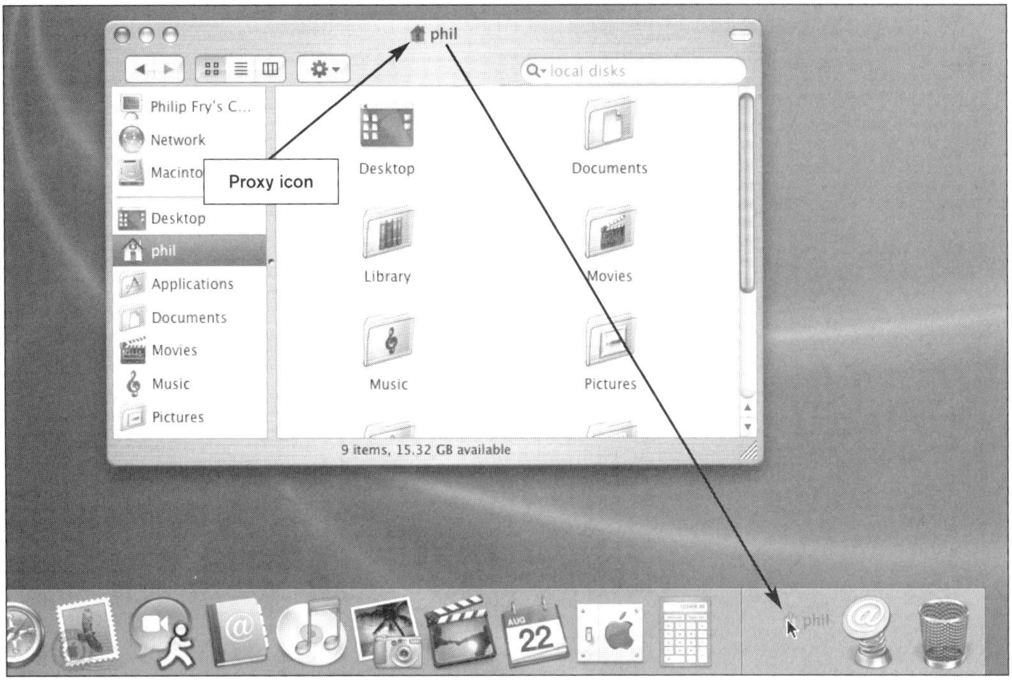

12. Drag the open window's icon (also known as the **proxy icon**) in the title bar directly to the **Dock**. There's a trick to this: Click and hold your mouse down on the icon (not your name, but the icon itself), then wait a moment before dragging. If you drag right away, you'll move the entire window. If you click, pause, and then drag, you should be able to pull the icon and its name right off the title bar and onto the **Dock**. Because this is a folder, it must be placed to the right of the **Dock's** dividing line.

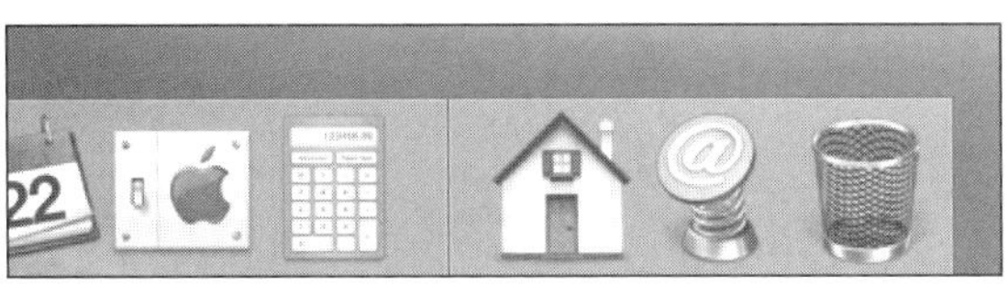

With the Home folder added to the Dock, you now have a way to immediately access its contents.

13. Close the **Home** window and any other windows that may be open.

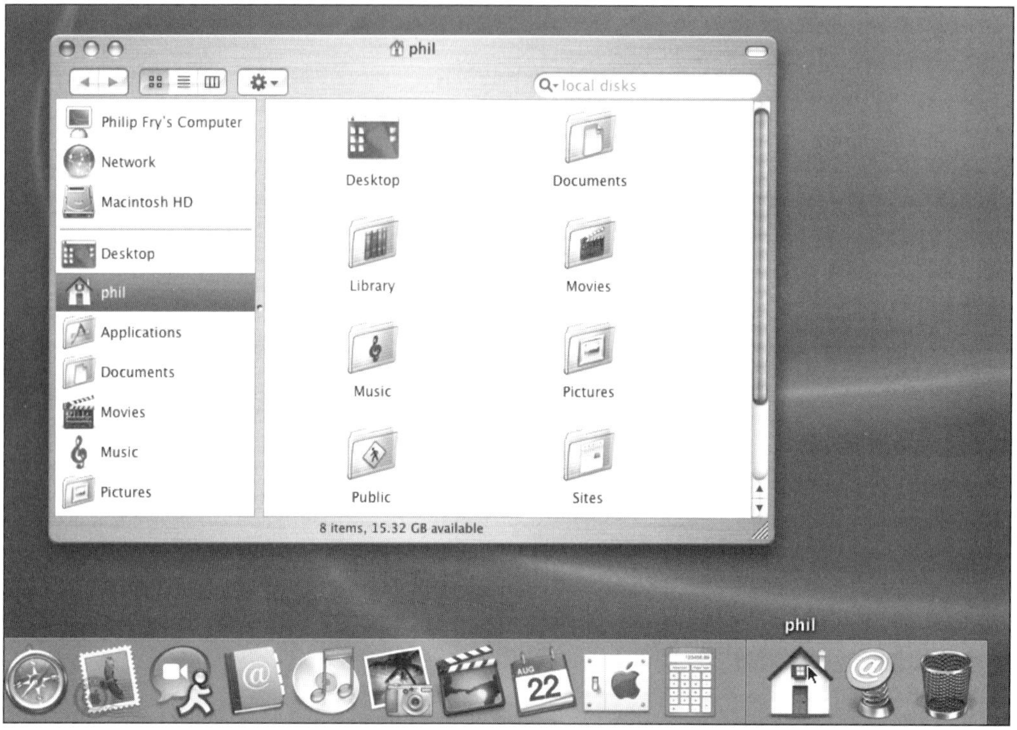

14. Click on the **Home** folder to view its contents in a **Finder** window. Obviously, you could now continue to double-click on the folders in this window to find the items you need. But in addition to quick access, another advantage of working with docked folders is the ability to navigate them using contextual menus.

15. Close the **Home** window.

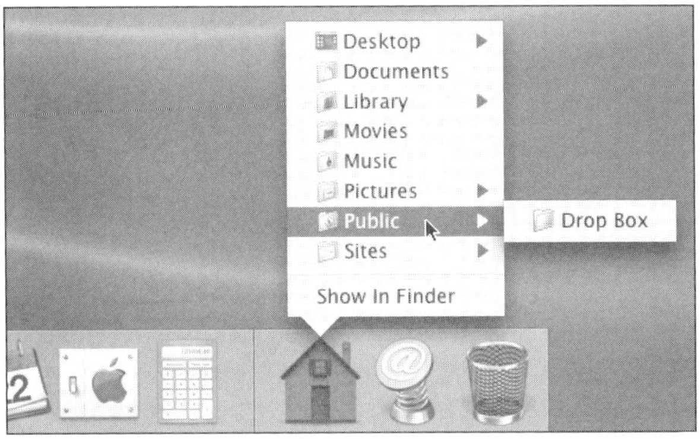

16. Click on the **Home** icon in the **Dock** and keep the mouse button pressed down. In a moment, the contextual menu appears showing you the contents of this folder. You can now search the folder simply by moving your mouse up and down the list.

*Tip: You can **Ctrl+click** a docked folder to immediately open its contextual menu.*

---

17. Click anywhere on the **Desktop** to close the contextual menu.

By now, you should have a pretty good idea of what the Dock is all about and how it can be used. The next exercise will show you how you can customize the behavior and appearance of the Dock to best suit your needs.

NOTE | Question Mark in the Dock

When you delete a file, folder, or application on your hard drive that has an icon in the Dock, the icon changes to a question mark, indicating that the Dock can't find the item. To remove this icon, just drag it off the Dock.

3. Setting Dock Preferences

In this exercise, you'll learn which options are available for customizing your Mac's Dock. Upon the initial release of Mac OS X, Apple understandably wanted to show off the visual capabilities of the Dock. The Dock's default actions had its icons magnifying and moving and generally eating up a lot of processor cycles, especially on older Macs. Although these visual treats are all still available in Panther, they're no longer the default preferences.

To see and alter the Dock options, you need to open the Dock Preferences control panel.

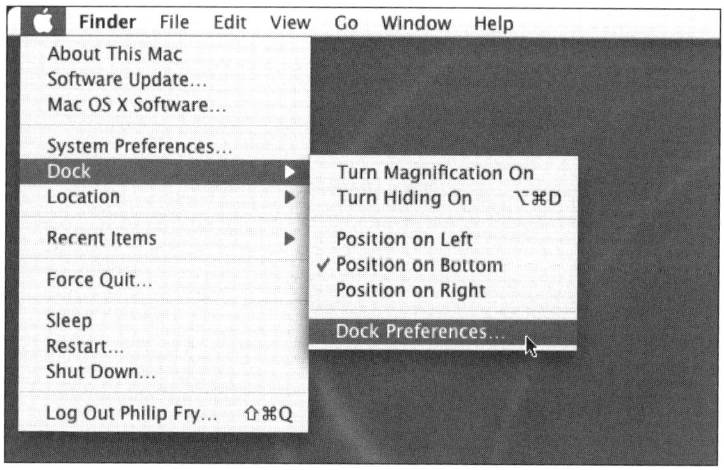

1. From the **Apple** menu in the menu bar, choose **Dock > Dock Preferences**. Although the **Dock** menu does contain some commands for modifying the **Dock**, **Dock Preferences** shows you all of the available **Dock** options. (This command actually opens the **Dock** pane of the **System Preferences** application. You'll learn all about system preferences in the next chapter.) This exercise walks you through each option so you can get some hands-on training in Dock customization.

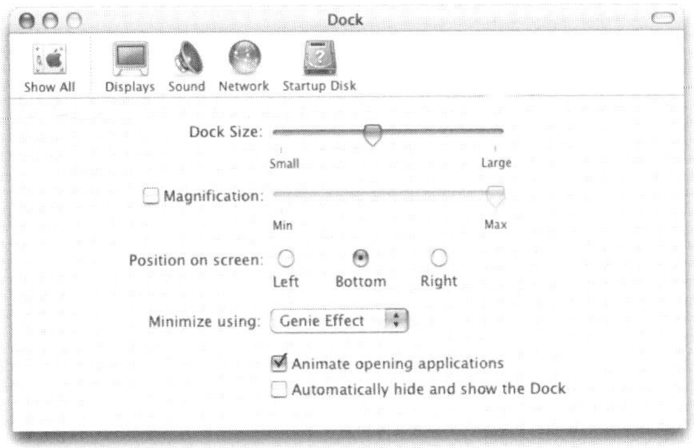

The great thing about working with the Dock Preferences panel is that you can immediately see the effects of your changes without having to first close the control panel. The next few steps will explain the different options available.

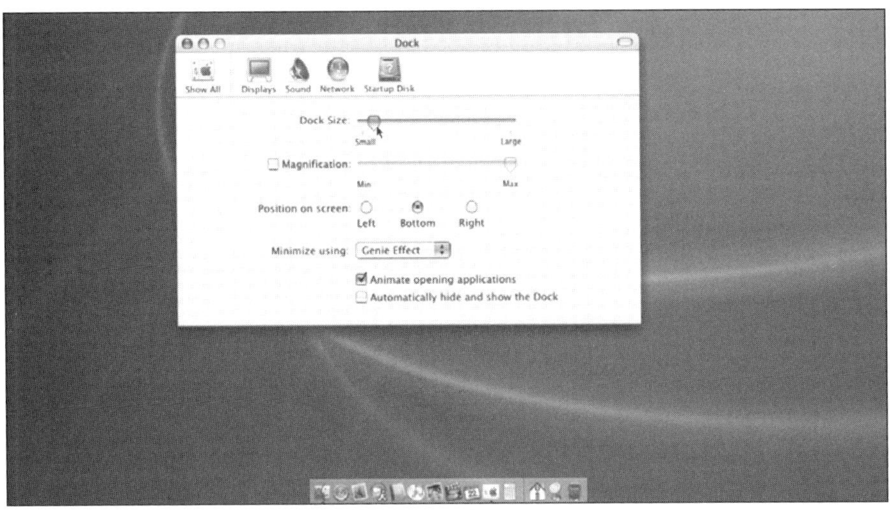

2. Move the **Dock Size** slider back and forth. Notice that the **Dock** immediately changes sizes based on the position of your slider. Many users prefer to keep the **Dock** as small and as unobtrusive as possible; others like to have big honkin' icons to click. Size the **Dock** any way you like–you can always resize it again later if you change your mind. (Note: "Big honkin' icons" do not actually honk.)

If you do decide to keep the Dock small, you may find turning on the Magnification setting to be useful. The magnification setting enlarges the size of each icon as the mouse rolls over it to make it easier to click. In previous versions of OS X, magnification was on by default, but in Panther, it has been turned off. Some people find this effect annoying and feel that it actually makes it more difficult to click the icon you want. You'll have to judge for yourself.

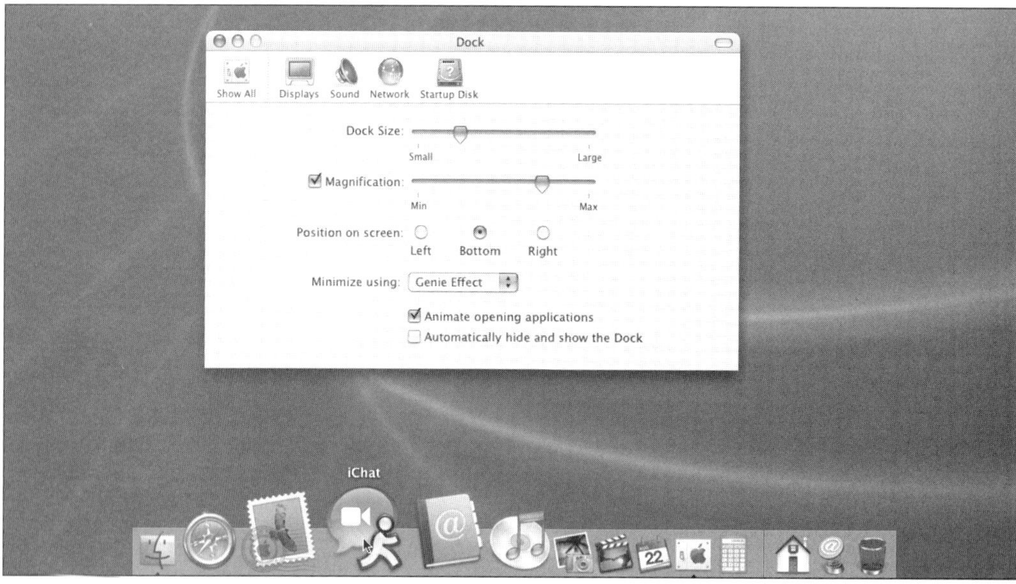

3. Check the **Magnification** check box and place the slider so that it is further to the right than your **Dock Size** slider (otherwise, you won't see any magnification at all) The more distance between the two sliders, the more dramatic the magnification effect will be. Now roll the mouse over the **Dock** to see the magnification effect.

Whether you're a fan of Magnification or not, you still have to admit that OS X does an amazing job of keeping the icons smooth and sharp even at the largest settings.

The next option for the Dock allows you to change its location on your screen. You may find that the Dock sometimes gets in your way at the bottom of the screen or that you simply don't like it there. You have the choice of moving the Dock to a vertical position on either the left or right side of your screen.

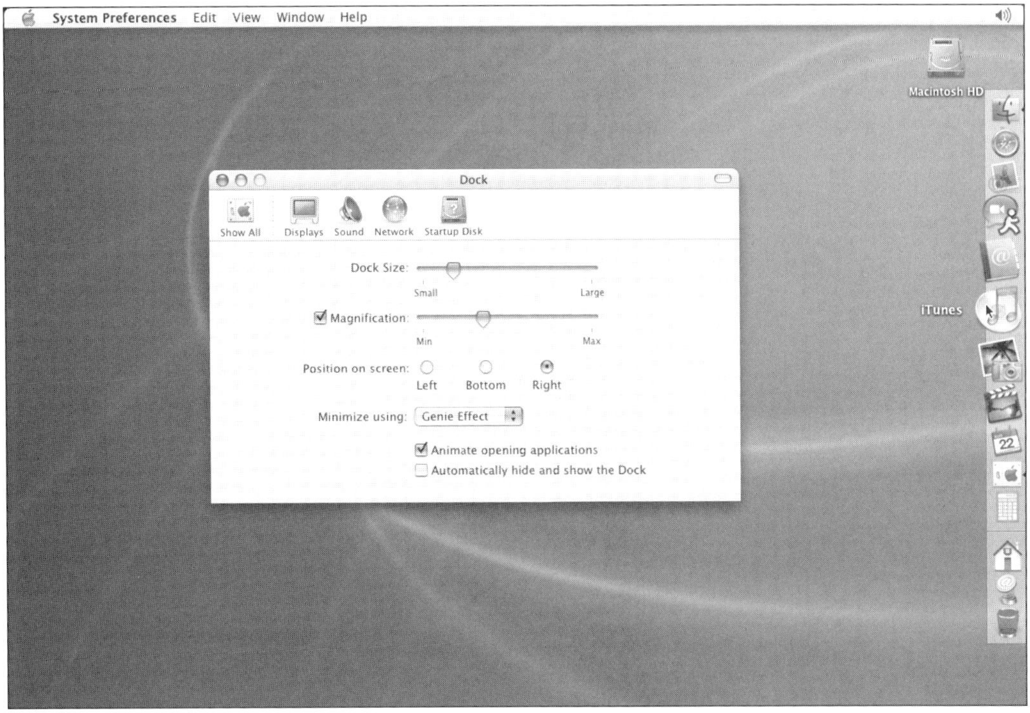

4. Click either the **Left** or **Right** button next to the **Position on screen** setting. Notice that your **Dock Size** and **Magnification** settings remain unchanged and still work the same as they did when the Dock was on the bottom of the screen. You may find, however, that you now need to tweak these settings to adjust to the **Dock's** new location.

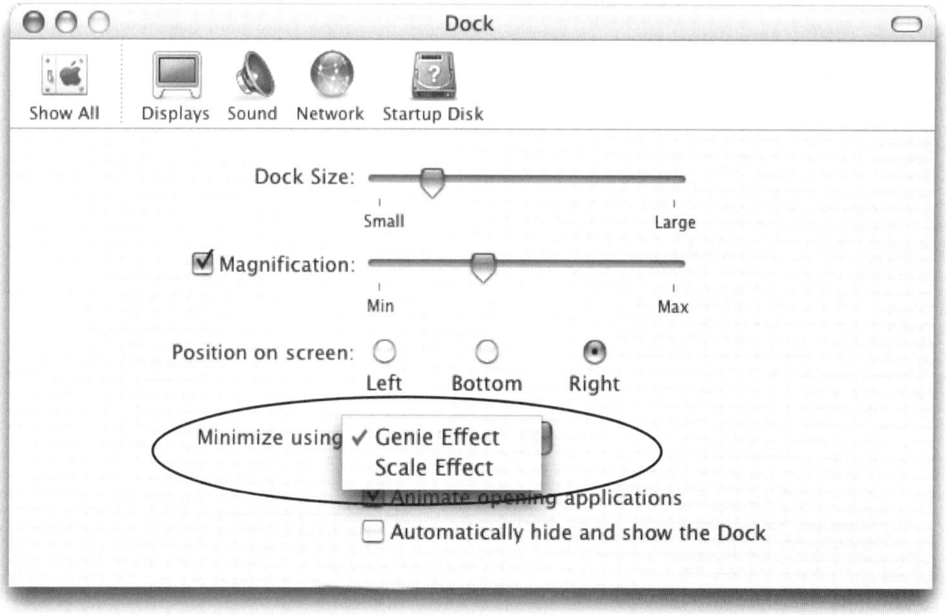

The next option in Dock Preferences is the Minimize effect. You have a choice of two options here: ***Genie Effect*** *and* ***Scale Effect****. You already saw the Genie effect in Chapter 2,* "Working with Files and Folders," *when you clicked a window's minimize button to see the window get "sucked" into the Dock. Granted the Genie effect looks pretty cool, but it's also fairly processor-intensive. If you're using an older Mac, or if you feel the Genie effect "sucks" in more ways than one, you can switch to the Scale effect.*

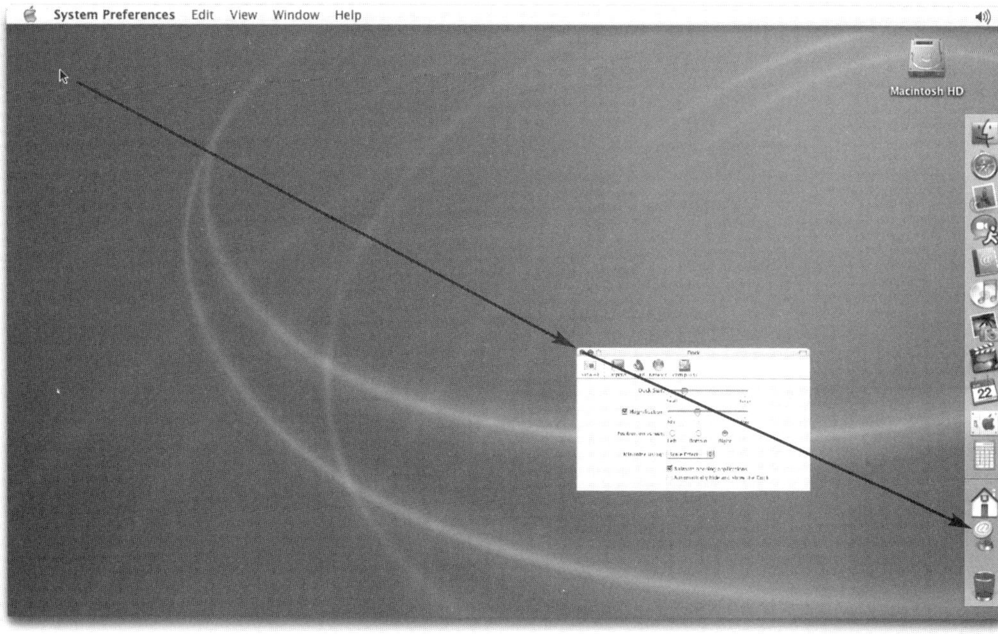

5. Select **Scale Effect** and click the **Minimize** button at the top of the window. The window quickly shrinks into the **Dock** without any showy display. Click the minimized icon to bring the **Dock Preferences** window back.

There are two remaining options in Dock Preferences:

- *The* ***Animate opening applications*** *selection determines whether or not you see the icon bounce in the Dock when you start up an application. Unchecking this selection leaves the icon perfectly still with no indication that the program is starting. (You will still see the black triangle under the icon when the application opens.)*
- *The* ***Automatically hide and show the Dock*** *selection is there for the people who really, really think the Dock gets in the way.*

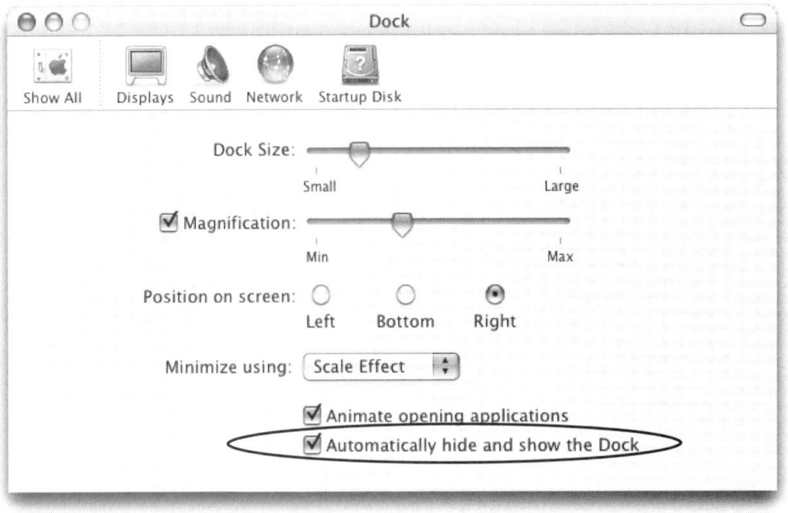

6. Check **Automatically hide and show the Dock**. The **Dock** immediately disappears. The **Dock** will now appear only when you move your mouse to the side of the screen where the **Dock** was positioned.

7. Roll the mouse to the area where you last placed the **Dock**. The **Dock** appears to slide into view. Move your mouse away, and the **Dock** retreats from view again.

So now you know all the things you can do to the Dock to make it easier for you to work with. It's really a matter of personal choice: There's no one right way to set up your Dock.

8. Take a moment to reset the preferences any way you like. When you're done, choose **System Preferences > Quit System Preferences**.

MOVIE | dock.mov

See the movie **dock.mov** on the **H•O•T CD-ROM** for a demonstration of the exercises in this chapter.

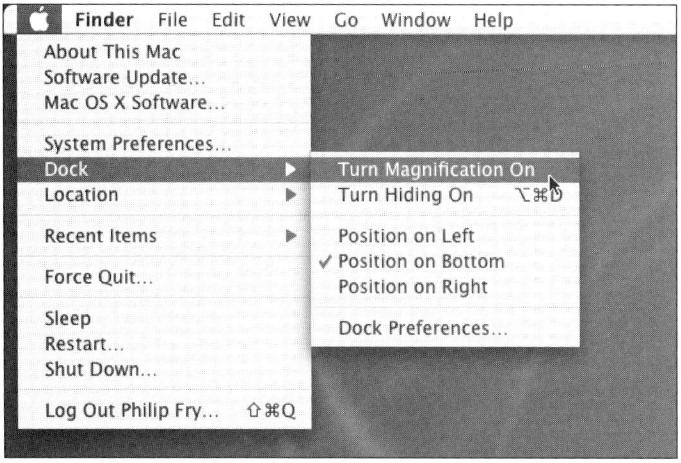

Tip: *As you probably noticed earlier, you can access some of the Dock options directly from the Apple menu without opening Dock Preferences. Choose* ***Apple menu > Dock*** *to turn Magnification and Hiding on and off, and to change the location of the Dock.*

More Dock Tricks

Here are some other ways you can use the Dock to make your life easier.

- **Option+click** an active application's icon in the **Dock** to hide all of its open windows. Click the icon again to bring the windows back.
- Drag documents and files directly onto application icons. For instance, if you have an image that you want to open in Adobe Photoshop instead of Apple's Preview application, drag the file's icon directly over the Photoshop icon to launch Photoshop and open the file.
- From your **Home** folder, drag the **Desktop** folder icon to the right side of the **Dock**. This will give you easy access to any items contained on your Desktop when it's obscured by other applications. This is a very useful trick if you often download items from the Internet onto your Desktop.

This chapter provided you with the most important information concerning the Dock, but as you progress through the book, you'll continue to learn many of the Dock's other capabilities.

---

4. System Preferences

Opening System Preferences	Appearance Preferences
Desktop & Screen Saver	Exposé
Burning a Data CD	Energy Saver	Keyboard and Mouse
Sound	QuickTime	Accounts	Classic	Date & Time

no exercise files

Mac OS X Panther
H•O•T CD-ROM

If you're a pre–OS X Mac user, you're most likely accustomed to adjusting system preferences by selecting Apple menu > Control Panels to choose from a long list of options. OS X has streamlined managing your preferences by placing them all in one central application called **System Preferences**. System Preferences contains the panes for adjusting nearly every aspect of your Mac's day-to-day operating behavior and appearance. The changes and adjustments you make here affect all aspects of your Mac. Panther has added several new panes to System Preferences, so even if you're familiar with earlier versions of System Preferences, be sure to read through this chapter to find out what's new.

In this chapter, you'll be taking a look at each System Preference pane. Although not every pane has its own step-by-step exercises, each one is addressed and described. In certain cases, a brief description is all that's needed. You won't be working with some of the panes, such as the ones for setting Internet preferences and sharing settings, just yet; they will be covered in their own chapters later in the book. But by the time you reach the end of this chapter, you will have a clear understanding of exactly what the System Preferences application allows you to do.

I. Opening System Preferences

Whether you're working on a fresh-from-the-box G5 or you've just installed OS X on your old PowerBook, sooner or later you'll have to open System Preferences to change some settings. In this exercise, you'll learn how to open System Preferences and how to call up and dismiss preference panes.

There are three ways to get to your System Preferences. One way is to double-click your hard drive, navigate to your Applications folder, and double-click System Preferences. This is known as the Slow Way. Alternately, you could choose Apple Menu > System Preferences, which is a little quicker. But the fastest and easiest way to get to you System Preferences is to simply click the System Preferences icon in the Dock.

1. Since you want to be as efficient as possible (right?), click the **System Preferences** icon in the **Dock** to open the **System Preferences** application.

*In the initial release of OS X, the System Preferences window was cluttered with alphabetically arranged icons for all of the available control panes. In Panther, the icons are organized into four specific categories: **Personal**, **Hardware**, **Internet & Network**, and **System**, making it much easier to find the pane you're looking for.*

In another example of OS X's clean, efficient user interface, clicking on any of the icons here does not open a new window; instead, all the other icons disappear and the System Preferences window resizes to fit the contents of the selected control pane. Try it out:

2. Click the **Dock** icon. (You've seen this one before.)

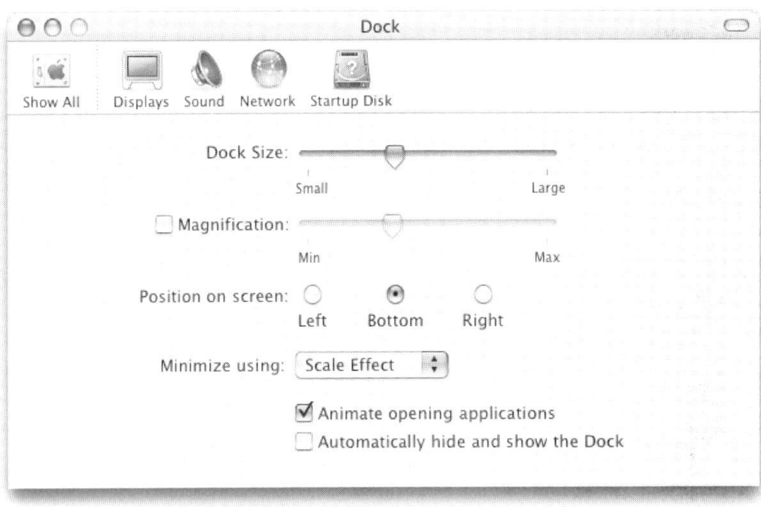

You'll see a brief animation of the window resizing itself, and then the current Dock settings will appear. You're now free to alter any settings you wish.

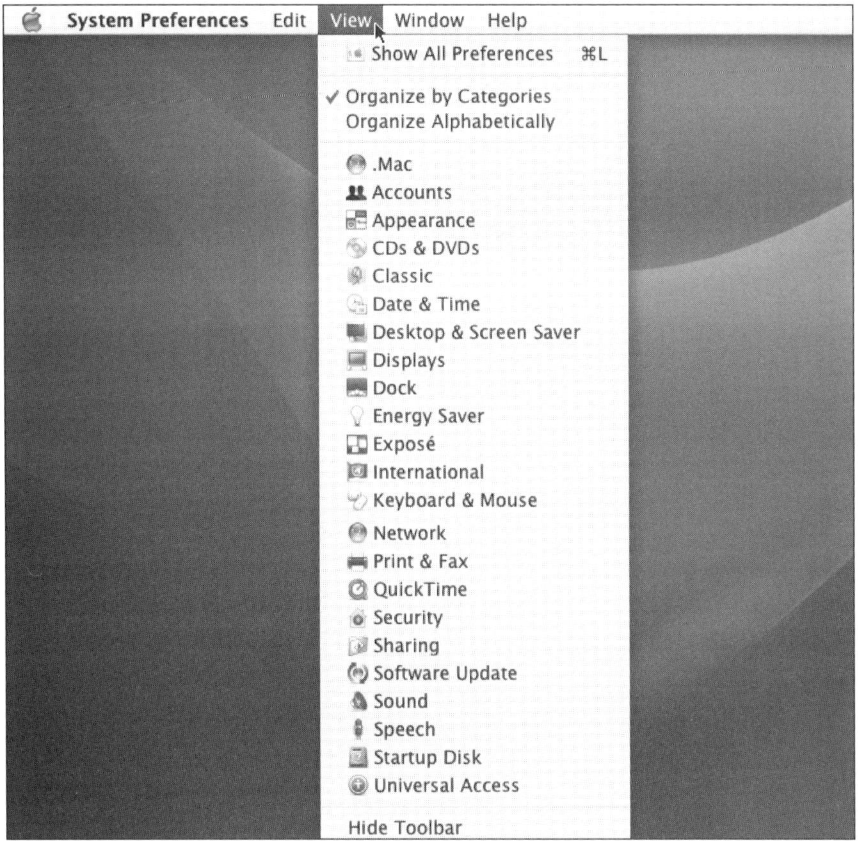

***Tip:** Alternatively, you can jump to any specific control pane from the **View** menu in the menu bar. Choosing any of the items listed here will open its individual control pane. (By the way, if you want to see how the System Preferences window used to be arranged in OS 10.0, choose **View > Organize Alphabetically.** Then choose **View > Organize by Categories** to return to the categorical listing.)*

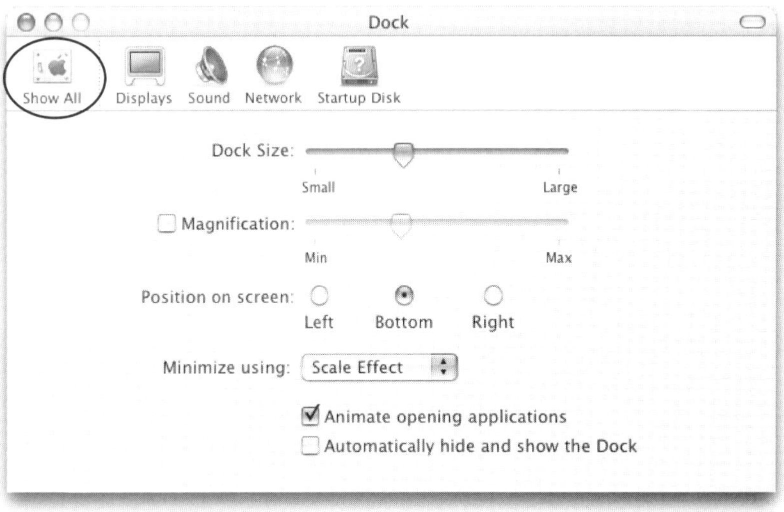

3. To return to the main System Preferences window, click the **Show All** button on the left side of the toolbar at the top of the window. The window again resizes to accommodate all of the preference icons.

Note: *Be sure to click Show All, not the Close button, if you want to return to the main System Preferences window. In Panther, clicking the Close button actually quits System Preferences, unlike earlier versions of OS X where clicking Close would close the window but leave System Preferences running.*

Now that you know how the System Preferences window works, in the following exercises you'll learn about the specific control panes it contains.

The System Preferences Toolbar

Clicking icons in the System Preferences window is an easy way to jump to a collection of settings, but if you find that you're always going back to a certain preference pane to make changes, it's probably a good idea to add that pane's icon to the System Preferences toolbar. For example, if you're always changing your Energy Saver settings, you might want to add its icon to the toolbar.

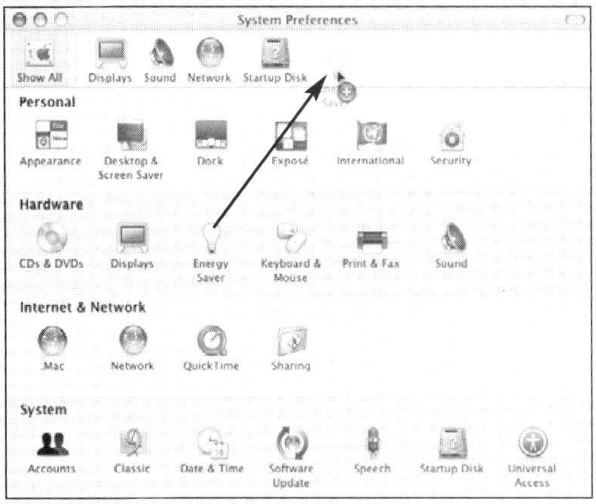

To do so, simply drag the control pane's icon into the toolbar and release.

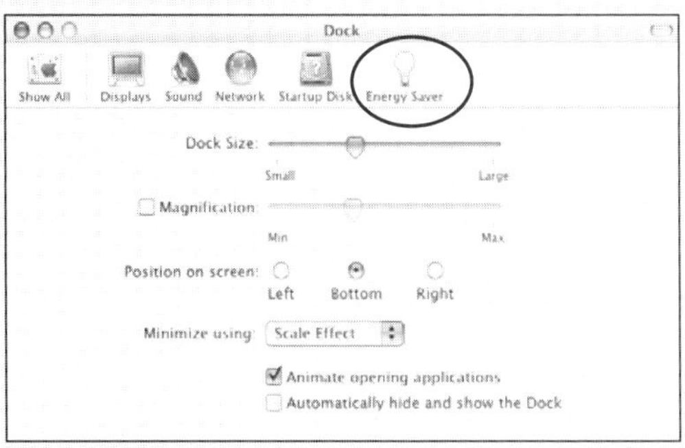

The icon is now accessible at any time, no matter which control pane you're currently working with.

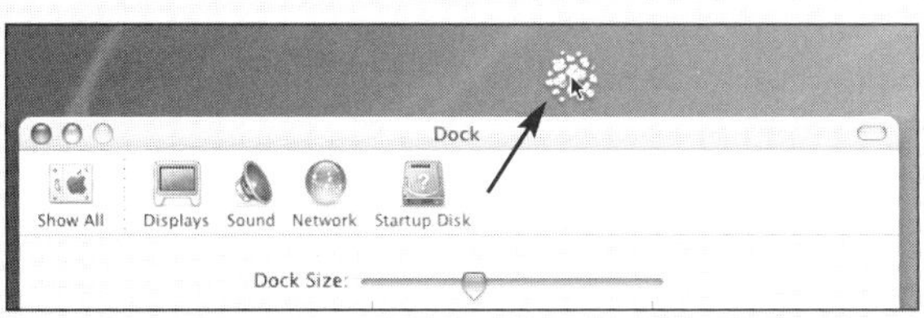

To remove the icon from the toolbar, just drag it out of the window.

2. Appearance Preferences

The control panes found in the Personal category of System Preferences are the keys to customizing your Mac and molding its appearance to suit your tastes. This exercise will show you how to use the **Appearance** and **General** control pane to personalize the look of the operating system's key elements.

Note: The choices you make under the Personal category go into effect only when you're the one logged onto your Mac. When other users log in on the machine, they can change their own preferences without altering your settings. You'll learn how to manage multiple users in Exercise 10.

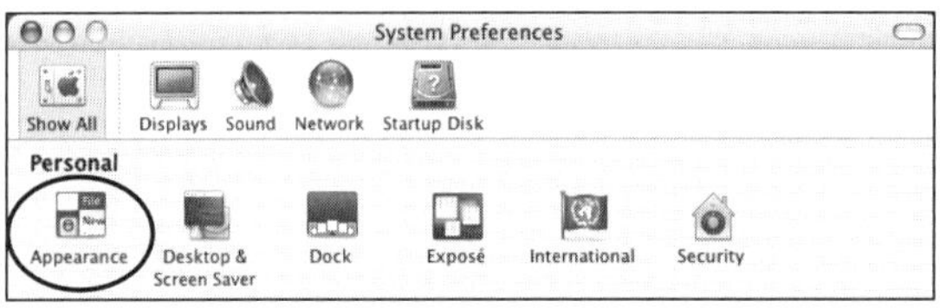

1. Click the **Appearance** icon.

The Appearance preferences allow you to control, to an extent, the look and behavior of the interface elements of OS X.

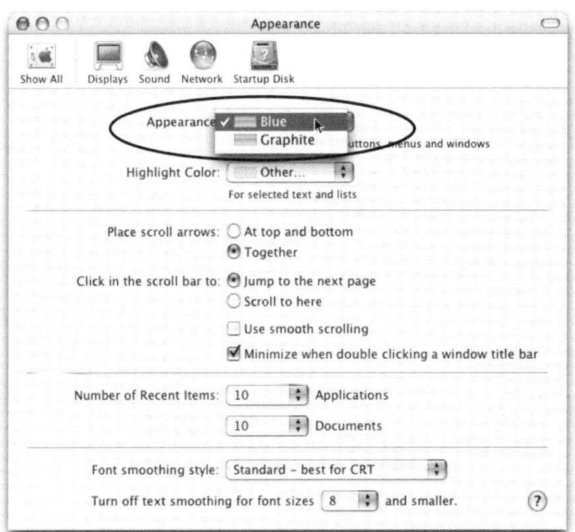

The first selection in this preference pane, Appearance, contains two choices: ***Blue*** *and* ***Graphite****, which determine the appearance of buttons, scroll bar handles, menus, and the close, minimize, and zoom buttons of windows. The default selection is Blue, which is what gives OS X its shiny blue appearance. If you're a tad put off by all this colorfulness, you can choose Graphite to give everything a flat gray appearance.*

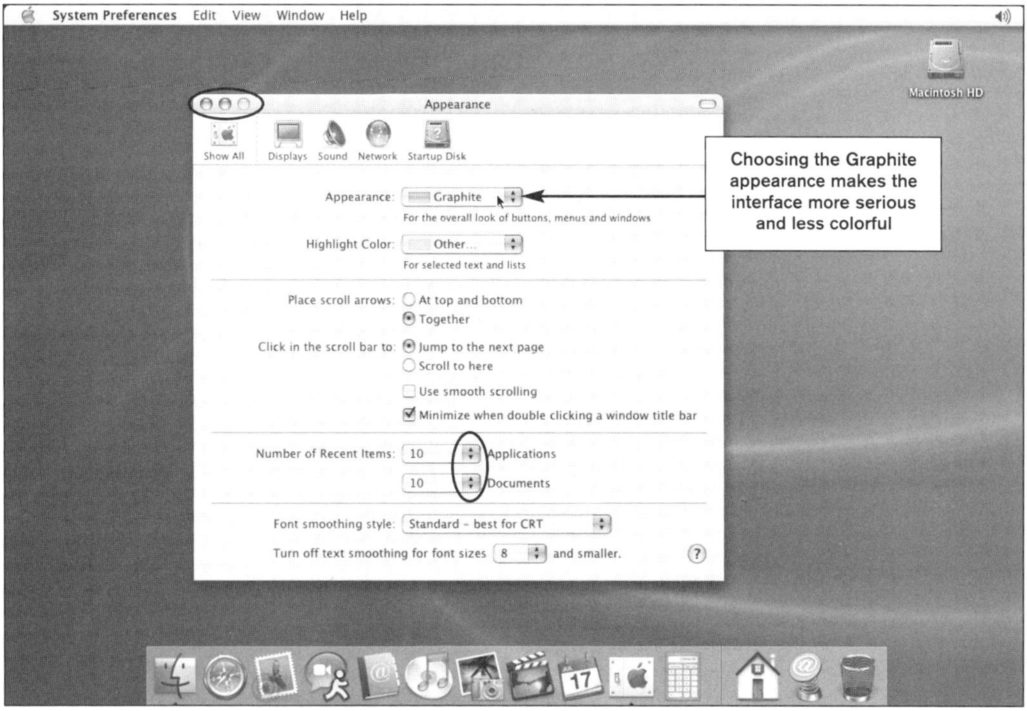

2. Choose **Graphite** from the **Appearance** menu. You'll instantly notice the change. All the buttons and menus in the window have turned gray (including the Close, Minimize, and Zoom buttons), and the Apple menu in the upper-left corner of your screen has also become a muted gray. When you click menu bar items, the items are highlighted in gray instead of blue. If you like this look, feel free to leave it this way. Otherwise, switch the **Appearance** back to **Blue**.

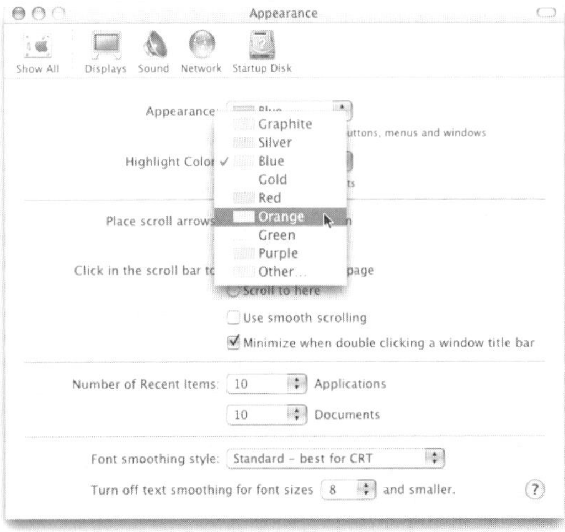

*The next selection is **Highlight Color**, which determines the color that appears behind text when it's selected. Again, the default selection is **Blue**, but you can choose from a list of several different colors.*

3. Select a color from the **Highlight Color** menu.

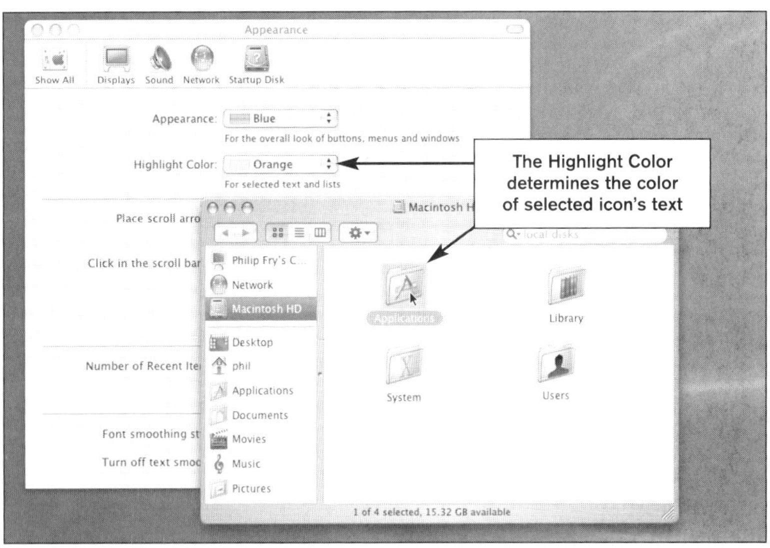

4. Double-click your **hard drive** icon to open a **Finder** window. Click once on any icon. (It doesn't matter whether you're in Icon, List, or Column view.) Notice that its name is now highlighted in the color you chose. The **Highlight Color** also affects the color that appears around any text you select in OS X and its applications.

5. Close the **Finder** window and click anywhere in the **Appearance** pane to bring it back to the front.

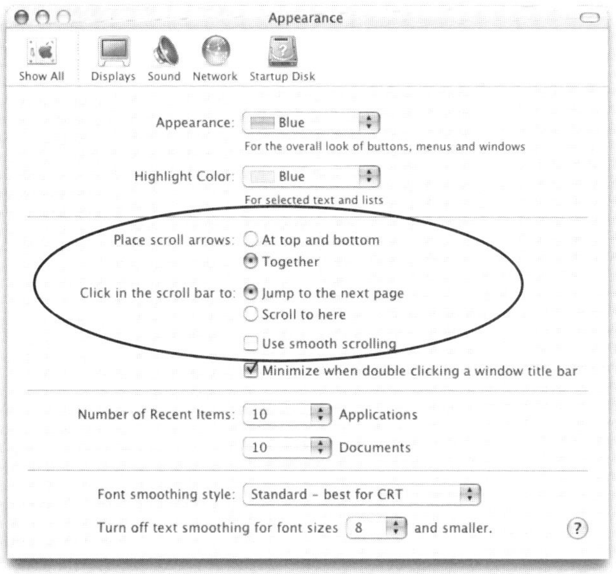

The next section of this pane deals with the appearance of scroll bars. Here you can choose where the arrows in the scroll bar appear and how the scroll bar will react when you click in it.

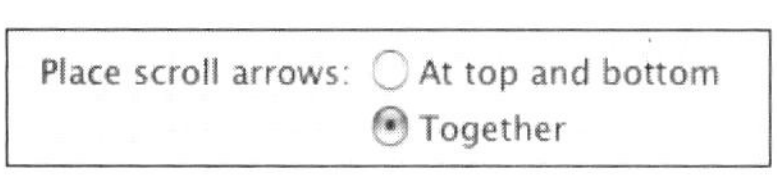

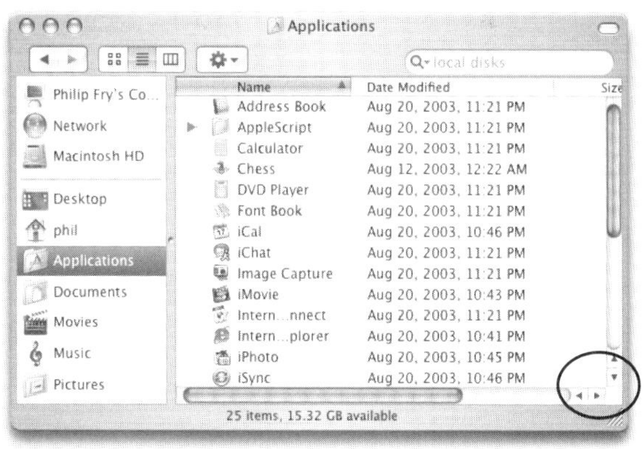

*Next to **Place scroll arrows**, you can choose either **At top and bottom** or **Together**. The default choice is **Together**, which places the up and down arrows together in the scroll bar (and also joins the left and right arrows if a window or document needs to be scrolled left or right). Many people find it easier to scroll when the arrows are placed back to back. As you can see in this example, you would only need to move your mouse pointer a short distance to scroll in any of the four directions.*

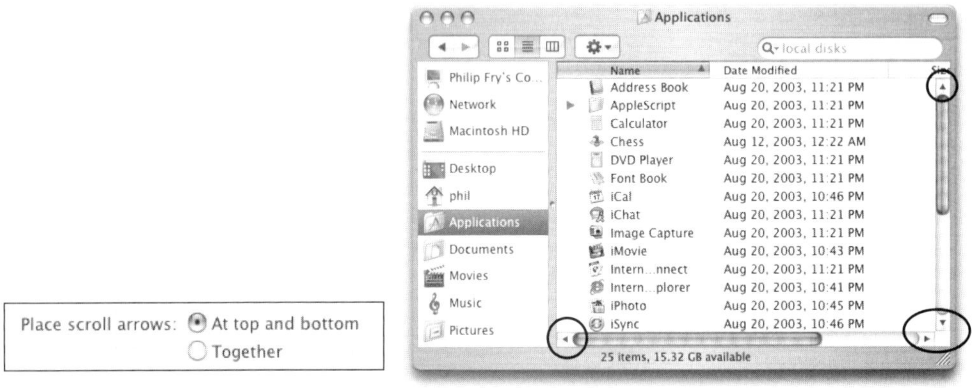

On the other hand, if you choose to place the scroll arrows at the top and bottom, the arrows are moved to opposite ends of the scroll bar. Most users feel this makes it more difficult to scroll up and down in a document. But in the end, these are all preferences, so you'll have to decide what works best for you.

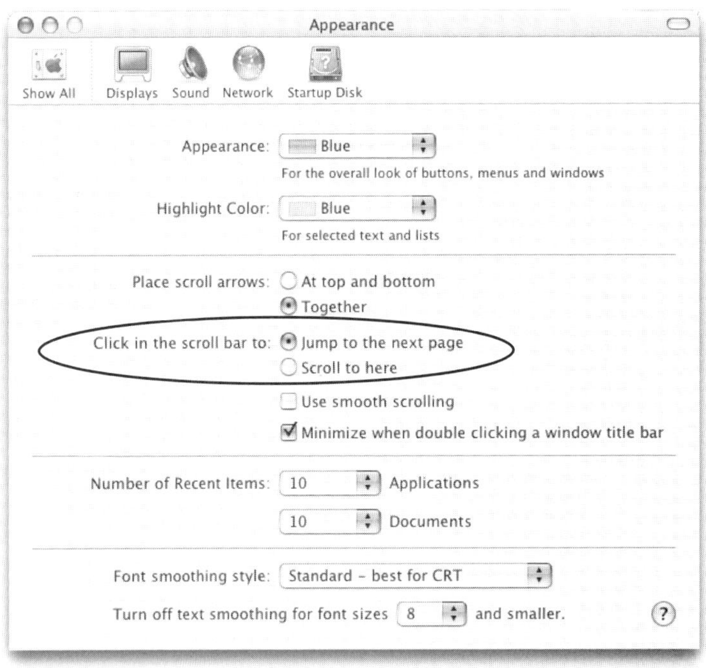

The next selection in the General pane determines how the scroll handle moves when you click on the scroll bar.

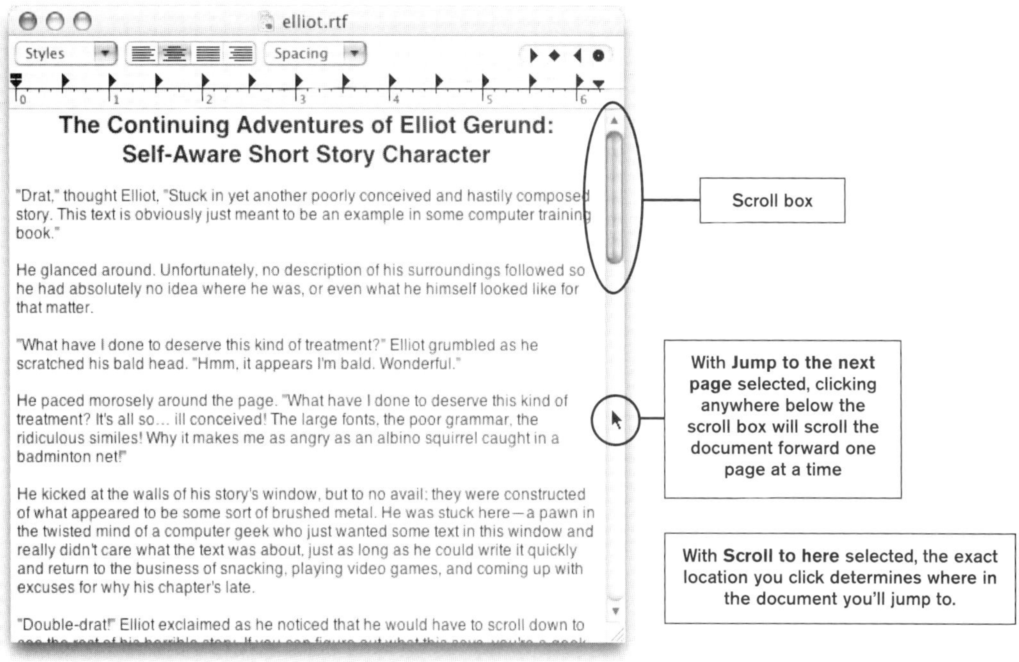

Jump to the next page *means that clicking in the scroll bar on either side of the scroll box will only move the document forward or backward one page at a time no matter where you click. Choosing* ***Scroll to here*** *means that the scroll handle will move to the exact location in which you click; clicking closer to the scroll box jumps you ahead just a few pages. Clicking farther away jumps you several pages ahead.*

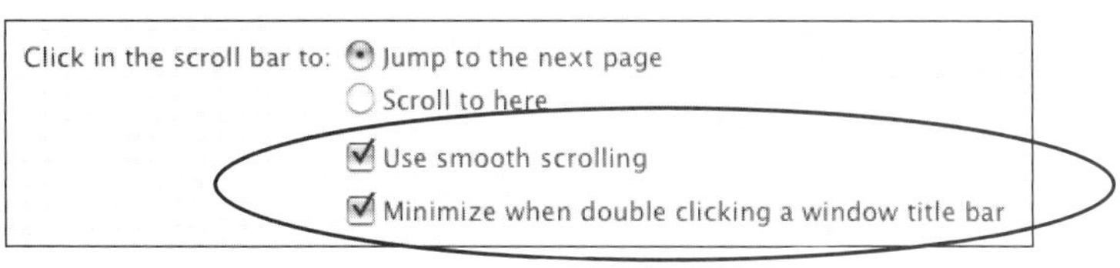

New to Panther is the ***Use smooth scrolling*** *option. If you have this option selected when clicking in a scroll bar, you'll see your page quickly scroll up or down, rather than jumping immediately to the new location. Also new here is the* ***Minimize when double clicking a window title bar*** *option. This item is checked by default, so when you double-click the title bar of any window, the window is sent to the Dock, just as if you had clicked the Minimize button. If you prefer not to minimize windows this way and want to prevent accidental minimizing, uncheck this option.*

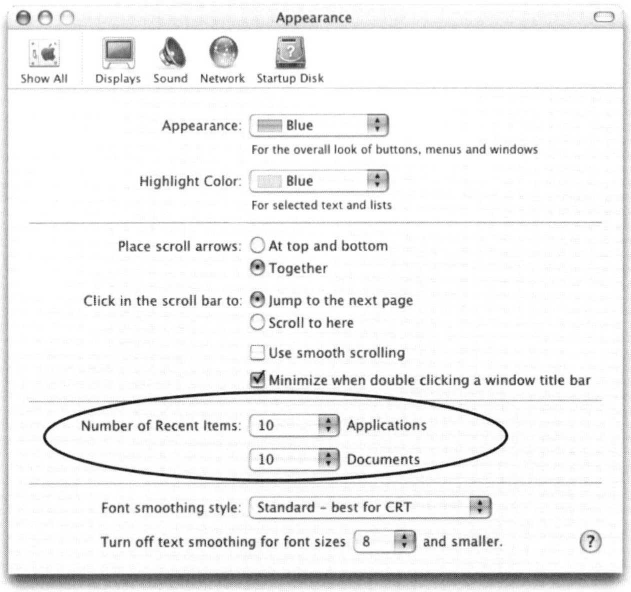

The next section of the Appearance pane determines how many recently used items Panther will remember for you. This is a convenient feature that can really save you time if you find yourself working with the same documents or applications over and over during the course of the day. If, after you quit an application or close a document, you realize that you still need to make another change, you can use your Apple menu to find the item rather than hunting through your hard drive.

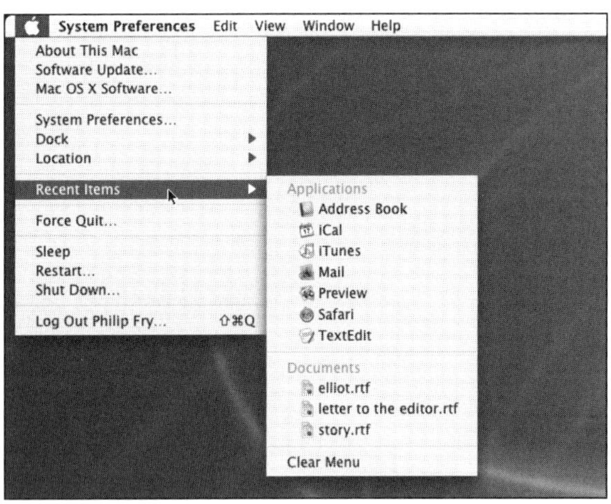

6. Click the **Apple** menu and place your mouse over **Recent Items**. You'll see a listing of all the applications and documents you've recently worked with.

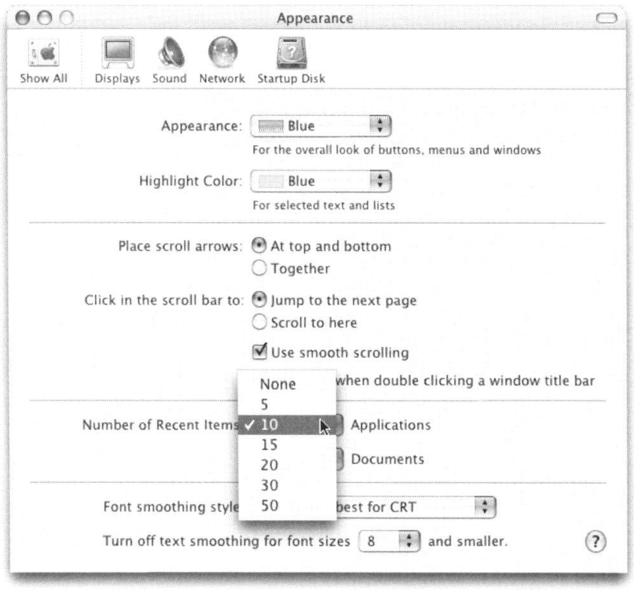

*In the Appearance control pane, you can determine how many items will be listed here. For both **Applications** and **Documents**, you can choose from the range **None** (if you don't want Panther to keep track of any items) to **50**.*

***Tip:** Anyone wandering by your unattended computer could easily find out which documents and applications you've recently been working with by checking your Recent Items menu–not an ideal situation if you've been writing your Great American Novel on company time. If you want to erase the current list of items that Panther's remembering for you, choose **Apple menu > Recent Items > Clear Menu.** This does not delete the items themselves from your computer; it just deletes them from the Recent Items menu.*

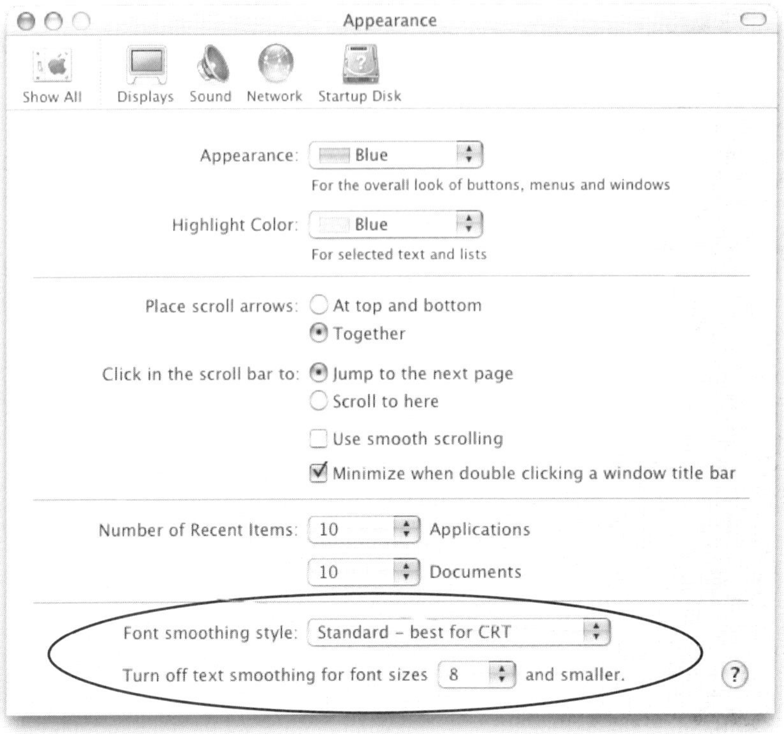

The final section of the Appearance control pane deals with the look of text in the OS. If you're a veteran Mac user, you've probably already noticed that the text on your screen looks smoother than text used to look in OS 9 and earlier operating systems. OS X uses an imaging technology known as "Quartz" to create the smooth textures and details you see on your screen. Part of what Quartz does is to create text that–in some people's opinions–is cleaner and easier to read. But not everyone agrees. Those who use LCD monitors often find text with font smoothing just the opposite: sloppy and illegible. With Panther, Apple has provided options to allow you to control the amount of smoothing that is applied to the text on your screen.

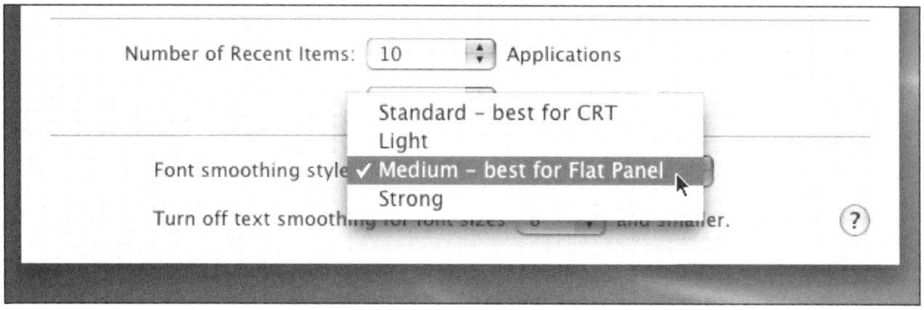

*In the **Font smoothing style** menu, you can choose from four different levels of smoothing:*

- ***Standard***
- ***Light***
- ***Medium***
- ***Strong***

*As you can see, Apple has suggested that the **Standard** setting be used for CRT (**C**athode **R**ay **T**ube) monitors (if your monitor is more than six inches thick, you most likely have a CRT), and that the **Medium** setting be used for flat panel monitors. But it's really up to you to determine which setting works best for you.*

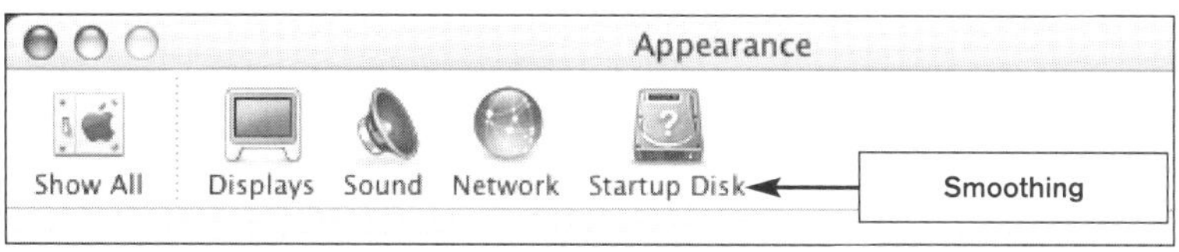

One aspect of font smoothing on which most users seem to agree is that smoothing actually makes smaller text more difficult to read. Again, you'll have to be the final judge, but at least Apple has made it possible to determine when and to what degree smoothing is applied to text.

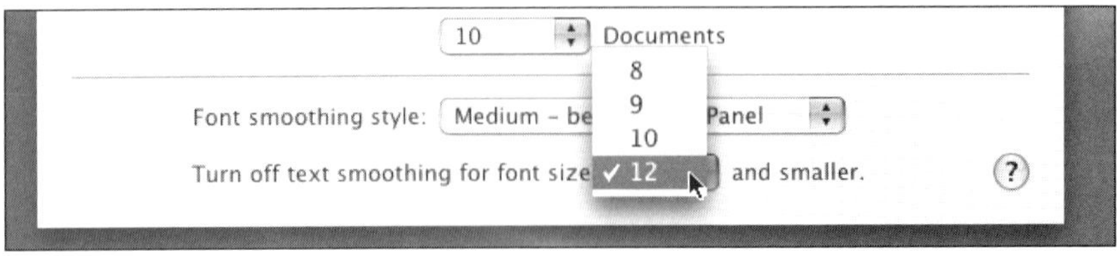

If you find that you're having trouble reading some text at smaller sizes, you can use ***the Turn off text smoothing for font sizes XX and smaller*** *menu to let OS X know that you don't want text below a certain size smoothed. For instance, if you're having trouble reading your word processing documents when using a 10-point font size, turn off font smoothing for 10 points and below. You'll probably find it much easier to read your documents.*

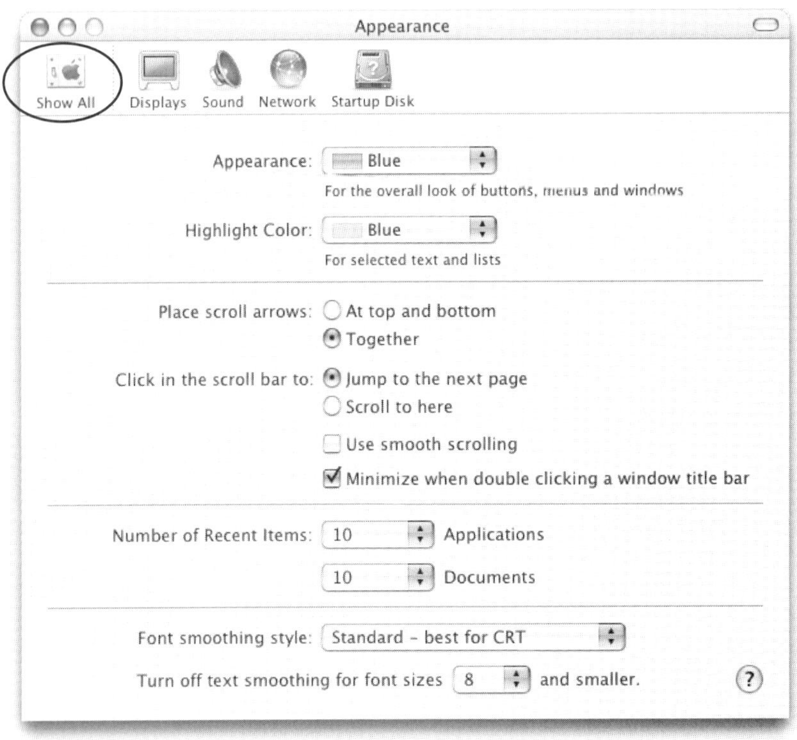

7. Take a moment to set the preferences in the **Appearance** pane to your liking and then click the **Show All** button in the toolbar to return to the main **System Preferences** pane.

3. Desktop & Screen Saver

The next preference pane in the Personal category is **Desktop & Screensaver**. This control pane has less to do with the way your Mac runs and more to do with your own personal sense of style.

1. In the main **System Preferences** window, click the **Desktop & Screen Saver** icon under **Personal**.

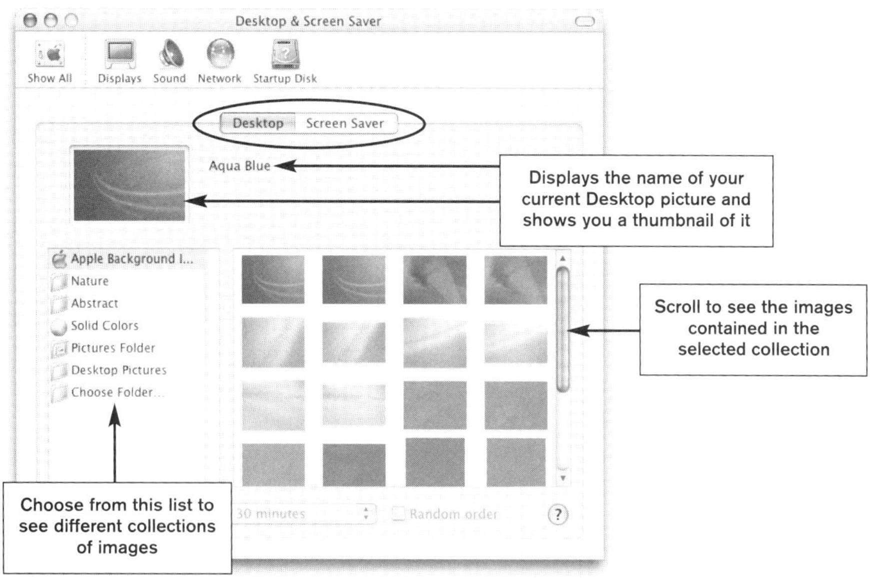

This control pane is divided into two sections: ***Desktop****, for selecting images or colors to display on your Desktop's background, and* ***Screen Saver*** *to select from a collection of animations to play when you're not using your computer. By default, the Desktop options are displayed. Here you can choose from a large selection of images to display on your Desktop. OS X's preinstalled images are organized into collections that can be viewed in the Collection menu. You can preview the contents of each collection by scrolling through the thumbnails at the bottom of the window. Next you'll take a look through these different collections.*

Note: *You might first want to note which image is currently being used for your Desktop picture in case you want to switch back to it following this exercise.*

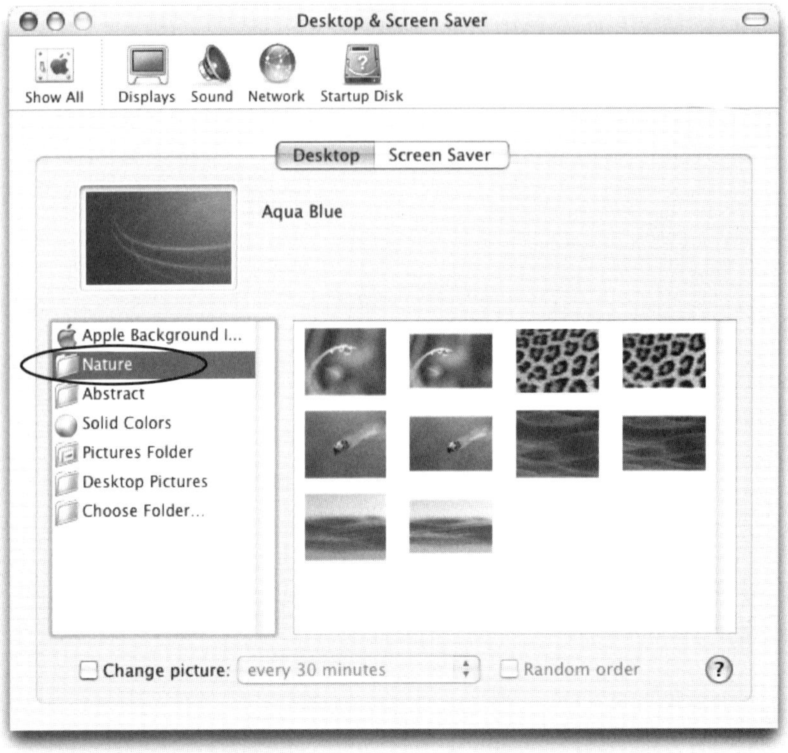

2. From the list of image collections, select **Nature**. This collection features images of leaves, dew, insects, water, and–a pattern introduced in Mac OS 10.2–a Jaguar pattern.

You'll notice that there are two versions of each image in this collection. The wider of the two images is for users of Apple's Titanium PowerBooks, 17-inch iMacs, or widescreen displays. If you don't have a Mac with a wide screen, you can still choose the widescreen images, but they'll be slightly cropped.

Don't throw red paint on your screen! It's not real fur!

3. Click the **Jaguar** pattern. (Its official name is **Faux Fur**, so don't worry: No large cats were harmed in the making of this Desktop picture.) As soon as you click the thumbnail, the **Desktop** picture changes, and the **Current Desktop Picture** thumbnail reflects your choice.

That's all there is to selecting a Desktop picture. Spend some time looking through the other collections to find one that suits your mood. ***Note:*** *See the upcoming sidebar "Adding Your Own Pictures" to learn about the* ***Pictures Folder*** *and* ***Choose Folder*** *options.*

The only other option here is the ***Change picture*** *check box, which you can use to have your Mac automatically swap in a new picture every few seconds, minutes, hours, or days.*

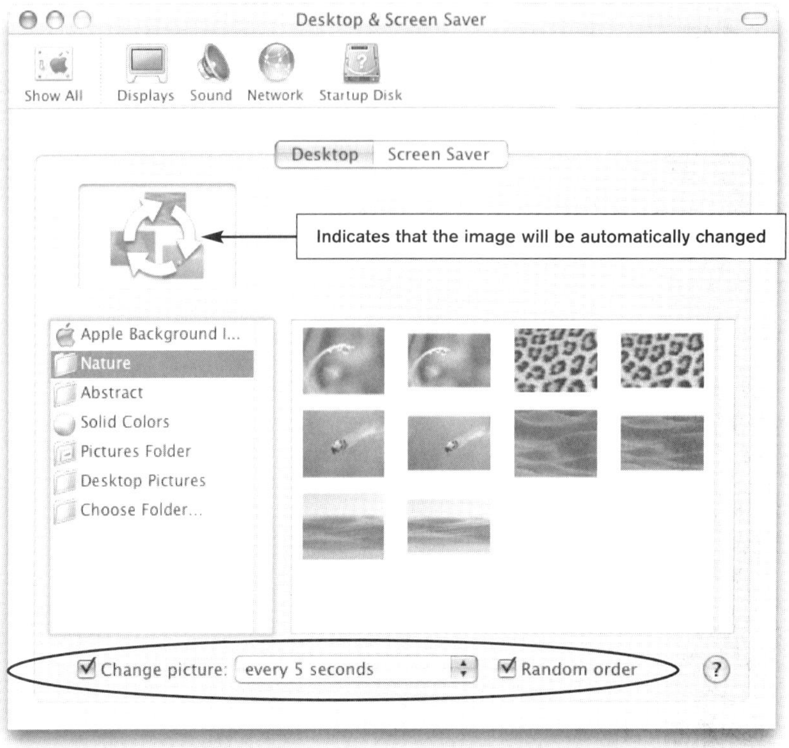

4. See this feature in action right now by checking **Change picture**, and selecting **every 5 seconds** from the menu. You can also check **Random order** to prevent the images from appearing in alphabetical order.

If you can actually work while your Desktop image changes every five seconds, feel free to leave ***Change picture*** *selected. Otherwise, either uncheck* ***Change picture*** *or choose a larger interval, such as every day, that won't drive you crazy.*

Adding Your Own Pictures

OS X provides you with four collections of images to suit your own sense of style: **Apple Background Images** (soft patterns in muted colors), **Nature** (green and/or furry and/or wet images), **Abstract** (possibly created while under the influence of recreational narcotics), and **Solid Colors** (for when it's time to get down to business). But if none of these collections fit your taste, it's an easy matter to add your own images to this control panel.

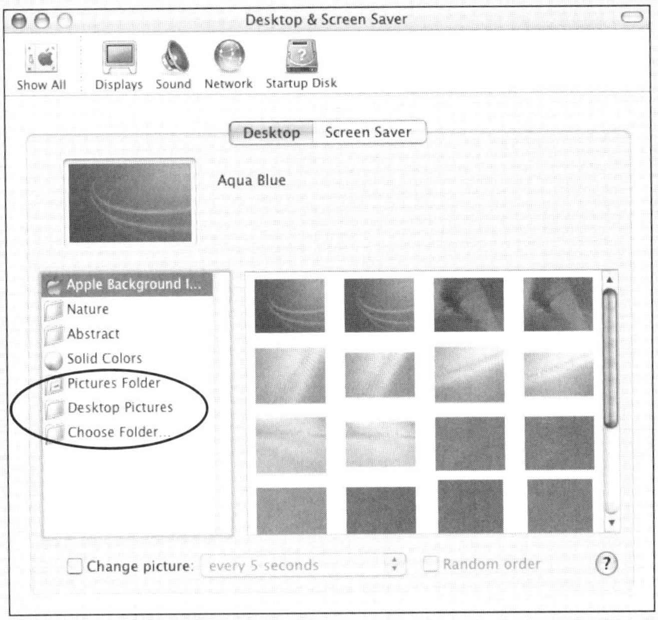

In the list of image collections, you'll notice that in addition to the four main choices, you can also select from **Pictures Folder**, **Desktop Pictures**, or **Choose Folder**.

Select **Pictures Folder** to display any images currently stored in the Pictures folder in your Home folder. Images stored in your Pictures folder are inaccessible to other users, so you can keep your embarrassing personal photos here without fear of them being seen by anyone else.

Select **Desktop Pictures** to display images located in the Desktop Pictures folder in your Mac's main Library folder. The Desktop Pictures folder is an excellent place to store images that you want other users to have access to.

Or select **Choose Folder** to specify another folder on your hard drive that contains images.

If you're not sure how to get your own images into your Mac, don't worry; you'll learn all about importing images in Chapter 15, "*iPhoto 2*."

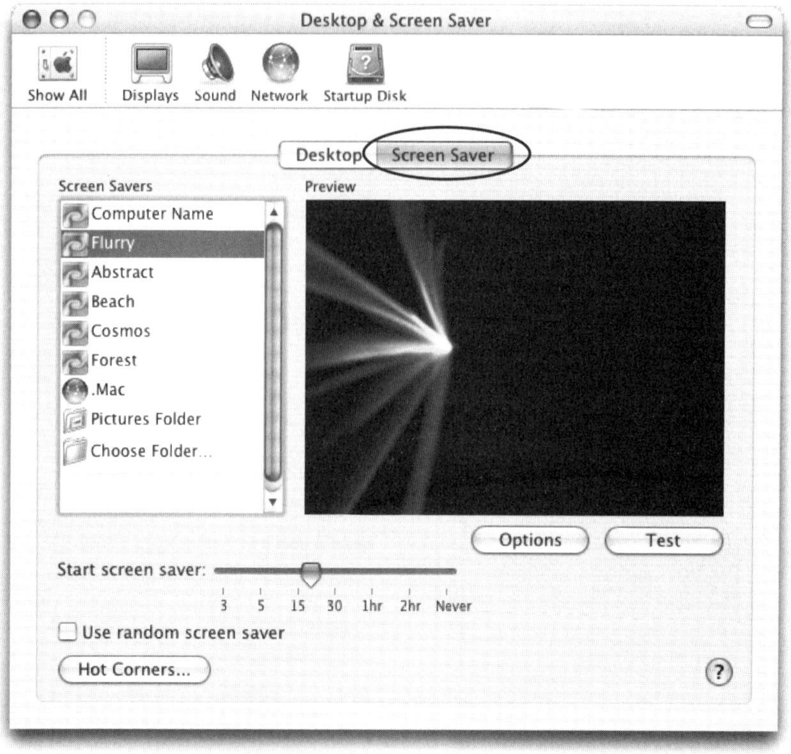

5. Take a moment to choose a Desktop picture you can live with and then click the **Screen Saver** button near the top of the pane.

*Prior to OS 10.2, this preference pane was known as **Screen Saver**. In Jaguar, it became **Screen Effects**. And now in Panther, it's called **Screen Saver** again, probably because everyone you know says "screen saver," and you've never heard anyone talk about their "screen effects."*

Computers originally needed screen savers to prevent the "burn-in" effect that was created if the same image was left onscreen too long (sometimes several hours did the trick) and burned out the monitor's pixels, leaving a ghost of the image on the screen. But screen savers are purely for show and fun these days because modern monitors really don't need any saving unless you leave them on for several months without changing the image on the screen.

In Panther's Screen Saver pane, you can choose from nine different modules for your screen saver (including the option of choosing your Pictures folder or another folder containing your own images). With the exception of Computer Name and Flurry, the screen effects modules are collections of images that zoom in and out and softly dissolve into one another. Computer Name just displays the Apple logo and your Mac's name as the screen saver; Flurry generates colorful dancing light waves.

6. Click any of the screen savers listed on the left side of the panel. A preview of the effect appears to the right.

Although the Preview window gives you a pretty good idea of what the screen effect looks like, it is much more impressive to view the effect at full size. You'll learn to do this next.

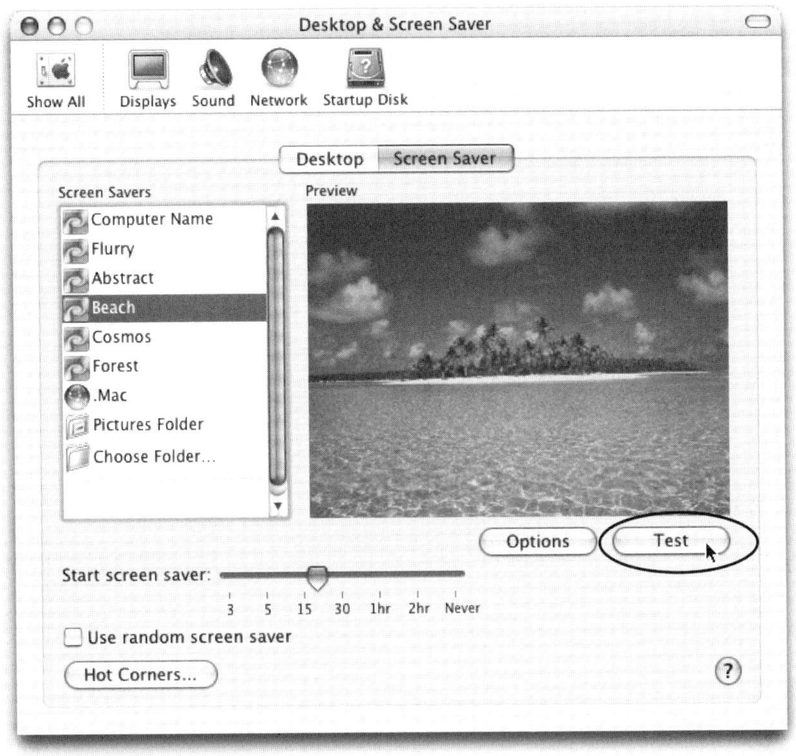

7. Click the **Test** button to view the currently selected screen saver at full size. Be careful not to slip into a hypnotic trance while staring at your screen.

8. Move the mouse or press any key on the keyboard to stop the screen effect and return to the **Screen Saver** window.

Tip: *If you wish, you can also click the* ***Options*** *button to tweak the settings of any module. The preview window will show you the results of any changes you make.*

Of course, you don't want to open the Screen Saver pane and click Test every time you want to see the screen effect. Instead, use the ***Start screen saver*** *slider to determine exactly when the screen saver turns on.*

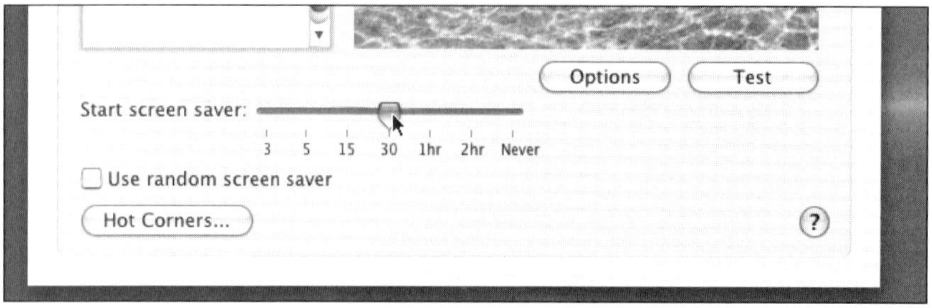

9. Move the slider to specify when you want the screen effect to turn on. For example, based on the settings shown in this screen shot, the screen effect will turn on after **30** minutes of inactivity. If you never want the screen effect to turn on, move the slider to the far right above **Never**.

You most likely don't want to sit there and wait 30 minutes every time you want your screen saver to turn on (unless you're getting paid by the hour at work). The ***Hot Corners*** *button allows you to specify an area of your screen where you can manually activate the screen saver.*

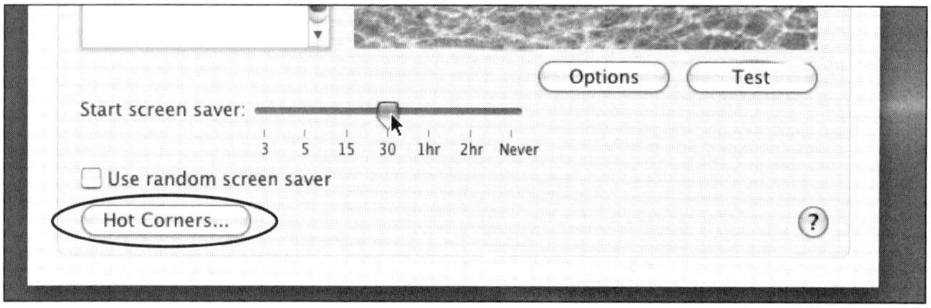

10. Click the **Hot Corners** button.

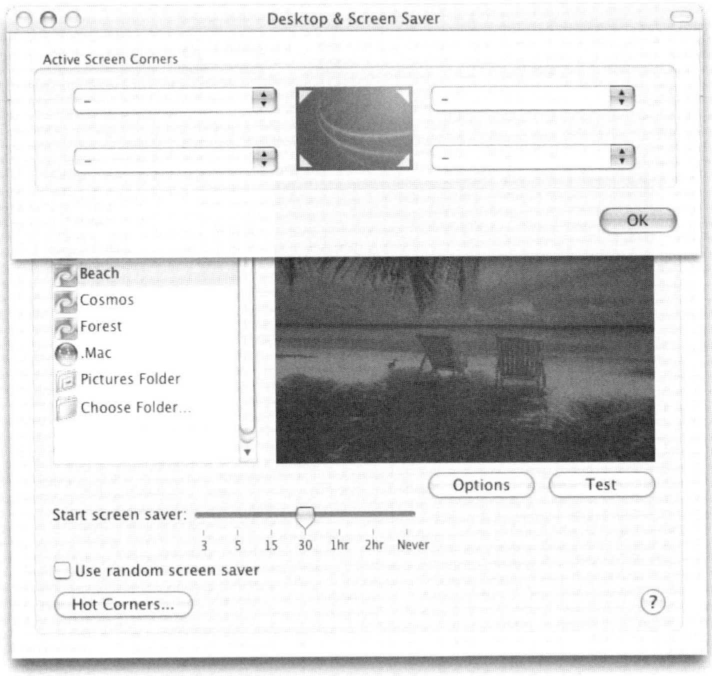

A sheet slides down containing a rectangle that represents your screen. Each of the fours corners has a corresponding pop-up menu. By clicking a corner's pop-up menu, you can specify an action to occur when you move your mouse to that corner of your screen.

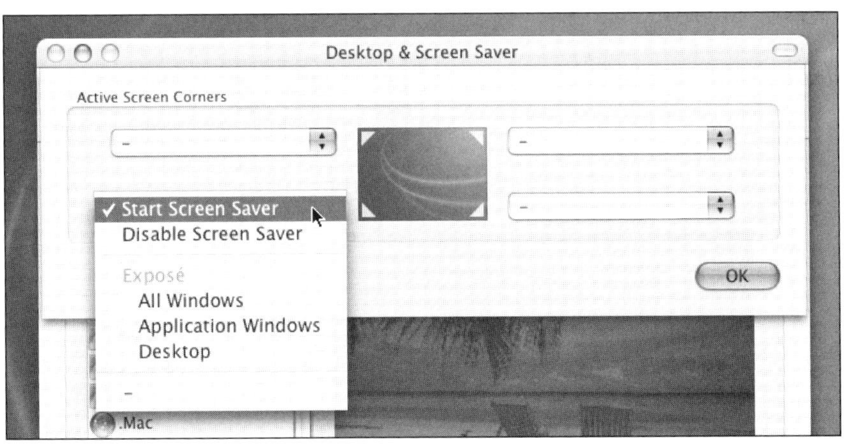

11. Click the menu in the lower-left corner and select **Start Screen Saver**. Note that you can also assign Exposé actions with this menu. (Exposé is covered in the next exercise.)

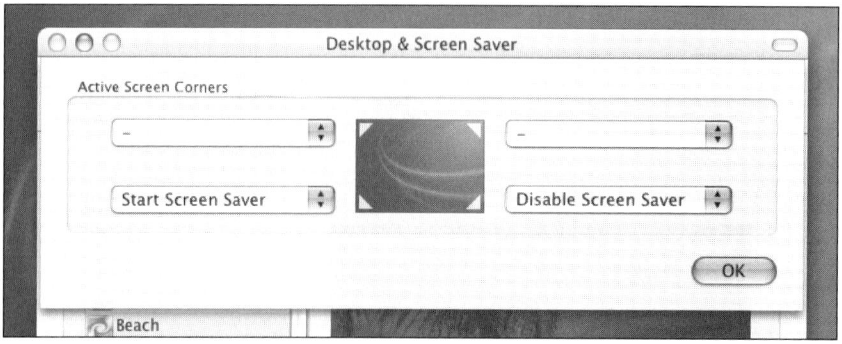

12. Now click the menu in the lower-right corner and select **Disable Screen Saver**. You've now set up two **Hot Corners** for your screen saver. Click **OK**.

13. Move your mouse to the lower-left corner of your screen and leave it there. (The mouse cursor should be nearly hidden from view in the very corner.) After a moment, your screen saver activates. Once you've confirmed that it's working, move the mouse to deactivate the screen saver.

14. Now move your mouse to the lower-right corner and leave it there. Sit and stare at your monitor for a few hours and notice how your screen saver never turns on.

Just kidding.

Take my word for it: The screen saver will never appear as long as the mouse is in that corner. This is a useful tip for times when you don't want the screen saver to activate. For instance, you might be keeping an eye on a large file you're downloading from the Internet but not doing anything else with your computer. It would be annoying if the screen saver kept turning on every few minutes and requiring you to give the mouse a shake. Instead, just drag the mouse into the lower-right corner to prevent the screen saver from appearing.

***Note:** In previous versions of OS X, the Screen Saver pane allowed you to check an option that would require a password to deactivate the screen saver once it turned on. In Panther, this option has been moved to the Security pane under the Personal section of System Preferences.*

15. Take a moment to set up different hot corners if you like. When you're done, click the **Show All** button in the toolbar to return to the main **System Preferences** window.

4. Exposé

Making its debut in OS 10.3, **Exposé** is arguably one of the most useful concepts ever implemented in a computer operating system. As you go about your day-to-day business in OS X and learn to appreciate how many applications you can run at once, at some point you'll probably find that you have more than a dozen windows open. In the past, you could click an application's icon in the Dock to bring all of its windows forward, but then you might still need to move several windows around to find the one you want.

The idea behind Exposé is simple: With a single key or mouse movement, you can instantly scale down all open windows to find the one you need. Click that one window and all the windows return to their previous sizes and positions, with the one you clicked in front. This exercise shows you how to set your Exposé preferences.

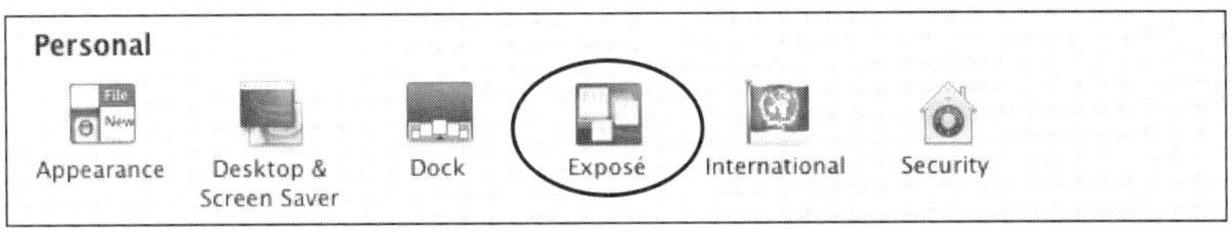

1. In the main **System Preferences** window, click the **Exposé** icon under **Personal**.

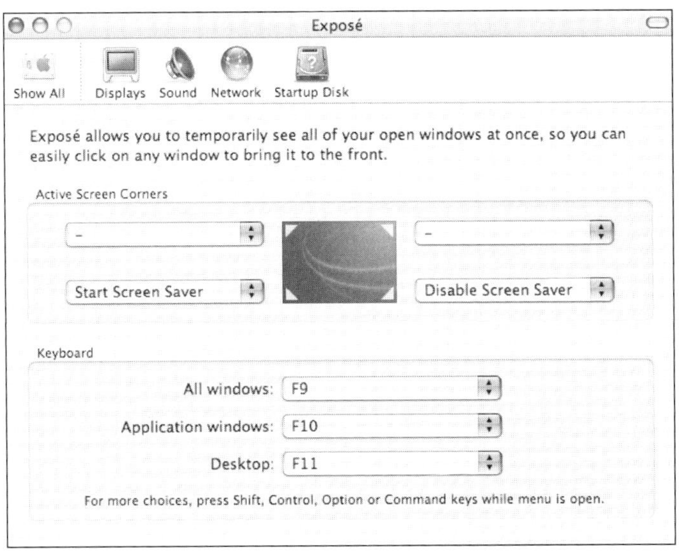

This top half of this preference pane looks a lot like the Hot Corners section of the Screen Saver pane you worked with in the last exercise. In fact, you can see the ***Start Screen Saver*** *and* ***Disable Screen Saver*** *hot corners you set up earlier. You can trigger Exposé with a keyboard command or a hot corner or both–you just can't assign an Exposé hot corner to a corner that's already been assigned to activate or disable your screen saver.*

The bottom half of this preference pane contains the menus used to select the keys that activate Exposé. Exposé gives you the option of viewing all open windows, viewing just the windows in the active application, or momentarily hiding all windows to give you a clear view of your Desktop. You'll take a look at all three of these options in the following steps.

2. Make sure the **Keyboard** keys for Exposé are set to **F9**, **F10**, and **F11**, as shown in the previous picture.

Now you'll open several windows and a few applications to clutter your screen a bit.

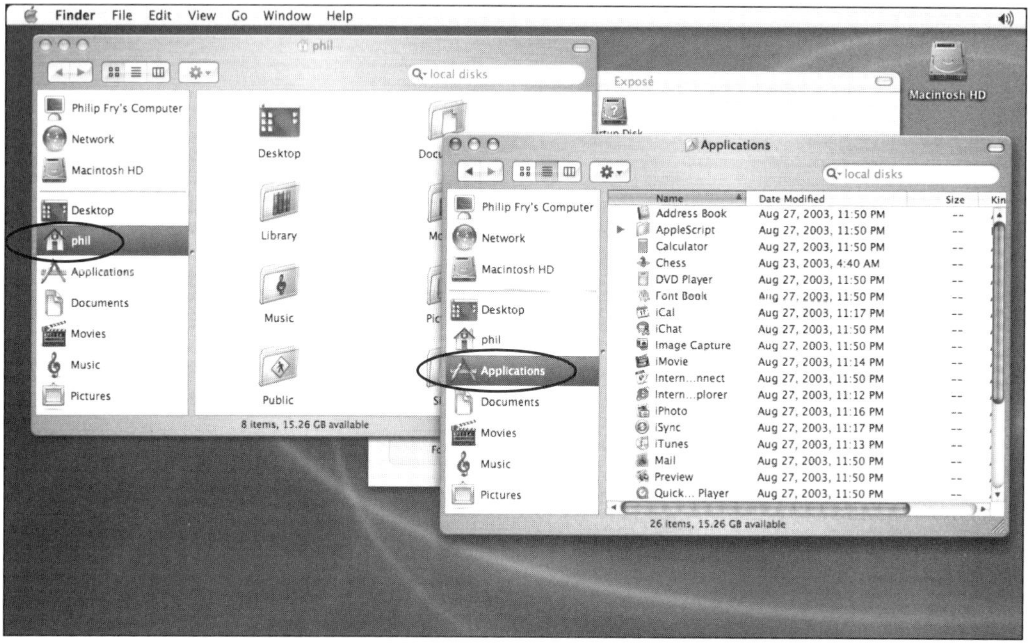

3. Keep the **Exposé** preference window open and click anywhere on your **Desktop**. Press **Cmd+N** to open a new **Finder** window. If it's not already selected, click your **Home** folder icon in the **Places** sidebar. Then press **Cmd+N** again to open another window and click **Applications** in the **Places** sidebar.

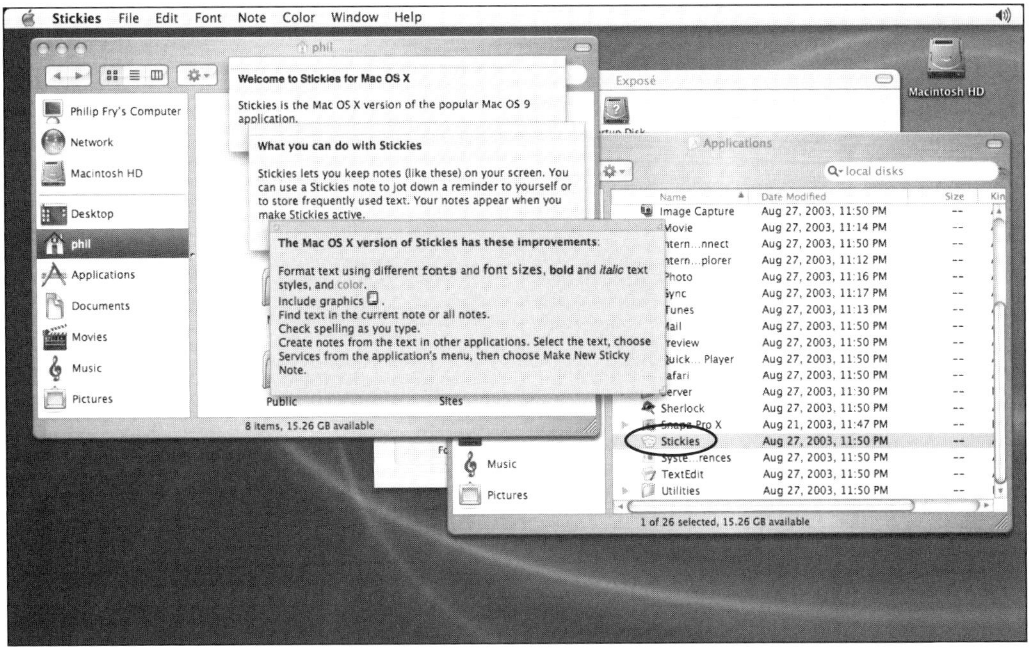

4. In the **Applications** window, locate and open **Stickies**, which is an application you can use to leave yourself onscreen notes and reminders, much like you might use a Post-It note. When you open Stickies, three default windows open containing information about the program. If the windows shown here don't appear, choose **File > New Note** three times to create some new note windows.

5. Now click the **Applications** window again and open **TextEdit**. In the blank document that opens, type a line or two of text.

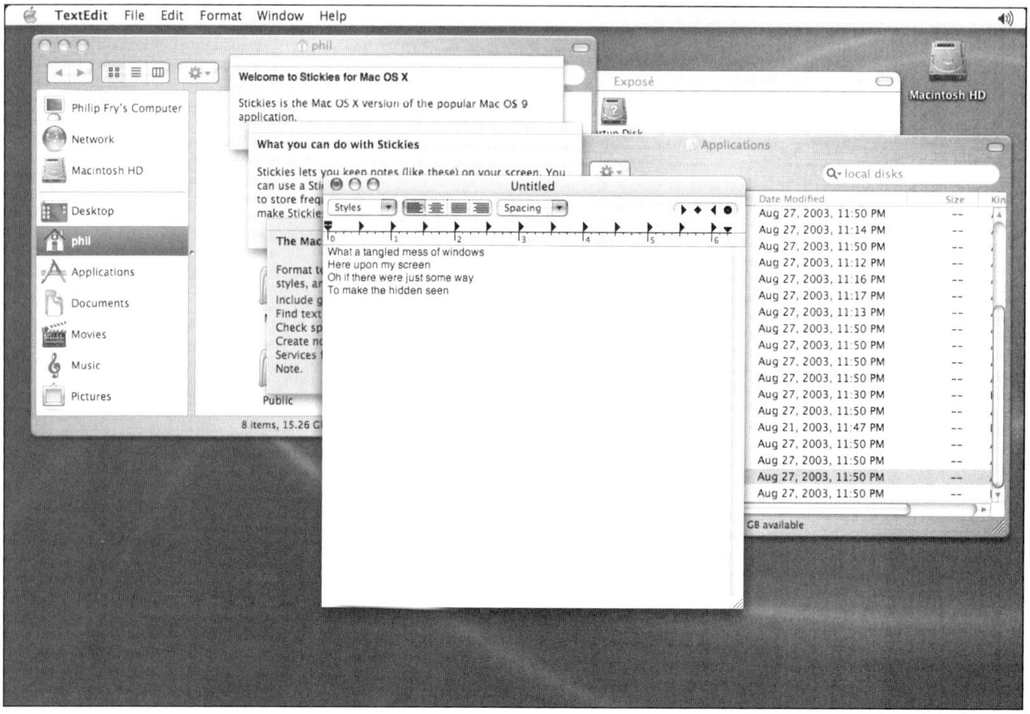

By now, your screen should be pretty cluttered. (Your own day-to-day Desktop might be even messier at times.) In pre-Panther versions of OS X you could bring groups of windows to the foreground by clicking on their respective icons in the Dock. But with Exposé, you can see all windows instantly and click the one you need.

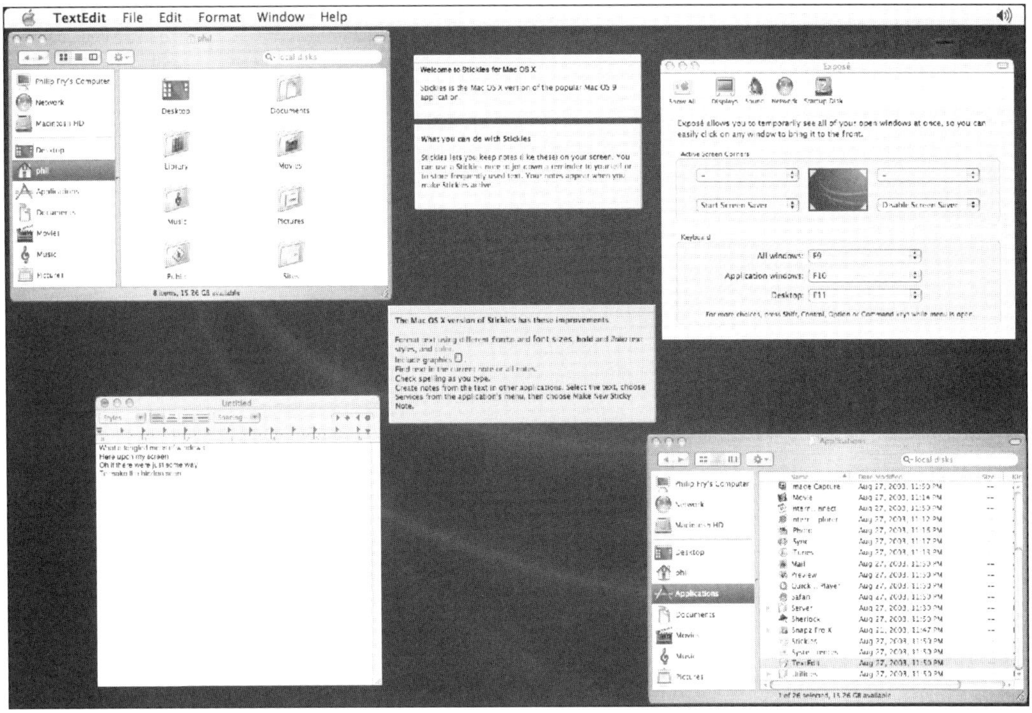

6. Press **F9** once and immediately release the key. At once, all your open windows scale down to a size where all windows are completely visible, and the rest of the screen dims. Roll your mouse over each window to see its name. Click the **Exposé** preference window to bring it to the front and to return all the windows to their original sizes and positions. That's it! That's how easy it is to use Exposé.

Tip: *If you hold down **F9** for more than a second, the windows will return to their original size and position as soon as you release the key. If you want them to "stick" in their scaled-down positions, be sure to immediately release **F9** after pressing it.*

Note: *Applications running in Classic mode are not shown when you use Exposé. You'll learn about Classic later in this chapter.*

*Based on your settings in the Exposé window, pressing F9 scales down all open windows. But sometimes you may find it more useful to search through just the windows open in a single application. For instance, you might be working with half a dozen Word documents and need to switch quickly among them. In this case, the **F10** key provides a more helpful function.*

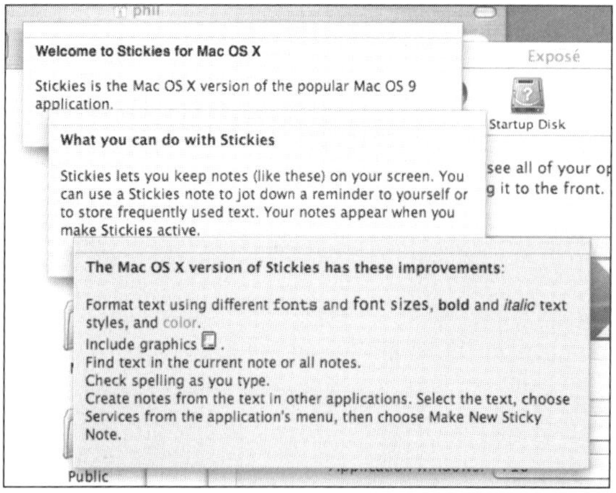

7. Click the **Stickies** icon in the **Dock** to bring the three Stickies windows forward. They should overlap each other.

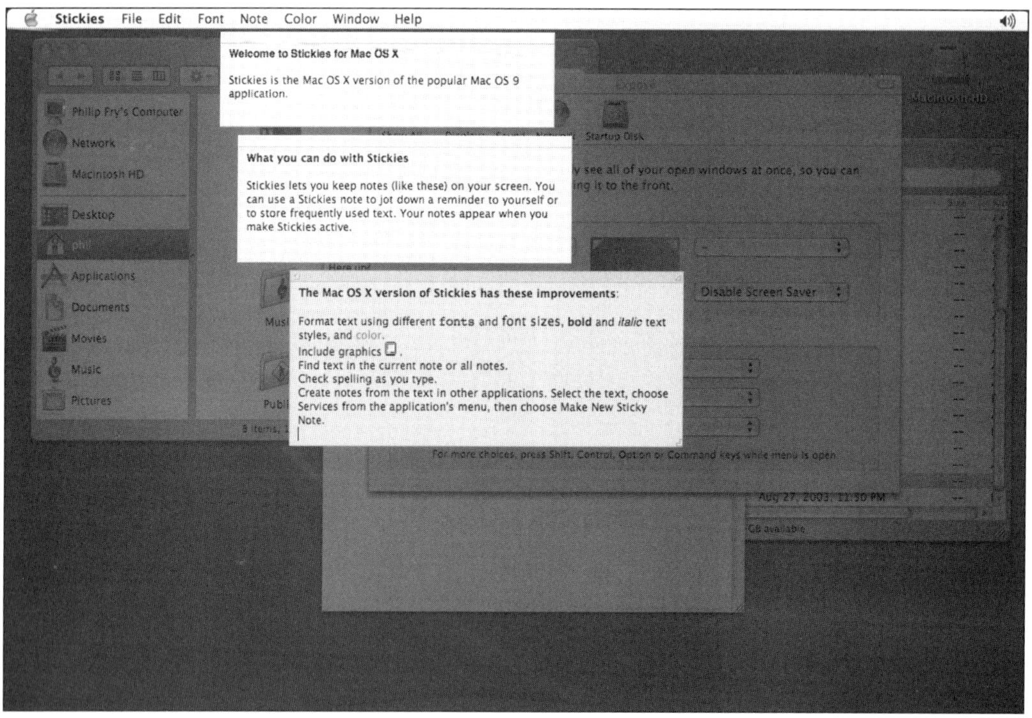

8. Press and immediately release **F10**. Notice that this time only the three **Stickies** windows shrink while the other open windows stay in place. The screen still dims to highlight the clickable windows. Click any of the three windows to bring it to the front.

The third capability of Exposé is the option to move all open windows out of the way so you can have an unobstructed view of your Desktop. If you're like me, your Desktop is a virtual dumping ground for all sorts of files, and sometimes finding a specific file under a dozen open windows can be a real chore.

9. Press and immediately release **F11**. All your windows shoot off to the sides of the screen, leaving you a clear view of the **Desktop**. If you have any files stored here, you could easily double-click them to open them now. Click anywhere in the dimmed border around your screen (or press **F11** again) to bring the windows back into position.

NOTE | Reassigning Keyboard Keys and Using Hot Corners

If you use the F9, F10, and F11 keys in other applications, they may not be the best choice of keys to invoke Exposé. You can easily reassign the keys in the Exposé preference pane.

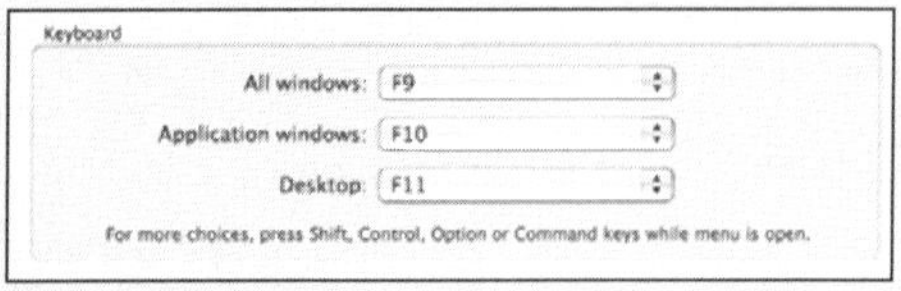

Simply select another F-key from the pop-up menus next to **All windows**, **Application windows**, or **Desktop**. You can also hold **Shift**, **Ctrl**, **Option**, **Cmd**, or any grouping of the four keys (while the pop-up menu is open) if you want to have the choice of combining these keys with the F-key. For example, you might want **Cmd+F9** to invoke **All windows**.

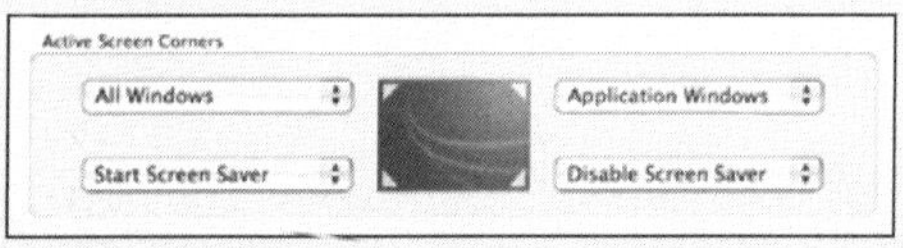

As mentioned earlier, you can also assign Exposé actions to Hot Corners. In the **Active Screen Corners** section of Exposé preferences, click the pop-up menu for the corresponding corner and choose **All Windows**, **Applications Windows**, or **Desktop**. Once selected, moving your mouse to that corner will invoke the Exposé action you chose. **Tip:** You might want to avoid assigning the upper-left corner an Exposé action because any time you go to click the Apple menu and overshoot just a little, Exposé will activate. If you're not using them to activate your screen saver, you'll probably find the bottom corners to be the most convenient for Exposé.

10. Close all open windows and applications, with the exception of the **Exposé** preferences window.

11. Click **Show All** to return to the main **System Preferences** window.

Note: *Exposé also makes it easier to attach files to emails. Be sure to see the exercise "Adding Attachments and Signatures" in Chapter 10,* "Address Book, Mail, and iChat AV" *for steps on using Exposé for file attachments.*

MOVIE | Exposé

To see a demonstration of Exposé and its preference settings, see the movie **exposé.mov** on the **H•O•T CD-ROM**.

International Preferences

The next Personal Preferences pane is the **International** pane. Unless you plan on using your Mac in multiple languages, you don't really need to mess around in here. For the most part, this pane is for determining things such as which language will be displayed in the Finder and other applications, how the Date and Time will be displayed (such as 11/17/02 vs. 17/11/02), and how numbers and currency are displayed. Here's some information on changing the language your Mac speaks just in case you're interested in internationalizing your Mac experience.

You may or may not know this, but your Mac has the capability to switch among more than a dozen different languages on the fly, without having to restart your computer.

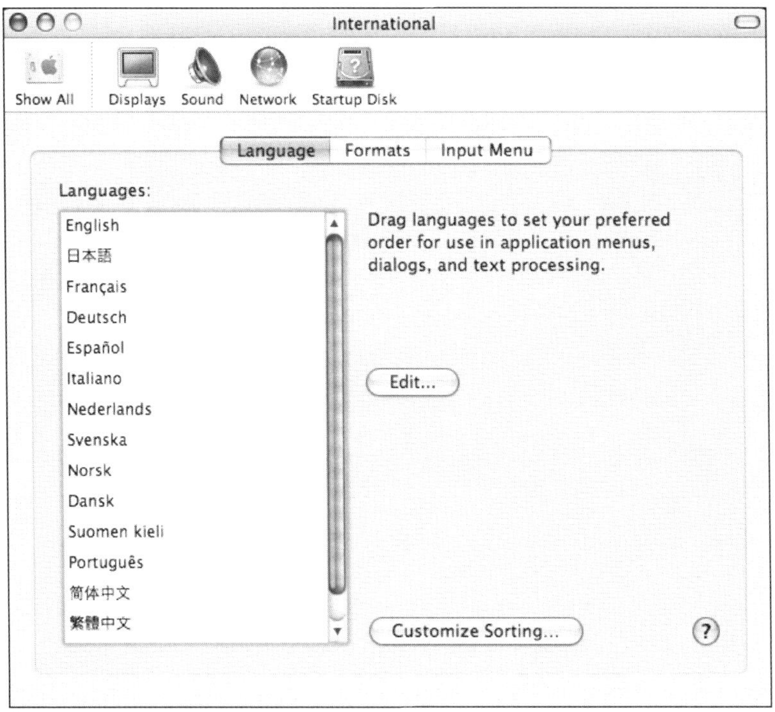

If you click the **International** pane and look under the **Language** section, you'll see a list of all the languages in which your Mac is fluent.

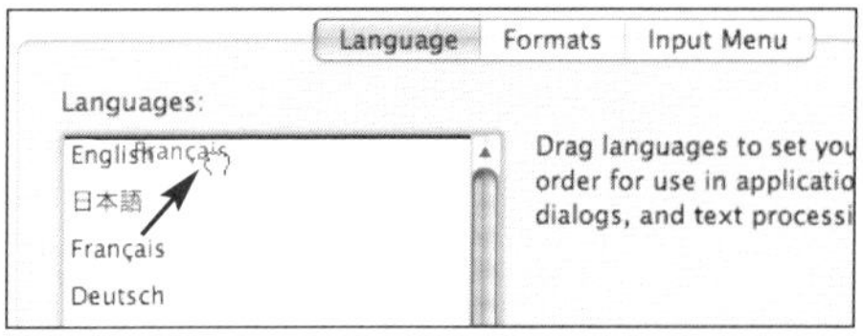

If you feel like working in French, strap on your beret (or any other horribly stereotypical accoutrement) and drag **Français** to the top of the **Language** list. A black line will appear letting you know you can release the mouse button. A message will appear in the pane telling you that changes to the Finder won't take effect until the next time you log in, and changes to applications will not take effect until the next time you open them.

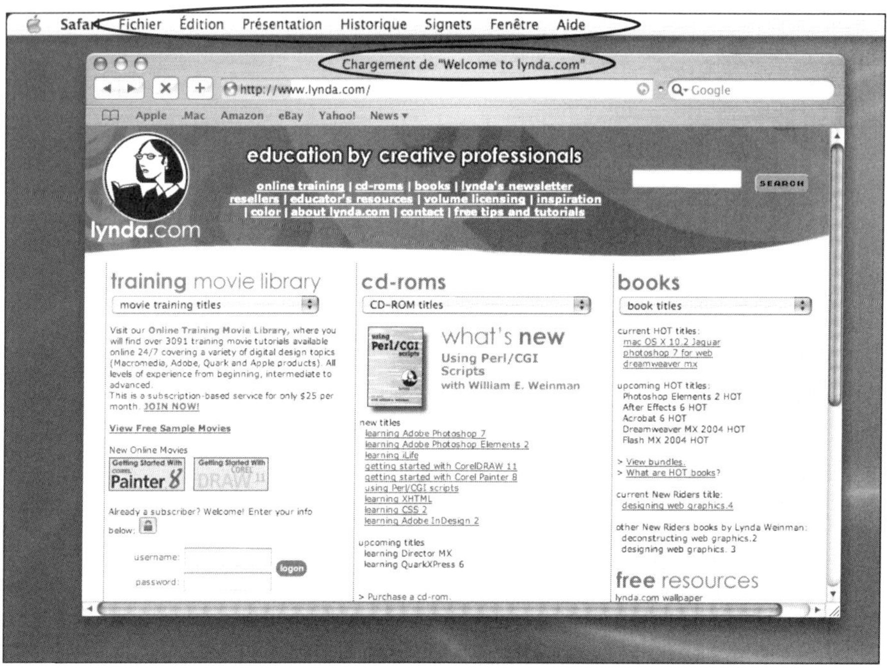

Now any application you open will use French as the default language in its menu bar and interface elements (if that application supports multiple languages). If the application doesn't support the language at the top of your list, it will continue moving down the list until it finds one it can use. If you restart your computer, the Finder itself will also be in French.

Note: It always helps to know a second language, but if you accidentally restart your Mac in a language you're not exactly fluent in, just click your System Preferences icon and then click the icon for the International pane to revert back to your native tongue. It's a cool trick to use your Mac in multiple languages, but you might just want to be sure that you know enough of the language you choose before you go selecting commands like *effacez mon ordinateur.*

Security

The final preference pane under your Personal Preferences is **Security**, which also happens to be a new feature making its debut in Panther. Also known as **FileVault**, this pane allows you to protect the contents of your Home folder using 128-bit AES (**A**dvanced **E**ncryption **S**tandards), the same level of encryption used on Web sites when you make credit card purchases. In other words, FileVault really locks your personal stuff down tight, which can be a silver lining if your Mac is ever lost or stolen.

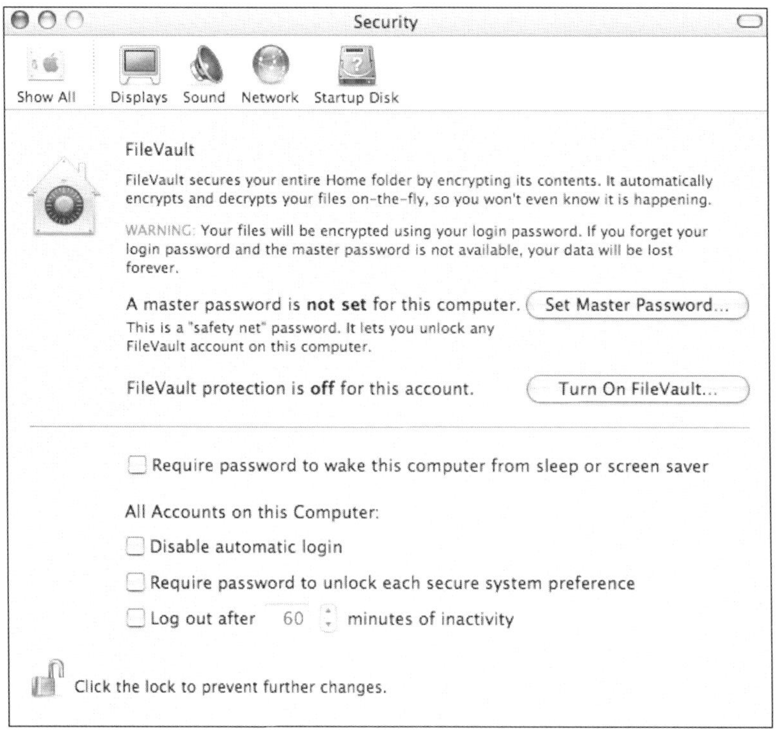

And don't let the word *encryption* intimidate you. FileVault does all its security-related encrypting and decrypting (scrambling and unscrambling data) for you. All you have to do is come up with a master password and decide just how secure you want your Mac to be. The following chart describes the options available in this preference pane.

Security Preference Pane Options	
Item	**Description**
Set Master Password	Click this button to create a master password for your Mac. You're required to do so if you want to use FileVault. As it says to the left of this button, the master password is a "safety net" in case you or another account holder on your Mac has forgotten his or her password. All users can unlock their Home folders with their personal account passwords, but the master password can be used to unlock any FileVault account on your Mac. When you click this button, you'll be asked to create a password, verify it, and create a hint for yourself in case you ever forget it. **Warning:** If you ever forget both your account password and your master password, the information in your Home folder will be forever lost.
Turn On FileVault	Click this button to activate FileVault. You'll be asked to enter the master password. Panther will then begin to encrypt your Home folder. This process could take some time, depending on how many files you have in your Home folder. When the encryption is complete, you'll be logged out of your account.
Require password to wake this computer from sleep or screen saver	With this option checked, you'll need to enter your password after each time your screen saver activates or your Mac goes to sleep (You'll learn about putting your Mac to sleep later in this chapter.) If you know that your Mac is fairly secure from prying eyes around your home or office, you can leave this unchecked. But if you travel with a PowerBook or iBook, you might want to check this option. Many users of portable Macs leave their computers in Sleep mode when not using them so they can quickly get back to work without having to wait for the computer to reboot. In the event that your Mac is lost or stolen, no one will be able to wake it from sleep without your password.
All Accounts on this Computer	The three options below this heading affect every user's account on your Mac.

continues on next page

Security Preference Pane Options *continued*

Item	Description
Disable automatic login	Check this option to require all users to enter their passwords before accessing their accounts.
Require password to unlock each secure system preference	Check this option to keep other users from changing some of the system-wide settings in System Preferences (such as Energy Saver or Network). With this option selected, an administrator password is required before any changes can be made to any of secure system preferences.
Log out after *XX* minutes of inactivity	With this option selected, you'll be automatically logged out of your account once your selected number of minutes of inactivity have elapsed. This can be useful if you're often called away from your computer and want to make sure your Mac is secure if left unattended for too long.

That's it for the Personal System Preferences. The next section starts introducing you to the Hardware Preferences.

CDs and DVD Preferences

The preferences found under the Hardware category of System Preferences affect how your Mac handles the various devices that are connected to it. Many of these preferences don't require actual step-by-step instructions, so detailed descriptions of the items in each preference pane are provided instead.

The first of the hardware preferences is the **CDs & DVDs** pane. You use this control pane to tell your Mac what to do when you insert CDs or DVDs into its drive.

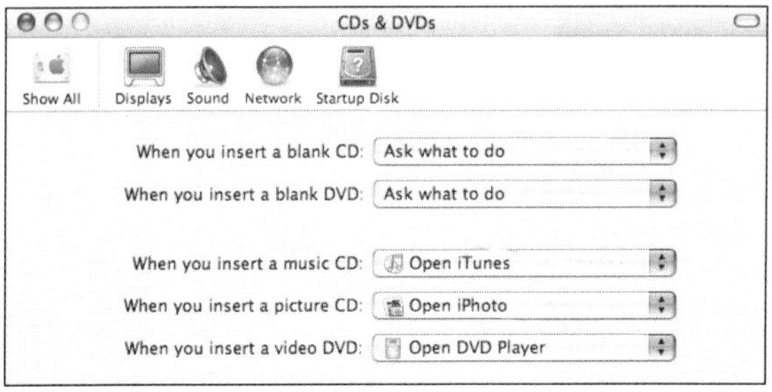

This pane presents you with several menus, each addressing the different types of media you might insert into your Mac. The first two menus deal with blank media and how your Mac will react when you insert a blank CD or DVD into your drive.

Note: Your Mac must have a CD-RW or a Combo drive to use blank CDs. A SuperDrive is required for using blank DVDs. If you're not sure which equipment you have, check the literature that came with your Mac.

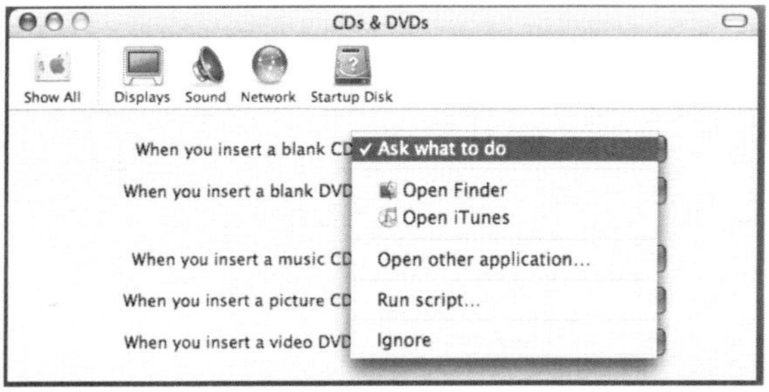

When you insert a blank CD or DVD, your Mac will want to know what action to take to prepare the media for you. With one exception, choices for blank CDs and DVDs are the same. The following chart explains each of the menu options.

Blank CD & DVD Options

Option	Description
Ask what to do	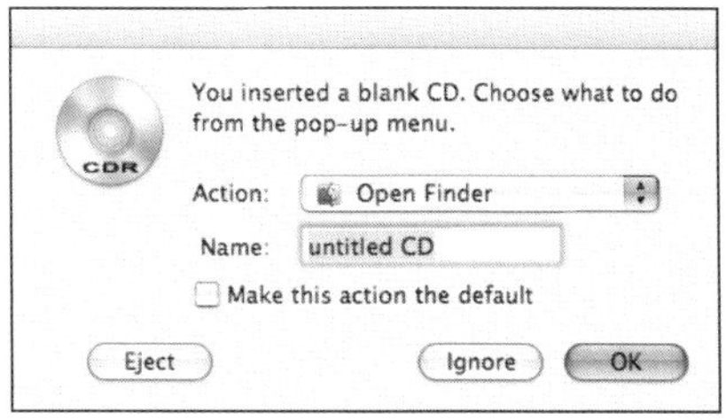 This option is a good choice if you use blank CDs or DVDs for various purposes but don't want a specific application to open each time you insert a blank disc. Choosing this selection will cause a dialog box to appear when you insert a blank disc, presenting you with the same choices that are offered here in the CDs & DVDs control pane: **Open Finder**, **Open iTunes**, **Open iDVD**, **Open other application**, and **Run Script**. Clicking **Eject** will eject the CD from your drive; clicking **Ignore** will leave the CD in the drive but will not mount it (you won't see its icon appear on the Desktop); clicking **OK** will confirm whichever action you've selected from the **Action** menu.
Open Finder	This selection will mount the CD or DVD and place its icon on the Desktop, at which point you're free to copy items to the disc for burning. Use this option if you want to copy files, folders, and other items to a CD or DVD. See Exercise 5 for information on copying files to blank CDs or DVDs.
Open iTunes (blank CDs menu)	With this selection chosen, the CD's icon will not appear on the Desktop. Instead, iTunes will open, and you'll be able to burn your music to the CD. You'll learn how to do this in Chapter 14, "*iTunes 4.*"
Open iDVD (blank DVDs menu)	This selection will open the iDVD application, which you can use to burn your own personal movies to a blank DVD. You'll learn how to do this in Chapter 17, "*iDVD 3.*"

continues on next page

Blank CD & DVD Options *continued*

Option	Description
Open other application...	If Open Finder, Open iTunes, or Open iDVD don't serve your needs, you can choose to have a different application open when you insert a blank CD. For instance, if you're one of the many users of Roxio's Toast CD- and DVD-burning software, you can choose **Open other application** and select Toast from your Applications folder.
Run script...	This option allows you to automatically run an AppleScript when a blank CD or DVD is inserted. A script is a series of commands written in the AppleScript language that tells your Mac to perform certain tasks. AppleScript is beyond the scope of this book, but you can visit **http://www.apple.com/applescript** if you're interested in learning more about it.
Ignore	If this option is selected, nothing will happen when you insert a blank CD or DVD. No dialog boxes, no prompts, no icons on the Desktop. Choose this selection if you plan primarily on using third-party software to work with your CDs or DVDs (such as Toast).

As you can see, Panther offers you several options for handling blank disks. The CDs & DVDs control pane also provides options for handling music and picture CDs as well as video DVDs. The options in these menus are self-explanatory: When you insert a music CD, for instance, you can have your Mac open iTunes or another application, run a script, or ignore it. For the most part, the default choices here are the best ones. (Why wouldn't you want DVD Player to open when you insert a video DVD?)

5. Burning a Data CD

Apple has made copying files, folders, and documents to a CD so easy that it's really not that much different from copying items from one folder to another. There aren't any specific files associated with this exercise. It contains the steps to create a data CD; if your Mac comes equipped with a CD burner, or if you've added a compatible external CD burner to your Mac, you can follow these steps to copy files onto a blank CD.

1. To copy files to a CD, first make sure that your preference for inserting blank CDs is set to either **Open Finder** or **Ask what to do**, and then insert a blank CD into your CD-RW drive, Combo drive, or SuperDrive. If you have **Ask what to do** selected, choose **Open Finder** from the dialog box that appears.

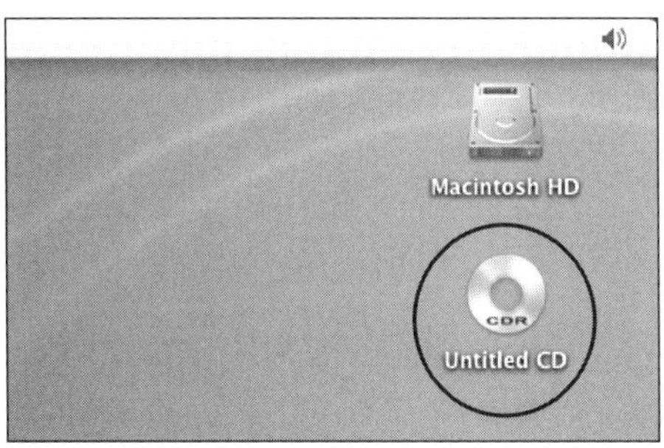

*After a moment, the icon for the blank CD appears on the Desktop. If the icon doesn't appear, choose **Finder > Preferences** from the **Desktop** menu bar. Under the **General** section of the **Finder Preferences**, make sure **CDs, DVDs, and iPods** is checked.*

2. Because this will be a data CD, click once on its name (**Untitled CD**) and title it appropriately.

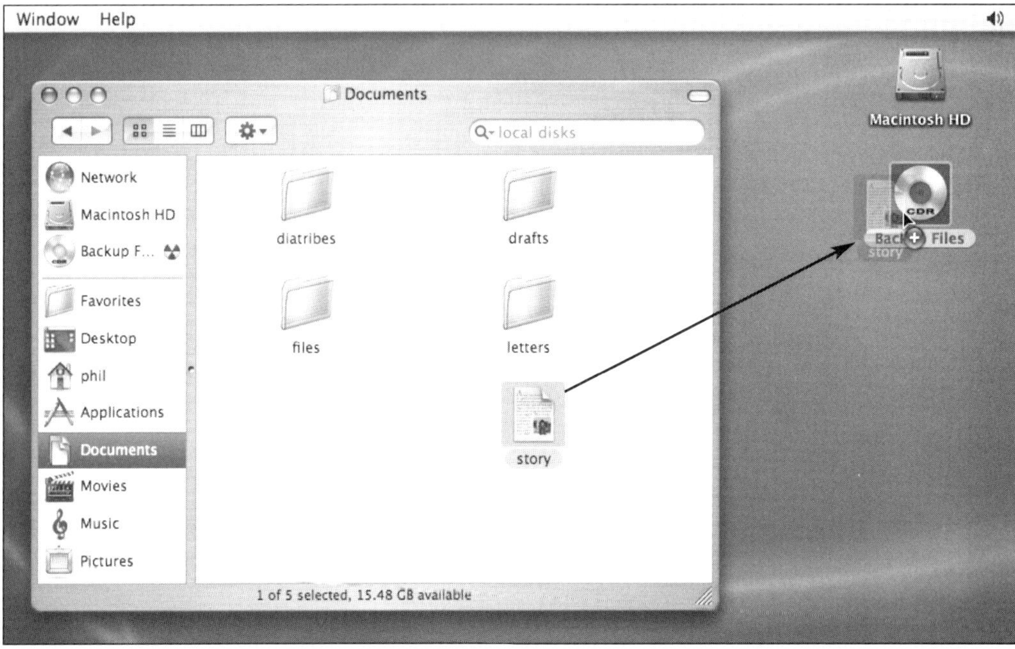

3. Drag the items you want to copy to the CD icon. You can double-click the CD icon to view its contents in a Finder window and create folders within the CD to organize your files. The important thing to remember is that when you drag items to the CD, you aren't burning them on the fly. You're just telling your Mac which files you want to place on the CD when you eventually burn it.

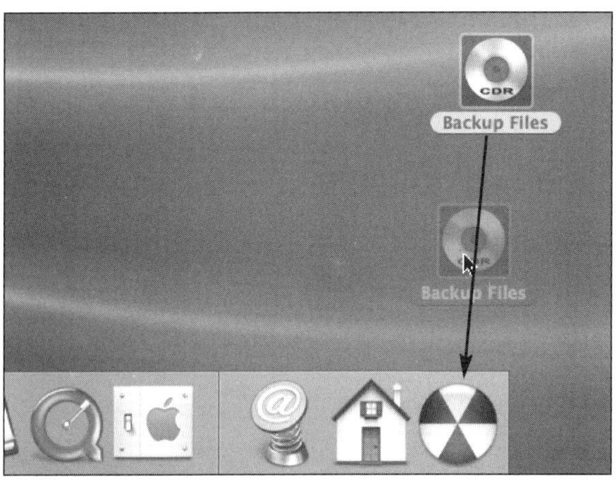

4. After you've moved your files to the CD and you're ready to burn, drag the CD icon to the **Trash**. The **Trash** icon turns into the **Burn** symbol.

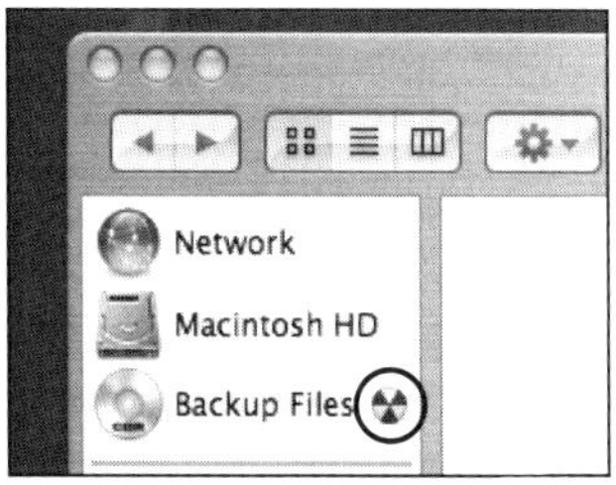

*Alternately, you can also click the **Burn** icon next to the CD's name in the **Places** sidebar of any open **Finder** window.*

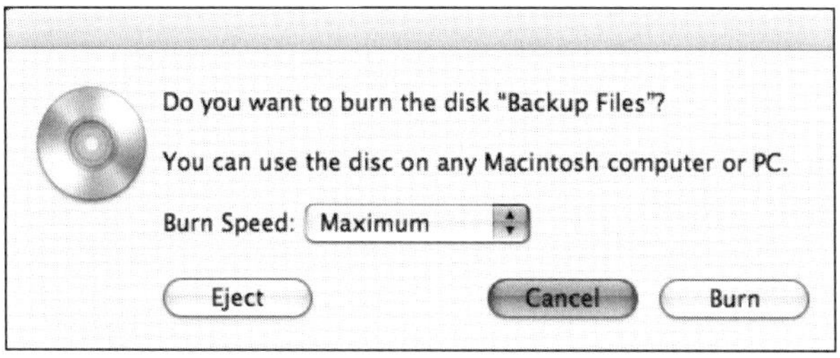

*A dialog box will open asking if you want to burn the CD. At this point, you can still choose to eject the CD without writing anything to it, or you can click **Cancel** if you want to add a few more items to the CD before you burn it. But if you're ready to go, click **Burn**.*

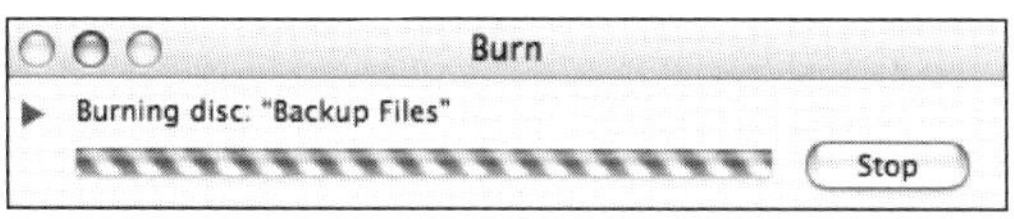

The disk's icon will disappear from the Desktop, and a window will appear letting you know that the CD is burning. When it's finished, the CD will appear on your Desktop as a regular data CD, at which point you can eject it or use it just as you would any other CD.

Displays

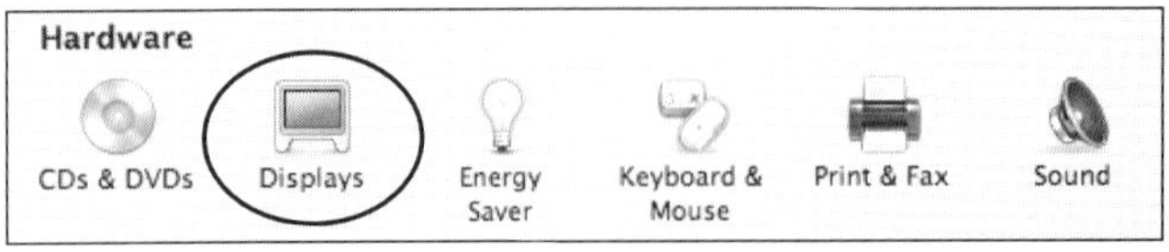

The **Displays** control pane contains the settings for the monitor (or monitors) you have connected to your Mac. Here you can adjust your monitor's resolution, determine the number of colors it displays, and calibrate its color settings.

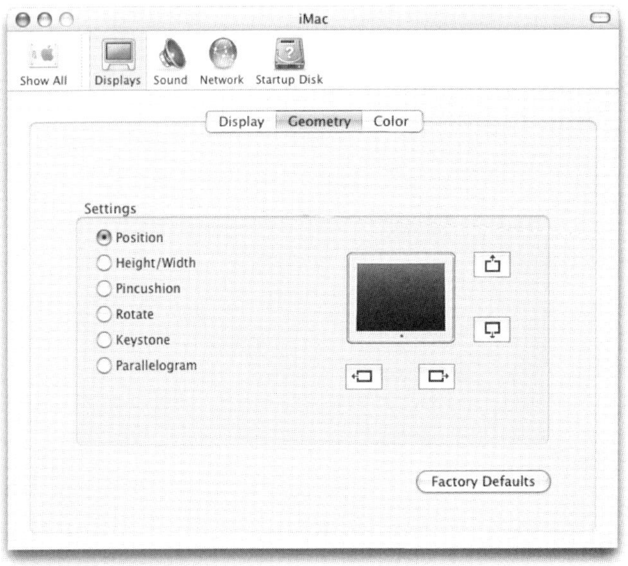

Depending on the model of Mac you're using, you may see different sections in this pane. For example, on an eMac or older iMac, you'll see the buttons **Display**, **Geometry**, and **Color**.

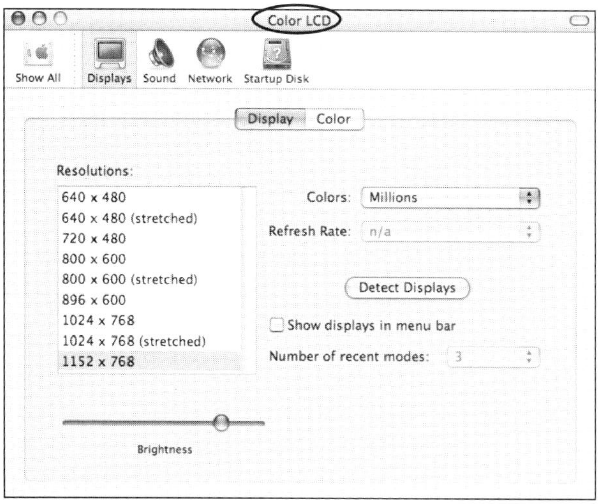

On other Macs, you'll see just **Display** and **Color**. Note that the title bar displays the type of monitor you're using. This screen shot was taken on a 15-inch PowerBook.

Regardless of which Mac you have, the two main tabs of the Displays control pane are Display and Color. The Display tab is where you can choose the resolution of your monitor and how many colors it displays. The following chart describes the options available under this tab.

Display Tab Options

Setting	Description
Resolution	All monitors today support multiple resolutions so that you can easily change the size of what appears on your screen. Selecting the proper screen resolution is all about finding the balance between the amount of screen real estate and the size of the objects onscreen. For example, if your resolution is currently set to 800 x 600, this means that your Mac is displaying 800 pixels horizontally and 600 pixels vertically. If you were to change the resolution to 1024 x 768, you'd be increasing the number of pixels onscreen and making your pixels smaller, thereby making everything onscreen slightly smaller, but at the same time you'd be increasing the amount of available work space. It's up to you to determine which resolution works best for you. Note that even though LCD flat panel monitors support multiple resolutions, they produce the best-looking image when set to their *native* resolutions. Unlike CRT (Cathode Ray Tube) monitors, LCD monitors can't change the size of their pixels, so when you choose a lower screen resolution, the LCD mimics the larger pixels that would normally appear in a CRT, resulting in a "fuzzier" looking image. Check the documentation that came with your monitor to find your flat panel's native resolution.

continues on next page

Display Tab Options *continued*	
Setting	**Description**
Colors	In the Colors menu, you can choose between thousands and millions of colors. If you're a veteran Mac user, you know that displaying more colors used to slow down your Mac, but with OS X, you shouldn't notice any speed difference whether displaying thousands or millions of colors, so feel free to keep Colors set to Millions.
Refresh Rate	The Refresh Rate menu lets you determine how many thousands of times per second your screen is redrawn. If you have a Mac with a flat panel monitor, this menu is disabled.
Detect Displays	Click this button to have OS X perform a check to recognize any other connected monitors.
Show displays in menu bar	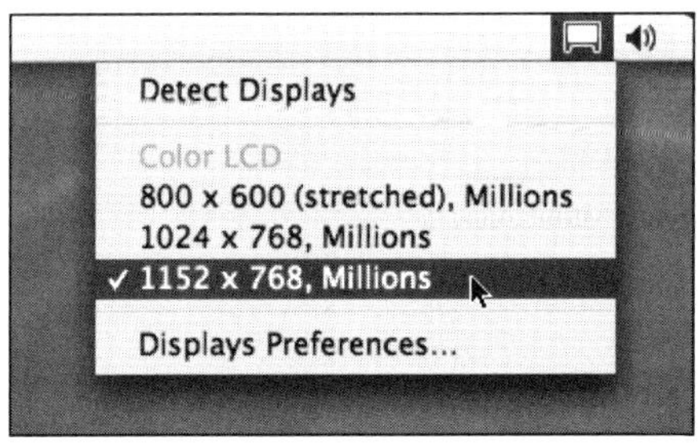 Checking this option will place a small Displays icon in your menu bar. If you often need to change resolutions or the color depth of your monitor, select this option. You'll then be able to change these settings without opening the Displays control pane each time.
Contrast/Brightness	Depending on your Mac and the type of monitor you have connected to it, you may or may not see Brightness and Contrast sliders. These days you can adjust brightness and contrast directly from Apple keyboards or on the monitors themselves, so there's really very little need for you to use these sliders here unless you're using an old iMac.

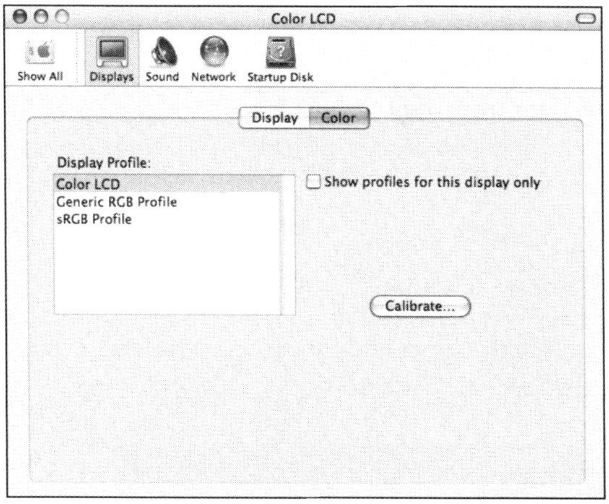

The Color section in the Displays pane is for calibrating the color profile of your monitor. You most likely won't have to worry about changing any settings here, but if you install a new monitor that's not recognized by OS X (if its name isn't listed here after you hook up the monitor) and you haven't been able to find or download a color profile for it, you can click the **Calibrate** button here in the **Color** tab to open the **Display Calibrator Assistant**, which will walk you through the process of creating a color profile for your monitor.

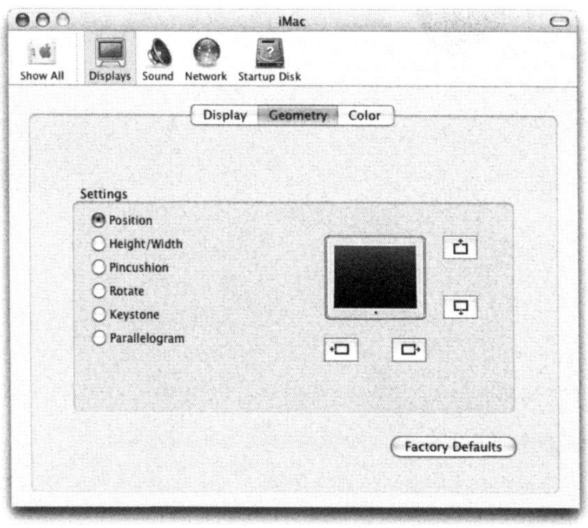

If you have an older iMac or an eMac (basically any Mac with a built-in CRT monitor), you'll also find the **Geometry** section in the Displays preferences. This collection of tools is for helping you to readjust the shape and position of the image on your screen if things start to look a little weird as the monitor ages. Just click the different **Settings** on the left side of the pane and then use the buttons surrounding the image of the monitor to the right. If you get a little overzealous and find that your screen is starting to look like it's melting, click the **Factory Defaults** button to return to the original settings and try again.

6. Energy Saver

You learned in Exercise 3 that using screen savers doesn't really save on the wear and tear of your monitor. If you're concerned about conserving electricity and prolonging your monitor's life, the **Energy Saver** control pane is the place to go.

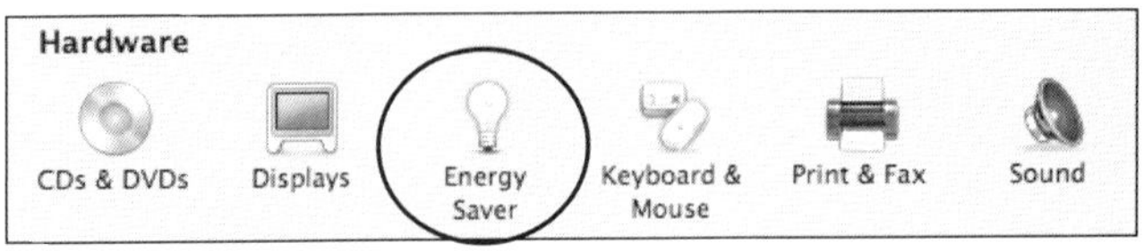

1. Click the **Energy Saver** icon.

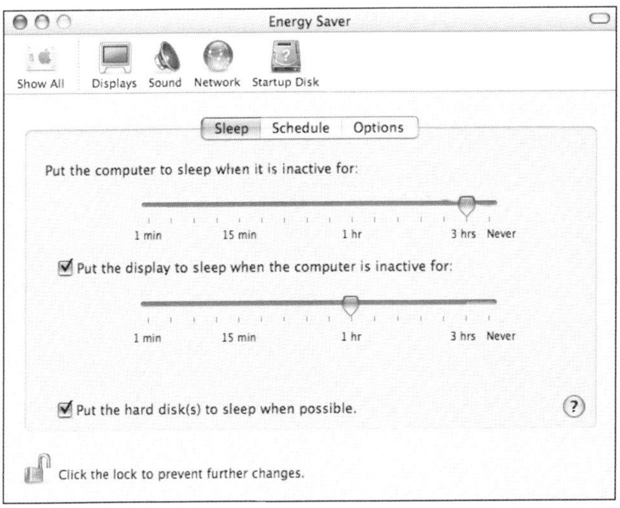

Here you can tell your Mac to sleep after a certain period of inactivity. ***Sleep*** *is a low-power mode in which your Mac turns off the signal to the monitor, stops the hard drive from spinning, and eliminates all but the most essential processor activities. The result is that your sleeping Mac uses only a fraction of the power that it needs when it's wide awake and running.*

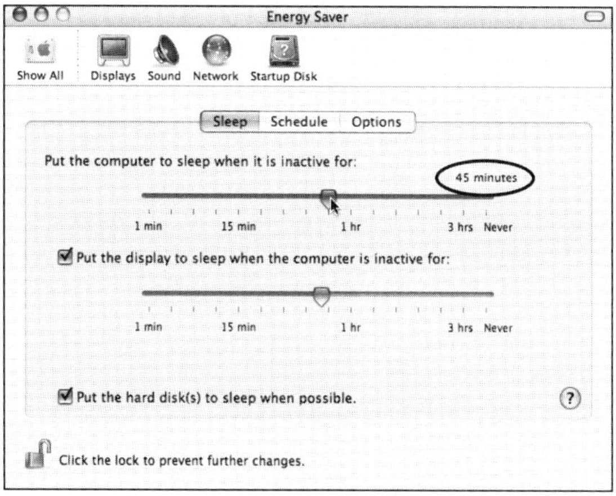

2. Drag the slider around **Put the computer to sleep when it is inactive for** and place it wherever you like. Notice that the exact time in minutes shows up in the upper-right corner while you drag.

If you prefer to have your monitor sleep before the computer itself goes to sleep, check ***Put the display to sleep when the computer is inactive for*** *and drag its slider to your preferred location. Having your monitor sleep more quickly than your Mac is sometimes advantageous because it takes a little longer to wake up your entire computer than it does to wake up just the monitor.*

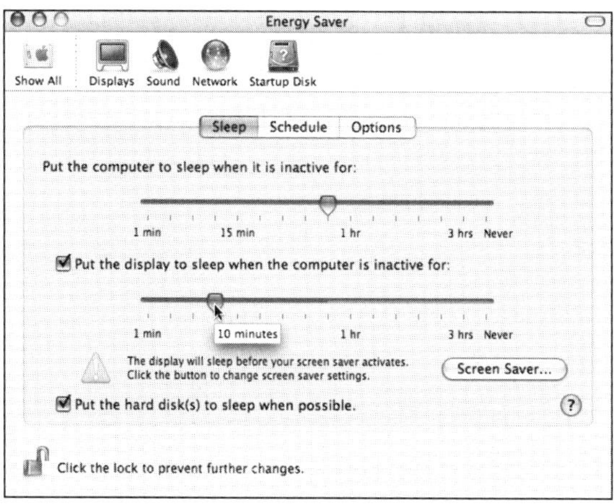

Just be aware that you can't drag the monitor slider past the position of the main sleep slider. Also, if you drag the monitor slider too far to the left, you may see a message informing you that your display will sleep before your screen saver activates.

Also found in this section of the Energy Saver pane is the ***Put the hard disk(s) to sleep when possible*** *check box. With this option selected, your Mac will spin down the hard drive whenever it detects that the drive hasn't been needed in some time. You cannot, however, specify an exact amount of time.*

PowerBook and iBook Energy Saver Settings

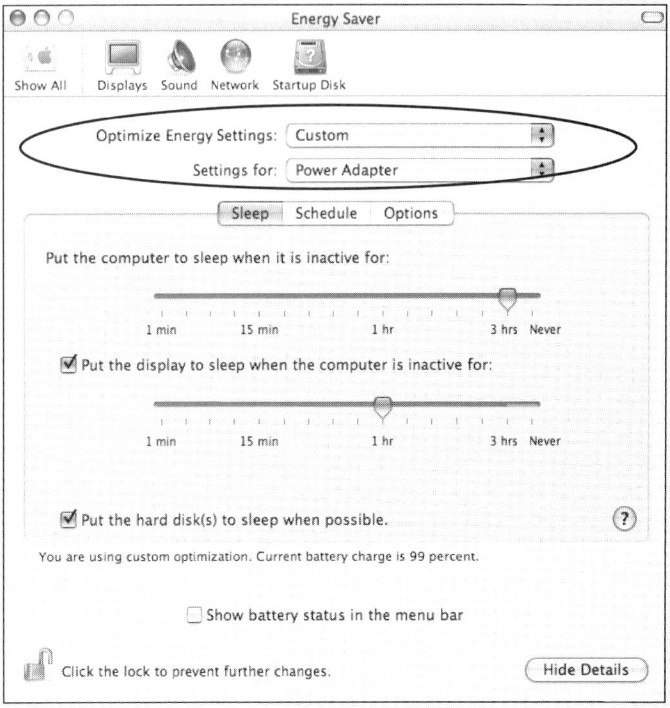

If you use a PowerBook or iBook, your Energy Saver pane contains some additional menus that allow you to customize your settings to get the best performance or longest battery life out of your Mac.

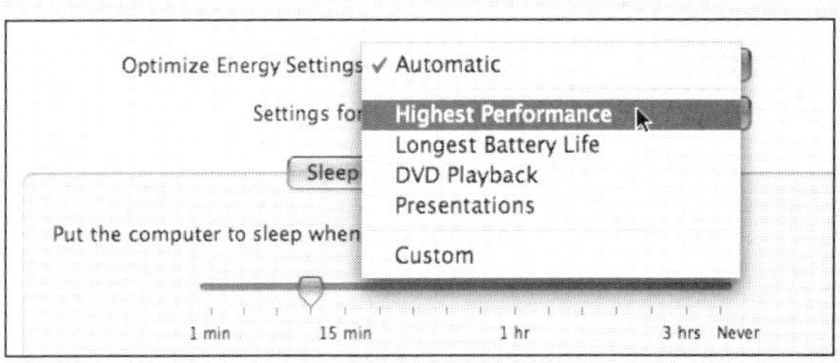

From the **Optimize Energy Settings** menu, you can choose among **Highest Performance**, **Longest Battery Life**, **DVD Playback**, and **Presentations**, as well as **Custom**, for creating your own settings, and **Automatic**, which sets your computer for highest performance when its plugged in and longer battery life when it's not. (Click the **Show Details** button to see the results of selecting each of these settings.)

continues on next page

PowerBook and iBook Energy Saver Settings *continued*

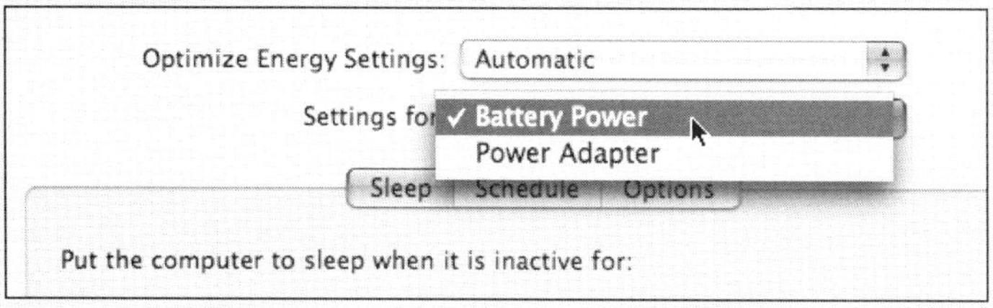

You can also create one configuration of settings that apply when your Mac is plugged in to a wall outlet and another configuration that applies when you're running off your battery. Just click the **Settings for** menu and choose either **Battery Power** or **Power Adaptor** and then choose a setting from the **Optimize Energy Settings** menu or create you own custom setting.

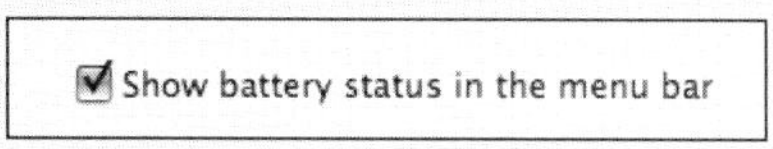

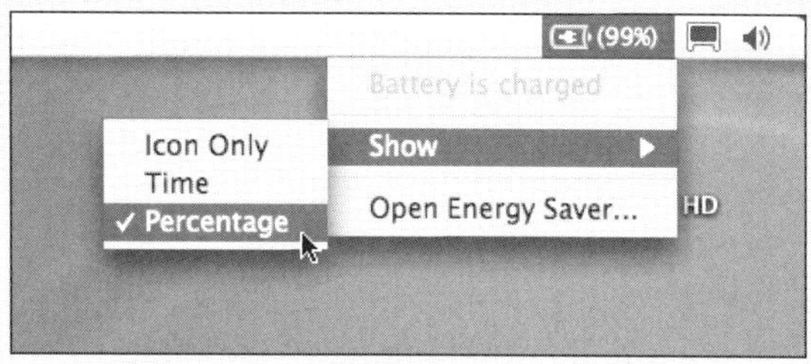

One more option found in the Energy Saver pane on PowerBook and iBooks is **Show battery status in the menu bar**. Checking this selection places a small battery icon in your menu bar, which allows you to monitor your Mac's energy use. This icon indicates the level of your battery's charge or, if your Mac is plugged into an outlet, whether the battery is charging or fully charged.

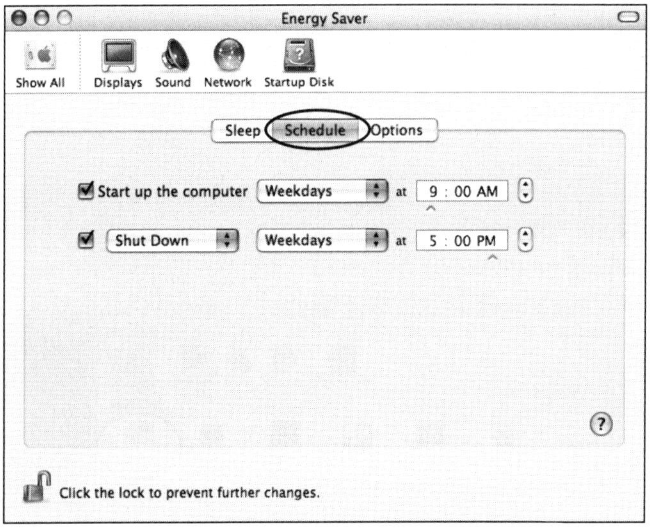

3. Click the **Schedule** button, which is new to Panther. Here you can schedule your Mac to start up, shut down, or sleep at specific times. It's simple to do: All you need to do is check either one or both of the check boxes and select the times you want these actions to occur.

4. Click the **Options** button.

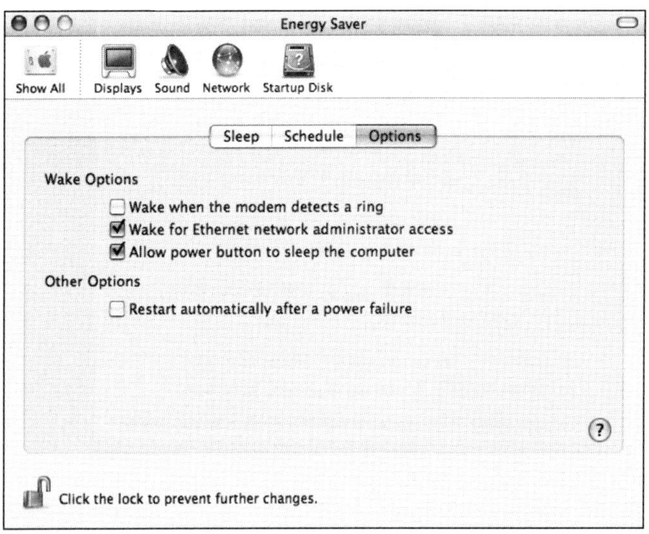

*The **Options** section offers you a handful of selections to determine what will cause your Mac to wake up and what it will do after a power failure. The following chart describes these options.*

Energy Saver Options	
Option	**Description**
Wake when the modem detects a ring	Checking this tells your Mac to wake up from sleep when the modem detects an incoming call.
Wake for Ethernet network administrator access	Checking this tells your Mac to wake up from sleep when it detects incoming requests over your Ethernet network.
Allow power button to sleep the computer	This option appears only on some Macs. Checking this option allows you to put your computer to sleep by pressing the power button once.
Restart automatically after a power failure	Check this option if you want to make sure your computer turns back on after a blackout. This can be an especially useful option if you're going to be away from your computer or accessing it from an off-site location. In the event that a blackout causes your Mac to shut off, it will turn itself back on once power returns.

5. Take a moment to personalize your **Energy Saver** settings and then click **Show All** in the toolbar.

*Tip: You can put your Mac to sleep at any time by choosing **Apple menu > Sleep.***

7. Keyboard & Mouse

Prior to Panther, the **Keyboard** and **Mouse** settings were two separate preferences panes. OS 10.3 has now joined them together and added some new features to this control pane.

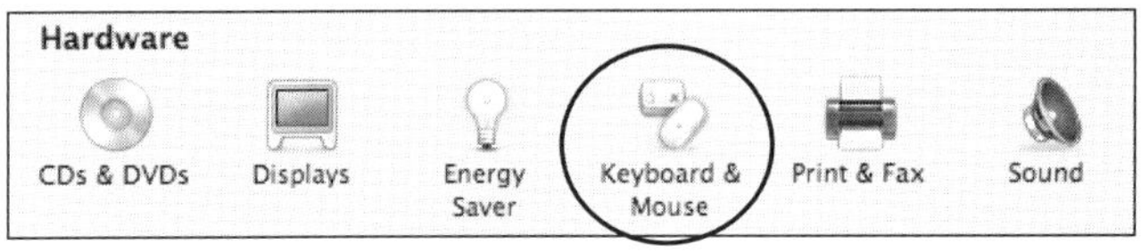

1. Click the **Keyboard & Mouse** icon.

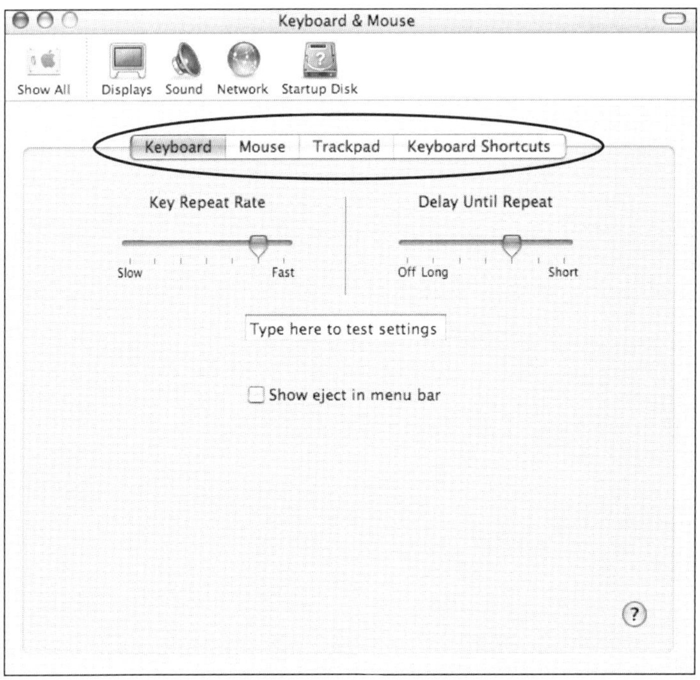

Depending on whether you're using a desktop or laptop Mac, this pane is divided into either three or four sections: ***Keyboard****,* ***Mouse****,* ***Trackpad*** *(if you're using a laptop), and* ***Keyboard Shortcuts****.*

2. If it's not already selected, click **Keyboard**.

The Keyboard section contains two sliders: Key Repeat Rate and Delay Until Repeat.

Say you wanted to express how bored you were with your friend's last email about his antique shoelace collection by typing "zzzzzzzzzzzz." Instead of pressing the Z key 12 times, you would simply hold the key, and it would start repeating the letter on your screen. You can adjust the sensitivity of this action by using the two sliders found here. Used together, the sliders determine how quickly the keyboard will react when you press and hold down a key.

*The **Key Repeat Rate** slider adjusts how quickly the letters are repeated, and the **Delay Until Repeat** determines how long the key must be held before it starts repeating. You can test your settings by clicking in the **Type here to test settings** field and pressing and holding any key. (By holding any key that results in a character appearing onscreen, wise guy.)*

*Also found under the Keyboard section on some Macs is the **Show eject in menu bar** option. Checking this selection puts a little Eject icon in your menu bar from which you can choose to eject discs from your Mac's CD or DVD drive. This is a useful option if you have an older Mac that lacks a keyboard with an eject button.*

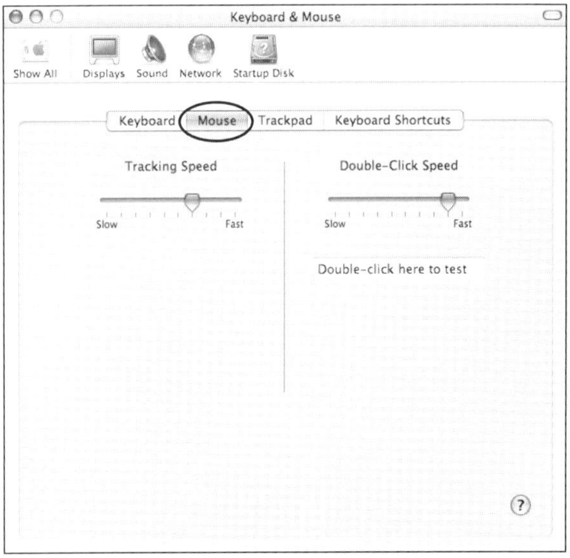

3. Click the **Mouse** button.

*In the Mouse section of **Keyboard & Mouse**, you'll also find two sliders. The **Tracking Speed** slider controls how much distance the mouse covers when you move it. Finding the proper tracking speed for your work takes some experimentation. The mouse cursor's movement onscreen doesn't depend as much on how far you move the mouse itself, but rather on how quickly you move the mouse. Moving the mouse quickly over a few inches of your screen covers more space than moving the mouse the same distance slowly. Play around with the settings to find a Tracking Speed that works for you.*

*The **Double-Click Speed** slider determines how quickly you must double-click your mouse for the double-click to register.*

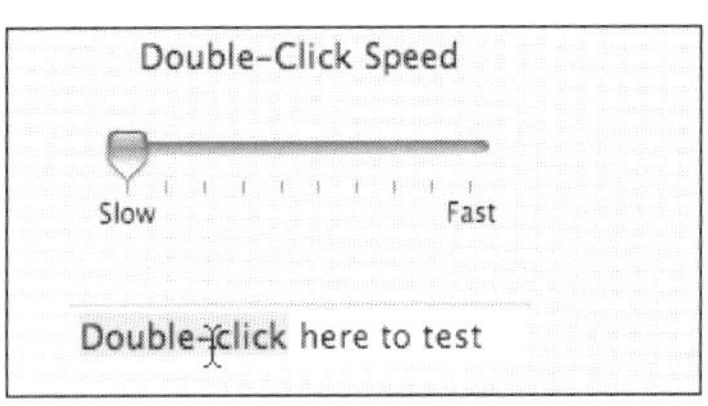

4. Drag the **Double-Click Speed** slider to **Slow**. Now test it by clicking once on the word **Double-click** below the slider; wait two seconds and click it again. You should still have been able to select the entire word. If you aren't able to double-click at least that fast, you need to be drinking more coffee.

5. Take a moment to experiment with the **Double-Click Speed** slider to find a speed that matches your clicking style.

Trackpad Settings

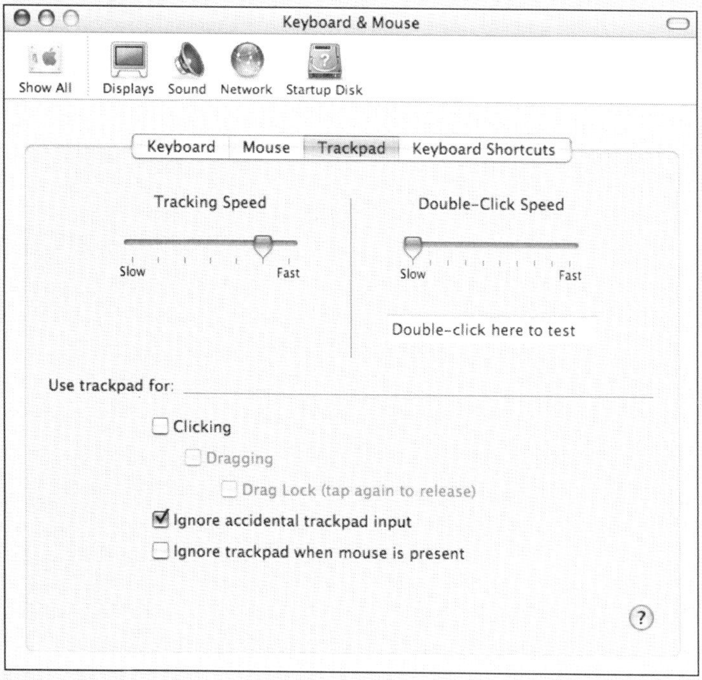

As mentioned earlier, if you're using a laptop Mac, your Keyboard & Mouse control pane features a **Trackpad** section. The two sliders found here are identical to the ones found in the Mouse section. The bottom half of the Trackpad section contains additional options for using your trackpad to click. No, there's nothing wrong with using the button below your trackpad, but some users find it easier to tap the trackpad itself rather than clicking the button. The following chart details the options available here.

Trackpad Options

Option	Description
Clicking	This turns on the trackpad's clicking capability. Instead of clicking the button below the trackpad, tap the trackpad itself. Double-tap to double-click. If the **Clicking** option is not selected, you cannot select the **Dragging** or **Drag Lock** options.
Dragging	This option allows you to use the trackpad as if you were holding down the mouse button and moving the mouse. You can use this option to drag icons, select from menus, draw marquees, highlight text, and anything else you normally accomplish through dragging. To drag an item, double-tap the trackpad, but immediately begin dragging on the second tap. You can continue dragging, and even lift your finger off the trackpad for a second if you run out of room, until you've moved the item to your preferred location. Once your finger leaves the trackpad for more than a second, the move is complete. The **Dragging** option must be selected to select the **Drag Lock** option.
Drag Lock	If you're having trouble with the dragging thing, this option "locks" the item you're dragging so you're free to move it around without fear that you'll take your finger off the trackpad for too long and end up dropping the item at the wrong location. With the **Drag Lock** option checked, double-tap and drag as you normally would when dragging an item, but then single-tap to release the item.
Ignore accidental trackpad input	This option is here for users who often find themselves accidentally touching the trackpad while typing, which can be pretty annoying if you're in the middle of typing a sentence and the cursor gets moved to a different location in the document. Check this option to prevent this aggravation.
Ignore trackpad when mouse is present	If you prefer to connect an actual mouse to your laptop instead of using the trackpad, check this option and your Mac will automatically disable the trackpad whenever you plug in the mouse. Leaving this option unchecked will allow both the trackpad and the mouse to control the pointer, which is totally unnecessary unless you want to mess with someone who's trying to use the trackpad by jiggling the external mouse around every time he or she tries to select some text.

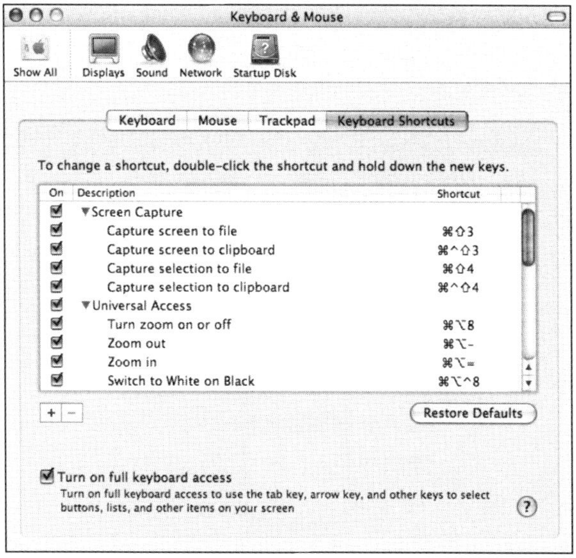

6. Click the **Keyboard Shortcuts** button. Here you'll find a list of several keyboard shortcuts that let you control your Mac almost entirely from the keyboard. You'll learn about this control pane in the next chapter, "*Universal Access and Speech*." For now, just take a quick sneak peak at the items listed here.

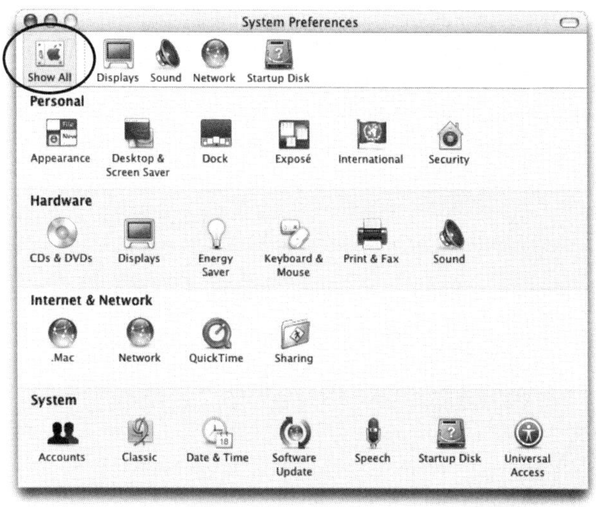

7. Click the **Show All** button to return to the main **System Preferences** window.

The next control pane in System Preferences is ***Print & Fax****. You'll skip this for now, but don't worry, you'll learn all about printing and faxing in Chapter 6,* "Printing, Fonts, and Faxing."

8. Sound

This exercise shows you how to manage the sounds coming out of and going into your Mac.

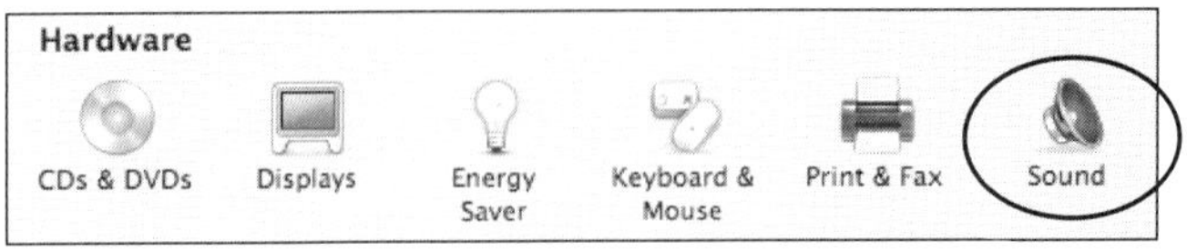

1. Click the **Sound** control pane icon.

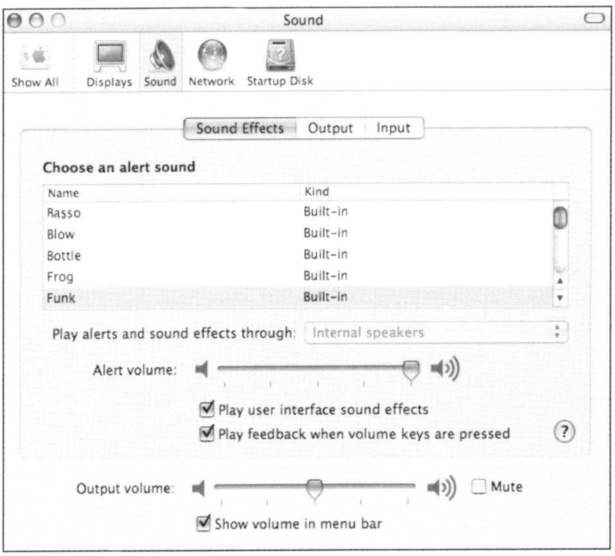

The Sound pane contains three sections: ***Sound Effects****,* ***Output****, and* ***Input****.*

The Sound Effects tab contains choices for your Mac's alert sound, which is the sound it makes when some dialog boxes pop up, when you click in a wrong location, or anytime the Mac needs your attention.

2. Click through the list of alert sounds and find one you like or can live with. Unfortunately, the ability to record your own alert sounds is no longer available in OS X, so you're stuck with what's in this list. Note to Classic Mac enthusiasts: The only sound that's survived since the old days is the ubiquitous **Sosumi**. All the other sounds were created for OS X.

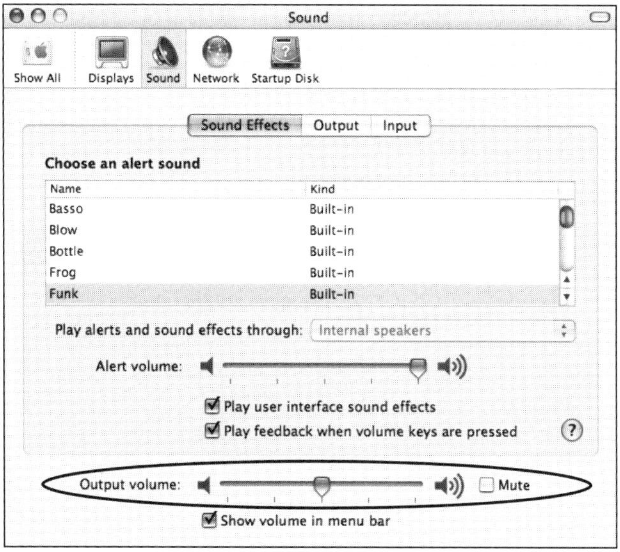

At the bottom of the Sound control pane is the ***Output volume*** *slider. This slider is for adjusting the level of the overall volume coming out of your Mac, and it remains visible no matter which of the three Sound sections you're working in.*

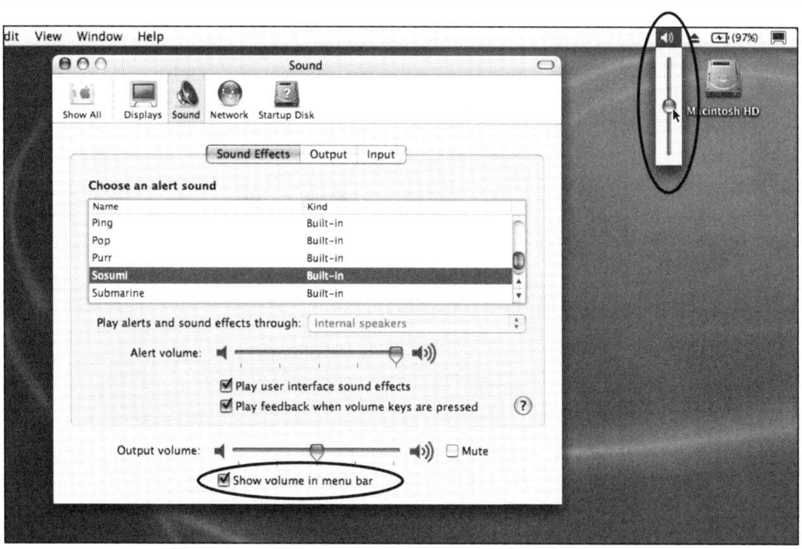

Keep ***Show volume in menu bar*** *checked if you want to be able to control your output volume without having to open System Preferences each time.*

The four remaining options under the Sound Effects tab are explained in the following chart.

Sound Effects Options	
Option	**Description**
Play alerts and sound effects through	By default, all alert sounds are sent through your Mac's built-in sound card (the built-in audio controller). If you have more than one audio output device, you can select one from this menu and route your alert sounds through your preferred device.
Alert volume	This controls the volume level of the alert sound. Bear in mind that it does not control the overall volume of all the sounds coming out of the Mac—that's what the Output volume slider at the bottom of the control pane is for.
Play user interface sound effects	Having this option selected will cause sound effects to play when you perform certain actions such as dragging an item off the Dock or throwing something into the Trash.
Play feedback when volume keys are pressed	With this option selected, your Mac will beep every time you increase or decrease the volume with the volume keys on your keyboard, giving you a pretty good idea of the overall volume level setting. If your keyboard doesn't have volume keys, you don't have to worry about this option.

3. Click the **Output** button.

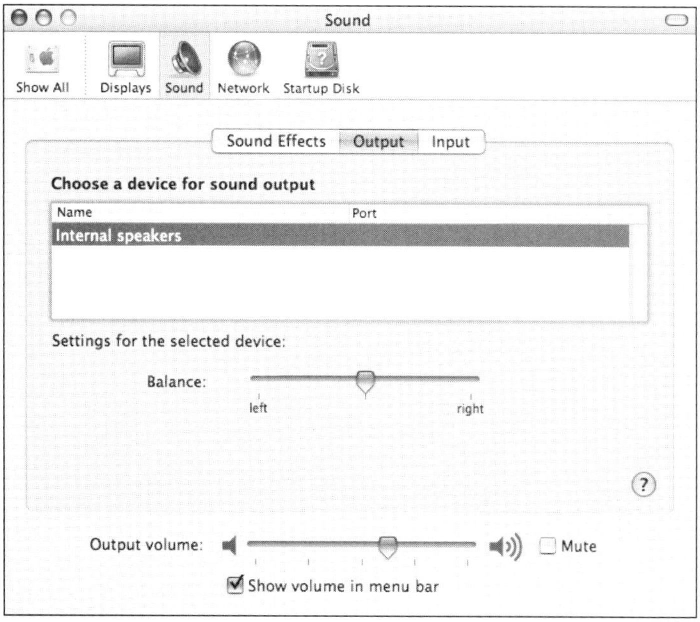

This tab lists any audio controller devices currently hooked up to your computer that are capable of outputting sound. (An audio controller is sometimes referred to as a "sound card.") Depending on your Mac, you may see ***Internal speakers*** *(if your Mac has built-in speakers) or* ***Line Out*** *(if your Mac has external speakers) listed here. If you have any other devices capable of outputting sound connected to your Mac, they'll be listed here as well.*

For Ultra-Geeks Only

As you just saw, the Output tab routes the audio, leaving your Mac through the built-in sound card or any other audio controller connected to your Mac. But you also saw in the Sound Effects section that you can select from a list of audio controllers through which you can route the Mac's alert sounds. You don't have to choose the same sound card for both alert sounds and output. If you have two audio controllers, it's possible to have your alert sounds leaving your Mac through one sound card and all other sounds leaving through a second sound card. Why would you want to do this? Because you can.

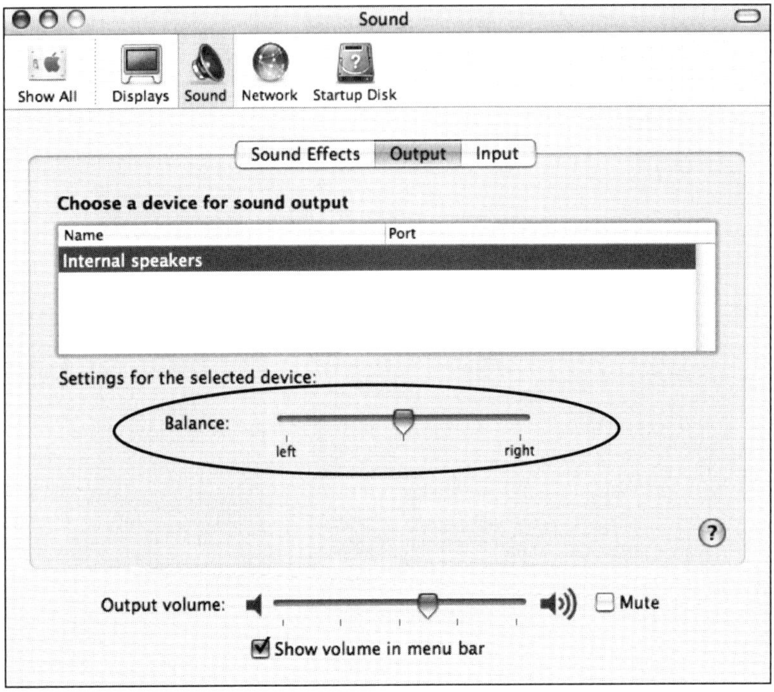

The only other option under the Output tab is the ***Balance*** *slider, which allows you to adjust the balance between the left and right output channels. In most cases, you'll want to keep this right in the center.*

4. Click the **Input** button.

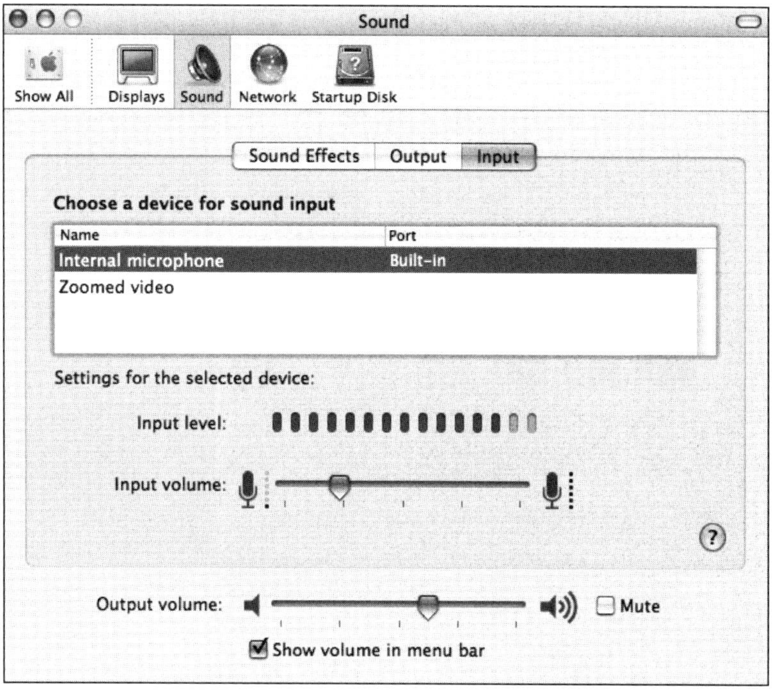

In this section of the Sound control pane, you can choose which input device the Mac will use to bring sound into the computer.

5. If your Mac has a built-in microphone, select **Internal microphone**. Or if you have a different input device, such as an iSight camera, select it. Now clap your hands, sing something, or scream. You'll see the **Input level** meter fluctuate, letting you know how much sound is coming into the computer. Don't get too excited though–there's no way to record any sounds from the Sound control pane. All you can do here is pick an input device and slide the Input volume slider around to adjust the level. You'll need third-party software to record audio into your Mac. (Well, technically you can use iMovie to record your voice through your built-in microphone, but you'll have to wait for Chapter 16, "*iMovie 3*" to learn how to do that.)

6. Take a moment to make sure all your Sound preferences are the way you want them, and then click the **Show All** button in the toolbar to return to **System Preferences**.

Inkwell

If you're a graphic designer or a technology junkie, it's possible that you may have one more Hardware icon in your System Preferences.

Users with a Wacom graphics tablet connected to their Macs will see the **Ink** icon listed under **Hardware** preferences. "Ink" is short for "Inkwell," the current name for Apple's handwriting recognition technology. Inkwell first debuted in the mid-'90s on Apple's short-lived Newton handheld device. The Newton may be gone, but the handwriting technology has returned and can add some cool functionality to your Mac.

For the uninitiated, a graphics tablet is a flat device that sits on your desktop (your actual desktop, the thing your Mac and/or monitor is sitting on) and looks kind of like a mouse pad. A special pen allows you to draw freehand in programs such as Adobe Photoshop. Unlike drawing with the mouse, which provides all the grace and finesse of drawing with a bar of soap, graphic artists often prefer drawing with the graphics tablet because it gives them more control. You can also use the graphics tablet to write longhand and import your handwriting into a word processing program. When you plug a drawing tablet into a Mac running Panther, the Ink icon automatically shows up under Hardware preferences, where you can turn on and tweak Inkwell's handwriting recognition settings.

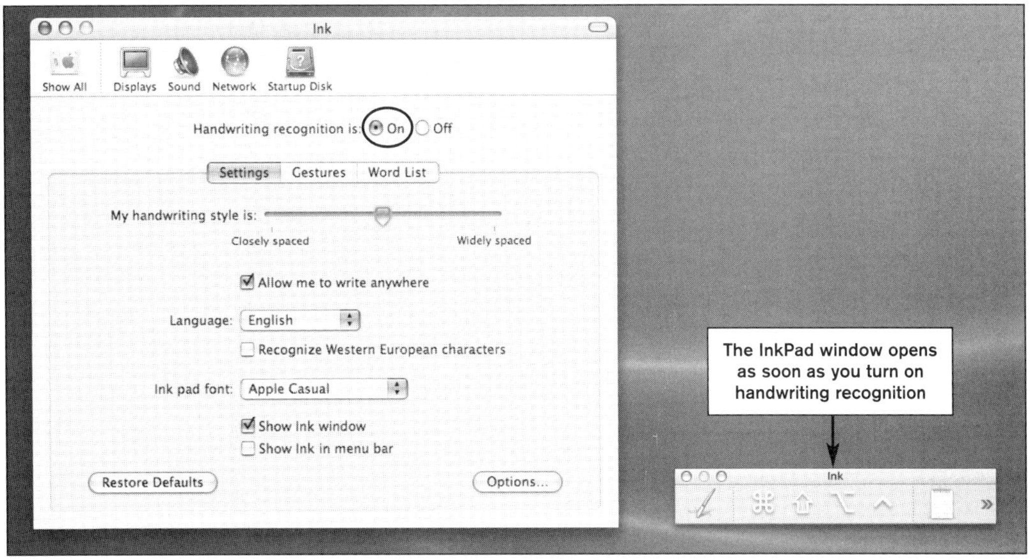

To turn on handwriting recognition, click the **Ink** icon to open the **Inkwell** control pane and then click **On**. This will open InkPad, a floating window that stays visible in all applications, which you can use to write or draw within any application that accepts text or images.

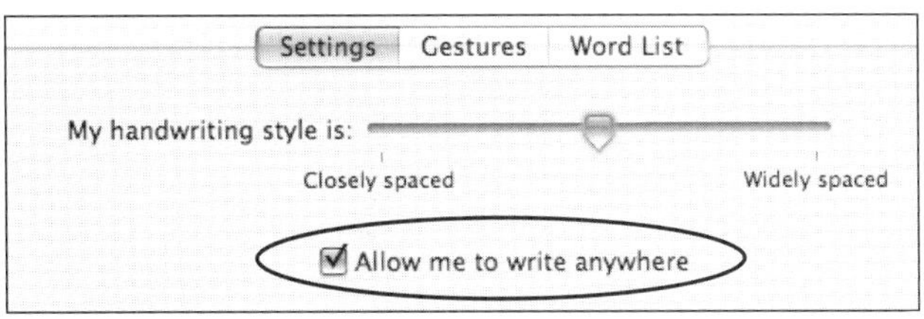

But before you start writing, determine whether you want Inkwell to accept your handwriting anywhere or just within the InkPad window.

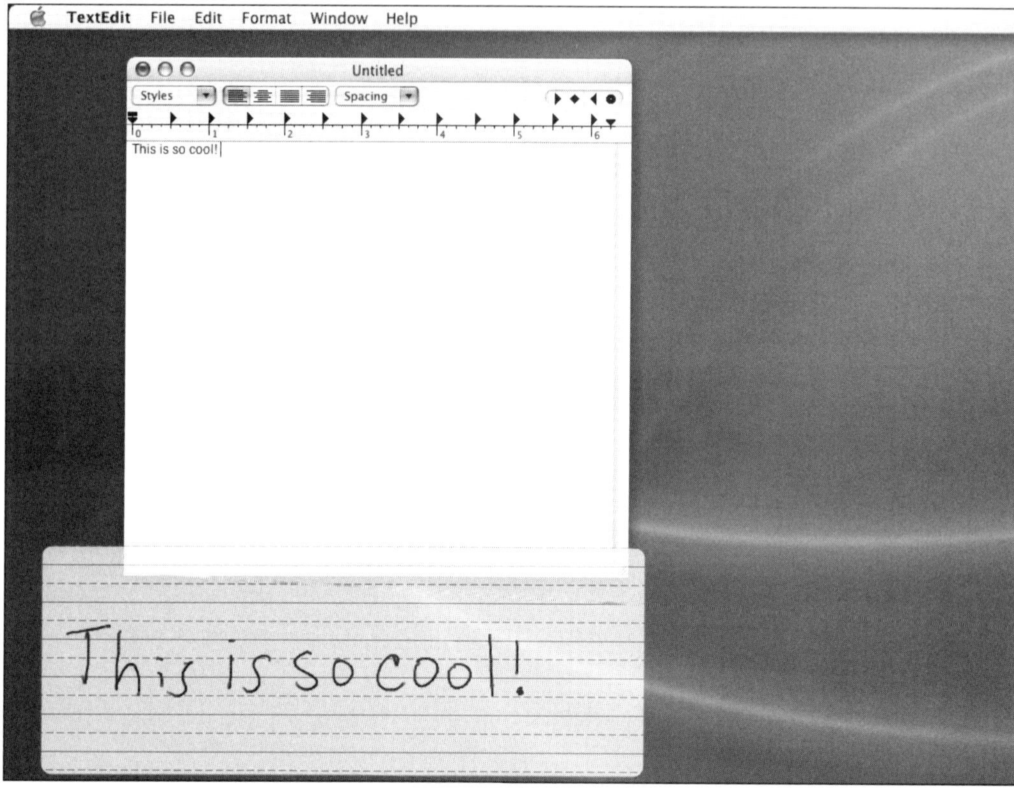

With **Allow me to write anywhere** selected, you can start writing in any application that accepts text or images. As soon as you start moving the pen, a semi-transparent window resembling a yellow legal pad will appear to show what you're writing. The moment you stop writing, your handwriting is interpreted and placed into the document at the current location of the cursor.

Being able to write anywhere and anytime is a great feature, but if you often use your pen as a mouse, it can also be inconvenient. You don't want Inkwell thinking that you're trying to write something when all you want to do is highlight some text.

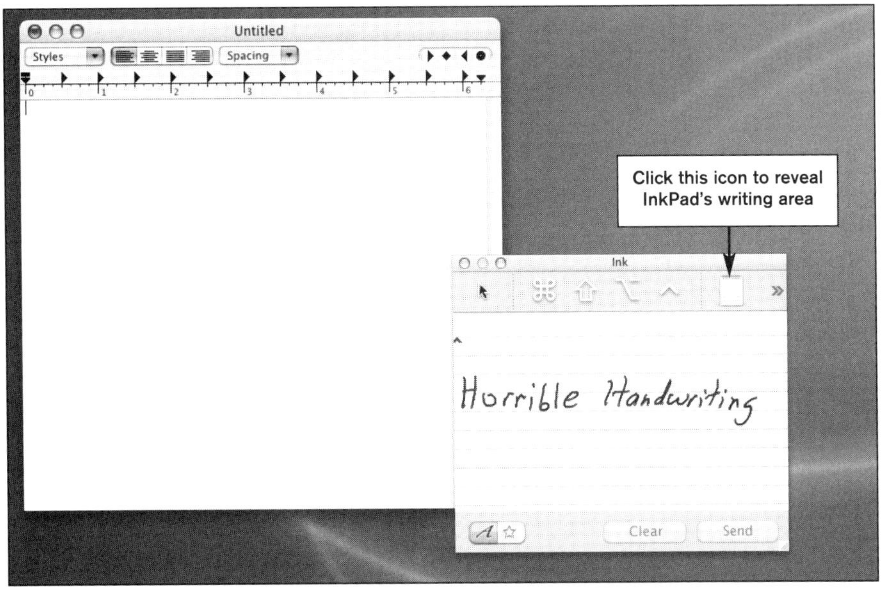

With the **Allow me to write anywhere** option unchecked in the **Ink** control pane, handwriting recognition is limited to the boundaries of InkPad.

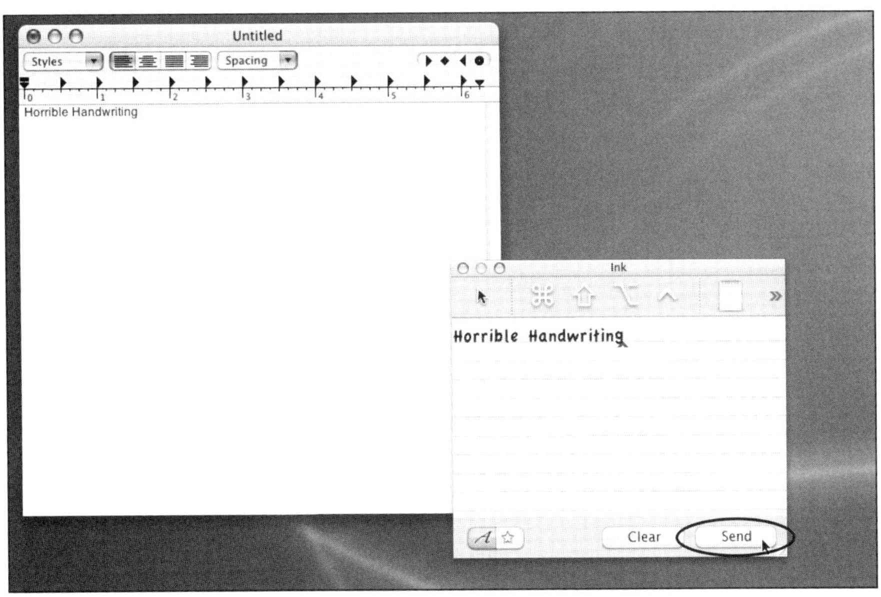

When you move your pen away, Inkwell interprets your writing. Click **Send** to place the text into your document. Limiting your handwriting to InkPad prevents Inkwell from accidentally assuming that you want to write whenever you use your pen as a mouse.

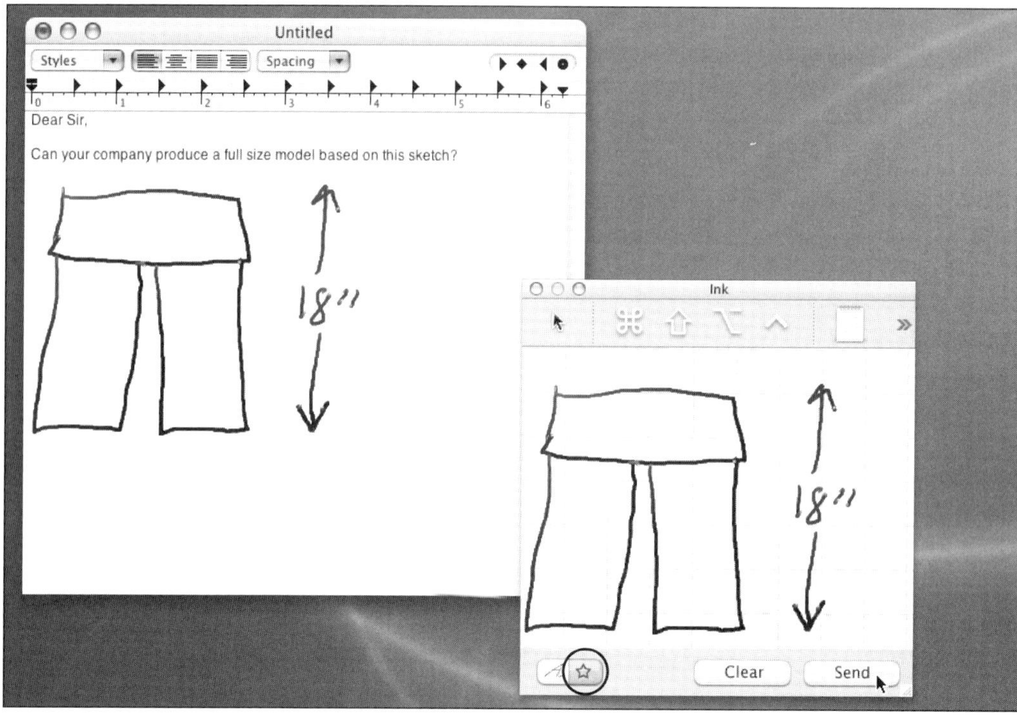

InkPad can even be used to insert a sketch into a document. Click the **star** icon in the lower-left corner to tell InkPad you want to draw. Create your drawing and then click **Send** to place your masterpiece in your document.

Inkwell technology is not quite to the point where it's going to replace the keyboard for anyone, but it is useful for writing small amounts of text. Your success with Inkwell will also depend on how neat or messy your handwriting is. To help Inkwell recognize your writing, keep these key points in mind:

- Don't use cursive. Inkwell can only recognize printing.
- Use the slider in the Ink control pane to let Inkwell know whether your handwriting tends to be closely spaced or more widely spaced.
- Exaggerate the difference between capital and lowercase letters.

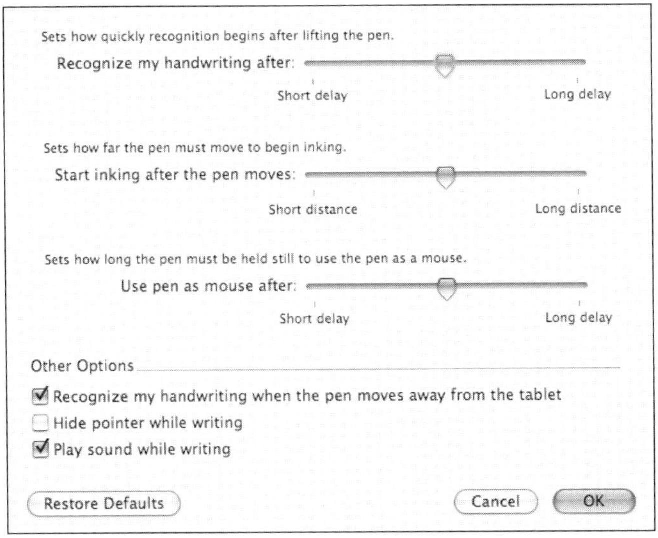

Click the **Options** button in the **Settings** section of the **Ink** control pane to find even more controls that help you adjust Inkwell to your writing style.

Use the **Word List** section to teach Inkwell any uncommon words (such as proper names or technological terms) that you may use often.

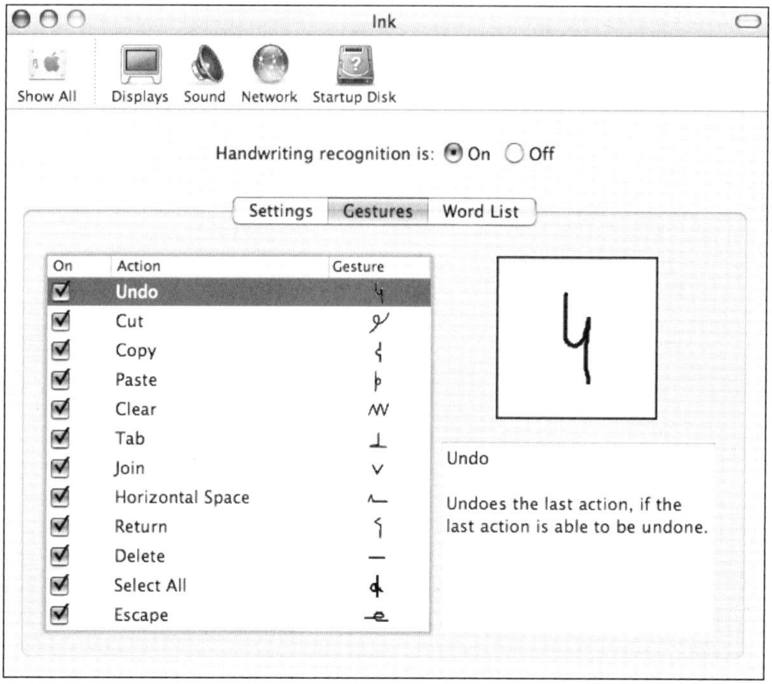

If you find that you're really starting to get the hang of working with Inkwell, you might want to take some time to learn **Gestures**, the collection of squiggles that acts as shorthand representations of specific actions such as copy, paste, undo, space, and so on. If you're familiar with writing in Palm OS devices, you shouldn't have any problem mastering Gestures.

Whew! You made it through the Hardware preferences. Take a well-deserved break and then move on to the next exercise and the next set of preferences.

Note: If you have a Bluetooth enabled device connected to your Mac, you may find a **Bluetooth** icon under your **Hardware** preferences. You'll learn about Bluetooth in Chapter 13, "*iCal and iSync.*"

Internet & Network

The Internet & Network preferences have a broad range of different settings that depend largely on how your computer is connected to the Internet. Because properly setting up your computer for Internet access is such an important issue, Chapter 8, "*Getting Online*," is devoted entirely to this topic. For now, you'll just examine the one control pane that at first glance seems to be a bit out of place here: the QuickTime control pane.

9. QuickTime

QuickTime is Apple's all-purpose media player. It can play music, videos, and even open most types of images. For the most part, QuickTime requires very little configuration–just tell it which file to play and it plays it. The QuickTime control pane in System Preferences deals mainly with how QuickTime handles video over the Internet.

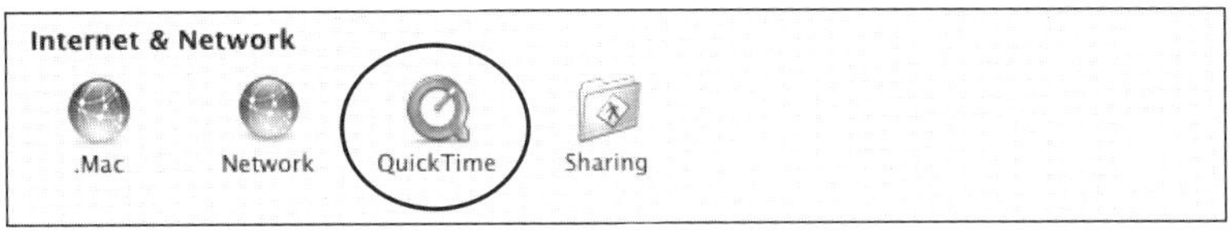

1. Click the **QuickTime** icon to open its control pane.

The QuickTime control pane contains five sections, but you'll most likely find only two or three of the sections to be useful to you.

2. If it's not already selected, click the **Plug-In** button. The options here determine how QuickTime will handle video and music streams from the Internet. The following chart describes these settings.

QuickTime Plug-In Settings	
Setting	**Description**
Play movies automatically	With this option checked, you won't have to wait until a movie has been completely downloaded to your computer before viewing it. As soon as QuickTime determines that enough of the movie has been buffered into memory, it will start playing the movie. Of course, if your Internet connection experiences higher traffic during the download, and the download slows down, you may experience pauses and skips in playback until the entire movie is downloaded.
Save movies in disk cache	With this option checked, downloaded movies are saved in the browser's cache memory. Essentially, this means that the browser will "remember" the entire movie even if you close the browser window or browse onto another page or site. If you return to the movie's page (via the Back button in your browser for instance), you won't have to wait for the entire movie to download again. Your browser will just reload it from its memory and play it back for you right away. If you quit your browser application, or if your browser's memory cache gets too full, the movie will be removed from memory and will have to be downloaded again when you wish to view it.
Enable kiosk mode	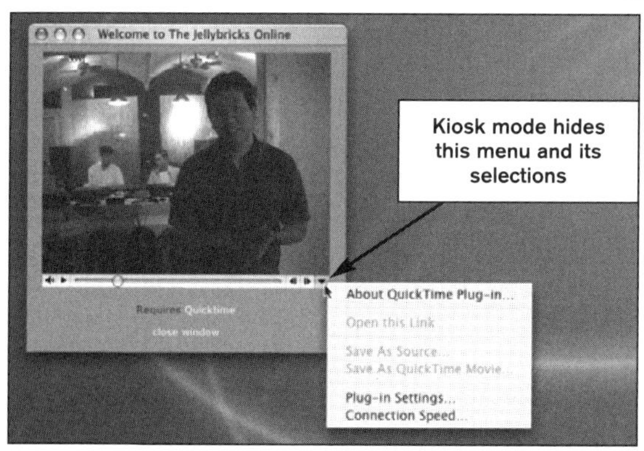 With this option selected, when movies are played in a browser window, the menu used for saving the movie to disk and adjusting QuickTime settings will be hidden.

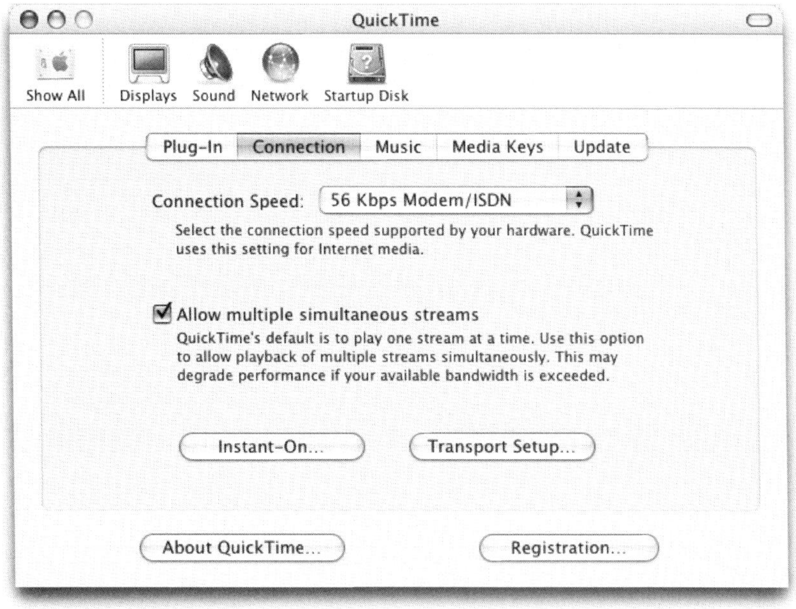

3. Click the **Connection** button. The following chart describes the options available here.

QuickTime Connection Settings	
Option	**Description**
Connection Speed	Use this menu to let QuickTime know the speed of your Internet connection. Some Web sites actually provide movies of different sizes for slower or faster connections. When you load a movie into your browser, the Web site first checks to see how fast your connection is and then serves up the appropriate size movie. If you find that your movies are taking too long to load, you can always return to this control pane and change your connection speed.
Allow multiple simultaneous streams	This option allows you to play back more than one downloading movie at a time. If you experience any decrease in speed while attempting this trick, be prepared for some hiccups and pauses in playback.

continues on next page

QuickTime Connection Settings *continued*	
Option	**Description**
Instant-On	Clicking this button will open a dialog box where you can enable Instant-On, which forces movies to begin playing back as soon as you start downloading them. However, to increase your chances of smooth and uninterrupted playback, you're better off ignoring this option and instead checking **Play movie automatically** under the QuickTime **Plug-In** tab.
Transport Setup	If you don't know what this is, you don't need to worry about it. But since you asked: Transport Setup is used if your Mac is behind a firewall that prevents Real Time Streaming Protocol (the technology that QuickTime uses to send content over the Internet) from being viewed. If you're having trouble viewing movies behind your company's firewall, you can click this button and then click **Auto Configure.** If you still can't view movies over the Internet, contact your network administrator for assistance or to be told to stop screwing around and get back to work!

*The next two tabs in the QuickTime control pane are **Music** and **Media Keys**, and can be summed up in a few sentences. The Music tab is for selecting a music synthesizer for playing back music and MIDI files, but there's only one choice available. If you're a musician and have installed your own MIDI controller, you'll be able to select it from the list here. Otherwise, the default QuickTime Music Synthesizer is all you need. The Media Keys tab is where you store passwords or keys that are supposed to unlock specially protected QuickTime files, but you'll be hard pressed to find anyone who uses these passwords to lock their movies.*

4. Click the **Update** tab. This tab contains some options for making sure that you always have the latest version of QuickTime.

*If you're connected to the Internet, clicking **Update Now** will scan Apple's site for any updated components of QuickTime. Selecting **Install new 3rd-party QuickTime software** and then clicking **Update Now** will search for non-Apple updates and then ask if you want to install them. You can also select **Check for updates automatically** to search for updated components each time you open the QuickTime application.*

Going Pro

With QuickTime, you're able to view and listen to all kinds of media files on the Web. But to be able to save or edit these files requires forking over $30 to Apple for a QuickTime Pro registration key. QuickTime Pro gives you the ability to save downloaded movies to your hard drive (if the movie's creator hasn't locked that feature). It also gives you some pretty impressive editing capabilities, such as trimming movie clips, adding and removing audio and video tracks, and joining separate movie files together. If you decide to go Pro, click the **Registration** button at the bottom of the **QuickTime** control pane and then click the **Register Online** button to go to Apple's Web site and register. Apple will send you your registration information, which you can then enter into the QuickTime control pane by clicking the **Registration** button again.

5. Click the **Show All** button in the toolbar to return to **System Preferences**.

10. Accounts

The final category of System Preferences is **System**. This category contains a lot of important options for setting up user accounts and running the Classic Mac environment. Many of the control panes in this section can be changed only by users with administrative privileges. Don't know how to give a user administrative privileges? Lucky you, that's the first thing you'll learn to do in this exercise.

1. Click the **Accounts** icon under **System**.

As you learned in Chapter 2, "Working with Files and Folders," *Mac OS X is a multiple-user operating system. Even if you're the only person using your Mac, you're still using your own personal account; it's just not obvious because when you turn on your computer, OS X doesn't ask you for a password (unless it has been set up to do so). But when you add more users to your Mac, the procedure for logging onto your Mac changes. After your Mac starts up, you're presented with a login screen where you can select your own account and enter your password (unless you've deactivated the login screen, which you'll also learn to do in this exercise).*

The major advantage of having a multiple-user environment is that all users get to keep their accounts and preferences exactly the way they like them without interfering with other users' accounts. When you log onto your Mac after someone else has used it, items such as your Dock settings, Desktop icons, and Web browser bookmarks remain unchanged. It's as if no one else has used your Mac at all.

There are two types of user accounts you can create: administrator and standard. Unless you enable some specific options, a standard user has complete access to his or her own personal user folder (the Home folder and its contents) and can view files and user applications found on the main hard drive, but cannot create or delete files, folders, or any other items outside of his or her Home folder. A standard user can change some preferences in System Preferences, such as Desktop images, Dock settings, and Login Items, but most System Preferences are off-limits. Off-limits System Preference control panes are marked with a lock icon found in the lower-left corner of the control pane. If a standard user wants to change one of these preferences, he or she must click the Lock icon and have an administrator enter his or her password.

An Administrator has complete access to the Mac's hard drive and has all the privileges necessary to create new folders, install applications, and make changes to all System Preferences. So unless you mean to give full access of your Mac to other users, make sure that you create standard accounts for them.

Next, you'll create a new user account.

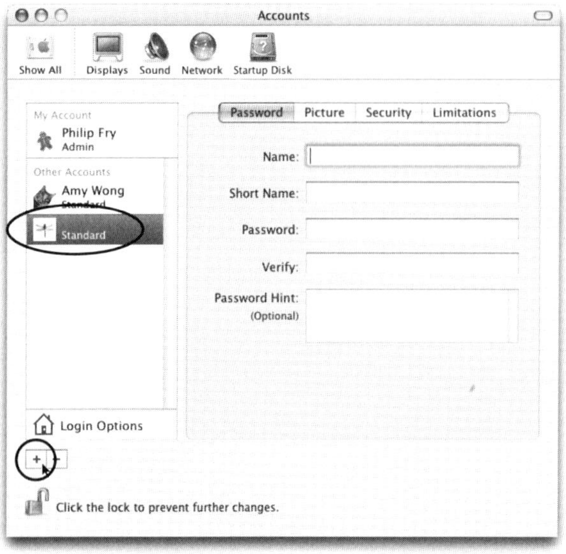

2. Click the **New User** (+) button. A new standard account appears in the list of users along the left side of the pane.

3. In the **Name** field, type **Garrick Chow** and then press **Tab**. A suggested short name will automatically appear in the **Short Name** field. The short name is the name that's applied to the user's Home folder, and should ideally be shorter than the user's full name.

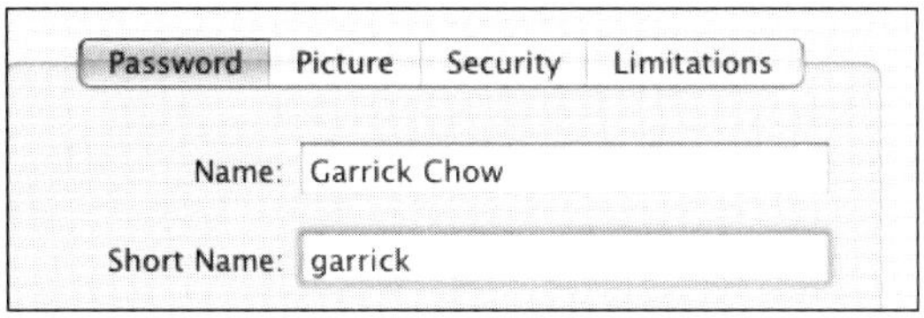

4. Change the **Short Name** to **garrick** and press **Tab**.

Next you'll create a password for this user.

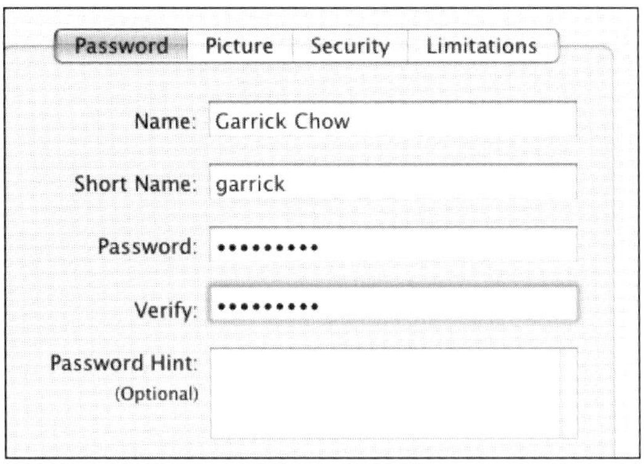

5. In the **New Password** field, type **woodchuck**. It will appear as a series of nine bullet points rather than letters. To make sure you typed it correctly, retype **woodchuck** in the **Verify** field.

*Notice that adding a **Password Hint** is optional. If you want to make sure that the user has some help in case of a forgotten password, add a hint here, but don't make it too obvious if security is a serious issue.*

---

6. In the **Password Hint** field, type **What happens when a beaver swallows too much bark?**

***Tip:** If the purpose of creating multiple-user accounts on your Mac is just so everyone in your household can have the Mac set up with his or her own preferences (that is, you're not worried about people getting into other people's accounts), you can leave the password fields blank to avoid the necessity of a user having to enter a password every time he or she wants to log in.*

7. Click the **Picture** button. Here you can select an image for this user by choosing from the list of pictures. This picture will be used to represent this user in the login window, the Address Book application, and in iChat.

Using Your Own Pictures

If you feel that none of the standard Apple Pictures really capture your dynamic personality, you can select any of your own pictures to represent yourself. If you have a Web cam (such as Apple's iSight camera) or video camera attached to your Mac, you can even take a snapshot of yourself to use as your user picture.

Next to your currently selected picture, click **Edit**.

continues on next page

Using Your Own Pictures *continued*

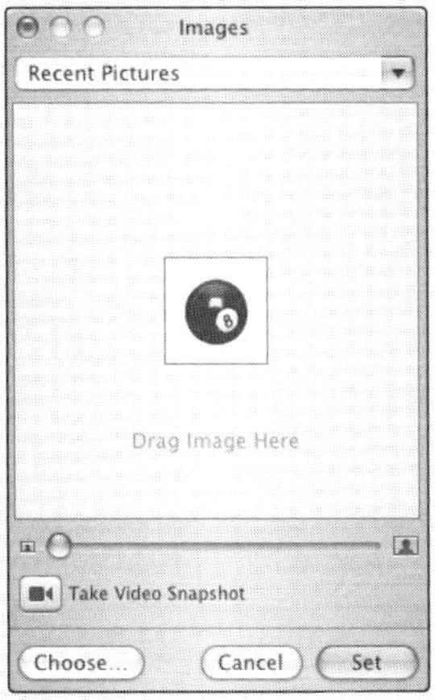

This opens the Images window. Here, you can drag in a picture of your choice from elsewhere on your Mac. For the best results, your image should be 64 x 64 pixels in size. If your image is larger than that, you can use the slider below the image to resize, reposition, and crop the image. Your image can be in just about any graphics format: GIF, JPEG, TIFF, PNG, or PDF formats all work well.

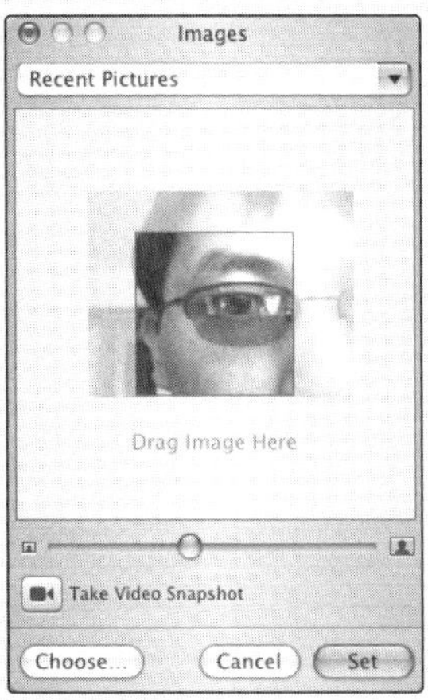

If OS X detects a camera attached to your Mac, you can also click the camera button next to **Take Video Snapshot**. Once clicked, you have a few seconds to primp and prepare before your picture is taken. If you're not happy with the result, just take another one–the original won't be saved.

Once you've chosen your own picture or taken a snapshot you're satisfied with, click **Set**. Incidentally, this same **Images** window appears when you take your picture in iChat AV. You'll learn more about this in Chapter 10, "*Address Book, Mail, and iChat AV.*"

8. Click the **Security** button in the **Accounts** preference pane. This area should look a bit familiar. Here you can turn FileVault on and off, just like in the Security pane of System Preferences. For the moment, however, it's more important to note that this is the area where you can check **Allow user to administer this computer** if you want this user to have full access to your Mac. Since you don't want to trust this Garrick character with complete access to your computer, you'll leave this unchecked.

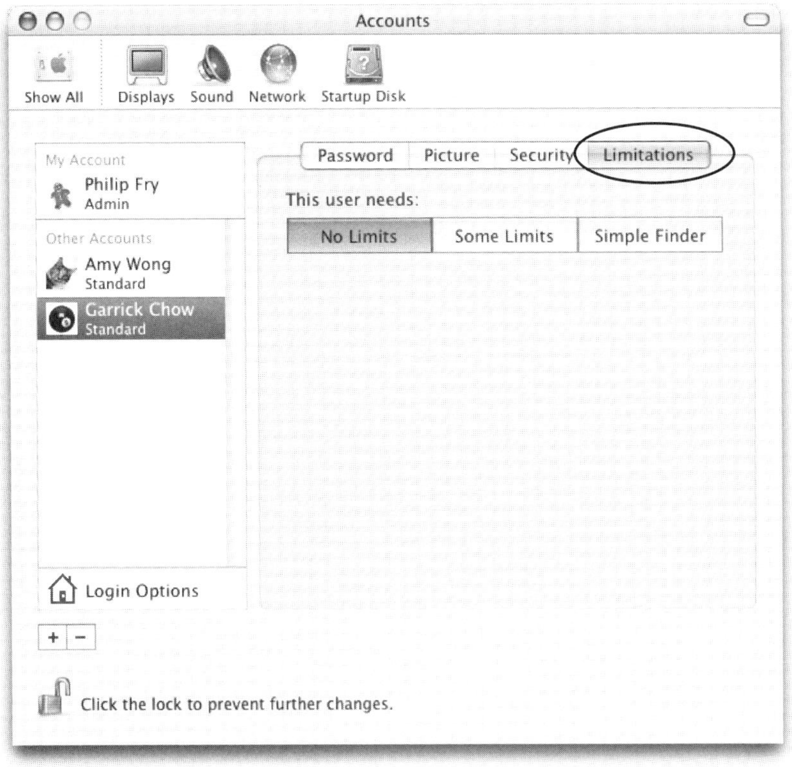

9. Click the **Limitations** button. (This button is not available if the selected user has administrator privileges.) Depending on the user, you may or may not want all standard accounts to have identical privileges. Although it's true that it's nearly impossible for standard users to damage the files on your hard drive, some users need a little protection from themselves. That's where the Limitations button comes in. Here you can choose from three categories: **No Limits**, **Some Limits** (also referred to as **managed**), and **Simple Finder** (also referred to as **simplified**). With **No Limits** selected, standard users can perform tasks such as running applications, adding and removing items from the Dock, and burning CDs. However, they still can't perform administrator tasks such as changing certain System Preference settings and installing or removing applications. If you feel that you need to further limit a standard user, choose either **Some Limits** or **Simple Finder**.

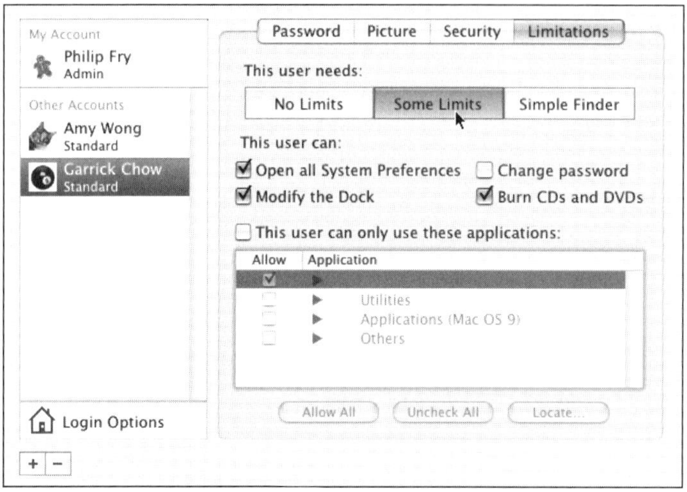

10. Click **Some Limits**. The following chart describes the options found here.

User Account Limitations: Some Limits

Option	Description
This user can	You can elect any combination of the five check boxes.
Open all System Preferences	This option allows the user to view all the System Preference panes, but the user will still not be able to change the settings of key system preferences such as Date & Time and Energy Saver.
Modify the Dock	The user is free to move items to and from the Dock. Remember, each user gets his or her own Dock preferences, so his or her changes won't affect the Docks of other users.
Change password	Gives the user the ability to access the Accounts preference pane and change his or her password. As an administrator, you can always change your users' passwords even if they've created their own.
Burn CDs or DVDs	This option allows the users to burn CDs or DVDs. Unchecking this option will prevent the user from writing any sort of information (data, audio, or otherwise) to CDs or DVDs.
This user can only use these applications	If you want to limit the user's access to only certain applications, check this option and then in the area below, check only the applications that you want to allow the user to use.

*As you can see, the **Some Limits** button gives you a fair amount of control over the selected user's capabilities.*

*If you want to even further restrict the user's access, click the **Simple Finder** button. But you should only choose this option if you* really *want to limit the user's Mac experience. With this option selected, the user has access to only the exact files and folders that you select from the window at the bottom of this control panel. Only a single Finder window is ever seen; multiple windows cannot exist. Icons and folders can be opened with only a single click. The best way to find out how Simple Finder acts is to see it for yourself. Set up a dummy account with Simple Finder privileges and then log out of your administrator account (by choosing **Apple menu > Log Out**) and then log in to the dummy account to see how limited the Mac experience can be. You'll most likely agree that Simple Finder should be reserved only for the most inexperienced users.*

***Important:** Make sure the level of access you want a user to have (No Limit, Some Limits, or Simple Finder) is selected before you close the Accounts pane. The button that's selected is the one that's in effect.*

Now that you've created an additional user on your Mac, you'll examine the Users folder to see what OS X has created.

11. Leave the **Accounts** pane open and double-click the hard drive icon on your **Desktop**. Then double-click the **Users** folder.

12. In the **Users** folder, along with your **Home** folder and any other users' folders that may have already been created, you'll find the **garrick** folder. Double-click it to view its contents and notice that OS X has created all the standard folders each user finds in his or her **Home** folder. Close the window.

*With multiple users on your Mac, sharing the computer is a simple matter of logging in to your account when you want to use the Mac, and logging out when you're done. When you first turn on the Mac, you'll be presented with a login screen where you can select your account, sign in, and get to work. When you're done, you can choose **Apple menu > Log Out**. This will take you back to the main login screen where other users can then log in to their own accounts and start using the computer.*

But what if the other users only use your Mac occasionally? You might not want to be bothered with the hassle of logging in to your computer every time you turn it on. If you're not overly concerned with the possibility that someone might turn on your computer and start messing around with your files, you can set OS X to automatically log in for you each time you turn on the computer. You'll learn to do this next.

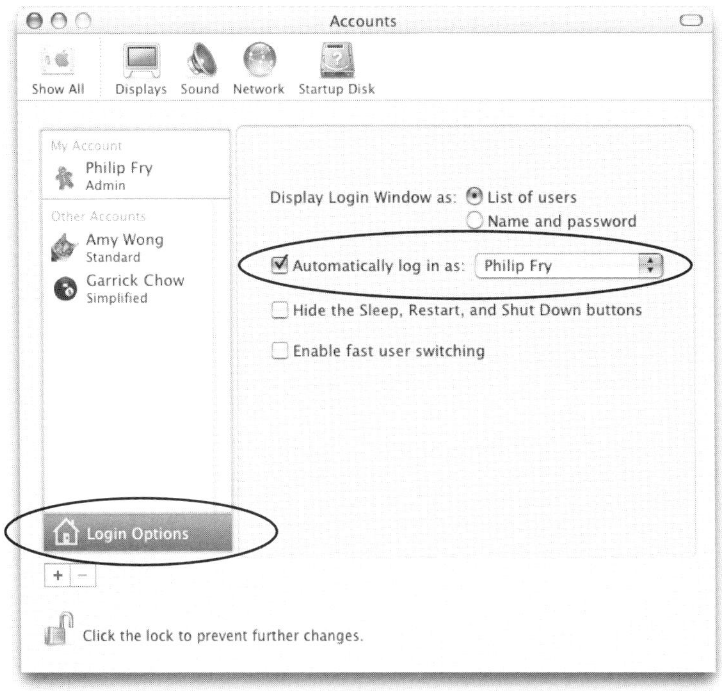

13. In the **Accounts** control pane, click **Login Options**. Check **Log in as [your name]** if it's not already selected. This will prevent the login window from appearing when you turn on your Mac.

Note: *You'll still be able to get to the login window by choosing **Apple menu > Log Out.** You'll need to do so in order to let other users access their accounts when you're done working.*

*While you're in here, you can also determine how the login window appears by selecting either **List of users** (which lists all the user accounts and their pictures) or **Name and password** (which only provides name and password fields, preventing anyone from knowing which users have access to this Mac). Additionally, you can check **Hide the Sleep, Restart, and Shut Down buttons** to prevent these buttons from appearing in the login window, and you can also check **Enable fast user switching** (see the following sidebar).*

Fast User Switching

New to OS 10.3 Panther is Fast User Switching. Prior to Panther, switching from one user to another required the first user to log out, which meant all running applications and documents would be closed, connected servers would be disconnected, and generally all activities would be shut down–all so the second user could log onto his account and check some email or copy a file in his User folder. Thankfully, Apple has introduced Fast User Switching, which allows a other users to log into their accounts without first forcing (sometimes physically) the first user to log out.

To turn on this capability, check **Enable fast user switching** in the **Login Options** of the **Accounts** preferences pane. You'll see a warning advising you to turn on this option only if you trust the other users of this computer. Click **OK** if you trust them.

Your account name now appears in the upper-right corner of your screen. Clicking on your name lists all the other users' accounts. Any of these other users can select their names from this list to quickly switch to their accounts, but you won't have to worry about losing your work; all of the applications you have open will keep running in the background. (And if you have a Mac that was built in the past year or two, you'll see a cool 3-D cube effect to visually emphasize the changing of accounts.) When the other user logs out of his or her account, you can log back into yours and get right back to work without having to worry about restarting programs or reopening files. Pretty nifty, huh?

At some point, for any number of reasons, you'll probably need to delete a user account. In early incarnations of OS X, getting rid of all traces of a former user was a complicated task to say the least. Thankfully in Panther, removing a user is a snap.

14. In the **Accounts** control pane, select **Garrick Chow** from the list of users. Click the **Delete User** (–) button.

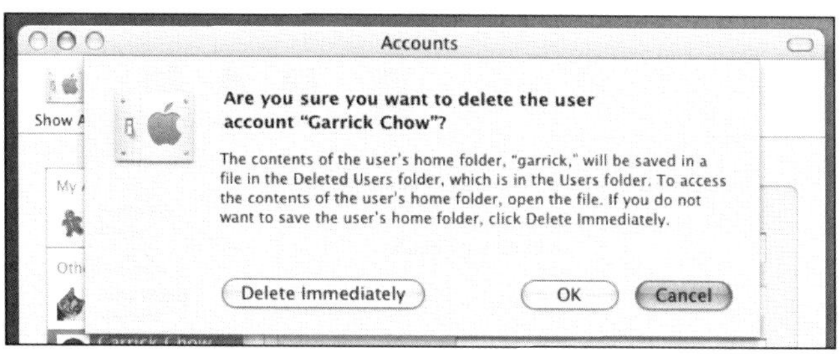

You'll be asked to confirm that you really want to delete this user. Also notice that this dialog box is informing you that the contents of the user's **Home** *folder will be placed in a folder called* **Deleted Users***. Unless you click* **Delete Immediately***, you're really only deleting the user's account information. The user's files and folders will remain intact.*

15. Click **OK**. OS X takes a moment to package up the contents of the user's **Home** folder, and then deletes the account information.

16. Double-click the **hard drive** icon on your **Desktop** and open the **Users** folder.

17. Notice that a folder called **Deleted Users** has been created. Open **Deleted Users**.

When you delete an account, the contents of the user's Home folder get packaged into a single compressed file called a Disk Image, which is extremely useful for archiving the user's files and folders. (You'll learn more about Disk Images in Chapter 7, "Installing Applications."*) You can copy this Disk Image onto a CD to give to the user or you can keep it where it is in case you need to re-create the user's account. If you did need to reinstate the user's account, you would simply create a new account in the Accounts control pane and then drag the contents of the user's Disk Image to his or her proper folder in the new Home folder. In this case, though, you'll just delete this Disk Image.*

18. Drag **garrick.dmg** to the **Trash** in the **Dock**. **Ctrl+click** the **Trash** and choose **Empty Trash** from the contextual menu. You've now completely deleted all traces of this user's account.

19. In the **Accounts** control pane, click **Show All** to return to **System Preferences**.

Startup Items

If you've used pre-Panther versions of OS X, you might have noticed that the Login Items preference pane has disappeared. The Login Items pane was used to designate applications and files to automatically open each time you log onto your computer. In Panther, this option has been moved into the Accounts preference pane and renamed **Startup Items**.

To access Startup Items, click your own name in the accounts pane and then click the **Startup Items** button. Here you can select applications and files to open each time you log into your Mac. For instance, if you use your Mac primarily for surfing the Internet and reading email, you probably use Safari and Mail all the time. Rather than manually starting these applications each time you turn on your computer, you can add them to your list of Startup Items.

To do so, just click the (+) button, navigate to the applications and select them. (You can also simply drag applications into this pane.) Check the application's Hide check box if you want the application to be hidden when it starts up. For example, you may prefer to check your email before you surf the web; checking Hide next to Safari means even though the application is running, it will be hidden from view so you don't have to worry about moving its browser window out of the way of your email.

To remove items from the **Startup Items** list, just select them and click the **Remove** (–) button.

II. Classic

In one aspect of Apple's vision of the perfect world, all Mac users would boot up their computers in OS X and happily remain there with no need to ever boot up in OS 9. In the real world, however, there are still many programs that operate only in a pre–OS X environment (although their numbers are dwindling). Users who continue to rely on non–OS X compatible software must either reboot their computers in OS 9 (which you'll learn how to do later in this chapter) or use the Apple-preferred method of Classic mode.

When Apple first introduced OS X to the world, they knew that Mac users would be hesitant to adopt a brand new operating system that so few applications were compatible with. To help ease the Mac community into OS X, Apple included Classic, which is essentially an application that emulates the previous Macintosh operating system, OS 9.x. With this emulator running, you can switch back and forth between OS X applications and Classic applications with ease. Just keep in mind that when you're running Classic, it's not running as an operating system because it's not controlling your computer. Mac OS X is always in control, and Classic exists as an application within OS X.

If you're new to the Mac, running in Classic may require you to pick up some additional instruction to learn the ins and outs of OS 9. However, if you're a Mac veteran, you should be able to use Classic with relative ease. This section of the exercise will show you how to get Classic up and running on your Mac.

The first thing to do is to make sure that you have a Classic operating system installed on your Mac.

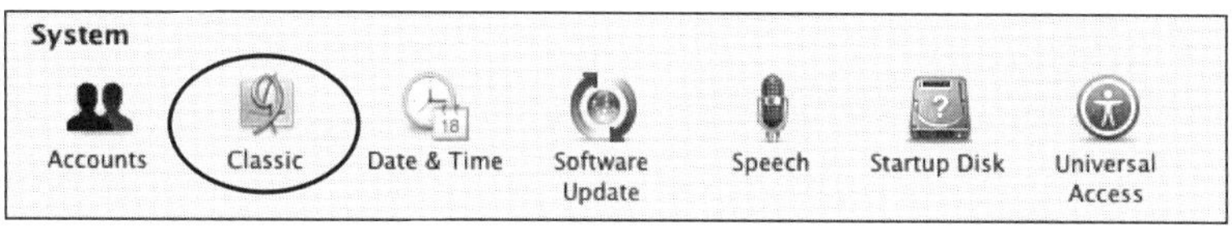

1. In **System Preferences**, click the **Classic** icon.

When you click Classic for the first time, OS X will perform a quick scan to see if OS 9.1 or later is installed on any local drives. Two things can happen at this point:

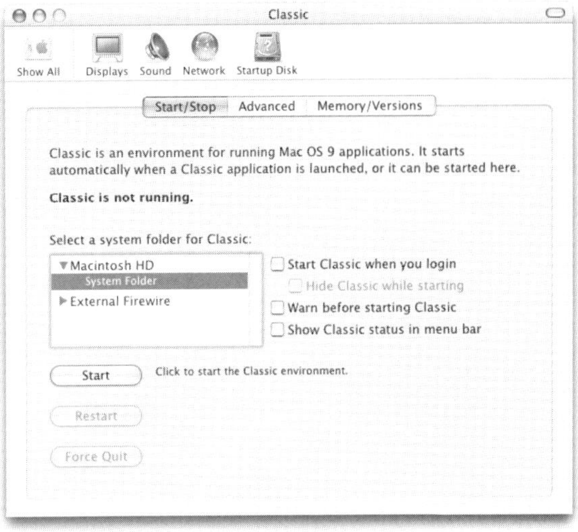

If you upgraded your Mac from OS 9.1 or later to OS X, you already have the necessary components to run Classic. If you have OS 9 installed on more than one drive connected to your Mac, you'll need to select the copy of OS 9 that you want to run for this user account.

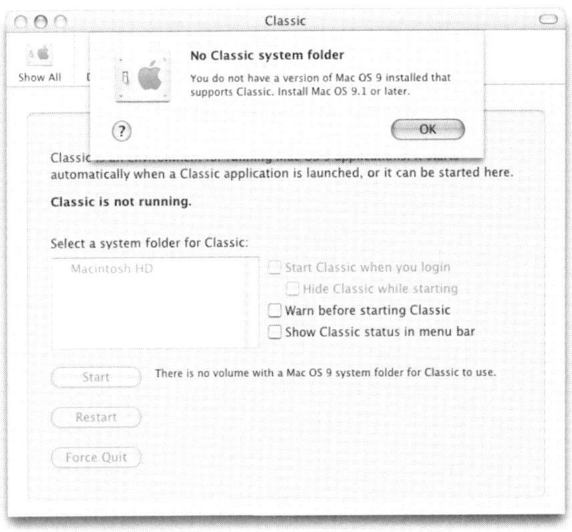

*If you installed OS X on a "clean" hard drive, meaning a drive that contained no information, OS X will obviously not find a version of OS 9 installed on your system (OS X is not bundled with Classic), meaning that you'll have to install OS 9 before you can continue. If you see the message shown in this screen shot, click **OK** and install OS 9.1 or later before continuing. See the sidebar "Acquiring OS 9" for more information.*

Acquiring OS 9

If you upgraded your Mac from OS 9 to OS X, you already have OS 9 installed (unless you did a clean install and erased your hard drive when you installed OS X). If you purchased the full version of Panther and need to run OS 9 in Classic mode, you can participate in Apple's OS Fulfillment Program, which allows you to purchase a copy of OS 9 for $19.95 if you can provide proof of purchase of OS 10.3. See **http://www.apple.com/macosx/upgrade/** for more details.

Once OS 9 has been installed on your Mac, you can run Classic.

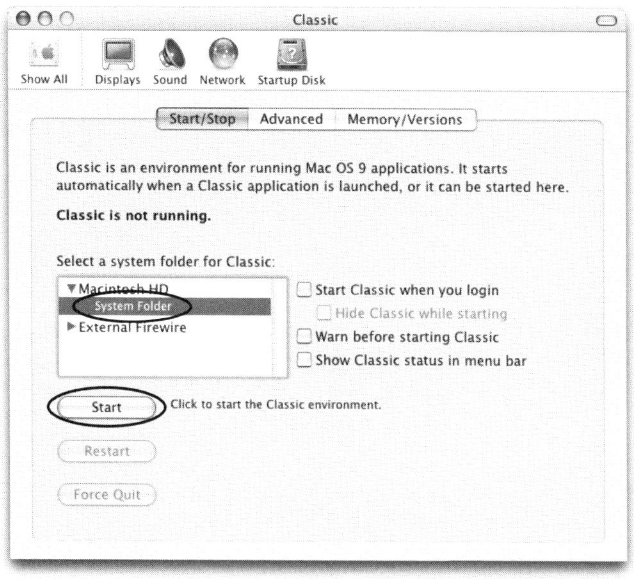

2. If you haven't already done so, select a system folder for Classic from the **Classic** control pane. (Unless you have more than one drive containing OS 9 connected to your Mac, you should have only one choice here.) Click **Start** to begin running Classic.

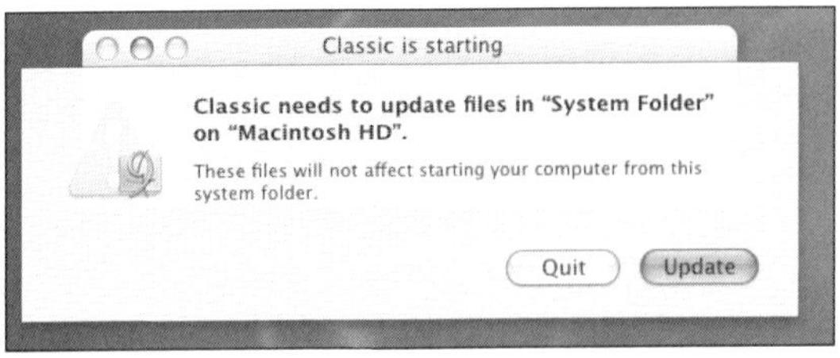

*If this is the first time you've started Classic, you'll probably see this message informing you that OS X needs to make some modifications in order to run Classic properly. Click **Update** if this message appears.*

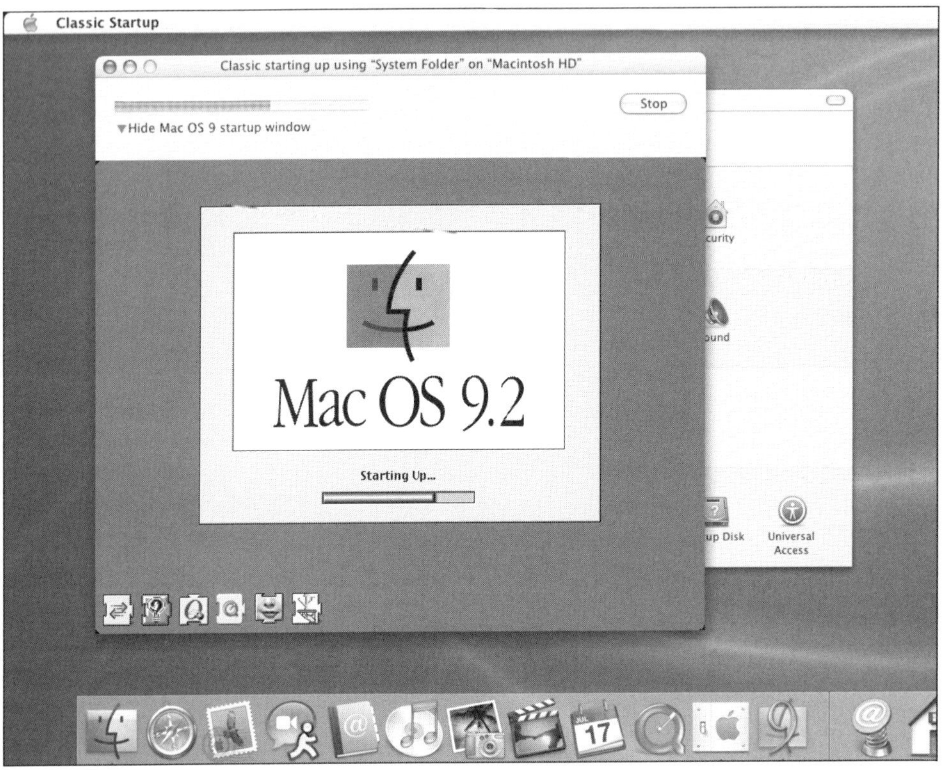

While Classic is loading, a window will appear detailing the progress of the Classic startup, and the Classic icon begin to appear in the Dock (if you look closely, you'll see that the "9" in the icon fills up with color as Classic loads). If you click the triangle next to Show Mac OS 9 startup window, you can watch OS 9 load, complete with the smiling Mac logo and the extension icons appearing across the bottom of the screen. (Of course, if you're completely new to the Mac, this all means nothing to you, but trust me, it's a nostalgic trip for veteran Mac users.)

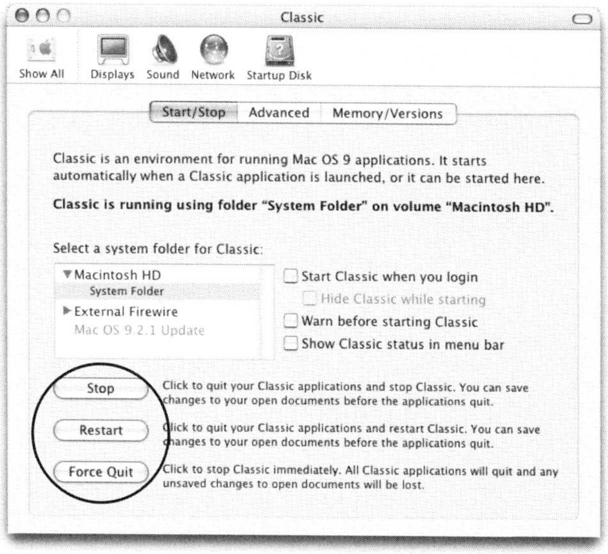

*Once Classic finishes loading, its icon will disappear from the Dock and nothing else will happen. Apple has tried to make working in Classic as unobtrusive as possible, so the only hint you have that Classic is in fact running is the fact that the **Stop**, **Restart**, and **Force Quit** buttons are now active in the Classic control pane. You can click any of these buttons to perform the specified task anytime Classic is running.*

Now you'll run a Classic application to see how it behaves in OS X.

3. Double-click your hard drive icon. With OS 9 installed on your Mac, you should have a folder on your hard drive called **Applications (Mac OS 9)**. Double-click this folder to view its contents.

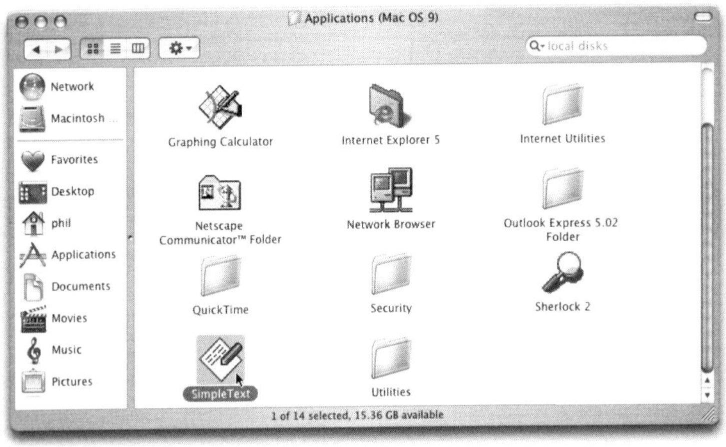

4. Locate and double-click the application **SimpleText**. SimpleText is a basic word processor, much like OS X's TextEdit, but SimpleText is a Classic application.

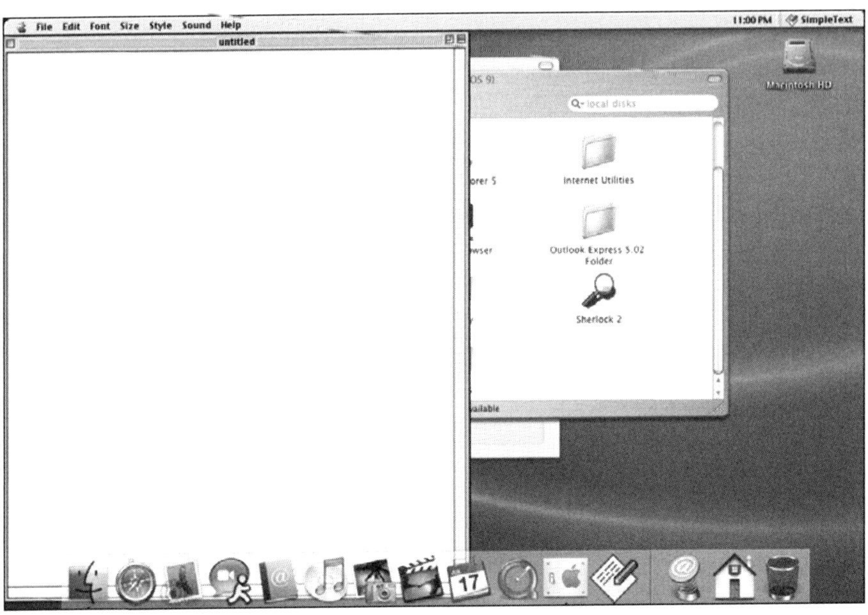

With SimpleText running as the active application, you're instantly entered into Classic mode. The menu bar has taken on the appearance of OS 9 menu bar, and includes all of its functionality: The Apple menu still works just like it did in OS 9, and the application menu still appears in the upper-right corner of the screen. The SimpleText icon appears in the Dock, but it looks jagged and rough compared to the OS Dock icons. You might also find that the Dock covers part of the SimpleText document. Many users prefer to hide the Dock when working in Classic.

At this point, you can work in SimpleText just like you would if it were truly running in OS 9. To switch back and forth between a Classic application and OS X, you can either click icons in the Dock, or click any unobscured portion of the Desktop.

---

5. Choose **File > Quit** to quit **SimpleText**. When you quit a Classic application, Classic itself remains running in the background. You don't have to worry about it consuming too many system resources though; when it's not running any applications, Classic itself takes up very little memory.

When you want to quit Classic, you can do so through the ***Classic*** *control pane.*

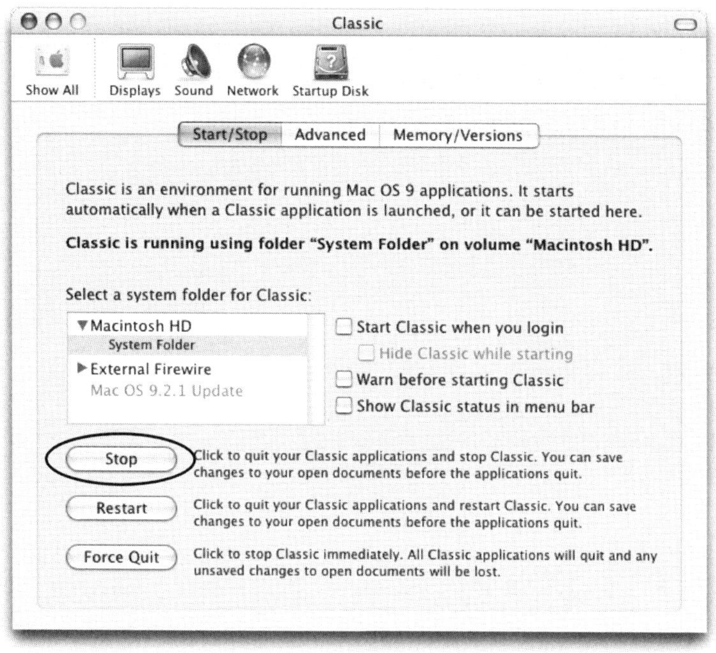

6. In the **Classic** control pane, click **Stop**. Clicking **Stop** is the equivalent to shutting down your Mac in OS 9. All presently running Classic applications will quit, and you'll be asked to save any unsaved changes to documents.

The Classic Menu Bar Item

New to Panther, you now have the option starting and stopping Classic from your menu bar, which can be quite useful if you use Classic a lot.

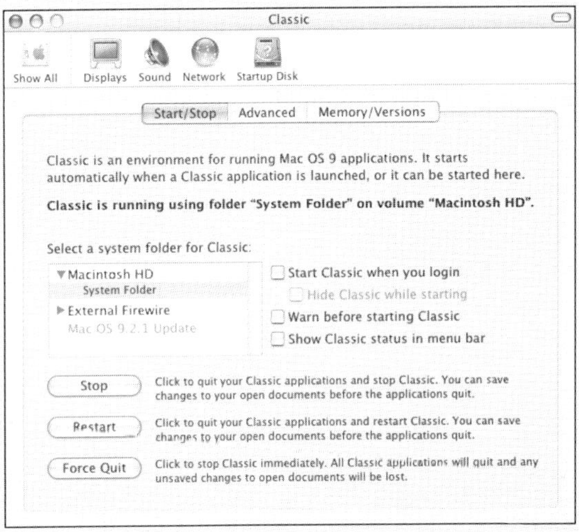

In the **Start/Stop** section of the **Classic** preference pane, check **Show Classic status in menu bar**.

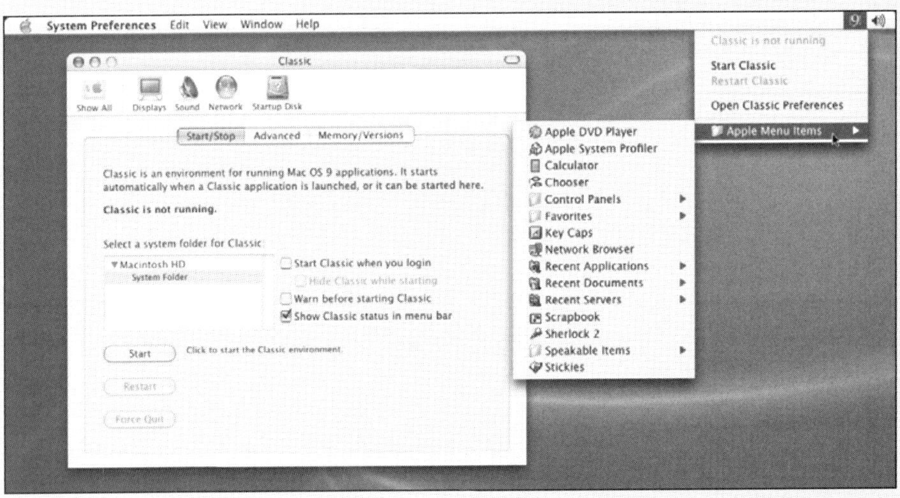

This places an icon in the menu bar that you can click to quickly start or stop Classic. It also gives you the advantage of being able to access Classic's Apple Menu Items without first running a Classic application. If you're still stuck splitting your time between OS X and Classic, you'll probably want the Classic status button in your menu bar.

Again, if you're familiar with OS 9, working in Classic should be a snap for you. If you've had no pre–OS X experience, you may have some initial trouble switching between OS X and Classic, but, quite possibly, you may never have any reason to go into Classic at all. More and more users are actually removing the Classic system folders from their Macs as more and more software becomes OS X–compatible.

Tip: *If you find yourself using Classic frequently, you can have it automatically start up when you turn on your computer by checking* ***Start Classic when you log in.*** *You'll be adding some time to your initial startup process, but at least you won't have to manually start Classic each time. Also, checking* ***Warn before starting Classic*** *will display a dialog box anytime you double-click a Classic application, asking you if you want to start Classic. Some users get annoyed when they double-click an icon just to see what it is only to have Classic start loading.*

If you're not experienced in working with OS 9, the following advanced steps will be of little value to you. Feel free to skip ahead to the Date & Time control pane exercise.

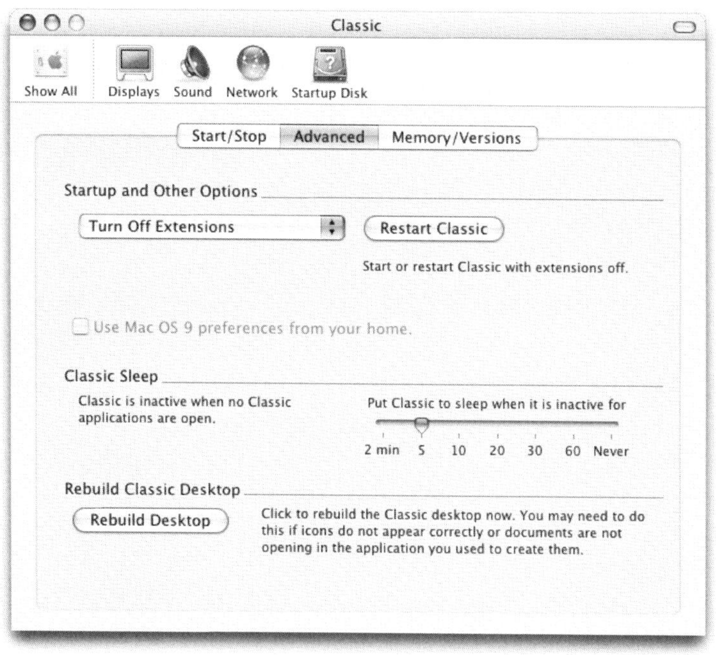

7. Click the **Advanced** button. Since Classic is an emulator running OS 9, unfortunately it does a pretty good job of emulating some of the system problems that OS 9 occasionally experienced. One of the cornerstones of troubleshooting pre–OS X systems was restarting your computer with the extensions turned off. Under the Classic Advanced tab, you can do just that.

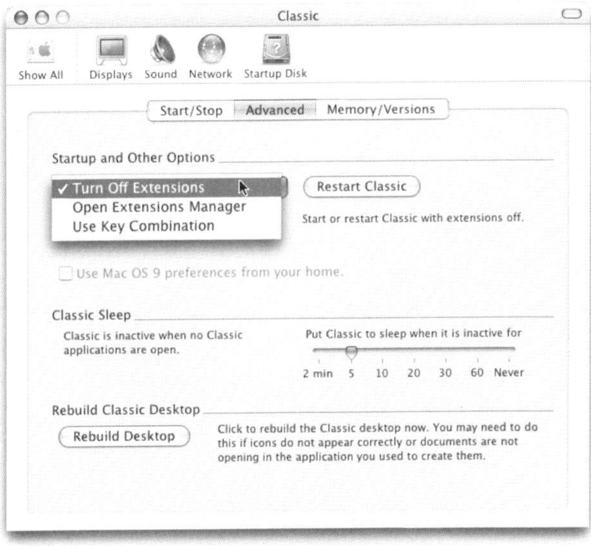

Under Startup Options, you can choose to restart Classic with extensions off, or to have the Extensions Manager application open after startup, or even to have Classic "press" any combination of keys during startup (for instance, pressing C to have the system start up from a CD). Note that any of these three actions will occur only when you click the Restart Classic button here under the Advanced tab. The remaining items under Advanced are detailed in the following chart.

Classic Advanced Options	
Option	**Description**
Use Mac OS 9 preferences from your home	For programs such as Word 2001 and Photoshop 7, which run in both OS 9 and X, checking this option will maintain your user preferences for these programs. For instance, your preferred palette locations from Photoshop will remain intact if you run Photoshop in Classic mode. It's sort of a moot point, however, since most Carbon programs (programs that run in both OS X and OS 9) work faster and are more stable in OS X.
Put Classic to sleep when it is inactive for	Use the slider to determine how long Classic must be inactive before it sleeps. A sleeping Classic uses even fewer system resources than an inactive Classic. Starting Classic applications will take a little longer, but not as long as it would take to start up Classic.
Rebuild Desktop	Remember this from the old days? Well, it's still here. If you're experiencing general errors in Classic, try optimizing the Desktop file by rebuilding it.

8. Click the **Memory/Versions** button.

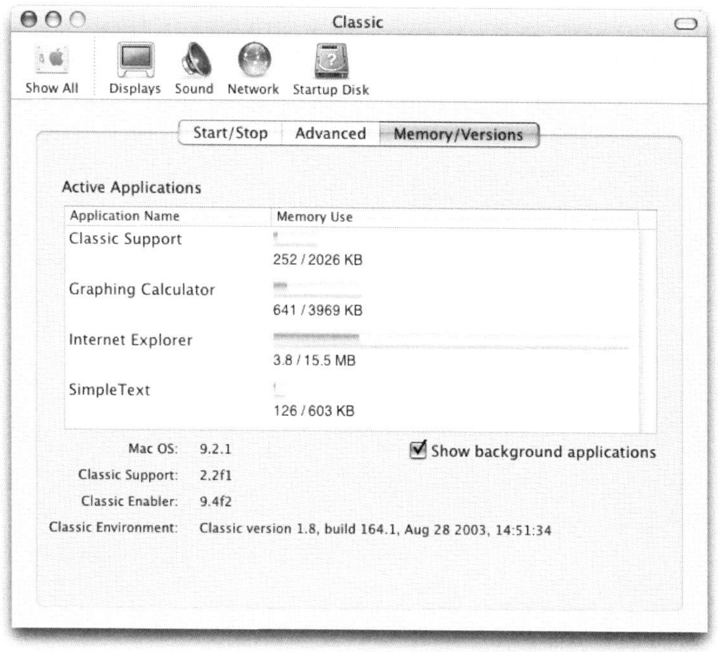

This area is similar to the About This Mac command you used to be able to select from the Apple menu in OS 9. Check ***Show background processes*** *to see exactly which applications are running in Classic and how much memory they're using. (This screenshot is just an example of what you'd see if you were running various Classic applications.) The information at the bottom of the pane tells you which versions of OS 9 you're running and which version of Classic is running it.*

9. Click the **Show All** button to return to **System Preferences**.

12. Date & Time

This exercise shows you how to make sure your Mac is running on the correct date and time. Having an incorrect date or time can result in problems like making yours emails appear as if you sent them several years ago. Also, if you have multiple revisions of a document, you might want to check the date each version was created to find the most recent revision.

1. Click the **Date & Time** icon.

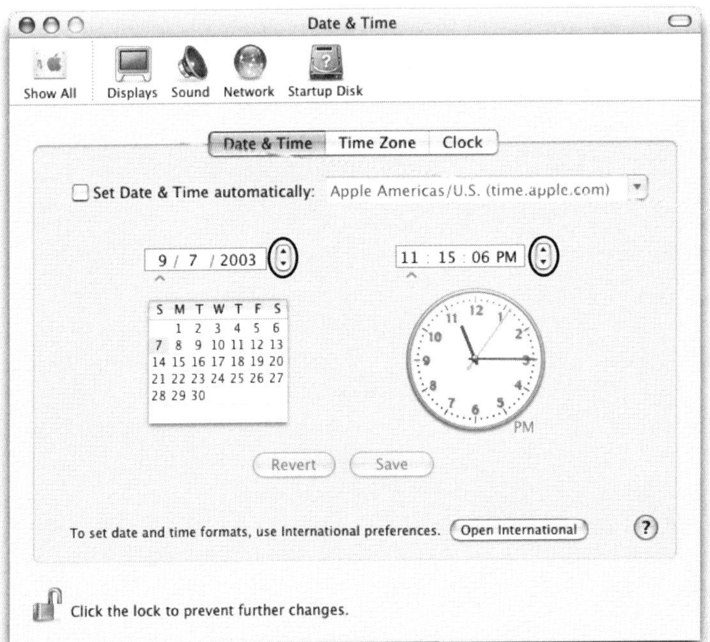

In this control pane, you can make sure your Mac is running on the correct date and time for your time zone, which is especially important if you keep track of files and projects by the date they were created or modified. Under the Date & Time tab, you can manually adjust everything by clicking on the appropriate arrows. If you don't see the arrows, it means your Mac has been set up to use a Network Time server.

2. Check **Set Date & Time automatically**.

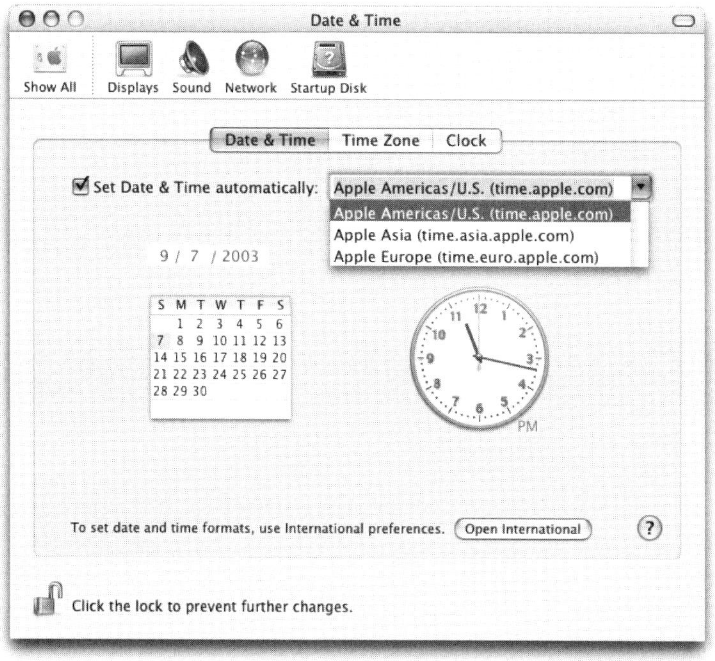

If you're connected to the Internet, you never have to worry about setting the time manually. All you have to do is check ***Set Date & Time automatically****, and select a server from the NTP Server list for the continent you're currently on. Your Mac will connect to the specified server and synch its clock with the one on the server. With this option selected, you won't be able to manually set the time in the Date & Time section.*

Of course, getting the correct date and time also depends on which time zone your Mac thinks it's in.

3. Click the **Time Zone** button.

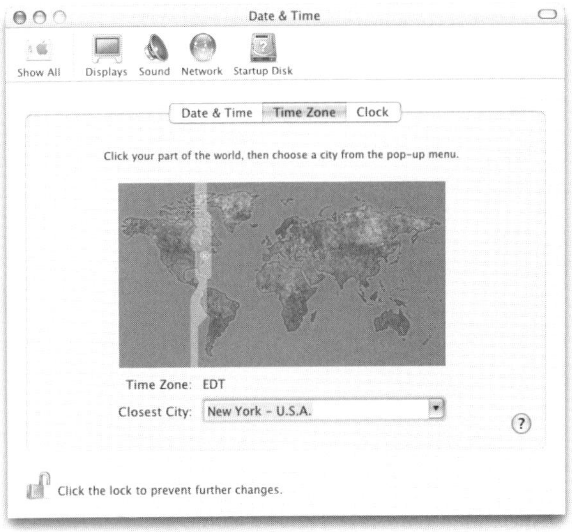

In this area, you can either click in the map within the time zone in which you reside, or you can choose from a list of major cities from the menu at the bottom of the pane to find one from your time zone.

4. Make sure your time zone is selected.

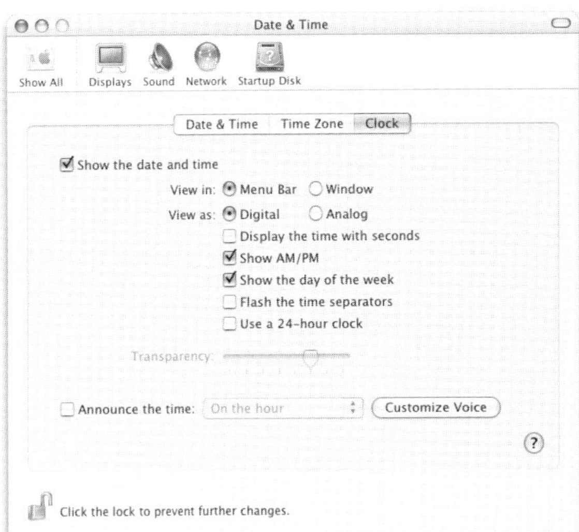

5. Click the **Clock** button. This area contains options for displaying the date and time in the menu bar or in a floating window. The following chart explains the options available here, although it's much easier to see what each option does by selecting it and observing the changes.

Menu Bar Clock Options

Option	Description
Show the date and time	Check this option to display the time and activate all the options found underneath this option.
View in	  Selecting **Menu Bar** displays the time in the menu bar. Selecting **Window** displays the time in a floating window.
View as	Selecting **Digital** displays the time in digital form. For example: 11:24:36. Selecting **Analog** presents the time as a small picture of a clock.
Display the time with seconds	This option is only available if **Menu Bar** and **Digital** are both selected or if **Window** and **Analog** are both selected.
Show AM/PM	Displays either AM or PM along with the time. This option isn't available if **Menu Bar** and **Analog** are both selected or if **Window** and **Analog** are both selected.
Show the day of the week	Precedes the time with an abbreviation of the current day. This option only affects the **Menu Bar/Digital** combination.
Flash the time separators	Flashes the **:** symbol between the hour and minute (and seconds if they're displayed) when **Digital** is selected
Use a 24-hour clock	Displays digital time in military time (for example, 8:00 PM becomes 20:00).
Announce the time	Check this box to have your Mac speak the time every hour, half hour, or quarter hour. Click **Customize Voice** to select your Mac's voice. You'll learn more about OS X's speaking capabilities in the next chapter.

***Tip:** Although there isn't a way to display the date in the menu bar, you can view the date by clicking the time in the menu bar. The date will be displayed in the menu below the time.*

6. Click the **Show All** button in the toolbar.

Software Update

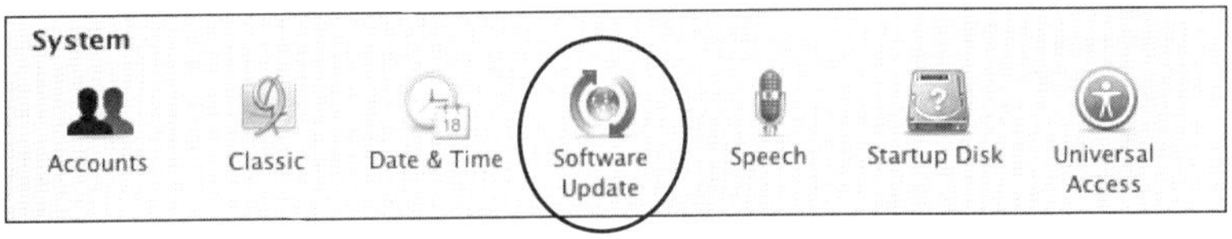

The **Software Update** control pane is an extremely useful tool for making sure that your Mac's software is kept as current as possible. Using this pane requires an Internet connection.

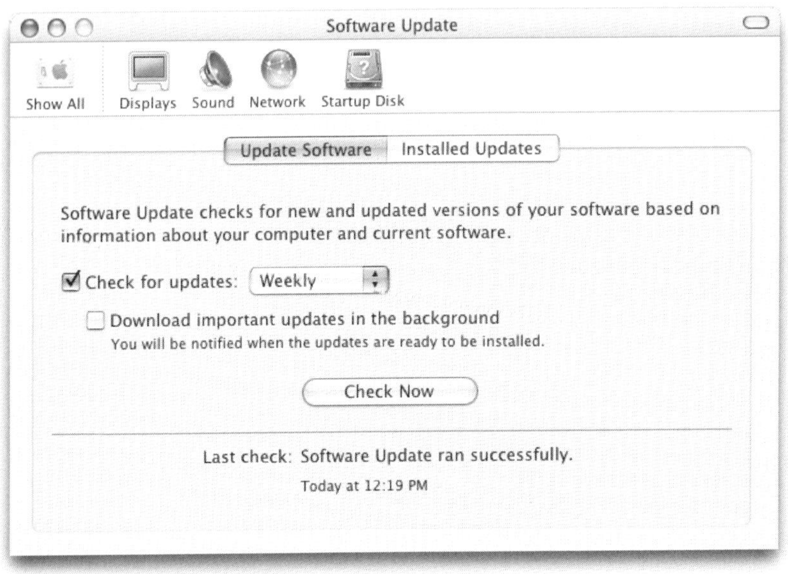

As it says at the top of this pane, Software Update checks for new and updated versions of your software based on its information about your current software version. You can choose to have Software Update run automatically every day, week, or month by selecting **Check for updates** when you have a network connection. If you want your Mac to download what it considers to be "important" updates without first asking you, check **Download important updates in the background**. When the update finishes downloading, you see a message asking if you want to install the update. If you uncheck **Check for updates**, Software Update will never check for updates.

However, you can always check for updates manually by clicking **Check Now**. As long as you're connected to the Internet, Software Update will connect to the closest server and compare any potential updates with what you already have on your computer.

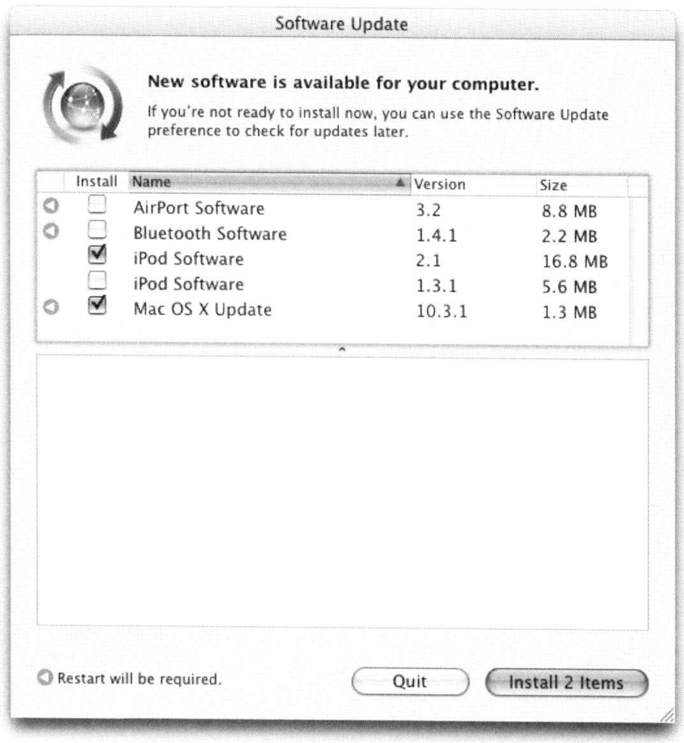

If any updates are found, Software Update will list them for you in a window. Software Update will never install any updates without your permission, and you'll always be provided with a description of each update and what it will do to your computer. In some cases, Software Update will even provide a link to a Web page that will give you even more information about the new version of the software.

Apple's recommended updates will appear with checks in the Install column. You can check or uncheck any items as you see fit. If you don't want to install any updates, you can just quit Software Update, leaving your Mac and its software unchanged.

If you do choose to install any updates, check the ones you want and click Install. You'll be asked for an administrator password. After entering your password, Software Update will download and automatically install your new software; no more manually installing updates for you! Go enjoy a beverage while you wait.

Depending on the software being updated, you may be required to restart your computer after the installation is complete.

Software Update Won't Stop Bugging Me

Being the helpful utility that it is, Software Update will inform you of every possible item whose installation could possibly be of benefit to you. For instance, Software Update informs you that the Italian Language software has been updated, which is great except that maybe you don't speak Italian and never intend to use it on your Mac. So you ignore it, install your other updates, and get on with your life. Only the next time you run Software Update, there it is again: the Italian Language update. To prevent the reoccurrence of items you've already dismissed, select the item and choose **Update > Ignore Update** from the menu bar. Now you'll never be bothered with this update again. But if you ever have a change of heart and decide that you were a fool for ever dismissing Italian, become fluent in the language, and/or change your nationality, you can view a list of your inactive updates by choosing **Software Update > Reset Ignored Updates**, which will display a list of all the updates you've ever ignored. If an ignored update is no longer listed, it may have been replaced by a newer update.

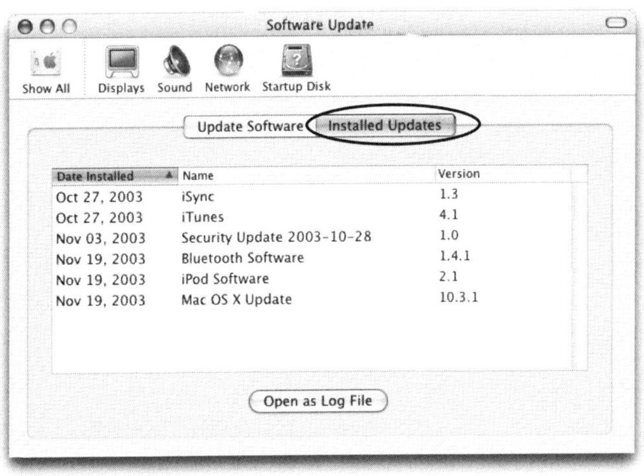

There won't be much to see under the **Installed Updates** section of **Software Update** if you've never installed any updates, but this is where you'll find a log of all the updates ever installed by Software Update, which can be a good troubleshooting resource in some cases.

Tip: Software Update checks only for updates to software that was installed with OS X. An excellent resource for checking for updates to your other programs and utilities is **versiontracker.com**, a Web site dedicated to keeping track of the most current versions of just about any application you can think of.

Speech and Universal Access

The **Speech** and **Universal Access** control panes will be covered in depth in the following chapter. Apple has put a lot into OS X for those who have trouble accessing and using their Macs with just a mouse and keyboard, and the next chapter will deal specifically with these issues.

Startup Disk

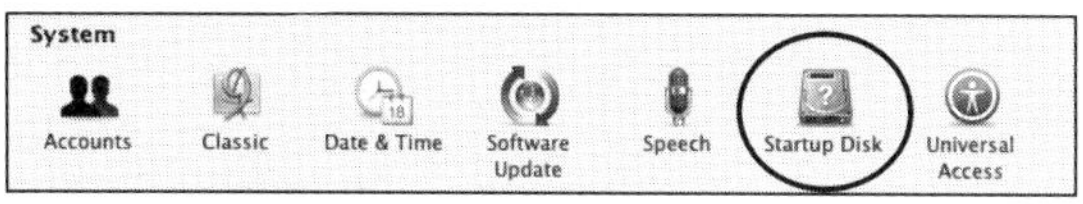

The final control pane you'll examine in this chapter is the **Startup Disk** pane.

The Startup Disk control pane is used to let your Mac know which disk or system folder you want it to use when it starts up. This pane can be used to reboot your Mac in OS 9 or for booting up your Mac from a system folder over your network.

When you click the Startup Disk icon in System Preferences, your Mac will scan all available drives, including your CD or DVD drive, for any system folders that it can use to be operational. You can also select **Network Startup**. Choosing this icon will have your Mac search your network for a startup disk when you turn it on. For those times when you absolutely need to run a Classic application in OS 9 instead of Classic, you can use the Startup Disk control pane to select the OS 9 system folder and then click **Restart**. The caveat here is that if you purchased a new Mac after January 2003, you can no longer boot up your Mac in OS 9. Apple has made new Macs OS X–only, and Classic is your only option for running Classic applications.

Note: If you clicked on anything in the Startup Disk pane while reading through this description, make sure you select your OS X folder to make it your startup disk. Otherwise you may find yourself booting into OS 9 the next time you start up your Mac.

Easy Access to Preferences

Remember in the pre–OS X operating systems how you could access any control pane by simply clicking the Apple menu and selecting the pane you needed from the Control Panes submenu? (If not, believe me, it was a real convenience.) You can regain this functionality in OS X by some simple maneuvering of items.

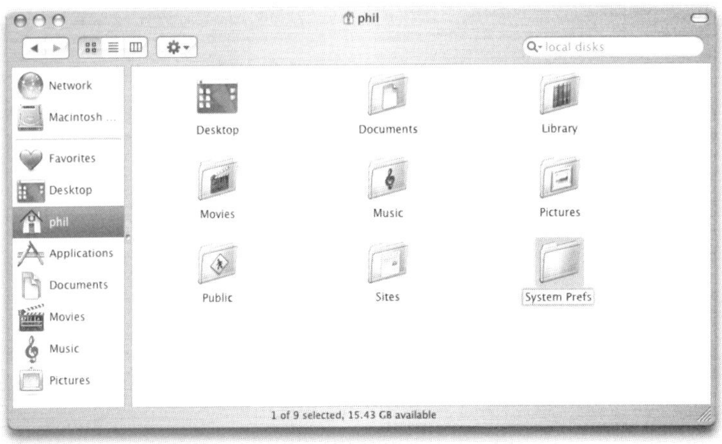

First, create a new, empty folder (preferably somewhere in your **Home** folder) and name it something like **System Prefs**.

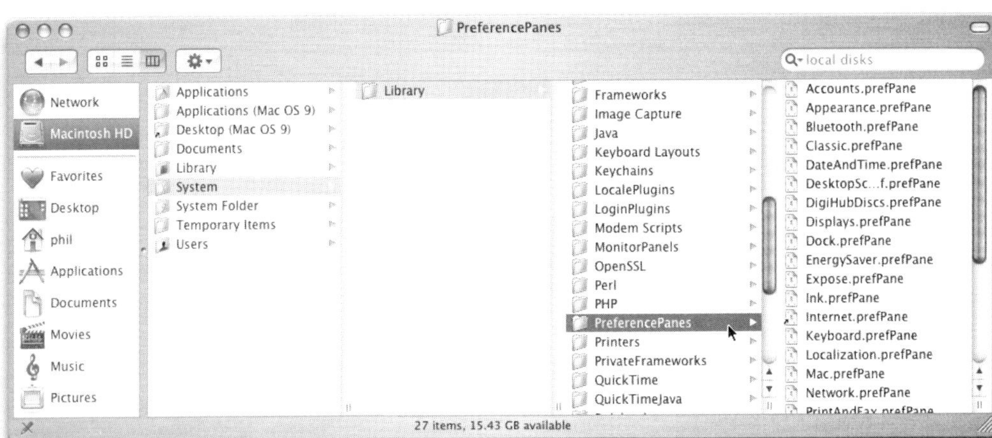

Now, from your hard drive navigate through the following folders: **System** (make sure it's System, not System Folder) **> Library > PreferencePanes**. (The path is shown in Column view here to help you locate this folder, but either Icon or List view will work just as well.) The PreferencePanes folder is where each control pane found in System Preferences is stored.

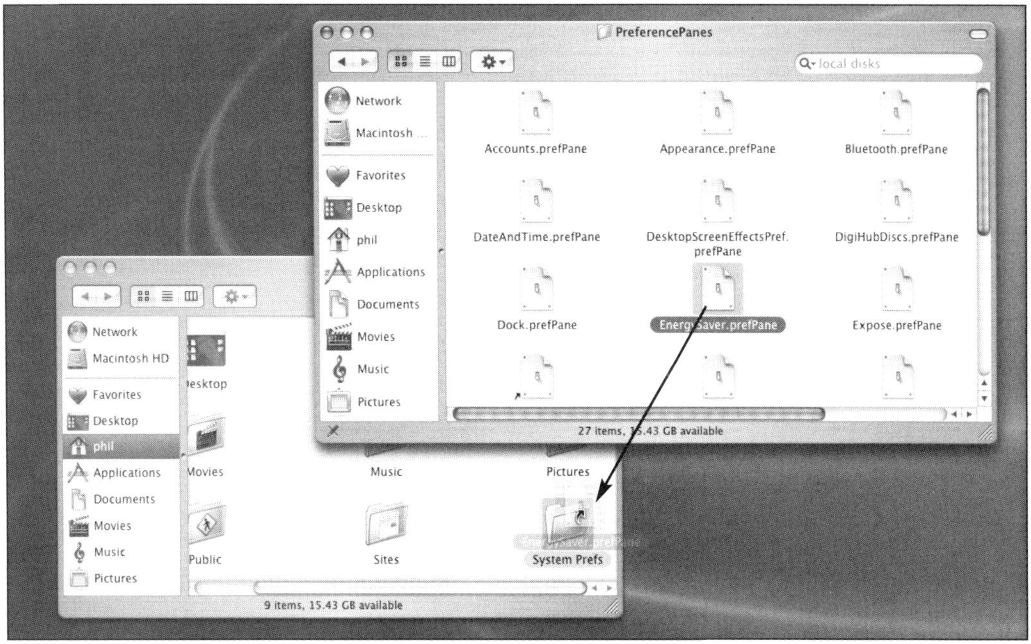

Make sure you can see the **System Prefs** folder you created and the contents of the **Preference Panes** simultaneously. Now hold **Option+Cmd** and drag any preference pane you want into the **System Prefs** folder. Holding **Option+Cmd** creates aliases of the preference panes. If you don't hold these keys, you'll end up copying the preferences panes, which won't work for what you're trying to accomplish here. Drag preference panes that you think you'll need often–Energy Saver, Dock, Accounts, and so on.

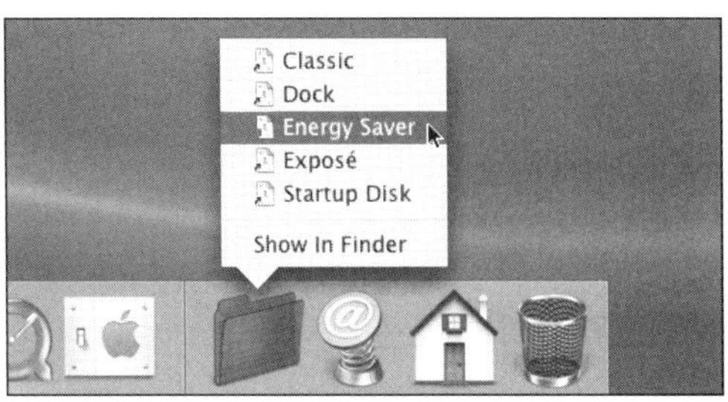

When you're done making aliases, drag your **System Prefs** folder to the right side of the **Dock**. Now all you have to do is **Ctrl+click** this folder any time you want direct access to one of your preference panes. You can even rename the aliases inside the folder however you like and they'll still work properly.

Whew! You made it through this chapter, and should now have a much broader understanding of how OS X controls your Mac. Take a well-deserved break and then move on to Chapter 5.

5. Universal Access and Speech

| Universal Access | Full Keyboard Access |

| Speech | Speech Recognition |

no exercise files

Mac OS X Panther H•O•T CD-ROM

Computers in today's workplace are as commonplace as desks, chairs, and coffee. It is essential, therefore, that computer manufacturers make their products accessible to everyone, regardless of physical capabilities. Some users, for example, have trouble discerning objects on monitors, while others struggle with using the mouse to control their computers. With OS 10.3, Apple has taken major leaps forward in its effort to make the Mac easier to use for people with disabilities. In this chapter, you'll learn how the Universal Access and Speech preference panes can be used to adjust the way your Mac accepts commands and displays information. And although Apple designed most of the features covered in this chapter to benefit people with disabilities, everyone has the potential to find some of these features useful in their day-to-day work.

I. Universal Access

In this exercise, you'll examine the options found in the Universal Access pane, and you'll try your hand at controlling your Mac without the mouse.

1. Click the **System Preferences** icon in the **Dock**.

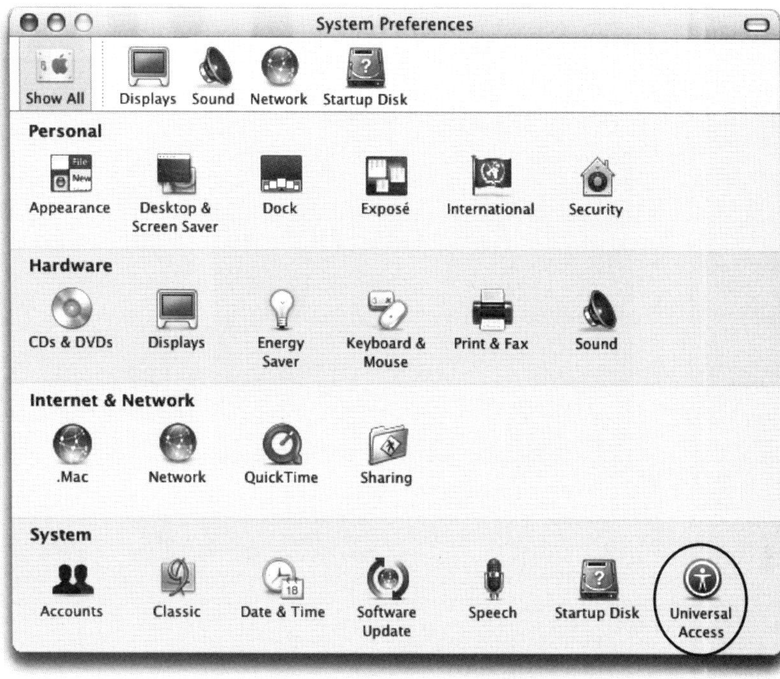

2. In **System Preferences**, click the **Universal Access** icon.

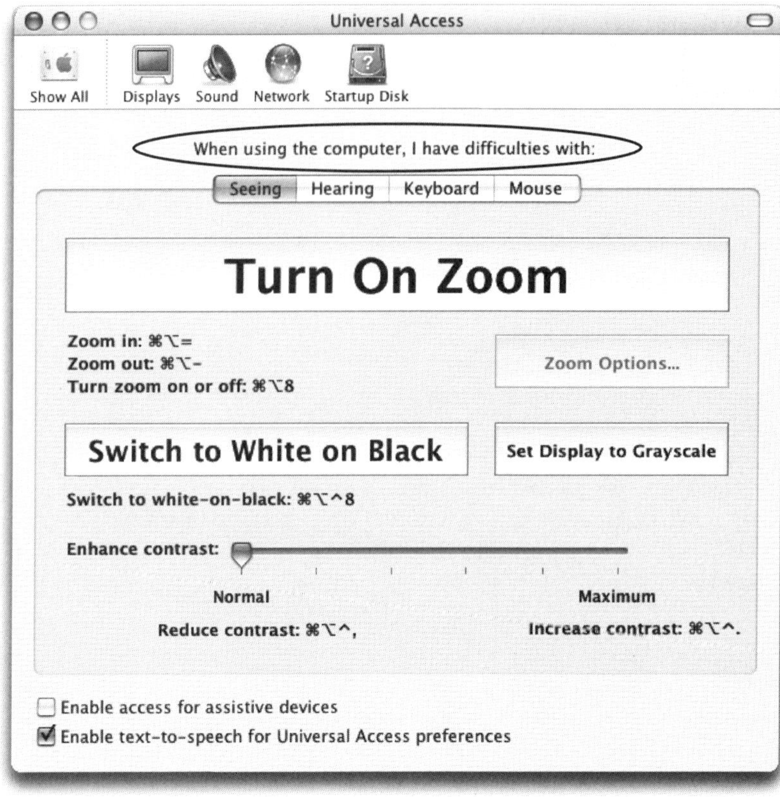

Notice the text at the top of the pane that reads, "When using the computer, I have difficulties with." Below this line are four tabs under which you can adjust settings to provide better access to the Mac: ***Seeing****,* ***Hearing****,* ***Keyboard****, and* ***Mouse****.*

3. Place the mouse cursor over any of the tabs in the control pane (but don't click). After a second or so your Mac reads the item to you. In fact, your Mac will read anything in the **Universal Access** control pane that you place your mouse over. This can be a great benefit for users with vision disabilities. But if you find this feature distracting during this exercise, uncheck **Enable text-to-speech for Universal Access preferences** at the bottom of the control pane.

4. If it isn't already selected, click the **Seeing** tab. As you've probably guessed, the items under this tab are for assisting those with vision disabilities.

One option for users who have trouble seeing items on the screen clearly is to enlarge the objects themselves. As you saw in the previous chapter, it's possible to enlarge the screen display by opening the Display preference pane and selecting a lower resolution for your monitor. But the Display pane can only enlarge the screen display so far. The ***Zoom*** *feature found in Universal Access gives you an incredible amount of control over enlarging an area of the screen.*

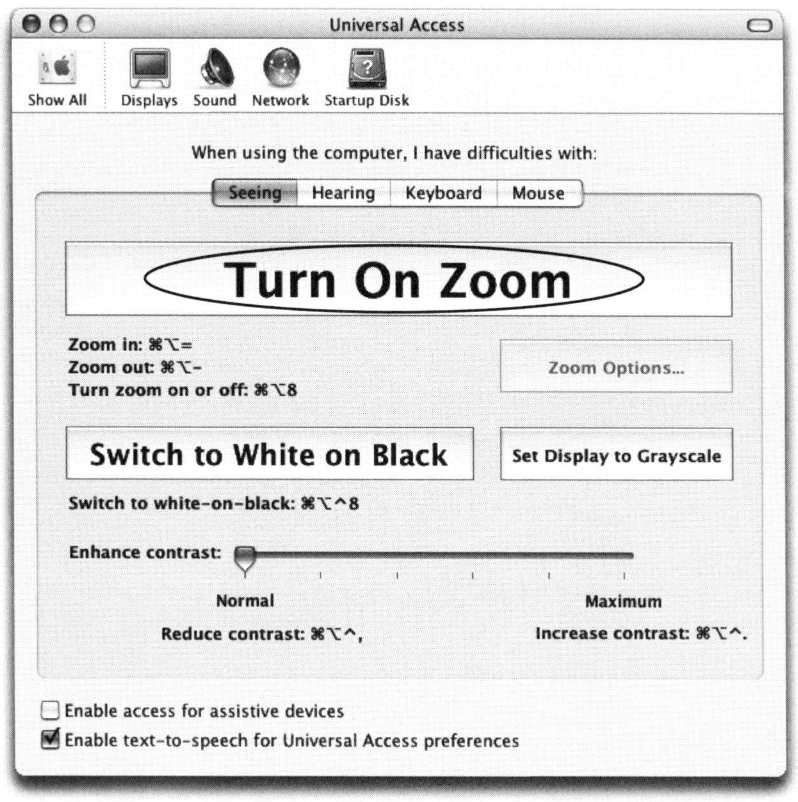

5. Click the **Turn On Zoom** button (if it's not already on). (The button will change to **Turn Off Zoom** when **Zoom** is on).

By invoking the keyboard commands listed under Universal Access shortcuts, you can incrementally zoom in or out on the area centered around the mouse cursor. Pressing **Option+Cmd+=** *(the equals key) zooms in; pressing* **Option+Cmd+–** *(the minus, or hyphen, key) zooms out. You can toggle the zoom function off and on at any time (whether the Universal Access control pane is open or not) by pressing* **Option+Cmd+8***.*

Note: *Previously in OS X, the zoom in keyboard command was listed as* **Option+Cmd++** *(the plus symbol), the logic being that, while holding* **Option+Cmd***, you could press the minus symbol to zoom out and the plus symbol to zoom in. But some people were mistakenly pressing the* **Shift** *key, as you're normally required to do to type a plus symbol. So Apple has changed the description of the zoom in keyboard command to* **Option+Cmd+=** *to avoid confusion, even though the keys you actually press have not changed.*

---

6. With **Zoom** turned on, hold down the **Option** and **Cmd** keys and press the = key to zoom in. Press the = key about five times to get the idea. Release the keys and move your mouse. Notice that you can now scroll to any portion of your screen simply by moving your mouse; the zoomed area always remains centered around the mouse. Because of OS X's Quartz graphics rendering, the enlarged area remains legible and smooth.

You can now zoom in and out of the screen as needed by pressing **Option** *and* **Cmd** *together and then pressing either the = or – keys.*

Tip: *Hold the = or – key down to zoom in or out quickly.*

---

7. Press and hold **Option+Cmd+–** until the screen returns to its normal size.

To further customize the zoom capabilities of OS X, Apple has provided the ***Zoom Options*** *button.*

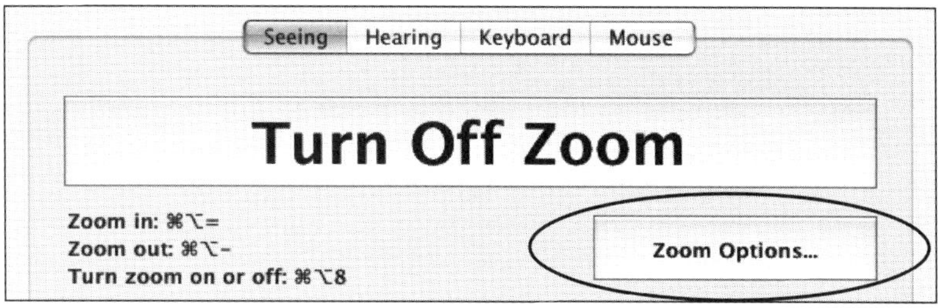

8. Click **Zoom Options**.

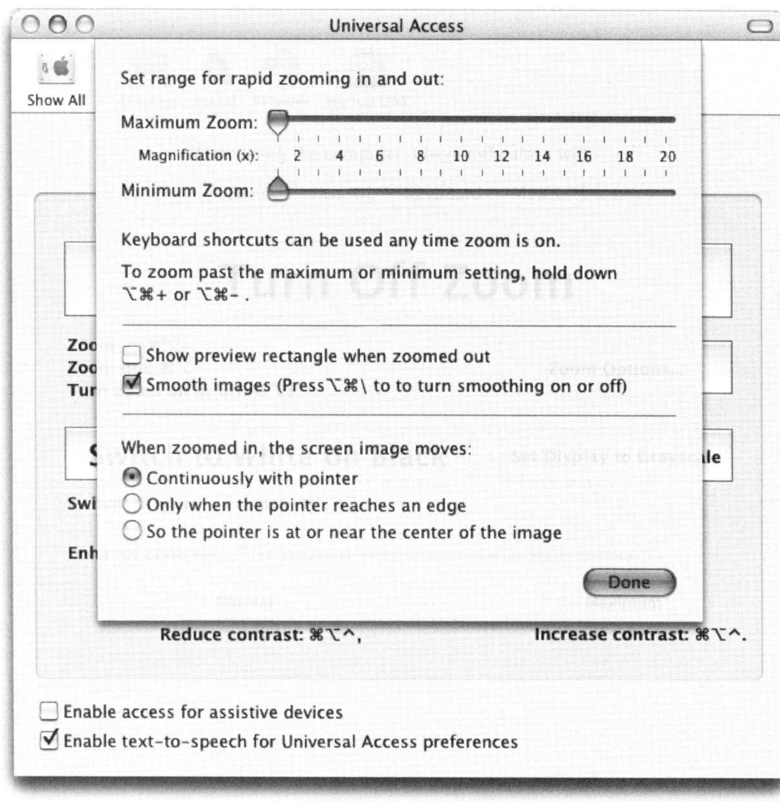

Some users might find it difficult or tedious to continually tap the + and – buttons to zoom in and out. For these users, setting a zoom range can be very useful.

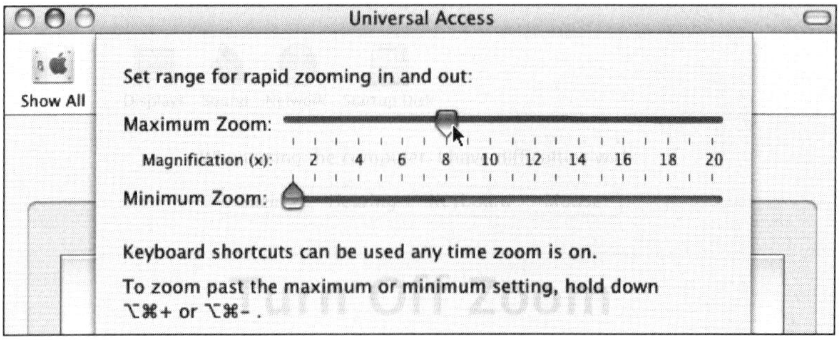

9. Drag the **Maximum Zoom** slider to **8x** magnification. Now press **Option+Cmd+=**. Notice that with just one press of the = key, the screen zooms into **8x** magnification (well, as far as you know, that's 8x). The term "Maximum Zoom" seems a bit misleading, because, at this point, you could continue pressing = to zoom in more. Just keep in mind that setting a **Maximum Zoom** level is a good way to get to a commonly used magnification size without having to press = multiple times. If necessary, the **Minimum Zoom** slider can also be used to set increments for zooming out.

---

10. Press **Option+Cmd+–** once to zoom back out.

*Near the middle of Zoom Options are two check boxes. Checking **Show preview rectangle when zoomed out** will draw a rectangle on the screen, indicating the area that will be enlarged when you zoom in. (You'll only see the rectangle if the Maximum Zoom slider is not set to the extreme left.) The **Smooth images** option keeps everything nice and clean when you zoom in. If unchecked, the more you zoom in, the more jagged and pixilated the images become (which can occasionally be useful if you have trouble distinguishing between certain colors).*

---

11. Set your **Zoom Options** however you like, and click **Done**.

For some users, the size of the screen display is not as much of an issue as the contrast between colors onscreen. For users with varying levels of color blindness, it's sometimes an incredible chore to just read text or see icons on certain backgrounds. The two remaining buttons under the Seeing tab can help these users to see and find items more easily. Take a quick look to see what these buttons do.

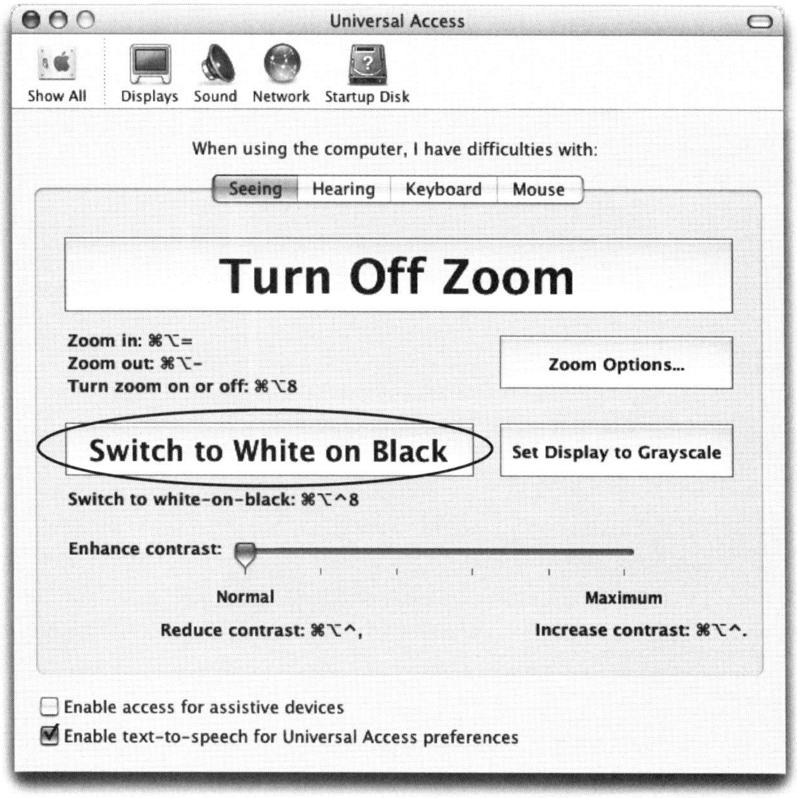

12. Click **Switch to White on Black**.

Black objects are now turned to white, white objects to black, and all other colors set to levels of gray.

---

13. Click **Switch to Black on White** to revert your screen back to its original colors.

Tip: To change to white on black at any time, press ***Ctrl+Option+Cmd+8.***

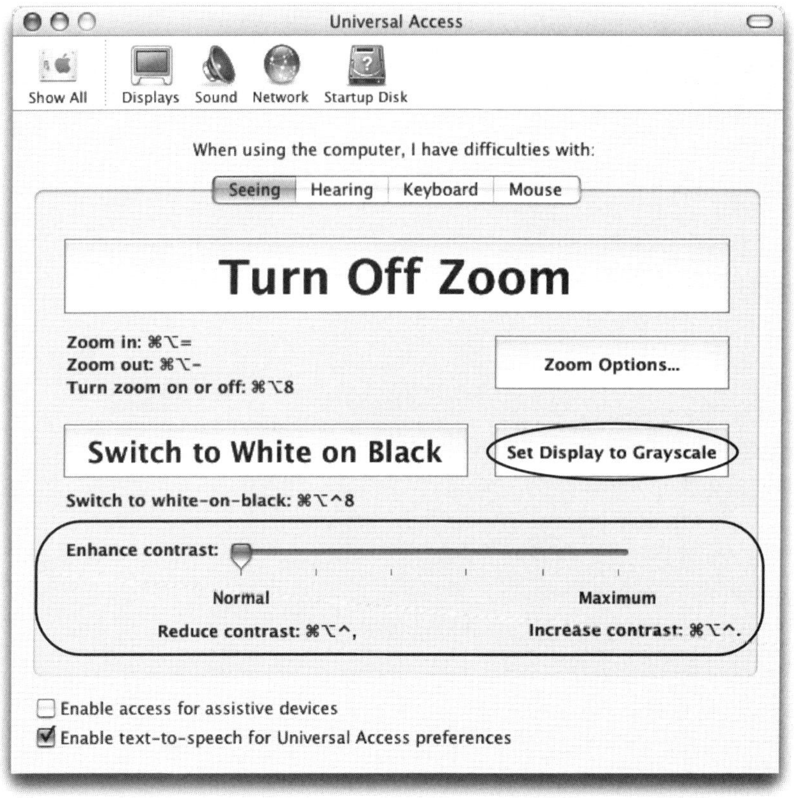

*Some users don't need quite as much contrast as white on black and may instead benefit more from clicking **Set Display to Grayscale**. Clicking this button once removes all color from the screen; clicking it again brings the color back. New to Panther is the **Enhance contrast** slider, which you can drag to the right to increase contrast, or to the left to reduce contrast (whether you're viewing the screen normally, in White on Black, or in Grayscale).*

14. Click the **Hearing** tab.

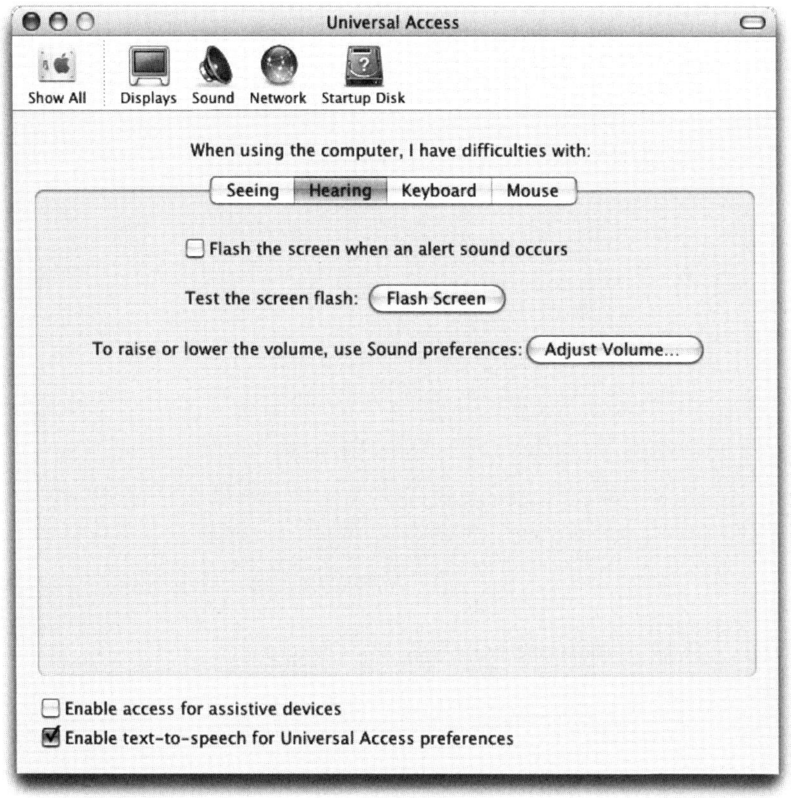

As you learned in the previous chapter, OS X comes with a collection of alert sounds that will play when your Mac needs your attention. For users who have trouble hearing, however, an alert sound doesn't do much good. You can increase the volume of the alert sound by clicking the ***Adjust Volume*** *button, which takes you directly to the* ***Sound*** *control pane, but you can still only increase the volume so much. Under the Hearing tab, you can choose to have your Mac flash the screen any time an alert sound plays.*

---

15. Click the **Flash Screen** button to see this effect.

If you feel that it will benefit you, you can check ***Flash the screen whenever an alert sound occurs,*** *so that any time the Mac sounds an alert, you'll also get a visual indication that your Mac wants your attention.*

The next two tabs under Universal Access deal with helping those who have trouble using the keyboard and mouse to control objects and select items.

---

16. Click the **Keyboard** tab.

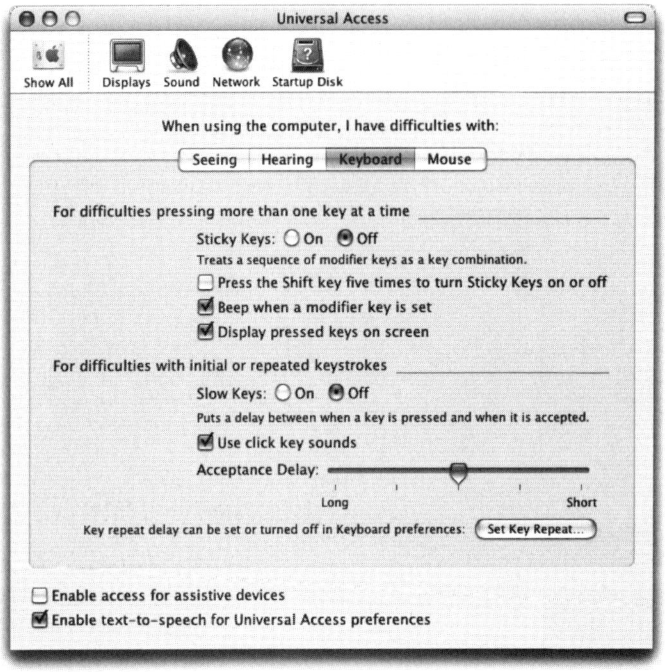

*The Keyboard section offers solutions for two different problems that some users may encounter: **Sticky Keys** for users who have trouble pressing more than one key at a time, and **Slow Keys** for those who have a tendency to accidentally press unwanted keys. You'll try out both of these features.*

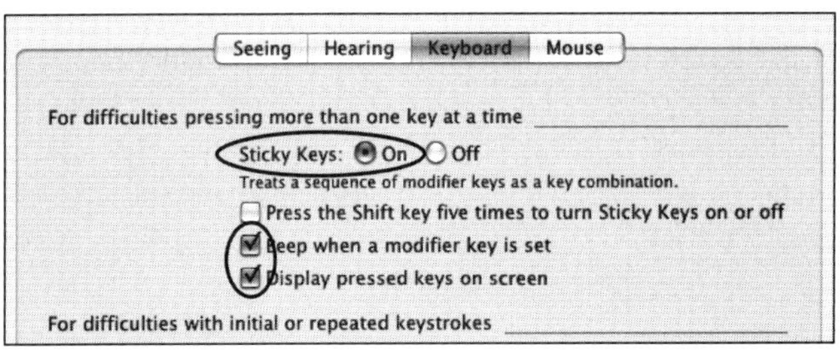

17. Turn **Sticky Keys** on. Also make sure **Beep when a modifier key is set** and **Display pressed keys on screen** are both selected. These two selections will give you both audible and visual feedback when you press the modifier keys.

*Sticky Keys work when any "modifier keys" are pressed. The modifier keys are **Ctrl**, **Option**, **Cmd**, and **Shift**. For instance, normally to open the **Force Quit** window, you need to press **Option** and **Cmd** simultaneously and then press the **Esc** key. With Sticky Keys turned on, you can press them one at a time.*

*You'll try out Sticky Keys by invoking the command for changing the screen to white on black, as you just learned to do under the Seeing tab. The keyboard command for changing the screen to white on black is **Ctrl+Option+Cmd+8**, which can be a difficult combination of keys for some users to press all at once.*

18. Press **Ctrl** and release. Because you selected **Beep when a modifier key is set** and **Display pressed keys on screen**, you hear a sound (although it's referred to as a "beep," it's actually more of a typewriter sound), and the **Ctrl** symbol appears on the screen.

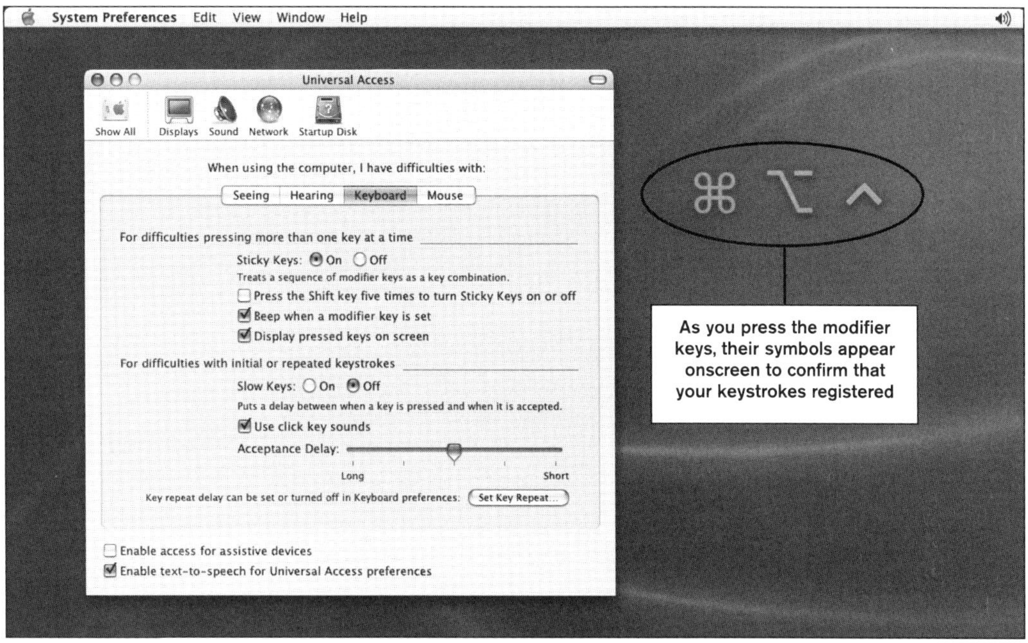

19. Now press and release **Option** and **Cmd**. Their symbols also appear onscreen. Now press the **8** key. Your screen switches to white on black.

20. Press **Ctrl**, **Option**, **Cmd**, and **8** again to revert back to color.

Sticky Keys can be a big help if you ever need to type with one hand or just have trouble getting the timing right to correctly press the modifier keys simultaneously.

Tip: *You can "lock" any modifier key by pressing it twice. When you press a modifier key twice, you hear a second, different click, and its onscreen symbol becomes an opaque white. Locking a key is useful if you need to use it for several successive commands and don't want to be bothered with holding down the key manually. For instance, you could press the* ***Ctrl*** *key twice to lock it and then click on any number of icons in the Dock or on the Desktop to view their contextual menus. Just press the locked modifier key once more to unlock it.*

---

21. Turn off **Sticky Keys**. You can decide for yourself later whether you want to leave it on for your day-to-day work.

Tip: *If you find Sticky Keys to be useful every now and then, you might want to check the* ***Press the Shift key five times to turn Sticky keys on or off*** *option. As you probably have guessed, with this option checked you can invoke Sticky Keys by pressing* ***Shift*** *five times, which is quicker than opening System Preferences and selecting the Universal Access preference pane.*

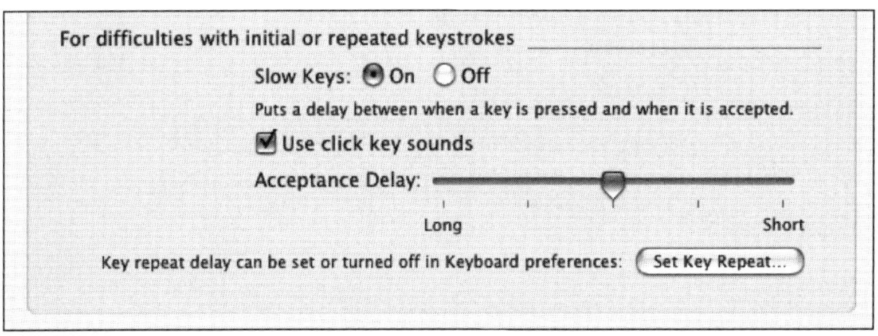

Users who have trouble with accidentally pressing keys can use the Slow Keys function to control how long a key must be pressed before it registers with the Mac. With Slow Keys turned on, dragging the ***Acceptance Delay*** *slider to the left increases the amount of time the key must be held before it appears onscreen; dragging to the right decreases this time. If you're a relatively fast typist, turning on the feature will actually be detrimental to your keyboarding. Use it only if you genuinely have trouble getting your fingers to the proper keys.*

---

22. Click the **Mouse** tab.

The settings in the Mouse section are used to control and adjust Mouse Keys, which allows you to use your keyboard to move the mouse cursor if you have trouble controlling a regular mouse. This control pane is also quite useful if your mouse is dirty, broken, or just acting funny.

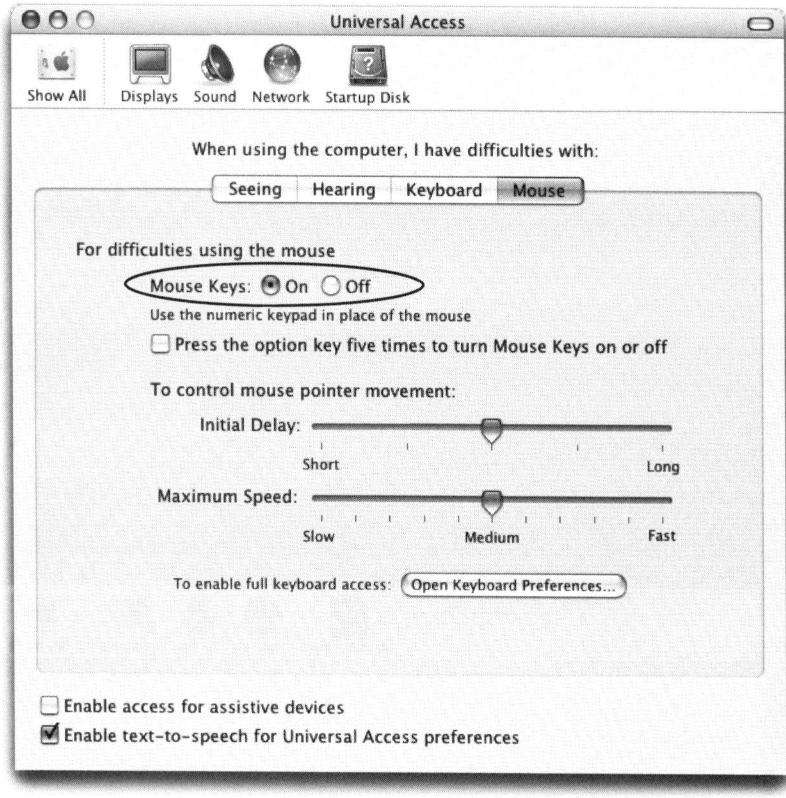

23. Turn on **Mouse Keys**.

To move the cursor with your keyboard, use the numeric keypad on your keyboard. Use ***2****,* ***4****,* ***6****, and* ***8*** *to move horizontally and vertically, and press* ***1****,* ***3****,* ***7****, and* ***9*** *to move diagonally. The* ***5*** *key acts as a mouse click; press it once to click, twice to double-click.*

---

24. Try moving the cursor around with the numeric keypad. If you have trouble getting it moving, press and hold one of the number keys.

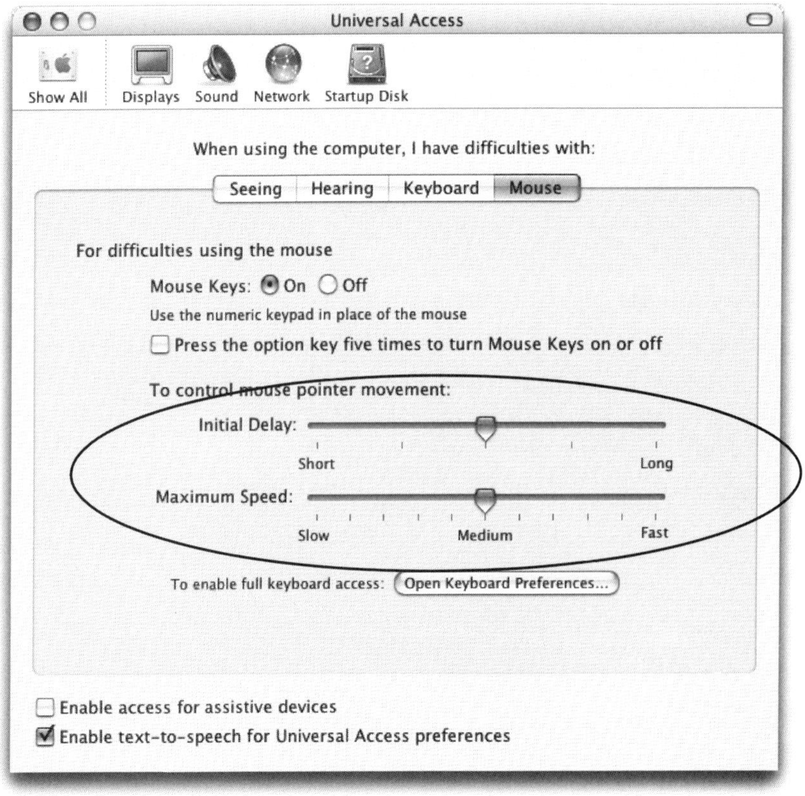

You can adjust the ***Initial Delay*** *slider to govern how long a number key must be held before it starts controlling the mouse. The* ***Maximum Speed*** *slider determines how fast the mouse cursor moves when you hold a number key down.*

Tip: *Mouse Keys can be useful in graphic editing programs when you need to move the mouse with single-pixel precision.*

Note: *Your regular mouse will continue to function even if Mouse Keys is on.*

25. Turn **Mouse Keys** off.

At the bottom of the Universal Access control pane are two check boxes. The following chart details these options.

Universal Access Options	
Option	**Description**
Enable access for assistive devices	Checking this option enables your Mac to verbalize text on your screen, much like it does in the Universal Access control pane. You'll learn more about this option in Exercise 3.
Enable text-to-speech for Universal Access preferences	As you've already seen, with this option selected, your Mac reads everything in the Universal Access control pane aloud to you.

26. Click the **Show All** button in the toolbar to return to **System Preferences** and keep it open for the next exercise.

*The Universal Access pane allows you to really customize your Mac experience to suit your personal needs. In the next exercise, you'll use the **Keyboard & Mouse** preference pane for a quick look at some other ways to control your Mac from the keyboard.*

2. Keyboard Shortcuts

As you continue on your lifelong journey down the path toward Mac Zen, you'll find that keyboard shortcuts are one of the keys to becoming one with your Mac. A true power user keeps his or her fingers on the keyboard nearly all the time, only moving the mouse when absolutely necessary. Whether you aspire to reach this state of geekiness or not, learning a few keyboard shortcuts can be a big timesaver. In the previous exercise, you learned how to use your keyboard to control the mouse cursor should your mouse ever break or wander off. In this exercise, you'll learn a few more tricks on controlling your Mac entirely from your keyboard.

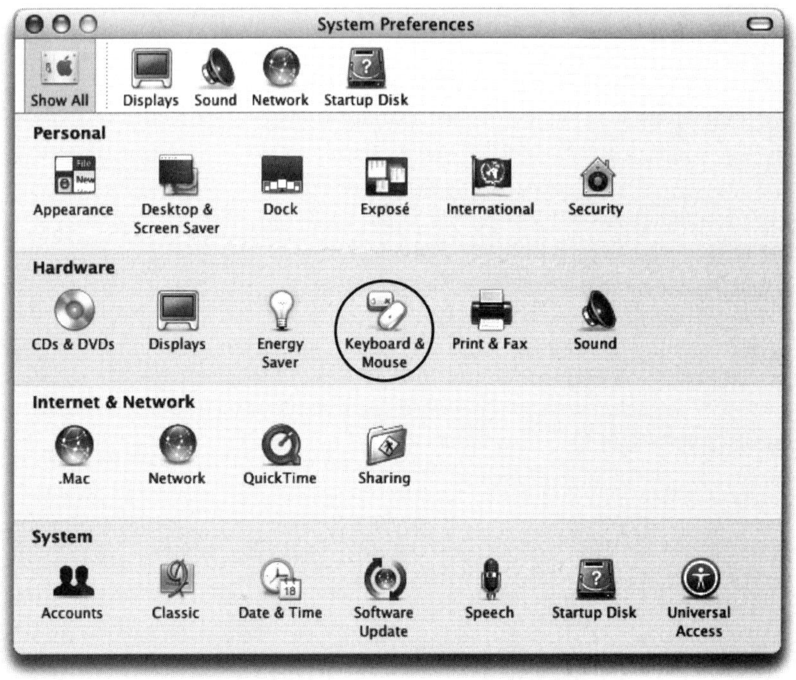

1. In **System Preferences**, click the **Keyboard & Mouse** icon.

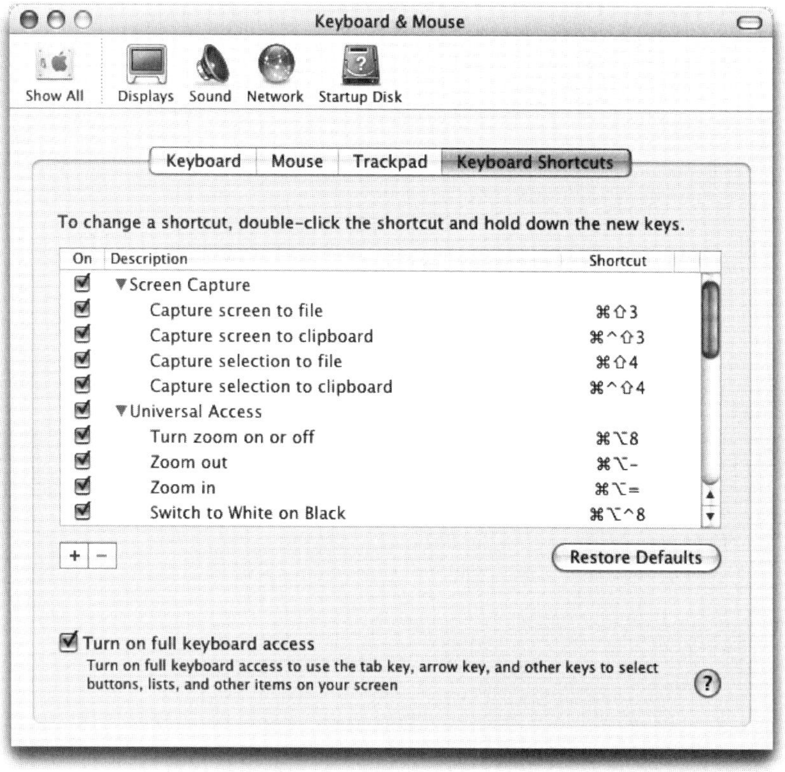

2. Under the **Keyboard & Mouse** preference pane (covered in the last chapter), click the **Keyboard Shortcuts** button. Here you'll find a list of some of the most common and useful keyboard shortcuts. The shortcuts are divided into categories such as **Universal Access**, **Keyboard Navigation**, and **Dock**. The shortcuts themselves are listed in the far-right column. You're free to check or uncheck any of these items to activate or deactivate them, but you'll probably visit this area more often to refresh your memory on the key combinations for single-use shortcuts.

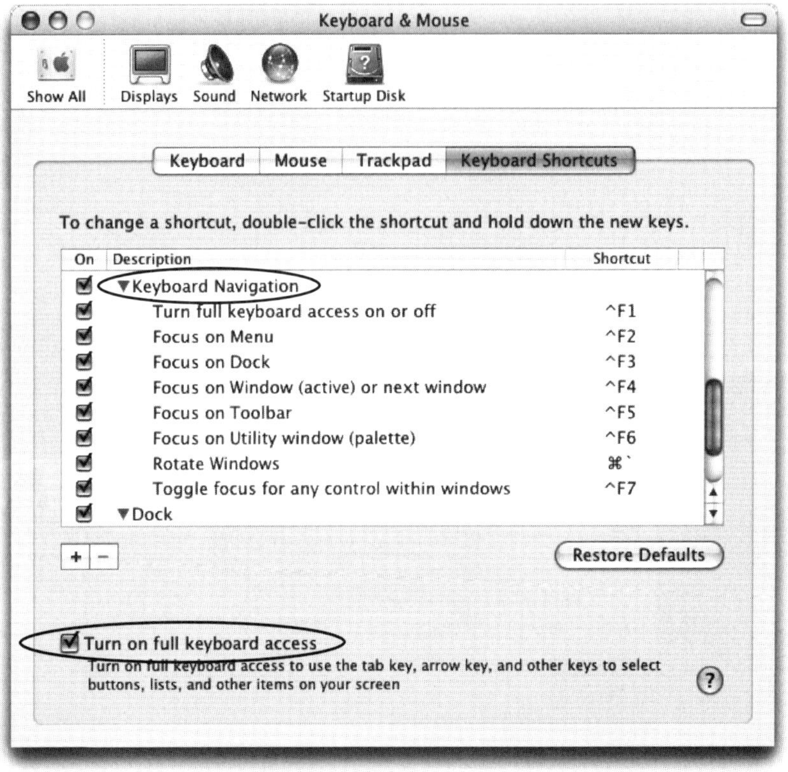

3. Make sure **Turn on full keyboard access** is checked, and then scroll through the list of shortcuts until you see the **Keyboard Navigation** section.

*Full Keyboard Access is the option that allows you to control your Mac from the keyboard. You can toggle Full Keyboard Access on and off at any time without opening the Keyboard & Mouse control pane by pressing **Ctrl+F1** (PowerBook and iBook users need to press **Ctrl+Fn+F1**).*

*The shortcuts listed under Keyboard Navigation give you access to the elements on your screen that you normally select by clicking them with your mouse. For instance, you can access the menu bar by pressing **Ctrl+F2**, and the Dock by pressing **Ctrl+F3**.*

---

4. Press **Ctrl+F2**. (If you're using a PowerBook or iBook, hold **Fn** as well). The **Apple** menu opens. Now you can navigate to any item in the menu bar by using the arrow keys on your keyboard.

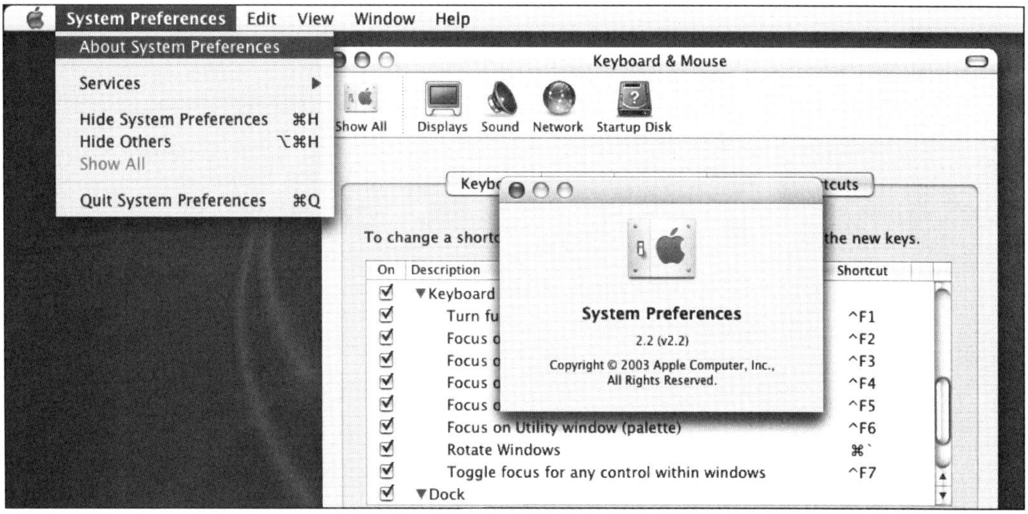

5. Using the arrow keys, navigate to **System Preferences > About System Preferences**, and press **Return** to "click" it. This will open a small window containing information about this version of System Preferences.

When you have more than one window open, the one in the front is said to be in "focus." With Full Keyboard Access on, you can use your keyboard to bring background windows into focus.

6. Press **Ctrl+F4** to bring the **Keyboard & Mouse** preference pane back to the front.

Depending on the position of your windows, it may appear as though the About System Preferences window has disappeared, but it's really only behind the Keyboard & Mouse pane.

7. Press **Ctrl+F4** a few times to toggle between the windows. (Isn't this fun?) Bring the **About System Preferences** window back to the front and press **Cmd+W** to close it. (**Cmd+W** is not a Full Keyboard Access–related command. It's the equivalent of choosing **File > Close**.)

*Take a moment to look through the other Keyboard Navigation shortcuts. As is the case with most preferences, it's up to you to decide whether or not Full Keyboard Access will benefit you. I personally like pressing **Ctrl+F3** to access the Dock and then using the arrow and Return keys to open applications that aren't running. If you play around with some of the shortcuts, you'll probably add them to your repertoire in no time.*

8. Click the **Show All** button to return to the main **System Preferences** window.

Switching Among Running Applications

As I just mentioned, you can use the Full Keyboard Access shortcut of **Ctrl+F3** to access the Dock and open programs that aren't running. You can also make use of a long-standing Mac capability by toggling through running programs by pressing **Cmd+Tab**. In previous versions of OS X, this would highlight the icons of the running programs each time you pressed tab. When you released the Cmd key, the highlighted application would come to the front.

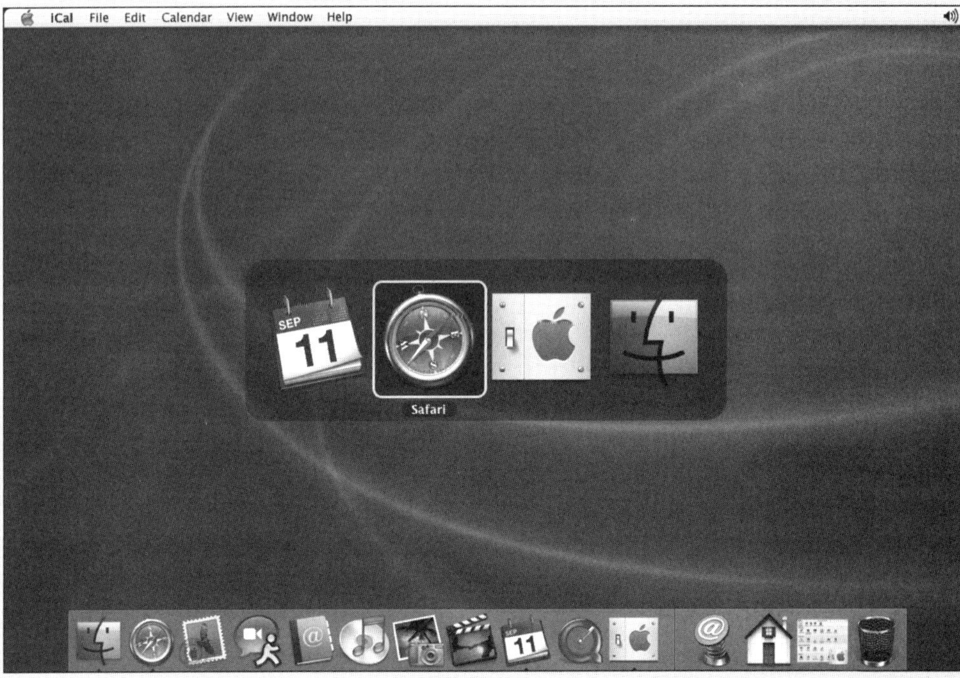

New to Panther, pressing **Cmd+Tab** now displays the icons of all running applications right in the center of your screen. Instead of having to find the application you want among all the other icons in your Dock, you now get a plain view of just the active programs, making it easier to select the one you want to bring to the front.

3. Speech

Although Macs have been able to speak for years, not too many people ever seem to take advantage of this capability. Many users view the Mac's speech and speech recognition capabilities as a novelty–something neat to show to friends. But with the proper adjustments, you may find yourself having entire conversations with your Mac. Well, maybe not entire conversations, but enough to get the people in the next room wondering who the heck you're talking to. This exercise will show you how to get your Mac talking.

1. Open the **Speech** control pane by clicking its icon in **System Preferences**.

The first thing to do here is to pick a voice for your Mac. OS X comes with 22 different voices to choose from.

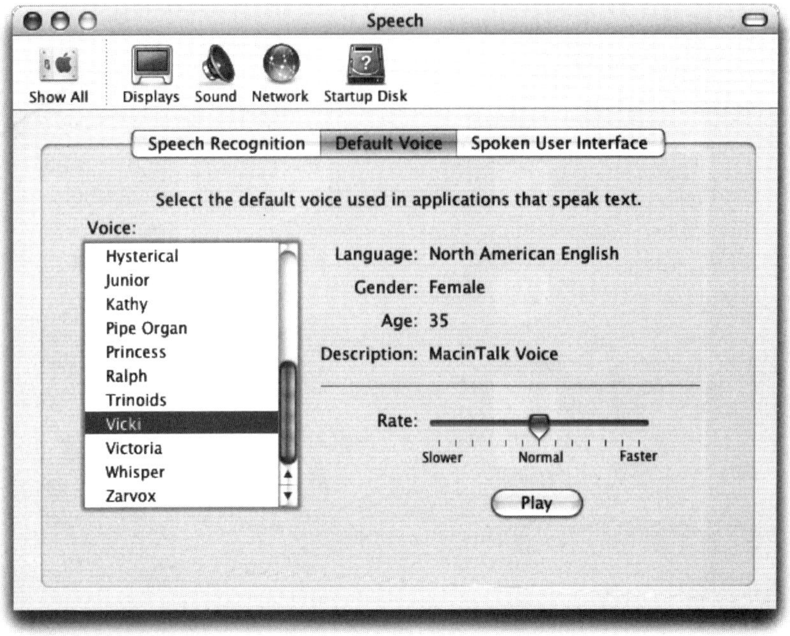

2. Click the **Default Voice** button (if it's not already selected) and scroll through the list of voices on the left. To hear a voice, simply click its name. Selecting a voice will bring up a description to the right of the list, but it doesn't really offer any particularly useful information. You can use the **Rate** slider to control how slowly or quickly the Mac speaks. Click **Play** to test your settings.

3. After you've listened to the selection of voices, pick one to be the default voice of your Mac.

Note: *Obviously, some of these voices are meant to be novelties, which is fine for adding some personality to your Mac. For the purposes of this exercise, however, select a nonsinging, nonwhispering, nonlaughing voice. The voices Agnes, Bruce, Fred, Kathy, Vicki, and Victoria will probably be the easiest for you to understand.*

Now that you've selected a voice, you'll learn how to get your Mac to use it. You already witnessed text-to-speech in the Universal Access control pane, which can be a big help to users who have trouble reading the items there. But your Mac can also be made to read just about any text that appears on your screen. To turn this feature on, you need to briefly revisit the Universal Access pane.

4. Click the **Show All** button in the toolbar, and then click the **Universal Access** icon.

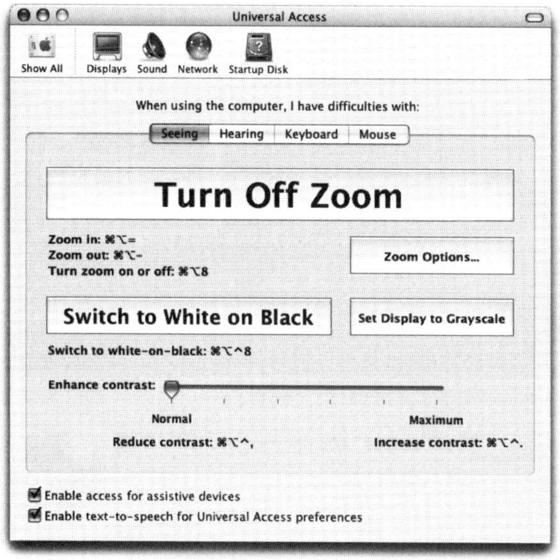

5. Check **Enable access for assistive devices**. This is the key to making text-to-speech work on your Mac. You'll be asked to enter your **administrator password**. Enter it and click **OK**.

6. Click the **Show All** button in the toolbar and return to the **Speech** control pane by clicking its icon.

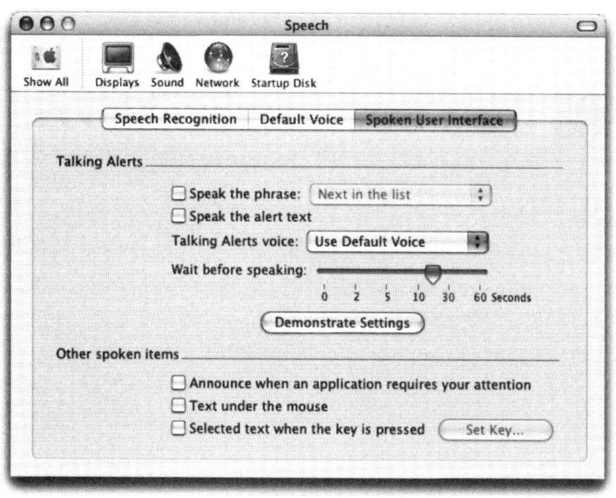

7. In **Speech**, click the **Spoken User Interface** button. This is where you determine how often you want the Mac to speak to you.

The following chart explains each of the options here.

Spoken Interface Settings

Item	Description
Talking Alerts	The options under this heading determine if and how the Mac speaks text in alert boxes. For instance, if an alert box appears asking you if you want to save a document, the settings here determine whether the Mac reads the alert box to you, and, if so, how it's read.
Speak the phrase	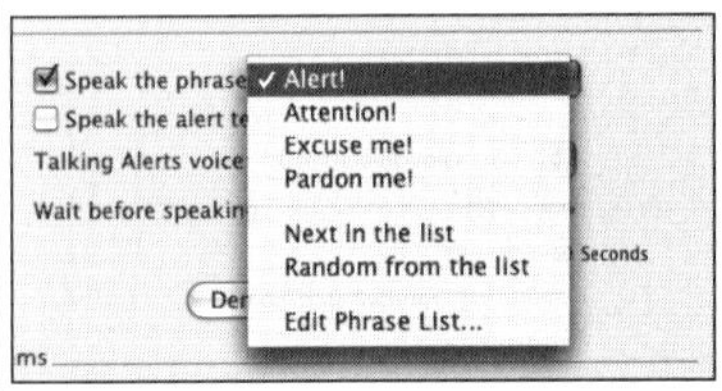 Select this option if you want the Mac to preface alert messages by speaking any of the four phrases in the menu: **Alert!**, **Attention!**, **Excuse me!**, or **Pardon me!**. Select **Next in the list** to have your Mac select the next phrase in the list each time it speaks an alert. Choose **Random from the list** to have it randomly select a phrase every time. You can also choose **Edit Phrase List** to remove a phrase or add one of your own (Yo Dude!, Hey!, Umm, and so on).
Speak the alert text	Check this option if you want the Mac to speak any alert dialog boxes that appear. Leaving this unchecked will nullify any other selections made under the Talking Alerts heading.
Talking Alerts voice	You can select a voice just for speaking alerts or leave the menu set to Use Default Voice to use the voice you selected under the Default Voice button.
Wait before speaking	Use the slider to specify how many seconds your Mac should wait before reading the alert. In most cases, you probably don't want the Mac to speak to you as soon as an alert dialog box appears. If you're sitting right there and can read the dialog box yourself, there's probably no reason for the Mac to read it to you. But if you tell your Mac to crunch some numbers or process a few dozen photos and then leave the room, it might be useful for your Mac to let you know if something goes wrong so that if you're within earshot, you can come back and get everything working again. There's nothing quite like leaving your Mac sitting in an adjacent room to process some files only to return an hour later to find that it got stuck on the first file.

continues on next page

Spoken Interface Settings *continued*	
Item	**Description**
Demonstrate Settings	Clicking this button will open a sample alert dialog box so you can see the effects of your current Talking Alerts settings.
OTHER SPOKEN ITEMS	
Announce when an application requires your attention	Normally, when an application needs your attention, its icon in the Dock jumps up and down. Checking this option will have your Mac give you a verbal alert in addition to the visual alert.
Text under the mouse	Checking this option reads the text of any interface item that you place your mouse cursor over. Check this option and your Mac will read buttons, tabs, menu bar items, icons, and file names. It will not read text in word processors or web browsers (see the next option for more on that).
Selected text when the key is pressed	This option allows your Mac to read text in any application. Word processing documents, spreadsheets, Web pages, email—if you can select the text, your Mac can read it. When you select this option, you'll be prompted to create a key combination that will have the Mac speak your text. Try to select a combination that's not used in any of your applications (**Shift+Option+Q** for instance). After the key combination has been set, you can select the text in any application and press this combination to hear the text read to you. To stop the reading after it starts, press the key combination again. If you ever need to change the key combination, click the **Set Key** button found here in the Speech control pane.

8. Leave the **Speech** control pane open for the next exercise.

4. Speech Recognition

Having your Mac speak to you can be a real convenience, especially if you aren't looking directly at the screen. But you can also speak to your Mac. Well, technically, you can always speak to your Mac–even if it's turned off; you'll just appear to be insane. But if you'd like to speak to your Mac and have it actually respond to your commands, read on.

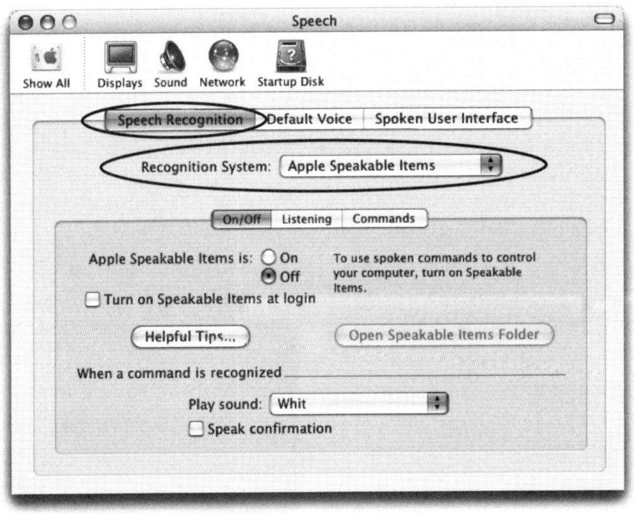

1. Click the **Speech Recognition** button in the **Speech** control pane. In this area, you control all aspects of your Mac's speech recognition. The menu that appears next to **Recognition System** shows that **Apple Speakable Items** is selected. This is the only speech recognition system available, so there's nothing to select here.

It should be noted here that the Mac's speech recognition technology does not allow you to dictate documents for it to type for you. Rather, speech recognition is used for the purpose of controlling and operating your Mac. You can use speech recognition to open applications, choose menu commands, close windows, and much more. This exercise will show you how to get your Mac listening to you.

***Tip:** If you are interested in dictating documents to your Mac, two applications you might want to look into are IBM's ViaVoice (**www-3.ibm.com/software/speech/mac/osx/**) and iListen (**www.macspeech.com**).*

***Note:** Your Mac must have a microphone for you to follow the remaining steps of this exercise. If you have a PowerBook, iBook, iMac, or eMac, you already have a built-in microphone. If you have a desktop Mac, you'll need an external microphone plugged into the back of your computer.*

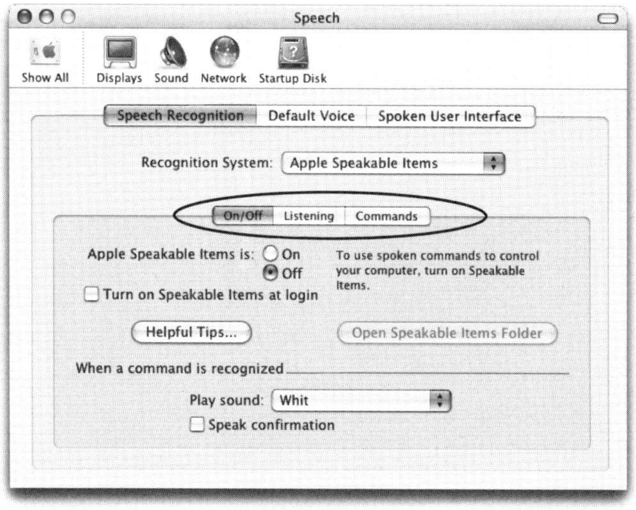

The Speech Recognition area itself contains three additional sections. As you learn to speak to your Mac in this exercise, you'll also learn which options are available to you when using your voice to control your computer. Speech Recognition is also referred to as ***Speakable Items****. Essentially, to command your Mac through speech, you must speak in phrases that it already understands. These phrases are known as* ***Speakable Items****.*

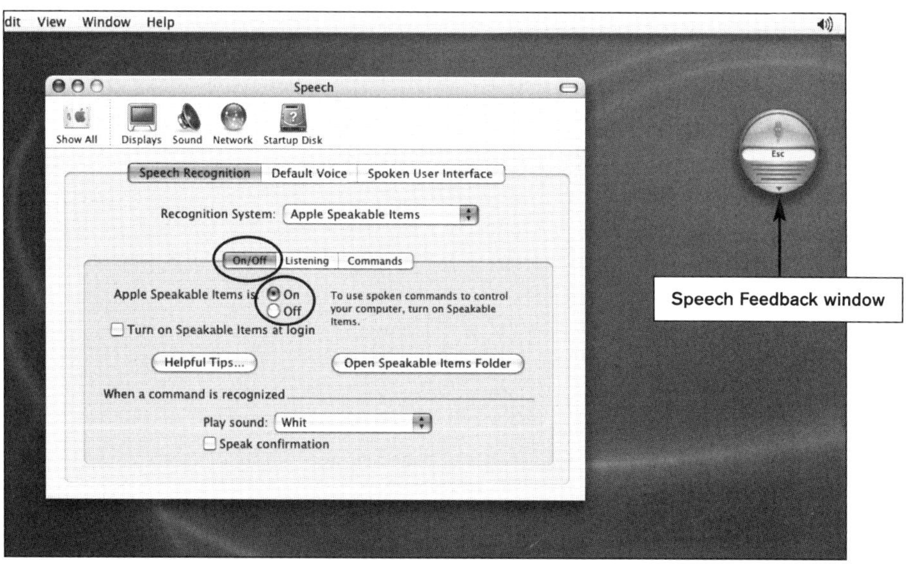

2. If it's not already selected, click the **On/Off** button. Turn **Apple Speakable Items** on. Turning Speakable Items on will cause the **Speech Feedback** window to open on the right side of your screen.

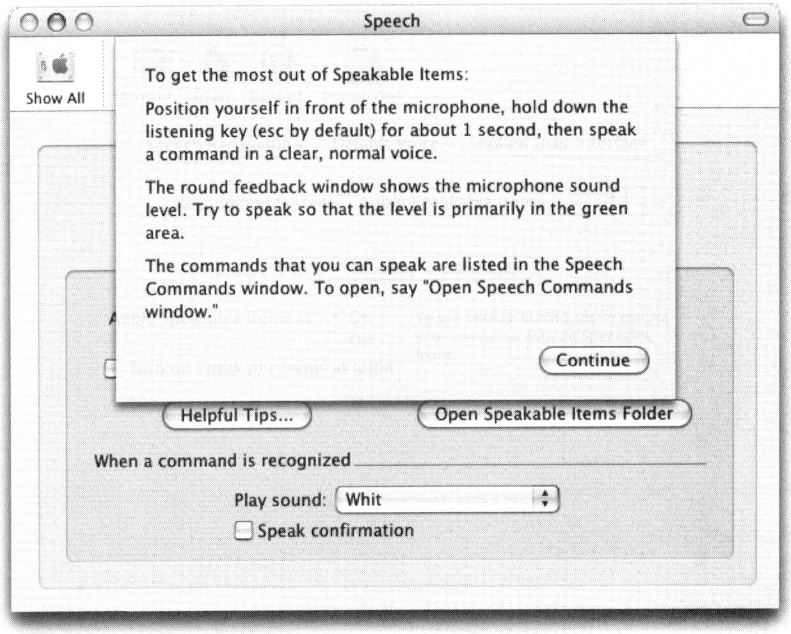

Note: *If this is the first time you've turned on Speakable Items, a tip sheet will descend from the top of the pane. If it appears, read the pane and then click* ***Continue.*** *If the window doesn't appear, you can still read the tips by clicking the* ***Helpful Tips*** *button.*

---

3. Under **When a command is recognized**, choose **Whit** from the **Play sound** menu if it isn't already selected. Your Mac will play this sound, called "Whit," whenever it recognizes a spoken command. Checking **Speak confirmation** will have your Mac repeat your command out loud. For now, keep this option unchecked.

At this point, Speech Recognition is up and running, but before you try it out, you'll first take a look at what makes your Mac listen to you.

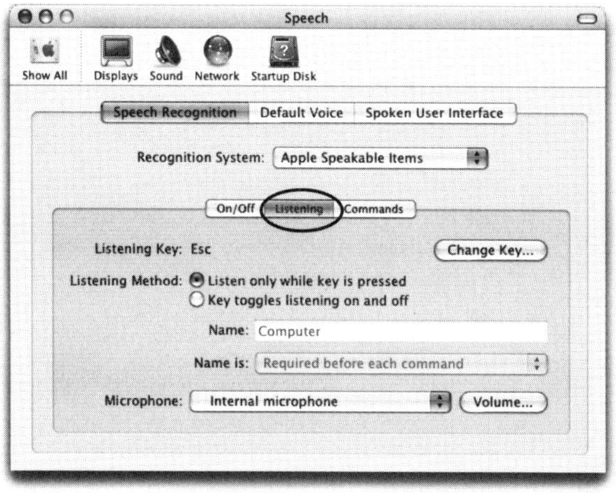

4. Click the **Listening** button.

You most likely don't want your Mac listening to you at all times. If someone pops into your room and asks you to empty the trash, it's possible that your Mac might respond by emptying its trash. Therefore, to make your Mac listen, you need to either press a specific "listening" key, such as the Esc key, or address the computer by name. You'll try both methods.

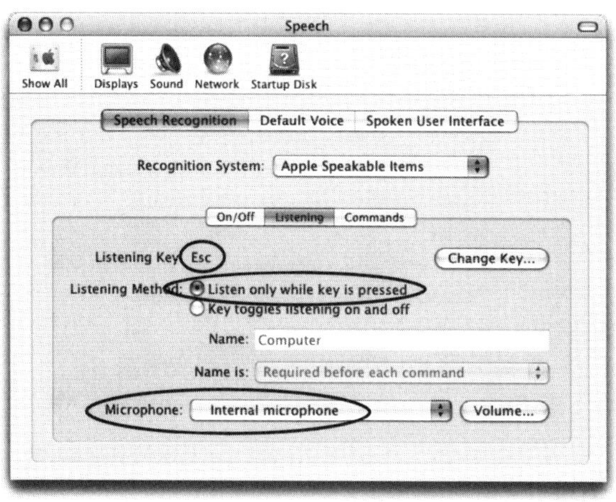

5. Make sure that the **Listening Key** is set to **Esc**. (If it's not, click **Change Key**, press **Esc**, and click **OK**.) Next to **Listening Method**, make sure that **Listen only while key is pressed** is selected. Lastly, make sure the proper microphone is selected. Unless you have a desktop Mac, **Internal microphone** should be the proper choice here. Choose **External microphone/Line in** if you have a desktop Mac.

Now you'll make sure that your Mac can hear you.

6. Observe the **Speech Feedback** window. Notice that the microphone icon is grayed-out and "Esc" appears below it. This tells you that the Mac is not currently listening and that the **Esc** key is used to activate listening.

7. Press and hold the **Esc** key. The microphone icon in the **Speech Feedback** window activates, and the "Esc" label disappears. Your Mac is listening. Wait about a second and then say "testing" a few times in your normal voice (there's no need to shout). This won't make your Mac perform any tasks, but if your Mac can hear you, you should see a series of arrows point to the microphone icon, and some blue and green bars should appear underneath it. The colored bars show how much sound your Mac is receiving. A blue bar is good, but two green bars are the best; if a red bar appears, you're either speaking too loudly or you're too close to the microphone. Release the **Esc** key after you've finished testing the microphone.

Note: *If you're not getting any reaction from the* ***Speech Feedback*** *window when you speak, make sure the proper microphone is chosen under the* ***Listening*** *tab.*

Now that you know your Mac can hear you, you'll try some commands. You'll be shown the entire list of commands later in the exercise, but for now you'll try a few basic ones.

8. Press **Esc**, wait a second, and then say, "What day is it?" and release the **Esc** key.

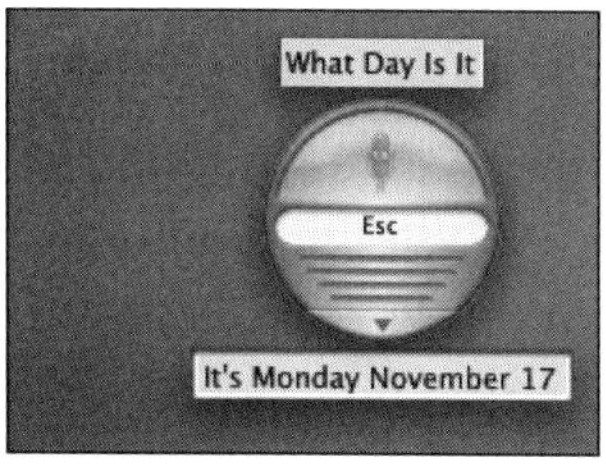

If your Mac understands you, you'll hear the Whit sound you selected and the phrase, "What day is it" will appear above the Speech Feedback window. Your Mac will respond by speaking the current day. The text it speaks appears below the Speech Feedback window. Now how cool is that?

9. Hold the **Esc** key and ask, "What time is it?" Your Mac should respond by telling you the time.

The advantage of the listening key method of speaking to your computer is that the Mac listens only when you have the Esc key pressed. The disadvantage is that you have to press a key to talk to your computer. Next, you'll try addressing the computer by name.

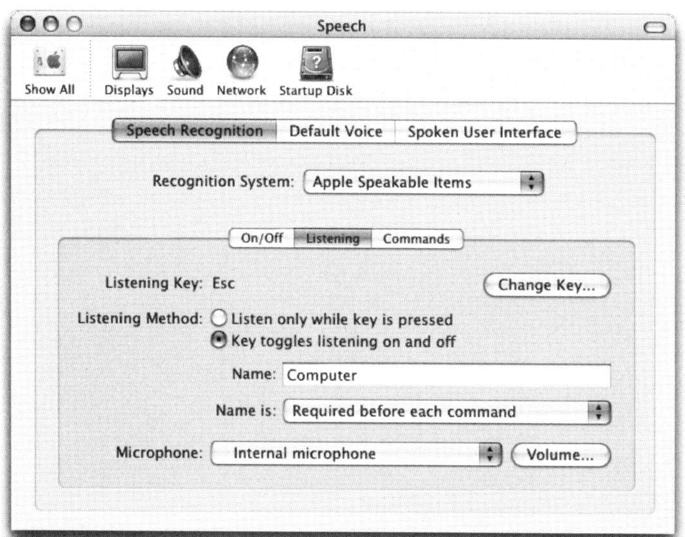

10. Under the **Listening** section in the **Speech Recognition** area, select **Key toggles listening on and off**. Now the **Esc** key acts as an on/off switch for listening. Press it once and the computer listens constantly; press it again, and it doesn't listen at all. Leave the **Name** as **Computer**. In the **Name is** menu, make sure **Required before each command** is selected.

With the preferences you just set, speaking to your Mac now requires that you say the name "Computer" before each command, but you no longer have to press the Esc key each time.

11. Make sure that the microphone icon in the **Speech Feedback** window is active (not grayed-out) and that you can see the name "Computer" in the window. If not, press **Esc**.

12. Say, "Computer" and pause for a second. Then say, "What time is it?" Your Mac should respond with the correct time.

13. Say, "What day is it?" You should get no response because you didn't preface the command with "Computer." Now say, "Computer, what day is it?" Your Mac should now respond.

If you have a series of commands to speak to the computer, saying "Computer" each time can get a little tedious.

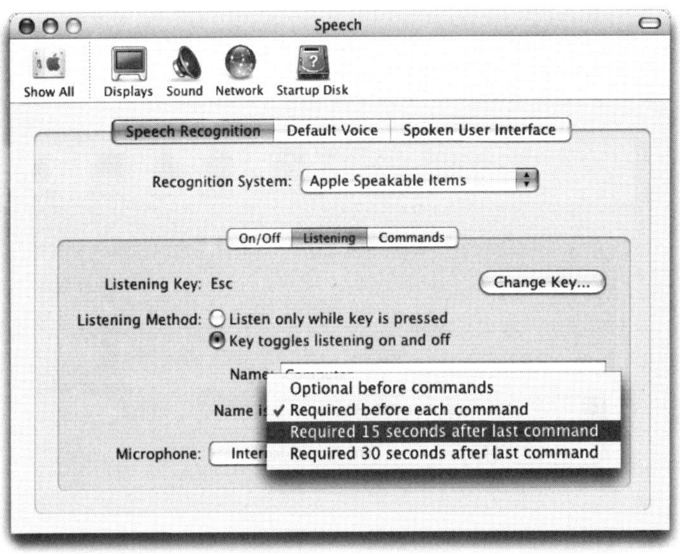

14. In the **Speech** pane, change the **Name is** menu to **Required 15 seconds after last command.** Now you can speak as many concurrent commands as you like without preceding all but the first one with "Computer," as long as each command comes within 15 seconds of the last one.

Try this one:

15. Say, "Computer, tell me a joke." The computer will respond with a lame knock-knock joke (as if there were any other kind of knock-knock joke). You fill in the "who's there" and "whatever-who" parts. The point is you don't have to say, "Computer, who's there?" because you already said "Computer" less than 15 seconds ago.

*You can also choose to let 30 seconds go by before needing to say the computer's name again. I strongly discourage you from choosing **Optional** before commands from the **Name is** menu. With this option on, your Mac is constantly listening and might possibly interpret background noises as commands.*

***Tip:** You don't have to keep calling your Mac "Computer," although the name does have that certain "Star-Trek: The Next Generation" feel to it. In the Listening section of Speech Recognition, you can name your Mac anything you like, though multisyllabic names work best. It might be amusing (depending on your sense of humor) to name your Mac "SimonSez," as in "SimonSez, empty the trash!"*

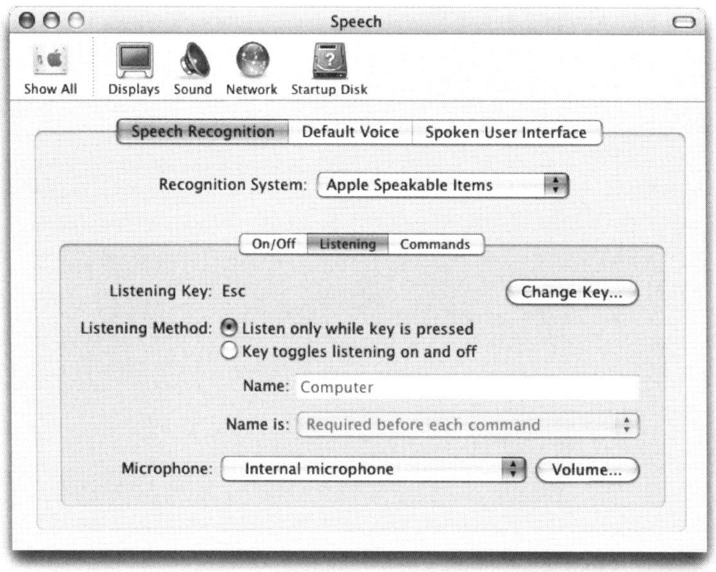

For the rest of this exercise, you'll switch back to using the Esc key to turn on listening.

16. Under the **Listening** tab, select **Listen only while key is pressed**.

Finding out the day and time and hearing an occasional joke are all great, but what can you really do with Speakable Items?

17. Press the **Esc** key and say, "Show me what to say."

The Speech Commands window opens below the Speech Feedback window. The top portion of the Speech Commands window lists all the commands you've spoken so far; the bottom portion lists all the currently available Speakable Items

Tip: *If you can't get the **Speech Commands** window to open by saying, "Show me what to say," click the arrow at the bottom of the **Speech Feedback** window and select **Open Speech Commands window.***

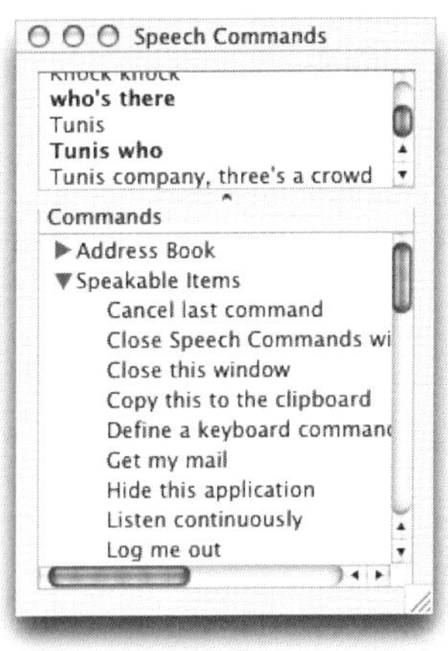

18. In the **Speech Commands** window, toggle the arrow next to **Speakable Items**. Scroll through the list of **Speakable Items**. When you're done looking, toggle the arrow again to hide the list of items.

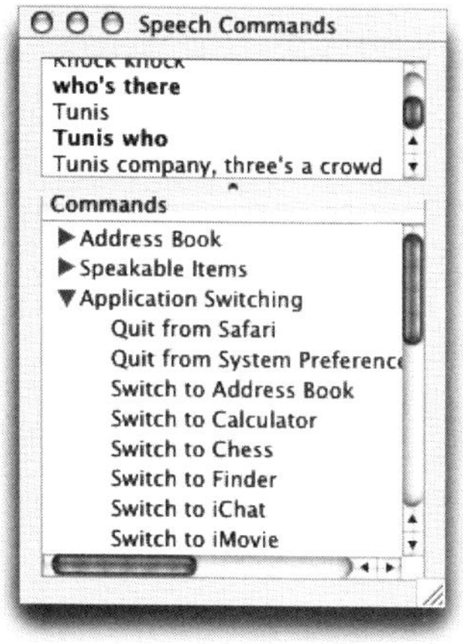

19. Toggle the arrow next to **Application Switching**. This list contains all the applications originally installed in your **Applications** folder. You can open any application by saying, "Switch to..." and the application's name. When you're done viewing this list, toggle it closed.

---

20. Hold the **Esc** key and say, "Switch to Chess." The **Chess** application opens.

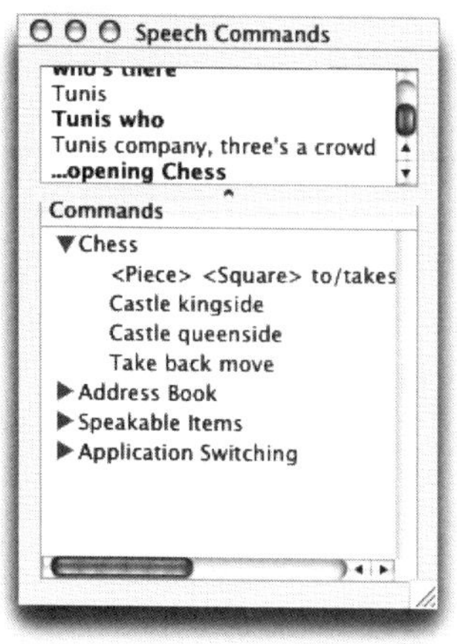

OS X's Chess game can be voice controlled as well, so it has some commands that now appear in the Speech Commands menu. For instance, you can say, "Pawn C2 to C4" to move the bishop's pawn.

---

21. To quit this application, hold **Esc** and say, "Quit this application." **Chess** quits.

As you can see, there are dozens of useful voice commands available to you already. And you can increase the amount of available Speakable Items by checking some items in the Speech control pane.

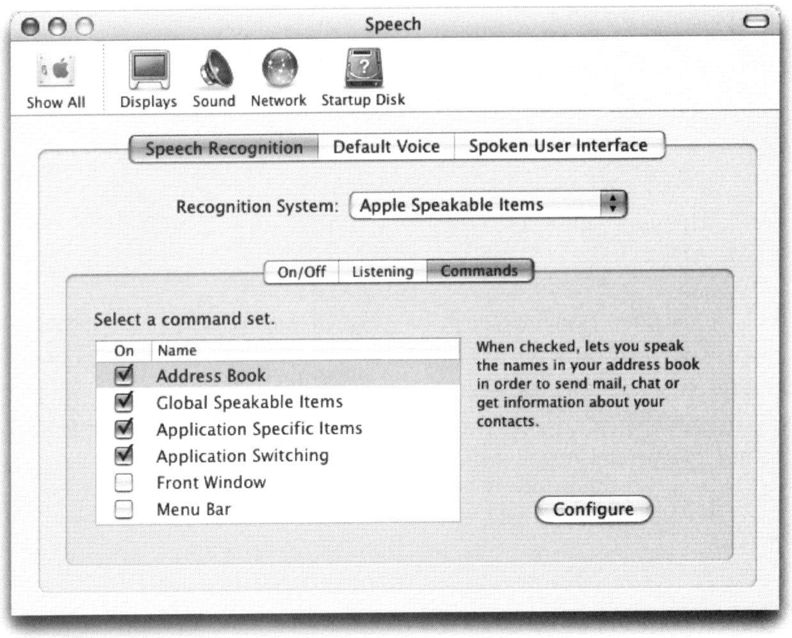

22. Under the **Speech Recognition** section of **Speech** preferences, click the **Commands** tab. Here you can specify which **Speakable Items** can be spoken. You've already seen the **Global Speakable Items** ("What time is it?", "What day is it?", and so on), **Application Switching** commands ("Switch to Chess"), and the specific application commands ("Pawn C2 to C4").

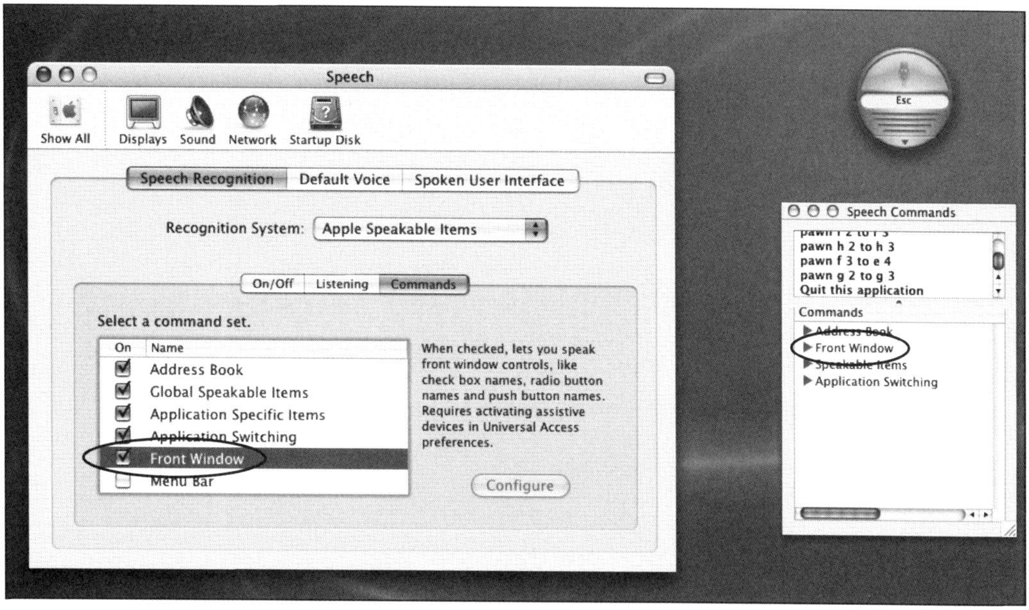

23. Check **Front Window** commands. Front window commands are specific to whichever window is active on your screen and allow you to speak the buttons, tabs, and other items that appear in that window.

Because the Speech window is active, you can speak its items.

---

24. Press **Esc** and say, "Default Voice." The **Default Voice** area becomes active. Press **Esc** and say, "Speech Recognition" to return to the **Speech Recognition** area. Press **Esc** and say, "On Off" and the **On/Off** area comes to the front.

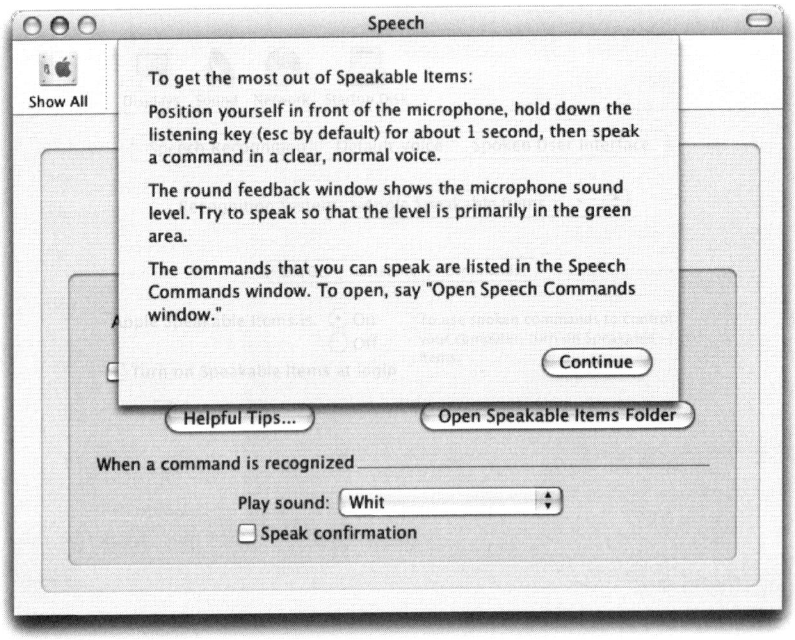

25. You can even speak the text on buttons to "click" them. Press **Esc** and say, "Helpful Tips." The **Helpful Tips** button flashes and the tips sheet appears. Hold **Esc** and say, "Continue" to dismiss it.

Take some time and scroll through the Speech Commands window to see what's available. If you feel like giving Speech Recognition a serious try, leave the Speech Commands window open while you work and check it often to see which commands can be used in which applications.

***Tip:** The menu bar command set (in the Commands area of Speech Recognition) provides access to menu bar items. Simply say the menu bar item (such as "Edit menu") and then speak the menu command (such as "copy" or "paste").*

---

26. Click the **On/Off** tab under the **Speech Recognition** tab and turn **Apple Speakable Items** off. (Alternately, you can press **Esc** and say, "Quit Speakable Items.")

---

27. Quit **System Preferences**.

Creating Your Own Speakable Items

If you install a new application and want to open it with a speech command, you can easily make it speakable in one of two ways. If Speakable Items is on, click the application's icon once to select it, then say, "Make this speakable" or "Make this application speakable." For example, if you select the icon for Adobe Photoshop 7 and say, "Make this speakable," from that point on you can say, "Switch to Adobe Photoshop 7" to open that application.

Additionally, you can manually drag application aliases into the Speakable Items folder. To do so, select the application's icon and choose **File > Make Alias (Cmd+L)**. Drag the alias into the **Speakable Items** folder, which is located in **Home > Library > Speech**. Obviously this method is much more involved than simply saying, "Make this speakable," but it's good to know where the Speakable Items are located if you ever want to change their names. For instance, if you're tired of saying, "Switch to Adobe Photoshop 7," you could find the Adobe Photoshop 7 alias in your Speakable Items folder and change its icon name to simply "Photoshop," allowing you to simply say, "Switch to Photoshop." Give Speakable Items a try in your work–you might be surprised how much you enjoy them.

Realistically, most Mac users–unless they have a disability and genuinely need the custom settings–probably don't use the Universal Access and Speech control panes. But after making it through this chapter, you might find some of these features to be useful in many different situations. For instance, if a friend sends you an image that's too small to discern certain details, you could use the Zoom feature to enlarge the image while keeping it smooth–it'll look much better than it would if you opened the image in Photoshop and increased its dimensions. Or if you need to step away from your computer, you can tell it to speak alerts so you'll know if it needs your attention. Keep these options in mind during your day-to-day work–they might help make things a little easier.

6. Printing, Fonts, and Faxing

Installing a Printer	Printing	Creating PDFs
Working with Fonts	Installing Fonts with Font Book
Managing Fonts with Font Book	Faxing

chap_06

Mac OS X Panther
H•O•T CD-ROM

One of the most problematic issues facing early adopters of OS X was its lack of compatible printer drivers. Many early users found themselves rebooting their Macs back into OS 9 every time they needed to print a document–hardly an efficient process. But as more and more printer manufacturers jumped onto the OS X bandwagon, more mainstream printer drivers became readily available. Today, Panther comes loaded with dozens of drivers from numerous leading printer manufacturers. In fact, when you plug a printer into a Mac running OS 10.3, there's a pretty good chance that you won't have to install any additional items in order to use it.

This chapter will show you how to install a printer on your Mac and how to get your Mac to recognize it. You'll also learn how to manage your printer and print jobs. Because the items that appear in dialog boxes when you print are specific to the application from which you're printing and the type of printer you're using, it's difficult to include explicit information. This chapter will cover printing in general terms, but will also present specific instructions for several common printing scenarios.

This chapter will also teach you how to install and manage the fonts on your computer using Panther's new Font Book application, and how to utilize OS X's new capability to send and receive faxes. There's a lot to cover, so let's get started.

I. Installing a Printer

In order for a printer to work with a computer, the computer must have the proper drivers installed. The driver is a piece of software that enables applications to communicate with the printer. The good news: If you bought your inkjet or laser printer in the past few years, the only thing you probably have to do to install the printer is to plug it into your Mac. OS X comes equipped to recognize printers manufactured by Hewlett Packard, Canon, Epson, and Lexmark. If your Mac recognizes the printer, you can start printing immediately. The steps in this exercise walk you through the process of hooking your printer to your Mac and making sure that your Mac sees it.

1. Plug the printer into your Mac. Depending on the model, printers can be plugged into your Mac through the USB, Firewire, or Ethernet ports. Be sure to check your printer's user manual if you're not sure which port to plug the printer into.

Note: *If you do not intend to connect a printer directly to your Mac, and instead plan on sharing a printer with another Mac over a network, see the section "Printer Sharing with Rendezvous" at the end of this exercise for more information.*

After plugging your printer into your computer, you need to make sure that your Mac recognizes it. To do so, you'll use Printer Setup Utility, an application that acts as the control center for all printers connected to your Mac.

---

2. Open **Printer Setup Utility**. It's located in the **Utilities** folder in your main **Applications** folder. You can also open it by opening **System Preferences**, clicking the **Print & Fax** button, and then clicking the **Set Up Printers** button.

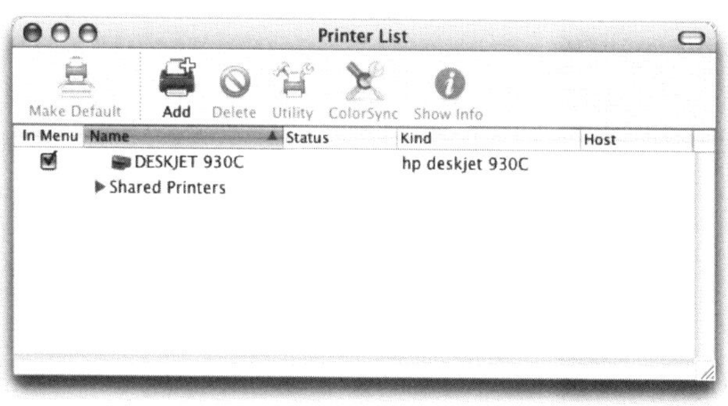

When Printer Setup Utility opens, you'll see a window called ***Printer List****. If you see your printer listed in this window, you're done! Your Mac recognizes this printer, and you're ready to print. You can quit Printer Setup Utility and disregard the rest of these steps. (If you have more than one printer listed here, see the sidebar, "Selecting a Default Printer," at the end of the exercise.)*

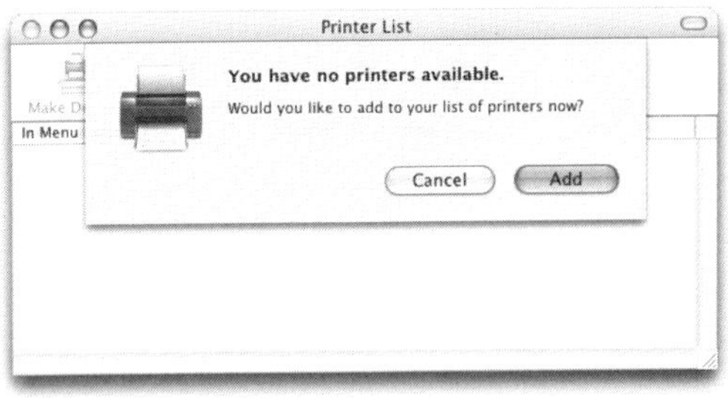

3. If your Mac didn't recognize your printer, you'll see this message informing you that no printers are available. If you see this message, click **Add**.

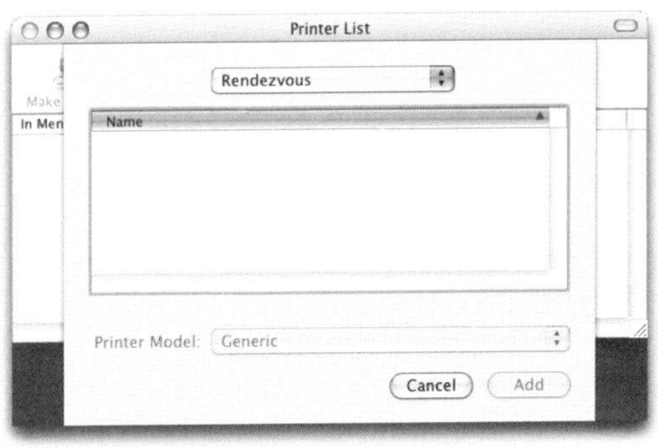

A sheet will descend from the top of the Printer List window. At the top of this sheet is a pop-up menu where you can select the type of connection your printer is using.

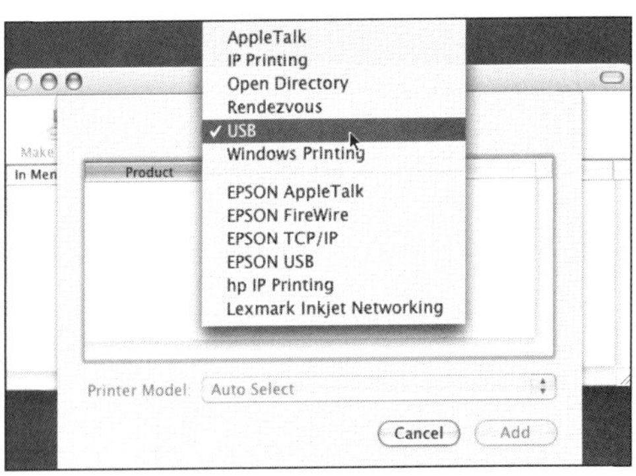

4. Select the proper connection type for your printer. For instance, if you're using an inkjet printer, it's most likely connected to your **USB** port. If you're using a laser printer that's connected to your Ethernet port, choose **AppleTalk**.

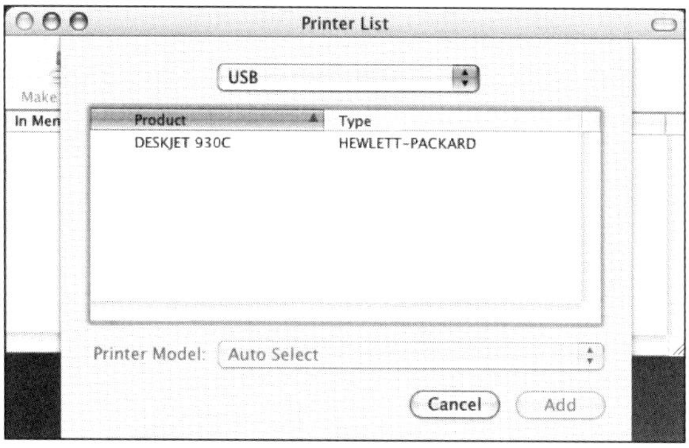

After choosing your connection type, any printers that are connected through that port (and are turned on) will appear in the window.

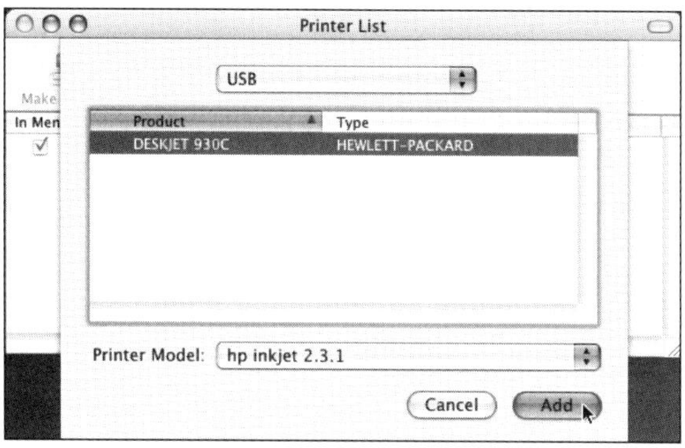

5. Click the name of the printer and then click **Add**. The printer will be listed in the main **Printer List** window along with any other printers you've added.

So what if your printer doesn't show up using any of these methods? If that's the case, OS X does not have a driver that will work with your printer, and you'll need to install the driver that came on the CD that shipped with your printer. If you don't have the driver, check the printer manufacturer's Web site. All major manufacturers provide their drivers for download on their sites; some have even written OS X drivers for older models, so if you have a vintage printer, you may still be able to use it in OS X.

---

6. Quit **Printer Setup Utility**.

Selecting a Default Printer

In OS X, you can easily print to any number of printers connected to your Mac. For instance, you might print drafts of your documents to an inkjet printer and print final copies on a laser printer. No matter how many printers you have connected to your computer, one of them has to be designated as the default printer. The default printer is the one that the Mac always assumes you want to print to unless you tell it otherwise.

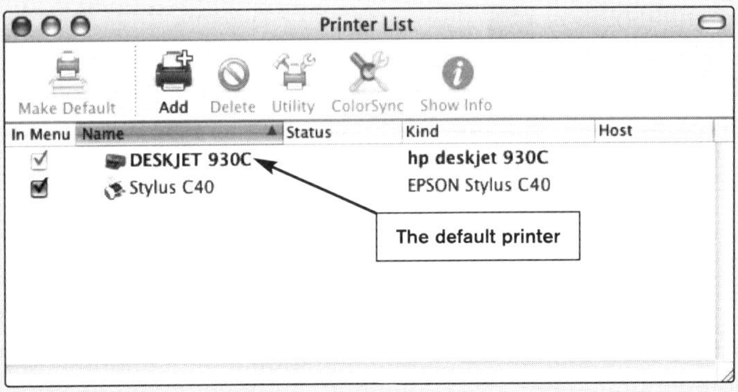

In Printer Setup Utility, your default printer is listed in bold.

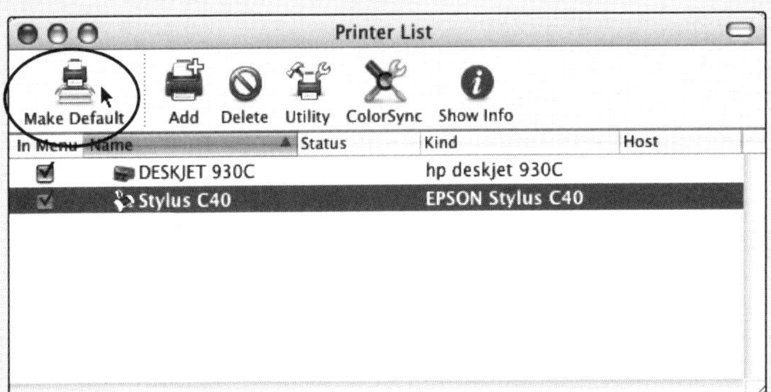

To change the default printer, click the printer's name, and then click **Make Default**. This is now your Mac's "go to" printer. You'll learn more about the importance of the default printer in the next exercise.

Printer Sharing with Rendezvous

Perhaps one of OS X's most exciting technologies is Rendezvous. Apple refers to Rendezvous as a "zero-configuration" technology because networked Macs automatically recognize other Rendezvous-compatible devices and require no other configuration to work with them. Most major printer manufacturers now sell Rendezvous-compatible printers. Your Mac will instantly recognize when one of these printers is connected to your network and will immediately be able to print to it.

Even if you don't have a Rendezvous-compatible printer, you can still use Rendezvous technology to print to any printer connected to any Mac on your network as long as both Macs are running at least OS 10.2.

On a Mac that's directly connected to the printer, open **System Preferences** and click the **Sharing** icon under **Internet & Network**.

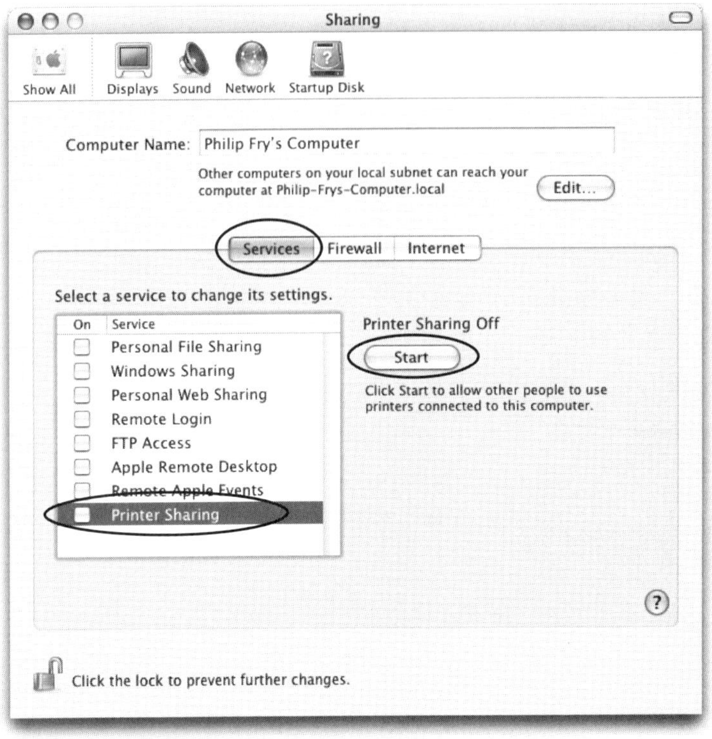

In the **Sharing** control panel, click the **Services** button. Turn on Printer Sharing by either clicking its check box or selecting it and clicking the **Start** button. This will allow any Macs on the network to see and use any printers connected to this Mac. Quit **System Preferences** when you're done.

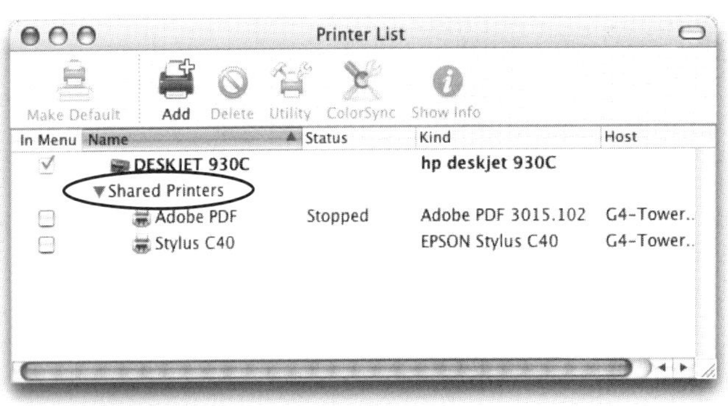

Open **Printer Setup Utility** on the Mac that you want to print from (the one not directly connected to the printer), and click the triangle next to **Shared Printers**. The shared printer (or printers) should immediately appear below. If you want to make it your default printer, you can do so by selecting it and clicking the **Make Default** button.

If the shared printer does not show up in the **Printer List**, click the **Add** button.

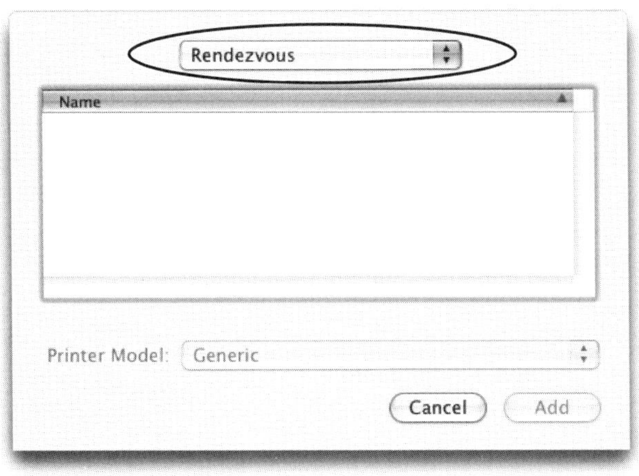

From the pop-up menu of printer connections, choose **Rendezvous**. The shared printer should appear in the list below. Click the printer and click **Add**. As long as the Mac that the printer is connected to stays on, you can print to this printer over the network.

2. Printing

Printing from OS X is no different than printing a document from a pre–OS X application, or any other application for that matter. To print from any application, choose **File > Print** from the application's menu bar. In the rare instances when Print is not available under the File menu, either the application does not have printing capability or printing is controlled through a button in the application itself.

What you see after you select Print will vary greatly and depends largely on the type of printer you're using and which application you're printing from. This exercise will present and explain the more common options that are available when you print.

1. Open **TextEdit** from your **Applications** folder. You'll use this application to examine basic print settings.

2. In the new document that opens, type some text. It doesn't matter what you type; just a sentence or two will do.

Before you print your masterpiece, you'll first examine the Page Setup settings. Generally, all applications that print have a Page Setup command, which allows you to make sure that you're printing to the correct paper size and at the proper orientation.

3. Choose **File > Page Setup** from the menu bar.

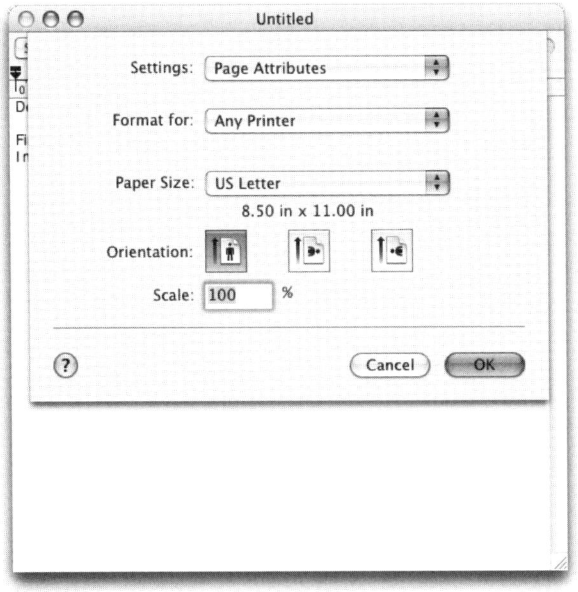

A sheet descends from the top of the document window. Page Setup settings are specific to the application; the selections you choose in this case will apply to any document opened or created in TextEdit.

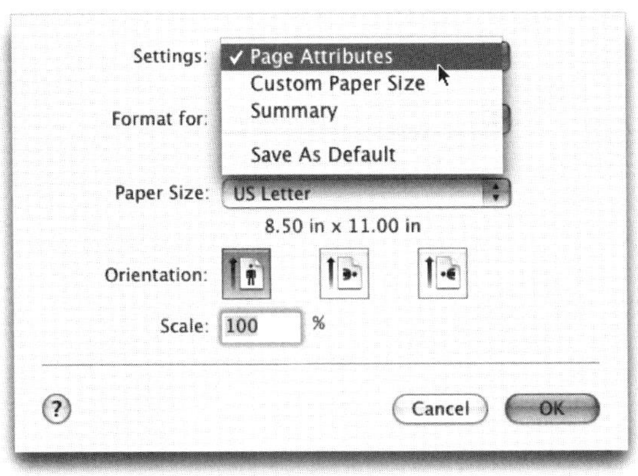

4. Click the menu next to **Settings** to view the options. The options in the rest of this dialog box will change depending on which Settings item you choose. Also, depending on the application in which you're working, you'll sometimes find a wider range of items in this menu than you see here.

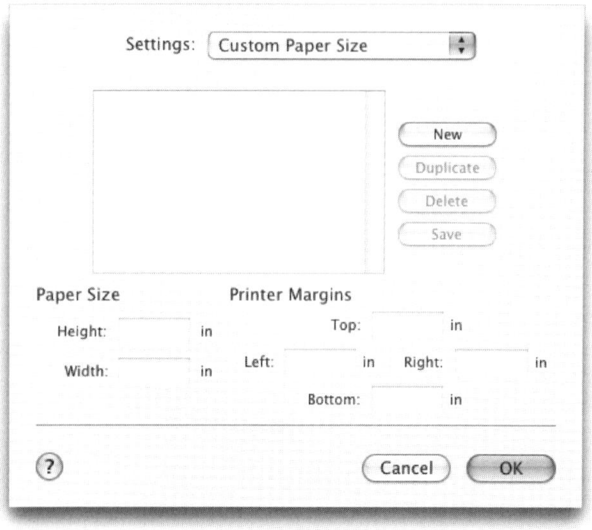

5. Choose **Custom Paper Size** from the **Settings** menu. The dialog box changes to allow you to enter your own measurements for paper size. You would use this area if you were printing to nonstandard-sized paper.

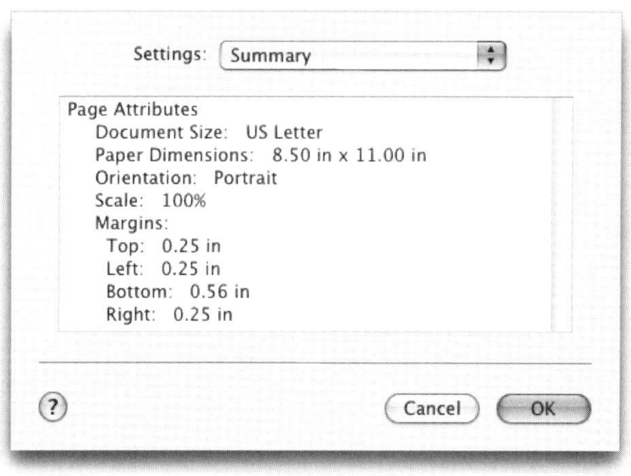

6. Choose **Summary** from the **Settings** menu. There are no choices to make in this area. You're simply presented with a summary of the current page settings, which can be useful if you need a quick rundown of your current page setup.

Most of the time, though, you'll use the Page Attributes area to alter the way your document will print.

7. Choose **Page Attributes** from the **Settings** menu.

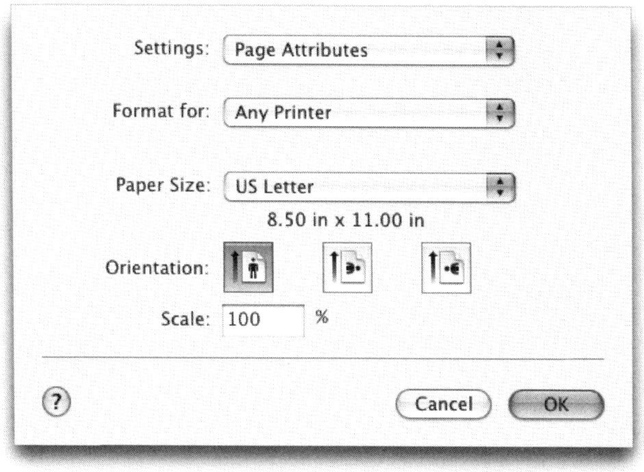

*The **Format for** menu allows you to decide which printer these settings will apply to; the **Paper Size** menu enables you to choose from a number of standard American and European paper sizes (if you don't see the size you need, you can always choose Custom Paper Size from the Settings menu and type in the dimensions of your paper); the **Orientation** menu allows you to decide which way the document will be rotated on the paper when it prints. The **Scale** input field lets you enlarge or reduce the size of the printed document.*

8. When you're done examining the **Page Attributes**, click **OK**.

You don't have to check your Page Setup settings each time you want to print. Unless you need to change a setting, you can generally ignore Page Setup after you've chosen your initial settings. In fact, if you're like many people, you'll only remember the Page Setup dialog box after you've mistakenly printed a document in the wrong orientation and wasted some paper.

Now you're ready to print this document.

9. Choose **File > Print**. This will open the **Print** dialog box.

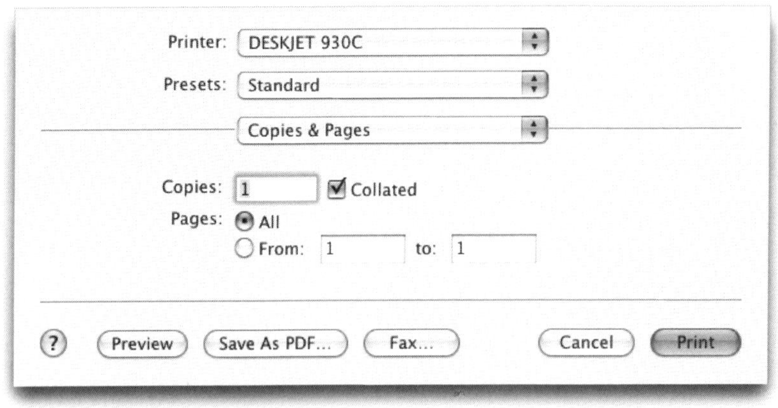

At the top of the dialog box, your default printer appears in the Printer menu. This is the printer that will print your document. If you have any other printers connected to your Mac, or if you have shared printers connected to other Macs on your network, you can select them from this menu if you wish.

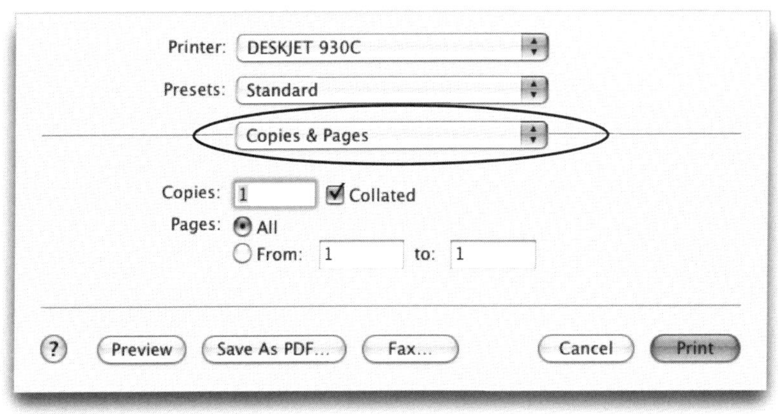

The contents of the unnamed pop-up menu circled here will vary depending on which printer you've chosen from the Printer menu. Here are some of the items you might find in this menu.

Common Print Dialog Box Options

<table>
<tr><th>Option</th><th>Description</th></tr>
<tr><td>Copies & Pages</td><td>This one appears in all print dialog boxes. With Copies & Pages selected, you can input the number of copies that you want printed when you click Print. You can use the page range selector to determine which pages of the document to print. Choose All to print the entire document, or From to specify a range of pages. Hint: Leaving the From or to box empty implies that you want to print from the beginning or to the end of the document. For example, typing 17 in the From box and leaving to empty means "print from page 17 to the end of the document." Similarly, leaving the From box empty and typing 17 in the to box means, "Print from page 1 to page 17."</td></tr>
<tr><td>Layout</td><td>
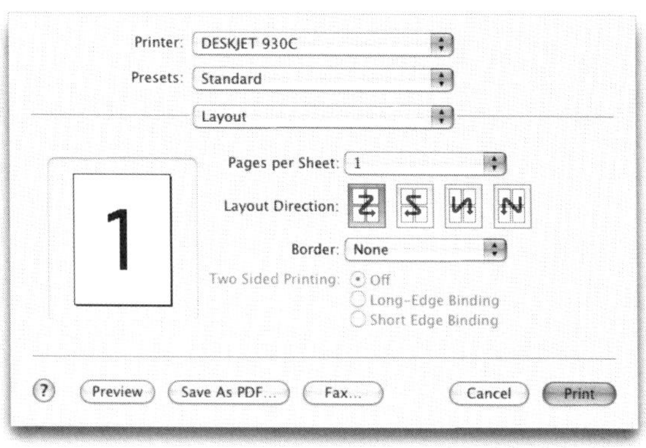

You can use this menu to print multiple miniature pages on a single piece of paper, which can be very useful and save a lot of paper if you just want to get an idea of how each page will look. Choose the number of pages to include on each sheet from the Pages per Sheet menu and then determine the Layout Direction. If you like, you can have the printer draw a border around each page by selecting a style from the Border menu.</td></tr>
</table>

continues on next page

<table>
<tr><th colspan="2">Common Print Dialog Box Options continued</th></tr>
<tr><th>Option</th><th>Description</th></tr>
<tr><td>Output Options</td><td>
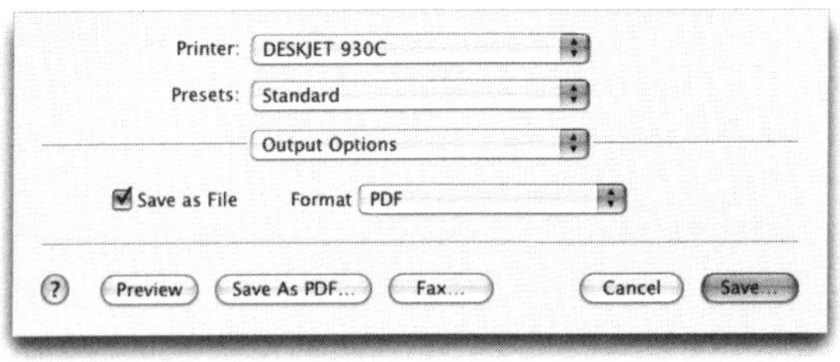

Here you can check Save as File to save your document as a PDF (Portable Document Format) file rather than printing it to paper. This is no different than clicking the Save as PDF button at the bottom of the dialog box (it, in fact, takes more steps). This native support of PDF is a major OS X feature—no other operating system for any computer platform has this capability. You'll learn more about creating PDFs in the following exercise.</td></tr>
<tr><td>Scheduler</td><td>New to Panther, you can choose to have a document print at a specific time. The default Print Document setting is Now, but you can select At to enter a time at which you want the document to print. You can also select On Hold to place the document in the printer queue, but not print it immediately. (See "Managing Print Jobs" at the end of this exercise.)</td></tr>
<tr><td>Summary</td><td>Provides a rundown of your current print settings.</td></tr>
</table>

Again, you'll probably find at least two or three more available sets of options in the print dialog box, such as Paper Type, Color Management, or Print Settings. Check the user manual that came with your printer for descriptions of these custom options.

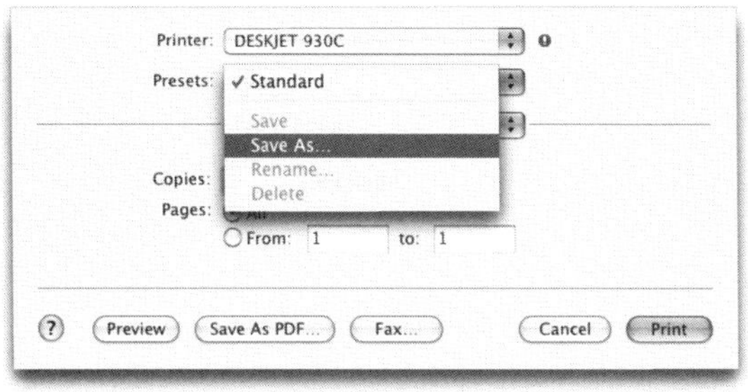

*Tip: OS 10.2 introduced the capability to save customized print settings under different names. By choosing **Save As** from the **Presets** menu, you can take a "snapshot" of your current print dialog box settings. Once you've named and saved this snapshot, you can call it up again at any time by choosing it from the Presets menu. This is an incredibly useful capability if you customize your print settings for different jobs.*

Once you've made your Print dialog box selections, you can click Print, which sends your document to the Printer Setup Utility.

10. Make sure you have paper in your printer and click **Print**.

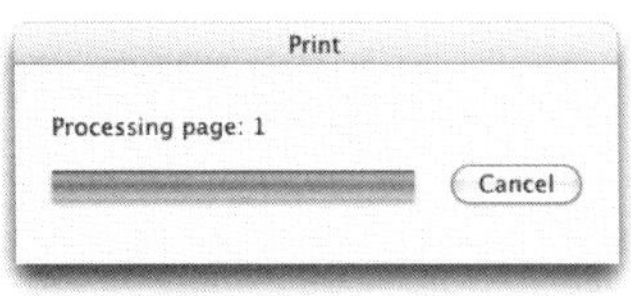

After clicking Print, your Mac will take a moment to process the job.

Then the icon for your printer will appear in the Dock. Prior to Panther, the Printer List window would open, but in Panther, a control panel for your printer opens instead. If you roll your mouse over the icon you'll even see the name of your printer. To be as unobtrusive as possible, your printer's control panel doesn't open any windows or give you any messages; it just receives the print job, sends the job to the printer, and then closes when the job's done. If you have a relatively fast Mac and a small print job, you might not even notice Printer Setup Utility opening at all. However, you can check on the progress of your print jobs by clicking your printer's icon. See "Managing Print Jobs" at the end of this exercise.

11. After your document prints, quit **TextEdit**. You don't need to save your document.

Managing Print Jobs

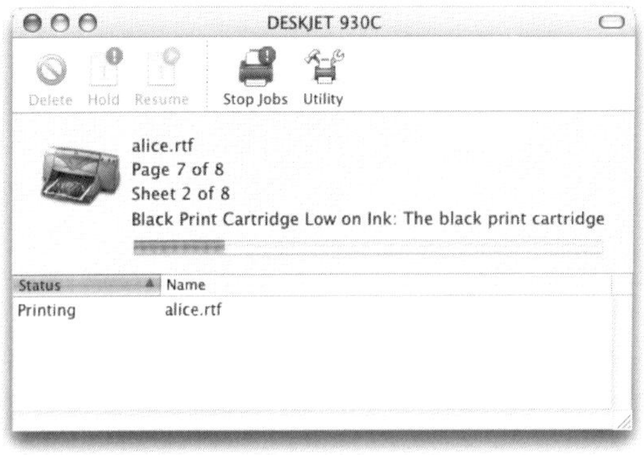

Printer Setup Utility does a pretty good job of keeping itself out of your way when it's printing a document. But if you want to check on the progress of a longer print job, you can click your printer's icon in the Dock to display its window. The Status column will let you know if the job is printing. You'll also be able to see which page is currently in process. Depending on your printer and its software, you may also see other information, such as messages letting you know that you're low on ink.

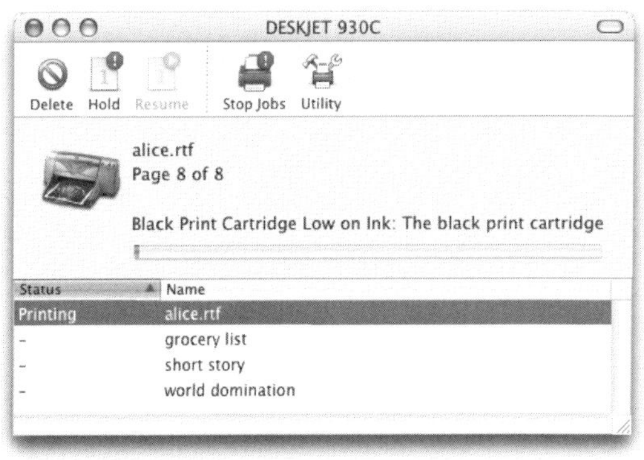

You can have multiple documents lined up, or "queued," to print. Your printer utility will print them one at a time.

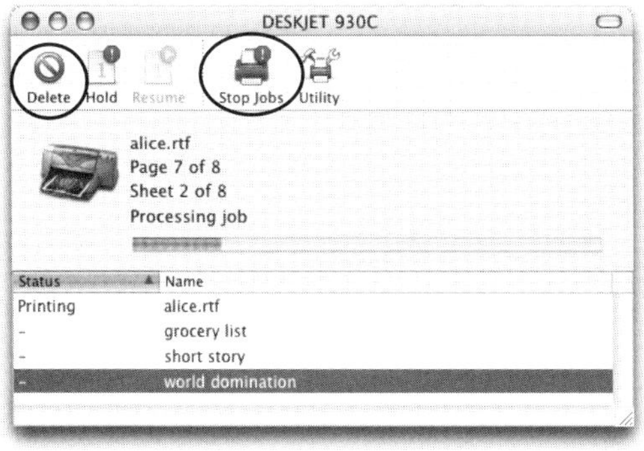

If you need to cancel a print job, select it from the list and click the **Delete** button to remove it from the queue. You can also "stop the presses!" by clicking the **Stop Jobs** button. Doing so will stop the current print job as well as any other documents in the queue.

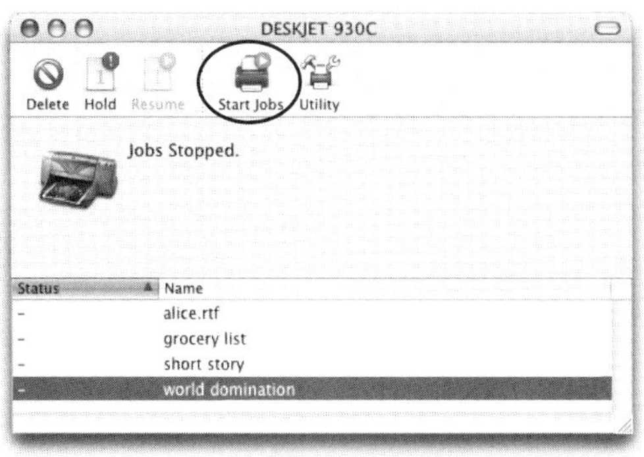

If you click **Stop Jobs**, the unprinted documents will all remain in the queue, but will not print until you click the **Start Jobs** button. If you choose **File > Print** from any application while the print queue is stopped, you'll see a dialog box alerting you to this fact.

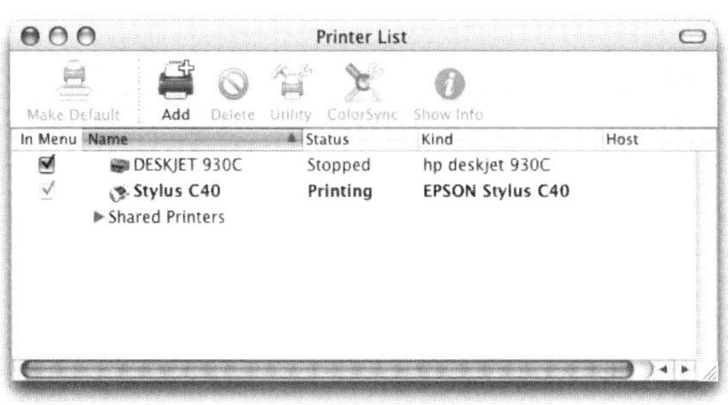

If you have more than one printer connected to your Mac, you can monitor the status of all printers by opening the **Printer Setup Utility** (located in **Applications > Utilities**).

3. Creating PDFs

If you've ever tried to open a Word file that someone e-mailed you only to find that you didn't have the proper fonts installed to read it, or if you've ever tried to send an InDesign document to someone only to find that he or she didn't own a copy of InDesign and couldn't open the file, you're well acquainted with the headaches of sharing documents electronically. To combat the problems that so many people encounter when they send files back and forth, Adobe developed the Portable Document Format (PDF) file. PDF files have the unique capability to maintain a document's original characteristics, regardless of whether the recipient has the application that created it or even whether the recipient is viewing the file on a PC or a Mac. As long as the recipient has a copy of the free Adobe Reader installed on his or her computer, any PDF file can easily be opened and viewed just as its creator intended. For these reasons, PDF files are the de facto standard when it comes to distributing and sending documents electronically.

But where do PDF files come from? As mentioned, the application used to view PDF files, Adobe Reader, is free. But to create PDFs, you have to pony up between $280 and $370 (or so) to get your hands on a copy of either Adobe Acrobat Standard or Acrobat Professional. That is, unless you're running Mac OS X, in which case you already have the ability to generate PDFs. This exercise shows you how to use this great built-in feature of your operating system to create files that anyone with Adobe Reader can view.

For this exercise, you'll open a document in TextEdit and then convert it into a PDF. This requires you to copy a file from the CD-ROM that came with this book.

1. Insert the **H•O•T CD-ROM** into your CD or DVD drive. After a moment, its icon will appear on your **Desktop**.

2. Double-click the CD icon to view its contents and then double-click the folder called **exercise files**.

3. Drag the **chap_06** folder to the **Desktop**. This will make a copy of this folder on your **Desktop**.

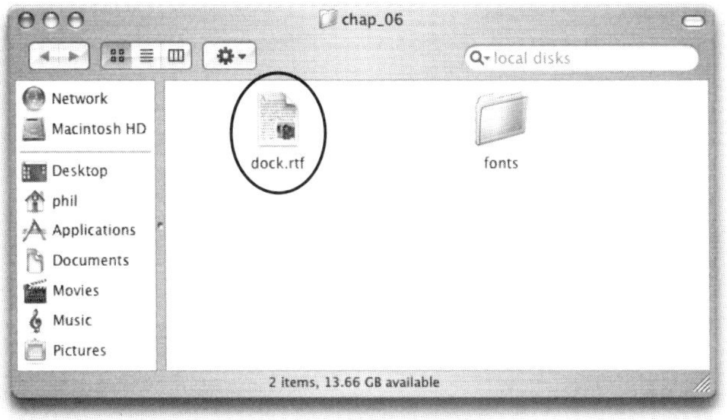

4. Open the **chap_06** folder and double-click the **dock.rtf** file found inside. The document will open in **TextEdit**.

3

Using the Dock

| Opening Applications from the Dock | Adding Items to the Dock | Setting Dock Preferences |

When Mac OS X debuted, one of the operating system's most prominent new features was the Dock. If you're familiar with pre–OS X versions of the Mac operating system, you'll notice that the Dock combines the features of both the old Apple menu and the old Application menu into the single strip of icons you see on your screen. Initially, some Mac users complained about the Dock: It takes up too much space on the Desktop, it looks clunky, it's new and different and I don't accept change very well, and so on. But after learning to use the Dock properly, most users can't believe that they ever got along without it.

In the previous chapter, you had some brief interaction with the Dock. You saw how application icons appeared in the Dock when the program was running and how they disappeared when you quit the application. You also learned to delete files by dragging them to the Trash icon in the Dock. This chapter takes a detailed look at the Dock. You'll not only learn how to use it, but you'll also find out how to customize it to best suit your purposes. As in the previous chapter, the exercises in this chapter use items already found on your Mac, so there are no files to copy from the **H•O•T CD-ROM**.

1. Opening Applications from the Dock

One of the primary purposes of the Dock is to provide you with a means of quickly opening applications and folders without having to double-click your hard drive icons and drill down through the various levels of folders until you find the item you're looking for. Although the addition of the Places sidebar in Panther makes it easier to get to many of your destinations quickly, you still have to open a Finder window to get to the sidebar. The Dock, however, is always on the Desktop, keeping your most important applications and files just one click away. In fact, once you get comfortable with the Dock and customize it to suit your needs, you may never need to double-click your hard drive icon again. In this exercise, you'll open some

This document is a copy of chapter 3 from this book. You'll convert this file into a PDF.

5. Take a moment to scroll through the document and note its length.

It would most likely take several sheets of paper if you were to print a hard copy of this document. One of the advantages of working with the PDF format in OS X is that you can use it to see exactly how many sheets a document will use to print, and exactly how the document will look on paper, without having to print it out first.

6. Select **File > Page Setup** from the menu bar.

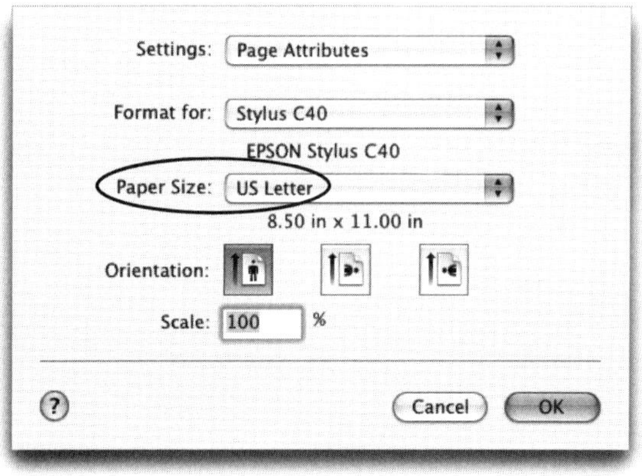

7. Make sure that the **Paper Size** is set to **US Letter** and that the page is set to the vertical orientation (also referred to as **portrait** orientation). Click **OK**.

8. Choose **File > Print**.

In Panther, there are actually three ways to convert a document into a PDF file from the Print dialog box. In the previous exercise, you learned that you can choose Output Options from the unnamed pop-up menu in the center of the dialog box. You can also click the Preview button or the Save as PDF button. All three methods create a PDF file, but clicking the Save as PDF button is by far the easiest technique.

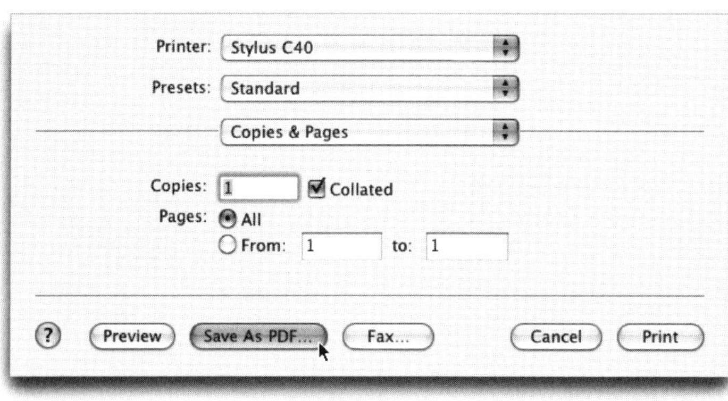

9. In the **Print** dialog box, click the **Save as PDF** button. This button is by far the easiest way to create a PDF in OS X.

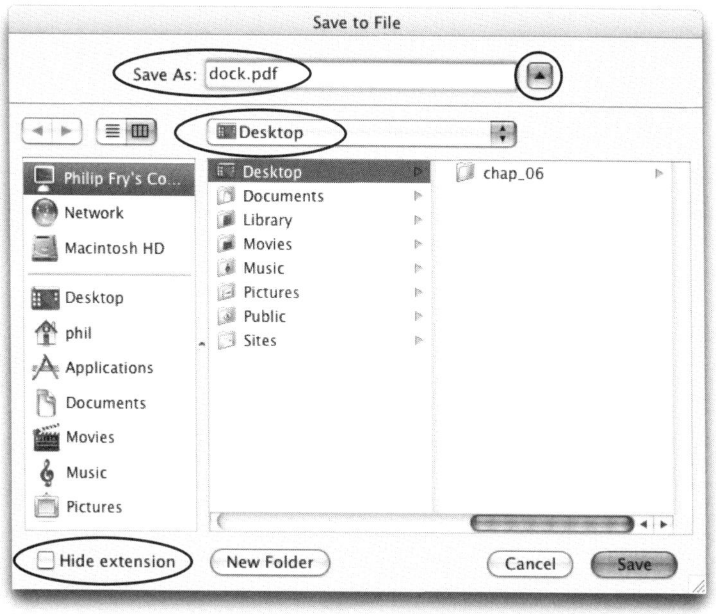

10. In the **Save to File** dialog box that appears, click the little triangle to the right of the **Save As** field to expand the dialog box. Uncheck **Hide extension**, which adds the **.pdf** extension to the end of the file name in the Save As field. (If you left this checked, the PDF would still be created–it just wouldn't have a visible extension at the end of its name.) Make sure the file is named **dock.pdf** and choose to save it to the **Desktop**. Click **Save**.

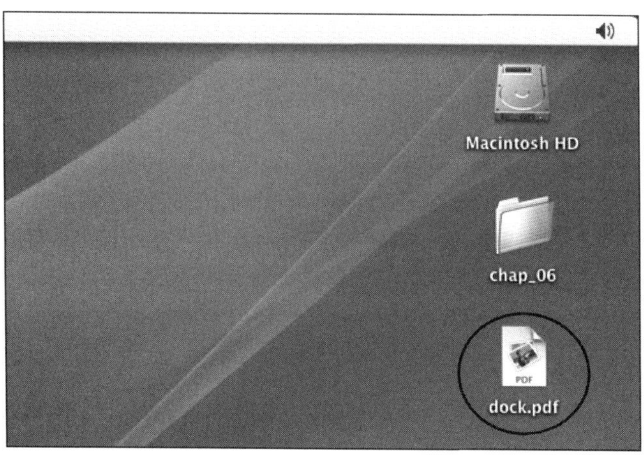

*After a moment, the **dock.pdf** file will appear on the Desktop.*

11. Double-click **dock.pdf** to view your PDF file. It will open in the application called **Preview**, Panther's built-in image and PDF viewer.

Note: *The file might open in Adobe Reader if you've installed it on your Mac. If it does, quit Reader and then open* ***Preview*** *from your* ***Applications*** *folder. Drag the* ***dock.pdf*** *icon from the* ***Desktop*** *to* ***Preview's*** *icon in the* ***Dock.*** *(See "Adobe Reader Versus Preview" at the end of this exercise for information on selecting a default PDF viewing application.)*

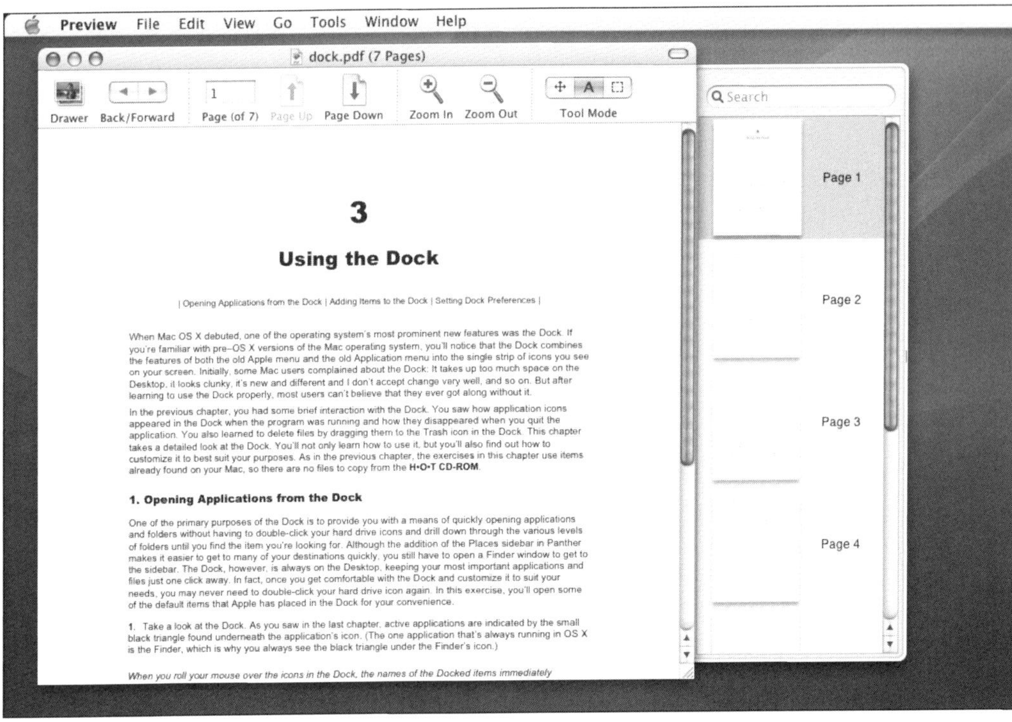

12. Take a moment to examine the PDF in **Preview**. Not only are you seeing what the document would look like if you were to print it out (including page and line breaks), but you're also seeing exactly what any other users would see if you sent them the **dock.pdf** file, which is the beauty of working with PDFs. In **Preview**, you can click the page thumbnails that appear to the side of the main window in an area called the **drawer**. Clicking a thumbnail displays its full-sized page in the main window.

13. Quit **Preview** and return to **TextEdit**.

14. Keep **dock.rtf** open for the next exercise.

Creating PDFs the "Old" Way

OS X has always been able to generate PDFs. Prior to version 10.2, you could click the Preview button in the Print dialog box to see how your document would look before you printed it.

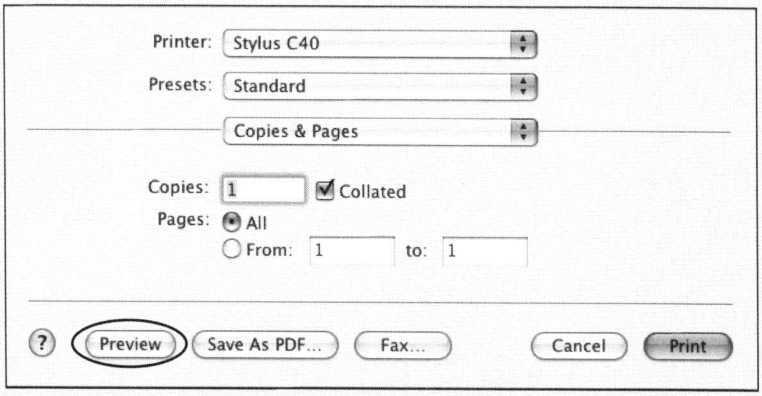

The Preview button still exists in OS 10.3, and it is still quite useful. If you want to see how the document will look when you print it out but don't need to save it as a PDF, you can use the Preview button to do just that. Clicking the Preview button creates a PDF version of your document but does not ask you to name and save the file (as it does when you click Save as PDF). Instead, the PDF is stored temporarily in your Mac's memory and displayed in Preview. After you've checked out the document, you can quit Preview without saving the PDF, or, if you change your mind about having a PDF of the document, you can choose to save the PDF to your hard drive.

Adobe Reader Versus Preview

If you've installed Adobe Reader on your Mac, depending on how you've set your preferences, it's possible that double-clicking your PDFs will open them in the Reader application rather than in Preview. Both applications are fine for viewing PDF files. Preview (found in your Applications folder) is OS X's default image-viewing application, and can be an extremely convenient tool.

When you view a PDF in Preview, you can zoom in and out of the page and rotate it, just like you can in Reader. When viewing a multiple-page PDF in Preview, a thumbnail of each page appears in the drawer to the side of the document window. Clicking a thumbnail displays that page in the main window.

When you double-click a PDF file, it will open in your default application–either Reader or Preview. It's up to you to decide which application you prefer to use when viewing PDFs.

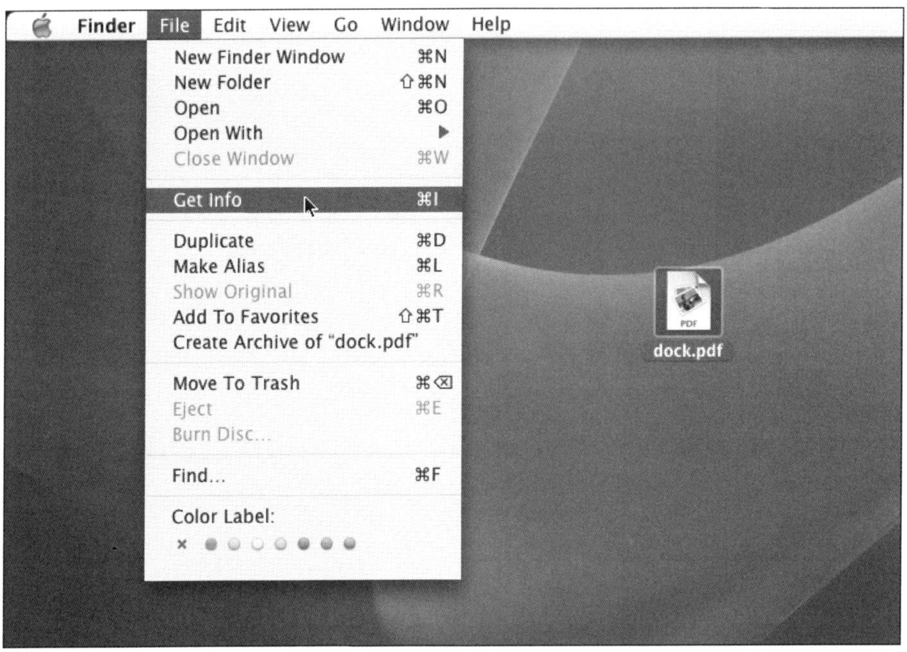

If double-clicking a PDF file does not open the file in your preferred application, you can change your default PDF-viewing program by single-clicking the PDF file and then choosing **File > Get Info**. Alternately, you can **Ctrl+click** the icon and choose **Get Info** from the contextual menu that appears, or just press **Cmd+I**.

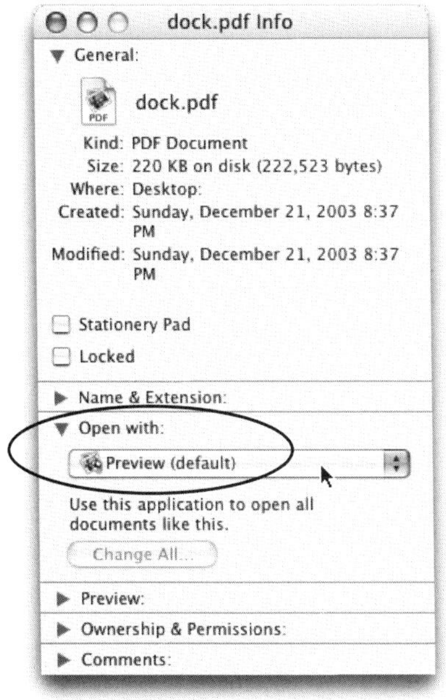

In the window that opens, toggle the triangle next to **Open with** and choose the application you wish to use when opening this document. If you're confident that you want all files of this type to be opened by the application you've selected, you can click **Change All**. Clicking this button will ensure that any file ending with **.pdf** will be opened by your preferred application when you double-click the file.

Note: You can use the Get Info window to change the default applications for any type of file. For instance, if you prefer to have JPEG images open in Photoshop rather than Preview, or for RTF documents to open in Word instead of TextEdit, you can use the Get Info window to set these preferences.

The capability to generate PDFs is a great built-in feature of OS X, and you'll probably find yourself using it a lot, especially if you need to share documents with co-workers or friends. One thing to keep in mind, however, is that OS X generates basic PDFs that are fine for printing on home or office printers, emailing, or viewing onscreen. But if you need to have your PDFs professionally printed, or if you plan to use your PDFs for more than just previewing your documents, you should purchase and install one of the full versions of Adobe Acrobat (either Standard or Professional). Acrobat comes with a program called Distiller, which gives you the maximum level of control over the quality of your PDF files. Acrobat also allows you to add interactivity to your PDFs and to protect them with security features. For more information about Acrobat, check out Adobe's Web site at **www.adobe.com/acrobat**. (And if you decide to install and use Adobe Acrobat, you'll of course want to pick up a copy of *Acrobat 6 Hands-On Training* [Peachpit Press], written by yours truly.)

4. Working with Fonts

Changing the font of your printed text in OS X works pretty much the same way it did in previous versions of the operating system: Just select the font and start typing or highlight existing text and then select a new font. What's new in OS X is that Apple has introduced the **Fonts palette**, which appears in OS X–native applications such as TextEdit. In this exercise, you'll learn how to use and customize the Fonts palette.

1. The file **dock.rtf** should still be open from the previous exercise. If it's not, double-click its icon on your **Desktop**.

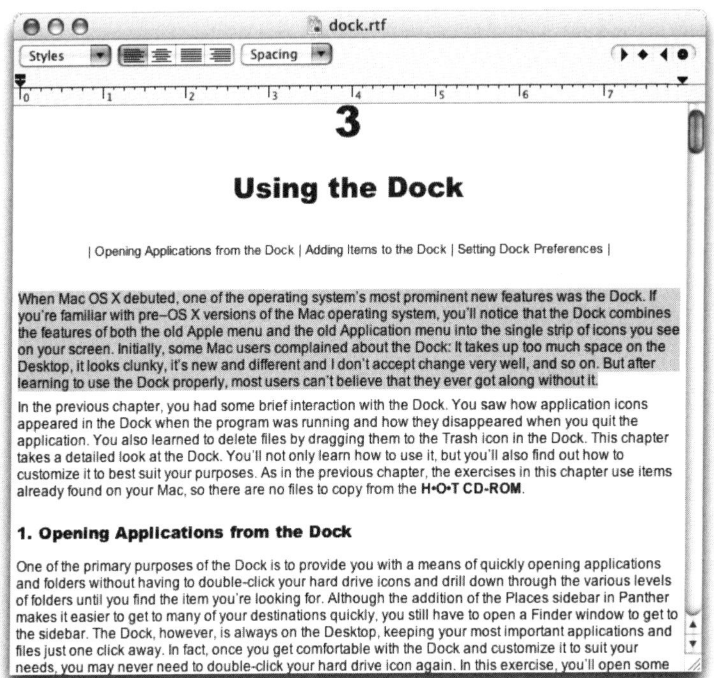

2. Highlight the first paragraph. You'll use this text to see what the **Fonts** palette can do.

3. From the menu bar, choose **Format > Font > Show Fonts**. This will open the **Fonts** palette.

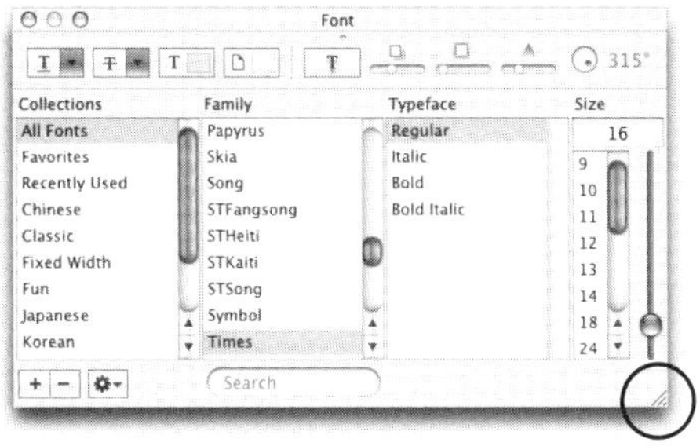

Tip: *If you don't see all four columns (**Collections**, **Family**, **Typeface**, and **Size**), drag the resize button in the lower-right corner of the Fonts palette to enlarge it.*

The Fonts palette offers a new way of viewing, selecting, and managing fonts. In pre–OS X applications, selecting fonts usually meant choosing your font face from a pop-up menu, choosing a size from another menu, and then choosing a style (bold, italic, and so on) from yet another menu. Although many programs still work this way, as time goes by you'll begin to see more and more applications using the Fonts palette for font selection. In the following steps, you'll examine the features of this versatile tool.

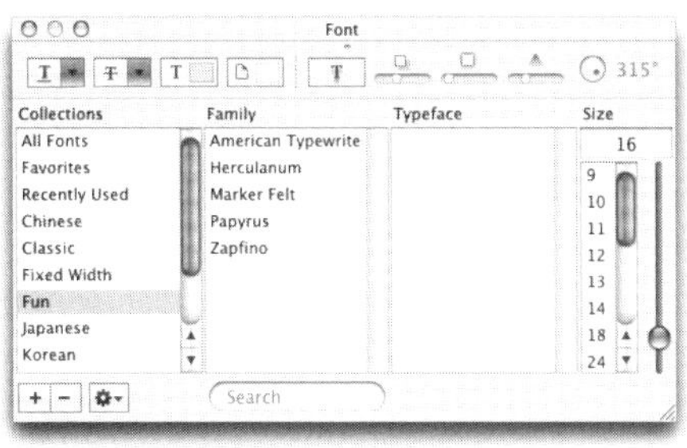

The Fonts palette is divided into categories to make font selection an easier, more logical process. You begin by selecting a collection in the left column. Selecting All Fonts, for instance, displays all the fonts available for use in the current application in the Family column. If you're one of those users who compulsively collects and hordes fonts (you know who you are), you might want to narrow down your choices by choosing among the other collections, which categorize the available fonts by their type. For example, if you were looking for a less formal font, you might select the Fun collection and choose from the fonts listed there.

Tip: *The Web collection contains fonts commonly found on both Macs and Windows machines. If you design Web pages, selecting from these fonts will ensure that visitors to your Web sites will see text in the font you intend. Similarly, the PDF collection contains fonts installed by Acrobat; so if you need to send a text file to a Windows user who needs to then convert your document into a PDF, choose from the PDF collection of fonts to ensure that the Windows user will have the necessary fonts to accurately create the PDF.*

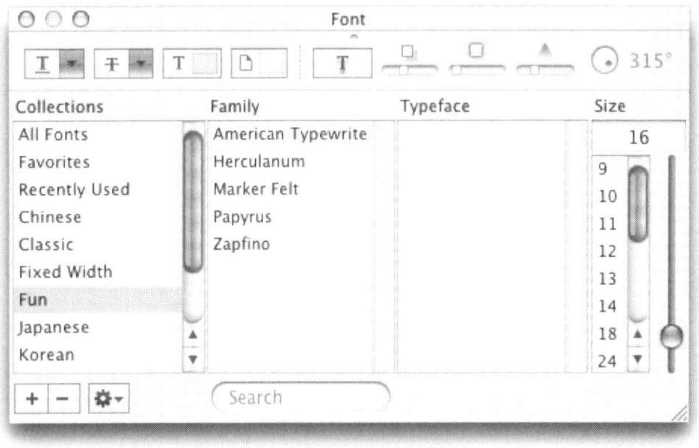

4. Select the **Fun** collection. The fonts found in this collection appear under the **Family** column.

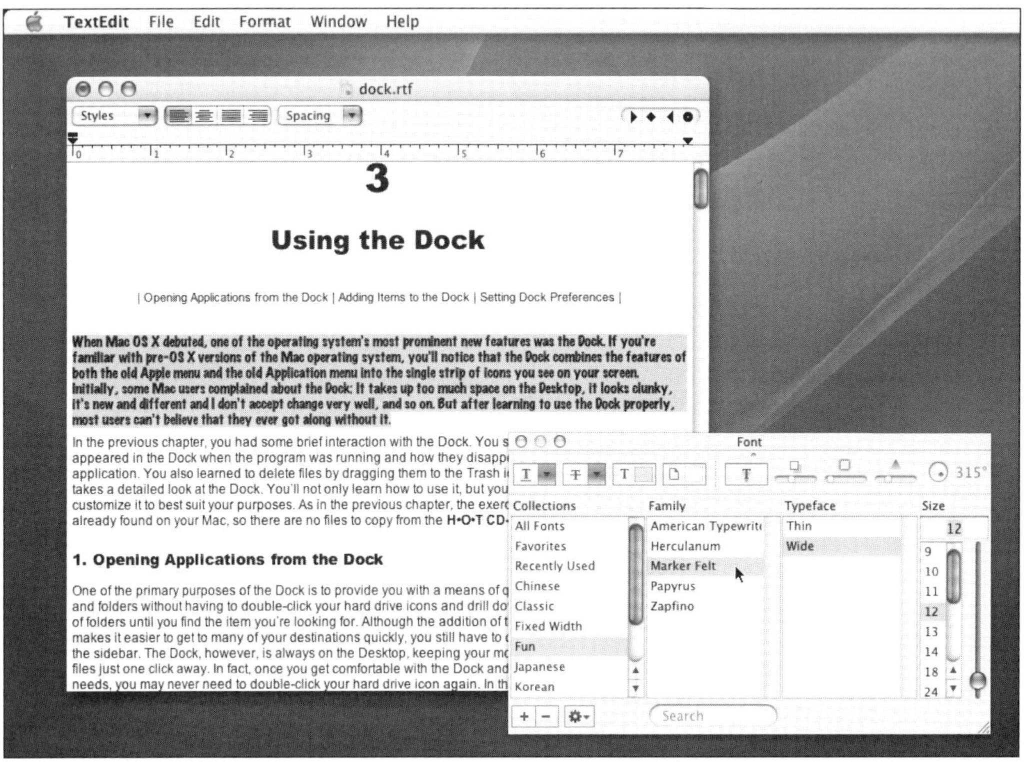

5. Take a moment to click each one of the fonts in the Family column and notice how the selected text changes each time.

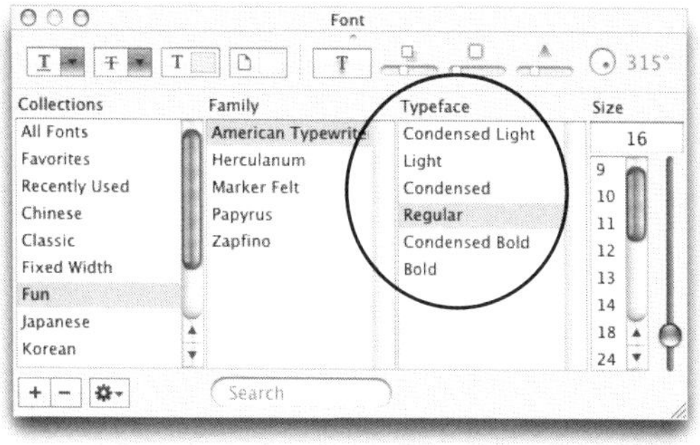

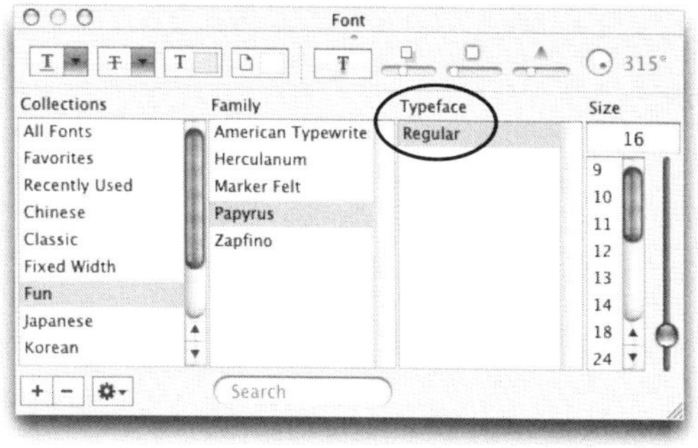

Observe how some of the font families (such as American Typewriter and Marker Felt) contain several typefaces (such as Condensed, Light, and Bold), but other families (Papyrus, Zapfino) contain only one typeface. One of the unique aspects of the Fonts palette is that it doesn't allow you to bold or italicize or otherwise alter a font's typeface unless that typeface actually exists. Professional printers and typesetters have long struggled to deal with fonts that were "bolded" by clients who simply clicked the "B" button in their word processing applications. The problem with this kind of artificial typeface is that it doesn't create a genuine bold font but merely thickens the strokes that make up the characters in a font family. Fake bold and italicized fonts look especially unprofessional when printed on paper. But now the only way to make text bold or italicized is to use a legitimate member of the font family. You can almost hear all those professional printers breathing a collective sigh of relief.

---

6. Select a few sizes from the **Sizes** column and observe how the size of the selected text changes.

Sometimes instead of selecting existing text and changing its font, you might want to know what a particular font face looks like before you start typing.

---

7. Click anywhere in the TextEdit document to deselect the text. (It doesn't matter if the font of the first paragraph doesn't match the rest of the document.)

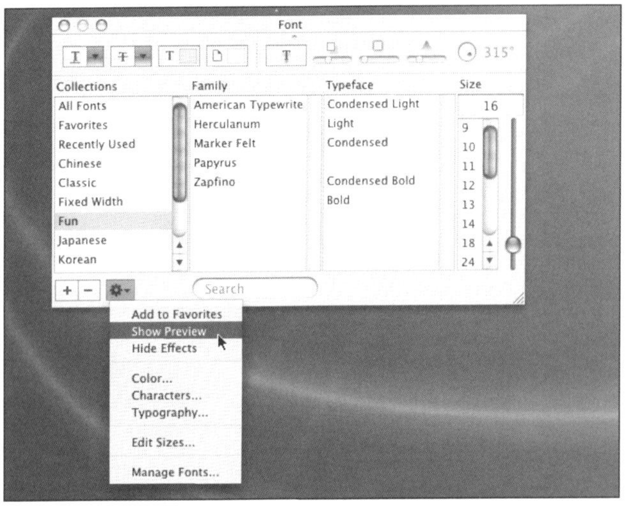

8. From the **action** button at the bottom of the **Fonts** palette, choose **Show Preview**. (The action button is new to the Fonts palette in Panther.)

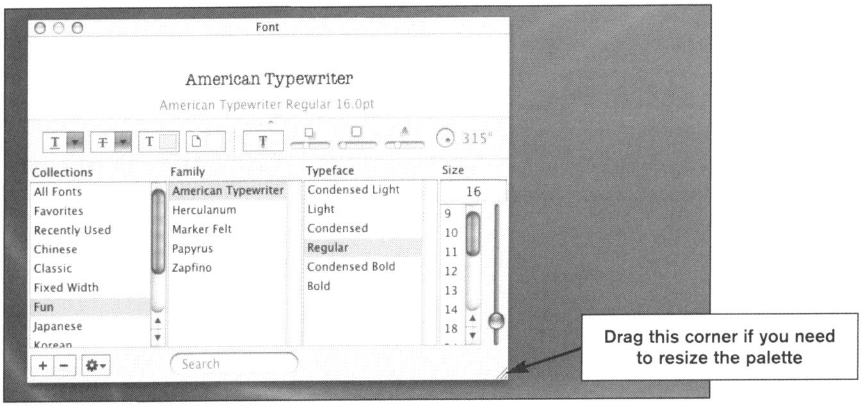

This will open up a pane at the top of the Fonts palette showing you the exact appearance of your currently selected font family, typeface, and size. You may need to resize the Fonts palette to get a better view.

9. Select a few more font collections and families to see the preview pane change accordingly.

After working with the Fonts palette for a while, you might be thinking the names of some the Collections columns to be a tad arbitrary. (What's so "fun" about Herculanum anyway?) Or you may often find yourself using fonts that don't appear together in a single collection. Fortunately, it's pretty simple to edit existing font collections or to create your own.

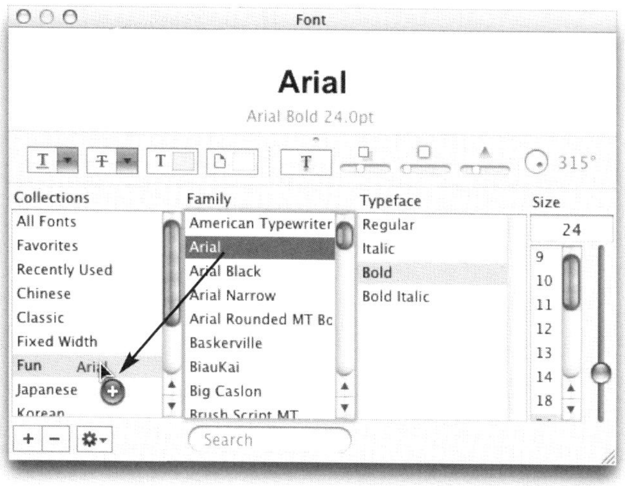

10. Click the **All Fonts** collection and locate **Arial** under the **Family** column. Drag **Arial** from the **Family** column into the **Fun** collection.

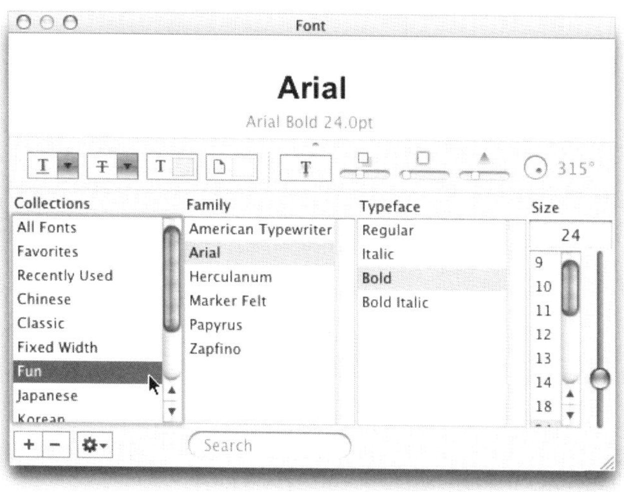

11. Click the **Fun** collection and notice that **Arial** is now listed under **Family**. That's all you have to do to move a font to a collection. Now you'll remove Arial from this collection.

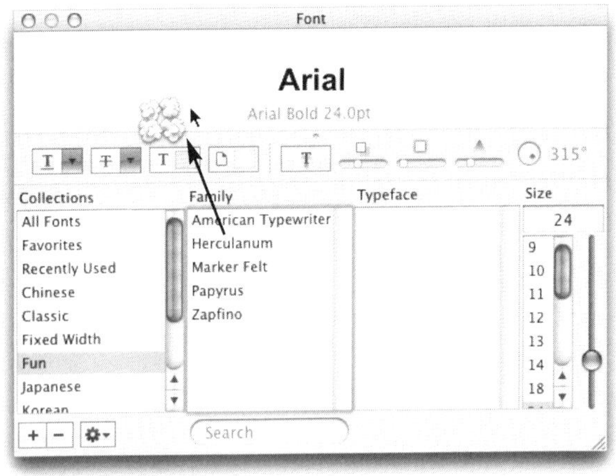

12. Drag **Arial** up and out of the **Family** column and release the mouse. It disappears in a puff of smoke. It's important to note here that you haven't deleted **Arial** from your computer; all you've done is removed it from the **Fun** collection. You can still find **Arial** under **All Fonts**.

Next, you'll create your own collection of fonts. Imagine that every time you wrote a report, you found yourself using three specific fonts, but these three fonts didn't appear together in any existing collection. You'll create a collection called ***Reports*** *to group these fonts.*

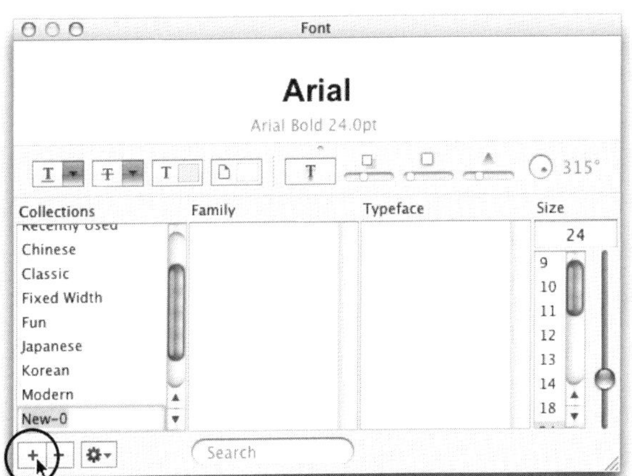

13. Click the + symbol in the lower-left corner of the **Fonts** palette. A new font collection called **New-0** (or similar) appears in the **Collections** column. **New-0** is highlighted, prompting you to rename it. Type **Reports**.

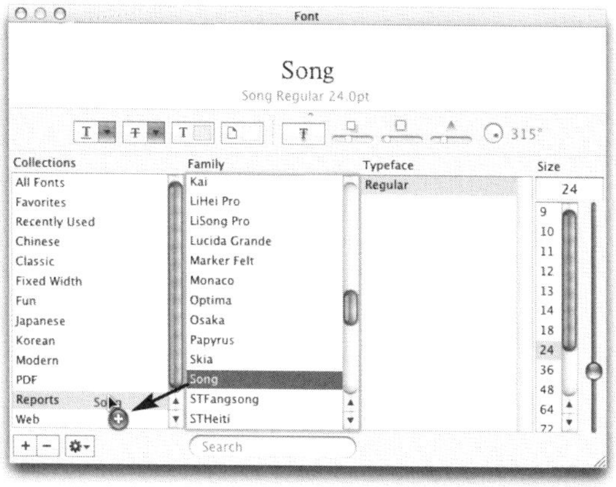

14. Click the **All Fonts** collection and expand the **Fonts** palette so you can see both the **All Fonts** and **Reports** collections. Locate the font called **Song** and drag it to **Reports**. (If **Song** isn't installed on your Mac, just pick any font.)

---

15. Locate the fonts **Optima** and **Futura** and add them to the **Reports** collection as well.

Tip: The information about the font collections you create is stored in your ***Home > Library > Font Collections*** *folder. Because font collection information is contained in your* ***Home*** *folder, each user can create his or her own font collections without interfering with other users' collections.*

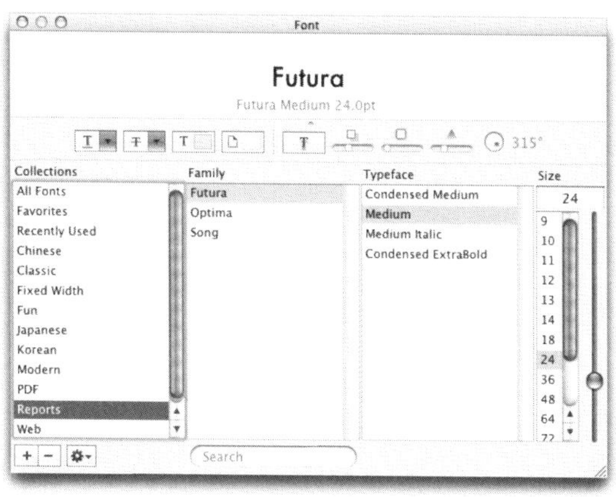

16. Click the **Reports** collection and observe the three fonts that are now conveniently grouped together. These fonts are now much easier to access, which will save time if you need to use them often.

Tip: Another way to group commonly used fonts together is to select a font and then choose ***Add to Favorites*** *from the* ***action*** *button. All fonts added to Favorites appear in the Favorites collection.*

Now you'll remove the Reports collection.

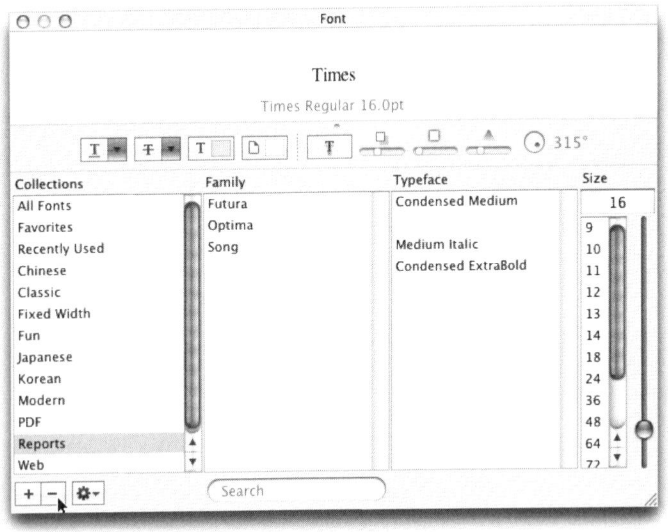

17. With **Reports** selected, click the – symbol in the lower-left corner of the **Fonts** palette.

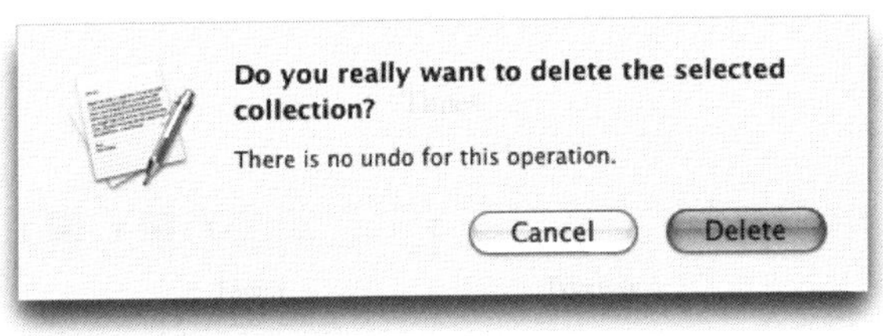

*You'll see a message warning you that deleting collections can't be undone. Click **Delete**. Again, you haven't deleted the fonts themselves; you simply got rid of the collection that grouped them together. All three fonts are still available in the All Fonts collection.*

18. Close **dock.rtf**. You don't need to save any changes. Keep **TextEdit** open for the next exercise.

As you can see, formatting text in OS X is pretty easy once you get used to the Fonts palette. The only problem is that not all OS X applications are using the Fonts palette yet. Many software manufacturers still prefer to use their own menus for font selection. In those cases, be sure to check the documentation that came with your software (if any came with it at all) to learn how to work with fonts in that particular application. In the next exercise, you'll learn how to install new fonts on your Mac.

TextEdit and Fonts Palette Tips

Although some people dismiss it as a low-end word processor, TextEdit is actually a powerful and functional application. If you create text documents only occasionally, or if you don't feel like shelling out a few hundred dollars for Microsoft Office, give TextEdit a try. These tips will help you get the most out of the application. (And remember that the Fonts palette tips work in any application that uses the Fonts palette, not just TextEdit.)

Turn on Page Wrapping

By choosing **Format > Wrap to Page**, you can have TextEdit display your document to show margins and page and line breaks, giving you a better idea of how your document will look when printed.

Have TextEdit Read to You

Many writers have found that having their work read to them helps them find grammatical errors and awkward sentences. You can have TextEdit read your document to you by choosing **Edit > Speech > Start Speaking**. (To select a voice, choose the **Speech** control panel in **System Preferences**. You learned about speech in Chapter 4, "*System Preferences*.") To stop the reading, choose **Edit > Speech > Stop Speaking**.

Select Special Characters from the Character Palette

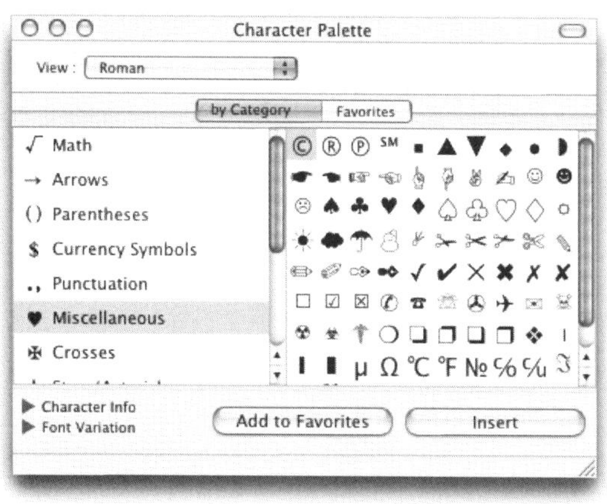

Special characters can be accessed from the keyboard if you know the proper key combinations. For instance, a © symbol is created by pressing **Option+G**. But if you don't know the keyboard combination for the character you need, you can choose **Characters** from the **action** button in the **Fonts** palette or select **Edit > Special Characters** to display the **Character** palette. From here, you can browse through the categories on the left to find the symbol you need to insert into your document.

Type Your Own Font Sizes

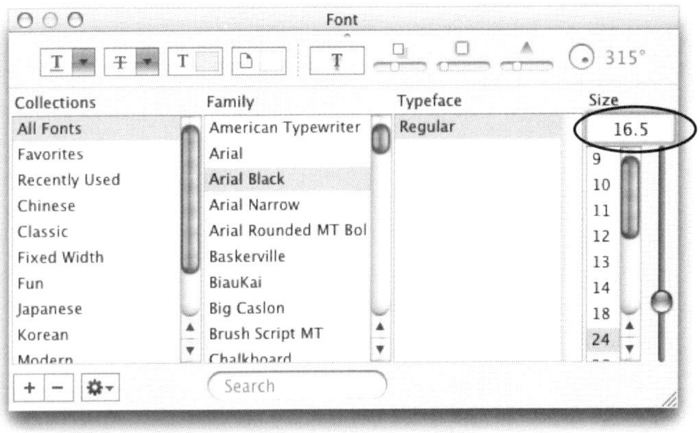

You're not limited to just the font sizes listed in the Size column of the Fonts palette. You can enter any font size you like–even half sizes are allowed.

Change the Color of Text

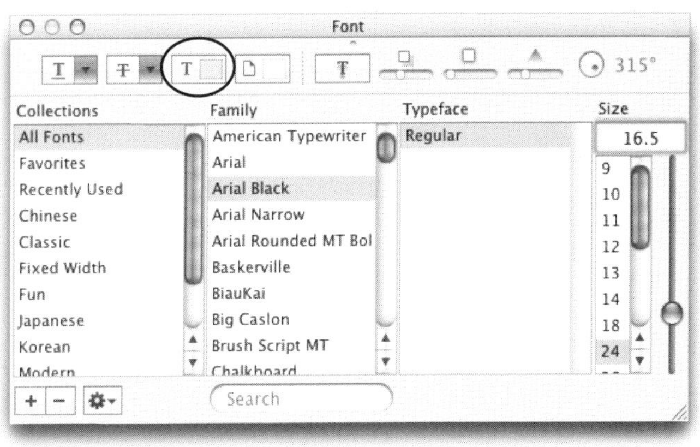

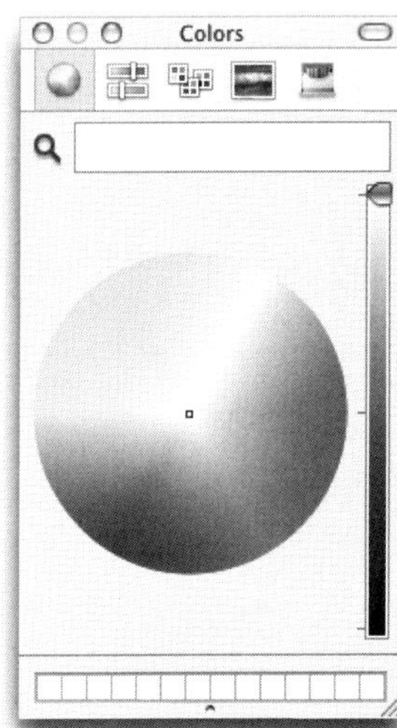

You can change the color of selected text by clicking the **Text Color** button. This will open the **Colors** palette, in which you can select from any range of colors from within five different color pickers. You can also choose the color of the page itself by clicking the **Document Color** button to the right of the **Text Color** button.

Underline Text or Strikethrough

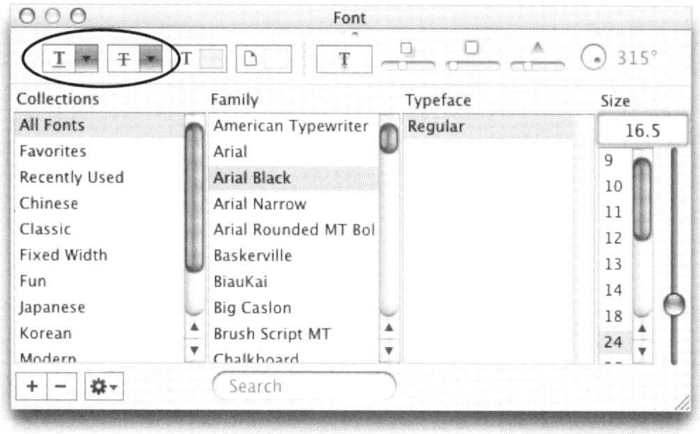

You can choose to underline or strike through text from the Fonts palette. Clicking the **Underline** or **Strikethrough** buttons reveals drop-down menus with these options: **None**, **Single**, **Double**, or **Color**. Choosing **Color** opens the **Color** palette with the same five color pickers, allowing you to select a color for your lines.

Create Drop Shadows

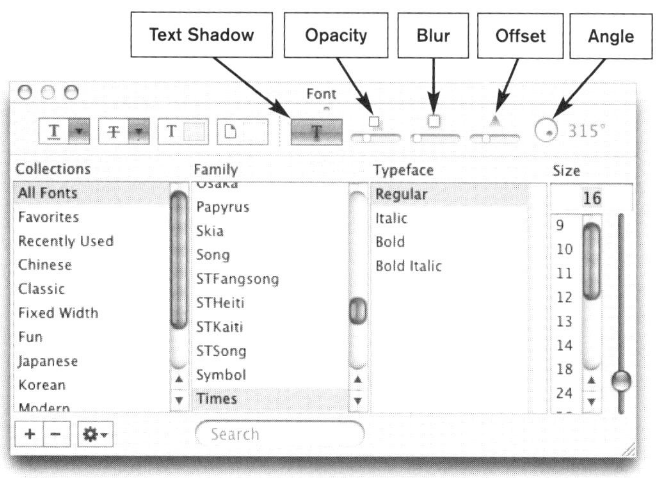

One of the neatest new features of the Fonts palette is its capability to add drop shadows to text. A drop shadow is an effect that makes it appear as though the text is hovering just above the surface of the page, causing a shadow to appear underneath it. You can add a drop shadow to any selected text by clicking the **Text Shadow** button. This activates the other four buttons to the right, which control the shadow's opacity, level of blur, offset (distance from the text), and angle (the direction of the "light" hitting the text and causing the shadow).

Use Pop-Up Menus in the Fonts Palette

Once you've created your own font collections and have set up the Fonts palette to your liking, you can reduce the screen space it occupies by resizing it into a more horizontal shape. The columns will automatically turn into pop-up menus, allowing you to conserve valuable screen real estate.

NOTE | Where Are Fonts Stored?

Before OS X, fonts were generally kept in **System Folder > Fonts**. Dragging new fonts into this folder would make them available to all applications. In OS X, however, fonts can be kept in any one of four different places on your hard drive. Here's a rundown of each of these locations:

Your Home Folder
Your personal **Home** folder contains a folder called **Library**, which in turn contains a folder called **Fonts.** Fonts stored in this folder are accessible only to you and are unavailable to other users. You can add as many fonts to this folder as you like without worrying about crowding other users' folders.

The Main Font Folder
Hard Drive > Library > Fonts contains the fonts that are available to all users. You must have administrator access to add items to this folder.

System Fonts
Located in **Hard Drive > System > Library > Fonts**, these fonts are the ones considered essential to OS X. These are the fonts OS X uses in menu bars, dialog boxes, icon names, Dock names, and so on. Because OS X absolutely needs these fonts, not even administrators can alter this folder. You can view its contents, but you can't add or remove items.

The Classic System Folder
If you've installed Classic (as discussed in Chapter 4, "*System Preferences*"), this is where OS 9 keeps its fonts. The fonts are located in **Hard Drive > System Folder > Fonts**. You can add fonts to this folder if you want them to be accessible to Classic applications.

So when you're working with the Fonts palette, OS X looks in each of these folders and presents you with the fonts available from all four. If two or more different fonts happen to share the same name but reside in different folders, OS X resolves this conflict by using the first one it comes across based on the order in which the folders are listed above. It ignores any repeated font names, even if the fonts are in fact different.

5. Installing Fonts with Font Book

In the previous exercise, you got to sample some of the high-quality fonts that come built in to Mac OS X. But eventually you may want to add some additional fonts to your collection. In this exercise, you'll learn how to use Panther's new program, **Font Book**, to install new fonts on your Mac. You'll also learn how to make these fonts available to other users, or, if you so desire, how to keep them to yourself.

*Special thanks to **www.fonthead.com** for providing the fonts for this exercise. Be sure to check out their Web site if you're in the market for some unique and great-looking fonts.*

1. In **TextEdit**, choose **File > New** to create a new blank document. If the **Fonts** palette isn't already open, choose **Format > Font > Show Fonts** to open it.

2. Type a line of text. It doesn't matter what you type or which font it's in.

Next you'll install some fonts into different locations to see if they show up in TextEdit.

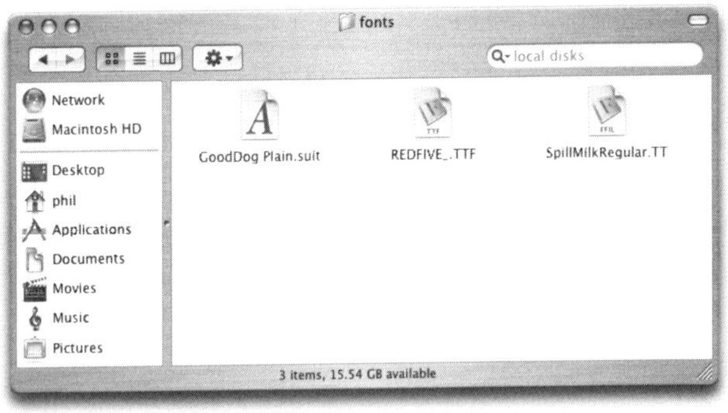

3. Open the **chap_06** folder that you copied to your **Desktop** in Exercise 3. Inside **chap_06**, open the folder named **fonts**. This folder contains three fonts that you'll install into your system. Unlike in previous versions of OS X, where you installed fonts by dragging them into folders, all you have to do in Panther is double-click a font.

4. Double-click the font **GoodDog Plain.suit**. This opens **Font Book**.

Note: *You don't need to double-click a font each time you want to run Font Book. Font Book is located in your Applications folder.*

*In Font Book, a window called **GoodDog Plain** opens, containing a sample of what this font looks like. If you've used previous versions of OS X, rejoice, for no longer must you install a font just to preview its appearance.*

*If the font contains various typefaces such as Bold, Oblique, Condensed, and so on, they'll appear as selections in the pop-up menu at the top of this window. The fonts in this exercise, however, have no variations, so you only see **Regular** listed in the menu.*

To install a font, just click the Install Font button. But before you do so in this exercise, you'll examine the Font Book preferences to see where this font will be placed when you install it.

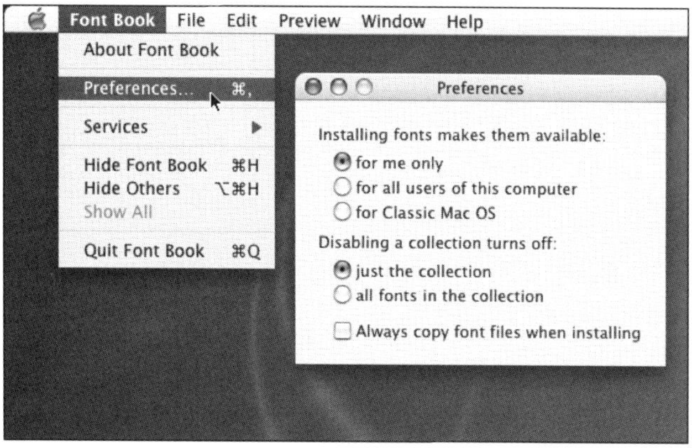

5. Choose **Font Book > Preferences** from the menu bar. This opens the **Preferences** window. The following chart describes the options found here.

Font Book Preferences	
Option	**Description**
Installing fonts makes them available	The selection you make under this heading determines where a font is placed when you install it. **for me only** places the font in your **Home > Library > Fonts** folder. **for all users of this computer** places the font in the **Hard Drive > Library > Fonts** folder. **for Classic Mac OS** places the font in the **System Folder > Fonts** folder in your Classic system folder.
Disabling a collection turns off	Here you determine whether disabling a collection of fonts makes the collection disappear from the list of collections in the Fonts palette, or if all the fonts contained in that collection disappear. You'll learn about turning fonts on and off in the next exercise.
Always copy font files when installing	Check this box if you prefer to place a copy of a font into your **Fonts** folder. Left unchecked, the font file is moved rather than copied. You'll see the results of leaving this unchecked in the next few steps.

6. Make sure that **for me only** is checked and **Always copy font files when installing** is unchecked. Close **Preferences**.

7. In the **GoodDog Plain** window, click **Install Font**.

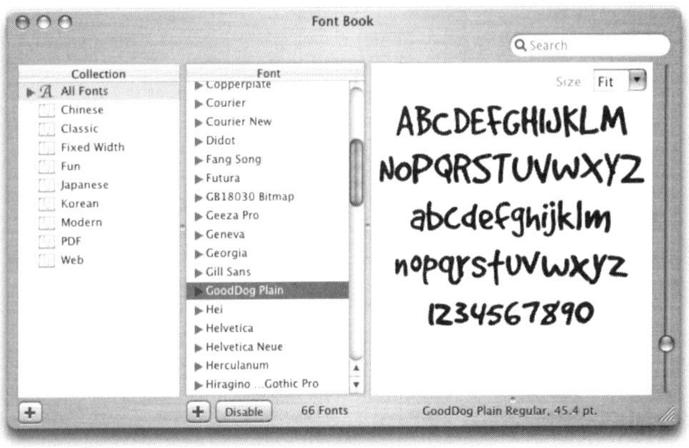

The main Font Book window opens with GoodDog Plain highlighted. This font has been installed on your Mac.

TIP | Customizing the Text in the Preview Pane

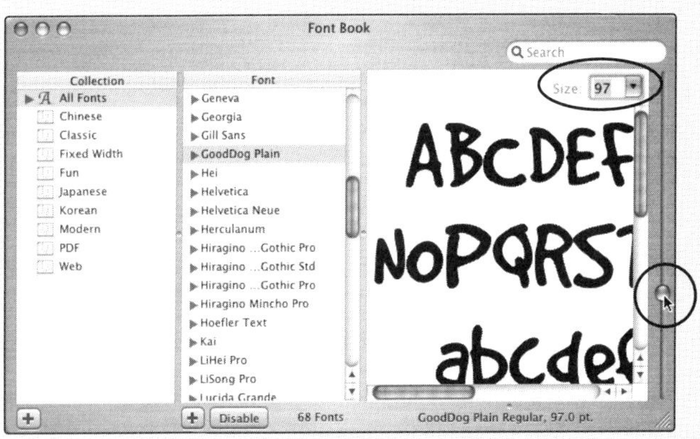

By default, the preview pane in Font Book displays the entire upper- and lowercase alphabet, as well as the numbers 0 through 9. You can change the size of the text displayed in the preview pane by either dragging the slider to the right of the window, or by making a selection from the **Size** menu in the upper-right corner. Choosing **Fit** from the **Size** menu ensures that the preview text appears as large as possible within the pane.

continues on next page

TIP | Customizing the Text in the Preview Pane *continued*

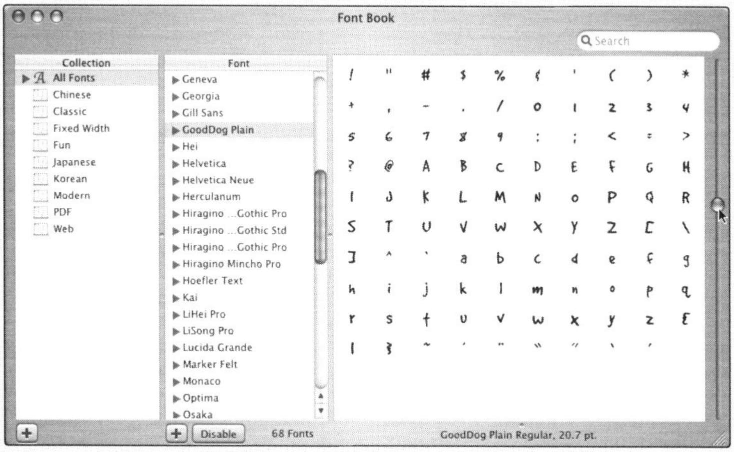

Additionally, you can choose **Preview > Repertoire** from the menu bar to display every single character found within the selected font. Again, you can use the **size** slider to zoom in and out on the text. (You'll be able to view more characters at once if you increase the overall size of the window by dragging out its lower-right corner.)

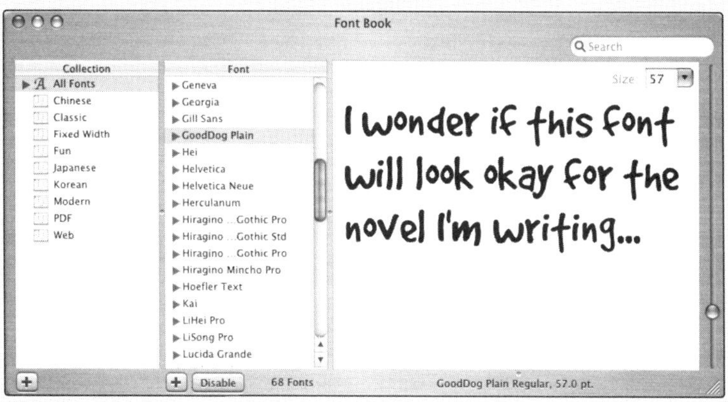

If you're still having trouble getting a sense of what a font will look like when you actually put it to use, choose **Preview > Custom**, which allows you to enter your own text.

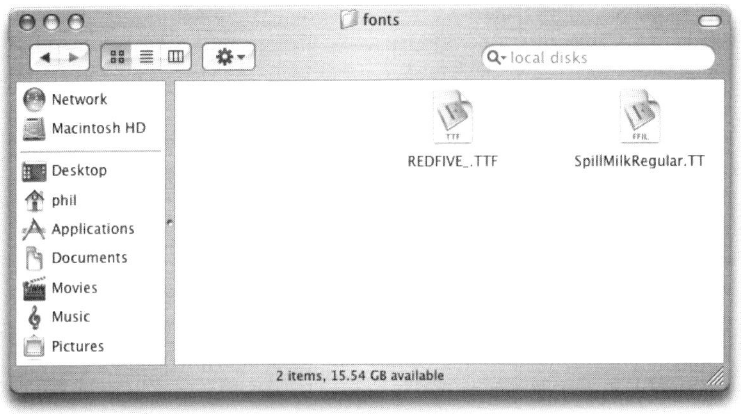

8. Click the **fonts** folder on your **Desktop** (where you originally double-clicked **GoodDog Plain**) and notice that the font file has disappeared. Well, it didn't really disappear–it was just moved because you left **Always copy font files when installing** unchecked in **Font Book's** preferences.

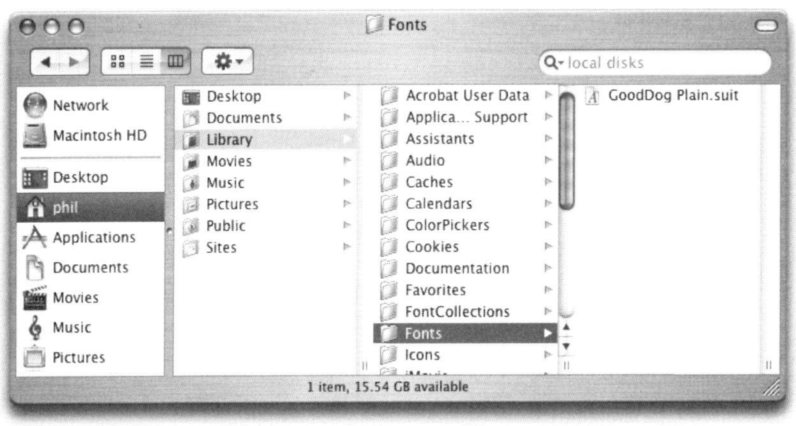

9. Click the **Home** icon in the **Places** sidebar of this window, and then switch to **Column** view. In the first column, click **Library** and then click **Fonts** in the second column. Here's where the **GoodDog Plain** font was moved (because you left **for me only** checked in **Font Book's** preferences). Since this font is located in your **Home** folder, it's unavailable to any other users on your Mac.

Now you'll check to see if your new font is available for use.

10. Click the **TextEdit** icon in the **Dock** to bring the application to the front.

11. In the **Fonts** palette, click the **All Fonts** collection and scroll through the **Family** column. You should see **GoodDog Plain** in the list. You can now begin using this font.

Another great thing about OS X is that you don't have to quit an OS X–native application before installing new fonts. The new fonts should become available to your apps as soon as they're installed.

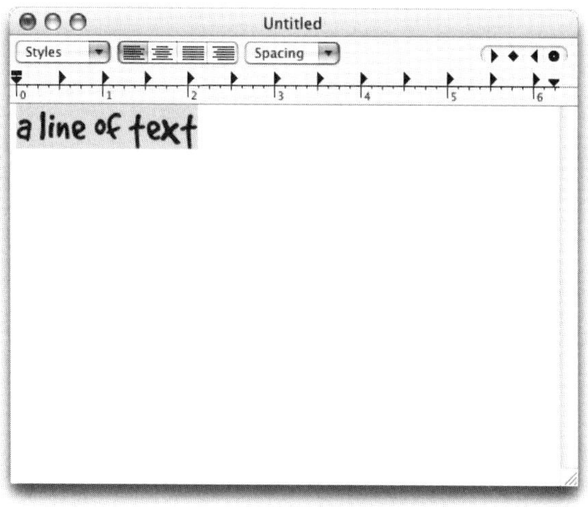

12. Highlight the text you typed earlier and select **GoodDog Plain**.

Again, because you installed this font into your Home Fonts folder, GoodDog Plain will be not accessible to any other users who have accounts on your Mac. If other users wish to install fonts, they can do so only into their own personal Library folders (unless they have administrator privileges). This allows each user to install as many fonts as he or she wishes without interfering with other users' folders. This also provides a way for you to keep your fonts all to yourself if you don't feel like sharing. Next, you'll add fonts to the main Library folder. This time, instead of double-clicking the fonts you want to install, you'll install them directly from Font Book.

13. Click the **Font Book** icon in the **Dock**. From the menu bar, choose **File > Add Fonts**.

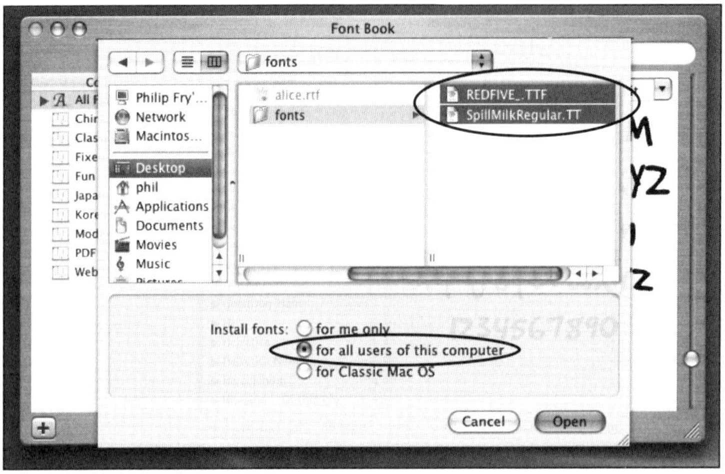

14. In the sheet that descends from the top of the window, navigate through **Desktop > chap_06 > fonts** and then **Shift+click** the two fonts here to select them both. Select **for all users of this computer** at the bottom of the sheet. Click **Open**.

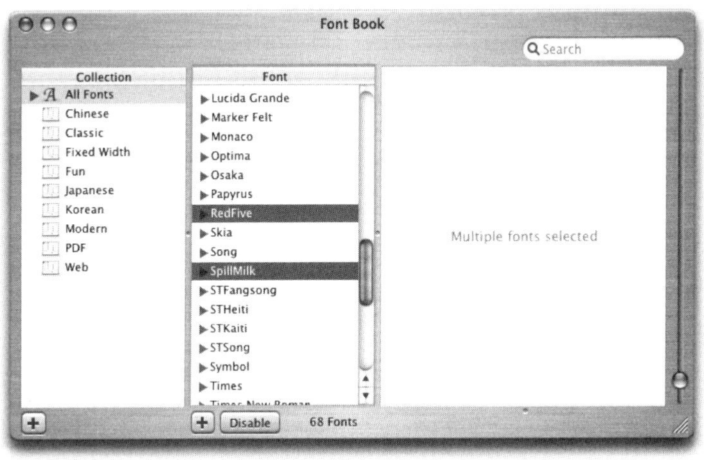

The fonts RedFive and SpillMilk have now been installed on your Mac. You can click either one individually to see what it looks like in the preview pane of the main Font Book window.

Now you'll take a look where Font Book installed these fonts. This time, instead of manually navigating through your hard drive, you'll use a simple command in Font Book.

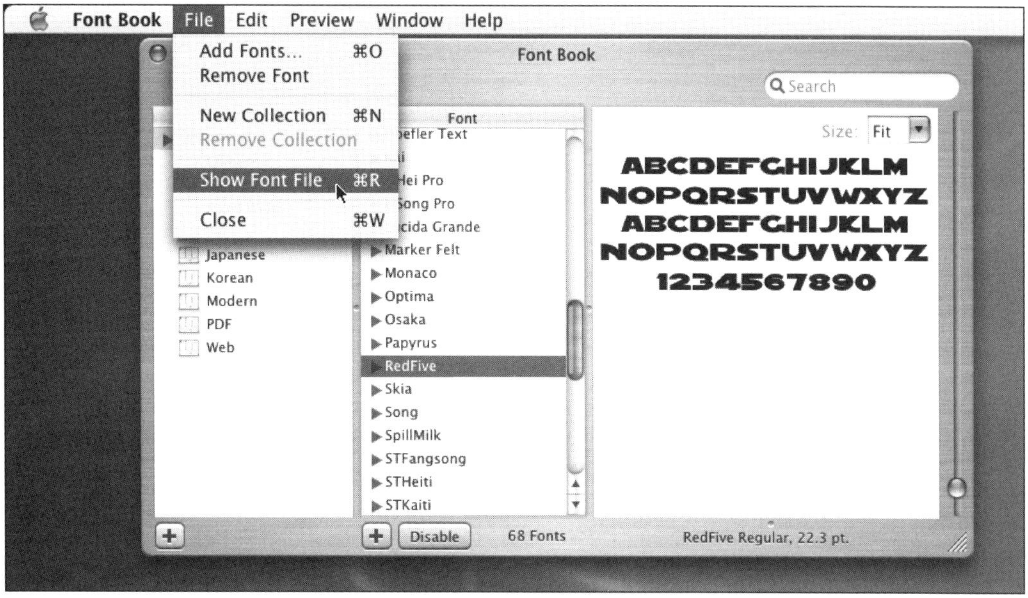

15. Click **RedFive** in the **Font** column and then choose **File > Show Font File** from the menu bar.

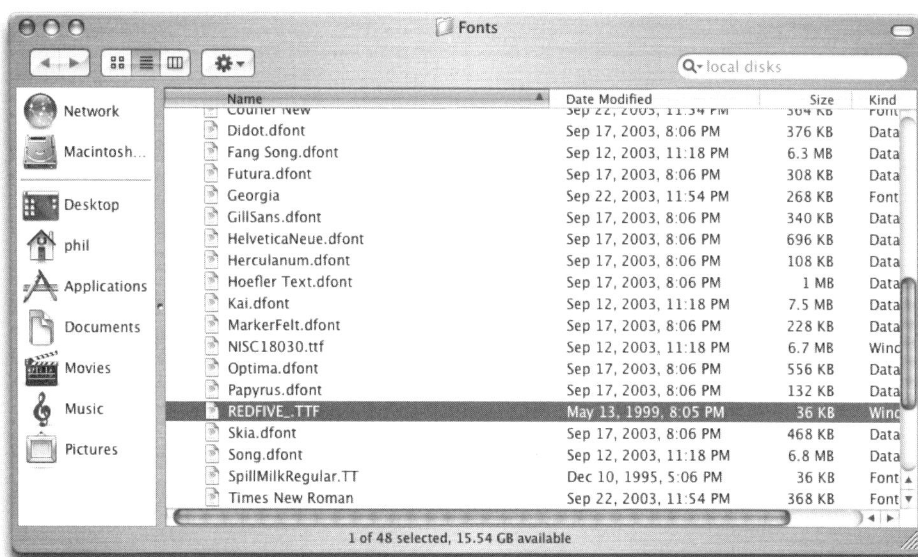

This opens the window of the folder containing this font. But it doesn't tell you where this folder is located.

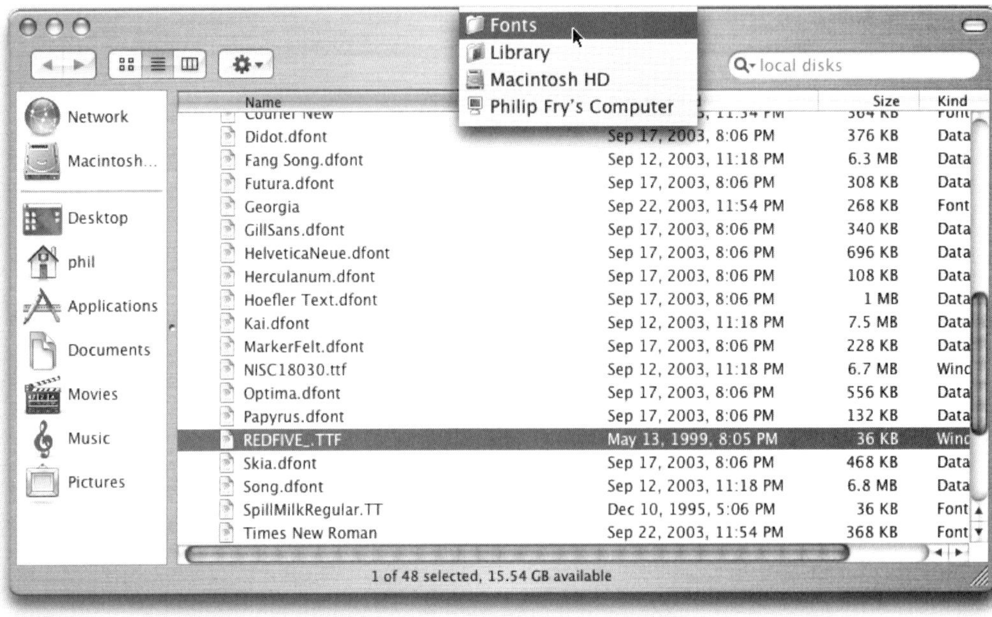

16. Cmd+click this window's name (**Fonts**). A menu appears, revealing the exact path, bottom to top, leading to this folder.

Tip: *You can perform this little trick with any open Finder window. Selecting a folder from this menu opens that folder.*

---

17. Close the window and click **TextEdit's** icon in the **Dock**. Scroll through the **All Fonts** collection in the **Fonts** palette and observe that **RedFive** and **SpillMilk** have immediately become available for you to use.

Note: *Although in this exercise the new fonts immediately appeared in TextEdit, you may encounter an occasional application where this is not the case. Just quit and restart your application–the font should then be available. If the font still doesn't show up, see the "A Brief Explanation of Font Types" sidebar.*

A Brief Explanation of Font Types

If you upgraded your Mac from OS 9 to OS X, you might find that some of your OS 9 fonts do not appear in OS X applications. Most likely these are bitmapped fonts, leftovers from the early days when fonts tended to look jagged and rough. The characters in bitmapped fonts were created by instructing Macs and printers to draw them with a series of dots. Back then, bitmapped fonts looked fine onscreen because monitor resolutions averaged 72 dots per inch (dpi) (and still do, for the most part), and the dot matrix printers that were available to most users also printed at a low resolution. However, the larger the font was printed, the more jagged its edges became–almost making it look like it was constructed with a stack of bricks. Any bitmapped fonts installed on your Mac are still available in your Classic applications, but OS X completely ignores them because they don't look good when printed on today's printers.

Bitmapped fonts were all but abandoned when Adobe introduced PostScript fonts. Instead of defining a font as a series of dots, PostScript fonts are described by their shape or "outline." The font contains the information for how it should look at any given size. When a user wants a font character to appear at a certain size, the character's description is merely multiplied by the requested point size. You get clean, crisp characters at any size. For many users, however, the downside of PostScript fonts is that they usually come in several different parts (the fonts, not the users): the regular bitmapped font for use onscreen, and the smooth PostScript versions for printing, which also come in several parts: you need a separate PostScript font for bold text, italic text, and any other styles that are part of the font family. To add to the confusion, these fonts are often named similarly, if not identically. When copying fonts to their Macs, some users fail to copy the entire collection, resulting in migraine-inducing complications. A font may look fine onscreen, but jagged when printed because the font's printer version is missing, or the user may clearly see the printer font in his or her Fonts folder but not be able to use it because he or she is missing the screen version. In order to successfully use PostScript fonts with OS X, it is essential to have a font's entire collection installed in your Fonts folder.

But unless you're a graphic designer, you most likely won't have to deal with bitmapped or PostScript fonts at all in OS X. The fonts that come installed with OS X are all TrueType fonts. TrueType fonts are single packages containing absolutely everything you'll need for that font. No separate files, no way to lose a part. And nearly all fonts released today come in a TrueType version. (The fonts you installed in this exercise were all TrueType fonts.) In fact, OS X can even handle most Windows versions of TrueType fonts–the RedFive font you installed was a Windows font. Being able to use Windows fonts on your Mac opens up a world of compatibility. No longer do you have to search for a Mac equivalent for a font that you need to use in a document.

6. Managing Fonts with Font Book

Font Book is used for more than just installing fonts on your Mac. It can also be used to enable and disable fonts and collections of fonts with relative ease, marking the first time the Mac OS has had its own built-in font-management software. If you're finding that your font collection is becoming too cluttered, you can use Font Book to turn collections on and off to remove fonts you don't use from the palette. This exercise shows you how to activate and deactivate fonts.

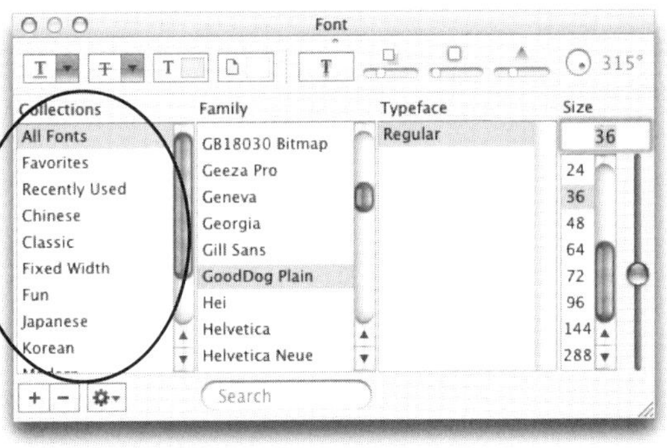

1. In **TextEdit's Fonts** palette, take a moment to note the name of the font collections found here.

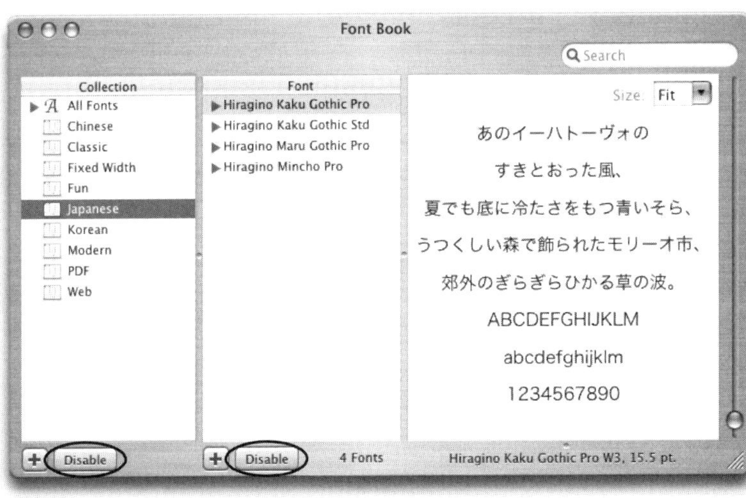

2. Keep **TextEdit** open and return to **Font Book**. Select the **Japanese** font collection in the first column. Notice that a **Disable** button appears under both the **Collection** and **Font** columns. You can choose to disable an entire collection or just a specific font. Click **Disable** under the **Collection** column.

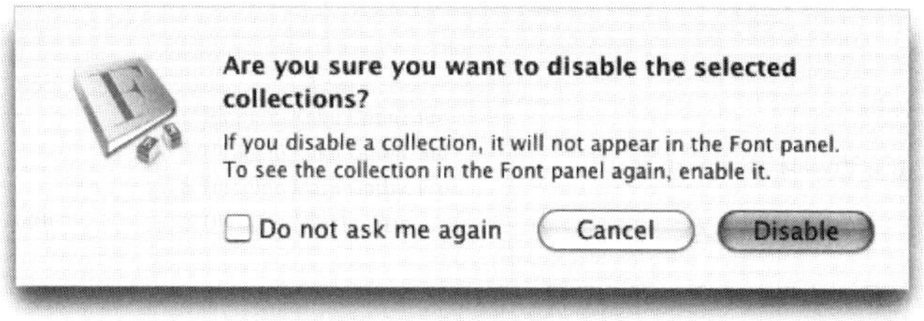

3. You'll see a message telling you what happens when you disable a collection. Click **Disable**.

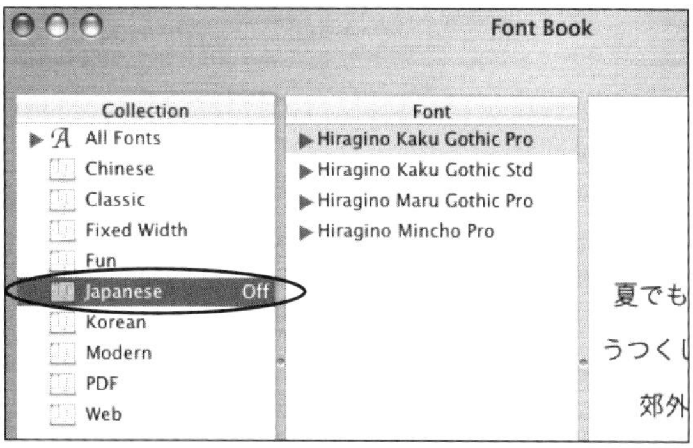

Notice that the word "Off" now appears next to the Japanese collection.

4. Switch to **TextEdit** by clicking its icon in the **Dock** and notice that the **Japanese** collection no longer appears in the **Fonts** palette–it's been disabled. Switch back to **Font Book**.

5. With the **Japanese** collection selected, click **Enable** under the **Collection** column to reactivate that collection.

Note: *Based on your Font Book preferences, disabling a collection either removes the collection only from your applications' Fonts palettes (leaving the collections fonts still available in the All Fonts collection) or disables all the fonts found in that collection (effectively removing them as a choice in all collections). To determine what happens when you disable a collection, open* ***Font Book > Preferences*** *and check either* ***just the collection*** *or* ***all fonts in the collection*** *under* ***Disabling a collection turns off.***

In addition to disabling and enabling collections, you can also disable and enable specific fonts. The important thing is to know whether you're disabling a font in a collection or disabling a font entirely. You'll learn the difference in the following steps.

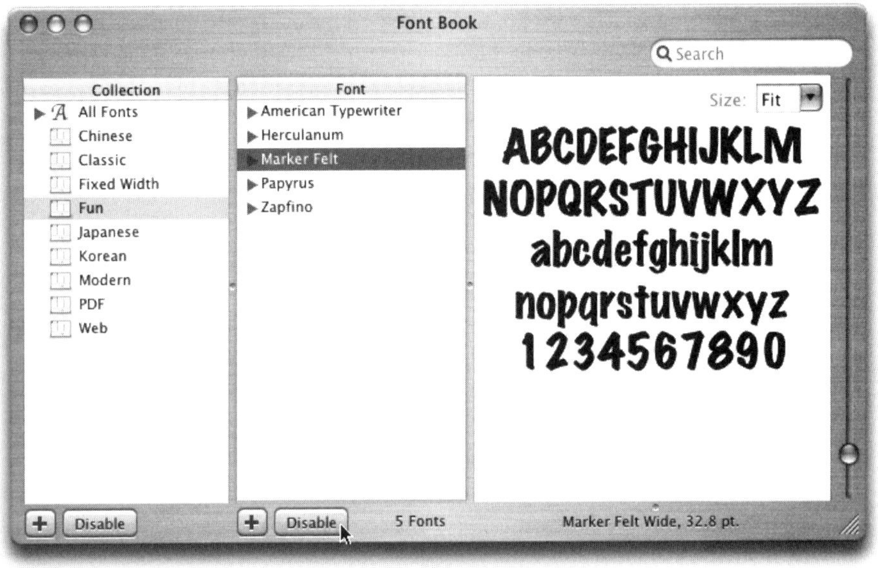

6. Select the **Fun** collection, and then select **Marker Felt** from the **Font** column. Click **Disable** under the **Font** column.

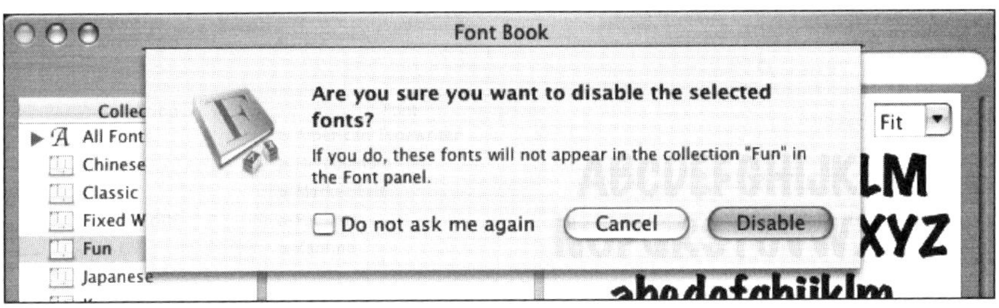

7. In the dialog box that appears, you're warned that the font will be disabled in the collection "Fun." Click **Disable**.

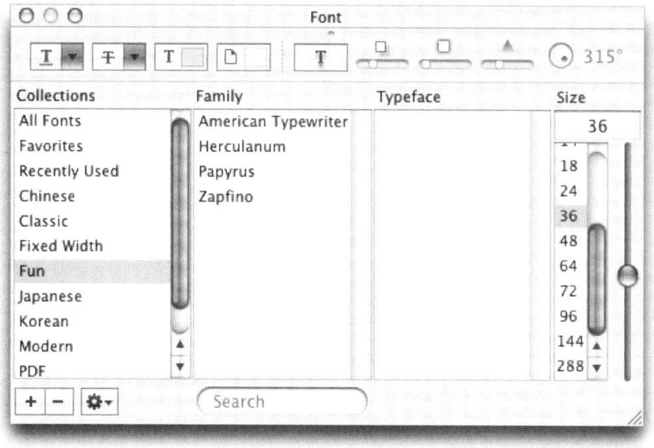

8. Switch to **TextEdit** and notice that **Marker Felt** no longer appears in the **Fun** collection in the **Fonts** palette.

9. Click the **All Fonts** collection and observe that **Marker Felt** still appears here.

When you disable a font in a Font Book collection (other than All Fonts), you disable only it within that collection. The font remains available through All Fonts and any other collection it's a part of. To disable a font entirely in Font Book, select the ***All Fonts*** *collection, select the font, and click* ***Disable****.*

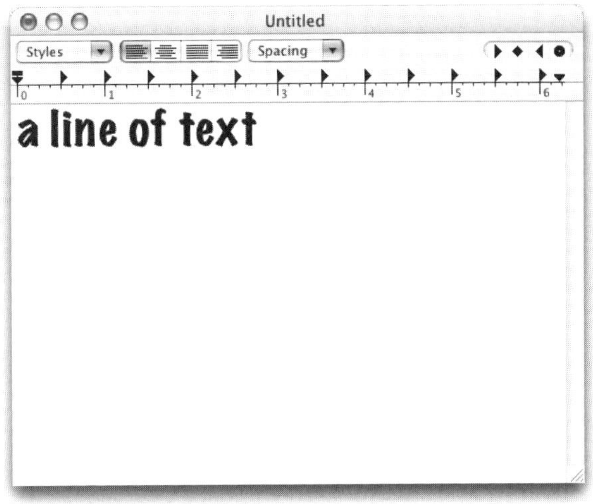

10. Highlight the text in your **TextEdit** window and change its font to **Marker Felt**.

11. Return to **Font Book**. Select **Marker Felt** in the **Fun** collection and click **Enable** to reactivate it in this collection.

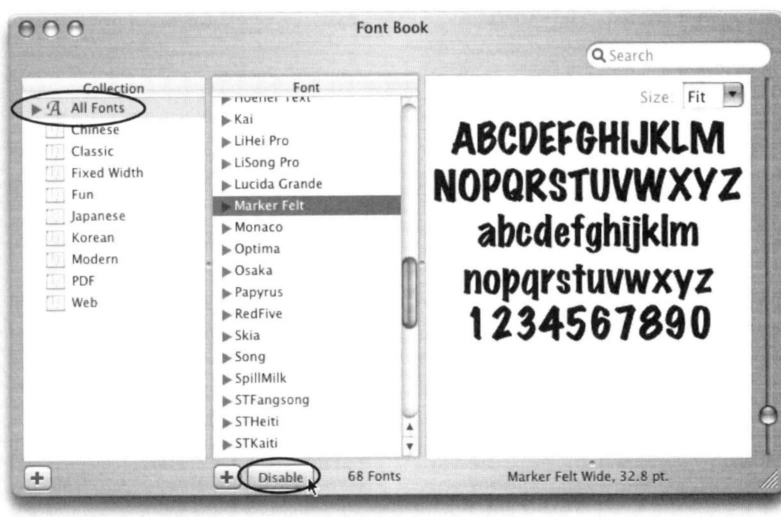

12. Click the **All Fonts** collection. Notice the **Disable** button no longer appears under the collections column (because you can't disable all your fonts at once). Locate **Marker Felt** in the **Font** column again and click **Disable**.

13. This time, you're warned that disabling this font will disable it in all collections in which it might currently appear. Click **Disable**.

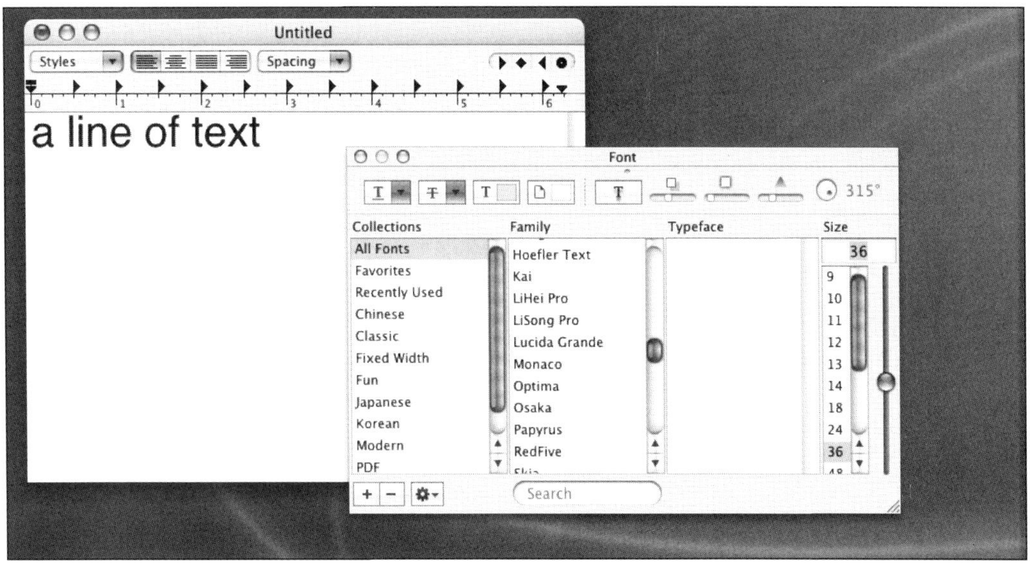

14. Return to **TextEdit** and notice that your text no longer appears in the **Marker Felt** font. Nor is the font to be found in any collections in the **Fonts** palette. With the **Marker Felt** unavailable, your text has reverted back to a default font.

15. Return to **Font Book** and enable **Marker Felt** once again. Click back to **TextEdit** and notice that the text has been restored to **Marker Felt**.

Managing fonts with Font Book is pretty easy once you get the hang of it. You'll find its management capabilities increasingly useful as you install more and more fonts on your Mac.

TIP | Searching for Fonts

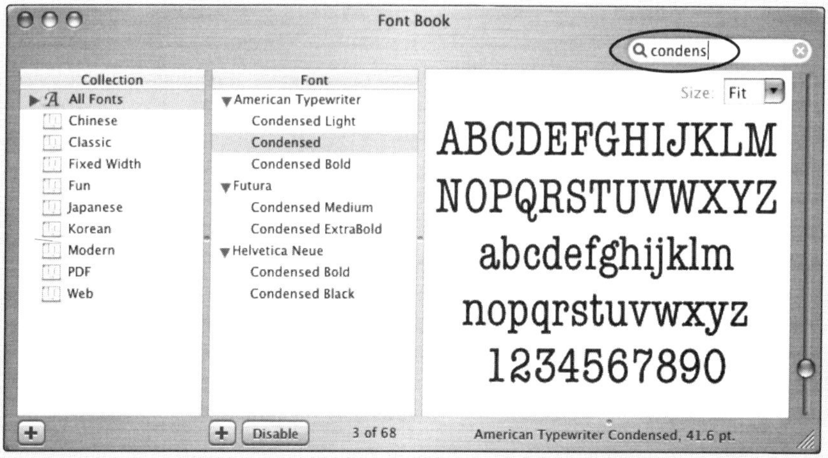

Another fantastic feature of Font Book is its integrated Search field. Simply select a collection (or All Fonts if you want to search trough all your fonts) and begin typing a font's name or style (such as bold or condensed) and the results begin appearing in the Font column. As you continue typing, the results continue narrowing down. This is a great way to find similarly named fonts or fonts of a specific style.

MOVIE | Font Book

For a demonstration of installing and managing fonts with Font Book, see the movie **fontbook.mov** on the **H•O•T CD-ROM**.

7. Faxing

New to Panther, you can now send and receive faxes on your Mac. In fact, you can send a fax from any application that prints because, as you might have noticed earlier, a Fax button appears in every Print dialog box. Being able to send and receive faxes on your Mac can save you lots of time and paper. This exercise shows you how to set up your Mac to act as a fax machine, but you'll need to provide your own fax numbers to actually send faxes. You'll also need to make sure that your Mac's modem is connected to an open phone line (meaning the modem and phone line can't be in use–connecting you to the Internet, for example–if you want to send or receive faxes).

First, you'll set up your Mac to receive faxes.

1. Click the **System Preferences** icon in the **Dock**. Then click **Print & Fax**.

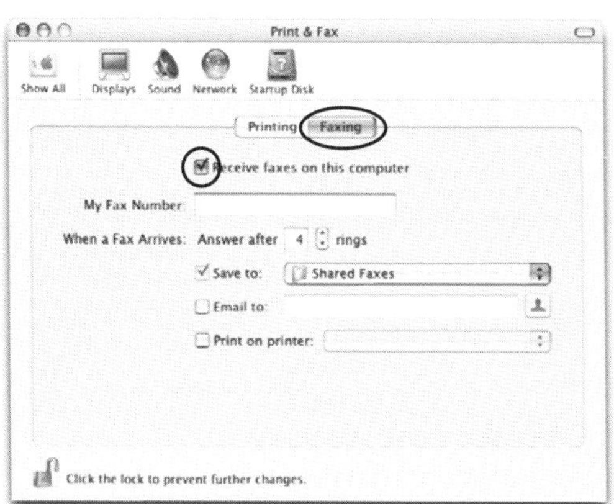

2. In the **Print & Fax** pane, click the **Faxing** button. Check **Receive faxes on this computer**.

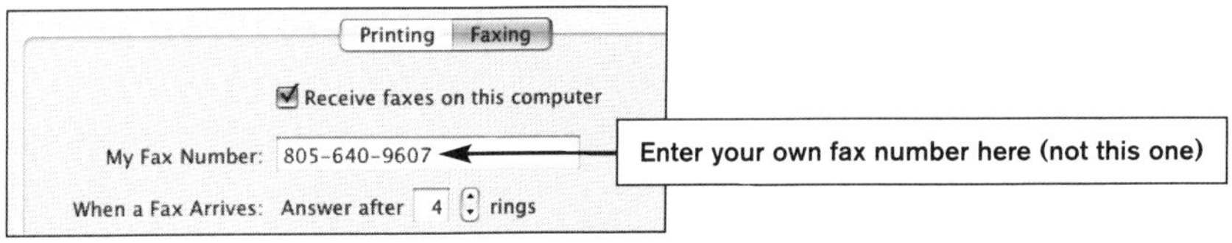

3. Enter your fax number in the **My Fax Number** field. This is the number of the phone line to which your Mac is connected and is used to identify your computer when you send or receive a fax. Select the number of rings allowed before your Mac answers the phone line. If you also receive voice calls at the phone number you entered, you should allow yourself three or four rings to pick up the phone before your Mac does.

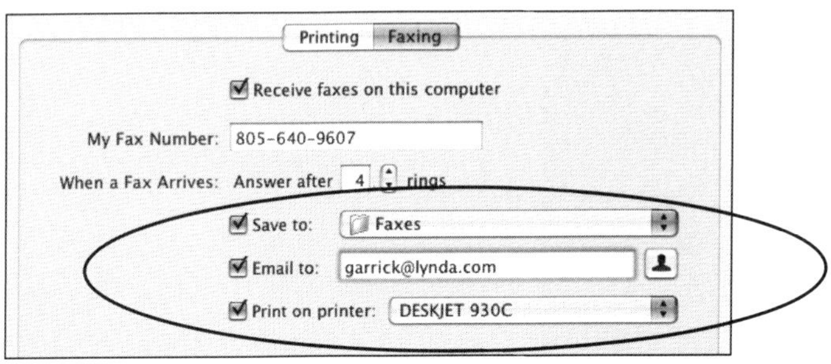

The next three check boxes allow you to determine what happens to the fax once it's received. You can check or uncheck any combination of the three choices, but you must check at least one choice to receive faxes.

Save to *allows you to specify a folder in which to save the fax. If you select the* ***Faxes*** *folder, faxes will be saved in your* ***Users > Shared > Faxes*** *folder, where they can be accessed by anyone with an account on your Mac. Choose* ***Other Folder*** *from this menu if you want to select a different folder.*

Email to *allows you to enter an email address to which your Mac will automatically forward incoming faxes. You can select an email address directly from Address Book by clicking the icon to the right of this field. (You'll learn how to enter information in Address Book in Chapter 10,* "Address Book, Mail, and iChat AV."*)*

Print on printer *allows you to select a printer connected to your Mac or on your network on which to print the incoming fax.*

4. Select one or more of these check boxes. You're now ready to receive faxes.

Note: *You don't have to be logged onto your account to receive faxes, but your Mac must be on. If your Mac goes to sleep, it can't receive faxes. To prevent your Mac from sleeping, open the* ***Energy Saver*** *preference pane, click the* ***Sleep*** *button, and drag the slider under* ***Put the computer to sleep when it is inactive for*** *to* ***Never.***

Now that you're Mac is ready to receive faxes, you'll take a look at how to send them.

5. Open the document you want to fax. Choose **File > Print** from the application's menu bar. (If the application can't print, you can't fax.)

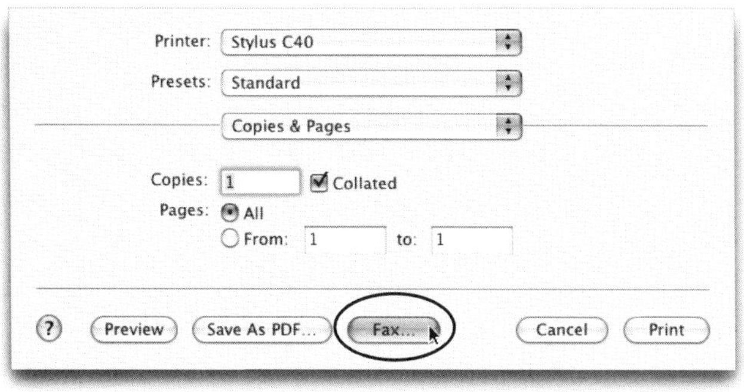

6. Click **Fax**. This opens another sheet in which your can enter information relevant to the fax you're sending.

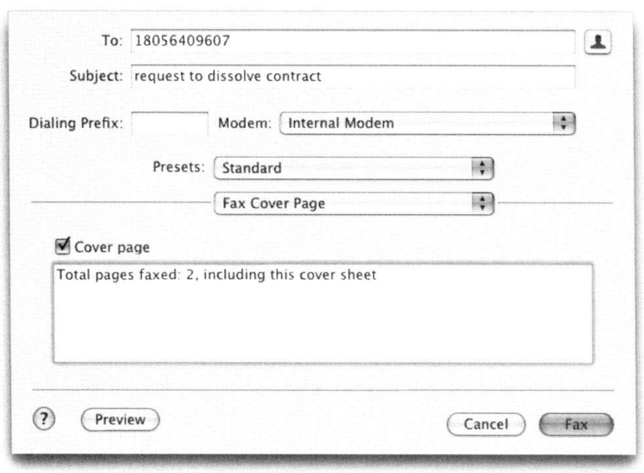

7. In the **To** field, enter the number to which you want to send your fax. If you wish, enter a **Subject**. If necessary, enter a **Dialing Prefix**. For example, if you need to dial **9** to reach an outside line, enter **9** in this field. If you have more than one modem connected to you Mac, you can select one from the **Modem** menu. Check **Cover page** to enter cover page information in the large text field.

Tip: If you have a combination of options you frequently use, click the ***Presets*** *menu and select* ***Save As*** *to save your options. You'll then be able to choose your saved combination from this menu anytime you fax.*

8. To see what your fax will look like, click **Preview**.

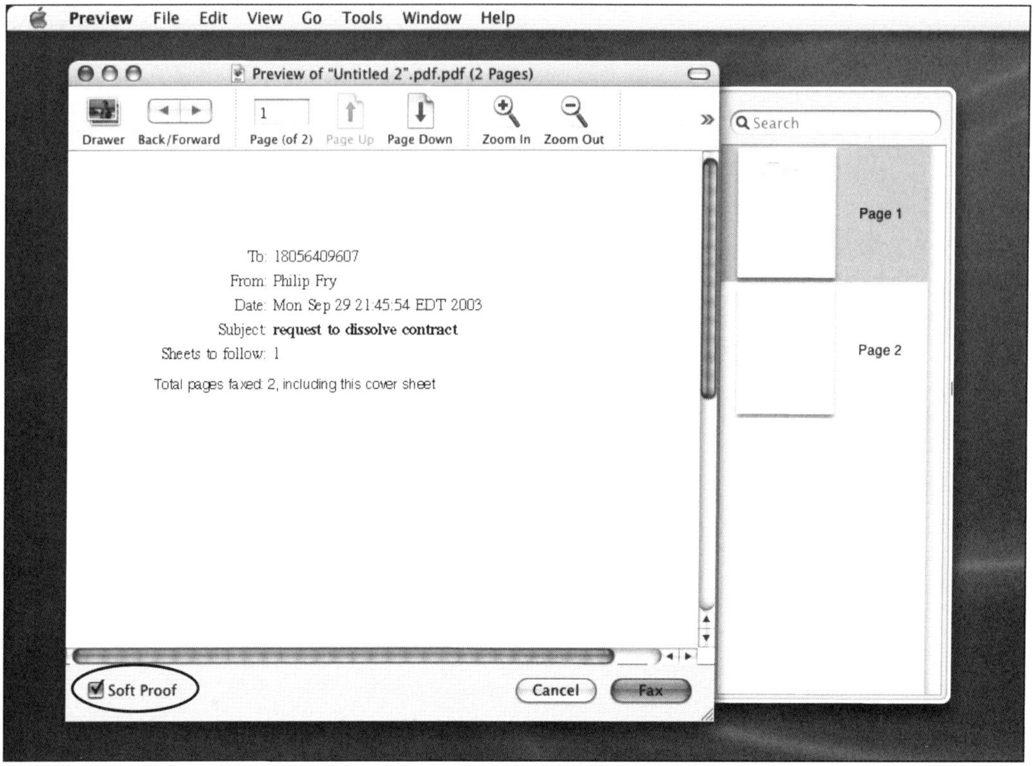

Your fax will open in Preview, with thumbnails for each page appearing in the drawer to the side of the main menu. Because most fax machines still print in black and white, Preview mimics the appearance of a black and white printer, giving you a better idea of what your fax is going to look like to its recipient. To disable this feature, uncheck ***Soft Proof.***

9. If decide that you want to make some changes, click **Cancel** to return to your original document. If you're satisfied with the appearance of your document, click **Fax**.

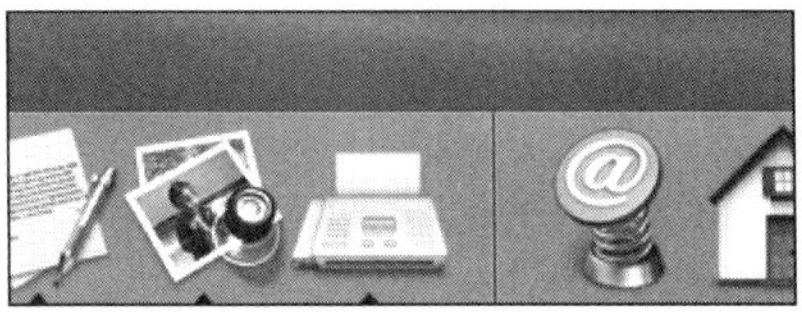

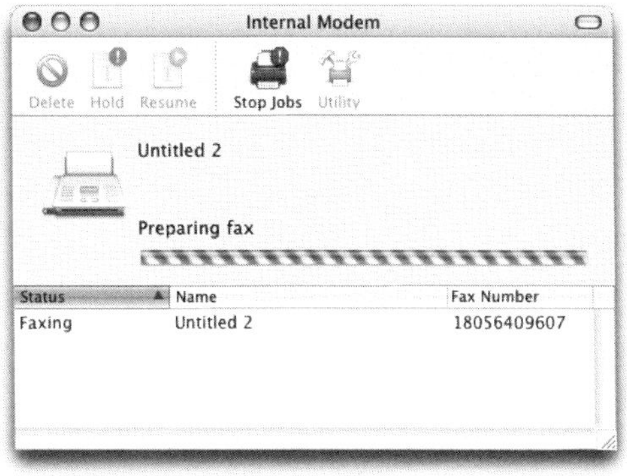

The fax icon will appear in the Dock. If you want to check on the status of your fax, click this icon to open the Internal Modem window–it resembles the window that shows you the status of your printing document, which you saw earlier in this chapter.

If your modem is already in use (if you're using it to connect to the Internet, for instance), your fax will be sent as soon as your modem becomes available.

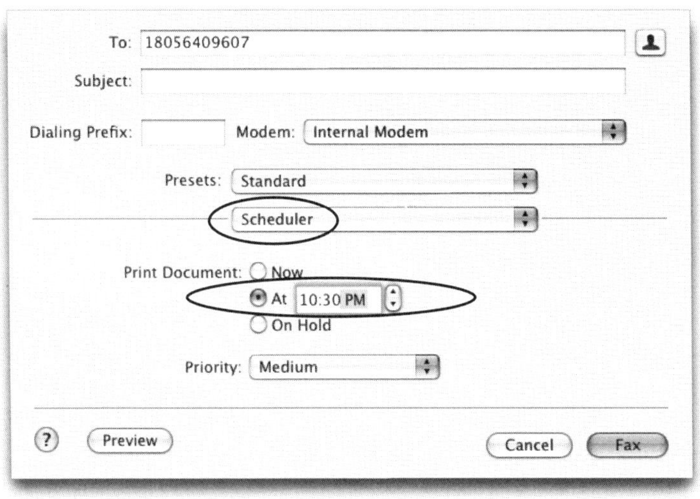

Tip: *To send your fax at a later time, choose* **Scheduler** *from the menu circled here and then select a time at which to transmit your fax.*

By now, you should be fairly comfortable with printing documents, managing fonts, and faxing in OS X. You'll be learning more about faxing from Mail and Address Book in Chapter 10, "Address Book, Mail, and iChat AV." *In the next chapter, you'll start the next section of the book and learn how to get your Mac onto the Internet.*

---

7. Installing Applications

| Decompressing, Mounting, and Installing an Application |

| Package Contents and Uninstalling Applications |

chap_07

Mac OS X Panther H•O•T CD-ROM

Up to this point, you've been learning about the features and applications that come built in to OS X. Although OS X comes with a vast array of really useful programs, eventually you'll probably have to install some additional software onto your Mac. Programs that edit images, or build Web pages, or display the weather in Tunisia–tons of applications are available for OS X. In this chapter, you'll learn about the different ways to install applications on your Mac and how to handle the different file types associated with software installers. This is a relatively brief chapter because, as you'll soon see, installing applications is a pretty easy task. However, there are some important things to know about where applications are installed, how to decompress their installers, and how to uninstall applications if you no longer need them.

StuffIt Expander

These days, you typically acquire software in one of two ways–either you download it from the Internet or you receive it on a CD-ROM. When you download an application from the Internet, you'll most likely be downloading a compressed version of the software. Compressing software allows the software developer to package the application's contents into a single file, called an **archive**. Archives make it easy to transport software because, regardless of the number of files or folders it contains, an archive remains a single file that's often smaller in size than the sum of its parts. Compressing a file is a simple way for a software developer to ensure that you get all the necessary pieces for the software to work properly. It can also decrease the file size, which is useful when downloading large applications from the Internet.

But before you can use a compressed file, it must first be expanded with special software that can interpret the type of compression that was applied to the file. Files can be compressed in more than one way. In fact, there are about as many types of compression out there on the Internet as there are types of pasta in a gourmet grocery store, and distinguishing among the different types can be similarly confusing (I still can't remember the difference between cannelloni and capellini). Fortunately, OS X comes with StuffIt Expander, a utility that can handle just about every kind of compression scheme available today.

With StuffIt Expander, you don't need to worry about distinguishing among compression types. Whether the file ends with .sit, .zip, .tar, .gz, or .tar.gz, StuffIt can open them all. The chart in Exercise 1 describes these different formats.

Disk Images

Once you've decompressed the software file, you'll often find that the software you wish to install is contained on a disk image. A disk image (.dmg) is a file that mimics the appearance and behavior of a hard disk or CD-ROM and provides a simple way for software creators to distribute their products.

Before a disk image can be accessed, however, it needs to be mounted on your Desktop, which, thanks to the **Disk Utility** that comes with OS X, is a relatively simple task. In the following exercise, you'll get some hands-on experience with installing software by using a compressed disk image.

I. Decompressing, Mounting, and Installing an Application

In this exercise, you'll install a copy of MacJournal, a fantastic piece of software by developer Dan Schimpf. MacJournal takes advantage of all the great OS X interface elements that are available to developers, such as spell checking, the Fonts palette, and the toolbar, and it's a excellent example of how great an OS X application can be. You can use MacJournal to keep a daily diary, job logs, or whatever. Of course, before you can use it, you first need to install it.

Note: You can find additional information and download the latest version of MacJournal from Dan Schimpf's Web site at **http://homepage.mac.com/dschimpf/**.

1. Drag the **chap_07** folder from the **H•O•T CD-ROM** to your **Desktop**.

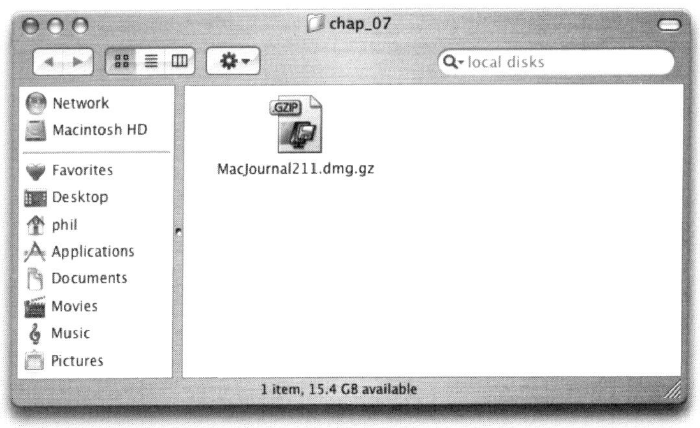

2. Open **chap_07**. Inside you'll find the file **MacJournal211.dmg.gz**.

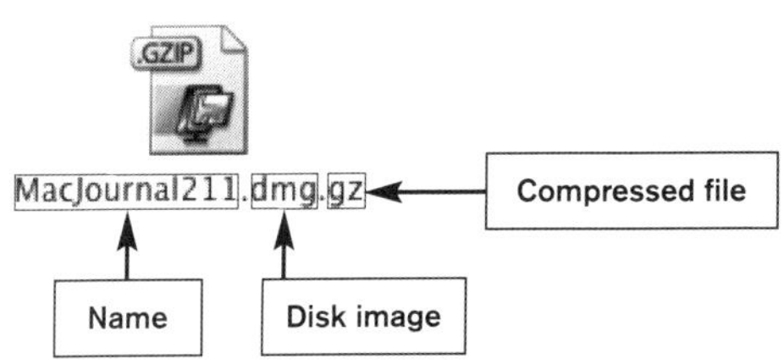

To understand what type of file you're looking at here, you should examine its name. ***MacJournal211*** *is the relatively arbitrary name that the software creator has given this file. In this case, the name indicates that this is version 2.1.1 of MacJournal. This name is followed by the extension* ***.dmg****, which indicates that the file itself is a disk image. But because the entire file ends with* ***.gz****, you know that this is a compressed file; therefore, the first thing you need to do is decompress it so you can have access to the disk image.*

Compression Types

As mentioned earlier, because StuffIt Expander takes care of compression for you, you generally don't have to worry about what type of compression has been applied to a file. But just in case you're curious, the following chart lists the most popular compression formats that can be decompressed by StuffIt. (For a complete list of file formats, visit **www.aladdinsys.com/support/techsupport/fileformats.html**.)

Compression Formats Supported by StuffIt

File Name Extension	Description
.sit, .seg, .sea	These are all types of StuffIt archives—archives that are created with the full version of StuffIt.
.hqx	This extension represents the BinHex (**Bin**ary **Hex**adecimal), a method for converting nontext files into ASCII, a plain text format. Some older email programs can only handle ASCII.
.bin	MacBinary. A form of compression developed in the '80s to use on files to be transferred between Macs.
.zip	A common (if not the most common) Windows compression format.
.gz	A Unix compression format.
.mim	Mime/base64. This is yet another common industry format for sending nontext files such as images, movies, and sound files.
.tar, .tgz, .tar.gz	Tape archive—an older Unix compression format.

Generally, whenever you download a compressed file from the Internet onto your Mac, StuffIt Expander will automatically decompress the file for you. But since you copied this file from a CD-ROM, you'll need to do it manually.

3. Double-click **MacJournal211.dmg.gz**.

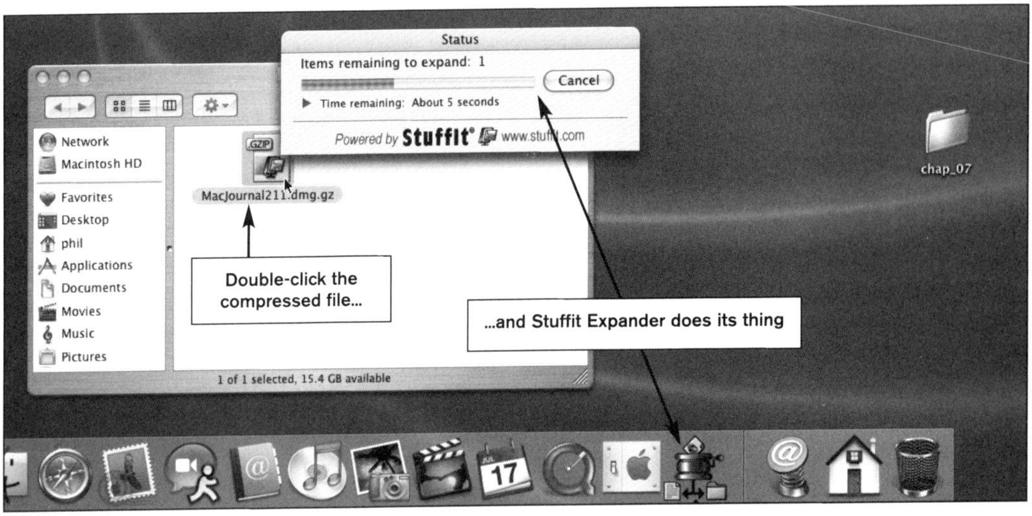

Instantly, StuffIt Expander opens and kicks into action.

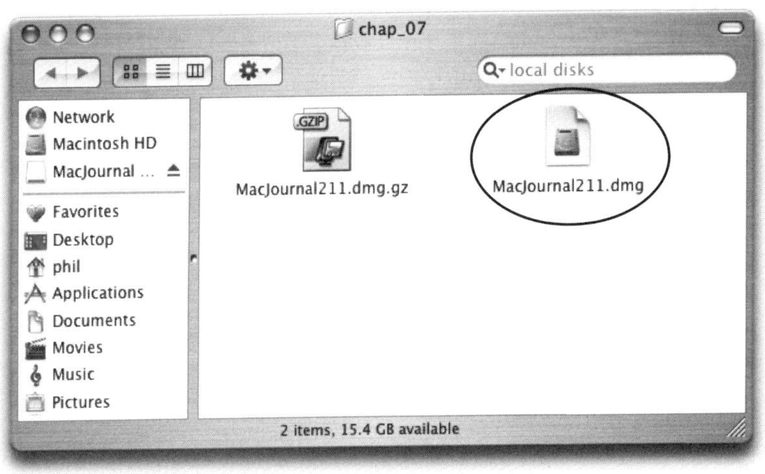

After the file has been decompressed (which takes only a few seconds), the file ***MacJournal.dmg*** *appears in the* ***chap_07*** *folder.*

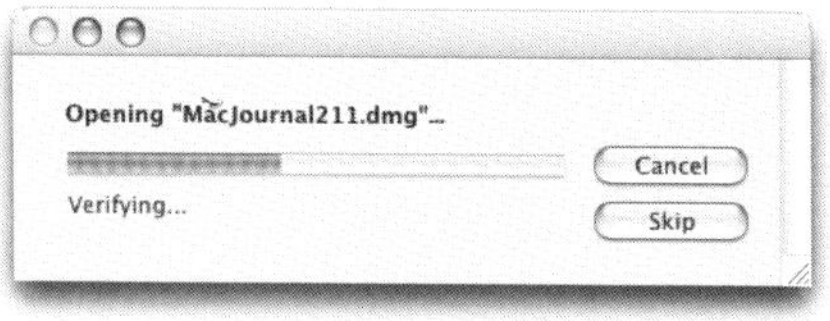

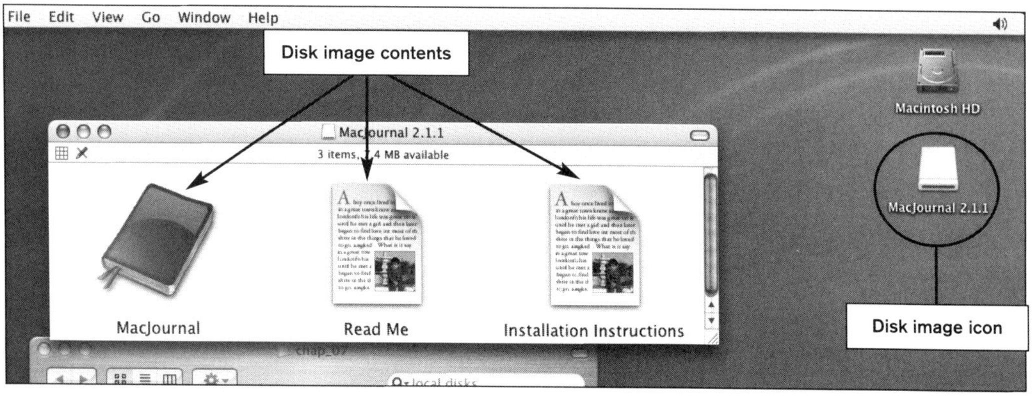

*Because OS X immediately recognizes this file as a disk image, it automatically runs **Disk Utility** for you, which mounts the disk image's icon on your Desktop and displays its contents. And all you had to do was double-click the compressed file! (If for some reason Disk Utility doesn't run, just double-click the DMG file.)*

***Note:** To be as unobtrusive as possible, StuffIt and Disk Utility automatically close when they're done doing their jobs. However, StuffIt has a feature that automatically detects if you have an active Internet connection. If you do, StuffIt checks in with **www.stuffit.com** to see if there are any newer versions of itself available.*

Here on the disk image is the MacJournal application and two TextEdit files containing information about this release. At this point, these files still exist only on the disk image sitting on your Desktop. If you were to eject the disk icon, the files would be removed as well. To install MacJournal to your Mac, all you have to do is drag it to wherever you want it to be stored. In keeping with the spirit of proper organization, you'll drag this file to your Applications folder.

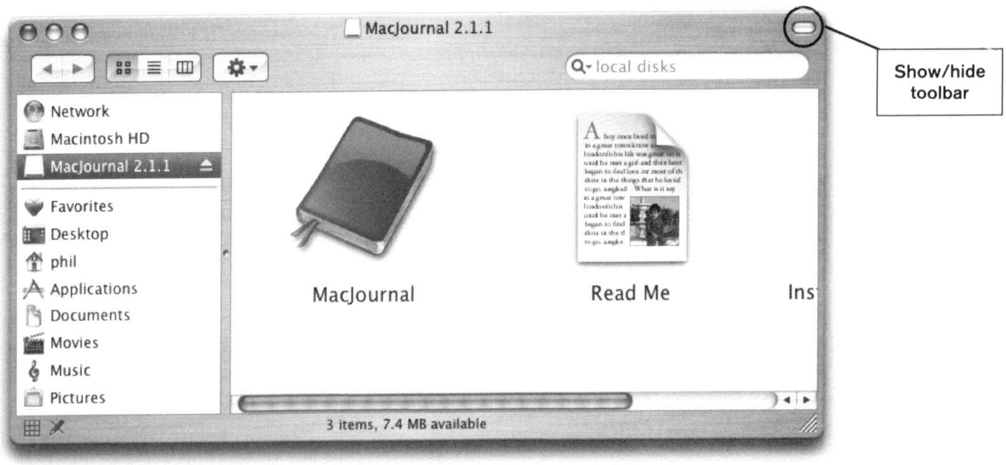

4. Click the **Show/hide toolbar** button in the **MacJournal 2.1.1** window. As you learned in Chapter 2, "*Working with Files and Folders*," this brings the **Places** sidebar into view.

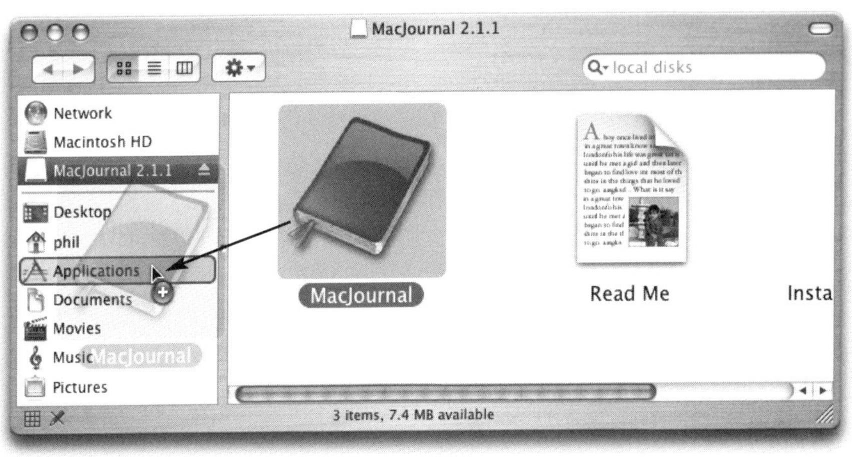

5. Drag the **MacJournal** icon onto the **Applications** folder in the **Places** sidebar. Notice the green plus sign (+) that appears, indicating that you're copying this file from one location to another.

That all there is to it! You now have a copy of MacJournal on your hard drive.

At this point, you still have the MacJournal 2.1.1 disk image icon sitting on your Desktop. Opened disk images remain on your Desktop until you shut down your Mac or eject the disk image. "Eject" may seem like a strange term to use here, but that's exactly what your Mac considers the act of putting away the disk image.

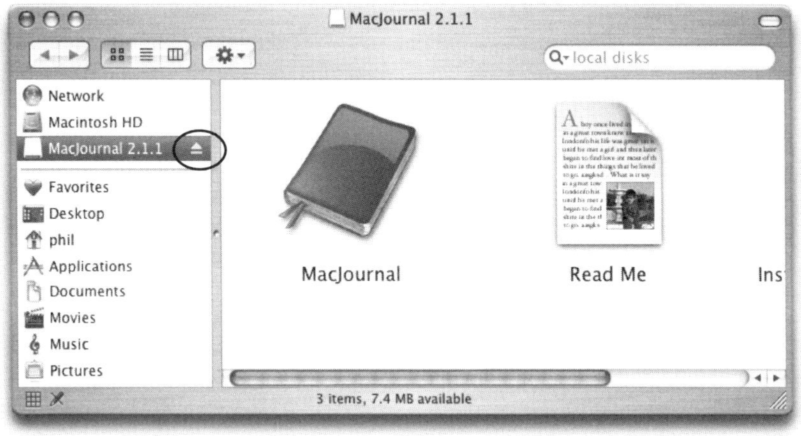

In previous versions of OS X, you would drag the disk image to the Trash in the Dock to eject it. Thanks to the Places sidebar in Panther, you can now also eject disk images from any open Finder window.

6. Click the **Eject** icon next to **MacJournal 2.1.1** in the **Places** sidebar. The window and the disk image disappear from your **Desktop**. Of course, nothing really gets ejected from your Mac; you just unmounted the disk image.

Now you'll run your copy of MacJournal.

7. The **chap_07** folder should still be open on your **Desktop**. If it's not, double-click its icon to open a window. Click **Applications** in the **Places** sidebar.

8. Locate **MacJournal** and double-click its icon.

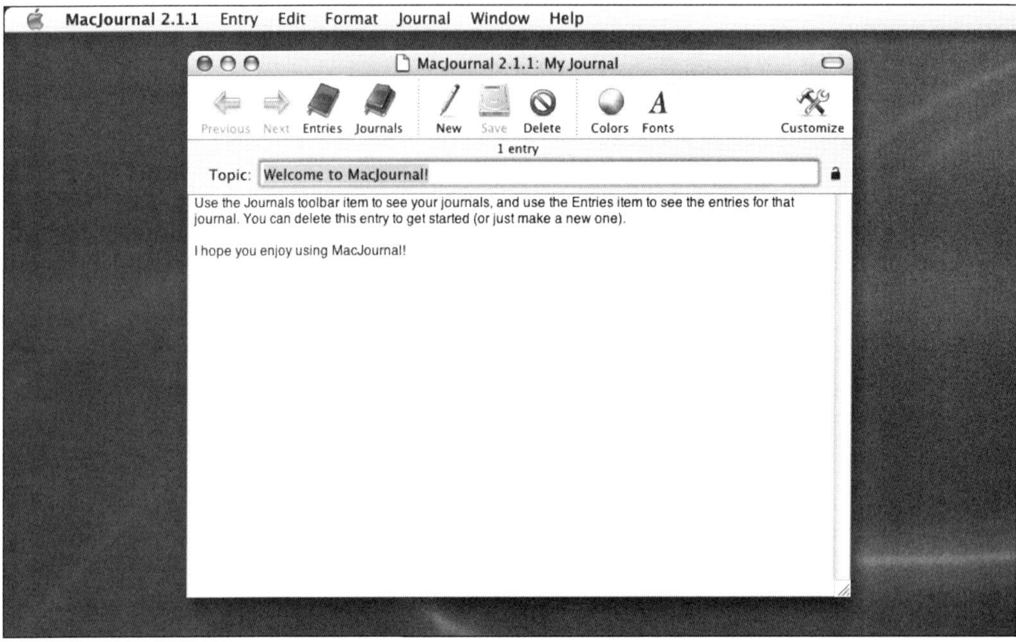

*If you see the welcome message, MacJournal is working properly. Feel free to take some time and play around with this great program. For information on how to use MacJournal, choose **Help > MacJournal** from the menu bar. If you have Internet access, you can also visit Dan Schimpf's Web site at **http://homepage.mac.com/dschimpf** for additional information and updates.*

---

9. When you're done examining the application, choose **MacJournal > Quit MacJournal** to return to the **Desktop**. Close any open windows.

So there you have it. As you've just seen, StuffIt and Disk Utility make it super easy to install applications from compressed disk images. The process shown in this exercise generally applies to most programs you download from the Internet. The files for Applications you acquire from CD-ROMs are usually not compressed; you can drag them directly to your hard drive without having to bother with StuffIt or Disk Utility, Some applications, however, require the use of a software installer, as described in the following sidebar.

NOTE | Software Installers

In this exercise, you witnessed how easy it is to install an application from a disk image–you simply drag the application to your preferred location. The majority of applications, especially those that can be downloaded from the Internet, are installed in this fashion. However, many commercial-grade, professional applications such as Adobe Photoshop and Illustrator or Macromedia Flash and Freehand require more complex installations than can be accomplished by simply dragging a single icon to your hard drive.

When an application needs to have certain components, such as a preferences panel or a startup item, placed in specific locations on your hard drive, or if installing the application requires administrator privileges, a software installer takes care of the details. A software installer is a small program designed to install the key elements of the main application in the proper locations on your hard drive.

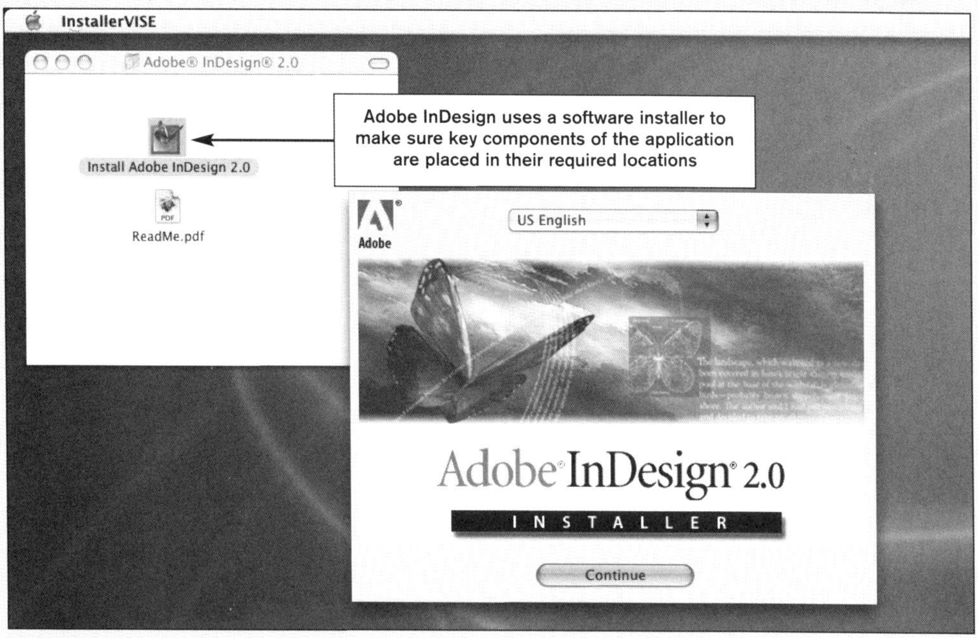

Using a software installer is no big deal. All you need to do is double-click the installer icon and you'll be walked through the steps to install the application, which can involve entering an administrator password, accepting a standard software license agreement, typing a serial or registration number, customizing the installation, and choosing a location for the application to be installed. Once these details have been established, the software installer takes care of the rest.

2. Package Contents and Uninstalling Applications

It happens. The magic is lost, the program isn't all you thought it would be, or you're simply running out of hard drive space. Somewhere down the line, you may want to remove an application from your Mac. This exercise shows you how to remove a program, which, in most cases turns out to be a fairly simply process.

But first, a little background about how applications exist in Mac OS X. If you're a veteran of Mac OS 9 or earlier operating systems, you might have noticed how OS X applications such as TextEdit, Chess, Preview, Safari, and MacJournal, pretty much just sit in your Applications folder without any apparent related files or folders. In earlier Mac systems, applications usually had their own folders, which meant that if you wanted to run, say, Adobe Reader, you'd have to first open your Applications folder, then open the Adobe Reader folder, and then double-click the Reader icon to run the program. The Adobe Reader folder contained not only the application itself, but also the essential files and folders needed to run Reader.

In OS X, applications still use collections of support files, but they're hidden from your view, so all you have to worry about is opening your Applications folder and double-clicking the application icon. The icon you're clicking is referred to as an application *package*. This package is in actuality a special type of folder that contains the elements required by the application to run properly. You'll be uninstalling MacJournal in this exercise, but before you do, you'll first examine the program to see exactly what you're deleting.

1. Choose **Go > Applications** from the **Finder** menu bar to open your **Applications** folder. Locate the icon for **MacJournal**.

Double-clicking this icon would start the MacJournal application, which is not what you want to do in this case.

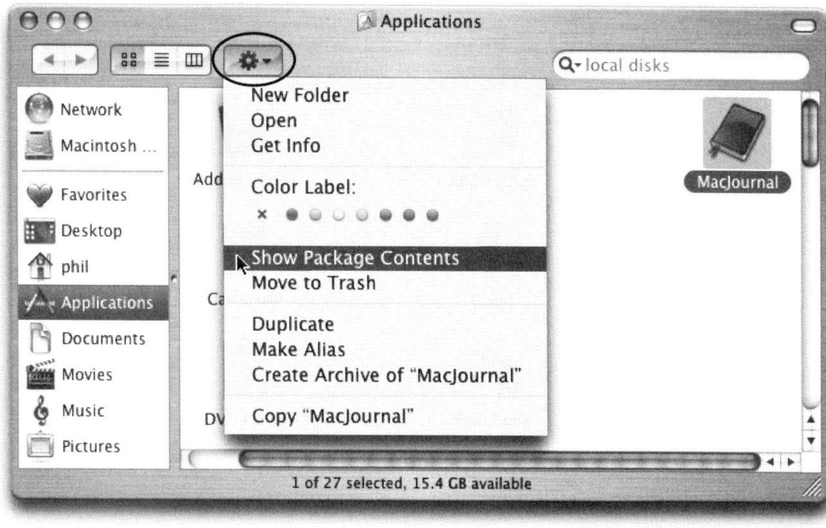

2. Instead, click the **MacJournal** icon once to select it and then click the **Action** button. From the **Action** menu, choose **Show Package Contents**. (You could also **Ctrl+click** the **MacJournal** icon to open its contextual menu and choose **Show Package Contents** from there.)

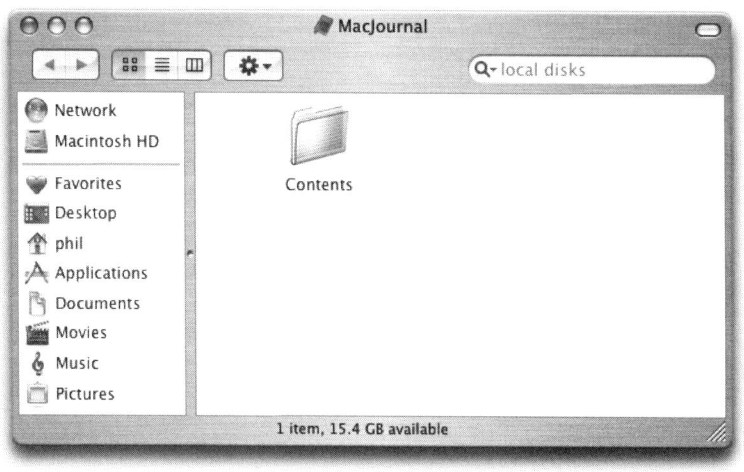

*This will open a new Finder window containing a folder called **Contents**.*

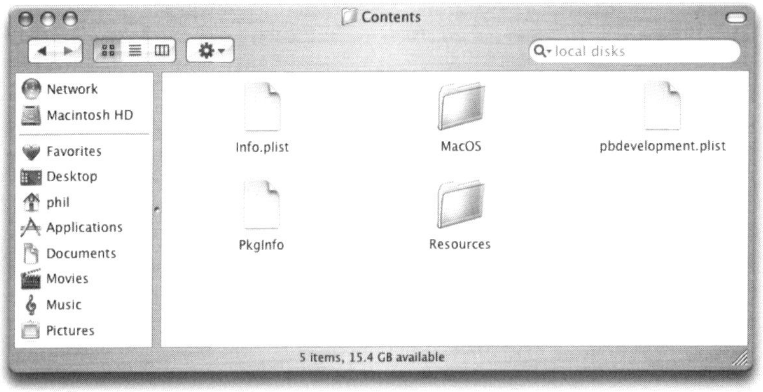

3. Double-click the **Contents** folder. These icons and folders you're seeing mean little to most users, but these are the key components that make the **MacJournal** program work. This is your backstage view of the applications.

4. Double-click the **Resources** folder. The **Resources** folder usually contains items such as the images for the application's **Dock** icon and for the graphics used in the program itself. As you can see, there's tons of stuff in here.

Tip: *If you know your way around image editing software, you can open the* ***Resources*** *folder of an application and create replacement images for the files found there. Many users like to customize their own buttons for their favorite applications. Just be sure to make a backup copy of any applications you intend to mess around with in case you really mess things up. You can easily copy an application by selecting its icon and choosing* ***File > Duplicate*** *from the menu bar. If you find that you develop a taste for modifying the appearance of applications and items in OS X, check out* ***www.resexcellence.com*** *for some samples and tutorials of other modifications you can make.*

5. When you're done examining the contents of the **MacJournal** program, close all open windows except for the **Applications** folder.

So what does the fact that applications come in packages have to do with uninstalling them? Application packages mean that users don't have to worry about a program's related files and folders in order to run the program. Packages also mean that users don't have to worry about an application's related files and folders when they want to throw the application away. All you need to do to get rid of most applications is just drag their icons to the Trash.

The following steps will uninstall MacJournal. If you've already started using MacJournal and want to keep your entries, don't perform these steps; just read through them.

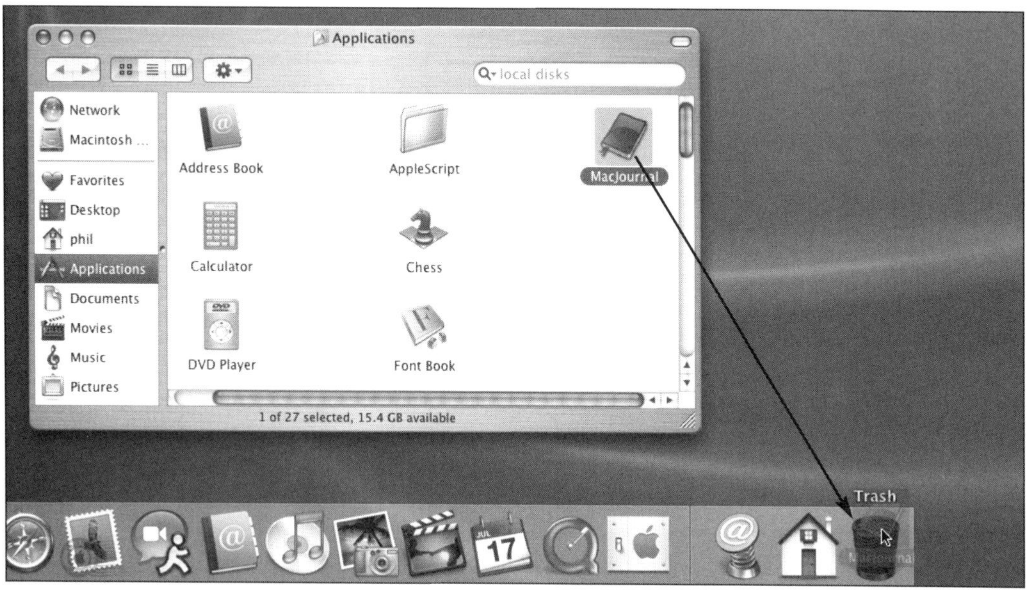

6. From the **Applications** folder, drag the **MacJournal** icon to the **Trash**.

Because MacJournal is a software package, you've now moved most of its related elements to the Trash and have prepared them for disposal–all in one move of your mouse. If you were to empty the Trash now, nearly all traces of MacJournal would be gone from your hard drive. However, there's usually at least one more place you should check if you want to make sure that you're removing all traces of an application.

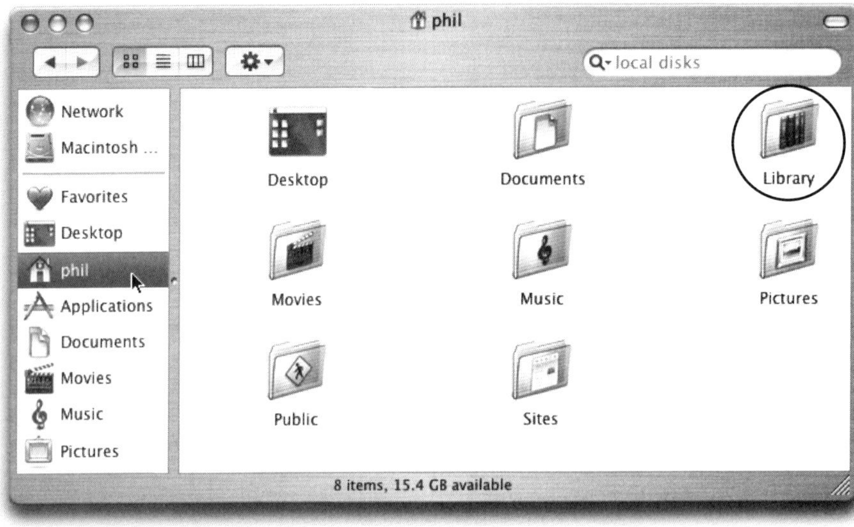

7. Click the **Home** icon in the **Places** sidebar to view your **Home** directory. Double-click the **Library** folder.

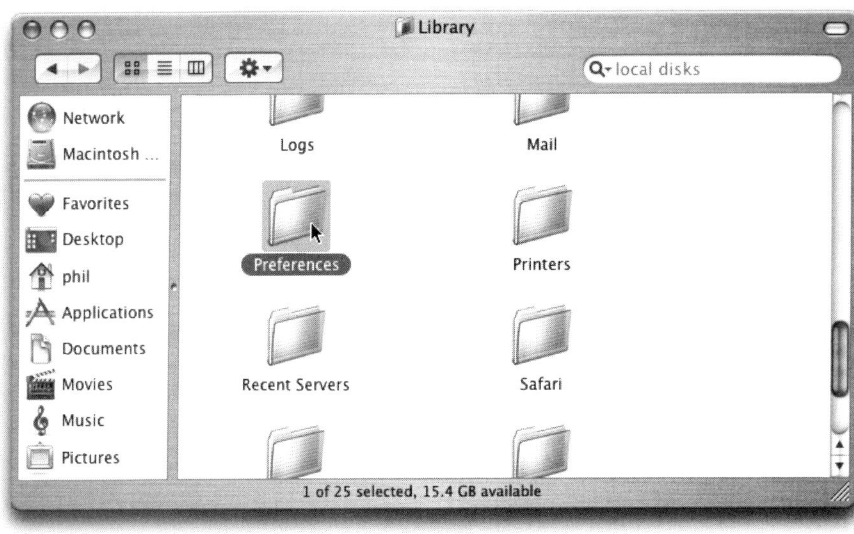

8. In the **Library** folder, find and open the **Preferences** folder, which is used to store your personal preferences for the applications you use. For example, in this folder you'll find any bookmarks you've saved in **Safari**. (You'll learn all about bookmarks in Chapter 9, "*Safari*.")

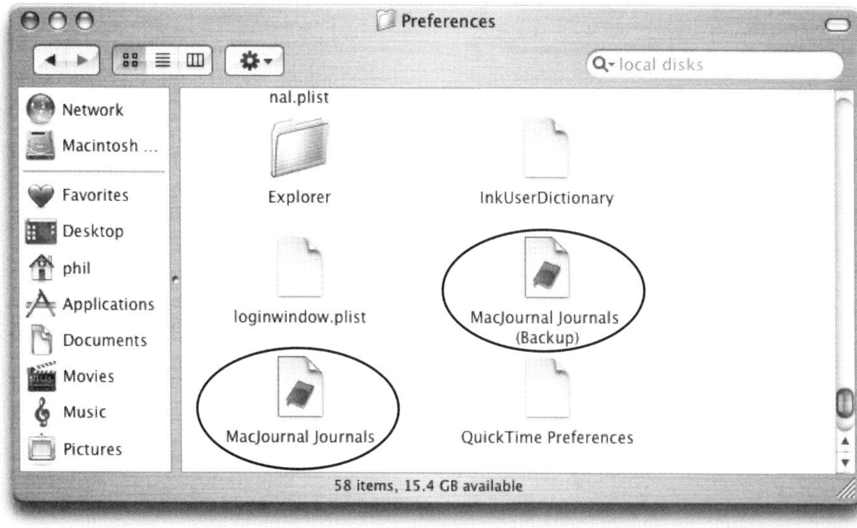

9. Scroll through the **Preferences** folder and locate the **MacJournal Journals**. As you can see, **MacJournal** created two preference files here: the journals themselves and a backup copy.

10. Drag the two **MacJournal** preference files to the **Trash**.

11. If you're sure you want to delete these items, **Ctrl+click** the **Trash** and select **Empty Trash** from the contextual menu. If you decide that you don't in fact want to delete MacJournal, it's an easy matter to drag the preference files back into the **Preferences** folder and the single **MacJournal** package back into the **Applications** folder. Close any open windows when you're done.

Uninstalling with a Software Installer

Although dragging an application and its preference files to the Trash will in most cases rid you of the application, programs that are installed with software installers (as described in Exercise 1) often place their components in multiple locations throughout your hard drive. Manually removing every piece of related software is sometimes difficult and can possibly cause problems if you don't catch everything. Before dragging a program that has been installed with an installer to the Trash, it's always a good idea to run the program's installer again to check if there's an uninstall option available.

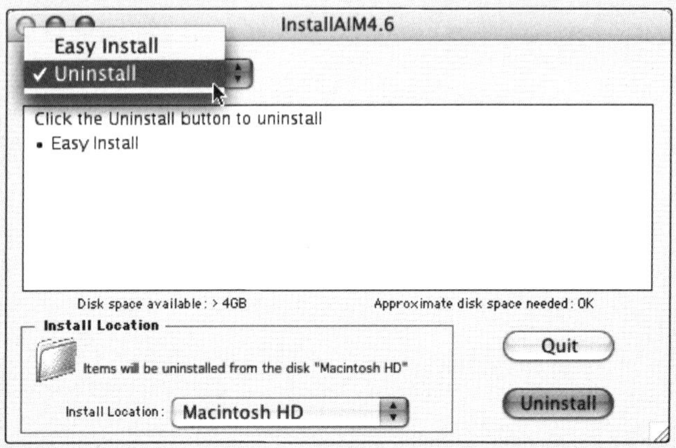

Many times, along with Easy Install or Custom Install, you'll find an Uninstall option that, when chosen, will go through your hard drive and eliminate all of the components related to the application, saving you the hassle of hunting down all the different pieces.

By now, you should have a pretty good understanding of how to install and remove applications from your Mac. The examples covered in this chapter will apply to most installation scenarios, but when in doubt, check the ReadMe file or, as a last resort, the manual that came with the software.

Section II

Working Online

An increasingly important aspect of the Macintosh Digital Hub is the Mac's capability to connect to the Internet and access the various services found online. Chapters 8 through 12 all involve using your Mac with the World Wide Web and other Internet-based services. First, you'll learn several ways to get your Mac online. From there, you'll learn to browse the Web, write and receive email, and manage your personal and business contacts—all with programs that come free with OS X. You'll also learn to use Sherlock, Apple's all-in-one Internet search tool. Finally, you'll sign up for a trial subscription to .Mac, Apple's online suite of tools and applications designed to enhance your Internet experience and discover what the Web has to offer.

8.

Getting Online

| Dial-Up Access | Setting Up an Ethernet Connection |
| Configuring a Wireless Connection |
| Sharing Your Internet Connection |

no exercise files

Mac OS X Panther
H•O•T CD-ROM

One of the most important aspects of owning a computer these days is the ability to connect it to the Internet. On the most basic level, Internet access enables you to send and receive e-mail, share files electronically, and access Web sites. And, as you've learned from previous chapters, most hardware and software companies—including Apple—provide updates for their products on their Web sites. Without a connection to the Internet, acquiring these updates would require contacting the manufacturer by phone and waiting for a delivery through the mail (if in fact the manufacturer provides such a service at all).

Navigating the various services the Internet offers is an important skill. Therefore, the next five chapters are devoted entirely to getting you online and then showing you what to do once you get there. You'll see that your Mac and OS X provide you with everything you need to become an active member of the online universe.

How Your Mac Connects to the Internet

These days there are many different ways to connect a computer to the Internet. Fortunately, current and recent Macs come equipped to handle just about any scenario you might encounter when preparing to get online. There are three main devices your Mac can use to connect to the Internet: a modem that utilizes a standard phone line, an Ethernet port that connects to a cable modem or DSL modem or to your company's network, or–if you have one–an AirPort card that connects wirelessly to a base station or router. (Don't worry if you didn't quite follow all of that. These terms will be explained more thoroughly later in this chapter.)

You can set up your Mac to connect to the Internet through any or all of these items, which are referred to as "ports." A **port** is a means of communicating data from your Mac to another device. Once you've set up your ports through network preferences, OS X will be able to correctly select an active port for you to connect to the Internet with. This process, technically referred to as multi-homing, simply means that your Mac is able to detect all active network connections and then automatically switches you to the fastest one. For instance, say you are working in an area near a wireless signal, and you're also plugged into your company's network through your Ethernet port. Although you have your AirPort card installed, OS X will most likely use the Ethernet connection because it's the faster of the two. But if the network connection should fail or drop in speed, OS X will automatically switch to the wireless network, without any input or changes needed from you.

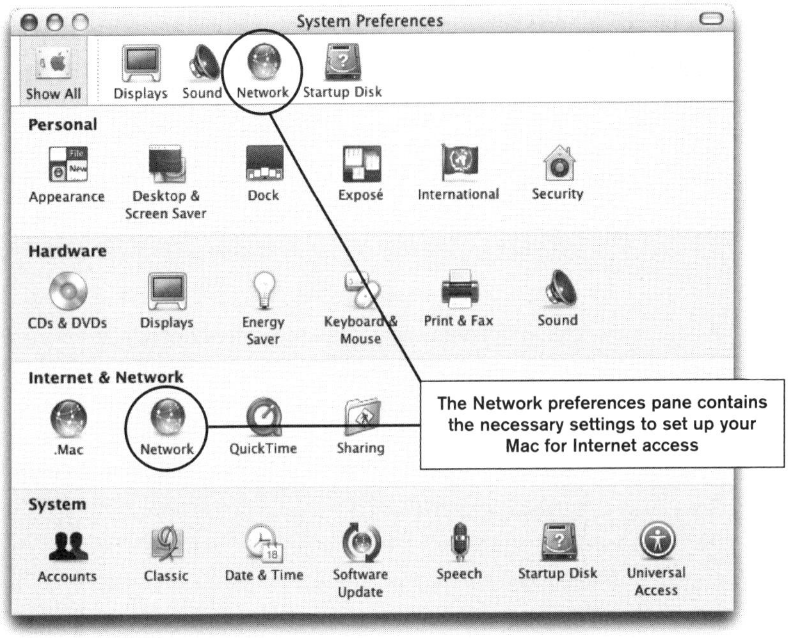

In order to set up your Mac to make these connections properly, you first need to open the Network settings found in System Preferences. The exercises in this chapter will show you how to use the Network panel to set up your Mac to connect to the Internet through your modem, your Ethernet port, and your AirPort card (if you have one). Even if you're only going to be connecting through one of the available ports, such as your modem, it's still probably worth your time to read through all of the exercises because important information about your Network settings is discussed in each section. Keep in mind that even if you usually connect to the Internet through a cable modem or DSL modem, it's still a good idea to know how to connect through your Mac's built-in modem just in case your broadband connection ever goes down.

NOTE | What Is an ISP?

Connecting to the Internet requires you to sign up with an Internet Service Provider (also known as an ISP). Your ISP will provide you with the necessary information to connect to its service. You will need to have this information on hand for the remaining exercises in this chapter. It's also possible that you or someone else already configured your Mac to connect to the Internet when OS X was first installed. If you're not sure, click the Safari icon in the Dock and try to access a Web page. If the page shows up, your Mac is already configured, and you don't need to worry about completing the next few exercises. You can jump ahead to Exercise 4 if you're interested in learning how to share your Internet connection with other Macs. Otherwise, move on to the next chapter.

I. Dial-Up Access

This exercise will show you how to connect to the Internet through your Mac's built-in modem. For this type of access, the modem dials a telephone number provided to you by your ISP. The call is answered by another modem, the connection is made, and you're online. A dial-up connection is the most common type of Internet service found in most homes. Although it is the slowest type of connection, dial-up does have some advantages over faster connection methods. If you travel, for instance, you're more likely to find dial-up service available than broadband or wireless services. When deciding on an ISP, check to see if local access numbers are available for the areas to which you frequently travel. Even if you have fast broadband service at home, it's good to know you can still get online when you're away from your home or office by dialing through your modem.

Note: If you are an America Online subscriber, the steps in these exercises will not apply to you. AOL provides its own setup program that you run when you first install the software on your Mac.

1. Click the **System Preferences** icon in the **Dock** to open **System Preferences**. (Or choose **Apple menu > System Preferences**.)

2. In **System Preferences**, click the **Network** icon.

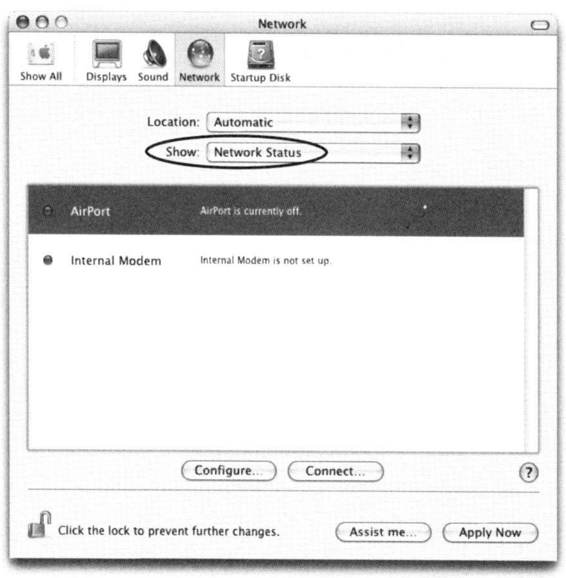

When you first open Network Preferences, you'll see the ***Network Status*** *of all active ports on your Mac. Depending on which ports are active, what you see in this screen shot may vary from what you see on your own Mac.*

3. Click the **Show** pop-up menu. This menu lists all of the ports that OS X can currently detect. You should have both **Internal Modem** and **Built-in Ethernet** available in this menu. If your Mac has an AirPort card installed, it will be shown here as well. (And if you have a PowerBook or iBook with an infrared port, you'll also see **IrDA** here.) Select **Internal Modem** if it's not already selected.

Finding Available Ports

If you didn't see the **Internal Modem** listed in the **Show** menu, choose **Network Port Configurations**.

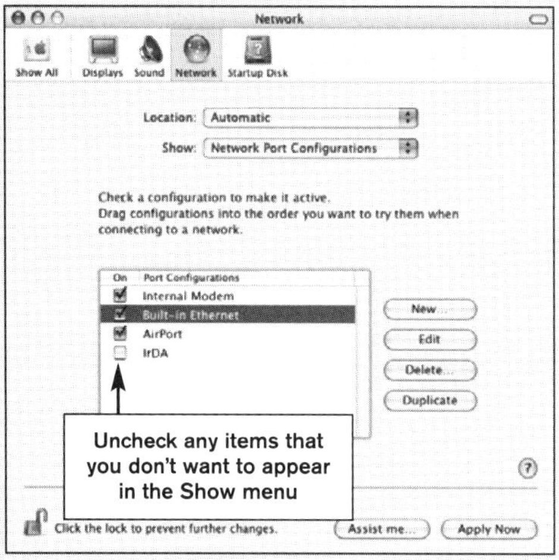

This panel controls which ports appear in the Show pop-up menu. You can uncheck any items you feel you won't need. For instance, if you're going to be using a dial-up connection and will not need your Ethernet connection, you can uncheck it here to prevent it from appearing in the Show menu. This is a simple way of reducing menu clutter, and it also prevents your Mac from wasting time checking for connections on ports you're not using.

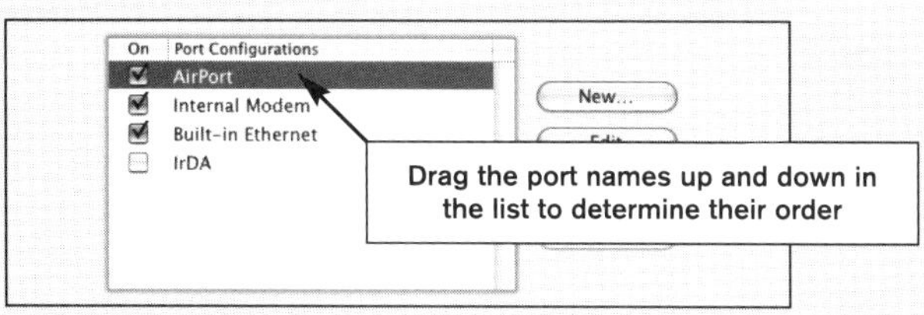

Additionally, the Network Port Configurations pane is used to determine the order in which OS X checks for an active network connection. For example, if your Mac is set up so you're able to connect to the Internet through your Ethernet port, an AirPort card, and through dial-up, you can drag the port names up and down in the list to designate which port takes precedence. Realistically, the Ethernet port would probably be the fastest and should therefore appear at the top of the list. If, however, that connection fails, OS X automatically checks for the next port on the list for an available connection–in this example, AirPort. Failing to find an AirPort connection would result in your Mac dialing up your ISP through the modem. While continuing through this chapter, be sure to check the Network Port Configurations pane if you can't find an item in the Show menu.

4. Now that you've selected **Internal Modem** from the **Show** menu, click the **TCP/IP** button and make sure **Using PPP** is selected in the **Configure IPv4** pop-up menu.

__PPP__, or __P__oint-to-__P__oint __P__rotocol, is a method by which computers transmit data when communicating through a modem, and is the most common way of connecting to a dial-up ISP. If your ISP is one of the rare service providers that requires you to configure your TCP/IP settings manually, you'll need to consult the specific documentation that was provided to you.

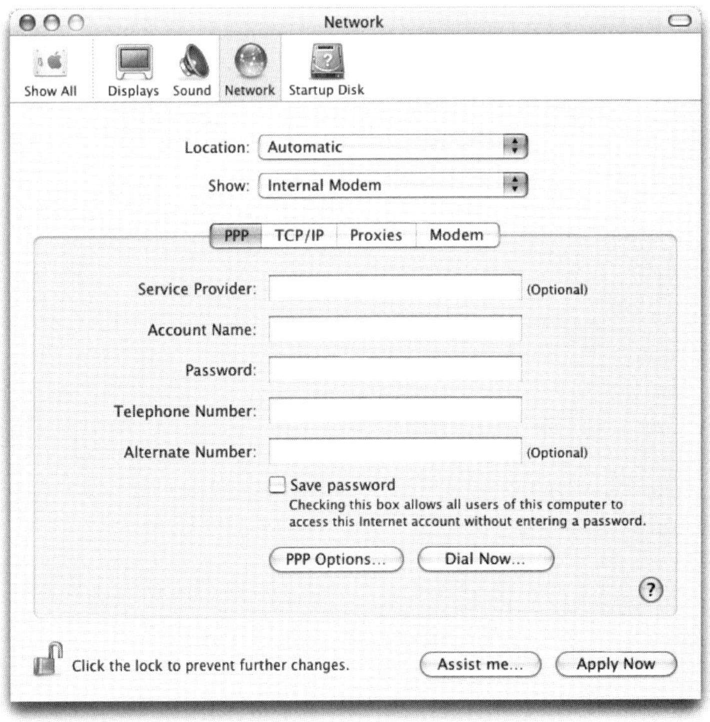

5. Click the **PPP** button. This is where you enter the information that was provided to you when you signed up with your ISP. The following chart describes the fields provided here.

PPP Settings	
Field	**Description**
Service Provider	You can type the name of your ISP in this field to remind you which service provider this information pertains to. This is an optional field, but it can be useful if you subscribe to more than one ISP. More information on setting up your Mac to access multiple ISPs appears in the "Using Multiple Locations" sidebar at the end of the chapter.
Account Name	This is the user name that you chose or was chosen for you when you subscribed to your service. For example, if your email address is **garrick@lynda.com** (it better not be!), you would type **garrick** into this field. (In some cases, you may be required to enter your entire email address into this field. Check with your ISP.)
Password	Enter the password that you created (or was created for you) here. Doing so automatically checks the **Save password** check box at the bottom of the panel. If you're concerned about other users accessing the Internet through your account, you can leave this field blank, but you'll be required to enter your password every time you want to go online.
Telephone Number	Enter the phone number that your ISP provided to you. This is the number that your modem will dial when you need to connect to the Internet. Be sure to enter all the necessary numbers here—if you're in a location where you need to dial the area code first, be sure to enter the area code (parentheses aren't necessary); if you need to dial a 9 or another number to access an outside line, type 9 followed by a comma. The comma provides a one-second pause before dialing the actual phone number, which should give the phone line enough time to access an outside line.
Alternate Number	ISPs will often provide you with more than one number to dial to connect to their services. If your ISP gave you an additional phone number, enter it here. If the number you entered in the Telephone Number field encounters a busy signal or other problem, your Mac will automatically try the Alternate Number.
Save password	This check box is automatically selected when you enter your password in the Password field. With this box checked, your Mac will automatically communicate all the necessary login information when you connect to your ISP. You won't have to type your password each time.

6. Take a moment to enter the proper information into the fields under the PPP tab.

7. Click the **PPP Options** button.

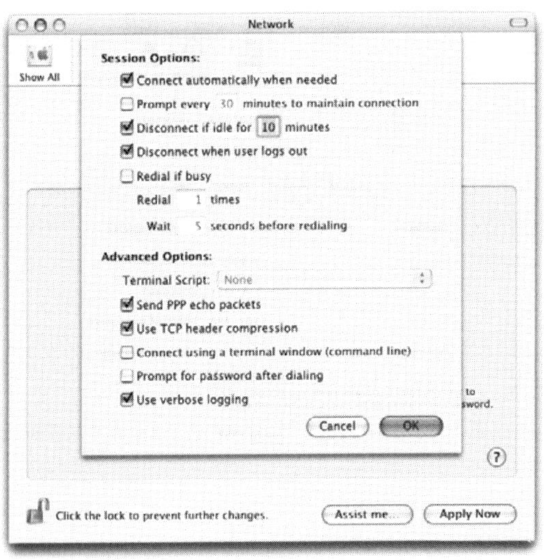

Clicking the PPP Options button will open a sheet from which you can select various options that relate to when your computer dials the ISP's number and how long it stays connected. Unless your ISP has specifically instructed you to do so, there is no need to change any of the Advanced Options, but you may want to customize some of the Session Options. Consult the following chart to find out what these different options do.

PPP Session Options	
Field	**Description**
Connect automatically when needed	Check this option if you want your Mac to automatically dial your ISP's number whenever it detects that you need to connect to the Internet. Actions you perform such as browsing for a Web page, checking your email, or setting network time will all cause your Mac to automatically dial your ISP. If you have Software Update set to automatically check for a new version of your software (as described in Chapter 4, "*System Preferences*"), your Mac will connect to the Internet anytime the Software Update check is scheduled (unless the computer is turned off). If you decided to leave this option unchecked, you'll need to use the Internet Connect program in your Applications folder every time you want to go online.
Prompt every *xx* minutes to maintain connection	With this option checked, you'll see a dialog box that periodically asks if you want to stay online. If your modem line is your only phone line, you may want to check this box to have your Mac remind you that you're still online.
Disconnect if idle for *xx* minutes	It's very easy to forget that you're connected to the Internet and go on with your non-online work, oblivious to the fact that your modem is still tying up your phone line. Check this box to have your Mac automatically close your connection if you don't perform any Internet-related tasks in *xx* number of minutes.
Disconnect when user logs out	Select this option to automatically disconnect from your ISP whenever you log out from your Mac's user account. If this box remains unchecked, other users logging on to the Mac after you've logged out will still have access to the Internet through your connection. This is not necessarily a bad thing; it just depends on how your household or office is sharing Internet access.
Redial if busy	Check this box to have your Mac retry a busy phone number. In the Redial field, enter the number of times you want your Mac to attempt a connection. In the Wait field, enter the number of seconds you want your Mac to pause before redialing (to give your phone line a chance to reset itself).

8. If necessary, customize your **Session Options** and then click **OK**.

9. Click the **Apply Now** button to activate your new settings.

You're now all set and ready to connect to the Internet.

---

10. To test your settings, first make sure that a working phone line is plugged in to your Mac's modem port. (The port has a small telephone handset symbol next to it.)

---

11. Click the **Safari** icon in the **Dock**. You should hear your Mac's modem dial. After a few seconds of modem screeching (and what a lovely sound it is), your default home page should appear. If it does, you've properly set up your Internet connection. You're now ready to surf the Web, check email, and so on. (If you've chosen not to store your password, you'll be prompted to enter it before your Internet connection is completed.)

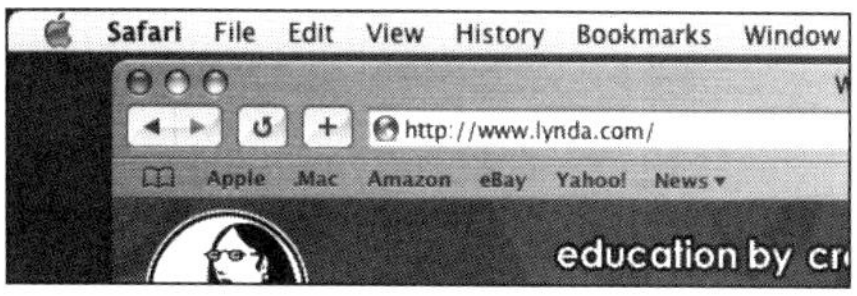

__Note:__ It's possible that you or someone else may have set up Safari to not automatically load a Web page when opened. If this is the case, type a Web address into the Address area of Safari (such as __www.lynda.com__) and press __Return__ to access the Web page. (You'll learn how to assign a home page to Safari in the next chapter.)

If for some reason your connection didn't work, go back to the __Network__ panel and double-check your settings. Remember to consult your ISP if you have specific questions regarding their service.

---

12. Quit **Safari** after testing your connection.

---

13. Quit **System Preferences**, unless you want to follow the next exercise on configuring your Mac to access the Internet through the Ethernet port.

Internet Connect

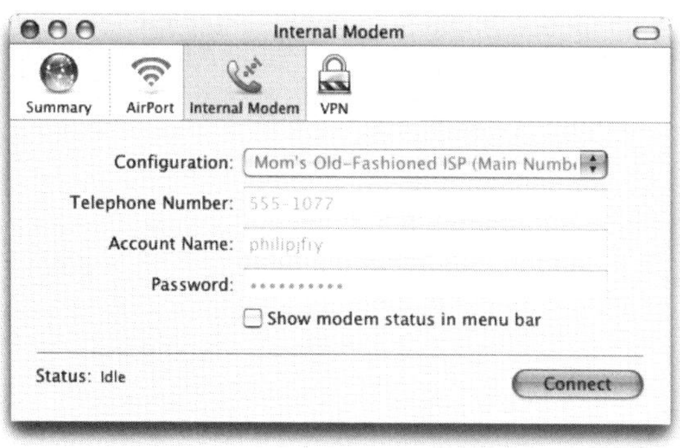

If you've chosen to not have your Mac automatically dial your ISP whenever it detects that Internet access is necessary, you'll have to use Internet Connect to manually connect. When you want to get online, open __Internet Connect__ from your __Applications__ folder. (You may want to add its icon to the __Dock__ for easier access. You can also click the new __Dial Now__ button found in the __PPP__ section of your internal modem settings in __System Preferences__.) If you haven't stored your password, enter it and then click __Connect__. Your modem will dial your ISP's number. Once connected, Internet Connect will show you the status of your connection, providing information such as how long you've been online and what your connection speed is. (Even if you're set up to automatically get online, you can always open Internet Connect to view this information as well.) When you're done, click __Disconnect__ to close the connection.

Proxies and Modem

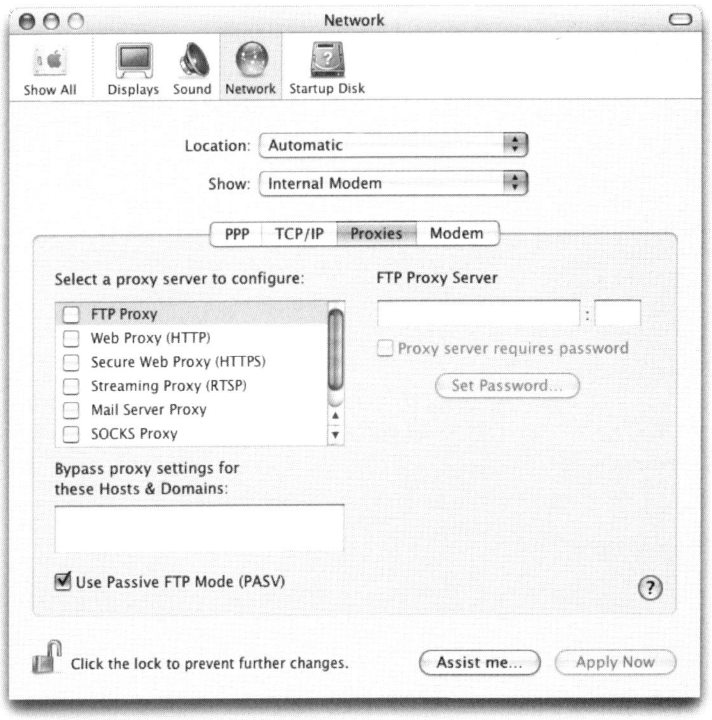

*The other two buttons that appear when you choose **Internal Modem** from the **Show** menu in your **Network** preferences are **Proxies** and **Modem**. In most cases, you'll never need to change anything under these tabs. The Proxies settings are used to configure your Mac if it's located in a workplace that uses proxy servers, which are computers that filter Internet data for content before it gets to the users. If your company does use proxy servers, it's highly unlikely that you're connecting to the Internet through a dial-up connection anyway. But if you do find yourself in a scenario where you need to use proxy settings with a dial-up connection: A) Wow; and B) Contact your network administrator to find out how you're supposed to set them.*

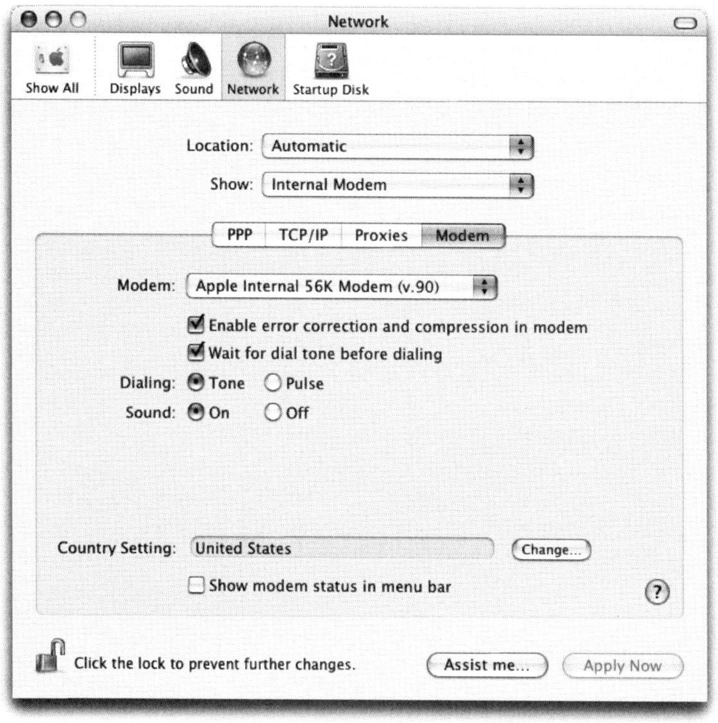

The Modem section is already set up with all the necessary information to use your Mac's built-in modem. If for some reason you've decided to replace the internal modem, you may need to configure it, but most likely the new modem will come with installation software that will handle this process for you. The only thing you might want to do in this panel is to switch the ***Sound*** *of the modem to* ***Off*** *if you're not fond of the modem's screeching sound. If you turn this sound off, however, you should check* ***Show modem status in menu bar*** *to give yourself visual feedback on whether the modem has successfully connected to your ISP.*

Dialing Modifiers

Sometimes when dialing a number from your Mac, it's necessary to give your modem special dialing instructions. For instance, it was mentioned earlier that adding a comma instructs your Mac to pause for a second before dialing the rest of the number. This can be useful if you need to dial a number to reach an outside line. You example, you might enter **9, 555-1234**. The following are some other special characters, known as **dialing modifiers**, that you might find useful when dialing an ISP or faxing from your Mac.

Modem Dialing Modifiers

Special Character	Effect
, (comma)	Adds a one-second pause. You can add more commas if you need a longer pause while dialing.
@	Wait for silence. The modem will listen for at least five seconds of silence before continuing with the number. This is useful if you have to dial an extension once the initial connection is made. For example, 5551234@5678 would cause the modem to dial 5551234, wait for the call to be answered, and then dial 5678.
&	Wait for credit card tone. The ampersand tells the modem to wait for a credit card tone before continuing with the number. This is useful if you need your Mac to automatically enter your credit card number when prompted.
W	Wait for dial tone. The modem will wait for a dial tone before dialing the numbers following the W.

Configuring a Broadband Connection

If you've decided to take the plunge and subscribe to a cable or DSL provider, congratulations! These two services are both referred to as broadband services because they provide you with access to a broader Internet bandwidth, meaning a much faster connection than a traditional modem. (Think of a dial-up connection as a garden hose and a broadband connection as a fire hose.) You're most likely paying more than a dial-up subscriber would, but you enjoy the benefit of a faster connection that, in the case of most services, is always on. Even if your service isn't constantly connected, your connection time is usually just a matter of a few seconds. You no longer have to wait for your built-in modem to dial your ISP over your phone line.

After signing up for either cable or DSL service, you should have received an external modem and an Ethernet cable. (An Ethernet cable looks a like a phone cable, but with larger connectors at either end.) Make sure you have these items before beginning the next exercise.

Tip: Your ISP may have sent you a "welcome kit" or similar package containing software that they suggest you install. For Mac OS X users, this software is usually unnecessary because OS X comes with everything you need to connect to a broadband modem. Usually the ISP's software reconfigures your Web browser to display the ISP logo and/or its home page. If you'd rather avoid having your browser settings changed, try following the steps in the exercise before you install your ISP's software. If your connection works after completing this exercise, you can safely ignore the software provided by your ISP.

NOTE | Hooking Up Your Cable Modem or DSL Modem

Your ISP should have provided you with instructions on connecting your modem to your computer, but here are the basic steps.

Cable modem service is offered by cable TV providers. If you have a cable modem, your broadband signal is provided by the same cable through which your television signal enters your home. Connect the cable from the wall to the modem they sent you. (You may have been provided with a signal splitter if you need to use a single cable to connect to both your computer and your TV.) Plug one end of your Ethernet cable into the modem and the other end into the Ethernet port on your Mac. Turn on the modem.

DSL (Digital Subscriber Line) modem service is offered by telephone companies. If you have DSL service, your broadband is provided through your phone line. Connecting to DSL through the phone line is different than accessing your ISP through your built-in modem, however, because the DSL signal travels on a different frequency than voice and standard modem signals. Because DSL does not interfere with your phone line, you can surf the Internet and talk on the phone at the same time. The DSL signal may sometimes cause interference on your phone line, but this can be easily remedied with filters that your ISP probably provided when you received your modem.

To connect your DSL modem, plug a phone line from the wall into the modem. Plug one end of your Ethernet cable into the modem and the other end into the Ethernet port on your Mac. Turn on the modem.

You're now ready to configure your Mac.

Tip: If you're still on the fence about deciding which service you want, or if you're not sure what's available in your area, check out **www.broadbandreports.com**, a site where you can enter your Zip code for a full report on available service, and where you can read reviews of broadband providers from other users in your area. (Of course, it's hard to check out a Web site if you don't have Internet service yet, so borrow some time on a friend's computer.)

2. Setting Up an Ethernet Connection

This exercise will show you how to set up your Mac to recognize and use an Internet connection through the Ethernet port. In addition to connecting to a cable modem or DSL modem, you can also use your Ethernet port to connect to your company's network or to a network router in your home or office. Both of these options will be addressed in this exercise.

1. In **System Preferences**, open **Network** preferences.

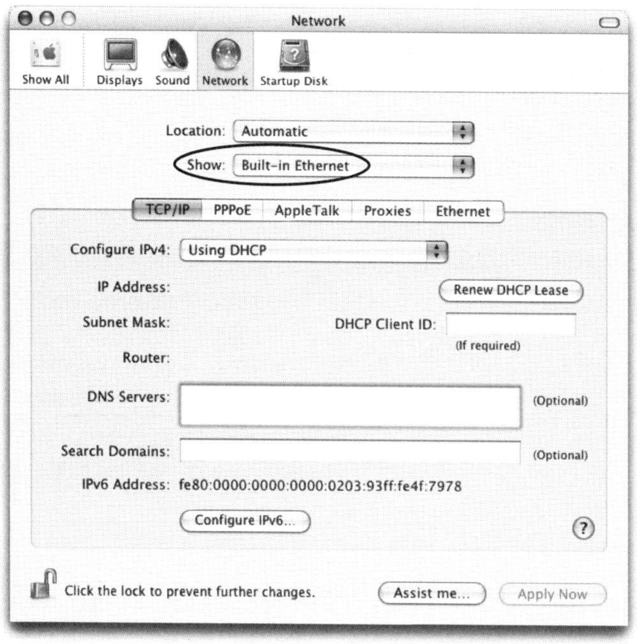

2. From the **Show** menu, choose **Built-in Ethernet** to display the settings related to your Ethernet port.

*When you connect to a broadband provider, your modem is assigned a unique Internet address referred to as an IP (**I**nternet **P**rotocol) address. Your IP address is your modem's identification number on the Internet. In most cases, your ISP is set up to dynamically assign you an IP address from a pool of available addresses every time you turn on your modem, meaning there's a chance that you won't have the same IP address each time. Sometimes, for an additional cost, you can purchase a static IP address, which can be useful if you want to use your computer as a Web server and need to have a permanent address so other users on the Internet can always find you. But in most cases, you'll be assigned a different IP each time.*

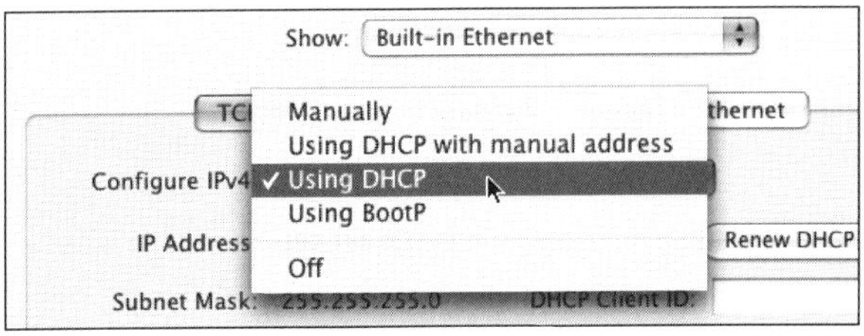

3. If necessary, click the **TCP/IP** button. From the **Configure IPv4** pop-up menu, choose **Using DHCP** to tell your Mac that your ISP will be dynamically assigning you an IP address and any other necessary network information. Click **Apply Now** to activate your changes.

Note: *If you're connecting your Mac to your company's network, you'll probably also choose DHCP. Check with your company's network person to make sure this is the case. It's possible that you may be assigned a static IP address, in which case a network specialist will most likely handle your configuration.*

If you're connected to a cable modem or to a network, in a few seconds you'll see some numbers appear next to the IP address field. Once your IP address shows up, your configuration is complete, and you're ready to surf the Net. As long as you keep your modem on, your connection to the Internet will be continuous (excepting [or should that be "accepting"?] the occasional system outage that all ISPs occasionally encounter). You'll never need to dial a number or enter a password. Your IP address may also appear if you're using a DSL modem, but in most cases you'll need to perform some additional steps.

Renewing Your IP Address

Occasionally, for any number of reasons, you may need request a new IP address from your DHCP server. For example, you may be on a network where many computers use the same DHCP server, which can occasionally cause address conflicts.

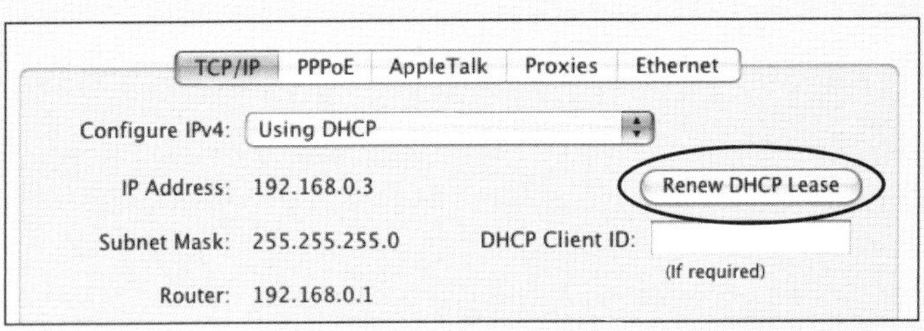

If you're having trouble connecting to your network or to the Internet, click the **Renew DHCP Lease** button (new to Panther) in the **TCP/IP** section of **Network** preferences. This forces your Mac to release its current IP and request a new one from the DHCP server.

*Cable broadband services are generally on all the time, but many DSL services require you to log onto their networks before you can connect to the Internet. The most common way of connecting with a DSL service is through a PPPoE application. PPPoE stands for **P**oint-to-**P**oint **P**rotocol **o**ver **E**thernet. Your provider may not call it by this name, but if they require you to enter a user name and password, it's most likely a PPPoE system. If this is the case, your ISP probably provided a software program to access its services. You don't need this software in OS X–use the following steps instead.*

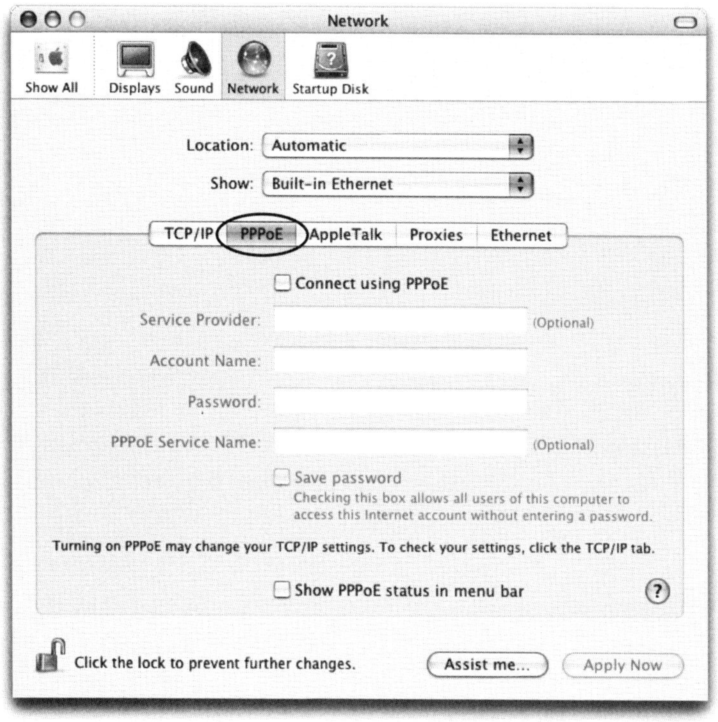

4. If you're using a DSL modem, and your IP address did not appear after following Step 3, click the **PPPoE** button.

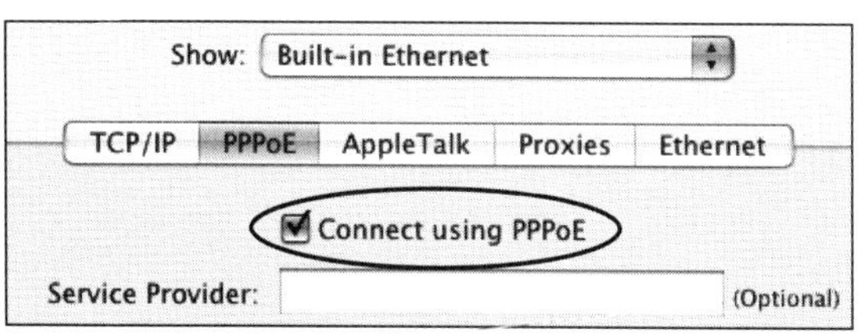

5. Check **Connect using PPPoE** to activate the fields below it.

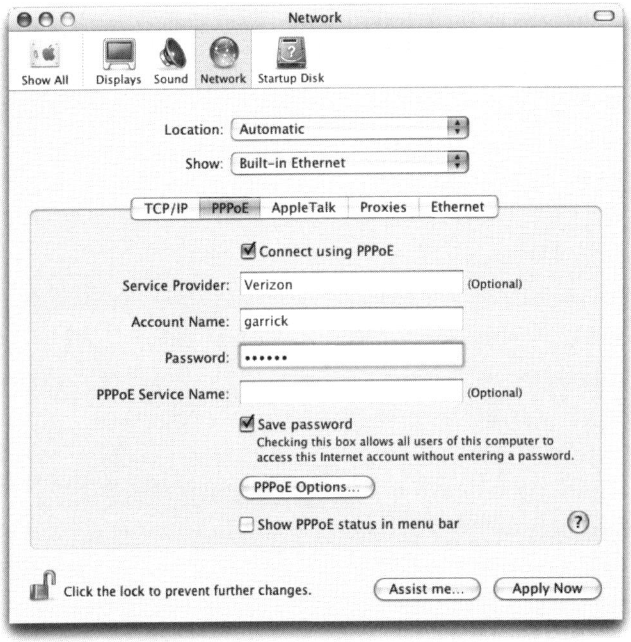

6. Enter the **Account Name** and **Password** you created (or were created for you). This is similar to the PPP setup from the preceding exercise. If you want, you can enter the **Service Provider's** name and the **PPPoE Service Name** in their respective fields, but this is unnecessary.

Tip: Much like setting up a dial-up connection, when you enter a password in the ***Password*** *field, the* ***Save password*** *check box is automatically selected. You can leave the* ***Password*** *field blank if you want to be prompted to manually type your password whenever you want to get online.*

---

7. Click **Apply Now** to activate your changes. Now whenever you need to get online, OS X will automatically use this information to log onto your DSL service. You'll never have to manually sign on (unless you chose not to include your password here).

---

8. Click the **TCP/IP** button and wait a few seconds to see if your dynamically assigned IP address appears. If it doesn't, you may have to open Safari to tell your Mac that you want to connect to the Internet.

If these steps didn't work, check the documentation that you received when you subscribed to your broadband provider. You may want to call your ISP if you have specific questions about configuring its service with OS X.

---

9. Quit **System Preferences**, unless you want to follow the next exercise on configuring your Mac to access the Internet through an AirPort card.

NOTE | Connecting Through a Router

As broadband becomes more and more popular, many people are also purchasing broadband routers, devices that allow you to share a single Internet connection with several computers.

As you saw in Exercise 2, when you connect to a cable modem or DSL modem, you're automatically assigned an IP address that becomes your computer's identity on the Internet. This IP address is referred to as a WAN (**W**ide **A**rea **N**etwork) address. When you connect a router directly to your modem in place of your computer, the router becomes the recipient of the WAN IP address. The router then assigns each computer connected to it a LAN (**L**ocal **A**rea **N**etwork) IP address, sort of a dummy IP to give each computer its own identity on your home network. One of the advantages of using a router is that you're much less vulnerable to hackers and other miscreants out there searching for computers that are constantly connected to the Internet. Neither your broadband provider nor anyone on the Internet has any way of knowing that you have a router connected instead of an actual computer, nor can they know how many computers you have hooked into the router.

If you're accessing your broadband connection through a router, follow the instructions that came with the router to set it up first. Then follow the steps in Exercise 2. (Unless you're setting up a wireless router, in which case follow Exercise 3.) The only real difference between configuring your Mac for use with a broadband modem and configuring it for use with a router is that the router will be assigning your Mac the dynamic IP address instead of your ISP.

You can buy routers in just about any electronics store that sells computers. These days most routers cost around $30 to $60, depending on how many available ports you want and the speed of the router. If you want a router with wireless capability (as described in the next exercise), you'll pay a little more. If paying money's not your thing, but you want to share an Internet connection with other computers in your workplace, Panther comes with a free built-in Internet sharing solution. Exercise 4 will tell you more about this great feature.

3. Configuring a Wireless Connection

One of the hottest Web and network-related technologies today is wireless networking, often called WiFi (short for **Wi**reless **Fi**delity). Apple calls its version of this technology AirPort. For the past several years, all Macs have been manufactured "AirPort ready." With the addition of a small card to your Mac, you can have wireless Internet and network access (if a wireless signal is within range). Going wireless offers the advantage of being able to connect multiple computers to the Internet and to each other without having to string Ethernet cables all over your home or office. And if you use a PowerBook or iBook, you'll enjoy the freedom of being completely untethered to cables. There's nothing quite like surfing the Net at high speeds from your porch, kitchen, or bed.

So where do these wireless signals originate? Normally the signal is transmitted by a wireless router, which is usually nothing more than a regular router with wireless capability. A wireless router is sometimes referred to as the base station. Apple manufactures an AirPort base station for use with AirPort cards, but the cards themselves are compatible with just about any base station on the market.

The Flavors of Wireless (Lots of Numbers Coming Up!)

Okay, so AirPort cards aren't really compatible with all base stations. The technical name for WiFi, and therefore AirPort, is 802.11b, which was the first and is still the most common wireless technology today. There are currently at least two competing technologies on the market: 802.11a and 802.11g. 802.11g has a faster transmission rate than 802.11b (WiFi), but it also transmits on the same frequency as WiFi (2.4 GHz, if you really must know) so it's compatible with AirPort cards. In fact, in January 2003, Apple announced AirPort Extreme, its new generation of AirPort base stations and cards that run on 802.11g and are compatible with older AirPort 802.11b devices. 802.11a on the other hand (don't you wish they all had nicknames like WiFi?) transmits between the 5 and 6 GHz range and is not compatible with AirPort (WiFi) and AirPort Extreme devices. Why does any of this matter to you? If you ever go shopping for a wireless router for your home network, make sure that you're buying either an 802.11b or 802.11g router if you want to use your Mac's AirPort or AirPort Extreme card.

This exercise will show you how to configure your Mac to access a wireless network. Of course, this requires that you've purchased and installed an Apple AirPort card and that you're within the range of a compatible wireless signal. Make sure to confirm these points before continuing with this exercise.

1. In **System Preferences**, open **Network** preferences.

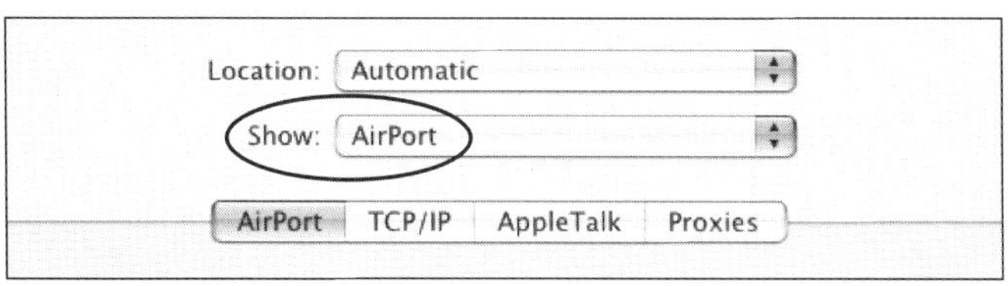

2. From the **Show** pop-up menu, choose **AirPort**. You won't see this option unless you have an AirPort card installed.

From this point, setting up an AirPort card is a lot like setting up an Ethernet connection to a network. In many cases, you'll be picking up a signal from a router that will dynamically assign you an IP address.

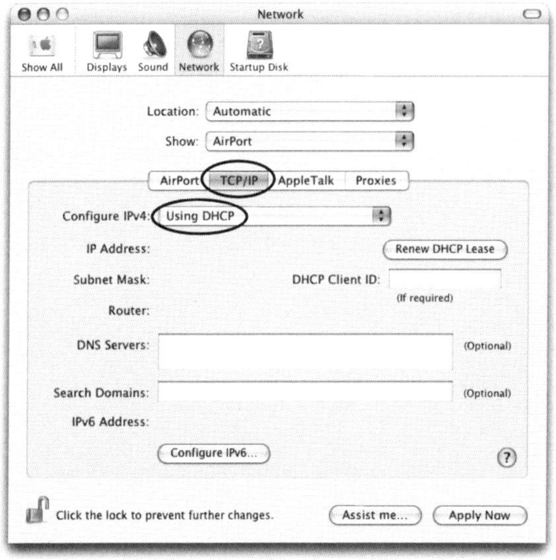

3. Click the **TCP/IP** button, choose **Using DHCP** from the **Configure IPv4** menu, and click **Apply Now**.

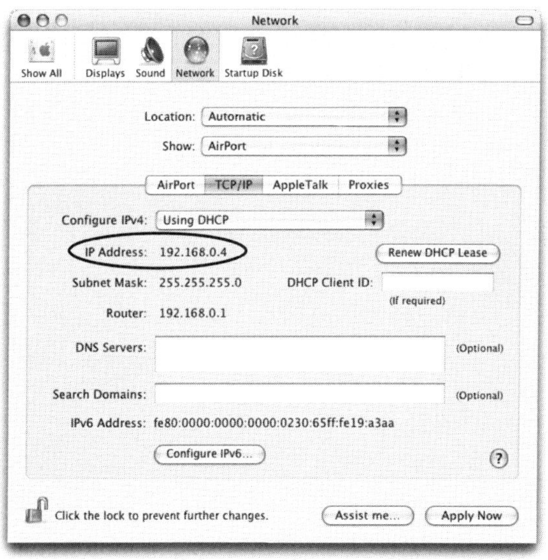

After a moment, you should see your IP address appear. This tells you that you have made a successful connection.

If you don't see an IP address appear, you're either out of range or you need to indicate to OS X which WiFi network you wish to join.

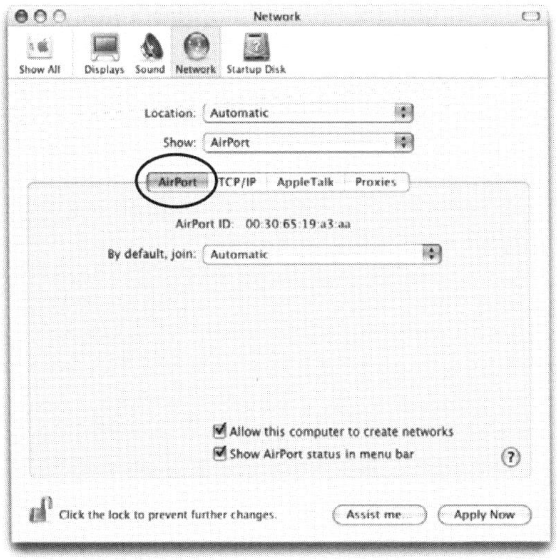

4. If your IP address didn't appear, click the **AirPort** button.

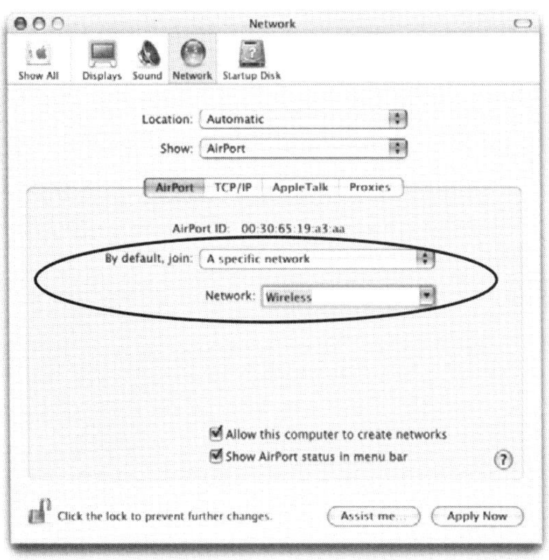

5. From the **By default, join** menu, choose **A specific network**. Your wireless network's name should appear in the **Network** menu. If there's more than one network available, select the one you want to join. If the network has been password protected, enter the **Password** in the provided field. Click **Apply Now** to activate your settings.

6. Click the **TCP/IP** tab. After a few seconds, your assigned IP address will appear.

7. Test your connection by opening **Safari** and visiting a Web site. If the Web site appears, you've successfully joined your wireless network.

***Note:** If you have both Ethernet and AirPort access available to your Mac, you might want to unplug your Ethernet cable from the Mac while testing the AirPort connection just to make sure that you're really receiving your Internet data through the AirPort card.*

8. Quit **Safari** when you're done testing your connection.

***Tip:** If you often find yourself traveling with your PowerBook or iBook, make sure to check **Show AirPort status in menu bar** if it's not already selected.*

*This option places an AirPort icon in your menu bar that shows the strength of the signal you're receiving. You can also click this icon to open a menu that displays all wireless signals within range. You can select a wireless network from this menu instead of opening System Preferences. Additionally, you can choose **Turn AirPort Off** from this menu when you're not using your card, which can save on the battery life of a PowerBook or iBook.*

9. Once you've configured your AirPort settings to your liking, quit **System Preferences**.

The AirPort Setup Assistant

If you're finding AirPort card configuration to be a bit baffling (or if you're like me and are just plain lazy), you always have the option of using the **AirPort Setup Assistant** utility.

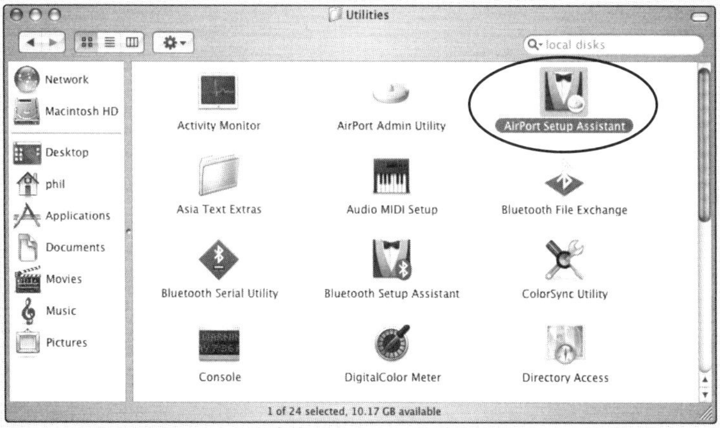

This handy item is found in the **Utilities** folder in your **Applications** folder, and walks you through the process of setting up your AirPort card.

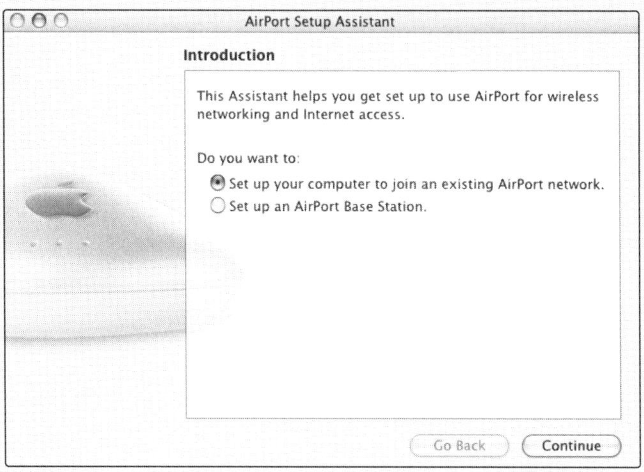

Double-click the **AirPort Setup Assistant** icon to start it, and then select **Set up your computer to join an existing AirPort network**. Click **Continue** and the Assistant will walk you through the remaining steps of configuring your AirPort connection. Once the wizard is completed, you can still go into the **Network** panel to customize your connection settings if you wish.

4. Sharing Your Internet Connection

The ability to share a single Internet connection among computers is a feature that was introduced in Mac OS 9, but then disappeared in the initial releases of OS X. Thankfully, this fantastic feature returned in OS X 10.2. Being able to share a single Internet connection is a big deal for homes and offices with multiple computers. Previously, in order to share an Internet connection in OS X, you had to purchase an Apple AirPort base station or similar network router. Panther, however, allows you to use one of your Macs as a base station, eliminating the need for a separate external routing device. For example, if your main Mac is connected to a broadband modem through its Ethernet port, you can broadcast the Internet signal through an installed AirPort card. Any other Macs with AirPort cards can then share the Internet connection.

To proceed with this exercise, make sure you have a Mac connected to the Internet through its Ethernet port. Because this Mac is going to act as a base station, it also needs to have an AirPort card installed. (Although it's possible to share a dial-up connection as well, you won't want to because dial-up connections are slow enough as it is without two or more computers sharing the connection. But if you get paid to sit there and stare at a computer screen, waiting for Web pages to load, go for it.)

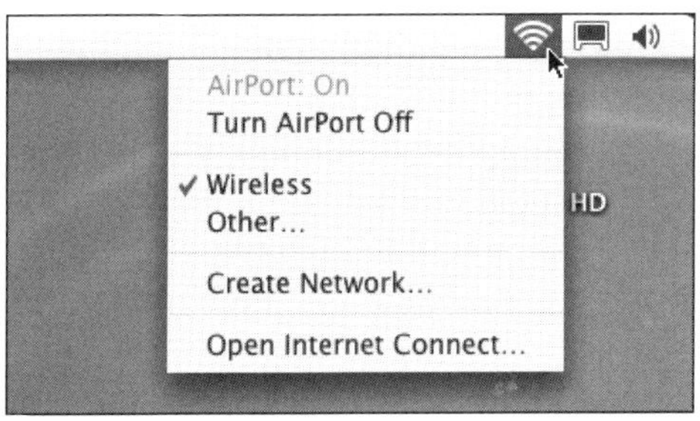

1. Make sure your AirPort card is on by clicking its icon in the **Dock**. If you see the option to **Turn Airport Off**, the card is on.

2. Open **System Preferences** and click the **Sharing** icon to open **Sharing** preferences.

3. Click the **Internet** button.

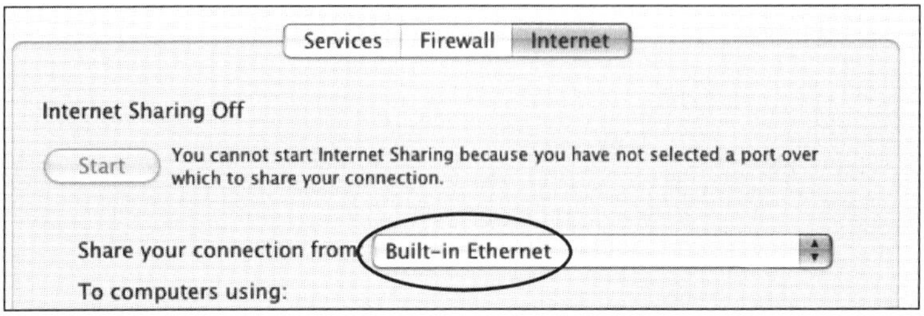

4. From the **Share your connection from** menu, choose **Built-in Ethernet**. This tells your Mac that you want to share the Internet access you're currently receiving over your Ethernet port. Now you have to tell your Mac which port to share this signal over.

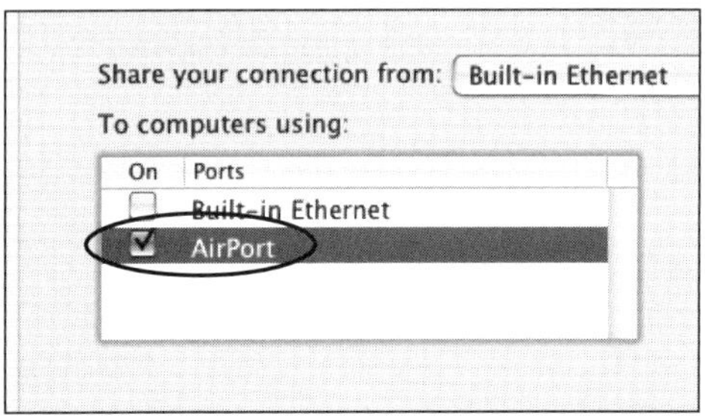

5. Under the **To computers using** section, check **AirPort** to send your Internet access out over your wireless card. This essentially turns your Mac into a miniature radio station, broadcasting your signal to nearby computers.

Note: *Do NOT check Built-in Ethernet. Because your Internet connection is coming in from your Ethernet port, you cannot share your connection through that same port. Selecting this option will create a paradox in the space-time continuum and possibly destroy the universe. Okay, probably not, but you'll definitely see this:*

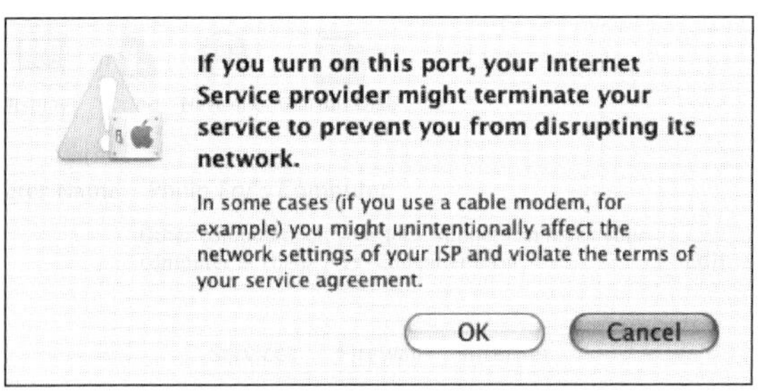

So make sure that AirPort is selected.

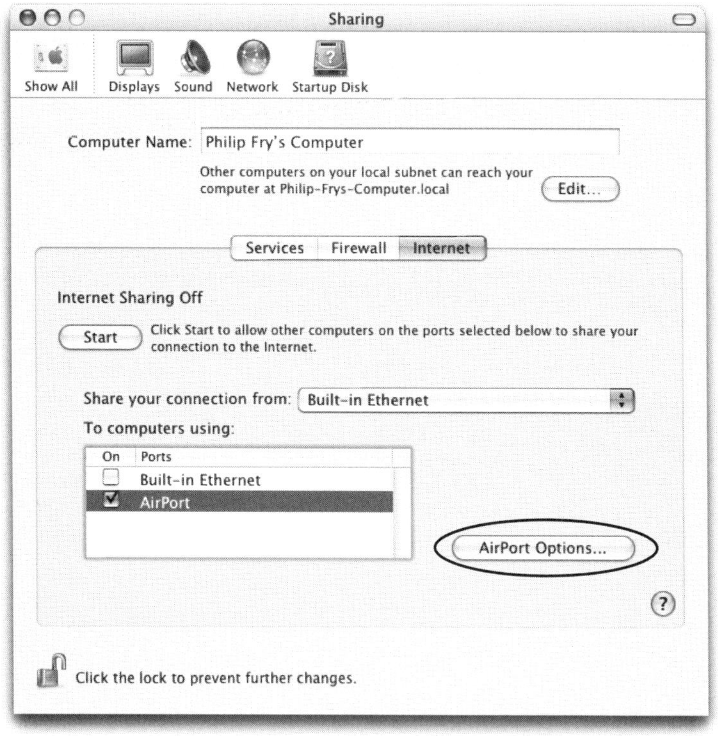

6. Click the **AirPort Options** button.

7. In the **AirPort Options** sheet, give your network a unique name so other users will be able to recognize it. If you wish, you can check **Enable encryption (using WEP)** and then create a password so only authorized users will be able to join your network.

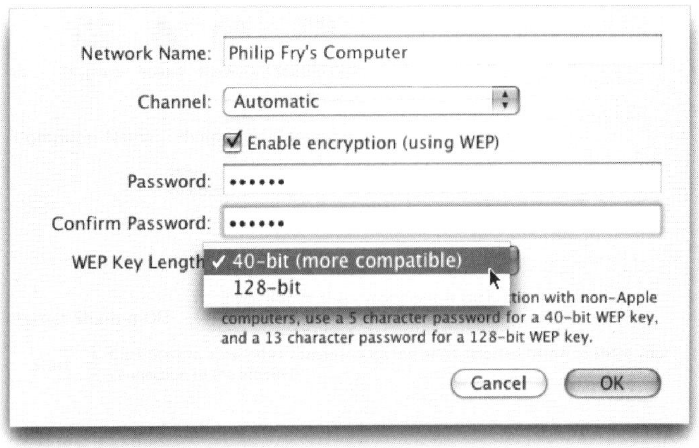

*If you do choose to use encryption, choose a **WEP Key Length** from the pop-up menu. 128-bit encryption is more secure than 40-bit, but can only be accessed by 128-bit compatible cards. 40-bit encryption is less secure, but both 128-bit and 40-bit cards can access 40-bit encrypted networks.*

WEP Encryption

WEP (**W**ired **E**quivalent **P**rivacy) encryption is a method of securing data that's transmitted over wireless networks. In a wired network, security is maintained through the physical Ethernet cables. But because wireless signals are transmitted through the air, technically anyone using a computer with a wireless card could access your data. With WEP, data is encrypted at the point of transmission (your base station or Mac that's acting as a base station) and then decrypted by the receiving device. Only users with the proper password will be able to access this encrypted information. WEP provides the same level of security to wireless networks as Ethernet cables provide to wired networks (hence the name "Wired Equivalent Privacy").

8. Once you've configured your AirPort options, click **OK** to return to the **Sharing** control panel.

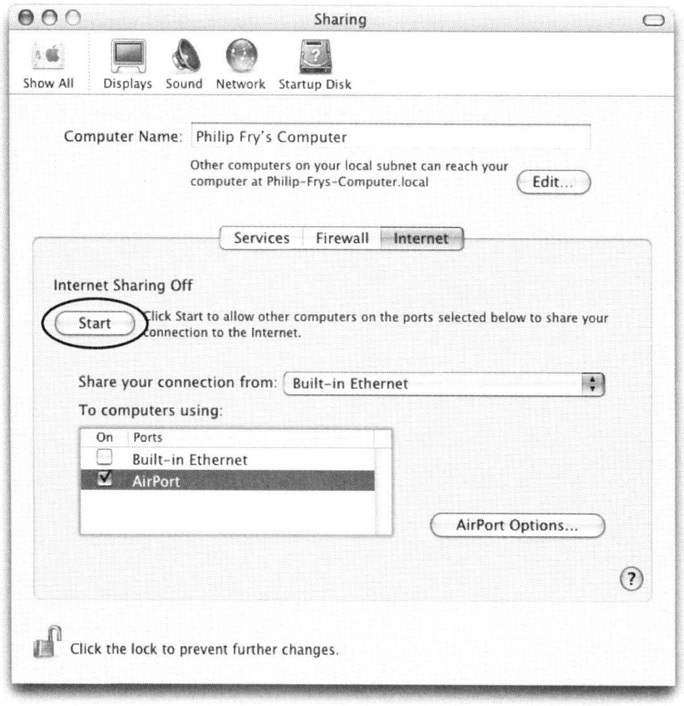

9. Click the **Start** button to begin sharing your Internet connection over AirPort. A sheet will descend asking if you're sure that you want to turn on Internet sharing. Click **Start**.

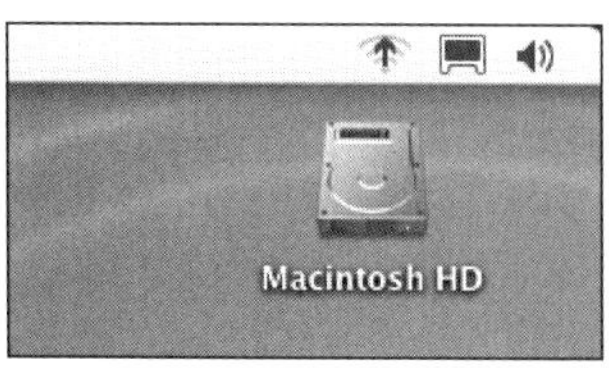

An arrow appears in the AirPort menu bar icon, indicating that you're now sharing your Internet connection.

You can now configure any other Macs within range by using the steps from Exercise 3 to join your new network. All Macs connected to your network will have access to the Internet as long as your base station Mac stays on. If your Mac is set to go to sleep after a certain period of time, you may want to open the ***Energy Saver*** *preferences to turn sleep off. If your Mac goes to sleep while sharing your Internet connection, any connected computers will lose their Internet access, and you'll have to restart Internet sharing after waking up your Mac.*

Note: *You're not limited to just sharing your Internet connection with Macs. Any PC with a wireless card will also be able to join your network.*

10. Quit **System Preferences**. If you ever want to stop broadcasting your signal, return to **Sharing** and click **Stop**.

Note: *You'll learn more about sharing data between computers in Chapter 18,* "Creating a Network."

Sharing the Other Way Around

In this exercise, you learned how to take an Internet signal that enters your Mac through the Ethernet port and then transmit it over your AirPort card. You can also share in the other direction–that is, you can take an Internet signal that originates from your AirPort card and send the signal to another computer from your Ethernet port. For example, imagine you're connected to the Internet through your Mac's AirPort card, but the computer at the desk next to you lacks an AirPort card and therefore can't connect to the Internet. If you run an Ethernet cable from the Mac with the AirPort card to the Mac without the card, you can share the Internet connection over the cable.

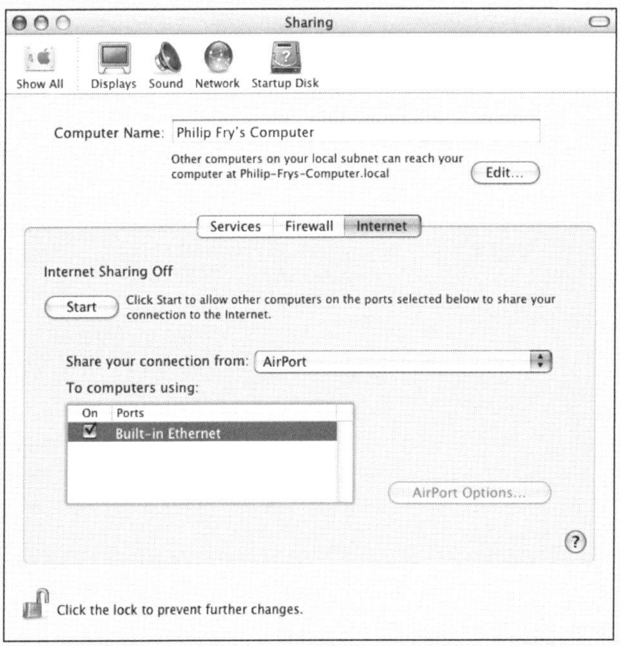

In the **Sharing** control panel, choose **AirPort** from the **Share your connection from** menu, and check **Built-in Ethernet** under **To computers using**. Of course, the downside to this is that you have only one Ethernet port and can therefore only share your connection with one computer. Sharing your connection with additional computers would require the purchase of an Ethernet hub, a device that contains multiple Ethernet jacks.

Using Multiple Locations

You might have noticed a pop-up menu called **Location** at the top of Network preferences.

If you have a desktop Mac or don't intend to carry your Mac around with you, you'll probably never have to touch this menu. For PowerBook and iBook users, however, the Location menu can be extremely convenient if you often have to change your network settings to get online from different places. For instance, you might have your Mac set up to connect through a router at home that dynamically assigns you an IP address, but when you go to the office and want to connect to your company's network, you need to manually create an IP address. Because you can have only one configuration setting for each port at once, the solution is to create an additional location.

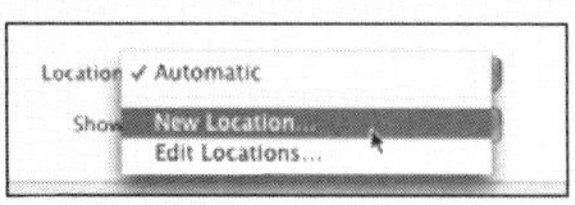

To do so, simply click the **Location** menu and choose **New Location**.

You'll be prompted to name your new location. Once you've given it a name and clicked **OK**, you'll be able to customize your settings for this location. For instance, you can configure your AirPort card to look for a specific network, different from the one you may use at home. Or if you travel a lot, you can create a location for each city you visit and enter a local dial-up number for your Internal modem in each location. You can make as many changes as you like to each location without worrying about messing up the settings used in other locations. Once you have your locations configured, all you have to do is switch back and forth between them as you move around.

By this point, you should be able to get online with your Mac. In the following chapters, you'll learn how to use OS X's included applications to surf the Web, write and receive email, and chat with friends.

9. Safari

| Safari Basics | New Window and Tabbed Browsing |
| Adding Bookmarks | The Bookmarks Library |
| Google Searching and SnapBack |

no exercise files

Mac OS X Panther H•O•T CD-ROM

The Internet offers many services: e-mail, newsgroups, and file-sharing, to name just a few. But to most people, the Internet means the Web. When someone tells you to go online and check out his or her Web page, you do so by firing up a Web browser. When you want to order new contact lenses or download some music, you will most likely do so from a Web browser. And when you're sitting at your desk, pretending to do work, you're most likely wasting time with your Web browser.

In June 2003, Apple released its own Web browser, called **Safari**, which was created and designed exclusively for OS X. Safari features elegantly simple windows that provide the maximum amount of space to the Web page itself (rather than to buttons and navigation panes). Safari also loads Web pages faster than any other OS X browser. This means less time sitting around waiting for pages to load and more time actually spent surfing.

If you're like most people, you probably know the basics of using a browser–you know how to click links to go from one page to another and how to use the Back and Forward buttons to navigate through pages you've already viewed. This chapter focuses more on the specific features of Safari that make surfing the Web an easier and more pleasant experience. You'll learn how to show and hide various interface elements of the Safari window and discover several ways to store the addresses of your favorite pages so you can access them more easily. You'll also practice "tabbed-browsing" to keep your window clutter to a minimum and learn a variety of tips and tricks involving Safari's built-in Google search bar. All this and more awaits you in this chapter, so get surfing!

Safari and Internet Explorer

Prior to Safari's release, OS X's default Web browser was Microsoft's Internet Explorer, the Mac version of the software giant's Windows/world-dominating browser. Many Mac users were happy and satisfied with Explorer, but people who used both Macs and Windows machines noticed that the Windows version of Explorer tended to load pages faster than its Mac counterpart. With Safari, Apple created its own browser software that has improved performance and features over Internet Explorer.

Although Internet Explorer is still installed as part of Panther's Applications folder, Safari is now the default browser of OS X. As a result, Microsoft announced in June 2003 that they were discontinuing development of Internet Explorer for the Mac. Although Microsoft will continue to support Explorer, future updates to the browser (if any) will contain primarily maintenance or security fixes, but no new features.

You might be tempted to throw Explorer away, but it's still a good idea to keep it in your Applications folder. Safari is a relatively young browser, and although it works fine with the majority of pages you'll encounter, you may occasionally run into a site that just doesn't display correctly. In such an event, it's handy to have an alternate browser available to help you view the troublesome page.

Alternative Browsers

Although Safari and Explorer both come with OS 10.3, there are several other browsers available for Mac OS X. But why would you want additional browsers on your Mac? An important point to keep in mind is that browsers display an interpretation of a Web page. That is, when you browse to a Web page, the browser reads the code that makes up the page and then visually presents the information. Each browser interprets code a little differently, so the same Web page might look slightly different in each browser. Some sites look better when viewed in certain browsers than when viewed in others. As I just mentioned, it's nice to have an alternative browser available in case you encounter a Web site that just doesn't look right in Safari or Explorer. More importantly, many commerce and secure (encrypted) sites don't always work in different browsers. Having an alternative browser ensures that you'll be able to access the information you need. The following chart lists some OS X–compatible browsers and the sites where you can download them.

OS X Web Browsers

Browser	Web Site
Netscape	**www.netscape.com** (click the **Browser Central** link under the **Tools** heading)
OmniWeb	**www.omnigroup.com/applications/omniweb**
Opera	**www.opera.com**
Mozilla	**www.mozilla.org/**

I. Safari Basics

This exercise covers the basics of surfing the Web while introducing you to Safari's interface and showing you how to customize its appearance to suit your needs.

Note: Make sure you have an active connection to the Internet before beginning these exercises. Also, due to the ever-changing nature of the Web, some of the sites you visit may look different than in the screen shots shown in this chapter, but this shouldn't prevent you from completing the exercises.

1. Open **Safari** by clicking its icon in the **Dock** or in your **Applications** folder.

Safari opens and displays its default home page. Although a home page can be a convenient way to view a page without having to type an address into the browser, it can also be a nuisance to have the browser start downloading a page that you might not necessarily want to view, especially if you're on a dial-up connection. Plus, the default home page (usually ***www.apple.com*** *or some Apple-related site) is probably not the page you want to see every time you start Safari.*

The first thing you'll do is decide whether you want to keep the current home page or have a different page of your own choosing appear whenever you open Safari or a new browser window. (Or, you might prefer to have no page load at all.)

2. Choose **Safari > Preferences** from the menu bar. Click the **General** button if it's not already selected.

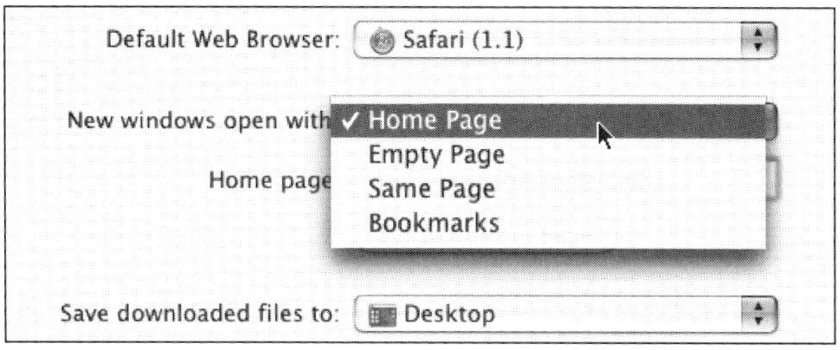

*From the **New windows open with** menu, you can select what appears whenever you open a new browser window (or Safari itself). The following chart describes these choices.*

Safari New Window Options	
Option	**Description**
Home Page	With this option selected, every time you open a new browser window, Safari automatically loads the page whose address appears in the **Home page** field below the **New windows open with** menu. You can click **Set to Current Page** to place the address of the currently displayed page into this field.
Empty Page	With this option selected, new browser windows open but don't automatically load a page. This option is useful if you constantly open new windows and don't want the annoyance of a particular page always appearing.
Same Page	This option opens the current page in the new window, giving you two copies of the same Web page in separate windows.
Bookmarks	Opening a new browser window displays your saved bookmarks. Bookmarks are covered starting in Exercise 3.

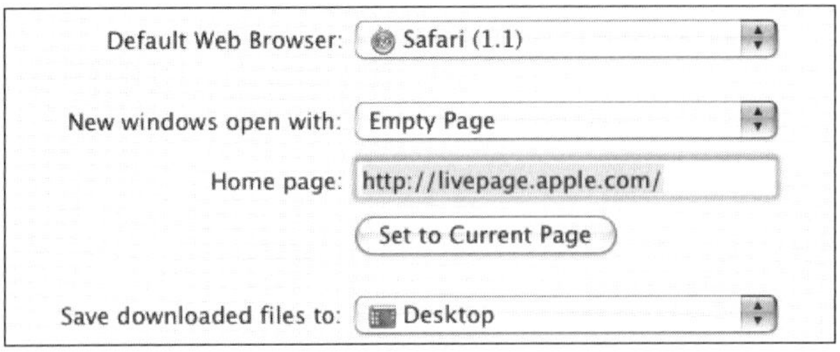

3. For this exercise, choose **Empty Page** from the **New windows open with** menu. If you want, you can select a different option after completing this chapter. Close the **Preferences** window.

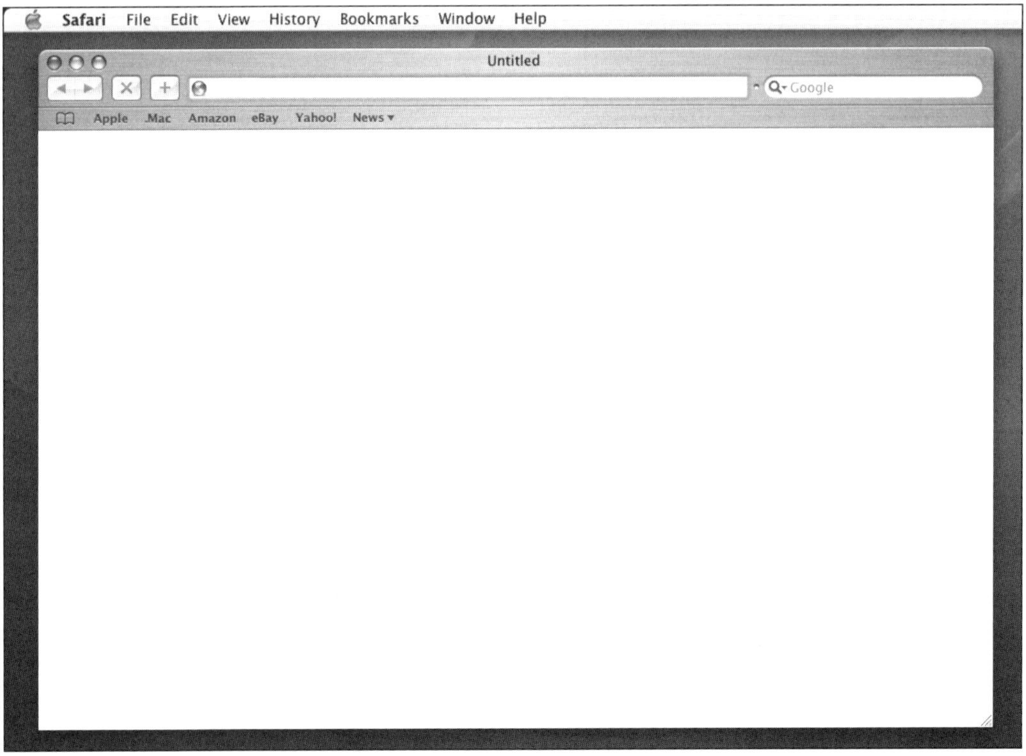

4. Close your current Safari window and open a new one (**File > New Window** or **Cmd+N**). Notice that it remains blank and doesn't load a Web page. (If you or other people have previously customized Safari, the window you see on your screen may not exactly match the one shown here. Don't worry, you'll still be able to follow along with this exercise.)

Next, you'll visit a Web page and click a few links to see how Safari handles them.

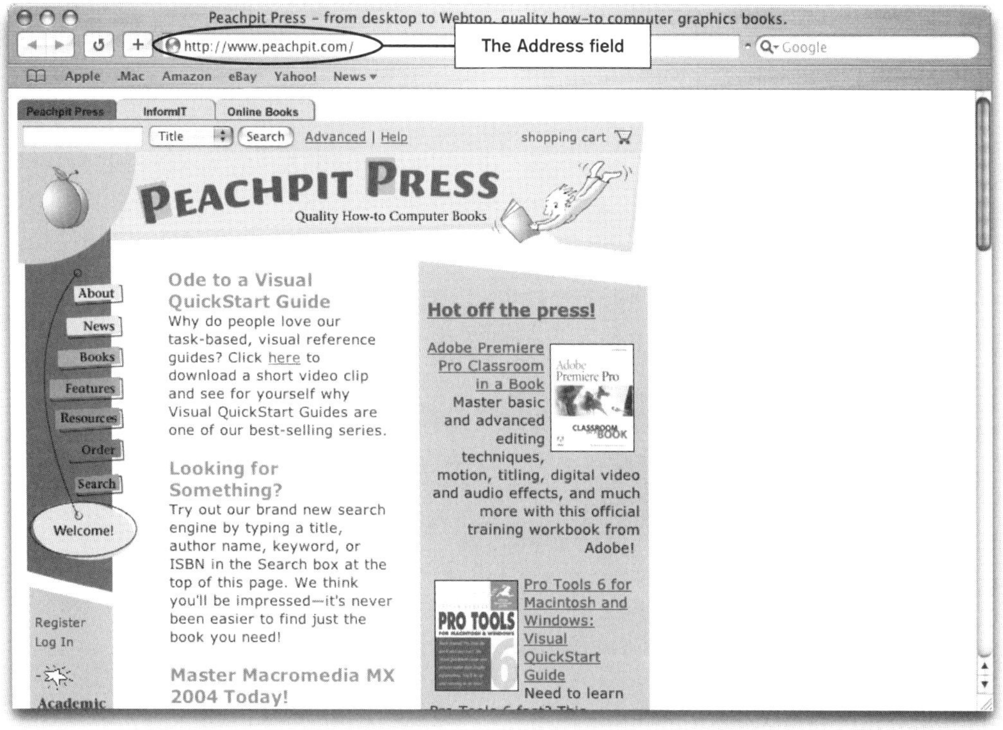

5. In the **Address** field, type **www.peachpit.com** and press **Return**. Peachpit Press's Web site loads into your Safari window.

NOTE | www and .com Not Necessarily Necessary

If the Web site you want to visit ends with **.com**, such as **www.lynda.com**, **www.peachpit.com**, and so on, you don't need to type the **www** or the **.com**. Just type **lynda** or **peachpit**. Safari assumes that these addresses end with **.com** and will place it in the address for you automatically. However, if the site's address ends with anything other than **.com** such as **.net**, **.org**, or **.edu**, you'll have to type that information as well.

6. On Peachpit's main page, roll your mouse cursor over the tab labeled **InformIT** at the top of the page. Your mouse turns into a pointing finger, indicating that you're hovering over a link. Click this link.

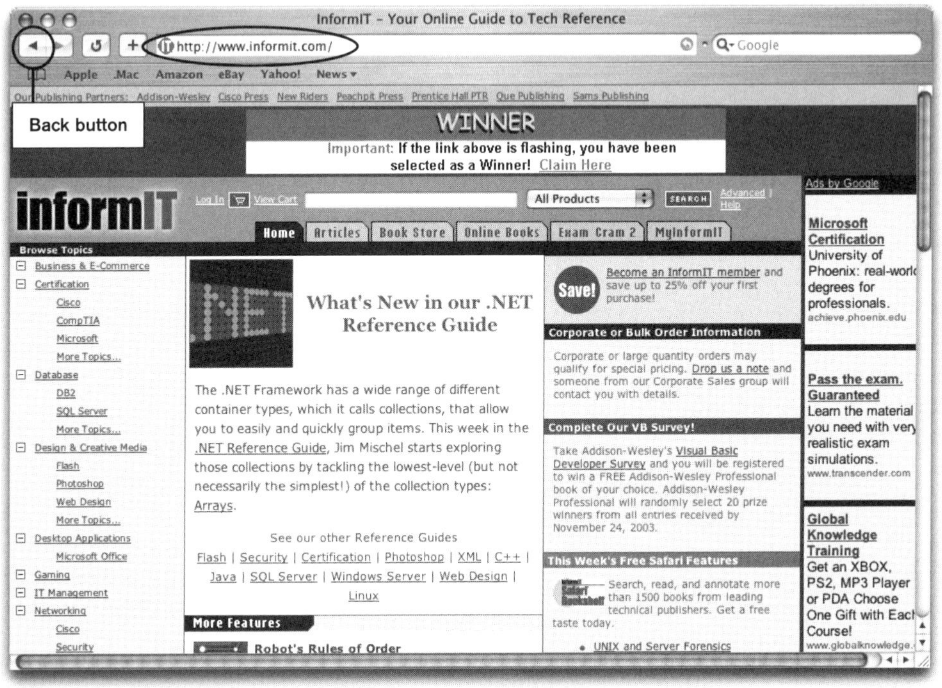

7. You are now viewing the page at **www.informit.com**. Click the **Back** button to return to **www.peachpit.com**.

NOTE | The Progress Bar

You might have noticed a blue bar growing in the Address field when you clicked the links in this exercise. This bar indicates the progress of the page as it's loading. When the bar disappears or reaches the end of the address, the page has fully loaded.

Although everyone occasionally blindly clicks links without regard to where the links are taking them, sometimes it's nice to know where you're going before you click a link. By turning on Safari's status bar, you can get instant feedback on a link's destination, as well as additional information about the page you're viewing. You'll do this next.

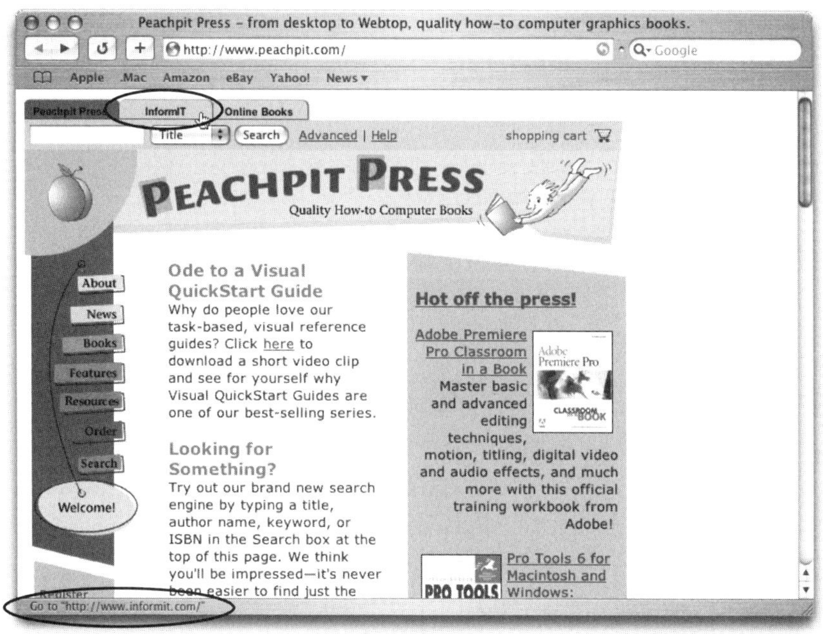

8. From the menu bar, choose **View > Status Bar** (if there's not already a checkmark next to it). This adds a small bar at the bottom of your browser window. Roll your mouse over some links on the Peachpit page and notice that the addresses of the links appear in the status bar. Now you'll always know where a link is taking you before you click it.

9. Keep Safari open for the next exercise.

TIP | The Pop-Up Blocker

Perhaps one of the most appreciated features of Safari is its built-in Pop-Up blocker. If you've spent any time at all on the Web, you're probably all too familiar with the annoying windows that pop up over and under the Web pages you're trying to view. Sometime these windows contain important information, but most of the time, they're occupied by advertisements. Safari allows you to ban irritating pop-up windows from your browsing experience with a single click. Simply choose **Safari > Block Pop-Up Windows** from the menu bar and say goodbye to unwanted advertisements.

Safari's pop-up blocker works so well that you may forget that pop-up windows even exist. But sometimes it works too well. Many sites these days post warnings on their main pages stating that you may miss information if your browser employs a pop-up blocker, but if you ever come across a Web site that doesn't seem to be working properly (for instance, if you're clicking a link that doesn't seem to be doing anything), try turning off Safari's pop-up blocker.

TIP | Increasing Text Size

It seems like Web designers these days are making the text on their pages smaller and smaller. Fortunately, Safari offers you a way to increase the size of text, making it easier to read. Simply hold the **Cmd** key and press the **+** key to enlarge the text or the **–** key to decrease the text.

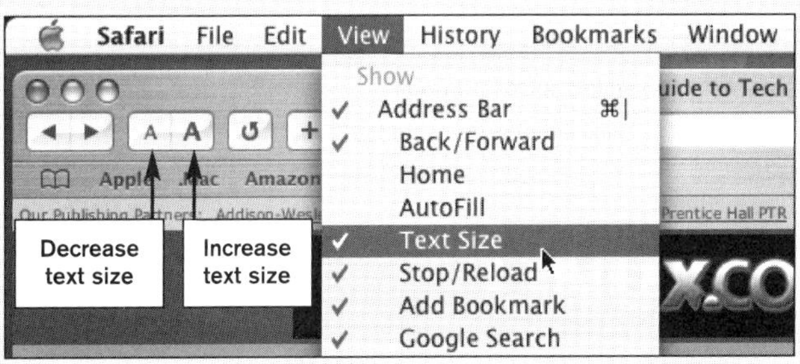

You can also choose **View > Text Size** from the menu bar to add two buttons to the Safari toolbar that you can then click to adjust the size of text. Bear in mind that this affects only real text, not text found in images.

2. New Window and Tabbed Browsing

In this exercise, you'll look at two alternate ways of working with links in a Web page. In most cases, clicking links results in a new page appearing in the current browser window, replacing the page where you clicked the link. Generally, this behavior is fine for most browsing, but there will be times when you'll find it convenient to open a linked page in a new window, keeping the initial page open in its original window. You'll look at two methods of accomplishing this.

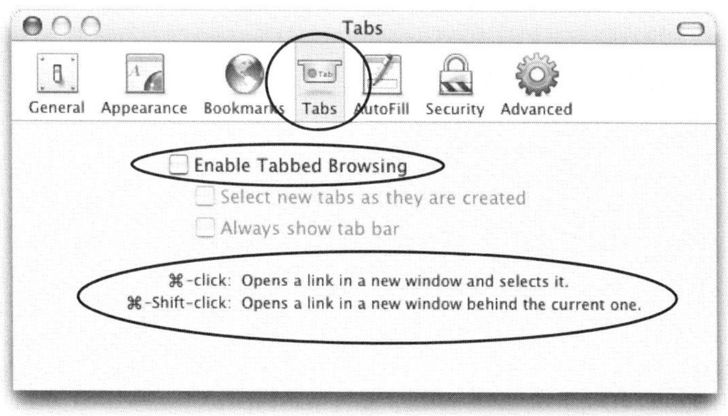

1. From the Safari menu bar, choose **Safari > Preferences** and click the **Tabs** button. Make sure **Enable Tabbed Browsing** is unchecked for now. Notice the information at the bottom of this window indicating what will happen if you **Cmd+click** or **Shift+Cmd+click** links. You'll explore these two keyboard commands next. Close the **Tabs** preferences window.

2. In a Safari window, go to **lynda.com**.

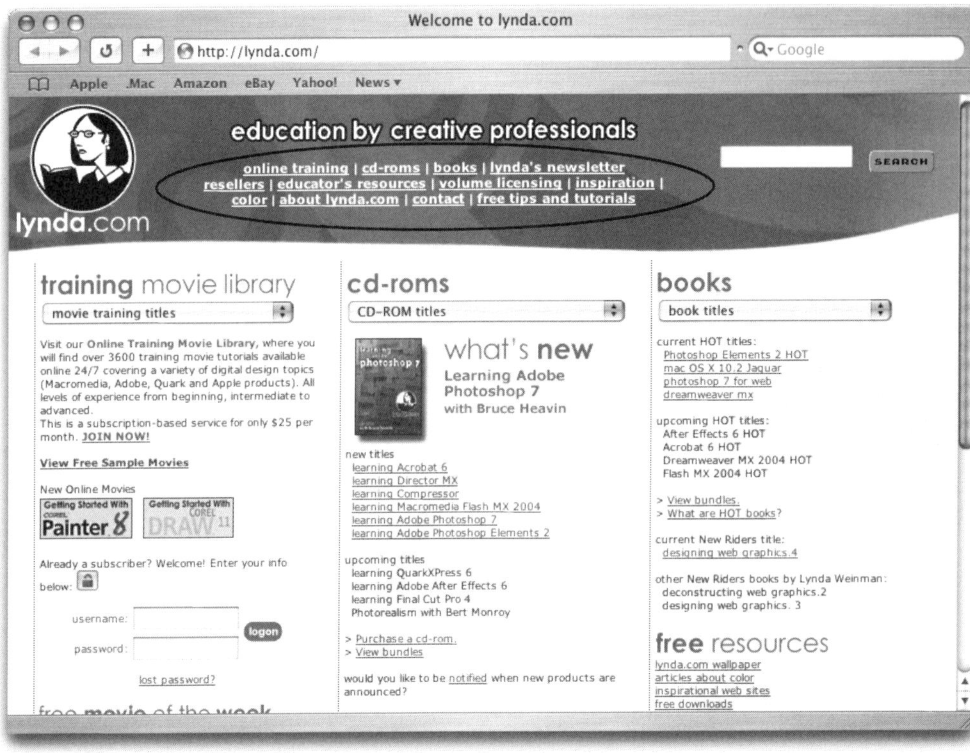

The top of this page contains links leading to several different sections of this Web site. For this exercise, assume you're interested in checking out the ***CD-ROMs*** *and* ***books*** *pages.*

---

3. Click the **cd-roms** link. You're taken to **http://lynda.com/products/videos**. Click one of the titles shown here to go to that product's page. Now you'll return to the first page. Click the **Back** button twice to return to the main lynda.com page.

---

4. Now click the **books** link. Again, you're taken to the appropriate page. Click a book cover to view its page and then click the **Back** button twice to return to the main page.

If you were really interested in the books, videos, and other products found here, you'd most likely spend some time in each section browsing through items. Clicking the Back button over and over again to return to the main navigation area would begin to get tedious, plus, because you are limited to viewing one page at a time, you might forget which products you were interested in exploring.

Next, you'll follow the same links you just clicked in the previous steps, but you'll have them open in new windows. Opening links in new windows is a great way to keep track of pages you want to look at without having to click the Back button each time you want to look at a different page.

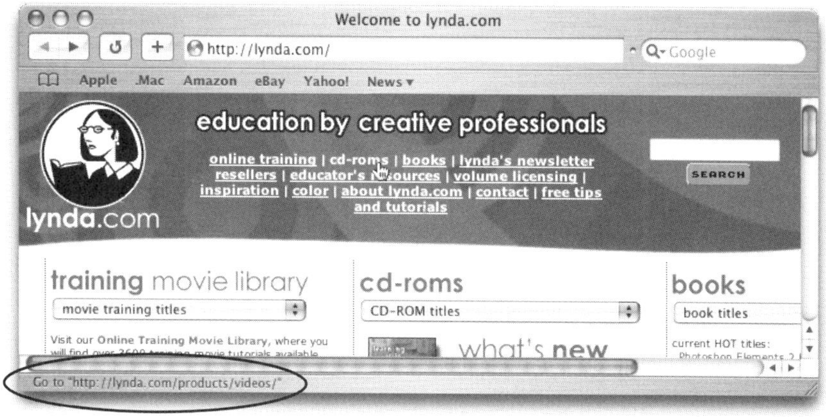

5. Place your mouse cursor over the **cd-roms** link, but don't click. Its address appears in the status bar.

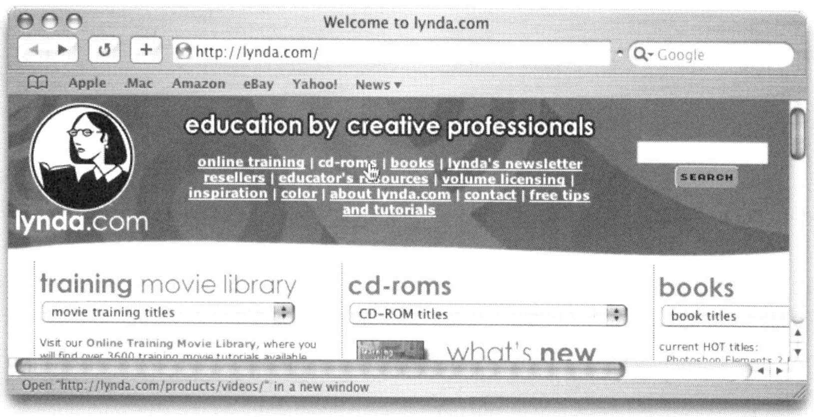

6. Keeping the mouse over the link, press the **Cmd** key. Notice that the status bar now indicates that the linked page will open in a new window. While holding down **Cmd**, click **cd-roms**.

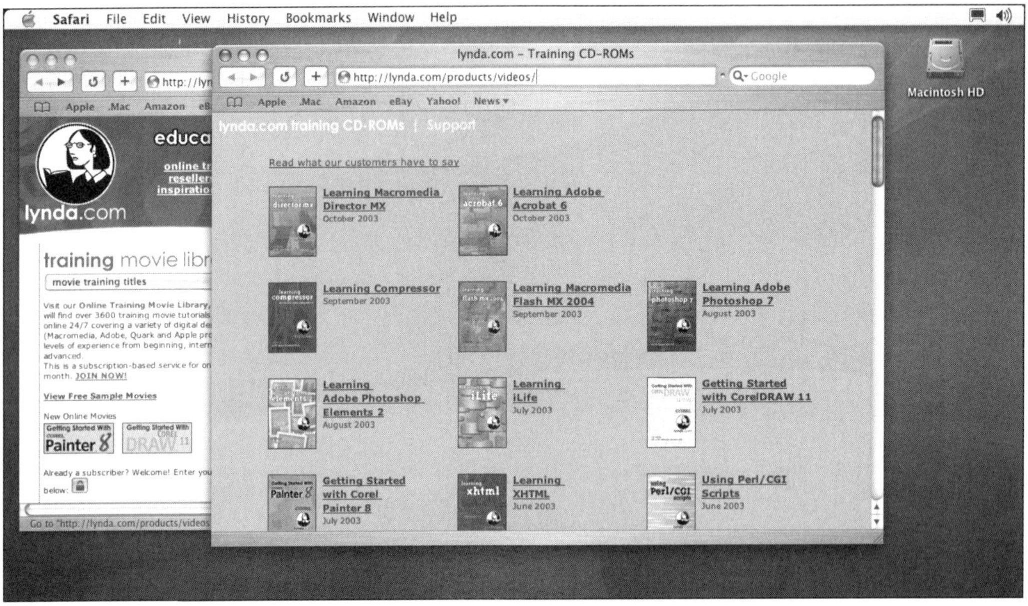

The CD-ROMs page opens in a new window on top of the original window. You can now freely browse through the CD-ROMs while the main page stays open in the background.

7. Click a link on the **CD-ROMs** page and continue clicking a few links on the subsequent pages. When you're done, close the window. The main lynda.com page remains open.

Another option you have for opening links in a new window is to automatically place the new window behind the current one. Sometimes you'll be reading a Web page and come across a link that you'll want to follow, but not right away. Opening the link behind the current window allows you to continue reading the original page without the new window obscuring the information you're trying to read.

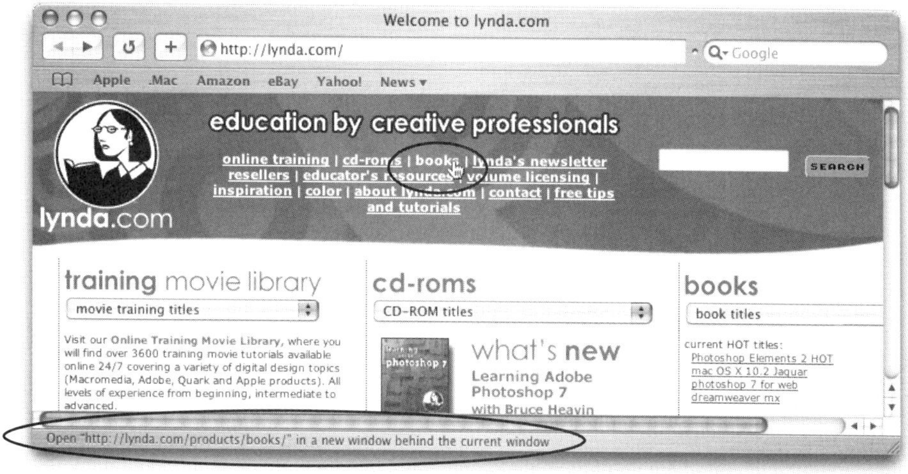

8. On the main lynda.com page, place your mouse over the **books** link. Press and hold **Shift** and **Cmd**. The status bar tells you that this link will open in a new window behind the current one. While holding **Shift** and **Cmd**, click **books**.

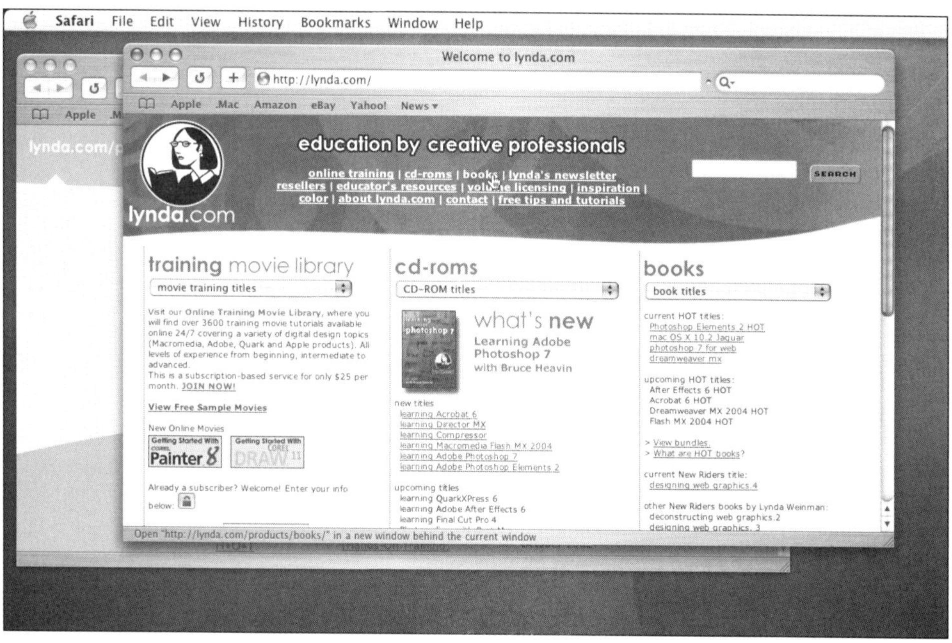

The books page opens behind the main page. Depending on the size and position of your front browser window, you might not even see the page, but it's there.

9. Hold down **Shift** and **Cmd** and click a few more links on the main lynda.com page. Each linked page opens in a new window behind the main one. Opening windows behind the front one can be really useful when you come across several links that you want to explore. Just open each one in the background and then bring them to the front one at a time to check them out.

Tip: *Each open window can be brought to the front by selecting it from the* ***Window*** *menu in the menu bar.*

---

10. Close all your open browser windows except for the main lynda.com page.

As you can see, opening links in new windows can be convenient, but some people prefer not to have a half dozen or so windows open on their screen at once. If you're one of these people, yet you would still like the ability to open several links at once, you'll want to enable tabbed browsing.

Tabbed browsing *allows you to open Web pages in the current window, rather than a series of new windows, with each page's title appearing in a tab near the top of the window. Clicking a tab brings the respective page to the front. In the following steps, you'll turn on tabbed browsing and try it out.*

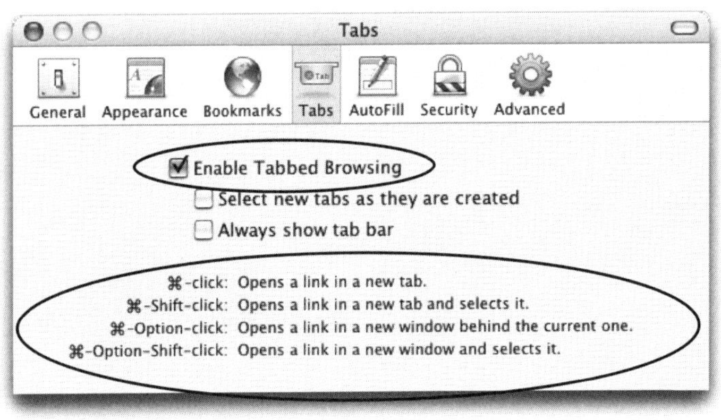

11. From the menu bar, choose **Safari > Preferences**. Under the **Tabs** section, check **Enable Tabbed Browsing**. Leave the other two items here unchecked for now. The information at the bottom of the window informs you that the **Cmd+click** and **Shift+Cmd+click** actions now open links in tabs, and that you can still open links in new windows with tabbed browsing enabled, but you have to add the **Option** key into the mix. Close the **Tabs** preferences window.

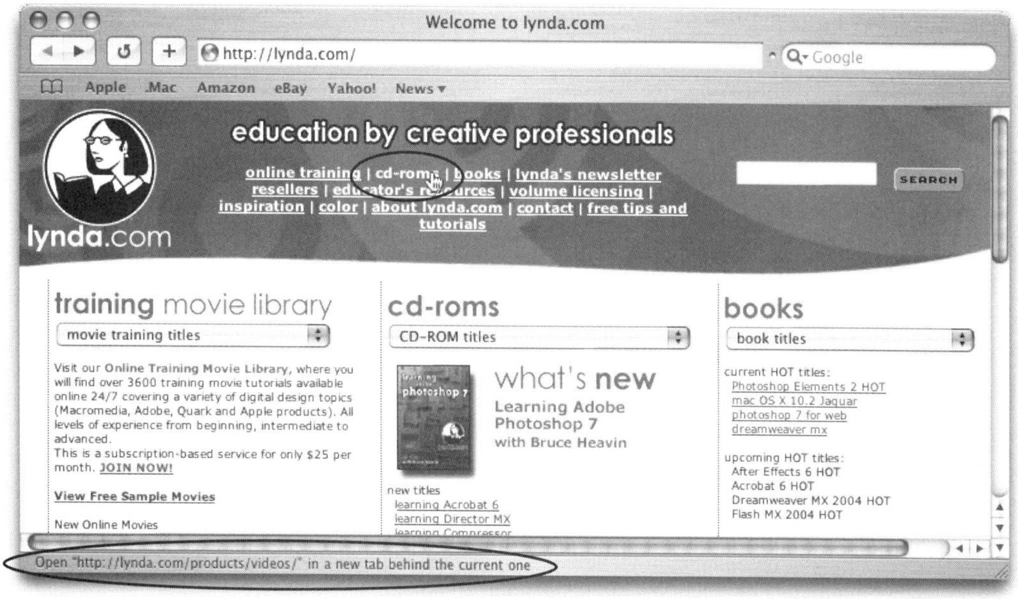

12. On the main lynda.com page, place the mouse cursor over the **cd-roms** link and press **Cmd**. The status bar indicates that the link will be opened "in a new tab behind the current one." Click the link while holding **Cmd**.

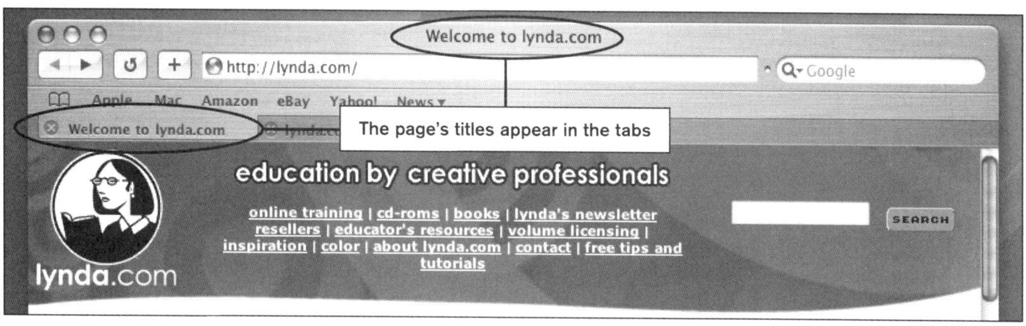

A tab bar appears near the top of the window, containing two tabs. The front-most tab represents the currently displayed window. The tab that appears slightly inset represents the link you just clicked. Before you check out this tab, you'll open another one.

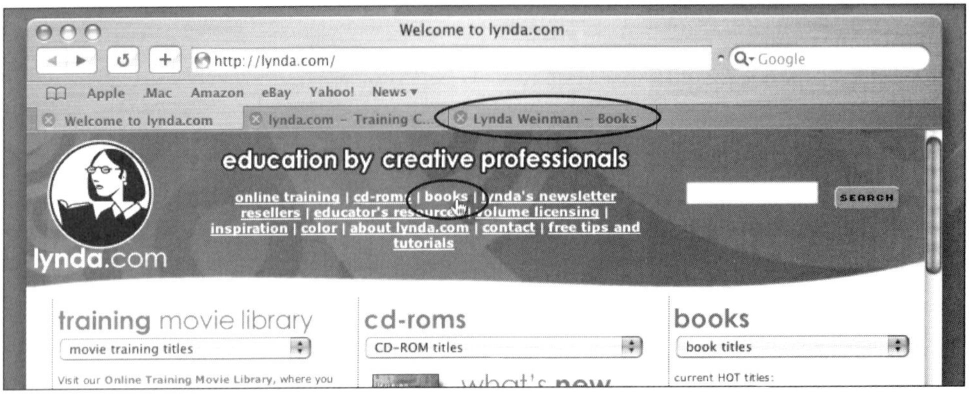

13. Shift+Cmd+click the **books** link. Because you held **Shift**, the linked page appears in a new tab and comes to the front (unlike the **CD-ROMs** link, which appeared in a tab behind the current page).

You could continue Cmd+clicking links in this fashion and each link would open in its own tab. The advantage here is that you're not cluttering up your Desktop with multiple browser windows.

14. Click the center tab to view the **CD-ROMs** page. When the page appears, its tab moves to the front-most position. Click among the three tabs to view each page.

To close a tab, click the little **x** *next to its name. (Don't click the regular Close button at the top of the window, or else you'll close the entire window and all the tabbed pages it contains.)*

---

15. Close the **CD-ROMs** and **Books** tabs. With only one page left to display, the tab bar disappears.

Opening links in new windows or in tabs is really a matter of preference—one is not necessarily better than the other. The following chart provides the keyboard commands for opening tabs and new windows.

New Window / Tabbed Browsing Keyboard Commands

Key Combination	Result
TABBED BROWSING TURNED OFF	
Cmd+click	Opens link in a new window in front of the current one
Shift+Cmd+click	Opens link in a new window behind the current one
TABBED BROWSING ENABLED	
Cmd+click	Opens link in a new tab, but keeps it hidden behind the current tab
Shift+Cmd+click	Opens link in a new tab and brings it to the front
Option+Cmd+click	Opens link in a new window behind the current one
Option+Shift+Cmd+click	Opens link in a new window in front of the current one

NOTE | Reversing the Default Tab Action

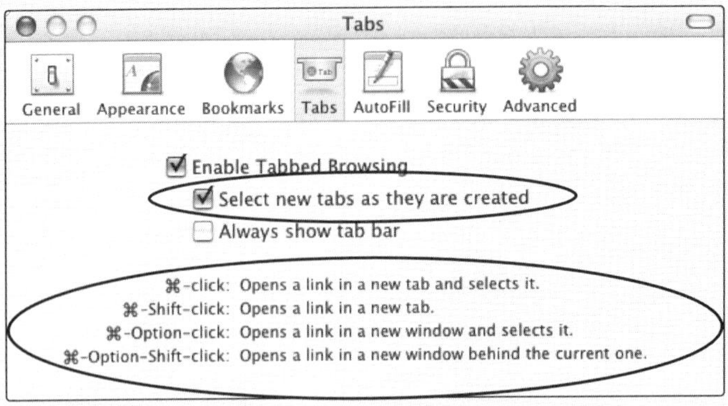

By default, **Cmd+clicking** links with tabbed browsing enabled opens them in tabs behind the current one. You can reverse this action if you prefer new tabs to immediately appear as the front-most page (and if you don't want to constantly **Shift+Cmd+click** links). To do so, choose **Safari > Preferences** and, under the **Tabs** section, check **Select new tabs as they are created**. Notice that this reverses the keyboard commands for determining whether tabs and new windows are opened in front of or behind the current page.

16. Keep Safari open for the next exercise.

3. Adding Bookmarks

If you spend a lot of time on the Web, there are probably numerous sites that you frequently visit. Like other browsers, Safari let's you create **bookmarks** (called "favorites" in some programs) to remember the addresses of Web pages so you can easily access them later. Bookmarks in Safari can exist in three different places: the bookmarks menu, the Bookmarks bar, and the Bookmarks Library. In this exercise, you'll learn how to add addresses to the Bookmarks bar and menu.

1. In Safari, click the **View** menu and make sure **Bookmarks Bar** is checked. The Bookmarks bar appears directly below the address field in your browser window, and contains some default bookmarks.

2. Click the **Apple** bookmark in the **Bookmarks** bar. **www.apple.com** loads in the window.

3. Click the **.Mac** bookmark in the **Bookmarks** bar. Then click the **Amazon** bookmark. Because the items in the Bookmarks bar are always visible, the Bookmarks bar is the quickest way to jump to your most frequently visited pages.

Now you'll add a few of your own bookmarks to the Bookmarks bar.

4. Go to **www.lynda.com**.

5. Click and drag the **globe** icon in the **Address** field straight down into the **Bookmarks** bar. Notice how the other bookmarks here move and make space. You can position the new bookmark anywhere you want in the **Bookmarks** bar (except to the far left side). Release the mouse button.

When you release your mouse, a sheet slides down giving you a chance to rename this bookmark. (The default name is the page's title.) In many cases, you'll probably want to rename the bookmark to remove any extraneous words. In this case, you don't need the "Welcome to" text.

6. Delete **Welcome to** so it just reads **lynda.com** and click **OK**.

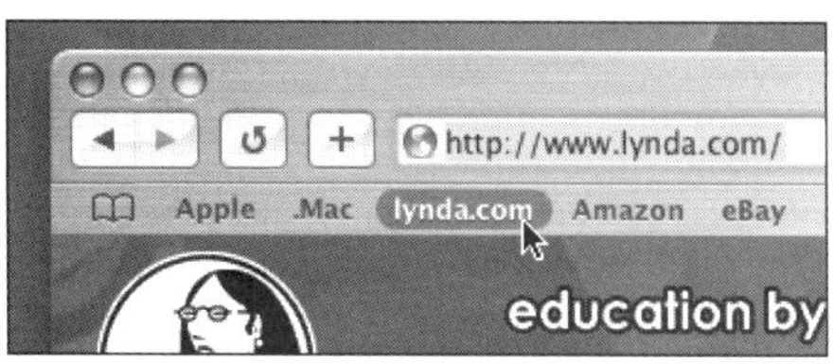

The bookmark lynda.com now resides in your Bookmarks bar. You can move this bookmark to the left or right to reposition it among the other bookmarks here.

But what if you want to get rid of a bookmark? The Bookmarks bar is a great way to quickly access pages, but you have a finite amount of space. Removing an item from the Bookmarks bar works in the same way as taking an item off the Dock.

7. Drag the **lynda.com** bookmark off the bar like you would drag an item off the Dock. It disappears in a puff of smoke. (You can undo this by pressing **Cmd+Z**.)

NOTE | Out of Space in the Bookmarks Bar?

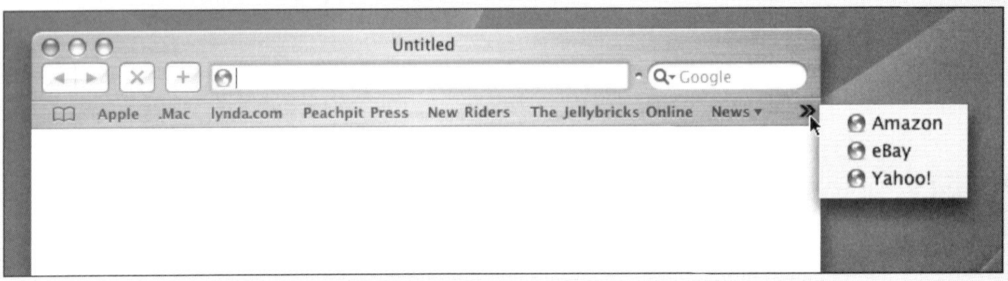

When your Safari window isn't wide enough to display all the items in your Bookmarks bar, the items that don't fit can be accessed from the >> icon that appears at the right end of the bar.

If you have some Web pages that you want to remember, but don't visit as frequently as others, you'll probably still want to save their addresses, but not in the Bookmarks bar. You'll add these pages to the Bookmarks menu.

---

8. www.lynda.com should still be displayed in your browser window. From the menu bar, choose **Bookmarks > Add Bookmark**.

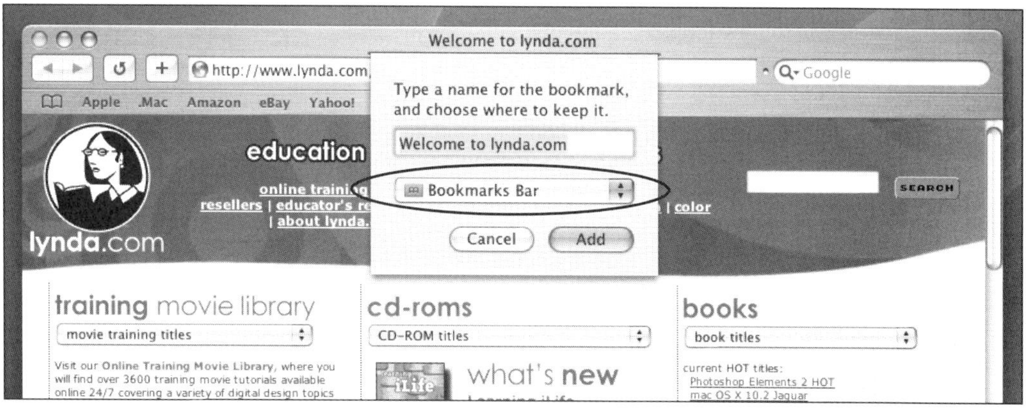

Again, a sheet descends from the top of the window. You can rename the bookmark as you did before. However, in this sheet, you can click the pop-up menu and choose to add this bookmark to the Bookmarks bar, the Bookmarks menu, or any existing bookmark folders in Safari. (You'll learn about these folders shortly.)

9. Rename this bookmark as **lynda.com**. Click the pop-up menu and select **Bookmarks Menu**. Click **Add**.

10. Close your browser window. Click the **Bookmarks** menu and see that **lynda.com** now appears here. Choose **lynda.com**. A new window opens and loads the page.

In this exercise, you learned how to add bookmarks to the Bookmarks bar and menu. In the following exercise, you'll learn how to organize your bookmarks.

4. The Bookmarks Library

The Bookmarks bar and menu are most likely where you're going to be accessing the majority of your saved addresses. But the place to store all your other bookmarks–the ones for pages that you might visit once in a blue moon, yet still want to keep track of–is the Bookmarks Library. The Bookmarks Library is the control center for all your favorite Web page addresses. All the bookmarks you save are stored in the library, where you can access, edit, and organize them.

1. To view your **Bookmarks Library**, click the icon at the far left of the **Bookmarks** bar. Alternately, you can choose **Bookmarks > Show All Bookmarks**, or press **Option+Cmd+B**.

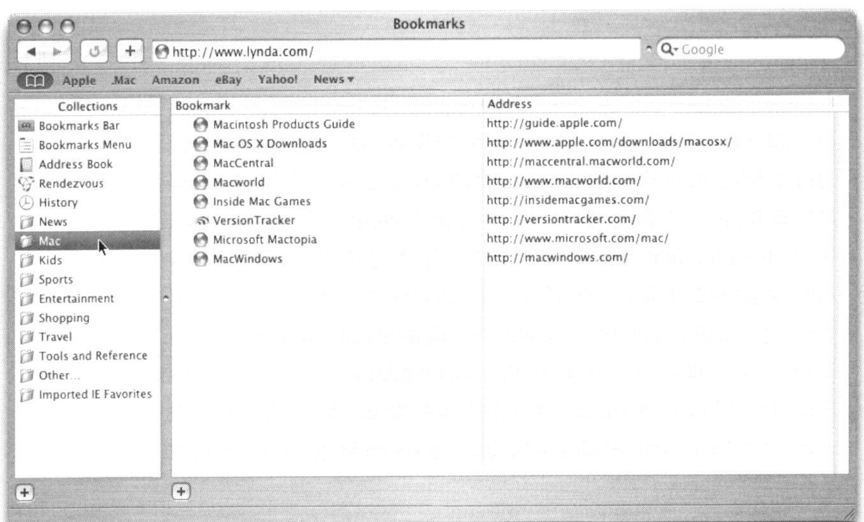

The Bookmarks Library works a lot like the Places sidebar in Finder windows. The left column of the Library shows your collections of bookmarks, including the Bookmarks bar and Bookmarks menu (listed at the top of the column), as well as several default collections of addresses such as Sports, Entertainment, Shopping, and so on. The right pane displays the contents of the selected collection. For instance, selecting Kids displays all the addresses stored in that folder. You can double-click addresses in the right pane to load their respective Web sites.

NOTE | Importing Bookmarks

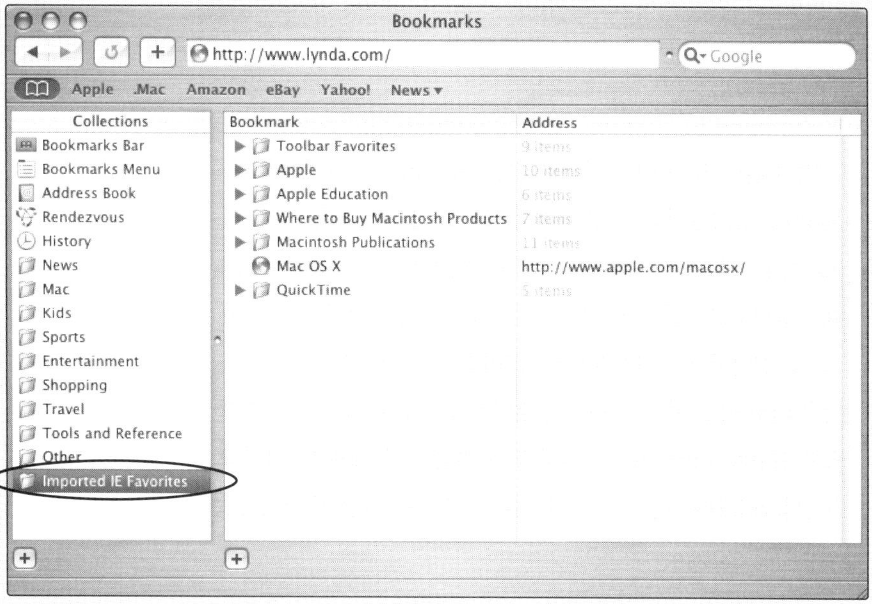

When you first open Safari, it automatically checks to see whether you have Internet Explorer, Netscape Navigator, or Mozilla installed on your Mac. If you do, Safari automatically imports your saved bookmarks and favorites and creates a collection in your Bookmarks Library called **Imported IE Favorites**, or **Imported Netscape/Mozilla Favorites**. You can then easily access the bookmarks you previously created in these other browsers.

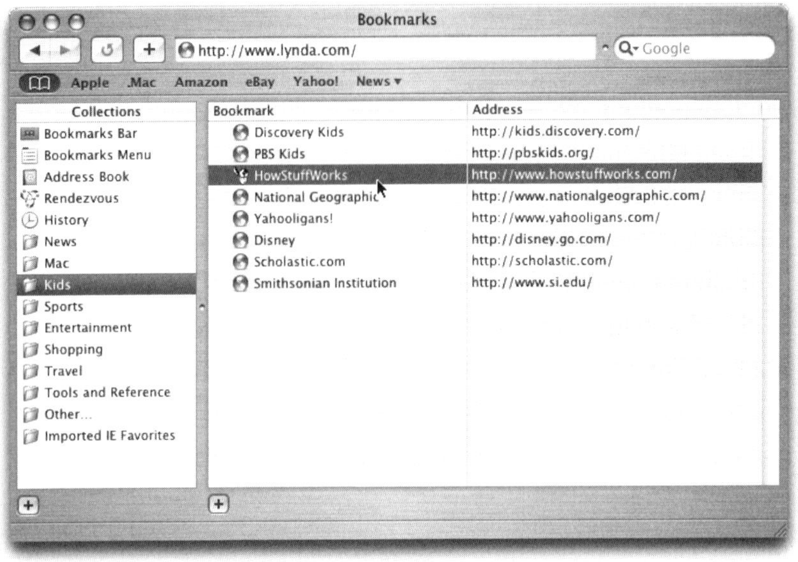

2. In the **Collections** column, select **Kids**. In the right pane, double-click **HowStuffWorks**. The **Bookmarks Library** disappears and is replaced with the Web site. Click the **Library** icon in the **Bookmarks** bar to return to the **Bookmarks Library**. If any additional windows popped up behind the current one, close them. (Remember, you can choose **Safari > Block Pop-up Windows** to prevent these windows from appearing.)

You can also use the Bookmarks Library to create your own collections and organize your bookmarks into custom categories. In the following steps, you'll create a collection of computer training sites.

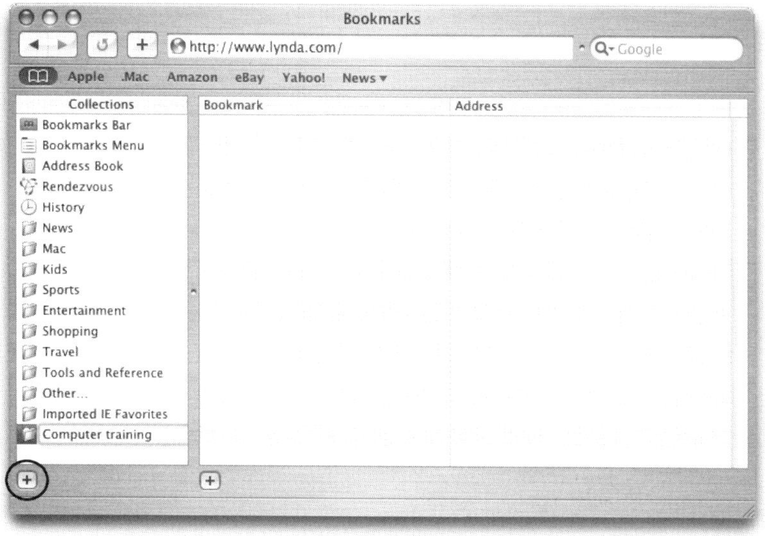

3. Click the **+** symbol under the **Collections** column to make a new folder. Name this folder **Computer training**. Now you'll add some addresses to this collection.

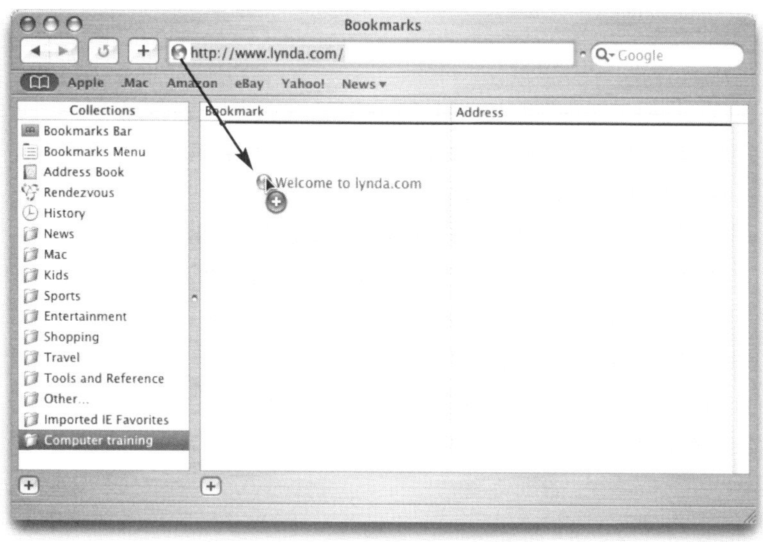

4. The **Address** field should still contain the address for lynda.com (if not, type in **www.lynda.com**). With the **Computer training** folder selected, drag the address down into the right pane. The page's title and address appear. Rename this bookmark **lynda.com** and press **Return**. You've added this address to the selected collection.

5. In the **Address** field, type **peachpit.com** and press **Return**. The **Bookmarks Library** is replaced with the Peachpit Web site. From the menu bar, choose **Bookmarks > Add Bookmark**.

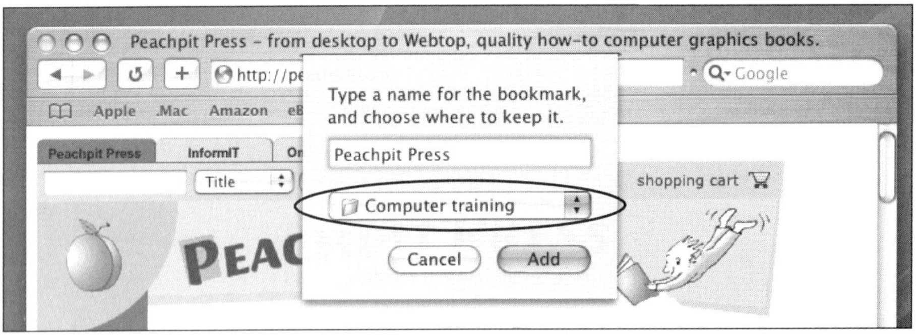

6. In the sheet that slides down, change the title to **Peachpit Press**. From the pop-up menu, choose **Computer training** to store this bookmark in that collection. Click **Add**.

7. Repeat Steps 5 and 6 for **www.newriders.com** and **www.informit.com**, making sure to appropriately rename the page titles and store them in the **Computer training** collection.

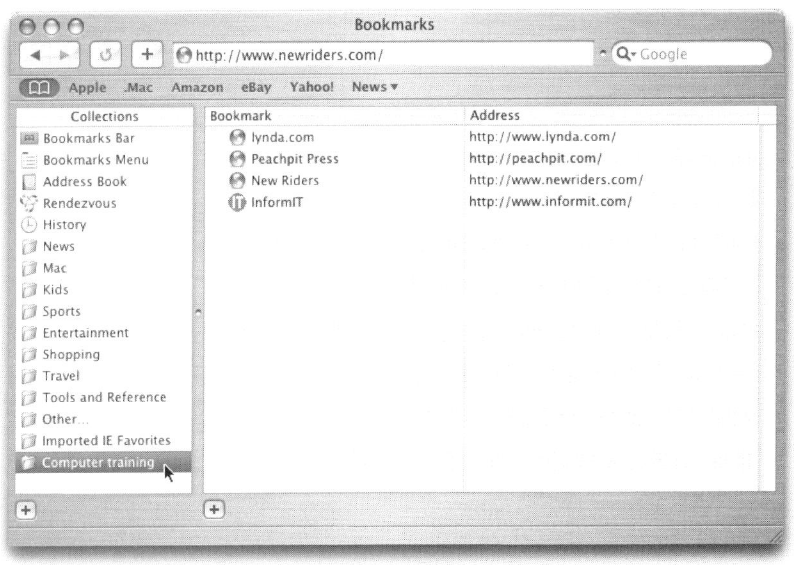

8. Click the **Bookmarks Library** icon in the **Bookmarks** bar and select **Computer training** if it's not already selected. Now that you've saved these addresses, you can access them at any time from your Library.

NOTE | Organizing Bookmarks and Collections

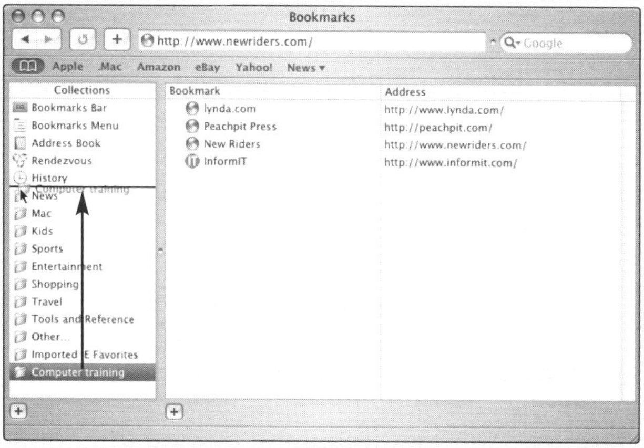

Once a folder has been added to your collections, you can drag it just about anywhere within the **Collections** column. Simply click and drag the folder up or down. A black line will appear between the other collections, indicating where the folder will be dropped when you release the mouse. The only place you can't drag your collections is among the **Address Book**, **Rendezvous**, and **History** collections. See the "Special Collections" section at the end of this exercise for information on these folders.

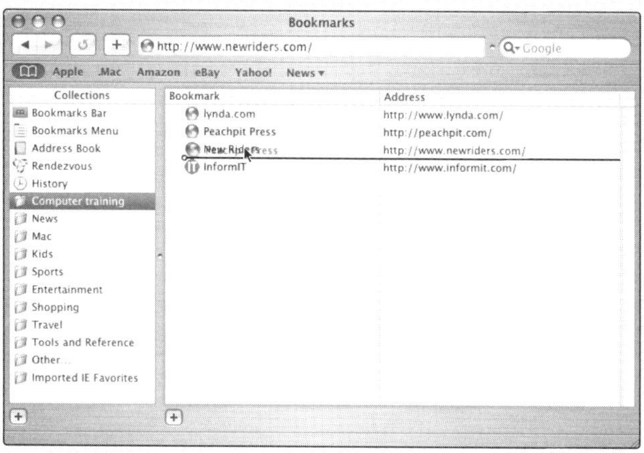

In addition to rearranging the order of collections, you can also rearrange the items in the collections themselves. Just drag addresses up and down to change their order. You may also rename the bookmarks and edit their addresses by clicking once on the text you want to change, and then clicking it again.

Opening your Library each time you want to access a bookmark is fine for the bookmarks you use only occasionally, but it can become inconvenient to access frequently used bookmarks in this fashion. As you saw in the previous exercise, the Bookmarks bar and menu are excellent places to store the pages you view most often. And, as you're about to learn, you can also drag entire collections into these areas.

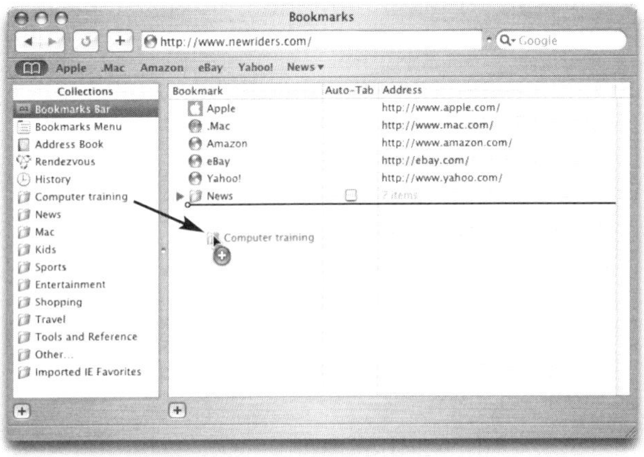

9. In the **Collections** column, select **Bookmarks Bar** to display its contents in the right pane. You'll copy your **Computer training** collection into the **Bookmarks** bar. Hold down **Option** and drag **Computer training** into the right pane.

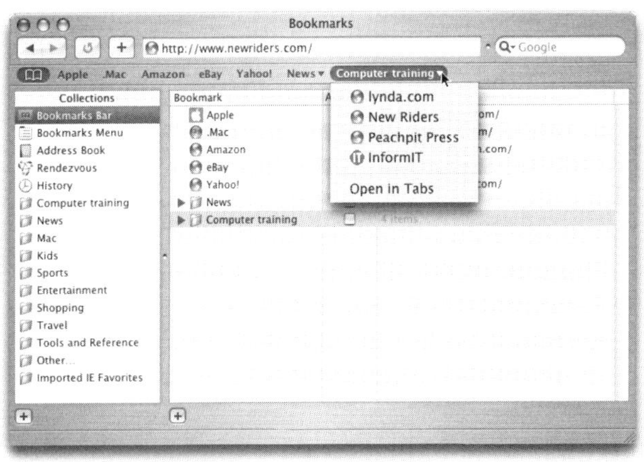

10. This collection of bookmarks now appears in the **Bookmarks** bar. Click the collection in the bar to view its items.

Note: *Collections in the Bookmarks bar are denoted by the little triangle next to the collection's name, which indicates that clicking the item will reveal hidden bookmarks.*

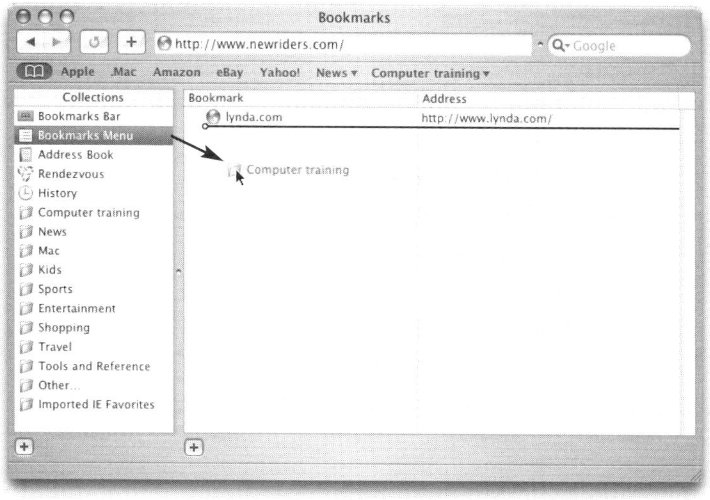

11. In the **Collections** pane of the **Library**, select **Bookmarks Menu**. Drag **Computer training** into the right pane to move this collection into the **Bookmarks** menu. **Computer training** disappears from the **Collections** column because you didn't hold **Option** to copy it this time.

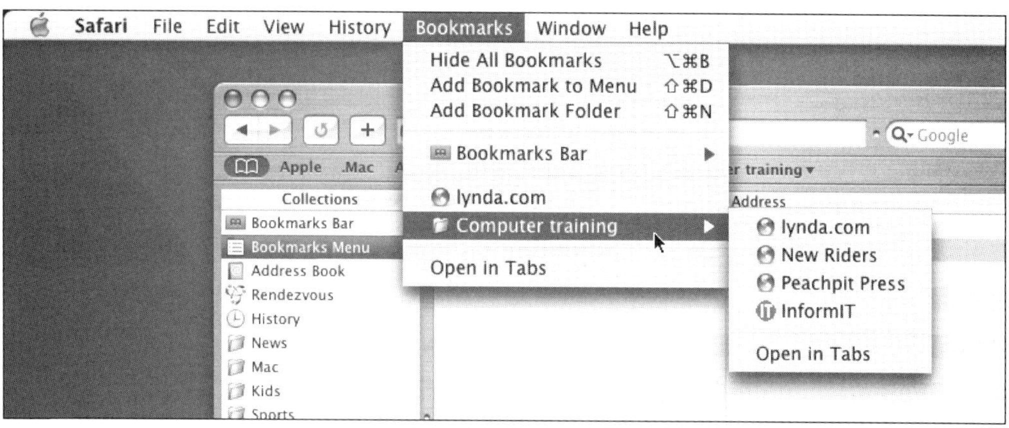

12. Click the **Bookmarks** menu in the menu bar and observe your collection.

As you can see, managing and organizing your bookmarks in Safari is a snap with the Bookmarks Library.

Auto-Tabbing Bookmarks

If you're like me, one of the first things you do when you sit down at your computer in the morning is surf through a series of favorite sites while telling yourself that you'll be getting to work in just a minute. (And sure enough, two hours later, you're ready!) One really cool feature of Safari that can help speed up your browsing time is its auto-tab capability. To take advantage of this feature, make sure tabbed browsing is enabled in Safari's preferences, and then create a collection in your Bookmarks Library containing all the sites you normally visit when you first sit down at your Mac. Then drag this collection into your Bookmarks bar.

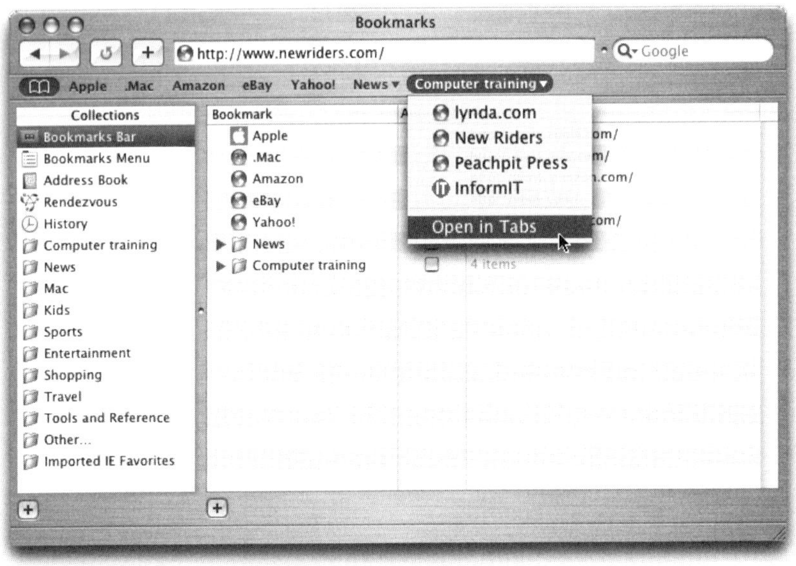

Now when you click this collection, you can choose **Open in Tabs** from the pop-up menu that appears.

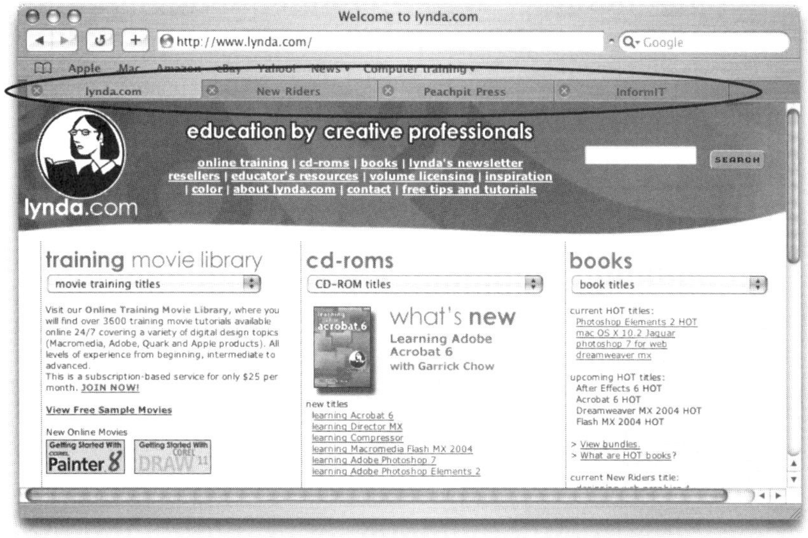

Safari will dutifully load each page into its own tab. You can start reading the first site that appears while all the other sites load in the background. To move on, just close the current tab and start reading the next one.

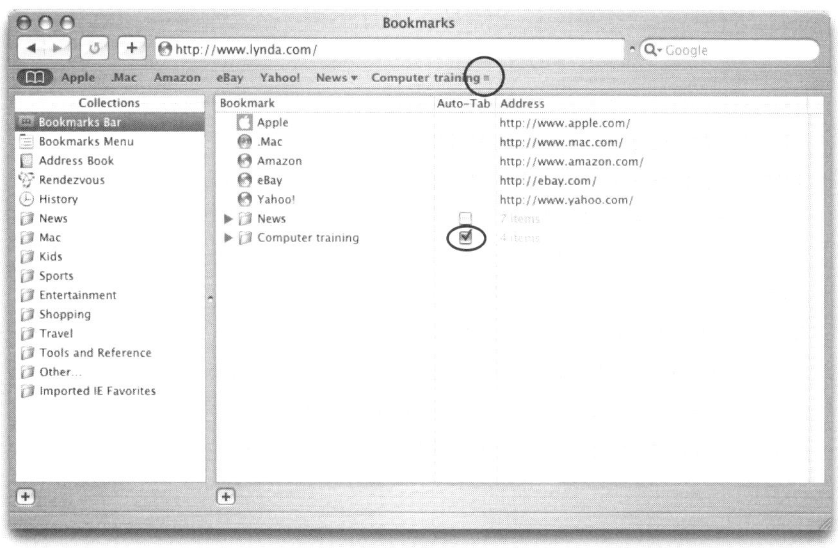

To save even more time, go to your **Bookmarks Library**, select **Bookmarks** bar, and check the **Auto-tab** box next to your collection. This places a small square next to your collection in the Bookmarks bar. Now when you click this item, all the bookmarks will automatically load in tabs–there's no longer a need to choose **Open in Tabs** from a pop-up menu.

Special Collections

Near the top of the collections column in the Bookmarks Library are three special collections whose contents can't be organized and rearranged like your other collections. Instead, the **Address Book**, **Rendezvous**, and **History** collections are automatically generated and change based on information you indirectly provide to Safari.

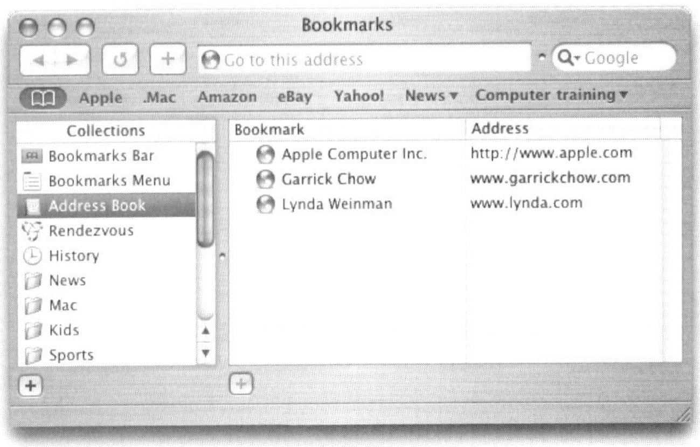

The Address Book collection contains the Web sites for any individuals or companies you have entered into Address Book (located in your Applications folder). You'll learn how to add contacts to your Address Book in Chapter 10, "*Address Book, Mail, and iChat AV*."

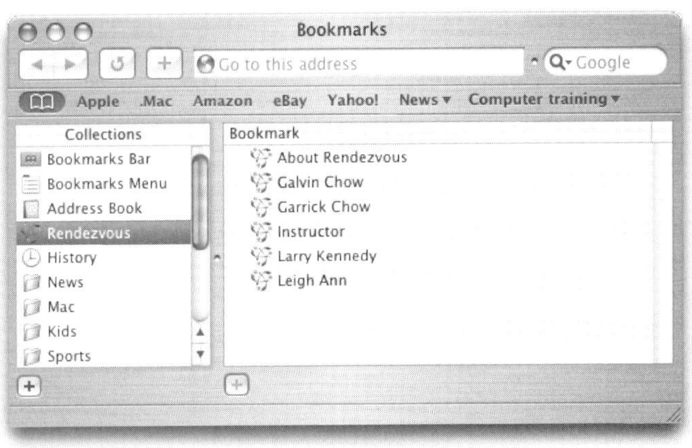

Using Rendezvous, Apple's zero-configuration technology (which you learned about in Chapter 6, "*Printing, Fonts, and Faxing*"), Safari automatically identifies any Web sites that are available on your local network and lists them in the Rendezvous collection. If anyone on your network is hosting a Web site from his or her computer, you can quickly access the site from here.

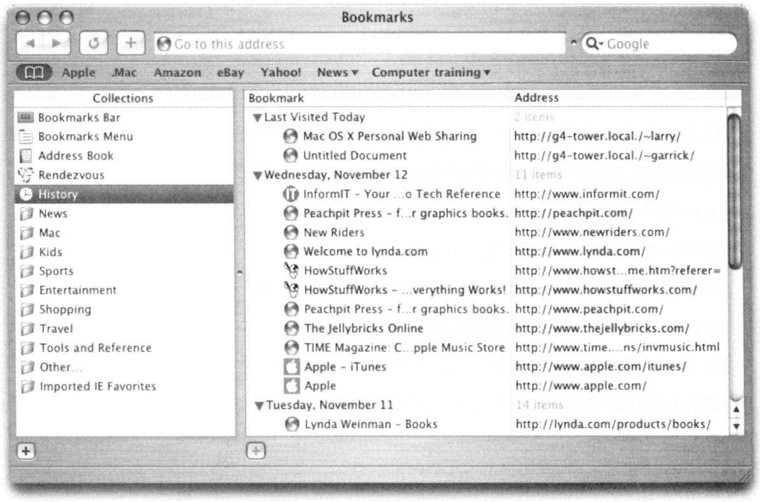

If you've ever tried to recall the address of a site you recently visited, but just can't remember it, you'll love the History collection. Safari remembers about a week's worth of Web pages that you've opened and lists them all here, arranged by date. Unlike the Address Book and Rendezvous collections, you can edit the History collection to some extent. If, hypothetically, you've visited a Web site that you don't want to show up in your History collection for others to see, (say, you were browsing a department store's Web site while looking for a gift for your spouse), you can select the incriminating address in the History collection and press **Delete** to remove it.

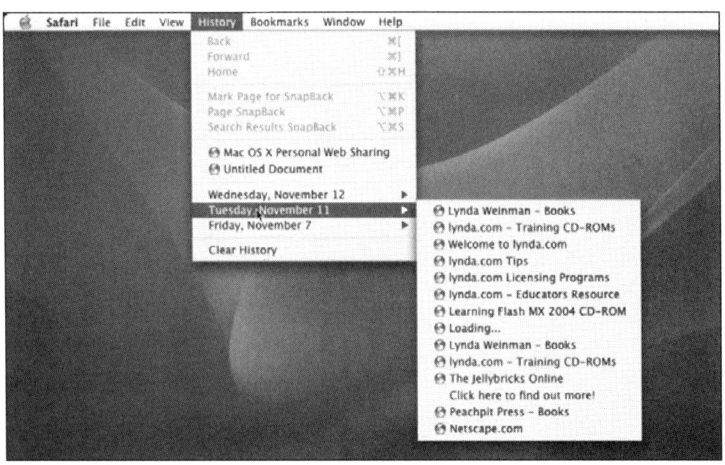

Because you'll probably use it more than the Address Book and Rendezvous collections, the History collection gets its own menu in the menu bar. Click **History** to access your list of recently visited sites. From here, you can also choose **Clear History**, to erase the entire list.

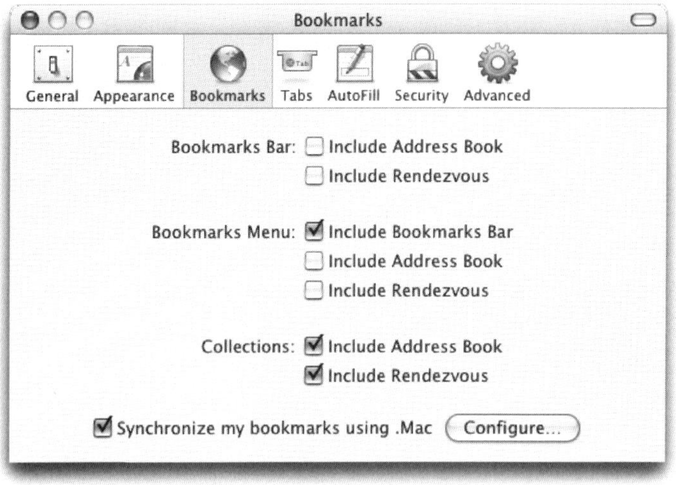

If you find yourself frequently using the Address Book or Rendezvous collections, you can make them more accessible by choosing **Safari > Preferences**. Under the **Bookmarks** section, select whether you want them to appear in the Bookmarks bar, the Bookmarks menu, or both. On the other hand, if you don't use these collections at all, you can remove them from the Bookmarks Library by unchecking them from **Collections**.

MOVIE | bookmarks.mov

To watch a demonstration of the different aspects of creating and managing bookmarks covered in this chapter, see the movie **bookmarks.mov** on the **H•O•T CD-ROM**.

5. Google Searching and SnapBack

Unless you're completely new to this whole Internet thing, you're probably already familiar with Google. In the past few years, google.com has become the de facto standard when it comes to searching the Web for information. With Safari, you don't even have to go to www.google.com first to perform your search. A Google Search bar is built right into every Safari window. In this exercise, you'll take a look at this very cool feature.

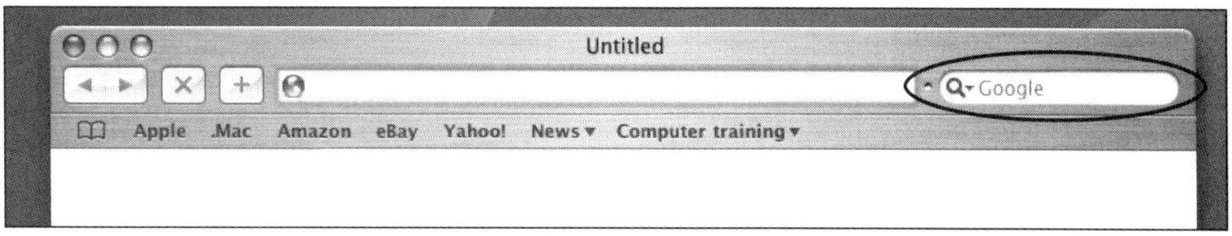

1. Open a Safari window (if you don't already have one open). The **Google Search** bar appears in the upper-right corner. If you don't see it, choose **View > Google Search** from the menu bar.

Imagine you wanted to find some information on setting up a wireless network.

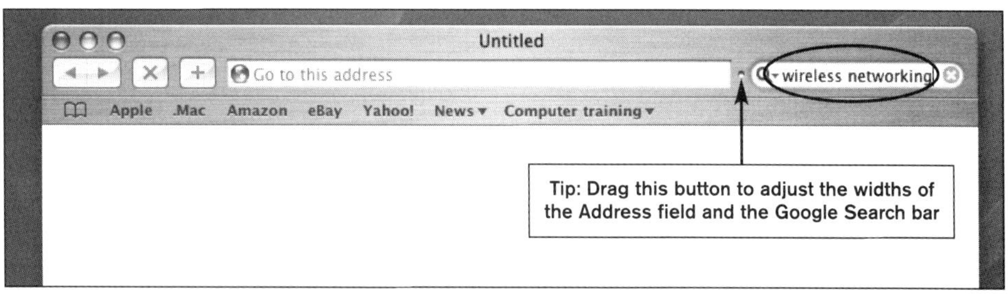

2. Click in the **Google Search** bar and type **wireless networking**. Press **Return**.

***Tip:** Pressing **Option+Cmd+F** will place a cursor in the Google Search bar, which is sometimes faster than moving your mouse and clicking in the bar.*

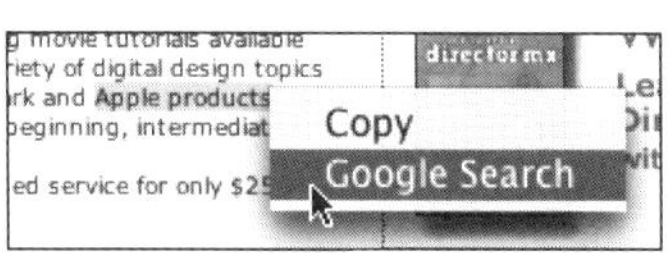

*Also, if the term you want to search for appears in a Web page you're viewing, you can highlight the term, **Ctrl+click** it, and select **Google Search** from the contextual menu that appears, rather than retyping the term in the Search bar.*

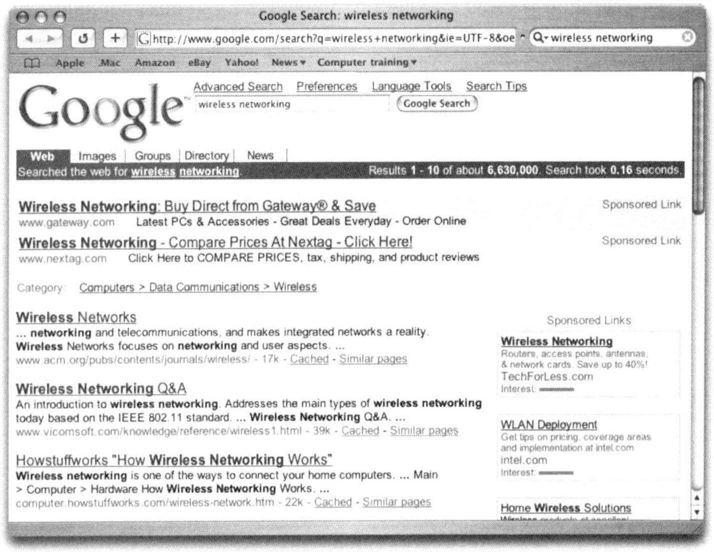

*After a moment, a Google results page appears. This is the same page that would appear if you had first gone to **www.google.com**, but Safari makes it unnecessary to start from Google's main page.*

3. Click one of your search results to view that Web page. (Your search results may be different than the ones shown in the previous screen shot.)

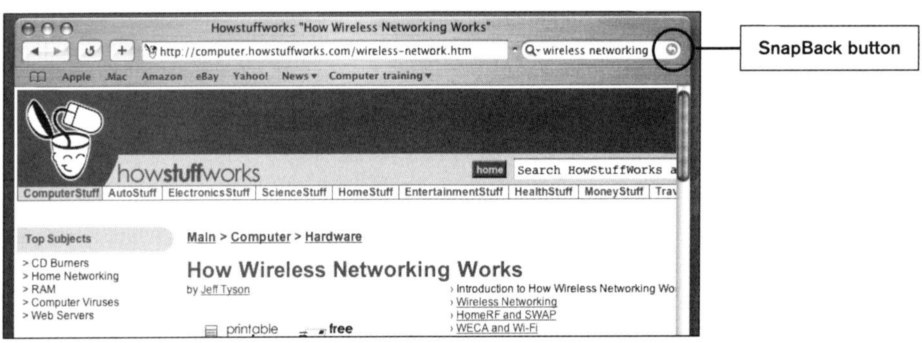

Once the page opens, take a look at the Google Search bar. The little orange arrow there is called the SnapBack button. If you've spent much time searching for information on the Web, you know how frustrating it can be to perform a search and follow links for several pages only to realize that the material isn't what you were looking for in the first place. Usually, you have to click your browser's Back button several times to return to the Google results page. This is where the SnapBack button comes in. As long as this window stays open, no matter how far into this site you explore, you can instantly return to the Google results page by clicking the SnapBack button.

4. Click any link on the page you're currently viewing. Then continue clicking other links and note how the SnapBack button remains in the Google bar.

5. Click the **SnapBack** button. You're returned to the Google results page. Pretty nifty, eh?

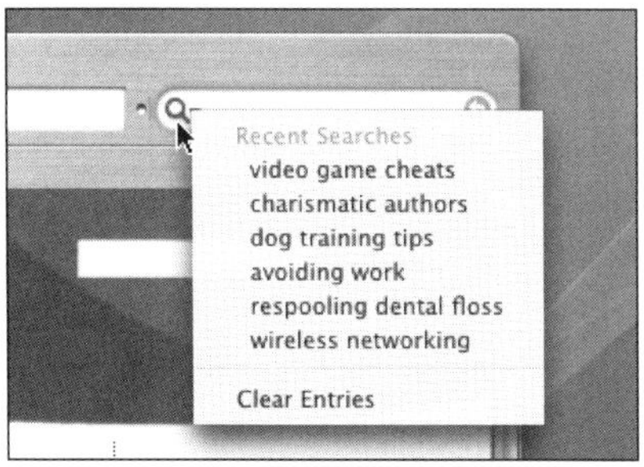

Tip: *Safari always remembers the last 10 searches you performed. Click the little magnifying glass icon in the search bar to see your recent searches. Select any item to search for it again. This list appears in any browser window you open, even if you quit Safari. You can select* ***Clear Entries*** *to delete the list if you share your computer with others and don't want them seeing what you've been searching for.*

NOTE | SnapBacks for Everyone

The SnapBack button isn't just for the Google Search bar. It also appears in the Address field anytime you type a Web address (or select a bookmark) and click a link. Clicking SnapBack will always return you to the page where you clicked your first link. (Note that if a link opens in a new window or tab, the SnapBack button won't appear.)

Additionally, you can assign SnapBack to any page you're viewing by choosing **History > Make Page for SnapBack**, which can be useful if you get the feeling that you're about to wander far away from the page you're viewing and want to be able to find your way back.

TIP | Google Calculations and Definitions

The Google search engine is constantly being improved and refined. One of the most recent additions to its repertoire is the capability to perform calculations. Safari's built-in Google Search bar makes this option even more convenient than opening OS X's Calculator application when you need to figure out some math.

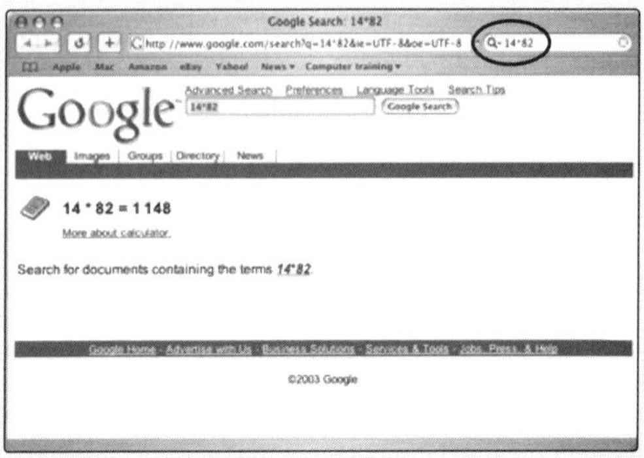

In the Google Bar, type something like **14*82** and Google will quickly return the correct product of **1148**. Not only that, but Google can also perform more complex calculations such as **(5+3)*2** (where the 5 and 3 need to be added before being multiplied by 2), or even conversions like **40 days in seconds** (to find out how many seconds make up 40 days). For a detailed list of Google's calculation capabilities, visit **www.google.com/help/calculator.html**.

Another new and useful feature of Google is **Definitions**. Now you have a dictionary built right into Safari. In the Google Search bar, simply type the word **define** preceding any word and the definition will appear in seconds, along with a list of related sites you might want to visit. Google will even offer spelling suggestions if you typed the word incorrectly.

The great thing about Safari's Google Search bar is that any improvements made to Google are automatically also improvements to Safari.

AutoFilling Forms

If you frequently use the Web to order products and services or to pay bills online, you most likely spend a lot of time filling out Web-based forms. Safari has a great feature called **AutoFill**, which, as its name implies, saves you the hassle of filling out a form by doing most of the work for you.

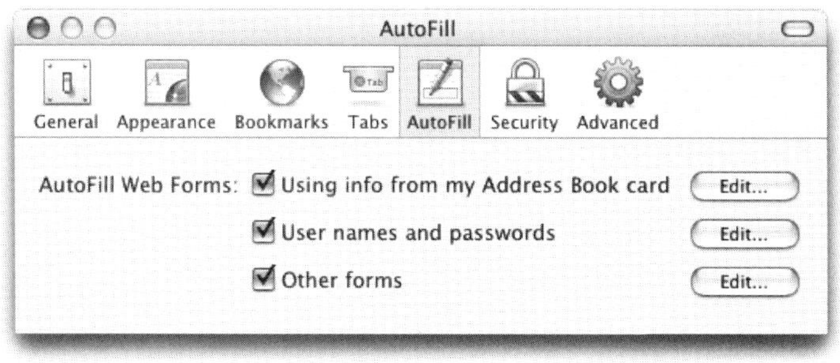

To turn on this feature, choose **Safari > Preferences** and click the **AutoFill** button. Check any of the items you want Safari to use. If you want Safari to AutoFill forms that ask for personal information such as name, address, phone number, email, and so on, check **Using info from my Address Book card**. Safari uses the information you entered about yourself in Address Book (covered in Chapter 10, "*Address Book, Mail, and iChat AV*") to complete forms. If you want Safari to remember your user name and passwords for the sites you visit, check **User names and passwords**. For all other types of forms, check **Other forms**, which makes Safari remember the information you type into any form field.

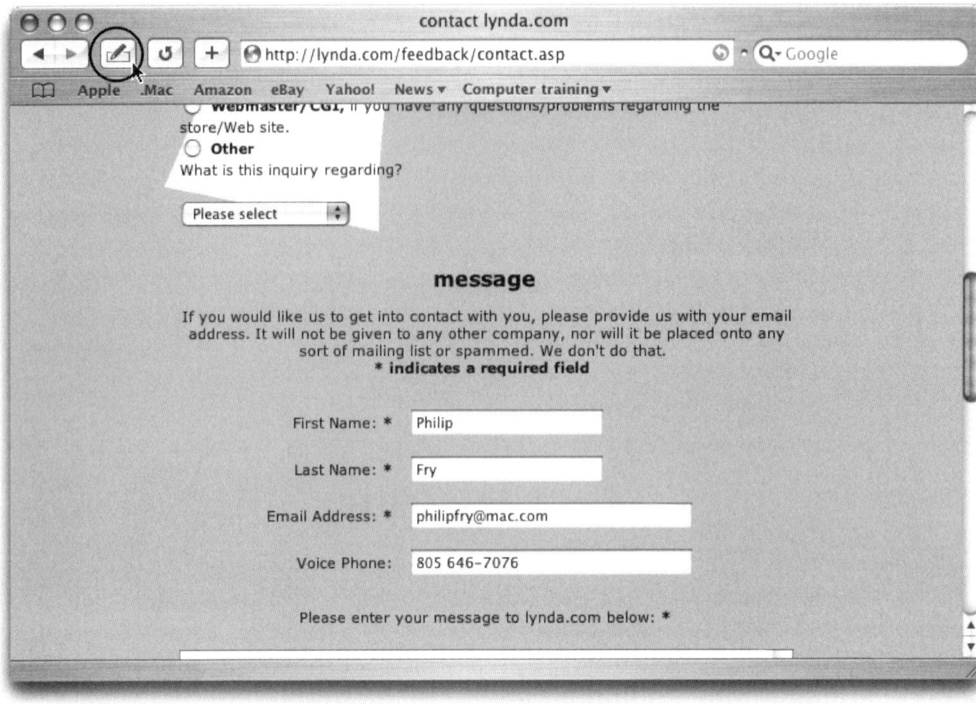

Once your preferences have been set, close the window and choose **View > Autofill** to place the AutoFill button in the Safari toolbar. Now, anytime you come across a form on a Web site, you can click this button to automatically fill in all the fields that Safari recognizes (and has the right information for). Fields that Safari completes are highlighted yellow so you can confirm their accuracy before submitting the form.

To complete individual fields, select a field and start typing. If Safari matches any of its saved information for the field, it finishes entering the text for you. If more than one item matches what you typed, a menu appears from which you can select the correct item.

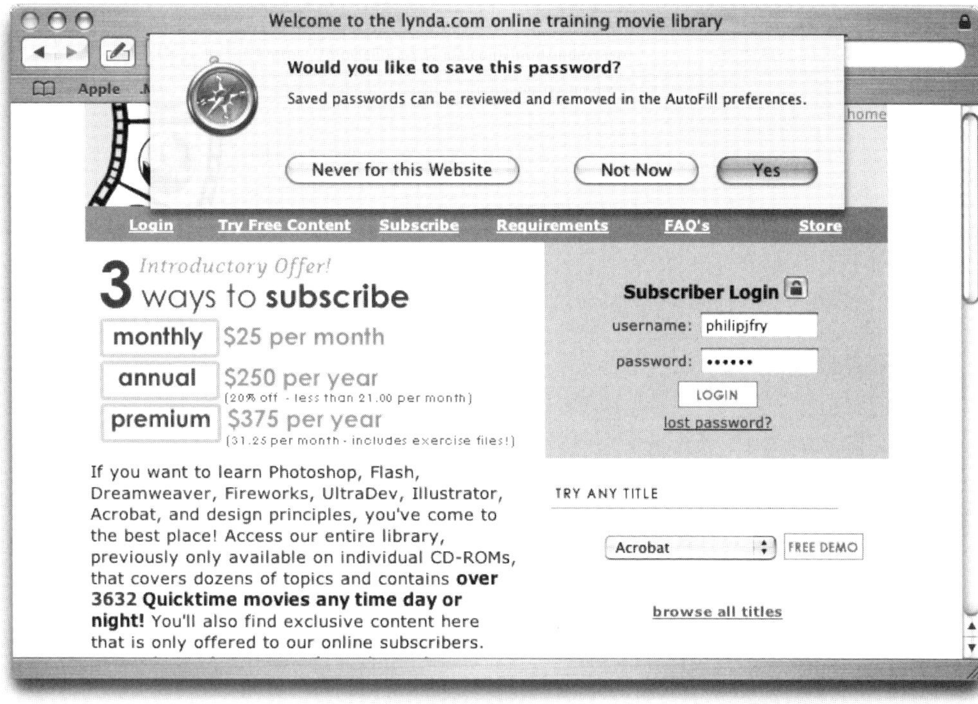

On sites where you enter a user name and password for the first time, Safari asks if you want to save this information. If you click **Yes**, you won't have to type this information each time you visit this site. Click **Not Now** if you might want to save the information at another time. Click **Never for this Website** to stop Safari from asking you if you want to save your information for the Web site again.

Finally, if you need to alter or remove your stored information, return to AutoFill under **Safari > Preferences** and click the appropriate **Edit** button to make your changes.

You should have a pretty good handle on browsing the Web at this point. In the next chapter, you'll learn about using the Address Book application you read about in this chapter, as well as how to send and receive email with OS X's Mail program.

10.

Address Book, Mail, and iChat AV

| Adding Contact Information to Address Book |

| Using Address Book | Setting Up Mail |

| Receiving Email | Composing and Sending Email |

| Adding Attachments and Signatures | iChat AV |

chap_10

Mac OS X Panther
H•O•T CD-ROM

The ability to communicate over the Internet through email is arguably the most important and useful Internet skill you can learn. If you're online, you likely have one or more email addresses of your own, as well as countless addresses for friends, family, and co-workers that you need to keep track of. Mac OS X comes with two free applications, **Address Book** and **Mail**, that will help you organize your ever-growing list of email addresses and manage the multitude of email messages you either already do or will eventually receive.

Also included in this chapter is a section on Panther's **iChat AV** program, in which you'll learn how to communicate in real time over the Internet through instant messaging services. **Instant messaging** is a great way of getting immediate responses to your messages, and it allows you to perform other tasks such as transferring files, sending Web links, and, with the right equipment, you can participate in video and audio chats.

Just because these are "free" applications, don't be fooled into thinking that they're not as good as programs you'd pay money for. Mac users have come to expect top-notch performance from the applications that come with OS X, and Address Book, Mail, and iChat AV do not disappoint. These are three extremely powerful and versatile tools you have at your fingertips. This chapter will show you how to use them.

I. Adding Contact Information to Address Book

OS X's Address Book is an incredibly useful application that you can use to organize and store information for your personal and business contacts. One of Address Book's main advantages is that it works in conjunction with other OS X applications, so once you've stored your contact information in Address Book, it's accessible from other OS X programs such as Mail, iChat AV, and Sherlock. This exercise walks you through Address Book's most useful features and will familiarize you with its interface.

1. Open **Address Book** by clicking its icon in the **Dock** or in your **Applications** folder.

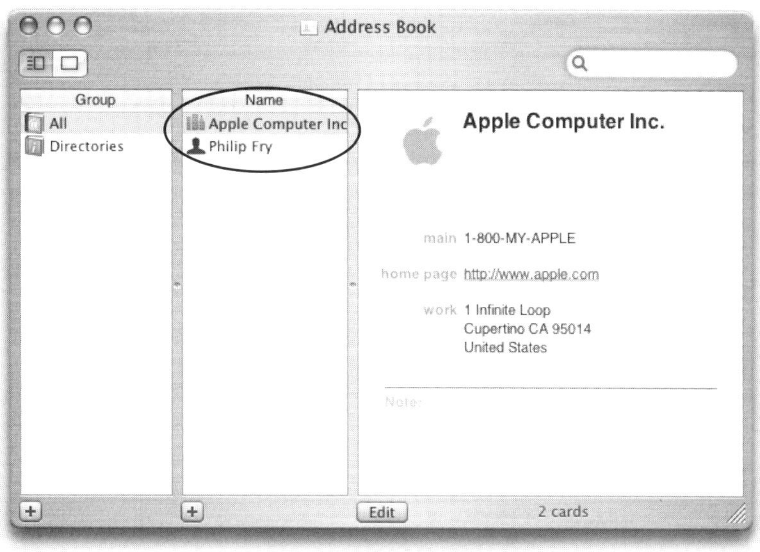

Unless you've already added contact information, only your own name should appear in the Name column along with Apple Computer Inc. Apple Computer Inc. is selected by default in this column, and the corresponding contact info appears in the right pane.

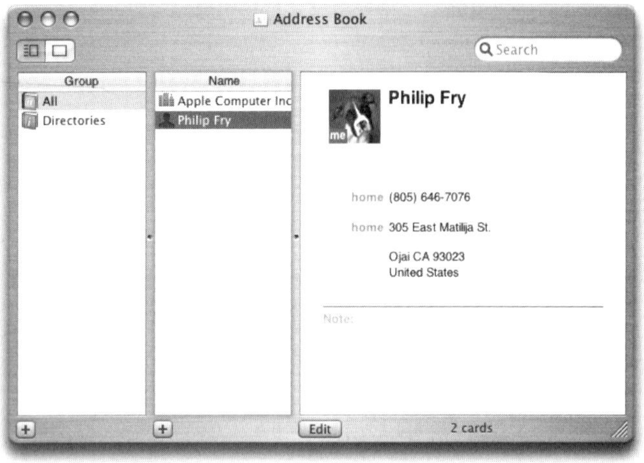

2. Click your name. If you're the person who originally set up Panther on your Mac, your contact information should appear in the right pane. This is the information that you provided after you installed Panther (or first turned on your new Mac) and went through the initial setup process. Notice that the picture you selected for yourself in the Accounts pane of System Preferences appears here as well. (You selected this picture in Exercise 10 of Chapter 4, "*System Preferences*.") If you're not the person who set up your Mac, the right pane contains nothing except your name and picture. But don't worry if it's empty; you're about to learn how to add contact information.

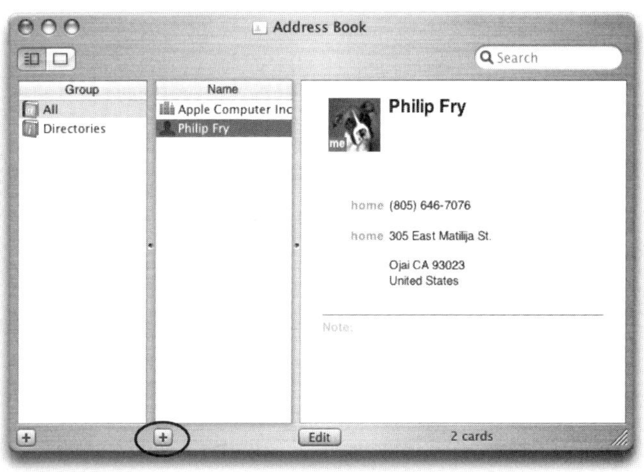

3. To add a new contact to your list, click the **+** symbol under the **Name** column. Alternately, you can choose **File > New Card** (each individual contact is referred to as a card) or press **Cmd+N** on the keyboard.

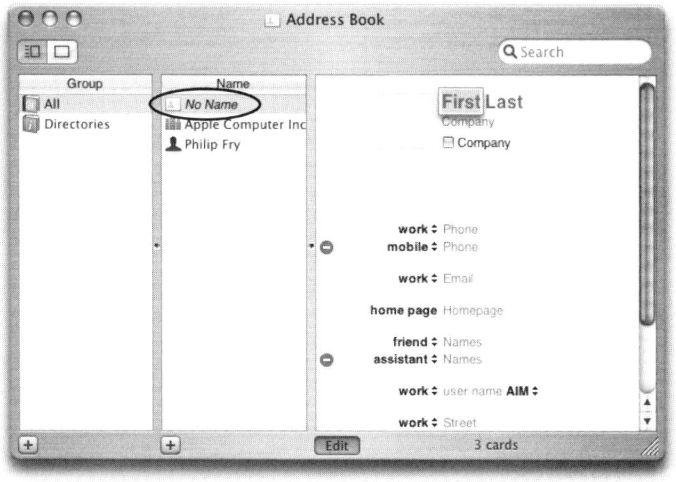

*When you create a new card, the generic entry **No Name** appears in the **Name** column and several empty fields appear in the right pane. You don't have to enter information into every field; just fill out the ones you want, and the empty fields will disappear when you're done.*

*You can now enter information about this contact, starting with the person's first name. Note that the **First** name field is already highlighted for you.*

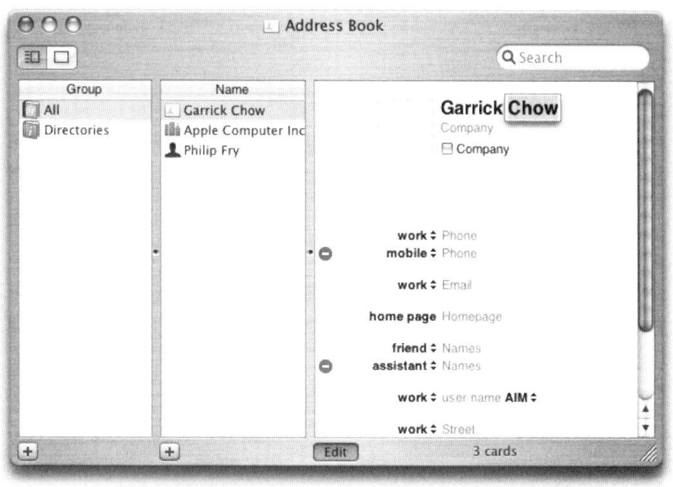

4. Type **Garrick** and then press **Tab** or **Return** to move to the **Last** name field. Type **Chow**. Notice as you type the name that it also appears in the **Name** column.

NOTE | How Do You Pronounce That Name?

Although it's handy to have the correct spelling of each contact's name in a central location like Address Book, sometimes you might need a little more help remembering how to pronounce it.

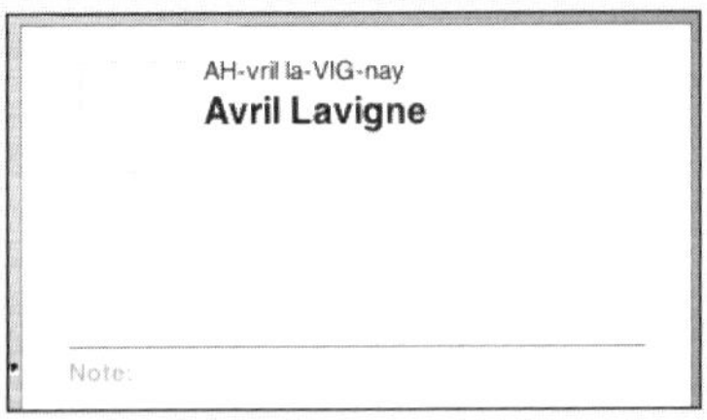

By choosing **Card > Add Field > Phonetic First/Last Name** from the menu bar, you can insert an additional field above the contact's name in which you can type the phonetic pronunciation of the name or any other words that might help you to remember how to pronounce it properly. You can use the same **Card > Add Field** menu to add several other types of fields such as one for the contact's birthday, which may be a good thing to have in case you do mispronounce their name and need to make up for it with a well-timed birthday present.

You can type as much or as little information as you have about each of your contacts. Information you may not have at the moment can always be added later. For now, you'll fill out a few more fields about yours truly.

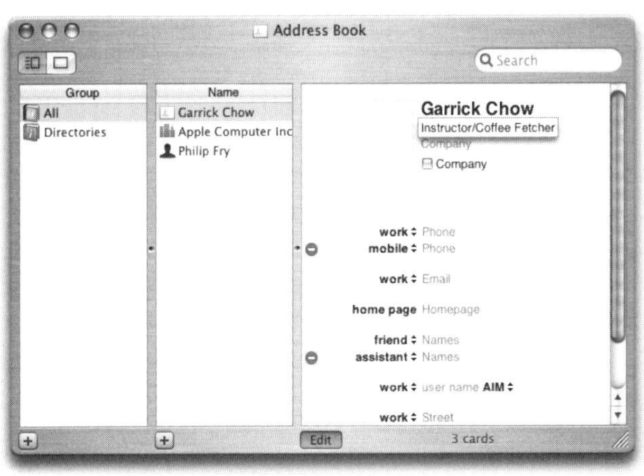

5. Choose **Card > Add Field > Job Title** from the menu bar. This places a field called **Job Title** under the name. In this field, type **Instructor/Coffee Fetcher**. Press **Tab** and, in the **Company** field, type **lynda.com**.

NOTE | The Company Check Box

New to Address Book in Panther is the **Company** check box. If you're adding contact information for a business or organization, check this box to ensure that this contact will be alphabetized by the company's name in the Name column, rather than by a person's last name. You can still add the first and last name of a person at that organization if necessary.

6. Press **Tab** and in the **work phone** field type **8056467076** and press **Tab**. Address Book automatically formats the number as **(805) 646-7076**.

Note: *If Address Book doesn't reformat the phone number, choose* ***Address Book > Preferences*** *and click the* ***Phone*** *icon. Make sure* ***Automatically format phone numbers*** *is checked and that your preferred format style is selected.*

You're not limited to just the work and mobile categories for phone numbers here, nor are you limited to just two types of numbers.

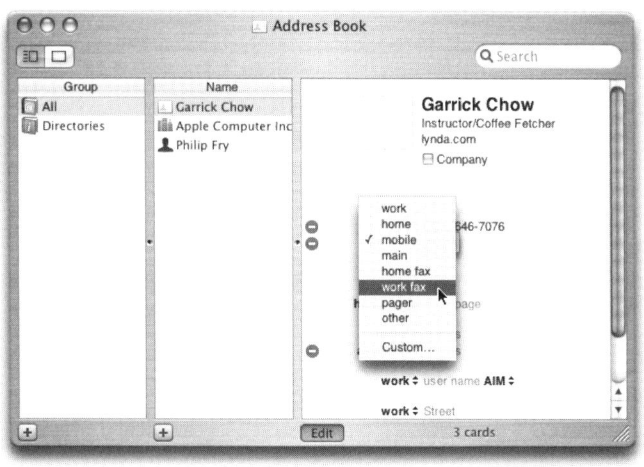

7. Click the little arrows next to **mobile**, which opens a list of phone categories to choose from. Select **work fax** from the list.

8. In the **work fax** field, type **(805) 640-9607**.

As soon as you start typing the fax number, a small green + symbol appears to the left of the field. Because you've now occupied the two available phone number fields, the plus symbol appears in case you need to add more phone numbers.

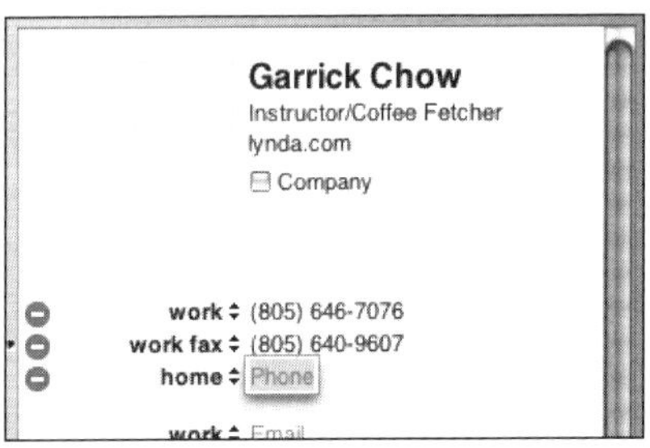

9. Click the + symbol. An additional phone field appears with the default name of **home**. As much as I'd like to print my home phone number in this book, um, I haven't paid the bill so it's not in service right now. You'll add lynda.com's toll-free 888 number here instead.

10. Click the **home** heading and choose **Custom** from the list of categories. A sheet called **Adding new custom label** descends from the window's title bar.

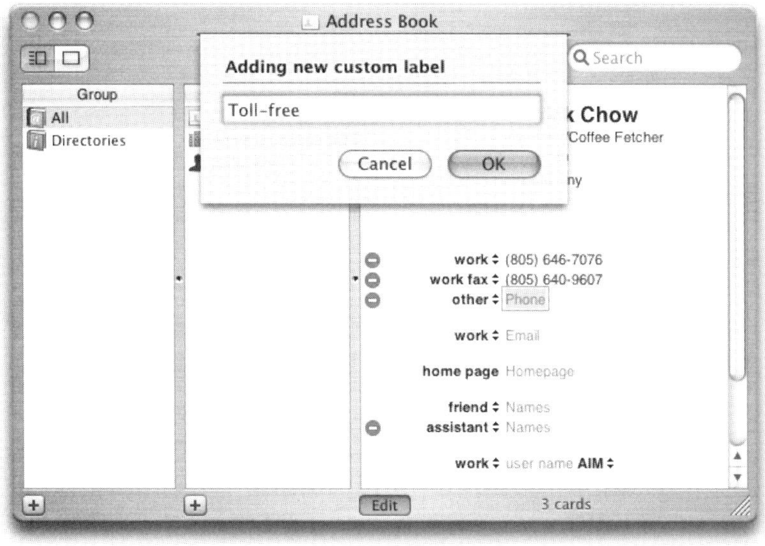

11. Type **Toll-free** in this field and click **OK** (or press **Return**).

---

12. In the new Toll-free field, type **1-888-33-LYNDA**. (Yes, letters are perfectly acceptable in the phone number fields.)

---

13. Continue adding information by typing **garrick@lynda.com** in the **work email** field. Notice that once you enter my email address, the + symbol appears to the left of the work email field in case you need to add more email addresses for this contact. Press **Tab** and enter **www.lynda.com** in the **home page** field. Press **Tab** twice to skip the **friend** and **assistant** fields. (If you click either of these fields, you'll observe that you can select from other titles such as father, mother, child, spouse, manager, and so on.)

The next field, work (AIM), is for the contact's instant messaging address. Instant messaging, the activity of chatting online with other people in real-time, has become an increasingly popular Internet service in the past few years. Some of the most popular services are America Online's Instant Messenger (AIM), Yahoo Messenger, ICQ, Jabber, and Microsoft Messenger. If your contact is a member of any of these services (or any other messaging service), you can enter his or her user name in the field. You'll be learning more about these messaging services later in this chapter.

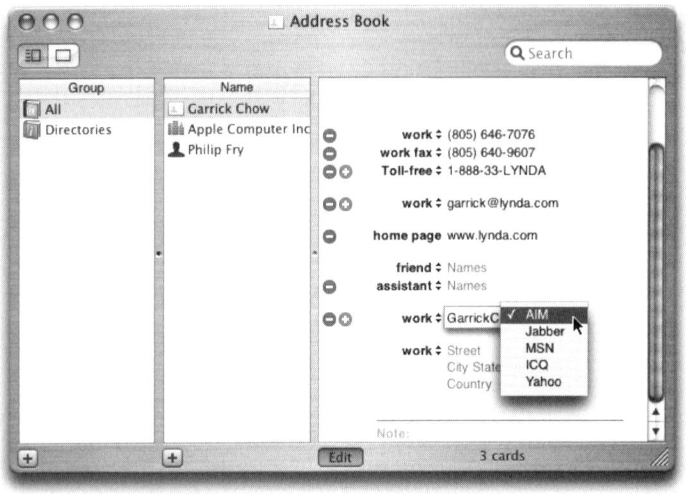

14. Type **GarrickCH** in the **work** field. This is an example of an instant messaging user name. Click **AIM** to see the list of other available instant messaging services. If your contact subscribes to a service other than AOL Instant Messenger, you can select it from this list. For this exercise, keep **AIM** selected.

Note: *If your contact subscribes to more than one service, just click the green + symbol to add additional instant message addresses.*

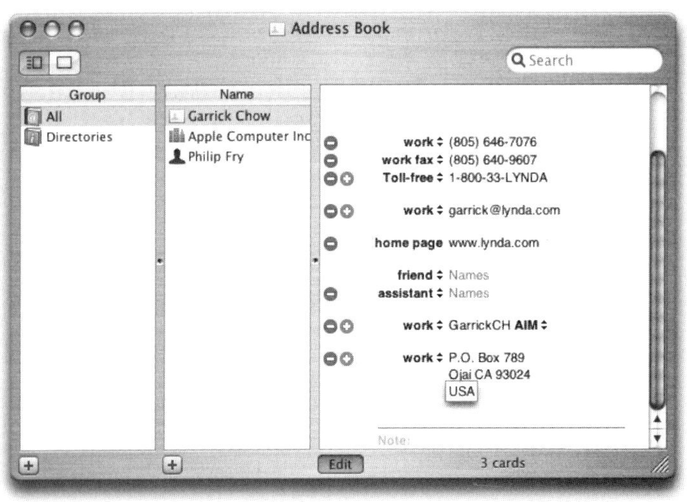

15. Enter the information shown here into the **work address** fields. Notice that there are separate fields for **street**, **city**, **state**, **ZIP**, and **country**, so there's no need for punctuation such as a comma between the city and state.

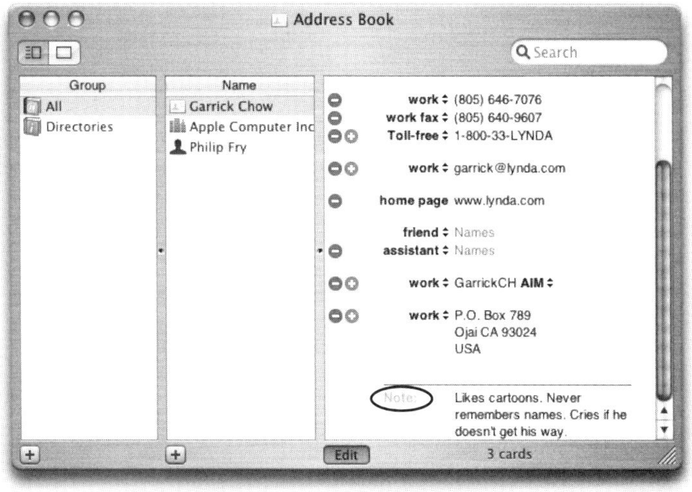

*The final field on this card is called **Note**. (Scroll down or increase the size of the Address Book window if you can't see this field.) If you click in this area, you can enter any information about this contact that you may need to remember, but which may not belong in any of the other fields.*

One of the coolest features of Address Book is its capability of putting a face with the name. If you have a photo of your contact (preferably a head shot, but any picture will do), you can easily add this photo to the contact's card.

16. Drag the **chap_10** folder from the **H•O•T CD-ROM** to your **Desktop**.

17. Double-click the **chap_10** folder to view its contents and locate the file **garrick.jpg**.

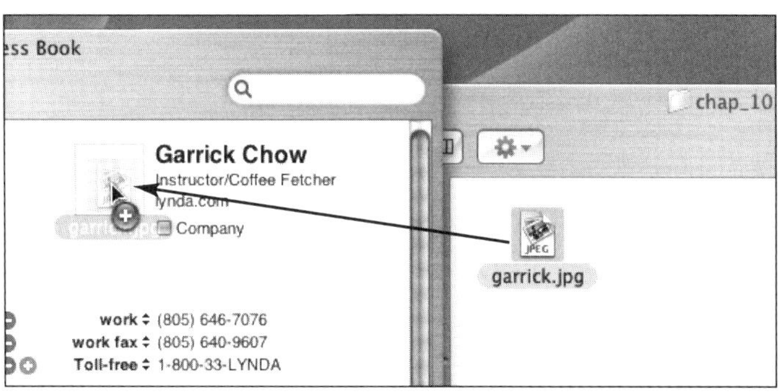

18. Make sure you can see both the **Address Book** window and the **garrick.jpg** file. If necessary, scroll up in the right pane of the **Address Book** window so you can see my name. Drag **garrick.jpg** onto the gray silhouette next to my name on the **Address Book** card.

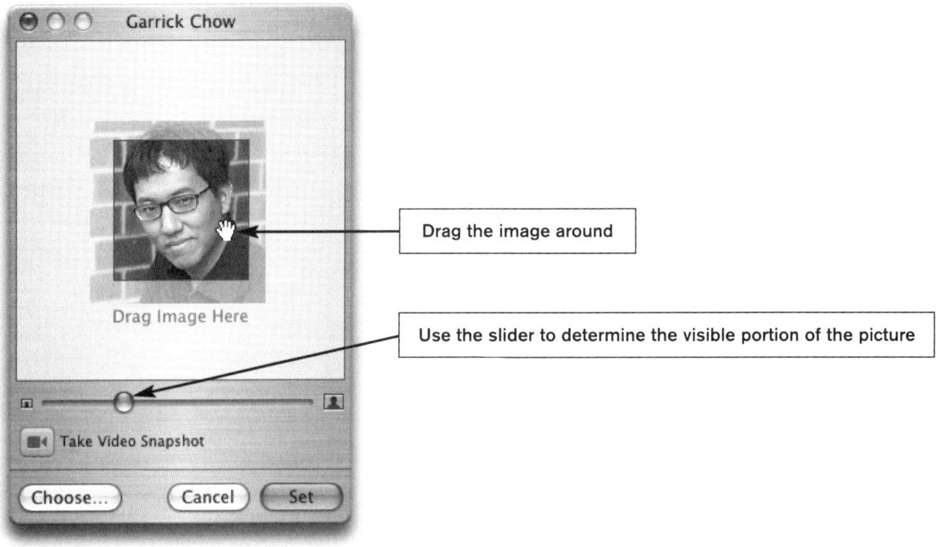

When you release the mouse, a window opens, allowing you to size the picture. You can use the slider to increase or decrease the visible portion of the picture. (The grayed-out portions of the image represent the areas you won't see after clicking ***Set****.) You can also use the mouse to drag the image around inside the visible area.*

19. Take a moment to position and size the image however you want. Then click **Set**. (You'll learn more about this picture window later in this chapter.)

My photo now appears next to my name. It's important to point out that the image has been copied into Address Book. You could delete the ***garrick.jpg*** *file on your Desktop without affecting the picture here on this card.*

Tip: *If you have pictures of your own friends and contacts, the images themselves should be as close to square as possible (around 64 x 64 pixels), and saved in JPG, GIF, TIFF, PDF, or PNG format.*

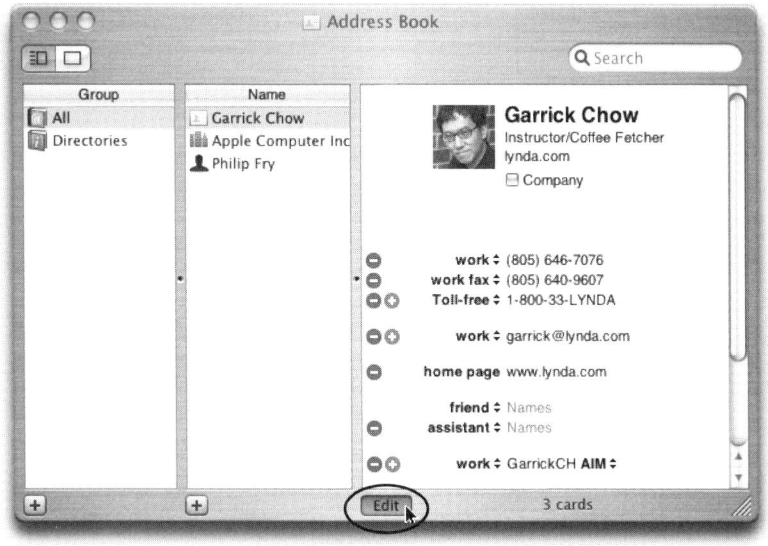

20. To stop editing this card, click the **Edit** button. Any empty fields disappear from the right pane along with all the minus and plus symbols. The information is now saved and can be accessed any time by clicking on **Garrick Chow** in the **Name** column.

Note: *To add or change information for a contact, select the name from the* ***Name*** *column and click the* ***Edit*** *button at the bottom of the window (or press* ***Cmd+L****). To delete a contact, simply select it in the* ***Name*** *column and press* ***Delete*** *on your keyboard. You'll be asked if you're sure you want to delete the contact. Click* ***Yes*** *if you're sure or* ***No*** *to change your mind.*

---

21. If you have any contacts of your own that you'd like to add, go ahead and do so at this time. If you don't have any contacts to add, go out and make some friends, get their names and phone numbers, and then come back and add them to **Address Book**. When you're done, keep **Address Book** open for the next exercise.

Creating Groups

As your number of contacts begins to increase, you'll probably find it useful to organize your contacts into groups. Grouping contacts together makes it easier to find certain people by searching for them in specific categories. If you use Mail as your email application, you can send an email to an entire group by dragging the group into Mail. To create a group, choose **File > New Group** from the menu bar (or click the **+** sign under the **Group** column) and give the group a name such as Friends, Family, Work, Enemies, and so on.

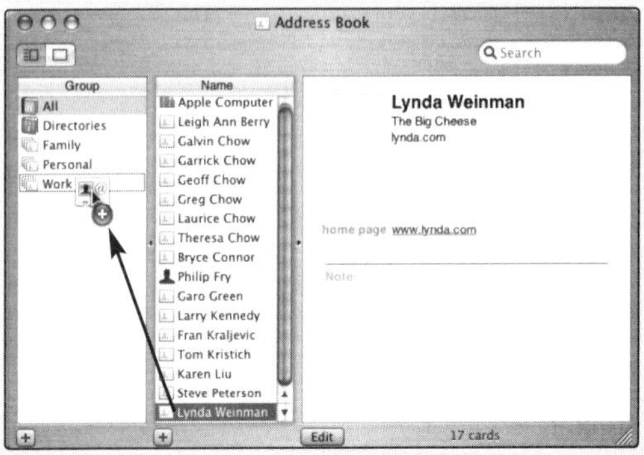

From there, it's just a matter of dragging names from the **Name** column into their proper groups. Alternately, you can select several contacts at once (by **Cmd+clicking** each name) and then choose **File > New Group From Selection** to automatically move multiple names into a new group at once.

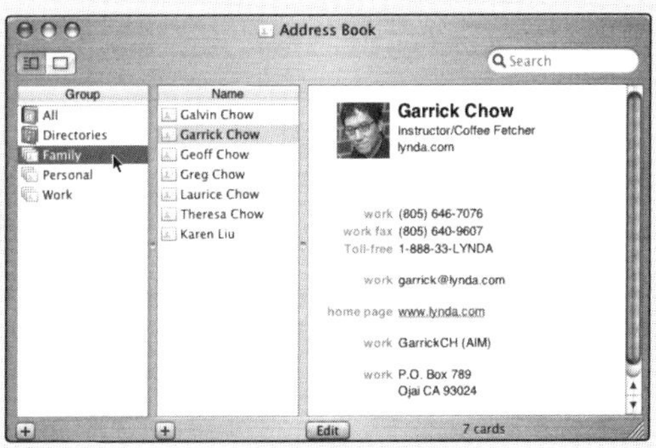

You can then select specific groups to view the smaller list of contacts within.

If a particular contact no longer belongs in one of your groups, select the group, then click the contact's name and press **Delete**. The contact will only be removed from the group, not your main collection. The only way you can permanently delete a contact is to have **All** selected under the **Group** column.

Importing Contacts from Other Applications

If you have contact information stored on your Mac in another application such as Microsoft Entourage, Outlook Express, Netscape, or Palm Desktop, you'll be happy to know that you can import this information into Address Book without having to retype it all. And if you're familiar with earlier versions of Address Book, you'll be extremely pleased to learn that this process has gotten much, much easier in the latest Panther release.

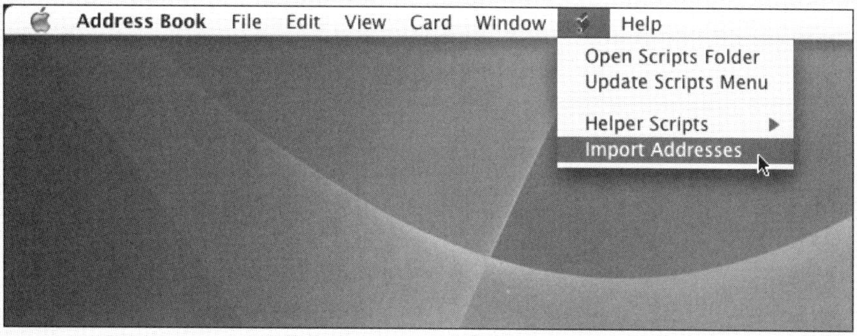

To import contacts from another application, click the **Script** icon in the **Address Book** menu bar and choose **Import Addresses**.

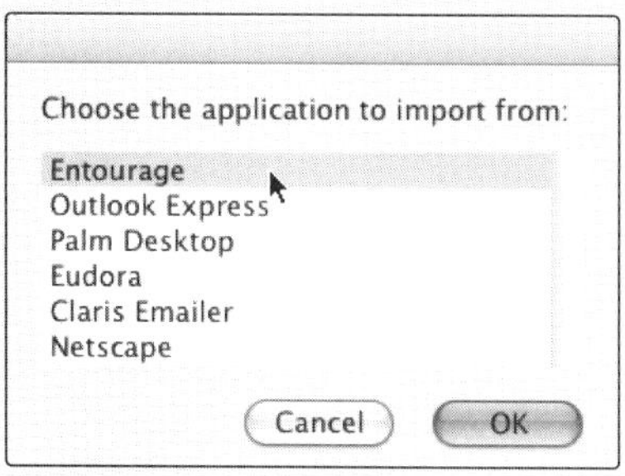

In the window that opens, select the application from which you want to import your contact information and click **OK**. The next steps vary depending on the application you chose. Just follow the instructions that appear to bring your contact info into Address Book.

2. Using Address Book

Now that you actually have some contacts in Address Book, you'll take a look at some of the cool things you can do with them. This exercise will take you on a short tour of some of the ways in which Address Book can function as the hub of your contact information.

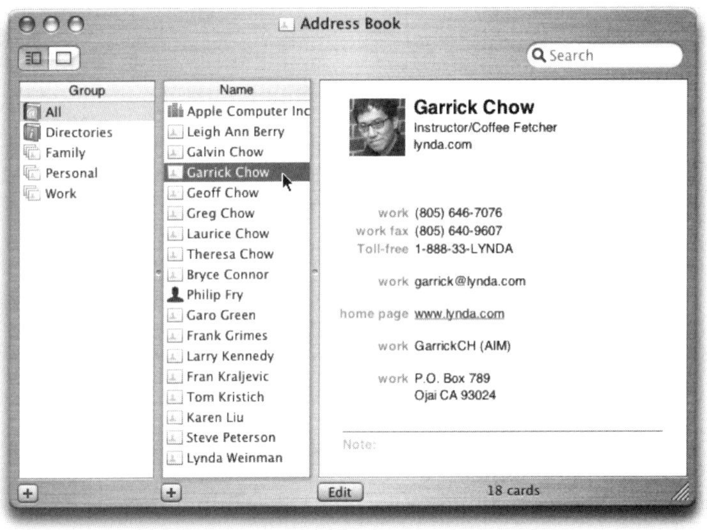

1. In **Address Book**, select **Garrick Chow** from the **Name** column.

Have you ever tried to read a phone or fax number off your monitor from across the room? Have you ever gone to the trouble of actually jotting down the number on a piece of paper just so you could take it across the room (thereby defeating the purpose of keeping your contact information digitally)? If you answered "yes" to either of these questions, has Address Book got a great feature for you! (If you answered "yes" out loud, seek therapy.)

2. Roll your mouse cursor over the **work**, **work fax**, and **Toll-free** headings on this card. Notice that a small capsule-like highlight appears around them. Anytime you see this highlight, you're being told that there is a menu selection available for this heading.

3. Click the **work fax** heading. A menu command called **Large Type** appears. Choose it.

Big enough for ya? You should now (I hope) be able to read this number from across just about any sized room. If your office is too big to be able to read this text clearly, just have one of your minions shout the number to you.

4. Click anywhere onscreen to make the large type disappear.

Tip: *This Large Type feature is available for any phone numbers listed on a contact's card. Of course, the big numbers are really only useful if you're within sight of your monitor. But what if the fax machine is around the corner? One possible solution is to have your Mac read the number to you. Make sure your Mac's volume is up loud enough, select the phone number on the card, and then choose* ***Address Book > Services > Speech > Start Speaking Text.*** *If you need more time to get to the fax machine before the number is read, just include some of the entries before the number when you make your selection. While your Mac is reading the contact's name, job title, and so on, you'll be hustling across the room to your fax machine.*

There are menus available for some of the other headings as well. For instance, if you have an active Internet connection, you can click the home page heading and select Go to Web Site, or you can click an instant messaging heading to open iChat AV (which you'll learn about later in this chapter).

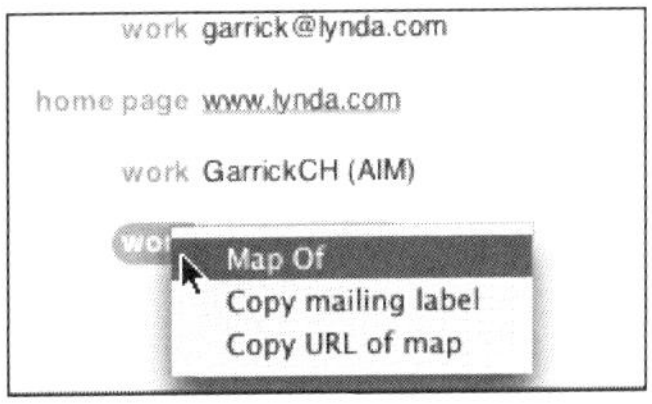

5. If you have an active Internet connection, click the **work** heading next to the **address** information and choose **Map Of**.

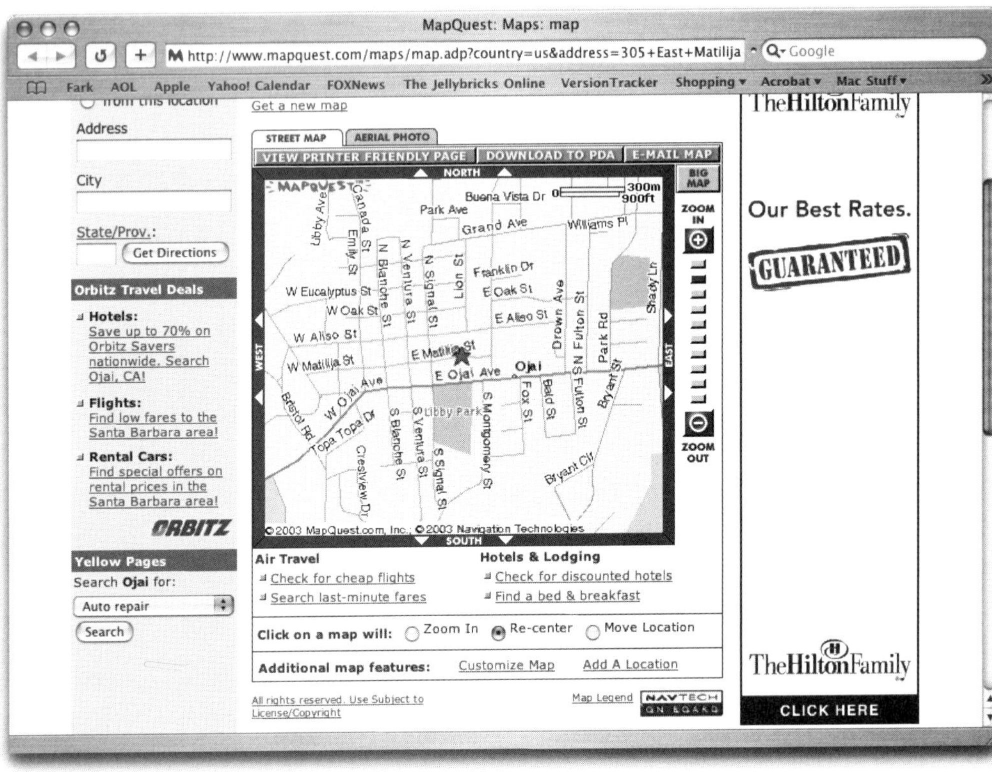

Your Web browser opens and takes you to mapquest.com, where a map of the address is displayed (among the wall-to-wall ads). From here, you can zoom in and out of the map, get directions to this address, or find nearby restaurants and businesses.

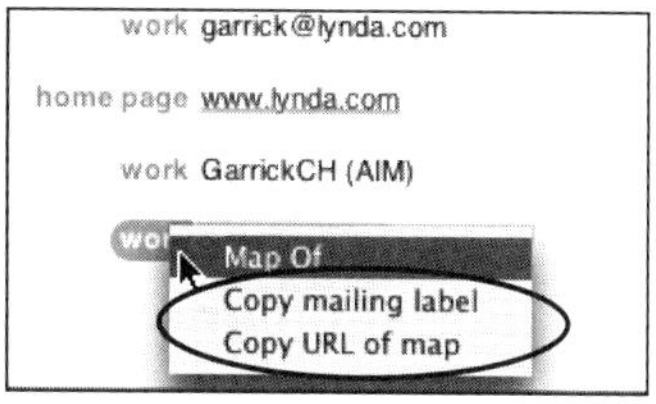

*Tip: New to this menu in Address Book are the selections **Copy mailing label**, which copies the address in its entirety so you can paste it into another application, and **Copy URL of map**, which copies the Web address of the Mapquest page so you can paste it into another application such as your email program.*

---

6. Quit your browser and return to **Address Book**.

The little contextual menus for the different card headings you've just examined can be extremely helpful, but they don't do you much good until you actually find the contact you're looking for. That's where the Search field comes into play. In the Search field, you can type a letter, number, name, word, or phrase–anything that might help you locate the card you need.

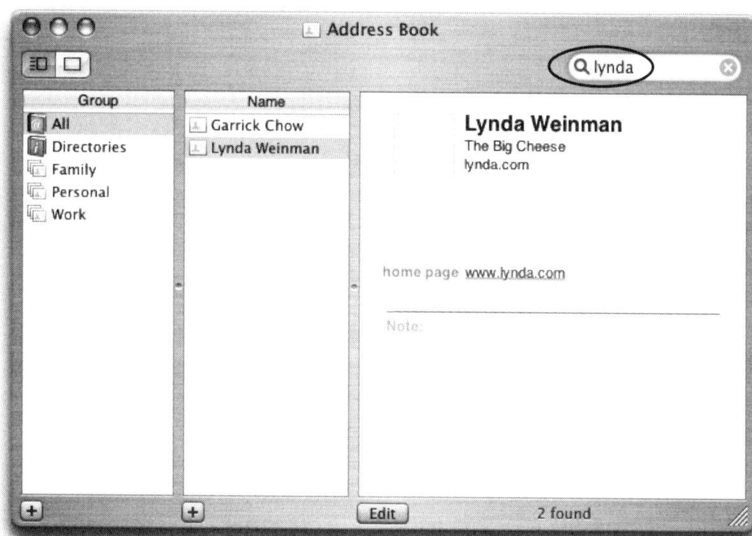

7. Type **lynda** in the **Search** field. You don't have to press **Return**; after a second, any cards with the word "lynda" in them will appear in the **Name** column. Of course, the Garrick Chow card is probably the only one that shows up in your list, unless you have a friend named Lynda, but you get the idea. If you added some of your own contacts into Address Book, enter some other names or words here to test this function.

NOTE | Minimizing Your View

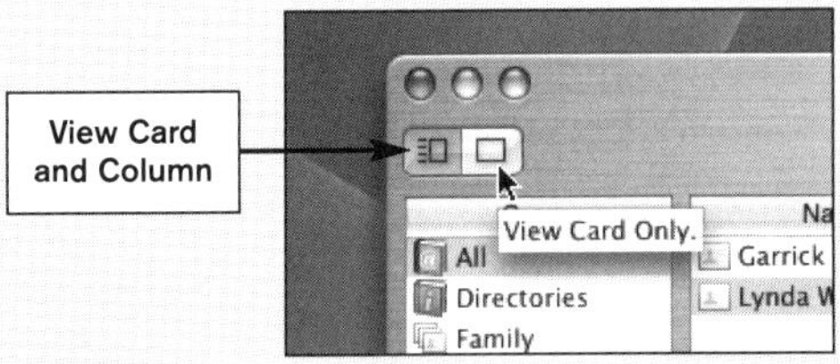

If you find that you prefer to use Address Book exclusively with the Search field instead of navigating through the Group and Name columns, you can minimize the Address Book window by clicking the **View Card Only** button in the upper-left corner of the window (or press **Cmd+2**).

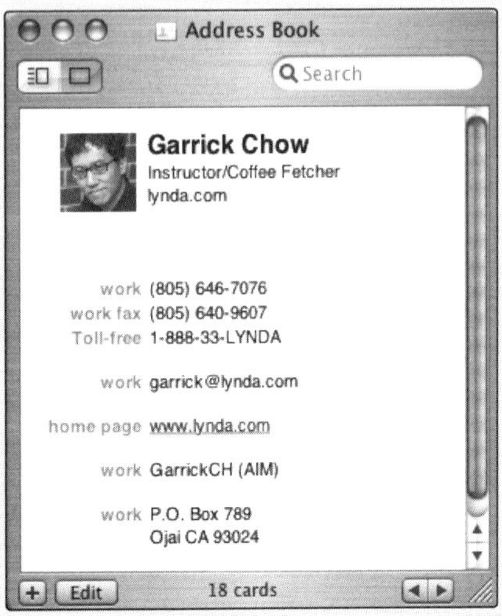

This will reduce the window to display just the card itself, which can save you valuable screen real estate. In this view, you can only find cards by typing search words into the Search field or by clicking the two arrows in the lower-right corner of the window to browse back and forth in your list of contacts.

To return to the original view, click the **View Card and Column** button (or press **Cmd+1**).

Tip: You can view any contact in its own window by double-clicking the contact in the **Name** column.

Other Cool Address Book Tricks

As you'll see in the next few exercises, Address Book incorporates itself nicely into other applications such as Mail and iChat AV. But you can also benefit from using Address Book if you own digital devices such as a Bluetooth-enabled cell phone or an Apple iPod.

The iPod, Apple's groundbreaking MP3 music player, gives you the ability to store contact information as well as music. To copy contacts to your iPod, connect the iPod to your Mac.

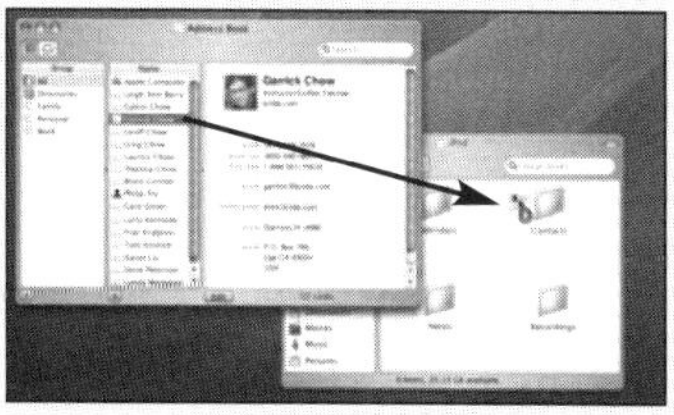

When the iPod icon appears on the Desktop, double-click it to view its contents. Among the items here, you'll find a folder called Contacts. Open Address Book and drag any of your contacts into this folder. You'll now be able to view these contacts from your iPod. In Chapter 13, "*iCal and iSync*," you'll learn how to move all your contacts to your iPod through Apple's iSync application.

Note that the act of dragging any contact out of Address Book instantly exports that contact as a vCard. vCards are an increasingly popular file format for contact information among the most popular address applications available today. Dragging your contacts out of Address Book is a simple way of preparing them for import into another application.

Perhaps one of the most exciting features of Address Book (well, exciting for geeks like me, anyway) is that it can communicate with Bluetooth-enabled cell phones. Bluetooth is a short-range wireless technology that allows enabled devices to communicate with each other. Check with your cell phone service provider to see if any of their phones are Bluetooth-compatible. With a Bluetooth phone and a Bluetooth USB adapter for your Mac (available at **store.apple.com**), Address Book takes on a whole new set of capabilities. For instance, once your Mac and your phone have been set up to recognize each other, you can click phone numbers in your contact cards and select Dial, which will automatically dial the number on your cell phone for you. All you have to do is pick up the phone and wait for the caller to answer. On the flip side, if your phone receives an incoming call, you can have the Caller-ID information appear in large type on your monitor so you don't have to pick up your phone to see who's calling.

What an age we live in.

8. Quit **Address Book**.

By this point, you should have a pretty good idea of the capabilities of Address Book. In the following exercises, you'll see how Address Book functions in relation to Mail.

3. Setting Up Mail

With the release of OS X, Apple introduced Mail, its own email application. Prior to Mail, Mac users had to rely on third-party programs such as Microsoft Entourage, Netscape, or Eudora. In general, most email programs work pretty much the same way, with a few differences in features and capabilities. One of the nice things about using Mail as your email application, however, is how seamlessly it integrates with other OS X applications such as Address Book and Safari.

Note: For this exercise, make sure that you have an email account and an active Internet connection. Depending on your email service, you'll have to set up Mail in a specific way. This exercise will cover the most common methods of setting up Mail to send and receive your email.

1. Open **Mail** by clicking its icon in the **Dock**. If you've removed its icon, you can find **Mail** in your **Applications** folder.

If this is the first time you've opened Mail, you may see this window. In order to use Mail, you need to configure it with your email account settings. The following chart describes the fields found in this window. (This window won't appear if you've already set up a .Mac account, as will be described in Chapter 12, ".Mac," and you can skip the rest of this exercise.)

Welcome to Mail Settings	
Field	**Description**
Full Name	The way your name appears here is how it will appear in the "From" field for people who receive your emails. It's up to you whether you want to enter your full name, just your first name, or a nickname. If your name is "Christopher" but you prefer to go by "Topher," feel free to change your name here. **Tip:** It's never cool to make up your own nickname.
Email Address	Enter your full email address in this field. This is the address that you have chosen or were given by your ISP or company.
Incoming Mail Server	Your ISP or company should provide the information for this field. It often takes the form of something like mail.your_isp.com or pop.your_isp.com. The incoming mail server info tells Mail the location of the server that stores emails addressed to you.
Account Type: **POP, IMAP, or Exchange**	Depending on the service you sign up for (or have been assigned to), you may encounter three different types of email servers: POP (also known as POP3), IMAP, and Microsoft Outlook Exchange. **POP**, arguably the most common type, is a server than sends your email to your Mac's hard drive for you to read. The advantage of a POP server is that all the emails you've read are stored on your Mac and can be accessed without having to connect to the Internet. The downside is that if you travel or have more than one Mac, you have to carry copies of any emails you want to keep with you. **IMAP**, on the other hand, is a Web-based email service that stores your email on a server allowing you access to your email from any computer connected to the Internet. The disadvantage to this service is that you must be online to work with your email. If you received your email address through your company, you may be using a Microsoft Outlook **Exchange** email server, which behaves similarly to IMAP, but uses a proprietary Outlook Web Access server. If you're not sure which type of email account you have, check with your ISP or network administrator. **Note:** Another type of email service is free Web-based email such as Yahoo or Hotmail. Email from these accounts is accessed directly from your Web browser, and Mail is completely uninvolved in the process.

continues on next page

Welcome to Mail Settings *continued*	
Field	**Description**
User Name	In most cases, your user name is simply your email address without the "@your_company.com." Some ISPs, however, use your entire email address as your user name. Check with your ISP.
Password	Enter the password you created for this account here.
Outgoing Mail Server (SMTP)	Again, your ISP or company should provide this information. The outgoing mail server info tells Mail the location of the server that handles all the outgoing email.
Outlook Web Access Server	This field appears only if you select **Exchange** as your **Account Type.**

2. Enter your information into the **Welcome to Mail** setup window.

Note: *If you have more than one email address, just enter your primary account's information here. You can add additional mailboxes to Mail later.*

Once you're done, the setup window should look something like this. (Be sure not to enter the information shown here though–it's fictional.)

3. Click **OK** when you're done. Mail will connect to the Internet and try to confirm your settings.

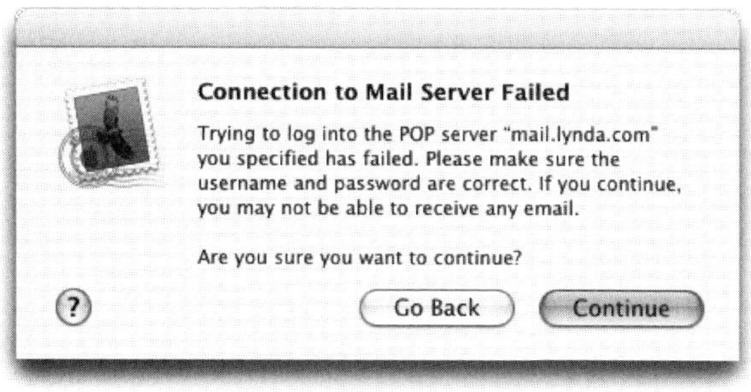

*If there's a problem with any of your information, you'll see this dialog box. Click **Go Back** to check your settings for errors.*

*If your settings were correct, you'll next be presented with this dialog box asking if you want to import any mailboxes from other applications you might have been using prior to Mail. If you click **Yes**, you'll be able to choose mailboxes from **Entourage**, **Outlook Express**, **Claris Emailer**, **Netscape**, or **Eudora**.*

4. If you want to import your old email folders, click **Yes** and follow the directions onscreen. If not, click **No**.

Note: *If you choose to say **No** now, and want to import your mailboxes from another application later, you can find this feature again by choosing **File > Import Mailboxes.***

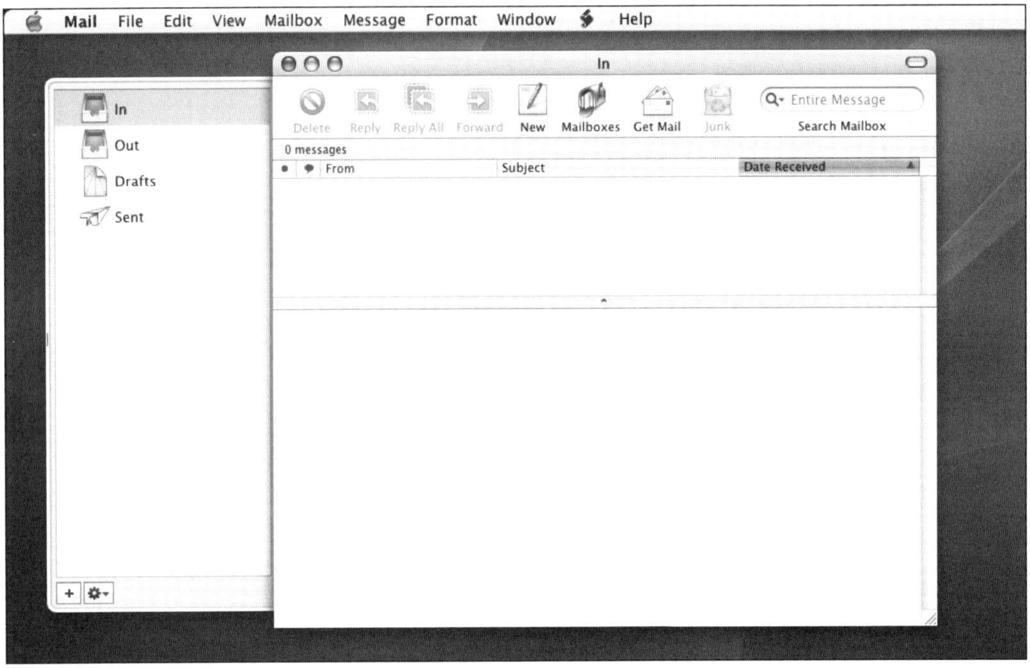

The main Mail window is now open, and you can start writing, sending, and receiving email. You'll do so in the next exercise.

---

5. If you see a dialog box asking if you want to see what's new in Mail, click **No**. (If you want to view this information later, choose **Help > What's New in Mail?** from the menu bar.) Keep Mail open for the following exercise.

---

4. Receiving Email

This exercise will take you through the basic act of checking for incoming email. By default, Mail is set to automatically check for new email every few minutes. The first thing you'll do is locate this setting and change it if necessary.

1. Choose **Mail > Preferences** from the menu bar.

2. If it's not already selected, click the **General** button in the toolbar.

In this area is a pop-up menu next to ***Check for new mail****. With this menu, you determine how often you want Mail to check for new email on your ISP's email server.*

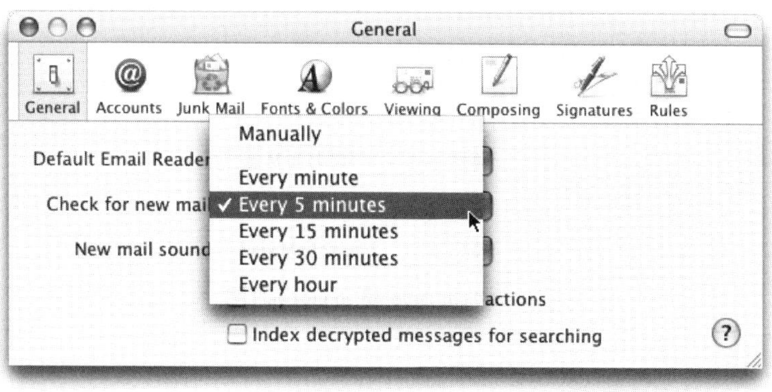

3. Select an interval from the **Check for new mail** menu. If you choose **Manually**, Mail will never check for email on its own–you'll have to click the **Get Mail** button each time you want to check.

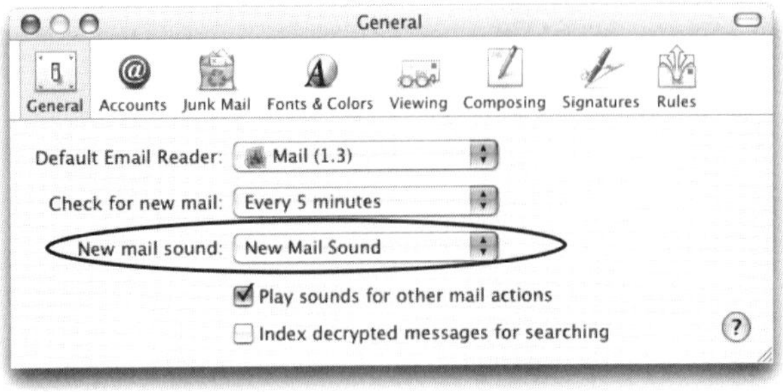

4. From the **New mail sound** pop-up menu, you can select a sound that will play to alert you when you have new mail. This is a useful feature if you've decided to have Mail automatically check for email; you'll be able to know when new mail arrives even if you're not looking at your screen at the time. Close the **General** window when you're done.

Even if you've set up mail to check automatically for new messages, you can always check manually at any time.

Adding Accounts

If you have more than one email address, you can add additional addresses to Mail by choosing **Mail > Preferences** and then clicking the **Accounts** button.

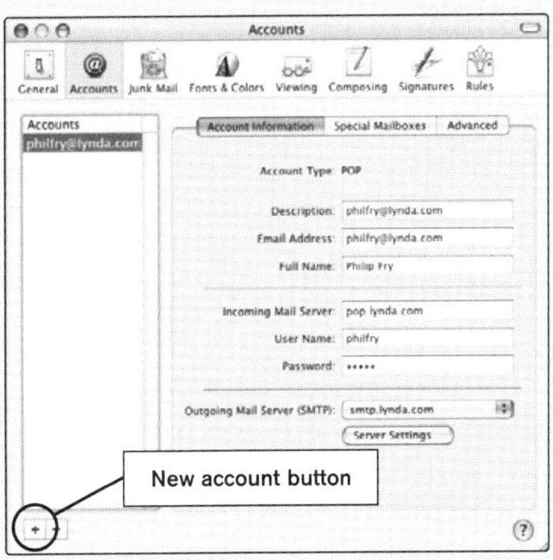

Click the + symbol in the lower-left corner to add a new account to Mail and then enter the necessary information under **Account Information**. Once completed, Mail will check for email under all your accounts, and when composing messages, you'll be able to choose from which account to send the email.

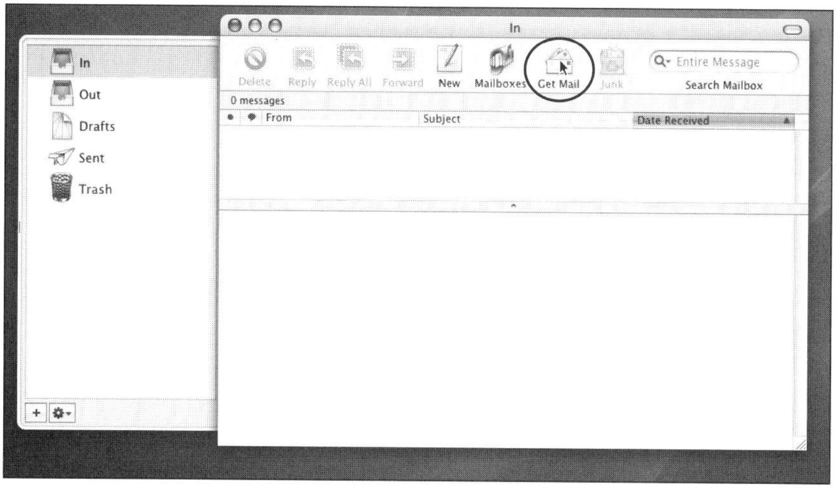

5. Click the **Get Mail** button in the toolbar.

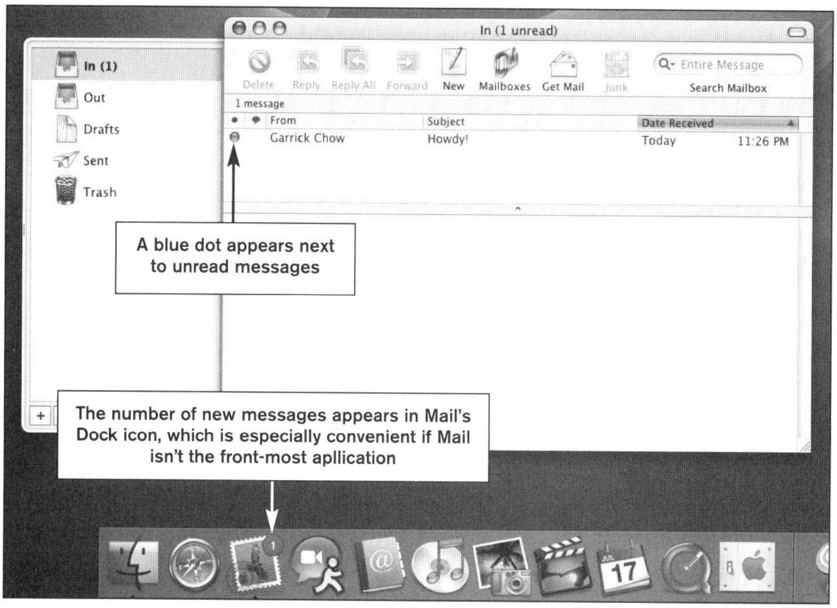

Mail will connect to your mail server, and in a moment, any new messages will appear in your ***In*** *box. Your In box is found in the panel to the right or left of the main window. This panel is called a "drawer," and you can show or hide it by clicking the Mailboxes button in the toolbar. Drawers can be found in many OS X applications. In Mail, the drawer contains the various mailboxes associated with your email account or accounts. The following chart describes these boxes.*

Mail's Mailboxes	
Mailbox	**Description**
In	Any mail you receive is stored in this folder. If you have more than one email account, you'll find separate folders within the In box for each account.
Out	Any mail you've written but haven't sent is stored in the Out box.
Drafts	Mail that you've started writing but haven't yet completed is stored in the Drafts box.
Sent	Emails that have been sent are stored in this box. Similar to the In box, emails sent from different accounts are stored in separate subfolders of Sent.
Trash	Mail that you delete or manually drag to the Trash icon is stored in this folder. Nothing is actually deleted, though, until you choose **Mailbox > Erase Deleted Messages** or press **Cmd+K.** If you change your mind about deleting a message, you can drag it from the Trash into other folders.
Junk	You'll see this mailbox if Mail has spotted any potential junk mail in your incoming messages. See the upcoming sidebar "Filtering Junk Mail."

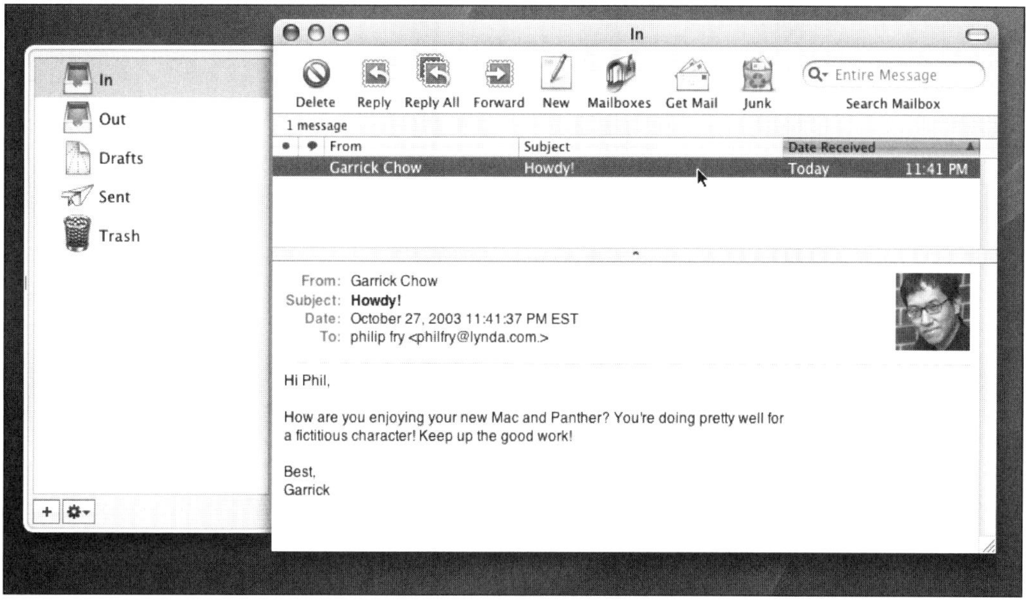

6. Click any incoming messages to display them in the lower pane of the window. (Alternately, you can double-click a message to display it in its own window.) If the email sender's address appears in Address Book, his or her picture appears along with the email (if you've previously added their pictures to Address Book).

Tip: *If you receive an email from someone who you haven't yet added to Address Book, select the email and choose* ***Message > Add Sender to Address Book*** *(or press* ***Cmd+Y****) to automatically create an Address Book card for them.*

What? You have no incoming email? Sounds like you need to write a few messages yourself, buddy. In the following exercise, you'll learn how to send emails from Mail to let your friends know you're still around.

---

7. Keep **Mail** open for the next exercise.

Filtering Junk Mail

Of course, you might have the opposite problem of not getting any email: getting way too much. Unsolicited email advertisements, known universally as **spam**, are the scourge of online life. If you've spent any time at all on the Internet, you've most likely ended up on some low-life's mailing list, resulting in a constant barrage of emails offering you the opportunity to purchase little spy cameras, enlarge your pectoral muscles, or go on a fabulous Caribbean cruise.

For the most part, spam is an unavoidable reality of being online; fortunately, Mail comes with a built-in junk mail filter. And you don't even have to turn it on. By default, Mail's junk mail filter is set to "training" mode, which means that when you receive email, Mail will try to determine which messages are spam and which are legitimate communications and deal with them accordingly.

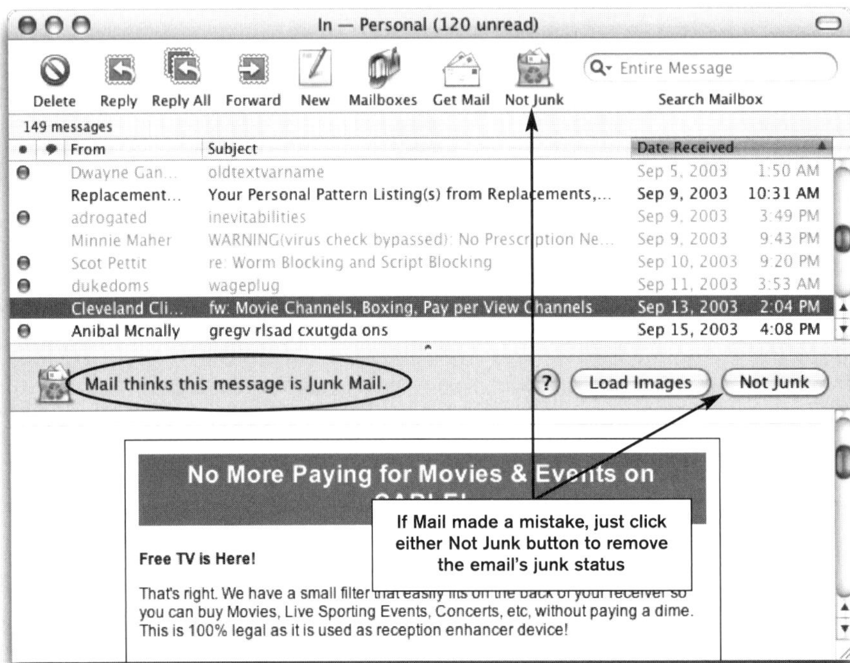

Any messages that Mail declares to be junk will be displayed, appropriately, in brown, making them easy to identify and delete. Mail does a pretty good job of picking out the junk, but you can train Mail to be even better at filtering by letting it know whether it accidentally labeled genuine email as junk, or if it missed some obvious spam.

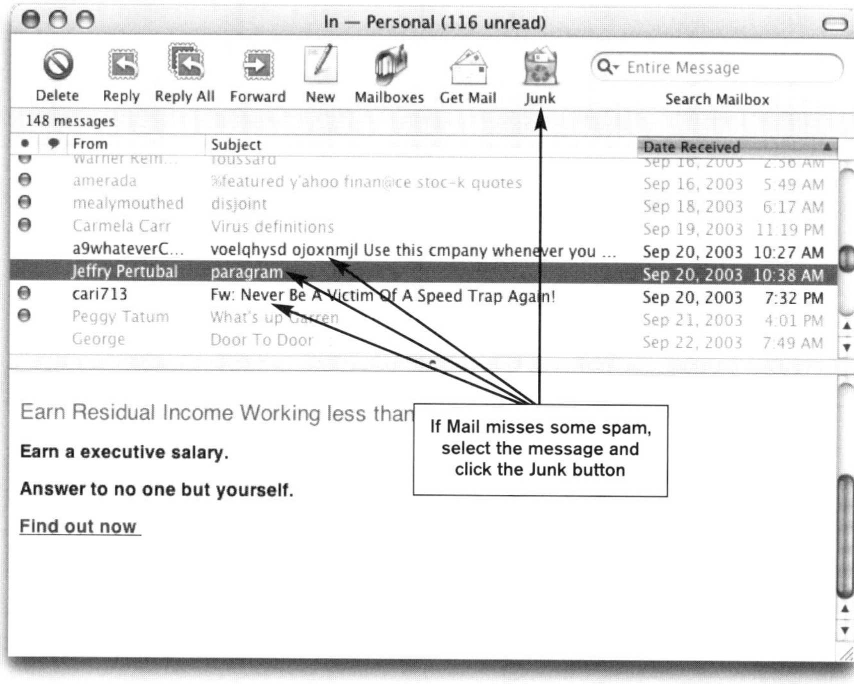

If a message tagged as junk is not in fact spam, just select it and click the **Not Junk** button; if Mail misses a spam email, select the email and click the **Junk** button in the toolbar. The more you help Mail, the better it will get at filtering out the junk.

You'll probably want to leave the junk mail filter in training mode for a few weeks or so while Mail learns what's junk and what's not.

Once you're satisfied with its performance, you can select **Move it to the Junk mailbox (Automatic)** from **Mail > Preferences**. Mail will then automatically send spam to a Junk mailbox it creates in the Mail drawer. You'll still be able to review the messages it sends there to check for mistakes, but having all the junk in one mailbox makes it that much easier to delete all at once. Just choose Edit > Select all and press the Delete key to send them all to the Trash.

The junk mail filter works pretty well for sorting out the spam, but it isn't much help in getting you off the list that you ended up on in the first place. One tactic you can try is to select spam that you've received and then choose **Message > Bounce to Sender** from the menu bar. This will return the spam to the originator and give the impression that your email address is no longer in service or does not exist. (If for some reason you enjoy receiving unsolicited offers, you can turn off the junk mail filter by choosing **Mail > Junk Mail > Off**. You're now free to improve your life and body via spam.)

5. Composing and Sending Email

This exercise shows you how to create new emails and send them out into the world.

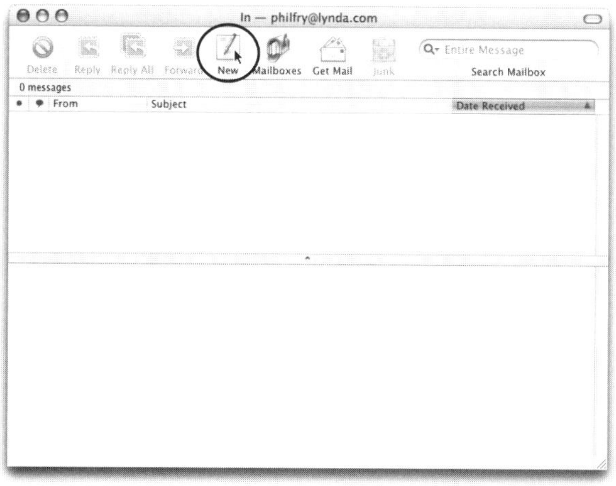

1. Click the **New** button in the Mail toolbar to open a **New Message** window.

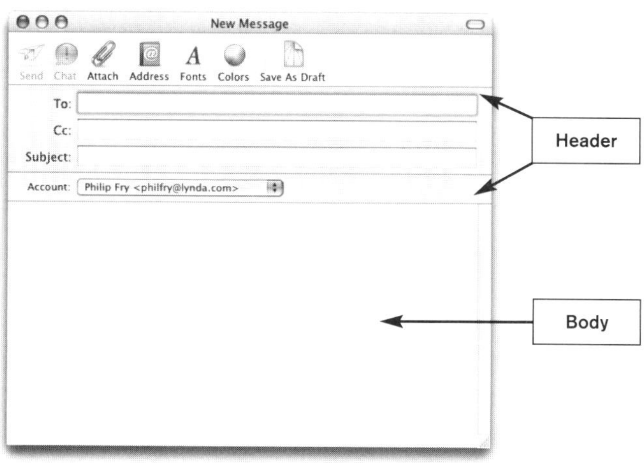

The top section of the New Message window is referred to as the ***Header****. The Header is where you enter the email address of this message's intended recipients and where you can type a subject for the email. The bottom portion of this window is known as the* ***Body****, which is where you type your actual message.*

Note: *If you created more than one email account in Mail, you'll also see a pop-up menu in the Header where you can select which account you'd like to send the email from.*

NOTE | Reply, Reply All, and Forward

As you just saw, you can create a new blank email window by clicking the New button in Mail. However, if you're responding to an email you received, you should select the email and then click **Reply**. Doing so creates a new email window that's already addressed to the sender of the original email, eliminating the need for you to type the address in yourself. Also, using the Reply button allows you to take advantage of Mail's new capability to keep track of message "threads." See "Viewing Email Threads" at the end of this exercise.

If you received an email that was addressed to you and several other people, you can click **Reply All** if you would like to send your response to everyone in that group. Just make sure you know which one you're clicking. Clicking Reply All when you only meant for the original sender to read your email can sometimes lead to embarrassing and awkward situations.

The **Forward** button in the toolbar allows you to send a copy of a received email to a completely different person. Clicking this button opens a new email window with the text of the original email already entered in the body. You can add your own comments before sending it off.

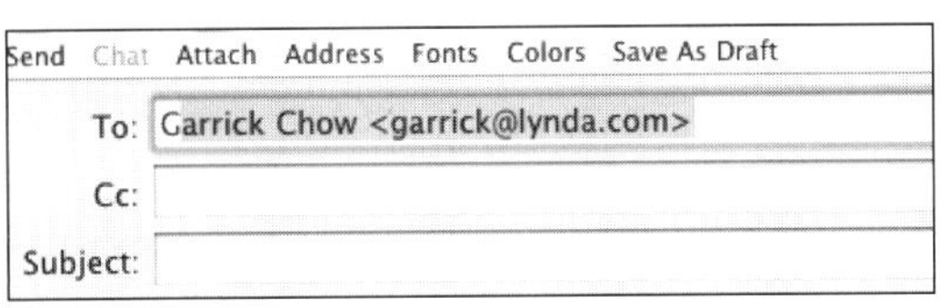

2. Click your cursor in the **To** field in the Header section. Type the letter **G**. Notice how the rest of my name and **<garrick@lynda.com>** immediately appears.

This is a great example of how well Mail and Address Book work together. As soon as you type a letter in the To field, Mail searches Address Book for possible matches and displays the first one that matches alphabetically. The characters you didn't type are highlighted, so if the address it displays is not correct, just keep typing. Mail will keep suggesting addresses until it can't find anything that matches what you're typing. But if the address that Mail displays is the one you want, you can stop typing and just press ***Tab*** *to move to the next field.*

3. Delete my email address and enter the email address of someone you know in the **To** field. (Or if you really want to drop me a line, go right ahead.) Press **Tab** to move to the next field.

*The **Cc** field is for carbon copying your email to someone other than the primary recipient shown in the To field. You'll leave this field blank for now.*

TIP | Blind Carbon Copying

When you Cc a recipient, both the primary recipient and the Cc recipient see each other's email address in the email and are made aware that the email went to both parties. If you prefer that the primary recipient not know that you sent a copy of the email to someone else, you can use the blind carbon copy, or **Bcc**. Bcc recipients see no addresses but their own in the email and have no way of knowing who else the message was sent to or that it was sent to someone else at all. (In some email applications, even the recipient's own address doesn't appear.) This is perfect for lazy thank-you note writers ("Thanks so much for your thoughtful gift!"). To add a Bcc field to your email window, choose **View > Bcc Header**.

Drag and Drop Addressing

New to Mail in Panther, you can now drag email addresses between the To and Cc fields if the address appears in Address Book. Also new, Mail now displays email addresses as just the recipient's name, rather than the name and email address.

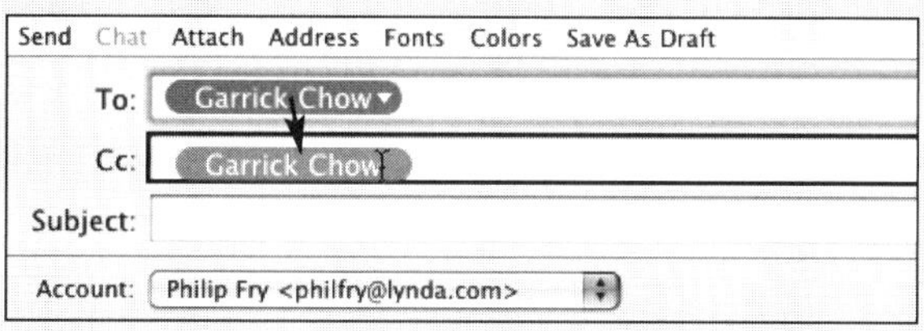

To change a To recipient to a Cc recipient, just drag his or her name from the To field into the Cc field. No more copying and pasting addresses! You can also drag someone's name to another email window. This is useful if you have a window open with many names in the From and Cc lines, and you want to respond to one person in the Cc line, but not everyone. You could create a new email document and drag the person's name from one window to another. You can also see a list of all your Address Book contacts by choosing **Window > Address Panel**. You can then drag individual contacts, or any groups of contacts you may have created, into the To, Cc, or Bcc fields in your New Message window.

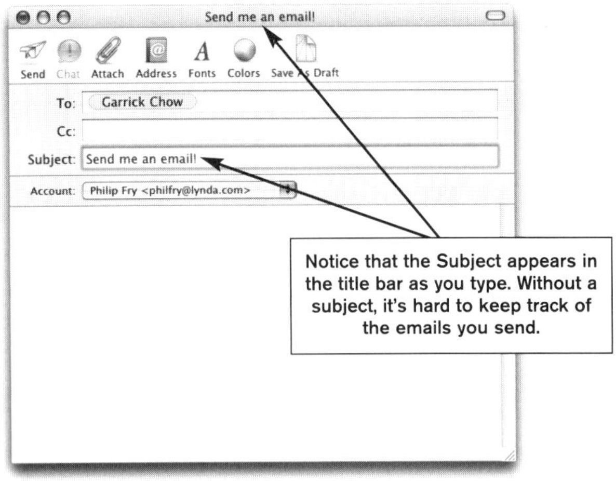

4. Press **Tab** to place the cursor in the **Subject** field. Type **Send me an email!** Although it's not necessary to include a subject with your emails, it's helpful to let your recipients know what your emails are about, and when they reply back to you, you'll know right away from the Subject line which email they're replying to.

5. Press **Tab** and type a short message to your recipient. Ask him or her to reply back to you so you'll have some new mail the next time you check for messages.

Tip: *As you type, Mail points out potentially misspelled words by drawing red dotted lines underneath them. If you know the word is correct, you can just ignore the line. If you're not sure you spelled the word right,* ***Ctrl+click*** *it to see a list of Mail's suggestions. (And yes, I'm well aware that it suggests replacing "Garrick" with "Garlic.")*

6. Now you're ready to send the email. Click the **Send** button in the toolbar.

The Out box in the Mail drawer will be briefly highlighted while your Mac connects to the mail server. After the mail has been sent, you'll hear the "mail sent" sound, and the Out box returns to normal.

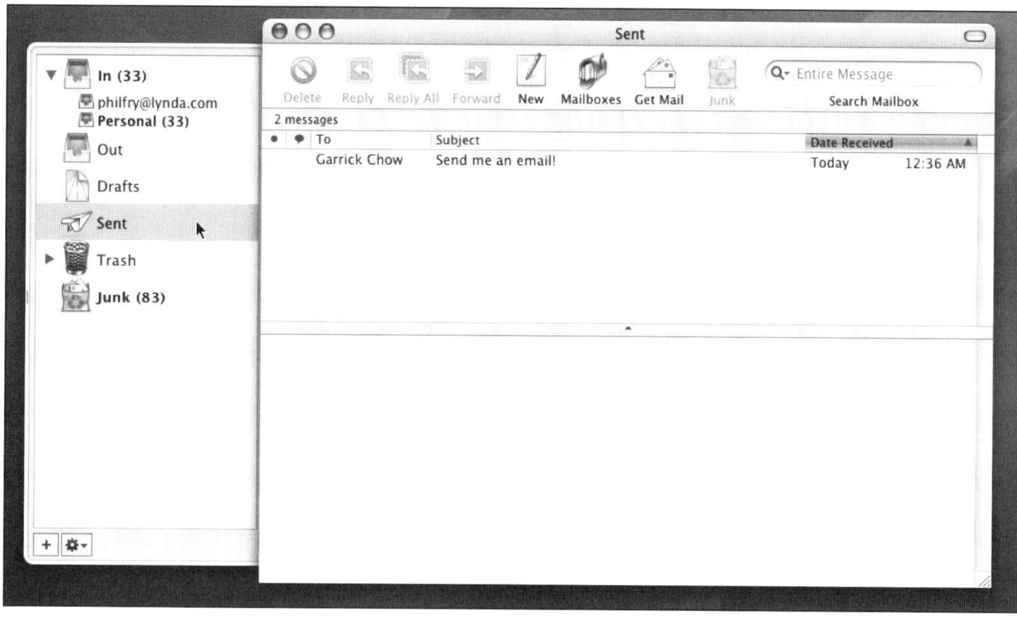

7. Click the **Sent** mailbox. The mail you sent is now stored here.

So that's composing and sending email in a nutshell. But it's certainly not all you can do with Mail. In the next exercise, you'll learn some tips and tricks for dressing up your messages before sending them out.

NOTE | Save a Draft

Occasionally you may need to write a lengthy email that could take more than one sitting to complete. If you need to take a break from writing, or if you just want to make sure that you don't lose your work, click the **Save As Draft** button in the toolbar. You email will be stored in the Drafts box and you can then take your break or even quit Mail; your email will be sitting safely in the Drafts box when you return. To resume writing, simply click the Drafts box and then double-click your email in the main window.

In actuality, Mail automatically adds new messages to the Drafts box after you've been typing for about twenty seconds or so. Clicking Save As Draft just ensures that the most recent version of your email is saved before you quit the program.

TIP | Viewing Email Threads

As you send and receive emails and your In box begins to grow, you may find it increasingly difficult to keep track of your email "conversations." There are times when you'll write a dozen or more messages back and forth with various people concerning a common topic. This chain of replies is commonly referred to as a message **thread**. Keeping track of these threads among all your other messages can be a frustrating experience, especially if you send and receive lots of email. Fortunately, Mail now features the capability to track email threads so you can quickly read through all related emails, even if someone decides to change the email's Subject line during the course of the correspondence.

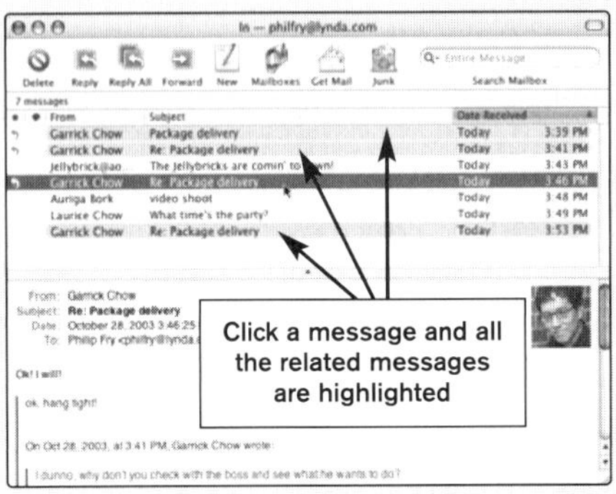

Mail helps you identify all of the messages in a thread by highlighting them in a color of your choice. Click any message in a thread to instantly highlight all related messages. You can select the color of the highlight by going to **Mail > Preferences** and clicking the **Viewing** button. From there, click the color well under **Message threading** to pick your color.

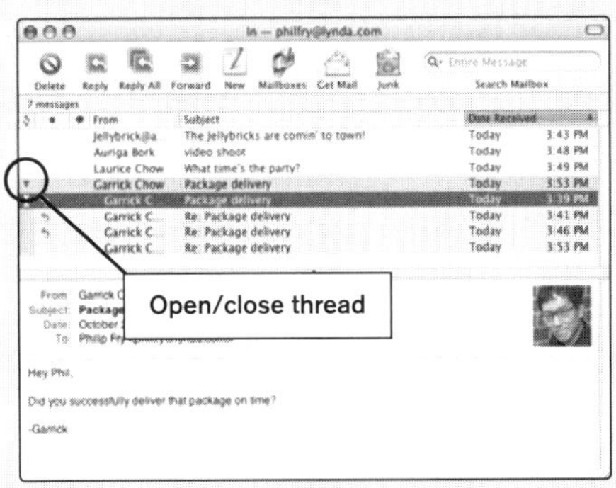

You can even choose to group messages together, sorted by date, under the original message that started the thread. To sort your email by thread, select a mailbox in the Mail drawer and choose **View > Organize by Thread**. All related emails will be grouped together. You can toggle threads open and closed by clicking the little triangle in the far-left column of the thread header. To return to your previous view, choose **View > Organize by Thread** again.

6. Adding Attachments and Signatures

Email is a great medium for sending notes, long letters, or jokes to friends and co-workers. But email isn't just about sending plain old text. There are several features that let you enhance and personalize your messages. For example, email offers you the advantage of attaching files such as documents, pictures, or folders to your email message. You can also add personalized signatures to the end of your messages that contain useful (or maybe not so useful) information such as your address or your favorite movie quote.

1. Create a new message window by clicking the **New** button in the **Mail** toolbar or by pressing **Cmd+N**.

2. Address the email to someone you know (or to yourself if you don't want to bother anybody). Add a **Subject** and type a short message.

3. To add a file to your email, click the **Attach** button in the toolbar.

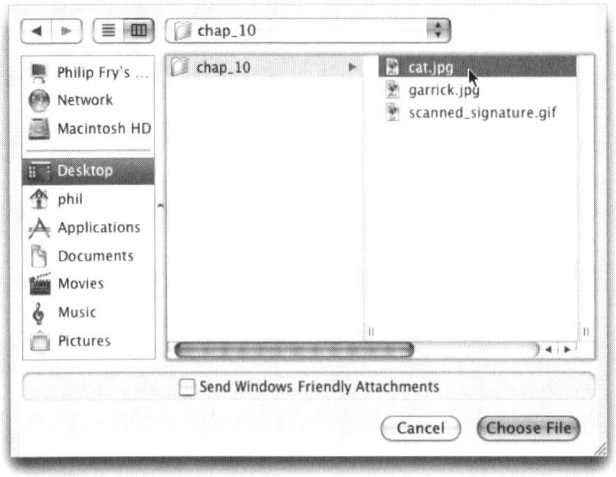

4. Navigate to the **chap_10** folder you copied to the **Desktop** in Exercise 1. Select **cat.jpg** and click **Choose File**.

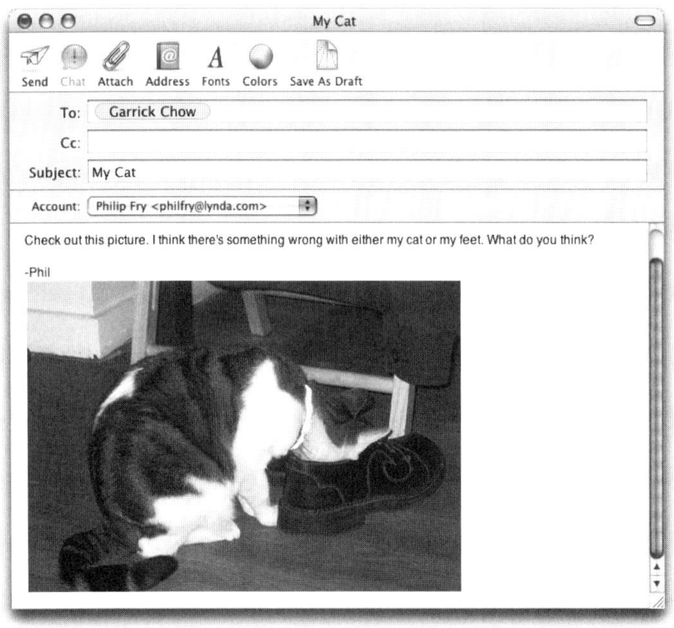

Because this is an image, it appears in the body of your email so you can make sure that you're sending the right file. It can be pretty embarrassing if you accidentally send someone the wrong picture. Believe me.

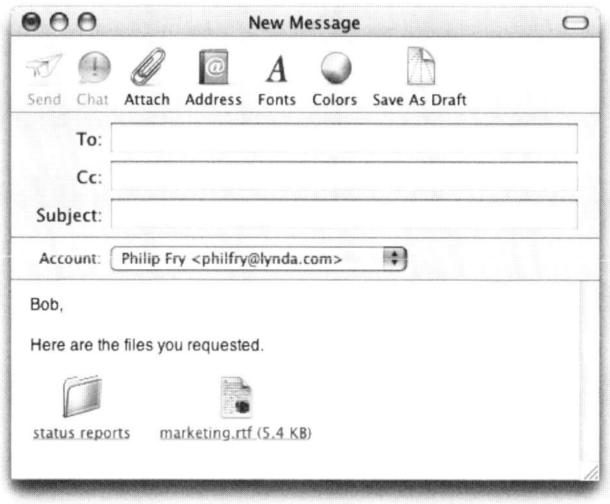

***Note:** Other types of file attachments such as text documents or folders appear as icons with their names underneath.*

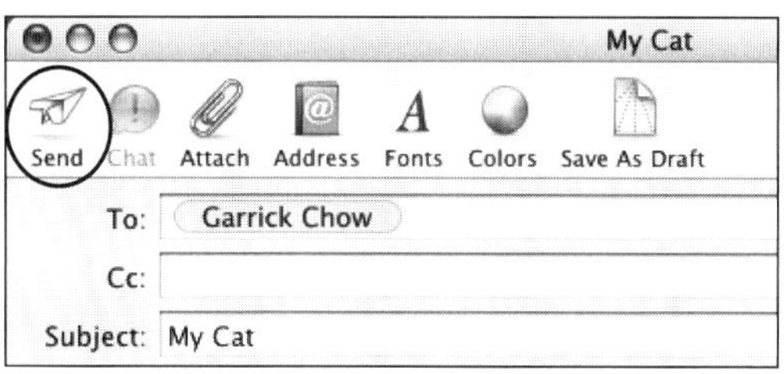

5. Now that you've successfully included the image file in your message, click the **Send** button to send the email and its attachment.

***Note:** You can attach as many files as you want to a single email. Just keep in mind that the more you add, the larger the total file size of the email will be (and that most email servers restrict the size of email attachments). If your recipient has a slow Internet connection (read "dial-up"), you may be dooming him or her to wait for hours while your attachment downloads. If you change your mind about an attachment and want to remove it, just highlight it and press **Delete.** You can also drag it to the **Trash** icon in the **Dock**. Either way, the body of your email will remain intact.*

TIP | Dragging in Attachments

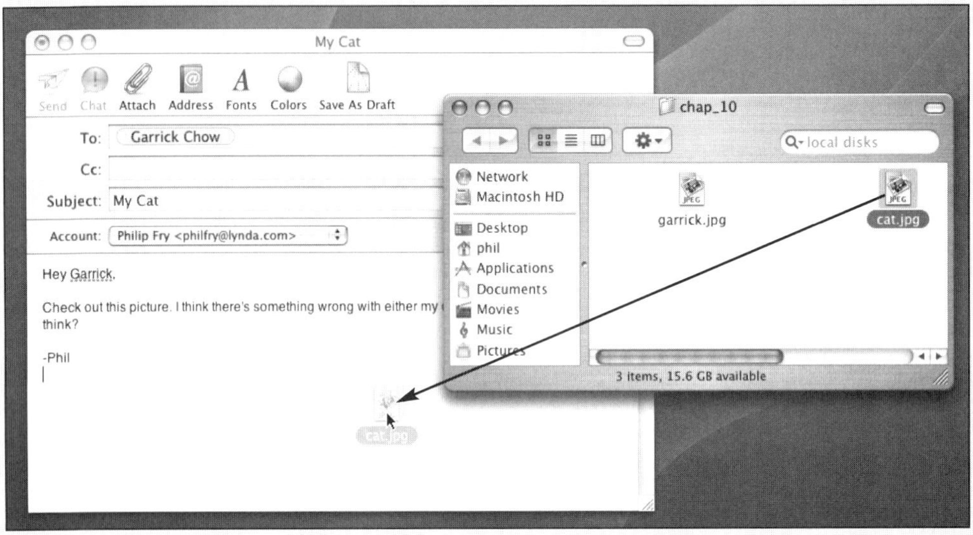

You just learned that attaching a file to an email is as simple as clicking the Attach button in your email message window. But you can also attach files by dragging them directly into your message, which is sometime more convenient than clicking Attach and then browsing for your file.

Sometimes the file you want to attach is sitting on your Desktop behind your Mail window, hidden from view. To get to the file in previous versions of OS X, you had to drag windows out of the way and uncover your file before you could drag it into your email message. Now, thanks to Panther and Exposé, you can easily get to concealed files.

To do so, press **F11** to reveal your **Desktop**. Then click and hold down on the file you want. Continue holding down on the file, press **F11** again to bring the Mail window back, and drop the file in your email window. (You learned about Exposé in Chapter 4, "*System Preferences*." If F11 doesn't reveal your Desktop, visit System Preferences and check your Exposé settings.)

See the movie **exposé_attachments.mov** on the **H•O•T CD-ROM** for a demonstration of this technique.

The rest of this exercise will show you how to add signatures to your emails. Signatures are a quick way of adding often-used information such as your mailing address or phone number to the end of your emails.

6. Choose **Mail > Preferences** from the menu bar and then click the **Signatures** icon in the toolbar.

7. Click the **Add Signature** button. A sheet for composing your signature descends from the top of the window.

You can create as many different signatures as you like. For instance, for emails to close friends, you might create a signature that includes a favorite quote or humorous saying; for formal emails, you might want a signature file that includes only your contact information. In this exercise, you'll create both a formal signature and one that includes an actual scanned image.

8. In the **Description** field, give this signature the name of **Contact Info**. In the body of the sheet, type your name, address, phone number, and anything that might help your recipients get in touch with you. You can include your email address here if you want, but it's superfluous because your recipients will already have it listed in the **From** field of any email you send them. Click **OK** when you're done.

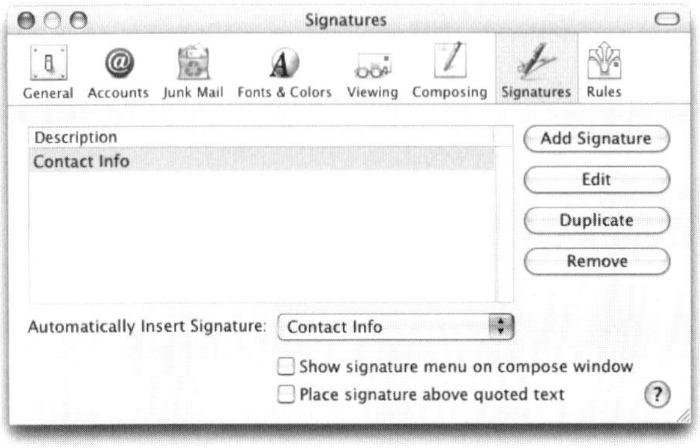

The Contact Info signature is now listed in the main Signatures window. You'll add a second signature now.

If you have a scanner connected to your Mac (and you know how to use it), you can scan a copy of your own signature to include in your emails. If you want, take a moment to prepare a scanned version of your signature and then continue with the exercise. If you don't have access to a scanner, you can use a practice signature that's been provided for these steps.

***Tip:** In scanning and preparing your signature image, keep the resolution at **72 dpi** and size the image exactly as you want it to appear at 100%. Save the image as a **JPEG** or **GIF** to keep the file size small.*

9. Click the **Add Signature** button again.

10. In the **Description** field, name this signature **Scanned**.

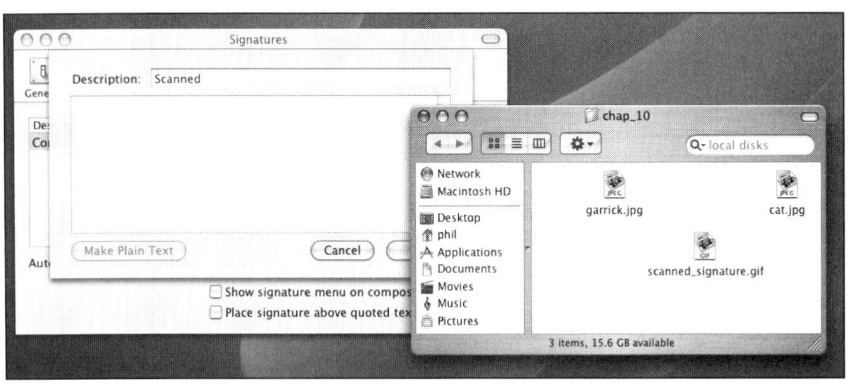

11. If you don't have a scanned copy of your own signature, open the **chap_10** folder on your **Desktop**. If you have a copy of your signature, open the folder containing it. In either case, make sure you can see both the **Signatures** window and the icon for the scanned signature.

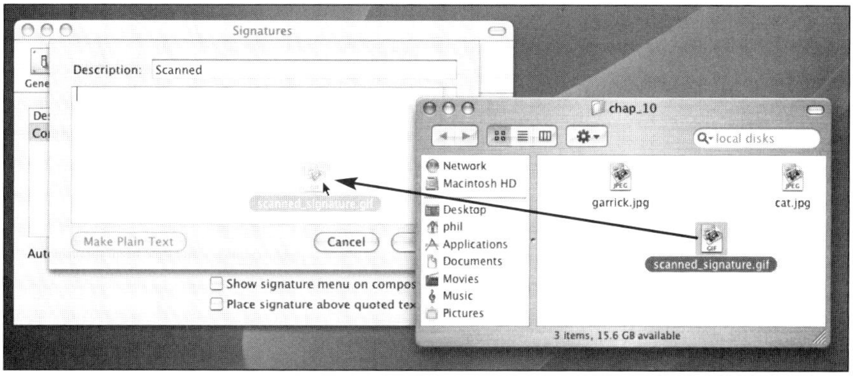

12. Drag **scanned_signature.gif** (or your own signature file) into the **Signatures** window.

13. The image is copied into the **Signatures** window. Click **OK**.

Note: *You don't have to worry about losing your signature if you move your original scanned image to another location on your hard drive. You signature is now safely copied into Mail.*

You now have two signatures ready for use. Now you just have to decide which signature you want to use most often or whether you want to have a signature on every email you send out. The ***Automatically Insert Signature*** *pop-up menu offers you several choices.*

You can select from either of the two signatures you just created, or you can choose ***In Random Order*** *to have Mail just pick one for you each time, or* ***In Sequential Order*** *to have the signatures take turns appearing in every other email message you send. (Of course, the more signatures you have, the more interesting randomly and sequentially become.) For this exercise, you'll give yourself the option of manually selecting a signature each time.*

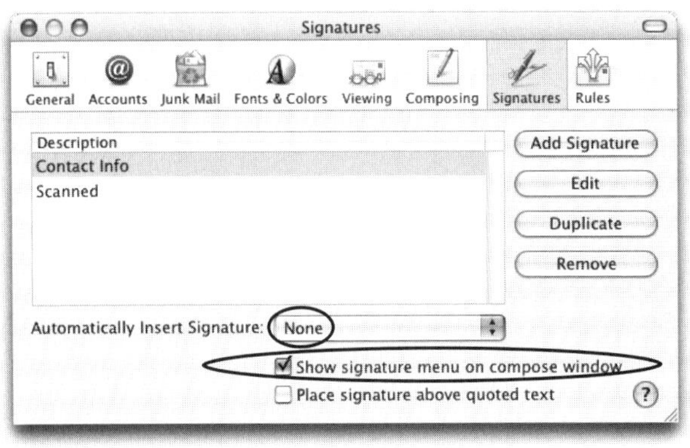

14. Choose **None** from the **Automatically Insert Signature** menu and check the box next to **Show signature menu on compose window**. This will place a signature pop-up menu in the window of each new email you write. Close the **Signatures** window.

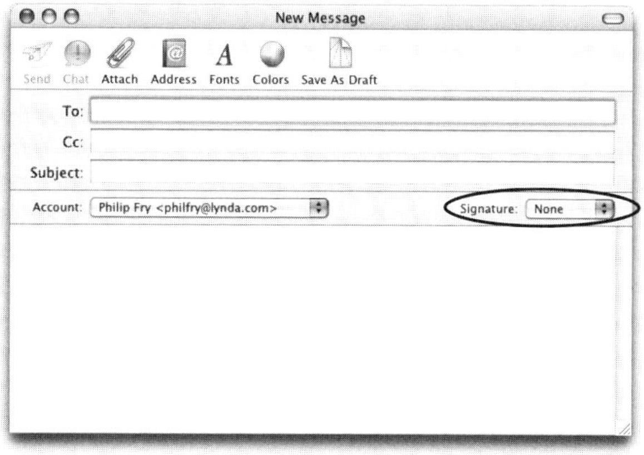

15. Press **Cmd+N** to open a new email composition window. Notice the **Signature** pop-up menu.

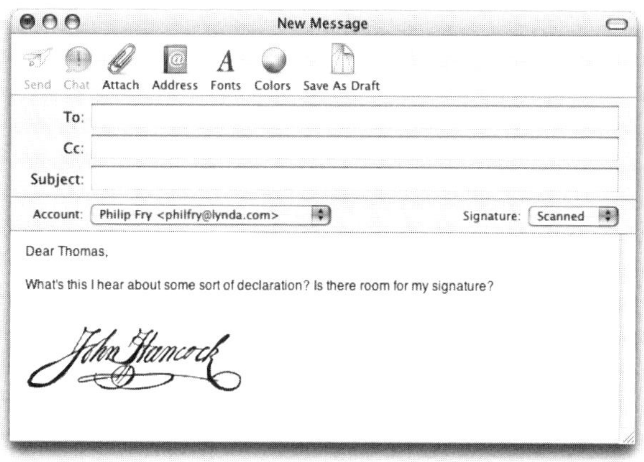

16. Write a short message and then try selecting between the different signatures. Notice that you can have only one signature per email.

17. When you're done playing with the signature menu, close the window. You don't need to save this email.

Note: *Although it's a neat trick to be able to attach your actual signature to an email, keep in mind that what you're really doing is sending an attachment of an image, just like you did earlier in the exercise with the picture of the cat. If you often send email to the same people, you might want to avoid attaching your signature to every email you send them, otherwise they'll end up with dozens and dozens of copies of the same image on their computers.*

18. If you used the sample signature from the **chap_10** folder and would like to delete it, open the **Signature** preferences (**Mail > Preferences**), select **Scanned**, and click **Remove**.

Formatting Email

The emails that you worked with in this chapter were all created in plain text format. Plain text, as its name implies, does not allow you to format text, which adds such characteristics as color, size variations, bold, and italics. But the advantage of plain text is that it keeps the file size of your emails small and therefore makes them fast to send and receive. Plain text is also compatible with every email program out there. Anyone can read a plain text email.

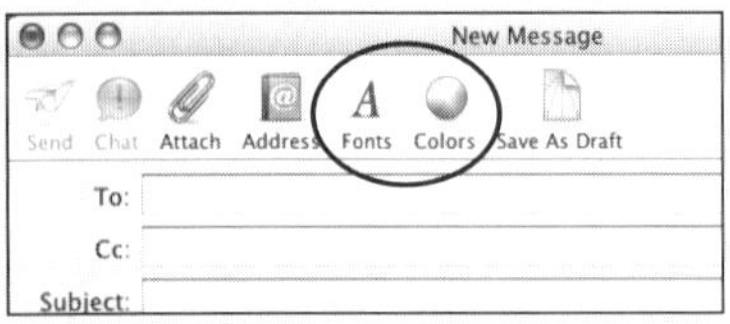

But if you just find plain text too boring, Mail has you covered. To format an email you've just written, click the **Fonts** and **Colors** icons in the toolbar. This will open, respectively, the **Fonts** palette (which you got plenty of experience with in Chapter 6, "*Printing, Fonts, and Faxing*") and the **Colors** palette.

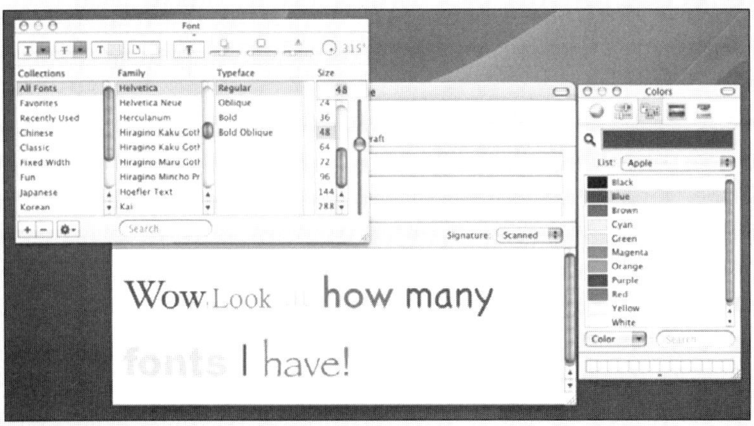

You're now free to highlight text and format it any way you like. The downside? Formatted text requires your recipient to have an email program that can interpret formatted text (referred to in most email applications as **HTML text**, but called **Rich Text** in Mail.). Even if your recipient's email application has HTML compatibility, there's often some formatting that doesn't look quite the way you intended. And any fonts you use in your email must also be installed on the recipient's computer; otherwise, a default font will be used. Some people consider these factors reason enough to shy away from sending emails in Rich Text. Formatted text is best used when you're fairly certain that the person on the other end will be able to see the email as you intend it to appear. For formal emails, it's much safer to stick with plain text.

Setting Mail as Your Default Email Application

Now that you've completed this exercise and have seen many of the great features that Mail offers, you may want to choose Mail as your default email program. To do so, open **Mail > Preferences** and click the **General** button in the toolbar.

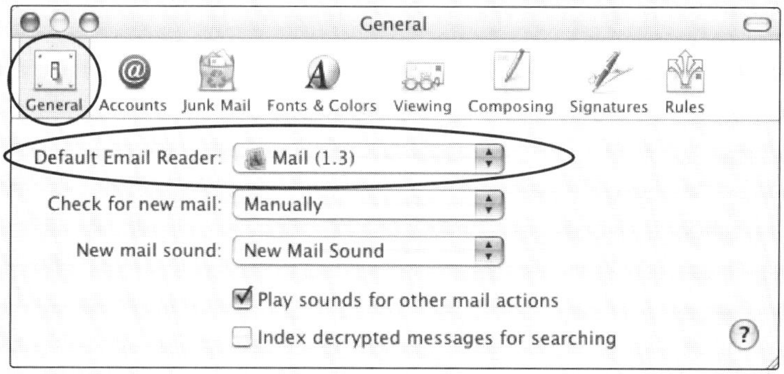

From the **Default Email Reader** pop-up menu, choose **Mail** (the most current version listed) if it's not already selected.

From now on, whenever you click an email link in your Web browser, Mail will start-up and open a new email window for you.

iChat AV

Although email offers the efficiency of electronic communication, there is still a waiting period between the time you send an email and the time you receive a response. Instant messaging, or IMing, is an Internet-based service that has become increasingly popular over the past few years. Instant messaging lets two or more users "chat" in real time, typing messages back and forth, with the only delay in response being the length of time it takes to type the message.

Apple's entry into the IM world is iChat AV, a free application that comes with OS X. As mentioned earlier in the chapter, there are several competing instant messaging applications available from companies such as Microsoft, Yahoo, and AOL, none of which are compatible with each other; in most cases, users must subscribe to the same service in order to chat with each other. Possibly the most compelling reason to use iChat AV is that it's the first IM application given permission to connect to AOL's Instant Messenger–a service over which 1.4 billion instant messages are sent each day. Using iChat AV gives you access to an enormous community.

And you're not limited to just typing your messages. As you might have guessed, the "AV" in iChat AV stands for "audio/visual," so, with the addition of a camera, you can now video chat with other similarly equipped iChat AV users, no matter where they are in the world.

But suppose you don't necessarily want to chat with people online; maybe you only want to IM with people over your local network at the office. iChat AV has you covered. In addition to being able to chat online, iChat AV allows you to chat over a network. If you and a co-worker both have iChat AV and are connected to the same network, you can chat with each other without being connected to the Internet, and without having to create an AOL or .Mac account (more on this shortly).

Because chatting requires interaction between two or more people, this section doesn't contain any step-by-step instructions. But it will provide everything you need to know to use iChat AV, so when you're ready to IM with a friend, you'll have all the information you need.

Setting Up iChat AV

You can start iChat AV by clicking its icon in the **Dock** or by opening it from your **Applications** folder. When you start iChat AV for the first time, you're presented with the **Welcome to iChat AV** window, which gives you some brief information on the new audio and video features. Once you click **Continue**, you'll see the **Set up a new iChat Account** window, where you need to enter your user information.

If you're only planning on using iChat AV for communicating over a local network and not the Internet, just make sure your **First Name** and **Last Name** are shown as you want them to appear and click **Continue**.

You'll be presented with a dialog box asking if you want to turn on Rendezvous messaging, which allows you to see other users on your network and also allows them to see you. Select **Use Rendezvous messaging** and then click **Continue**.

If you plan on using iChat AV on the Internet, you need to provide either a Mac.com or AOL user name. To create a Mac.com account, click the **Get an iChat Account** button, which opens your Web browser and takes you to the Mac.com free 60-day trial signup page. Chapter 12, "*.Mac*," will walk you through this process. Even if you decide not to subscribe to the .Mac service, you get to keep your .Mac user name and can continue using it even after your 60-day .Mac trial period ends. If you have an AOL or AOL Instant Messenger (AIM) user name, you can enter that here as well. You don't have to be a member of AOL to get an AIM screen name. You can register for a free screen name at **http://my.screenname.aol.com**. But before you do so, try to recall if you've ever created a screen name at any of AOL or Time Warner's other Web sites such as Netscape, Time, CNN, Entertainment Weekly, or any of the other sites that fall under the AOL/Time Warner empire's enormous umbrella. These screen names will work as well.

Once you've obtained a screen name from either .Mac or AOL, select the proper **Account Type**, enter your **Account Name** and **Password**, and click **OK**. You'll be asked whether you want to turn on Rendezvous messaging. Select either **Use Rendezvous messaging** (if you want to chat with people on your network) or **Do not use Rendezvous messaging** (if you're not on a network or just don't want to chat with people at work) and then click **Continue**. (You can always reverse your decision later.)

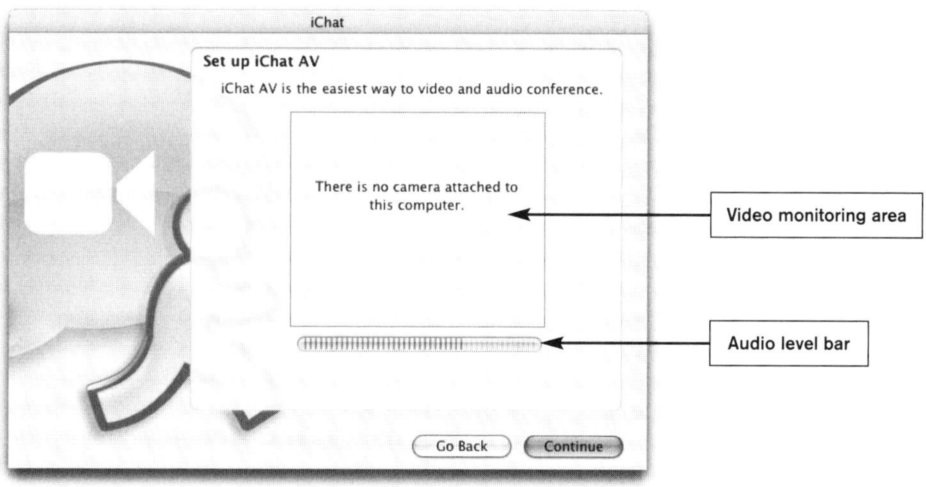

In the next screen, iChat AV checks out your audio/visual capabilities. If your Mac has a built-in microphone, you should see the audio level bar moving. If you have an Apple iSight or other FireWire camera connected to your Mac, you should see a picture as well. This gives you an opportunity to make sure your camera is working properly, but you don't have to set up your camera right now if you aren't ready to. You can attach it to your Mac later. (See the "AV Chatting" section later in this chapter.) Click **Continue**.

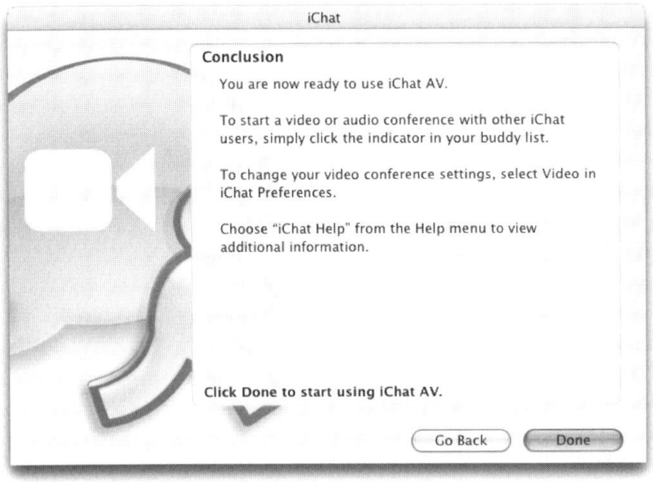

The last screen gives you some basic instructions on using iChat. Click **Done**.

Once you're in iChat AV, you need to set up your **Buddy List**, a list of the people you know who have screen names. If you're an AOL subscriber or have used AIM in the past, your Buddy List will automatically appear. If you're new to this whole IM thing, you need to add some names to create your list.

If you see a message telling you that AOL Instant Messenger is disabled, click **Enable**. If your Buddy List window didn't appear when you started iChat AV, choose **Window > Buddy List**. (Make sure it says "Buddy List" at the top of the window and not "Rendezvous." You'll learn about Rendezvous messaging shortly.) To add to your Buddy List (or create it) click the + sign at the bottom of the **Buddy List** window.

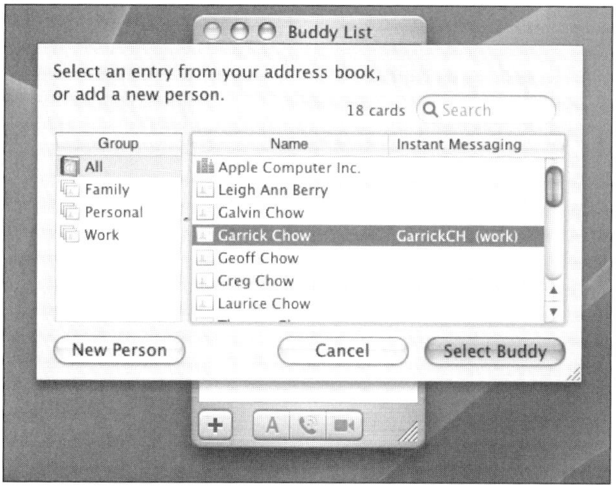

A sheet appears from the top of the window listing all the entries from your Address Book. If you entered an AIM address for any of your buddies in Address Book, you can choose it here and then click **Select Buddy**. If the person you want to add doesn't appear in your Address Book, click **New Person**.

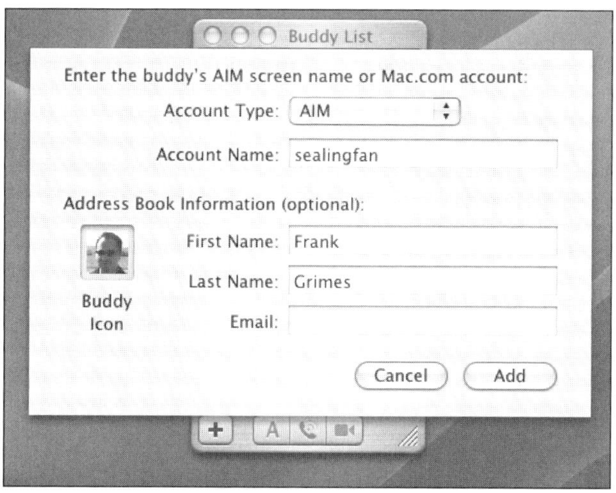

A different sheet will appear in which you can enter the information for your new buddy. All you really need to add is your buddy's screen name. If you want information about this buddy added to Address Book for you, enter his or her **First Name**, **Last Name**, and **Email** address. If you have a picture you'd like to use to represent your buddy, drag it to the **Buddy Icon** area. Click **Add** when you're done.

Chatting

Names that you've added to your Buddy List appear grayed-out until the person they represent signs on to either AIM or iChat AV.

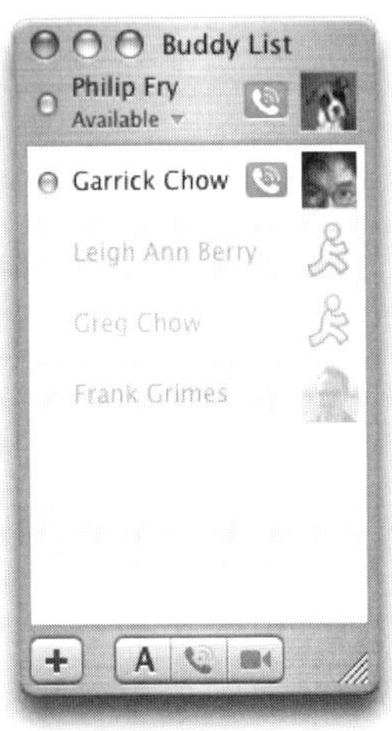

When a buddy signs on, you'll hear a brief sound effect, sort of a "whooshing" sound, and his or her name will appear at full opacity and move above all the faded-back names in your buddy list. You can now begin a chat with this buddy by double-clicking his or her name.

Type your message in the bottom field of the window that opens and press **Return**.

When your buddy responds, his or her text will appear in its own word balloon.

That's all there is to it. Continue chatting until neither of you can think of anything to say anymore. To end the chat, just close the window. As long as you both are still signed onto iChat AV or AIM, you can chat again at any time.

TIP | Inserting Line Breaks

A complaint that some users had about the original version of iChat was that the text entry field displayed only one line of text at a time and that you couldn't force your text to start on the next line–pressing Return would just send your message.

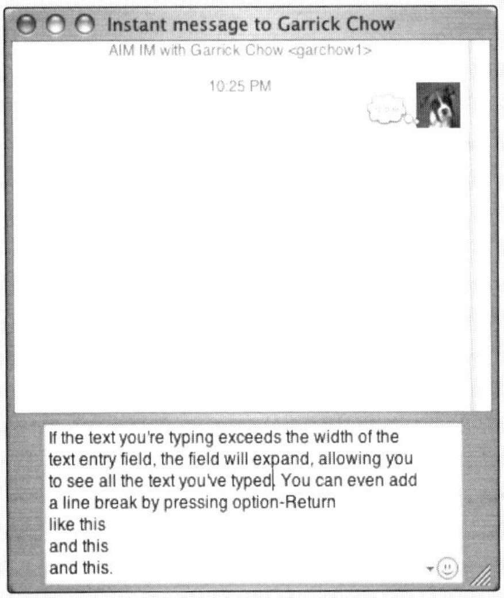

In iChat AV, however, the text entry field automatically expands as necessary as you type and you can insert line breaks by pressing **Option+Return**.

Chatting over a network is very similar to chatting over the Internet. The main difference is that you don't have to set up a Buddy List to chat over your network. Because of Rendezvous, Apple's zero-configuration communication technology (described in Chapter 6, "*Printing, Fonts, and Faxing*"), iChat AV automatically recognizes when other Macs running iChat AV are connected to the network.

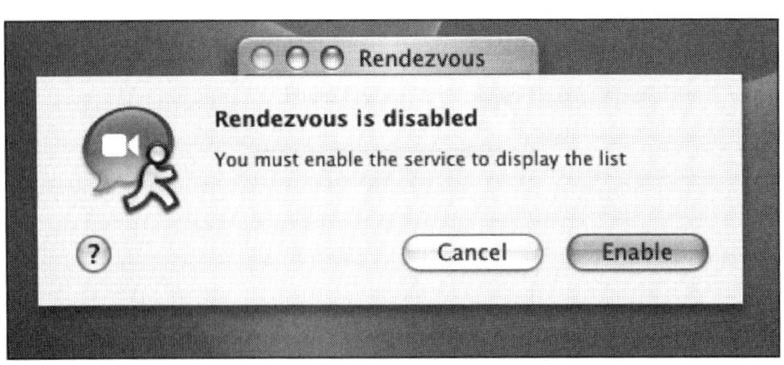

To see who's running iChat AV on your network, choose **Window > Rendezvous**. If this is the first time you've run iChat AV, you'll need to click **Enable** to start Rendezvous.

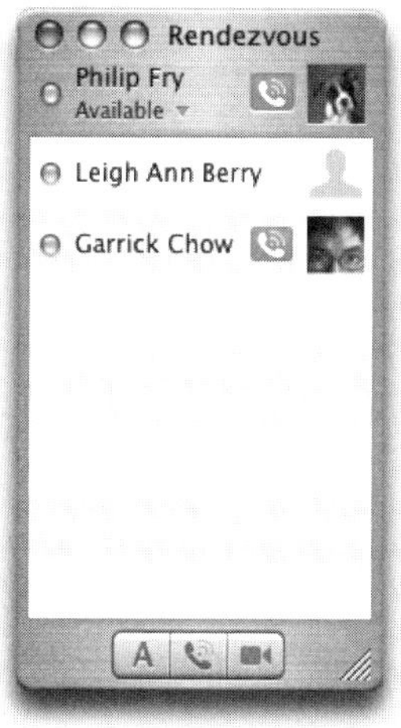

Once enabled, any users running iChat AV on their Macs will appear in your Rendezvous window. To chat with someone, double-click his or her name and proceed just like you would with someone on your Buddy List.

Of course, you're not always going to be the one starting the chat. If other users notice you in their Buddy Lists, they might send you messages first.

When someone wants to chat, the first line of his or her text appears in a new window, accompanied by a "popping" sound effect. If you want to chat, click **Accept** and type your message. If you really don't want to talk to the person and don't want them to know you're still there, click **Block**. You will disappear from their Buddy List. To give the user the privilege of seeing you again, choose **iChat > Preferences** and click the **Privacy** button. Click **Edit List** next to **Block Specific People** and then select the blocked user's name and click the **–** (minus) symbol to remove him or her from the list of blocked users.

Status Indicators

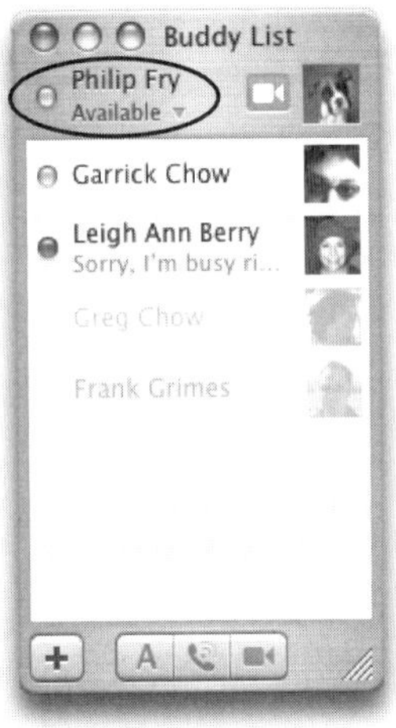

Your iChat status lets people in your Buddy List know your current availability. Your status appears under your name at the top of your Buddy List window. When your status is set to **Available**, others who have you in their Buddy Lists assume that you're at your computer and can respond to their messages. Your available status is indicated by a green dot. Others in your Buddy List who are available also have green dots next to their names.

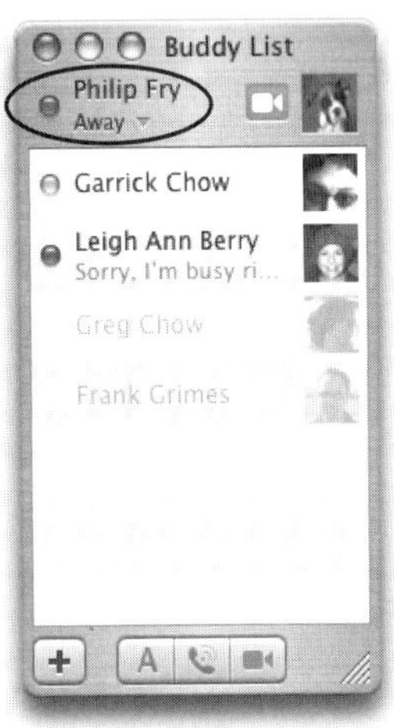

If you want your buddies to see that you're online, but you don't want to chat or are going to be away from your computer, set your status to **Away** (indicated by a red dot). People will still be able to send you messages that will appear in windows on your screen, but your Away status lets them know that you might not respond to them immediately.

By selecting **Custom** under Available or Away, you can create your own messages to go along with your status indicator. For example, under Away, you might create a more specific message like "Walking the dog," or "Out to lunch."

TIP | Responding to Emails Over iChat

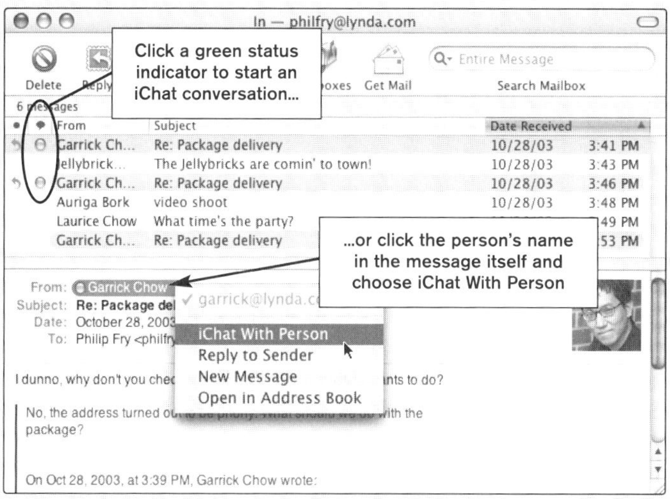

Here's yet another example of the tight integration between Panther's applications. If you're logged onto iChat and you receive an email in Mail, Mail displays a green "available" status indicator next to messages from people in your iChat buddy list who are currently online and whose addresses are in Address Book. You can send the person an instant message, rather than replying to the email by clicking the status indicator.

In order to see the person's status, his or her email address and iChat name must match the information in Address Book. If you don't see the Buddy List column in Mail, choose **View > Columns > Buddy Availability**.

Enhancing Your Chat

iChat AV doesn't limit your text communication capabilities to just chatting with plain text. You can dress up your chats with formatted text, Web links, and pictures. Here's how.

Formatting Text

You can perform basic text formatting within the chat window itself by selecting text and then pressing **Cmd+B** or **Cmd+I** to apply bold and italic styles to your text for emphasis.

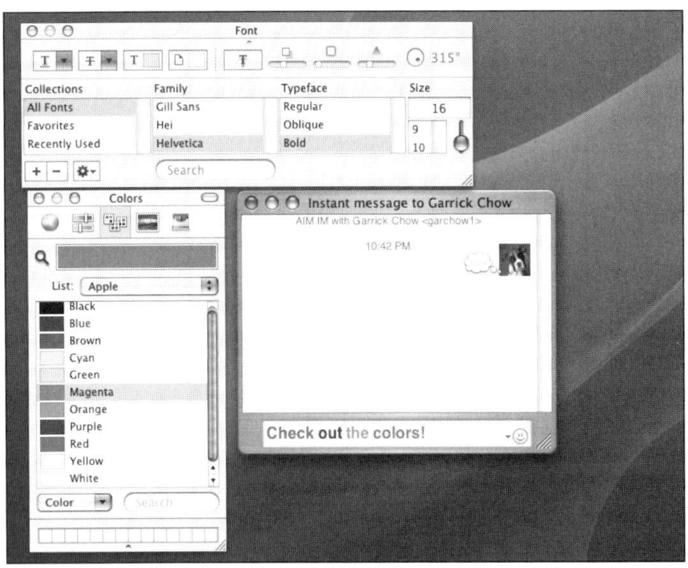

For additional formatting choices, you can open the **Fonts** and **Colors** palettes by selecting them from the **Format** menu. Keep in mind that, as with sending formatted email, the fonts you select will only appear on the user's computer if he or she has the same fonts installed. The colors you choose, on the other hand, will show up fine on any recipient's computer.

Attaching Files

Another similarity that IMing shares with email is the capability to send file attachments. Unlike email, however, file attachments sent through instant messages are sent directly from your computer to the recipient's computer, instead of being stored on their ISP's email server until they're downloaded.

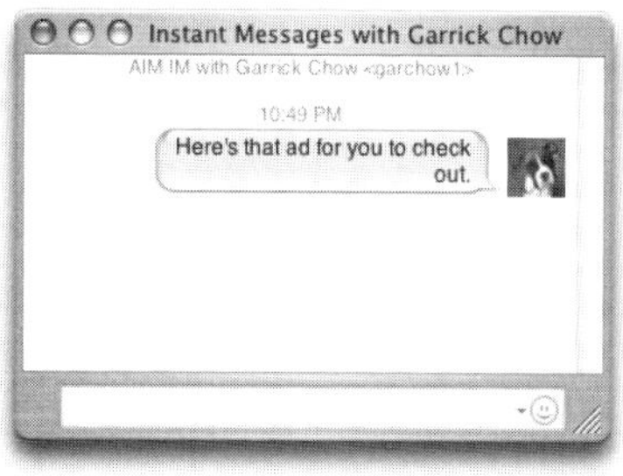

To send a file to someone through iChat AV, start a chat with your recipient and then choose **Edit > Attach File**. You'll be given a dialog box to locate the file you want to send.

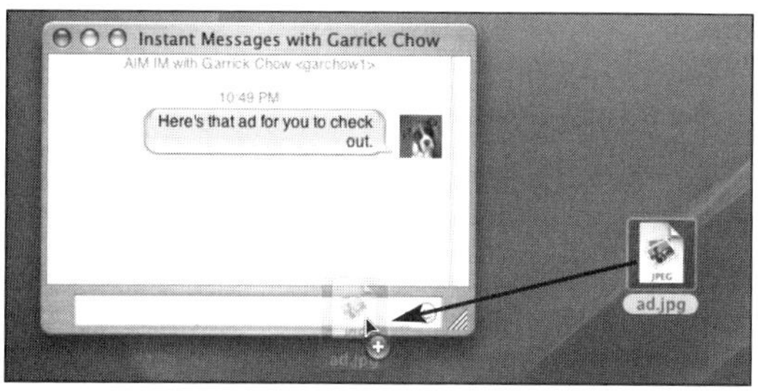

Tip: You can also drag files into the chat window's text entry field to send them to your recipient. Additionally, you can drag a file onto the recipient's name in your Buddy List if you don't want to send a text message first.

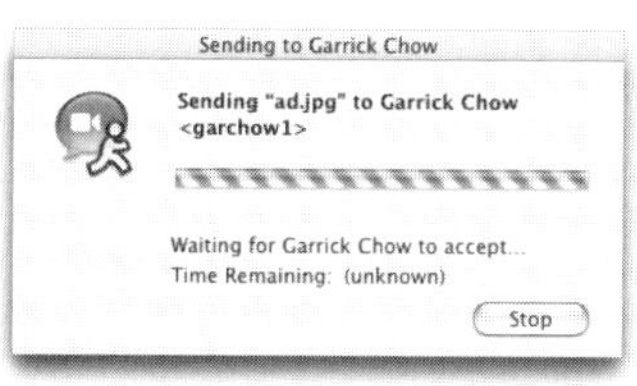

Once you send the file, your recipient must accept the file to begin the transfer. The status bar shown here will show you the progress of the transfer, during which time you can continue chatting with each other.

Many ISPs limit the size of files that can be transferred through email to about 5 or 10 MB. If the file you want to send is larger than the allowed email size, sometimes sending the file through instant messaging is a viable option. If both you and your recipient have broadband Internet connections, just start up an IM session and send your file.

Adding Web Links

Occasionally, there will be times when you want to send your chat buddy a link to a Web site.

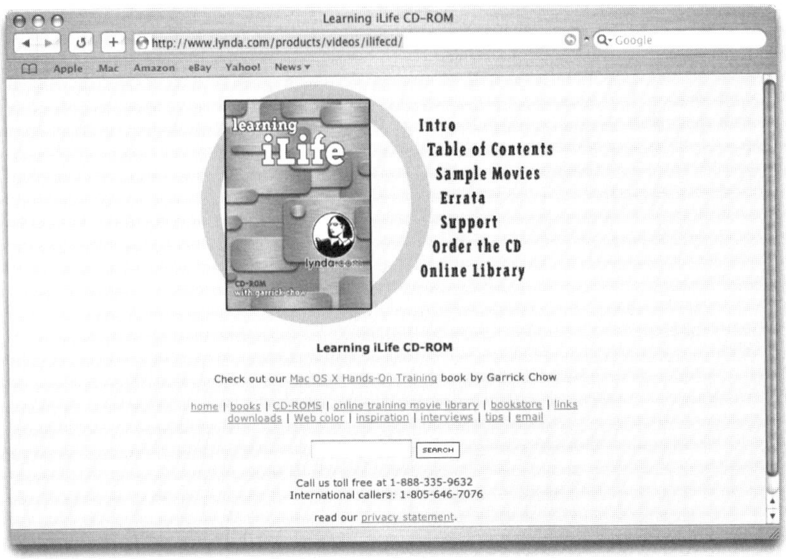

To do so, navigate to the site in your Web browser, highlight the address, and choose **Edit > Copy** (or press **Cmd+C**). Return to iChat AV.

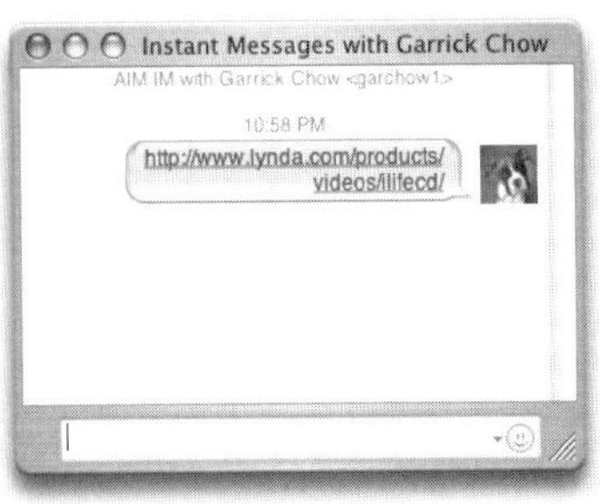

You can just choose **Edit > Paste** to send the link to your buddy.

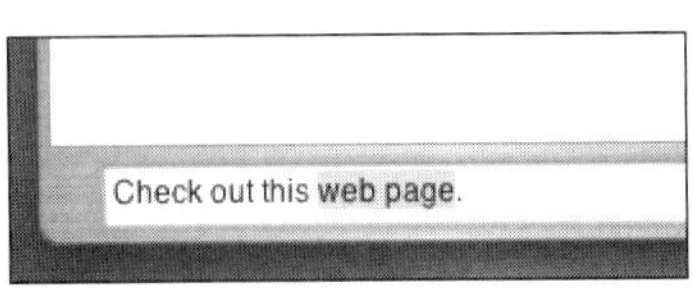

But if you'd like the link to look a little less cluttered, just type a brief sentence like, "Check out this web page" and then highlight the words "web page." From the **Edit** menu, choose **Add Hyperlink** (or press **Cmd+K**).

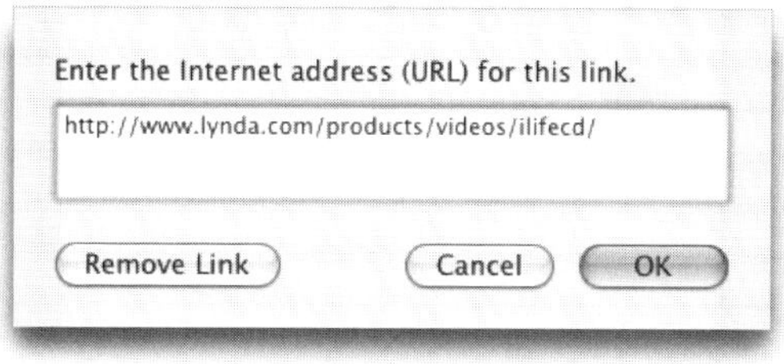

In the dialog box that appears, paste the Web address and click **OK**.

You now have a clean working Web link to send to your buddy.

Changing the Appearance of Your Chat

Finally, if you're not a big fan of the cartoonish word balloons that appear in the chat window, iChat AV gives you a few options for changing the way your chat is displayed.

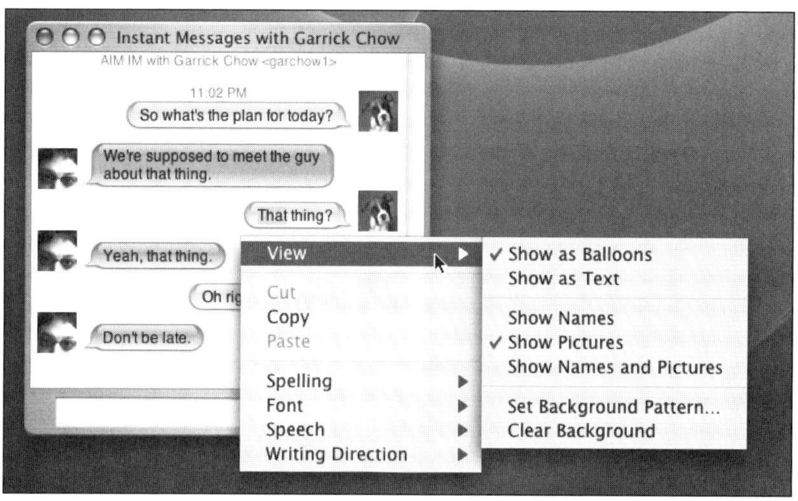

Ctrl+click anywhere in the area of the chat window that displays the conversation and roll your mouse over the **View** menu. To remove the word balloons, choose **Show As Text.**

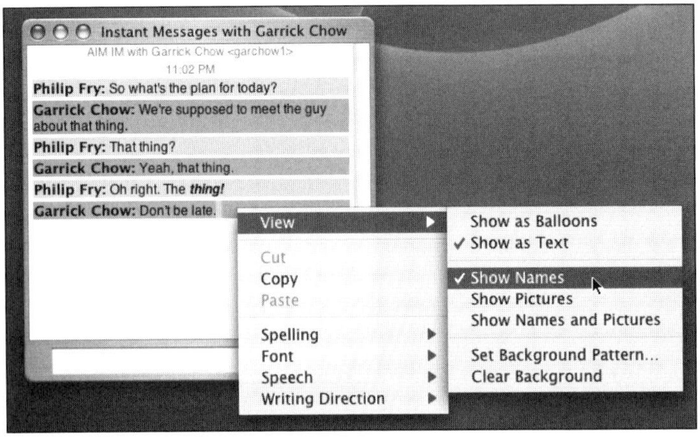

Notice that you can also choose to display just the name of your chat buddy, or both the name and picture in the chat window. If you really want to get fancy, choose **Set Background Pattern** from the contextual menu and select an image to use as the background for your chat.

To change the color of the chat balloons (or the color of the text background if you got rid of the balloons), choose **iChat > Preferences** and click the **Messages** button in the toolbar. Here you can change the appearance of both your outgoing and incoming messages.

Tip: At the bottom of the Messages preferences, you can check Automatically save chat transcripts to keep copies of all your chats. Click the Open Folder button to open the Finder window containing your saved transcripts.

AV Chatting

Now that you know how to text chat, you'll take a look at how to use iChat AV to perform audio and video chats. In order to audio chat, that is, speak back and forth with someone over iChat, both you and your buddy must be using iChat AV, and you both need microphones connected to your Macs. Video chatting requires you both to have cameras and microphones.

If you have a FireWire camcorder, you can use it as your iChat camera/microphone, but you may be reluctant to use your expensive video camera as a Web cam. You can find several reasonably priced FireWire cameras on the market that are created specifically for video conferencing. At the time of publication of this book, Apple's iSight camera is hands-down the best choice for using with iChat AV. iSight is a tiny camera with a built-in microphone that you can mount on your monitor or laptop. It was designed specifically for use with iChat AV. You can find out all about this great little camera at **www.apple.com/isight**.

In addition to the camera, video chatting with iChat AV requires you to be using a Mac with a G5, G4, or a 600 Mhz or faster G3 processor, and a broadband Internet connection.

When you connect your camera to your Mac, a video camera icon appears next to your name at the top of your buddy list, indicating that you have video chat capability. If you see a phone icon here, you have only voice chat capability. Others in your Buddy List with voice or video chatting capability will also have the corresponding icon next to their names. If neither icon appears, you can only communicate with that particular person via plain old text chatting.

To begin a video chat, click the video camera icon next to your buddy's name. A preview window will open while you wait for your buddy to respond. This is your chance to primp before anyone sees you.

When your buddy answers your call (which sounds like a ringing telephone on his or her end), his or her camera's image will appear in the video window and yours will shrink down into one of the four corners. You can drag your image around in the video window to prevent yourself from covering your friend's image. At this point you can both start talking. Depending on your connection, there might be a slight delay between the time your friend speaks and the time you actually hear his voice, but Apple has figured out a way to ensure that the video and audio signals stay synched together, so the delay should be barely noticeable.

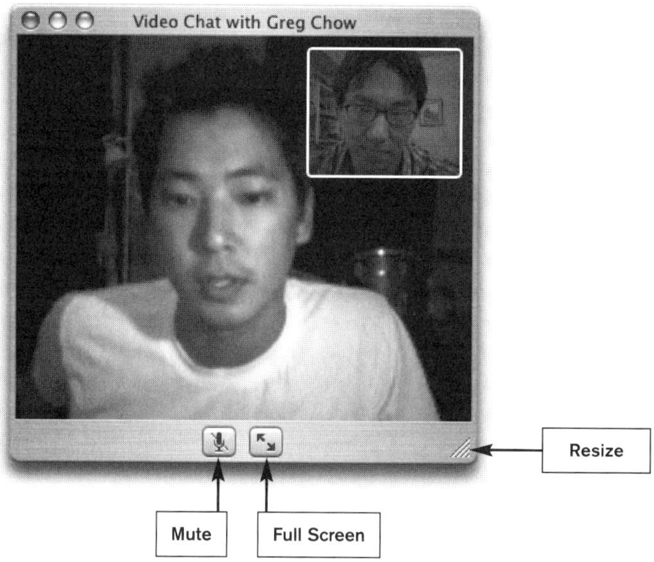

While you're chatting you can click the Mute button to temporarily prevent your buddy from hearing you (if you have to answer the phone on your end or talk to someone else in the room, for instance). You can also click the Full Screen button to have your buddy's image fill your entire monitor. If that's a little too much for you, you can instead drag the window's resize corner to size the window to your liking.

TIP | One-Way Audio or Video Chatting

If your buddy doesn't have a microphone or camera, you can invite him or her to a one-way audio or video chat. To do so, select your friend's name in the Buddy List window and then choose **Buddies > Invite to One-Way Audio Chat** or **Invite to One-Way Video Chat**. (If these options aren't available, your friend can't support audio or video chat.) If you can select either of these options, your buddy will be able to hear and/or see you, but will have to type his or her responses—not the greatest thing for your buddy, but you get to keep your hands free to do other things.

Great job! You're quickly becoming a Mac master of Internet services. You'll continue adding to your Internet skills in the next chapter.

11.

Sherlock and Searching Your Mac

The Internet Channel	The Pictures Channel	The Stocks Channel
The Movies and Phone Book Channels	The eBay Channel
The Flights Channel	The Dictionary and Translation Channel
The AppleCare Channel	Searching Your Mac

no exercise files

Mac OS X Panther H•O•T CD-ROM

If you're a veteran Mac user, you're probably familiar with Sherlock. Introduced in Mac OS 8.5, Sherlock was created to search for items on your Mac based on specific information such as a file's name, type, or the date it was created. Essentially, the first version of Sherlock was a slightly enhanced, renamed version of the Find application, used for locating files on your hard drive. What Sherlock added to the Mac was the capability to search the Internet as well as its own hard drive. When Sherlock 2 debuted in Mac OS 9, Apple added even more Internet search capabilities. But when users encountered noticeable lags while searching, some began to feel that Sherlock might have bitten off more than it could chew.

Sherlock 3, introduced in Mac OS 10.2, is an entirely new beast. This version searches only the Internet, leaving the task of searching the Mac's hard drive to the reincarnated Find application, which has been greatly enhanced in Panther. This chapter will show you how to use Sherlock's "channels" to search the Internet as well as how to use the much-improved Find application to search your Mac.

Channel Surfing in Sherlock

The World Wide Web contains an amazing wealth of information. The problem is finding the information you need. With the incredible volume of material available on the Internet, most people have come to rely on Web-based search engines such as Google, Yahoo, or AltaVista, to sift through it all. So with advanced Web search engines freely available, why should you use Sherlock? Well, for one thing, Sherlock gives you the ability to search the Web through several search engines at once, instead of a single search engine at a time. Sherlock also allows you to search particular categories, called "channels," such as stock reports, movie listings, phone book listings, or reference books, all without ever opening your Web browser. This is not to say that there isn't a time and place for Google searches, but you might want to consider using Sherlock for its specialized services.

In the following exercises, you'll be taken on a guided tour of Sherlock's multitude of channels. In order to open Sherlock, you must have an active connection to the Internet. Make sure you're connected to the Internet before beginning this exercise.

I. The Internet Channel

This exercise introduces you to Sherlock and explains its channels, providing you with the necessary information to quickly get up and running. You'll first examine Sherlock's interface, and then you'll perform a search using the Internet channel.

1. From the **Finder** menu bar, choose **Go > Applications** (or press **Shift+Cmd+A**) to open your **Applications** folder. Locate and double-click the **Sherlock** icon.

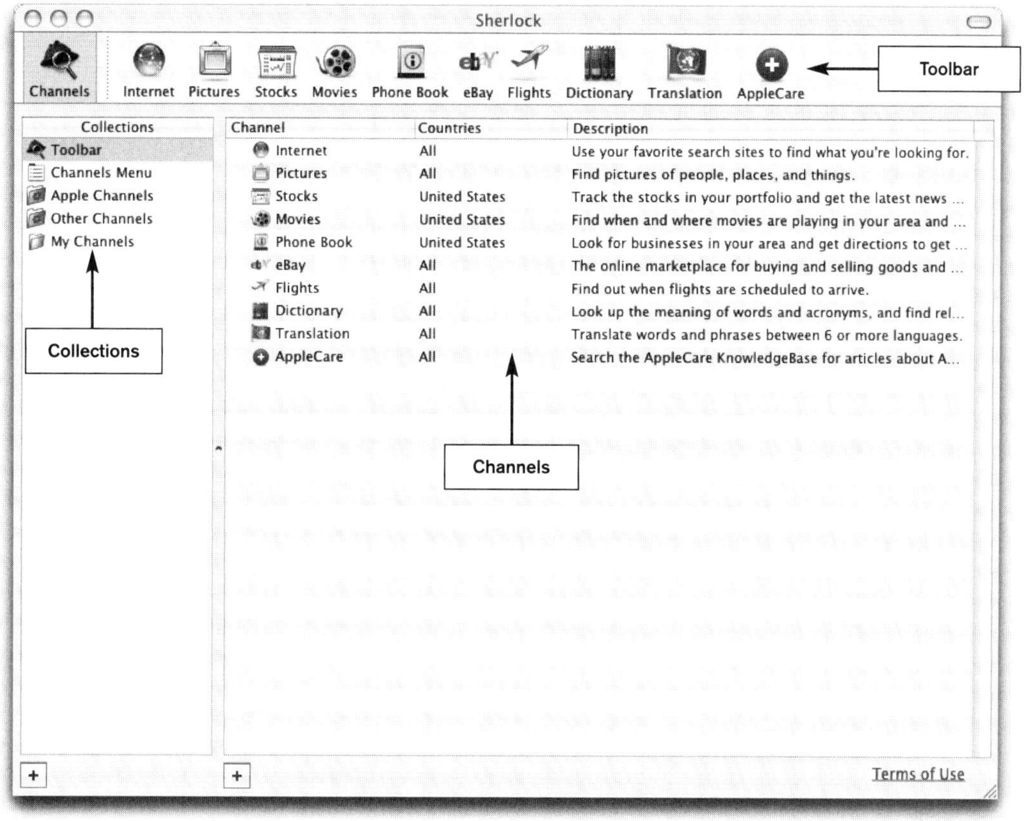

*When Sherlock first opens, it checks to make sure you're connected to the Internet. Once it finds the connection, the main window opens and displays a rundown of each available channel and its purpose. You can access a channel by double-clicking it in the **Channels** pane, or by clicking its icon in the toolbar.*

2. Click the **Internet** icon.

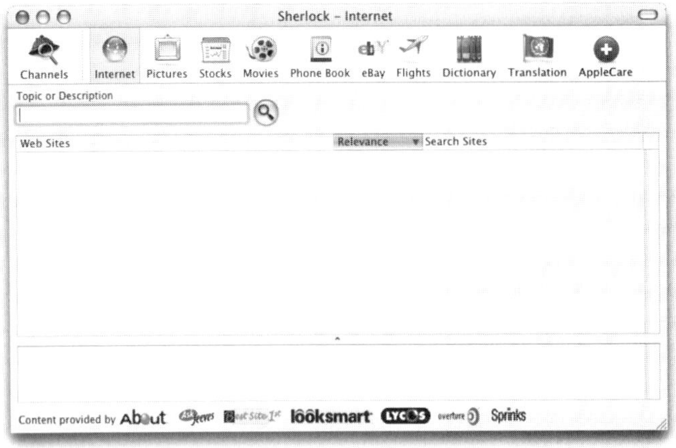

*The **Internet** channel searches the seven Web sites whose icons appear at the bottom of the window: **about.com**, **ask.com**, **bestsitefirst.com**, **looksmart.com**, **lycos.com**, **overture.com**, and **sprinks.com**. Never heard of some of these? I hadn't either, but clicking on any of their icons will take you to the search engine's home page, where you can learn more about the specific types of information it searches for.*

The Internet channel is used to find Web sites containing information about whatever topic or description you're searching for. Now you'll give the Internet channel a try.

---

3. In the **Topic or Description** field, type **powerbook G4** and press **Return**.

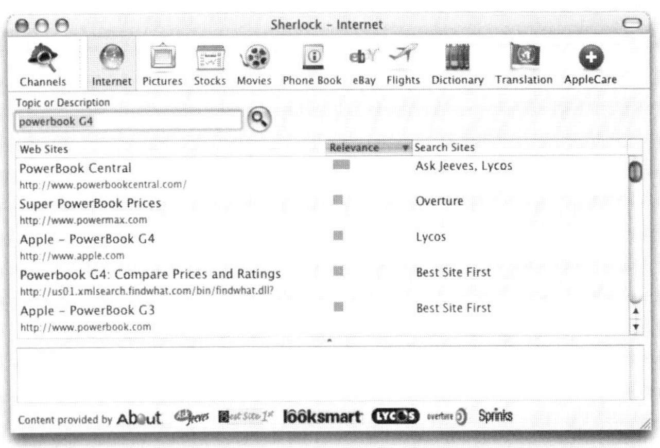

Sherlock immediately begins searching the Internet. As the results of your search are returned, they're sorted by order of relevancy (the default sort setting). You should see Sherlock reorganizing the search results for several seconds.

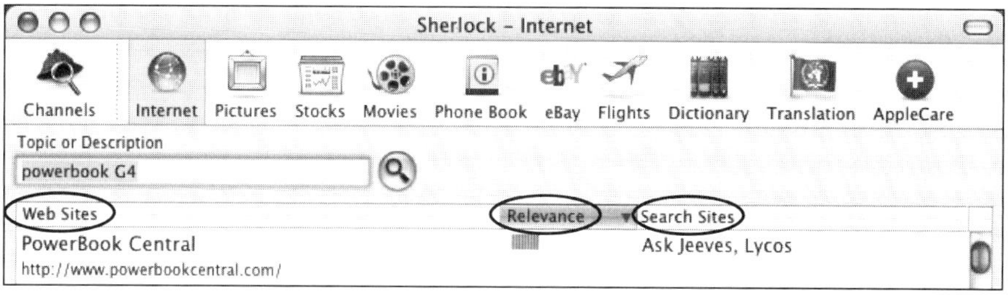

Tip: In addition to sorting the results by relevancy, you can also sort them by Web site name or by search site. Just click the column headers to change this default. Clicking an already-selected header reverses the order of the list. (The little triangle in the header indicates the direction the list is currently sorted.)

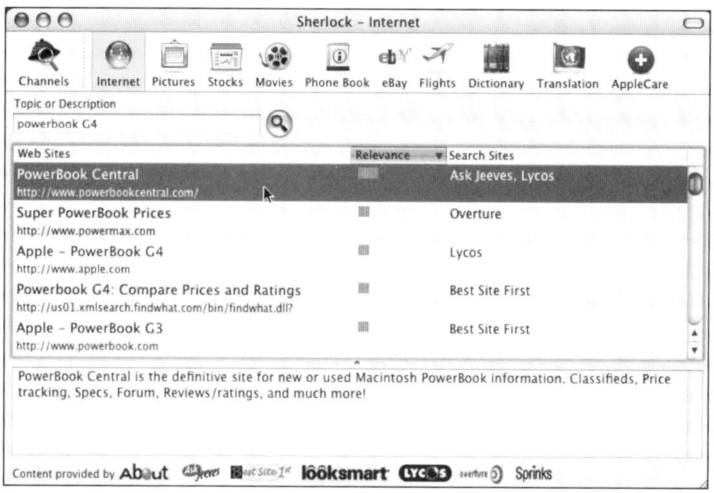

4. Click once on any search result to select it. A description from that site appears in the lower pane of the window. (If the site's Webmaster didn't include a description, the first few sentences of text from the site will appear instead.)

5. Double-click any of the sites listed to view the actual Web page. Your Web browser will automatically open. When you're done viewing the Web page, close it and return to Sherlock. One of the best aspects of searching with Sherlock is that your search results all remain in the single Sherlock window, allowing you to view the Web pages it finds in your browser window.

Sometimes you'll have too many results to check out all at once, or you may come across a search result listing a Web page that you'll want to check out later. Sherlock allows you to easily create a "location file," a small icon that will open the specified Web page when you double-click it.

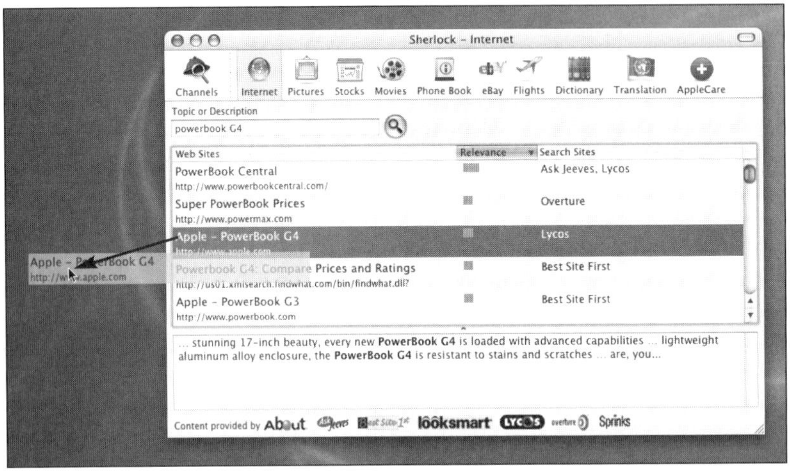

6. Select one of the search results in the main window and drag it to your **Desktop**.

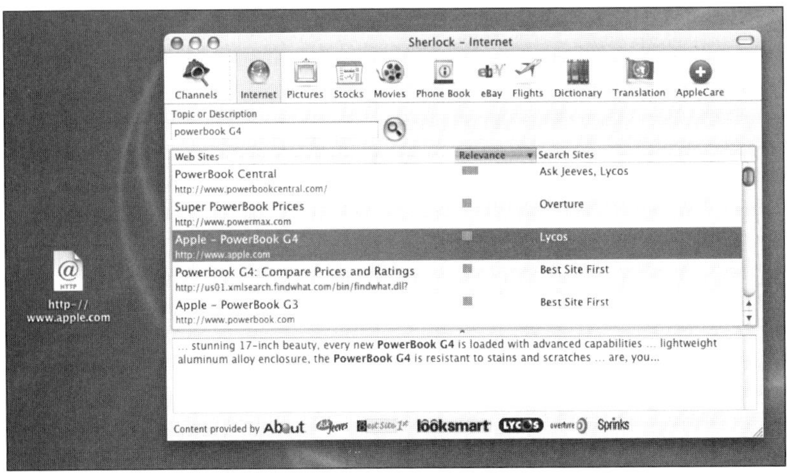

7. The **location file** icon appears, and you now have a convenient shortcut to this Web page. Double-click this icon to test it. Once the Web page opens in your browser, close the browser window. Creating a location file is a good way to keep track of pages you want to visit but might not necessarily want to add to your browser's list of Favorites.

8. Drag the **location file** icon to the **Trash**. Click Sherlock's window to make it the front-most application.

You can perform a new search in the ***Internet*** *channel at any time by typing a new word or phrase in the* ***Topic or Description*** *field. In the next exercise, you'll take a look at the Pictures channel, which works a lot like the Internet channel.*

2. The Pictures Channel

Sherlock's **Pictures** channel works much in the same way the Internet channel does, except that instead of returning Web pages, your search results bring back images. The Pictures channel searches **creative.gettyimages.com** and **multimedia.lycos.com**, and is great for people who need to locate and purchase high-quality, professional images.

1. Click the **Pictures** icon in Sherlock's toolbar.

2. In the **Picture Topic or Description** field, type **beagles** and press **Return**. In a moment, several pictures matching your description appear.

Note: *If more results are available for your search, the phrase* ***Click again for more pictures*** *will appear next to the magnifying glass icon. You can continue clicking this icon for more pictures until* ***Click again for more pictures*** *no longer appears.*

The images your search returns are thumbnails that, when double-clicked, will take you to a Web page where you can view larger and higher-quality versions of the pictures.

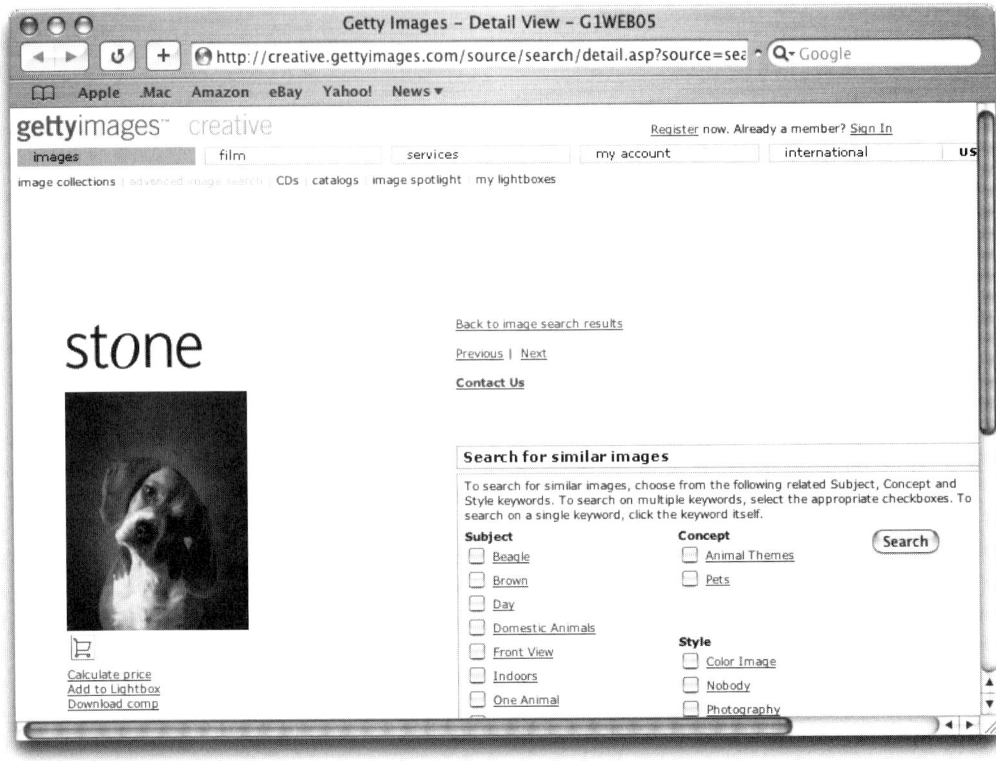

3. Double-click any of the search results. Your Web browser opens and takes you to either a Getty Images or Lycos Web page.

So what's the downside to the Pictures channel? You have to pay for the images you find if you want to use them in your own work. The Pictures channel is a great way to find images if you're a professional graphic designer in need of some stock photos, but if you're just looking for some standard pictures of various things, you're much better off using the Image search function at www.google.com. Although Google won't bring back as many printable, high-quality images, it will locate lots of Web-ready images. Still, you should be sure to check with the owner of each picture for permission to use any images you find on the Web.

---

4. Close your browser and return to Sherlock.

---

3. The Stocks Channel

With Sherlock's **Stocks** channel you can keep track of your stocks, read news about them, and see graphs of your stocks' recent performances.

1. Click the **Stocks** channel in the toolbar.

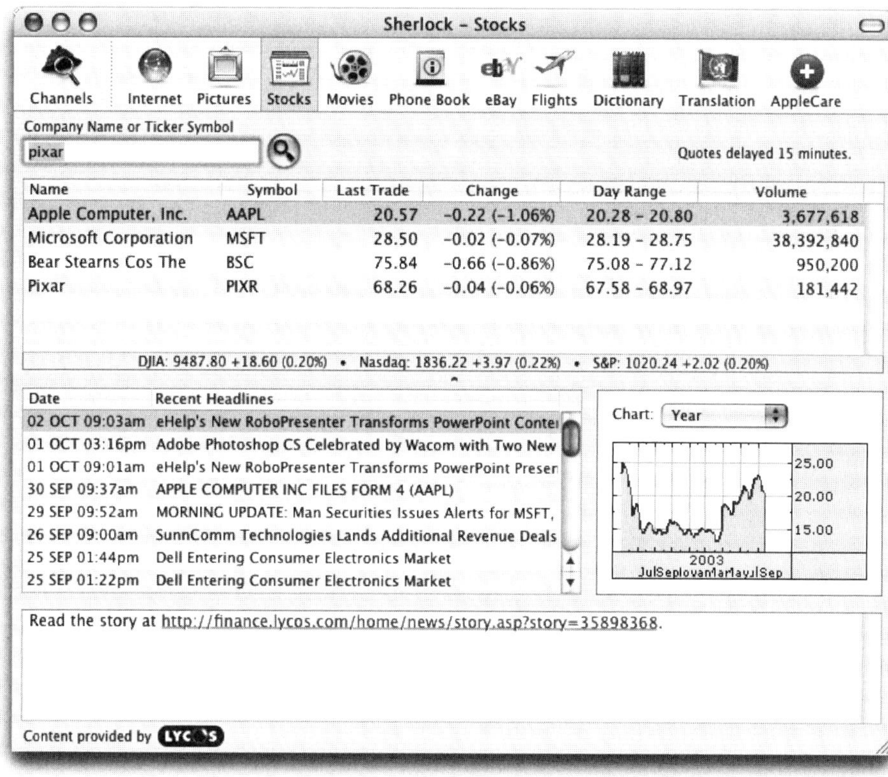

The Stocks channel is a great tool for keeping an eye on several stocks at once. All you need to do is type the company's ticker symbol into the field at the top of the window to track its stock. If you don't know the ticker symbol, just type the company's name. If Sherlock isn't sure which company you're looking for, it will present a list of possible matches from which you can choose.

2. In the **Company Name or Ticker Symbol** field, type **AAPL** and press **Return**. After a moment, Apple's stock information appears. If you know the ticker symbols for any other companies, feel free to type them in.

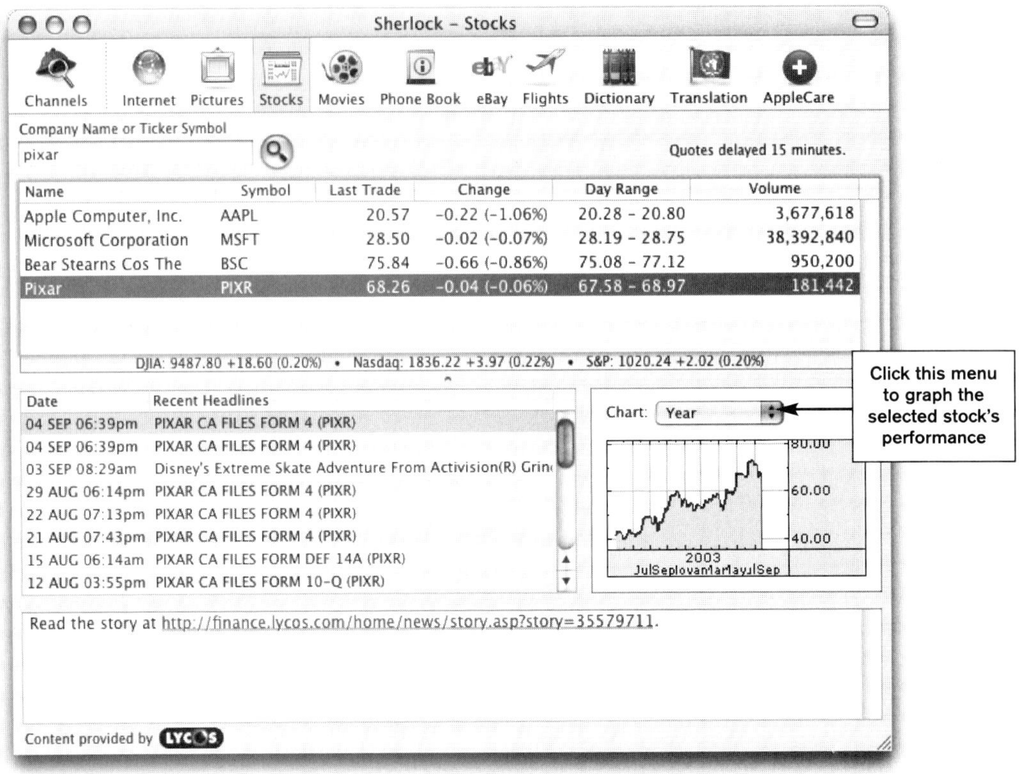

*Once a stock is listed in the top panel, clicking it will display its performance chart, which you can view by **Year**, **Week**, or **Intraday**.*

***Note:** Stock prices are delayed by 15 minutes in Sherlock, so be sure to check with your broker for the actual prices.*

3. Click the **Chart** menu and choose **Year**, **Week**, or **Intraday** to view different charts.

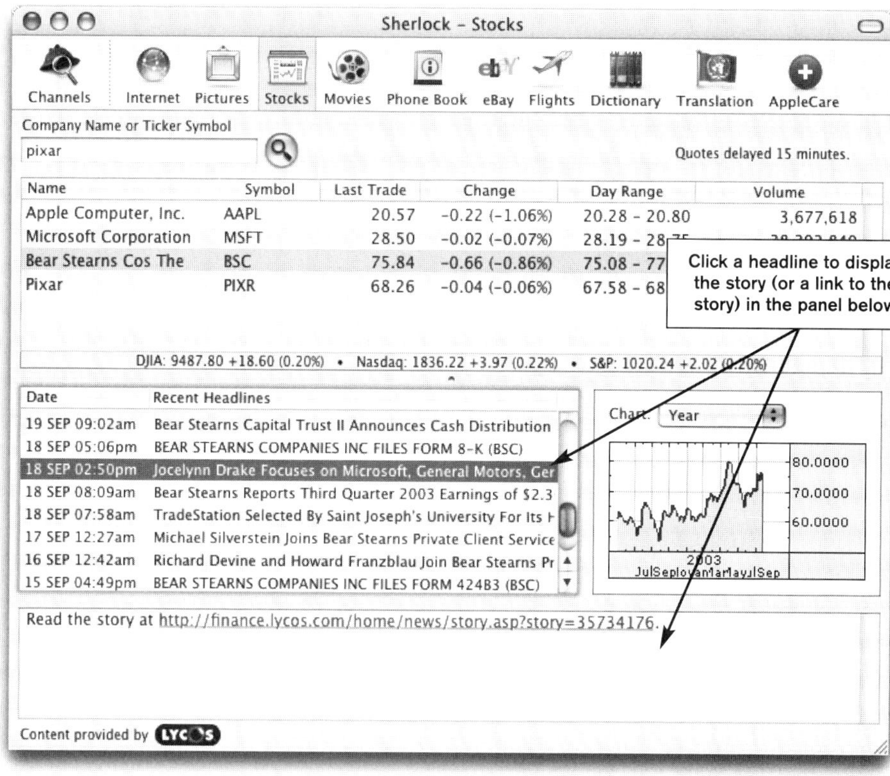

Sherlock also fetches recent news reports containing any information about the company.

4. Click any headline to display the story in the bottom panel of the window. (Some stories provide only a link to a Web site; others display the entire story in Sherlock.)

5. If this channel interests you at all, take some time to type in a few stocks and see how they're doing. If you have no interest in stocks whatsoever, say, "Huh!" and move on to the next exercise.

4. The Movies and Phone Book Channels

Now here's what being online is all about: movie listings for every theater in your area. Using the **Movies** channel, you can search for local theaters as well as for specific movies to see where they're playing.

1. Click the **Movies** icon in the toolbar.

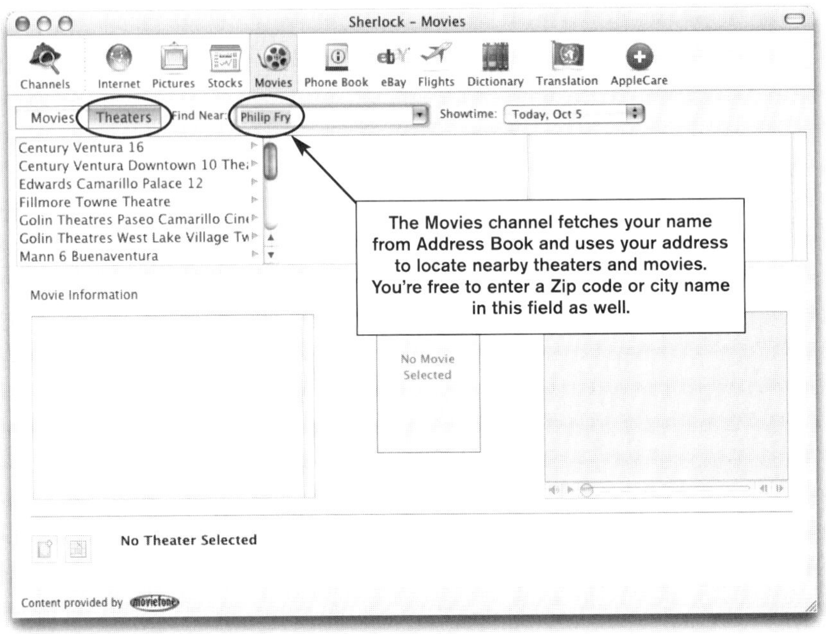

2. New to Panther, the Movies channel now works in conjunction with Address Book (covered in Chapter 10, "*Address Book, Mail, and iChat AV*"). Sherlock fetches your name from Address Book, inserts it in the **Find Near** field, and uses your address to automatically search for movies and theaters near you. If you haven't entered your address information in Address Book yet (although you should have if you've gone through Chapter 10), just type your **Zip code** in the **Find Near** field. Click the **Theaters** button to the left. In a moment, Sherlock lists all the theaters in your vicinity (if there are, in fact, any theaters in your vicinity). Note: The Movies channel works only for theaters in the United States.

Tip: *Also new to the Movies channel in Panther, you can type a city's name into the Find Near field to make Sherlock begin guessing possible matches to the name you're typing.*

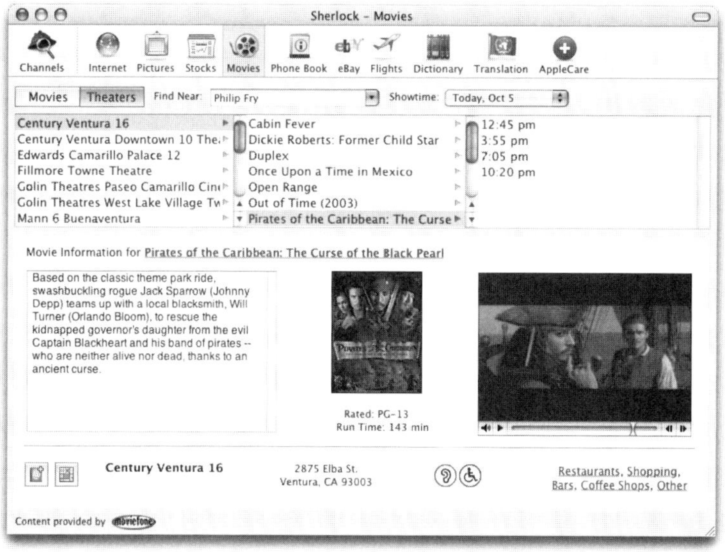

3. The layout of the Movies channel acts a lot like OS X's column view. Click a theater in the far left column. The movies currently showing appear in the next column. Select a movie, and the showtimes appear to the right. Not only that, but once you select a movie title, the bottom pane displays a description of the film and a poster, and it downloads the movie's trailer in QuickTime format. How cool is that? This feature is great when you don't know what a movie is about, or if you're a preview junkie and just love watching trailers.

*Tip: If you're more interested in knowing which movies are showing, you can click the **Movies** button (instead of **Theaters**) to see a list of films in current release. Selecting a movie will display a list of local theaters playing it. Additionally, you can click the **moviefone** icon in the lower-left corner to go to **www.moviefone.com** and purchase tickets online.*

You've probably noticed that the selected theater's address appears at the very bottom of the window. If you're not sure where the theater is, no problem. Sherlock's Phone Book channel can find it for you (along with other local businesses) and provide directions.

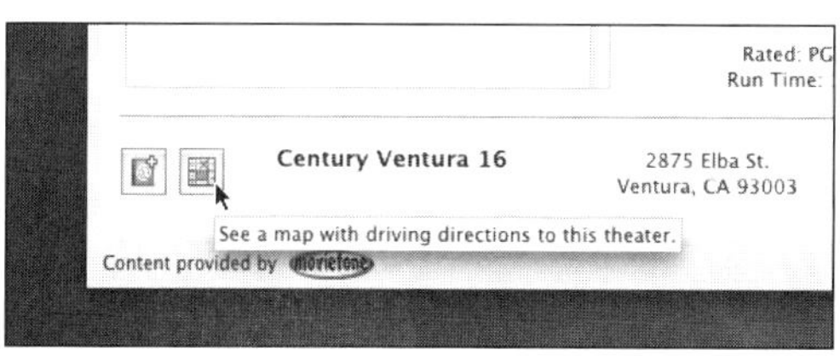

4. Click the **map** button in the lower-left corner of the window. This button is new to the Panther version of Sherlock. Clicking it opens the **Phone Book** channel.

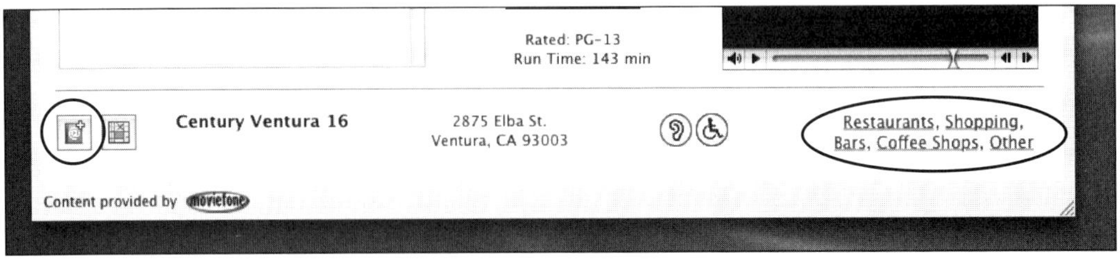

Tip: *You can click the* ***Address Book*** *icon to the left of the* ***map*** *button to add the selected theater's address to* ***Address Book.*** *Additionally, you can click the* ***Restaurants, Shopping, Bars, Coffee Shops,*** *and* ***Other*** *links to the right to locate nearby businesses (using the* ***Phone Book*** *channel).*

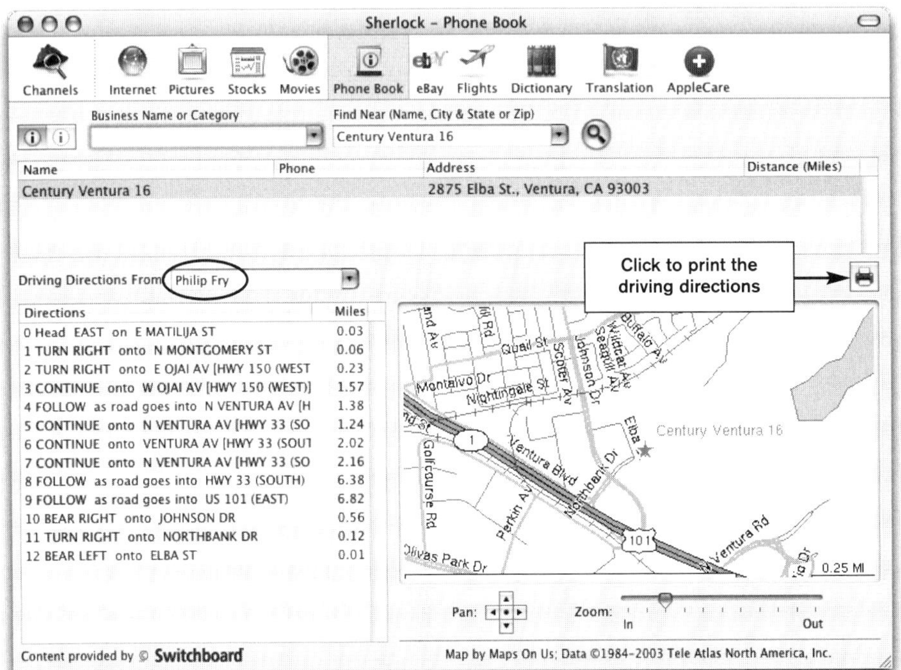

After clicking the map button in the Movies channel, the selected theater's address is displayed in the Phone Book channel along with a map of its location. Again, Sherlock uses your address as it appears in your Address Book and automatically provides driving directions to the theater. You can obtain directions from other locations by typing a name or address that appears in your Address Book into the ***Driving Directions From*** *menu, or by entering a* ***Zip code*** *in this field. You can even print the driving directions by clicking the* ***Print*** *button that appears above the map.*

Note: *Like the Movies channel, the Phone Book channel is only good for addresses in the United States.*

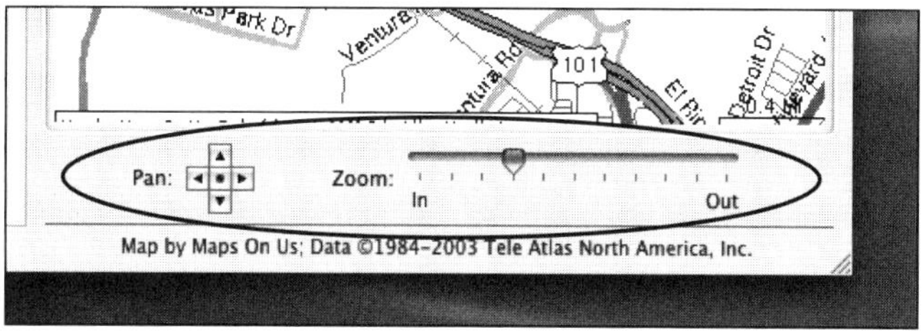

Tip: *You can use the* ***Pan*** *buttons and the* ***Zoom*** *slider to adjust the display of the map and help you get your bearings.*

Finding Businesses, Finding People

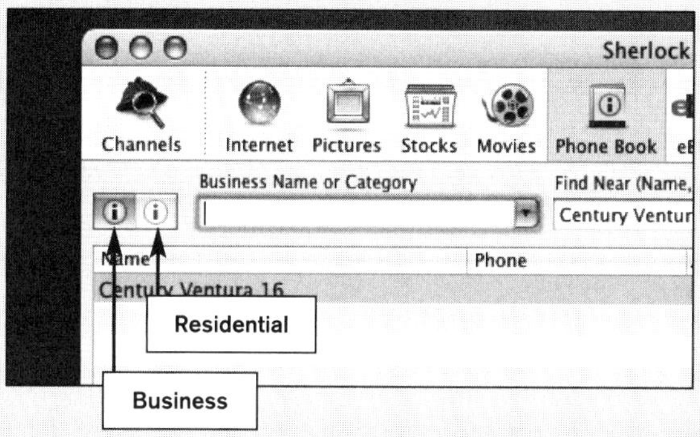

New to Panther, the Phone Book channel now allows you to find information for both business and residential addresses. While searching for businesses, you can select from a list of categories (such as Coffee Shops, Hotels & Motels, Parks, and so on), or enter the business's name in the **Business Name or Category** field. Switching to residential allows you to search for a specific person by name and location.

As you can see, the Movies channel and the Phone Book channel are well-integrated with each other, but either channel can also be used independently if you just want to watch a trailer or find a local business.

---

5. The eBay Channel

The **eBay** channel caters to the ever-growing number of people who participate in eBay auctions. Rather than going to eBay.com in your browser, you can use this channel to quickly search for items on which you're interested in bidding. You can even use this channel to track specific items to monitor their current bids.

Since the items on eBay are constantly changing, this exercise provides general instructions for searching eBay.

1. Click the **eBay** icon in the toolbar.

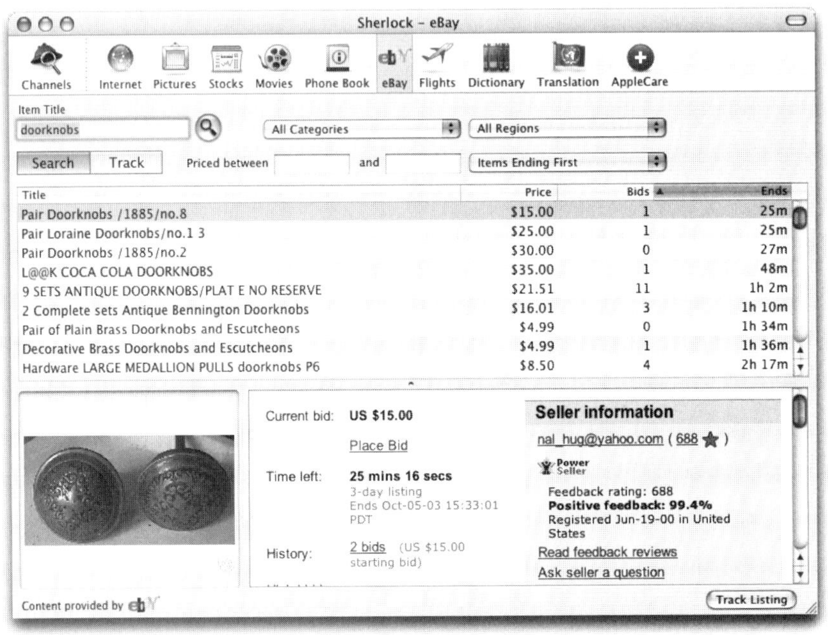

The eBay channel is exclusively for finding and tracking auctions on eBay.

2. To use it, type in an item you're looking for and press **Return**. You can narrow down your search by selecting a specific category or a region (for local auctions) to search in.

3. When your search results return, click any item to see an image (if the seller has provided one) and to view the current status of the auction. To bid on an item, double-click its listing and you'll be taken to the eBay page in your Web browser.

Tip: *By default, search results are listed in the order of the auctions that are ending soonest. You can further sort your results by the auction's title, price, or its number of bids by clicking on the proper column headers.*

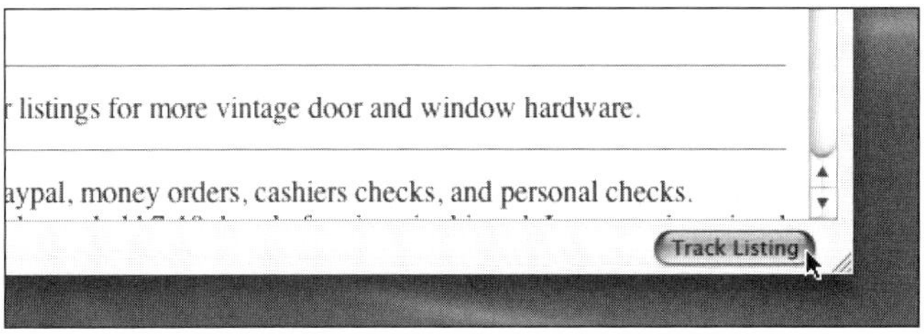

If an item interests you, you can follow the auction by selecting it and then clicking ***Track Listing*** *in the lower-right corner of the window.*

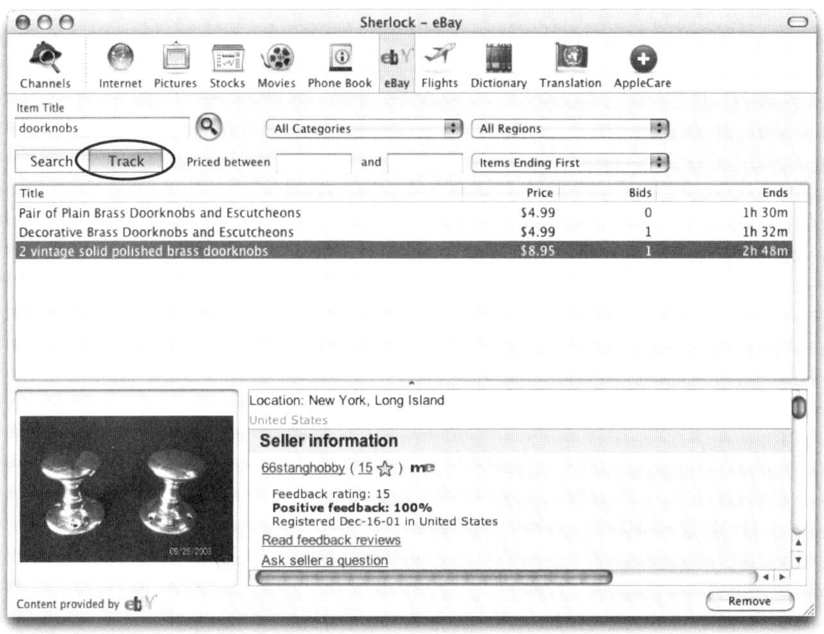

View your tracked items by clicking ***Track*** *in the upper-left corner of the window. You can clear tracked items by selecting them and clicking* ***Remove*** *at the bottom of the window.*

6. The Flights Channel

You can use the **Flights** channel to track flights if, for instance, you've been the lucky person selected to pick up a friend at the airport and you need to check the current status of his or her flight. As in the previous exercise, the steps in this exercise provide general information on using this channel.

1. Click the **Flights** icon in the toolbar.

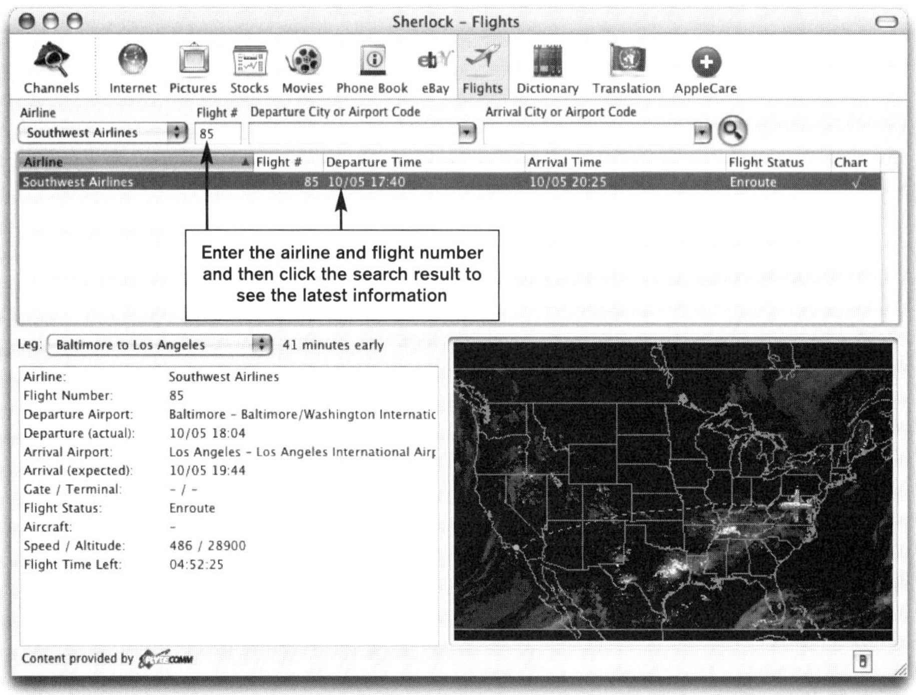

2. To track a flight, just enter the airline and flight number, and Sherlock will give you up-to-date information on when the flight is landing, at which terminal it is arriving, and its current position (if a map is available).

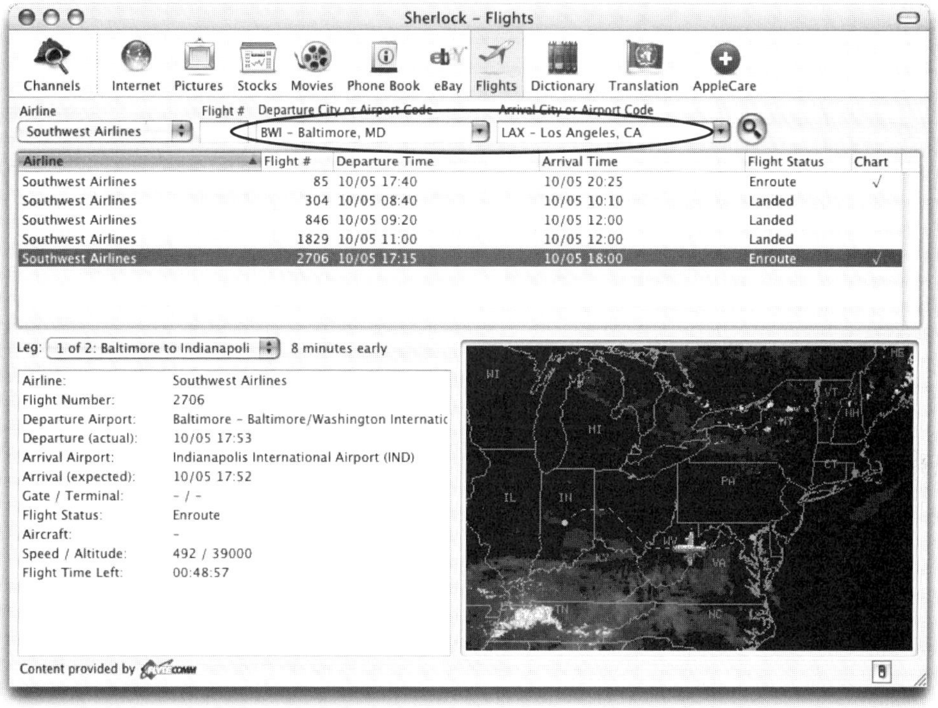

If you don't know the flight number, just enter as much information as you can, such as the airline and the flight's departure and arrival cities. Sherlock will display all flights matching your data.

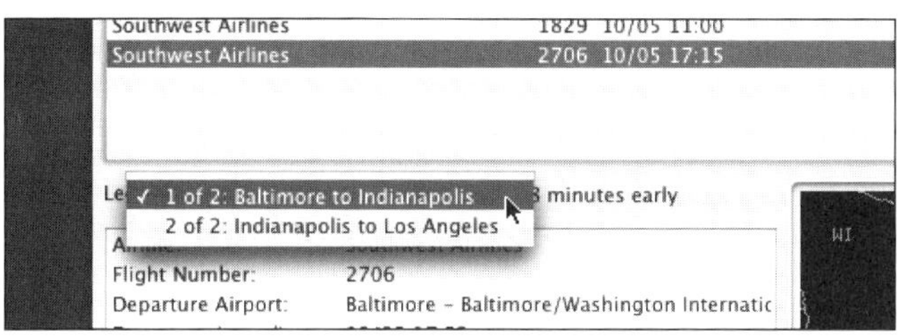

3. If the flight you select includes multiple stops, choose the part of the flight you want to track from the **Leg** menu.

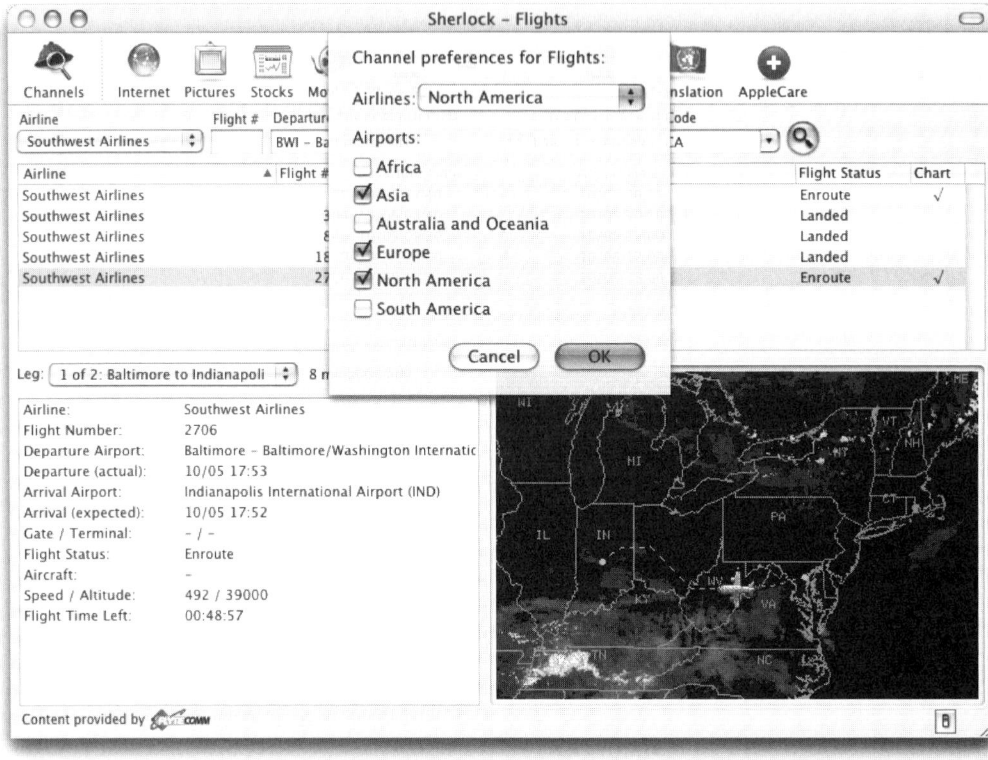

Tip: *If you're more of an international traveler, you can tell Sherlock to search airlines and airports based in other continents by clicking the small switch icon in the lower-right corner of the window.*

7. The Dictionary and Translation Channels

In this exercise, you'll take a look at the **Dictionary** and **Translation** channels, which come in handy when you run across words you might not be familiar with.

1. Click the **Dictionary** icon in the toolbar. Now here's a straightforward channel.

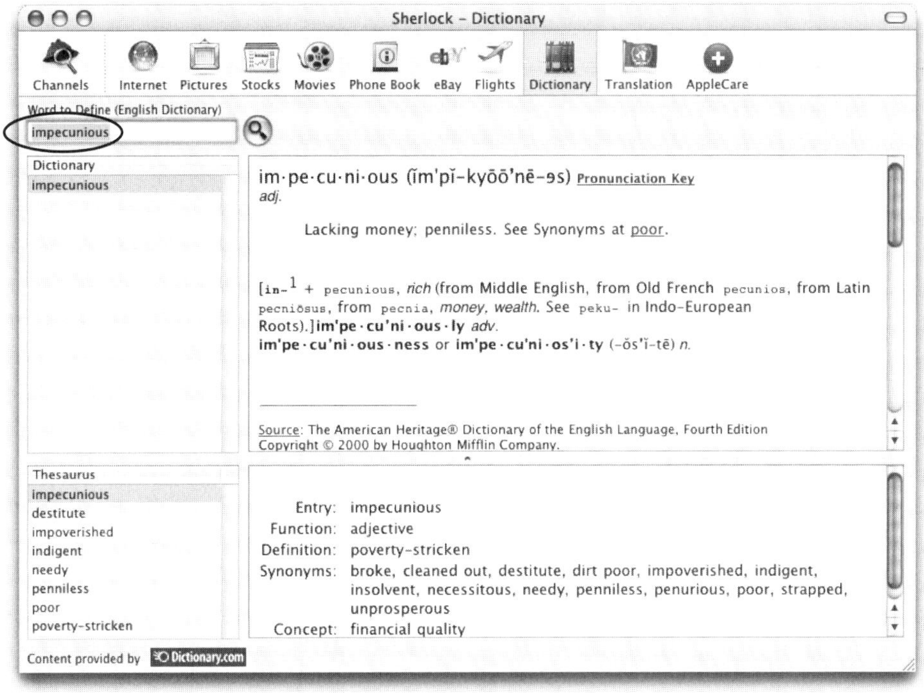

2. Type **impecunious** into the **Word to Define** field and press **Return** to search for its definition. Sherlock searches Dictionary.com for the word's definition and displays it in the top pane of the window. If Sherlock finds any synonyms for the word, they will appear in the **Roget's II Thesaurus** pane. Clicking on a synonym will display its definition along with even more words that have a similar meaning.

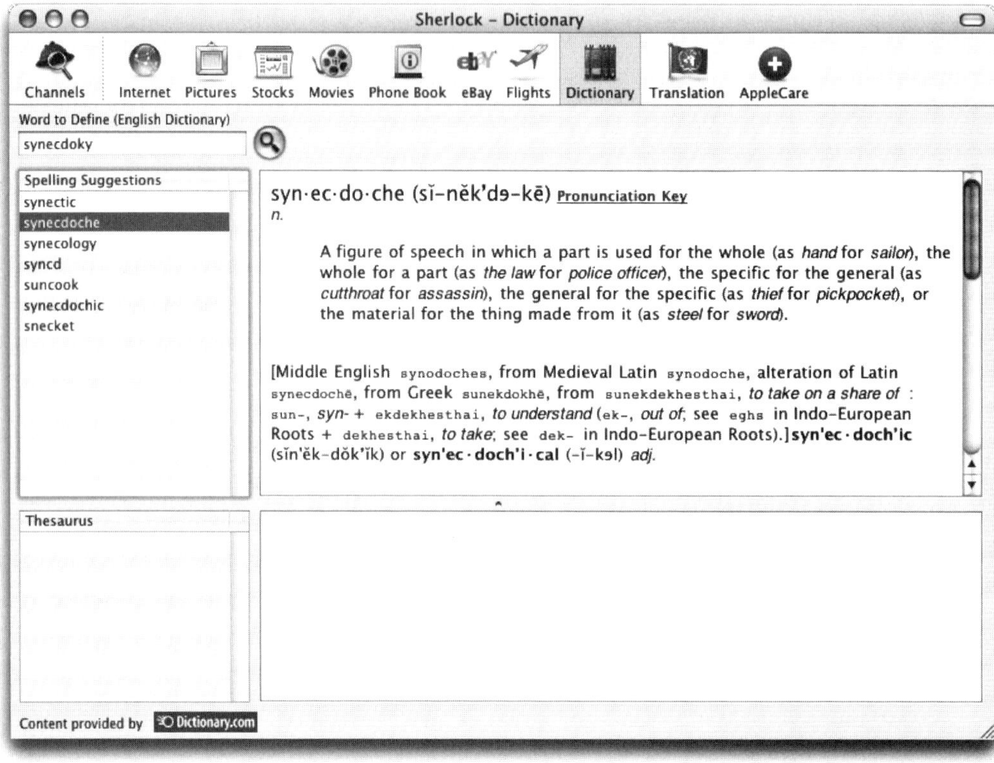

*If you misspell a word or if Sherlock can't find the word you typed, a list of alternatives may appear in a **Spelling Suggestions** column. Click any of the alternatives to see their definitions.*

***Tip:** The Dictionary channel can be very useful for those times when you run across words in your Web browser or word processing program that you might not recognize. Select the word in question and choose **Edit > Copy** from the menu bar (or press **Cmd+C**). Then open Sherlock's Dictionary channel, make sure the cursor is flashing in the **Word to Define** field, and then choose **Edit > Paste** from the menu bar (or press **Cmd+V**). Press **Return** to see the word's definition.*

The Dictionary channel does a great job finding definitions and synonyms for English words. But for non-English words you may occasionally come across, you'll probably find Sherlock's Translations channel to be much more useful.

3. Click the **Translation** icon in the toolbar.

Sherlock can translate whole paragraphs of text, not just single words, from English into several other languages, as well as being able to translate other languages into English. This channel is especially helpful when you surf onto foreign-language Web sites and need a translation of some text.

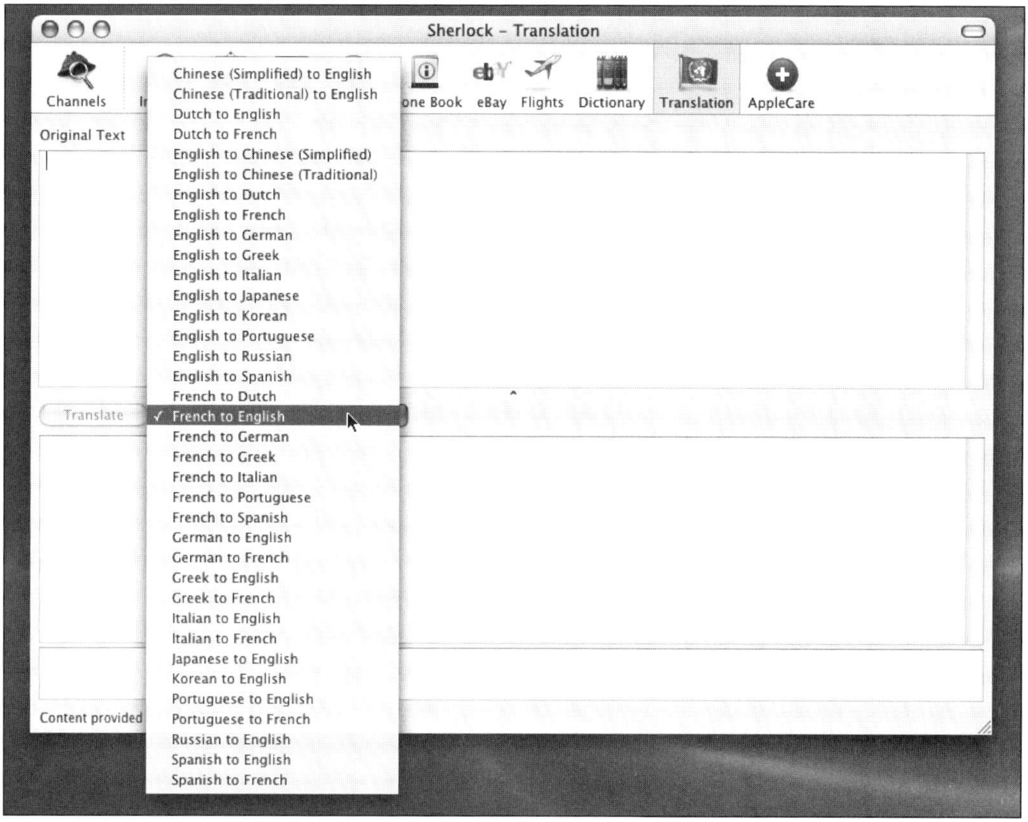

4. Click the pop-up menu in the middle of the window to see a list of all the available translations that Sherlock can perform. Select **French to English**.

5. In the **Original Text** field, type **Il y a une poisson dans votre bibliotheque** and then click **Translate**. In a moment, the English translation of the phrase appears.

Note the disclaimer at the bottom of the window, indicating that this translation was generated automatically without any human involvement other than your own. The Translation channel is well-suited to giving you the gist of a foreign phrase you might stumble across in your Web surfing or reading, but because of the potential for unintentionally amusing (or embarrassing) translations, you probably don't want to use it as a tool if you're, say, a diplomat to a foreign country writing a letter to the nation's top leader. ("Mr. President, we acknowledge you with waving limbs and toothsome faces!")

Fun with Translations

Start with a simple phrase in English like, "I fell on my bottom," and translate it into another language such as French. Copy the French translation and paste it into the Original Text field and translate it from French to German. Copy the German translation and turn it back into English. The phrase "I am on my soil please" should give you a pretty good idea of why you shouldn't use this channel for professional translation.

8. The AppleCare Channel

The **AppleCare** channel provides a central point from which to search Apple's immense **Knowledge Base**, the source for troubleshooting and finding information about all of Apple's products. Normally, searching the Knowledge Base involves firing up your Web browser, going to Apple's site, clicking on Support, typing your search terms, and then browsing through several Web pages to find the information you need. The AppleCare channel works in a similar fashion, but has the advantage of keeping your search results in plain view so you can quickly browse among them to find what you're looking for.

1. Click the **AppleCare** icon, the last channel in the toolbar.

---

2. For instance, pretend you were wondering about a strange sound emanating from your G4 Power Mac. Type **G4 noise** into the **Topic or Description** field and press **Return**.

In a moment, a list of matching articles from Apple's Knowledge Base appears, sorted in order of relevancy.

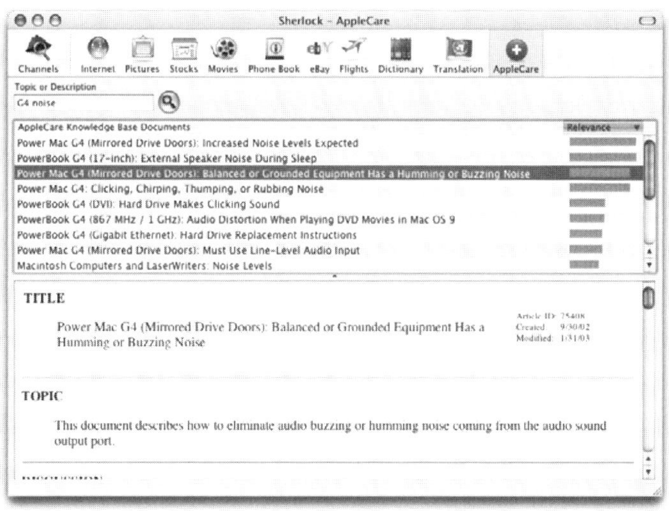

3. Select any article to view it in the lower pane of the window. You might want to increase the size of the window to see more of the article at once.

***Tip:** You can also drag the horizontal divider between the two panes to increase the size of the article window.*

So now you have a complete rundown of Sherlock's channels. Now just remember that it's there and don't forget to use it. Naturally, you'll probably find yourself using some channels more than others, but if you keep Sherlock running, you'll always have quick access to any of its channels.

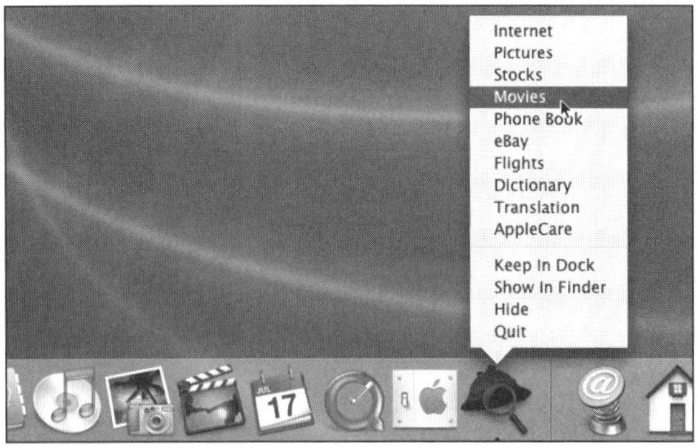

Tip: If Sherlock is running, you can quickly jump to any channel by ***Ctrl+clicking*** *on its icon in the* ***Dock.*** *Select a channel from the contextual menu that appears. This shortcut works as long as Sherlock is already running, regardless of whether it's the front-most application.*

Customizing the Toolbar

Much like the toolbar in Finder windows, Sherlock allows you to customize its toolbar to best suit your needs. Choose **View > Customize Toolbar** to open a sheet from which you can select items to add to the toolbar.

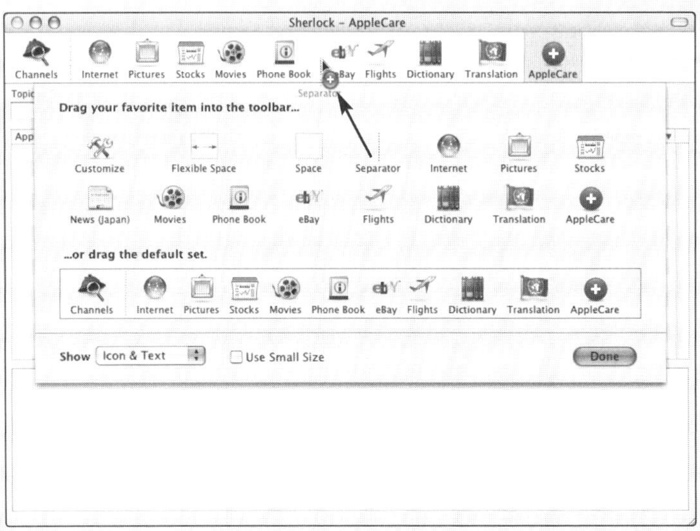

To add an item, simply drag it onto the toolbar to your preferred location. You may also remove items that you don't use by dragging them into the sheet below. To return the toolbar to its original configuration, drag the default set into the toolbar. When you're finished customizing the toolbar, click **Done.**

Customizing Your Channels

Sherlock was created to accept new channels created by Apple or by third-party developers. In Panther, Apple has made it super easy to add more channels to Sherlock and to create custom collections of channels. To customize your channel collections, click the **Channels** button in the toolbar.

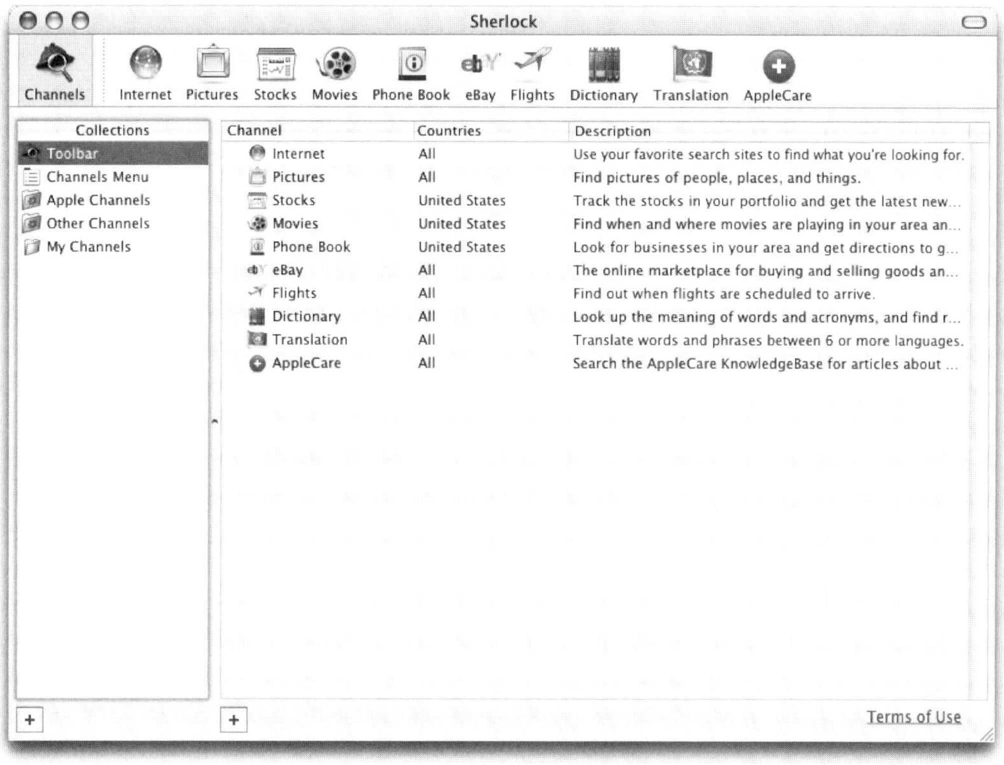

Here you can click the items listed in the Collections column to view all the available channels. The following chart describes the collections.

Sherlock Collections

Collection	Description
Toolbar	This collection displays all the channels that appear in the toolbar. Here, you can select items to delete them or to drag them up and down in the list to rearrange the order in which they appear in the toolbar. If you accidentally delete a channel, get it back by choosing **View > Customize Toolbar** and then dragging the icon for the channel into the toolbar.
Channels Menu	This collection displays the channels found under the Channels menu in the Sherlock menu bar. Drag channels to this collection if you prefer to select among channels from the menu bar.
Apple Channels	These are the default channels that appear in Sherlock—the channels covered in this exercise.
Other Channels	Here you can view and access channels that have been created by third party developers. Double-click any channel to access it. If you find yourself using some of these channels often, you might want to drag the channel into the Toolbar or Channels Menu collections for quick access. More and more channels are constantly being developed, so check back here often for new ones.
My Channels	This is an empty collection into which you can drag your favorite channels. You can also create new collections by clicking the **+** symbol at the bottom of the collections column.

At this point, you should have a pretty good idea of what Sherlock is capable of. But for all of the specific searching it can perform, the one thing it can't do is look for things on the Mac itself. The next exercise will show you how to search and find things on your own computer.

4. When you're done exploring Sherlock, either quit the application, or feel free to keep it running if you think you might want to start using it more often.

9. Searching Your Mac

As mentioned earlier, when Sherlock was introduced in OS 8.5, it replaced the Find application that had previously been used to locate items on your Mac. As you just saw, the current incarnation of Sherlock is used exclusively to search Web resources; it doesn't search your Mac at all. For this reason, Apple has reintroduced the **Find** command into the Mac OS. Apple also introduced the Search field into Finder windows, which is a handy searching tool that's new to OS X. This exercise will show you how to use both the Search field and the Find tool to locate the things you may have lost track of on your Mac.

Tip: The fastest way to search for a file is to use the Search field in a Finder window.

1. Double-click your **hard drive** icon to open a **Finder** window.

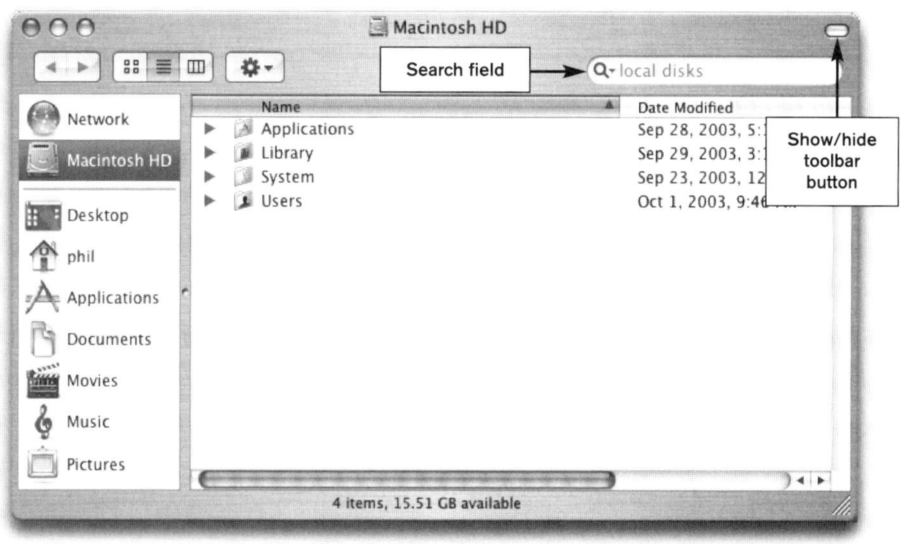

2. Make sure you can see the **Search** field. The toolbar must be visible in order to see the Search field. Click the **Show/hide toolbar** button if you don't see the toolbar. It may also be possible that you've customized the toolbar to not include the Search field. If this is the case, choose **View > Customize Toolbar** from the menu bar to reinsert the Search field.

The Search field is a quick and convenient way to search for an item by its file name. This feature has been greatly improved in Panther. Previously, you could only search the Finder window in which the Search field appeared (including any folders within that window, but ignoring folders outside the window), but now you can tell OS X exactly where you want to search.

3. Click the **magnifying glass** icon in the **Search** field to select a location to search and choose **Local Disks** (if it's not already selected). The following chart describes the choices found in this menu.

Search Field Locations	
Search Location	**Description**
Local Disks	Restricts your search to just the hard drives directly connected to your Mac
Home	Searches just the contents of your Home folder
Selection	Searches just the disk, server, or folder whose window you're currently viewing
Everywhere	Opens your search to all the locations mentioned in this chart

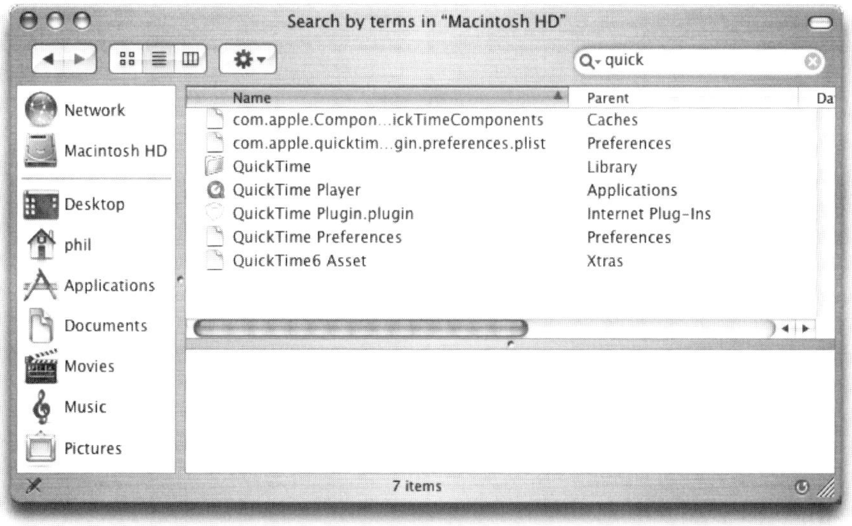

4. In the **Search** field, type **quick**. New to Panther, you immediately see a list of all the files and folders that match what you're typing. You know longer need to press **Return** to begin your search. This feature, known as **Fast file search**, first premiered in applications like iTunes and Address Book, and Apple has now integrated it into the Finder.

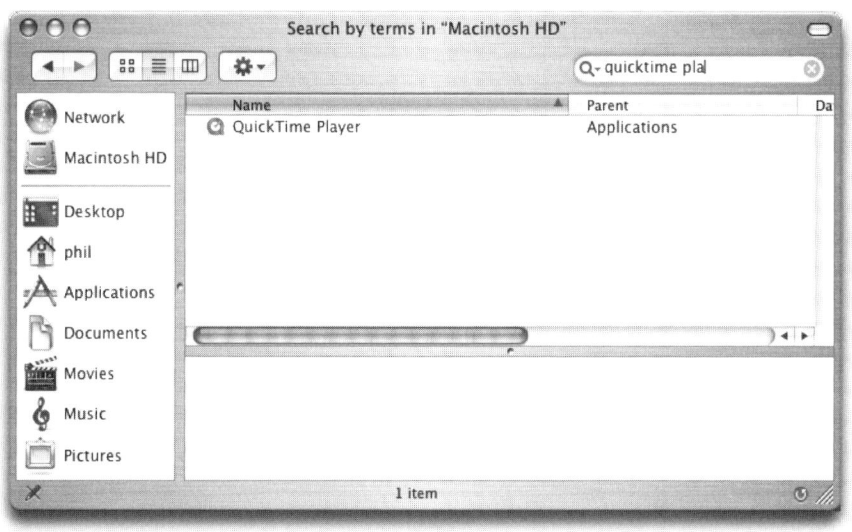

5. Continue typing to create the search term **quicktime player**. Notice that the result list continues to narrow itself down as you type. By the time you type **quicktime pla**, only one result should appear.

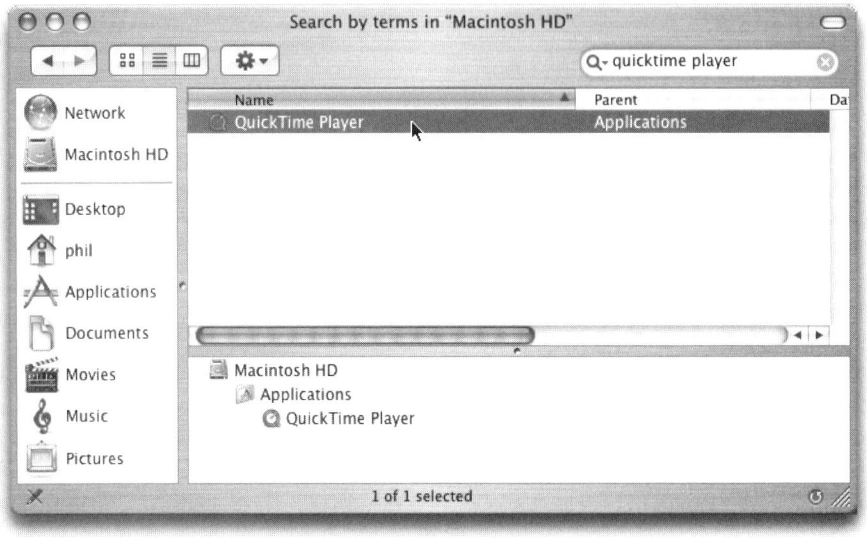

6. Click the **QuickTime Player** search result (just single-click or else you'll open QuickTime Player), and its exact location appears in the lower pane of the window.

At this point, you can do several different things with your search results:

- Double-click the **hard drive** icon in the lower pane to display its contents in a new window.
- Double-click the **Applications** folder in the lower pane to open it in a new window.
- Double-click **QuickTime Player** in either pane to run that application.
- You can rename files in the top pane by clicking them once and then keeping your mouse over them. If you have privileges to rename the file, the file's name will become editable.
- Additionally, you can drag items from the **Search** window to the **Trash** in the **Dock**.

7. Double-click **QuickTime Player** in either pane to launch the application. Once you've observed that you can open programs directly from the **Search** window, quit **QuickTime Player**.

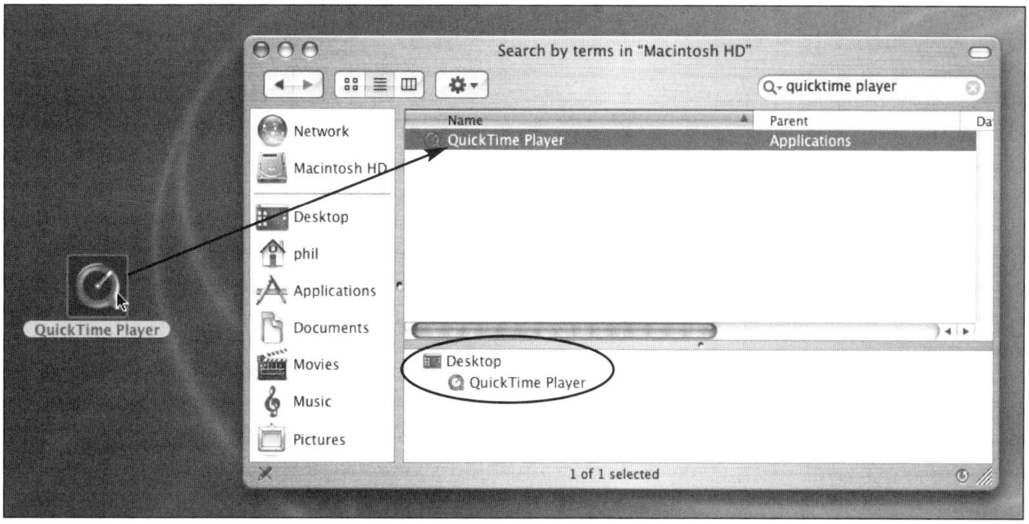

Tip: *You can drag items directly from the top pane of the **Search** window onto the **Desktop**, the **Places** sidebar, or into other folders. The information in the lower pane will immediately change to reflect the file's new location. This can be convenient if you want to move a file without having to open a series of folders in order to get to it. Holding down the **Option** key while you drag will create a duplicate of the file in the new location rather than moving the file.*

*The Search field is a great tool if you're looking for an item based on its name. But let's face it; you won't always remember what you named a file. Sometimes you might only remember part of its name, or maybe just the approximate date you created it. If you need to search for files based on less specific criteria, it's time to pull up the **Find** application, which lets you perform searches based on a file's type, content, date, or other criteria.*

8. Close any open windows. Choose **File > Find** from the menu bar (or press **Cmd+F**).

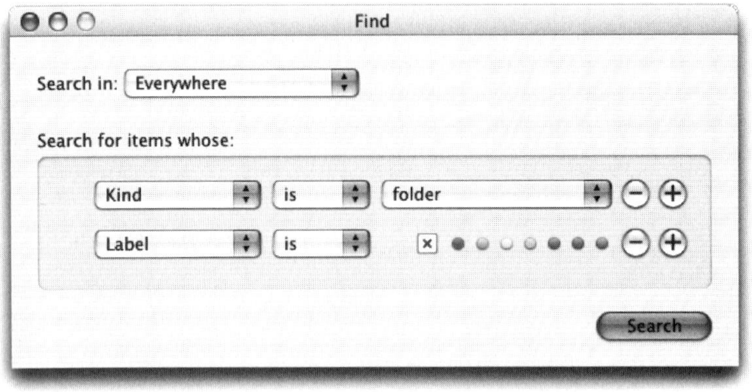

*This opens the **Find** window. Here you can perform a search based on whatever information you know about the file you're looking for. You can click the **Search in** menu to select the same four search locations found in the Finder window's Search field. Under the **Search for items whose** section, you can add or remove criteria for your search.*

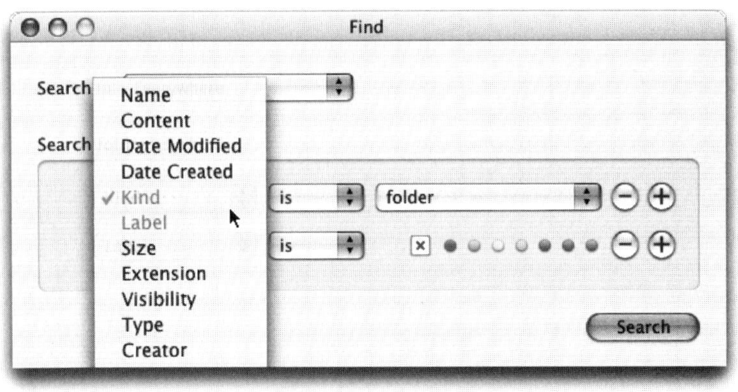

9. Click the first menu under **Search for items whose** to observe the available search criteria. As you can see, there's a wide range of options when it comes to searching for items on your Mac.

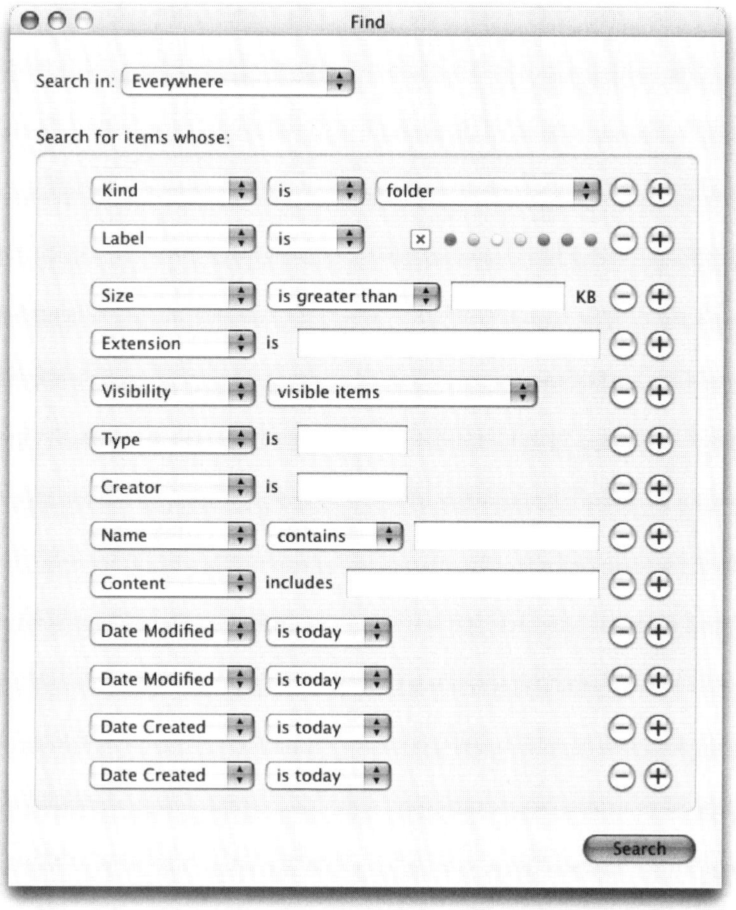

By clicking the – and + symbols on each line, you can add or remove specifications in any combination necessary to find the item you're looking for. The following chart explains all the criteria and their search options.

Find Window Criteria	
Item	**Description**
Search in	This menu allows you to specify the location in which you want to perform your search. **Home** searches only your own home folder, ignoring the other contents of your hard drive. **Local disks** searches all drives connected to your Mac. **Everywhere** searches all drives, including those that you may have mounted over your company or home network (searching everywhere naturally may result in a long search time). Choosing **Specific places** opens an additional pane in the window, allowing you to click an **Add** button to stipulate exactly which folders or drives you want to search.
Name	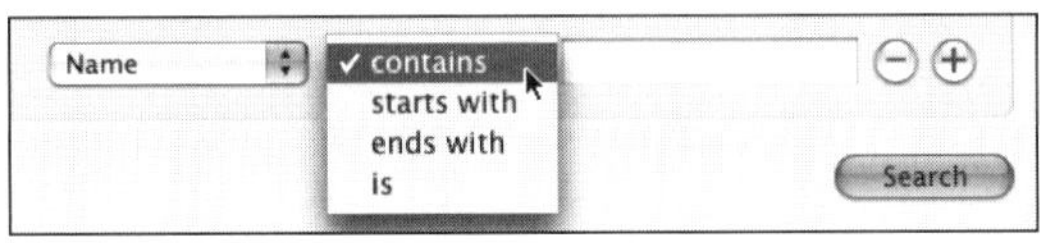 Much like the Search field covered earlier in this exercise, the file name criterion allows you to search for an item based on its name. But this criterion allows you to be more specific than the Search field does: By clicking the pop-up menu in this field, you can specify that the file name **contains**, **starts with**, **ends with**, or **is** the phrase you type in the field to the right.
Content	This amazing criterion actually searches the content of your files. For example, if all you know about a document is that somewhere in it is the word "guacamole," you could type that word here to track down the file, even if you don't remember what the file itself is called. (See the sidebar "The Importance of Indexing" for an important caveat.)
Date Modified	The word "modified" here really means saved. Select an item from the pop-up menu based on the date you last saved the file you're looking for. **is today** will list all files created today. **is within** reveals an additional pop-up menu from which you can select a range of dates to search from anywhere between one to six months. **is before**, **is after**, and **is exactly** allow you to enter an exact date from which to start your search.
Date Created	This criterion's pop-up menu contains the same items as date modified, but the search is based on which date the file was created and ignores when the file was last saved.

continues on next page

Find Window Criteria *continued*	
Item	**Description**
Kind	This criterion allows you to perform a search based on what a file is or is not. From the first pop-up menu, select **is** or **is not.** Then from the second pop-up menu, choose a kind of file (**alias**, **application**, **folder**, **document**, **audio**, **image**, or **movie**).
Size	If you're aware of the relative size of a file (for instance, if you know that you have a huge video file sitting somewhere on your drive), you can use this criterion to display all files within a certain range of sizes. From the pop-up menu, select either **is less than** or **is greater than** and then type a file size in the text field. This is also a great way to track down really large files that you may never use but are eating up your hard drive space.
Extension is	If you know the extension type (.jpg, .doc, .psd, and so on) of the file you're looking for, type it here.
Visibility	In addition to the files you can see on your Mac, there are thousands upon thousands of invisible files residing in each folder as well. These files are usually essential to the operation of OS X and are invisible so that you don't accidentally move or delete them. For the most part, you'll probably only be looking for visible files (**visibility items**) rather than invisible files (**invisible items**). If you want to look for both types of files, however, select **visible and invisible items**, from the pop-up menu here.
Label	Allows you to search for items that you've labeled by color. You learned about labels in Chapter 2, "*Working with Files and Folders.*"
Creator is	**Creator** refers to a four-character code that tells the Finder what application goes with what document. Typing a code in this field tells your Mac to find documents that can be opened by this application. Typically, the majority of users never have to worry about this "creator" thing; it's used mostly by Mac developers.
Type is	This is another criteria that most people don't need to search for. Like **creator**, **type** is a code associated with a file. It identifies the format of a file, but it doesn't necessarily associate an application with the file. Entering a **type** code in this field displays all the files that match the code. Again, you'll probably never need to use this criteria.

*By combining different criteria, you can really narrow down your search. For instance, you could find all files over 5 MB in size created yesterday. Once you've added all your known criteria to the Find window, click **Search**. Results will be displayed in the same two-paned window that you observed when using the Search field.*

***Note:** You won't be able to search for items located in the Home folders of other users. Because OS X is a multiuser operating system, each user's Home folder is still off-limits to all other users. Therefore, you can't go searching for phrases like "birthday presents" in your spouse's folder.*

The Importance of Indexing

So how does your Mac know where everything is? The Find command and Search field rely on an index of all the various files, folders, and icons on your hard drive that your Mac automatically creates.

In pre–OS X versions of the Mac OS, indexing was scheduled by default to occur at a time when you and your Mac's other activities were likely to be at a minimum (usually at midnight). The main problem with this indexing method was that night-owl Mac users had to put up with an indexing dialog box floating on their screens while the multi-hour process ran its course. In OS X, indexing occurs constantly, but you never notice it. It happens in the brief moments between the keystrokes and commands you're performing in other applications. OS X just waits until a free moment appears, indexes a few files, and then stops whenever you start working again.

Although your Mac can pretty much find any application or item based on its file name, without an index file you wouldn't be able to search for files based on their content. The index files that OS X creates contain the information about word processing documents, PDF files, Web pages, and generally any file containing text.

If you ever unsuccessfully search for a file that you're sure exists on your hard drive or in a particular folder, the problem may be that the folder in which the file resides has not yet been indexed. For example, if you're searching for a document by its contents (as described in the previous chart), you won't be able to find the document unless OS X has already indexed it.

To check whether a folder has been indexed, select it in the **Finder** and then choose **File > Get Info** from the menu bar, or press **Cmd+I**. (Alternately, you can **Ctrl+click** the folder and choose **Get Info** from the contextual menu).

continues on next page

The Importance of Indexing *continued*

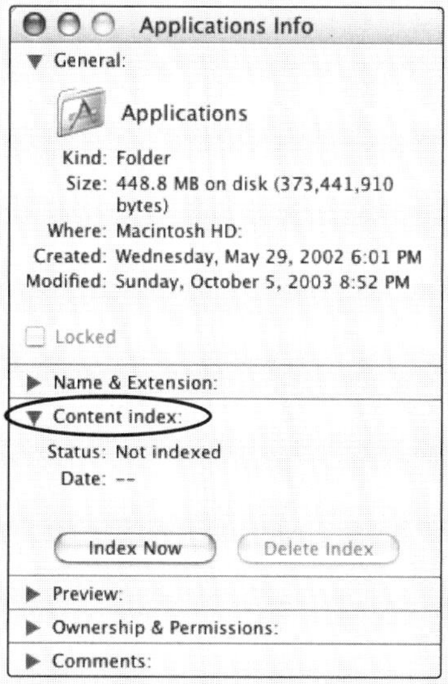

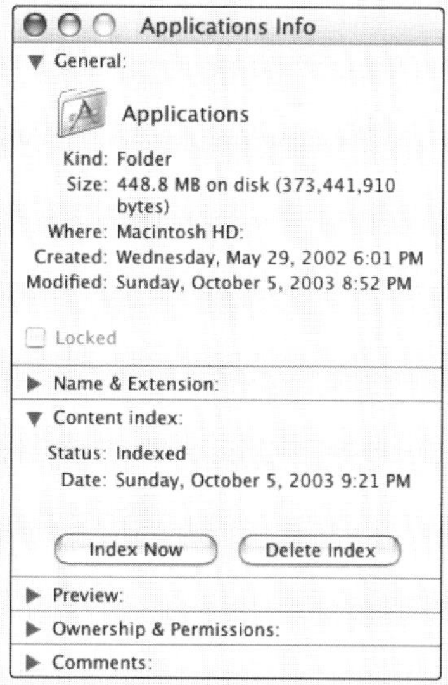

In the info window that opens, click the toggle triangle next to **Content Index** to see if the folder has been indexed yet. If the file has been indexed, you can also see the date it was last indexed. In either case, you can click **Index Now** to create an updated index file. The file that's created when a folder is indexed is an invisible file, and the great thing is that this invisible file is placed into the folder that it indexes. This means that when you copy or move the folder, the index goes with it. If you want to remove this invisible file (if you're short on hard drive space, for instance), you can click **Delete Index** in the **Get Info** window.

10. When you're done examining the **Find** application window, click the minus (–) sign next to any of the criteria you don't think you'll need in the near future. (You can always activate them again by clicking the **Add criteria** pop-up menu.) Close the **Find** window.

The Find command in OS X is a powerful search tool that can help you locate just about any file on your computer. When you need to perform a search, you might want to start with the Search field, since it's immediately accessible from any Finder window's toolbar. If your Search field hunt turns out to be unsuccessful, you can then move onto the Find application.

Now that you've made it through this chapter, you should be able to find pretty much anything, whether it's on your Mac or on the Internet. In the next chapter, you'll look at one more Internet-based tool.

12.

.Mac

| Signing Up | .Mac Mail | Address Book |
| iDisk | HomePage | Backup |

chap_12

Mac OS X Panther
H•O•T CD-ROM

In July 2002, Apple introduced **.Mac** (pronounced "dot-mac"), a $99-per-year subscription service that provides its members with features such as email, Web site hosting, and storage space, as well as several downloadable applications and utilities. Although .Mac is not technically an element of Panther, this book devotes a chapter to it in order to introduce .Mac's features and to explain how they relate to Panther and your computer. .Mac's tools are more tightly integrated in Panther than ever before; applications such as Address Book, iCal, iSync, and iPhoto all have features that you can take advantage of as a .Mac subscriber.

Whether or not .Mac is worth its price is a determination only you can make. Fortunately, Apple provides a free 60-day trial period for you to put .Mac through its paces. This chapter will walk you through .Mac's services, but in the end, you will have to decide whether you want to keep your account when the trial period expires.

What Do You Get for Your $99?

Your purchase of a .Mac account entitles you to a Web-based email account (your_name@mac.com), iDisk for storing files for yourself and others, space for a Web page, Backup (an application for backing up important files to an online server or onto a CD-R, Virex virus checking software, plus several other features and services. To decide whether .Mac is worth $99 a year, you'll have to determine if you'll use any of these services often enough to justify the expense. Probably one of the most compelling reasons to use .Mac is that it gives you Web-based access to your email and some of your most important files (that you store on your iDisk). As long as you're some place with an Internet connection, you can log into **www.mac.com**, check your email, send messages to people in your Address Book, download files from your iDisk, and even access the addresses for your favorite Web sites. This chapter will walk you through the features of .Mac to help you to decide whether to take the plunge.

I. Signing Up for the Free Trial

The first step to using .Mac services is to sign up for the free 60-day trial. This should give you enough time to determine whether you'll use the services enough to get your money's worth. The nice thing about this is that there's no financial commitment–no credit card number is required to secure the trial. Plus, if you decide not to keep your account after the 60 days, you'll still be able to keep the account name you created, which can be used as your screen name when using iChat AV (covered earlier at the end of Chapter 10, "*Address Book, Mail, and iChat AV*").

1. Connect to the Internet and open **Safari**. (You'll need to be connected to the Internet for every exercise in this chapter.) Go to **www.mac.com** and click the **Free Trial** link on the left side of the screen. (The Web page might not exactly match the screen shot shown here.)

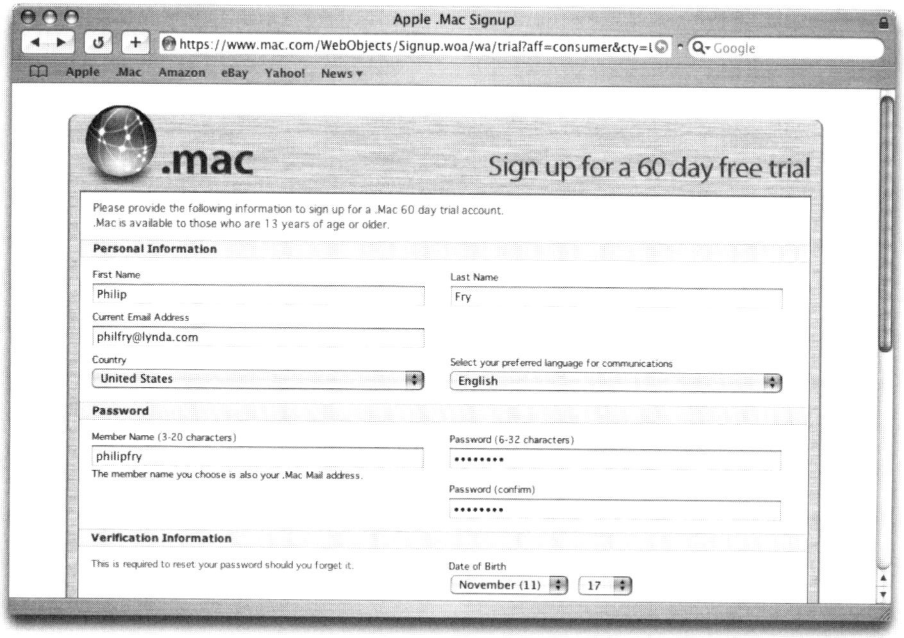

2. Fill out the required information here. Pick a member name that you think will be unique. Bear in mind that you might not get the first one you try–over 400,000 people have created .Mac accounts before you. After you've completed the information on this page, click the **Continue** button at the bottom.

---

3. If your member name and password are acceptable, you'll be presented with a page displaying your account information, letting you know what your email address is and when the trial period expires. Print this page for your reference. If you don't have a printer hooked up to your Mac, copy down the information here:

(If you use this space, don't loan this book to any untrustworthy characters. Buy them their own copies. In fact, buy them several copies.) Click **Continue** when you're done.

*If there was anything wrong with your signup information, you'll be returned to the signup page and prompted to create a new member name or password. If this happens, enter your new information and click **Continue** to try again. (If you selected a name that's already taken, you'll see a page offering several variations on the name, prompting you to select one from the list or to enter a new one.)*

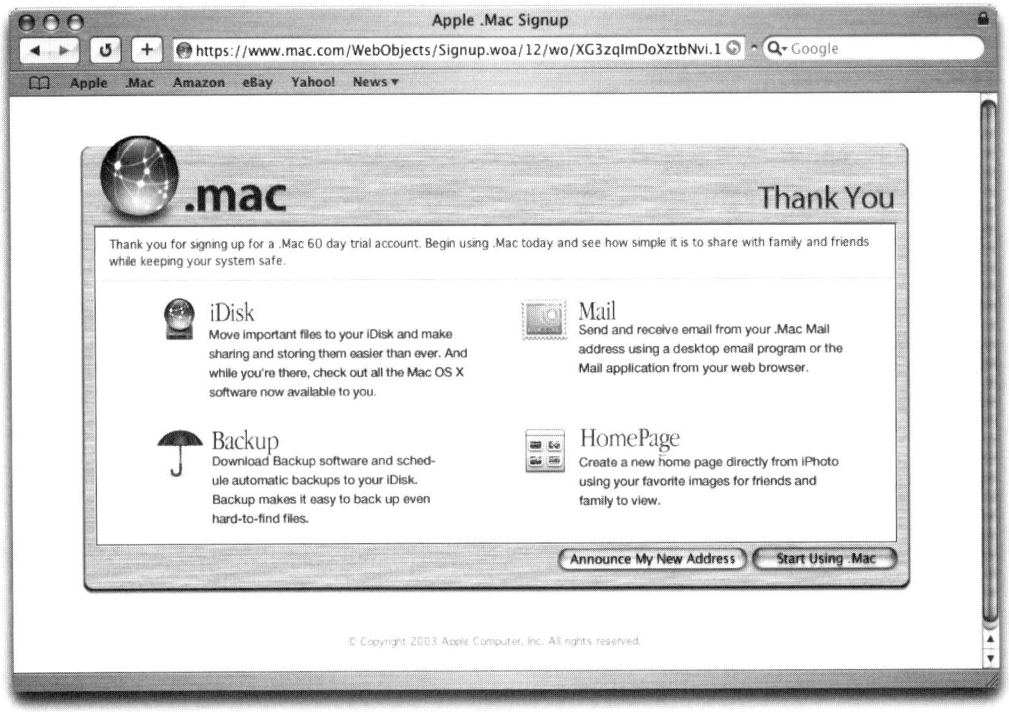

You'll see a thank-you-for-signing-up page informing you of all the wonderful stuff that's now available to you.

---

4. Click the **Start Using .Mac** button to go to the main .Mac members page.

That was easy, wasn't it? You're now ready to explore all that .Mac has to offer. The first stop is .Mac Mail, which is covered in the next exercise.

---

2. .Mac Mail

As a subscriber (or trial subscriber) to .Mac, you're immediately issued an email address at **www.mac.com**. Your .Mac email is accessible from any computer connected to the Internet, regardless of whether it's a Mac or a Windows PC. Just go to **www.mac.com**, click the **Mail** button, and enter your password. In many ways, .Mac Mail behaves much like OS X's Mail application (covered in Chapter 10, "*Address Book, Mail, and iChat AV*"), so this exercise should seem familiar to you.

1. To access your .Mac mail, locate and click the **Mail** icon in the toolbar of the main .Mac members page.

Note: *Apple frequently redesigns this page, so the layout you see might not match the one shown here.*

Even though you're already logged into your .Mac account, you may be asked to verify your password. This extra security measure can be especially valuable if you use a public or shared computer because it ensures that others won't be able to use your .Mac account in case you forget to log out of your .Mac session.

2. Enter your password and click **Enter** (or press **Return**). This will take you to your **Inbox**, the place where all your new email messages are stored.

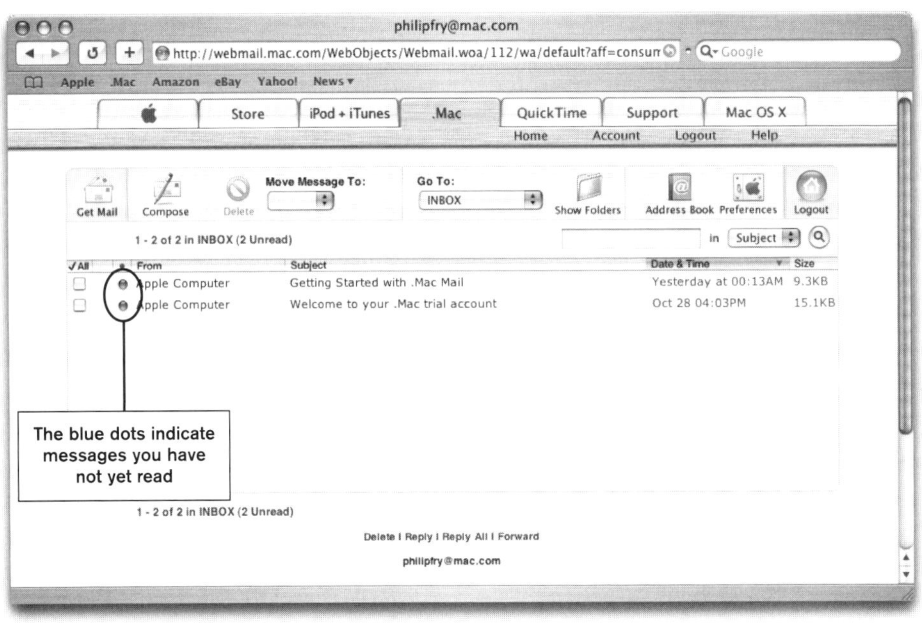

*You should have at least two email messages waiting for you, both from Apple Computer. (Click **Get Mail** if you don't have any messages. In some cases, it may take several minutes for the emails to be sent to you.) To read a message, simply click the text under either the **From** or **Subject** column.*

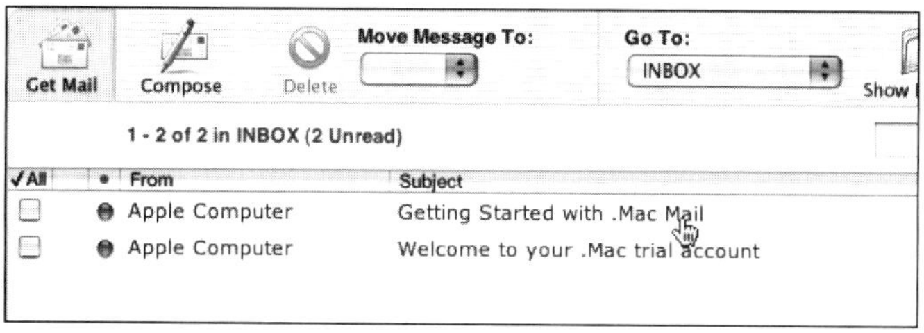

3. Click **Getting Started with .Mac Mail**. (If this email hasn't yet appeared, just click the **Welcome to your .Mac trial account** message.)

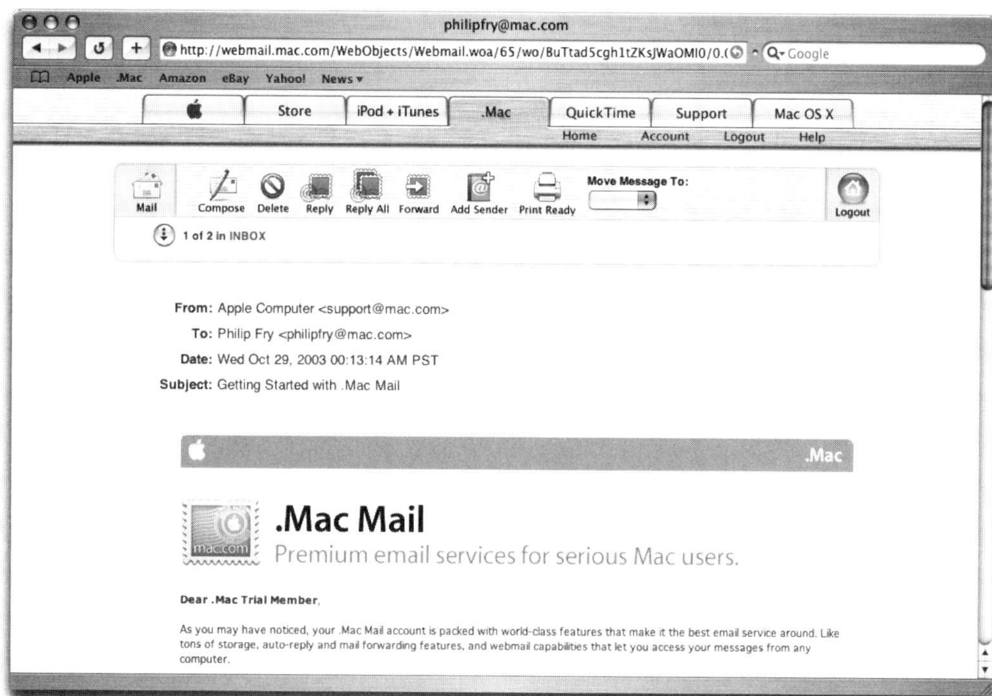

The email message is displayed in your browser window. This particular message from Apple highlights some of the features of .Mac Mail and tells you how to perform tasks such as adding email addresses to your online Address Book and adding your picture to your emails.

4. Take a moment to read through this email.

When viewing a message in .Mac Mail, you'll always have the same toolbar available at the top of each page. The following chart explains each button in the toolbar.

.Mac Mail Toolbar Items	
Item	**Description**
Mail	Takes you back to your Inbox.
Compose	Takes you to a page where you can write and send new email.
Delete	Sends the current message to the Deleted Messages box, but does not actually erase it. This is similar to moving a file into the Trash icon in the Dock; the file is in the Trash, but you can retrieve it if you change your mind.
Reply	Takes you to a page where you can compose an email to the sender of the current message. This is essentially the same as the Compose button, but the **To** and **Subject** fields will already be filled in.
Reply All	Sends your reply to each recipient of the current message (if the message had multiple recipients).
Forward	Allows you to send a copy of the current message to another email address.
Add Sender	Adds the sender to your online Address Book.
Print Ready	Creates a printer-friendly version of the current message by displaying it in its own browser window without the toolbar or any other interface elements. You can then choose **File > Print** to print the message.
Move Message To	From this pop-up menu, you can select **Inbox**, **Deleted Messages**, **Sent Messages**, or any other mailbox you may have created.
Logout	Signs you out of Mail and returns you to the main .Mac page.

5. Once you've read the email, click the **Mail** button in the toolbar to return to your **Inbox**.

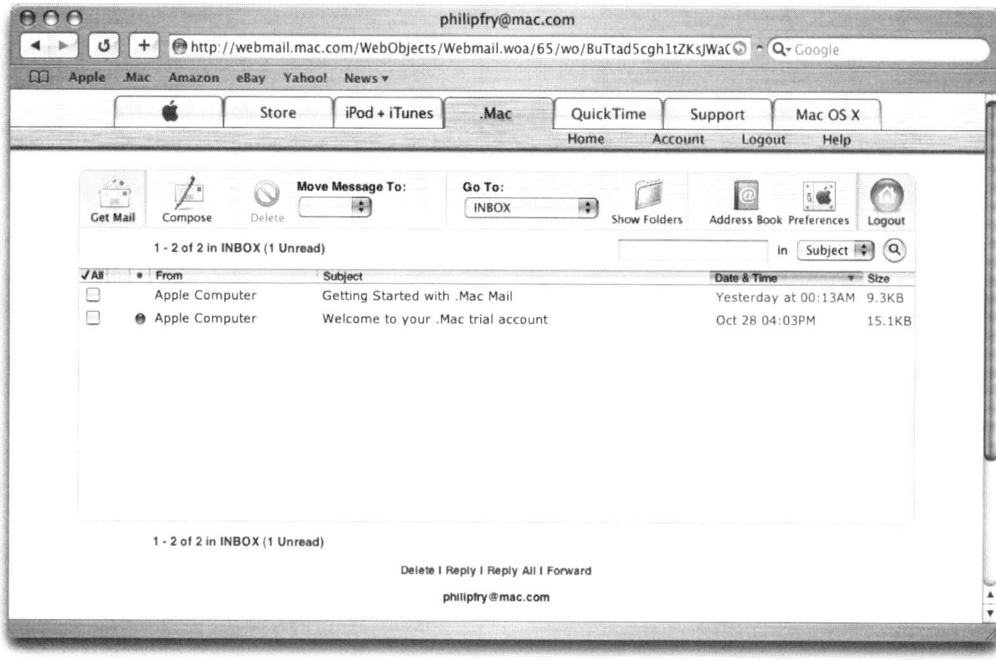

Notice that the message you just read no longer has a blue dot next to it, which indicates that you have already seen this email.

6. If you want, click the other email from Apple (**Welcome to your .Mac trial account**). When you're done reading it, return to your **Inbox** by clicking the **Mail** button in the toolbar.

When viewing any of your mailboxes in .Mac Mail, the toolbar looks slightly different than it does when viewing an actual message. The next few steps will show you how to perform various tasks from the mailbox toolbar.

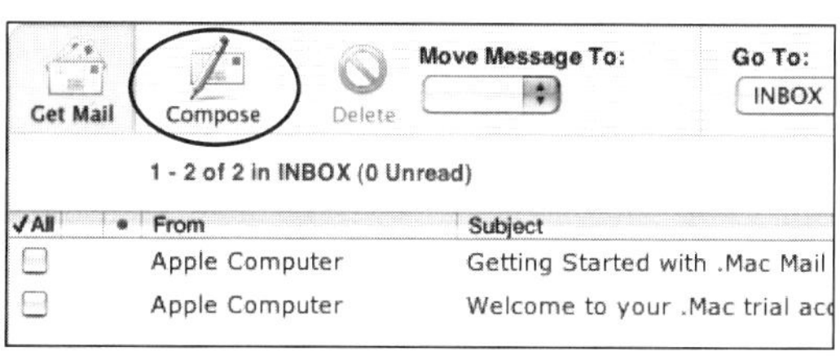

7. Click the **Compose** button. You'll write yourself a short message to practice sending email.

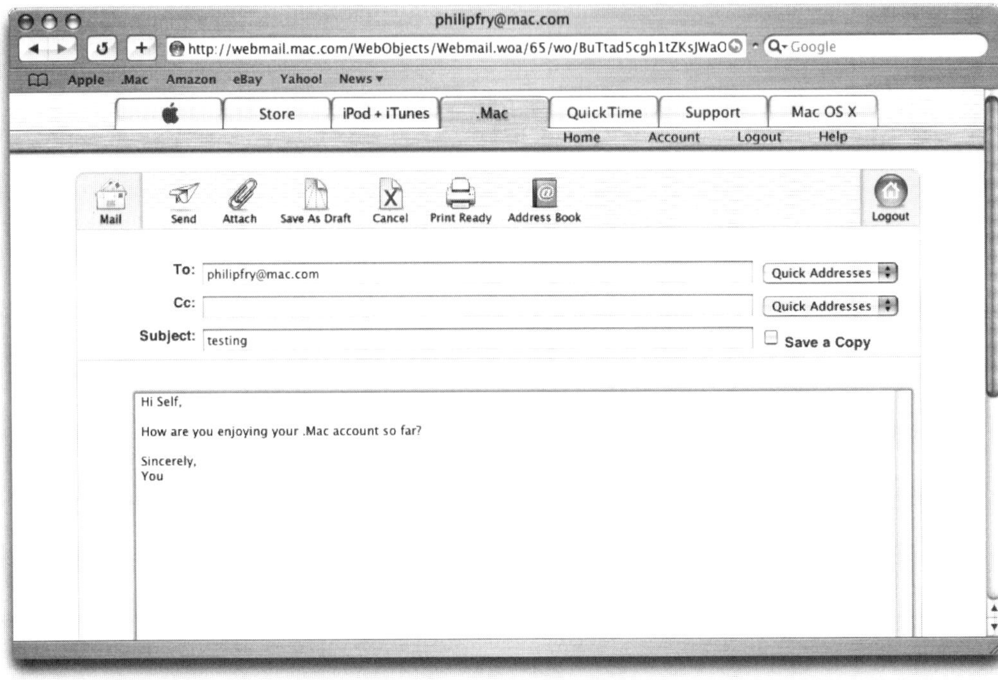

8. In the **Compose** window, enter your own .Mac email address in the **To** field (your_account_name@mac.com). Type **testing** in the **Subject** field, then type a short message. When you're done, click the **Send** button in the toolbar. You'll be returned to your **Inbox**, but the message you just wrote may not appear there yet.

Note: *You may have noticed that the other buttons in the toolbar are similar to the buttons found in OS X's Mail application. You can click* ***Attach*** *to attach a file to your email;* ***Save As Draft*** *will create a folder called* ***Drafts*** *and store your email there until you want to work on it again;* ***Cancel*** *will close the Compose window without saving anything you may have written;* ***Print Ready*** *displays your email in a window without toolbars; and* ***Address Book*** *gives you access to your online Address Book, where you can locate saved email addresses. You'll learn more about using the Address Book in the next exercise.*

9. If the message you wrote to yourself hasn't appeared in your **Inbox**, click the **Get Mail** button to force Mail to check your **Inbox** for new messages.

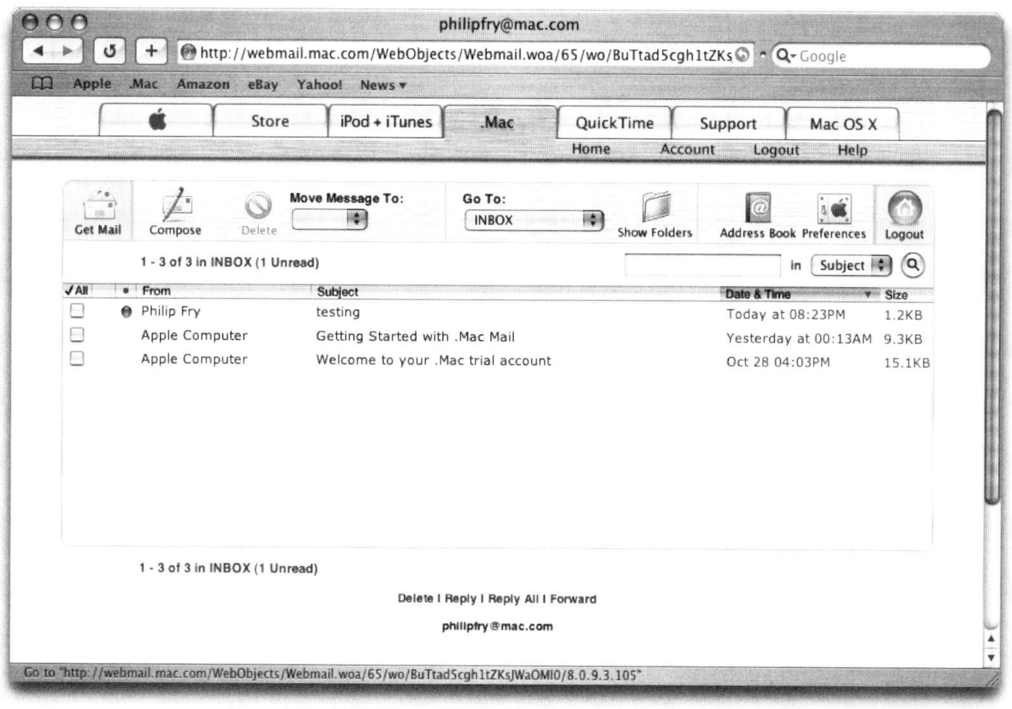

Your message to yourself should appear in your Inbox.

10. Click your new email to read it.

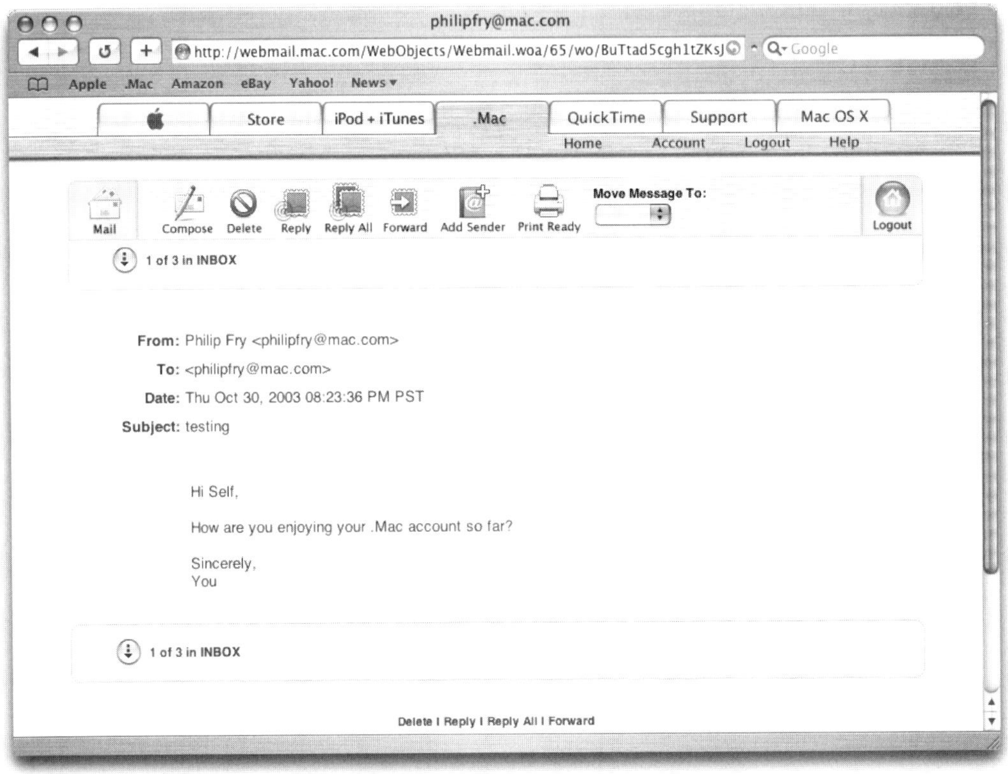

Now that you've seen this email, you'll send it to the Deleted Messages folder.

11. Click the **Delete** button in the toolbar.

Your message is moved from your Inbox to the Deleted Messages folder, and your browser automatically displays the next message from your Inbox.

12. Click **Mail** to return to your **Inbox**.

You can also manage and move email messages directly from any of your mailboxes, instead of opening each message individually.

13. Check the boxes next to the two emails from Apple Computer.

*Tip: You can click the **All** column header to check or uncheck all messages.*

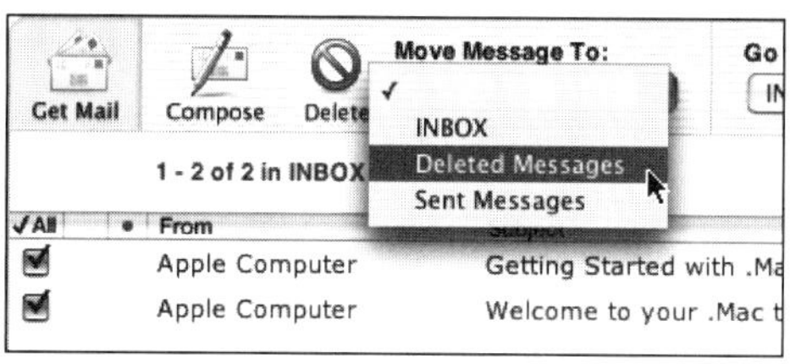

14. From the **Move Message To** pop-up menu in the toolbar, select **Deleted Messages**. This will move the selected emails into the **Deleted Messages** folder. Don't worry, if you want to save these emails, you'll still have a chance.

Your Inbox should now be empty. Next you'll take a look inside your Deleted Messages folder to determine which messages you really want to eliminate.

15. From the **Go To** pop-up menu in the toolbar, select **Deleted Messages**.

You're now seeing the contents of your Deleted Messages folder.

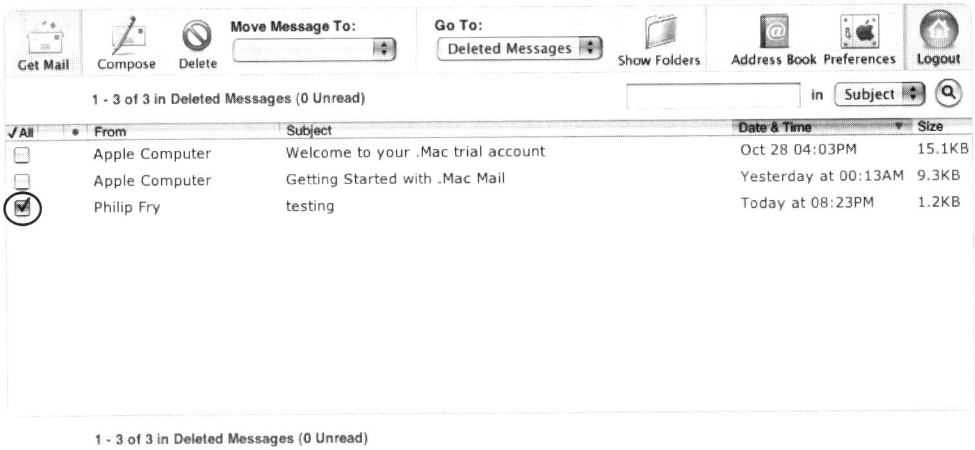

16. Check (as in "check the little box next to") the message you wrote to yourself.

Note: *Any message that you delete from the Deleted Messages folder will be permanently deleted, so be sure you really want to get rid of an email before deleting it.*

17. Click the **Delete** button in the toolbar. The email is erased.

18. If you want to delete the two messages from Apple, check them and click the **Delete** button. If you'd prefer to keep them, check them and choose **Inbox** from the **Move Messages To** pop-up menu to send them back to your **Inbox**.

19. Keep your browser window open for the next exercise.

Using .Mac Mail is pretty easy once you get the hang of it. In the next exercise, you'll take a look at your .Mac Address Book and learn how to store your contact information online.

Creating Additional Folders

In addition to the Inbox, Draft, Sent Messages, and Deleted Messages folders, you're free to create as many additional folders as you like. For instance, you may want to create folders called Work Messages or Personal Messages to sort and store the various email messages you receive.

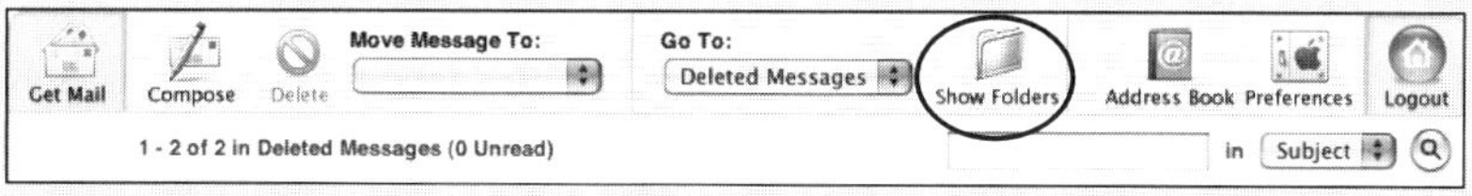

To create a new folder, click the **Show Folders** button from the toolbar of any of your existing folders.

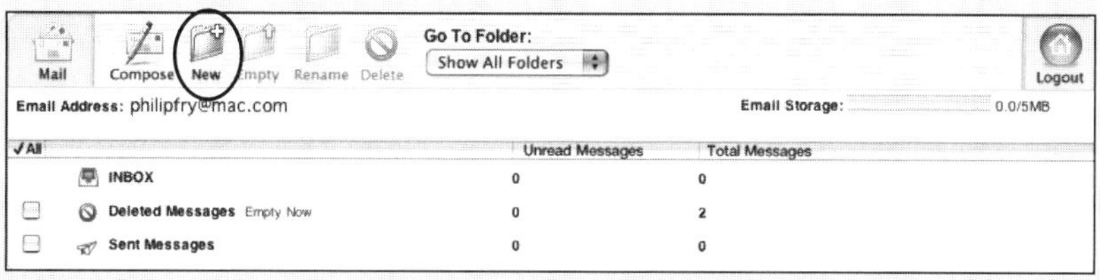

Click the **New** button in the toolbar of the next window.

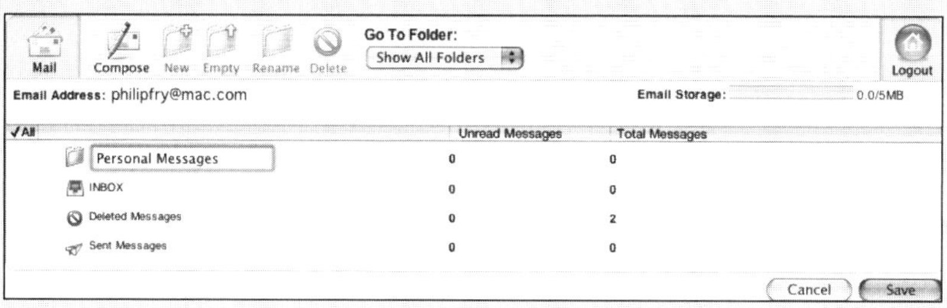

Name your new folder and press **Return** (or click **Save**). Your new folder is now accessible from both the **Move Messages To** pop-up menu and the **Go To** menu.

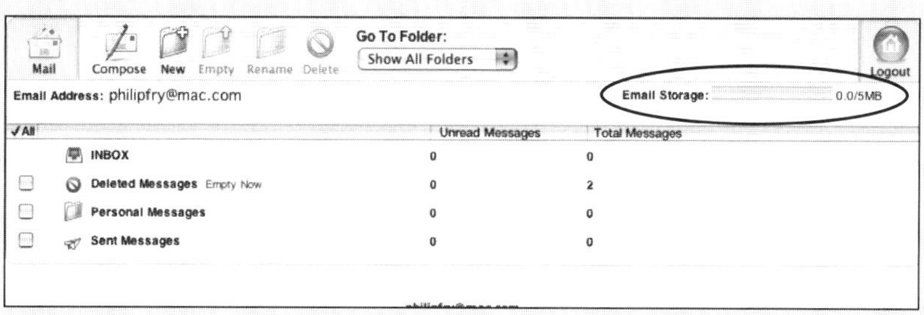

Tip: You can also use the **Show Folders** button to check how much of your allotted email storage space you're using. Your trial account has 5 MB, but full .Mac members get 15 MB.

Accessing .Mac Mail from Mail

Probably the greatest advantage of .Mac Mail is that it makes your email accessible from just about any computer that's connected to the Internet. If you travel frequently, it's especially nice not to have to worry about carrying your email messages and address book around with you. However, OS X's Mail application is more fully featured than .Mac Mail, so when you're at home, you may prefer to download your email to your own computer rather than storing your messages on the Web.

To download your .Mac Mail to your Mac, you need to create a new account in Mail.

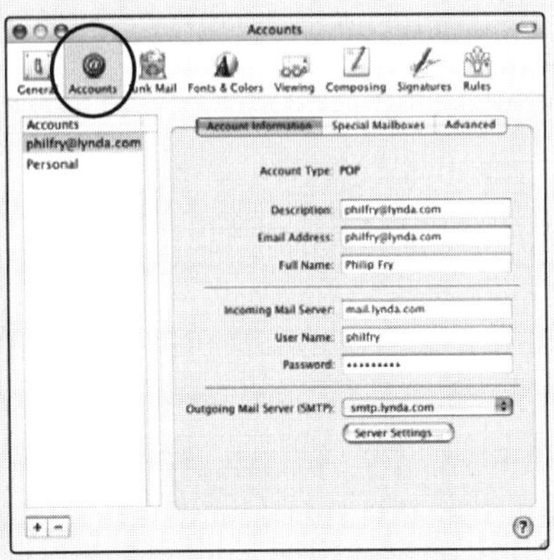

Start **Mail** and choose **Mail > Preferences**. Click **Accounts** on the toolbar and click the **+** button.

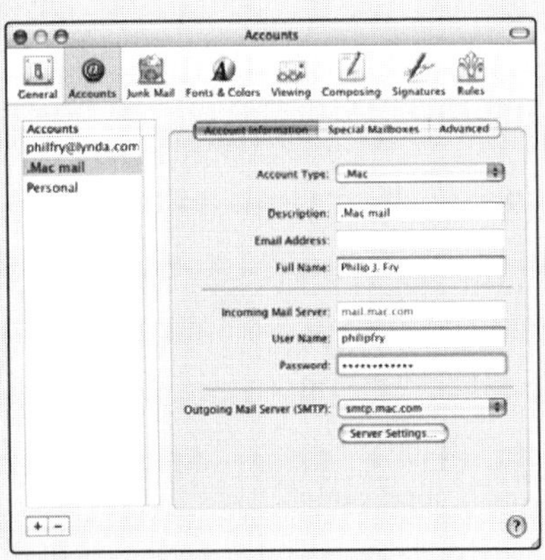

For **Account Type**, choose **.Mac**. The only other information you need to enter is your **Full Name** as you would like it to appear in your emails, and your **User Name** and **Password**. (You can add a **Description** such as **.Mac mail**, too, if you wish.) Close the window when you're done and save the account info when prompted.

That's all there is to it. You can now click **Get Mail** to retrieve your .Mac email.

3. Address Book

Much like the Address Book application on your Mac complements the Mail application, your .Mac Address Book complements your .Mac Mail. In this exercise, you'll learn how to add contacts to your .Mac Address Book and how to use them when composing email.

1. Click **Home** in the main toolbar of the .Mac browser window. If you closed your browser window, open a new one and sign in at **www.mac.com**.

2. In the main .Mac window, locate and click the **Address Book** button.

3. If prompted, enter your password. If you see a message offering to tell you about using iSync with your online Address Book, click **Ignore**. You'll be learning about this in Chapter 13, "*iCal and iSync.*"

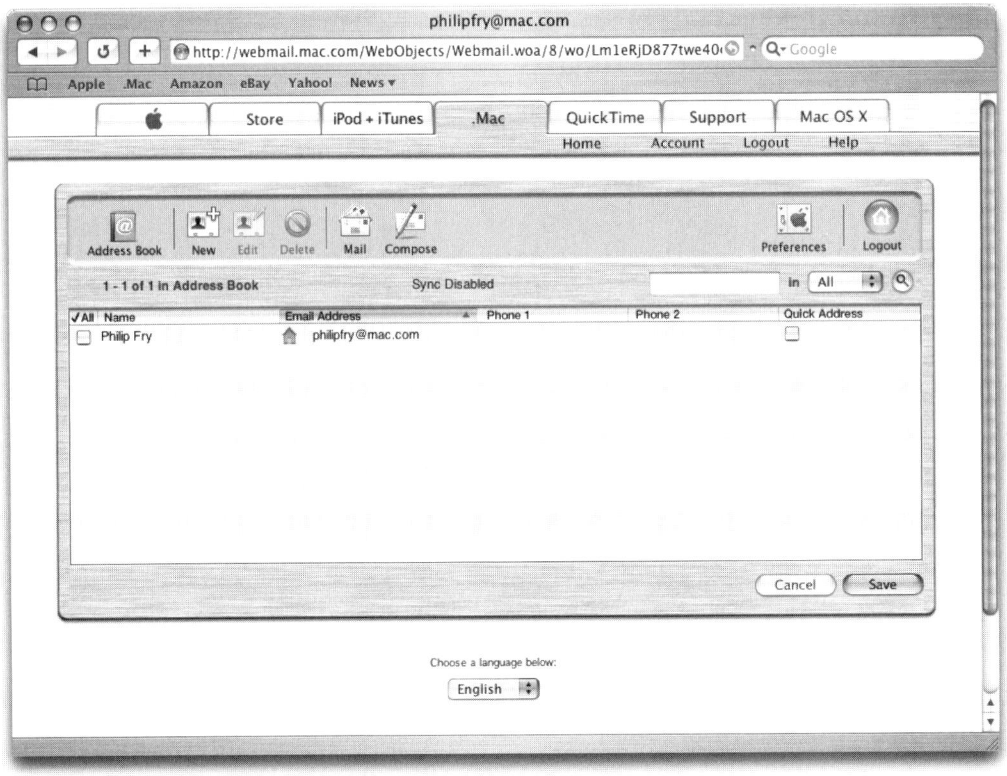

At this point, you most likely have only your own information listed in your Address Book.

4. Click the **New** button in the toolbar to add another address.

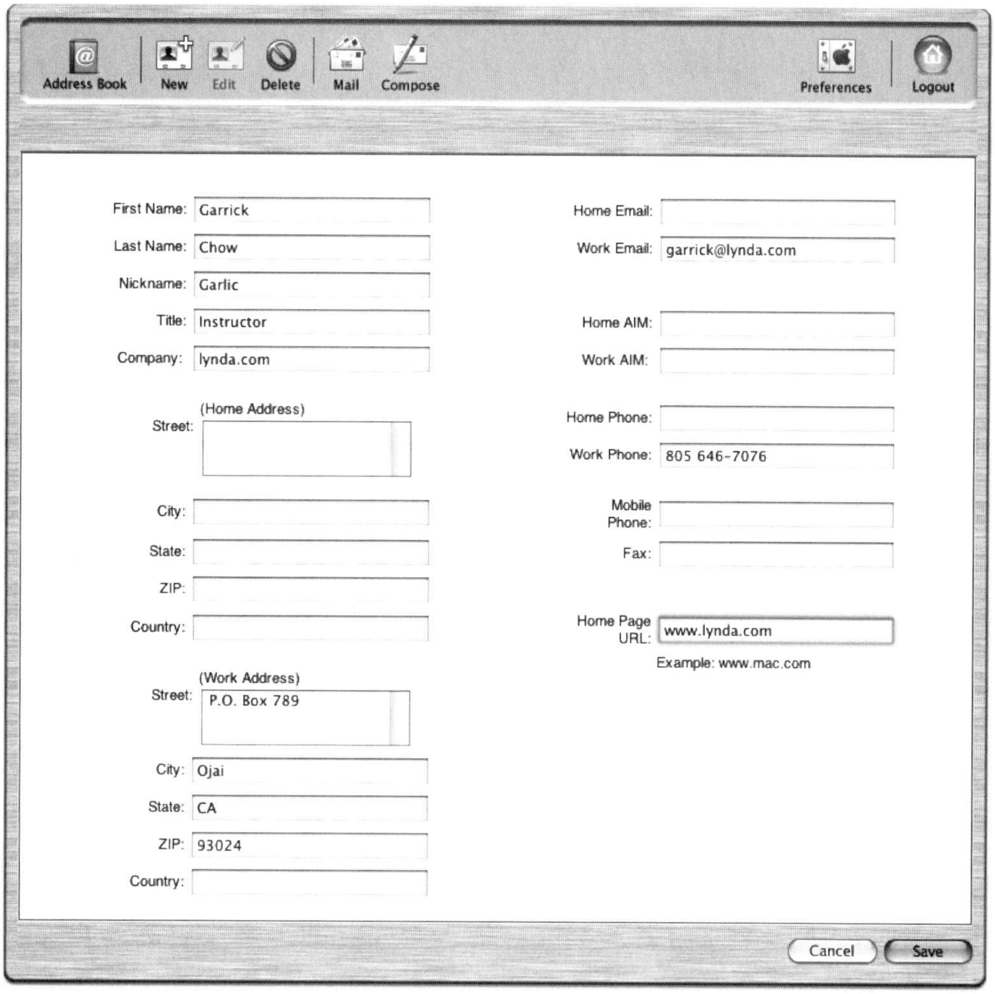

5. Enter the information for a friend or co-worker. Make sure that you include at least a name and email address. Click **Save** when you're done.

You'll be returned to the main Address Book window.

---

6. Enter two or three more contacts by clicking the **New** button in the toolbar each time.

Tip: *Wait–don't enter all your contacts now! You'll learn how to import contacts from your Mac's Address Book into your .Mac Address Book in Chapter 13,* "iCal and iSync."

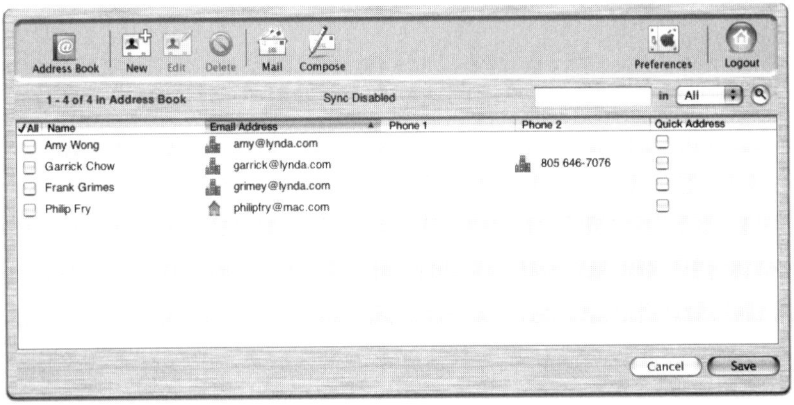

Now that you have some contacts stored in your .Mac Address Book, you'll be able to view their information from any computer connected to the Web by logging on to ***www.mac.com***.

7. Click on any name in your **Address Book** to display the detailed information.

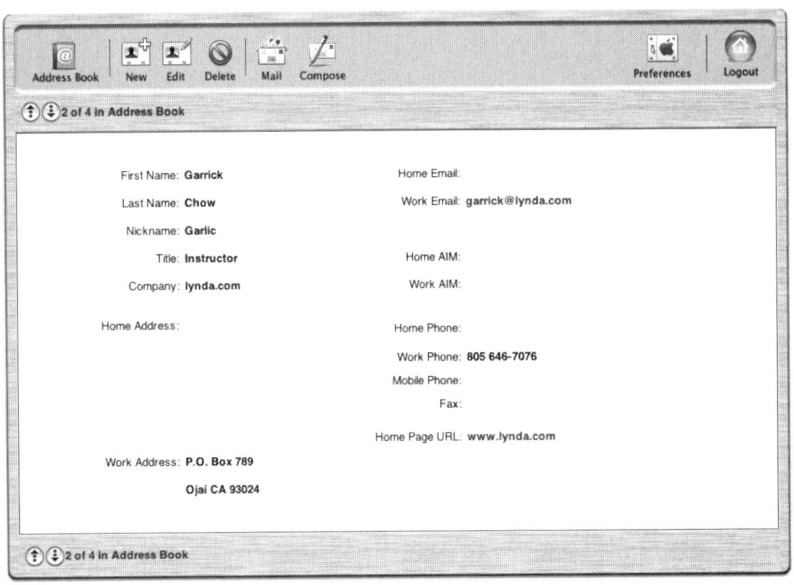

From this window, you can view your contact information. The icons in the toolbar allow you to edit the information and add additional contacts.

8. Click the **Address Book** icon in the toolbar to return to the main **Address Book** window.

*One of the main advantages of having your Address Book online is that you can send email to anyone without having to remember his or her email address. In fact, Address Book offers a feature called **Quick Address**, which allows you to designate the email addresses you use most often. You'll take a look at how this works next.*

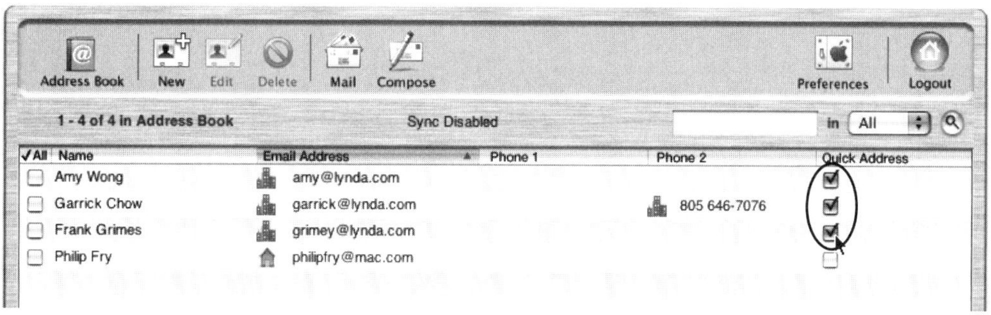

9. Under the **Quick Address** column of the main **Address Book** window, click the check boxes next to any one to whom you often send email. (For the purposes of this exercise, make sure you check at least two or three.) Click **Save**.

10. Click the **Compose** button in the toolbar (just like you did earlier to write an email to yourself).

Notice the Quick Addresses pop-up menus next to the To and Cc fields.

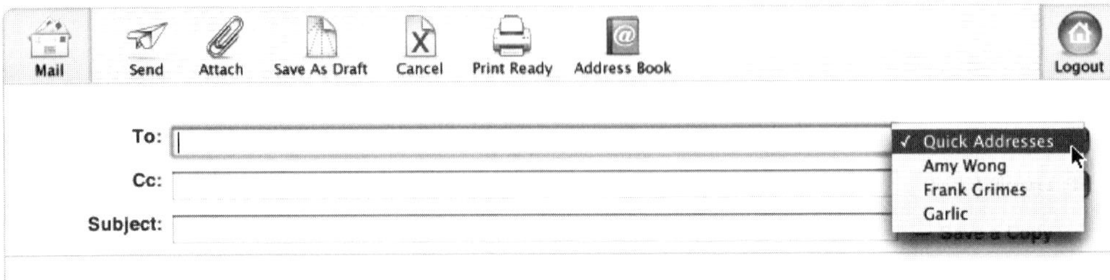

11. Click the **Quick Addresses** menu next to the **To** field and observe how all the names you checked in **Address Book** appear here.

When using this menu, you can select as many names as you like. Each one will get added to the adjacent field.

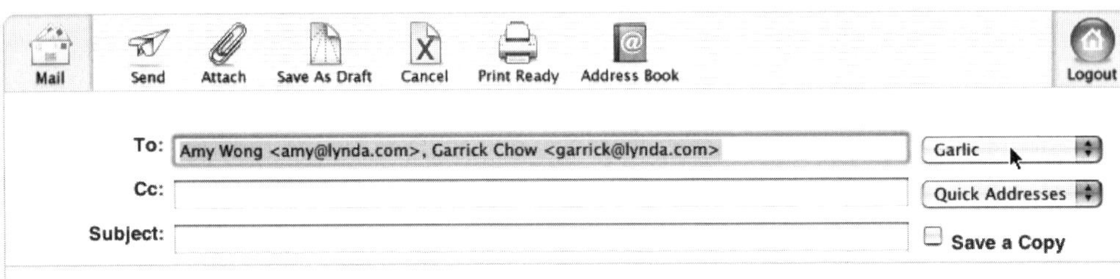

12. Select a name or two from the **Quick Addresses** menu.

You can also access and select names from your Address Book that you didn't designate as Quick Addresses.

13. Click the **Address Book** icon in the toolbar to access your entire list of contacts.

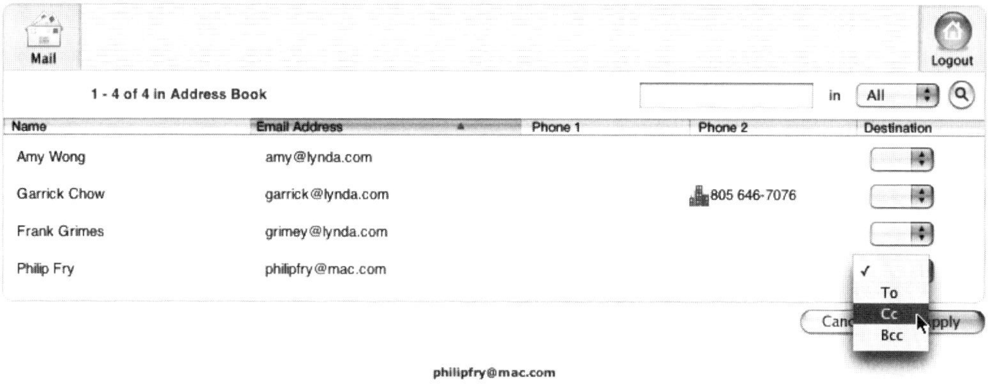

From here, you can click the Destination field for the contact's email address.

14. Select **Cc** from the menu by your own name and then click **Apply**.

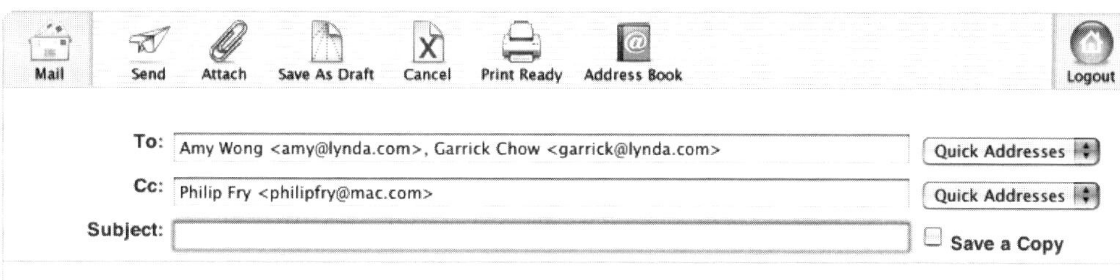

15. If you feel like dropping a line to the people you've selected, go ahead and do so. Otherwise, you're done with this exercise. Click **Home** in the navigation bar at the top of the page to return to the main .Mac page.

4. iDisk

For many users, one of the most persuasive reasons to subscribe to .Mac is **iDisk**. iDisk acts as a virtual hard drive, giving you 100 MB of server space to store files, music, videos, or anything else you want to upload. (Note that your trial subscription limits you to 20 MB.) Because your iDisk storage is Web-based, you can access your iDisk from any computer–Mac or PC–that's connected to the Internet, which can be a great convenience if you need to move large files from one computer to another, or if you want to back up important files offsite of your main computer. Your iDisk's Public folder can also play an important role when you need send files that are too large for email. This exercise will show you how to connect to your iDisk and transfer files between it and your Mac.

Tip: With a .Mac membership, you can purchase up to an additional 1 GB of storage space.

The first step to using your iDisk is to mount it on your Mac's Desktop. Unlike .Mac's Mail and Address Book, iDisk is not primarily accessed through your Web browser. Instead, your iDisk appears as an icon on your Desktop.

---

1. If your Web browser is still open, press **Cmd+H** on the keyboard to hide it; you won't need it just yet.

2. Click the **System Preferences** icon in your **Dock** and then click the **.Mac** icon under **Internet & Network**.

3. Your .Mac username and password should already be entered here, but if it's not, enter it now. Close the **System Preferences** window.

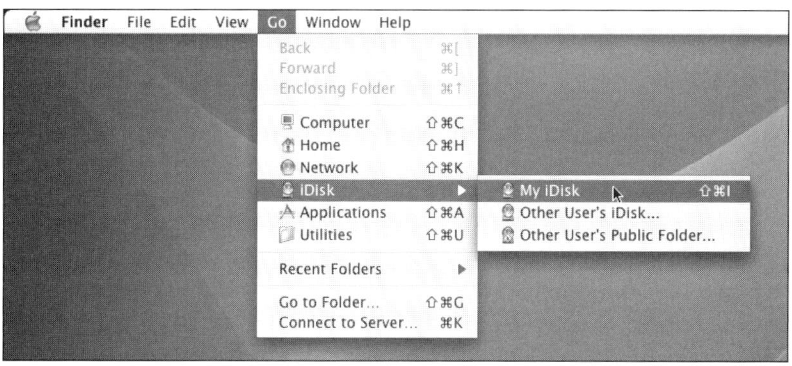

4. From the **Finder** menu bar, choose **Go > iDisk > My iDisk**.

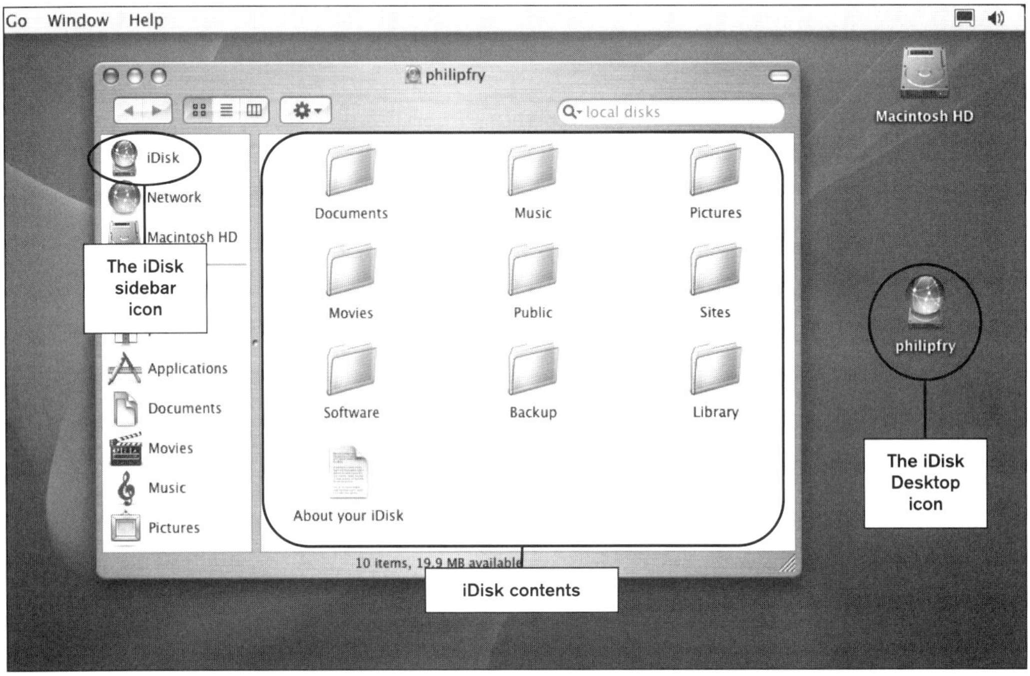

*After a moment, the iDisk icon appears on your Desktop, and a Finder window opens displaying its contents. The iDisk icon also appears in the Places sidebar. Notice how your iDisk is already organized into several folders for you. The folders named **Documents**, **Music**, **Pictures**, **Movies**, **Sites**, and **Public** mimic the contents of the Home folder on your Mac. Your iDisk also contains folders called **Backup** and **Software**. Clearly, Apple wants you to keep yourself organized.*

***Note:** If you don't see the iDisk icon on your Desktop, choose **Finder > Preferences**, click the **General** button, and make sure **Connected Servers** is checked. If you don't see the iDisk icon in the Places sidebar, choose **Finder > Preferences**, click the **Sidebar** button, and make sure **iDisk** is checked.*

Your iDisk behaves just like a hard drive, albeit a particularly slow one. You can view its contents by double-clicking its Desktop icon, you can navigate its contents by opening its folders in a Finder window, and you can copy files to it by simply dragging them into an iDisk folder. Once mounted, your iDisk remains on your Desktop until you unmount it by dragging it to the Trash or by shutting down your computer. Before you move any files to your iDisk, you'll first take a look inside one of its folders.

5. Double-click the **Software** folder.

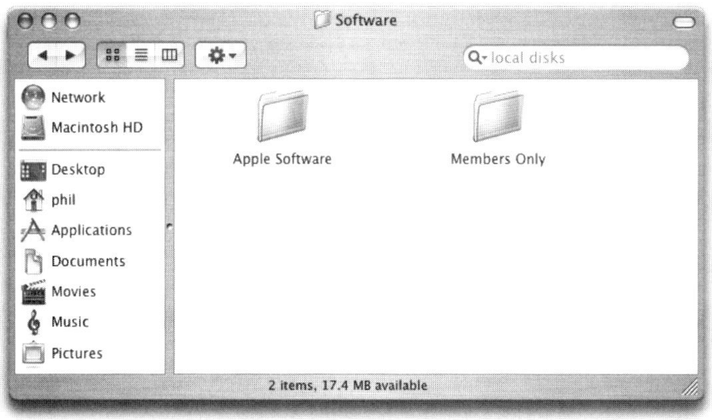

*The Software folder contains two folders: **Apple Software** and **Members Only**. The Apple Software folder contains the latest versions of all the free software that you can normally download from apple.com. The Members Only folder contains the various free third-party software packages that Apple periodically offers to .Mac members, and, as you might have guessed, is available only to full .Mac subscribers. Nothing in this folder counts against your iDisk space allotment. It's just a way to access software without having to download it from the .Mac or Apple Web site.*

6. Double-click the **Apple Software** folder.

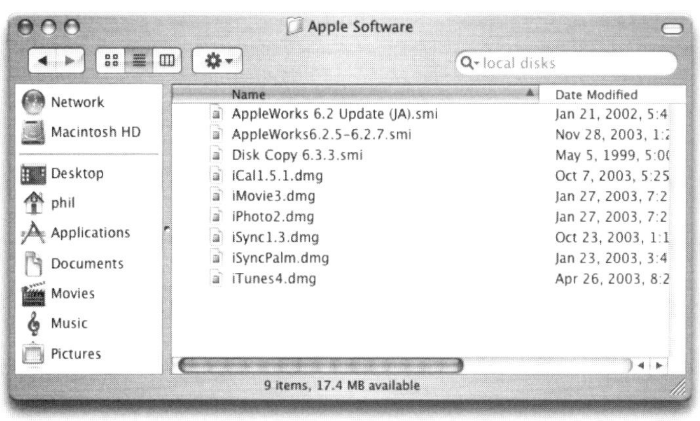

From here you can download the installers for Apple's free applications such as iCal and iSync, as well as three of the four iLife apps: iTunes, iPhoto, and iMovie. (All of which should already be installed in Panther, but it's good to know you can always get a fresh copy if something happens to yours.)

7. Click the **Back** button to return to the main **Software** folder and then click the **Members Only** folder **Applications**.

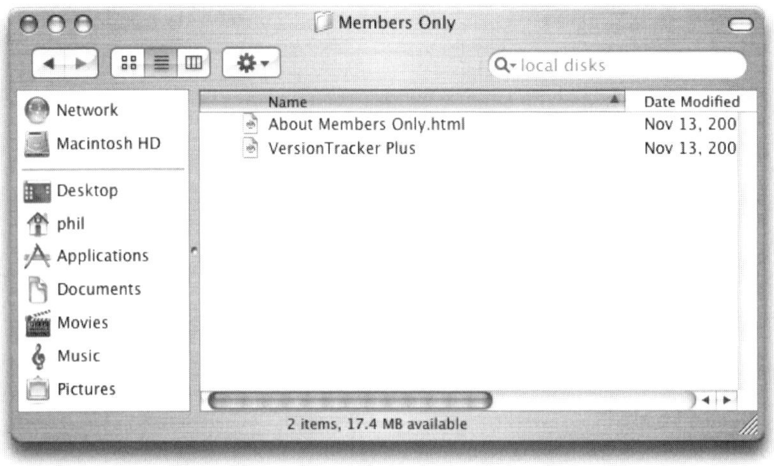

As a trial .Mac subscriber, opening this folder only displays an icon that takes you to a page in Safari, detailing the benefits of becoming a full subscriber. (You may see another Safari icon or two in here.)

If you held a full account, however, you'd see folders for all of the current .Mac and third-party software programs available to you.

8. Click the **Back** button in the toolbar twice to return to the main iDisk window (or just close this window and double-click the **iDisk** icon on your **Desktop**).

As mentioned before, the contents of the Software folder don't count against your allotted iDisk space, therefore you can't copy anything to this folder–you can only copy things from it (the same goes for the Backup folder, but we'll be getting to that later). But the rest of the iDisk is all yours. To copy a file to your iDisk, just drag it into any of the folders other than Software or Backup and use the folder names to keep yourself organized (music into the Music folder, images into the Pictures folder, and so on). The only other rule is that you have to store your files inside a folder–they can't be placed in the main iDisk directory, nor can you create new folders in the main iDisk directory.

In addition to storing your personal files, you can also use your iDisk to share files with others. By placing files into your Public folder, you can make them available to any user who knows your .Mac account name. You'll upload some files into your Public folder next.

---

9. Drag the **chap_12** folder from the **H•O•T CD-ROM** onto your **Desktop**. Double-click the **chap_12** folder and open the folder named **iDisk**. Inside you'll find three image files. You'll copy these files to your iDisk's **Public** folder.

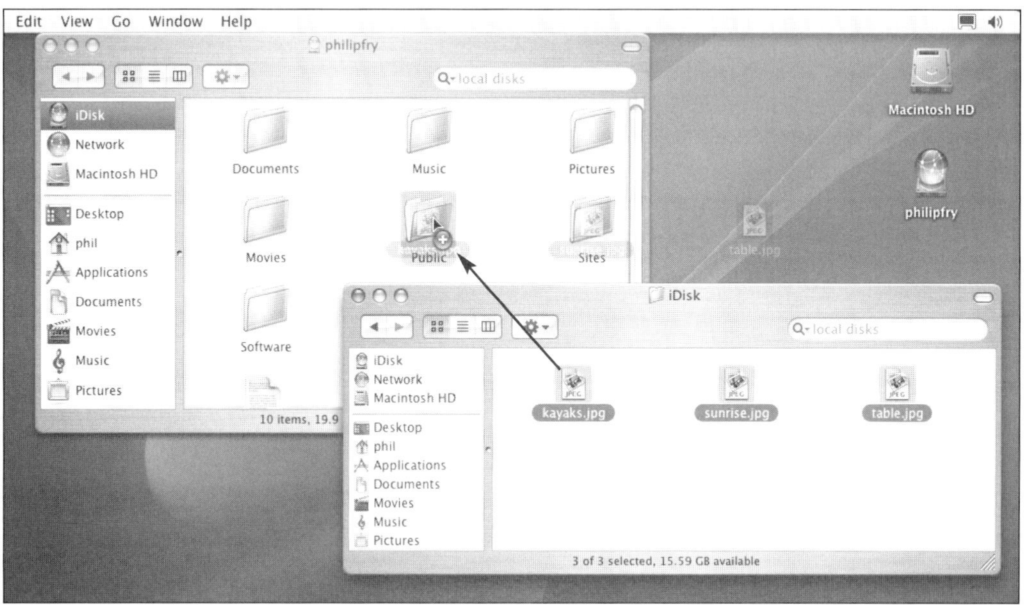

10. Select all three images by drawing a selection marquee around them with the mouse. Then drag them into the **Public** folder on your iDisk.

It'll take a few seconds for each file to be copied.

Congratulations, you've just copied your first files to your iDisk. You'll be viewing these files from your Web browser in the next exercise.

Creating a Local Copy of your iDisk

The iDisk icon on your Desktop represents your personal storage space on Apple's Internet servers. Copying a file to your iDisk can be a time-consuming process, largely depending on your connection speed and the size of the file, because you're actually uploading files via the Internet to your iDisk space. New to Panther, you can now create a copy of your iDisk on your computer. This means that you can now quickly copy files to your iDisk even when you're not connected to the Internet. Once you connect to the Internet, any changes made to the iDisk on your computer are automatically synched with the iDisk on your .Mac account.

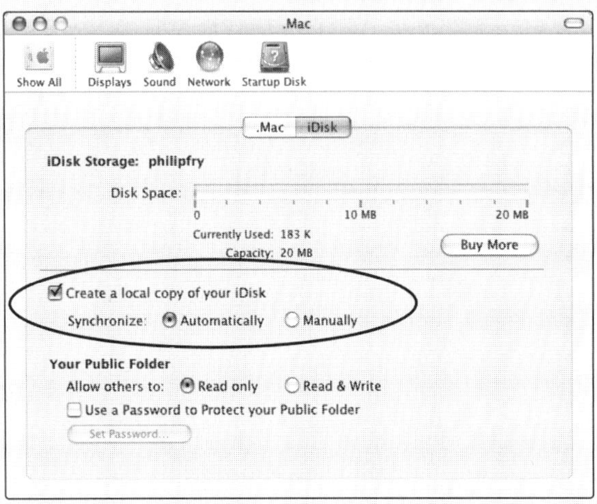

To create a copy of your iDisk on your Mac, open **System Preferences** and click **.Mac**. Then click **iDisk** and check **Create a local copy of your iDisk**. Then choose whether you want to synchronize your iDisks **Automatically** or **Manually**. Close **System Preferences** to begin the copying process.

continues on next page

Creating a Local Copy of your iDisk *continued*

You can see when your iDisk was last synchronized by selecting it in the **Places** sidebar of any **Finder** window. If it's currently synching, you'll see a progress bar at the bottom of the window. If it's done synching, you'll see the time and the date of the last sync. If you chose automatic synchronization, your iDisk will sync itself periodically whenever your Mac is on and connected to the Internet. If you chose manual synchronization, you can click the **sync** icon to the right of the **iDisk** icon in the Places sidebar any time you want to make sure that the most current version of your iDisk is online.

11. Close the **iDisk** window (the one from the **H•O•T CD-ROM**, not your actual iDisk). Double-click the **Public** folder to confirm that the files made it there. You can now access these files from any computer connected to the Internet. And because they're in your Public folder, so can anyone else who knows your .Mac account name. (See "Connecting to a Public Folder from Various Operating Systems" at the end of this exercise.)

Password-Protecting Your Public Folder

Although the majority of your iDisk is available only to you, your Public folder is accessible to anyone who knows your .Mac member name. Your Public folder is a great tool for sharing files with friends, family, and co-workers. You can place files in there to share with other users, and other users can drop files in there to share with you. But if the information you're sharing is sensitive in nature, you'll probably want to password-protect your Public folder just in case someone else stumbles across it or figures out your member name.

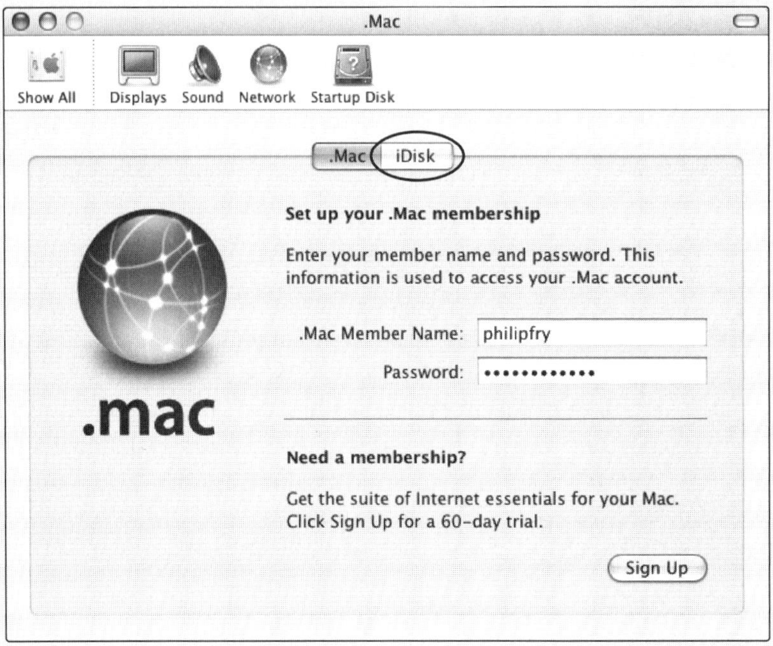

To password-protect your Public folder, click the **System Preferences** icon in the **Dock** and then click the **.Mac** icon. Click the **iDisk** button.

continues on next page

Password-Protecting Your Public Folder *continued*

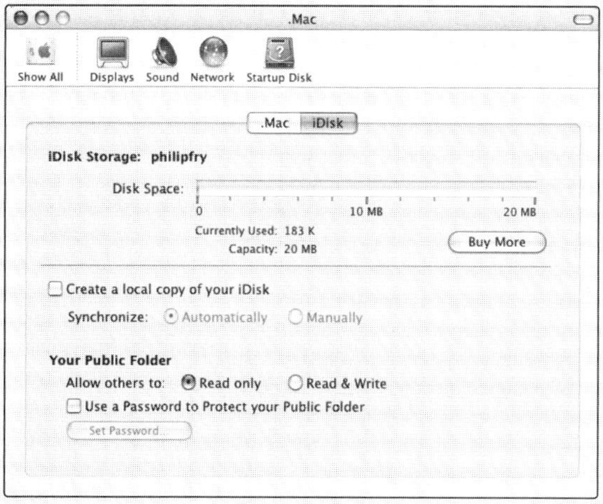

The top section of the iDisk tab shows you how much of your iDisk space you're currently using–this is a convenient way of visually checking how much space you have left. Under the **Your Public Folder** section, selecting **Read only** allows other users to download files from your Public folder, but prevents them from placing any files there. **Read & Write**, on the other hand, allows users to both download and upload files to your Public folder.

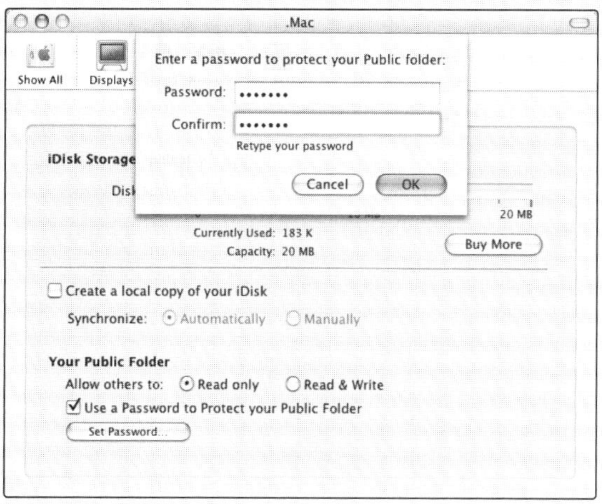

In either case, you can prevent access by unwanted visitors by checking **Use a Password to Protect your Public Folder**. Check this box and then click **Set Password** to enter a password. Quit **System Preferences** when you're done. From that point, only users who know the password will be able to access your Public folder.

Connecting to a Public Folder from Various Operating Systems

The steps other users must follow to connect to your Public folder vary depending on which operating system they're using. The following chart details the process of connecting to a Public folder from various operating systems, without using any special software. Even if you're the only one who's going to use your iDisk, be sure to read through this chart in case you ever need to access your iDisk from a different operating system.

Connecting to a Public Folder

Operating System	Method
Mac OS 10.3	From the **Finder** menu bar, choose **Go > iDisk > Other User's Public Folder.** Enter the user's account name in the dialog box that opens.
Mac OS 10.2	Choose **Go > Connect to Server** from the **Finder** menu bar. In the Address field of the dialog box that opens, type **http://idisk.mac.com/member_name/Public** and click **Connect** (make sure you use a capital "P" in "Public"). A Public icon will appear on the user's Desktop. The user can then freely copy files to and from your Public folder.
Mac OS 9	Choose **Apple menu > Chooser.** Click **AppleShare** and then click the **Server IP Address** button. Enter **idisk.mac.com** and click **Connect**. Enter the .Mac member's account name and use **Public** as the password (unless the .Mac member has password-protected his or her Public folder, in which case, enter the real password). The Public folder will appear as an icon on the OS 9 Desktop.
Windows XP	Open **My Network Places** and choose **Add a network place.** In the **Add Network Place Wizard**, enter **http://idisk.mac.com/member_name-Public?**. (Yes, that's a question mark at the end of that line.) Click **Next** until you finish with the wizard. The iDisk folder will appear in your Network Places.
Windows 2000	Open **My Computer** and choose **Tools > Map Network Drive** from the menu bar. Click **Web folder or FTP site.** Enter **http://idisk.mac.com/member_name-Public?** and press **Enter**.
Windows 98	Open **My Computer** and double-click the **Web Folders** icon. Double-click **Add Web Folder.** Enter **http://idisk.mac.com/member_name-Public?** and press **Enter**.

The steps shown in the chart are for connecting to a .Mac user's Public folder with the intention of both downloading and uploading files. As you can see, each operating system has its own method, and (except perhaps for the Mac OS 10.3 method) none of them are particularly simple, especially if you're trying to explain to your octogenarian grandmother how to download some pictures from your iDisk.

If other users often need to access your iDisk to upload and download files, you might suggest to them that they install the free iDisk Utility, a small program that makes connecting to an iDisk much easier than going through the rigmarole in the chart. iDisk Utility can be downloaded from **www.mac.com/1/idiskutility_download.html** and is available for Mac OS 10.1.2 and above, as well as Windows XP.

But there's even much easier way to set up your iDisk for people who only want to download items and have no interest in uploading files via a Public folder icon. The next exercise shows you how to create a simple Web page that users can visit through their Web browsers to download your files.

5. HomePage

Another benefit of having a .Mac account is the free Web-hosting space. If you know how to build a Web site, you can upload it to the Sites folder of your iDisk and share it with the rest of the world. Even if you don't know how to build a Web site, you can use the .Mac **HomePage** themes to have one automatically built for you. In this exercise, you'll kill two birds with one stone by using one of HomePage's themes to create a page that gives users access to your iDisk's Public folder.

1. Open your Web browser and go to **www.mac.com**. Click the **HomePage** icon in the toolbar.

2. Enter your password if you're prompted to do so.

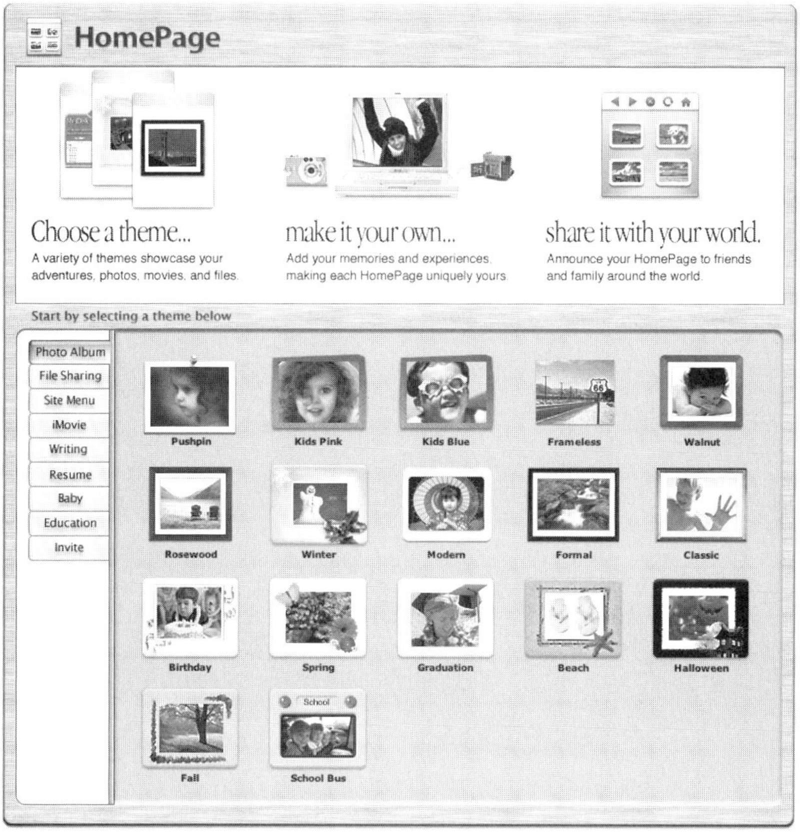

If you've never built a .Mac Web site before, the main HomePage window shows you the three basic steps for creating one: You select a theme, add your content, and upload it. That's what you'll be doing in this exercise.

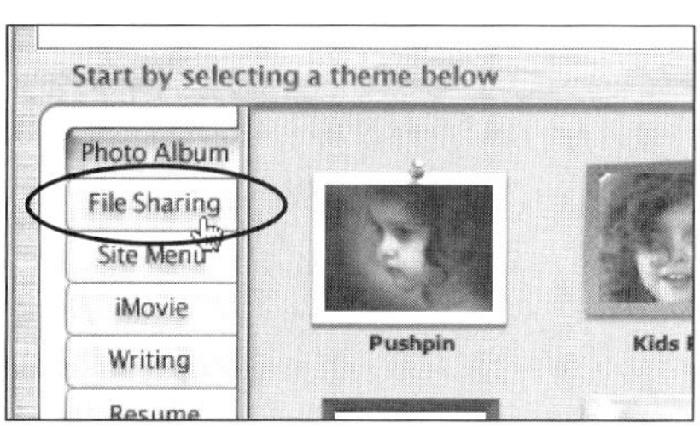

3. Click the **File Sharing** theme. Building a File Sharing page allows you to provide other people access to your iDisk's Public folder without them having to mess with all the steps outlined in the "Connecting to a Public Folder from Various Operating Systems" sidebar.

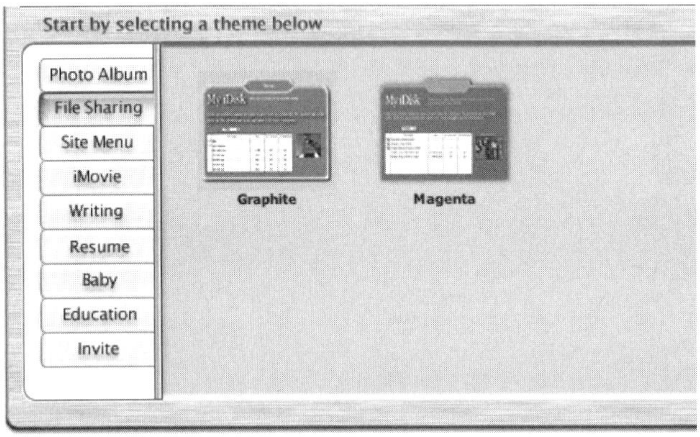

4. Click a theme: **Graphite** or **Magenta**.

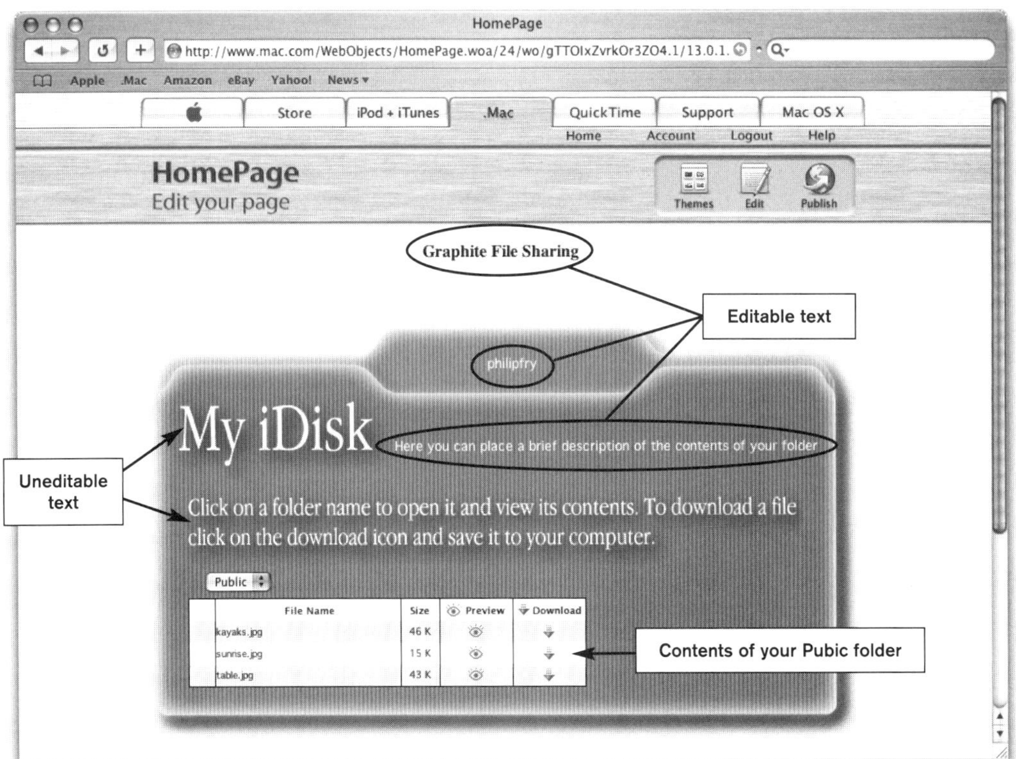

This next page shows you what your Web page will look like. You're free to edit the title of the page, the text that appears in the tab of the "folder," and the description below it.

5. Click the **Edit** button in the upper-right corner.

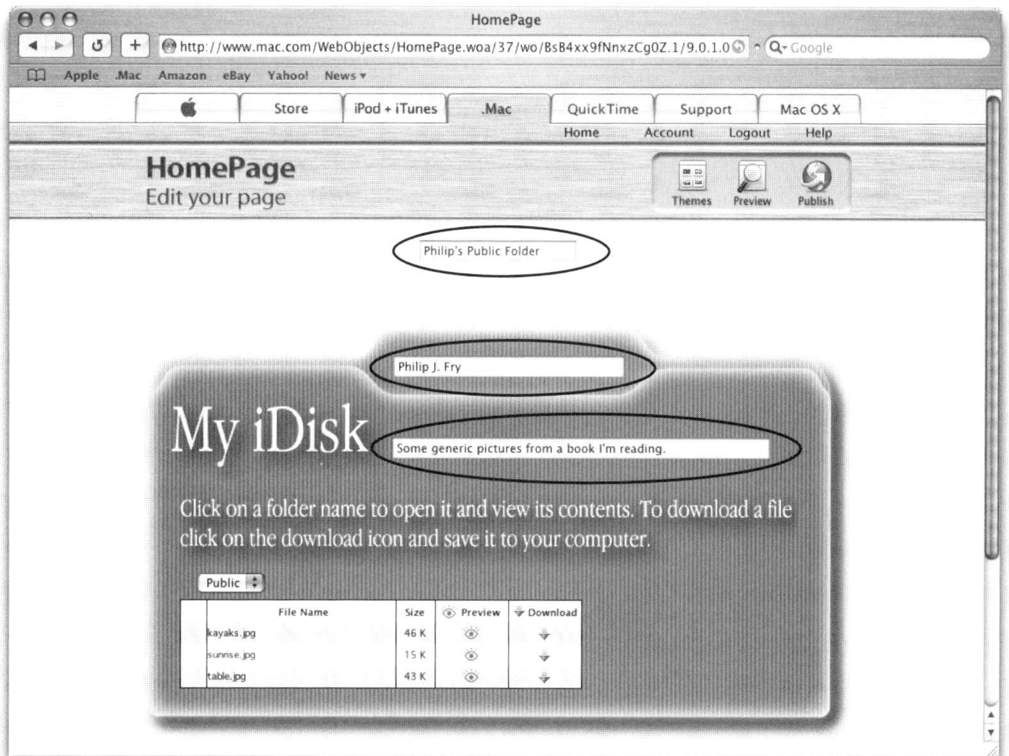

6. Change the title of the page to **[Your Name's] Public Folder**. Change your account name to your full name or nickname. Type a brief description of your Public folder. Type anything you want–you can always come back and change it when you're done with this exercise. When you're done, click the **Preview** button in the upper-right corner to see how this page will look.

7. If you made any typos, you can click the **Edit** button to make your changes. Otherwise, click **Publish**.

*You'll see a page confirming that you've successfully published your site. Note that your page is now located on the Web at **http://homepage.mac.com/your_member_name/FileSharing1.html**. You can give this address to other users to invite them to download files from your Public folder.*

8. Click your Web page address to view your page.

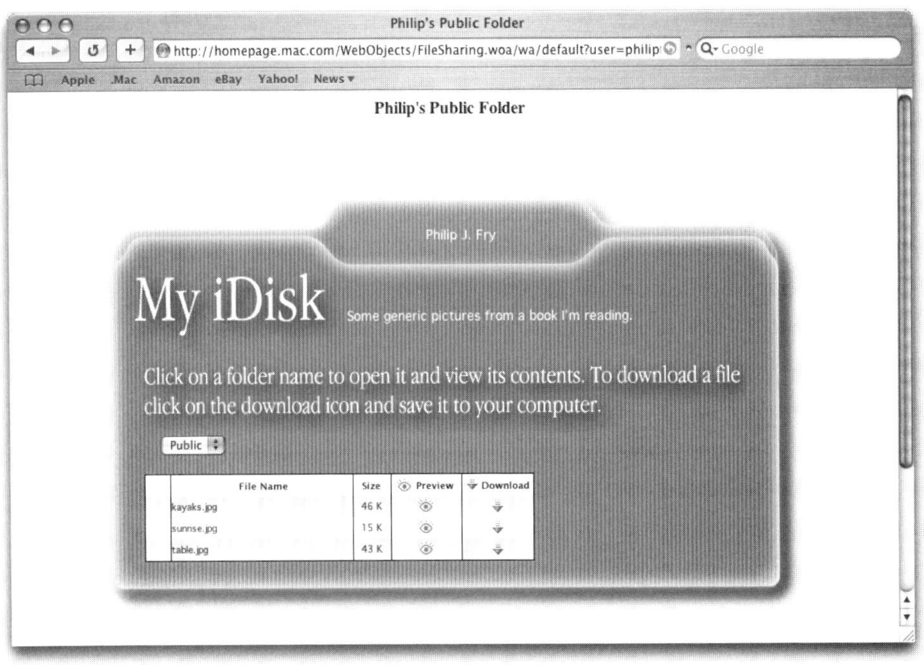

*It doesn't get much easier than this. Visitors to your page see the custom text that you entered. In the File area below it, they can click the **Preview** icon next to a file to see a thumbnail of the image there. If they want to download one of the files, they can click its **Download** icon.*

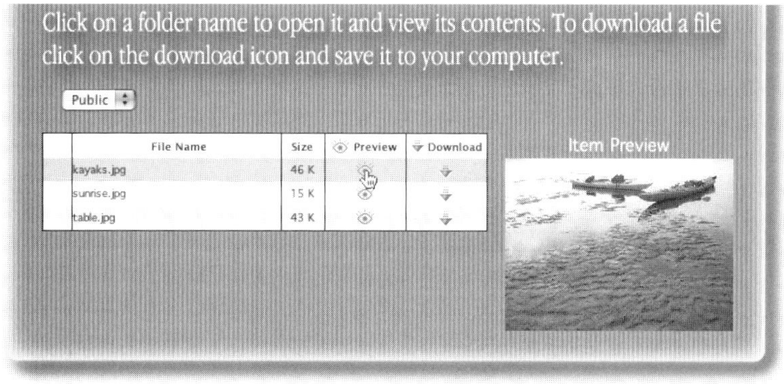

9. Click the **Preview** icon for all three of the JPG files. If you want, click on one of the **Download** icons to download the image to your hard drive. You now have a way to share files with friends and family without having to teach them to connect to a server or network place.

Tip: *If your file sharing page is the only page you have on your .Mac account, you and others can view the page by typing* ***homepage.mac.com/your_member_name*** *in the browser instead of* ***http://homepage.mac.com/your_member_name/FileSharing1.html.*** *Because you have only one page published, your .Mac account automatically defaults to this page.*

---

10. In your browser, return to **www.mac.com** and click the **HomePage** icon at the top of the page again.

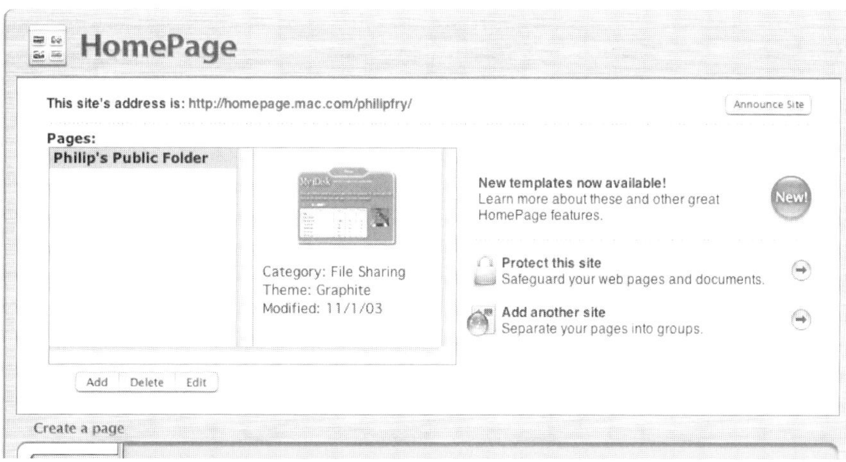

Now that you've published your first page, the HomePage main window displays the page's name. From here you can select your page and click the ***Edit*** *button to change its appearance or the* ***Delete*** *button to delete the page entirely. Click the* ***Add*** *button to build another page; you'll be walked through the steps to create a page based on one of the many available themes.*

11. If you want to delete the page you just created, select it and click the **Delete** button. But if you think that you might want to use this page to share files with friends, keep the page and just delete the files from your **Public** folder by opening your **iDisk** on your **Desktop**, opening your **Public** folder, and dragging the three images to the **Trash**.

12. When you're done viewing this page or deleting files, whichever the case may be, return to **www.mac.com** in your browser and keep it open for the next exercise.

Publishing Your Own Web Pages

If you don't know how to design Web pages from scratch, you can get along just fine with .Mac's themes (and ignore the rest of this sidebar). If you're not the theme-using type, however, you can always design your own Web pages in the program of your choice such as Dreamweaver, GoLive, FrontPage, or good old HTML. Once your page is ready, simply drag it into the **Sites** folder on your iDisk.

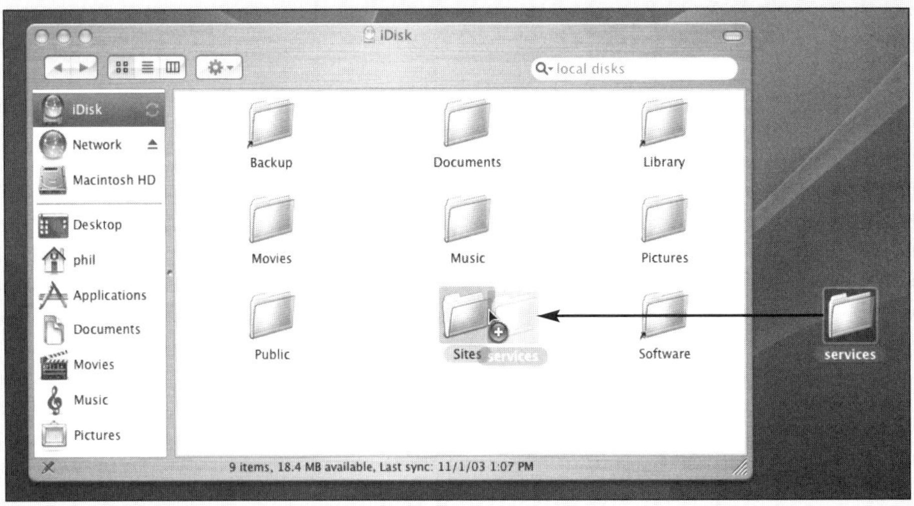

For example, if your Web site is stored in a folder called **services** on your hard drive, just drag the entire folder into **Sites**. The Web address of your Web site will now be **http://homepage.mac.com/your_member_name/services**. (Like most Web servers, .Mac automatically displays the **index.html** or **index.htm** file inside the **services** folder.) Bear in mind that anything placed in your Sites folder counts as usage of your 100 MB of allotted iDisk space (20 MB if you're using the trial version).

6. Backup

Backup is an application that comes with your .Mac subscription and is used for (ready for this?) backing up files on your Mac. Most of us have at one time or another lost important documents due to hardware-related problems or human error (and if you never have, don't worry, you will). With Backup, you can copy vital files to CD, DVD (if you have a full .Mac membership), your iDisk, or an external hard drive, so that you'll always have an extra copy of your important files in case anything unfortunate should happen to your computer. This exercise will walk you through backing up some files to your iDisk.

Although Backup is considered a component of .Mac, it's actually a stand-alone application that can be used without being online (if you're backing up to CD or DVD) or can be integrated with .Mac (if you're backing up to your iDisk). In either case, you first need to download Backup to your Mac.

1. If your browser isn't already displaying the .Mac main page, go to **www.mac.com**. Click the **Backup** umbrella icon in the toolbar.

2. If you're prompted, enter your password.

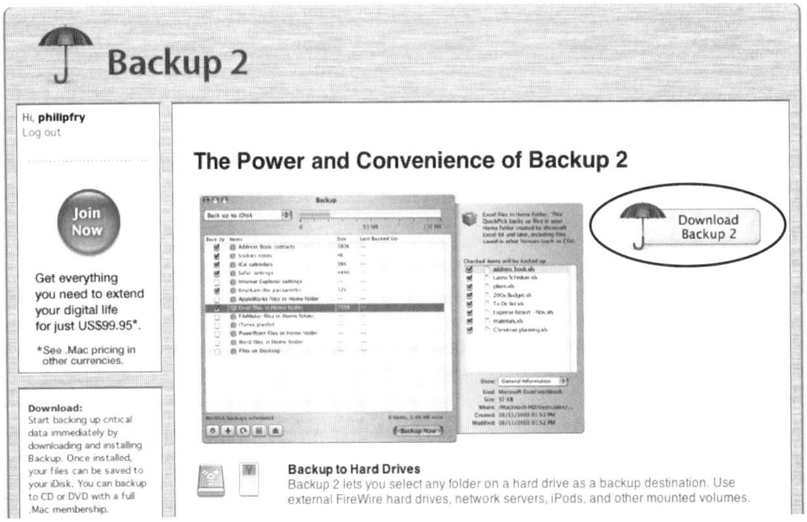

3. Click **Download Backup 2**.

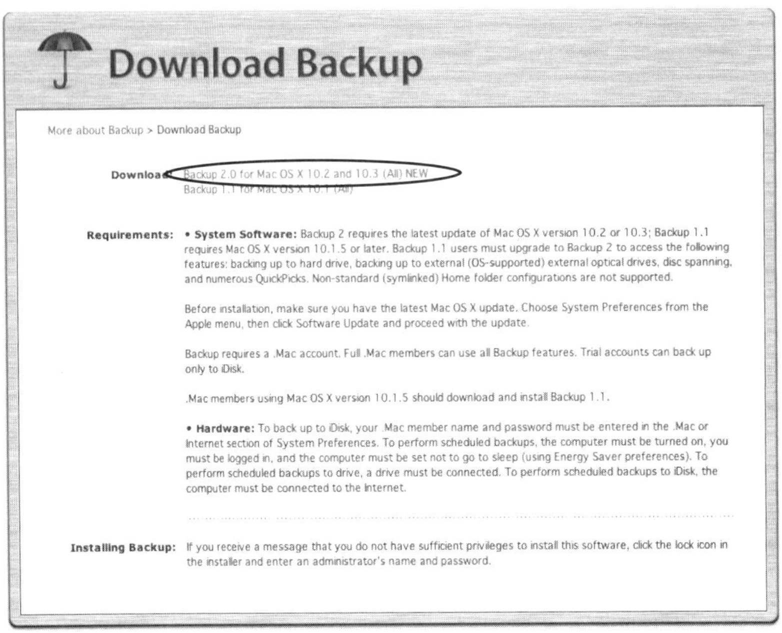

4. In this next window, click the **Download** link for **Backup 2**. Backup is a relatively small 2.2 MB, so the download shouldn't take too long.

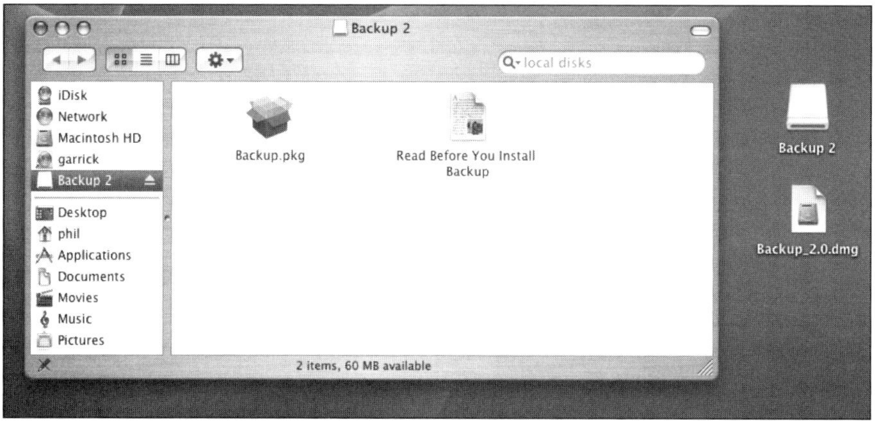

5. When the download is complete, press **Cmd+H** to hide the Web browser. Locate the **Backup 2** disk image on your **Desktop**. OS X should have already opened the contents of this disk image. (Your Desktop should be the default download location for your Web browser. If you don't find Backup, check your browser's preferences to see where your downloaded file went.)

Tip: *Instead of downloading Backup from the .Mac Web page, you also could have copied it from your iDisk's* ***Software*** *folder in* ***Apple Software.***

---

6. Double-click **Backup.pkg** to begin the installation.

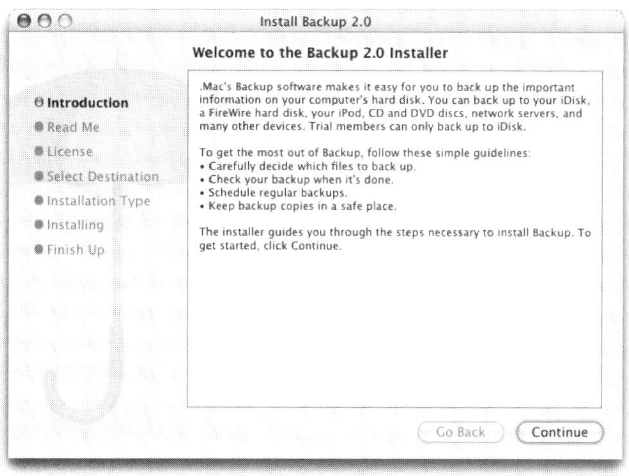

7. Follow the steps in the installer program by clicking the **Continue** button, agreeing to the software agreement, and selecting your hard drive as the installation drive. The installation will take a few minutes to complete.

---

8. When the installation is finished, click the **Close** button to close the installer.

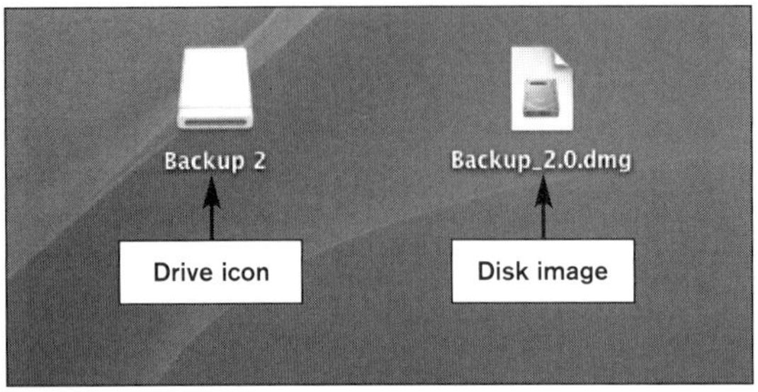

9. Drag the **Backup** drive icon to the **Trash** to unmount it. You can keep the Backup disk image where it is or move it to one of your folders if you want to save it in case you need to reinstall Backup at some point. Otherwise, you can drag it to the Trash.

You're ready to run Backup.

10. Click **Applications** in the open **Finder** window's sidebar (or press **Shift+Cmd+A**). Locate and double-click **Backup**.

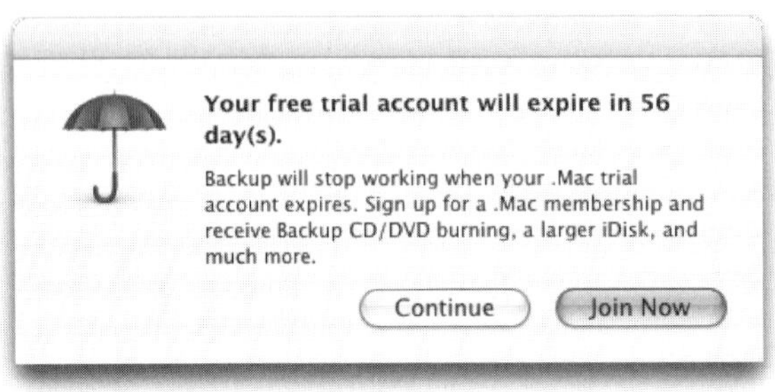

11. Click **Continue** when you see the free trial expiration message (if you're using a trial account).

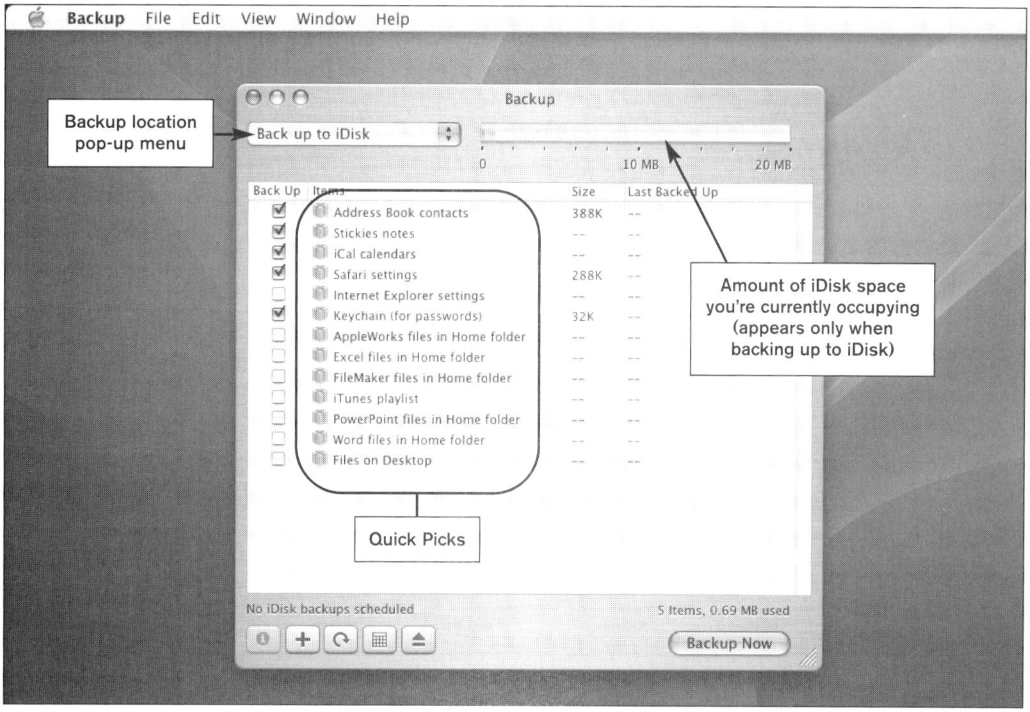

Backup's interface is, like most Apple software products these days, pretty simple. All you need to do is decide which files you want to back up, and they'll be displayed in the main part of the application window. The items that are already listed there are called Quick Picks–files that are usually pretty personalized, such as your Address Book contacts, Safari settings (including bookmarks and preferences), and iTunes playlists. By checking any of these items, you can quickly pick to back them up.

You've probably already spent some time adding your contacts to your Address Book and setting bookmarks in Safari–it would be a pain to go back and enter all that information again if it somehow got lost.

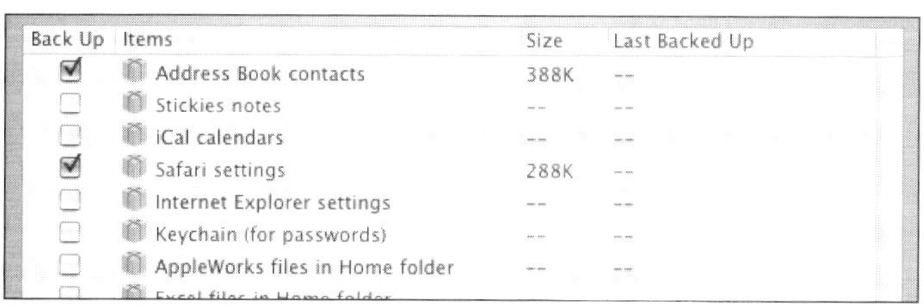

12. Check **Address Book contacts** and **Safari settings**. Uncheck the other Quick Picks for now.

Next you'll back up some additional, non–Quick Pick files.

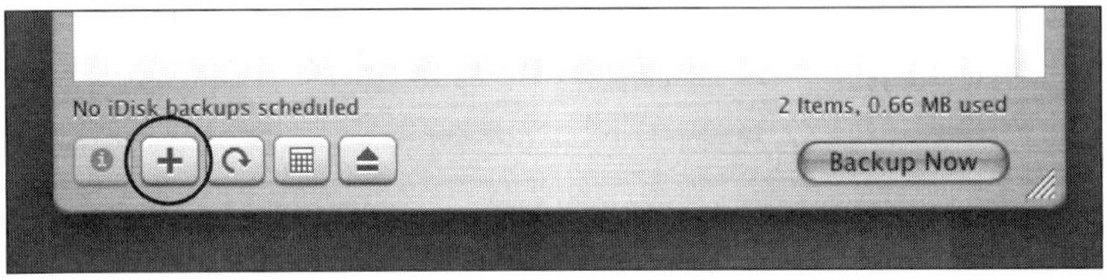

13. Click the + button in the lower-left corner to choose more files to back up.

You can choose to back up individual files or entire folders.

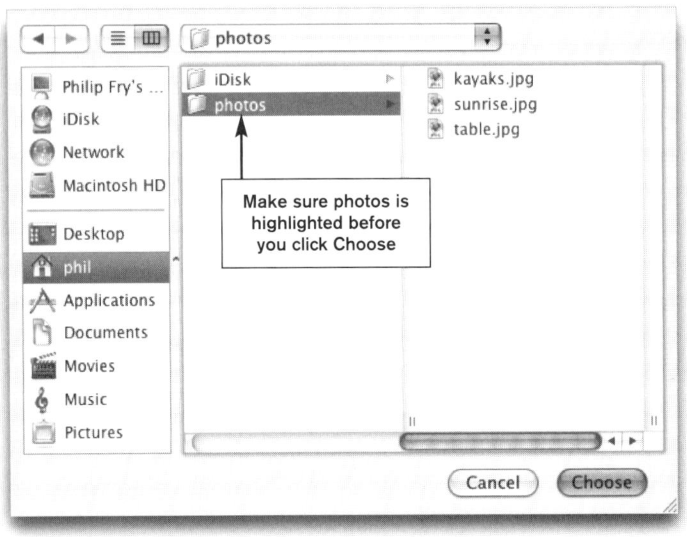

14. Navigate to your **Desktop** and locate the **photos** folder inside **chap_12**. This folder contains the same three images you used in Exercise 4. For this exercise, you'll back up this entire folder. (Although you could also select the three images individually, you might as well select the whole folder.) Select **photos** and click **Choose**.

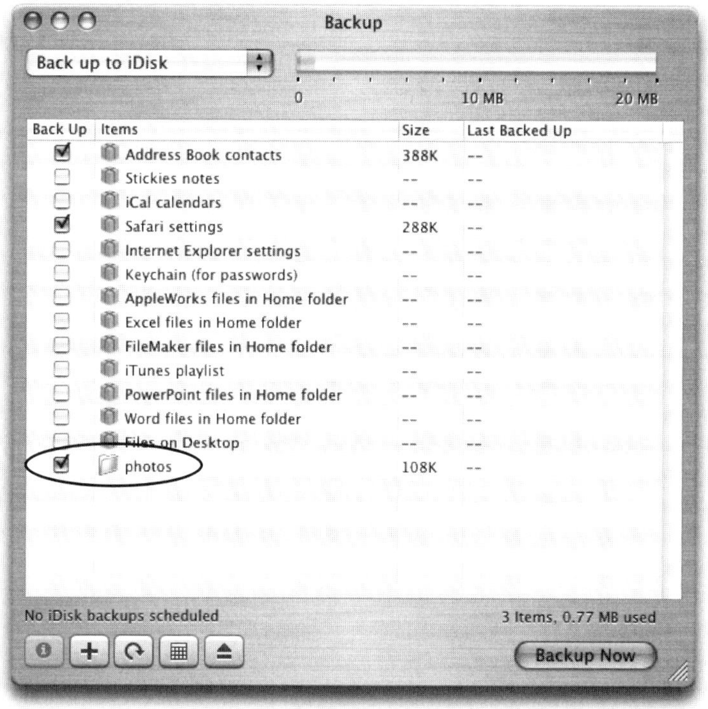

*The **photos** folder has been added to your list of items to be backed up. Now you're ready to send these items to your iDisk.*

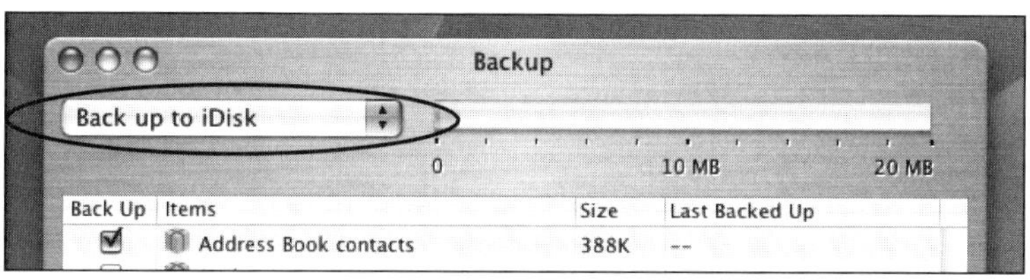

The pop-up menu in the upper-left corner of the window is for choosing your backup location. Because you're using a trial version of .Mac, your only choice is to back up to your iDisk. If you forked over the cash for a full account, you'd also have the option of backing up to a CD or DVD, as well as to any hard drives connected to your Mac. Still, having your important files stored on your iDisk, away from your computer, provides some peace of mind in the case of fire, thievery, or clumsiness. (I'm talking to you PowerBook-droppers out there.)

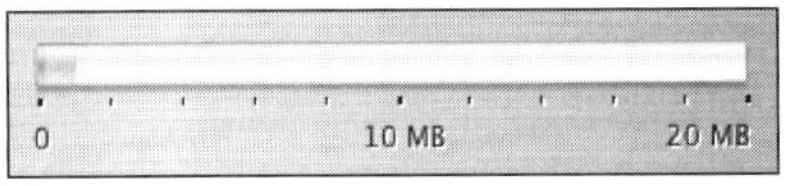

The bar shown here tells you how much of your iDisk space you're currently using. Look closely and you'll see that green part of the bar is actually two different shades of green. The dark green tells you how much is actually being used; the light green represents how much additional space your selected backup items will take up.

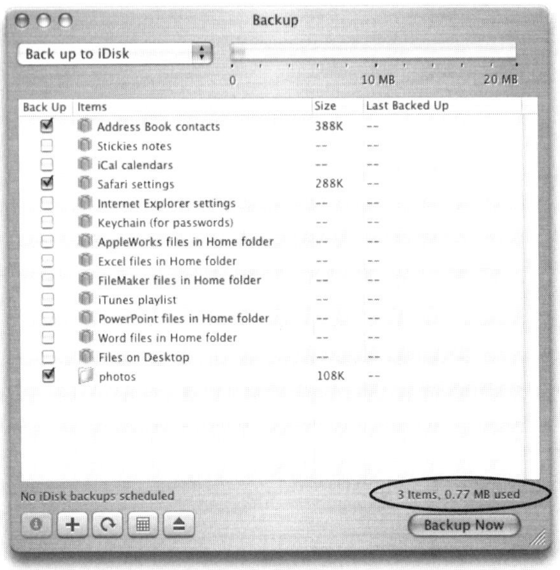

For an exact measurement of file size of your selected backup items, look to the lower-right corner of the window.

15. Click **Backup Now** to copy the selected items to your iDisk.

Backup takes a few moments to create the proper directories on your iDisk and then copies the files to them.

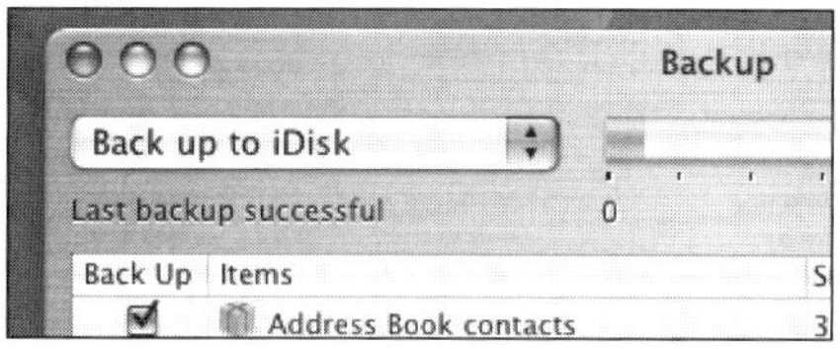

When it's done, you'll be returned to the main application window, and "Last backup successful" will appear in the upper-left corner.

NOTE | Where Exactly Do My Backup Files Go and How Do I Get Them Back?

When you use Backup to store your files on your iDisk, they're placed within the folder called **Backup** on your iDisk. Like the Software folder, the Backup folder is read-only, meaning you can't copy files to it by dragging them on the folder. The only way to place items in this folder is through the Backup application. But you can still drag copies from the folder if you need to access them. All of your backed up items are located in **iDisk > Backup > Users > [Your Account Name]**. In most cases, however, you don't need to manually copy files from your Backup folder.

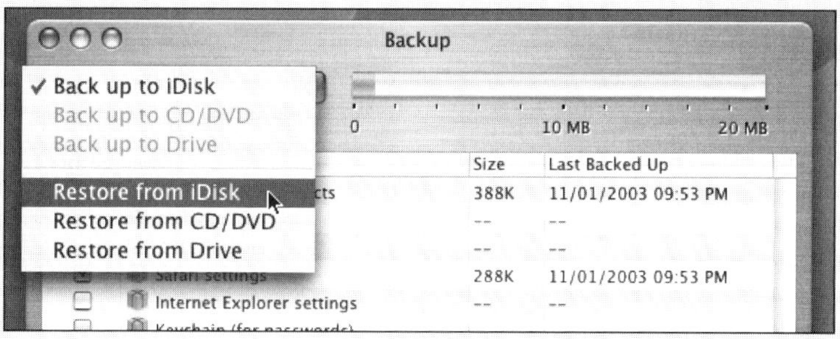

To restore backed up items, simply choose **Restore from iDisk** from the pop-up menu in the upper-left corner of the application window. Backup will copy the files from your iDisk to your hard drive and place them in the exact locations they originally came from.

One of the main problems with the concept of backing up files is that most of us don't do it often enough. Fortunately, you can schedule automatic backups with Backup. (Apple's software titles are infinitely logical, but they sure make for some awkward sentences.)

16. Click the **Schedule** button in the lower-left corner of the window.

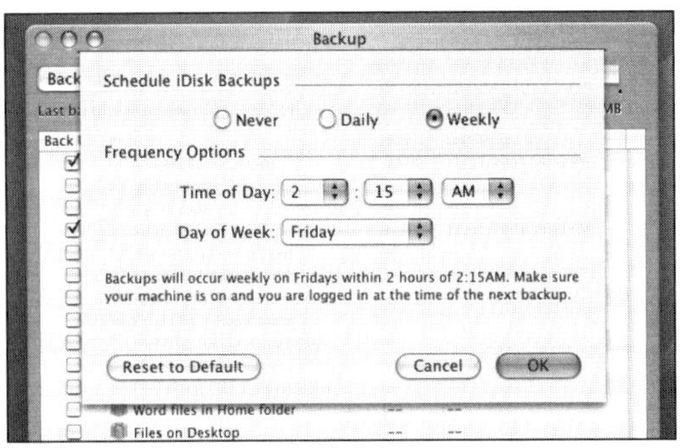

In this sheet, you can determine when and how often you want Backup to run. Once you set your backup schedule, the only thing you have to worry about is making sure that your computer is on and logged onto your user account.

17. Schedule a backup if you want, then click **OK**. Or click **Cancel** if you don't want to schedule one at this time.

18. Quit Backup.

*If you think Backup is useful, remember that signing up for a full .Mac account enables you to back up to CD or DVD (if you have a CD or DVD writer) and external hard drives. If you're looking for even more versatile backup software, check out Dantz Retrospect (**www.dantz.com**) or Lacie SilverKeeper (**www.silverkeeper.com**).*

The Other Stuff

That pretty much covers the major free applications and features you get with your trial .Mac subscriptions. In case you're curious, these are some of the other items in the .Mac toolbar that weren't covered in this chapter:

Bookmarks: You'll be learning about this feature in the next chapter. Using iSync and your .Mac account, you can keep a copy of your Safari bookmarks online so you can access them from the road.

iCards: Anyone can send iCards; you don't need a .Mac subscription, trial or otherwise. iCards lets you select from a collection of photos and drawings and send them to friends along with personalized greetings. Conveniently, each card also contains a tiny Apple logo to let your friends know where the card came from. iCards are free to you, and they give Apple free advertising. Everybody wins! If you do upgrade to a full .Mac account, you gain the additional ability to select your own photos from your computer to send as iCards.

iSync: You'll learn all about iSync in the next chapter.

Virex: One of the advantages of using an operating system that nearly 95 percent of the world doesn't use (other than the obvious air of superiority it gives you) is that Macs are much less frequent targets of computer viruses. Viruses aimed at the Mac do exist, however, and although they are much less malicious than their PC counterparts, it's still a good idea to occasionally scan for them. A full .Mac subscription gives you a downloadable copy of McAfee's Anti-Virus utility, Virex, which normally sells for about $30. Using Virex, you can manually or automatically scan your Mac for known viruses. You can download monthly updates from McAfee's Web site to keep your copy of Virex up to date. Obviously, if anti-virus protection is the most attractive feature of .Mac for you, it makes more sense to spend $30 on a stand-alone copy of Virex than $100 on a .Mac account.

iCal: iCal is not a .Mac application. It comes free with Panther, but it can be used in conjunction with .Mac. iCal is covered in the next chapter.

Member Benefits: To entice new subscribers (as well as to keep current subscribers), Apple constantly offers specials gifts to its members that run the gamut from free software to online tutorials to discount coupons for various products. Clicking the Member Benefits button takes to you a page listing all the currently available freebies.

Support: This is a link to a page that contains links to other support pages around Apple's Web site, most of which are accessible to all users, .Mac subscribers and nonsubscribers alike. As a .Mac subscriber, you can post questions to a discussion board that's moderated by Apple employees, but don't expect to get live telephone support.

After finishing this chapter and seeing what .Mac has to offer, it's up to you to decide whether it makes sense to upgrade to a full account. Use your remaining trial subscription days and see if .Mac becomes part of your daily routine. You can upgrade your account at anytime from the main .Mac page. If you don't think .Mac is for you, just let your subscription run out and that will be that. Your .Mac email account will become inactive, and any Web pages you've uploaded and any files you've copied to your iDisk will be erased. But remember, as mentioned in Chapter 10, "Address Book, Mail, and iChat AV," *that you get to keep your account name if you want to use it for iChat.*

Section III

The Digital Hub

Chapters 13 through 17 cover the major "i" applications available for Mac OS X. These are the applications that truly help you manage all the aspects of your digital lifestyle. Chapter 13 shows you how to use iCal to manage your personal schedule and iSync to keep your schedules and contacts up to date on your iPod, Palm organizer, or wireless phone. Chapters 14 through 17 cover the applications found in the iLife suite: iTunes for managing and playing your music collection; iPhoto for storing, organizing, editing, and sharing your digital pictures; iMovie for editing and assembling the video you shoot with your digital camcorder, and iDVD for putting everything–music, pictures, and video–onto one convenient DVD.

13.
iCal and iSync

| Entering Schedule Events |

| Publishing and Subscribing to Calendars |

| Syncing with an iPod | Syncing with a Palm Device |

| Syncing with a Bluetooth Phone | Syncing with .Mac |

| Syncing with Your .Mac Address Book |

no exercise files

Mac OS X Panther H•O•T CD-ROM

This chapter begins the section of the book covering OS X's various "i" applications. All of the i-apps share the common purpose of helping you to organize your digital life. This chapter will introduce you to iCal, Apple's simple and elegant personal calendar application. iCal allows you to keep track of your personal and work schedules in one convenient program and to share your calendar online with friends and co-workers.

This chapter will also show you how to use iSync, an application that helps keep the contact and schedule information on your Palm organizer, cell phone, and iPod up to date. You'll also learn how to use iSync and iCal in conjunction with your .Mac account.

I. Entering Schedule Events

This exercise shows you how to add your schedule information into iCal.

1. Start iCal.

Tip: The iCal icon in the Dock displays the actual date while iCal is running.

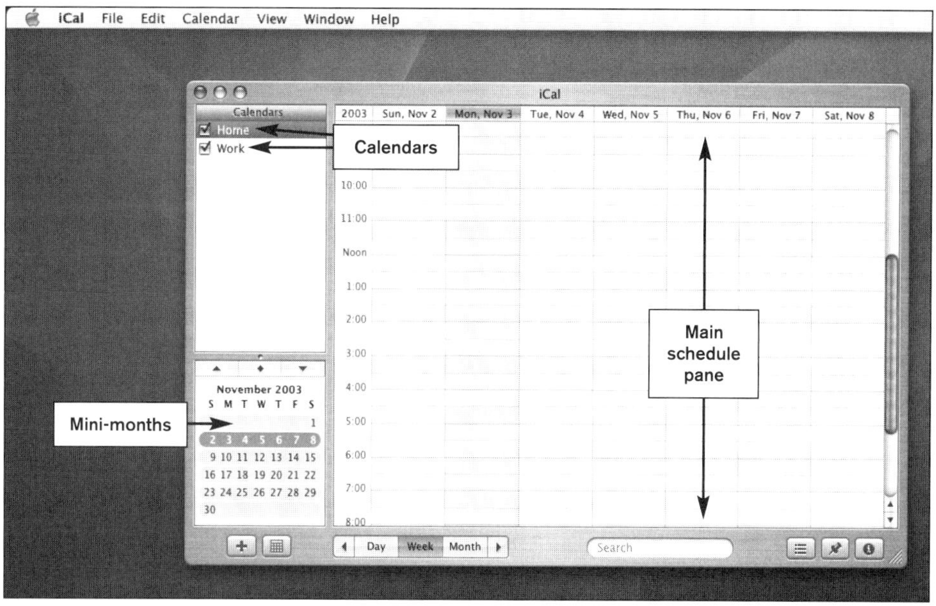

When you first open iCal, its main window is broken into three sections: calendars, mini-months, and the main schedule pane.

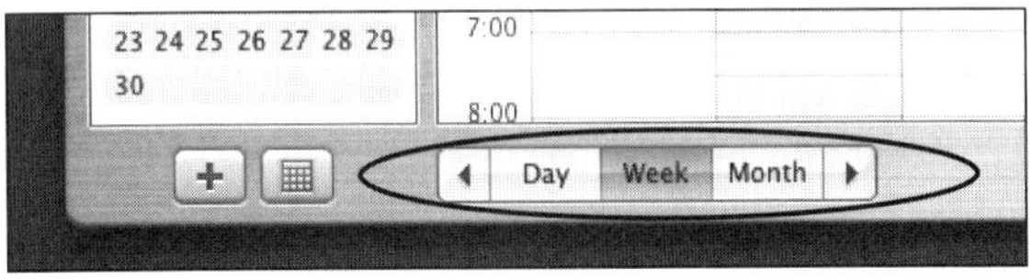

*You can change the view of the main schedule pane by clicking the **Day**, **Week**, and **Month** buttons at the bottom of the window. The arrows on either side of these three buttons take you to the previous day, week, or month, depending on the current view.*

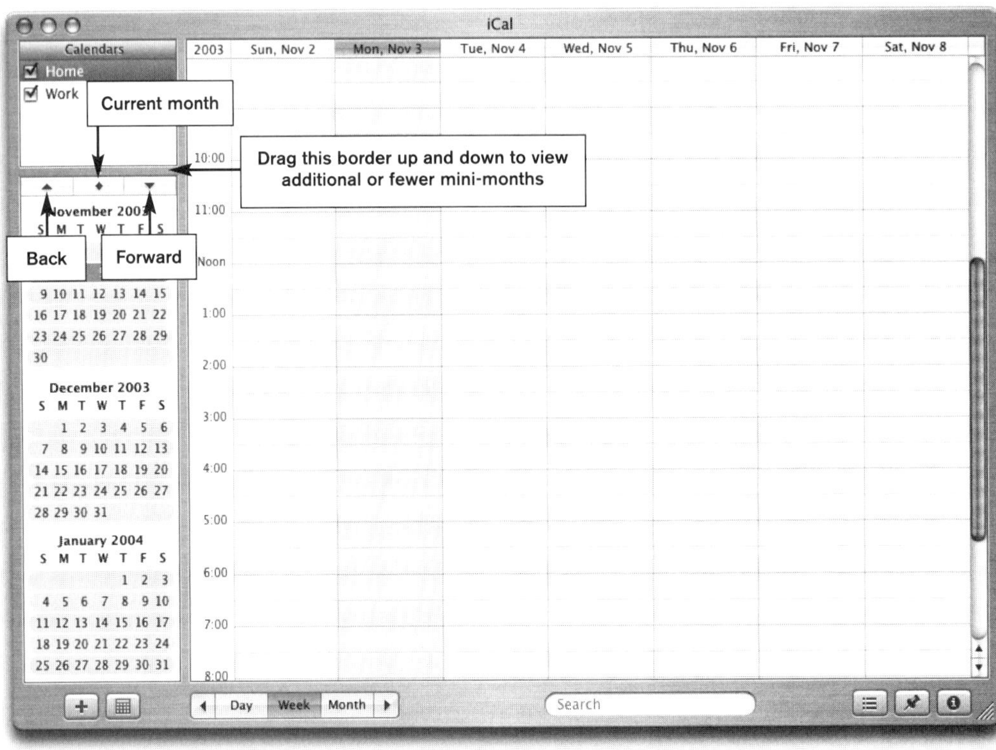

The mini-months provide a quick way to jump back or forward, month by month. You can drag the border above the mini-calendar pane to increase or decrease the number of visible mini-months. Click the up and down arrows at the top of the pane to move backward and forward, respectively. Clicking on a date in a mini-month will display that date in the main schedule window based on the currently selected view (Day, Week, or Month). You can click the diamond icon in the center to return to the current month.

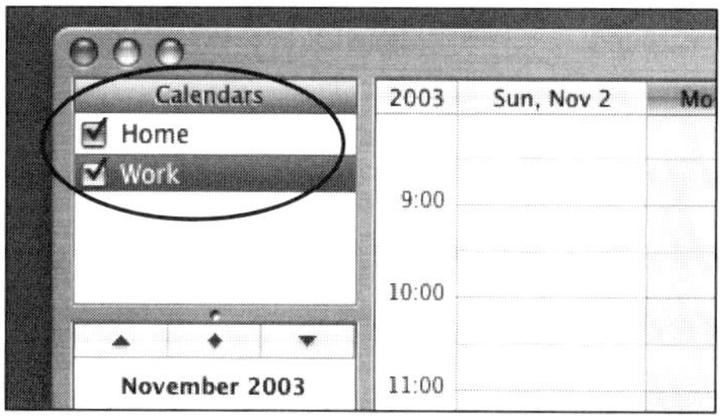

*iCal makes it easy to maintain several calendars of activities at once. For instance, by default, you already have a **Home** and **Work** calendar created for you. You might use your Home calendar to keep track of events such as family get-togethers or trash pickup days, and your Work calendar may contain dates for meetings or seminars. iCal lets you view each calendar individually or both simultaneously to check for possible scheduling conflicts. To see multiple calendars in action, you first need to add a few events to your schedule.*

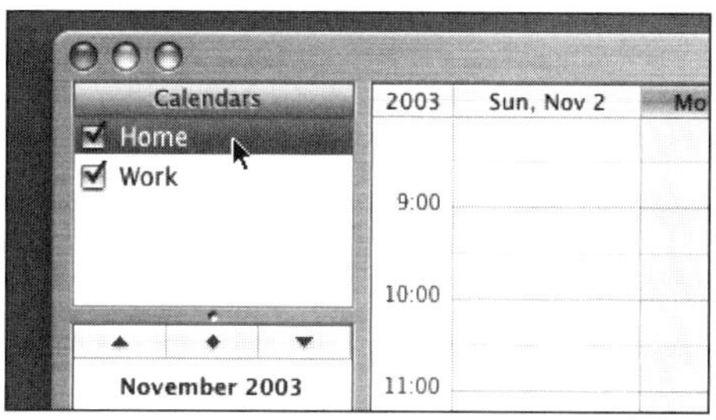

2. Click the **Home** calendar to select it. (Click the word "Home" itself; don't uncheck it. And be sure you just single-click–a double-click highlights the calendar name, allowing you to rename it.) It's a good idea to have the right calendar selected before you add an event to your schedule (although you can change the calendar associated with an event if it becomes necessary later).

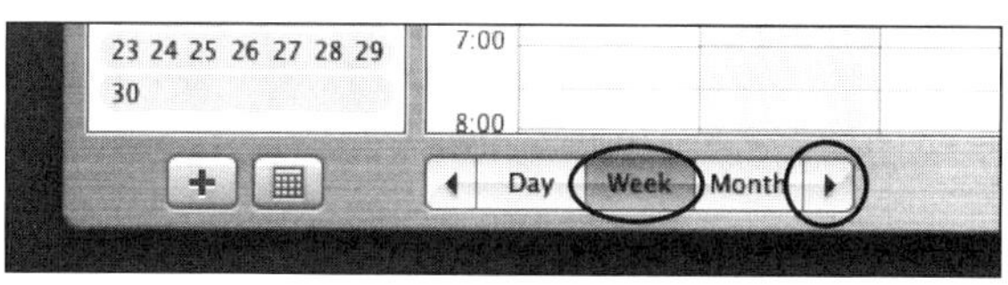

3. For the purposes of this exercise, make sure you're in **Week** view and then jump ahead to next week by clicking the right arrow.

Let's imagine that you're planning to repaint the kitchen next Tuesday. You plan on starting around 10 a.m. and figure that it will take about three hours.

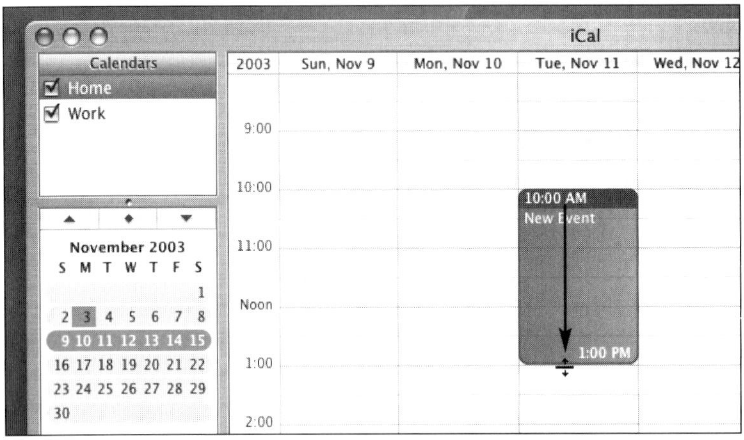

4. Under the column for next **Tuesday**, click and hold your mouse over the line representing **10 a.m.** and then drag down to **1 p.m.** A colored box appears (the same color as the check box next to **Home** in the **Calendars** pane).

Note: *Be sure to click right on the 10 a.m. line or you may end up choosing 10:15 or 9:45. If you draw the box incorrectly, just let go of the mouse and press* ***Cmd+Z*** *to undo the box and try again.*

Once you release the mouse, a text box marked ***New Event*** *appears.*

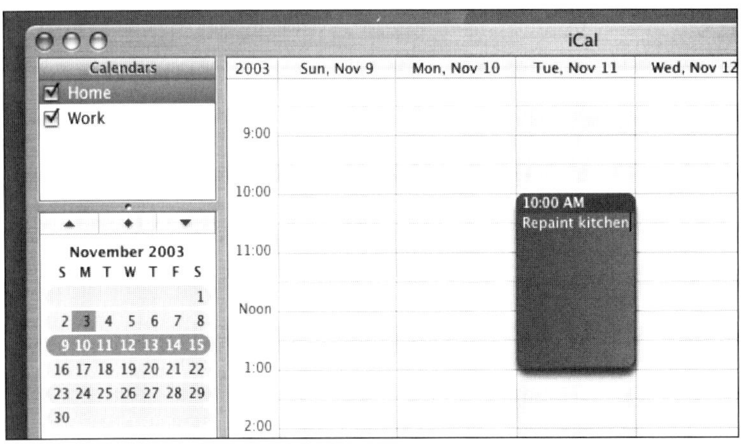

5. In the **New Event** text box, type **Repaint kitchen** and press **Return**. The event has now been added to your **Home** calendar.

But wait, you just remembered that you're supposed to spend Tuesday morning drafting a proposal for your company. You'll have to put off the painting until the afternoon.

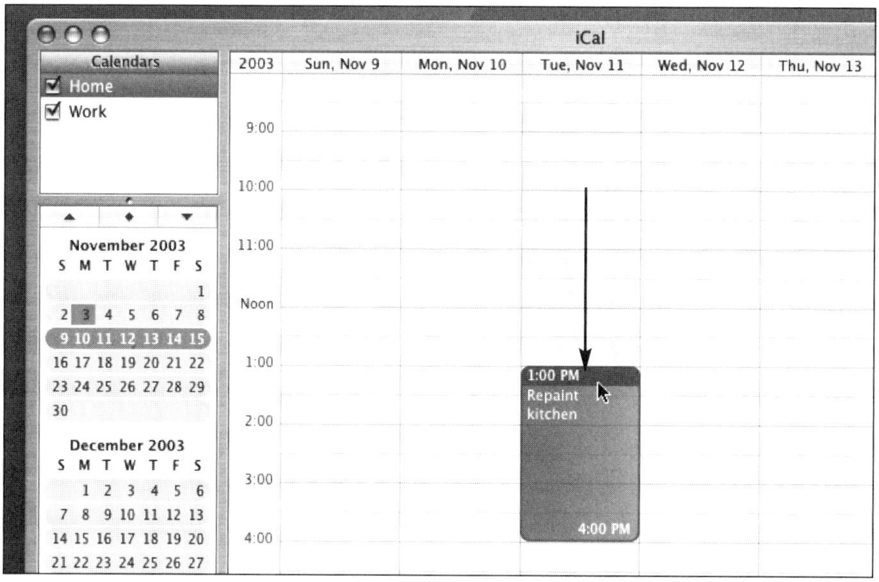

6. No problem, simply click the event box's title bar and drag the box down to **1 p.m.** Notice how the time in the title bar changes as you drag down.

Now you'll add the proposal to your schedule.

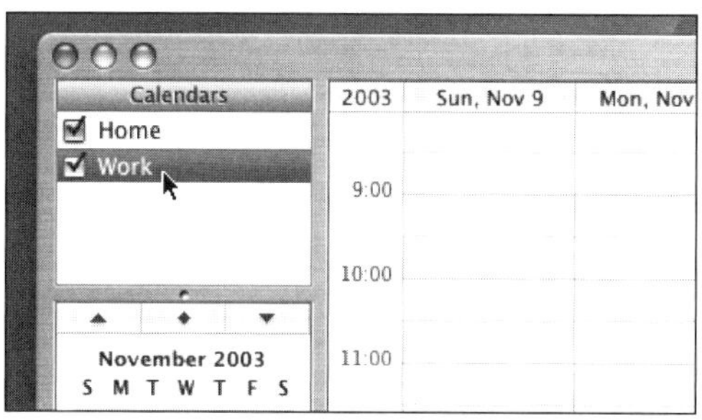

7. Since this is work-related, click the **Work** calendar.

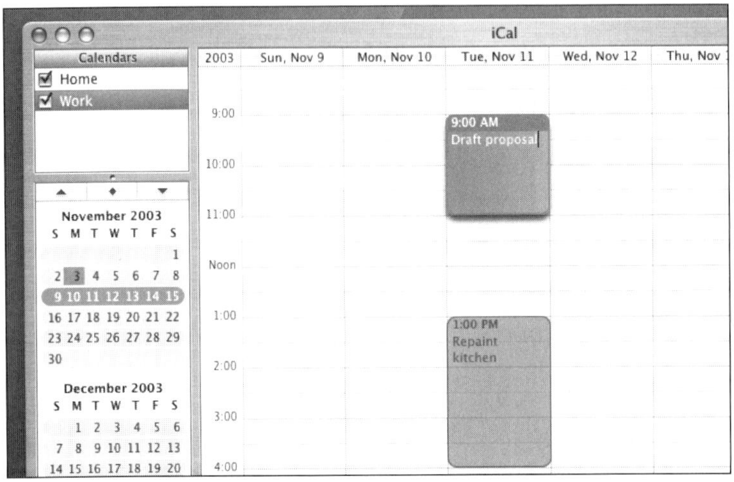

8. Drag a box from **9 a.m.** to **11 a.m.** on **Tuesday**. Notice that it appears in the color associated with **Work**. Type **Draft proposal** in this box and press **Return**.

You can now see two events from two different calendars appearing on the same day. You can check and uncheck the Home and Work calendars to show and hide each one as necessary.

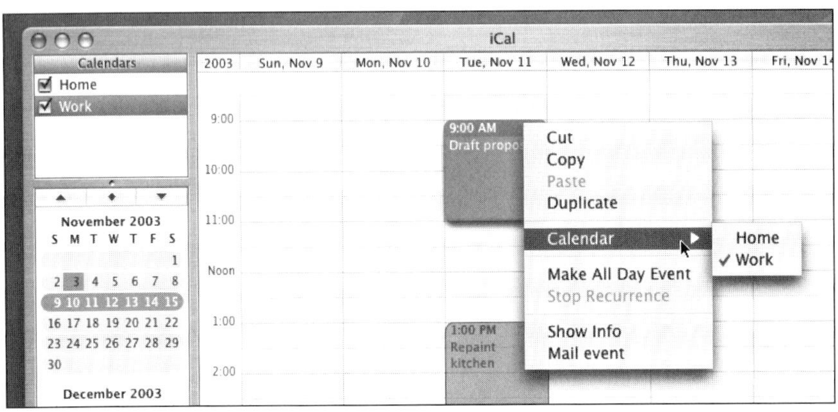

Tip: *You can quickly change an event from one calendar to another by* ***Ctrl+clicking*** *the event box's title bar and choosing the calendar from the contextual menu that appears.*

Next, imagine that the cable guy is coming next week to install your new digital cable. The cable company has narrowed down his arrival time to sometime between Wednesday and Friday, within the hours of 8 a.m. and 8 p.m. To note this on your schedule, you could select the Home calendar and drag a box from 8 a.m. to 8 p.m., but because this is, for all intents and purposes, an all-day and multiday event, it's much easier to use the Month view to add this item.

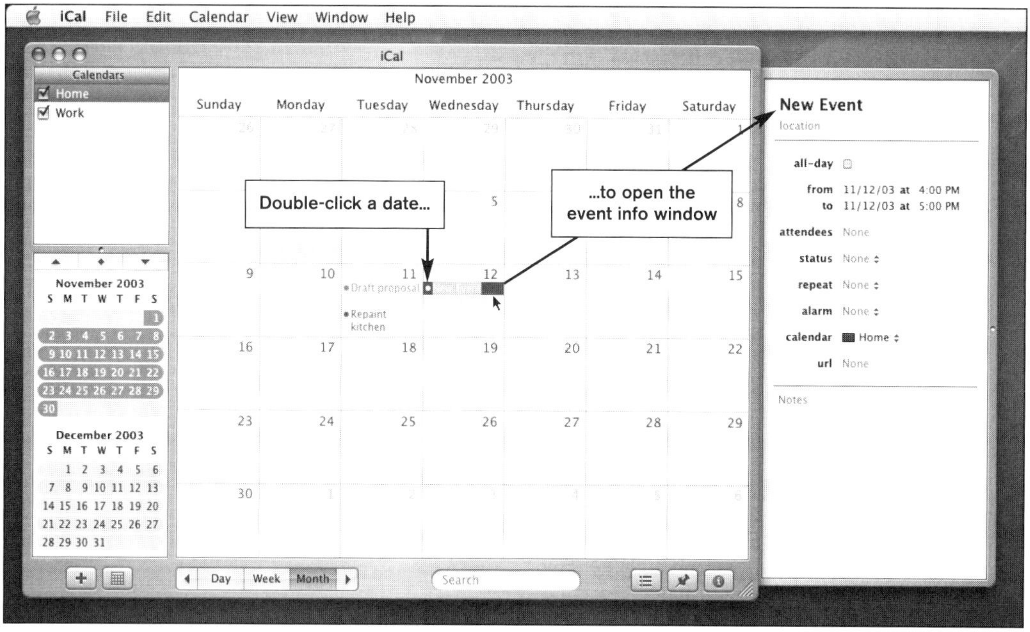

9. Click the **Home** calendar to activate it and then click the **Month view** button to switch to that view. Double-click the box representing next **Wednesday** to open the **Info Drawer**. Double-clicking any event, date, or To Do item will cause the **Info Drawer** for that item to slide out from the right or left side of the calendar. (You can show and hide the **Info Drawer** by pressing **Cmd+I**.)

Note: *Be sure to click somewhere in the box under the date. If you click on the same line as the date, you'll be switched into Day view. If this happens, just switch back to Month view and click a little lower in the date's box.*

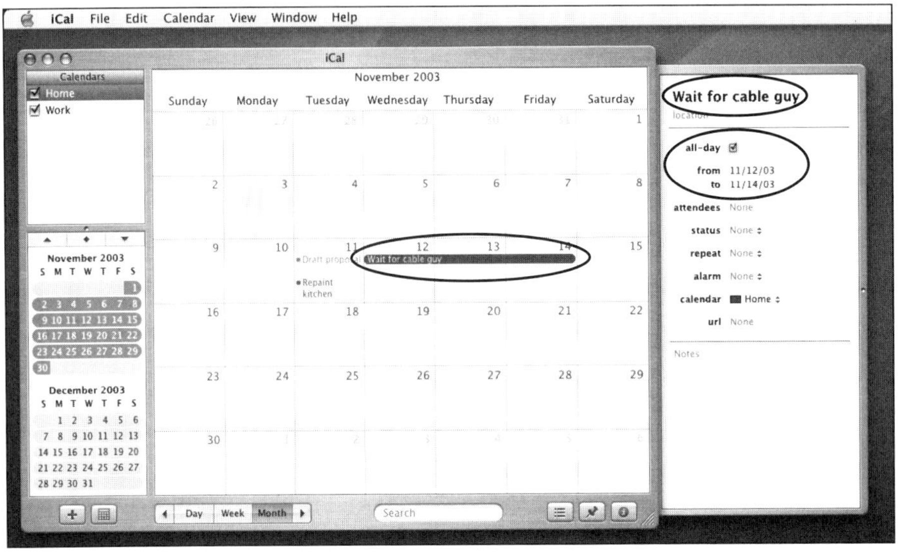

10. In the **Info Drawer**, delete the text "New Event" and type **Wait for cable guy**. Check the **all-day** check box. The **from** date already reflects next **Wednesday's** date. Change the **to** date to next **Friday's** date. Notice that the event in the main schedule pane now stretches from Wednesday to Friday.

The Info Drawer is convenient for adding all-day events, but can also be used to add or edit other events.

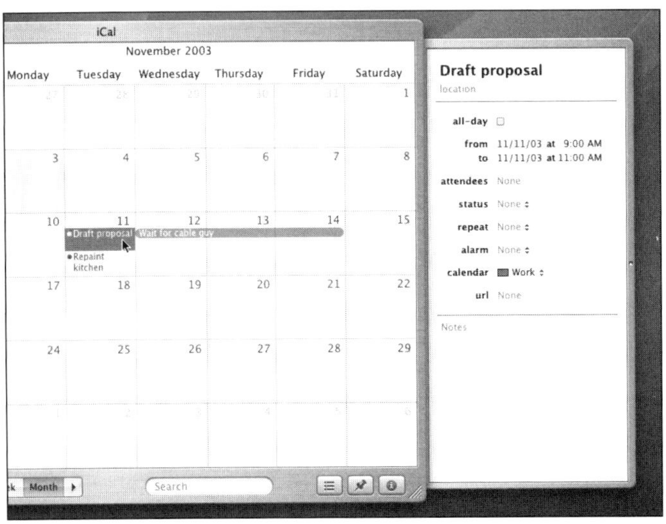

11. Click the **Draft proposal** and **Repaint kitchen** events on **Tuesday** and notice how their details appear in the Info Drawer.

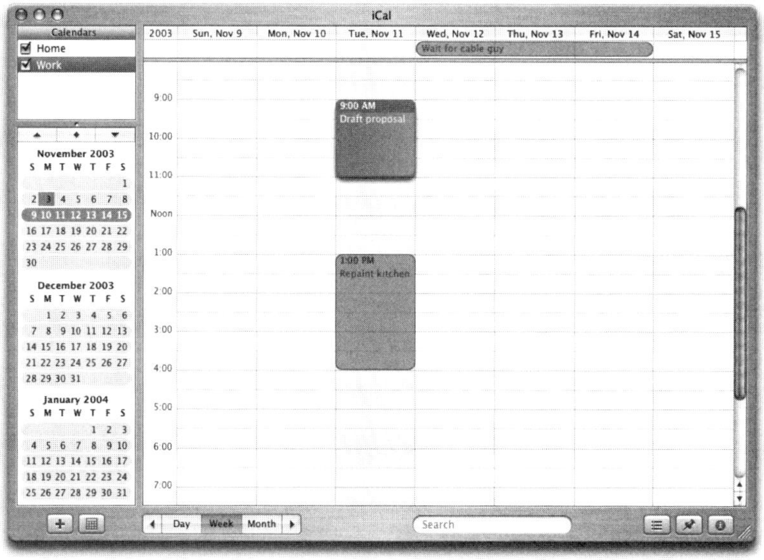

12. Click the **Week** button at the bottom of the window to switch back to **Week** view. Notice that a new row has been added to the top of the week. This row indicates all-day events. (An all-day event row appears in the **Day** view as well.)

*Tip: By default, iCal displays the Daily and Weekly hours from midnight to midnight. If you do not need to schedule every waking (and sleeping) moment, you can select **iCal > Preferences** from the menu bar to decrease the number of visible hours per day.*

As you can see, it's pretty easy to add events to your schedule. But what about the events on your schedule that repeat daily, weekly, or monthly? iCal makes it easy to repeat events without having to re-enter them. You'll add some repeating events to a new calendar.

13. Click the **Add a new calendar** button (the + symbol) in the lower-left corner of the window (or choose **File > New Calendar**).

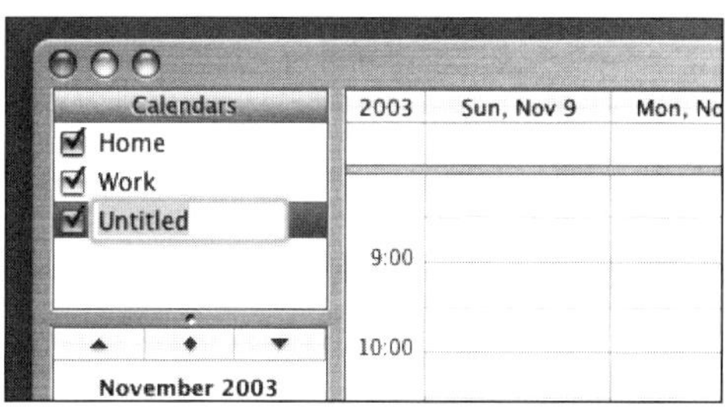

A new, untitled calendar appears in the Calendars pane along with a new colored check box.

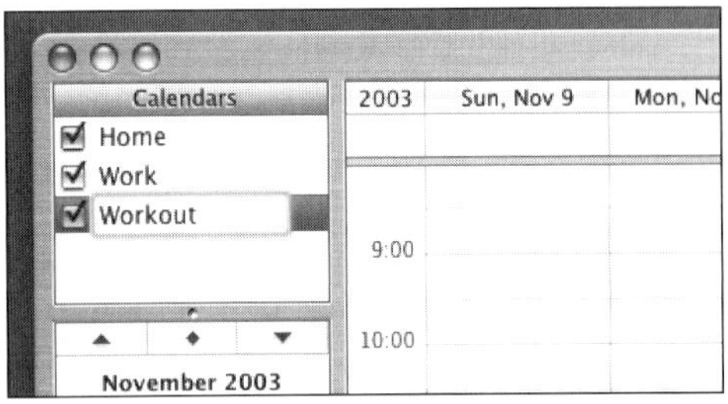

14. Name this calendar **Workout**.

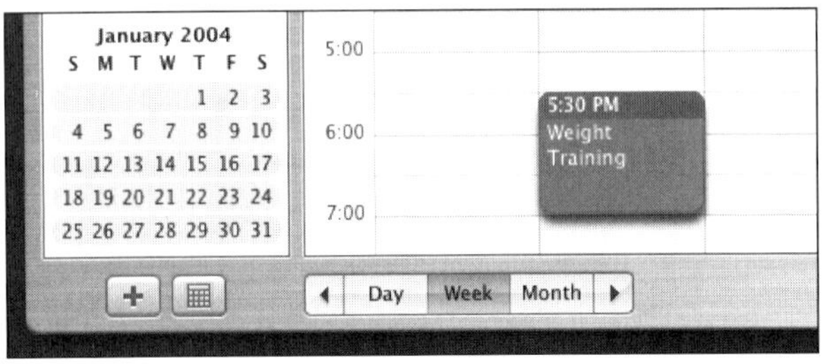

15. With **Workout** selected, draw a box from **5:30 p.m.** to **7 p.m.** on next Monday's schedule. (You should still be in **Week** view.) Name this event **Weight Training**.

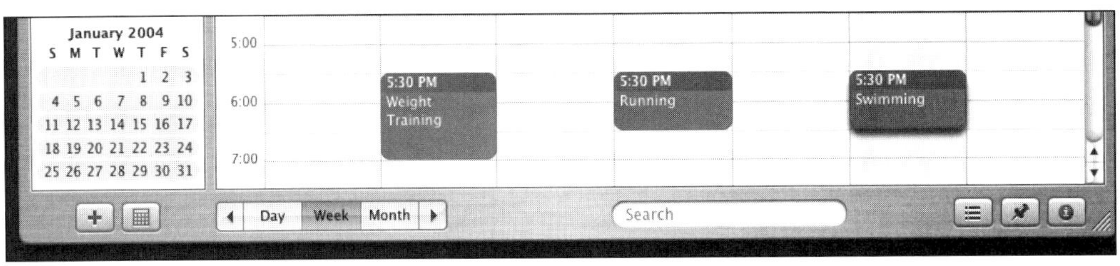

16. On **Wednesday**, create another **Workout** block called **Running** from **5:30** to **6:30 p.m.** On **Friday**, also from **5:30** to **6:30 p.m.**, create one more **Workout** block called **Swimming**. (We'll assume you have your own in-home treadmill and swimming pool to use while waiting for the cable guy.)

You'll want to repeat this workout schedule each week. (Hey, it's fictitious–you can repeat it as much as you want!)

17. Click once on the **Weight Training** event and make sure the **Info Drawer** is still open. If it's not open, click the **i** button in the lower-right corner of the window, or press **Cmd+I**.

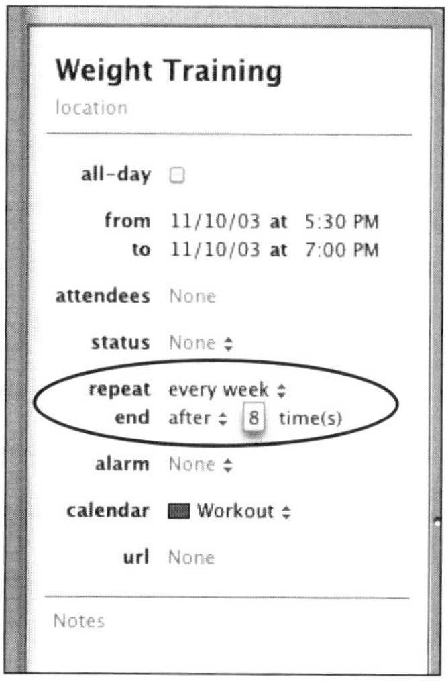

18. In the **Info Drawer**, click the arrows next to **repeat**. Choose to have this event repeat **every week**. After doing so, the **end** menu will appear below **repeat**. Click the arrows and choose **after** and type **8** in the adjacent **time(s)** field. This will tell iCal to stop repeating the event after eight weeks, which should be enough time for you to evaluate whether or not your training schedule is working for you.

Notice that the reoccurrence icon has appeared in the corner of the Weight Training event to let you know that this event repeats.

19. Click the **Running** event and have it repeat **every Wednesday for 8 weeks**, then do the same for **Swimming** on **Fridays**. Close the **Info Drawer** when you're done by clicking the **i** button or dragging the pane border toward the main calendar window.

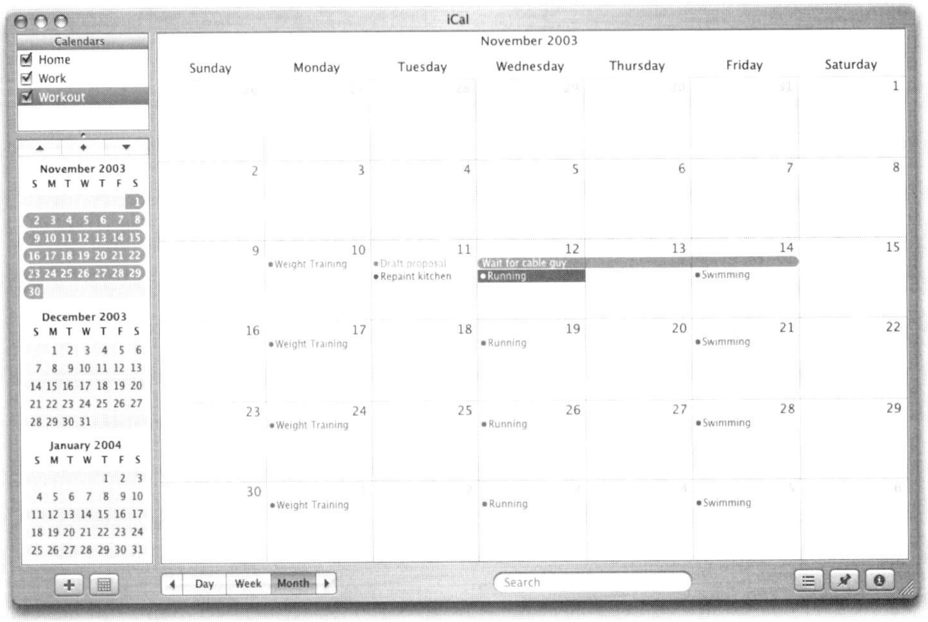

20. Switch to **Month** view and observe how your workouts now appear every week for the next eight weeks. (You might have to advance forward a month to see the multiple listings if you're currently near the end of the month.)

But what if you decide that one of these activities–swimming, for instance–isn't for you? It's easy to remove events whether they're repeated or not.

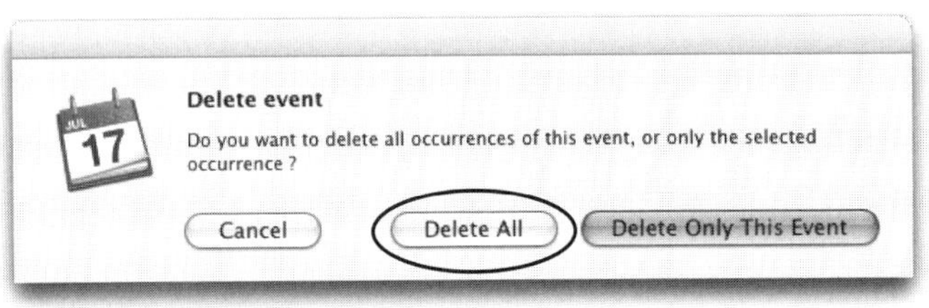

21. Click the first occurrence of **Swimming** and press **Delete**. A dialog box appears asking whether you want to delete all occurrences of this event, or just the one you clicked on. Click **Delete All** to remove all appearances of **Swimming** from your calendar.

Tip: *If you click any occurrences of an event other than the first one, you'll be given the choice to delete them all or just the ones following the occurrence you selected.*

Finally, let's assume you were a little overly optimistic with your Schwarzeneggerian plan of lifting weights for an hour and a half every week. (I won't mess with your cinematic or political aspirations here.)

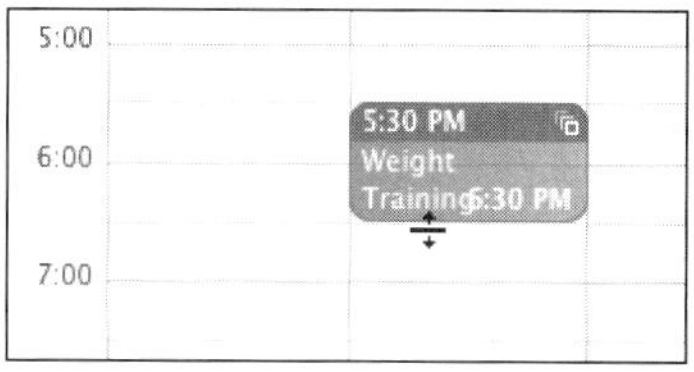

22. Switch back to **Week** view and locate the first **Weight Training** event. Drag the bottom border of the event up until it reaches **6:30 p.m**.

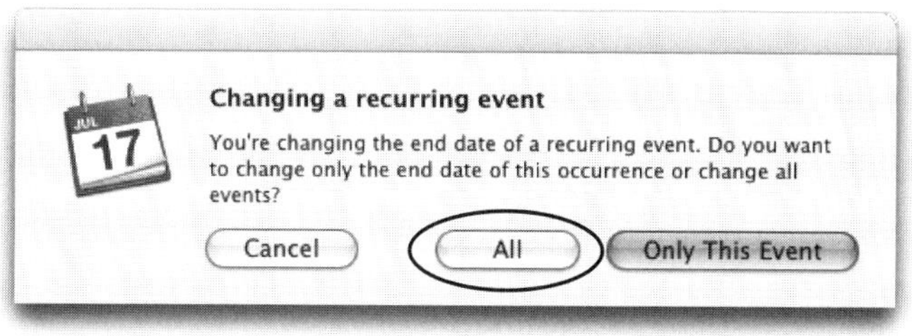

23. Because this a is a recurring event, a dialog box appears asking whether you want to change just this instance or all instances of **Weight Training**. Click **All** to chop a half-hour off each occurrence.

24. Keep iCal open for the next exercise.

This exercise showed you how to add and remove events to and from multiple calendars. In the next exercise, you'll learn how to share your calendars with others.

MOVIE | iCal.mov

See **iCal.mov** on the **H•O•T CD-ROM** for a demonstration of the steps covered in this exercise.

Setting Up Reminders

You can keep as many events in as many calendars as you like in iCal, but if you don't remember to check for upcoming events such as important meetings, social events, or birthdays, you may find yourself in trouble. Fortunately, you can instruct iCal to display periodic reminders that will appear at a set time to jog your memory about important events.

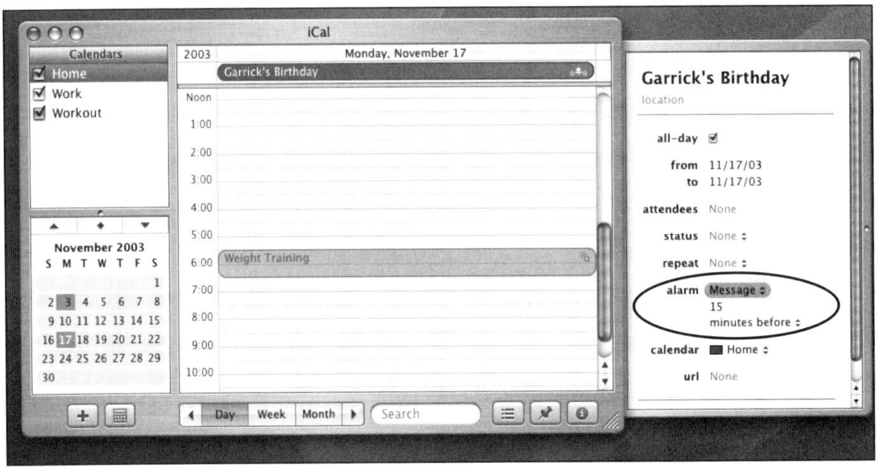

To add a reminder to an event, select the event and click the **arrows** next to **alarm** in the **Info Drawer**. There are four different alarms to choose from: **Message** (for iCal to display a dialog box), **Message with sound** (to have iCal play an alert sound when displaying the dialog box), **E-mail** (to have iCal automatically send an email to your email address as it appears in your Address Book), and **Open file** (to have iCal open an iCal calendar or another application file).

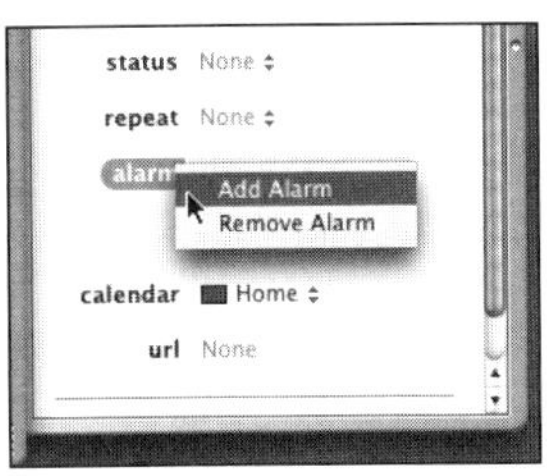

You also have the option of adding multiple alarms. After choosing one alarm, click on **alarm**, and you are given the choice to remove the alarm or add another alarm. There is no limit to the amount of alarms you can add, so if you suffer from a weak short-term memory, this is the program for you.

For each of these reminders, you can choose to have them activate minutes, hours, or days before the selected event. Just make sure you select an interval that will give you enough time to prepare for the event, but not so much time that you forget about it again. When the appointed time arrives, the alert will be sent whether iCal is running or not.

To Do Lists

If you use iCal to manage your schedule, it makes sense that there should be a way for you to keep track of all the various tasks you need to accomplish. iCal's To Do list provides a place for you to record the chores and errands that may not require a specific slot of time on your schedule but need to be completed nonetheless.

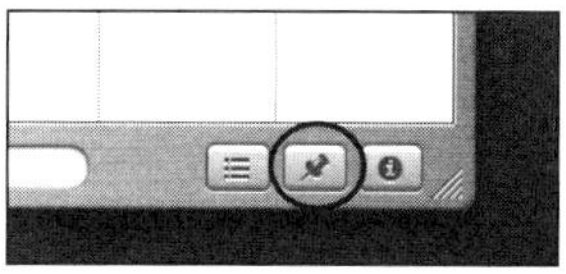

To view your To Do list, click the **pushpin** icon in the lower-right corner of the window. This will open the **To Do** pane on the right side of the window.

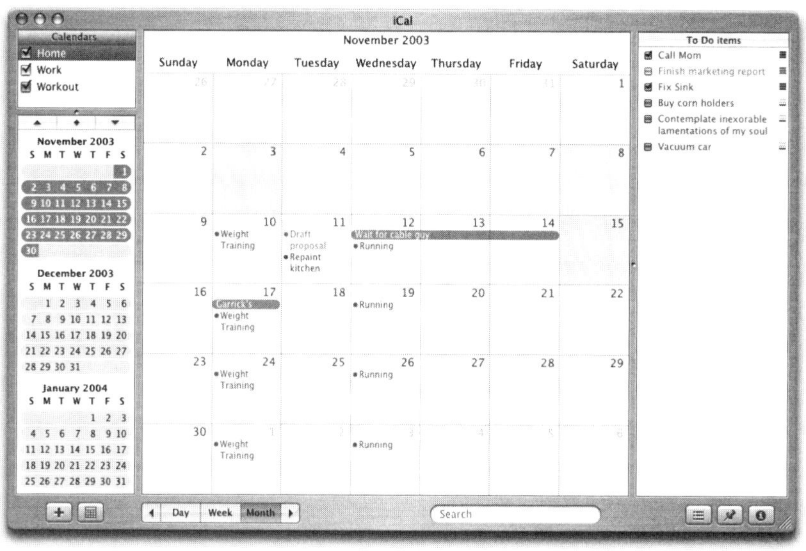

Double-click in this pane to add items to your list. Each To Do item corresponds with whichever calendar you have selected at the time, and includes an adjacent check box for you to check off items as you accomplish them. You can completely remove items from your list by selecting them and pressing **Delete**. The icon to the right of each To Do item indicates its priority level. Double-clicking the check box of any of the To Do items opens the Info Drawer. Here, you can check the **completed** box, set the **priority** to **Important**, **Very important**, or **Not Important**; select a **due date**; add an **alarm**; change which **calendar** each To Do item is associated with; and enter a **url** address to the To Do item. Once you've set your priority levels or due dates, **Ctrl+clicking** in the To Do pane opens a menu from which you can determine the order in which the items are listed.

You can shirk your responsibilities, or at least put them out of view, by clicking the **pushpin** icon again.

2. Publishing and Subscribing to Calendars

If you often find yourself using computers other than your own, or if you frequently have to inform other people of your schedule, you'll be glad to know that iCal makes it easy for you to publish your calendars to a Web site. If you have a .Mac account (covered in the preceding chapter), you can post your calendar to your Web space, where it can be viewed by anyone with a Web browser and an Internet connection. This handy feature is also perfect for checking your schedule when you're on the road. Additionally, when you publish your calendar, other iCal users can then subscribe to it, meaning that your calendar will be loaded into their copies of iCal, where they can view all its details. This exercise shows you how to publish your own calendars and how to subscribe to other people's iCal calendars as well.

You can publish as many of your calendars as you want, but you can only publish them one at a time.

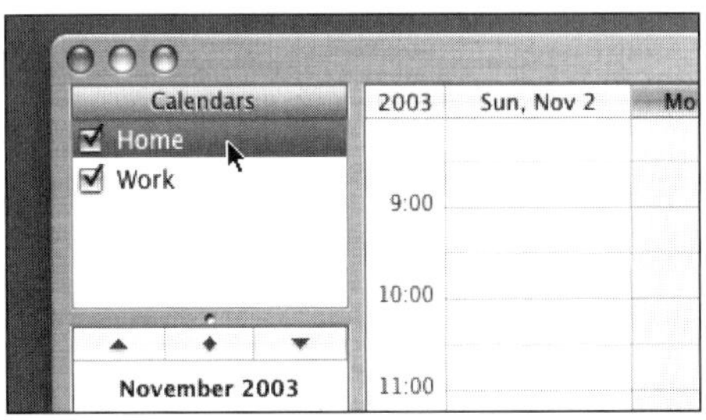

1. Select **Home** in the **Calendars** pane.

2. Choose **Calendar > Publish** from the menu bar.

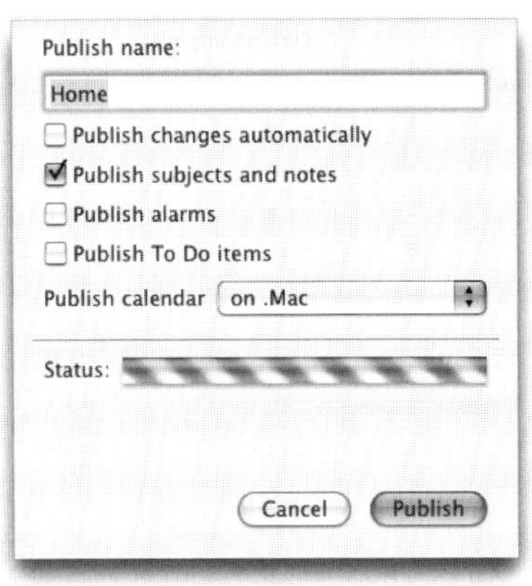

The dialog box that appears has several options for you to choose from. The following chart describes these options.

Calendar Publishing Options	
Option	**Description**
Publish name	Enter the name of your calendar in this field. Bear in mind that you're publishing this to the Web for others to view or subscribe to; you might want to choose a more descriptive name than Home or Work.
Publish changes automatically	With this option checked, anytime you make a change to your calendar, iCal will automatically connect to the Internet and update the changes to the calendar online, ensuring that the most current version of your calendar is available on the Web.
Publish subjects and notes	This option publishes any notes you may have included with your events. (Notes are found in the event Info Drawer.)
Publish alarms	This option includes any event reminders you may have set. For instance, if you set a reminder to appear on your screen two days before an event, the reminder will also appear on the screens of any iCal users who have subscribed to your calendar. Other users can turn off alarms in the calendars they subscribed to.
Publish To Do items	Checking this option will include any To Do items you may have created in the calendar you're publishing.
Publish calendar	**on .Mac:** Publishes your calendar to your .Mac account (based on the account info in the .Mac panel of System Preferences). This is necessary for other users to view your schedule through a Web browser. **on a WebDAV server:** If you decided not to publish your calendar on a .Mac account, you can select this option to specify the location of a WebDAV (Web-based **D**istributed **A**uthoring and **V**ersioning) server. To publish to a WedDAV server, you must enter the Base URL address of the server, and then provide a login and password.

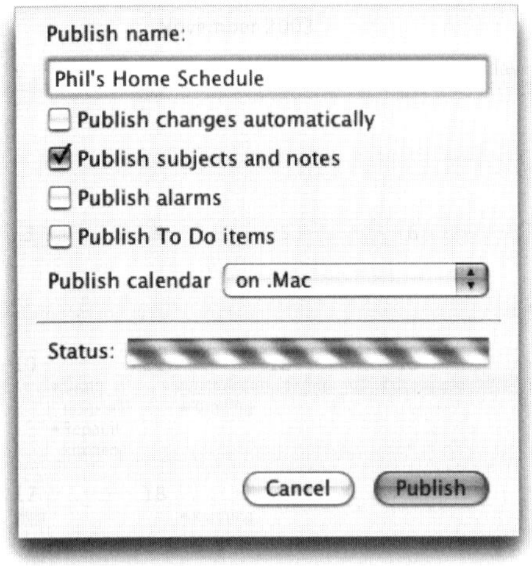

3. In the box that opens, name this calendar after yourself (**Phil's Home Schedule**, for example). Choose .**Mac** from the **Publish calendar** menu. (You still have your trial account from the last chapter, right?). Click **Publish**.

After a few seconds, a dialog box appears telling you that your calendar has been successfully published and where it's located. Don't worry about noting the address provided to you here. There are easier ways to access your published calendar than copying down this information.

4. Click **Visit Page**.

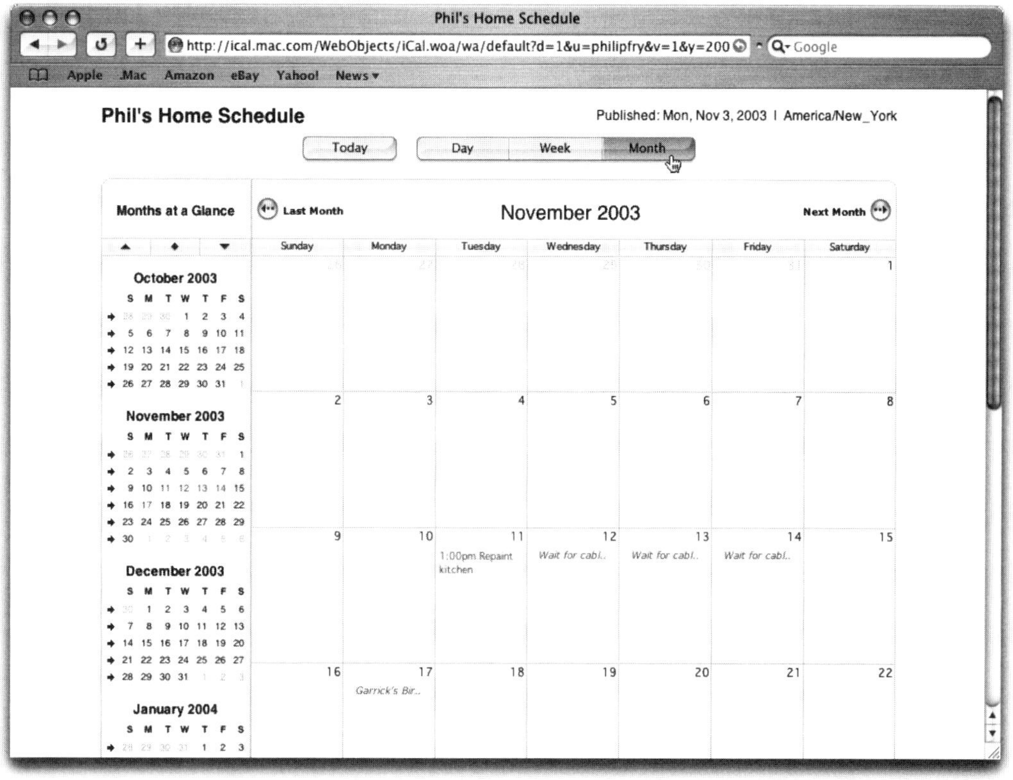

Your Web browser opens and takes you to your published calendar. This Web calendar acts much like iCal itself. You can click the ***Day****,* ***Week****, and* ***Month*** *buttons at the top of the screen to change views, and you can advance forward and backward by clicking the arrows on either side of the upper portion of the window. You can even click on events to see their details.*

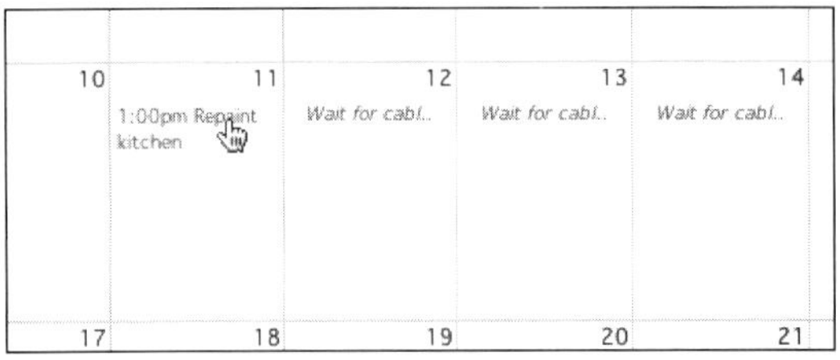

5. Browse through this calendar and find the dates you created in the preceding exercise. Click the **Repaint kitchen** event.

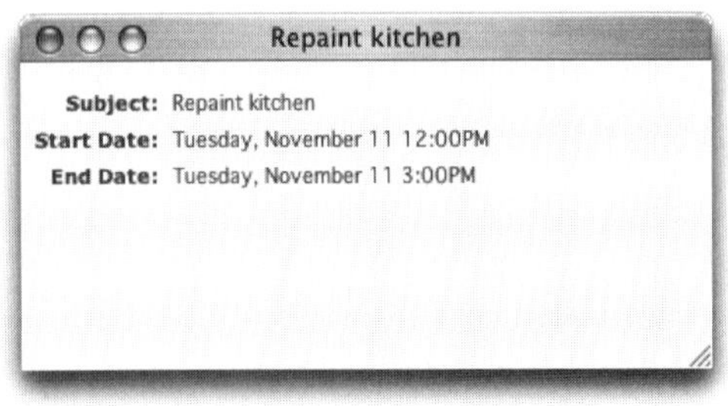

A new window opens up displaying the specifics of the event.

6. Close any open windows in your browser and return to iCal.

Being able to publish your calendar online is a great convenience if you often find yourself using computers other than your own. Another advantage of publishing your calendar is the ability to share it with others. In order to share your calendar, you have to let people know where it is.

7. In iCal, the **Calendar Published** dialog box should still be open. Click **Send Mail**. (If you already closed the dialog box, choose **Calendar > Send publish email** from the menu bar.)

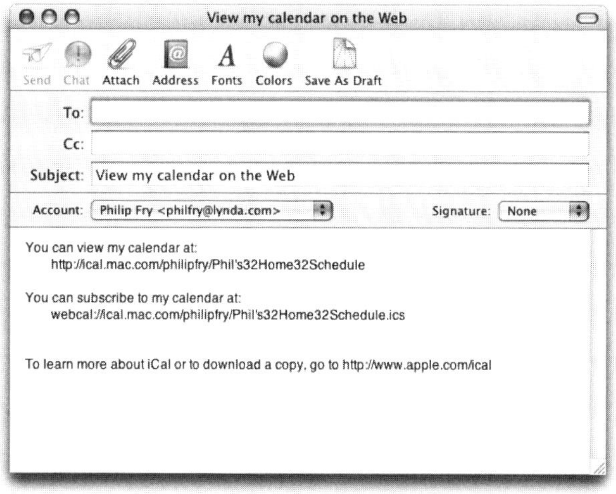

*Mail opens and automatically composes an email for you, detailing the location of your calendar for users who wish to view it from their browsers and providing instructions for those who might like to subscribe to your calendar through their own copies of iCal. All you have to do is supply the addresses of your recipients in the **To** field and then send it off.*

NOTE | Spaces in Calendar Names

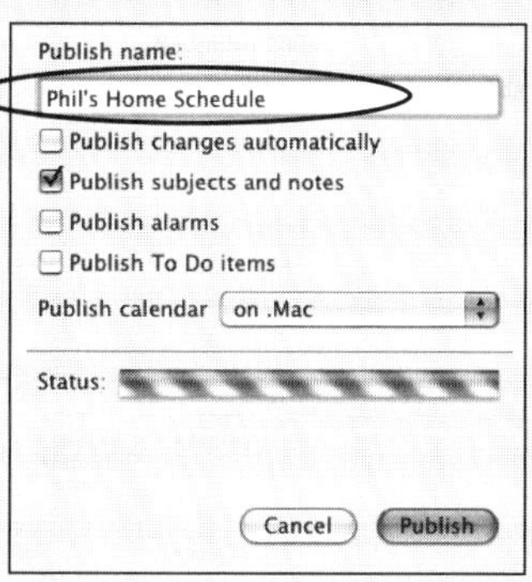

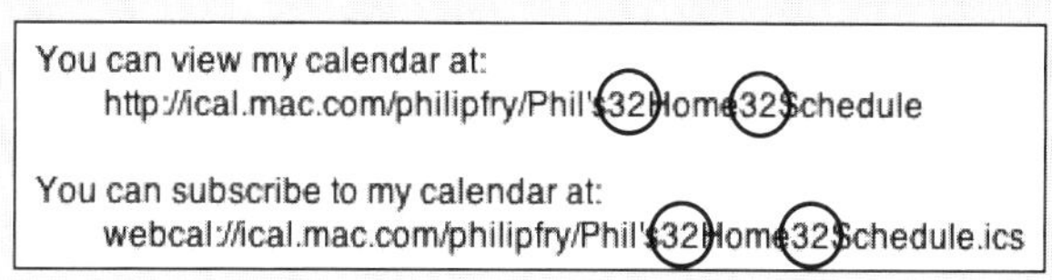

You might have noticed that the number 32 appears a few times in the address for your calendar. In the language of Web addresses, 32 represents blank spaces in the name of your calendar. For instance, if you named your calendar **Phil's Home Schedule** when you published it, its Web address name became **Phil's32Home32Schedule**. If you don't like having the 32s in your iCal address, you can prevent them from appearing by not using spaces when you name your calendar: **Phil's_Home_Schedule**, for instance. Not that any of this is really that big an issue–your calendar will appear correctly either way. But at least now you know what the deal is with 32.

8. There's no need to send an email announcing your calendar right now. Quit **Mail** and return to **iCal**.

9. Choose **Calendar > Unpublish** to remove the calendar you published from the Web. Click **Unpublish** in the dialog box that opens. You can always republish it once you get your real information in your calendar.

TIP | Alternatives to .Mac for Calendar Hosting

If you like the idea of publishing your calendar for others to see but aren't crazy about the idea of paying $99 for a .Mac subscription, sites such as **www.icalx.com** and **www.icalworld.com** offer free hosting of iCal calendars along with many other iCal-related services.

Next, you'll subscribe to an iCal calendar to experience the other side of publishing.

10. Choose **Calendar > Subscribe**.

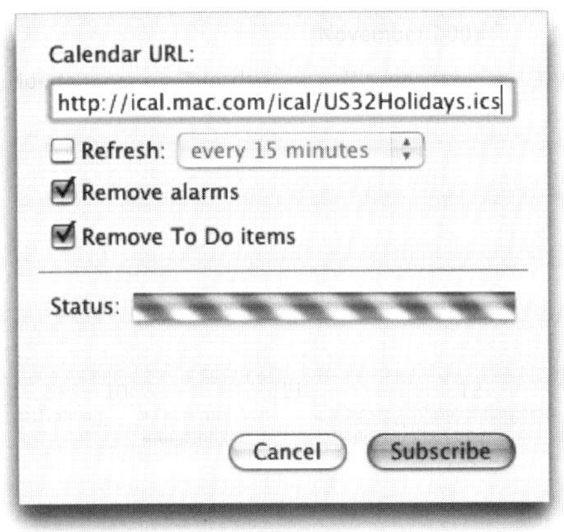

11. In the Calendar URL field, enter **http://ical.mac.com/ical/US32Holidays.ics** and make sure that **Remove alarms** and **Remove To Do items** are both checked. This will ensure that you won't get any alarm reminders from the calendar you're subscribing to. The **Refresh** check box allows you to specify how often you want iCal to automatically check for updates to this calendar. Keep this box unchecked for now. Click **Subscribe**.

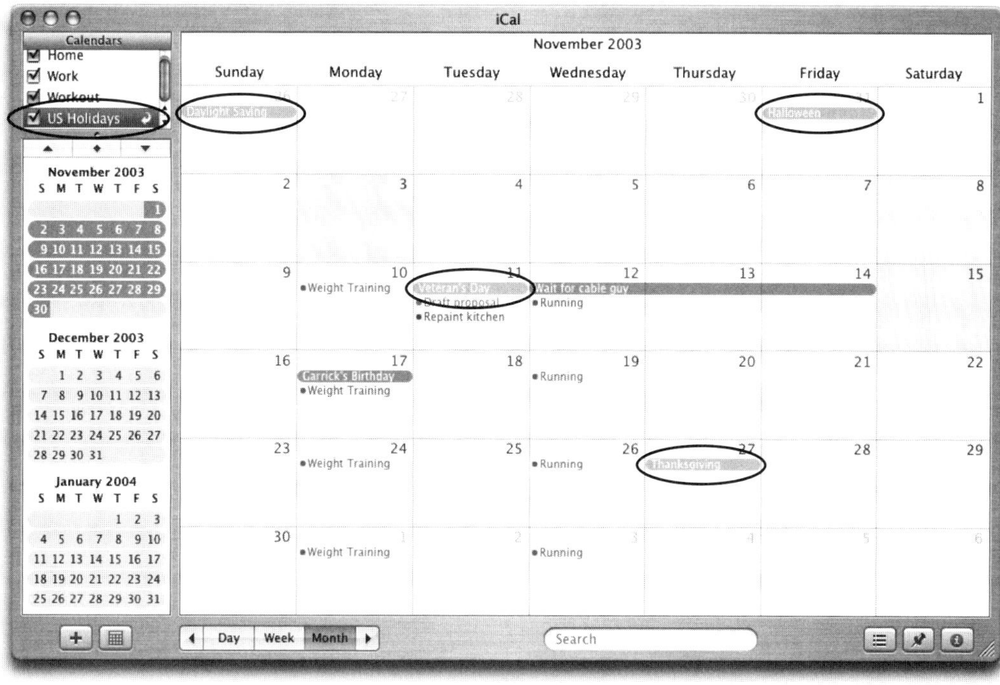

*You've just subscribed to a calendar called US Holidays. Once the calendar has been downloaded, the **US Holidays** appear alongside all your other calendars, and its events display in the main iCal pane.*

Tip: *This calendar, along with dozens of other useful calendars such as sports schedules, movie release dates, and SAT dates can be found and subscribed to directly from Apple's Web site at **www.apple.com/ical/library.** For a truly expansive collection of calendars, check out **www.icalshare.com**, where you can subscribe to nearly 1,000 different calendars (as well as publish your own). They even offer a Sherlock channel that you can download and install that allows you to search for calendars through Sherlock.*

*Calendars that you subscribe to are read-only, meaning they can't be changed. If you no longer need a calendar that you subscribed to, or any other calendar you might have created, for that matter, simply select it in the **Calendar** pane and press **Delete**.*

Searching Your Calendars

If you're one of those overscheduled social butterflies who has trouble finding specific events in your overflowing calendar, iCal's search bar makes it easy to locate the item you're looking for.

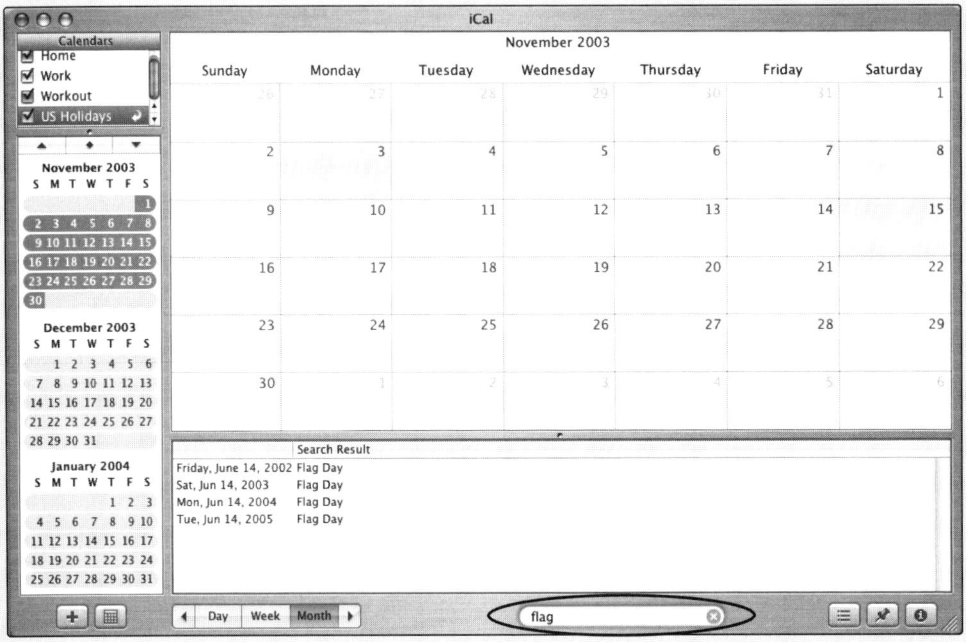

Simply type any word related to the event in the search bar, and the search pane will immediately open at the bottom of the window and display your search results. Click any result to view it in the main schedule pane.

12. Once you've finished viewing the US Holidays in your calendar, you can delete this menu, or keep it if you find it useful.

13. Quit iCal.

iSync

If you're a gadget junkie, chances are that you have two or three devices capable of storing calendar and contact information. Chances are also pretty good that up until now you've manually entered the same information into said devices (especially phones) because there hasn't been a good way to sync the information on all of your devices together. Until now. Apple has created iSync to help you manage contacts and schedules on all your digital devices.

Using iSync is pretty easy. Of course, in order to use it, you need something to sync with. iSync works by taking the data from Address Book and iCal and copying it to your iPod, Palm organizer, Bluetooth cell phone, or .Mac account. If you have only one Mac and no other electronic organizers, you don't need iSync at all. (You do, however, need a serious injection of geek DNA.)

Unless you own all the devices I just mentioned, you don't need to go through each of the following exercises. Just read the ones that apply to your own syncing needs.

3. Syncing with an iPod

The iPod, Apple's breakthrough portable music player, allows you to store your contacts and calendars as well as music. With the iPod's built-in software, you can view your addresses, phone numbers, and schedules directly on its screen. Many people have found that the iPod is all they need in the way of a personal digital device.

Unlike other types of devices you can sync with, syncing with an iPod is a one-way transaction; you can copy your latest contact and schedule updates from your Mac to your iPod, but since there's no way to edit this information on your iPod, there's no need to send info from your iPod to your Mac.

Note: iSync syncs your iPod with Address Book's contacts and iCal's calendars, but does not handle your music files. To sync your music collections, you'll use iTunes, covered in the next chapter.

1. Connect your **iPod** to your **Mac**. Locate **iSync** in your **Applications** folder and start it up. (When you connect your iPod to your Mac, iTunes may start up. You can leave iTunes running or quit it–it won't affect iSync either way.)

2. Click the **iPod** icon to view your sync options. (If your iPod doesn't show up in iSync, choose **Devices > Add Device** from the menu bar, and follow the instructions in the window that opens.)

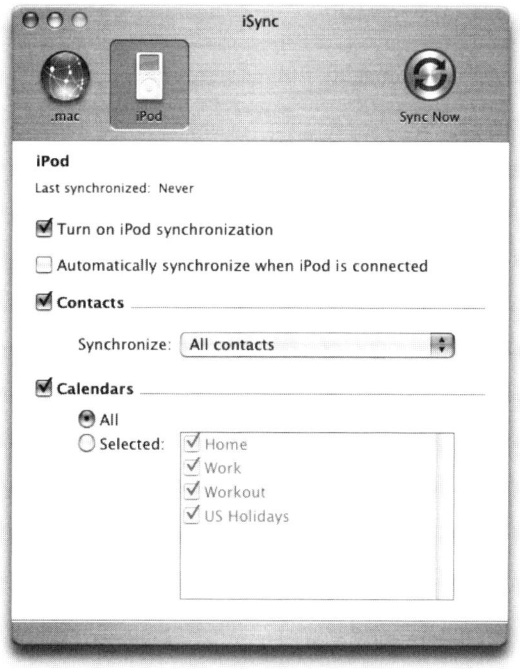

The following chart describes the options available here.

iPod Syncing Options	
Option	**Description**
Turn on iPod synchronization	Checked by default. With this option unchecked, your iPod won't be included when you sync your devices.
Automatically synchronize when iPod is connected	Syncs your iPod as soon as you connect it to your Mac.
Contacts	You can choose to move all your contact information from Address Book to your iPod, or pick specific groups (such as Work, Home, Friends, Family, and so on) from the **Synchronize** pop-up menu.
Calendars	Click **All** to copy all your iCal calendars to your iPod, or click **Selected** to copy only certain calendars.

3. Once you've made your selection, click **Sync Now**.

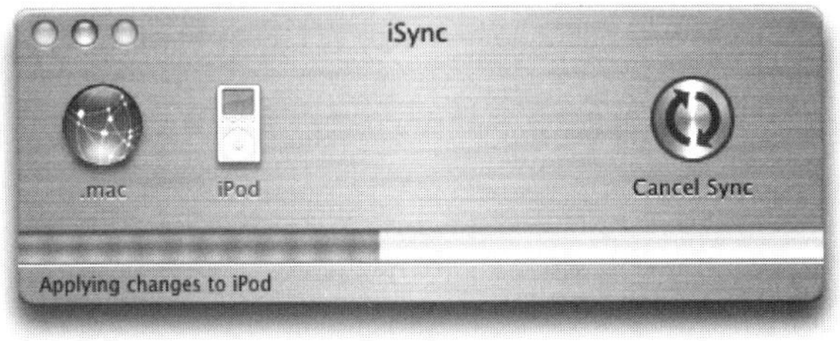

iSync begins copying the information from Address Book and iCal into your iPod. Depending on how many contacts and calendars you have, this may take a few minutes. Once iSync completes the transfer of information, you can quit and disconnect your iPod to browse your contacts and calendars.

TIP | Removing Synced Items from Your iPod

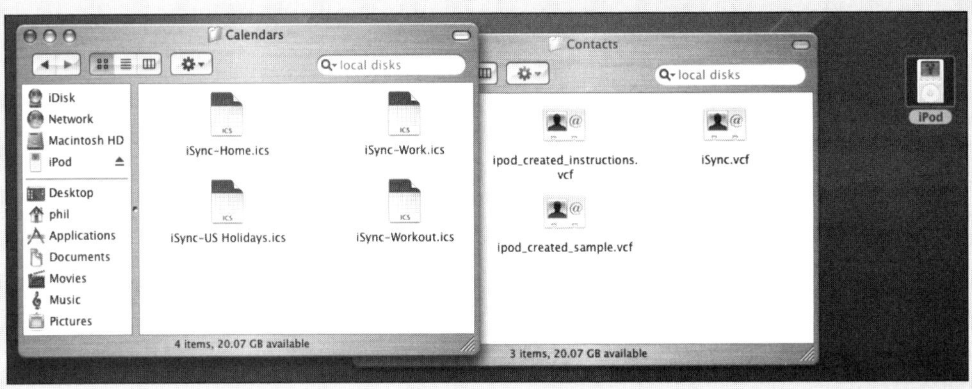

Items synced to your iPod are easy to remove manually. The contact and calendar information on your iPod is stored, appropriately, in the folders called **Contacts** and **Calendars**. To view these folders, connect your iPod and double-click its icon once it appears on the Desktop. Your iCal calendars appear in the **Calendars** folder and can be removed individually (**iSync-Home.ics**, **iSync-Work.ics**, and so on). Your contacts are all stored in a single file called **iSync.vcf**, which means that deleting this file deletes all your synced contacts from your iPod. If you want to delete only selected contacts, do so in Address Book and then resync your iPod. Incidentally, you can also delete the files **ipod_created_instructions.vcf** and **ipod_created_sample.vcf** to remove the instructions and sample contacts that came installed on your iPod.

4. Syncing with a Palm Device

If you have a Palm or Palm-compatible organizer, you may have already used Palm Desktop software to sync your Palm with your addresses, schedules, to do lists, and all the other features of your Palm device. But Palm Desktop doesn't sync the info from Apple Address Book or iCal to your Palm. If you'd like to move the contacts and calendars in Address Book and iCal to your Palm, you need to use iSync.

Syncing with a Palm organizer requires you to have Palm Desktop 4.0 or later and Hot Sync Manager 3.0 or later installed on your Mac. (Hot Sync 3.0 comes installed with Palm Desktop 4.0.) You can download the latest version from **www.palmone.com/support/macintosh/mac_desktop.html**. At the time of publication of this book, the most current version of Palm Desktop was 4.1. You'll also need to download and install the iSync Palm Conduit software from **www.apple.com/isync/download** before you can sync your Palm device with your Mac.

Once you've installed all the necessary software, you must set up Hot Sync Manager. Hot Sync actually does all the work; iSync simply serves as the interface for the syncing operation.

1. Open **Hot Sync Manager** (located in the **Palm** folder in your **Applications** folder).

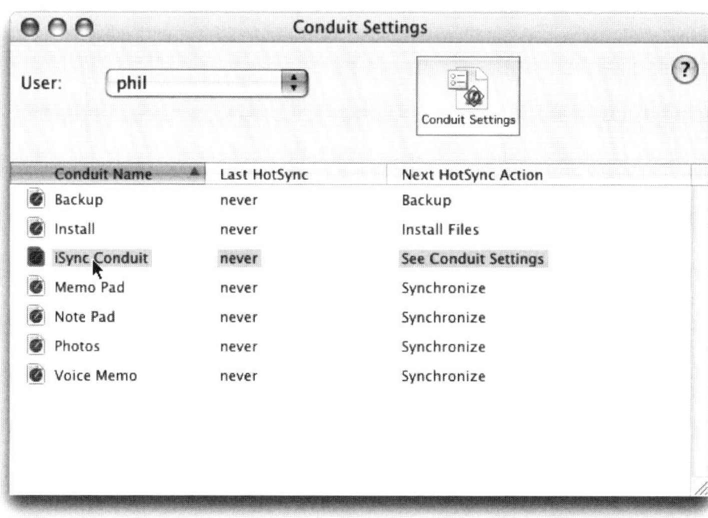

2. Select **Hot Sync > Conduit Settings** from the menu bar and then double-click **iSync Conduit**.

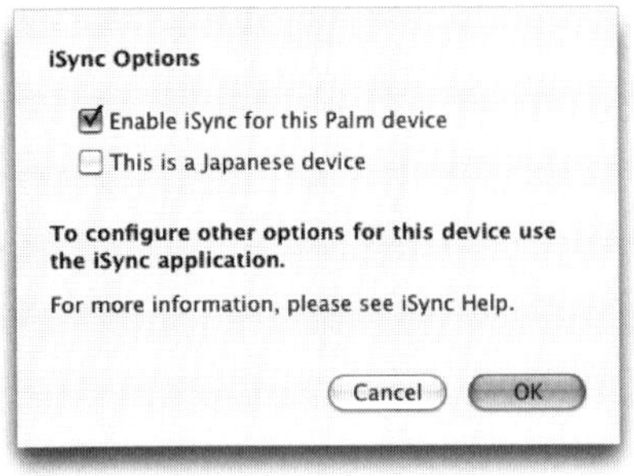

3. Choose **Enable iSync for this Palm device** and then click **OK**. (If your Palm device is localized for use with Japanese, check **This is a Japanese device** as well.)

4. Open iSync. A Palm icon (named "phil" in this example) should now appear there.

5. Click the Palm icon to view its synchronization options.

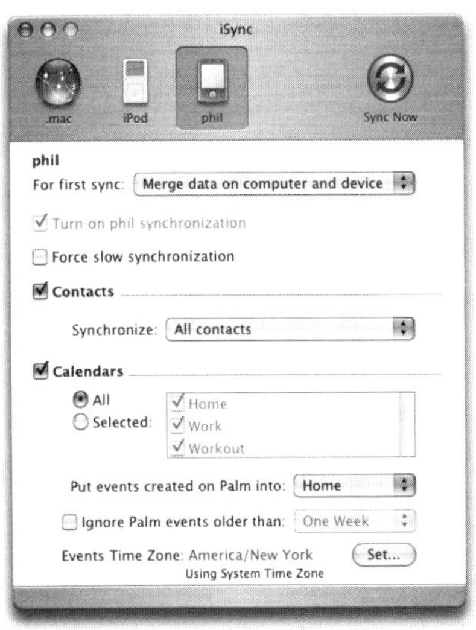

The Contacts and Calendars options are the same as the iPod options explained in Exercise 3. The following chart describes the options specific to Palm syncing.

Palm Syncing Options	
Option	**Description**
For first sync	This menu appears if this is the first time you've synced your Palm with your Mac. You can choose **Merge data on computer and device** to copy the newest information from either device to the other one, or **Erase data on device then sync** to delete the Address Book, Calendar, and To Do list from your Palm device and replace it with all the current info from your Mac.
Force slow synchronization	Check this option if you're having trouble syncing your Palm device with your Mac or if some of the data synced between the two doesn't match up. Slow synchronization forces iSync to analyze all the information on your Palm to make sure it's the most current.
Put events created on Palm into	If you've added an event to your Palm's calendar, you can choose to add these events to one of your iCal calendars (Home, Work, and so on). If your events fall into different calendars, just move them into one calendar and then open iCal, where you can **Ctrl+click** on individual events to change their calendar association.
Ignore Palm events older than	If you've had your Palm organizer for a while now, you might have events dating back several months or years. You can prevent these items from being copied into iCal by checking this option and then selecting a period of time from the pop-up menu.

6. Once you've made your Palm synchronization choices, you're ready to sync. Don't click **Sync Now**, which is for syncing all devices except your Palm. Sync your Palm by pressing the **Hot Sync** button on its cradle or by using the **Hot Sync** software.

Hot Sync will do its thing, and then iSync will start moving info back and forth between your Mac and Palm as well.

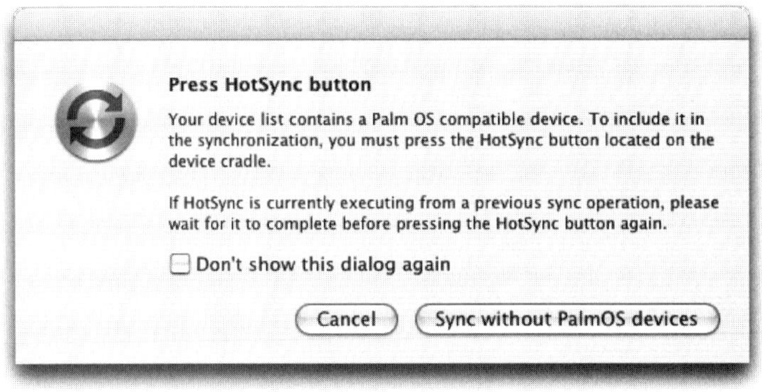

Note: *Don't worry: If you do click **Sync Now** by mistake, you won't mess anything up. You'll just see this message.*

Once the synchronization is complete, you can check your Palm for the updated information. From now on, anytime you press the Hot Sync button on your Palm's cradle, iSync will automatically start up and sync your device.

Note: *iSync synchronizes only your contacts, calendars, and to do lists. Your notes or memos on your Palm will continue to be synced with Palm Desktop. If you want to disable iSync and return to syncing exclusively with Palm Desktop, open **Hot Sync Manager**, choose **Hot Sync > Conduit Settings**, double-click **iSync Conduit**, and uncheck **Enable iSync for this Palm device.***

---

5. Syncing with a Bluetooth Phone

Bluetooth is a short-range wireless protocol designed to communicate between your computer and the various electronic devices you own. With a range of about 30 feet, it's not to be confused with Airport or Airport Extreme, which have much longer ranges, but Bluetooth is a great technology for clearing the cable clutter off your desk. The number of Bluetooth devices has been growing steadily over the past few years. Today you can purchase Bluetooth keyboards, mice, Palm devices, digital cameras, phones, and headsets.

This exercise shows you how to set up your Mac to recognize and sync with a Bluetooth phone that can store your contact and calendar information. Syncing with a Bluetooth-compatible phone (or any Bluetooth device) requires your Mac to have Bluetooth capability as well. If you purchased your Mac recently, you might have Bluetooth capability built-in. If not, you can purchase a Bluetooth USB adapter from **http://store.apple.com** (perform a search for "Bluetooth"). For a list of phones and other devices that work with iSync, check **www.apple.com/isync/devices.html**.

Once you have Bluetooth capability and a compatible phone, you need to set up the devices to recognize each other. This is known as "pairing," an authentication process that ensures that only your Mac and your phone can share with one another. (You wouldn't want to be using your phone in an airport and have someone download your information onto his or her computer.) The process of pairing will vary depending on the phone you're using, but the Mac side of things is pretty much the same. This exercise will show you how to get your phone and your Mac talking to one another.

1. If you're using a Bluetooth USB adaptor, plug it into a USB port on your Mac. If you have built-in Bluetooth, move onto Step 2. Unlike your Windows counterparts, you don't need to install the Bluetooth software that came with your adapter. OS X has all the necessary software built in.

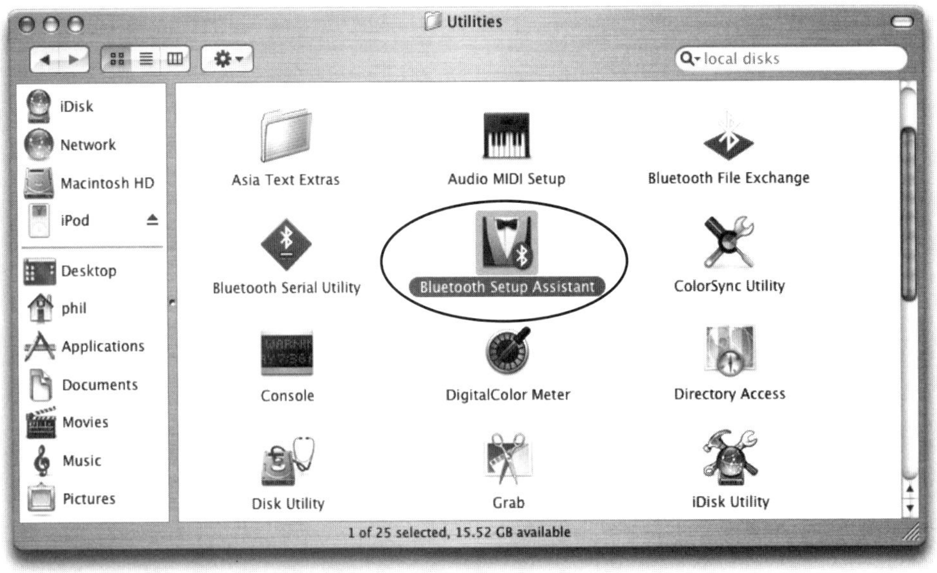

2. Open the **Utilities** folder located in your **Applications** folder. Locate and double-click the **Bluetooth Setup Assistant**. This utility walks you through the process of pairing your Mac with your Bluetooth devices.

3. The first window of the **Bluetooth Setup Assistant** confirms that your Mac has Bluetooth capabilities. (You won't see this window if you don't have the right hardware.) Click **Continue**.

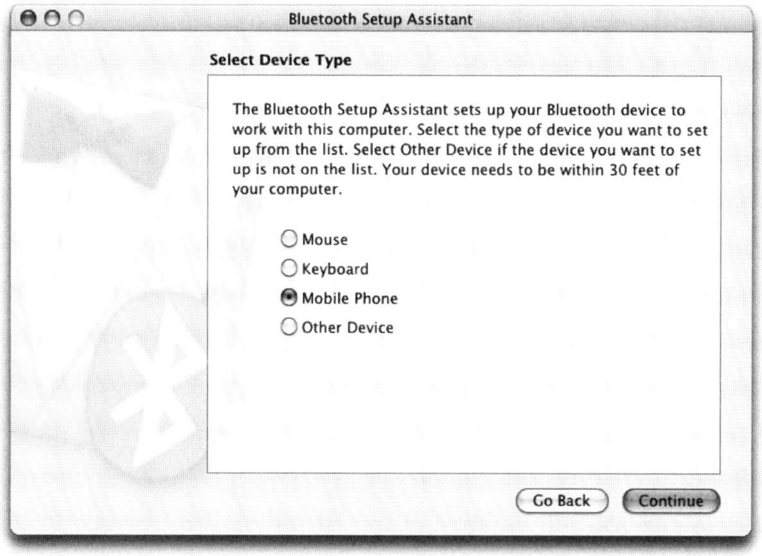

4. In the next window, select the type of device you want to set up. In this case, select **Mobile Phone**. Before clicking Continue, set your Bluetooth phone to "**Discoverable**" mode. Check your phone's user manual for instructions on how to do this. Click **Continue** when you're ready.

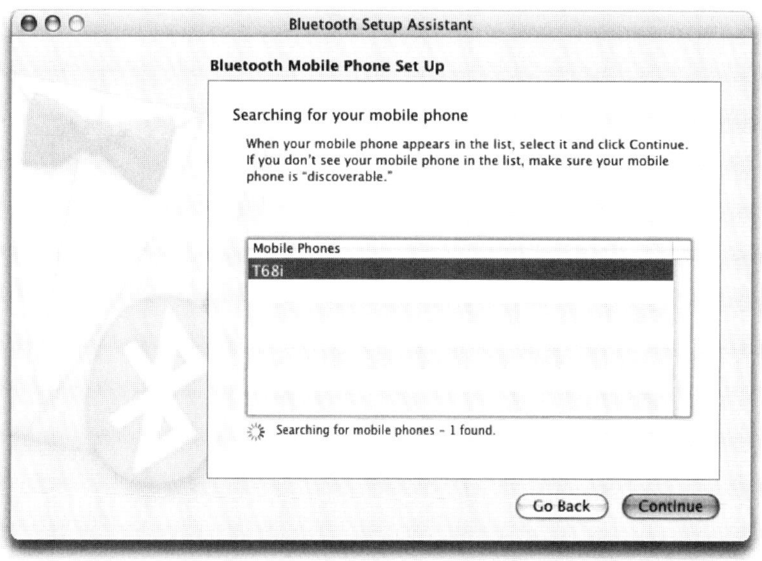

5. Your Mac scans for nearby mobile phones. Your phone should appear in the list. Make sure it's selected and click **Continue**.

6. Next, you'll be asked to enter a passkey to use with your phone. Type a numerical passkey (up to 16 digits) such as **1234**, but not so obvious, and click **Continue**.

7. Your phone will prompt you to enter this same passkey to validate this pairing. When prompted, enter the passkey on your phone.

8. If the pairing was successful, the next window appears, asking which services you'd like to use with this phone. Check **Set up iSync to transfer contacts and events** and click **Continue**. The last page of the **Bluetooth Setup Assistant** congratulates you on successfully setting up your Bluetooth features. Pat yourself on the back or head (your choice) and click **Quit**.

9. Open **iSync**.

10. Your phone's icon appears in iSync. If it doesn't, choose **Devices > Add Device**. Your phone should appear in the **Add Device** window. Double-click your phone to add it to iSync (or drag it to the iSync window).

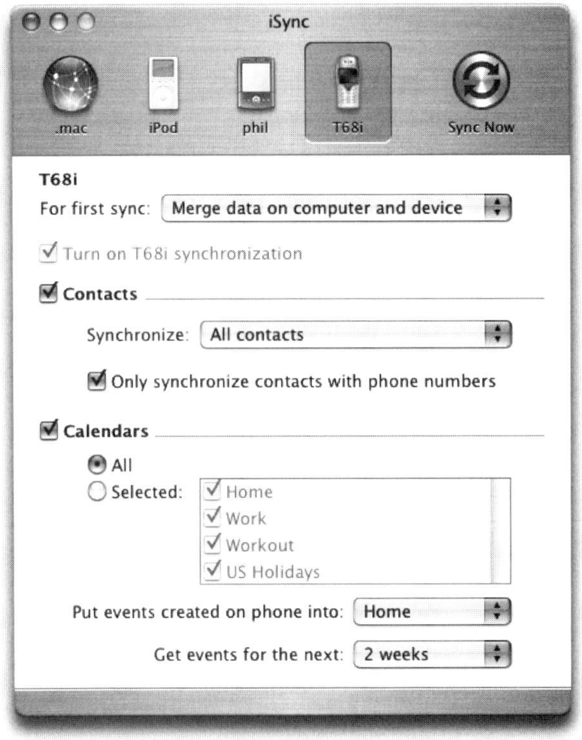

You can now sync your phone much like you can your iPod or Palm organizer. In fact, the options here are the same ones found in the Palm sync options. Refer to the chart in the preceding exercise for descriptions of these items.

Note: *The only two options unique to syncing your phone are* ***Only synchronize contacts with phone numbers****, which moves only the contacts that have actual numbers associated with them to your phone, and* ***Get events for the next****, which allows you to determine how much of your schedule you want to download to your phone. Your phone's memory might not be as large as your Palm's, and/or you may not want to store events that take place several weeks or months from now.*

---

11. Click **Sync Now** to transfer your information to your phone.

For more information on Bluetooth and its capabilities, choose ***Help > Mac Help*** *from the* ***Finder*** *menu bar and perform a search for "Bluetooth." You'll find instructions on how to dial your phone through Address Book and how to connect to the Internet through your phone for those times when you're stranded in an airport lounge and need to get on the Web or check your email.*

---

6. Syncing with .Mac

An important point to note about using iSync is that you shouldn't sync your iPod, Palm, or phone with more than one Mac. Doing so can confuse iSync and result in errors. I've known some users who have tried to use their Palms or phones as the middleman between two Macs to move information from one Mac to another. This just doesn't work very well.

In yet another attempt to convince you that .Mac is worth your money, Apple has made it possible to use .Mac to sync the contact and calendar information between two or more Macs. This can be useful for making sure you have the most up-to-date information on all your Macs.

1. To sync with .Mac, click the **.Mac** icon.

If this is your first time syncing with .Mac, you need to register your computer. Registering enables .Mac to distinguish your different Macs.

2. Click **Register**.

3. Give your Mac a name to identify it on the .Mac server, like **Office** or **Home**. Giving your Mac a unique name is necessary if you want to sync its information with another Mac. Click **Continue**.

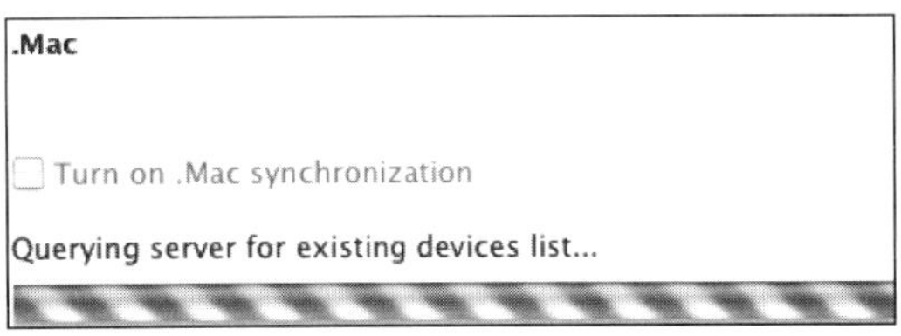

iSync will check to see if you have any other Macs synced to your .Mac account.

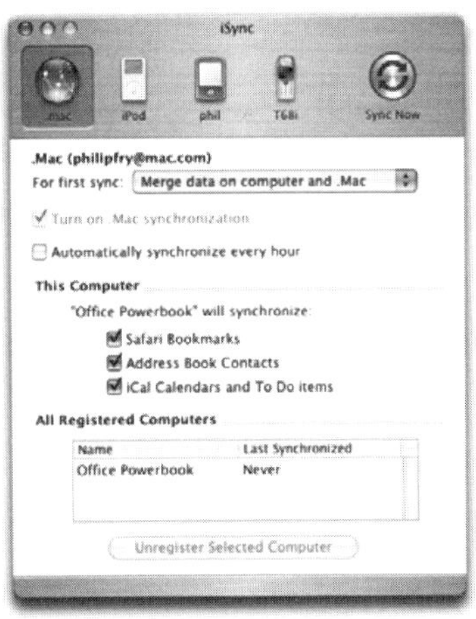

The following chart details the options available here.

.Mac Syncing Options	
Option	**Description**
For first sync:	This pop-up menu gives you three choices for your first sync: **Merge data on computer and .Mac**, **Erase data on .Mac then sync**, and **Erase data on computer then sync.** This menu will no longer appear after your first sync.
Turn on .Mac synchronization	Checking this option includes .Mac syncing when you click **Sync Now.**
Automatically synchronize every hour	Check this option and your Mac will connect to the Internet every hour and synchronize your contacts and calendars with .Mac. This is a very useful option if you have two or more Macs with this option turned on—you can ensure that each Mac always has the most up-to-date info.
This Computer	Under this section, you can choose to synchronize your Safari Bookmarks, Address Book contacts, and iCal calendars and To Do items.
All Registered Computers	This area lists any other computers you have registered under this .Mac account. Click a computer and then click the **Unregister Selected Computer** button to remove it from this list.

4. If this is the first computer you're syncing to .Mac, select an option from the **For first sync** pop-up menu and then click **Sync Now**. iSync will send your Address Book and iCal info to your .Mac account.

*Once you've synced one computer to .Mac, you can then open iSync on a second Mac and register it to your .Mac account. Click **Sync Now** and both your Macs will be in sync with each other.*

---

5. Quit iSync when you're done with syncing.

.Mac Bookmarks

Once you've synced your Safari bookmarks to your .Mac account with iSync, you'll be able to access your bookmarks from any computer with an Internet connection. Just go to **http://bookmarks.mac.com**.

The first time you visit this page, you'll be asked if you want to turn on bookmark syncing. Click **Sync Now**. It will take a few moments for .Mac to sync your bookmarks.

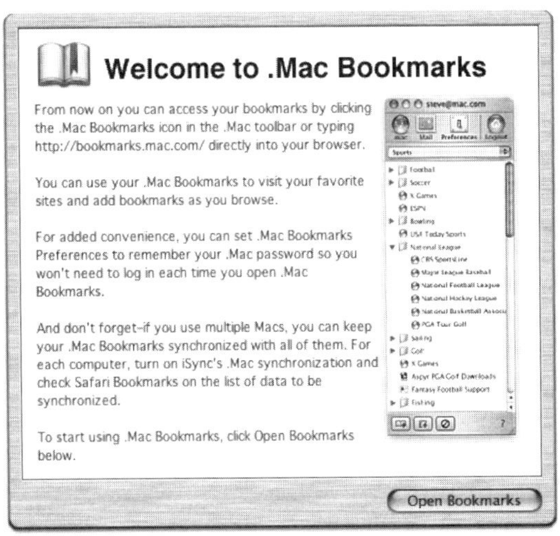

Once the syncing completes, return to **bookmarks.mac.com** and click **Open Bookmarks**.

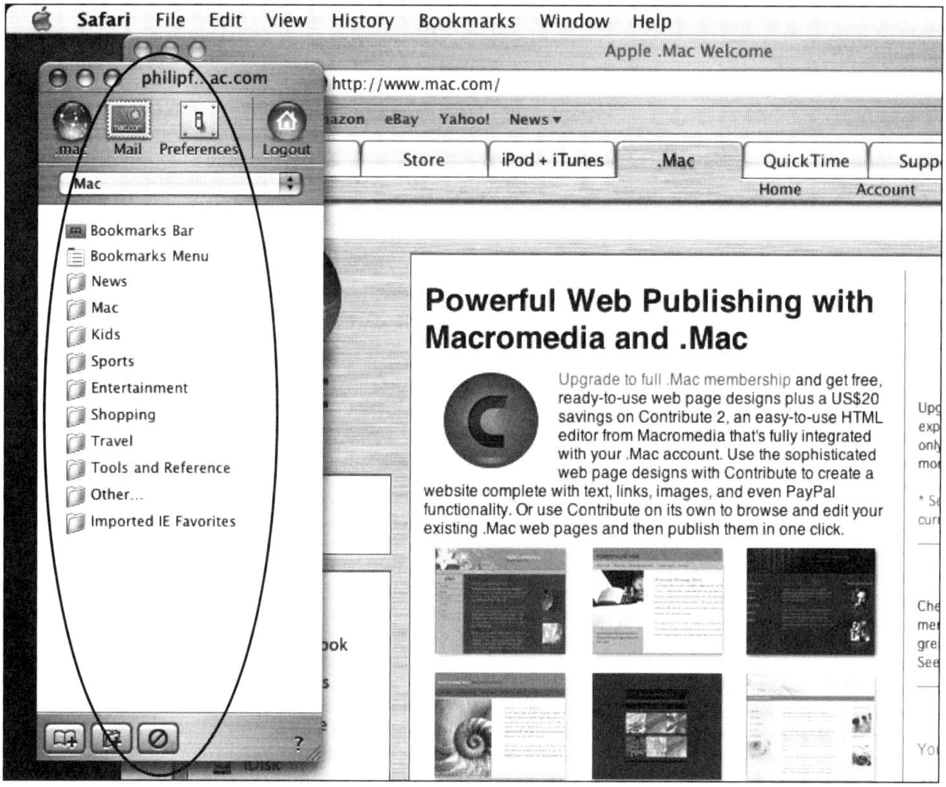

This opens a narrow browser window containing all your Safari bookmarks, including the ones in your Bookmarks bar and Bookmarks menu. Click any bookmark to open that page in a new window. Synched bookmarks can be a real blessing when you're on the road and trying to remember the name of that one site that has the information you need.

7. Syncing with Your .Mac Address Book

Once you've synced your Mac with your .Mac account, you have the additional ability to sync your Address Book with your .Mac Address Book. (Even though you already synced your Address Book with .Mac, your online Address Book is not changed unless you intentionally sync it.) You need to have synced with .Mac at least once before you can do this.

1. Log onto your .Mac account and click the **Address Book** icon. Verify your password if prompted.

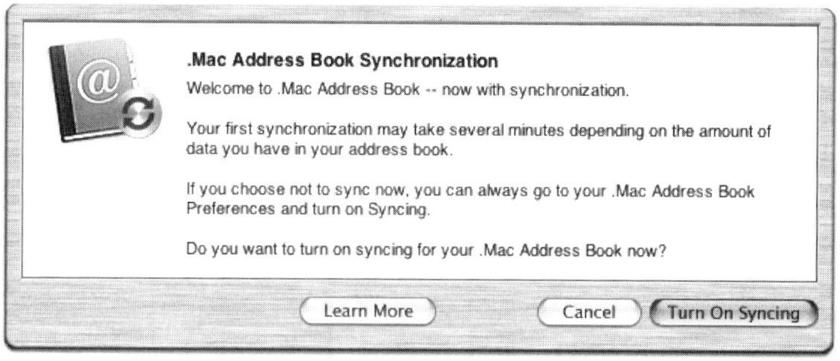

2. If you see this **.Mac Address Book Synchronization** window, click **Turn On Syncing**.

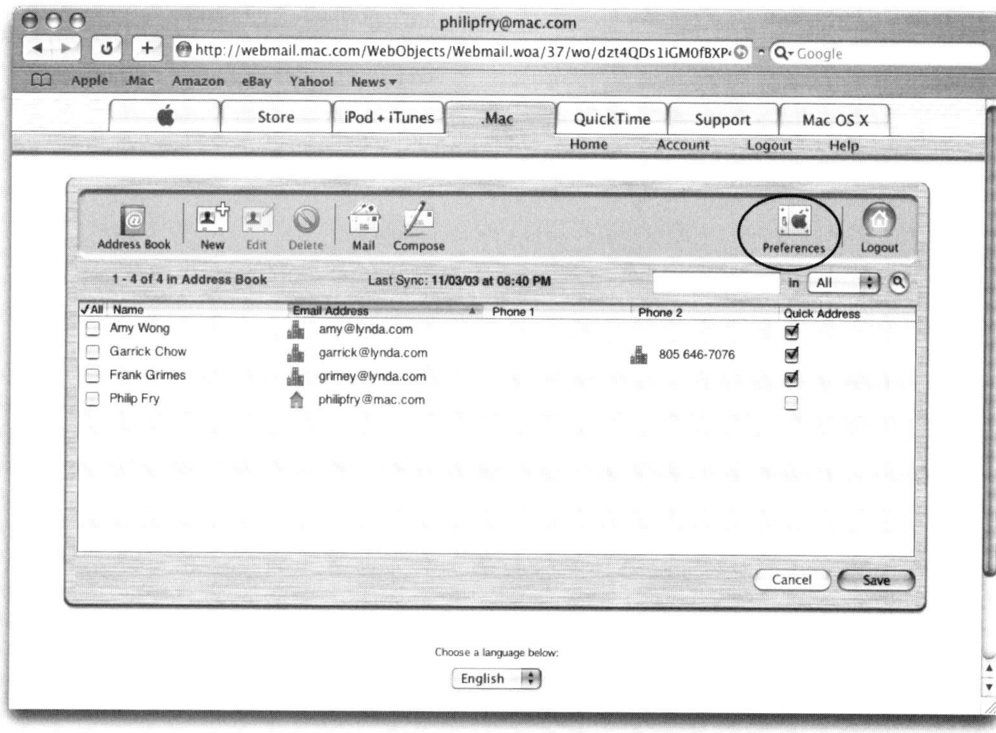

3. If you didn't see the **.Mac Address Book Synchronization** window, click the **Preferences** button.

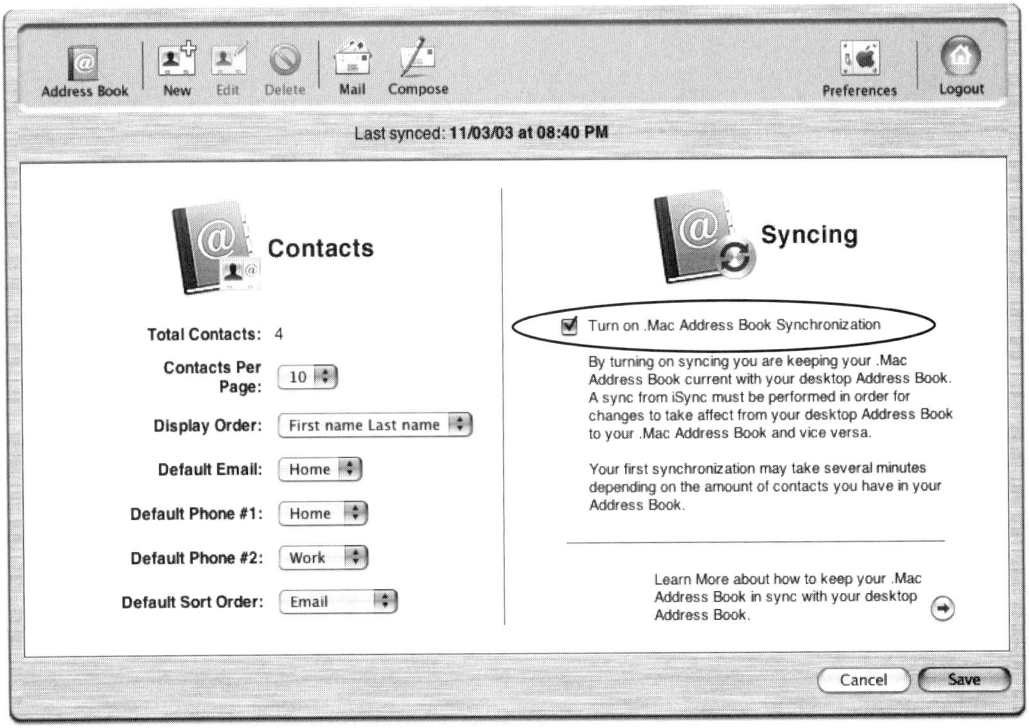

4. Under **Syncing**, check **Turn on .Mac Address Book Synchronization**. Click **Save**.

Your Address Book items will be synced with your .Mac Address Book and will now be accessible to you from any computer that can connect to .Mac. As long as .Mac Address Book Synchronization is turned on in your preferences, your online Address Book will be updated every time you sync your computer with .Mac via iSync. This is especially convenient for those times when you're away from your Mac but need to send an email from your .Mac account. Just log onto .Mac from any computer with an Internet connection. Your entire Address Book will be available to you online.

As you can see, iSync makes it easy to share Address Book and iCal information between your Macs and your digital devices. In the next chapter, you'll continue learning about your Mac's "i" applications with a look at iTunes.

14.
iTunes 4

| Ripping an Audio CD | Importing MP3s |
| Playing Your Music | Playlists | Burning CDs |
| The iTunes Music Store |

chap_14

Mac OS X Panther
H•O•T CD-ROM

iTunes, the first application from the **iLife** suite that you'll examine, makes your Mac a powerful audio control center. With this one free application, you can play and burn audio CDs, copy them to your hard drive, play Internet radio, and store and manage hundreds, if not thousands, of songs.

iTunes is the perfect place to start when learning about iLife: not only is it an incredible program when used on its own, but you can also use the music you've saved in iTunes to enhance projects in iPhoto, iMovie, and iDVD. In this chapter, you'll learn to use the functions of iTunes as a stand-alone application. Later, you'll see how well iTunes integrates into the other iLife applications.

I. Ripping an Audio CD

Don't you love the terminology associated with transferring files from CD to hard drive? It's not enough to copy a file from a CD–you have to **rip** it! And you don't write CD-ROMs–you **burn** them! In this exercise, you'll learn how to rip songs from an audio CD to your hard drive with iTunes. Along the way, you'll be introduced to several interface elements of iTunes. This exercise requires you to have at least two or three music CDs to copy. (Of course, you should own the CDs you intend to copy.)

iTunes 4 is included with Mac OS X. If you don't have it for some reason, you can download it from **www.apple.com/itunes**. Make sure you're using iTunes 4 (not an earlier version) before continuing.

1. Start **iTunes** by clicking its icon in the **Dock** or by opening it from your **Applications** folder.

*If this is the first time you've run iTunes, you'll see a **Software License Agreement** window. Click **Accept** to move on.*

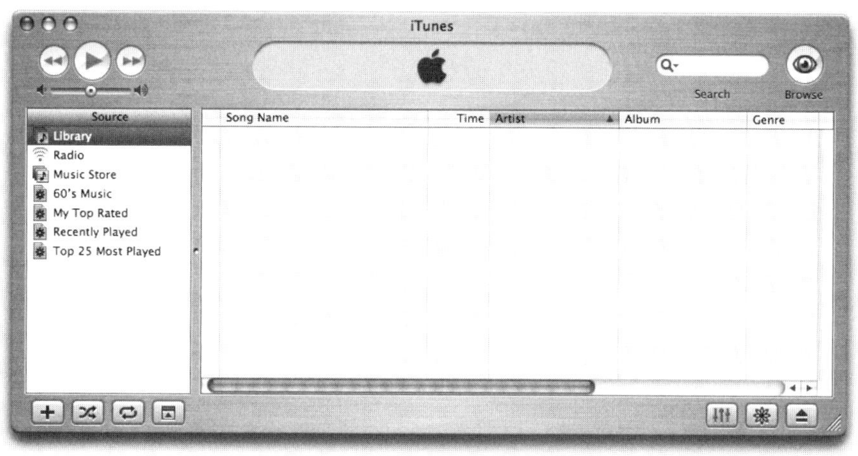

Depending on whether you bought a new Mac with iTunes pre-installed or if you installed iTunes on an older Mac, you may or may not see any songs listed in the iTunes window. Some Macs come with a few dozen songs pre-installed. If you don't have any music listed here, no matter; you'll have some songs on your Mac soon enough. First, you'll set up some preferences to make sure iTunes behaves the way it should.

2. Choose **iTunes > Preferences**, or press **Cmd+,** (**Cmd+comma**).

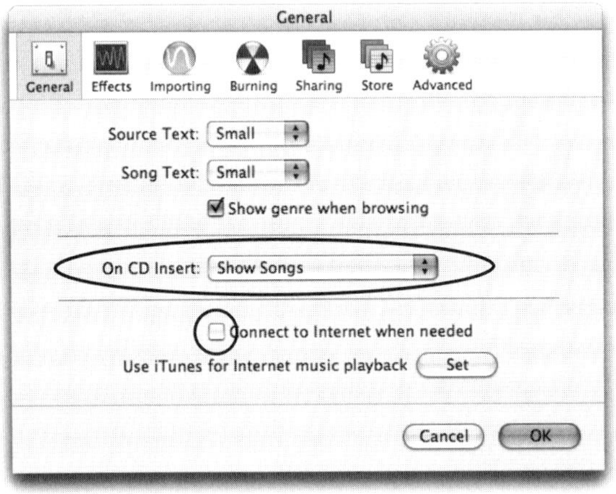

3. Click the **General** button and make sure **Show Songs** is selected in the **On CD Insert** pop-up menu. This selection ensures that iTunes won't start playing the CD right away or start copying the songs to your hard drive. Uncheck **Connect to Internet when needed**. This is an option you'll probably want to keep checked in the future, but for this exercise, you'll leave it unchecked. Click **OK**.

Note: *For complete descriptions of all of iTunes' preferences, see the charts at the end of the chapter.*

4. Pick a music CD from your collection and insert it into your Mac's CD or DVD drive.

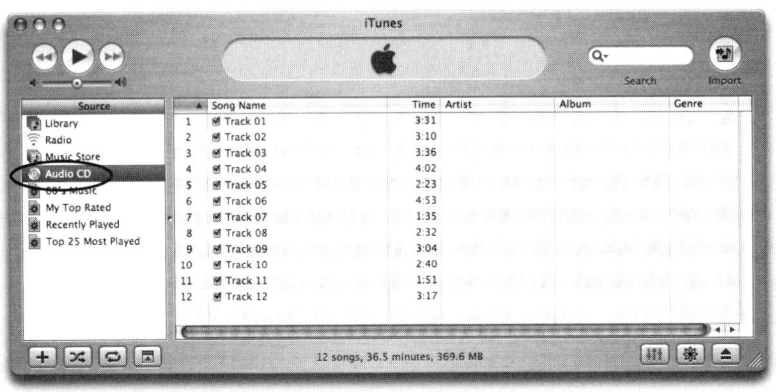

As your Mac automatically reads the CD, tracks will appear in the iTunes window, and ***Audio CD*** *will appear in the* ***Source*** *pane. From here, you can see the number of tracks on the album and the length of each. This is all well and good if this is your favorite CD and you've memorized the order and title of the songs. But wouldn't it be better to actually see the titles of the songs? Thanks to the wonder of the Internet, you can display the song titles quickly and easily. But first, you'll enter one track's details manually just so you'll know how to do it in case an Internet connection isn't available (and so you'll appreciate the Internet method all the more).*

Note: Normally, iTunes immediately connects to the Internet to download the CD's information, but you turned off that option when you unchecked ***Connect to Internet when needed*** *in Step 3. Be sure to turn this option back on when you're done with this chapter.*

5. Ctrl+click Track 1 and select **Get Info** from the contextual menu. This opens the **Song Information** window.

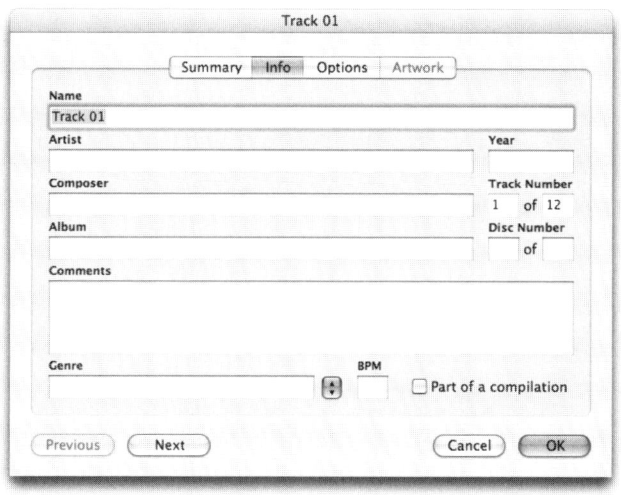

6. Click the **Info** button at the top of this window. Type the name of the song at the top of the window (where **Track 01** is highlighted). Using the CD case as a guide, enter the **Artist**, **Year**, and **Album** information. (You can press the **Tab** key to move from field to field. Just don't press **Return** or you'll close the window.) If this is a piece of classical music, you can enter the **Composer** information as well. Click **OK** when you're done.

The track information now appears in the iTunes window. You could take the time to manually enter the information for each track, but it's much easier to take advantage of the **Gracenote CDDB** *(CD Database), an online directory containing information on more than 2.1 million CDs. Chances are good that if you have a nationally released CD (or even a regionally released CD by your favorite local band), the CDDB will have the information for that CD. Next you'll check to see if the track info for your CD appears in the CDDB.*

7. Choose **Advanced > Get CD Track Names** from the menu bar.

Your Mac will automatically connect to the Internet (if you've set this up in advance per the instructions in Chapter 8, "Getting Online"), and after a few moments, all the song titles will appear in the iTunes window. Not only that, but the Audio CD icon on your Desktop will change to reflect the album's title.

If the tracks for your CD weren't found in the CDDB, see the sidebar, "My Songs Weren't Found!" at the end of this exercise.

Note: *Although you don't have to have all the track information in place before you rip a CD, if you omit the track names, you'll end up with iTunes listings that are identified as Track 01, Track 02, and so on. It's worth checking with the CDDB to add song titles to tracks. Once a CD has been identified by iTunes, your Mac will always remember it. From now on, anytime you insert this CD into your drive, the album title will appear along with the CD icon on the Desktop, and the track details will appear in iTunes.*

You're almost ready to copy the songs to your hard drive. Before you do so, you need to make some decisions about what kind of quality you want for the copies of the songs.

*When you copy music from CDs, the default action of iTunes is to convert the tracks to AACs. AAC stands for **A**dvanced **A**udio **C**oding, a new form of audio compression that can produce CD-quality sound while keeping file sizes smaller than the older MP3 format. Because of their tiny size, you can keep an incredibly large collection of AACs (or less efficiently compressed MP3s) on your Mac. Once you take the time to copy your CDs to your Mac, you might find that you rarely pull the actual discs out again; you can just use iTunes as the jukebox for all the music you own.*

The main factor determining the file size of AACs and MP3s is the bit rate. The higher the bit rate, the better the sound quality. But a higher bit rate also means a larger file size.

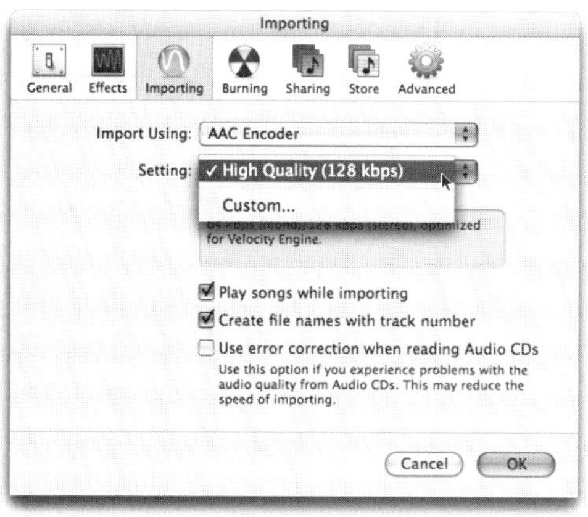

8. Choose **iTunes > Preferences** and then click the **Importing** button at the top of the window.

*The **Setting** pop-up menu gives you two choices for your AAC bit rate. The default setting is **High Quality (128 kbps)**. This means that every second of an AAC that's been encoded at this rate will be 128 kilobytes in size. A three-minute song would be approximately 23,040K or 2.3 MB. The bit rate you choose really depends on your own opinion on sound quality versus file size. **High Quality** (128 kbps) is considered to be acceptable by many people, but you can select **Custom** if after listening to the song file you're pretty sure that you can hear the difference between a CD and a 128 kbps AAC. (You're probably one of those people who can hear the difference between regular and gold audio connectors, too.) After choosing **Custom**, you can bump up the bit rate to 360 kbps, but keep in mind that the file size will increase.*

9. For this exercise, keep the configuration set to **High Quality**. You can always go back and change these settings later. Also make sure **AAC Encoder** is selected in the **Import Using** pop-up menu and that **Play songs while importing** and **Create file names with track number** are both checked. Click **OK**.

Now you're ready to rip.

10. Make sure the CD is still selected in the **Source** column and then click the **Import** button.

Tip: *If you don't want to convert all the songs on a CD to AACs, clear the check box of tracks you don't want converted. The check box is a toggle. If it has a checkmark, clicking it will clear it; if it is empty, clicking it will display the checkmark. Pressing* ***Cmd*** *before clicking any check box turns all the check boxes in the current list on or off.*

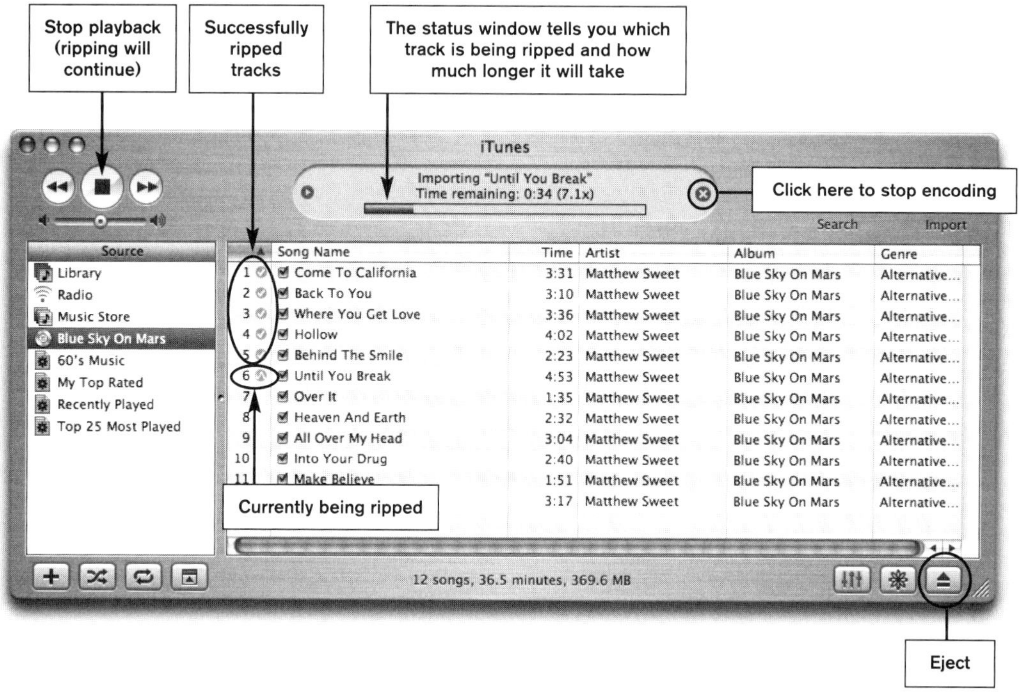

*iTunes begins to convert the CD tracks into AACs. After enough of Track 1 has been encoded, it will start to play (because you checked **Play songs while importing** in the Importing preferences). What you're hearing is the AAC itself, so if you have a decent set of speakers hooked up to your Mac, you can get a pretty good idea of the sound quality of the tracks. You can click the **Stop** button if you don't want to listen to the tracks while you're ripping them.*

---

11. Once all the songs are ripped, eject the CD by clicking the **Eject** button in the lower-right corner of the iTunes window.

The songs you just copied are now stored in your iTunes ***Library****. The Library is where you'll find the listings of every single track that has been imported into iTunes. Later, you'll learn how to create playlists to manage collections of tracks, but for now, just remember that you'll always be able to find any song you've ever imported into iTunes in your Library.*

12. Before you move on to learn more about iTunes' features, take the time to rip two or three more CDs by some different artists. Remember to check the CDDB for track listings and info. When you're done, keep iTunes open for the next exercise.

Tip: *You can choose* ***iTunes > Preferences*** *and check* ***Connect to Internet when needed*** *under the* ***General*** *tab to have iTunes automatically retrieve the CDDB info for you when you insert a CD.*

Where Exactly Is My Music Being Saved?

Unless you've changed your preferences, music you import into iTunes is saved into the **Music** folder in your **Home** folder.

Click the **Advanced** button in iTunes Preferences to see that the location of your music is **Home > Music > iTunes > iTunes Music**. The option **Keep iTunes Music folder organized** ensures that the music you copy will be copied into appropriately created folders.

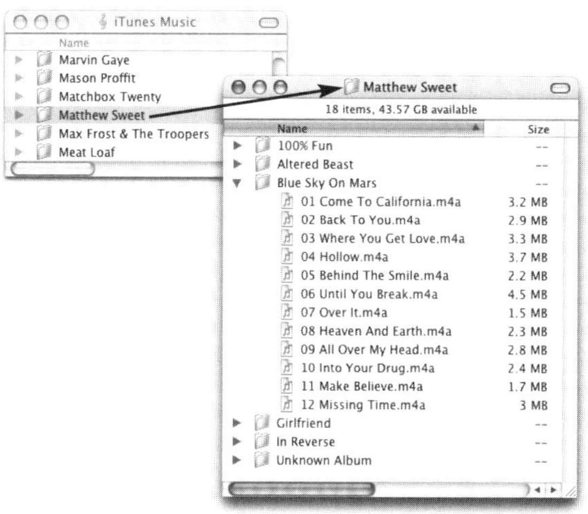

With **Keep iTunes Music folder organized** checked, music is organized by artist and album, making it easy to find specific AAC and MP3 files from the Finder. Without this option checked, music is just tossed into your iTunes folder. Although this makes no difference to iTunes, it makes it considerably more difficult for you to locate songs by looking in your iTunes Music folder. This is another good reason to name your tracks with the CDDB–CDs without track names or titles are stored in folders called **Unknown Artist** and **Unknown Album**.

TIP | Forgot to Check the CDDB Before Ripping?

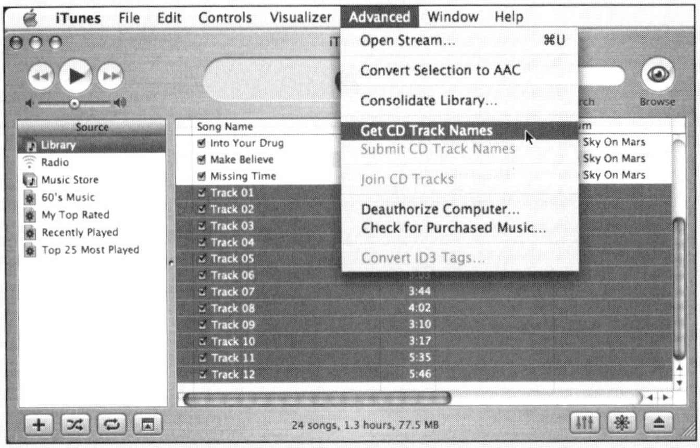

If you forget to enter the track information before ripping the CD, you can still select the songs in your Library and choose **Advanced > Get CD Track Names**, even if the CD isn't in the drive. iTunes will update the listings of these songs in the Library, and create newly-titled folders to keep these tracks properly organized by artist and album. (In Exercise 2, you'll see how iTunes automatically renames folders when you change or add song information.)

My Songs Weren't Found!

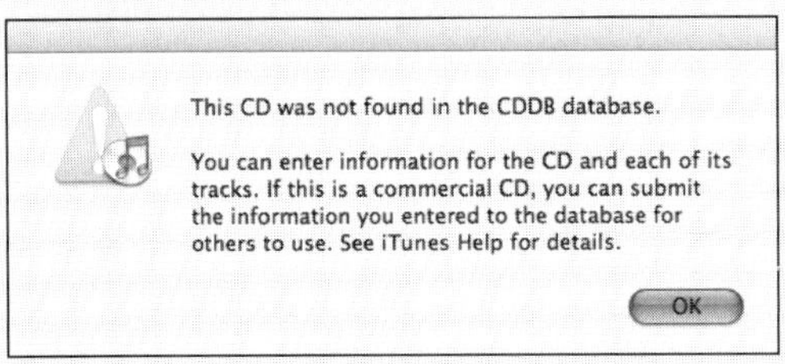

If iTunes can't find a CD's information on the CDDB, you're obviously listening to some too-cool-for-school music there, buddy. You'll have to enter the track information manually, but there is a trick to making this process a little easier on you.

Click a track to select it and then press **Cmd+A** to select all the tracks. **Ctrl+click** any track and choose **Get Info** from the contextual menu.

continues on next page

My Songs Weren't Found! *continued*

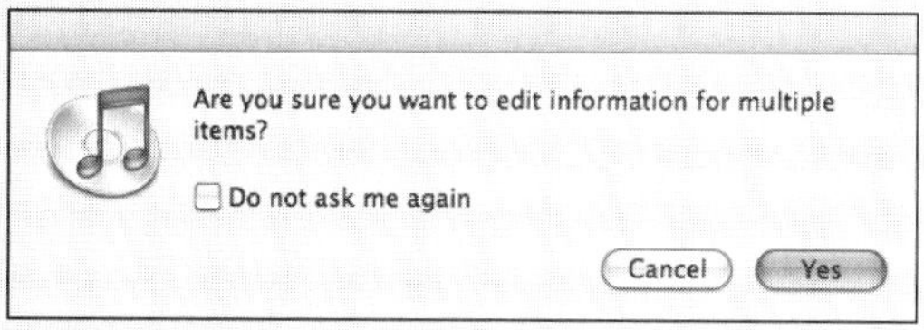

You'll be asked if you're sure you want to edit the information for multiple items. Click **Yes**. (You can check **Do not ask me again** if you want.)

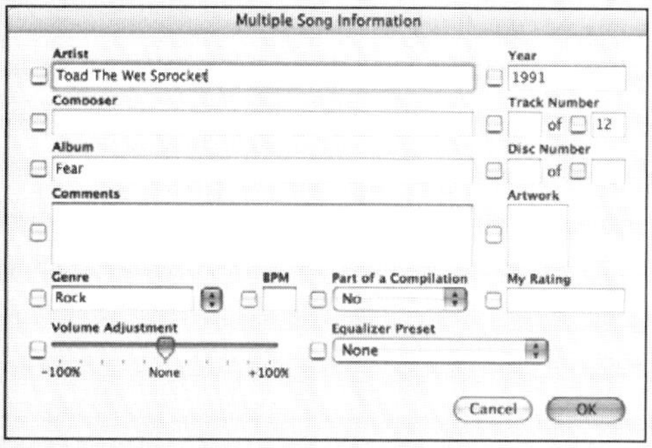

This window allows you to enter global information for all the selected tracks. The only thing you can't enter here is the individual track names. You'll still have to enter each track name one at a time, but you can save yourself a lot of work by entering as much information here as possible.

Once you're done, the information you entered will be listed with each track. You can now **Ctrl+click** each track to enter the song titles. If you're feeling generous, you can choose **Advanced > Submit CD Track Names** from the menu bar to submit your track info to the CDDB so other people with this album can benefit from your hard work.

2. Importing MP3s

There will occasionally be times when you'll come across an MP3, on a Web site for example, that you'll want to play in iTunes. In the previous exercise, you saw how easy it is to convert an audio CD to MP3s. This exercise shows you how to take existing MP3s and move them into iTunes.

*Special thanks to Cliff Hillis (**www.cliffhillis.com**), ike (**www.ikeonline.net**), and The Jellybricks (**www.thejellybricks.com**) for contributing music for this exercise.*

---

1. Copy the **chap_14** folder from the **H•O•T CD-ROM** to your **Desktop**. This folder contains some MP3s that you'll import into iTunes.

2. Choose **iTunes > Preferences** from the menu bar and click the **Advanced** button. Make sure **Keep iTunes Music folder organized** and **Copy files to iTunes Music folder when adding to library** are both checked. These two options ensure that songs you import into iTunes will be copied and properly placed into existing folders (if the artist already has a folder on your system) or into a new folder if you don't yet have any songs by that particular artist. Click **OK**. You'll watch iTunes create some folders in the following steps.

---

3. From the **Finder** menu bar, choose **Go > Home** to open your **Home** folder. From there, open **Music**, **iTunes**, and **iTunes Music**, in that order.

You should now be looking at the folders for the artists you imported into iTunes in the previous exercise. Although it might seem logical that you should be able to drag music files into the iTunes Music folder, iTunes won't recognize them if you do. To play music in iTunes, you must import the music directly into iTunes itself.

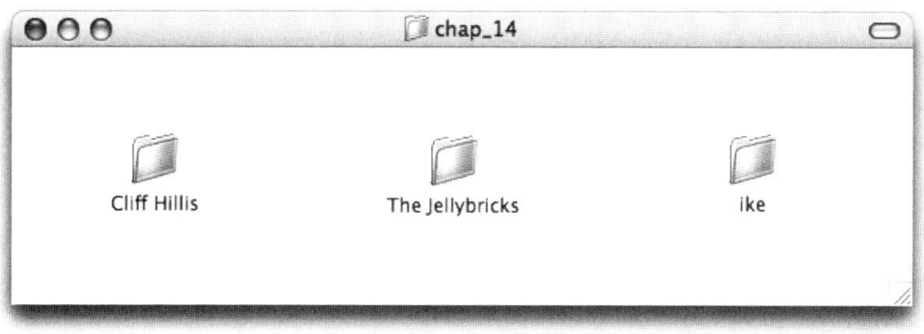

4. Keep the **iTunes Music** window open (with your **Library** selected) and double-click the **chap_14** folder on your **Desktop**. This folder contains three additional folders, each containing MP3s of songs by each band. You'll import these songs into iTunes now.

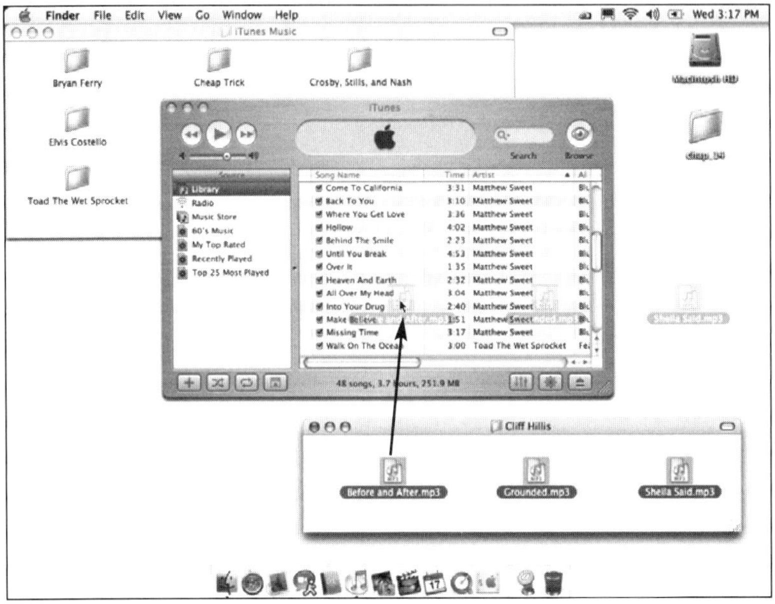

5. Double-click the folder labeled **Cliff Hillis**. Position this window so that you can see the iTunes window behind it. Drag a marquee selection around the three songs in the **Cliff Hillis** folder and drag them into the song list pane of the iTunes window.

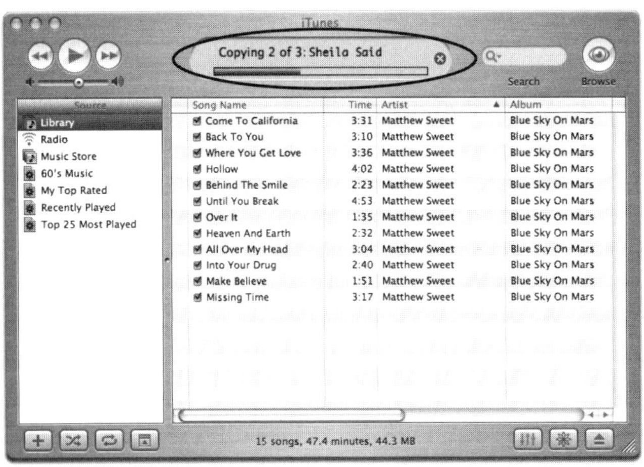

The songs are copied into iTunes. Note that the songs are copied, not moved. This means that once you import MP3 or AAC files into iTunes, you can discard the original if you want to save space (if your preferences are set to copy songs into iTunes, as mentioned in Step 2 of this exercise). Before you delete files, however, it's always a good idea to make sure that they were copied correctly.

6. Keep iTunes open and bring the **iTunes Music** folder in the **Finder** back to the front (the one you opened in Step 2). It should now contain a folder called **Cliff Hillis**. Switch to **List** view so you can see the contents of this folder without double-clicking it. Toggle the triangle next to the **Cliff Hillis** folder to find another folder called **Be Seeing You**, which is the name of the album all three of the songs came from. iTunes automatically generated these folders to keep the songs organized.

iTunes is able to create folders because most AACs and MP3s are created with ID "tags" that contain information about the artist, album, song, and so on. You saw how to enter this information in the "My Songs Weren't Found" sidebar in the previous exercise. Occasionally, though, you may encounter MP3s that were created without ID tags. In those instances, iTunes won't be able to create properly named folders. The next few steps will show you how to correct improperly tagged AACs and MP3s.

---

7. Keep the **iTunes Music** window open and bring the **Cliff Hillis** window back to the front. Click the **Back** button to return to the **chap_14** folder. (If you accidentally closed this window, just double-click the **chap_14** icon on your **Desktop**.) Double-click the **ike** folder.

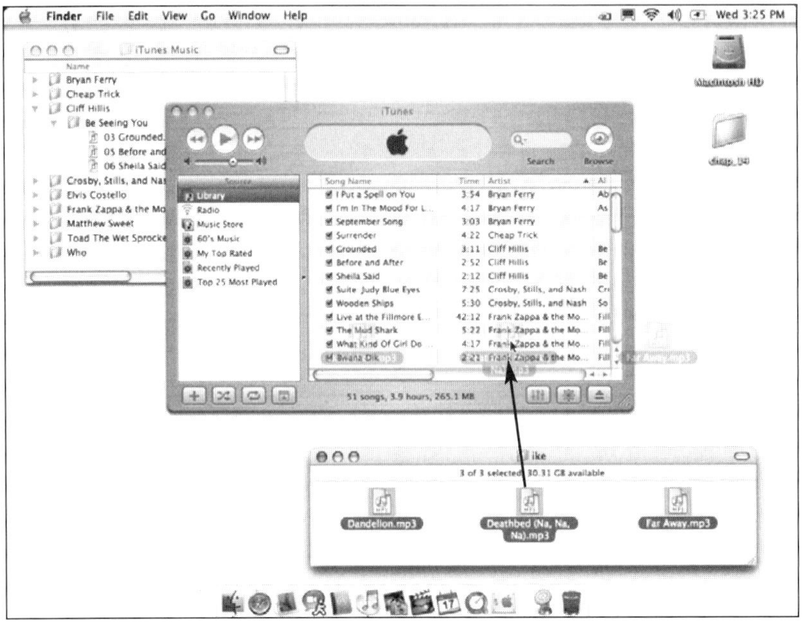

8. Select the three MP3s in **ike** and drag them into the iTunes song list pane. Although they will be copied into iTunes, these particular MP3s don't include the tags that identify the artist or album they came from.

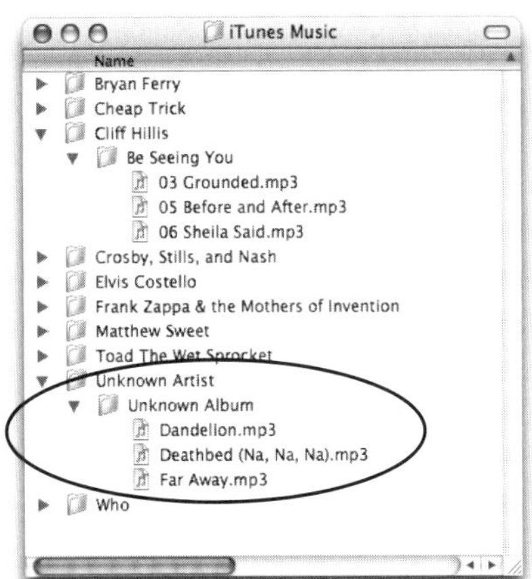

9. After the copying is complete, click the **iTunes Music** window to bring it to the front. Notice that a folder called **Unknown Artist** has been created. Toggle this folder open to observe the **Unknown Album** folder inside. In here, you'll find the copies of the three songs you just imported. iTunes automatically creates these folders to store songs without ID tags.

10. Bring iTunes back to the front and scroll down to the bottom of the song list, where you'll find the three songs you imported. Notice how all three are missing the **Artist** and **Album** information. You'll add this information now.

11. Hold **Shift** and click all three songs one at a time to select them. **Ctrl+click** your selection and choose **Get Info** from the contextual menu. Click **Yes** if a dialog box opens asking whether you want to edit multiple items.

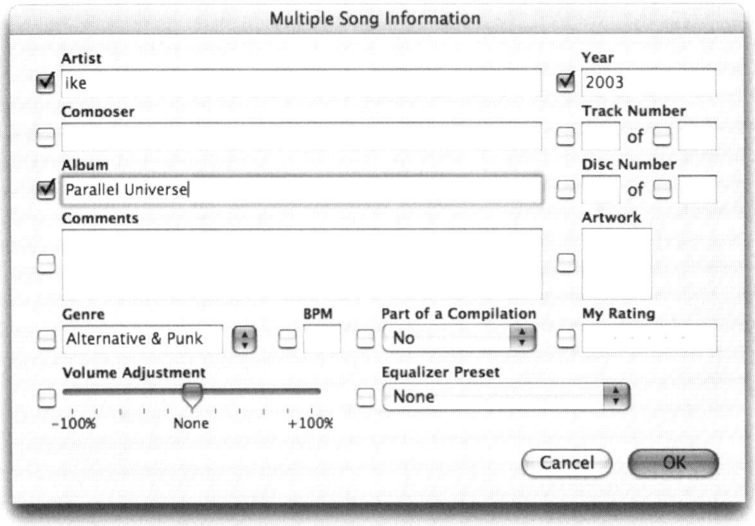

12. In the **Multiple Song Information** window, enter the band's name, **ike**, into the **Artist** field. Then type **2003** in the **Year** field and **Parallel Universe** as the **Album** title. Click **OK** when you're done.

Now that the proper tags have been added to these tracks, they're placed properly into the song list.

13. Scroll up and find the three ike songs. (Make sure the list is sorted by **Artist**.)

Now let's see how iTunes has handled this new information.

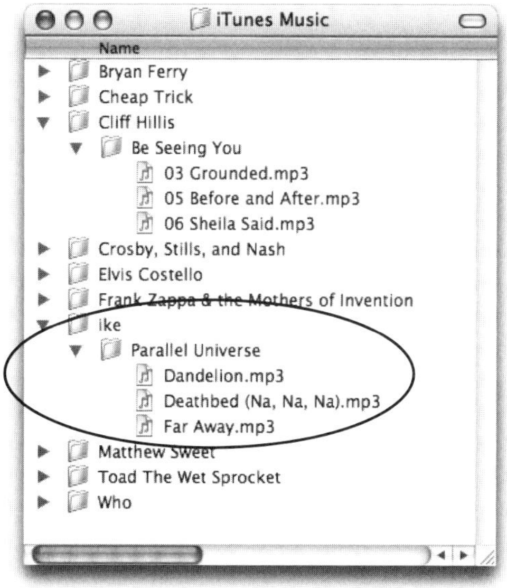

14. Bring the **iTunes Music** window to the front. Observe how iTunes has now created a folder called **ike**, containing the folder **Parallel Universe**, and the **Unknown Artist** and **UnKnown Album** folders have been deleted. Pretty nifty, huh?

Keeping your music organized in this fashion makes it easier for you to keep track of your collection in case you want to back up music to another drive or to a disc. You'll take a look at one more scenario for importing music next.

---

15. Bring the **ike** window back to the front and click the **Back** button to display the **chap_14** contents. Double-click **The Jellybricks**.

So here you have three MP3s from a band with a weird name you've never heard of, and you're not sure you want to copy them to your iTunes collection.

You could open your iTunes Advanced preferences and uncheck ***Copy files to iTunes Music folder when adding to library*** *to prevent the song from being copied. But if you prefer to have files copied to your iTunes folder most of the time, it's inconvenient to open this window every time you want to play an AAC or MP3 you might not want to keep. Instead, use the following keyboard shortcut for those times when you just want to play a song in iTunes without adding it to your Library.*

---

16. Select the three songs in **The Jellybricks** folder. Hold down the **Option** key and drag the songs into the iTunes Library window. The Option key prevents the songs from being copied by iTunes.

Tip: Holding the ***Option*** *key when dragging songs into iTunes does the opposite of whatever your current copying preference is. For example, if* ***Copy files to iTunes Music folder when adding to library*** *is checked, holding* ***Option*** *prevents the files from being copied. If that preference is unchecked, holding* ***Option*** *copies the files to your iTunes Music folder.*

---

17. Bring the **iTunes Music** window to the front and observe that no folder for **The Jellybricks** has been created here.

---

18. Bring **iTunes** to the front and locate **The Jellybricks'** songs. These songs are now playable in iTunes, but they remain in their original location in the **chap_14** folder on your **Desktop**. If you move or delete the **chap_14** folder, the songs will remain listed in the iTunes window until you delete them, but iTunes won't be able to play them. This is why it's a good idea to copy any songs you plan to listen to again.

So what if, after listening to these three songs, you change your mind and decide that you want to have them as part of your permanent collection? Do you delete them from the list and then drag them in again without holding Option? Nope.

---

19. From the iTunes menu bar, choose **Advanced > Consolidate Library**. This command will copy any music files that don't currently reside there into your **iTunes Music** folder. (Unfortunately, you can't pick and choose, so if there are songs you don't want to copy, don't select this command. You'll have to drag your songs in manually again.)

*Click **Consolidate** when iTunes tells you that this command cannot be undone (which just means that you can't choose **Edit > Undo** after selecting this command.) Now you'll test to see if this worked.*

20. Drag the **chap_14** folder to the **Trash**.

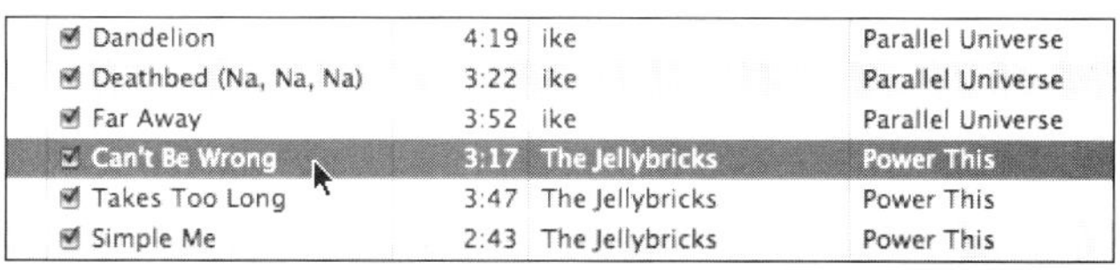

21. Return to **iTunes** and double-click the song "Can't Be Wrong" to play it. Press the **spacebar** to pause the song once you've confirmed that it's playing (or take a few minutes to listen to your new music, if you like). Keep iTunes open for the next exercise.

3. Playing Your Music

As you saw at the end of the last exercise, it's pretty simple to play a song in iTunes–just double-click it and it plays. But iTunes is not your run-of-the-mill digital audio player. It includes many powerful features that not only help you keep your music organized, but also help you control how your music is played. This exercise shows you many of the features related to music playback.

1. Locate the song "Grounded" by Cliff Hillis (which you imported in the preceding exercise) and double-click it to play it.

Double-clicking a song is probably the fastest way to play it, but iTunes also comes with standard playback controls, located in the upper-left corner of the window.

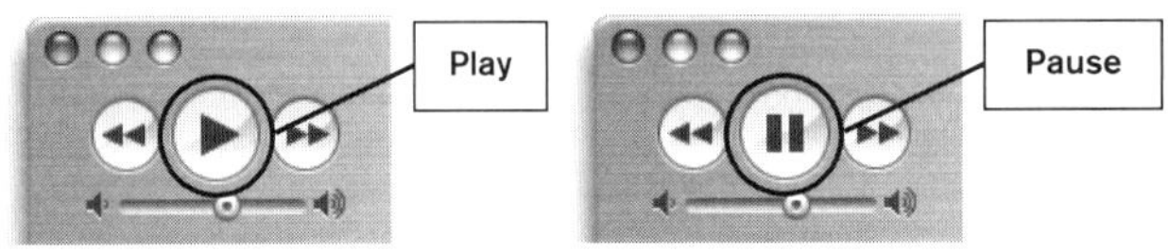

2. Clicking the **Play** button also plays the song. While the song is playing, notice that the **Play** button turns into the **Pause** button. There is no **Stop** button when playing music in iTunes, except when importing songs or listening to Internet radio (more on this later).

If you need to adjust the volume of the playback, move the iTunes volume slider. This slider behaves independently from your Mac's main volume (which is controlled from your Mac's menu bar, System Preferences, or from your keyboard if you have a relatively new Mac).

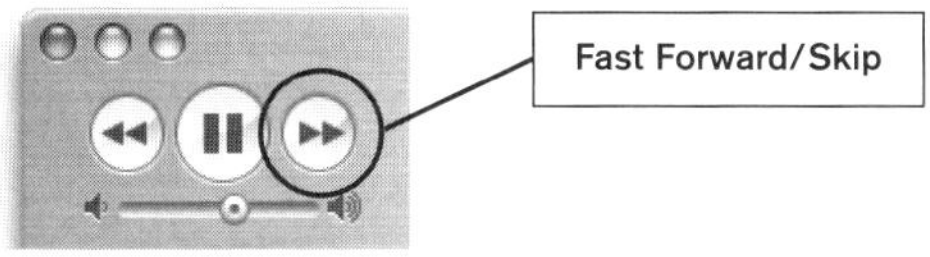

To fast forward through a song, click and hold down on the right arrows next to the Pause button. You can also click and release this button to jump ahead to the next song in the list. Clicking the left arrows will jump you back to the beginning of the song, or to the previous song if you click it twice. Holding this button will rewind the song.

You can also move forward and backward in a song by dragging the diamond marker in the status pane. This is referred to as "scrubbing." Scrubbing allows you to visually determine which point of the song you want to jump to.

Changing the Time Display

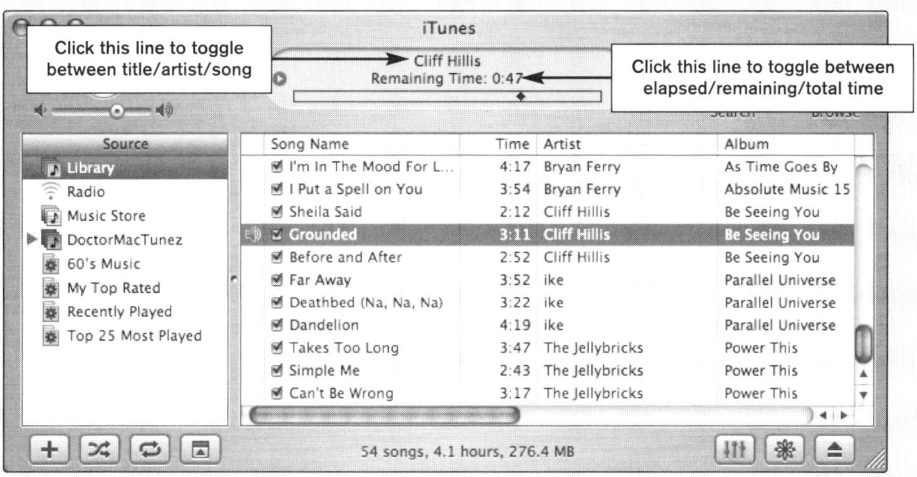

The bar in the status pane gives you a visual indication of how far along you are in the current song. The status pane also scrolls through the song's title, album, and artist, and provides the exact time of the song. You can switch between total, elapsed, and remaining time by clicking the time display itself. Similarly, you can quickly see the title, album, and artist by clicking the top line of text in the display.

3. Click the **Pause** button to stop playback.

In addition to the controls within the iTunes window, you can also control playback via the keyboard, which often is more convenient than using the mouse. The following chart lists iTunes' keyboard commands.

iTunes Playback Keyboard Shortcuts

Keystroke	Action
Spacebar	Play/pause selected song.
Return	Play selected song from beginning.
Right arrow	Next track.
Left arrow	If the song is playing, or paused midsong, returns to the beginning of the song. If the song is stopped at the beginning, jumps to the previous song.
Cmd+Option+right arrow	Fast forward.
Cmd+Option+left arrow	Rewind.
Up arrow/down arrow	Selects songs up and down the list.
Cmd+up arrow/Cmd+down arrow	Volume up/volume down.
Cmd+Option+up (or down) arrow	Mute; if currently playing, the song will continue to play, but no sound will be heard.

4. If you haven't done so already, take a few moments to try out the keyboard commands. Once you have committed them to memory, which shouldn't be too difficult, you'll most likely find yourself using them instead of the mouse controls.

Next, let's take a look at iTunes' built-in graphic equalizer. In the world of audio equipment, an ***equalizer*** *(EQ) is a device that allows you to adjust the level of specific ranges of frequencies, which can enhance the sound of different types of music or compensate for limitations in your sound system.*

5. Select a song from your **Library** and play it.

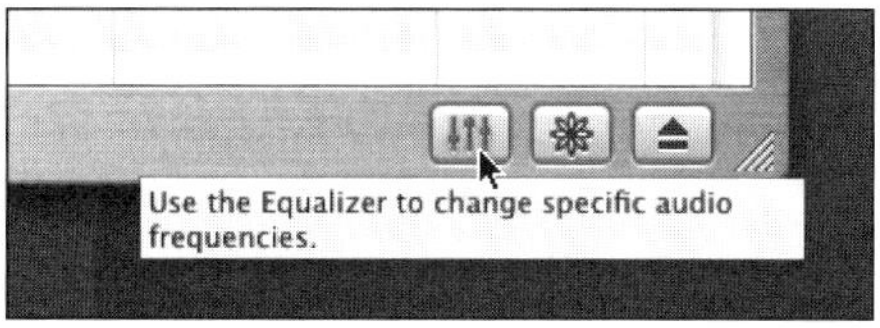

6. Click the **Equalizer** button in the lower-right corner of the iTunes window.

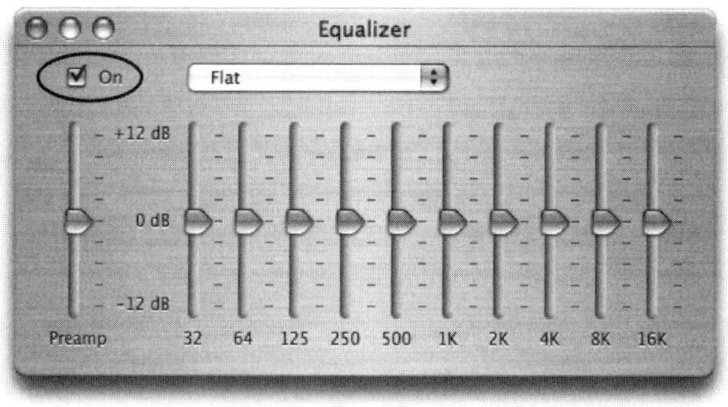

7. Make sure the **Equalizer** is checked **On**.

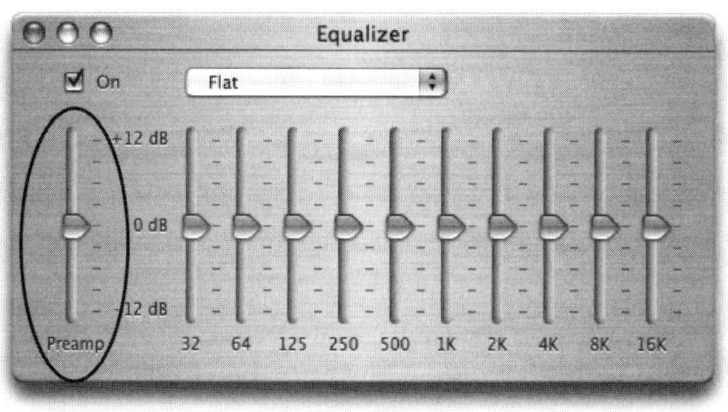

*The **Preamp** slider in this window controls the level of volume before it reaches the volume slider. This can be a useful feature if you're trying to listen to a particularly low-level recording and need to raise the volume to a level higher than you can achieve by cranking the iTunes and Mac volume levels to their fullest. Just be aware that setting the Preamp level near its highest setting at +12 dB can cause distortion in playback, which won't necessarily damage your equipment, but it sounds pretty horrible.*

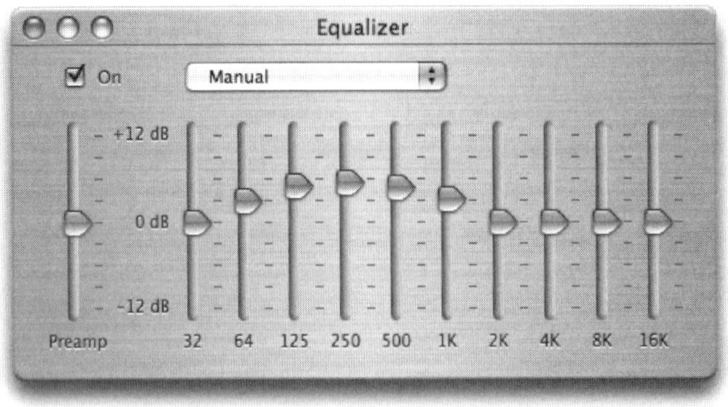

The other ten sliders each control a separate range of frequencies. The sliders to the left control the low, bass frequencies, and as you move to the right, progress to the higher frequencies. Being able to adjust specific frequencies gives you the ability to boost aspects of the audio that might be difficult to hear or to reduce other sounds that are too overbearing. For example, if you're listening to your music on a PowerBook or iBook, you'll probably find that the bass from your Mac's tiny speakers sounds a little weak. By manually adjusting the sliders to the left of the equalizer, you can increase the low-end response. You won't get booming bass, but the audio will sound a little fuller.

Tip: *If you click the triangle in the Status panel while a song is playing, you'll see a live meter showing you the song's frequency response. If you're playing a stereo track, you'll see two sets of meters: one for the left channel and one for the right. You can use them to see which frequencies are particularly high and which ones may be lacking, and you can adjust your EQ settings accordingly. Or you can ignore what this display means, and simply appreciate how cool it looks.*

Manually adjusting the EQ takes some experimentation to get the optimum sound out of your Mac. If you're the impatient type or just don't feel like messing with the sliders, you'll be happy to know that iTunes comes with 22 preset EQ settings.

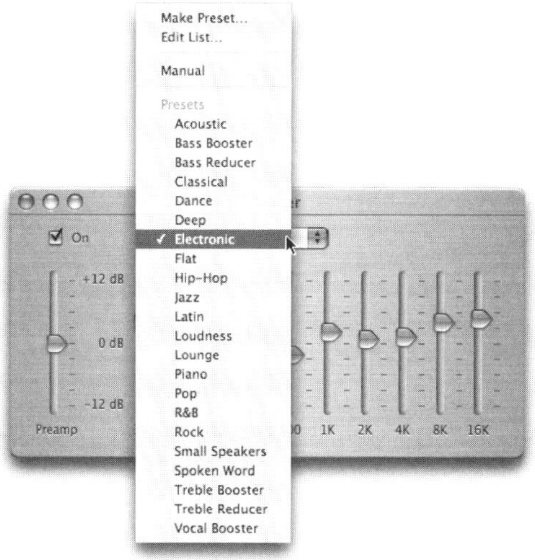

8. With music playing, click the pop-up menu at the top of the **Equalizer** window and select a preset EQ setting. Once selected, you should hear a change in the overall sound of the playback after a second. Pick a few more presets to hear the difference between the settings.

Tip: *Don't let the names of certain presets discourage you from trying them. For instance, depending on your Mac and speakers you're using, you may find that the Dance preset sounds pretty good with Classical music. Your best bet is to try several presets to see which one best enhances the sound of your music. If you decide against using the Equalizer altogether, you can uncheck the* ***On*** *button, or choose the* ***Flat*** *EQ preset.*

Creating Your Own Presets

If you've taken the time to manually adjust the EQ and have found a setting that you like, you can save it by choosing **Make Preset** from the pop-up menu and giving your setting a name. You'll then be able to select this setting from the pop-up menu at any time. You can also remove presets by choosing **Edit List** from the pop-up menu.

9. Set the EQ back to **Flat** for now and keep it open. Pause the music playback if it's playing.

If you have a large collection of music stored in iTunes, you'll probably find that a single EQ setting won't be the best setting for every song. iTunes lets you associate EQ settings to individual songs, which can be useful if you have a song that always sounds a little off with your regular EQ setting.

---

10. Locate the song "Can't Be Wrong" by The Jellybricks. **Ctrl+click** this song and choose **Get Info**.

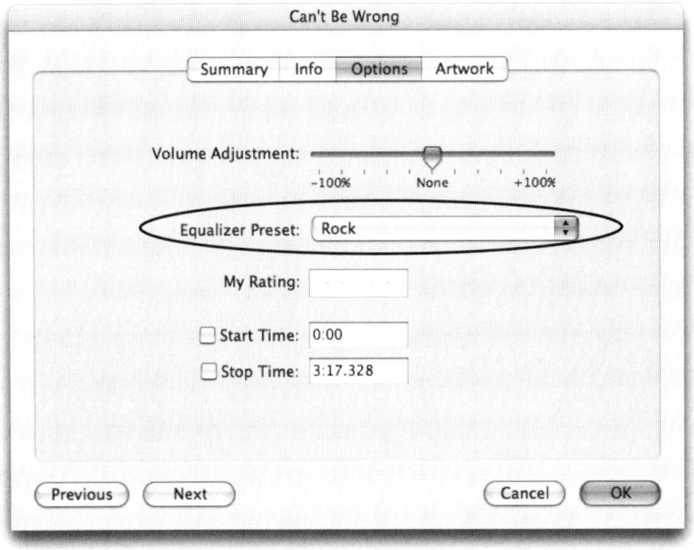

11. In the window that opens, click the **Options** button. Choose **Rock** from the **Equalizer Preset** pop-up menu. (Notice that you can also adjust the song's individual volume, which is great for songs that are too quiet or too loud.) Click **OK**.

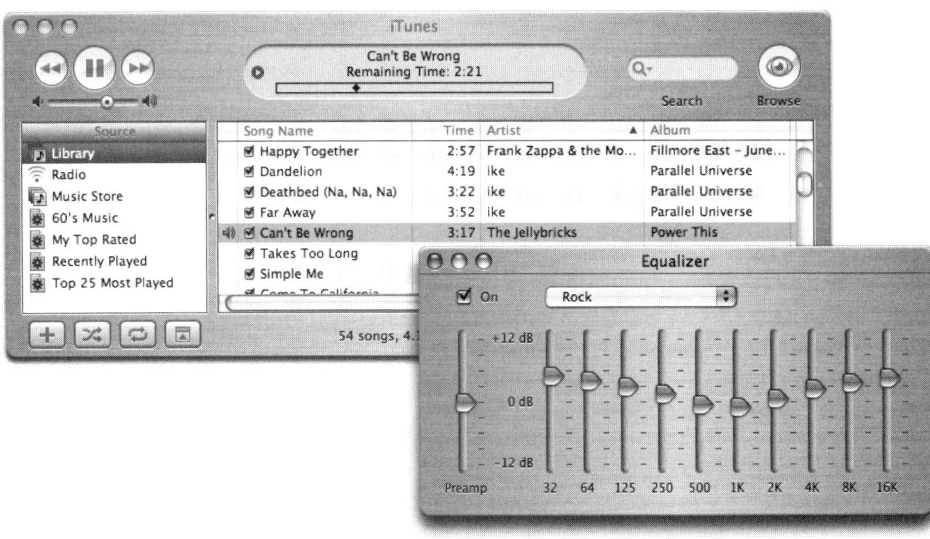

12. Make sure you can see the EQ window (which should still be set to **Flat**) and double-click "Can't Be Wrong" to play it. Watch the EQ automatically adjust itself to the **Rock** setting.

---

13. Now double-click any other song, and the EQ returns to the **Flat** setting (unless you've placed a preset EQ on the song you just clicked). Pretty cool, huh? Applying a preset EQ to individual songs may take some time, but if you're particular about the way your music sounds, it's well worth it. Bear in mind that you can select multiple songs by **Shift+clicking** or **Cmd+clicking** them and then apply an EQ setting to them simultaneously through the **Get Info** contextual menu command. For instance, I selected all of my jazz MP3s and applied the **Jazz** presets to them, so now anytime these songs are played, the EQ automatically adjusts for them.

Sound Check

As your collection of music begins to grow, you may notice that some recordings are louder or quieter than others. It can get annoying if you have to constantly adjust your volume settings to compensate for the variation in volume levels. Although you could manually adjust each song's volume level through its Song Information window, iTunes 4 comes with **Sound Check**, a feature that automatically analyzes and adjusts the volume of your songs, increasing the volume for quieter songs, and decreasing the volume for louder songs. Turn on **Sound Check** by choosing **iTunes > Preferences** and then select **Sound Check** under the **Effects** settings.

So now that you have your music playing, what else can iTunes do? If you're the type of person who likes music, but can't stand to be without visual entertainment as well, iTunes' visual effects have you covered.

14. Choose **Visuals > Large** from the menu bar. Make sure that **Full Screen** is not checked for now.

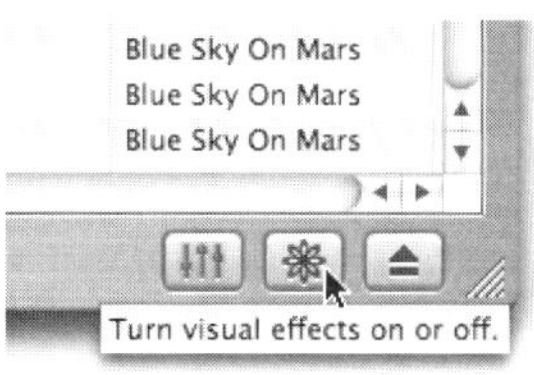

15. Play a song and then click the **Visual Effects** button in the lower-right corner of the window (or use the keyboard shortcut: **Cmd+T**).

Whoa. iTunes launches into a flurry of color, shapes, and movement that reacts to the music you're playing. Be careful not to stare at it for too long without blinking your eyes.

Believe it or not, you can actually exercise a modicum of control over this psychedelic hodge-podge you're seeing. The following chart gives you the keyboard shortcuts.

iTunes Visual Effects Controls

Keystroke	Action
Q/W	Rotates forward or backward through iTunes visual waveforms. Watch the upper-right corner of the display to see the names of the waveforms.
A/S	Rotates through variations of the selected waveform.
Z/X	Changes the color scheme.
C	Displays the current waveform/style/color configuration.
I	Shows info about the current song, MTV-style in the lower-left corner.
B	Displays the Apple logo so you can display your brand loyalty.
?	Displays a list of additional keyboard commands related to visual effects.

16. To get the full effect of the visuals, choose **Visuals > Full Screen** from the menu bar (or press **Cmd+F**). Try to snap out of it after a few seconds and press the **Esc** key or click the mouse to return to the iTunes window.

Tip: *If you found the full-screen visuals to be slow and choppy, try choosing **Small** or **Medium** from the **Visuals** menu.*

For the last part of this exercise, let's look at some different ways you can locate music in your list of songs. This becomes increasingly important as your collection grows.

*In addition to organizing your song list by **Artist** (iTunes' default setting), you can also quickly rearrange your list by clicking the column headers for **Song Name**, **Time**, **Album**, **Genre**, **My Rating**, **Play Count**, and **Last** (Most Recently) **Played**. (See the sidebar "Rating the Songs" for information on the **My Rating** column.)*

***Tip:** If you find all these different columns unnecessary or overwhelming, choose **Edit > View Options** to display a window that allows you to select which columns will appear in the main song list window.*

In most cases, sorting your music by artist makes it the easiest to find the song you're hunting for. But scrolling through hundreds or thousands of songs can still take some time. An alternative is to browse for the songs.

17. Click the **Browse** button in the upper-right corner of the window. This further divides the iTunes window into separate panes for **Artist**, **Albums**, and **Songs**. Now you can click any artist's name to display his or her albums, and by clicking an album, you can display its song titles below. Take a moment to browse through your collection this way and then click the **Browse** button to return to the original window configuration.

Of course, browsing really works only if you can remember the name of the artist, album, or song. If you can't quite remember who performed the song you're thinking of or which album the song came from, the Search field might be able to help you out.

18. In the **Search** field, type a word or two that you know appears in at least one of the titles, artists, or songs in your collection. (Hint: If you have lots of rock or pop songs, try typing or "Baby," or "Girl.") iTunes displays a list of all songs that match this word or phrase. Once a song has been located in this manner, you can double-click it to play it.

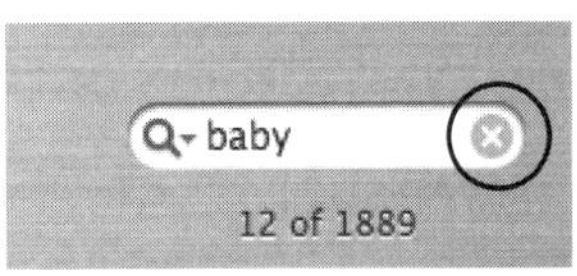

19. Click the **x** in the search field to delete the search term and to display your full song list again. Keep iTunes open for the next exercise.

In this exercise, you learned to play songs from your entire music Library. In the following exercise, you'll learn to create and manage playlists.

Rating the Songs

iTunes 4 includes a feature that lets you play music critic and apply star-based ratings to every song in your collection. This is totally optional, but it can be useful if you want to organize your songs or create a playlist based on your ratings.

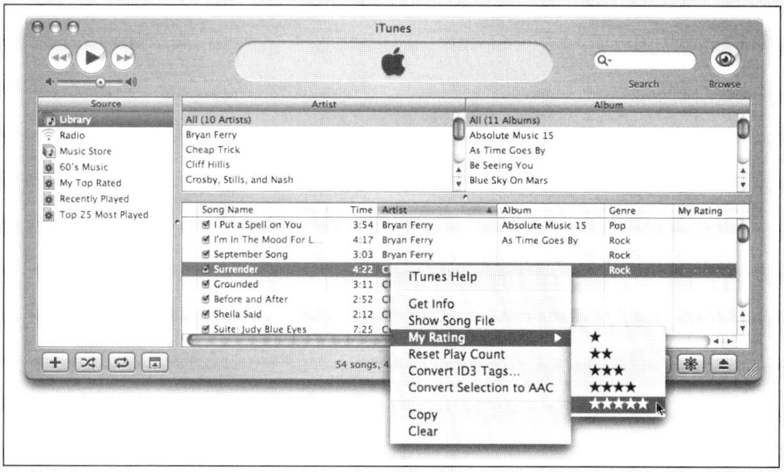

There are two ways to rate a song. You can **Ctrl+click** it, choose **My Rating**, and choose between **1** to **5** stars.

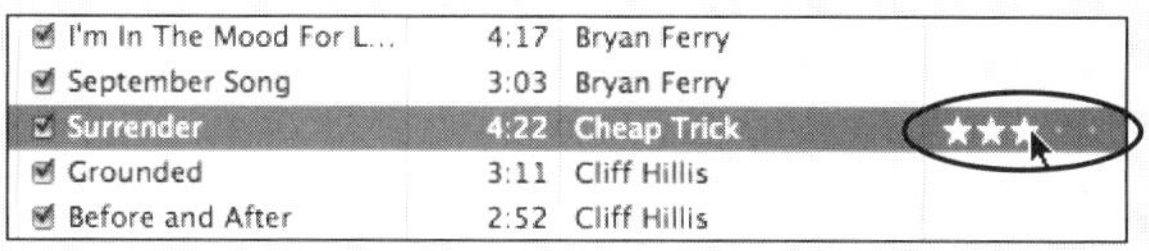

Or you can scroll to the song's **Rating** column and drag horizontally within the column to place stars.

Once you've rated enough songs, you can then click the **My Rating** column header to sort your songs by rating.

TIP | Minimizing iTunes

While iTunes is playing music, you may want to do other work on your Mac. Click the green **Zoom** button in the upper-left corner of the iTunes window to collapse iTunes to just the essential information. You can then drag this window to a corner of your screen where you can keep an eye on the track information, control playback volume, or skip around your songs.

Tip within this tip: You can make this window even smaller by dragging the lower-right corner to the left.

Click the **Zoom** button again to return the iTunes window to full size.

4. Playlists

Sometimes instead of playing an album straight through from beginning to end, you may want to hear just a few select songs from several different albums. By creating playlists in iTunes, you can make your own "mix tape" of songs to suit your various moods (or personalities). You may have a playlist called "Workout Tunes" or "Tunes to Snack By" or "Gettin' Busy." This exercise shows you how to create a basic playlist, as well as how to use and create iTunes' Smart Playlists.

This exercise focuses heavily on the Source column of your iTunes window. The Source column determines what is displayed in the main song list pane. For instance, if you have an audio CD inserted in your drive, its icon appears in the Source column and, when selected, its songs appear in the song list pane. Your Source column contains the Library icon, the Radio icon (discussed in the "Internet Radio" sidebar at the end of the exercise), an icon for any CDs you may have inserted, your iPod icon (if you have one and it's connected to your Mac), and four Smart Playlists (which are discussed later in this exercise). First, you'll create a playlist of your own.

1. Click the **New Playlist** button in the lower-left corner of the window (or press **Cmd+N**).

2. An untitled playlist appears in the source column. Name it **Garrick's Favorites** and press **Return**.

3. If it's not already selected, select the **Library** in the **Source** column.

Now you'll drag some songs to the empty playlist you've just created.

4. Locate the three songs by **Cliff Hillis** (this will be easiest if your song list is sorted by **Artist**). Select all three songs and drag them to **Garrick's Favorites** in the **Source** column.

5. Locate the three songs by **ike** and drag them into the **Garrick's Favorites** playlist. Then drag the three songs by **The Jellybricks** into that playlist as well.

6. Click **Garrick's Favorites** and observe that the nine songs now appear in this playlist.

Tip: *You can double-click a playlist to view it in its own window. This can be convenient if you have several playlists and can't see both the one you need and your Library in the Source column at the same time. With two windows open, you can easily drag songs from your Library into the separate playlist window.*

When you create a playlist in iTunes, you're not copying songs or moving them. All you're doing is organizing them into a specific group. The songs themselves remain in your main Library, while references to the songs appear in your playlists. This means that you can add the same songs to multiple playlists without worrying about increasing the overall file size of your Library.

Once you have your songs in a playlist, you can arrange *them in any order you like. For example, let's say you've decided that you want to hear the three ike songs first in this playlist.*

7. Select the three **ike** songs and drag them to the top of the list. You'll see a black line appear between the tracks as you drag upwards. Release the mouse when the line is at the very top of the list. If you didn't get the songs to the very top, just drag them again until you've placed them properly.

That's all there is to creating a playlist. You can now click the ***Play*** *button to play the songs in this order.*

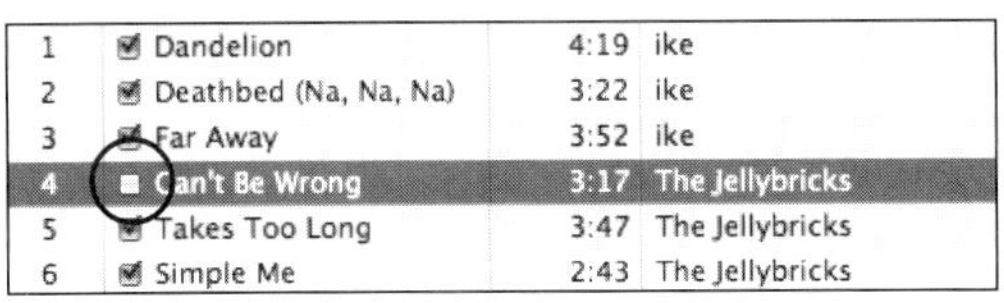

Tip: *If you don't feel like listening to a certain song in your playlist, but want to keep it in the playlist, simply uncheck the song and iTunes will skip it.*

Shuffle and Repeat

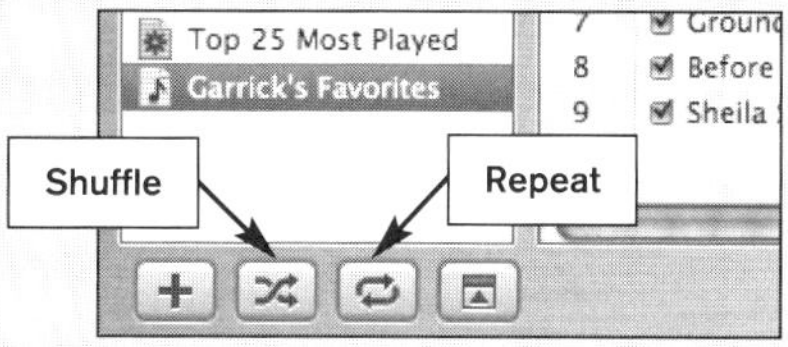

In the lower-left corner of the iTunes window are two buttons that allow you to shuffle the order of the songs in the main song list pane and to repeat songs or playlists. Clicking the **Shuffle** button will play the songs in the song list pane in a random order. (If a playlist is selected, you'll be able to see the order of the shuffled songs. If the Library is selected, it remains sorted by the column headers, but the songs will still play randomly.) Clicking the **Repeat** button once will repeat the entire playlist; clicking it a second time will repeat only the selected song.

Next, you'll take a look at how to create a Smart Playlist. Unlike regular playlists, which you have to create yourself and never change unless you alter them manually, Smart Playlists automatically generate lists and update themselves based on rules that you establish.

*iTunes comes with four prebuilt Smart Playlists to get you started. Clicking the **60's Music** Smart Playlist will display all the songs that were released during the 1960s. **My Top Rated** will list the songs in the order of your ratings. I'll let you guess what **Recently Played** and **Top 25 Most Played** do.*

8. Hold the **Option** key, which turns the **New Playlist** button into the **New Smart Playlist** button. Click it.

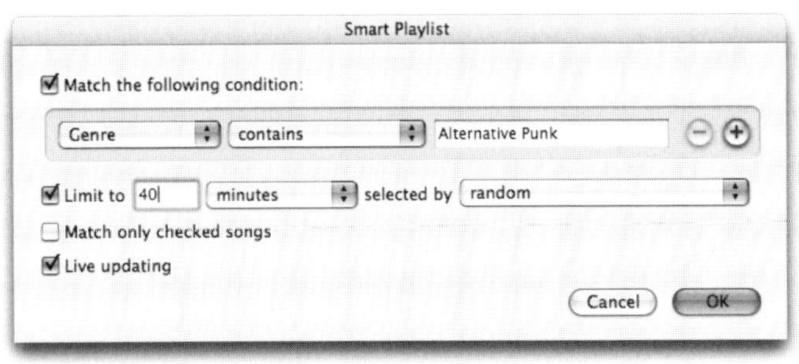

*In the **Smart Playlist** window, you can determine the criteria for your Smart Playlist. The options here allow you to select songs by **Artist**, **Composer**, **Genre**, **Length**, **Size**, or any other attribute. Additionally, you can choose to limit the playlist to a set number of minutes, hours, or songs, or limit it by file size. For example, this screen shot shows how to create a Smart Playlist that will collect 40 minutes worth of songs that have either the words "alternative" or "punk" listed in the Genre information.*

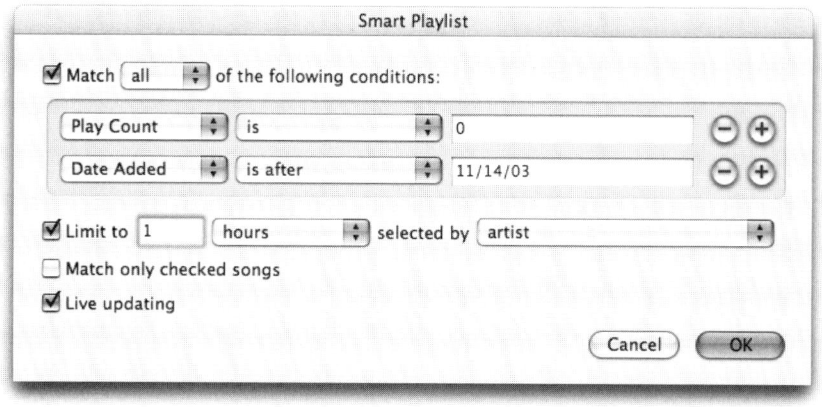

*If you want to get really specific, click the + button on the right side of an item to add even more criteria, including **Size**, **Sample Rate**, **Time**, **Year**, **BPM** (beats per minute) and so on. In this example, the playlist is set to collect one hour of songs that I added to iTunes after November 14, 2003, but have never played.*

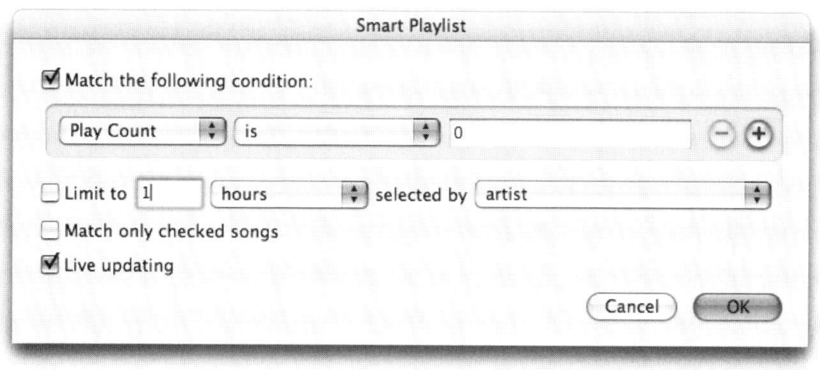

9. Set up a Smart Playlist to collect all songs that have never been played in iTunes. Your setup should match the screen shot shown here. Make sure **Live updating** is checked. Click **OK** when you're done.

10. Your Smart Playlist appears in the **Source** column. Name it **Never Played**. You should see all the songs you haven't played in iTunes yet. (Songs don't count as played until you reach the end of the song. If you don't have any songs that haven't been played, you'll need to import some new music before you can complete this exercise.)

11. With **Never Played** selected, double-click any song to play it and let it play through to the end.

*Because you checked **Live updating** in the Smart Playlist setup window, once the song reaches the end, it disappears from the list because now it's officially been played.*

***Tip:** If you don't feel like waiting through an entire song to see it disappear from your Smart Playlist, you can cheat by scrubbing forward in the status window to a point near the end of the song and letting it play to the end from there.*

Because Smart Playlists can update automatically, they're ideal for people who are really serious about keeping their music organized.

MOVIE | smart_playlists.mov

For a demonstration and further details on creating Smart Playlists, see **smart_playlist.mov** on the **H•O•T CD-ROM**.

Deleting Playlists and Songs

Once you grow tired of a playlist, you can easily delete it by selecting it and pressing the **Delete** key. Because the playlist is just a way to organize songs, not the files for the songs themselves, only the playlist is deleted. The songs remain intact on your hard drive and can still be found in your Library. (If you do want to delete a song, select it from the **Library** and press the **Delete** key.)

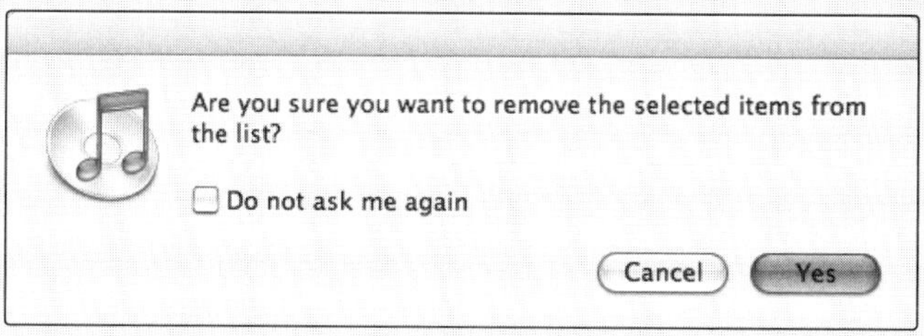

You'll be asked if you are sure that you want to remove the item from the list. Note that you're only removing it from the list in this step. Click **Yes** if you're sure.

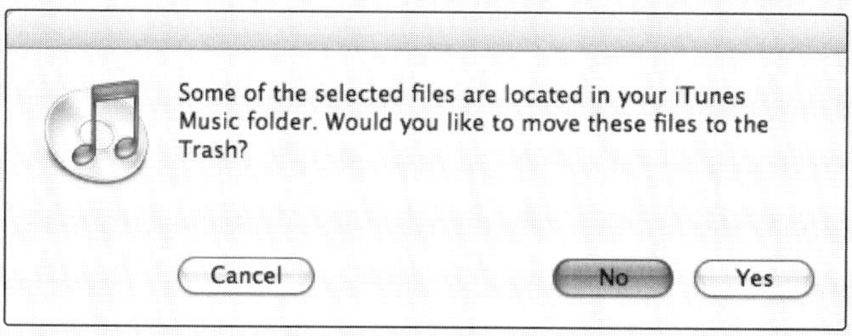

If this song is stored in your iTunes Music folder, you'll see another dialog box asking if you also want to move the song file itself to the Trash. If you click **No**, the song will remain in your **iTunes Music** folder but will no longer appear in the song list. Click **Yes** to move the file to the Trash.

Internet Radio

If you have a fast Internet connection, the **Radio** source can provide you with a break from everyday commercial radio.

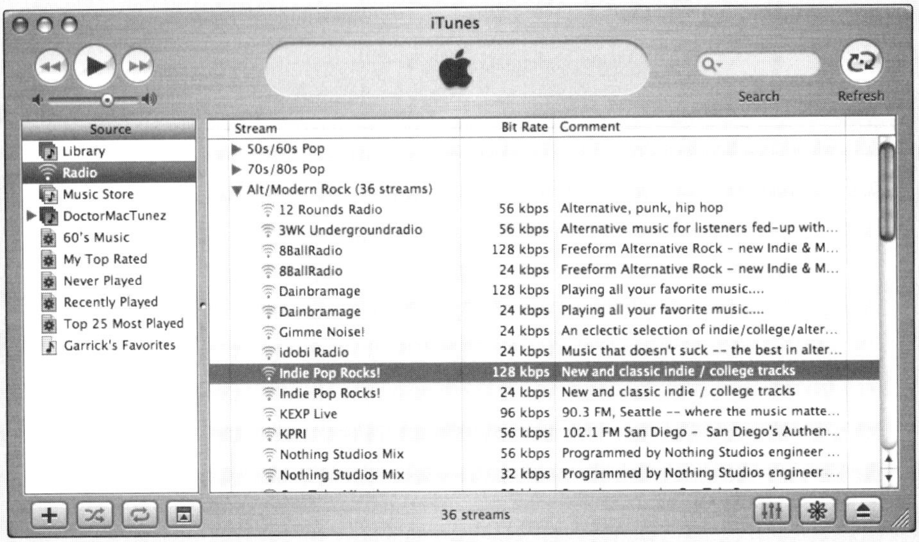

Clicking **Radio** will display a list of genres. Toggling open any of these genres will display a list of Internet radio stations; the stations include an incredibly diverse, nearly commercial-free selection of music. If you have a dial-up Internet connection, try to select only the stations with a bit rate of 56 kbps or lower. With a fast Internet connection, you can select any stations you want, but the higher the bit rate, the higher the sound quality. Many stations even broadcast a different bit rate to accommodate different connection speeds.

5. Burning CDs

In addition to sorting your music, you can also use playlists to gather songs you want to burn to a CD. Audio CDs created in iTunes can be played on any retail CD player that accepts CD-Rs. This exercise requires you to have a CD-Recorder. Use these steps as a guideline for burning your own CDs.

1. To burn a CD, first collect your songs into a playlist. Most CDs can hold 74 minutes of music. The display at the bottom of the window lets you know how long your CD will run.

2. Once you have collected and arranged the songs in the running order you prefer, click the **Burn Disc** button in the upper-right corner of the window. If you haven't already done so, iTunes will prompt you to insert a blank CD.

3. Once iTunes has confirmed that your playlist will fit on the CD, you'll be prompted to click **Burn Disc** again to start copying the songs to the disc.

4. Once the disc is complete, it will appear in your **Source** column. You can eject it from your Mac by clicking the **Eject** button in the lower-right corner of the window.

The iPod

If you own an iPod, Apple's portable music player, you can connect it to your Mac via a FireWire cable. The iPod's icon shows up in the Source column and behaves much like an audio CD. You can select the iPod to view the songs it contains and double-click any of the songs to play them. But unlike a CD, you can copy songs and playlists to your iPod by dragging them from your Library to the iPod icon. The only thing you can't do is drag songs from your iPod into your Library. This is Apple's way of preventing music piracy, but you shouldn't be copying any music you don't own anyway, right?

iTunes also works with several other audio players. For a list of compatible players, search for "iTunes compatible MP3 players" in the **AppleCare** Sherlock channel, covered in Chapter 11, "*Sherlock and Searching Your Mac*."

6. The iTunes Music Store

In April 2003, Apple launched the **iTunes Music Store**, a revolutionary, subscription-free service for purchasing and downloading music over the Internet. Although copycat services have appeared since, Apple set the standard by offering songs for just 99 cents and albums for $9.99, with no monthly subscription fee. And unlike some online music services that stream the music you purchase over the Internet, forcing you to sit in front of your computer to listen to the music you paid for, songs purchased from the iTunes Music Store can be copied to multiple iPods or CDs and can be played on up to three computers (Mac or Windows) at a time. This exercise takes you on a tour of the iTunes Music Store and shows you how to browse for and purchase music.

Note: You must be connected to the Internet to access the iTunes Music Store. Also, make sure you're running at least iTunes version 4.2, which you can download from **www.apple.com/itunes**.

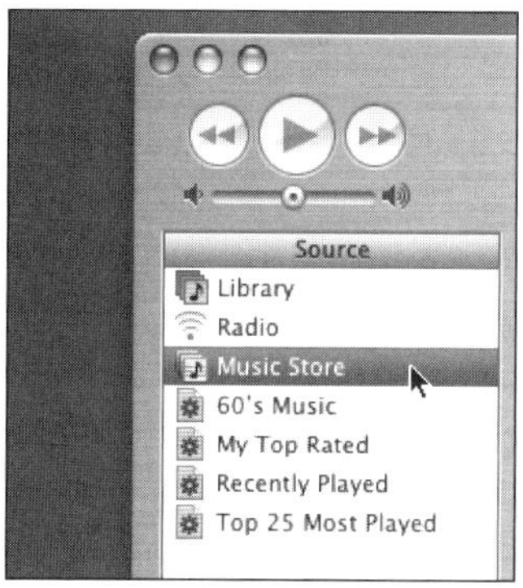

1. In the **Source** pane, click **Music Store**.

Tip: In iTunes version 4.2 or later, you can double-click ***Music Store*** *to view the store in its own window.*

*The iTunes Music Store is laid out a lot like a Web page. You're presented with several different areas for accessing music or particular artists. The categories are fairly self-explanatory–**New Releases**, **Exclusives**, **Staff Favorites**, and so on. Also listed are **Today's Top Songs** and **Today's Top Albums**, to let you know what everyone else is listening to.*

The music store is a flat-rate service. Most songs cost $.99 to download, and entire albums can be purchased for $9.99, meaning that even if the album you want to download has 22 tracks, you will still pay only $9.99 (so long as you specify that you want to download the entire album). You'll learn more about purchasing and downloading music later in this exercise.

2. The central area of the main Music Store page lists several featured albums. Browse through them by clicking on the arrows on either side of each row. The rows will eventually loop around to the beginning.

3. Click one of the featured albums under **Staff Favorites**. (The albums you see in your iTunes window will most likely differ from the ones shown above.)

*You're taken to the album's information. In addition to the available tracks, iTunes also gives you the release date information, the number of songs available, the genre, and–so you know who's getting your money–the music label that releases the music. In the middle of the top pane, you'll also see a list of the top downloaded songs by the artist you've chosen. The **Listeners also bought** column, gives you a list of other songs purchased by people (presumably with musical tastes similar to yours) who downloaded this selection. This is a great way to discover new music. You can click any one of these songs to view its information page.*

Album Notes

In addition to the basic release information, some of the albums in the iTunes Music Store are displayed along with **Album Notes** to help you get a better idea of what you're purchasing. The album notes are similar to the liner notes traditionally printed on LP and CD booklets, and provide further information about the release such as the musicians' names, where the album was recorded, or background history of the artist or album.

You can first listen to a 30-second sample of any song available on the Music Store to decide if you actually want to download it. If, after listening to the sample, you decide to buy the track, you can simply click ***Buy Song****, and you will be taken through the purchasing process, which you'll examine later in this exercise.*

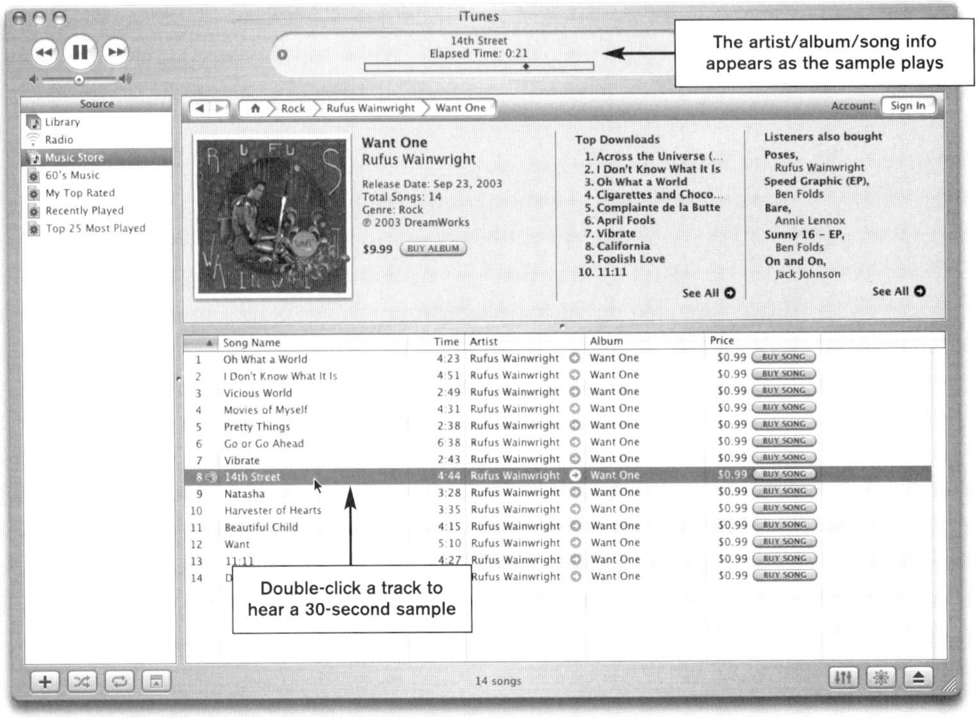

4. Select one of the album's songs and click the **Play** button (or just double-click the song). After a few moments, you'll hear the 30-second sample.

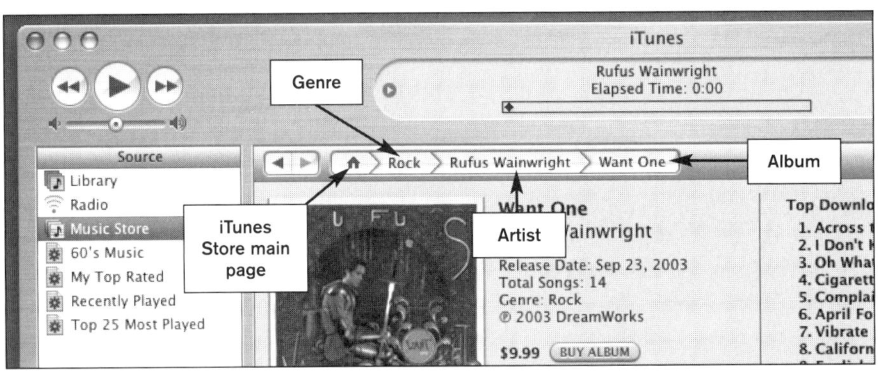

iTunes offers several different methods for navigating around the Music Store. At the top of the information pane, you can view the path the Music Store has taken to get to the current selection. You can use this path to work your way back to the artist, genre of music, or to the Music Store home page. If you want to find out what else is available by the same artist, you need only click the artist's name.

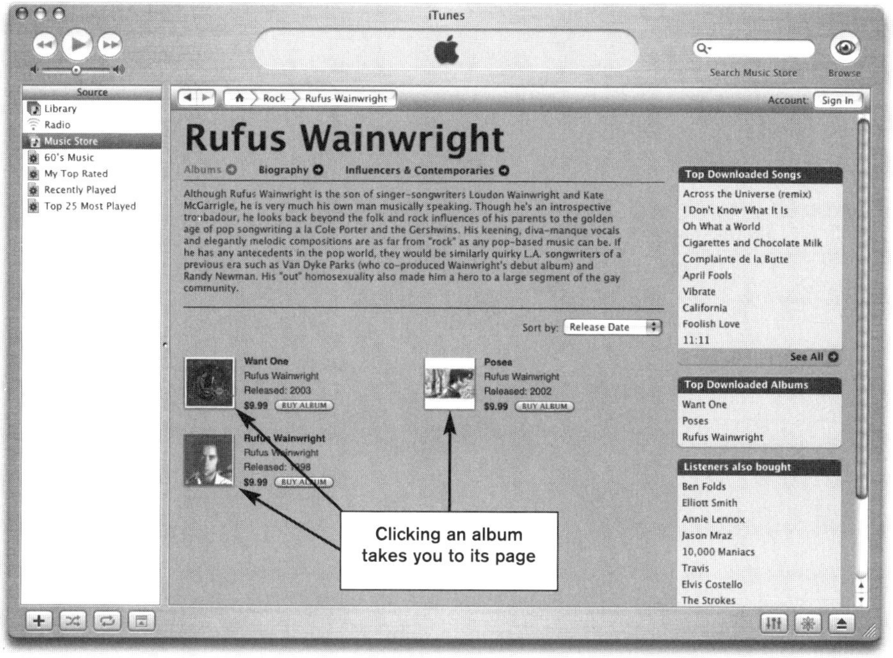

Once you click an artist's name, you can click any of the albums to sample the songs from the artist's catalog. (Or if you're ready to buy the album and don't want to first listen to some samples, you can click the corresponding ***Buy Album*** *button, which you'll learn about shortly.) For many artists, a short* ***Biography*** *may be provided to give you further insight into the mind behind the music. You may also find a link to* ***Influencers & Contemporaries****, which displays a special page listing albums and artists in a similar vein.*

Use the right and left arrows to navigate back and forth between pages. If you search for an artist or band and then browse to one of their albums, you can just use the left arrow button to return to the artist's page, rather than searching or browsing for that artist again. The right arrow button will only be available if you've clicked the left arrow at least once.

Now you'll take a look at different ways to search for music in the iTunes Music Store.

5. Click the **Home** button to go to the main Music Store page. In the upper-left corner, you can use the **Choose Genre** drop-down menu and choose among any of the categories listed. Choose **Alternative**.

This takes you to the front page of the Alternative music section. The layout here is the same as the Music Store home page, except all the listings in each category are from alternative artists. (Bonus question: Alternative to what? Discuss.) Each available genre has its own page laid out in this fashion.

Another way to search for music is to use the ***Browse*** *button.*

6. Click **Browse** in the upper-right corner of the window. This is very similar to browsing your personal iTunes Library, only now you're searching all of the online songs available in the Music Store.

7. Under the **Genre** column, click **Alternative**, which displays all the alternative artists in the next column. In the **Artist** column, locate and select **Belle & Sebastian**. In the next column, you're given a listing of every album by Belle & Sebastian available in the iTunes Music Store. Clicking on **All** in the **Album** pane will display every song in one list in the bottom pane.

*You can double-click any listing under the **Genre**, **Artist**, or **Album** columns to jump to that specific page. Or you can click the little arrows next to the artist's name, album, or genre in the bottom pane. Double-clicking a song in the bottom pane plays the 30-second sample.*

You can also search the Music Store the same way you would search your iTunes Library.

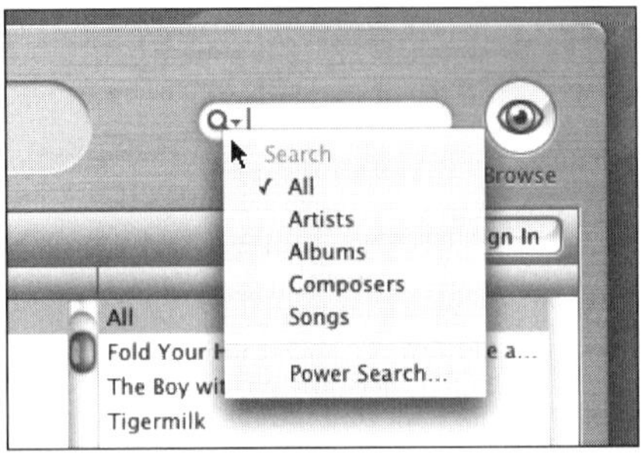

8. Click the magnifying glass in the search bar in the upper-right corner of the iTunes window. By clicking on the triangle, you can choose to search the entire store (**All**), or by **Artists**, **Albums**, **Composers** (useful for searching for classical music), or **Songs**.

Tip: Choosing ***Power Search*** *allows you to search a combination of these items simultaneously.*

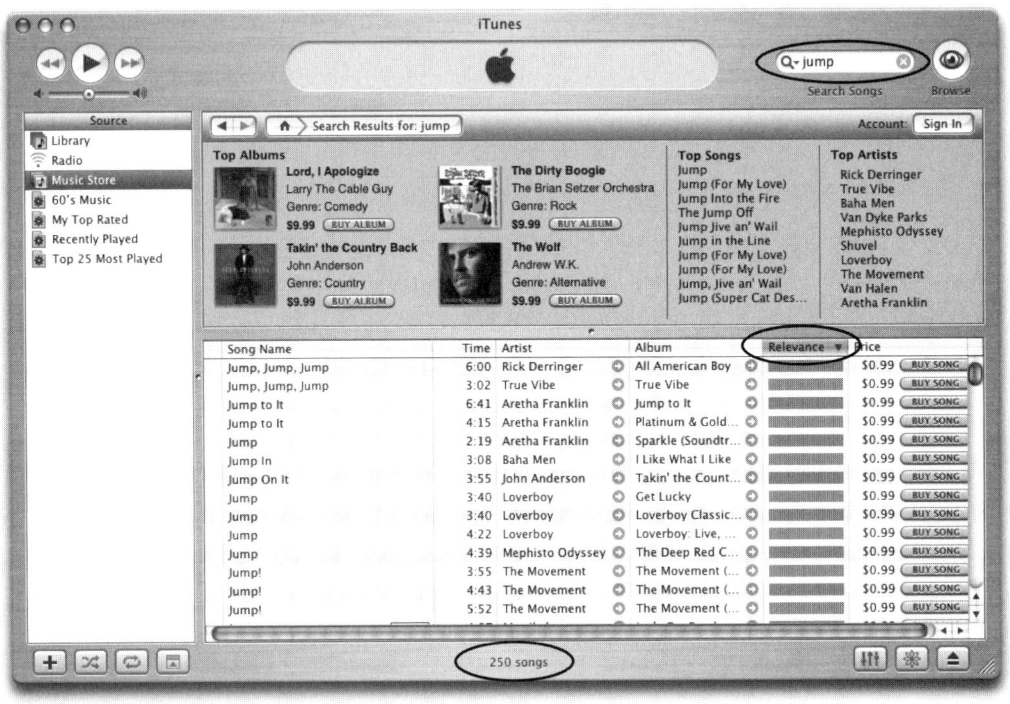

9. Choose **Songs** and type **jump** in the search bar. The search yields (at least) 250 results, all with the word "jump" in their titles, and listed by relevance. The top pane of the window features the most popular songs and artists related to this search.

10. To pare your results down, choose **Power Search** from the search bar's drop-down menu. In **Power Search**, you can enter other information in order to find what you're looking for, which is helpful when you're looking for a song containing a common word or phrase. Enter **jump** in the song field and **van** in the artist field. Click **Search**.

Now the search yields just three songs, two by Van Halen and one by Van Dyke Parks. (The Music Store continually updates its song catalog, so your results may vary, and might include songs from Van Morrison, Bran Van 3000, Townes Van Zant, and so on.) Once you've narrowed down your search, you can click around to listen to samples and view the artists' pages or albums.

NOTE | Clean/Explicit Versions

Many artists who use "colorful" language and lyrics often offer two different versions of their albums–explicit and clean. Explicit versions usually bear the Parental Advisory warning on the album cover, which cautions you that the music contains potentially offensive language. To appease restrictive parents and family-friendly retailers, some artists also release a clean version of the record, with the objectionable material changed or removed. In the iTunes Music Store, you have the option of downloading clean versions of albums as well as their explicit counterparts.

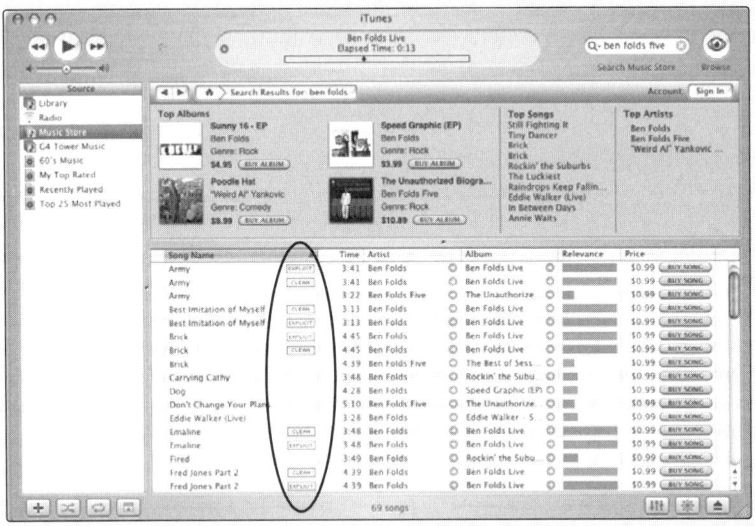

When you find a song you're looking for, a red box stating "explicit" indicates that the song contains explicit lyrics. A box showing "clean," designates an edited version, but also means that an explicit version exists, should you desire to download that instead.

Note: If you want both the clean and explicit versions of a song, you must download and pay for both.

Now you'll look at the actual process of buying a song. Let's pretend you just had to have the live version of Van Halen's "Jump," which you saw in the search results from the last step. Again, you could click the arrow by the album to see the other songs on this album, but let's say you want only this particular song.

***Note:** If you don't really want to purchase this song, you may just want to read through the rest of the steps in this exercise and apply them later when you actually want to purchase a song for yourself. Or, if you prefer, browse around and find a song you'd like to own and follow the rest of the steps to purchase that song instead.*

11. In the row containing **Jump (Live)**, click **Buy Song**.

A window appears, prompting you to sign in or create an account. If you have a .Mac address, use that ID and password to sign in. If you still have the trial .Mac account you created in Chapter 12, ".Mac", you may use that. With iTunes 4.2, you can also now use an America Online screen name to purchase music and have it charged directly to your AOL account. Otherwise, you'll need to click ***Create New Account****, which will walk you through the account setup process.*

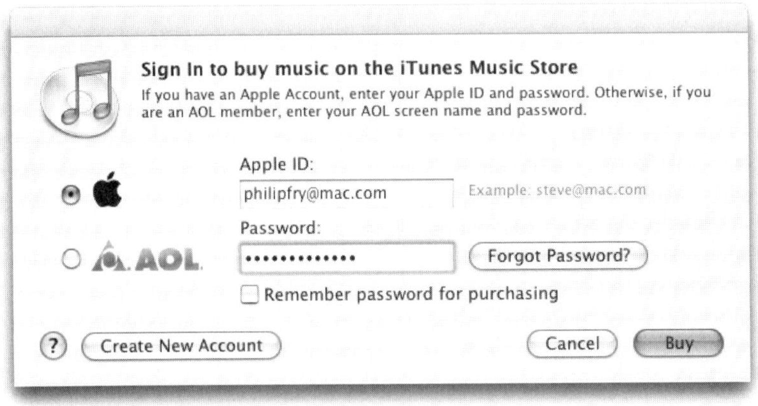

12. If you don't have a .Mac account, click **Create New Account** and follow the steps to sign up for an Apple ID. If you have a .Mac or AOL account, select either the Apple or AOL icon, enter your .Mac user name or your AOL screen name, and type your password in the **Password** field. Click **Buy**.

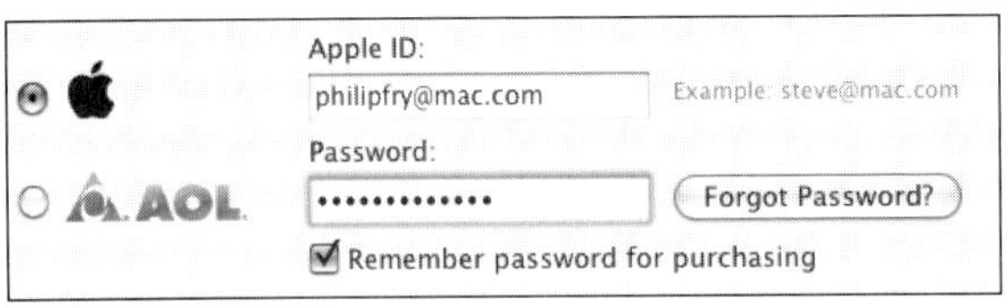

Tip: You can check ***Remember password for purchasing****, which will allow you to buy songs or albums simply by clicking the Buy button. Of course, this has its disadvantages as well. If you're worried that someone else might buy songs using your computer, or if you simply need another step to stop yourself from buying every song you see on a whim, leave this option unchecked.*

13. If this is your first time signing in to the iTunes Music Store, you will get this window stating that this ID has not been used to purchase music yet. Click **Review**. (You'll only have to do this the first time you decide to purchase music.)

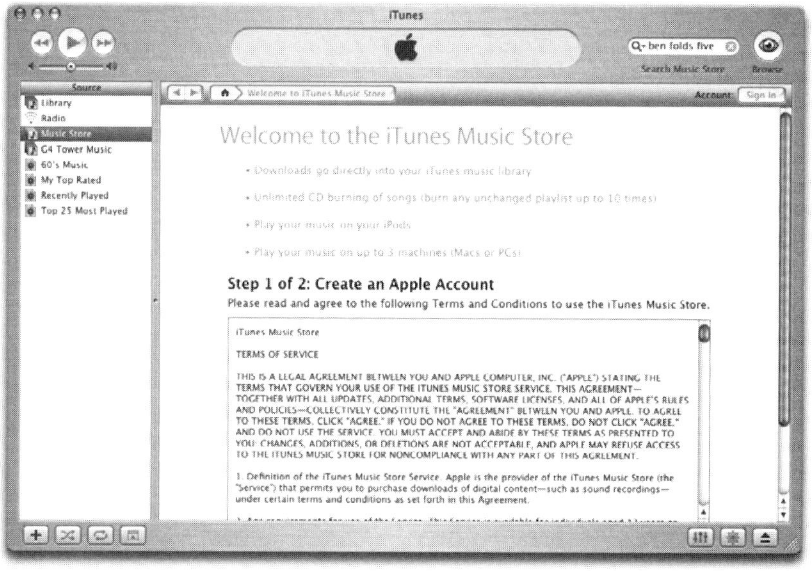

14. In the first step, you'll be asked to review the iTunes Music Store's terms of service. Read through the agreement and then click **Agree**.

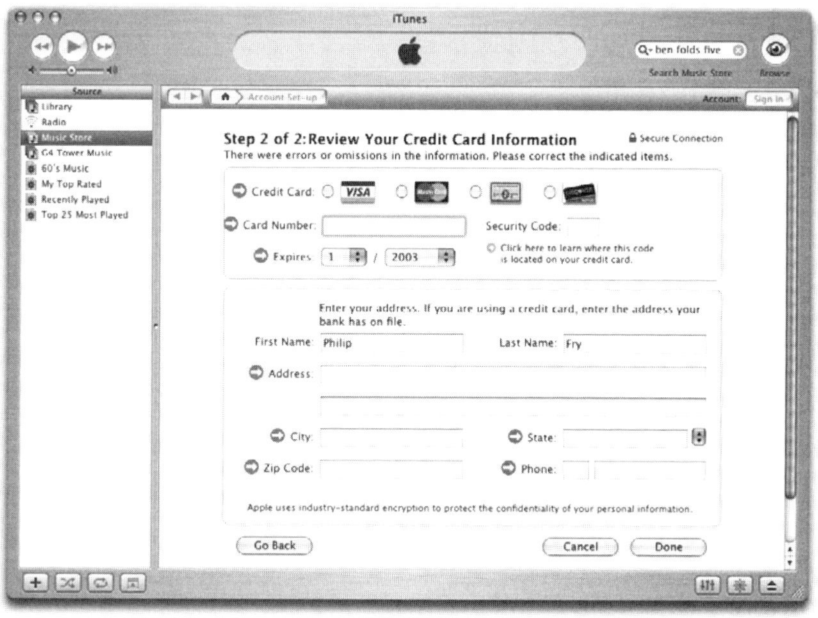

15. In the second step, verify or enter your credit card information in the appropriate fields and click **Done**.

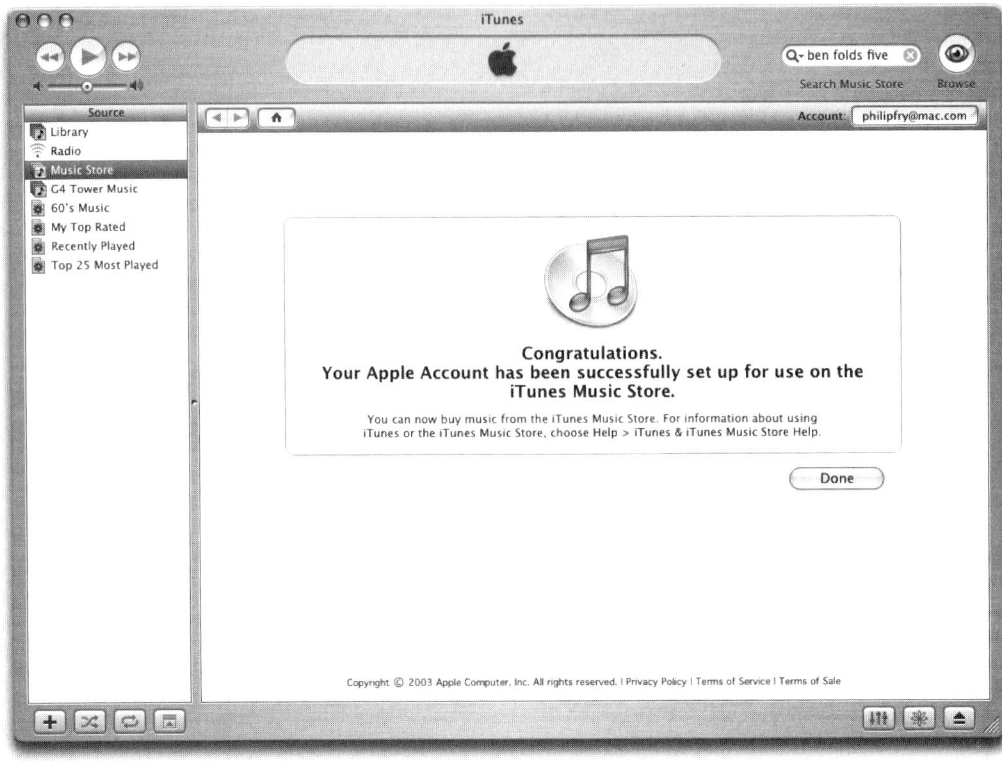

16. Once your account information has been verified, you'll see a confirmation message. Click **Done** to return to the page you were viewing before you clicked **Buy Music**. In this case, you'll be taken back to the **Jump**-related search results.

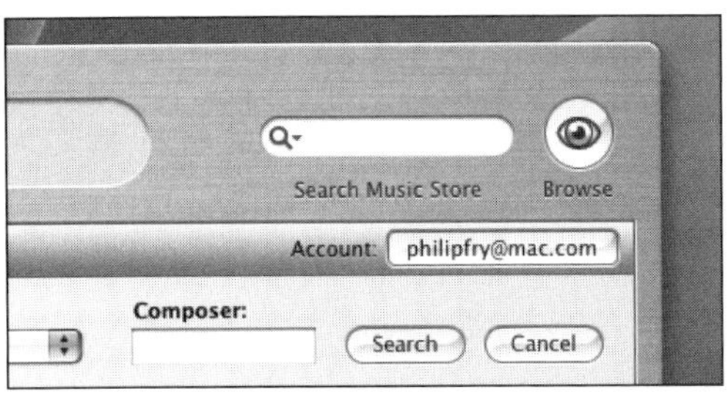

Your information will be displayed in the upper-right corner, by the ***Account*** *line, letting you know that you are signed in to the Music Store and that you may now purchase music.*

17. Now click **Buy Song** in the **Jump (Live)** row.

*The alert window appears asking you to confirm the purchase, telling you that once you click **Buy**, you will be charged and the music will download to your Mac. You can choose to deactivate this alert by checking **Don't warn me about buying songs again** in this window. If you do so, anytime you click Buy Song, the music will automatically be downloaded, and your credit card will be charged. If you lack self-control, mouse precision, or a large credit line, you may want to keep this alert active.*

18. Click **Buy** to purchase this song.

*Once click **Buy**, the download begins. The progress of your download is displayed in the status pane at the top of the iTunes window.*

***Note:** You'll receive an email receipt for every song you purchase. In case you're purchasing several songs at one time, the iTunes Music Store doesn't immediately charge your credit card, so they can all be itemized in a single transaction. Therefore, it may take several hours before your card is charged and you receive a receipt.*

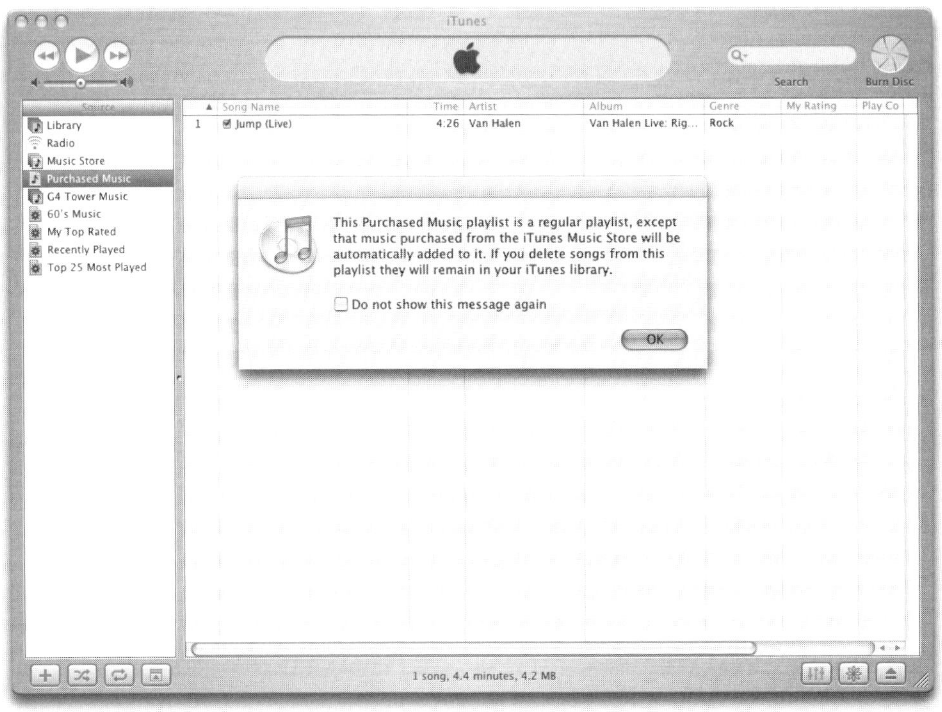

19. Notice in the **Source** pane, that a new playlist, called **Purchased Music**, has been added. Click this playlist. To make it easier to locate the music you've purchased, all downloaded music can be found in here. Note the dialog box that appears telling you that this is just a regular playlist, meaning the songs listed here can be deleted without fear of removing them from your Mac. You'll still be able to find the songs in your main Library. Click **OK** to dismiss this dialog box.

20. Double-click the downloaded song to listen to it in its entirety.

I've Downloaded Some Music—Now What?

Once a song has been downloaded, you can add it to as many of your own playlists as you like and copy it to an unlimited number of iPods. The songs that you download are in AAC format, just like the format you used in when ripping CDs into iTunes. The difference with music purchased from the iTunes Music Store is that the files are security encoded. For protection purposes, Apple has limited the number of times you burn the song to CDs to 10 times. But all you have to do is create a new playlist containing the song to burn it another 10 times if you want.

You can also copy and play your purchased music on up to three different computers (Mac or Windows running iTunes).

The first time you try to play a purchased song on a computer other than the one you originally downloaded it on, you'll see a dialog box asking you to enter you account information to authorize this computer to play the song. Enter your password and click **Authorize**. ITunes will connect to the Internet and confirm that you haven't exceeded your limit of computers and then allow you to play the song. You only have to authorize a computer the first time you play the song. If you've exceed your limit of three computers, you'll need to deauthorize one of them before you'll be able to play the song on another computer. To do so, choose **Advanced > Deauthorize Computer** from the iTunes menu bar and enter the account info you originally used to purchase the song. Just be aware that this deauthorizes every song purchased with this account.

Buying a Whole Album

Purchasing an entire album from the iTunes Music Store isn't much different than buying a single song. Just click the **Buy Album** button next to the album's name. The album will be downloaded one song at a time, and you'll be able to find them in the **Purchased Music** playlist.

Album Artwork

In addition to the usual tags containing information about a song's artist, album, genre, and so on, Music purchased from the iTunes Music Store also contains the cover art of the album from which the music originated.

To view the album cover, click the **Show or hide song artwork** button in the lower-left corner of the iTunes window. This pane displays either the artwork for the currently selected song or the currently playing song. Click the top portion of the pane to toggle between these two options.

If you ripped a CD or imported selected songs from your own collection into iTunes, you can add the artwork data to these tracks as well. To do so, you'll need to either scan in your copy of the album artwork or find a copy on the Internet. Use Safari to check **amazon.com** or **allmusic.com** for good, clean scans of thousands of album covers. **Ctrl+click** the image in Safari and choose **Download Image to Disk** to save it on your hard drive. Once you have a copy of the artwork, you can add it to the appropriate songs in your collection.

To add artwork to a single track, **Ctrl+click** the song in your **Library** and choose **Get Info**.

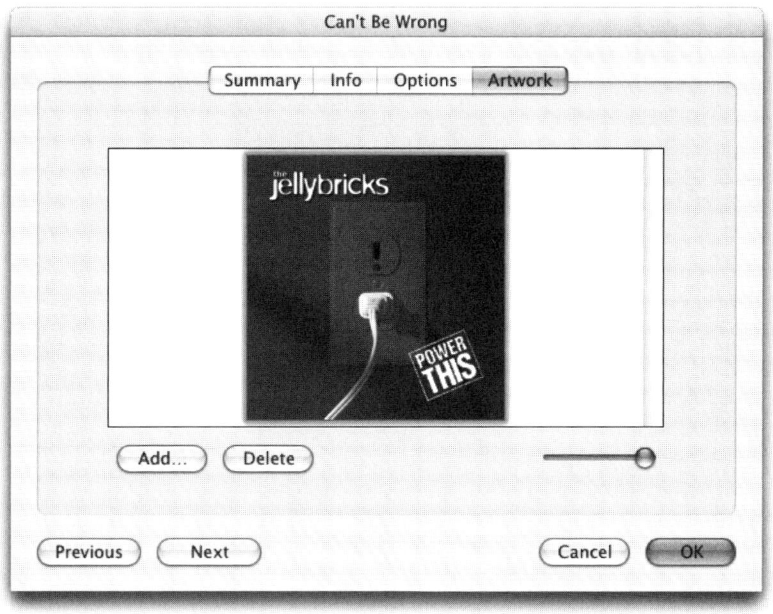

In the window that opens, click the **Artwork** button, click **Add**, and then locate the artwork file your Mac. You can use the slider in this window to resize the artwork if necessary. Click **OK** when you're done.

You can also add artwork to multiple songs simultaneously, which is useful when you've imported an entire CD. The easiest way to do this is to place the artwork file on your Desktop, making sure the iTunes window doesn't cover it. Also, make sure the artwork pane is visible and set to **Selected Song**. **Shift+click** all the songs from the album and then drag the cover art into the artwork pane. iTunes will add the artwork data to each track.

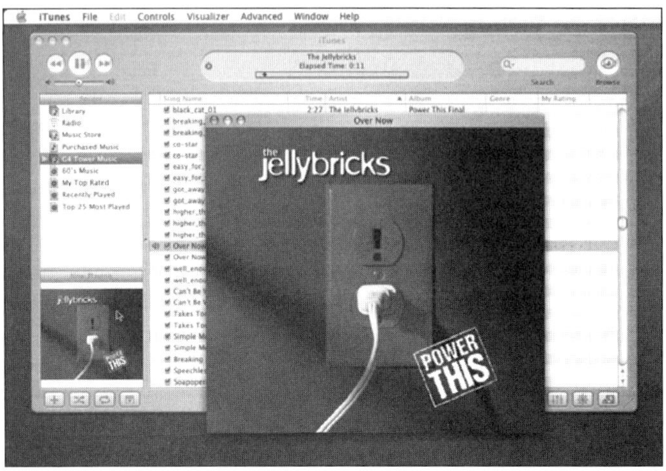

Clicking the image in the artwork pane opens it in a larger window, allowing you to appreciate the finer details of the cover.

Tip: You can add multiple images to songs by simply dragging them into the artwork pane. For instance, if you have both the front and back covers of an album, dragging both files into the artwork pane makes arrows appear at the top of the pane, allowing you to toggle between them.

Other Music Store Features

Given the popularity of the iTunes Music Store, Apple has added a few functions that make purchasing music easier, as well as providing a way to control your spending, or the spending of children or teens who may run amok with downloading.

Allowances

On the main Music Store page, click **Allowances** to jump to a page that allows you to set up an iTunes Allowance. Here you can buy allowances for friends and family as a gift or for yourself as a way to control your own spending. You can set allowances in $10 increments from $10 to $200. To purchase an allowance, you must be signed in, and the recipient of the Allowance must have iTunes and an Apple ID. If your recipient does not have an Apple ID, you can even set one up for him or her.

Gift Certificates

Gift certificates work similarly to Allowances. The main difference is that the recipient does not need to have an Apple ID. Also, from a gift-giving standpoint, the gift certificate is more of a formal present: the recipient will receive an attractive electronic gift certificate from Apple. To buy a gift certificate, click **Gift Certificates** on the main Music Store page. In order to redeem it, the recipient must access the **Gift Certificates** area in the Music Store and click the **Redeem** button and enter the confirmation number that appears on the certificate.

Audiobooks

One of the more recently added features of the iTunes Music store is the addition of audiobooks. You can access the audiobooks section the same way you search for other music. Choose **Audiobooks** from the **Choose Genre** menu on the main page, or enter a search in the search field. The main difference between the music and books section of the Music Store is the price. Most songs and albums in the Music Store share a uniform pricing scale, but audiobook prices vary from book to book.

iTunes Preferences

This chapter touched on several of the options found in iTunes Preferences. The following charts provide detailed descriptions of all the options. Each collection of preferences is accessed by selecting **iTunes > Preferences** from the menu bar and then clicking the icons at the top of the window.

iTunes General Preferences	
Option	**Description**
Source Text/Song Text	Choose from **Large** or **Small** to determine the size of the text in the source column and the main song list pane.
Show genre when browsing	When checked, a third column for genre appears when you click the **Browse** button in the upper-right corner of the iTunes window.
On CD Insert: Show Songs	When an audio CD is inserted into your Mac, iTunes lists the tracks.
On CD Insert: Begin Playing	When an audio CD is inserted into your Mac, iTunes lists the tracks and begins playing the CD.
On CD Insert: Import Songs	When an audio CD is inserted into your Mac, iTunes lists the tracks and begins converting the tracks and importing them into your music Library.
On CD Insert: Import Songs and Eject	When an audio CD is inserted into your Mac, iTunes lists the tracks and begins converting the tracks and importing them into your music Library. When finished, it ejects the CD.

continues on next page

iTunes General Preferences *continued*	
Option	**Description**
Connect to Internet when needed	When checked, iTunes will connect to the Internet whenever it needs to access Web-based services, such as accessing track titles on the CDDB. When unchecked, you have to select **Get CD Track Names** yourself from the **Advanced** menu.
Use iTunes for Internet music playback	Click **Set** to make iTunes the default program for playing music off the Internet. For instance, if you subscribe to **www.audible.com**, where you can download audio books, you need to set this option to use iTunes to play back the content you download.

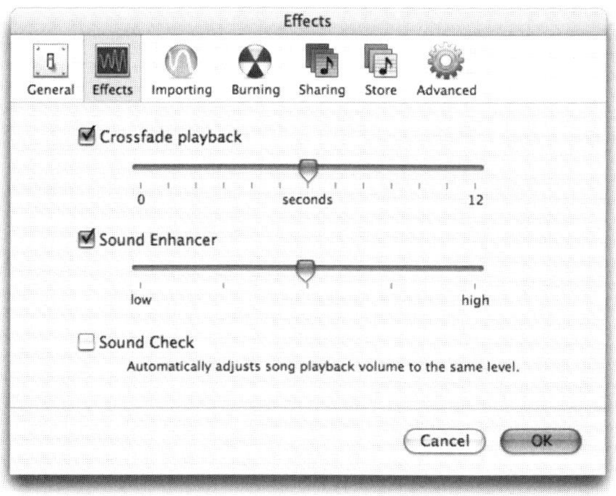

iTunes Effects Preferences	
Option	**Description**
Crossfade playback	This effect creates a seamless transition between songs by fading out the end of one song while the next song fades in. Use the slider to control how many seconds of overlap the two songs will have.
Sound Enhancer	This effects tweaks the songs to add depth and create a richer overall sound. Drag the slider to determine how much to enhance the music. **Note:** Dragging the slider all the way to **high** may cause distortion in playback.
Sound Check	As described earlier, this effect adjusts the volume of each song so that the overall volume of playback doesn't change from song to song.

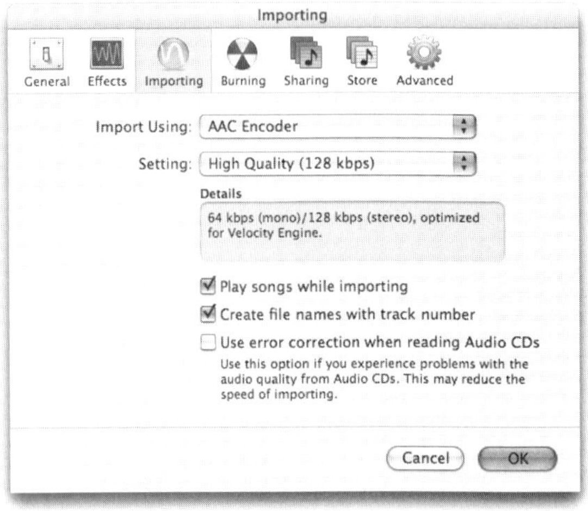

iTunes Importing Preferences

Option	Description
Import Using	Use this pop-up menu to choose among **AAC**, **MP3**, **AIFF**, and **WAV** encoding. AAC is the default because it keeps the file sizes the smallest; MP3 keeps them almost as small. AIFF and WAV produce large files because they don't compress the sound. You'll probably only use AIFF and WAV if you're importing music that you'll be using in a professional sound editing application. Then again, if you're doing professional sound editing, you most likely won't be using iTunes to import music.
Setting	This menu changes based on the selection chosen in the **Import Using** pop-up menu. For MP3s, you can choose among **Good** (128 kbps), **Better** (160 kbps), **High Quality** (192 kbps), or **Custom**. For AACs, your choices are **High Quality** (128 kbps) or **Custom.** For AIFF and WAV, your choices are **Automatic** and **Custom**.
Details	This area gives you a summary of your currently selected encoding configuration.
Play songs while importing	When checked, the songs you import will play as soon as enough of the first song is encoded. This gives you a chance to hear the quality of the playback and stop the encoding if you feel the quality isn't good enough.

continues on next page

iTunes Importing Preferences *continued*	
Option	**Description**
Create file names with track number	When checked, this option automatically adds a song's track number to its name. For instance, the sixth song on the Beatles' album Revolver would appear as "06 Yellow Submarine" instead of just "Yellow Submarine." This is a useful option for ensuring that the album will be played in order if you copy your MP3s to another location and use a different MP3 player for playback.
Use error correction when reading Audio CDs	When checked, this option may help if you experience errors or other problems with audio quality when you import music from CDs, but using it may reduce the speed of importing.

iTunes Burning Preferences	
Option	**Description**
CD Burner	Displays the model of the CD recorder iTunes will use to burn your CDs. If you have more than one CD recorder connected to your Mac, a pop-up menu will appear here from which you can choose the CD burner you want to use.
Preferred Speed	Use this pop-up menu to choose the speed at which you'd like the CD to be burned. In most cases, **Maximum Possible** is the best choice. Choosing higher speeds such as **24x** won't make your CD recorder burn at that speed. You can only burn as fast as your CD burner is designed to burn, which is why **Maximum Possible** is the best choice. However, if you notice glitches or errors in the music you burn, lowering the preferred speed may produce better results.

continues on next page

iTunes Burning Preferences *continued*	
Option	**Description**
Disc Format	You can choose to burn your disc as an **Audio CD**, **MP3 CD**, or **Data CD.** Audio CDs (the default setting) hold approximately 74 minutes of music and can be played in nearly all CD players manufactured in recent years. (Some older CD players can play CD-Rs.) MP3 CDs, on the other hand, are a type of data CD, which means they can hold up to 650 MB of information, enough to hold hundreds of songs. Only certain newer models of CD players can play MP3 CDs, but if you have one of these players (check the information that came with your player), you can create MP3 CDs that contain hundreds of your favorite songs and play them all on one CD. The media for Audio and MP3 CDs is the same (CD-R). Your selection in this preference window determines which type will be created. Data CDs can contain all the audio files in a playlist including MP3, AAC, AIFF, WAV, and Audible files. If the playlist contains more songs than will fit on one CD or DVD, iTunes will burn as many songs as will fit on one disc, and then ask you to insert another disc to continue burning the remaining songs. Data CDs play on your computer, but may not play in some CD or DVD players.
Gap Between Songs	With **Audio CD** selected, you can use this pop-up menu to determine how much silence you want to appear between tracks on your CD. This menu is disabled for MP3 and Data CDs.
Use Sound Check	This option allows you to apply the Sound Check effect to your burned CDs to ensure that the overall volume of playback doesn't change from song to song.

iTunes Sharing Preferences	
Option	**Description**
Look for shared music	When checked, music shared by other iTunes users on your local area network will appear in your Source list, allowing you to listen to songs shared by others without first copying the song file to your computer.
Share my music	When checked, your songs are shared with other iTunes users on your local area network. You can choose to either share your whole library or only selected playlists.
Shared name	What other iTunes users on your local network will see in their Source list if you've chosen to share your music.
Require password	When checked, other iTunes users on your local network are required to supply a password before they can listen to the music you've shared.

Note: Shared music is not copied to the other computers on your network. Instead, the music is streamed from one computer to another, like an Internet radio station, so you don't have to create multiple copies of the same songs on each computer.

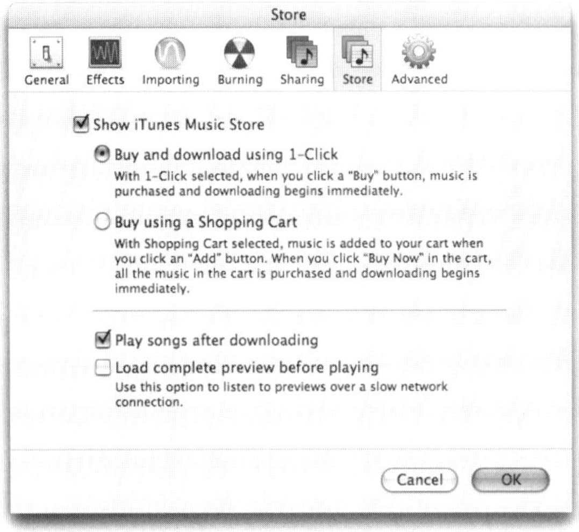

iTunes Store Preferences

Option	Description
Show iTunes Music Store	When checked, the iTunes Music Store will appear in your Source list.
Buy and download using 1-Click	When selected, music is immediately purchased and downloaded when you click a **Buy** button.
Buy using a Shopping Cart	When selected, music is added to your shopping cart when you click an **Add** button. Click **Buy Now** in the shopping cart to purchase and download its contents.
Play songs after downloading	Plays the song as soon as the download completes.
Load complete preview before playing	Forces iTunes to download the entire 30-second preview before it starts playing. This setting is particularly useful if you have a slower dial-up connection.

iTunes Advanced Preferences	
Option	**Description**
iTunes Music Folder Location	Displays the current location of your Music Library. If you decide to store your music elsewhere on your Mac, click the **Change** button to select a new location. If you change your mind, the **Reset** button selects your iTunes Music Library folder again.
Streaming Buffer Size	This pop-up menu determines how much of a Radio audio stream needs to be downloaded before iTunes starts playing the stream. The larger the buffer, the less chance of the stream playing back intermittently. But also, the larger the buffer, the more latency (time lag between playback and actual broadcast).
Shuffle by	Select either **Song** or **Album** to determine the effect of clicking the **Shuffle** button (in the lower-left corner of the iTunes window).
Keep iTunes Music folder organized	As described in this chapter, this option creates folders organized by artist and album in your Music folder.
Copy files to iTunes Music folder when adding to Library	With this option checked, dragging music into the iTunes window creates a copy of the file in your iTunes Music folder.

This chapter covered the major features and capabilities of iTunes. The next three chapters will show you how well iTunes can integrate into the other iLife applications.

15.

iPhoto 2

| Importing Photos and Creating Albums |
| Viewing and Editing Pictures | Creating a Slideshow |
| Emailing Photos | Publishing Photos via .Mac |
| Copying Your Photos to CD or DVD |
| Ordering Prints and Books |

chap_15

Mac OS X Panther
H•O•T CD-ROM

If you have a digital camera, iPhoto can do for your pictures what iTunes does for your music. Not only does iPhoto help you store and organize your photos, but it also enables you to accomplish just about anything else you might want to do with them once they're on your Mac. Whether you want to email pictures, post them on a Web page, print them, or copy them to a CD, you can do it all from iPhoto. iPhoto 2 also includes tools for editing and enhancing your pictures and for copying them to CD or DVD.

As part of the iLife suite of applications, iPhoto also integrates seamlessly into the other iLife applications. As you'll see later, the photos you import and the albums you create in iPhoto are available for use in iMovie and iDVD. But first, you need to get some pictures into iPhoto.

I. Importing Photos and Creating Albums

This exercise shows you how to import pictures into your iPhoto library. Once you've imported some pictures, you'll learn to organize them into albums.

1. Start iPhoto.

If this is the first time you've run iPhoto, you'll see this dialog box, giving you a brief rundown of iPhoto 2's features. At the bottom, it asks if you want iPhoto to start up whenever you attach your digital camera.

2. Click **Use iPhoto** to continue. (If you click **Decide Later**, you'll be asked this question again the next time you run iPhoto. Clicking **Use Other** will prevent iPhoto from starting up when you connect a camera. You can always start iPhoto manually to import pictures no matter which button you click here.)

*Now you'll import some photos. For this exercise, you'll import pictures from the **H•O•T CD-ROM**. If you have a digital camera, read the "Importing from a Digital Camera" section at the end of this exercise for information on moving pictures from a camera into iPhoto.*

3. Copy the **chap_15** folder from the **H•O•T CD-ROM** to your **Desktop**.

4. In **iPhoto**, choose **File > Import**.

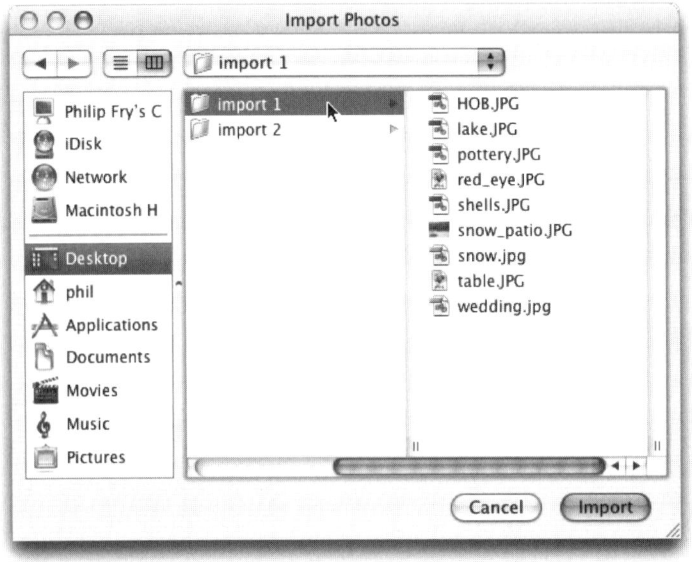

5. In the **Import Photos** dialog box, navigate to the **Desktop**, into the **chap_15** folder, and click the **import 1** folder to select it. You want to import the entire contents of this folder, so don't select any individual images within it. Click **Import**.

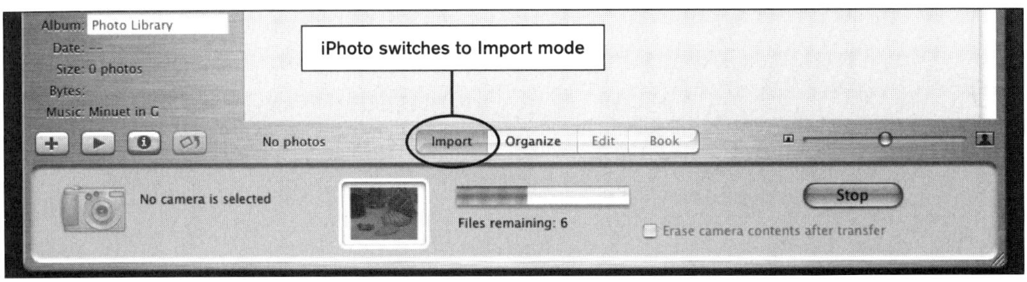

*In the lower portion of the iPhoto window, you can watch as the pictures are imported. These pictures are being copied to the **iPhoto Library** folder in the **Pictures** folder of your **Home** directory (much like iTunes imports music into the Music folder of your Home directory). The original photos remain in the **chap_15** folder on your Desktop.*

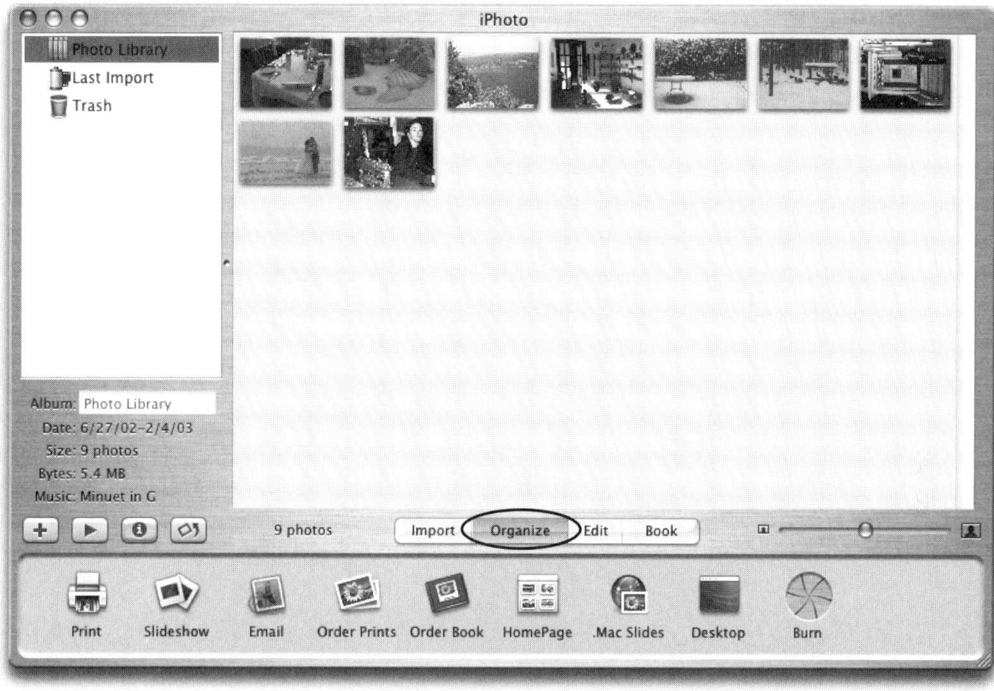

Once the pictures have been imported, iPhoto switches back to Organize mode, which gives you access to the variety of actions you can perform by clicking the buttons at the bottom of the window. You'll learn about these buttons later in the chapter. First, you'll import another batch of pictures.

Another way to import images that are already on your computer is to drag them to the main photo viewing area.

6. Double-click the **chap_15** folder on your **Desktop** to view its contents.

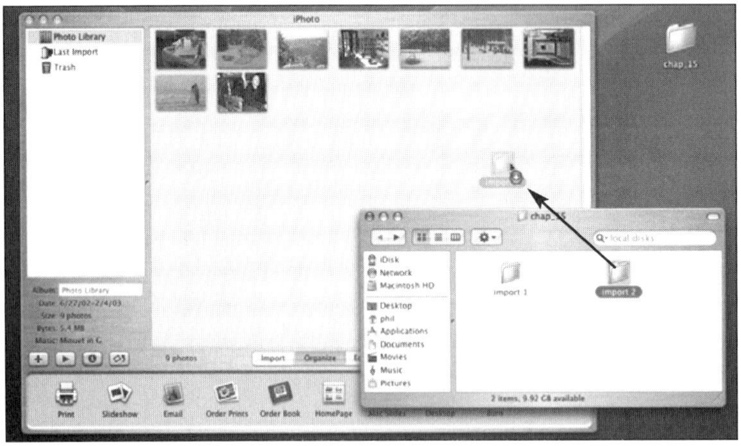

7. Position the window so you can see the iPhoto window behind it. Drag **import 2** into the photo viewing area of iPhoto. The images in this folder are copied into iPhoto.

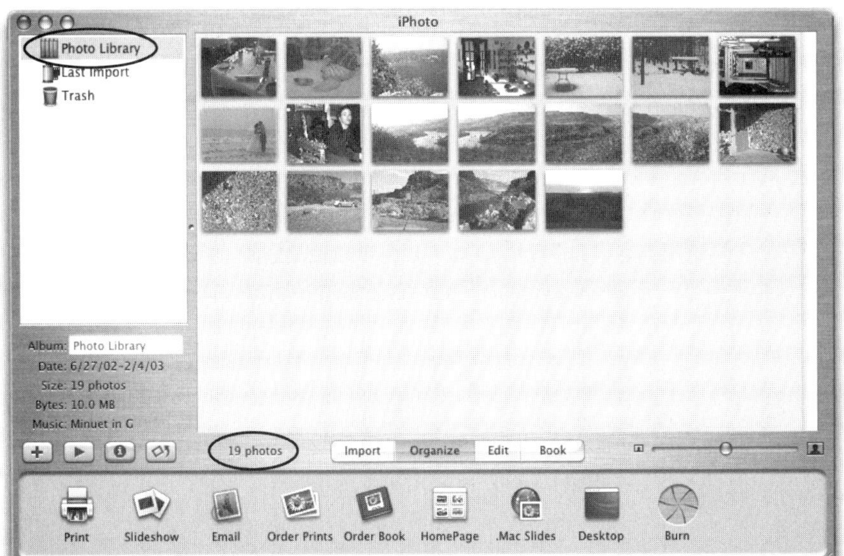

You should now have 19 photos in iPhoto (indicated near the bottom of the window). Viewing your photos in iPhoto is a lot like viewing your music library in iTunes. The column to the left of the iPhoto window determines which collection of photos is displayed in the main photo view area. You can create your own collections, or ***albums****, in this column to organize your photos into different collections (which you'll be learning to do shortly). Currently, your* ***Photo Library*** *is selected, which always displays all the photos in your collection.*

8. Select **Last Import** from this column. This album always displays the pictures that were imported most recently. Here you can see the 10 pictures you just dragged into iPhoto.

*The choices **Photo Library** and **Last Import** are always available no matter how many other albums you create. The **Trash** album choice is used for photos you no longer want, though, much like the Trash icon in the Dock, images in the iPhoto Trash are not permanently deleted until you do so manually.*

It's a good idea to create your own albums, especially as your collection of photos begins to grow. Albums allow you to organize and arrange your pictures in the order you want. They're especially useful for separating pictures from different events or for collecting the photos of friends or family, no matter when the picture was taken.

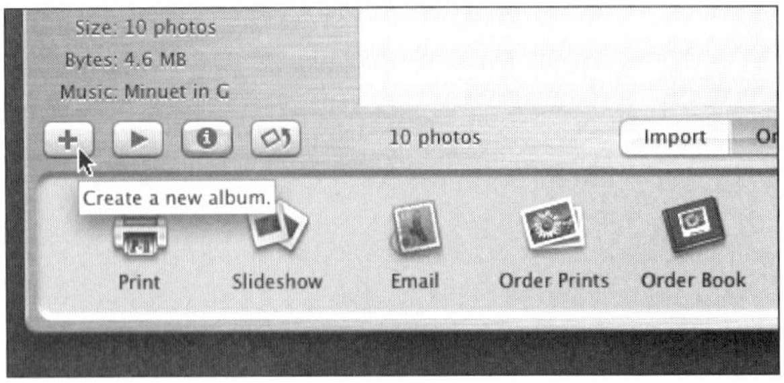

9. Click the **New Album** button in the lower-left corner of the window. A dialog box appears, asking you to enter a name for this album. Type **Snake River** and click **OK**.

The album now appears in the album column. Even though the name appears, the album is currently empty, so next you'll drag some of the pictures from your Library into it.

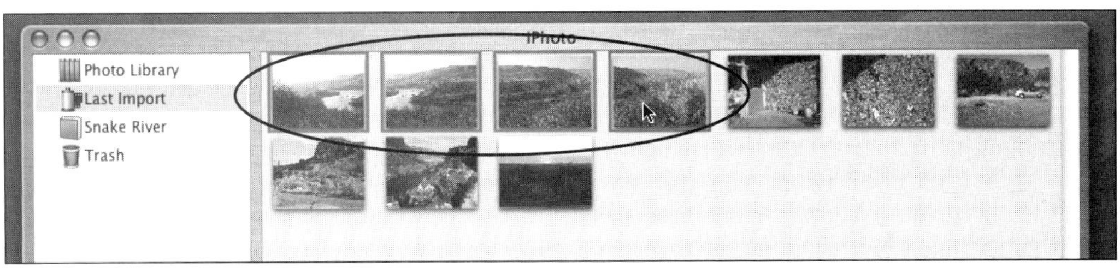

10. Hold the **Cmd** key and click the four pictures of the Snake River. (Refer to the screen shot if you need help locating them.) Release the **Cmd** key after all four are selected.

11. Click and drag any one of these four images to the **Snake River** album. A plus symbol appears, letting you know that you're adding these pictures to an album, and a small number four lets you know how many pictures you're moving. Make sure a rectangle appears around the **Snake River** album before releasing the mouse.

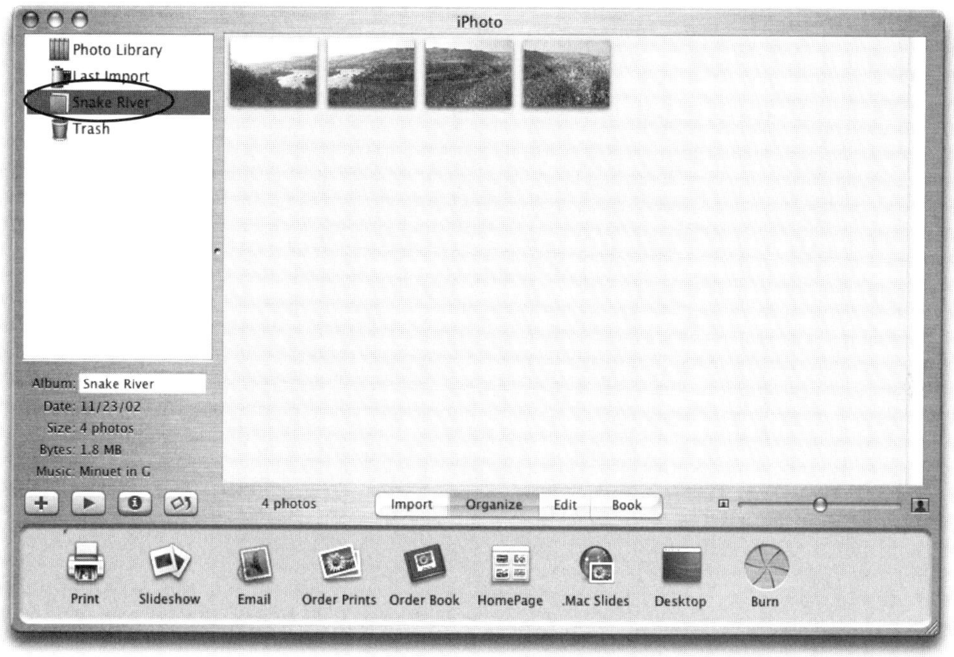

12. Click the **Snake River** album to see the images it contains.

TIP | Insta-Album

Instead of clicking the **New Album** button, you can create an album on the fly by selecting a group of photos (or even a single photo) and dragging them into the blank area in the album column.

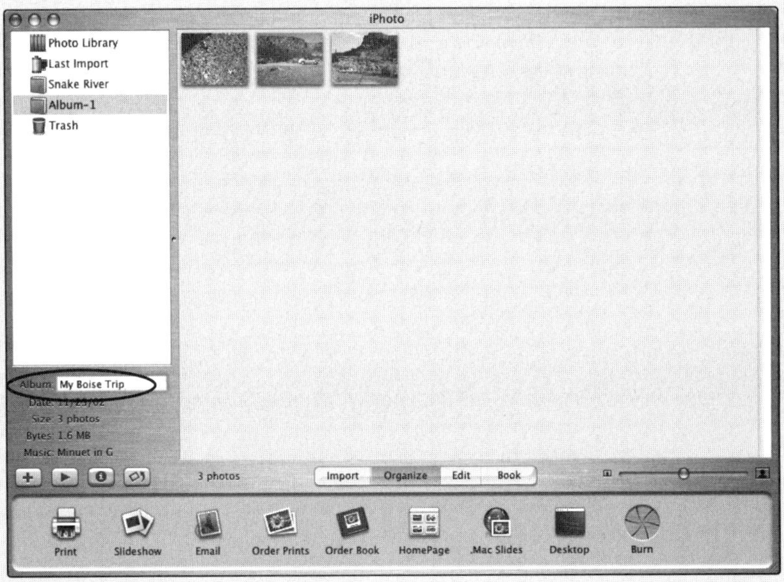

A new album will appear containing the pictures you dragged. You can give the album a more fitting name in the **Album** field.

In the previous chapter, you learned that dragging songs into a playlist you've created does not duplicate the song file itself. Similarly, the pictures you move into albums are not duplicated; rather, iPhoto creates a reference to the pictures in your main Library. Because the pictures are not copied, you can drag the same picture into multiple albums without increasing the overall file size of your photo collection. Also, as you're about to see, deleting a photo from an album or deleting an entire album itself does not delete the original pictures.

13. With the **Snake River** album selected, click the first picture on the left in the photo viewing area and press the **Delete** key. The photo disappears instantly. (You could have also dragged the picture to the **Trash** icon under the **Snake River** album.)

14. Click the **Photo Library** to view your entire collection. Notice that the image you deleted from the **Snake River** album is still here in the **Photo Library**. If you wanted to, you could drag the picture back into the **Snake River** album.

15. Select the same picture here in your **Photo Library** and press **Delete**.

The image disappears again, but this time, notice that the Trash icon has changed to indicate that a photo has been deleted. Because you selected the image in your Photo Library, iPhoto assumes that you really want to delete it, not just remove it from an album. The Photo Library serves as the master collection file; the Snake River grouping represents an album that uses images from the Photo Library. To use the iTunes comparison again, the Photo Library is the equivalent of importing an CD, and the Snake River collection is the equivalent of a playlist.

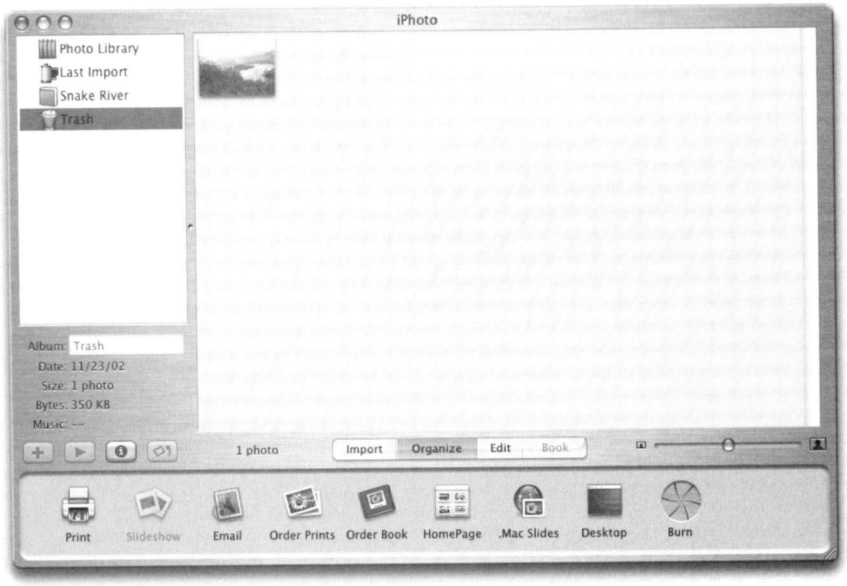

16. Click the **Trash** icon.

*At this point, you could **Ctrl+click** the **Trash** and choose **Empty Trash** to permanently delete this picture from iPhoto. Just be aware that this action can't be undone if you change your mind.*

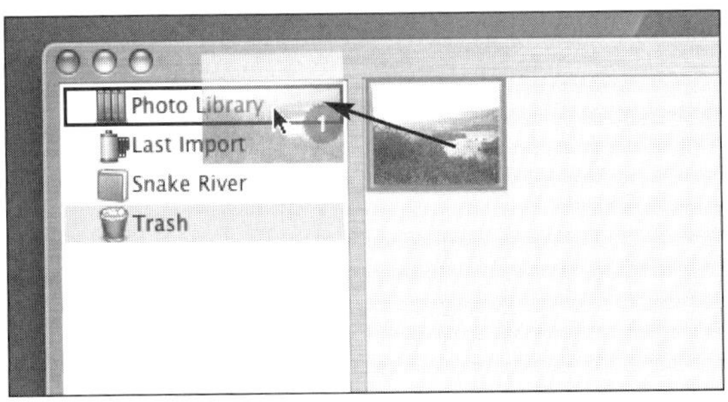

17. Instead, drag the picture's thumbnail back into the **Photo Library**. This is a good way to recover a file that you accidentally threw in the Trash.

18. Keep **iPhoto** open for the next exercise.

Now that you know how to import and organize photos in iPhoto, move onto the next exercise to learn how to edit and enhance your pictures.

Importing from a Digital Camera

In real life, you probably won't be doing that much importing of images that already reside on your hard drive. iPhoto exists you so can easily transfer the pictures you snap on your digital camera onto your Mac. And the process couldn't be easier. iPhoto works with most of the popular digital cameras available today. iPhoto even works with most card readers (the USB devices that read your camera's media cards). Check **www.apple.com/iphoto/compatibility** to see if your camera is compatible. Even if it's not listed, there's still a good chance that it will work with iPhoto.

To copy pictures from your camera into your Mac, connect the two devices using the cable that came with your camera. If iPhoto is running, it will switch to Import mode. If iPhoto isn't running, and you chose to have iPhoto open when connecting a camera (explained in the first step of Exercise 1), iPhoto will automatically run and switch to Import mode. If iPhoto doesn't open when you connect your camera, start it up yourself and click the **Import** button.

In Import mode, iPhoto displays the model of your camera and how many photos it contains. Click the **Import** button to copy the pictures to iPhoto. You can also check **Erase camera contents after transfer** if you want to clear your camera's memory card after the pictures have been imported.

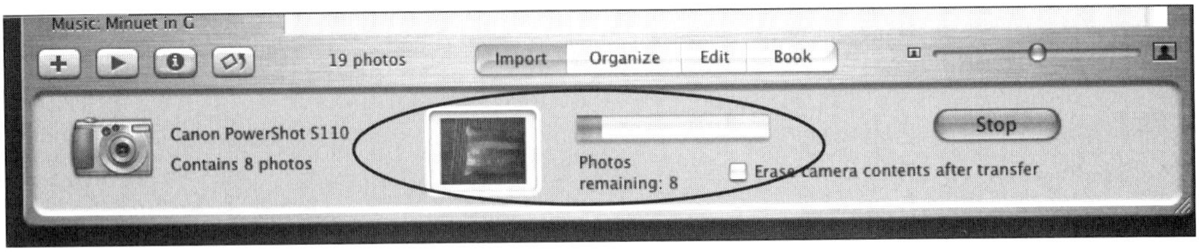

iPhoto displays thumbnails for each image as it's imported onto your Mac.

Once the photos have been imported, iPhoto switches back to Organize mode and you can begin working with the pictures.

NOTE | Image Capture

Before iPhoto came along, copying pictures from your digital camera to your Mac in OS X required using a program called Image Capture. Image Capture still comes with OS X and can be useful when you want to copy a photo to your Mac but you don't want it as part of your iPhoto Library. For example, maybe you'd like to email a friend a photo that's on your camera, but you don't need to keep a copy for yourself.

To use Image Capture, connect your camera to your Mac. If iPhoto starts up, just ignore it (or quit). Open **Image Capture** from your **Applications** folder.

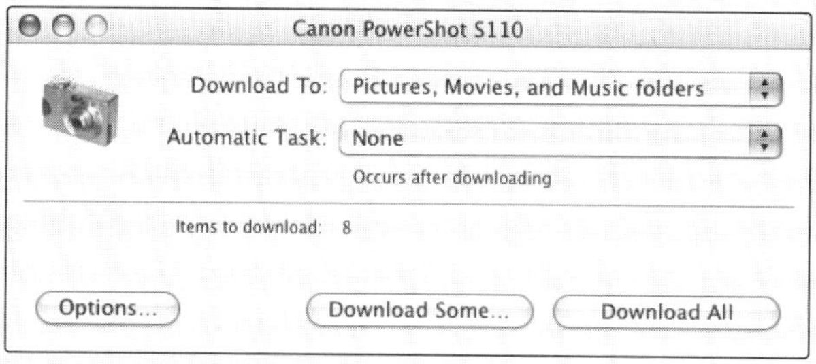

Your camera's model appears in the title bar of the Image Capture window. From here, you can select a location from the **Download To** menu to store your images. Click **Download All** to copy all the pictures to your Mac.

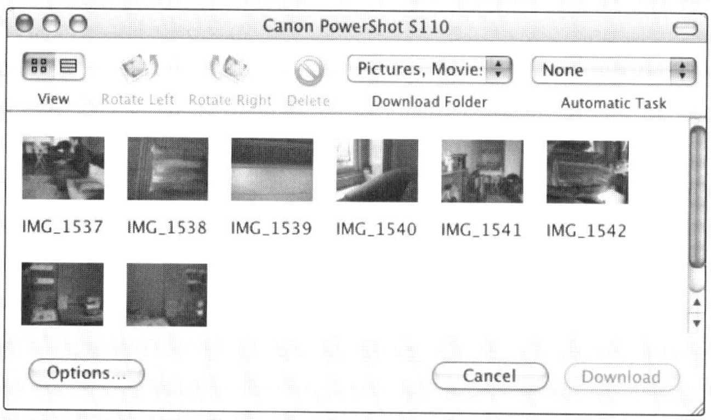

You can also click **Download Some** to select specific thumbnails for the images on your camera–something you can't do in iPhoto.

iPhoto is by far the more powerful program of the two, but Image Capture is a great app for quickly grabbing some pictures that you don't want to store in iPhoto. If you change your mind, you can always drag or import the pictures into iPhoto later using the methods you learned in Exercise 1.

2. Viewing and Editing Pictures

Once you've imported your pictures into iPhoto, you can do any number of things to and with them. This exercise shows you how to name, edit, and touch up your pictures.

When you snap a picture with your digital camera, your camera creates a file, and in most cases, gives the picture a cryptic name like **IMG_20029BA.jpg** or something like that. If you've ever imported images from a digital camera onto a Windows PC, you've probably seen this type of naming convention firsthand. iPhoto gives you an easy way to rename your image files with names an ordinary person can understand.

1. Click once on some of the thumbnails in iPhoto. (You should be in **Organize** mode right now.) Under the **Albums** column to the left, notice how some of the images have titles like **IMG_0038** and **STB_0023**, while other images have already been renamed with easy-to-comprehend titles like **table**, **shells**, and **lake**.

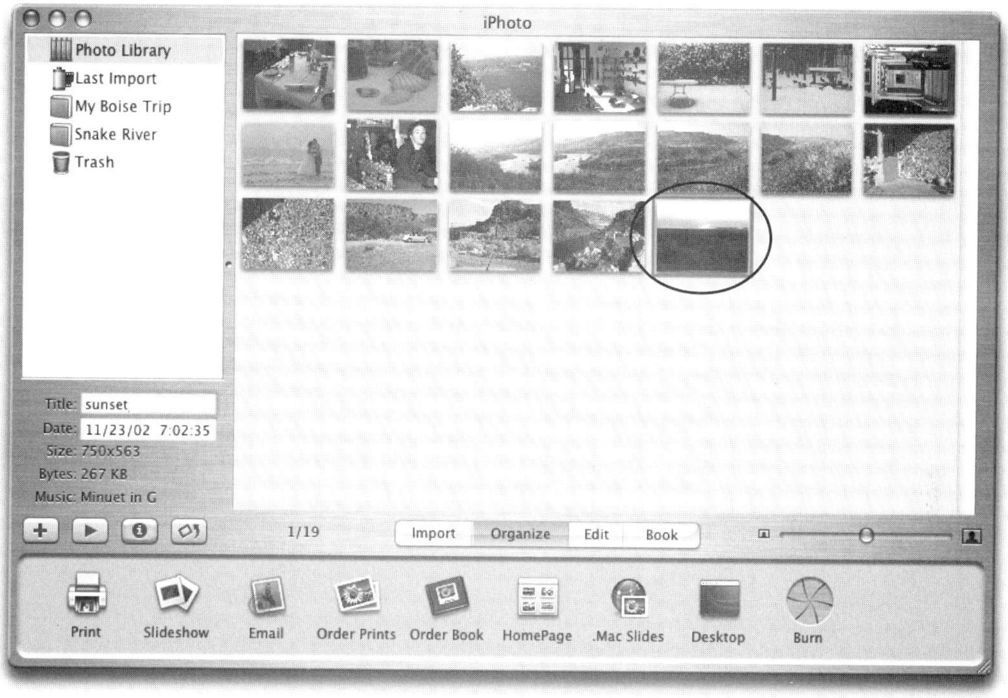

2. Select the image of the sunset (it should be the last image). Currently its title is **IMG_0047**. Rename it as **sunset**.

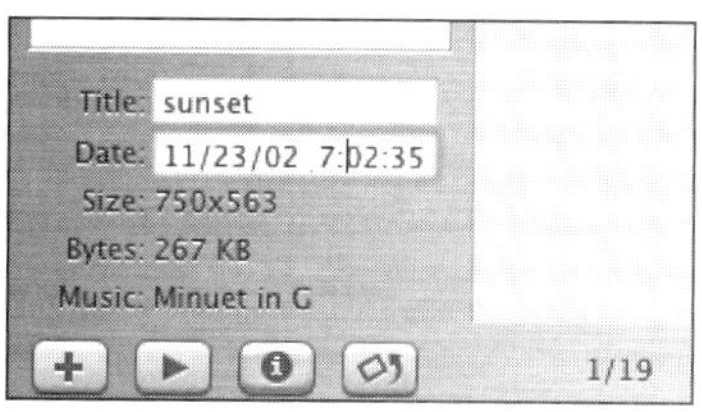

Using a plain-English title gives you a way to identify a picture without enlarging it onscreen. You can make the title as detailed as you like. Note also that you can change the Date information as well if the time in your camera was set incorrectly when you took the photo.

TIP | Searching

One of the main advantages of giving your photos easy-to-understand titles is that it will make it easier to locate them through iPhoto's Search function later. To find a photo you've titled, choose **Edit > Keywords** (or press **Cmd+K**).

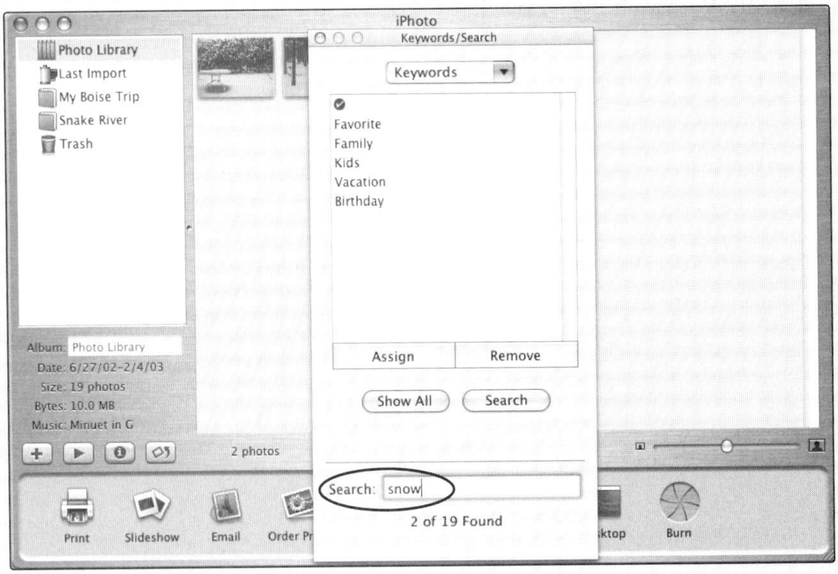

In the **Keywords/Search** window, type your search term in the **Search** field. iPhoto instantly displays any photo names that match your search. If you have trouble locating the images mentioned in the rest of this exercise, use the Search function to locate them.

You can also assign keywords to images here. For more information, see the "Adding Keywords" section at the end of this exercise.

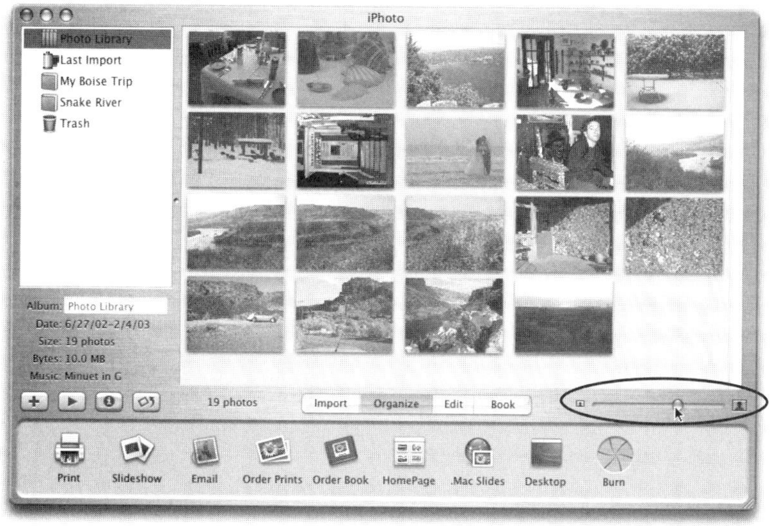

Note: *If you have trouble identifying your pictures, you can increase the size of the thumbnails by moving the* ***magnification*** *slider to the right. But keep in mind that these are called thumbnails because they're supposed to be smaller, more manageable versions of the full-sized images. If you want to work with an image at full size, you need to enter Edit mode.*

To enter Edit mode, select a thumbnail and click ***Edit****, or just double-click the thumbnail.*

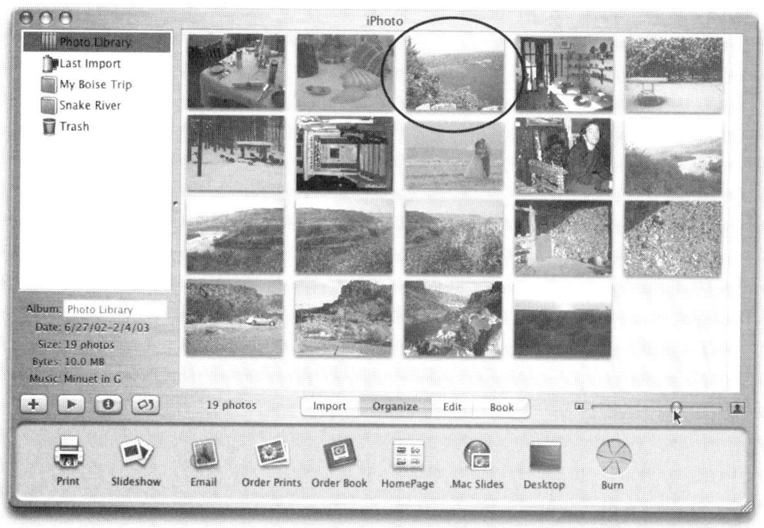

3. Locate and double-click the image called **lake**. It opens in **Edit** mode.

In Edit mode, iPhoto's editing tools all appear at the bottom of the window in the form of buttons and sliders. They can all be used to alter the appearance of the currently selected photo. For example, you can adjust the brightness and contrast of the image by moving their sliders until you are satisfied with them.

NOTE | Important Editing Information

In this exercise, you're going to be changing the appearance of several of the photos you've imported. Editing a picture changes it in your main Photo Library and, therefore, in every album in which it appears. If you're unhappy with the result of an edit, you can always undo any changes by pressing **Cmd+Z**. If you've made several contiguous edits to your image, iPhoto allows you to press **Cmd+Z** multiple times. You can also choose **File > Revert to Original** if you want to scrap your changes and start over with the original version of the image. You can revert to the original even if you've quit iPhoto and restarted it since making the changes.

If you want to edit a picture without changing it in all albums in which it appears, select its thumbnail in the main iPhoto Library and choose **File > Duplicate** to create a copy of the file to work with.

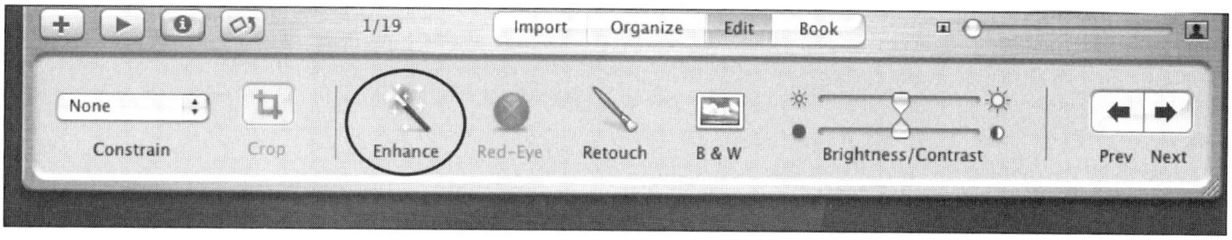

*A feature that debuted in iPhoto 2 is the **Enhance** button, which can dramatically improve the appearance of your photos. When you click the Enhance button, iPhoto examines the selected image and automatically adjusts the brightness, contrast, and color saturation to create a richer, more vibrant rendering of the picture. At least that's what it's supposed to do. You'll have to judge whether it does a good job or not.*

---

4. With the **lake** image still in **Edit** mode, click the **Enhance** button. After a moment, you should observe a distinct change in the photograph. The greens and blues have become deeper, and the overall reddish cast has been reduced. But does it look better? That's for you to decide.

Tip: *You can click the **Enhance** button multiple times to increase the effect. After enhancing a photo–or after using any of the other editing tools–pressing the **Ctrl** key lets you compare the altered version with the original image. If you prefer the original, press **Cmd+Z** to undo the edit.*

Next, you'll enhance another picture with a decidedly different set of colors.

5. Click the **Organize** button to return to the thumbnail view of your **Photo Library**. Locate and double-click the image called **snow_patio**. It's a picture of a snow-covered patio table.

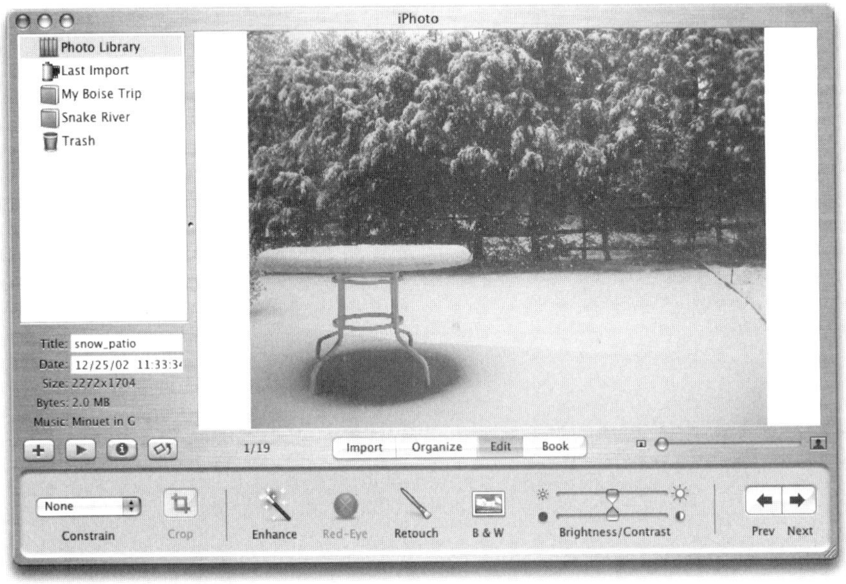

Snow scenes are always tricky to photograph because of the extreme whiteness of snow mingled with the light and color of the other elements of the picture. This image, for instance, has a hazy, gray cast.

6. Click the **Enhance** button. The result should be a sharper-looking picture in which the snow looks white and the trees in the background are a nice deep green. (Again, you can press **Ctrl** to compare this with the original image.)

Next, you'll take a look at another editing tool.

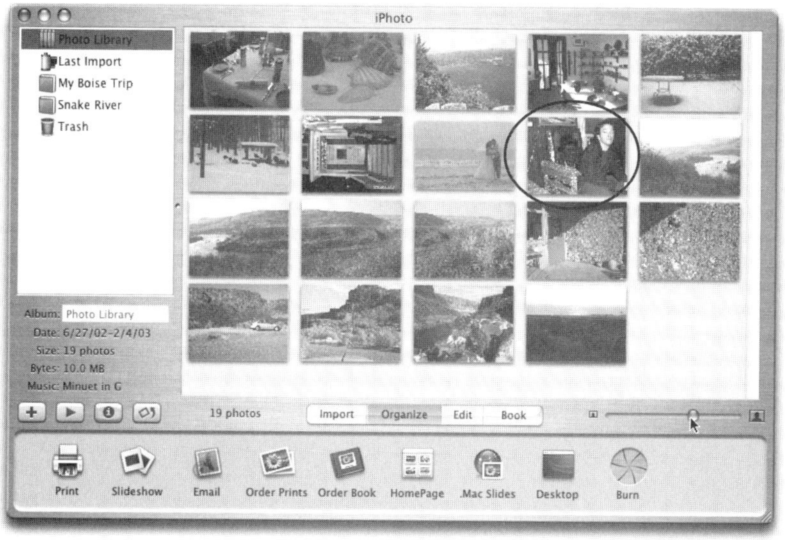

7. Click the **Organize** button to return to the **Photo Library**. Locate and double-click the image called **red_eye**.

Redeye occurs in flash photography when the light from the flash is reflected off the blood vessels lining the back wall of the subject's eyes. This pesky problem can ruin an otherwise great photo. In this picture, the subject's eyes look just slightly demonic. Fortunately, iPhoto has a pretty good red-eye correction effect. To get a better look at this effect in action, you'll first magnify this image.

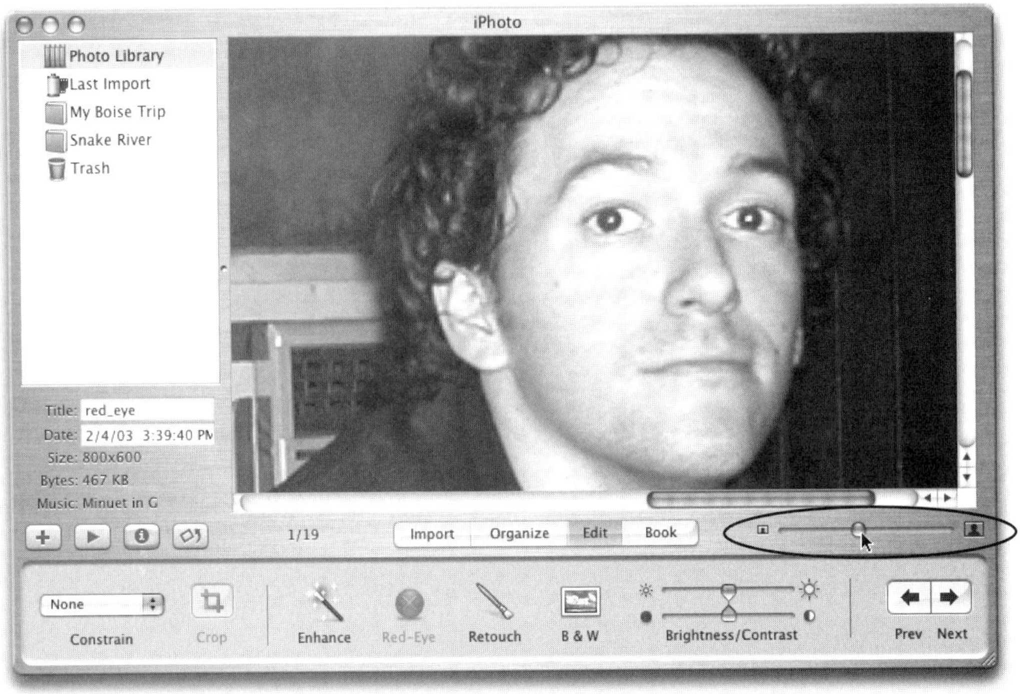

8. Drag the **magnification slider** towards the right, just about to the middle point. Use the vertical and horizontal scrollbars to center the subject's head in the window.

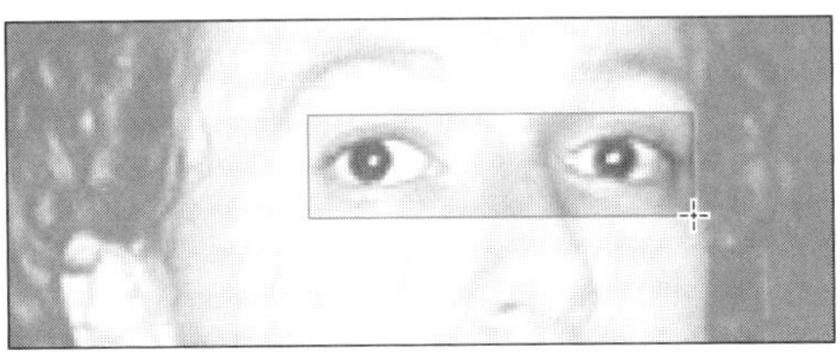

9. Place your cursor over the photo and notice how it becomes a crosshair. Using the crosshair, draw a rectangle as tightly as you can around the subject's eyes. This activates the **Red-Eye** button at the bottom of the window.

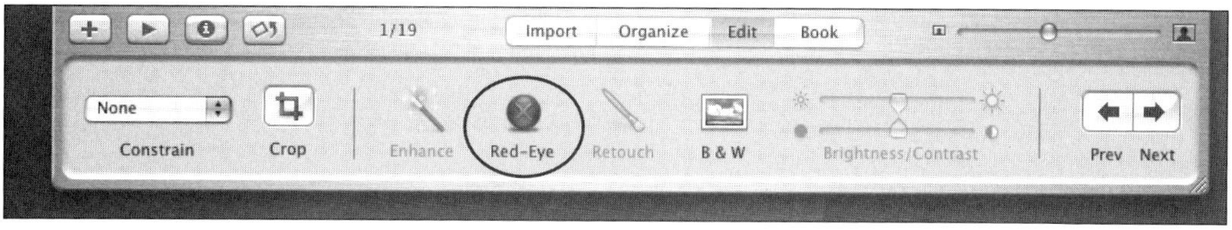

10. Click the **Red-Eye** button. iPhoto scans the selected area for shades of red and eliminates them. Pretty amazing, huh? Drag the photo size slider back to the far left and notice how much more natural the subject's eyes look. While you're at it, click the **Enhance** button to see if you can liven up the photo a little more.

*Another one of iPhoto's new editing tools is the **Retouch** button. Often, when working with a scanned picture, you might notice scratches or dust present in the image. Rather than rescanning the picture, first give the Retouch tool a try to see if it can fix the problem for you.*

11. Click the **Previous picture** button in the lower-right corner of the window to display the picture that immediately precedes the currently selected image in your library. You should see a picture of a couple standing on the beach. (If not, click the **Organize** button to locate and double-click this image.)

This image may look okay initially, but it actually contains a few imperfections.

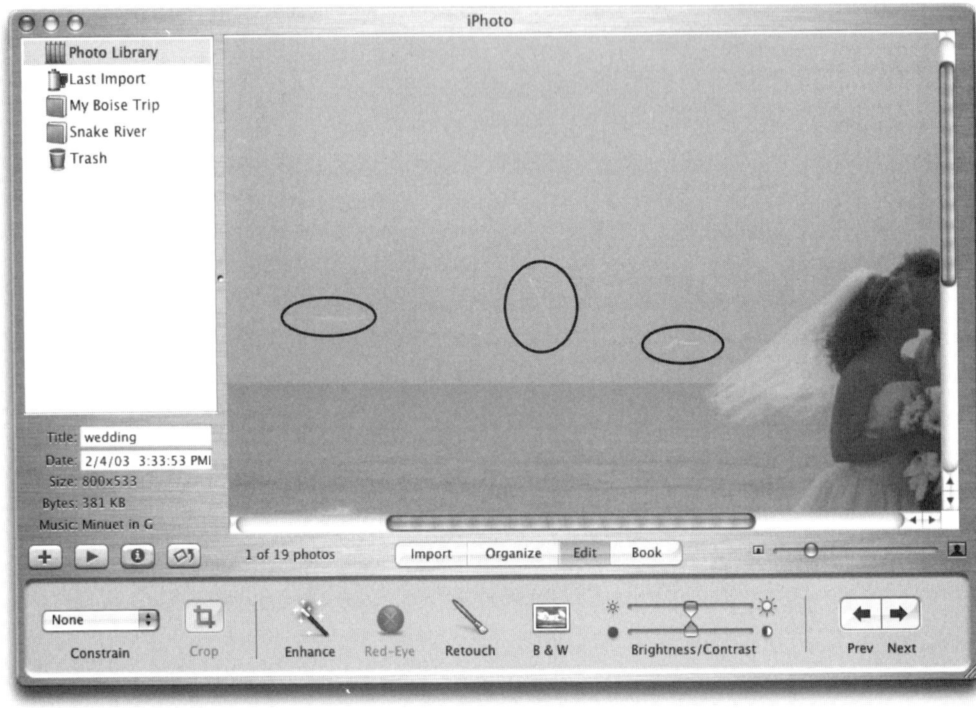

12. Drag the **magnification** slider slightly to the right and use the scrollbars to position the couple to the right of the window. Use this screen shot as a guide. Notice the scratches and dust in the skyline. These may seem like minor flaws, but there's no sense leaving them there if iPhoto can easily fix them.

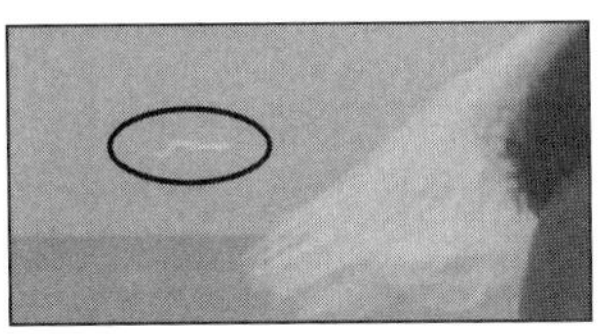

13. Click the **Retouch** button. If necessary, further enlarge the image with the **magnification** slider. Place the cursor over the dust mark near the bride's veil and brush the cursor back and forth over it while holding down the mouse button. After a few passes, the dust should disappear. Use the scrollbars to examine the skyline for other imperfections to retouch. When you're done, drag the **magnification** slider back to the left to display the entire photo.

The picture should look a little better now. But what else can you do to improve it? Well, the photo looks as if it was taken on an overcast day, which you can't do much about. But what if you were to convert the picture to black and white? For some photos, black and white conveys a timeless, sophisticated quality, and in this case, it may relieve the flatness of this image.

14. Click the **B & W** button. After a moment, iPhoto converts the picture to shades of gray. But it still looks kind of washed-out.

15. Click the **Enhance** button. There! That looks much better. Good enough to be found on a postcard on the impulse item rack at your local bookstore.

iPhoto also allows you to crop your pictures to eliminate unnecessary background, encouraging the viewer's eyes to focus on the subject.

16. Using the cursor crosshair, draw a rectangle like the one shown here.

Tip: *If you're having trouble positioning the rectangle, just draw the approximate shape. You can then place your cursor within the rectangle and drag it into position.*

17. Click the **Crop** button. You now have a nice, cropped black and white photo.

Let's take a look at one more photo.

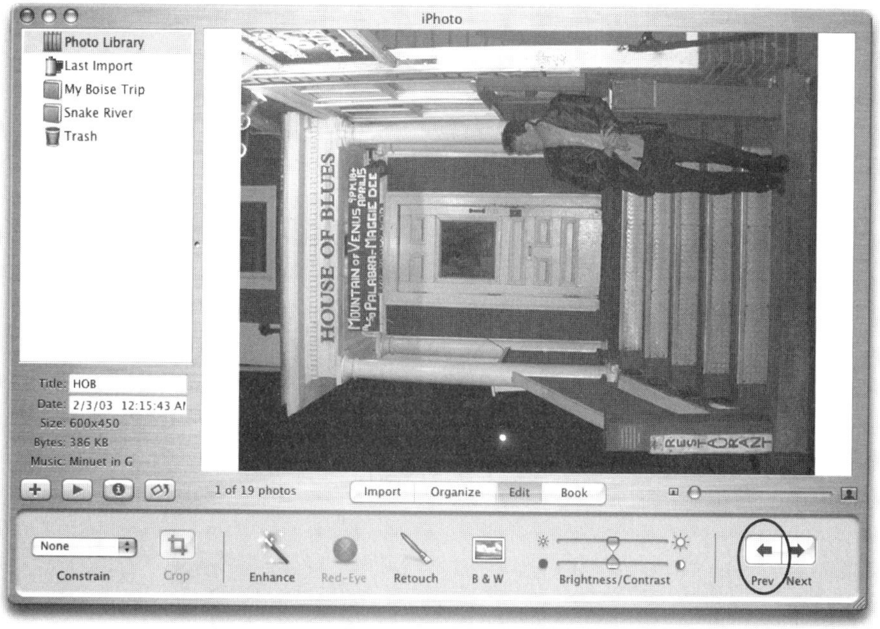

18. Click the **Previous picture** button to view the picture preceding the current one. This image was shot vertically, but iPhoto has no way of knowing that. You might want to rotate this picture 90 degrees clockwise (or 270 degrees counter-clockwise if you're opposed to typical clockwise-centric snobbery.)

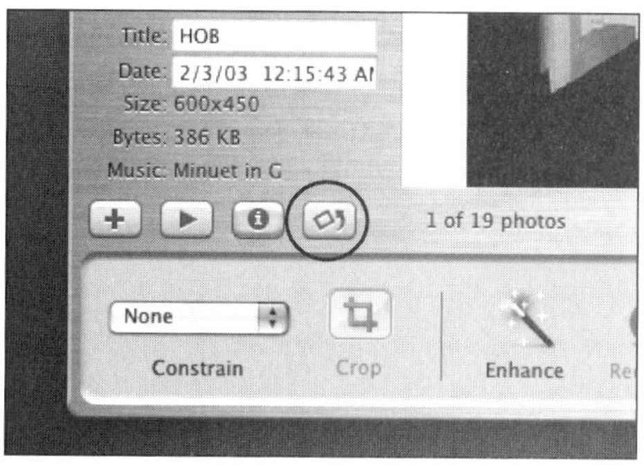

*The **Rotate** button is located in the lower-left corner of the window, but notice that its icon indicates that the picture will be rotated counter-clockwise. No one's saying that you couldn't just click this button three times, but there's an easier way.*

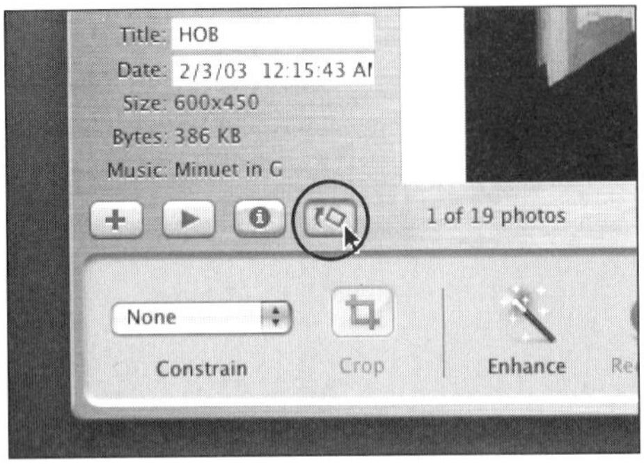

19. Press the **Option** key. The **Rotate** button reverses direction. Click it to turn the image right side up. As a final touch, click the **Enhance** button to improve the picture's color balance.

Tip: You can also rotate a picture by ***Ctrl+clicking*** *on the picture and choosing either* ***Rotate > Clockwise*** *or* ***Rotate > Counter Clockwise*** *from the contextual menu.*

20. Click the **Organize** button to return to the main **Photo Library**. The thumbnails here should now reflect the altered wedding photo and the rotated vertical photo. Keep **iPhoto** open for the next exercise.

Although there are other, more powerful photo editing applications available for OS X, if you're just a photo hobbyist, you'll probably find that iPhoto's editing tools handle most of the tasks needed to alter the appearance of your images.

Adding Keywords

In addition to grouping your photos together into albums, iPhoto also lets you add **keywords** to your pictures so you can easily find all the photos in a specific category. For example, you can label any vacation-related photos, regardless of which vacation or album they're from, and call them all **vacation**. Or take all the photos you shot at concerts and label them with a **concerts** keyword.

To add a keyword to a photo, select the image or images you want to label, and then select **Edit > Keywords (Cmd+K)**. Select a keyword from the list (or create a new keyword from the pop-up menu at the top of the window) and click **Assign**. You can assign more than one keyword to an image if you feel the picture falls into multiple categories. You can also keep the **Keyword/Search** window open to assign keywords to additional photos by selecting them, clicking a keyword, and then clicking **Assign**.

Tip: If you can't come up with a name for a group of photos, but you still want to make them easier to find, assign them the check symbol from the list of keywords. This will add a small checkmark to the lower-right corner of the image's thumbnail.

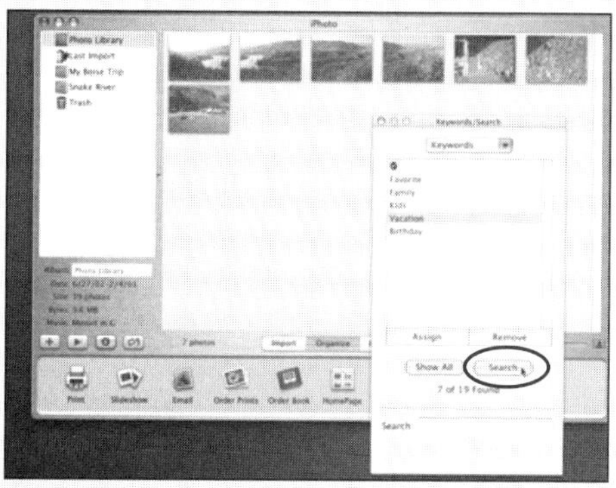

Once you've assigned keywords to your pictures, you can quickly find all the pictures from a specific category, including checked photos, by selecting a keyword and clicking **Search**.

iPhoto Preferences

If you look closely at the thumbnails in the main photo viewing area of iPhoto, you'll notice that each one has a small "drop shadow." A drop shadow is a fake shadow designed to make the image above it appear to hover over the background. It's a nice effect, but it does tend to be processor-intensive, and on older Macs you may find that iPhoto begins to slow down as your Photo Library grows. Turning off the drop shadow effect can help iPhoto run faster.

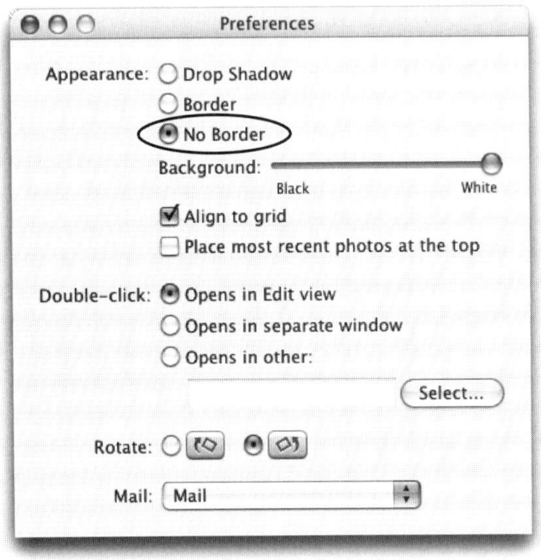

To turn off drop shadows, choose **iPhoto > Preferences** from the menu bar and click the **No Border** button. You'll see the drop shadows disappear right away.

The Preferences dialog box offers several other ways to customize the behavior of iPhoto. The following chart describes each item found here.

iPhoto Preferences	
Option	**Description**
Appearance	**Drop Shadow** places a soft shadow behind the thumbnails; **Border** places a white border around each thumbnail that can't be seen unless you change the background color (see the following description for **Background**); and **No Border** removes all decorations from the thumbnails.
Background	This slider allows you to adjust the color of the main photo viewing area. You can have black, white, or any level of gray. As you move the slider, the background color changes simultaneously.
Align to grid	When checked, keeps the thumbnails in line with each other, regardless of whether images are turned vertically or horizontally. When unchecked, the thumbnails are spaced evenly across in rows, but not in columns.
Place most recent photos at the top	Unchecked by default, so the most recently imported images appear at the bottom of the photo viewing area. Check this option to reverse the order.
Double-click: Opens in Edit view	This is the default setting you saw in action in this exercise. Double-clicking a thumbnail switches iPhoto to Edit mode within the same window.
Double-click: Opens in separate window	Double-clicking still opens the image in Edit mode, but in its own window. Opening a picture in its own window allows you to view it at a larger size without the constraints of the main iPhoto window.
Double-click: Opens in other	If you prefer to edit your images in another application, such as Adobe Photoshop, check this option. Then click **Select** to locate your image-editing application.
Rotate	These two buttons allow you to select the default action of the Rotate button. For instance, if you know that you always need to rotate your vertical pictures clockwise, select the clockwise rotation button here.
Mail	Use this pop-up menu to select the default mail program iPhoto uses to email your pictures. You'll learn more about emailing pictures shortly.

MOVIE | photo_edit.mov

See the movie **photo_edit.mov** on the **H•O•T CD-ROM** for a demonstration of the tools covered in this exercise.

3. Creating a Slideshow

Once you've imported and edited your photos, you'll probably want to share them with friends and relatives. iPhoto offers several ways for you to share your pictures, such as printing them, compiling them into a slideshow, burning them onto a CD, and publishing them on the Web. The next few exercises walk you through each of these activities. First, you'll learn how to create a slideshow.

If you observe the bottom portion of the iPhoto window while in Organize mode, you'll see nine buttons, each representing different ways to share your photographs.

*For instance, to print a picture, choose **File > Page Setup** to configure iPhoto for your printer, then click once on the picture's thumbnail and click the **Print** button. From there, it's a pretty straightforward process of selecting your printer and clicking **Print**. (If you need a refresher on printing, see Chapter 6,* "Printing, Fonts, and Faxing."*)*

Printing a Contact Sheet

One useful option in iPhoto's Print dialog box is the capability to print a **contact sheet**. A contact sheet is a photographic term for a single sheet of thumbnails for photos on a roll of film. In iPhoto, you can print a contact sheet of your library or album so you can have a paper copy for yourself to refer to or to show others.

To print a contact sheet, select your library or an album and make sure that no thumbnails are selected. (Click in a blank area of the picture viewing area to deselect any selected thumbnails.) Then click **Print** (or choose **File > Print**).

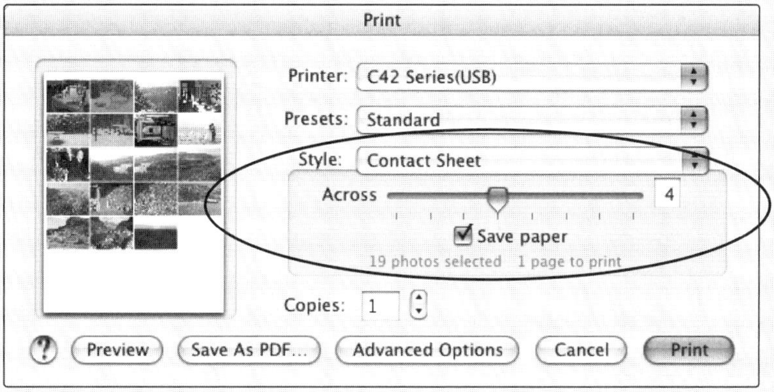

This is iPhoto's version of the **Print** dialog box. Click **Advanced Options** to view the regular print dialog box for your selected printer.

In the **Print** dialog box, choose **Contact Sheet** from the **Style** pop-up menu. You can use the slider below it to determine how many thumbnails will be printed in each row. The preview of the page to the left gives you an idea of how the printout will look. Check **Save paper** to create smaller margins between the images, which allows you to fit more thumbnails on the page. Click **Print** when you're done making selections.

Of course, printing your pictures is not always the ideal way to show them to friends and family. For one thing, printing can get pretty expensive. So, the next time you have friends, family, or any other type of captive audience visiting, why not revive the lost art of the slideshow? iPhoto's Slideshow function is an elegant way to present your pictures, especially if you can hook up your Mac to a TV or projector. (But there's nothing wrong with having everyone crowd around your computer either. It brings people closer together.)

1. Select the **Photo Library** and click the **Slideshow** button at the bottom of the window. This opens the **Slideshow Settings** dialog box.

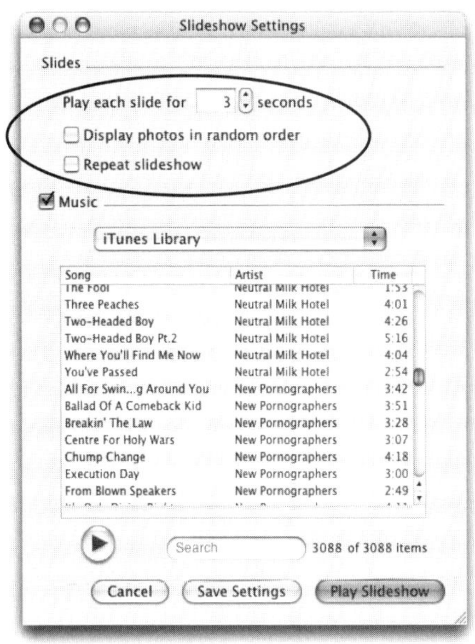

2. Configure the slideshow to play each picture (slide) for **3** seconds, and uncheck **Display photos in random order** and **Repeat slideshow** if they're selected. This will display each picture from your Library in order for three seconds each, and stop the slideshow after the last image is displayed.

Note: *The length of time for each slide to be displayed is completely arbitrary. If you're the kind of person who likes to narrate as the pictures go by, you might want to increase the time between slides for your own slideshows.*

New to iPhoto 2 is the integration of your iTunes library in this window.

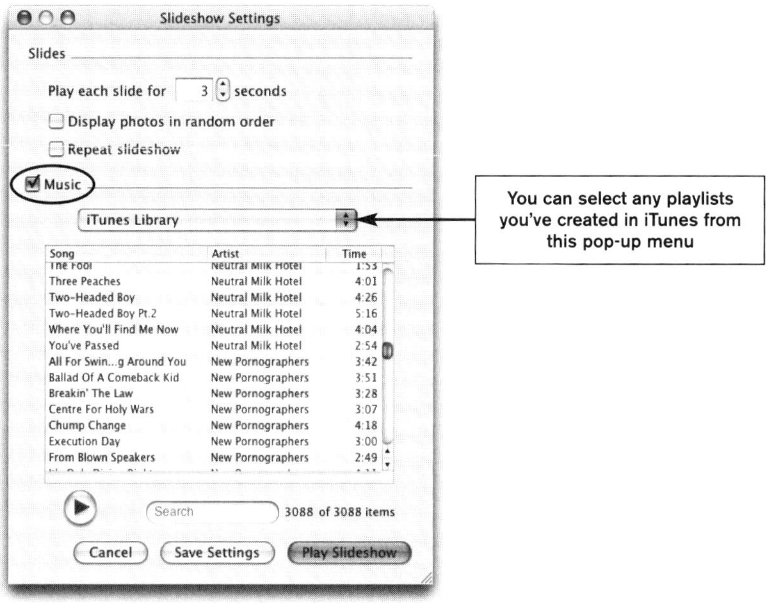

3. Check **Music** and select a song from the list.

Tip: *Use the* ***Search*** *field to find a specific song, just like in iTunes. Use the* ***Play*** *button to hear the song to make sure that you want to use it for your slideshow.*

4. Once you've selected a song, click **Play Slideshow**. iTunes drops into **Full Screen** mode and starts showing your slides with nice cross-fade transitions, accompanied by your selected music.

Tip: *If your slideshow outlasts your selected song, the song will repeat. You could also create a special playlist of songs in iTunes to try to match the length of your slideshow, and then choose it from the pop-up menu in Slideshow Settings.*

When the show is finished, iPhoto returns you to the main library.

Creating an Album Slideshow

In most cases, you won't want to use your entire Photo Library for a slideshow. To display only certain pictures, create an album as you learned to do in Exercise 1. Creating an album also gives you the ability to arrange your photos in any order you wish.

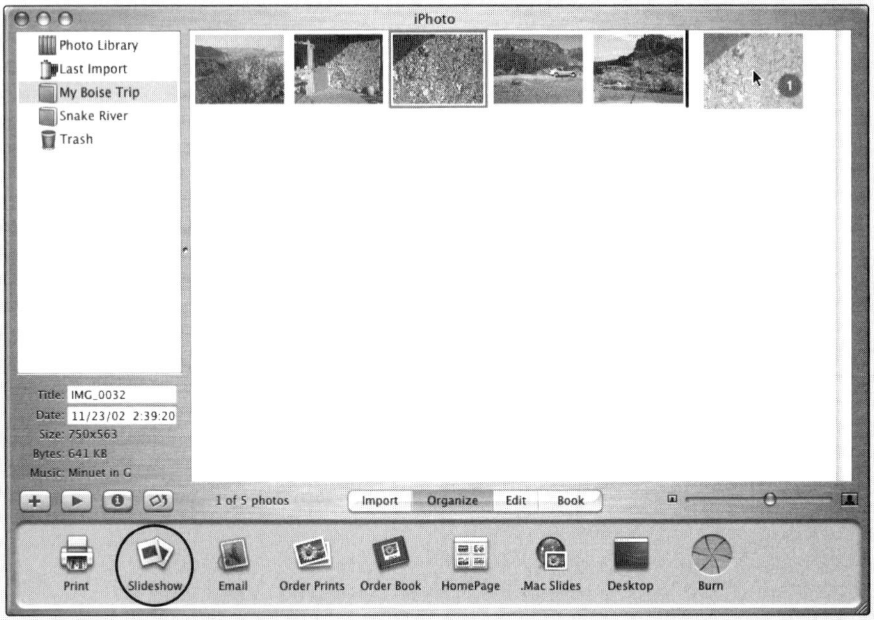

Simply drag photos around until they are displayed in the order you want them to play. Then click the **Slideshow** button, adjust any settings you want, and click **Play Slideshow**.

Tip: If you're happy with your slideshow settings, click the **Save Settings** button so you don't have to make changes every time.

Using Slideshow is a great way to show your pictures on your Mac. Another, more permanent way of creating a slideshow is to use iPhoto's capability to generate a QuickTime movie.

5. With your main **Photo Library** selected, choose **File > Export** from the menu bar.

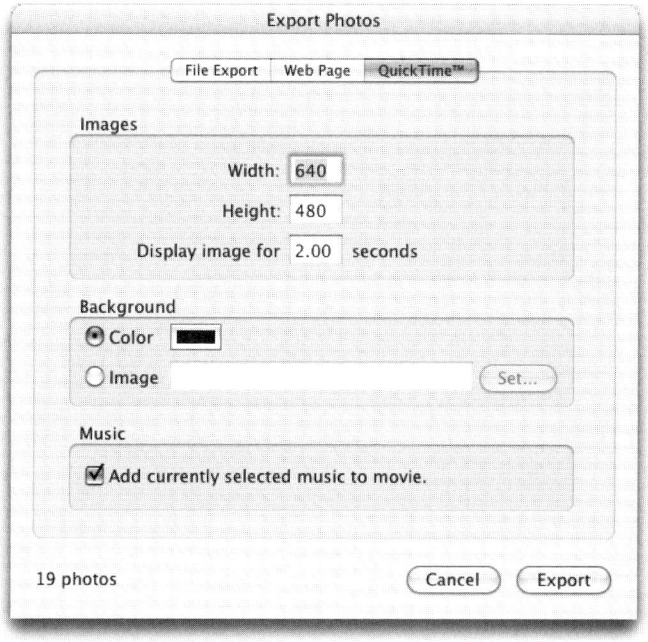

6. In the **Export Photos** window that opens, click the **QuickTime** button. Leave the default settings of having the movie sized at **640 x 480** pixels with each image being displayed for **2** seconds. The **Background Color** should be black and make sure **Add currently selected music to movie** is checked. Click **Export**.

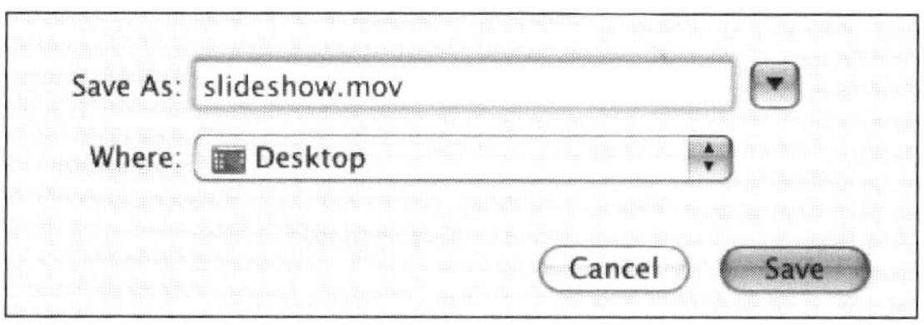

7. Name the file **slideshow.mov** and choose the **Desktop** as the location. Click **Save**.

*iPhoto takes a few moments to export the pictures. The file **slideshow.mov** should appear on your Desktop when it's done.*

8. Find **slideshow.mov** on your **Desktop** and double-click it. When QuickTime opens, click the **Play** button. You now have a QuickTime version of your slideshow, complete with transitions and music in a file that's only about 2.2 MB in size. You could email this to a friend or post it to a Web site. Quit **QuickTime** and return to **iPhoto** when you're done watching the movie.

4. Emailing Photos

Speaking of email, another option for sharing pictures with friends is to email them. iPhoto gives you a one-click method of doing this.

1. Select any thumbnail in your **Photo Library** and click the **Email** button at the bottom of the window.

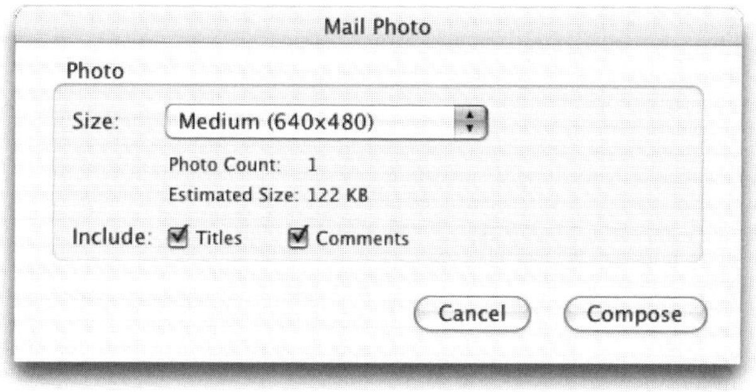

*In the **Mail Photo** dialog box that opens, you can select the size for the image you're sending (**Small**, **Medium**, **Large**, or **Full Quality**). With the exception of Full Quality, iPhoto applies compression to the image based on the size setting you choose, making it small enough to email even to friends with dial-up Internet connections. The Full Quality setting applies no compression, so if you have a high-resolution image, you might want to make sure that your recipient has a fast connection. The **Estimated Size** display can help you to determine which Size setting to select. If you know your friend uses iPhoto, you can also include **Titles** and **Comments** so that they'll appear in his or her copy of iPhoto as well.*

2. Choose **Medium** as the **Size** and click **Compose**. iPhoto takes a moment to compress the photo and then opens your default email program. (Your default email program is determined in **iPhoto > Preferences**, as described in the chart at the end of Exercise 2.)

Once your email program opens, a new message window is automatically created with the picture already attached. From here, you just need to address this email to someone, maybe compose a short message, and send it off.

---

3. Quit **Mail** (or whichever email program iPhoto opened) without sending this email, and return to **iPhoto**.

*The next two buttons along the bottom of the iPhoto window are **Order Prints** and **Order Book**. These two options are covered in Exercise 6. But first, you'll continue examining other methods of sharing your photos.*

---

5. Publishing Photos via .Mac

If you have a .Mac account, iPhoto allows you to publish your photos as a .Mac Web page and as .Mac slides. These next few steps show you how to do this.

Note: You need an active .Mac account to perform these steps. You should still have the trial account you created in Chapter 12, "*.Mac.*" If not, go to **www.mac.com** to create a new free trial account if you want to work along with this section of the exercise.

1. Press **Cmd** and select five or six photos from the main library. Click the **HomePage** button at the bottom of the window. iPhoto connects to the Internet and your .Mac account.

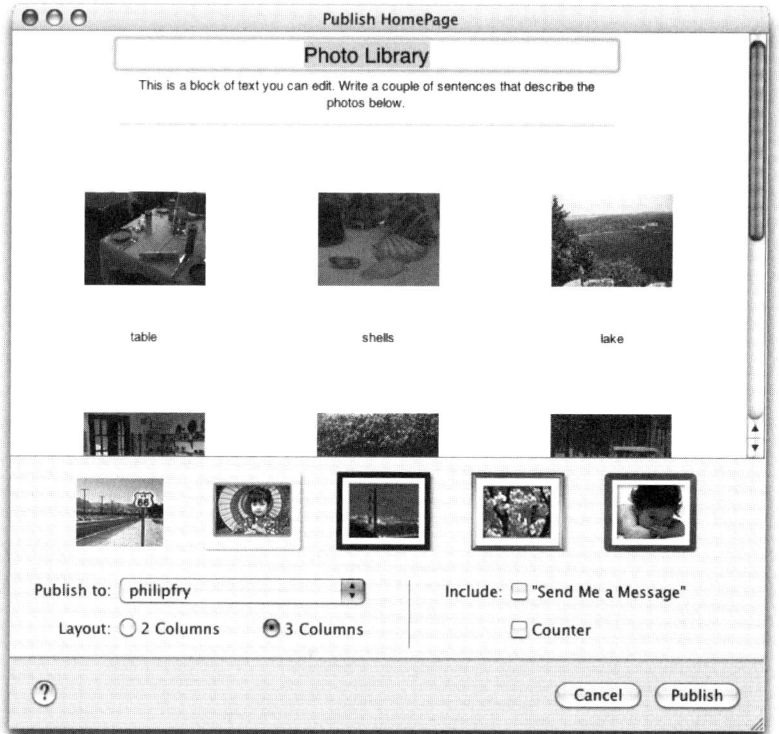

*After a few moments, the **Publish HomePage** window appears. This is an incredibly easy way to create a Web gallery of photos.*

2. Highlight the "Photo Library" text at the top of the page and change it by typing **iPhoto HOT Gallery**. Then highlight and replace the text below it with, **These are some photos from chapter 15 of Mac OS X Hands On Training**

Tip: You can also rename the titles under each picture. Any changes you make are exclusive to this Web page and won't be reflected in your iPhoto library.

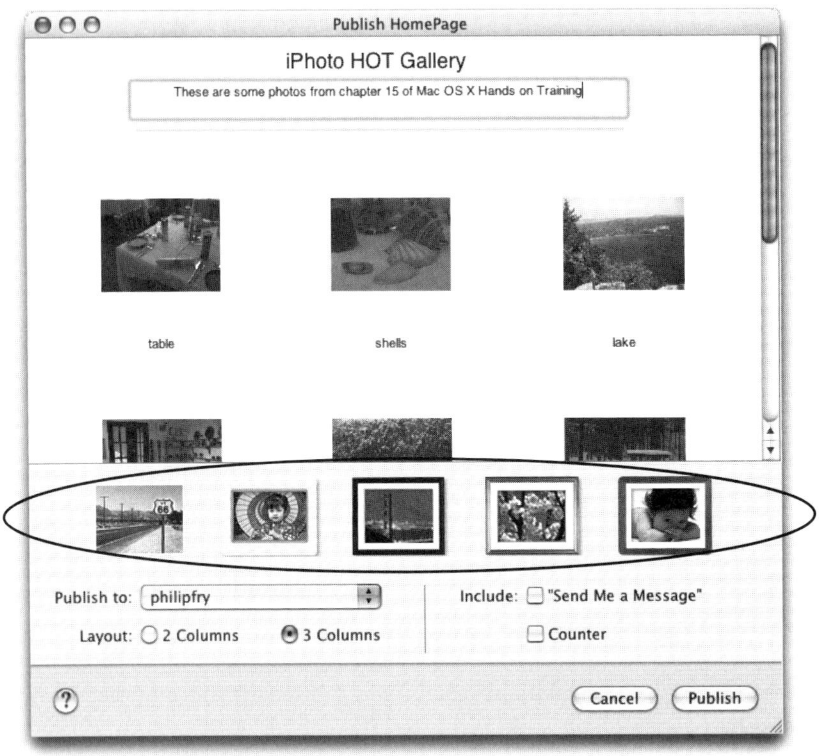

3. In the lower section of the window are five different styles of frames for your images. Click each one to see what it looks like and then pick your favorite.

4. Scroll down to the bottom of the thumbnails, where you'll see the **Created using .Mac** logo. Check **Send Me a Message** and **Counter**. This adds two items to the bottom of your page: a counter for tracking the number of visitors to your page, and a button visitors can click to email you a message. Click **Publish** when you're done.

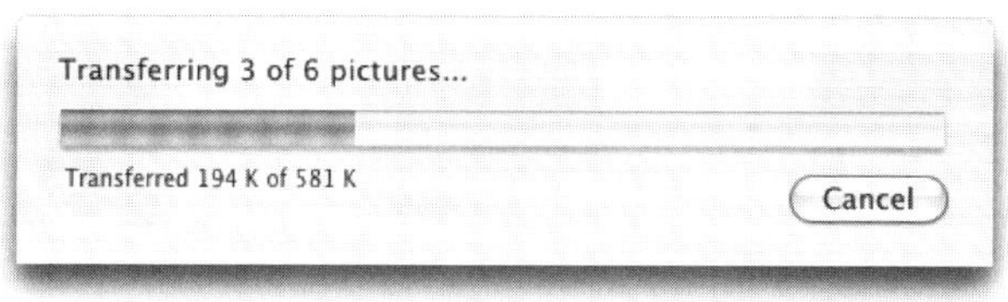

iPhoto connects to your .Mac account and begins uploading the pictures.

5. When the transfer completes, iPhoto provides the page's address for you. Click **Visit Page Now** to open your Web browser and view the photo gallery. (You can also highlight and copy the address in this dialog box to paste it into an email or text document.)

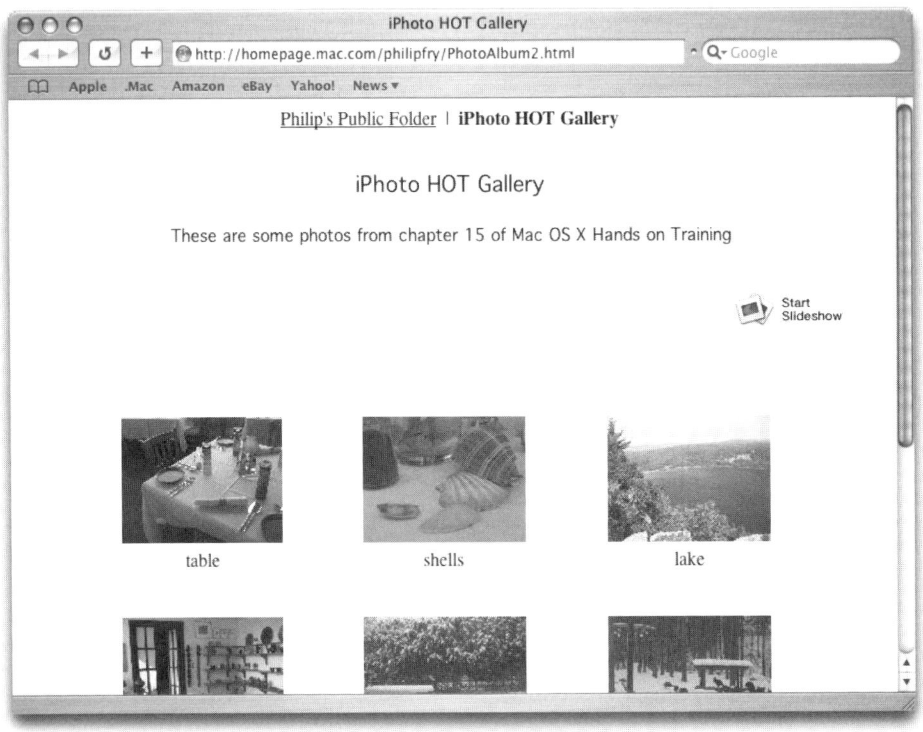

*The Web gallery on your .Mac account is displayed based on the settings you chose. Clicking on any thumbnail displays the image in **Slideshow** mode, where you can navigate from picture to picture using the arrows at the bottom of the window.*

6. Take a moment to click a thumbnail and view your gallery of pictures. When you're done, quit the browser and return to **iPhoto**.

Tip:** If you want to remove this gallery from your .Mac account, sign in to .Mac and click the **HomePage** button. Select **iPhoto HOT Gallery** from your list of pages and click **Delete.

*Yet another option for sharing your photos through .Mac is iPhoto's .Mac Slides publisher. The **.Mac Slides** button gives you a quick way to copy selected pictures to your iDisk, where other OS X users can then use them as their own screen savers. (You learned about screen savers in Exercise 3 of Chapter 4, "System Preferences.")*

7. If it's not already selected, click the main **iPhoto Library**. Select four or five images (by holding the **Cmd** key and clicking thumbnails) and then click the **.Mac Slides** button at the bottom of the window.

*iPhoto takes a moment to connect to your .Mac account. (If you're using a trial account, you may see a message asking if you want to upgrade to a full account. Click **Continue** if this dialog box appears.)*

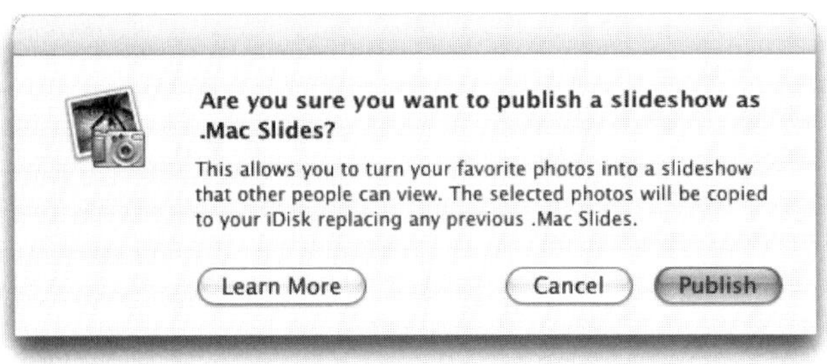

8. When the dialog box appears asking if you're sure you want to publish a slideshow, click **Publish**. Note that you can publish only one set of slides at a time.

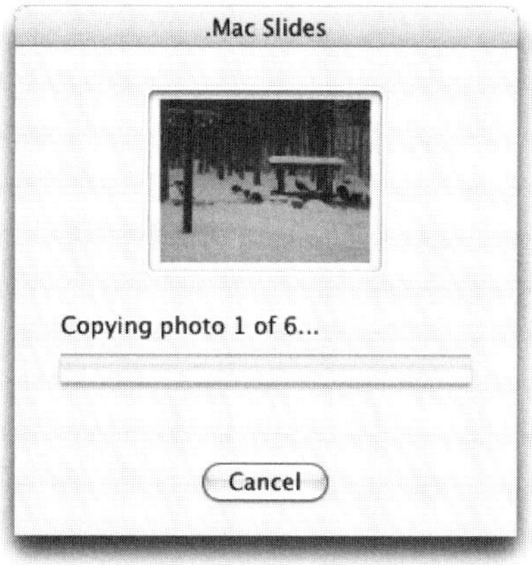

The photos you selected are uploaded to your iDisk.

Note: *In case you're wondering, your images are saved on your iDisk in* ***Pictures > Slide Shows > Public.***

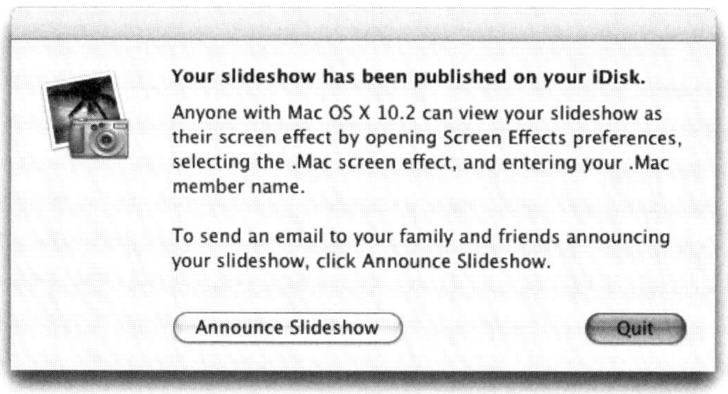

When the upload is complete, a dialog box appears giving you instructions on how you and other OS X users can access your slideshow. If you click ***Announce Slideshow****, your email program will open and automatically generate a message with detailed instructions that you can send to friends.*

9. Click **Quit**. You'll set up your screen saver in the next few steps.

10. Keep **iPhoto** open and click the **System Preferences** icon in the **Dock**. (Or choose **Apple > System Preferences** from the menu bar.) Click the **Desktop & Screen Saver** icon.

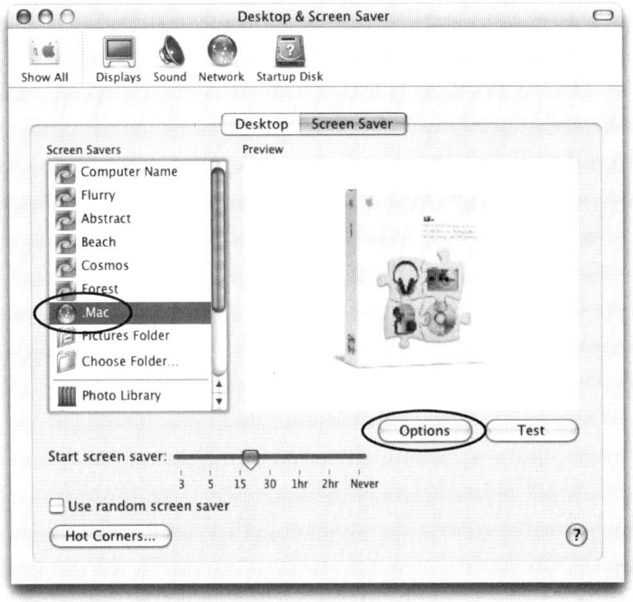

11. Click the **Screen Saver** button, select **.Mac**, and then click the **Options** button.

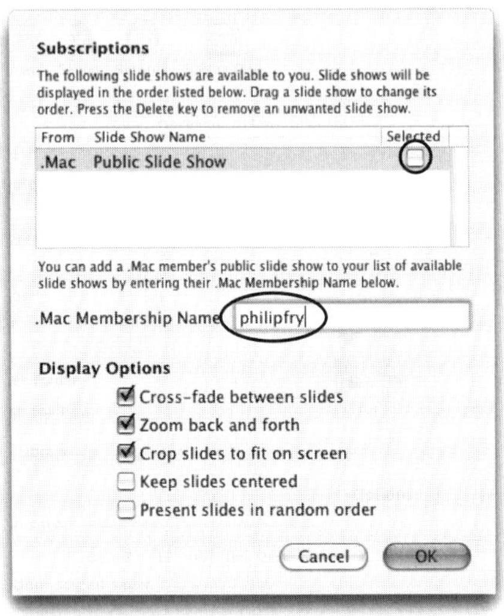

12. In the **Subscriptions** sheet, enter your **.Mac Membership Name** (your account name). Uncheck the **Public Slide Show** box, which will temporarily deactivate the default .Mac slides from playing. Click **OK**.

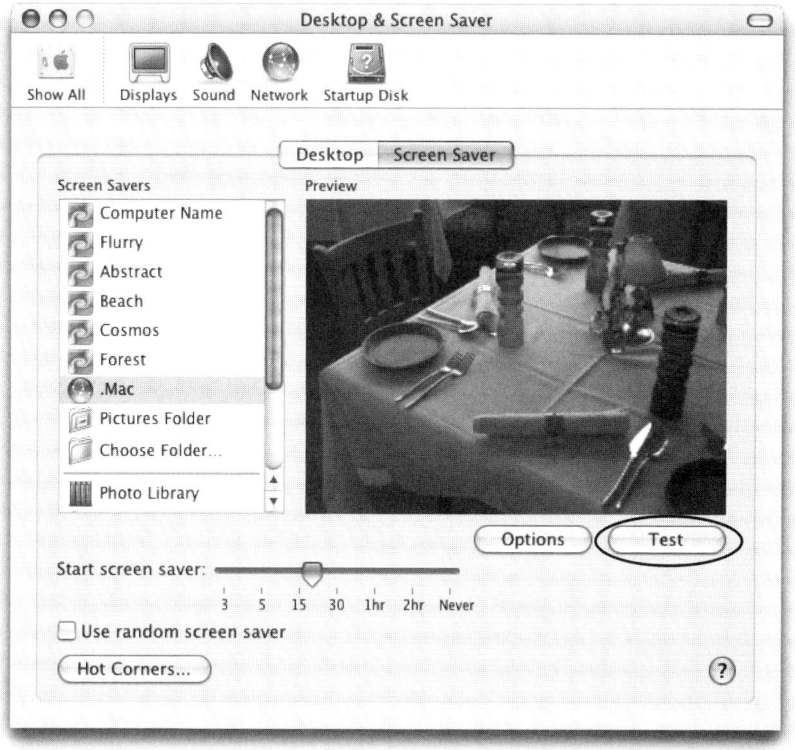

13. Back in **Screen Saver** preferences, click **Test** to view your .Mac slideshow.

Note: *Depending on the speed of your Internet connection, you may get a message saying your selected pictures folder is empty. If you see this message, wait a minute or two and then click the* ***Test*** *button again.*

---

14. Once you're done watching the slides, move the mouse or press a key to deactivate the screen effect. If you want, switch back to your preferred screen saver. Quit **System Preferences** and return to **iPhoto**.

Setting Your Own Screen Saver and Desktop Pictures

If you'd like to use your photos for your own screen saver or Desktop picture, and you don't intend to share them with others, there's no need to upload your pictures to a .Mac account.

To use your photos for your screen saver or Desktop pictures, create an album and move the pictures you want to use into it. Then click the **Desktop** button at the bottom of the iPhoto window.

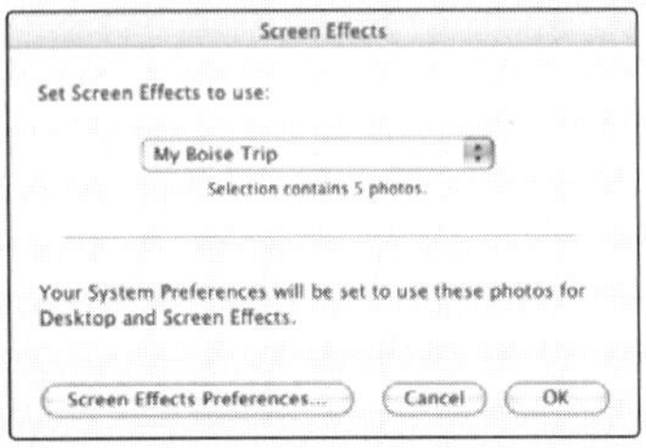

In the **Screen Effects** window that opens, select your album from the pop-up menu and click **OK**. Your screen saver preferences will be automatically set to display your album. If you want to customize your screen saver and Desktop picture settings, click **Screen Effects Preferences**.

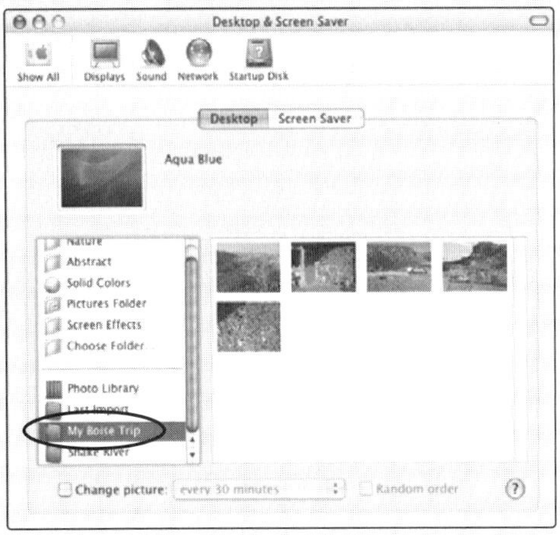

In the **Desktop** preferences, your iPhoto albums are listed along with the Panther's default picture collections. Select your album and click the photo you want to set as your Desktop picture. Click the **Screen Saver** button to customize your screen saver settings.

If you need a refresher on your Desktop & Screen Saver preferences, refer back to Exercise 3 of Chapter 4, "*System Preferences*."

15. Keep iPhoto open if you want to follow along with the next sections on burning CDs or ordering prints.

Copying Your Photos to CDs or DVDs

One of the best new features of iPhoto 2 is its capability to copy your pictures to CD or DVD. This allows you to copy groups of pictures to CD for backup or to send to friends and family. It's also a great way to archive old photos that you no longer need to store in your iPhoto library but also don't want to delete. (iPhoto tends to get sluggish after a few thousand photos have been imported, so it's good to go through and clean house every now and then.)

To burn a CD or DVD of photos, select the library, album, or individual photos you want to copy to a disc, and then click the **Burn** button. If you haven't done so already, iPhoto will prompt you to insert a blank disc.

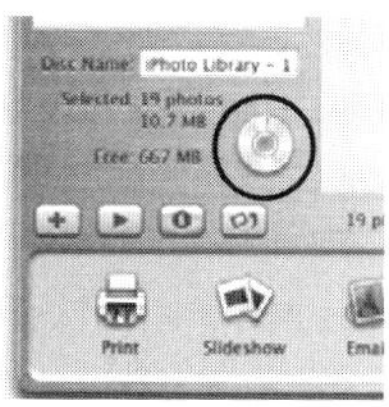

In the information area of the window, a disc icon containing a green bar will appear. The green bar indicates how much disc space the selected photos will occupy on the disc. If you have too many photos selected to fit on the disc, deselect some and burn them to a second disc.

When you're ready, click the **Burn** button again. A **Burn Disc** dialog box will appear, giving you your last chance to cancel. Click **Burn** to copy the selected photos to the disc.

Once you've burned your photos to disc, you can delete them from your iPhoto library if you need to free up some space. You can always access these photos by inserting the CD you burned; it will show up in iPhoto's album column. Although you won't be able to modify the photos or albums on the CD, you can copy any of the photos to your main iPhoto Library by dragging them there.

6. Ordering Prints and Books

One of the reasons some people are still hesitant to adopt digital photography is because there's still something very satisfying about the look and feel of pictures on real photo paper. The inkjet photo printers on the market today come pretty close to reproducing the quality of film photos printed on photo paper, but if you don't want to invest in a new printer, or only occasionally might want to have some prints of the pictures you've taken, you can take advantage of iPhoto's options for ordering prints over the Internet. From within iPhoto, you can order individual prints of your photos in various sizes. You can also collect several pictures into an iPhoto "book" and then order a bound, hardcover album.

Because you probably don't want to order and pay for prints of the photos used in this chapter, just read through the following steps for now and use them as a guide if you ever decide to order prints or books through iPhoto.

Ordering Individual Prints

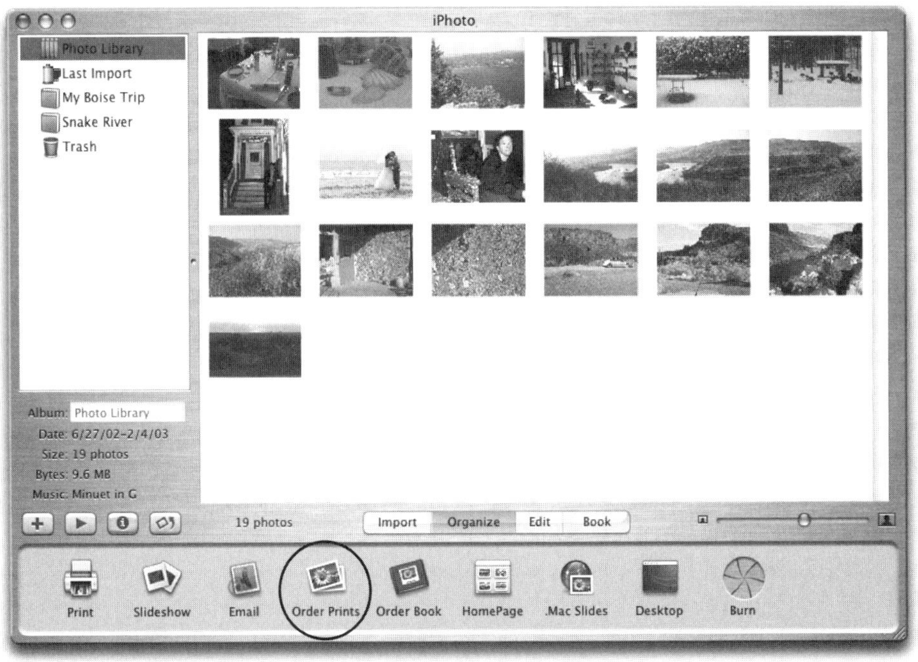

1. To order individual prints, select the photos you want to order and click the **Order Prints** button.

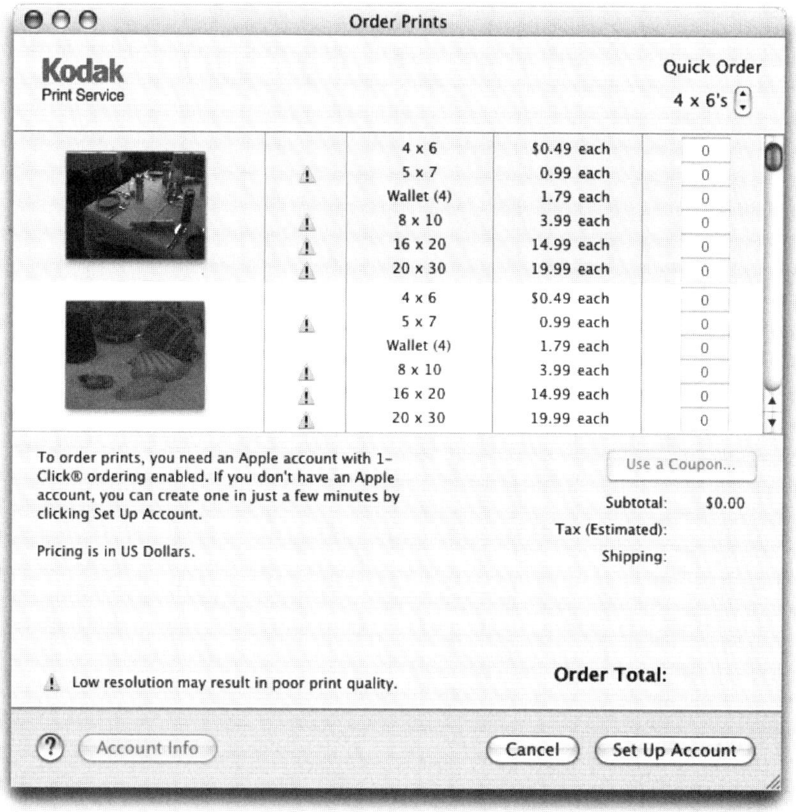

iPhoto connects to the Internet and then the ***Order Prints*** *window appears.*

---

2. If this is your first time ordering prints, click **Set Up Account**. You'll be guided through the necessary steps to set up an Apple ID and password, which are required for ordering prints. If you already have an Apple ID, continue to the next step.

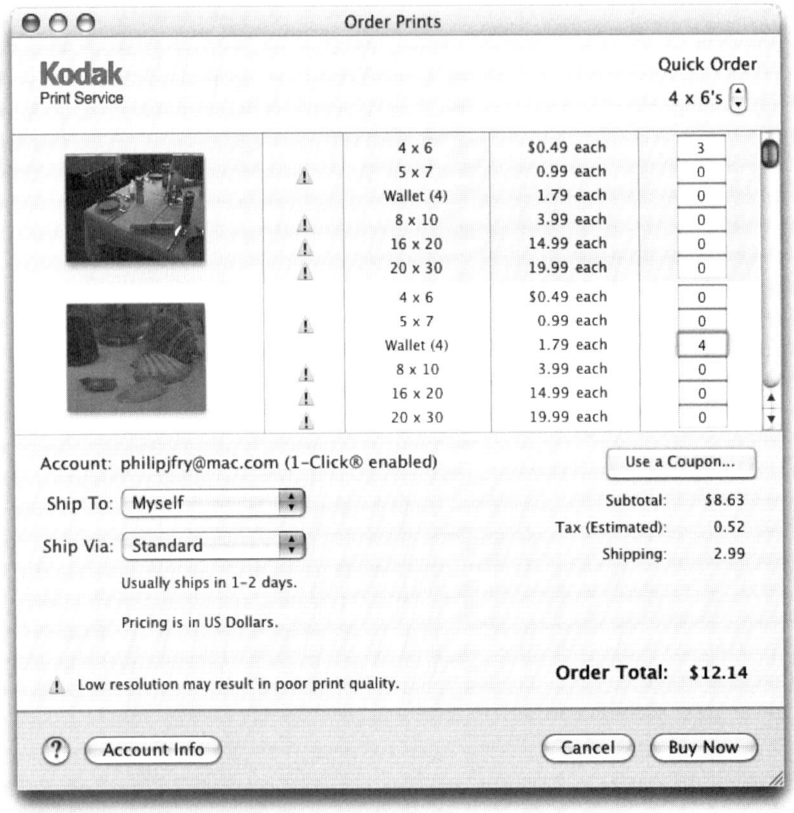

3. Select the size and quantity of each photo you want to order. If you want to order only 4 x 6 prints, use the **Quick Order** arrows in the upper-right corner to specify the number of sets you want. Any sizes marked with a yellow triangle containing an exclamation point indicate that the image is of low resolution and may result in a poor quality print at that size. If you see this icon, you may want to choose a smaller print size.

4. Select a shipping destination and method from the **Ship To** and **Ship Via** pop-up menus.

5. When you're done with your selections, click **Buy Now**. Your photos will be uploaded from your computer to the Apple servers, and depending on the shipping method you selected, your prints will arrive in a few days.

Ordering Books

If ordering individual prints isn't enough, iPhoto offers you the option of creating an album, preparing it as a book, and then ordering the book online. A few days later, you receive a beautifully bound book containing color prints of your pictures accompanied by any text you've added.

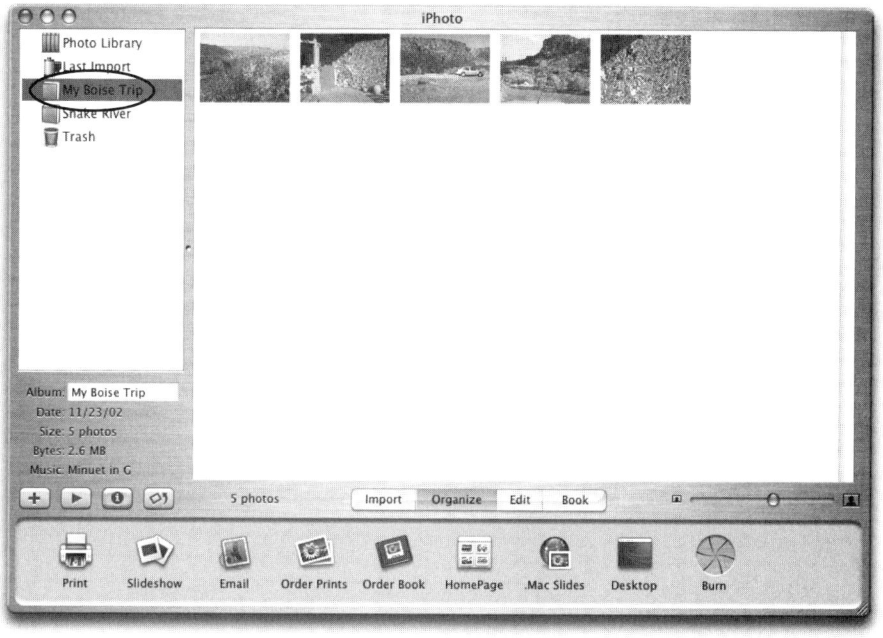

1. To create a book, first create an album and copy all the photos that you want in the book to the album. See Exercise 1 of this chapter if you need a refresher on creating albums.

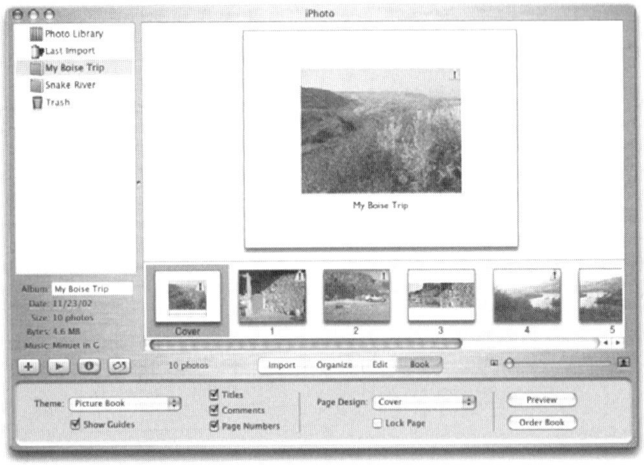

2. Select the album and then click the **Book** button. In **Book** mode, the main picture viewing area is split into two areas. Thumbnails of each page of the book are numbered and displayed horizontally along the bottom of the viewing area. Above the thumbnails is an enlargement of the page. Selecting a page's thumbnail displays it in the area above. You can go through and customize each page by adding text or changing the layout.

3. Begin by choosing a **Theme** from the pop-up menu in the lower-left corner. Each theme has its own type of layout, which is shown in the viewing area when you select the theme.

Tip: *Uncheck* ***Show Guides*** *if you want to see how the layout looks without the distracting borders on the page, which indicate where you can enter text. You can also check or uncheck the other items here (**Titles**, **Comments**, and **Page Numbers**) to determine which elements will appear in the book.*

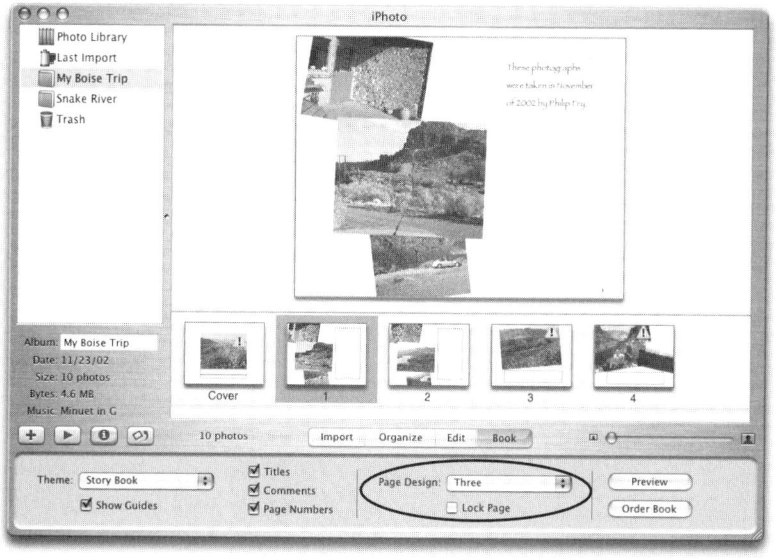

You can further customize the layout of a page by clicking the ***Page Design*** *pop-up menu. Check* ***Lock Page*** *to prevent accidental changes to the selected page.*

Note: *You cannot customize the page design for the cover page.*

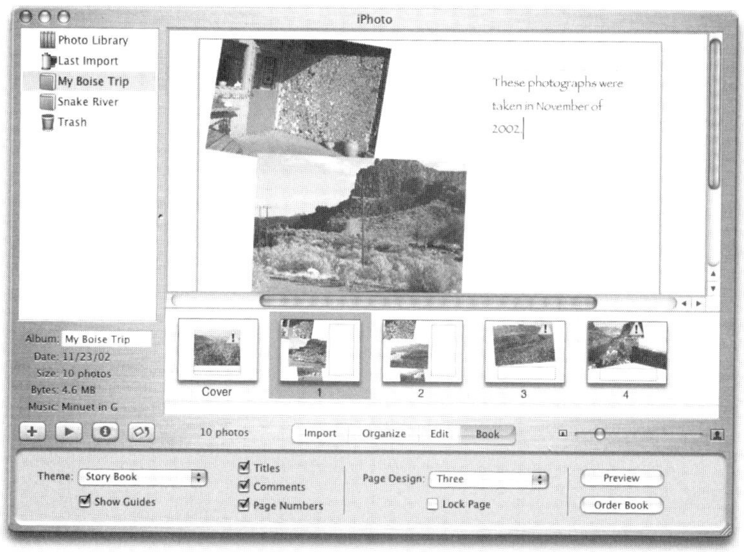

4. You can also click each page's thumbnail and add text to the page.

---

5. After you've set up your book, click **Preview** to browse through it and check for any mistakes.

You can browse from page to page by clicking the arrows in the upper-left corner of the Preview window.

6. Close the **Preview** window when you're done browsing the book. If you have no further changes to make, click **Order Book**.

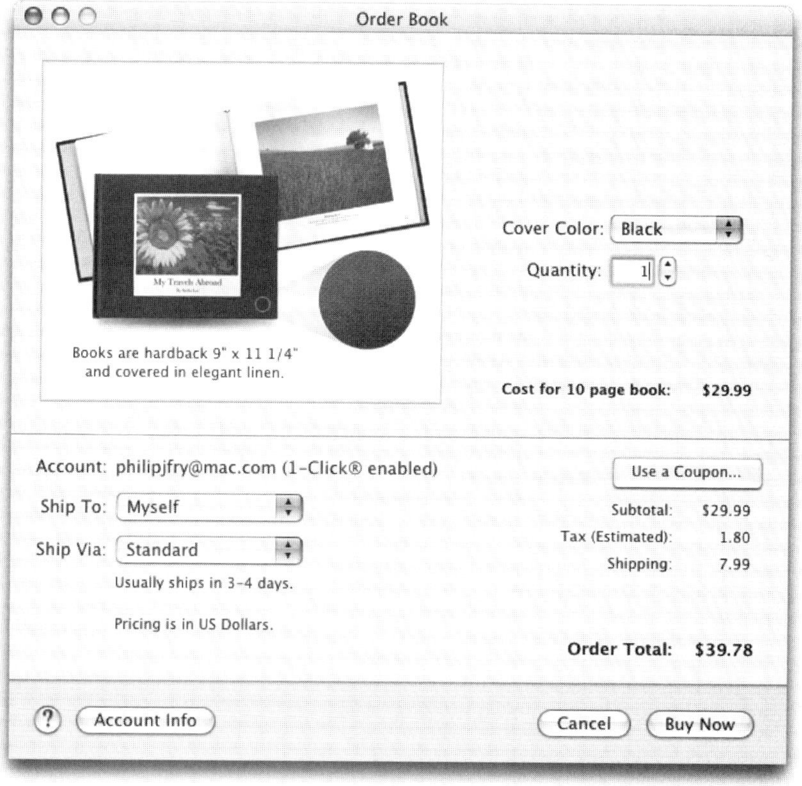

7. In the **Order Book** window, select the number of books you want to order. Choose a **Cover Color** as well. The books are hardbound and covered, in Apple's words, "in elegant linen."

***Note:** If you haven't yet set up an Apple ID, you'll need to click the **Set Up Account** button before you can continue.*

---

8. Choose a shipping destination and method from the **Ship To** and **Ship Via** menus.

---

9. Click **Buy Now** to place your order. Your book will arrive in a few days.

By now it should be obvious how richly featured a program iPhoto is. As you saw in this chapter, iTunes integrates nicely into iPhoto for adding music to slideshows. In the next chapter, you'll see how both iTunes and iPhoto integrate into iMovie.

16.

iMovie 3

Importing Footage	Editing and Arranging Clips
Adding Transitions	Working with Sound
Adding Titles	Adding Still Photos
Effects and Finishing Touches	Exporting Your Movie

chap_16

Mac OS X Panther
H•O•T CD-ROM

On a list of Apple's most innovative recent applications, iMovie definitely belongs somewhere near the very top. iMovie puts sophisticated video editing tools into the hands of people who don't "do lunch" or worry about focus groups. For free.

Before iMovie, videotaping an event or special occasion usually resulted in a tape of the important moments surrounded by lots of boring, uneventful ones. Anyone who's ever owned a video camera knows what it's like to fast-forward through the tedious stuff while searching for the scenes you really want to see, or having to, on at least one occasion, sit through a seemingly endless tape of someone else's vacation footage. ("Here's the inside of the elevator on the way up to our room!")

With iMovie you can edit out all the filler and focus on the interesting stuff. Not only that, but you can also dress up your video with effects, captions, music, and still photos. With a little practice, you can take an hour's worth of video and transform it into a short and snappy 10-minute highlight reel that your friends and family will be happy (or at least more willing) to sit through.

Make sure you're using the latest version of iMovie 3 before beginning the exercises in this chapter. You can download the most current version for free from **www.apple.com/imovie**.

Note: You'll need to complete the project in this chapter in order to perform the exercises in Chapter 17, "*iDVD 3.*"

DV Cameras

Although you'll be working with the video clips provided on the **H•O•T CD-ROM** in this chapter, it's important to know what kind of equipment you'll need when you set out to shoot your own footage. To import video footage into your Mac, you need to have a DV (**D**igital **V**ideo) camera that includes a FireWire port. Nearly all DV cameras today sport FireWire ports, although some manufacturers may refer to FireWire as IEEE-1394, DV Terminal, DV In/Out, or, in the case of Sony camcorders, "i.Link."

You may be thinking, "But I already have a video camera. Why should I get a new one?" For one thing, DV cameras store video and audio information as digital code and produce high-quality results that, unlike VHS tapes, don't lose quality as the footage is copied from tape to tape or from tape to computer. More importantly, you can't use iMovie unless you shoot your footage on a DV camera.

NOTE | Make Sure You're Getting a DV Camera

If you go shopping for a camera, don't be confused by the multitude of tape formats available. You may find formats such as VHS, VHS-C, S-VHS, 8mm, or Hi-8. None of these kinds of cameras includes the necessary FireWire ports. Only cameras that record to "DV" tapes can be used with iMovie. The only exception to this rule is the Digital8 camera manufactured by Sony. Like DV cameras, Digital8 cameras record a DV signal, but they use 8mm tapes rather than DV tapes. A Digital8 camera is a good choice for people who want to make the jump to digital and use iMovie, but have lots of old 8mm tapes in their collections.

Once you've decided on a camera, you're now ready to shoot your video and import it into iMovie for editing. This chapter contains several tips on shooting your footage to achieve the best results in iMovie. If you're a novice with a video camera, you may want to complete this exercise before taping your own footage.

I. Importing Footage

In this chapter, you'll be working on one project over several exercises to complete a single movie. Each exercise has been designed to teach you the basics of iMovie's most useful features. By the end of this chapter, you'll have learned enough to be able to import, edit, and export your own videos.

1. Drag the **chap_16** folder from the **H•O•T CD-ROM** to your **Desktop**.

2. Open **chap_16** and double-click the file **completed.mov**. It opens in QuickTime.

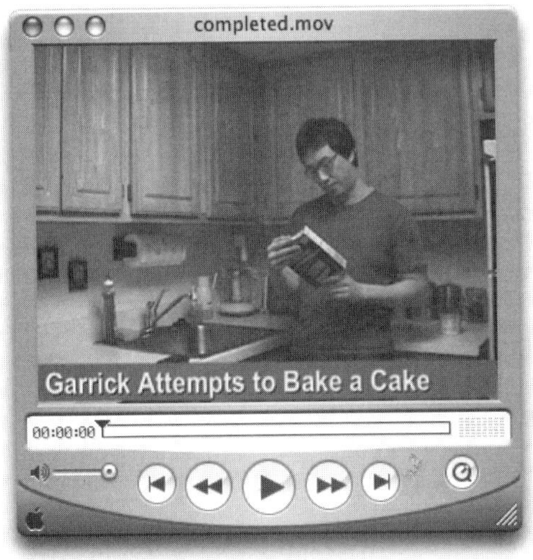

This is a completed version of the movie you'll be editing in this chapter. I shot this video with a single camera mounted on a tripod. The movie shows me doing a horrendous job of baking a cake from store-bought mix. I make absolutely no claims about my abilities as a baker, but I take pride in the fact that I'm probably the first computer book author who's been able to use cake mix as a tax write-off.

3. Click the **Play** button and watch the entire movie.

This movie contains numerous shots and scenes that have been edited together to produce the illusion of time passing quickly. It also contains text overlays at the beginning and end. You'll learn how to do these things in the exercises later in this chapter. But first, you need to get the raw footage of the movie into your Mac.

4. When the movie's over, quit QuickTime and open **iMovie** by clicking its icon in the **Dock** or in your **Applications** folder.

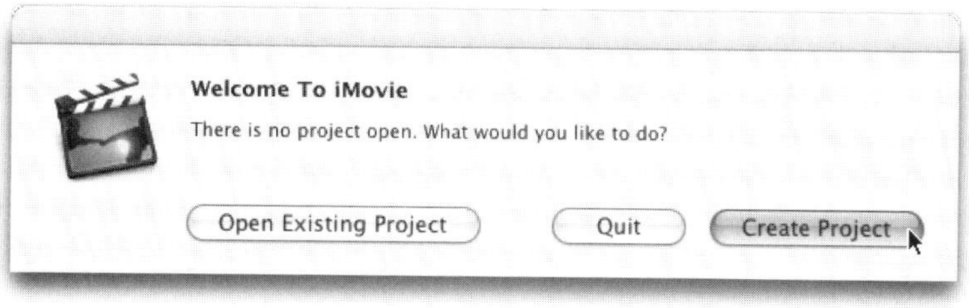

If you've never used iMovie before, you'll be asked if you want to open an existing project, create a new one, or quit.

5. Click **Create Project**. (If you have used iMovie before, it automatically opens the last project you were working on. If this happens, choose **File > New Project**.)

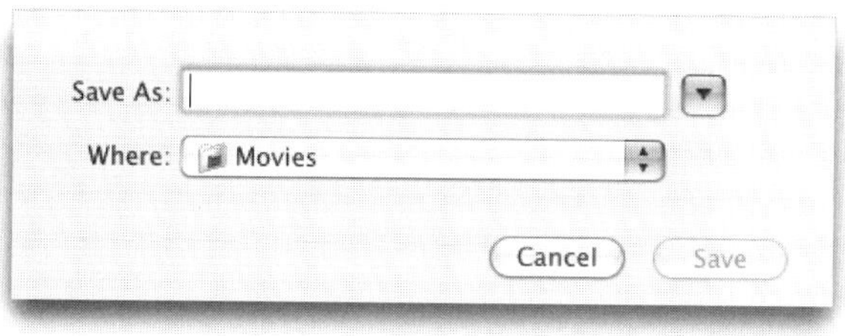

*By default, iMovie wants to save your iMovie projects in the **Movie** folder of your **Home** directory, but for this exercise, you'll save the project in the **chap_16** folder so you can easily delete all the related files when you're done with this book.*

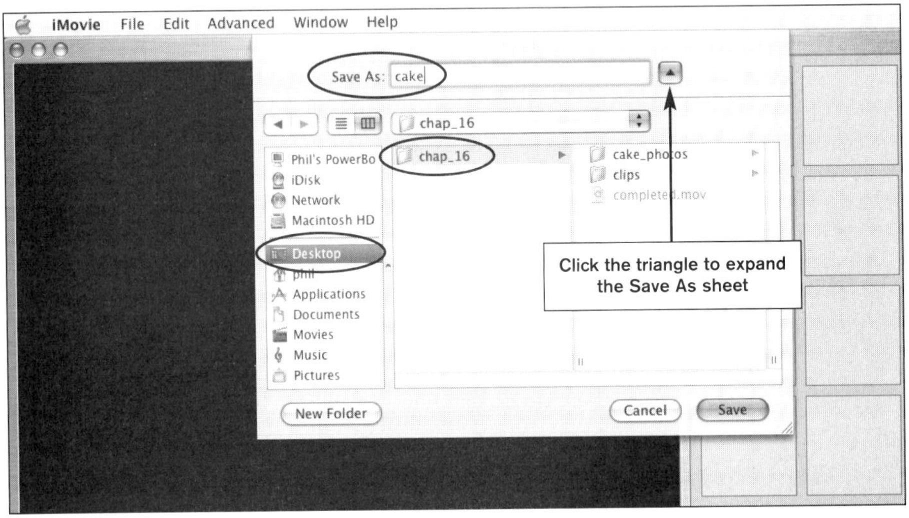

6. In the **Save As** sheet, name this project **cake** and then navigate out to the **chap_16** folder on your **Desktop**. Click **Save**. This creates a folder called **cake** that stores all the files related to your movie.

You're now ready to import video clips into your project. In iMovie, a clip is a segment of footage that you combine with other clips to build and produce your final movie. Each individual section of footage is called a clip. For your own projects, you'd normally be importing clips from your video camera, but for this exercise, you'll import pre-created QuickTime movie clips. See the "Importing Clips from Your Camera" section at the end of this exercise for information on transferring footage from your camera to iMovie.

***Tip:** If your iMovie window is partially covered by the Dock, press **Option+Cmd+D** to temporarily hide the Dock. Press this combination again to bring it back when you're done with this chapter.*

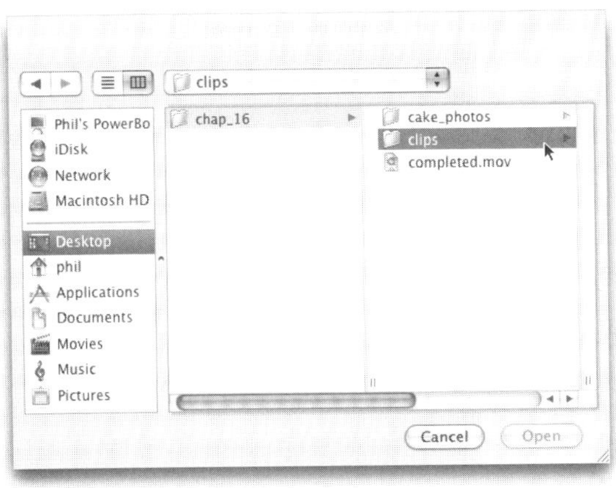

7. Choose **File > Import** and navigate to the **chap_16** folder on your **Desktop**. Click the **clips** folder.

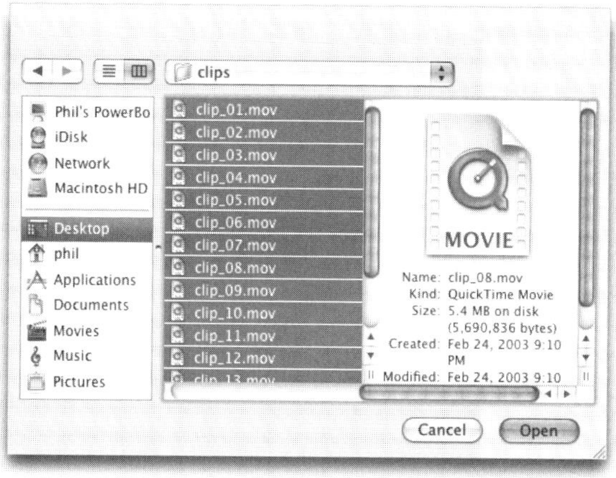

8. Click the file **clip_01.mov** to select it, and then press **Cmd+A** on your keyboard to select all 16 clips in this folder. Click **Open**.

iMovie begins importing the selected clips. This may take several minutes (or more than an hour) depending on how fast your Mac is. You'll see the clips appearing to the right of the window in the area known as the ***Clips*** *pane.*

9. Once the files have all been imported, choose **File > Save Project** and keep iMovie open for the next exercise.

Importing Clips from Your Camera

Although iMovie is capable of importing and using most QuickTime-compatible formats such as the clips for the exercises in this chapter, the majority of the footage for your own projects will come from your DV camera. After shooting the video for your project, connect your camera to your Mac via a FireWire cable.

If your camera didn't come with a FireWire cable, you'll have to purchase one. Specifically, you'll need a 4-pin-to-6-pin cable. (As mentioned earlier, be aware that FireWire products may be sold under different names like IEEE 1394 or i.Link.) The smaller, 4-pin end goes into your camera, and the larger, 6-pin end gets plugged into a FireWire port on your Mac. Once the camera and your Mac are connected, set your camera to VCR mode and start iMovie.

In iMovie, select **File > New Project** (or click the **Create Project** button if iMovie doesn't open a previous project). Save your new project to your hard drive.

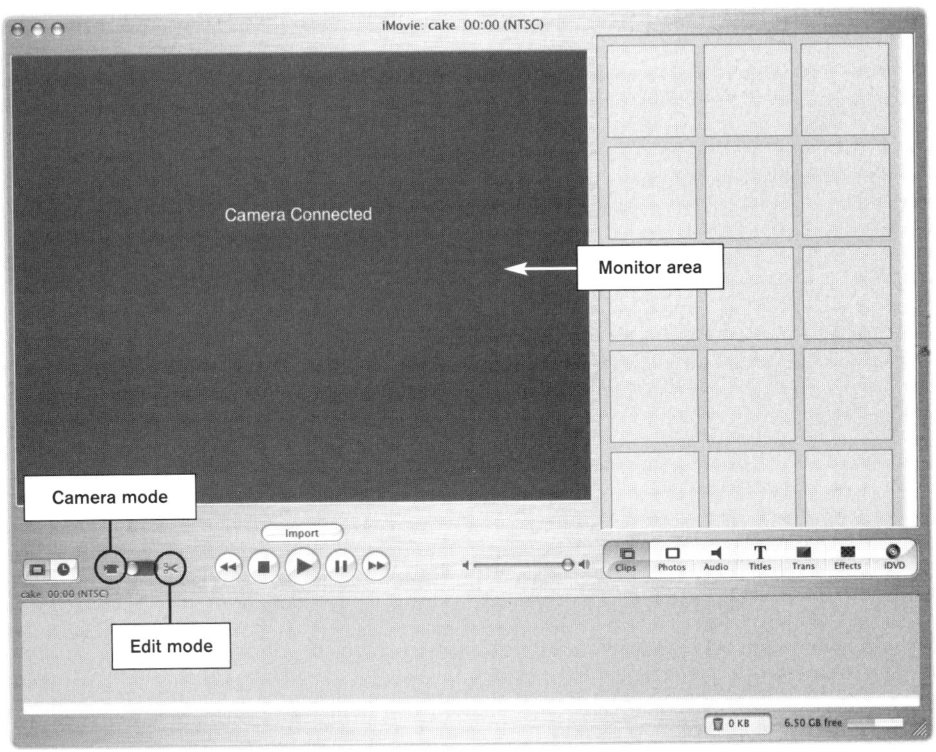

Once the project has been saved, iMovie switches to **Camera** mode and the words "Camera Connected" appear over a blue screen in the monitor area.

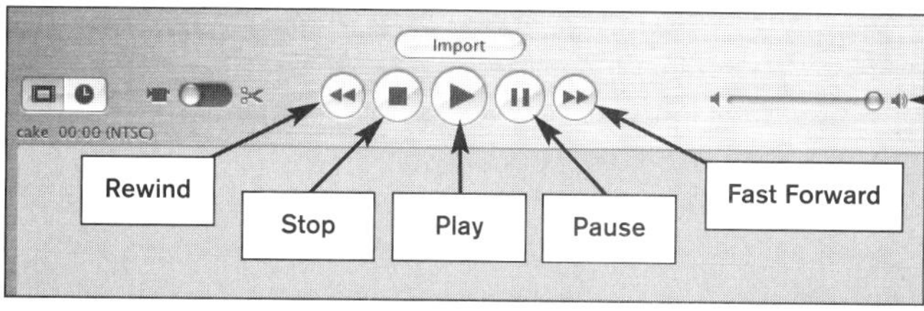

You can use the VCR control buttons below the monitor area to play your video and locate the footage you want to import. When the footage you need appears, click the **Import** button to begin copying it to your Mac. Click the **Import** button again to stop copying video. You can continue clicking **Import** to bring selected video clips into your Mac, or if you want iMovie to import all the footage from your camera, you can simply click the **Import** button without first clicking **Play** to begin importing all the footage from your camera right away.

If the footage you're importing includes scene breaks, iMovie automatically generates separate clips of each shot rather than bringing everything in as one long, continuous shot. When you are shooting footage, scene breaks are created each time you press the camera's Record button. Having iMovie automatically create separate clips can make the editing process much easier, but if you prefer to import everything in one long clip, select **iMovie > Preferences** and uncheck **Automatically start new clip at scene break**.

NOTE | DV Footage Size

An extremely important point to consider when importing video from your DV camera is that digital video takes up a massive amount of hard drive space. Each second of DV footage requires just under 3.6 MB of space, meaning that importing an entire 60-minute DV tape worth of raw footage requires nearly 13 gigabytes of storage. So before you begin your project, be sure that you have enough space for all your footage.

You can keep an eye on how much space is left on the hard drive to which you're copying your video by watching the bar in the lower-right corner of the iMovie window.

Once you've imported the video from your camera, you're ready to edit and manipulate your clips into a coherent movie. (Or an incoherent movie, if that's your intent as the video auteur.)

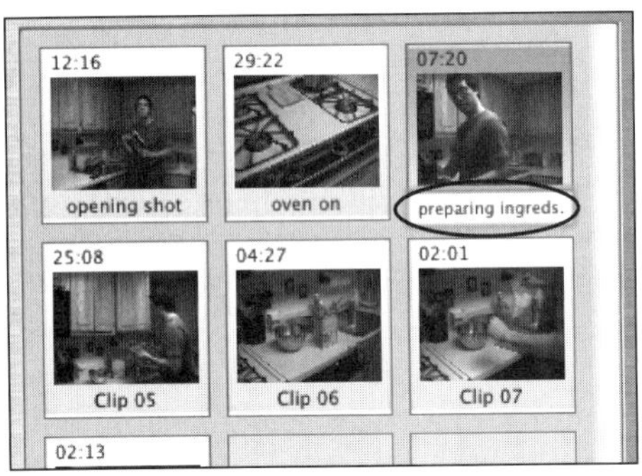

Tip: If you feel it helps you to keep organized, you can rename your clips by double-clicking their names and then typing your preferred clip name.

2. Editing and Arranging Clips

Now that you have some footage to work with, you'll assemble the clips you imported into something resembling the completed movie you watched in the first exercise.

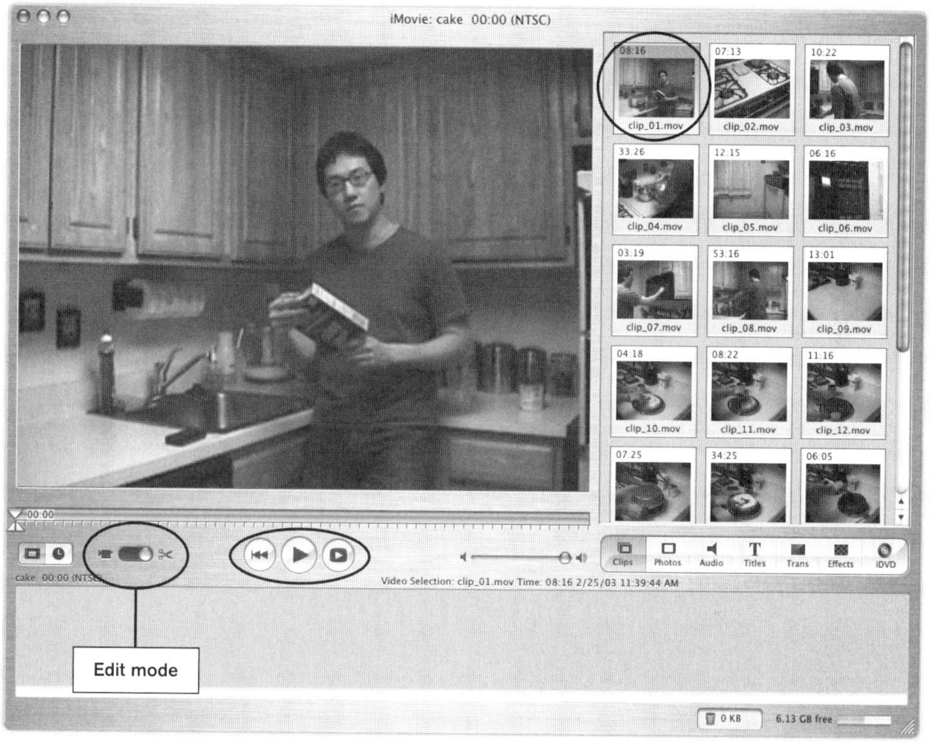

1. In the **Clips** pane, click **clip_01.mov**, which should be the first clip in the upper-left corner of the pane. Once you click the clip, it becomes highlighted to indicate that you've selected it, and the monitor area switches from **Camera** mode to **Edit** mode and displays the first frame of the clip. You'll also notice that there are now only three buttons below the monitor area, rather than the full complement of buttons you saw in **Camera** mode.

2. Click the **Play** button to watch this clip in its entirety.

Note: *In order to fit them onto the* ***H•O•T CD-ROM****, these clips had to be compressed, so the quality of the video you'll see in this exercise is not as high as the quality you'd be viewing if you imported clips directly from your DV camera.*

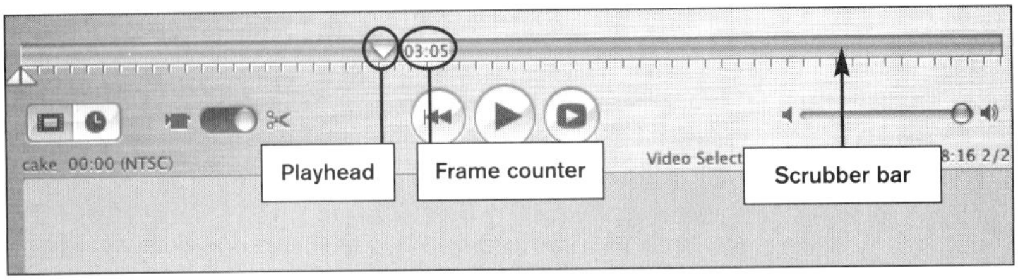

As the clip plays, the playhead (circled above) moves along the scrubber bar (see above), letting you know which section of the clip you're watching. A frame counter (see above) also appears next to the playhead indicating its exact point along the scrubber bar. The frame counter displays its information in terms of minutes, seconds, and frames. For example, a display of 03:05 indicates that you're 3 seconds and 5 frames into the clip; a display of 02:04:17 indicates 2 minutes, 4 seconds, and 17 frames. In North America, video runs at 29.97 frames per second (although many people just say 30 fps to avoid the fractions), so the far-right number in the frame counter counts up to 29 before flipping back to 00. For example: 03:28, 03:29, 04:00, 04:01, and so on.

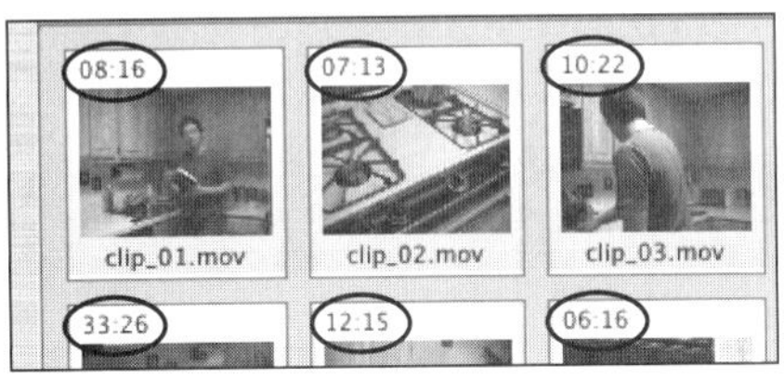

Note: *The total length of each clip is also displayed in its upper-left corner in the Clips pane.*

While watching clip_01, you probably noticed that, unlike in the completed version of the movie, the clip starts with me looking directly at the camera. When I was shooting this clip, I was looking at the camera to make sure it was recording before I started "acting." You'll cut this "behind-the-scenes" part out of the clip so that the movie opens with me examining the box of cake mix.

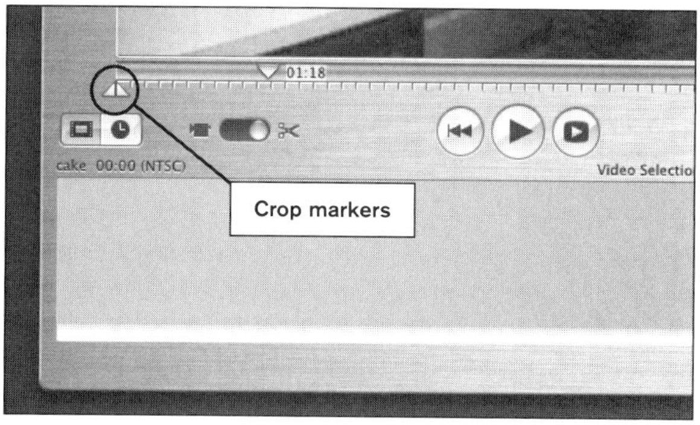

*Cutting out a section of a clip is referred to as **cropping**. To crop out footage, you need to position the crop markers that appear directly below the scrubber bar.*

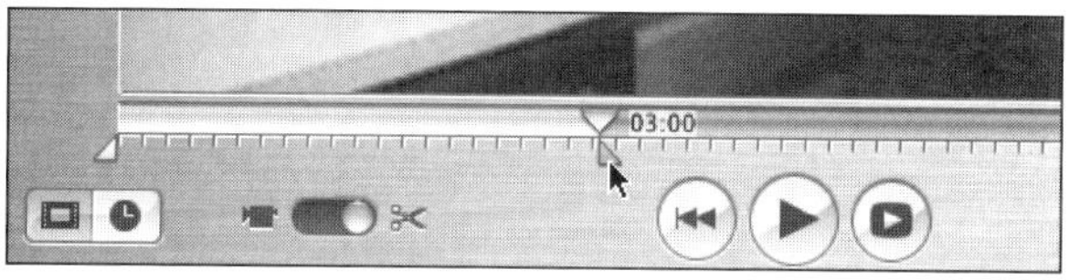

3. Drag the **right crop marker** to the **03:00** point of the **scrubber bar**. The scrubber bar turns yellow between the two crop markers, indicating the selection to be cut. If you have trouble positioning the crop marker at exactly 03:00, use the **right** and **left arrow** keys on the keyboard to move a frame at a time. Once the marker is placed properly, press **Delete**. The highlighted section is removed from the clip.

*The clip is now three seconds shorter. The clip's thumbnail in the Clips pane has updated to display the new first frame of the clip, and the frame count now says **05:15**. Additionally, the iMovie Trash now indicates that it contains **10 MB** of data. All deleted footage is stored in the **Trash** until you choose **File > Empty Trash**.*

***Tip:** Until you empty the Trash, you can restore any cropped clip to its original length by selecting it and then choosing **Advanced > Restore Clip.** Even if you quit iMovie and restart it, you can still restore deleted clips. Once you've emptied the Trash, however, the clip is gone for good.*

Now that the first clip has been cropped, you can add it to your movie. Clips in the Clips pane are not considered part of your movie until you add them to the clip or timeline viewer (which I define in the next step).

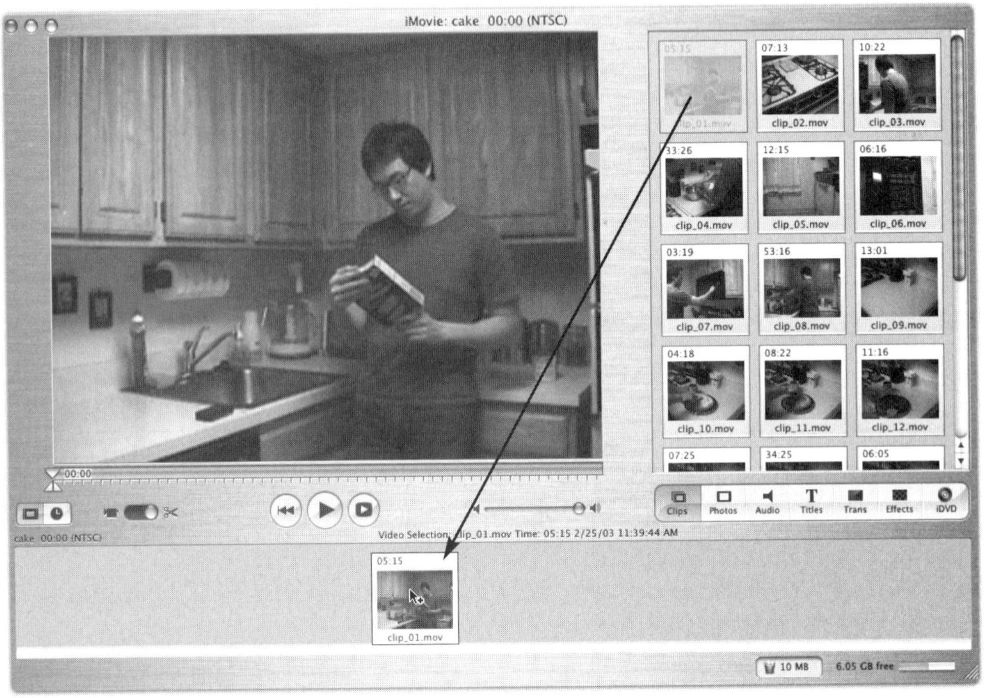

4. Drag **clip_01** to the bottom pane of the iMovie window.

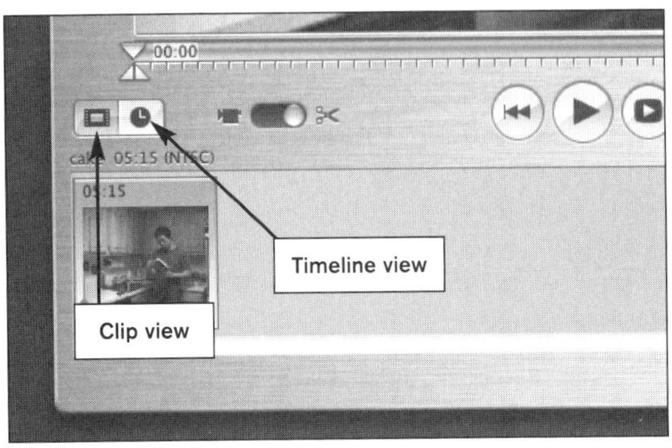

When you release the mouse, the clip appears to the far left of the clip viewer (and disappears from the Clips pane). There are two ways in which you can view your movie: the clip viewer or the timeline viewer. Currently, you should be in Clip view, which allows you to easily see each clip and drag it around to change the order of clips in your movie.

Tip: *If you* ***Option+drag*** *a clip to the clip viewer, you'll leave a copy of the clip in the Clips pane, which can be useful if you need to use the same footage in multiple areas of your movie.*

When playing your movie in Clip view, a red line crawls across each clip to indicate which point of the clip you're currently watching.

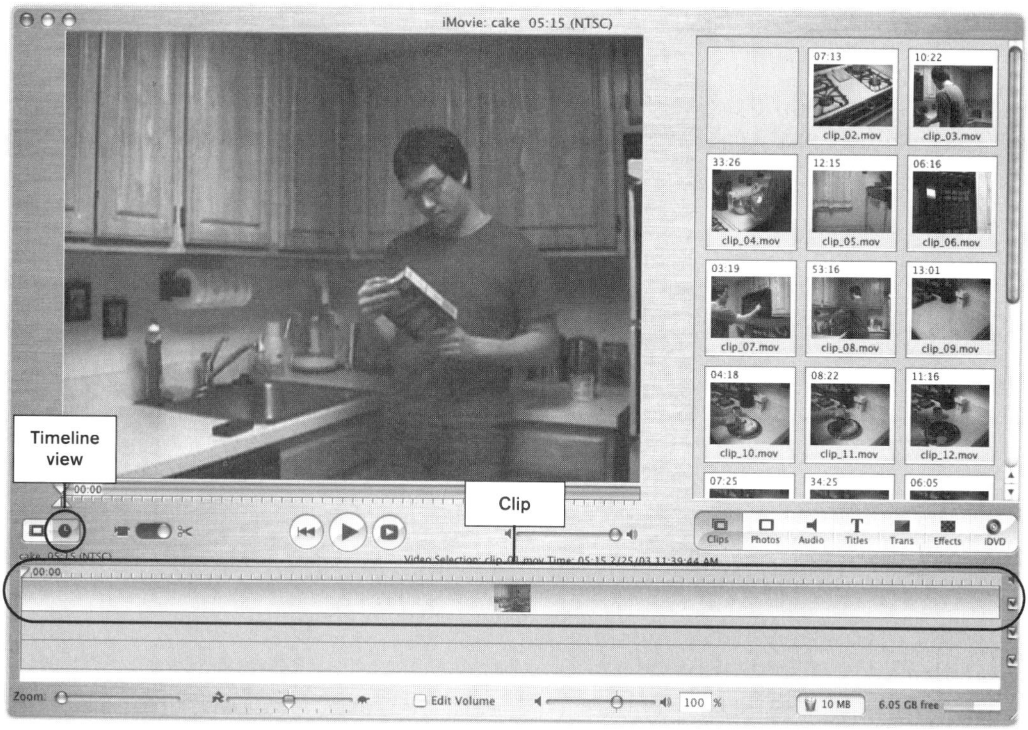

5. Click the **Timeline view** button to switch to Timeline view. In this view, each clip is represented by a colored bar whose width is based on the clip's size relative to the entire movie. Because you have only one clip in the movie right now, this bar runs the entire length of the window. Although Timeline view is useful when you need to work with a clip's video and audio track separately, you'll probably find Clip view much easier to work with when you're first organizing clips early in the creation of your movie.

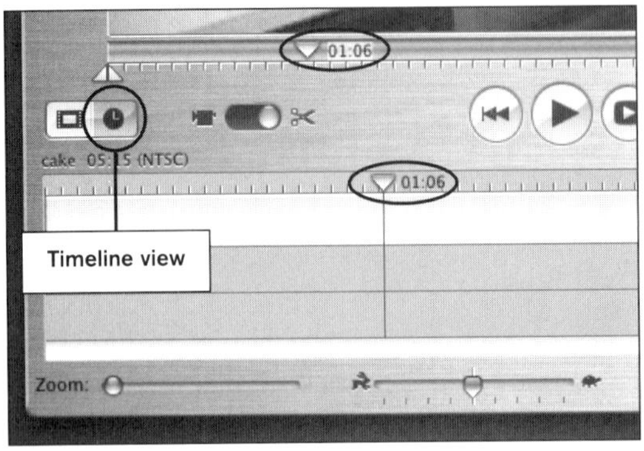

When viewing your movie in Timeline view, a playback head appears along the top clips in addition to the one that appears in the scrubber bar below the monitor area. You can drag either playback head to move to any point in the movie.

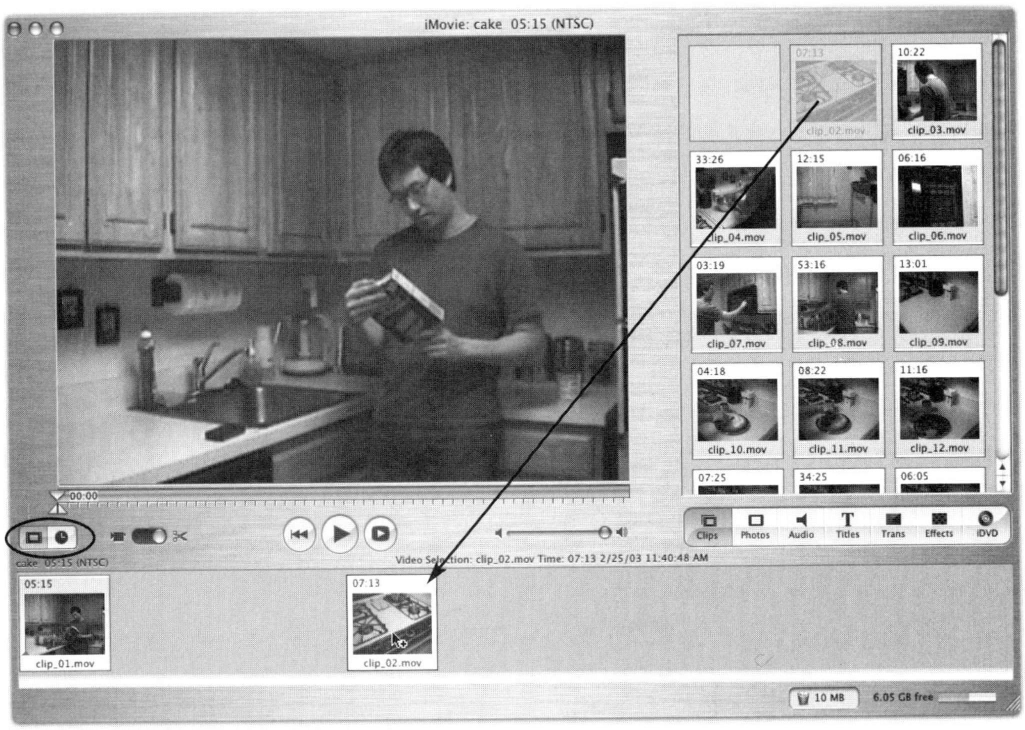

6. Switch back to the **Clip** view and drag **clip_02** into the **clip viewer**. You now have two clips in your movie. Let's see how they look together.

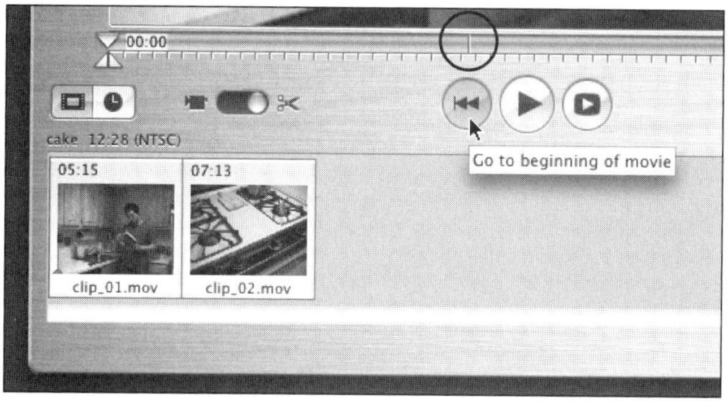

7. Click the **Rewind** button to take the playhead back to the very start of the movie. Note the indentation in the **scrubber bar**, which indicates where **clip_01** ends and **clip_02** begins. Click **Play** and watch the movie. (You can also click the **Play Fullscreen** button to the right of the Play button if you want to watch the movie at the largest possible size, but bear in mind that because this is a compressed video file, it won't look very good blown up to a large size.)

As you watch the movie, notice how the two clips play one after another with no pause or skipping between the action.

---

8. Drag **clip_03** to the right of **clip_02** in the **clip viewer**, giving your movie a total of three clips. Click the **Rewind** button to return to the beginning of the movie and play the entire movie again.

Recapping the movie action so far, our hero has checked out the back of the cake box, preheated the oven, and begun to assemble the necessary ingredients for his cake. Although these events can be easily understood by anyone watching this movie, the clips themselves could be tightened up a bit to make the overall action of the movie a little snappier. For instance, at the end of clip_01, you can see my right hand reaching out as if to turn a dial, but at the beginning of clip_02, there's approximately 1.5 seconds of inaction before my hand enters the screen. After my hand leaves the screen, there's nearly a three-second pause before clip_03 begins. This might seem like an insignificant amount of time, but cropping down clip_02 will make the movie flow much more naturally.

---

9. If you want, watch the entire sequence once more to note the unnecessary pauses in **clip_02**, then click **clip_02** in the clip viewer to select it.

When an individual clip is selected in the clip viewer, only the clip itself appears in the monitor area above. To edit a clip precisely, use the arrow keys on your keyboard.

10. With **clip_02** selected, press and hold the **right arrow** key on your keyboard until you see the tips of my fingers enter the screen (at approximately **07:04**). Since this is where the action really begins, you'll learn a new way to crop out all the footage before this point.

Earlier, you cropped a clip by dragging the right crop marker to the appropriate point and pressing Delete. Since your playhead is already at the point where you want to crop this clip, you can automatically move the right crop marker to this point by ***Shift+clicking*** *the playhead.*

11. Press **Shift** and click the **playhead**. The right crop marker jumps directly underneath it. (If you moved your mouse when you clicked the **playhead**, you might have moved it slightly right or left. Simply use the **arrow** keys to reposition both the **playhead** and the **crop marker** simultaneously. Press **Delete**. The cropped footage is sent to the **Trash**.

Now you'll crop out the unnecessary footage at the end of this clip.

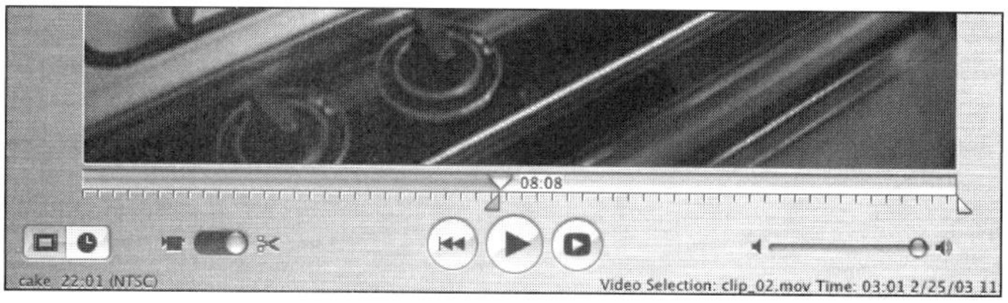

12. Drag the **right crop marker** to the far right of the **scrubber bar**. Now drag the **left crop marker** to the point just before my hand disappears from sight (at approximately **08:08**). Press **Delete** to remove the selected footage.

Tip: *If you ever change your mind about cropping a clip after you've positioned the crop markers, you can clear them by dragging them both back to the far left of the scrubber bar, or by clicking in a blank area in the timeline.*

NOTE | Make Sure You Crop Completely

When cropping off the end of the clip, make sure that the right crop marker is positioned completely to the right side of the scrubber bar.

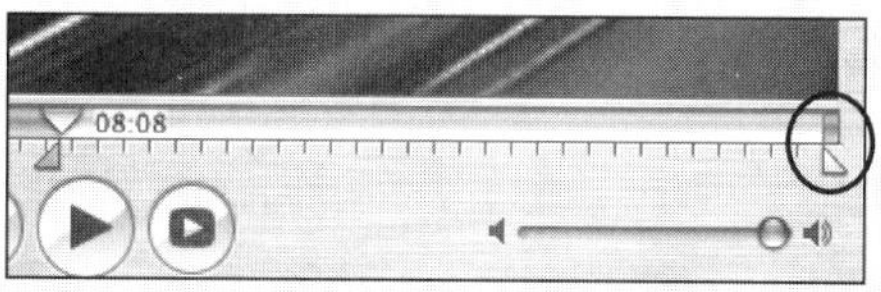

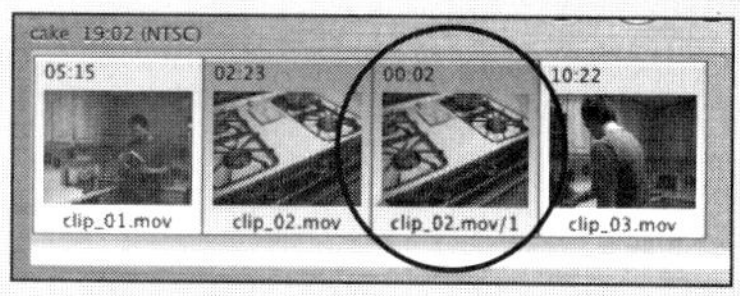

If you miss even a single frame from the end of the clip, iMovie assumes that you're removing a section from the middle of the clip and will place an additional clip in the clip viewer representing the one or two frames you failed to crop off the end. In the two screenshots above, two frames were missed at the end of the scrubber, so iMovie created a two-frame clip after the selected footage was cropped out. If this happens to you, you can either select **Edit > Undo** and try again, or just click the second clip and delete it.

This is also good information to know if you intend to crop out a section from the middle of a clip. Anytime you remove a section of footage from within a clip, you'll end up with three clips: the section preceding the crop, the cropped clip itself, and the section following the crop.

13. Now that you've cropped the ends of **clip_02**, watch the entire movie again. Notice how much more natural and smooth the action looks? It appears as though I'm continuously in motion throughout the movie, even though each shot was filmed separately. As you can see, good cropping can make a big difference.

Now you'll continue adding clips to the movie.

---

14. Drag **clip_04** to the right of **clip_03** in the **clip viewer**. With **clip_04** selected, click the **Play** button to watch it.

This clip consists of multiple shots that have already been edited together for you. Clip_04 consists of a sequence of quick cuts from one shot to another, with no single shot lasting more than one or two seconds. During the 33 seconds of the clip, you see all the ingredients added to the bowl and then mixed together. This rapid-fire method of moving from one shot to another enables you to convey a lot of information to your audience in a short period of time. The viewer knows that it takes longer than 33 seconds to do everything shown in this clip, but by showing just a snippet of each activity, you allow the viewer to fill in the blanks in his or her head. You'll get some practice with this technique using the next three clips.

15. Drag **clip_05** to the right of the other clips in the **clip viewer**. Click **Play** to view this clip.

In this clip, you see me walk into the shot, open the oven, place the pans on the rack, and close the door. To match the quick-cut sequence of clip_04, you'll edit clip_05 to include just the necessary information: the pans going in the oven, and the oven being closed. (If the pans are going into the oven, I obviously walked over to it and opened it, so there's no need to show these actions.)

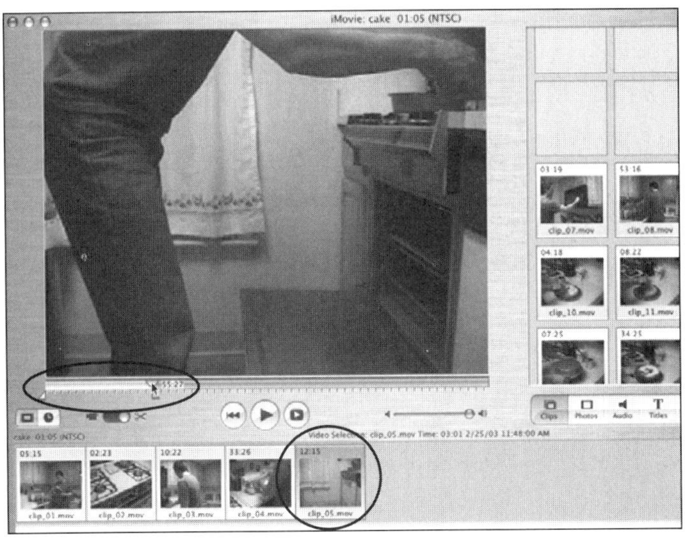

16. With **clip_05** selected, drag the **playhead** to the point where I'm lifting the first pan off the counter (right around **55:27**). **Shift+click** the **playhead** to place the **right crop marker** underneath it and then press **Delete** to remove the footage.

At the end of the clip, after closing the oven, my right hand begins to move up and out of screen toward the timer on the microwave oven above. You'll trim the end of this clip to better sync it with the following clip. This time, instead of placing both the right and left crop markers to trim the end of the clip, you'll position just the right crop marker and then use a menu command.

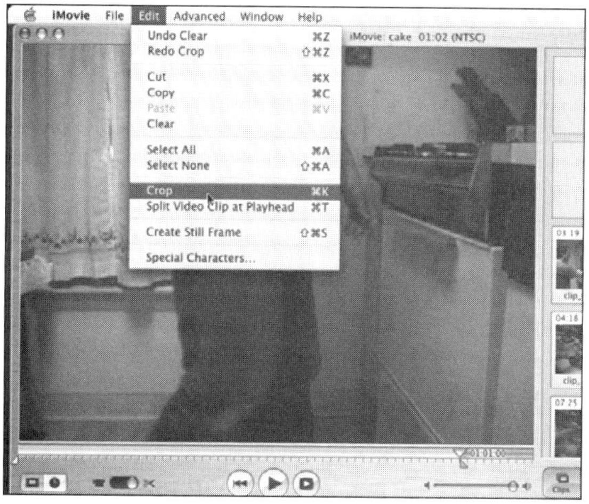

17. Drag the **right crop marker** to the point in the **timeline** just after my hand leaves the screen (around **01:01:00**). From the menu bar, choose **Edit > Crop** or press **Cmd+K**. This deletes the end of the clip, leaving just the selected yellow section of the clip.

Now you're ready for the next clips.

18. Shift+click clip_06 and **clip_07** to select them both, and then drag them to the right of the other clips in the **clip viewer**.

Note: *Make sure clip_06 precedes clip_07 in the clip viewer. If the two are reversed, drag clip_07 to the right of clip_06.*

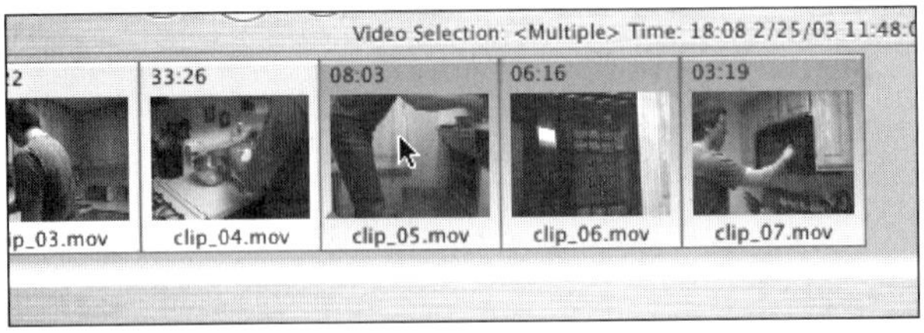

19. Shift+click clip_05. The last three clips in the clip viewer should be selected now. Click **Play**.

Clip_06 needs to be cropped at both the end and the beginning to make the motion between the clips look more natural.

---

20. Click **clip_06** and move the **right crop marker** to the point where my thumb enters the shot (**01:02:14**). Press **Delete**. Next, move the **right crop marker** to the point after my thumb presses the last button on the microwave and begins to pull off screen (**01:03:18**). Choose **Edit > Crop** or press **Cmd+K**.

---

21. Shift+click clip_05 and **clip_07** to select all three clips and click **Play**. The motion between the clips should seem much more natural now.

---

22. Choose **File > Save Project**. Keep iMovie open for the next exercise.

By this point, you should be fairly comfortable with placing clips in the clip viewer and cropping them. In the next exercise, you'll learn about adding transitions between clips rather than constantly relying on quick cuts.

---

3. Adding Transitions

In the previous exercise, you saw how proper clip cropping can produce a "seamless" effect, making the action appear as if it is happening in one take and in real time. You also saw how quickly cutting from clip to clip can convey a sense of time passing rapidly. In this exercise, you'll learn to use iMovie's built-in transitions, which allow you to apply an effect between clips to segue smoothly from one to clip to another.

1. Drag **clip_08** into the **clip viewer** to the right of **clip_07**. (**Clip_08** is another series of clips that have already been edited together for you.) Click **Play** to watch it.

Again, this clip uses a series of quick cuts to convey the passage of time. But another way to imply that time has passed is to use a transition effect. Transitions are appropriate for times when you don't want to jump from one shot to another, but instead want to provide a smooth, stylish changeover between action scenes.

You'll first add a transition between clips 07 and 08, and then you'll add some more within clip_08 itself.

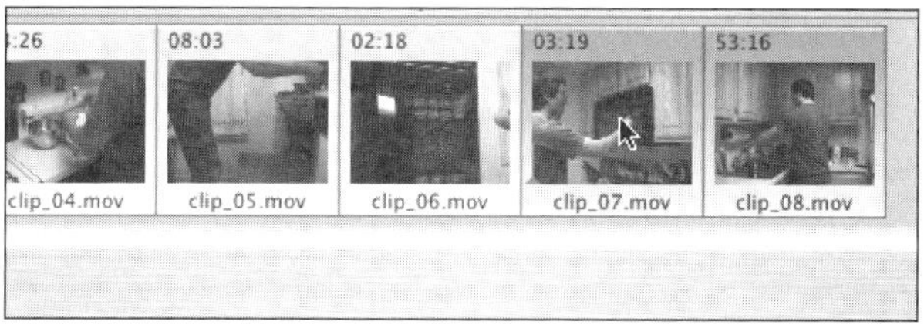

2. With **clip_08** still selected, **Shift+click clip_07** to select them both. Click **Play**. Notice that I've purposely left a few seconds of inaction at the end of **clip_07**. This will allow room for a transition effect between the two clips. Click the **Play** button again to pause the action if you don't want to watch to the end of **clip_08** again.

3. Click **clip_08** to select just that clip, and then click the **Trans** button under the **Clips** pane.

You're now viewing the Transitions pane. This pane contains a list of several transitions that you can apply to your clips. Each transition is pretty obviously named, but if you're not sure what a particular one does, just click it to see its effect. Clicking on any transition shows you a preview of the effect in the small thumbnail-sized monitor in the upper-right corner of the pane.

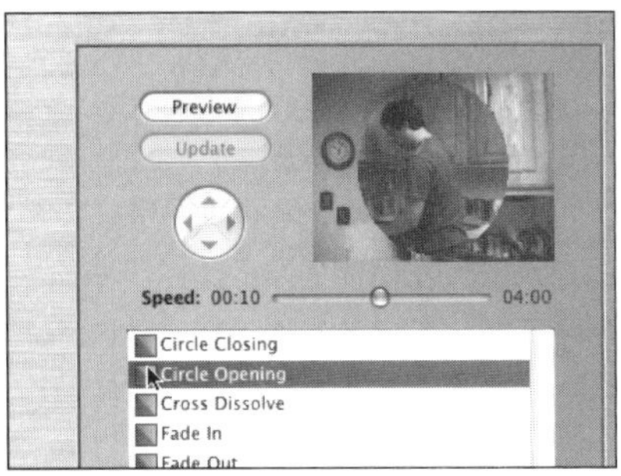

4. Make sure **clip_08** is still selected and click a few of the transitions to see how they are applied in the thumbnail monitor.

Note: *When previewing transitions, iMovie uses the currently selected clip. If no clips are selected, iMovie finds the start and end points of the two clips closest to the playhead and uses them for the preview.*

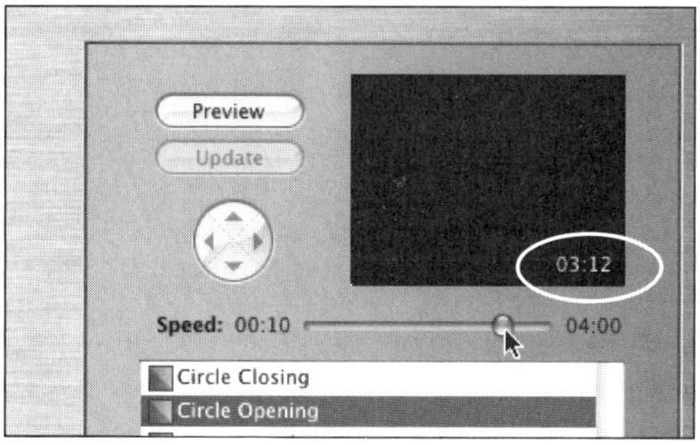

*The **Speed** slider allows you to adjust how long the selected transition takes to complete. You can drag it anywhere from 10 frames (00:10) to 4 seconds (04:00). The numbers in the lower-right corner of the thumbnail monitor let you know exactly how long the transition will last.*

NOTE | The Push Transition

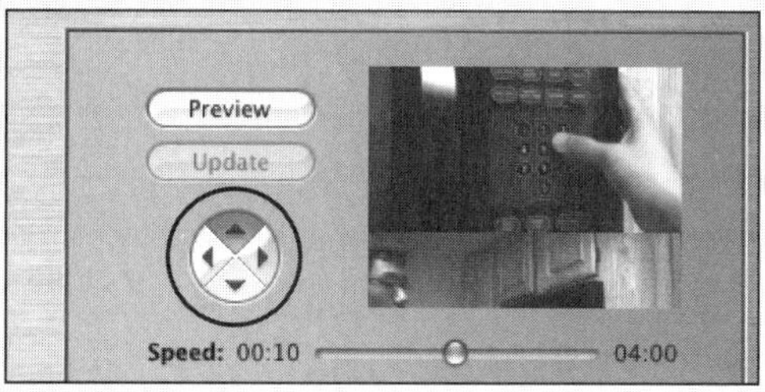

What about that oval with the four arrows? Have you noticed that it's grayed out for nearly all the transitions? These arrows are used to control the **Push** transition, which creates the effect of a clip "pushing" the previous clip off screen. When you select the Push transition, the arrows become active and you can choose to have the clip push in from the top, bottom, left, or right of the screen.

You can also see a larger version of the transition by clicking the ***Preview*** *button. Doing so will show you the transition in the monitor area, but be aware that this is just a preview and will look pretty choppy. In order to see a smooth transition, iMovie needs to render the transition, which is what you're about to have it do.*

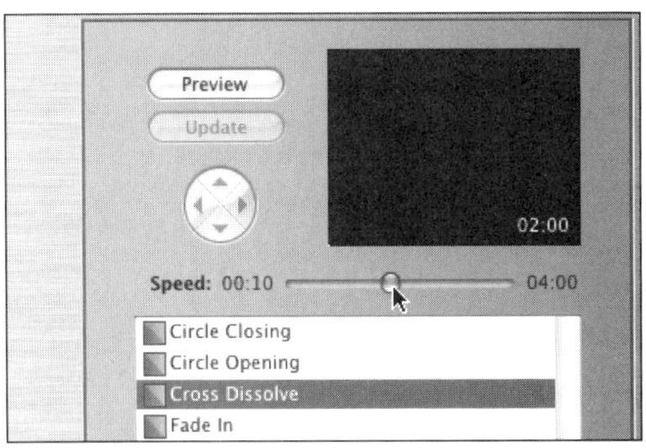

5. With **clip_08** still selected, click the **Cross Dissolve** transition, and then drag the **Speed** slider to **02:00** (to make the transition last two seconds).

6. To actually add the transition to your movie, drag **Cross Dissolve** down between **clip_07** and **clip_08**. They'll move apart to make room.

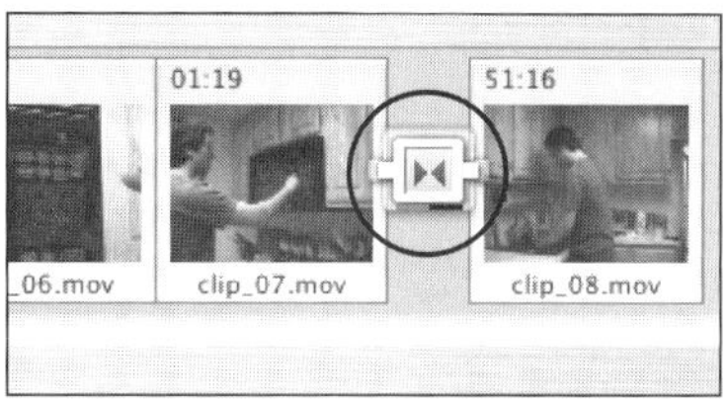

As soon as you release the mouse button, the transition begins to render, meaning that iMovie is performing the necessary calculations and actions to add the transition between the clips. The transition itself appears as sort of a mini-clip, and the red bar creeping along its bottom lets you know how far iMovie has progressed in the rendering process. If you were to watch the movie now, before the rendering is complete, the transition would still appear choppy, but once the red bar disappears, the transition will play in full, smooth motion.

NOTE | Transitions Shorten Your Movie

As you just saw, transitions you add to your movies appear as individual clips in the clip viewer. Any transition that joins two clips together (like Cross Dissolve, Circle Opening/Closing, or Scale Down) results in a slight reduction to the overall length of your movie. For example, you just applied a two-second Cross Dissolve transition to clips 07 and 08. When rendering this transition effect, iMovie took the last second of clip_07 and overlapped it with the first second of clip_08, resulting in the overall loss of one second to your movie. In many cases, this isn't a problem, and might actually be beneficial by helping to keep your movie short. But just be aware of this fact if you're working with a movie that's required to meet a certain time requirement.

Note: Some of the transitions are "single-clip" transitions that affect only one clip. They are Fade In, Fade Out, Overlap, Wash In, and Wash Out. Because these transitions are applied only to the beginning or end of a clip and don't affect the surrounding clips, they have no effect on the overall length of your movie.

7. Shift+click clip_07 and **clip_08** and click **Play** to see the transition you applied.

Notice how the Cross Dissolve gives the movie a smoother, more graceful changeover between clips? The Cross Dissolve is probably one of the most commonly used transitions in video editing. Unlike some of the wilder transitions such as Radial or Warp Out, Cross Dissolve is subtle enough that most viewers don't even notice its use. Of course, there's a time and place for each of the transitions, but you'll probably find that most of your projects will benefit most from straight cuts (no transitions) and Cross Dissolve transitions.

Next you'll apply another transition within clip_08.

TIP | Undoing and Removing Transitions

If you change your mind about a transition after it's been added and rendered, you can always change it by clicking its clip in the clip viewer and then making your adjustment in the Transitions pane. For example, if you applied a Cross Dissolve, but instead want to use a Scale Down transition, click the **Cross Dissolve** clip to select it, and then click the **Scale Down** transition in the **Transitions** pane. If necessary, adjust the **Speed** slider and then click the **Update** button. iMovie will render the new transition over the old one.

If, on the other hand, you decide that you don't want to use a transition at all, simply click the transition's clip in the **Clip** view and press **Delete**. iMovie removes the transition and restores the clip (or clips) to its original state.

8. Select **clip_08** and play the first 15 seconds or so. The clip opens with me washing some dishes and then cuts to a shot of the timer counting down. Adding a transition between these two shots would again help to convey the illusion of time passing. But because these two shots exist within the same clip, you can't add a transition between them. Transitions can only be applied to the end or beginning of a clip, not the middle. To add a transition between these two shots, you'll have to split the clip into two pieces.

9. Select **clip_08** and drag the **playhead** along the scrubber bar to **01:20:27**. This is the point immediately following the washing-the-dishes shot where the movie cuts abruptly to the microwave timer counting down. Use the **right** and **left arrow** keys on the keyboard to precisely position the playhead–you want to make sure you're looking at the very first frame of the timer. (It's okay if this frame doesn't fall exactly on **01:20:27**–it's more important that you have the **playhead** at the right place between the two shots.)

10. From the menu bar, choose **Edit > Split Video Clip at Playhead** (**Cmd+T**).

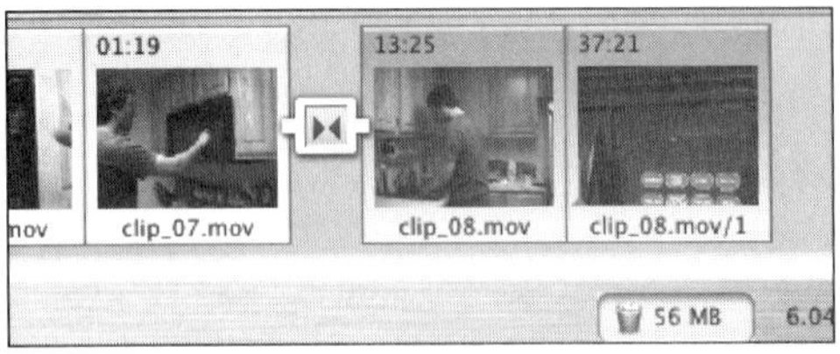

You now have an additional clip in the clip viewer: ***clip_08.mov/1****. clip_08.mov is now just the shot of me washing dishes. clip_08.mov/1 contains all the shots that followed. Because you've split clip_08 into two clips, you can now easily add a transition.*

11. Select **Cross Dissolve** in the **Transitions** pane and set the **Speed** slider to **2:00** (if it's not already there.) Drag **Cross Dissolve** to the **clip viewer** between **clip_08.mov** and **clip_08.mov/1**. Give the transition enough time to render and then select both clips and click **Play** to view the transition.

12. Choose **File > Save** when you're done watching the clips.

How you cut and edit your movie is really a matter of intent and personal taste. In most cases, you'll probably find yourself using cuts more than transitions–you don't want to place a transition between every single clip, unless, of course, you do. Tasteful use of transitions can add a professional look to your home movies. (Although your definition of "tasteful" may vary from others'.)

4. Working with Sound

In this exercise, you'll learn how to work with sound in iMovie. iMovie's audio controls allow you to work with and edit any existing audio that was recorded when you shot your footage as well as letting you insert additional sound effects and audio into your movie.

First, you'll work with some audio that's already in your movie.

1. Click **clip_04** and click the **Play** button. This is the clip containing the rapid-fire sequence of shots showing the cake's ingredients being mixed together. At the end of this clip, you see the electric mixer being used to blend the ingredients. It's pretty loud compared to the rest of the movie, so you'll bring the volume level down during this section of the movie.

To work with audio, you need to switch to Timeline view.

2. Click the **Timeline view** button. The clips become horizontal bars, each one sized to represent its overall length relative to the movie.

Because you don't want to adjust the volume of the entire clip, you'll need to split clip_04, much like you split the clip in the last exercise to insert a transition. (Splitting the clip is the easiest way to adjust the volume in this instance. See the section "Fade In, Fade Out" at the end of this exercise for information on altering a clip's volume without splitting it.)

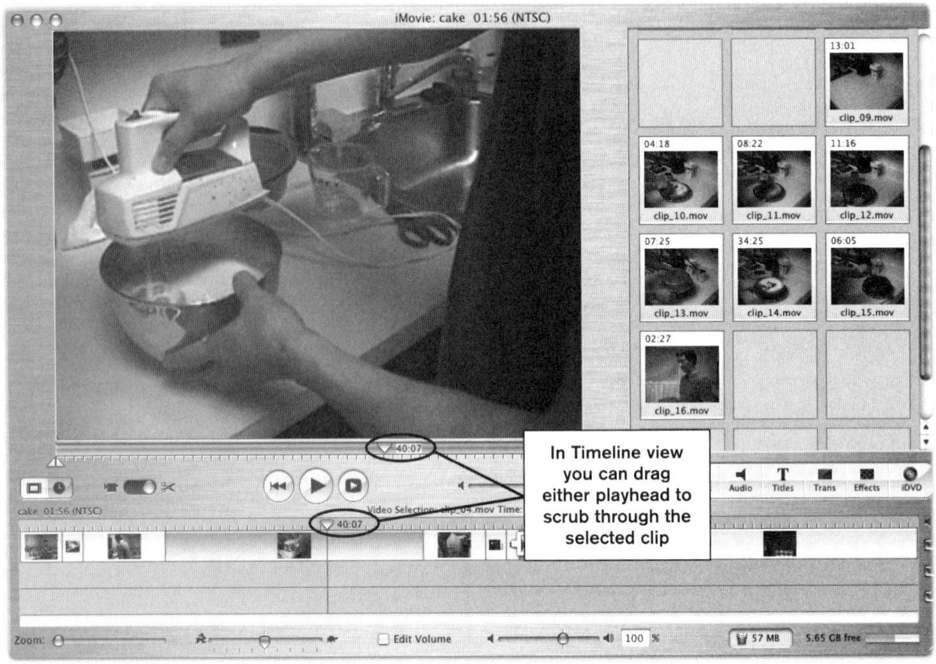

3. With **clip_04** selected, drag the **playhead** (either one) to the first frame depicting the electric mixer at **40:07**. Choose **Edit > Split Video Clip at Playhead (Cmd+T)**.

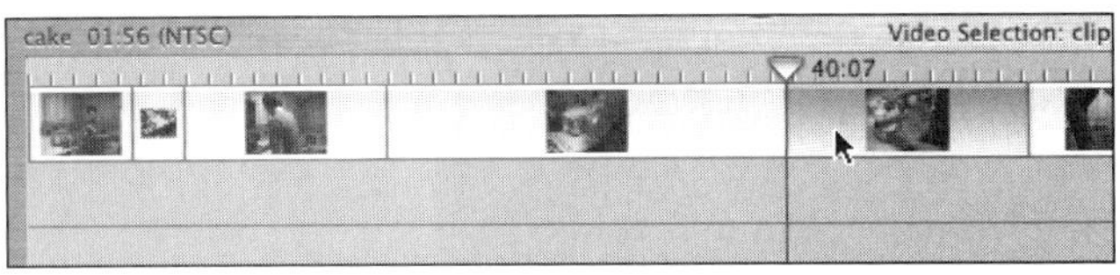

4. Click your new clip to select it. (Its name is now **clip_04.mov/1**, but you can't see its name unless you switch back to **Clip** view. Stay in **Timeline** view for now.)

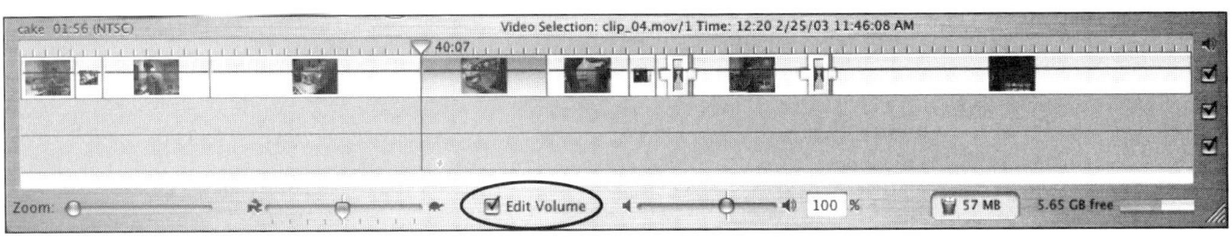

5. At the bottom of the iMovie window, check **Edit Volume**. Notice the horizontal line that appears through the clips. This line represents the volume level in each clip.

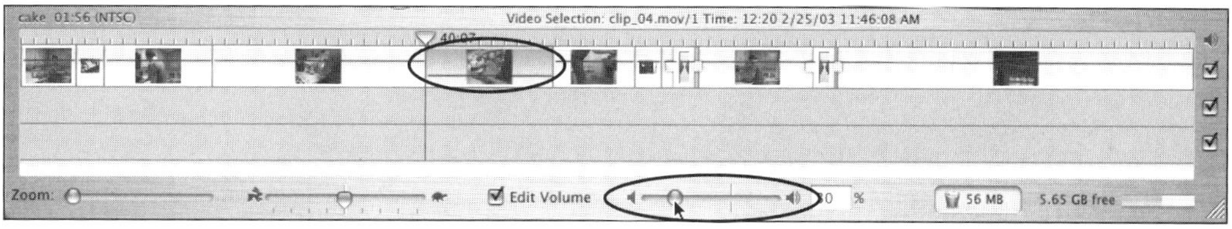

6. To reduce the selected clip's volume, drag the **volume** slider to the left. Notice that the horizontal line in the clip moves simultaneously. Drag the slider to **30%**. (You can also just type **30** into the field next to the slider.)

Tip: *How much you decrease or increase a clip's volume is entirely up to you and your ears. To help you find the level that suits a clip in your own project, you can adjust the volume while the clip is playing. Each time you move and release the slider, iMovie will adjust the volume based on your modifications.*

7. Uncheck **Edit Volume** to prevent any accidental volume changes, and then **Shift+click clip_04** (the clip immediately preceding the currently selected one) and click **Play** to check out the volume change you just made. The sound of the mixer should be a little less jarring to your eardrums now.

TIP | The Zoom Slider

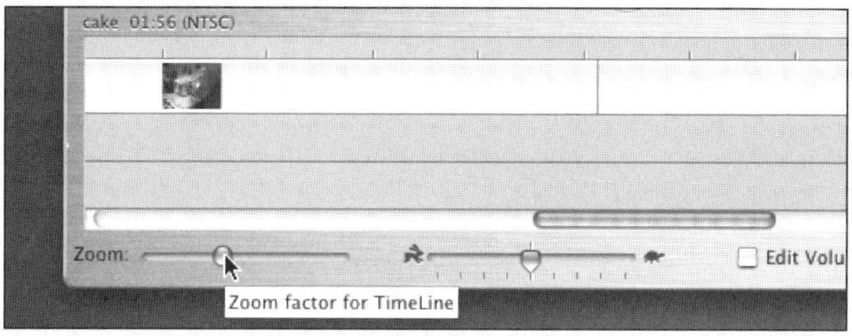

When in Timeline view, you might find it difficult to work with some of your shorter clips. If you're having trouble working with a particular clip, especially if you're trying to make precise adjustments to the volume, use the **Zoom** slider to increase the size of the bars in the timeline. Dragging the slider to the right enlarges even the smallest clip to a workable size.

In addition to working with your clips' existing audio, you can also add and manipulate other sounds from iMovie's library of sound effects or from your own collection of music you've imported into iTunes. You'll work with this feature, called iMovie Sound Effects, next.

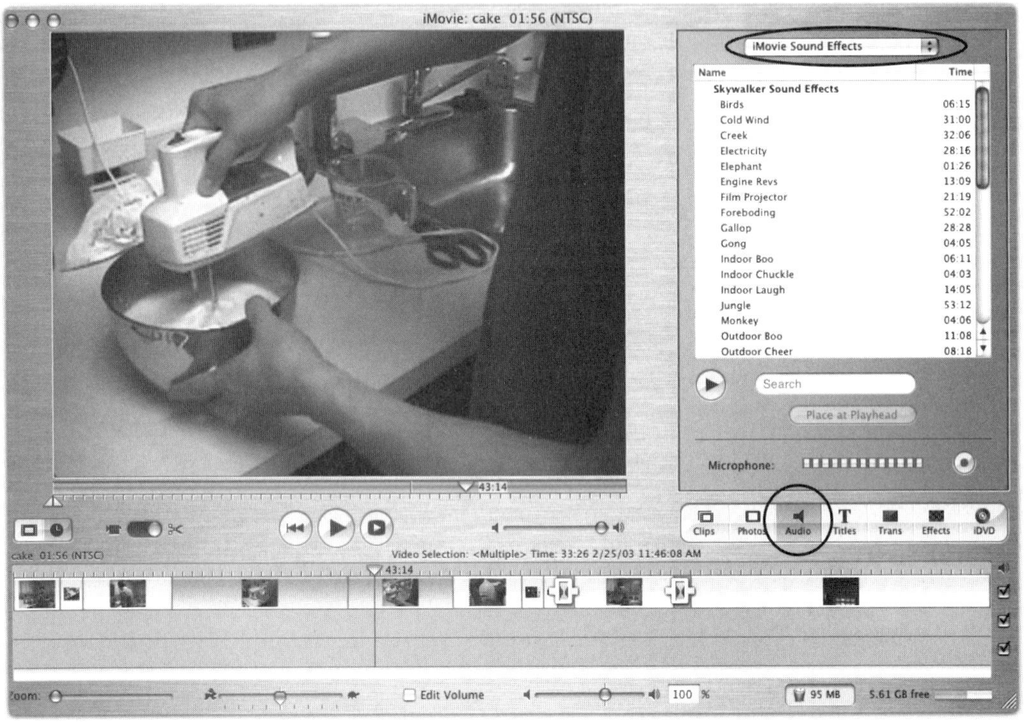

8. Click the **Audio** button under the **Clips** pane. From the pop-up menu at the top of the **Audio** pane, choose **iMovie Sound Effects**.

iMovie comes loaded with a great collection of professional sound effects created by Gary Rydstrom, sound designer and Director of Creative Operations at Skywalker Sound, the folks who brought you some small indie-flicks called "Star Wars" or something like that.

---

9. Double-click any of the sound effects to hear them.

In addition to the sounds of specific things like birds, a film projector, or a typewriter, you'll also find longer tracks of ambient music such as Foreboding and Suspense, which are perfect for adding to a scary movie (like one of a computer book author trying to bake a cake).

For this exercise, you'll add the Ticking Clock sound effect over the clip of me waiting for the cake to finish baking.

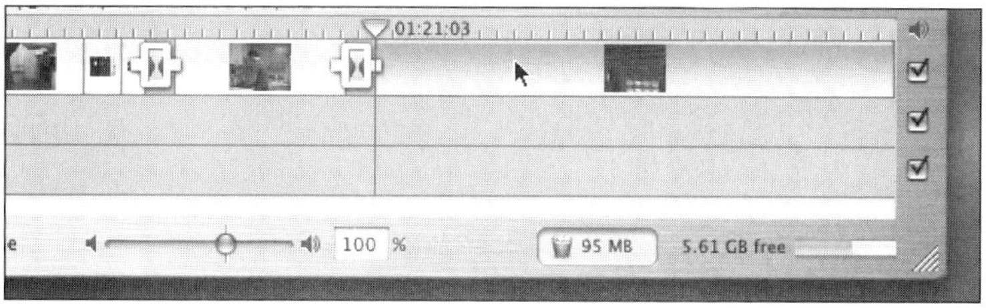

10. Click the last clip in the timeline. This places the **playhead** at the very beginning of the clip.

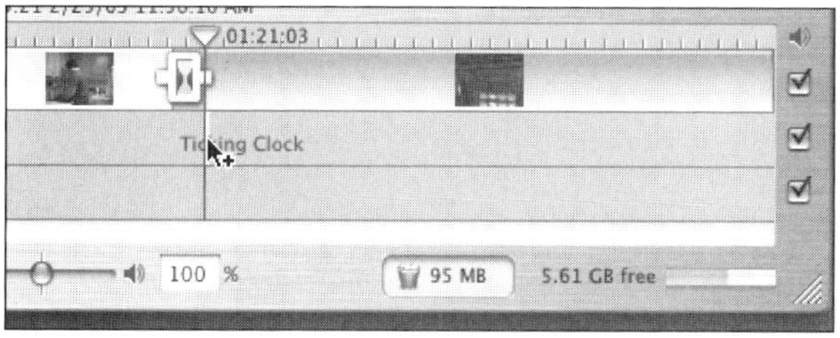

11. Locate and select the **Ticking Clock** sound effect in the list of iMovie sound effects. Drag **Ticking Clock** down into the **timeline** under the selected clip. You're dragging this effect into one of the two audio tracks available to you in iMovie. A yellow line appears; place it in line with the **playhead** (at the beginning of the video clip) and release the mouse.

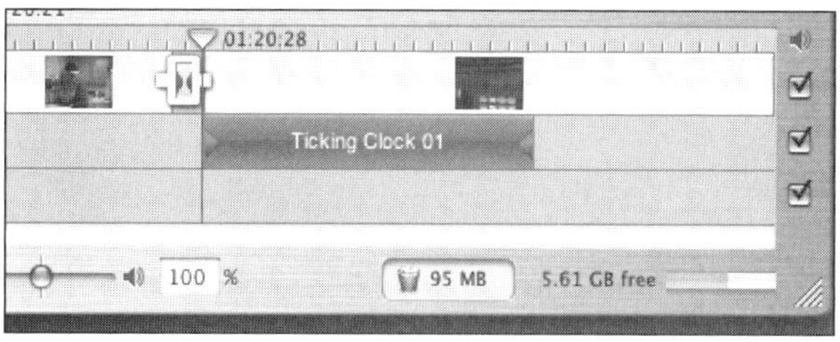

A bar representing the sound effect appears below the clip.

12. Click **Play** to hear the sound effect along with the video clip. Yeah, okay, the timer in the video is digital so you shouldn't hear any ticking. We'll just say the sound effect's there to reinforce the idea that time is passing.

In any case, the ticking clock sound effect isn't lasting long enough to fill out this clip. No problem, you just add the effect a second time.

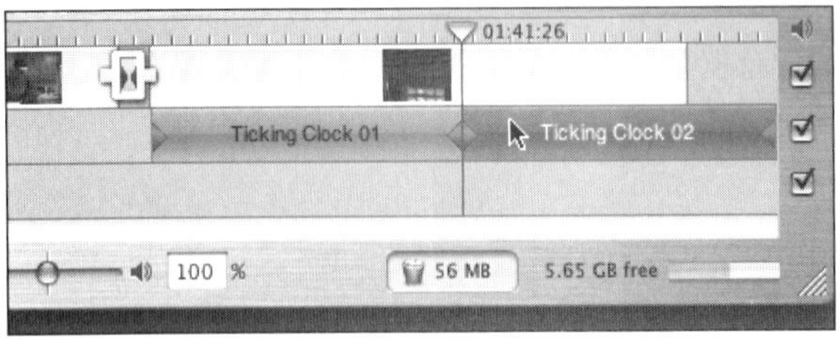

13. Drag **Ticking Clock** from the audio pane to the right of the existing effect. It should snap to the very end of **Ticking Clock 01**, but if you have trouble placing it, use the arrow keys on your keyboard to tap it into place.

Now you have the opposite problem; the sound effect lasts too long. You need to adjust the effect to make it stop when the digital timer in the video reaches the end of its countdown.

14. Drag the right end of **Ticking Clock 02** to the left until the **playhead** reaches **01:53:18**, or until you see the first frame of the microwave reading "PRESS" (if **01:53:18** doesn't exactly match up with your project).

15. Click the video clip and click **Play** to check your work and make sure that the sound effect stops just as the timer finishes.

Because the sound effects you added need to appear at very specific points in the movie, you should take the precaution of locking them to the clip. Locking prevents the audio and video from getting out of sync. In the previous exercise, you learned how adding transitions to your movie can shorten its length. If you've gone to the trouble of adding sound effects or other audio to your movie before adding your transitions, you'll definitely want to lock your clips, or else your audio tracks will stay in the same place along the timeline while your video tracks get shorter.

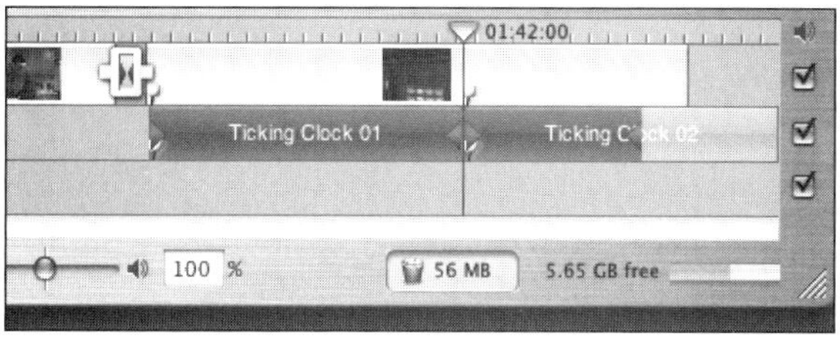

16. Click **Ticking Clock 01** and then **Shift+click Ticking Clock 02** to select them both. Choose **Advanced > Lock Audio Clip at Playhead** (**Cmd+L**). Pushpin icons appear at the beginning of both clips to indicate that you've locked them into position with the video clip above.

17. To make sure the audio clips are locked, select an earlier video clip on the timeline and press **Delete**. Notice how the audio clips shift to the left along with the video clip they're attached to. If they weren't locked, they would have stayed in place, and your audio would be out of sync with your video. Choose **Edit > Undo** to restore the clip your deleted. Choose **File > Save Project**.

Tip: You can download additional sound effects from Apple's Web site at ***www.apple.com/imovie/audio_effects.html.***

iMovie's sound-editing capabilities don't stop there. Here are some more cool things you can do with audio in iMovie:

Extracting Audio

There may be times when you don't want or need the audio you recorded when you shot your video footage. Or you may find yourself in a situation where you need only snippets of the sounds you taped. To edit your recorded sound independently of your video, select the video clip and choose **Advanced > Extract Audio**. The audio track appears in the track below the video, which allows you to edit the audio however you want without worrying about messing up your video.

Adding Music

With iMovie 3, your entire iTunes library is at your disposal for adding music to your movies.

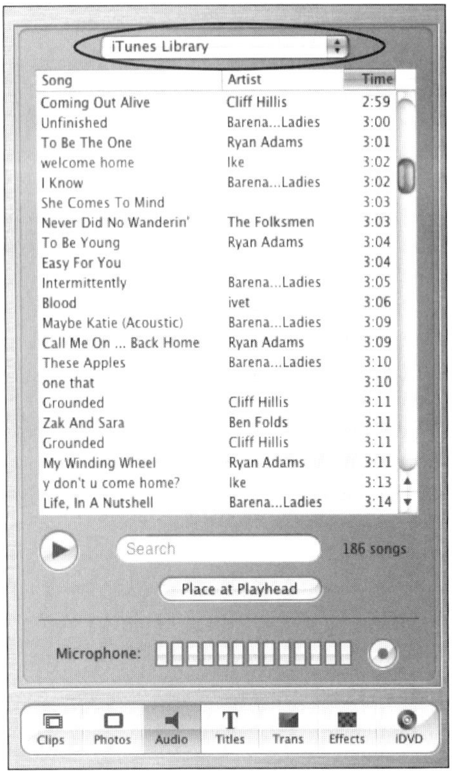

To access your iTunes music, click the **Audio** button in iMovie and choose **iTunes Library** from the pop-up menu at the top of the **Audio** pane. If you've created any playlists in iTunes, you'll also find them listed in the pop-up menu to make it easier to find your favorite tunes. You can also use the **Search** bar under the music list to quickly find a song by title or artist. Once you've located the music you want to use, either drag it into one of the audio tracks, or position the **playhead** at the point you want the music to start and then click **Place at Playhead** to automatically import the music to the exact location of the playhead.

Recording Live Audio

In addition to sound effects and music, iMovie has a feature that lets you record sounds with your Mac's built-in mic (or attached microphone) directly into your movie. This can be an extremely useful feature for creating voiceovers for your movies. For instance, after watching some of your footage, you might feel that parts of it would benefit from some narration.

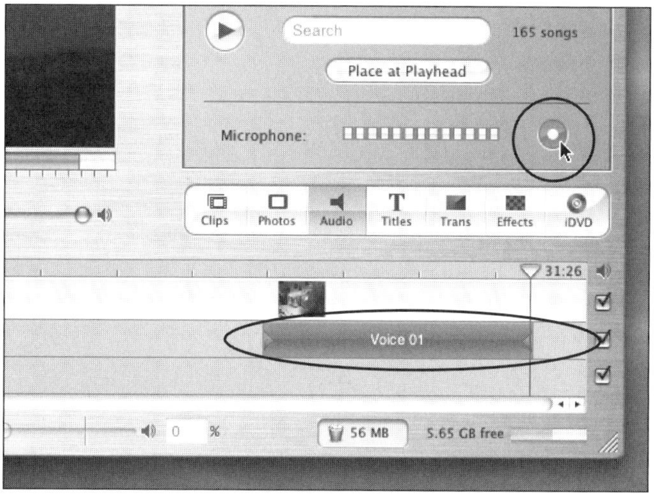

To add your voice, place the playhead where you want to start talking and click the **Audio** button. Click the **Record** button and start talking. You'll see an audio track appear as you begin to speak. When you're done, click the **Record** button again to stop recording.

Fade In, Fade Out

New to iMovie 3 is the capability to fade a clip's audio in and out at different points. At the beginning of this exercise, you learned to adjust an entire clip's volume, but there may be times when you want to adjust a clip's volume in a specific location without splitting the clip into separate pieces. For example, if you have a piece of music playing over a clip, you may want the music to diminish in volume at the end of the video or when someone speaks.

To adjust the volume level within a clip, check the **Edit Volume** box at the bottom of the window in Timeline view to make the volume level lines appear in each clip.

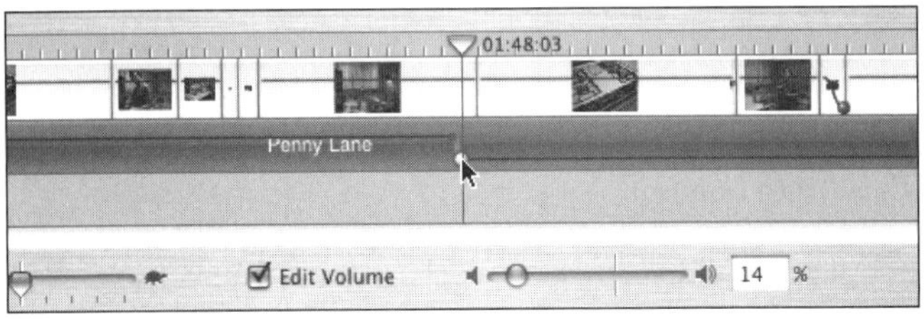

Click the volume level line at the point you want the volume to change and drag the marker that appears up to increase the volume or down to decrease the volume. You can drag the marker up or down at as many points as you need.

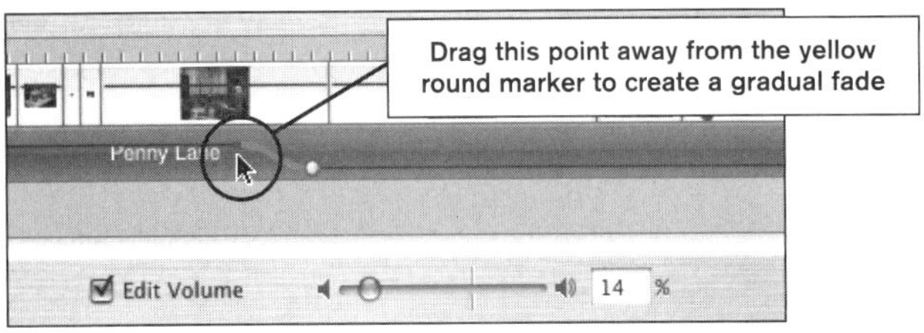

If you want a more gradual fade in or fade out, drag the square marker away from its corresponding round marker. This is a good technique to use when you need a slow audio fade, and it doesn't require splitting a clip into two.

MOVIE | fading.mov

See the movie **fading.mov** on the **H•O•T CD-ROM** for a demonstration of fading audio within a clip.

5. Adding Titles

Along with transitions, one of the elements of a well-edited video that makes it stand apart from the usual just-play-the-tape-off-the-camcorder video is the use of **titles**. The word "titles," at least in iMovie terms, refers to any text that appears in your movie–whether it's credits, subtitles, or words crawling up the screen reading "Chapter IV: A New Hope." This exercise shows you how to use iMovie's vast array of title effects to find the most appropriate look for your video.

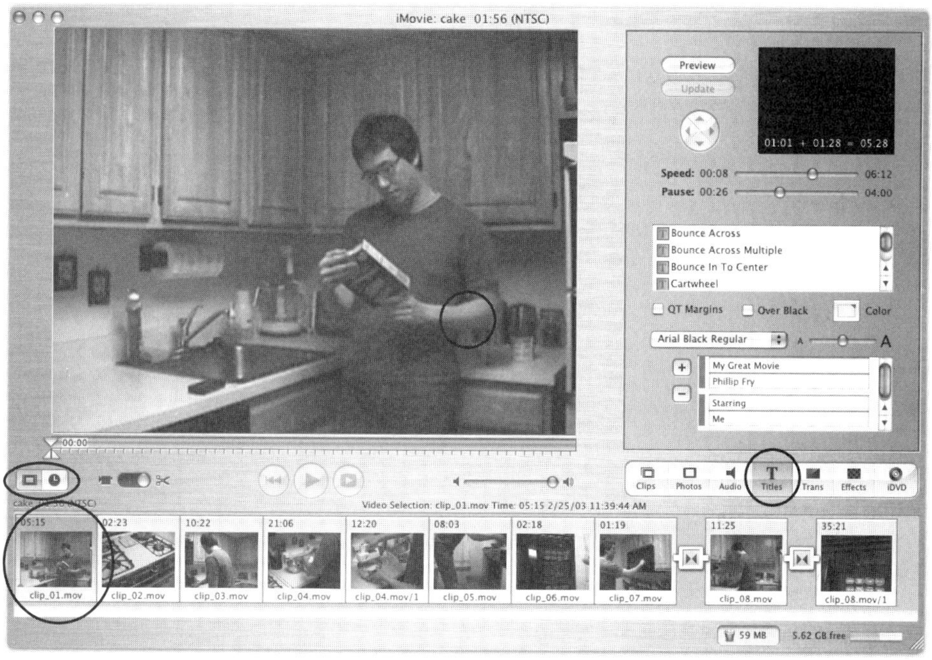

1. Switch back to the **clip viewer** and then click the **Titles** button to open the **Titles** pane. Select **clip_01** in the **clip viewer**.

You're going to add the opening text you saw earlier in the completed version of this movie, but first you'll take a look at the different features of the Titles pane.

2. The available title styles appear in the scrollable list at the middle of the **Titles** pane. Click any title to preview its appearance in the thumbnail monitor. Unless you've previously added titles to a movie project, the default text used for the titles is "My Great Movie" and your name.

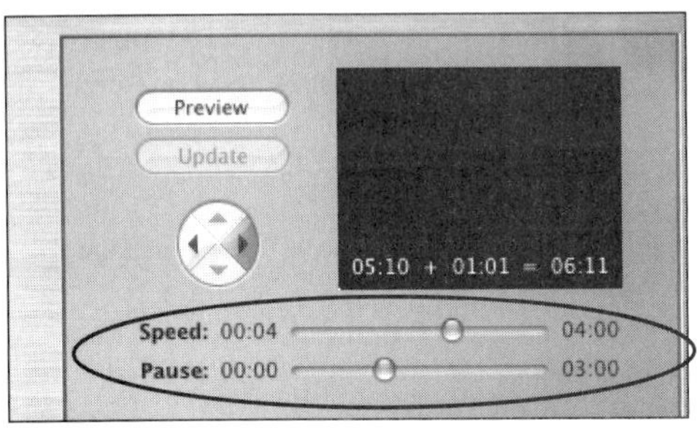

*Above the list of titles are the **Speed** and **Pause** sliders. Depending on the style of title you've selected, the Speed slider determines how quickly text fades in and out, rolls across screen, or bounces around. The Pause slider determines how long the text remains still after it has finished its entrance animation and before it begins its exit animation. For example, if you select the Cartwheel title style and set the Speed slider to 6:00 (six seconds) and the Pause slider to 2:00 (two seconds), your text will take three seconds to cartwheel onto the screen, then pause for two seconds, and then take the remaining three seconds to cartwheel off screen.*

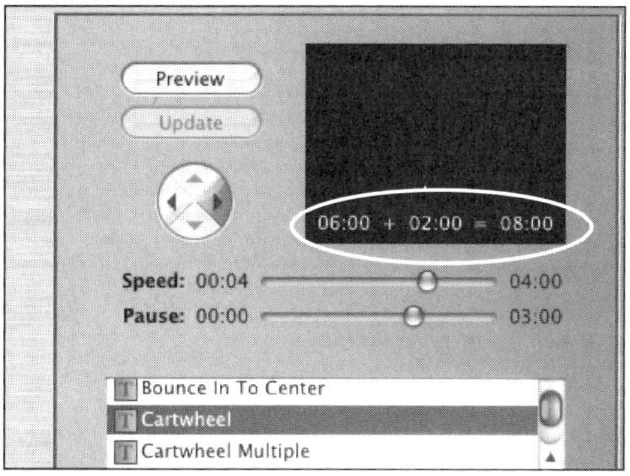

iMovie even does the math for you, so you know exactly how long your text will be onscreen. Note that some of the title styles, such as Drifting, Gravity, and Subtitle, don't use the Pause slider. For these styles, just use the Speed slider to determine how long the title will be seen.

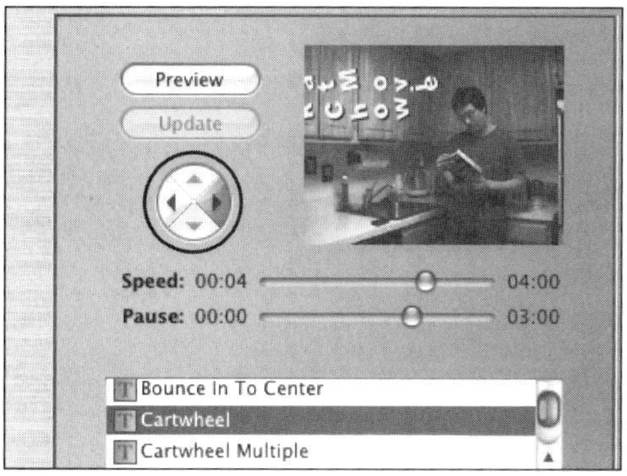

Several of the animated styles can be further customized by using the directional arrows to determine from which direction your text enters the screen.

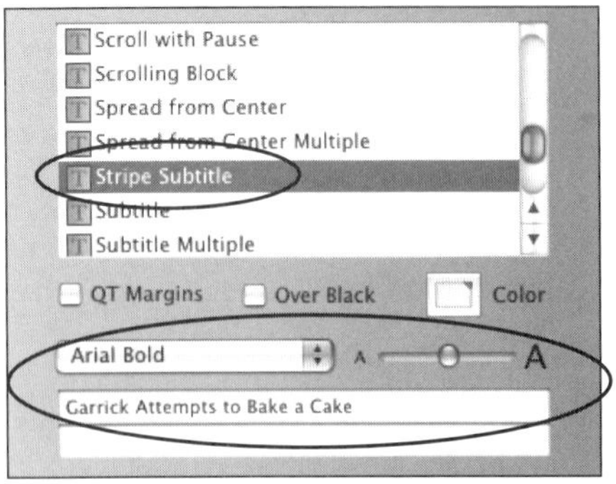

3. With **clip_01** selected, click the **Stripe Subtitle** style. In the top text field at the bottom of the **Titles** pane, type **Garrick Attempts to Bake a Cake**. Delete your name or any other text that appears in the lower text field. For the font, select **Arial Bold** (or a similar Arial font if you don't have Arial Bold) and set the text size somewhere in the middle of the slider.

4. Drag the **Speed** slider to around **3:25** (three seconds, 25 frames). This is an arbitrary period of time chosen for this particular exercise. For your own projects, you'll need to experiment to determine the amount of time you want your titles to appear onscreen.

NOTE | QuickTime Margins

An important decision to make when adding titles to your movie is whether you intend to present the completed project on your computer as a QuickTime movie or on a television through your camera.

Most TVs are designed to ensure that the picture appears from edge to edge on the screen, and, as a result, the margins of images tend to be cropped around the edges. iMovie compensates for this cropping by placing titles, such as Stripe Subtitle, slightly away from the bottom edge of the window into the so-called "safe area" to ensure that the entire title will be visible on a TV.

TV safe area

QuickTime margins

QuickTime movies, on the other hand, display the entire viewable area of your projects. If you're confident that your movie will be shown only with QuickTime and not on a TV, you can check the **QT Margins** box in the Titles pane to make your title appear flush to the edge of the screen.

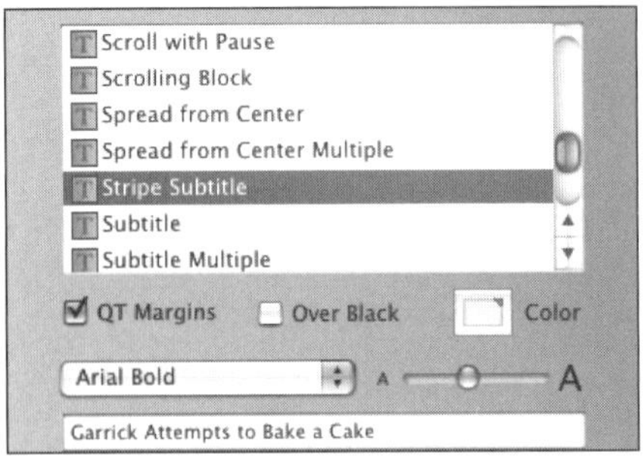

5. Since you'll only be viewing the final version of this project in QuickTime, check the **QT Margins** check box. The **Stripe Subtitle** now appears flush with the bottom border of the footage.

You're ready to add this title to you movie. Adding a title is just like adding a transition–simply drag the title where you want it to appear.

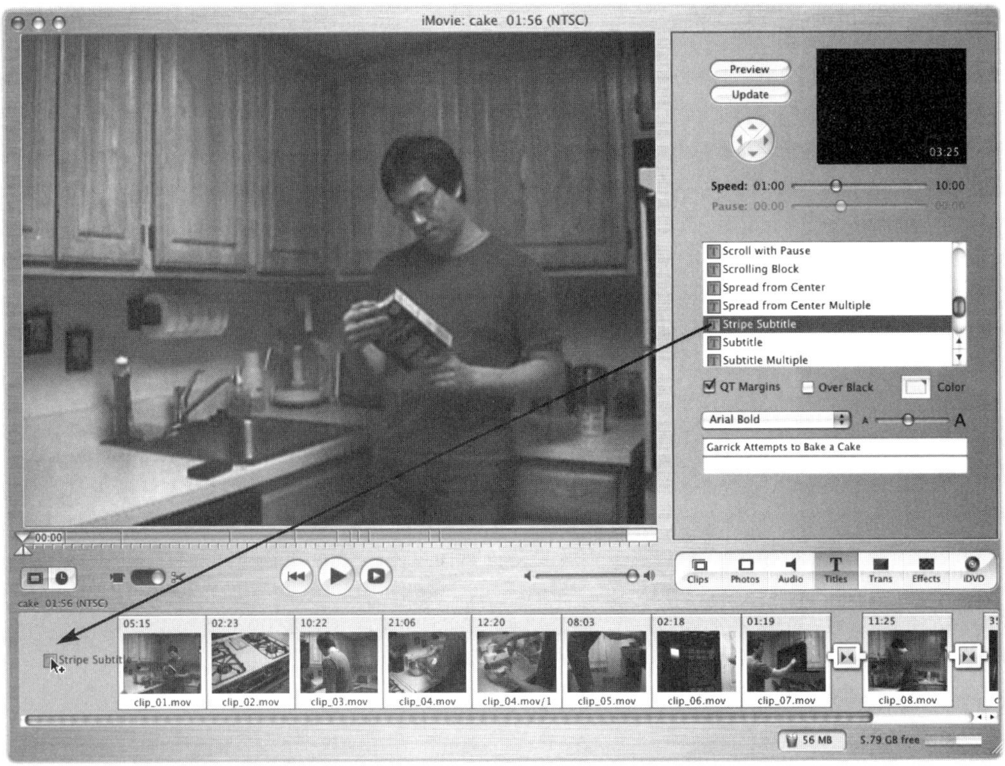

6. Drag **Stripe Subtitle** to the very front of the **clip viewer**, to the left of **clip_01**. **clip _01** will move out of the way for you.

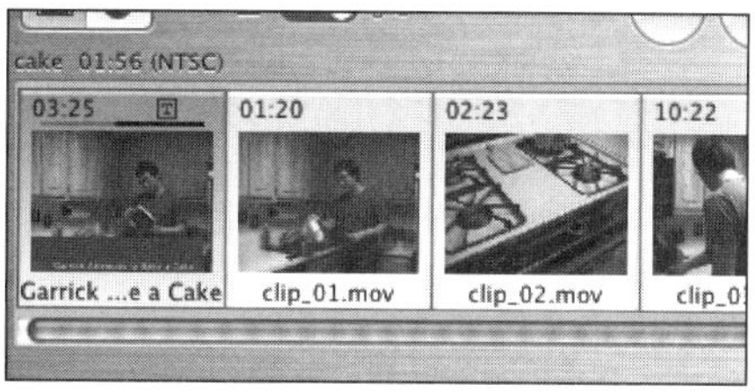

Once you release the mouse, iMovie begins to render the title into your movie. Much like transitions, titles need to be made into their own clips. When you dragged this title into the clip viewer in front of clip_01, the first 3 seconds and 25 frames of clip_01 were chopped off and turned into the title clip.

7. When the title is done rendering, **Shift+click** the first two clips and click **Play** to watch the title over the first scene of the movie.

8. Save your project and keep it open for the next exercise.

NOTE | Titles over Black

Depending on your project, you may want your titles to appear over a black screen rather than on top of the video. If this is the case, click the **Over Black** check box in the Titles pane to present your title with no background images. After setting title preferences, drag the title into the clip viewer the same way you just did in this exercise.

TIP | Editing Titles

If you need to edit or change any title that's been rendered, select its clip and make your changes to the title's style, text, speed, or whatever it is you need to change. When you're done, click the **Update** button at the top of the Titles pane. iMovie re-renders the title. To remove a title completely, simply select its clip and press **Delete**. If the title appears over a video clip (instead of over black), the video clip will be restored to its original state.

6. Adding Still Photos

In the next two exercises, you'll complete the video project by adding the remaining clips and some photos, and applying an effect from iMovie's Effects pane.

First, you'll insert the remaining clips into the clip viewer.

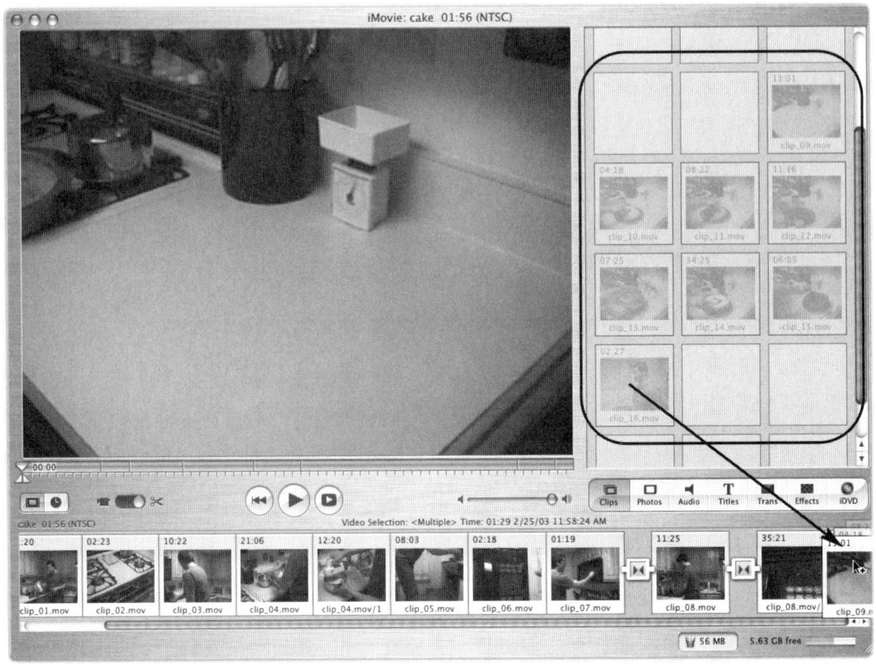

1. Click the **Clips** button to display the **Clips** pane. If necessary, scroll the clip viewer to the far right so you can see the last clip in the movie. Click **clip_09** in the **Clips** pane and then **Shift+click** the rest of the clips in order to select them all. Drag the clips to the right of **clip_08.mov/1** in the **clip viewer**.

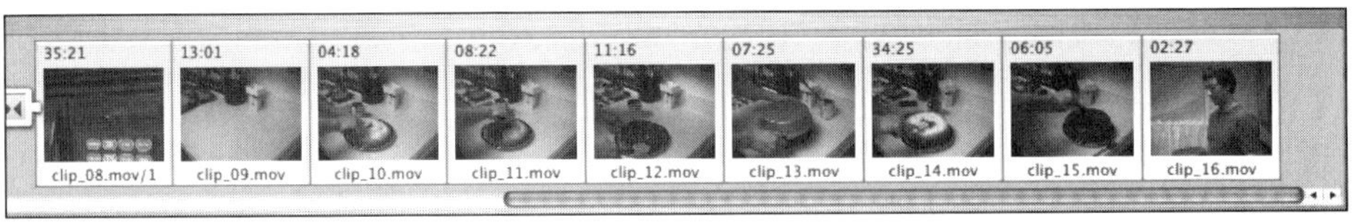

2. Check the clip titles to make sure they're all in order.

The video portion of the movie is now pretty much complete. Next you'll add some still photos to the end of the movie.

The Ken Burns Effect

iMovie 3 comes with a new effect for still images called the Ken Burns effect, named after the acclaimed director of documentaries such as "The Civil War," "Baseball," and "Jazz." In his films, Ken Burns frequently uses old photographs to accompany a narrator's anecdotes or to illustrate a point. But rather than just displaying a still picture, the camera zooms in and out and pans across the photographs to show a specific person or detail, drawing the viewer's eye to a particular portion of the image. Although Ken Burns popularized this effect, he didn't invent it. In professional animation circles, this technique is known as kinistasis, which means "moving still," and has been around for decades. iMovie 3 makes it easy for you to apply this same style to give your photos a heightened dramatic effect. You can create a pretty nifty slideshow of images in iMovie by applying the Ken Burns effect to a sequence of photographs.

3. Click the **Photos** button to view the **Photos** pane.

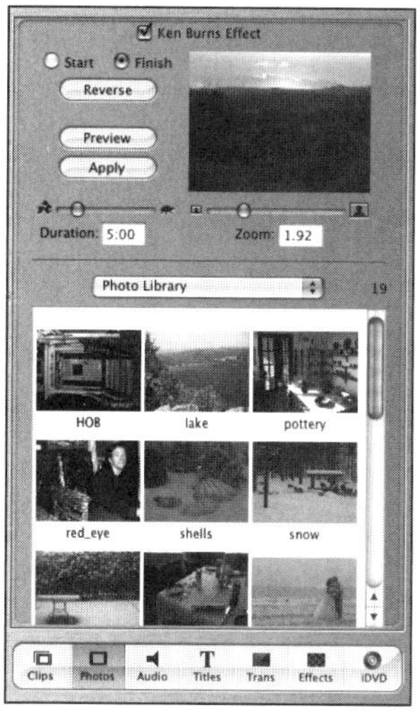

*From the Photos pane, you can access all the images stored in your copy of iPhoto. Here you'll see the images you used in Chapter 15, "*iPhoto 2*" (unless you've already deleted them), and any other photos you may have imported. You can use the pop-up menu to see all the photos in your iPhoto Library or to select specific albums to narrow down your search to a single collection of photos. You should also see the Ken Burns effect doing its thing in the thumbnail monitor. (If it's already stopped, just click any photo thumbnail and the effect will preview again.)*

*Although the Photos pane makes it super easy to grab pictures from iPhoto, images aren't required to be in iPhoto before you can use them in iMovie. For this exercise, you'll import pictures directly from the **chap_16** folder on your Desktop.*

4. Choose **File > Import** from the menu bar. Navigate to the **chap_16** folder on the **Desktop** and click **cake_photos**. Select **cake_01.jpg** and click **Open**.

The image is imported into iMovie and placed into the Clips pane. Notice the 5:00 in the clip's upper-left corner, indicating that the photo has been set to display for five seconds (5:00). By default, the Ken Burns effect immediately starts rendering.

5. Watch the red line creeping along the bottom of the clip and allow the clip to finish rendering.

Tip: *If you want to stop the Ken Burns effect, press* ***Esc*** *after importing a photo. When working with iPhoto pictures in the Photos pane, you can stop the KB effect by unchecking it at the top of the pane.*

6. Drag **cake_01.jpg** to the far right of the clip viewer, making it the last clip in the sequence. If you click the **Play** button with this clip selected, you'll see the playhead move across the scrubber bar, but since this is a still photo, nothing changes visually. Left as it is, this photo will display for five seconds. You'll make some changes to it now.

7. Click the **Photos** button to return to the **Photos** pane. Make sure **cake_01.jpg** is still selected in the **clip viewer**.

Setting up the Ken Burns effect is pretty simple. First, click the ***Start*** *button and decide how you want the picture to look when it appears, then click the* ***Finish*** *button and determine how you want it to look at the end of the effect.*

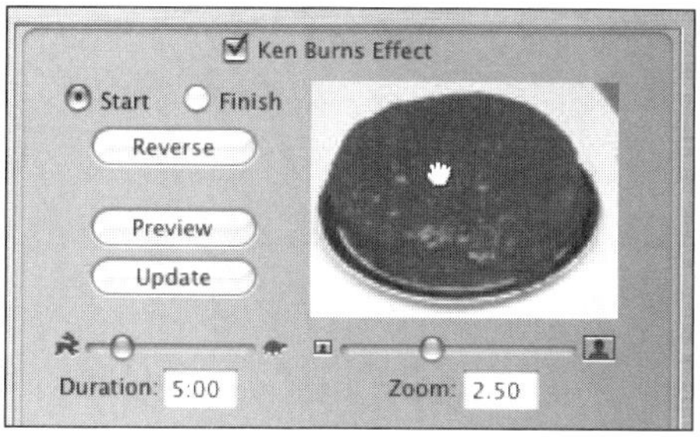

8. At the top of the **Photos** pane, click the **Start** button. Leave the **Duration** slider at 5 seconds (if it's not already there, set it to **5:00**), then drag the **Zoom** slider to **2.50** to magnify the image. Click inside the thumbnail monitor and drag the image until the cake is centered in the monitor. This is how the image will appear when the clip begins.

9. Now click the **Finish** button. Set the **Zoom** slider to **1.25** to apply a slight magnification to the image, then drag the photo in the thumbnail monitor just far enough to the right to hide the dirty dishes in the sink at the right of the image.

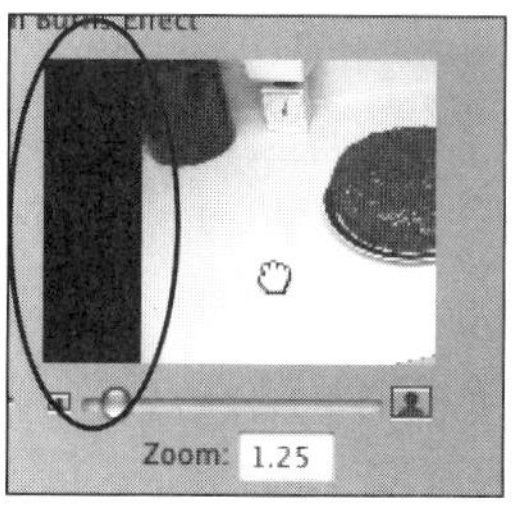

Tip: When dragging a zoomed photo, be careful not to drag the image too far in any direction, or you'll end up with a black border where the picture ends. What you see onscreen is a pretty good representation of what the final effect will look like, so keep an eye on the edges of your photos.

10. Now that you've set your preferences for the Ken Burns effect, click **Update** to render the effect to the clip. (For your own work, you'll probably want to click the **Preview** button a few times while making your adjustments to see what your settings will do.)

11. Watch the red rendering bar in the **cake_01.jpg** clip. When the rendering is complete, click the **Play** button to see the results. Pretty nifty, huh? If you need to make any adjustments, you can make your changes and then click the **Update** button again to re-render the effect.

Now you'll bring in a second image.

12. Choose **File > Import** and open **cake_02.jpg** from the **chap_16** folder.

13. Drag **cake_02.jpg** to the right of **cake_01.jpg** in the **clip viewer**. Click the **Photos** button and then click the **Start** button under the **Ken Burns Effect** check box.

The effect's settings should still be set from the previous picture.

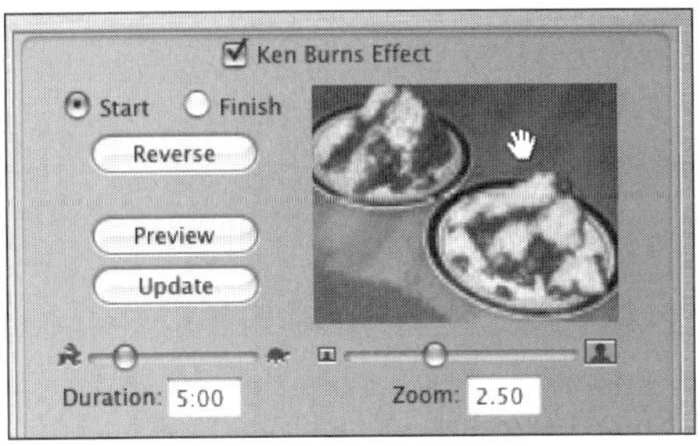

14. Drag the thumbnail image so the two slices of cake are centered in the monitor. (Once again, allow me to apologize for the horrible cake that you now have to view close-up.)

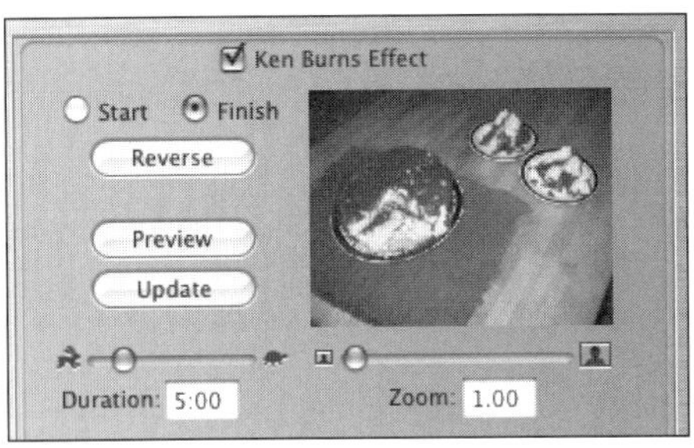

15. Click the **Finish** button and drag the **Zoom** slider to the far left so there's no magnification added to the image. Click **Update**.

16. Allow the effect to fully render and then click **Play** to observe the results.

As you can see, still images are pretty easy to work with in iMovie. You can even grab frames from your video footage to turn into still images, which can be useful if a particular frame captures an important moment that goes by too quickly.

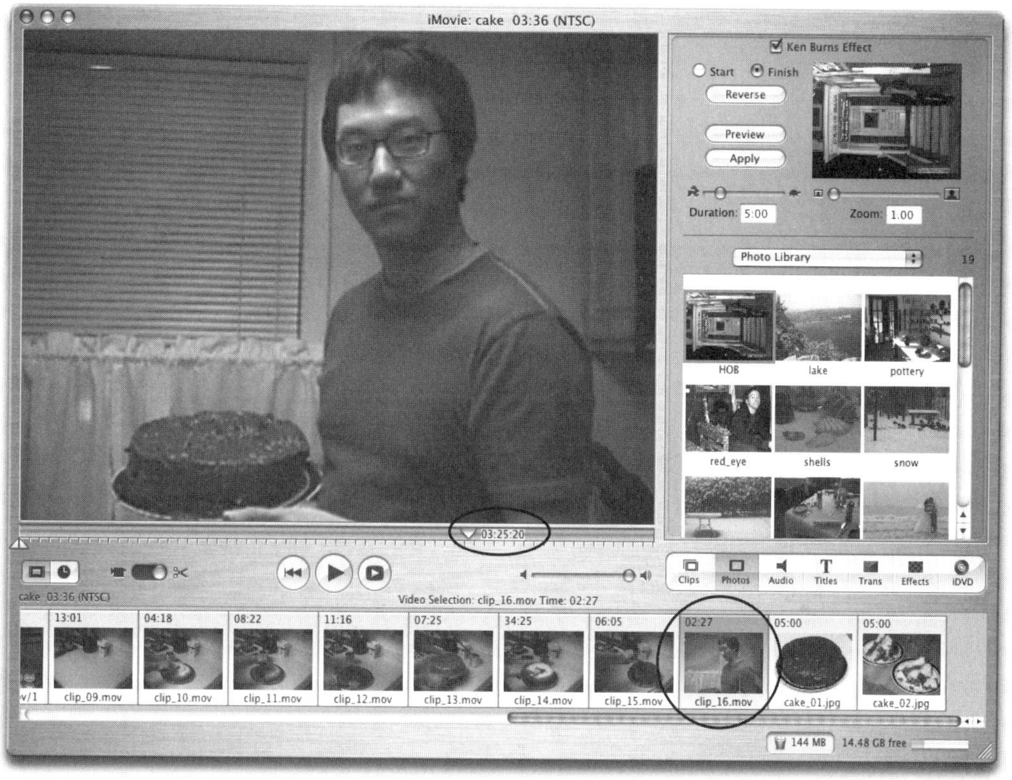

17. In the **clip viewer**, click **clip_16.mov** (the last video clip immediately preceding the first cake photograph). Drag the **playhead** to approximately **03:25:20**. You'll grab this frame and use it as the last image of the movie.

18. Choose **Edit > Create Still Frame**. This automatically turns the frame into a five-second clip and places it in the **Clips** pane.

Tip: You can also create still frames by choosing ***File > Export Frame As.*** *You can then save the frame to your hard drive as a JPEG (good for emailing) or a PICT file (for use in another iMovie project).*

---

19. Drag this clip to the far right of the **clip viewer**, making it the final clip of the movie. Because you created this still clip from your video, you can't apply the Ken Burns effect to it. The KB effect can only be applied to photos you import.

---

20. Shift+click cake_01.jpg to select the last three clips. Click **Play**. This sequence of clips could probably benefit from some quick Cross Dissolve transitions to soften the switching of images.

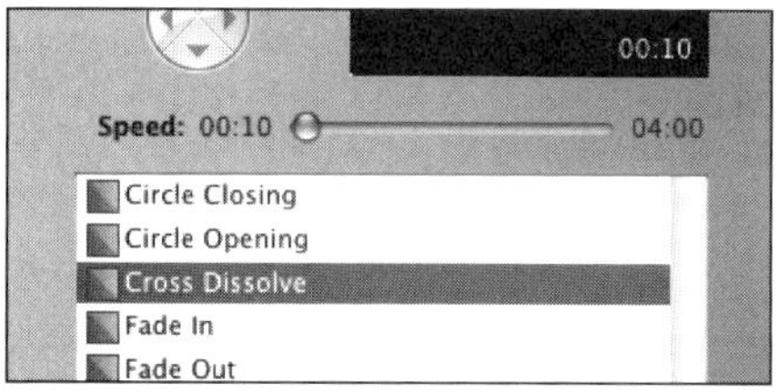

21. Click the **Trans** button to open the **Transitions** pane. Select **Cross Dissolve** and set the **Speed** slider to the far left.

Sometimes, quick Cross Dissolves between clips make transitions between shots easier on the eyes, and almost unnoticeable to most viewers.

22. Drag the **Cross Dissolve** transition between **cake_01.jpg** and **cake_02.jpg**, and allow the transition to render. Then drag a second **Cross Dissolve** between **cake_02.jpg** and your still image. After the transition renders, select all three clips again and click **Play**. See how much nicer the still image montage looks now?

Let's add one more Cross Dissolve.

---

23. Select **Cross Dissolve** in the **Transitions** pane and set the **Speed** slider to **1:00**. Drag **Cross Dissolve** between **clip_16.mov** and **cake_01.jpg**. This slightly longer transition will provide a nice segue from the video portion of the movie into the still images. After the transition renders, select the last four clips of the movie (not counting the cross dissolve clips between them) and click **Play** to get the full effect.

---

24. Save the movie when you're done and keep it open for the next exercise.

MOVIE | kburns.mov

See the movie **kburns.mov** on the **H•O•T CD-ROM** for a demonstration of applying the Ken Burns effect.

7. Effects and Finishing Touches

In this exercise, you'll take a quick look at some of the special effects built into iMovie. You probably won't find yourself using the Effects pane as much as you might use transitions or titles, but some of iMovie's effects can be useful in certain situations when you need a clip to look a particular way or when you just want to be silly. We'll go for the silly option in this exercise.

1. Click **clip_04.mov/1** in the **clip viewer**. This is the clip that begins with a shot of me using the electric mixer.

2. Click the **Effects** button to view the **Effects** pane.

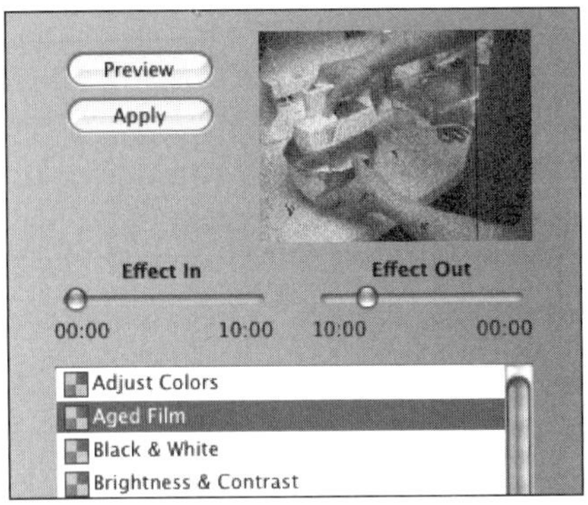

Here's where you'll find the special effects to apply to your video clips. To apply an effect, click its name and then adjust the Effect In and Effect Out sliders to determine how far into the clip you want to get before the effect appears, and how long you want the effect to last. Each of the effects has an additional set of sliders to adjust settings specific to that effect.

3. Click a few of the effects to see what's available here. Feel free to experiment with each effect's individual settings. Dragging in the thumbnail monitor can further control some effects like Electricity, Fairy Dust, and Lens Flare.

For the clip you have selected, let's say you want to emphasize that this is a really powerful mixer. You'll apply the Earthquake effect to the shots showing the electric mixer.

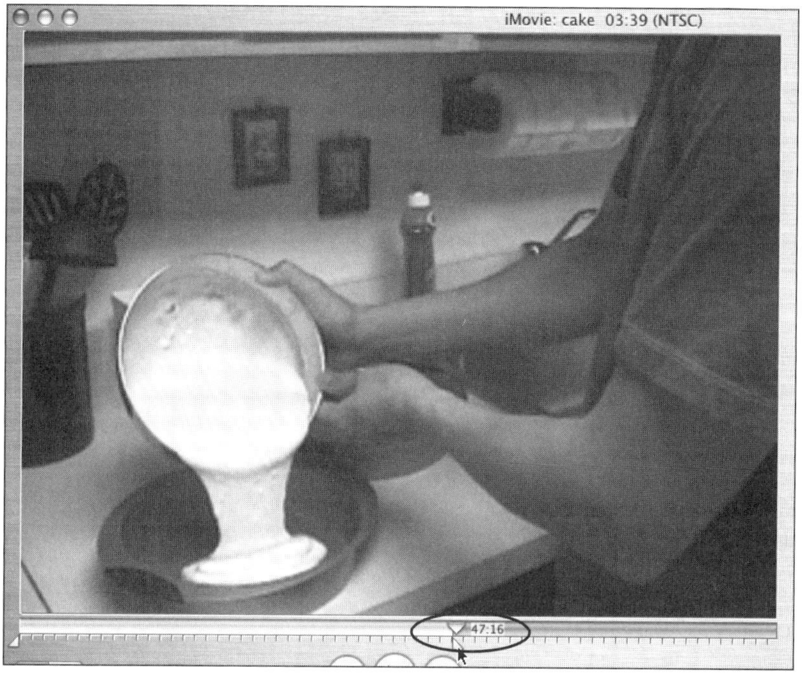

That batter's pretty lumpy for having been through the mixer.

4. With **clip_04.mov/1** selected, drag the **right crop marker** to **47:16**. This should be the first frame after the electric mixer shots.

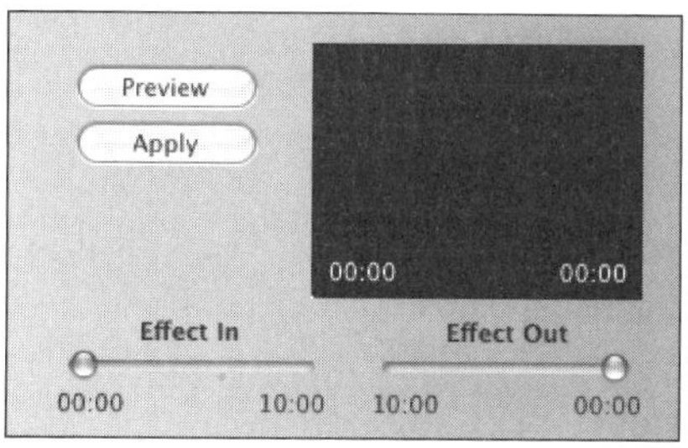

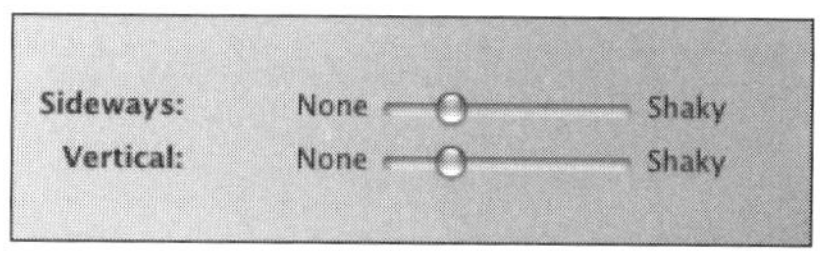

5. Click the **Earthquake** effect in the **Effects** pane. Drag the **Effect In** slider to the far left to apply the effect to the clip immediately. Then drag the **Effect Out** slider all the way to the right to make the effect last for the entire duration of the selected sequence. At the bottom of the pane, drag the **Sideways** and **Vertical** settings slightly to the left to reduce the amount of vibration to be created by the effect. (As is the case with transitions and titles, when working on your own projects, you'll have to play around with the sliders to determine the appropriate settings for the effects you use.) Click the **Apply** button.

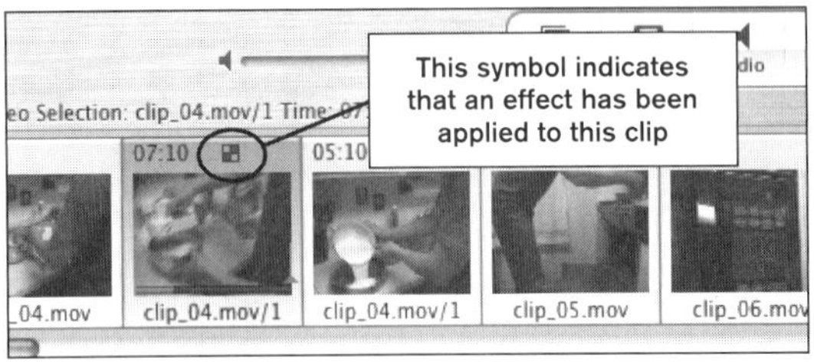

Because effects can only be applied to entire clips, iMovie splits the selected frames into their own clips.

6. Allow iMovie to completely render the effect, and then click the **Play** button to see the result. Depending on your Mac, rendering this effect could take several seconds or several minutes.

Although they don't appear in the Effects pane, there are a few other tricks you can apply to your clips to change their appearance. For instance, you can change the speed of a clip to make it faster or slower, which can be useful when you need to slow down an especially quick clip to show detail or speed up a tedious clip to make time pass faster. For example, let's speed up the embarrassing frosting scenes in this movie. Please.

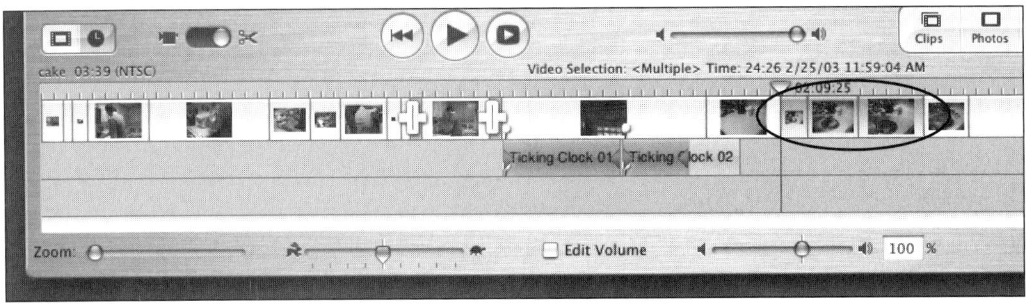

7. Click **clip_10.mov** and then **Shift+click clip_12.mov** to select the three clips of me slathering frosting on the first layer of the cake. Switch to **Timeline** view. The clips will remain selected.

In Timeline view, you can use the Speed slider to adjust how fast a clip is played.

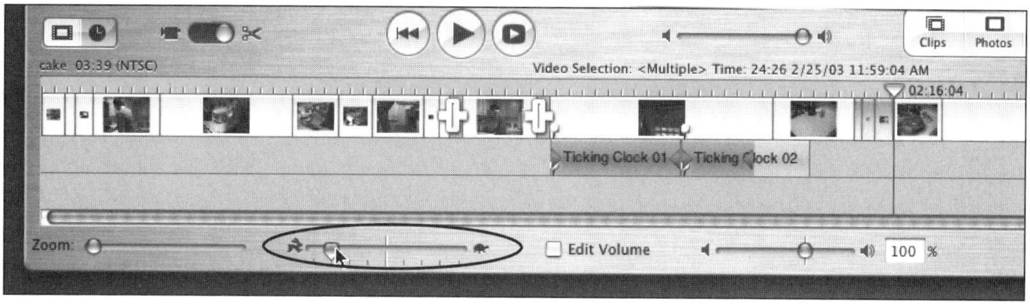

8. Drag the **Speed** slider to the second-to-last marker on the left to speed up the selected clips. Click the **Play** button to see the result, and then switch back to the **clip viewer**.

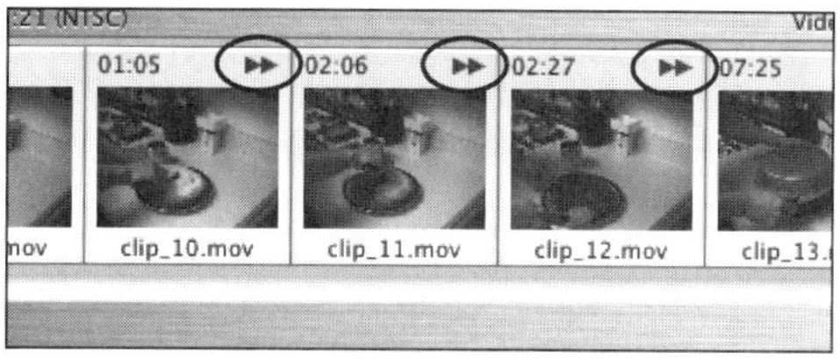

The marks in the corners let you know that you've messed with the speed of these clips.

You'll also speed up the clip that shows me frosting the second layer.

9. Select **clip_14.mov** and then switch back to **Timeline** view. Set the **Speed** slider to the same point you set in Step 8. This will make the frosting scenes more bearable to watch.

Playing Clips in Reverse

Another neat trick you can easily apply to your clips is to play them in reverse. Select a clip and choose **Advanced > Reverse Clip Direction**. Playing video in reverse is always good for a laugh, especially if it's footage of a sporting event, but you may also find this effect useful at times when you need to zoom out of a shot, but only have footage of the camera zooming in, or when you need the camera to pan from right to left instead of left to right. Just be aware that reversing a clip also reverses the audio, so you may want to extract a clip's audio into its own track (**Advanced > Extract Audio**, as described in Exercise 4), before reversing the video. That way, the sound will play properly over the backwards clip.

Now you'll apply one final title to this movie and call this a completed project.

10. Switch to the **clip viewer** and scroll to the last clip in the movie.

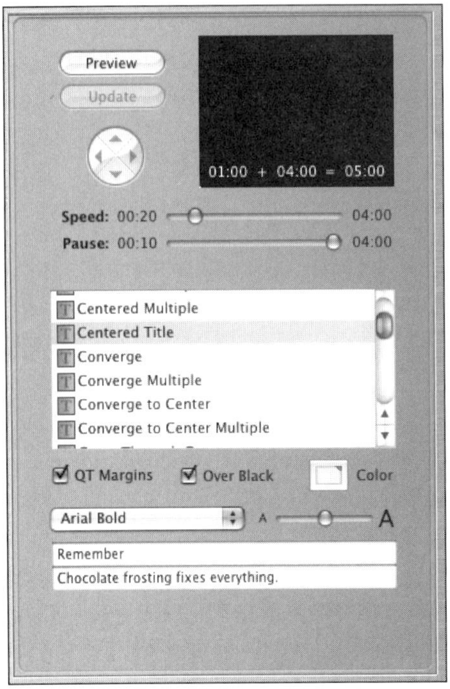

11. Click the **Titles** button to switch to the **Titles** pane. Select the **Centered Title** style and check **Over Black**, which will place the title over a black screen rather than over the still image at the end of the clip. In the top text field, type **Remember** and in the bottom text field type **Chocolate frosting fixes everything**. For the font, choose **Arial Bold** (or something similar) and leave the font size in the middle of the slider. Lastly, set the **Speed** slider to **1:00** and the **Pause** slider to **4:00**.

12. Once you've adjusted these settings, drag **Centered Title** to the end of the **clip viewer**, making it the last clip of the movie.

13. Once the title has rendered, click the **Rewind** button to send the **playhead** back to the beginning of the movie. Click **Play** to watch the entire movie. Use the **Full Screen** button if you want.

14. Good job! Now save the movie and keep it open for the next exercise, where you'll learn how to export your project out of iMovie.

8. Exporting Your Movie

Once you've finished editing your movie, you have to get in into a form that makes it easy to share with others. iMovie gives you three options for exporting your project: You can record it back to your camera, save it as a QuickTime file, or send it to iDVD to burn onto a DVD. In this exercise, you'll create a QuickTime file of the cake movie, but you'll also learn about the other two options.

1. Choose **File > Export** from the iMovie menu bar.

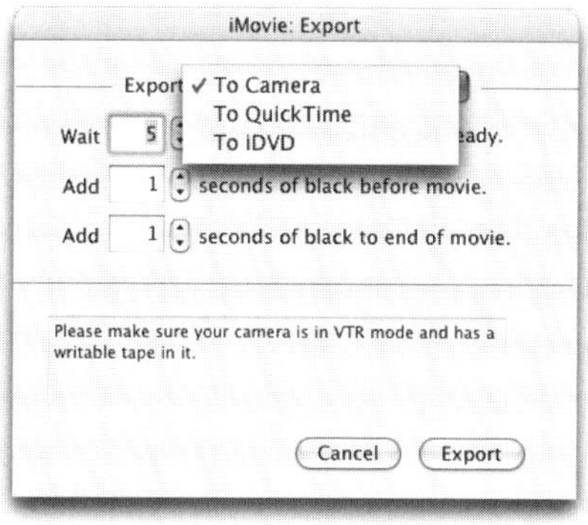

*This opens the **iMovie: Export** window. From here, you can click the **Export** menu to send your movie **To Camera**, **To QuickTime**, or **To iDVD**.*

2. Choose **To QuickTime** from the **Export** menu. This opens a second pop-up menu called **Formats**, from which you can choose the most appropriate setting for your movie. The selection you make depends on what you plan to do with the movie once it's saved. Each setting applies different levels of compression to your movie. The following chart gives you a rundown of each setting.

iMovie 3 QuickTime Formats

Format	Description
Email	**Size:** 160 x 120 pixels **Frame rate:** 10 fps (frames per second) **Audio:** Mono This format produces a relatively small file, which is necessary for sending to someone via email, but the quality of the picture and sound suffer. Your recipient needs QuickTime 4 or later to view a movie in this format.
Web	**Size:** 240 x 180 **Frame rate:** 12 fps **Audio:** Stereo This format is good for movies you want to publish to a Web site. A movie formatted with this setting will be larger than one formatted for email, but offers a larger picture and a faster frame rate. Your recipient needs QuickTime 3 or later to view a movie in this format.
Web Streaming	**Size:** 240 x 180 **Frame rate:** 12 fps **Audio:** Stereo This setting is very similar to the Web setting, but is optimized for posting on a QuickTime streaming Web server.
CD-ROM	**Size:** 320 x 240 **Frame rate:** 15 fps **Audio:** Stereo If you intend to save your movie onto a CD-ROM, you don't have the same space and size concerns as you do when you want to email your movie or post it to the Web. Therefore, this setting allows you to save your movie at a larger size and a faster frame rate, but also produces a larger file size.
Full Quality DV	**Size:** 720 x 480 **Frame rate:** 30 fps **Audio:** Stereo This setting applies no compression to your footage, giving your movie the same quality as your original DV footage. This setting is useful for importing your movie into other video applications such as Final Cut Pro, Premiere, After Effects, iDVD, or DVD Studio Pro.

continues on next page

iMovie 3 QuickTime Formats *continued*	
Format	**Description**
Expert Settings	This setting allows you to control the individual settings of your movie, down to compression type, frame rate, audio compression, and dozens of other options. To apply your own custom settings, choose **Expert Settings**, click **Export**, and then click **Options** to select your settings. If you're not familiar with customizing video output settings, you're better off selecting one of the other five options in the **Formats** pop-up menu. If you're interested in learning how to manually optimize your video and audio compressions, check out Sean Blumenthal's Compression Principles CD-ROM at **http://lynda.com/products/videos/cpcd/.**

For this exercise, you'll export your project as a CD-ROM movie.

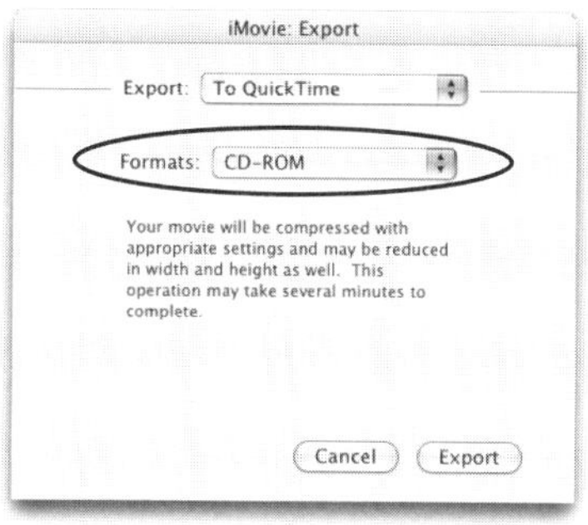

3. Choose **CD-ROM** from the **Formats** menu and click **Export**.

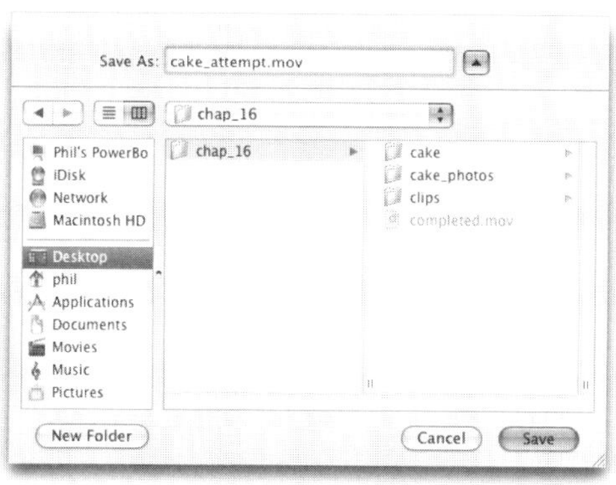

4. Name the movie **cake_attempt.mov** and navigate to the **chap_16** folder on your **Desktop**. Click **Save**.

It will take a few minutes for the movie to be exported. Go have a snack or take a walk.

5. Once the movie has been exported, choose **iMovie > Hide iMovie** from the menu bar and then open the **chap_16** folder on your **Desktop**. Double-click **cake_attempt.mov** to view your completed, compressed movie in QuickTime. (Remember that the clips you used in this project were already compressed, so the quality of this movie is slightly worse than the quality you'd get from your own projects.) Quit QuickTime when you're done.

***Note:** After you export a movie, the original iMovie project remains intact–no compression or changes were made to your clips themselves, so you can continue to edit the movie or make other changes as necessary.*

6. If you have a SuperDrive and a copy of iDVD, you can keep iMovie open for the next chapter. Otherwise, save your work and quit iMovie.

Exporting to Your Camera

In addition to exporting your completed movies to QuickTime, iMovie also gives you the option of sending your movie back to your DV camera. This provides an additional way to back up your project and offers the advantage of being able to show your movie to friends by hooking up your camera to a TV rather than burning a CD-ROM or emailing it.

To save your movie to your camera, put a tape (a blank or one that you want to record over) in your camera and connect it to your Mac with the FireWire cable. In iMovie, choose **File > Export** and choose **To Camera** from the **Export** pop-up menu. There are three text fields available here. The following chart explains them.

iMovie Export to Camera Options

Option	Description
Wait *x* seconds for camera to get ready	This field is here to allow your camera a few seconds to switch into record mode. Most cameras are not capable of recording the instant you press the Record button, so by delaying iMovie for five seconds or so, you're giving your camera enough time to start rolling so you won't inadvertently chop off the first few seconds of your movie. If you find that the default five seconds isn't enough, just type in a higher number the next time you export to your camera.
Add *x* seconds of black before movie	By adding a black screen before your movie begins, you automatically trigger the response in your audience's collective heads that something is about to happen. (In other words, the black screen subtly says, "Shut up and pay attention.") You'll probably find that three seconds or so of black is enough time to ease your audience into the movie.
Add *x* seconds of black to end of movie	Likewise, if your movie just stops abruptly at the end, and the TV screen starts displaying static (or the increasingly typical blue screen), you may lose the impact of your movie's gripping closing scene. A few seconds of black silence will give your message enough time to sink through the skulls of your audience.

Once you've made your selection in the Export dialog box, make sure your camera is set to VCR (or VTR) mode and click **Export**. iMovie will give the camera five seconds to get rolling (or however many seconds you selected), add however many seconds of black you chose, and then export the movie in real time–meaning that a 30-minute movie will take 30 minutes to export to tape. When the exporting is done, unhook your camera from your Mac and connect it to your TV to watch your movie in all its DV glory.

Exporting to iDVD

The third option available to you in iMovie's Export window is to export your movie to iDVD. This and iMovie's other iDVD-related options are discussed in the next chapter. If you have iDVD and plan to run through the exercises in Chapter 17, "*iDVD 3*," don't delete the files from this chapter–you'll need them again.

So if you have iDVD, move on to the next chapter. If not, jump ahead to Chapter 18, "Networking." *In either case, you might want to take a short coffee break first (and maybe enjoy a piece of cake).*

17

iDVD 3

| Preparing in iMovie and Exporting to iDVD |
| Working With Themes | Adding Your Own Pictures and Music |
| Adding Additional Movies | Creating a Photo Slideshow |
| Previewing and Burning Your Project |

chap_17

Mac OS X Panther
H•O•T CD-ROM

The fourth application in the iLife suite of programs is iDVD 3. When you fork over your $49 for iLife, it's iDVD that you're really paying for—not iTunes, iPhoto, or iMovie, which can all be downloaded for free. iDVD makes it easy to create your own high-quality DVDs that can be played in most set-top DVD players on the market today.

In this chapter, you'll import the video you created in Chapter 16, "*iMovie 3,*" into iDVD, so if you haven't yet completed that chapter, do so before starting this one. Once you get the movie into iDVD, you'll learn to work with iDVD's built-in themes to produce a complete DVD project that includes colorful menus, animations, and sound. You'll also learn how to build menus and add your own pictures and music to them.

NOTE | SuperDrive Required

As of this writing, iDVD does not support external DVD burners. In order to perform the exercises in this chapter, you need to have a Mac with a built-in SuperDrive. iDVD won't even install on a machine without a SuperDrive.

I. Preparing in iMovie and Exporting to iDVD

Before you send your video from iMovie to iDVD, you can take advantage of iMovie 3's iDVD pane to add **chapter markers** to your project. Chapter markers enable your audience to quickly jump to specific scenes of your movie, just like in professionally manufactured movie DVDs. iDVD recognizes the chapter markers created in iMovie and automatically generates scene selection menus when a project is imported. (iDVD also recognizes chapter markers created in other Apple video editing tools such as Final Cut Pro, Final Cut Express, and QuickTime Pro.)

1. Open **iMovie 3**. If the **cake** project you used in the previous chapter doesn't load, choose **File > Open Recent** and select it from the menu.

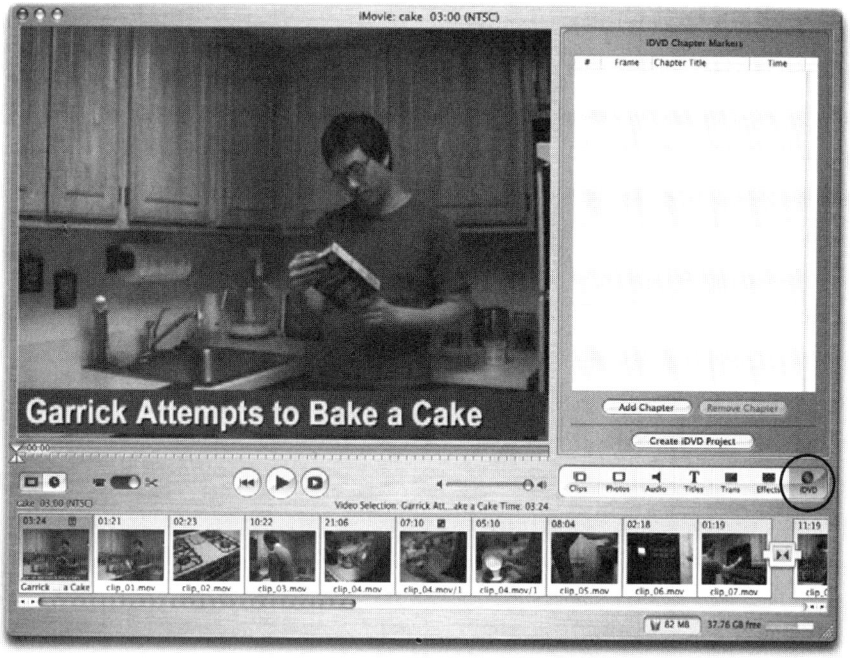

2. Click the **iDVD** button to view the **iDVD** pane. This is where you create the chapter markers in your movie.

Where (and whether) you create chapter markers is entirely up to you. Some logical places to place chapter markers are points in the movie when a new event begins, when a scene changes location, or any other significant moment someone watching your movie might want to access easily. In this exercise, you'll add chapter markers at a few of the stages in the cake's creation. You'll start by creating a chapter marker at the beginning of the first clip.

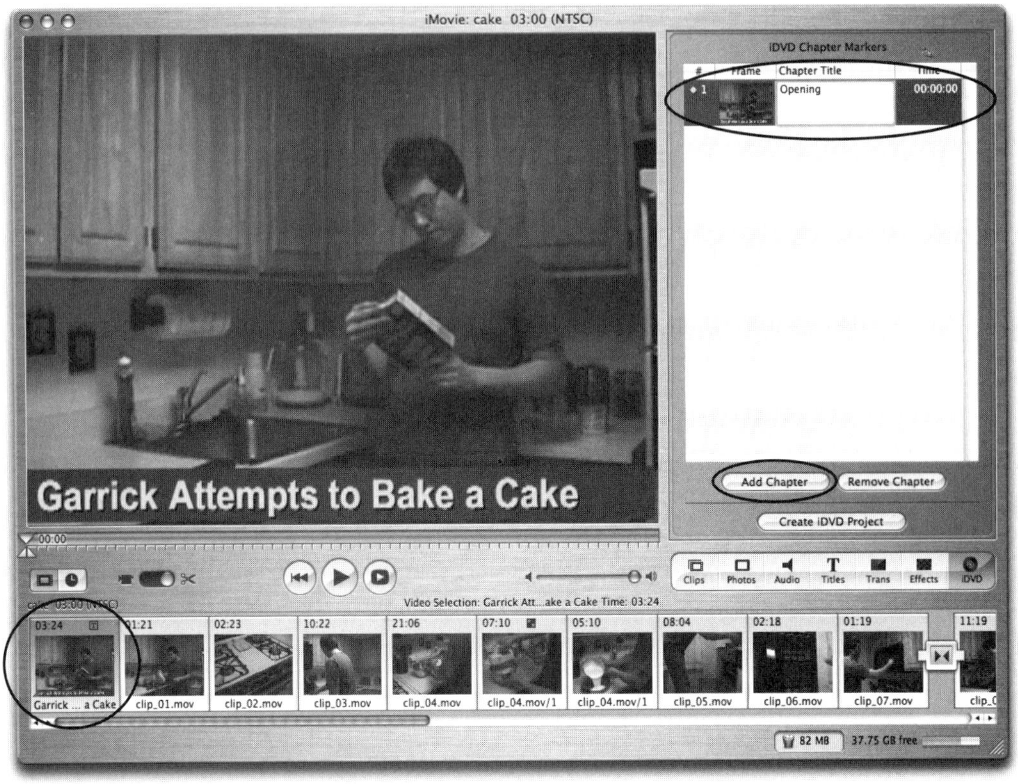

3. Select the very first clip in the **clip viewer** and then click **Add Chapter** in the **iDVD** pane. iMovie creates the chapter marker. Rename this marker **Opening**.

That's all there is to creating a chapter marker. You'll add several more now before sending this project to iDVD.

---

4. Select **clip_04**. This is the clip of the ingredients being mixed together. Click **Add Chapter** and name this marker **Combining Ingredients**.

---

5. Select **clip_05**, click **Add Chapter**, and name this marker **Into the Oven**.

---

6. Select **clip_08.mov/1** (the clip of me performing various activities while waiting for the cake to finish baking). Click **Add Chapter** and name this marker **Patiently Waiting**.

---

7. Select **clip_09**, click **Add Chapter**, and name this marker **Out of the Oven**.

---

8. Select **clip_10**, click **Add Chapter**, and name this marker **Fast Frosting**.

9. Select **clip_15**, click **Add Chapter**, and name this marker **The Final Result**.

TIP | Chapter Markers Can Be Placed Anywhere

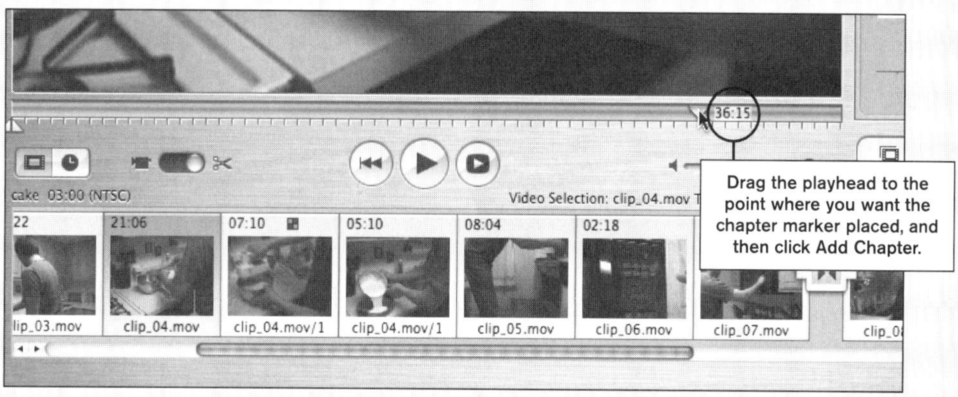

Chapter markers don't necessarily have to appear at the beginning of clips. To place a marker within a clip, select the clip and drag the playhead to the point where you want the clip to appear. Then click **Add Chapter** and name your chapter marker.

10. Choose **File > Save**. With the chapter markers in place, your work in iMovie is done and you're ready to send the project over to iDVD.

In previous versions of iMovie and iDVD, you had to export the project from iMovie (which could take from several minutes to several hours, depending on your Mac) and then import the project into iDVD. With the latest versions of these applications, all you need to do is click one button to open your project in iDVD–there's no need to export the movie first.

11. In the **iDVD** pane, click **Create iDVD Project**. If prompted, save your work.

Note: *You can also choose **File > Export**, choose **To iDVD** from the **Export** pop-up menu, and then click **Export**, but why do all that when you can get the same results by simply clicking the **Create iDVD Project** button?*

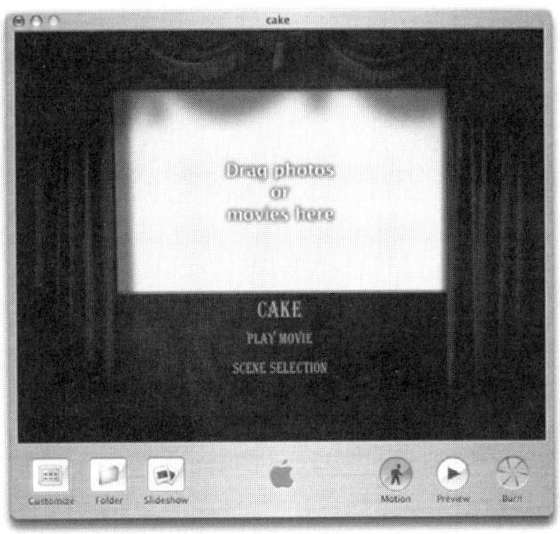

*iDVD starts up, and, after a few moments, your project opens the default theme, called **Theater** (which you will learn about shortly). The title **Cake** (named after your iMovie project) appears above the buttons **Play Movie** and **Scene Selection**. The Scene Selection option appears because your project contains chapter markers.*

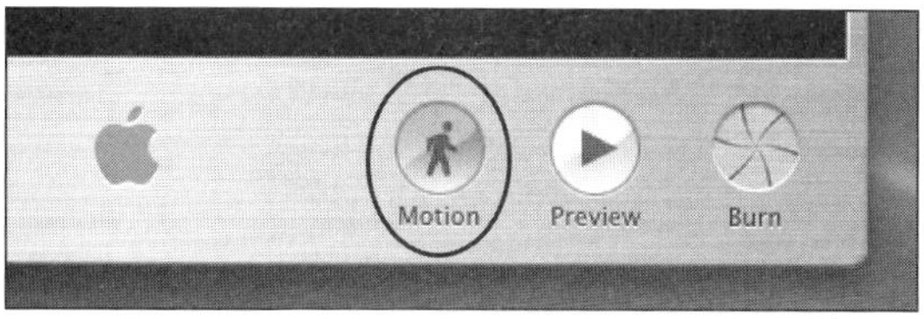

12. Click the **Motion** button to temporarily stop the theme's animation and music.

13. Choose **File > Save Project**.

14. If you want, you can **Ctrl+click** iMovie's icon in the **Dock** and choose **Quit** from the contextual menu. You won't need it again in this chapter.

In the next exercise, you'll customize your DVD project's appearance and behavior.

iMovie to iDVD: What Happens?

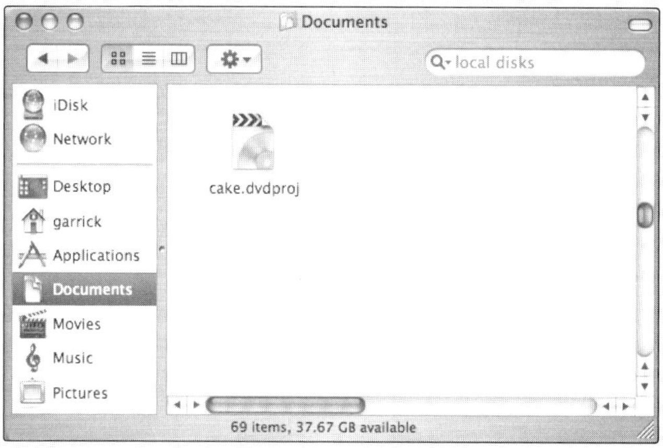

When you click **Create iDVD Project** in iMovie (or when you export your movie to iDVD by choosing **File > Export**), iDVD creates a project file and saves it in the **Documents** folder in your **Home** directory. You can identify the project file by its **.dvdproj** extension. This file is updated every time you save your DVD project, and it's the one you double-click when you want to edit your iDVD project. However, the movie itself is not copied into iDVD–instead, iDVD relies upon your iMovie files, so don't move or delete your project's iMovie folder if you want to continue working on your DVD project.

2. Working with Themes

iDVD 3 comes with more than three dozen ready-made themes that you can choose to apply to your DVD projects. Many of the themes are animated and/or accompanied by music. In this chapter, you'll learn to work with several of them. You'll also learn to add your own backgrounds and music to your project if you want to further personalize your DVD.

When you first opened your project, iDVD applied the theme called Theater. This theme is a great one to start learning with because it has animation, music, and a **drop zone**. A drop zone is an area of an iDVD theme into which you can drag pictures or movies to customize the look of the theme. You'll start by dragging a movie into this theme's drop zone.

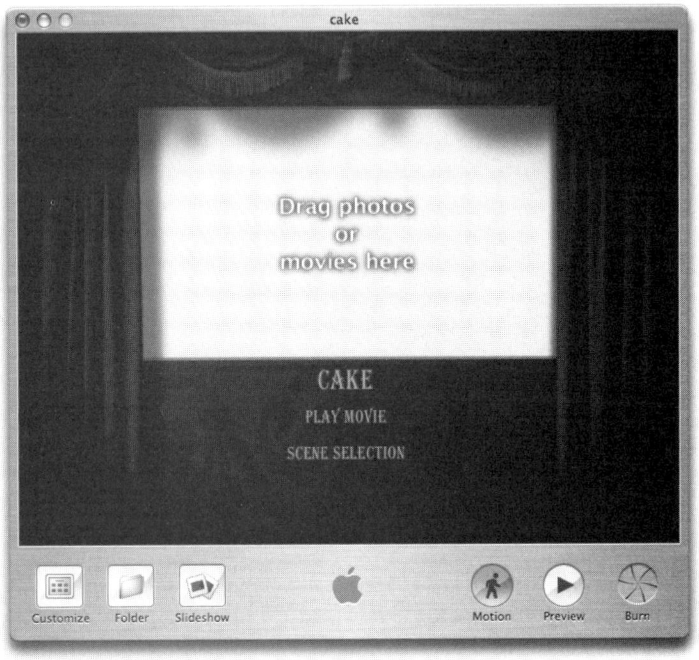

1. Click the **Motion** button at the bottom of the iDVD window to see the theater theme in action (if you stopped it at the end of the last exercise). Notice the area that says **Drag photos or movies here**? That's the drop zone. Next, you're going to drop a movie in here yourself.

Note: *You might want to turn down the volume of your Mac unless you have a high tolerance for repetitive instrumental music. Or just wait a few more steps and you'll learn how to mute the theme's music track.*

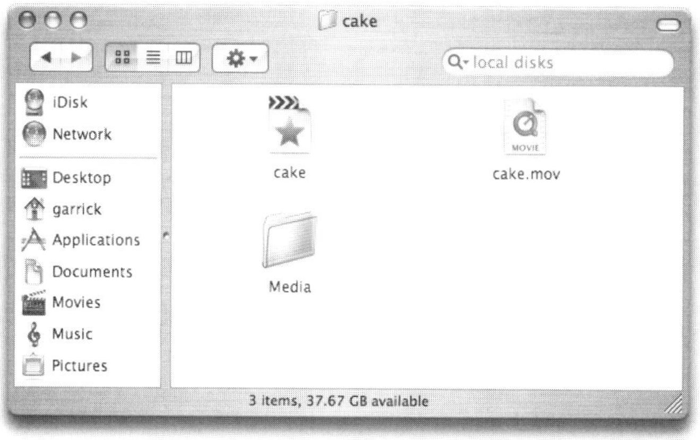

2. Keeping iDVD open, double-click the **chap_16** folder on your **Desktop** (yes, **chap_16** because you created the iMovie project in the previous chapter), and open the **cake** folder located inside. This is your iMovie project folder, which contains the file **cake.mov**, the reference file for this project.

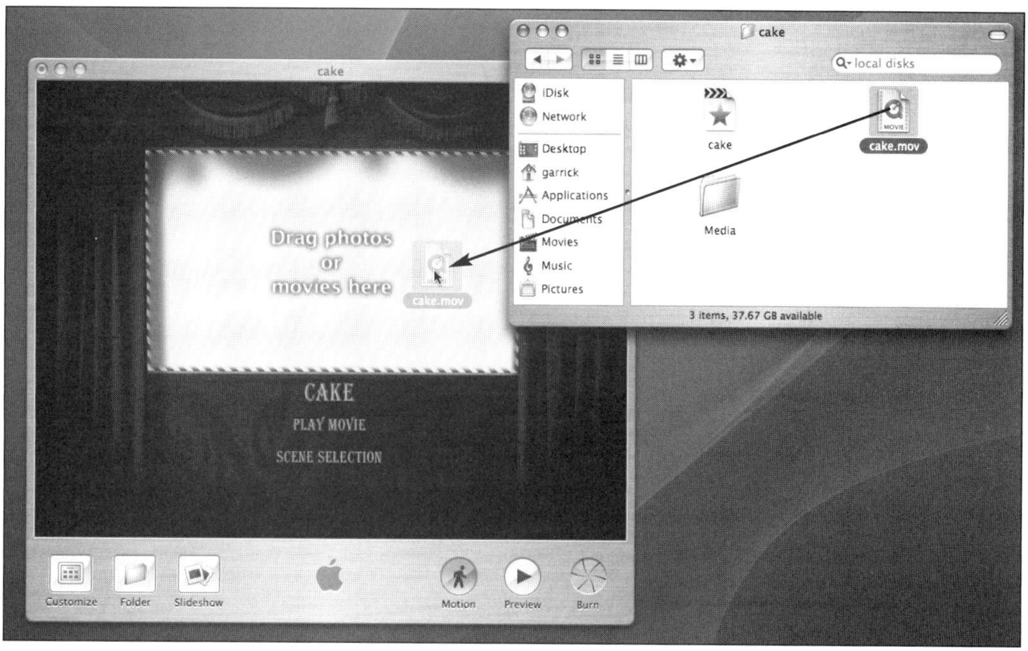

3. If necessary, drag the **cake** window so you can see the drop zone in iDVD. Drag **cake.mov** into the drop zone.

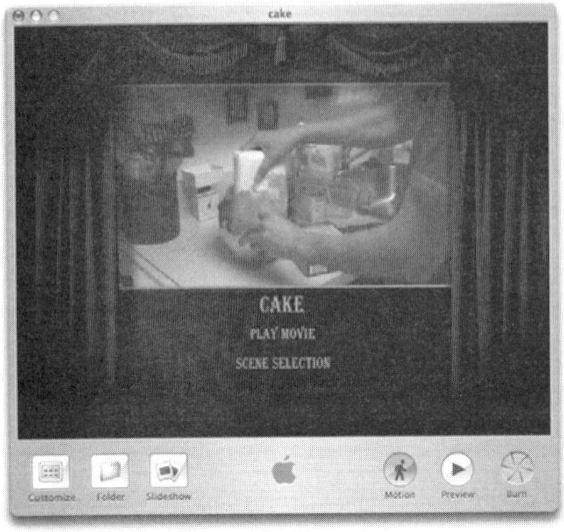

How cool is that? Your movie project is now playing within the drop zone. Each iDVD theme can play up to 30 seconds of video and music before repeating, so you'll see the first 30 seconds of this movie and then the animated curtains will close before the whole theme loops back to the beginning and starts over.

Next, you'll get a chance to see some other themes.

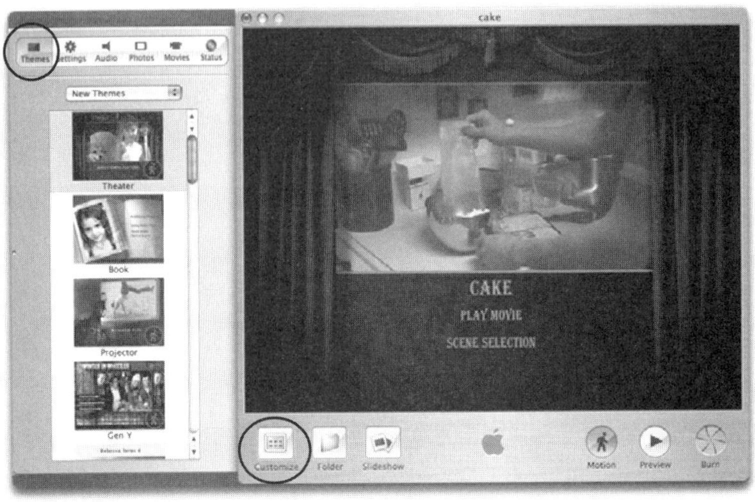

4. Click the **Customize** button in the lower-left corner of the iDVD window to open the **Customize** panel to the left of the window. If it's not already selected, click **Themes** at the top of the panel and choose **New Themes** from the pop-up menu below it.

This collection contains 24 different themes to choose from. As you can see, Theater is currently selected.

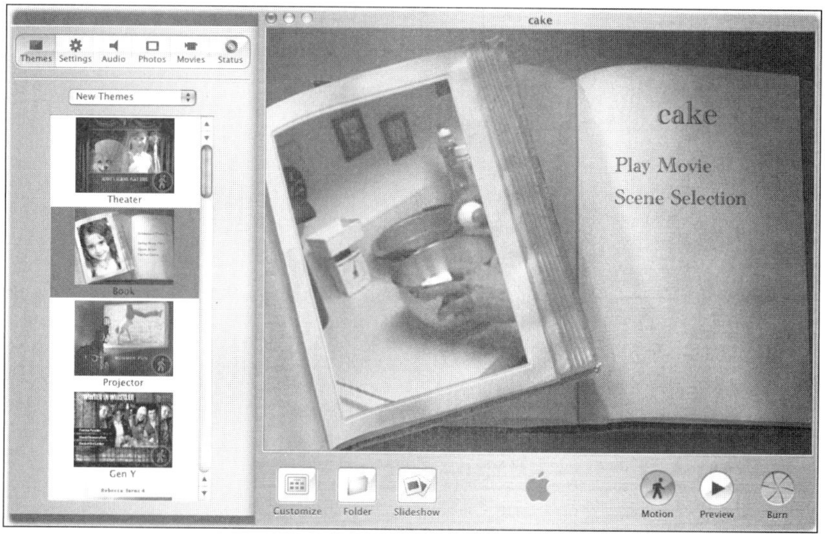

5. Click the **Book** theme. iDVD takes a few seconds to rework your project and then the new theme appears in the main window. It's that easy.

Repositioning Drop Zone Items

This book theme, like most of the other themes, also contains a drop zone where the reference movie you dragged into iDVD is playing. Many themes have irregularly shaped drop zones, so it's sometimes necessary to reposition the photo or movie in the drop zone to make sure the desired area of the video is visible.

To reposition the movie in the drop zone, place your cursor over it and drag left, right, up, or down. The arrows in the hand cursor let you know which directions you can drag the movie.

Every theme is different. To find one that fits your needs, click through them all to get an idea of what each one looks and sounds like.

***Tip:** Themes that include animations are identified by the little motion figure in the lower-right corner of the theme's thumbnail.*

---

6. Take a few minutes to explore the different themes. Feel free to select **Old Themes** from the pop-up menu at the top of the panel to look at those themes as well.

NOTE | Motion Buttons

Some themes, such as **Portfolio Color**, **Brushed Metal Two**, and **Green Linen Two**, have multiple areas in which to drop movies. These areas are known as **motion buttons**. Unlike regular drop zones, in a motion button, you can control at which point a clip begins playing by selecting the movie and moving the slider above it until you see the point where you want the clip to start.

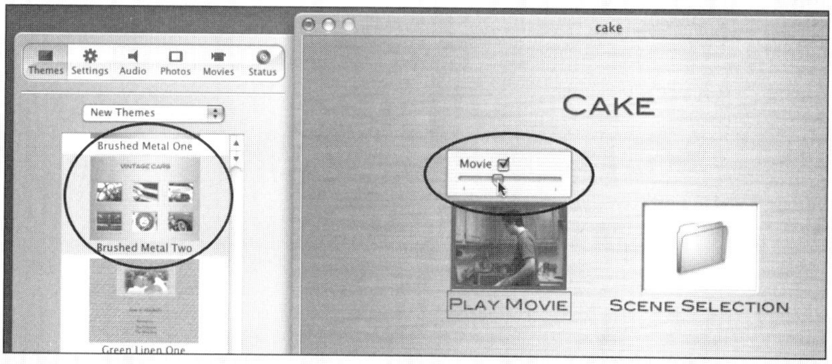

Once you've set the slider, the clip in the motion button will always begin at that point.

7. When you're done browsing the themes, select the theme **Blue** from the **New Themes** collection. This will be the theme you use for this exercise.

Now let's take a look at the text in your project. As mentioned earlier, your iDVD project originally took its title from the name of your iMovie project, but this doesn't mean you have to keep it.

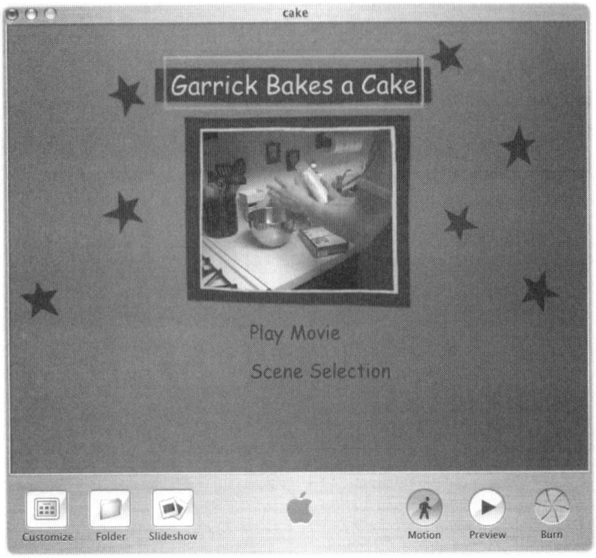

8. Select **cake** and type **Garrick Bakes a Cake**. Press **Return**.

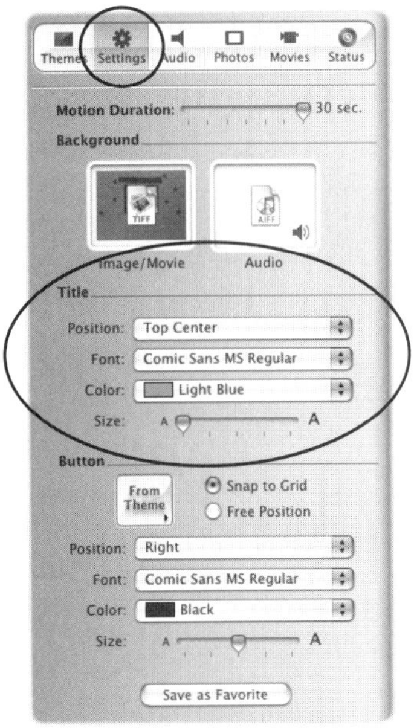

9. In the **Customize** pane, click **Settings**. Here's where you'll find the settings for your title's font face, size, and positioning, as well as several other settings you'll be examining shortly. You'll leave the title settings unchanged.

*Tip: You can silence a theme's music by clicking the **speaker** icon in the **Audio** well under the **Background** setting. Feel free to do so for this exercise. This is an alternative to stopping the sound and music altogether with the Motion button. Clicking the speaker icon mutes only the sound, but lets the video continue playing in your selected theme. You just have to remember to turn the sound back on when you're ready to burn your DVD (if you want the music to be included on the DVD).*

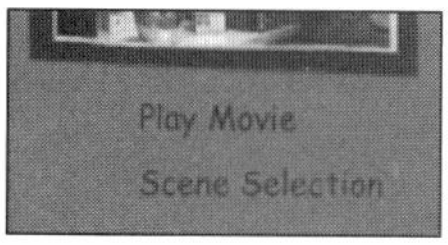

*The two pieces of text that say **Play Movie** and **Scene Selection** are actually buttons. When viewing your project on a DVD player or computer, selecting Play Movie will start the movie from the beginning, and clicking Scene Selection will open another menu from which you can choose from the chapter markers you created in iMovie. You'll take a look at the Scene Selection menu next.*

10. Double-click **Scene Selection**.

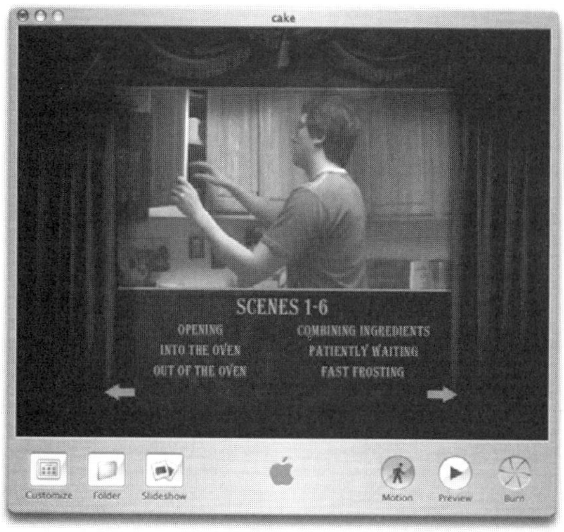

After a moment, you'll be looking at the list of chapter markers you created in iMovie. By default, this menu opens in the Theater theme.

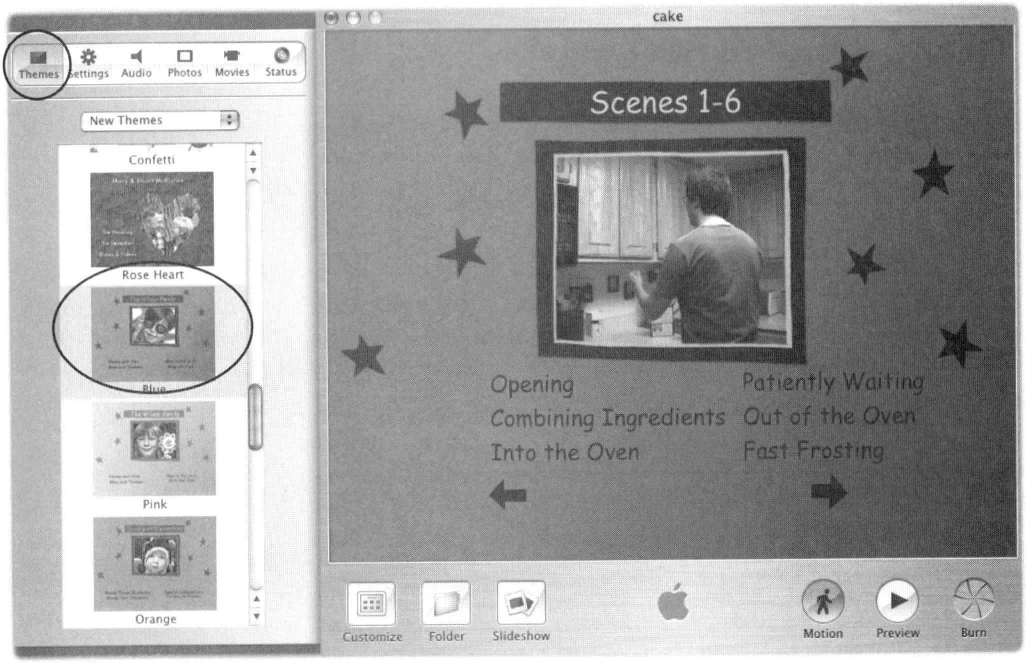

11. In the **Customize** panel, click **Themes** and then scroll down and select the **Blue** theme. Although you can use a different theme for each menu, for now you'll keep the theme consistent.

As you can see on this screen, the first six of the seven chapter markers you created in iMovie are listed. In every theme, you can have up to six buttons per screen. Because you have more than six chapter markers, iDVD has automatically created a right-pointing arrow to take the user to the next page of scene selection buttons. (The left pointing arrow takes you back to the main menu.) When someone viewing your DVD clicks on one of these buttons, he or she will be jumped directly to the point in the movie where you created the marker.

12. Click the **right-pointing arrow**.

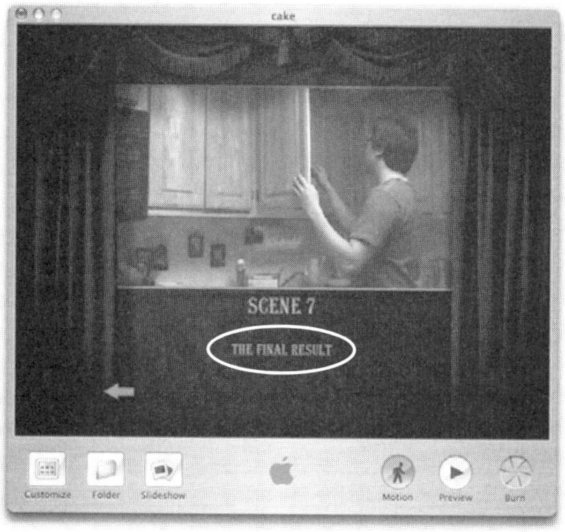

Here's the last chapter marker you created, sitting here all by itself.

---

13. Click the **Blue** theme in the **Customize** panel to make this menu match the rest of your project.

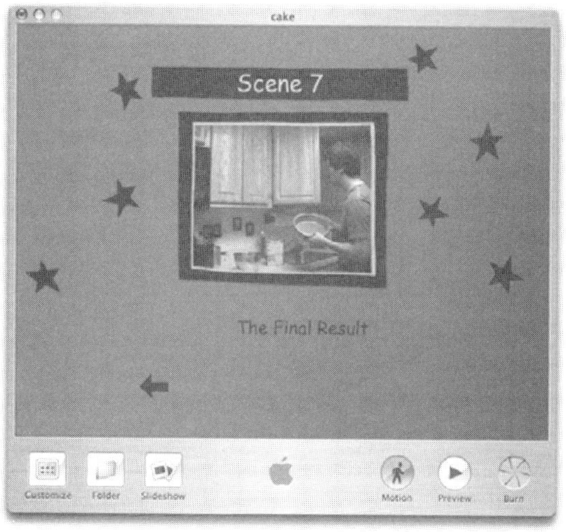

Although technically there's nothing wrong with having a single chapter marker sitting on a menu by itself, it does seem like an inefficient use of space. When creating chapter markers in your own projects, you'll probably want to keep in mind that you can have up to six buttons per menu screen. But in this project, you'll just move some of the buttons from the previous menu to this menu to balance out the screens.

---

14. Click the **left-pointing arrow** to return to the previous screen.

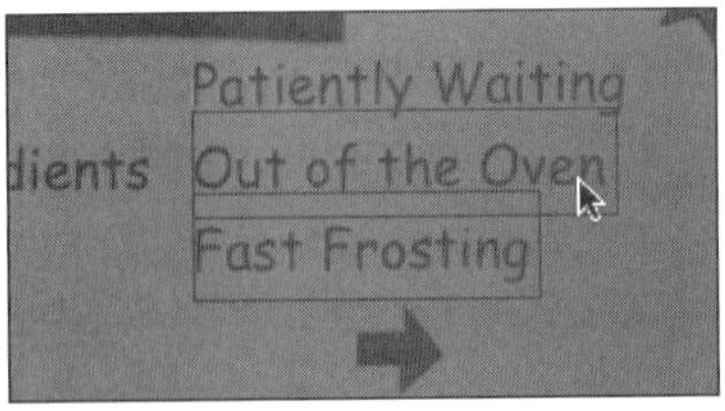

15. Shift+click Out of the Oven and **Fast Frosting** to select both buttons. Choose **Edit > Cut** (**Cmd+X**) to remove and copy the two items. The other four buttons neatly rearrange themselves to take up the empty space you just created. Click the **right-pointing arrow** to go to the next menu.

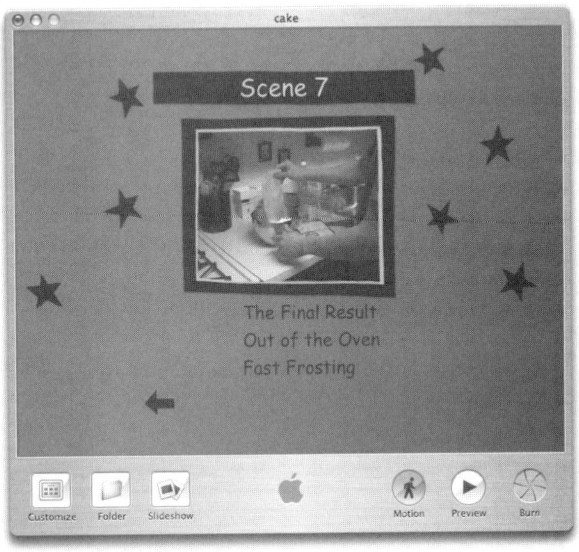

16. Choose **Edit > Paste** (**Cmd+V**) to add the two buttons to this menu. They're placed under the last chapter marker by default. You need to put them in the right order.

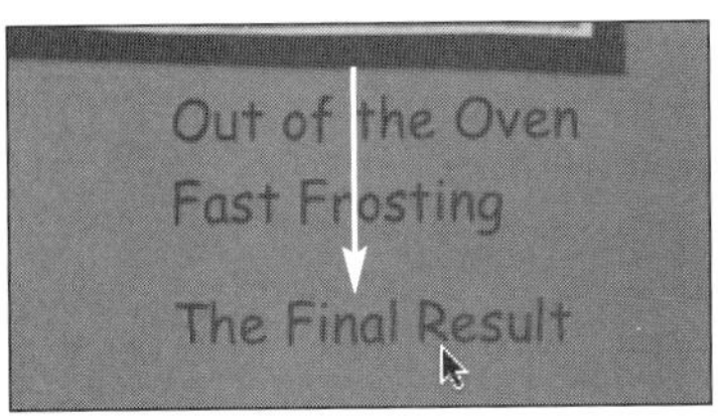

17. Drag **The Final Result** down below **Fast Frosting**.

NOTE | Dragging Buttons

As you just saw, dragging buttons around your iDVD menus is a snap, literally. By default, buttons snap into place and move out of the way of other buttons you may be dragging. There may be times, however, when you don't want your buttons to snap to a location.

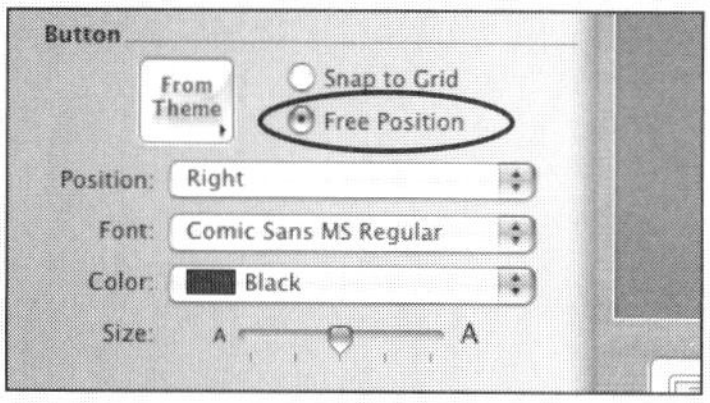

To give yourself total freedom over button placement, click the **Settings** button in the **Customize** panel and select **Free Position**. Once you select this option, you're able to place your buttons anywhere you want.

A word of caution: As you learned in Chapter 16, "*iMovie 3*," the "safe area" of your video project is the area where you can be pretty sure the important elements of your movie won't be chopped off by the edge of the TV screen.

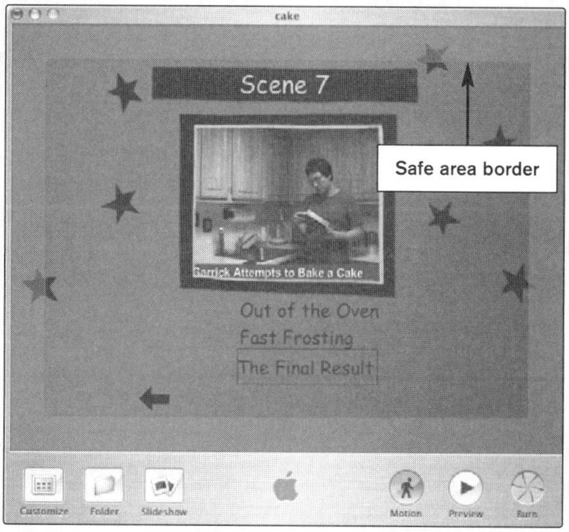

When your buttons are set to **Snap to Grid**, you don't have to worry about placing them outside the safe area because iDVD makes sure that every item is well within it. But when your buttons are set to **Free Position**, you might want to choose **Advanced > Show TV Safe Area** to make sure your buttons aren't going to get chopped off by the TV screen.

Now that you've moved some of your buttons around, the titles of the scene selection menus need a little editing.

18. Highlight the title **Scene 7** and change it to **Scenes 5–7**.

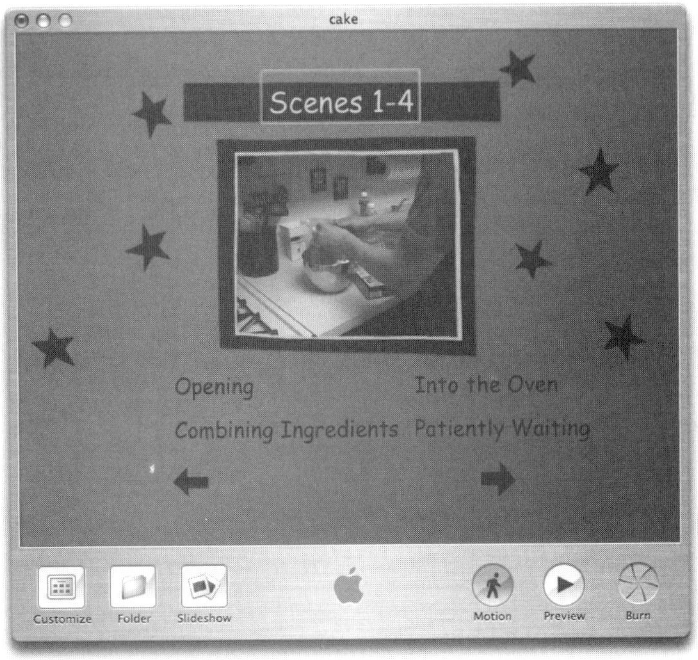

19. Click the **left-pointing arrow** on this screen to return to the previous menu. Change the title of this menu to **Scenes 1–4**.

You've probably noticed that the same movie is playing in the drop zone of each of the menus in this project. By default, any time you drop a movie into your project's main menu, the movie appears in each subsequent menu unless you manually change it. You'll throw another movie into the first Scene Selection menu just to change things up a bit.

20. Keep iDVD open and drag the **chap_17** folder from the **H•O•T CD-ROM** to your **Desktop**.

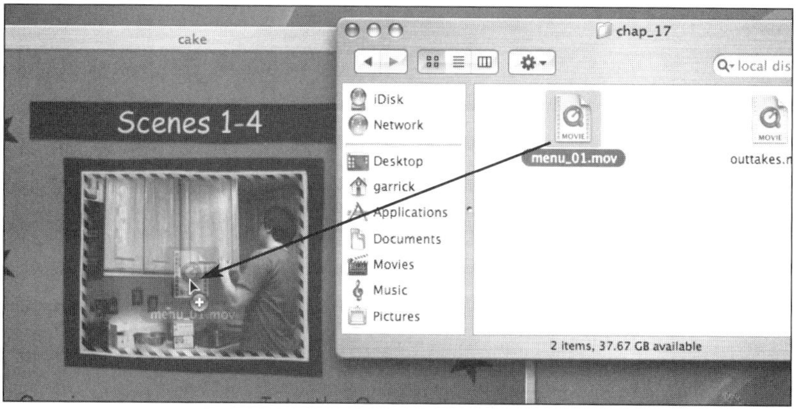

21. Open **chap_17** and drag the movie **menu_01.mov** into the drop zone of the scene selection menu. (Drag it right on top of the movie that's already playing there.)

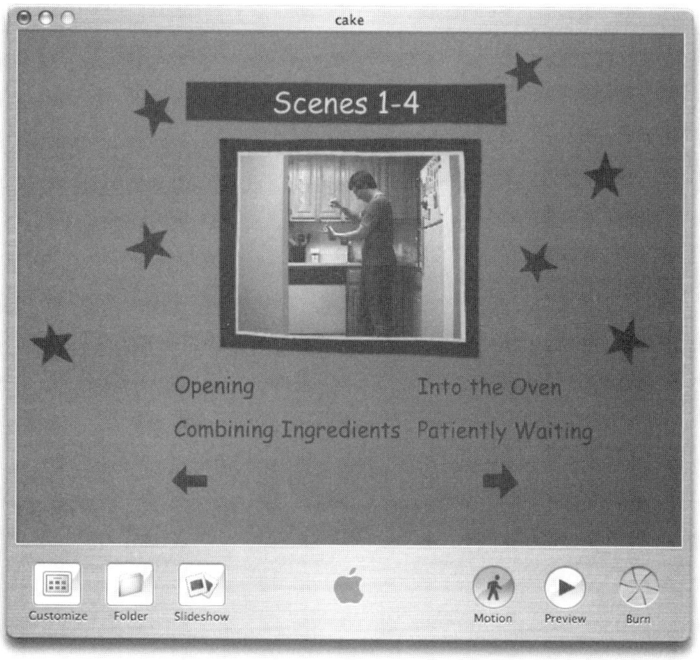

This 30-second movie was edited in iMovie and created for the purpose of placing into this menu. In your own projects, you'll first need to create and edit any movies that you want to drop into your menus yourself (unless you just want to use the reference movie created by iMovie like you did at the beginning of this exercise).

Note: Once you've dragged a movie into your iDVD project, don't move the original file or else iDVD won't be able to find it the next time you open your project, and you'll get the "broken link" icon shown above. If you absolutely have to move the file, you'll just have to drag it into the menu's drop zone again when you open your project.

22. Save your project and keep iDVD open for the next exercise.

Adding Your Own Pictures and Music

If you're more of a go-your-own-way sort of person, you might feel that using iDVD's themes, varied though they are, goes against your nonconformist nature. If you prefer to use your own pictures for the backgrounds of your various menus, you're free to do so. And best of all, it's really easy to do.

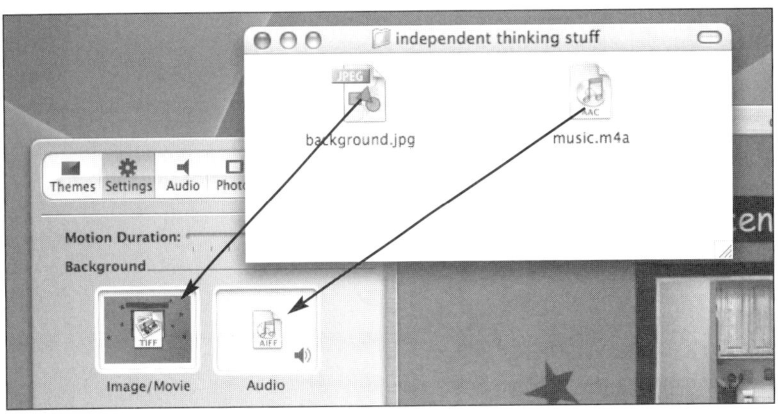

To place an image into your project menu's background, drag the file into the **Image** well under the **Settings** section of the **Customize** panel. You can even drag a movie in here if you want to have a full-sized video playing as the background for your menu. To add an audio track, drag your audio file into the **Audio** well. It will start playing immediately.

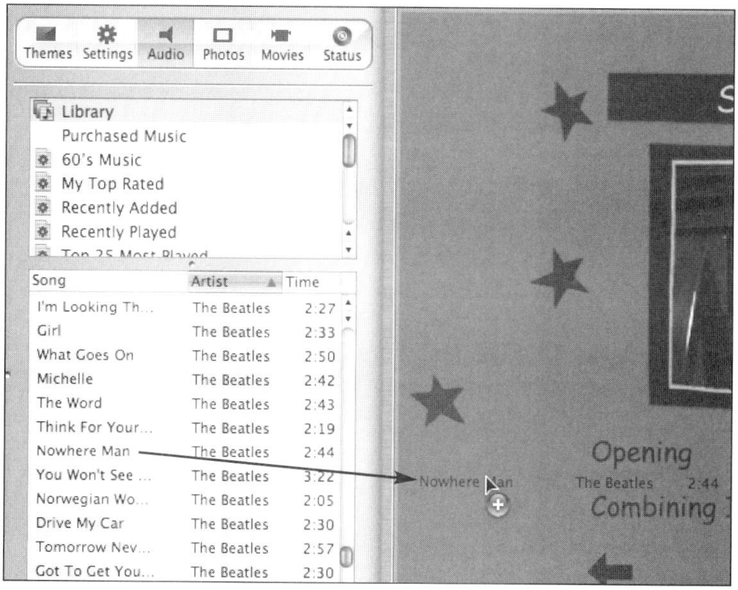

If the music or images you want to use already reside in your iTunes and iPhoto libraries, you can click the **Audio** and **Photos** buttons in the **Customize** panel, respectively, to locate the files and drag them into the main window.

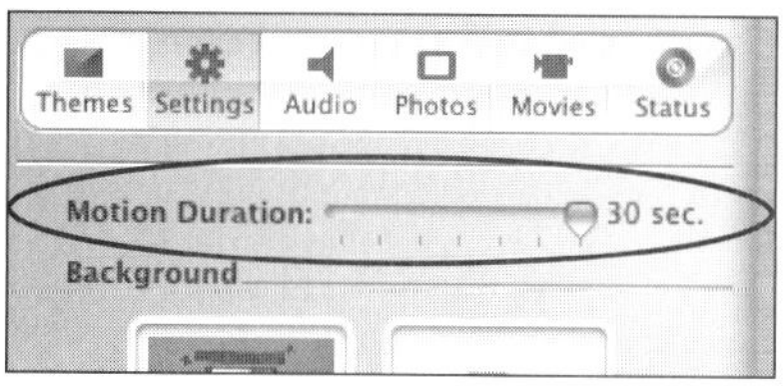

If necessary, you can use the **Motion Duration** slider to adjust how long the music will play (up to 30 seconds) before it loops back to the beginning and starts over.

3. Adding Additional Movies

As you saw in Exercise 1, sending a movie from iMovie into iDVD automatically generates a main menu and, if you included chapter markers, a scene selection menu or two. Sending a project directly from iMovie is probably the easiest method of setting up your iDVD project, but you can also add additional movies without first opening them in iMovie. In this exercise, you'll add an additional movie of outtakes to your DVD project.

1. Click the **left-pointing arrow** to return to the project's main menu. You're going to add another button to this menu that will take the viewer to a movie of outtakes from this video.

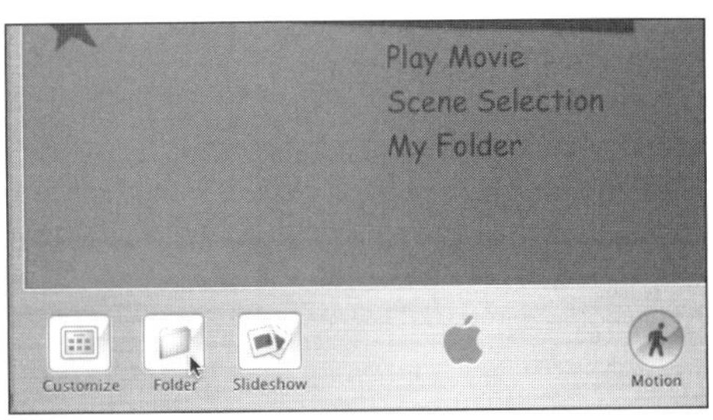

2. Click the **Folder** button in the lower-left corner of the iDVD window. This generates a new button called **My Folder**.

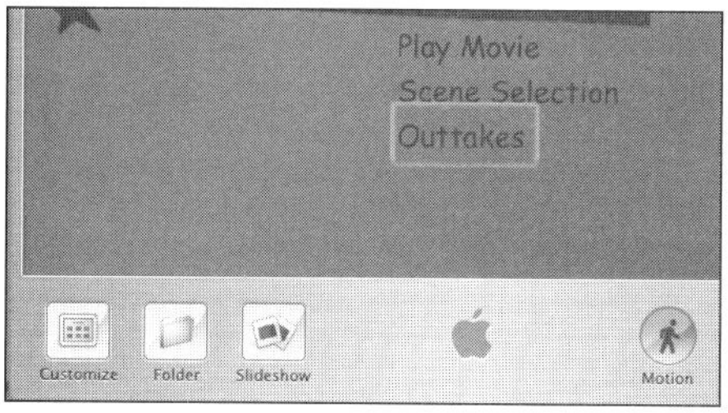

3. Click **My Folder** once. Pause a second and then click it once again to highlight the text (double-clicking too quickly opens the next menu instead of highlighting the text). Rename this button **Outtakes**.

4. Now double-click **Outtakes** to open the menu you just created.

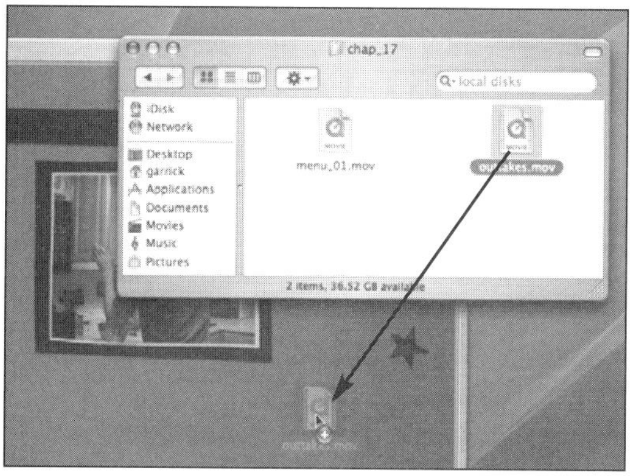

5. On this menu, rename the title **Outtakes**. From the **chap_17** folder on your **Desktop**, drag **outtakes.mov** into iDVD. iDVD automatically generates a button for this movie.

That's it. Adding additional movies to your iDVD project is as simple as dragging them into the window.

6. Click the **left-pointing arrow** to return to the main menu, and save your project. Keep iDVD open.

TIP | A New Folder Isn't Always Necessary

In this exercise, you first created a new folder button called Outtakes and then dragged the Outtakes movie into the resulting menu. If you had wanted to, you could have just dragged **outtakes.mov** directly into the main menu of your project–there really isn't any rule saying you can't have a direct link to more than one movie in your main menu. You just did it this way here to keep your menus organized and to learn how to generate additional menus by clicking the Folder button. In your own work, you can decide for yourself when a new folder is necessary.

Creating a Photo Slideshow

Another useful feature of iDVD is the capability to create slideshows from the pictures in your iPhoto library or any other photos you drag into iDVD.

To create a slideshow, click the **Slideshow** button. This generates a button called **My Slideshow** (which you can rename if you like). Double-click **My Slideshow** to begin editing the slideshow.

In the Slideshow window, drag pictures from the **Photos** section of the **Customize** panel. These are the photos stored in your iPhoto library. You can also drag pictures from your **Desktop** or other locations on your Mac into the main window.

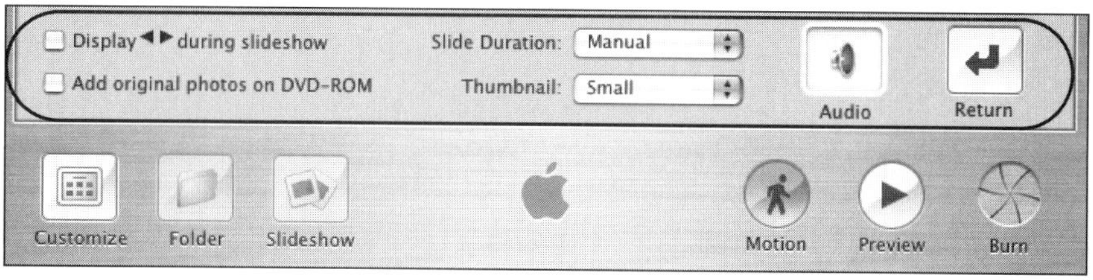

The lower portion of the Slideshow window contains several check boxes and pop-up menus. The following chart describes these options.

iDVD Slideshow Options

Item	Description
Display ◀▶ during slideshow	Checking this item places navigation arrows onscreen during your slideshow so viewers can move forward and backward with the DVD player's remote control. Without these arrows, they have no way to view previous pictures or to skip ahead in the slideshow.
Add original photos on DVD-ROM	When you create a slideshow in iDVD, the photos displayed are compressed and optimized for viewing on a TV screen. With **Add original photos on DVD-ROM** selected, iDVD will include the original full-resolution photos on the DVD-ROM you burn. Although your DVD recipients won't be able to watch these pictures through their DVD players, they can access the photos through a computer's DVD-ROM drive, so they can print out copies for themselves. **Note:** If you usually prefer to have your photos included in the DVD-ROM part of your DVD, choose **iDVD > Preferences**, and then click the **Slideshow** button and check **Always add original slideshow to DVD-ROM.**

continues on next page

iDVD Slideshow Options *continued*

Item	Description
Slide Duration	From this pop-up menu, you can select how long you want each picture to appear onscreen. You can choose from 1, 3, 5, or 10 seconds, or you can choose **Manual**, which requires the viewer to click the Next or Forward button on his or her DVD remote to advance to the next picture. If you've added audio to your slideshow, you can select **Fit to Audio**, which times your slideshow so that it matches the exact duration of the song you chose to accompany the pictures.
Thumbnail	Choose **Large** or **Small** from this pop-up menu to determine the size of the image thumbnails you see onscreen. This does not affect the appearance of your images in the slideshow; it merely makes the thumbnails in the slideshow window bigger or smaller so you can work with them more easily while you're creating your slideshow.
Audio	This is an audio well, just like the one found under Settings in the Customize panel. Drag an audio file here if you want your slideshow to be accompanied by some music.
Return	Click this button to return to the main menu when you're done arranging your slideshow.

Now that your DVD project has been assembled, the next lesson shows you how to preview it onscreen and then how to burn it to a DVD.

4. Previewing and Burning Your Project

As you lay out your DVD project, it's often helpful to see how it will really look when someone plays it on a DVD player. Previewing allows you to check the usability of your menu layouts and to find mistakes. Although recordable DVDs are becoming increasingly more affordable, they are still not cheap enough for you (or most people, anyway) to justify burning a DVD every time you want to see the effect of one little change to your project. Fortunately, iDVD allows you to preview your project with the click of a button.

If you turned off the audio in any menus while working on the previous exercises, now's the time to turn the music back on. Otherwise, you won't have any music in some menus (which may be the effect you want in some of your own projects, but not for this one).

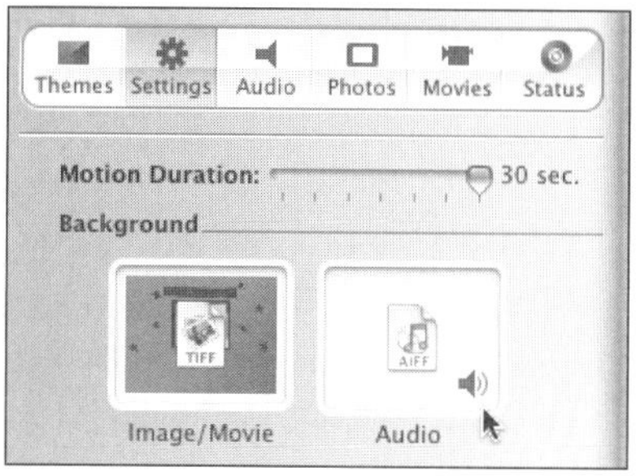

1. Click the **Settings** button in the **Customize** panel. Go through each menu and make sure the sound is on in each one. For example, double-click the **Scene Selection** button to go to the first scene selection menu. If you don't hear any music, click the **speaker** icon in the sound well. (You might also want to click the **Motion** button if you can't get any sound to play.) Once the music is playing, click the **right-pointing arrow** to move on to the next menu and repeat the process to make sure the music is playing. Then return to the main menu and double-click **Outtakes** to make sure the music is playing in the Outtakes menu. Finally, return to the main menu and make sure the music is on there.

Now that the music is playing in each menu, you're ready to test your project.

2. Click the **Preview** button in the lower-right corner of the iDVD window. The **Customize** panel retracts into the main window and a little remote control device appears onscreen. This remote control looks a lot like the remote controls you use for regular set-top DVD players and can be used to control your movie.

3. In the iDVD window, click **Play Movie**. The movie should start playing from the beginning.

Because you created chapter markers, you can use the remote control to jump ahead in this movie.

4. Click the  (**skip ahead**) button to jump to the next chapter. Click it a few more times to jump to your other chapter markers.

5. Now that you know the chapter markers are working, click the **menu** button on the remote to return to the main menu. (If something isn't working, go back and check the steps of the previous exercises.)

6. Click **Scene Selections** and try out the scene selection buttons. Use the **menu** button on the remote to return to the menu each time.

Note: *Because iDVD has to perform a lot of calculations on the fly while you're previewing your project, the menus aren't going to react and change as quickly as they would if you were really viewing this project on a burned DVD.*

---

7. Go back to the main menu and try the **Outtakes** button. Watch the Outtakes movie. When you're done, return to the main menu. Click the **Preview** button to leave preview mode.

After you've previewed your project and made sure that everything's working properly, you're ready to burn. You probably don't want to waste a good DVD-R on this exercise, so just read through the following steps (unless you really want to burn this project to a DVD).

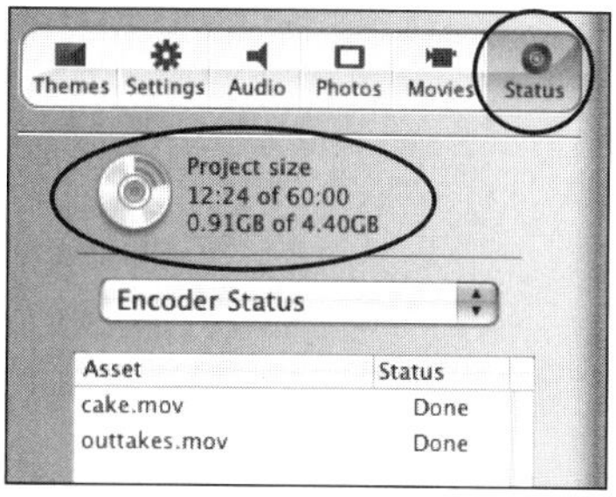

8. Click the **Status** button in the **Customize** panel. (If you don't see the panel, click **Customize** at the bottom of the window.) The **Status** area tells you how much space your project will take up on the DVD.

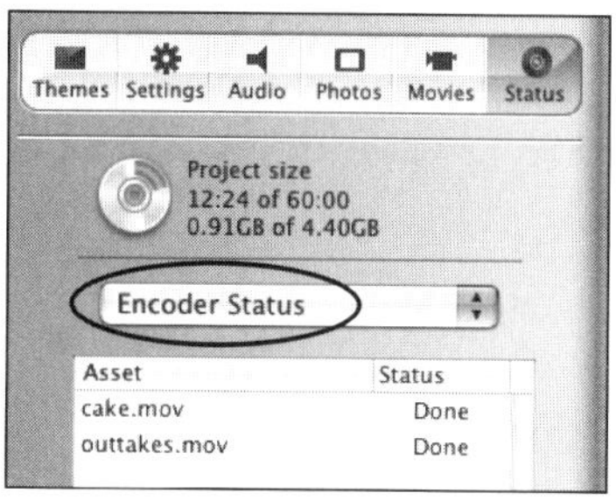

9. If it's not already chosen, choose **Encoder Status** from the pop-up menu.

When you drop a movie into your project, iDVD immediately begins encoding it for use on a DVD-R. iDVD performs this task in the background so you can continue working on other parts of your project. Before burning your DVD, you might want to check the Encoder Status menu to see if iDVD has completed encoding your movies. If not, the burning process may take a little longer than it would if the movies have already been encoded.

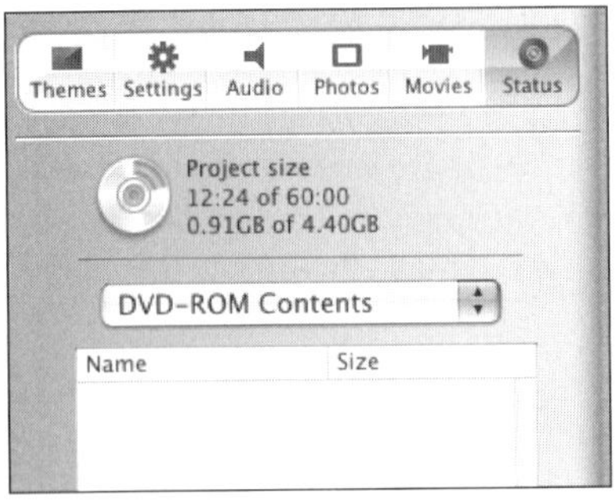

Note: *From the same pop-up menu, you can choose* ***DVD-ROM Contents*** *if you want to include any data that will be accessible on a computer DVD drive. You can drag files into this area and even click the* ***New Folder*** *button at the bottom of the panel to keep your files organized.*

Checking the Status area isn't really necessary when burning a DVD, but it's a good habit to get into if you really want to make sure everything's ready to go.

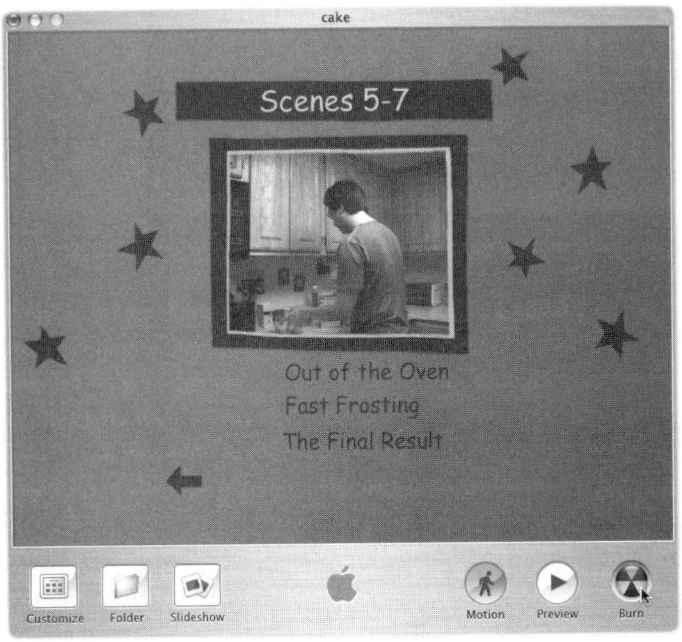

10. Click the **Burn** button in the lower-right corner of the window. The glowing, nuclear-radiation symbol **Burn** button appears. Click **Burn** again.

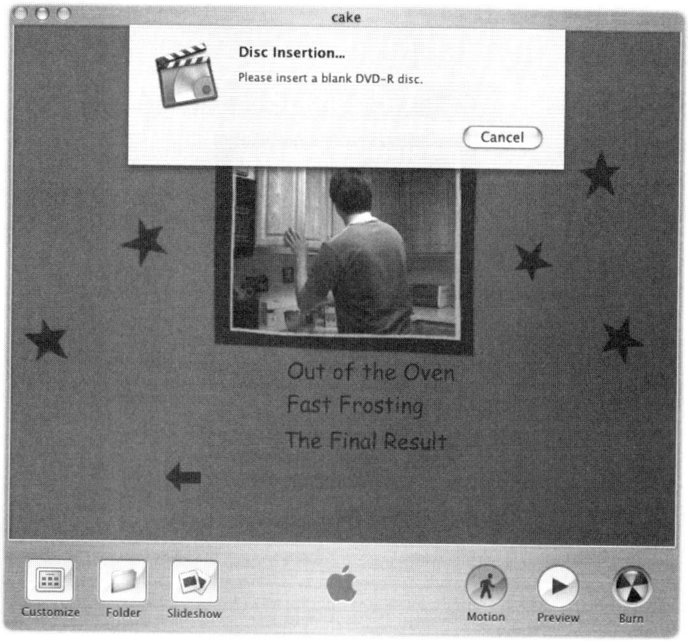

Unless you've previously inserted a DVD-R, you'll be prompted to insert a recordable disc.

11. Insert a DVD-R and take a break. iDVD will burn your disc. When it's done, you can play it using the **Apple DVD Player** application in your **Applications** folder, or pop it into your regular DVD player and watch it on your TV.

Note: *When the burning is complete, iDVD will ask if you want to burn another disc. If you want more than one copy, now is a good time to burn another one because iDVD won't have to go through the time-consuming processes of rendering and encoding your project again–it can just burn the disc. If you choose not to make another copy at this time, you'll still be able to burn an additional copy later, but you'll have to sit through iDVD's prep work all over again.*

Troubleshooting Tip

Several Mac discussion boards have documented cases in which some Macs don't complete the burning process properly. I have personally encountered this same problem: iDVD would go through the steps of rendering and encoding the movie, but it never actually burned the disc. I even left it running overnight, but it still never finished the project. After scouring Mac discussion groups online, I found this weird solution.

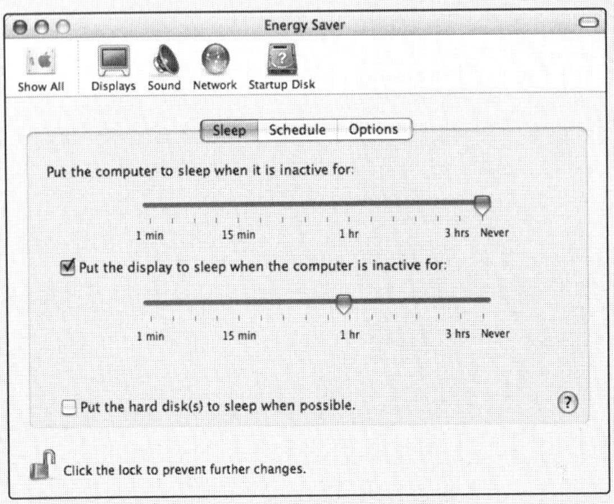

If your Mac seems to get hung up in the final stages of burning, restart the computer and open the **Energy Saver** panel in **System Preferences**. Under the **Sleep** section, drag the top slider to tell your Mac to never sleep. Then uncheck **Put the hard disk(s) to sleep when possible**. After performing these steps, my DVDs burned fine.

Player Compatibility

The DVD-R discs you burn in iDVD should be readable by any DVD drive manufactured within the last year or so. Still, you may run into a model here and there, especially an older model, that won't read DVD-Rs. Unfortunately, there isn't much you can do about this, other than telling the owner of the player to get with the times. Check Apple's Web site at **www.apple.com/dvd/compatibility** for a list of players that they have confirmed are able to read DVD-Rs.

So that's it for iLife. By this point, you should have a firm understanding of how well the four iLife applications integrate with each other, and you should have no trouble using some or all of them to manage your digital devices.

Section IV

Networking

| Chapter 18 – Networking |

By this point, you should have a pretty firm grasp of your Mac's capabilities and features. This last chapter takes you one step further by showing you how to hook up your Mac to a network so that you can share files and information with other computers, regardless of whether they're PCs or Macs. If you have only one Mac and don't need to connect to another computer, you can skip this section entirely.

18.

Networking

no exercise files

Mac OS X Panther
H•O•T CD-ROM

By now you should be comfortable with using OS X for both work and play. You've already learned a book's worth of tasks and activities that you can perform from your own Mac. But if you have more than one computer in your household or business, networking your computers together can greatly enhance the efficiency of your day-to-day operations. If you need to move files or documents from one computer to another, for example, you can simply copy them directly to the other computer rather than having to save them to a disk and transfer them the hard way.

This chapter shows you how to connect from OS X to other computers, whether they're running OS X or some version of Windows. You'll also learn how to connect to OS X from Windows machines as well as how to access your Mac over the Internet when you're away from your home or office.

Setting Up the Network

Before your Mac can communicate with other computers, you first need to install the proper hardware. Fortunately, nearly every Mac capable of running OS X has a built-in **Ethernet** jack. If you want to connect two Macs together, all you need is an Ethernet cable to run between them.

Note: Specifically, you need an Ethernet **crossover cable** to run between your two Macs. Although newer Macs like the PowerMac G4, Titanium PowerBook, or white iBook can use either crossover cables or regular Ethernet cables, you can't go wrong getting a crossover–it will work with all Macs. You can purchase Ethernet crossover cables at any computer or electronics store.

Alternately, if your two Macs both have **AirPort** cards installed, you can forget the cables and have them communicate with each other wirelessly. (More on this later.)

But if you have more than two computers that you want to connect to one another, you'll need to purchase an Ethernet **hub** or, if you're planning on connecting wirelessly, an AirPort **base station** or other type of **wireless router**.

Ethernet hubs are relatively inexpensive devices that feature anywhere between four and eight Ethernet jacks for connecting multiple computers together into a single network. (They aren't Mac- or PC-specific). If you want to share a single Internet connection among computers, you'll want to pick up a slightly more expensive Ethernet router, a device that distributes your Internet service to each computer on the network. (Basically, a hub connects computers on the same network; a router connects two networks together. In the case of sharing an Internet connection, you use a router to connect your home network to a much larger network: The Internet. Most routers are also hubs.) And if you want the option of connecting both conventionally and wirelessly, you can purchase one of several hybrid hubs on the market that have both Ethernet ports and wireless antennas.

Purchasing a Router

If you're looking for a wireless router, you can demonstrate your brand loyalty by choosing Apple's AirPort or AirPort Extreme base stations. But if you want to spend a little less, you can go with routers from other companies such as Linksys (**www.linksys.com**), Netgear (**www.netgear.com**), or Belkin (**www.belkin.com**). As mentioned in Exercise 3 of Chapter 8, "*Getting Online*," AirPort and AirPort Extreme run on the wireless standards 802.11b and 802.11g, respectively, and are completely compatible with one another. Whether you have an older AirPort card or a newer one, any router you purchase with 802.11b or 802.11g will work with your card. The only standard you want to avoid is 802.11a, which doesn't work with AirPort cards at all.

A word about 802.11b/g: The older 802.11b is by far the most popular and widely used flavor of wireless. It receives and transmits data at a theoretical speed of 11 Mbps (megabits per second). Realistically, you'll probably only get about 6 Mbps, which is still more than fast enough for Web surfing. Because the throughput of most home and small business cable and DSL services peak at around 1.5 Mbps, it's overkill to use the faster (and slightly more expensive) 54 Mbps 802.11g devices exclusively for Internet use. The higher speed is beneficial only if you want to transfer large files quickly between computers on your home or business network, bearing in mind that the speed is achievable only if all the computers involved have 802.11g cards installed. Even then, 54 Mbps is only a theoretical speed; in real-world situations, you'll probably get around 25 Mbps. When you're ready to decide on a router, you'll first need to determine whether you want to save some money with an 802.11b device or to spend a little more for 802.11g to get faster file transfer speeds.

Once you've purchased your router, follow the instructions to connect it to your Internet service and to all the computers on your network.

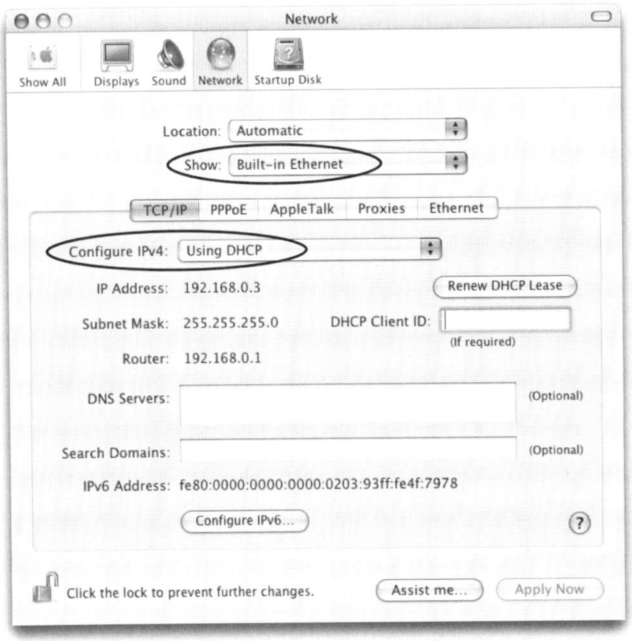

The setup for routers varies depending on the vendor, so be sure to follow the directions provided with the box. After your router is installed, you'll then need to set up each computer to connect to the router. Typically in OS X, you'll need to access your **Network** settings under **System Preferences**. From the **Show** pop-up menu, choose either **Built-in Ethernet** or **AirPort**, depending on which connection method you're using, and then choose **Using DHCP** from the **Configure IPv4** menu. Click **Apply Now** and your router will automatically assign you an IP (Internet Protocol) address, which is a series of numbers that distinguish this computer from others on the same network. At this point, you should be able to connect to the Internet by opening your Web browser. If these steps don't work for you, refer to the instructions that came with the router.

Once your computers are all connected to the network, you need to set them up to communicate with one another. Exercise 1 shows you how to prepare your OS X Mac for access by other computers. Be sure to perform the steps in Exercise 1 before jumping ahead to another exercise.

I. Preparing OS X for File Sharing

This exercise shows you how to prepare Macs running OS X to accept communications from other computers. Each Mac that you want to prepare should already be connected to the network router before beginning these steps (unless you're connecting two Macs together via their Ethernet ports using a crossover cable).

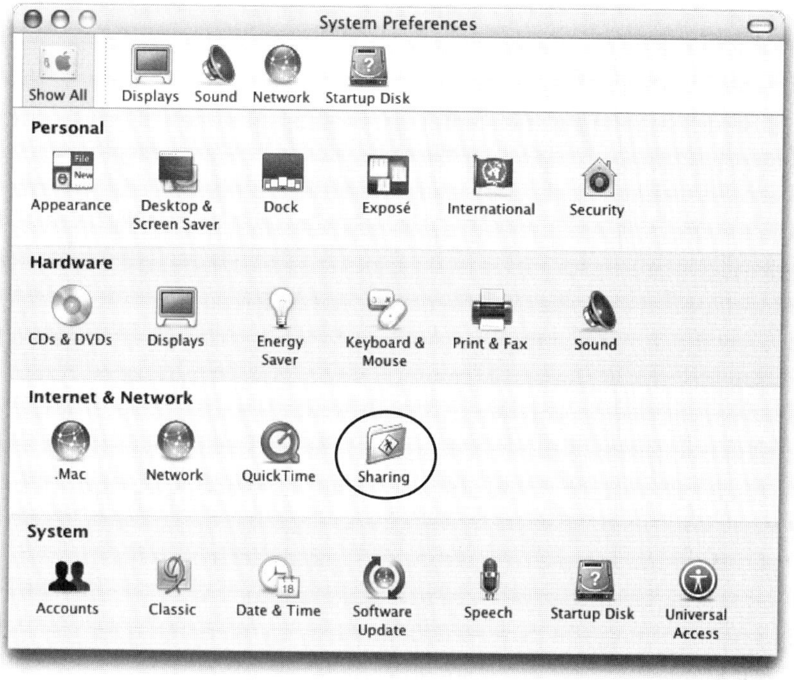

1. To prepare your Mac to accept a connection from another Mac, open **System Preferences** and click the **Sharing** icon.

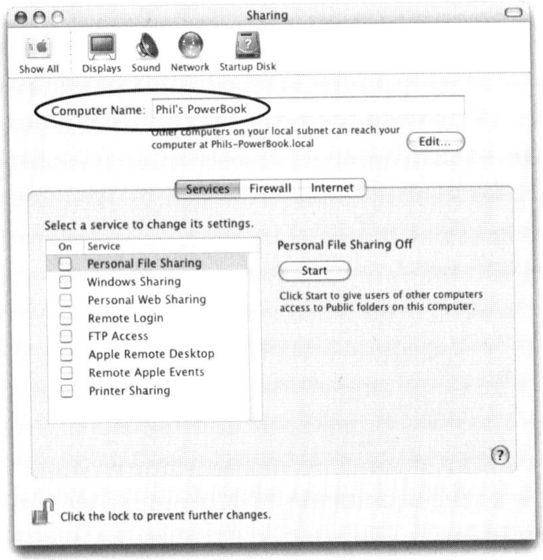

2. If necessary, enter a descriptive name in the **Computer Name** field. If you have several computers on a network, you need to be able to distinguish them from each other.

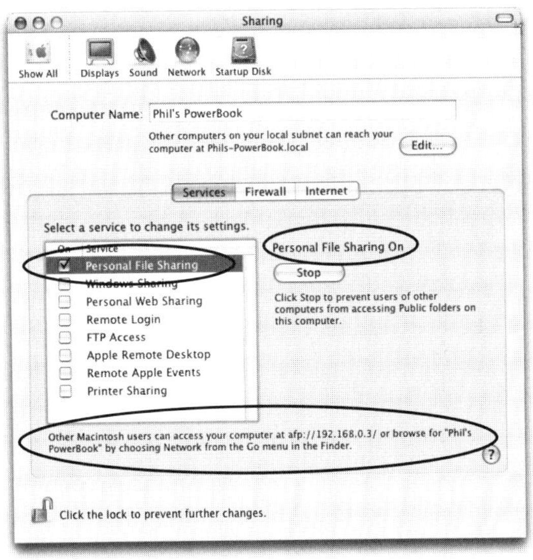

3. If it's not already selected, click the **Services** button. Check **Personal File Sharing**. It will take a few seconds to get started, and then the message **Personal File Sharing On** appears above the **Stop** button. Note the text near the bottom of the window that tells you how other Macs can access your computer. This information will be important shortly.

4. Close **System Preferences** and repeat Steps **1** through **3** on any other OS X Mac(s) that you want to be able to access from other Macs.

If your Macs are connected to a hub either wirelessly or via Ethernet, or if your two Macs are connected to each other via an Ethernet cable, you're done with the prep work. If you're using AirPort cards to communicate between two Macs, you have a few more steps to follow.

5. On the Mac you're prepping for access, click the **AirPort** icon in the menu bar and choose **Create Network**. If you don't see the AirPort icon or don't have the **Create Network** option, open the **AirPort** settings in the **Network** preference panel and check **Allow this computer to create networks** and **Show AirPort status in menu bar**.

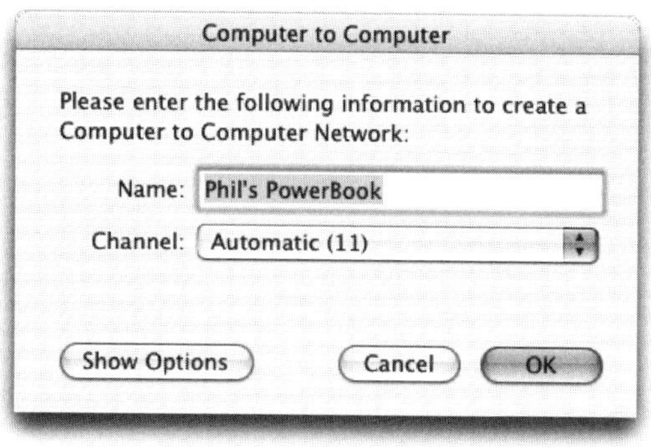

6. In the dialog box that opens, give your network a **Name** and then click **OK**.

Your Mac is now ready to be accessed by other computers. Consult the following exercises for the appropriate steps.

2. Connecting from Panther to Any OS X Version

The steps in this exercise show you how to connect from a Mac running OS 10.3 (Panther) to another Mac running OS X (any version). Make sure that you've completed the steps in Exercise 1 before beginning this exercise.

Imagine you're working on your Mac running OS 10.3 (called the **client** Mac in this exercise), and you realize you need a file that's stored on your other Mac in the next room (called the **remote** Mac in this exercise). If both machines are connected to a network, and you've turned on Personal File Sharing (as shown in Exercise 1), retrieving the file is a simple task.

AirPort Network Prep

If you performed Steps 5 and 6 of the previous exercise (creating an AirPort network without a wireless hub), you'll need to connect the client Mac to the AirPort network you previously created.

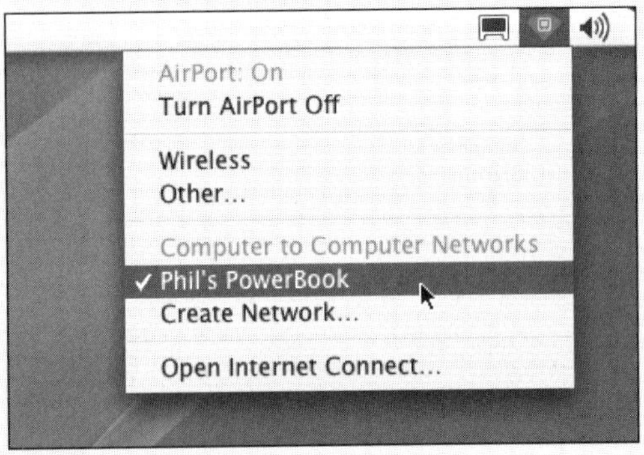

To do so, click the **AirPort** menu bar icon on the client Mac and choose the AirPort network's name. (If there are multiple wireless networks in your area, make sure you select the right one.) If you created a password, enter it and click **OK**.

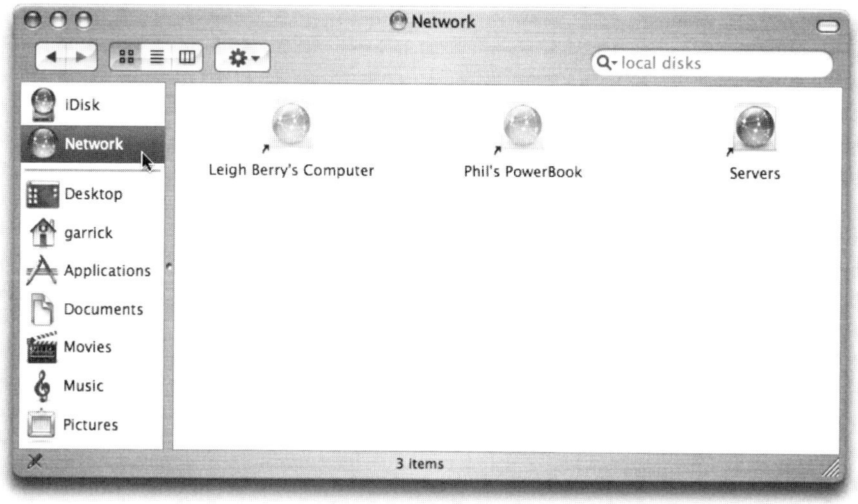

1. Open a new **Finder** window and click the **Network** icon in the **Places** sidebar. Your Mac will scan for and display the names of any other computers it finds on the network, including the one you're currently using (called **Servers**).

2. When the computer to which you want to connect appears, double-click its name.

Note: *If your Mac network happens to be a part of a larger network within your office, you'll see the names of each network workgroup appear in the left column of this window, rather than the individual computer names. If this is the case, select the name of the network on which your other Mac resides.*

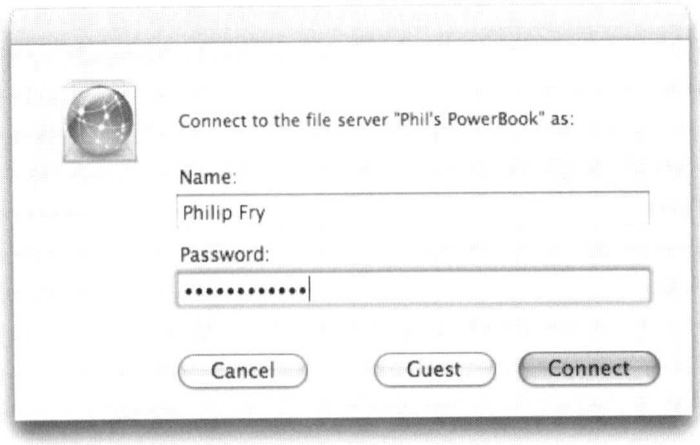

You'll be prompted to enter a name and password for the Mac to which you're connecting.

---

3. Enter your user name and password for your account on the remote Mac.

Note: *Other users can connect to your Mac only if you've created an account for them (or if you've provided them with your user name and password).*

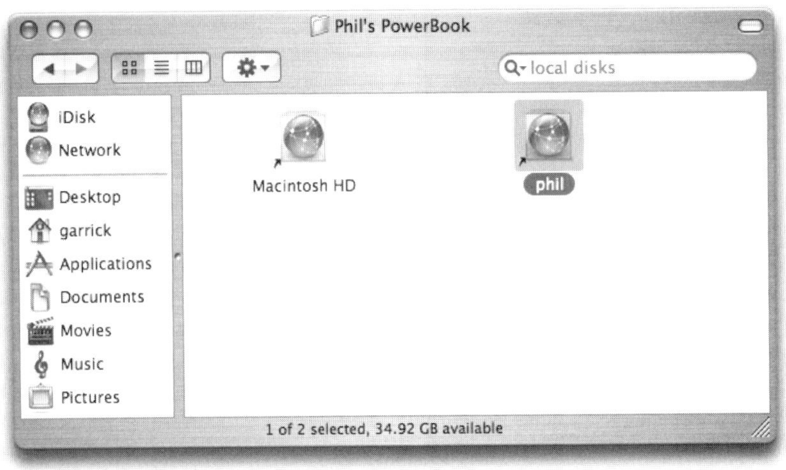

4. If the remote Mac has more than one hard drive or user account, select the drive or account you wish to access and click **OK**.

The remote Mac's drive icon appears in the Places sidebar. (If you don't see the icon, choose ***Finder > Preferences*** *and check* ***Connected Servers*** *under the* ***Sidebar*** *preferences.) You can now use this icon to view the contents of the remote Mac, and you're free to drag files to and from the remote Mac as needed if you have an Administrator account on the remote Mac or if the Administrator has given you privileges to move and copy files.*

NOTE | User Account Required to Make Changes

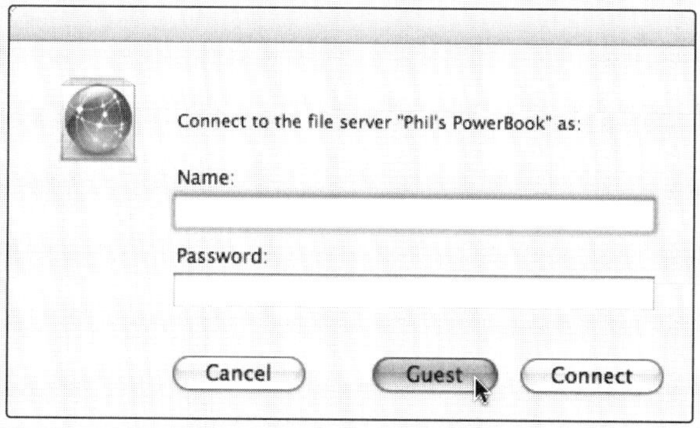

With Personal File Sharing activated on the remote Mac, anyone on the network can log onto it as a guest.

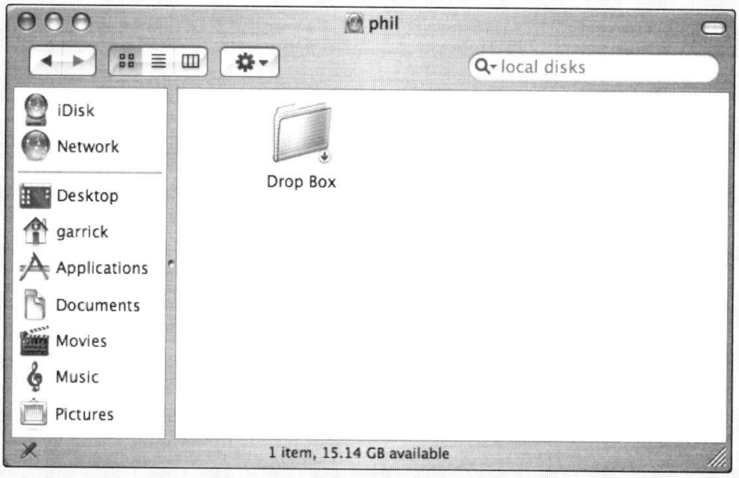

However, guests can only drop files into the **Drop Box** folder located in the **Public** folder of your **Home** directory. Guests cannot open the **Drop Box** folder, nor can they open any other files or folders on the remote Mac. If you want to give other users on your network the ability to access files on your Mac, you need to provide each user with his or her own account. See Exercise 11 of Chapter 4, "*System Preferences*," for information on creating additional accounts and controlling privileges.

TIP | Just Enter the Address

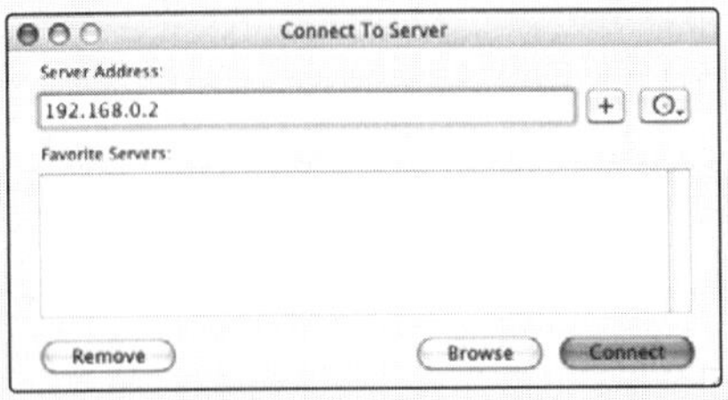

If you know the IP address of the remote Mac (which you saw in the **Sharing** preferences in Exercise 1), you can choose **Go > Connect to Server** from the **Finder** menu bar (or press **Cmd+K**) and just type the IP address in the **Server Address** field and click **Connect**. Enter your user name and password when prompted.

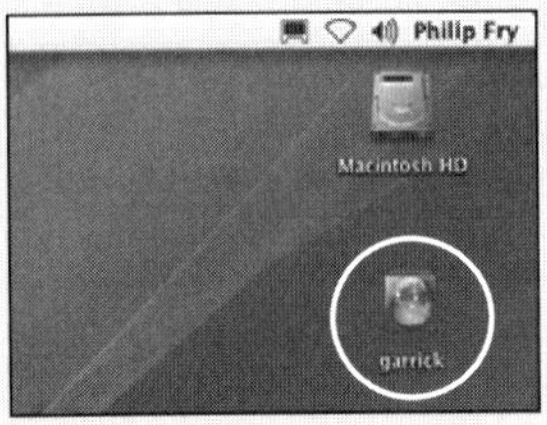

Connecting in this fashion places the remote Mac's icon on your Desktop, which you can leave there to remain constantly connected (at least until the remote Mac is shut down). Double-clicking this icon gives you quick access to the remote Mac. When you're done, you can drag this icon to the Trash to "eject" the remote Mac from your computer.

Note: If you don't see the icon appear on your Desktop, choose **Finder > Preferences** and check **Connected Servers** under the **General** preferences.

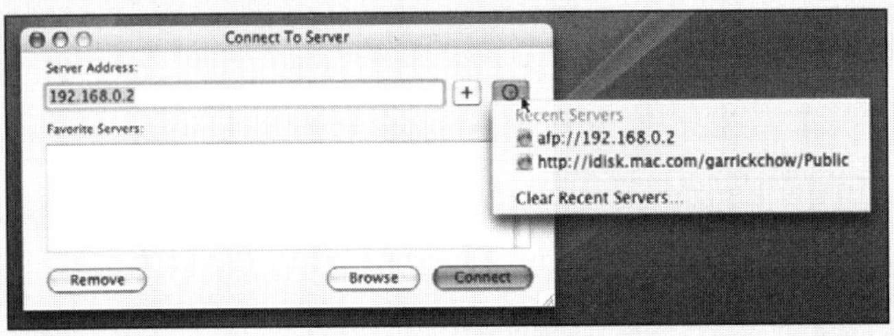

Once you've connected to the remote Mac using the Connect to Server command, you can access it again at any time by clicking the **clock** button at the right of the address field, which lists all your recently accessed servers. If you connect to the remote Mac all the time, click the + button to add it to your list of **Favorite Servers**. Afterwards, you'll be able to connect to this server quickly by double-clicking its address.

Connecting over the Internet

If you're a frequent traveler, you'll be happy to know that connecting to your home Mac from the road isn't all that different than connecting to it over your network. Being able to grab files from your Mac over the Internet saves you the time and hassle of copying all the files you think you might need before you hit the road. As long as you have a continuous Internet connection at home (a broadband connection is highly recommended), you can connect to your Mac from any other Mac with Internet access.

Depending on whether your Mac is directly connected to your broadband modem or whether it's connected through a router, the process of setting up your Mac for access over the Internet will vary.

Direct Connection

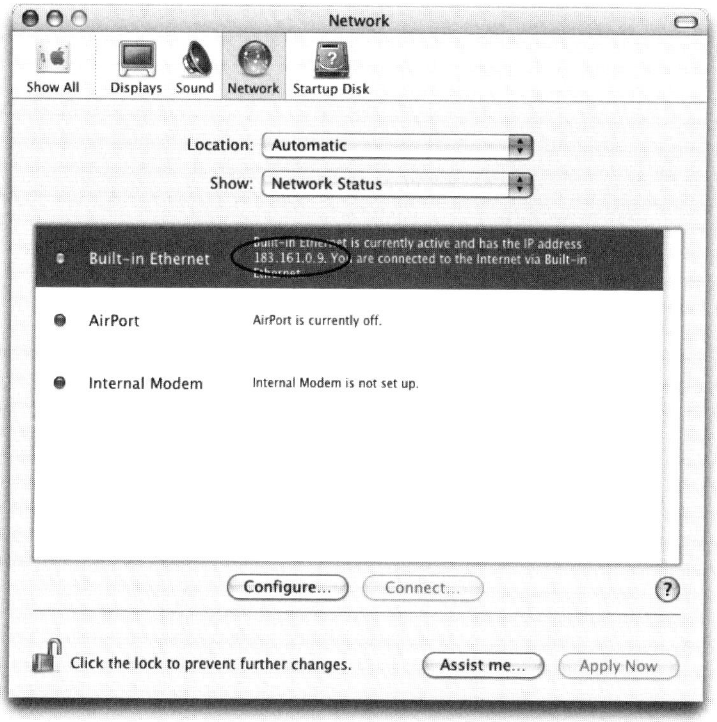

The first thing you need to do is to determine your home Mac's IP address. If your Mac is connected directly to your cable modem or DSL modem, this is an easy task. Simply click the **Network** icon in **System Preferences** and copy down your **IP address** as it appears next to your **Built-in Ethernet Port** port listing.

Note: Most broadband providers use DHCP (**D**ynamic **H**ost **C**onfiguration **P**rotocol), which means that each time you turn on your modem and/or computer, the IP address your ISP assigns you may not be the same address you had the last time you connected. So don't shut off or restart your modem or Mac between the time you copy the IP address and the time you depart on your trip, otherwise the address you take with you might not be the one currently assigned to your Mac.

Before your go, make sure that **Personal File Sharing** is on in the **Sharing** pane and that you've informed roommates, family members, or co-workers not to turn off your computer while you're gone. (You should also set your Mac to not sleep in the **Energy Saver** panel in **System Preferences**.)

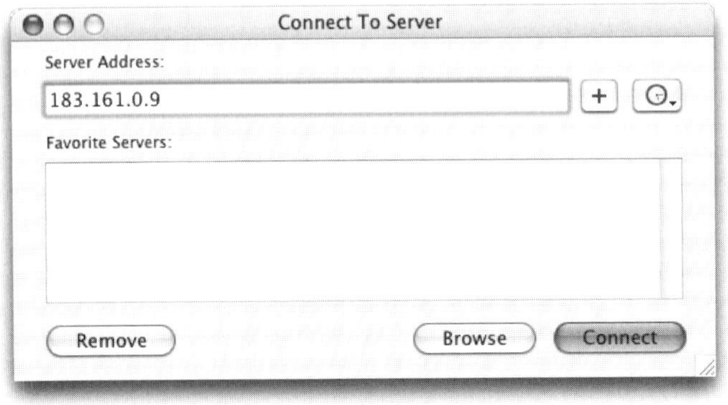

To access your home Mac from the road, first connect to the Internet through your PowerBook (or any other Mac running OS X), then choose **Go > Connect to Server** from the menu bar, and type your IP address into the **Address** field. After entering your user name and password, your home Mac's icon will appear on your **Desktop**. Get the files you need and then drag the icon to the **Trash** to sign off from your home Mac.

Connecting Through a Router

If your Mac is connected to the Internet through a network router, you'll need some information in addition to the IP address you see in the Sharing pane. If you want to connect to your Mac over the Internet while you're away from home, you need to know both your router's WAN (**w**ide **a**rea **n**etwork) IP address as well as your home computer's LAN (**l**ocal **a**rea **n**etwork) IP address. The WAN IP is the address for your router, assigned by your ISP (**I**nternet **S**ervice **P**rovider). The LAN IP is the address that your router assigns an individual computer on your home network. Think of the WAN IP as the street address of an apartment building and the LAN IP as the apartment number.

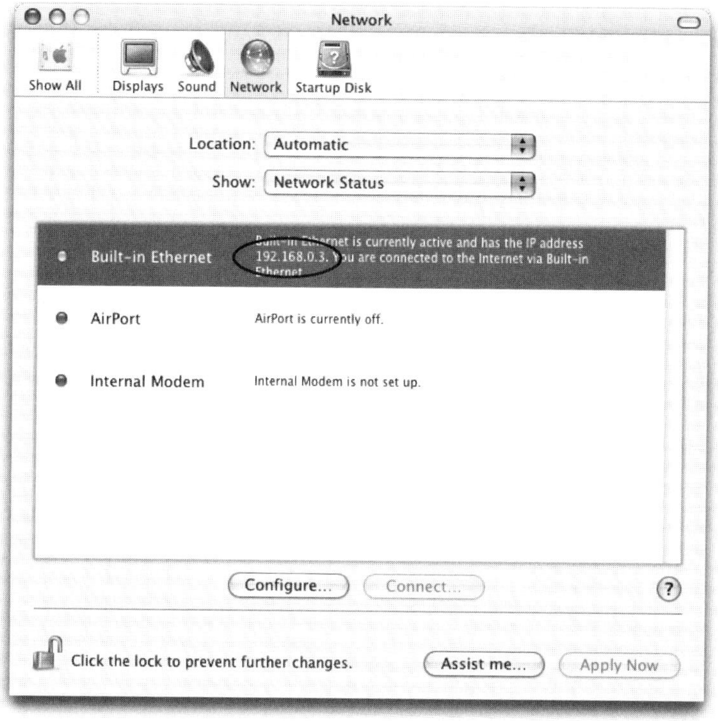

Open the **Network** pane in **System Preferences**. The address you see here (mostly likely starting with **192.168**) is the LAN address, the one your router assigns to individual computers on your network. All the computers on your home network are part of the LAN, and your router controls the distribution of IP addresses on this network.

In order to function on the network, each computer needs a unique IP address. The router assigns each computer a local IP address, which allows the computers on your network to see and communicate with one another, but because the router is the only device assigned an actual Internet address, the computers are invisible to anyone outside the router's network. This protects the computers on your LAN from hackers and other outside intruders.

Just as the computers in your home or business are connected to the LAN, the router itself is connected to a much larger network–the Internet. In this case, the Internet is known as the WAN. When you connect your router to the Internet through your broadband modem, your ISP assigns the router an IP address. This address is known as your WAN IP address. Check the instructions that came with your router for directions on finding your WAN IP address.

Tip: If you can't find the WAN IP, try visiting **www.whatismyip.com** in your Web browser. This site's main function is to tell you your IP address.

Now you have both your LAN IP address and your WAN IP address. But before you're able to connect to the Internet from the road through your router, you'll need to do one last thing. You need to let the router know which of the computers on your network you want to access. There are a couple ways of making sure that your connection requests from the road are directed to the right computer, but the easiest way is to tell the router to send all incoming requests to one Mac. Most routers can be set up with a DMZ (**dem**ilitarized **z**one) address. Don't let the term scare you; a DMZ address is simply the default IP address to which the router sends incoming communications. Check your router's instructions for entering a DMZ address and enter your Mac's LAN IP. This tells your router to send all incoming traffic to one particular Mac.

For example, let's say you have a WAN IP address of 79.24.35.124, and your router has assigned your Mac a LAN IP address of 192.168.0.3.

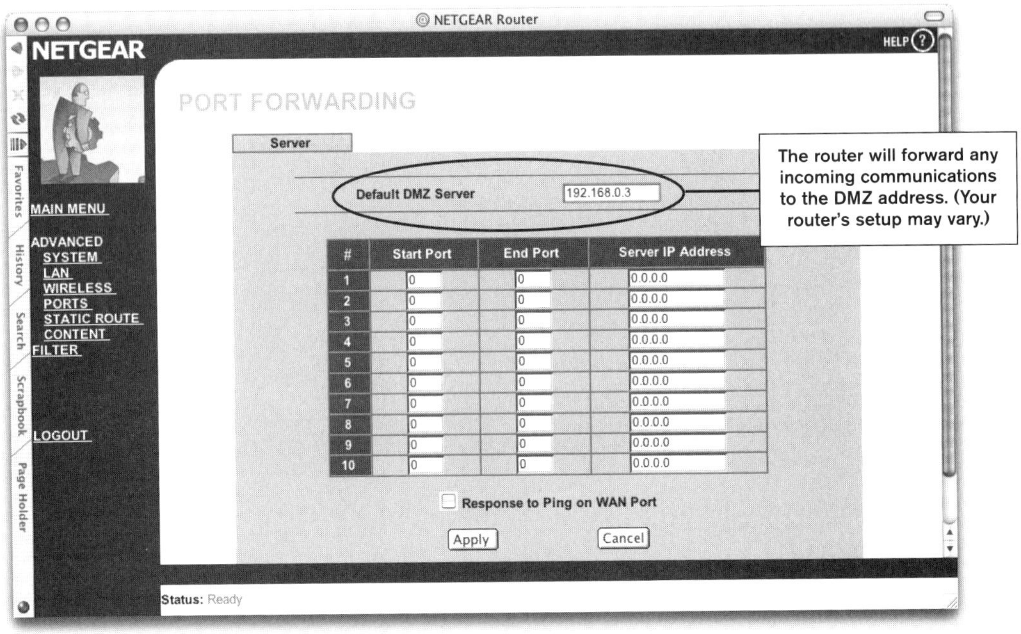

In your router's setup software, you would enter **192.168.0.3** as the DMZ address. To connect to your Mac from the road, choose **Go > Connect to Server** from the menu bar of the road Mac (after establishing an Internet connection, of course). In the **Address** field, type **79.24.35.124**, which locates your router on the Internet. Your router notices the incoming traffic and immediately routes it to your Mac at 192.168.0.3. From there, you enter your user name and password, the home Mac appears on your Desktop, and you're ready to transfer files back and forth.

Yes, this is definitely more complicated than accessing a single Mac directly connected to the Internet, but it's a small price to pay for the convenience of sharing an Internet connection through a router.

3. Connecting to OS X from Windows

With OS X, you're not limited to just accessing your Mac from another Mac, you can also connect to the remote Mac from a PC running Windows. This exercise shows you how to set up your Mac to be accessed from a Windows machine and how to perform the connection from Windows.

1. On the Mac, open **System Preferences** and click the **Sharing** icon.

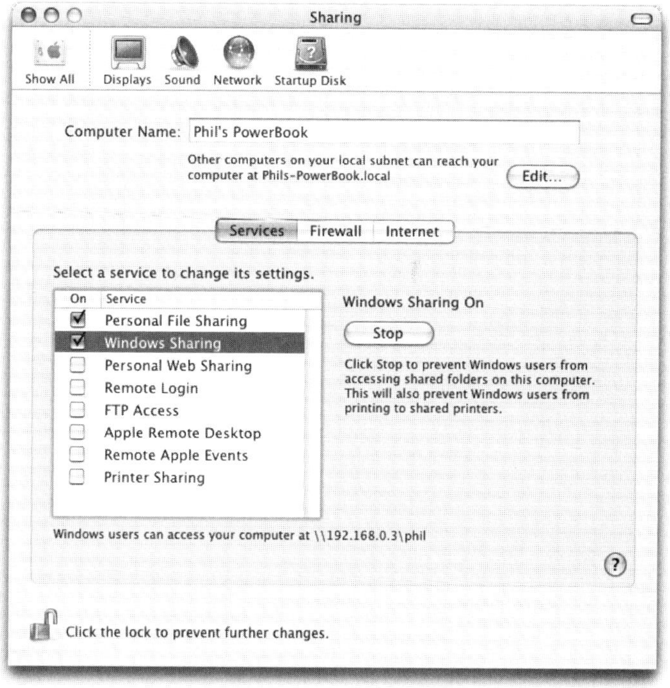

2. Under the **Services** section, check **Windows Sharing**. This opens the door for Windows users to access your Mac. (You can keep **Personal File Sharing** checked if you like, but it doesn't affect Windows users.)

To prevent unauthorized users from accessing your Mac from Windows, each person to whom you want to give access needs to have a user account that's been enabled for Windows access. Unlike accessing a Mac from another Mac, there is no guest account available for Windows users.

3. Close **System Preferences**.

Your Mac is now ready to host Windows users.

4. Move to a Windows machine on your network.

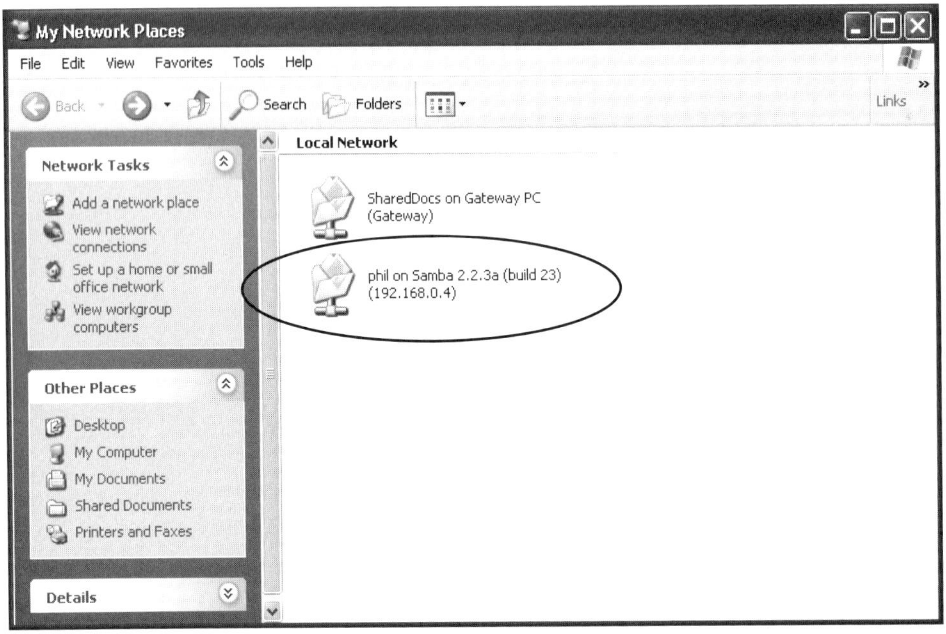

5. In Windows, open **My Network Places** (Windows 2000 and XP) or **Network Neighborhood** (Windows 98). The remote Mac's icon should appear in this window with a name like "phil on Mac OS X" or "phil on Samba 2.2.3a." (Samba is a Windows networking protocol.)

If your Mac's icon appears here, you're done. Double-click the folder to access its contents. You're free to copy files to and from this folder. Of course, this being Windows, there's a good chance that things didn't happen the way they were supposed to, and your Mac didn't show up yet. See the following steps for troubleshooting advice.

6. First, try restarting the Windows machine and then opening your **Network Places** again.

If your Mac still doesn't show up, you may need to change its workgroup. The term "workgroup" refers to a grouping of related computers under a meaningful name. For instance, on a single office network, you might have a workgroup called "sales" and a workgroup called "accounting." All the sales computers can see and interact with each other, but they cannot see the accounting computers.

OS X's default workgroup is called "Workgroup." If your Windows PC belongs to a differently named workgroup, you'll have to change your Mac's workgroup name in order for it to appear on your PC.

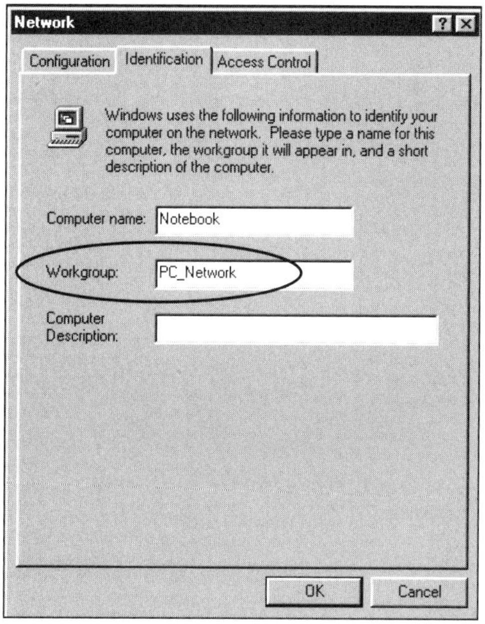

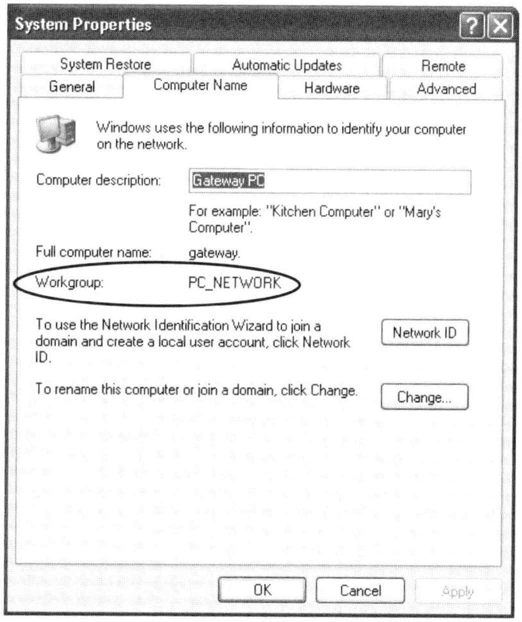

7. First, find and note your PC's workgroup name:

- **Windows 98:** Choose **Start > Settings > Control Panel** and then double-click the **Network** icon. (Or just right-click the **Network Neighborhood** icon on the **Desktop** and choose **Properties.**) Click the **Identification** tab to see the workgroup name.
- **Windows XP:** Click the **Start** button and choose **Control Panel.** Double-click the **System** icon and click the **Computer Name** tab in the window that opens to see the workgroup name.

8. On your Mac, open the **Directory Access** utility program located in **Applications > Utilities**.

9. Click the padlock icon in the lower-left corner and enter your administrator password when prompted.

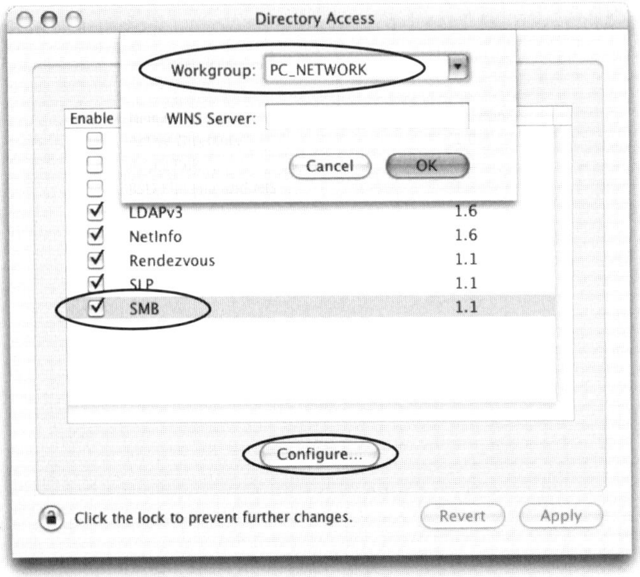

10. Select **SMB** from the **Services** list and click **Configure**. Locate your PC's workgroup name from the **Workgroup** pop-up menu (or, if it's not listed, type the name in the **Workgroup** field). Click **OK** when you're done and quit **Directory Access**.

---

11. Go to your Windows machine and follow Step 5 of this exercise to see if your Mac now appears.

*Tip: The workgroup change may take up to five minutes to be recognized by other computers on the network. To force a quicker update, stop and restart **Windows Sharing** in the **Sharing** preferences pane (shown in Step 2 of this exercise). You may also need to restart your Windows computer.*

The following steps show you how to manually search for your Mac if it's still not showing up in Windows XP.

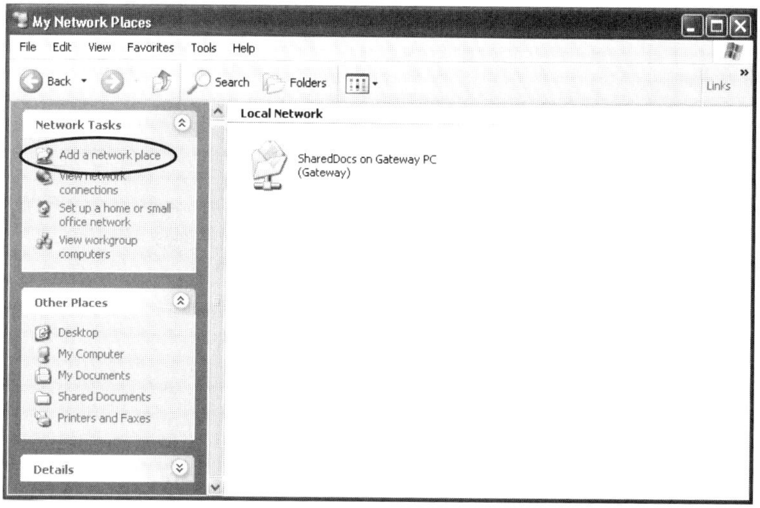

12. Find a large hammer and a blowtorch… just kidding. Well, kind of. In Windows XP, click **Add a network place** to open the **Add Network Place Wizard**. (If you don't see this option, choose **Tools > Folder Options** and check **Show Common Tasks in Folders**.)

---

13. Click **Next** on the first screen of the wizard.

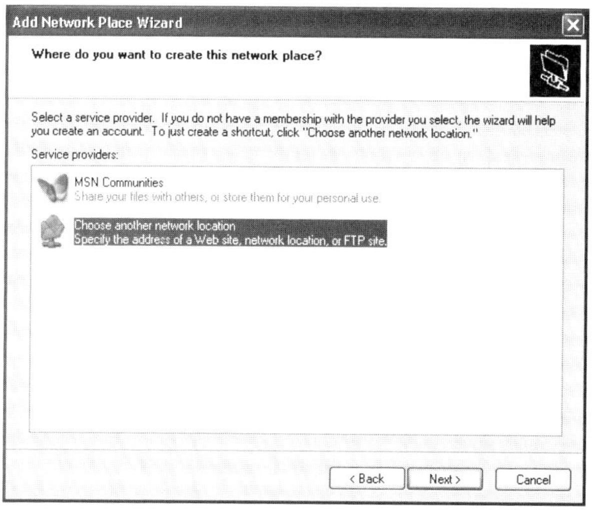

14. When asked, "Where do you want to create this network place?", select **Choose another network location** and click **Next**.

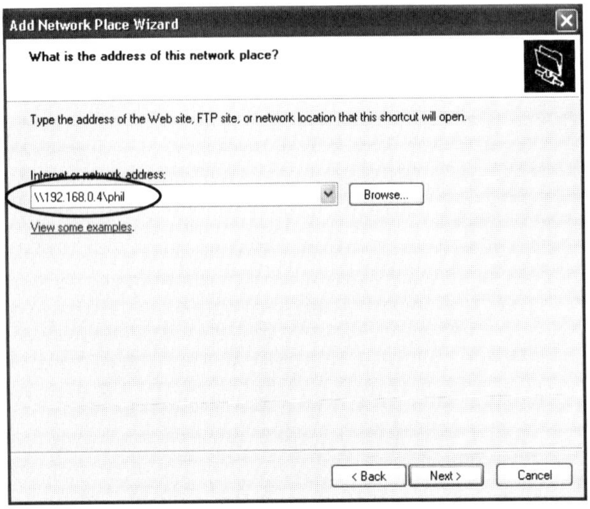

15. On this screen, type your Mac's IP address and account name as it appears in the **Sharing** pane of OS X's **System Preferences**. Note that the slashes in the address are backslashes (\), not forward slashes (/). Click **Next**.

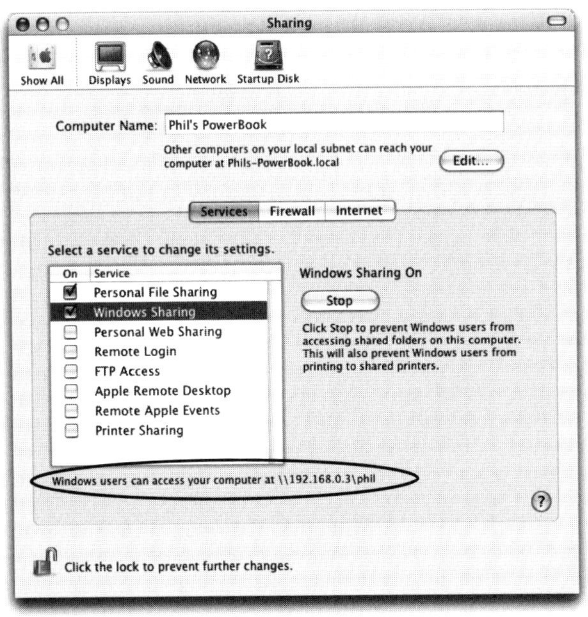

***Tip:** If you don't know your Mac's IP address, open **System Preferences > Sharing** on the Mac and click **Windows Sharing** to see the address written out for you.*

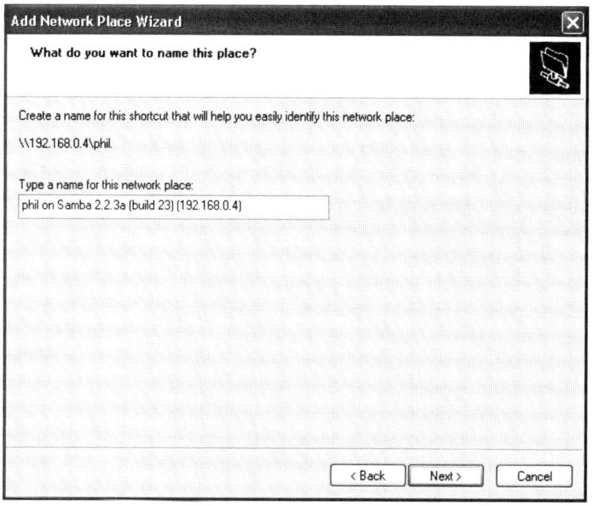

16. On the next screen, you can enter a less verbose name for your Mac if you like. Click **Next**.

17. Click **Finish**. Your Mac's folder should now appear in the **My Network Places** folder.

4. Connecting to Windows from OS X

Along with being able to access your Mac from a Windows machine on your network, you'll most likely want to access the Windows computer from your Mac at some point. This exercise shows you how to set up the Windows machine and then how to connect to it from your Mac.

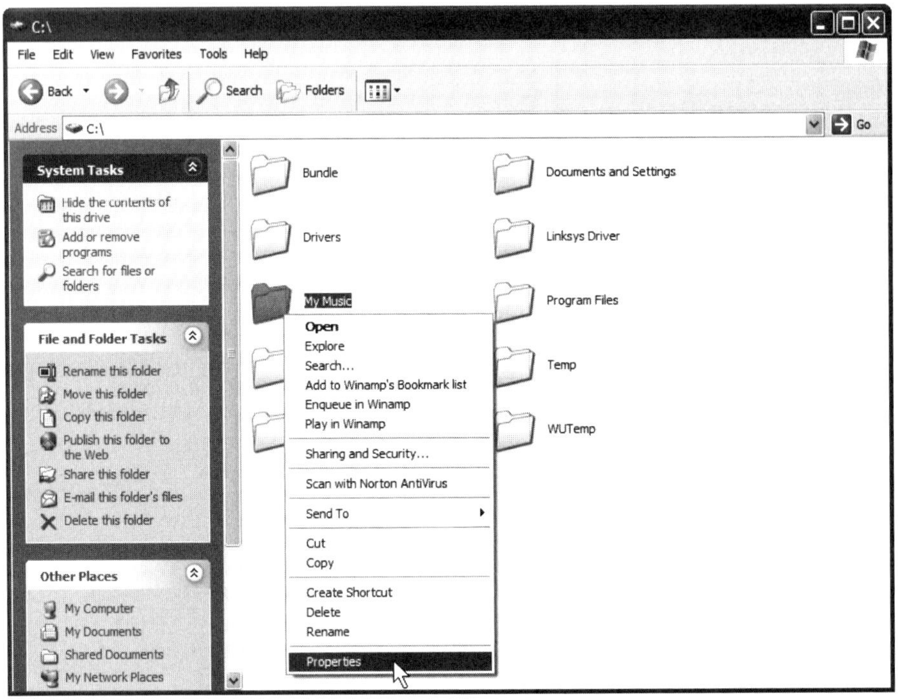

1. From Windows XP, ME, 2000, or 98, right-click the folder you want to share and choose **Properties** from the contextual menu. Each folder you want to access from your Mac has to be set up for sharing.

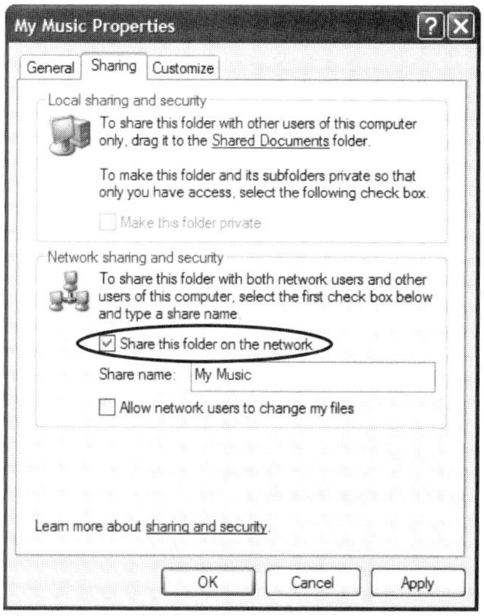

2. Click the **Sharing** tab and check **Share this folder on the network**. (Windows 98 users check **Shared as.**) If it will help you or others to discern its contents, you can give this folder a more descriptive name in the **Share name** field. Click **OK**.

Note: *If you've never shared a folder before, you may be prompted to run the* ***Network Setup Wizard.*** *Follow its directions, reboot your PC to enable sharing, and restart this exercise.*

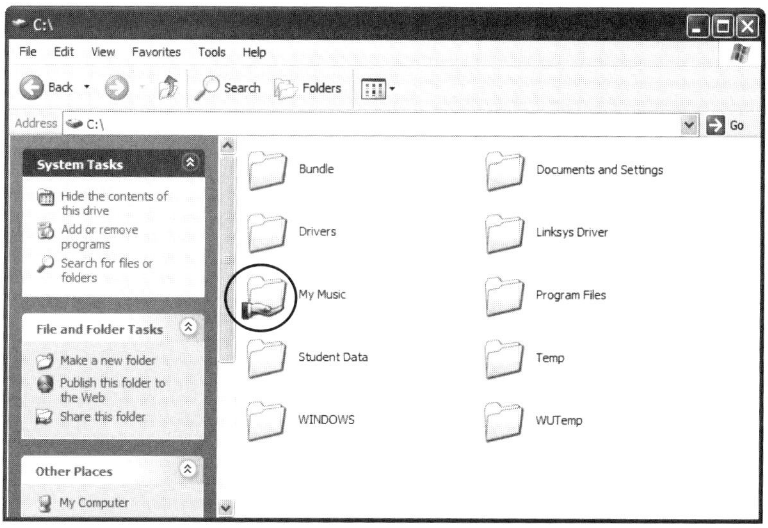

Once the folder has been successfully set up, its icon will change to indicate that it's being shared.

3. Repeat Steps 1 and 2 for any other folders you want to access from your Mac.

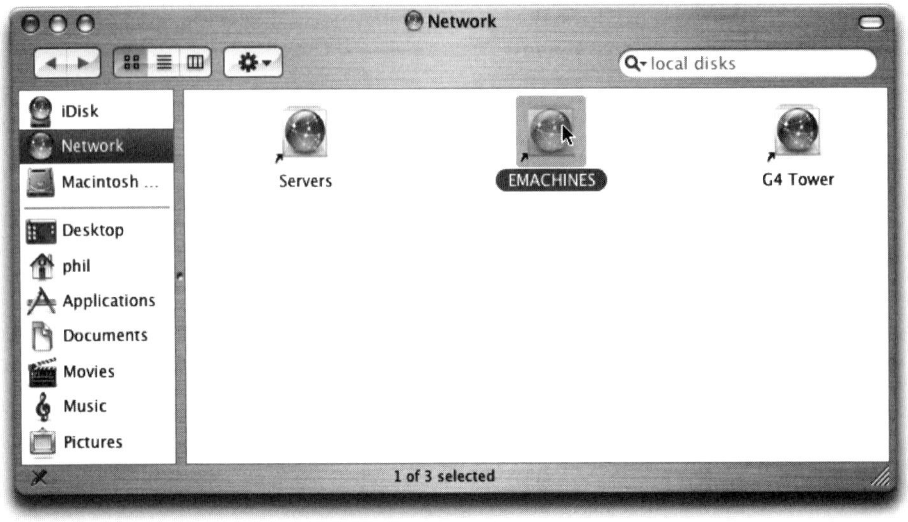

4. Switch to your Mac and open a **Finder** window. Click **Network** in the **Places** sidebar. Your PC's name should appear. Double-click its icon. (Your PC's name may differ from the one shown above.)

5. You'll be prompted to enter a user name and password (which you set up when you ran the **Network Setup Wizard** the first time in Windows). Type your **Username** and **Password**. You can check **Add to Keychain** if you want your Mac to remember your name and password in the future. Click **OK**.

6. The **Finder** window now displays all the shared folders on your PC, and you're free to move files to and from it.

So that's it! You made it through the book. Be sure to check out the Appendices for lots of useful tidbits about the applications and utilities that came with OS X and for a list of several resources you can use to further expand your knowledge of this fantastic operating system.

A. Applications and Utilities

H•O•T

Mac OS X Panther

When you first install Mac OS X, you soon notice that your Applications folder is already stuffed with programs that come with the operating system. This appendix lists and briefly describes most of the default items found in your Applications and Utilities folders. This list includes items in the OS X Applications folder, not the Applications (OS 9) folder you'll also see if you have Classic installed.

Applications

Address Book

An application for organizing phone numbers, addresses, and other contact information. Covered in Chapter 10, "*Address Book, Mail, and iChat AV*."

Calculator

A small, yet elegant calculator program that can be used as a basic or scientific (click **Advanced**) calculator. It can also perform several types of conversions such as currency, temperature, and weights and masses. Click the **Convert** menu to see a full list.

Chess

A challenging 3D version of Chess that allows you to play against the computer and another person. It's been newly updated for Panther to include features that allow you to rotate the board to change the appearance of the board and pieces.

DVD Player

This is the software required to watch DVD movies on your Mac (if your Mac is equipped with a DVD drive).

Font Book

Font management software, covered in Chapter 10, "*Address Book, Mail, and iChat AV*."

iCal

A personal calendar application, covered in Chapter 13, "*iCal and iSync*."

iChat

Apple's instant-messaging application. See Chapter 10, "*Address Book, Mail, and iChat AV*."

iDVD 3

This program will only appear in your Applications folder if your Mac is equipped with a built-in SuperDrive. See Chapter 17, "*iDVD 3*."

Image Capture

An application for importing images from your digital camera or scanner. Covered in Chapter 15, "*iPhoto 2*."

iMovie

Apple's video editing program. Part of the iLife suite. Covered in Chapter 16, "*iMovie 3*."

Internet Connect

Application for connecting to the Internet. Covered in Chapter 8, "*Getting Online*."

Internet Explorer
Microsoft's Web browser. A useful alternative if the Web page you're trying to view doesn't show up properly in Safari for some reason.

iPhoto
Apple's photo editing and organizing software. Part of the iLife suite. Covered in Chapter 15, "*iPhoto 2*."

iSync
Used for synchronizing address and scheduling information between your Mac and your other digital devices. Covered in Chapter 13, "*iCal and iSync*."

iTunes
Apple's digital music player/ripper/burner. Part of the iLife suite. Covered in Chapter 14, "*iTunes 4*."

Mail
Apple's email program. See Chapter 10, "*Address Book, Mail, and iChat AV*."

Preview
Apple's all-purpose default image viewer. This application can read and display nearly all image formats in use today, including PDF (**P**ortable **D**ocument **F**ormat) files.

QuickTime Player
Apple's media player. It can play most audio and video formats. To edit and save files in QuickTime, you must upgrade to QuickTime Player Pro, available at **www.apple.com/quicktime/download**.

Safari
Apple's Web browser. Covered in Chapter 9, "*Safari*."

Sherlock
An application used to find various information on the Internet. See Chapter 11, "*Sherlock and Searching Your Mac*."

Sitckies
A useful little program for leaving yourself colorful notes and reminders onscreen.

System Prefences
The command center for setting up the way your Mac behaves. See Chapter 4, "*System Preferences*."

TextEdit
A basic but useful word processing program. Covered in Chapter 6, "*Printing, Fonts, and Faxing*."

Utilities

Activity Monitor

New to Panther, Activity Monitor shows you every single activity or "process" that's currently running on your Mac and also lets you know how much of your Mac's processing capability each activity is taking up. You can use this utility to monitor the usage load of your Mac's processor, memory, disks, and network.

AirPort Admin Utility

Used to set up or update your AirPort base station and AirPort wireless card (if you have these devices installed).

AirPort Setup Assistant

An application that walks you step-by-step through the initial process of setting up your wireless AirPort network. After using this utility once, you can use it again to change settings, or you can use the AirPort Admin Utility instead.

Asia Text Extras

The stuff in this folder is only useful if you're designing Asian fonts.

Audio MIDI Extras

If you're a musician, this utility is useful for setting up your Mac to control MIDI (**M**usical **I**nstrument **D**igital **I**nterface) devices. The Audio Devices section is used to control all your audio inputs, and the MIDI Devices tab is for managing the various MIDI instruments that connect to your Mac.

Bluetooth File Exchange

You can only open this utility if you have a Bluetooth adapter connected to your Mac. If you do, you can use this utility to send files back and forth between your Mac and your Bluetooth devices.

Bluetooth Serial Utility

Certain Bluetooth devices require you to open specific "ports" or connections on your Mac to enable communication between your devices. This utility allows you to open these ports.

Bluetooth Setup Assistant

This utility walks you through the process of setting up your Mac to communicate with your Bluetooth devices. See Chapter 13, "*iCal and iSync*."

ColorSync Utility

You only need to use this utility if you're in the professional color printing business. This utility is used to repair ColorSync profiles that don't conform to ICC (**I**nternational **C**olor **C**onsortium) profile specifications.

Console

The Console lets you view all the behind-the-scenes communications between OS X and other applications. Not that any of these communications will make much sense to most people. This utility is here mostly for programmers and debuggers.

Digital Color Meter

This is a neat little utility that gives you the exact color value of any pixel you place your mouse over, which can be useful if you're trying to match a specific color on a Web page.

Directory Access

Used for setting up your Mac to access different network directory services. You'll most likely never have to open this unless you're having trouble connecting your Mac to a PC network. See Exercise 3 of Chapter 18, "*Networking*."

Disk Utility

This utility lets you repair, verify, erase, and format the drives connected to your Mac, and is also used for creating and managing disk images. Covered in Chapter 7, "*Installing Applications*."

Grab

A screenshot utility that lets you create images of your entire screen or of specific areas.

Installer

You don't use this utility directly. Other installation programs run this utility when you install applications on your Mac.

Java

This folder contains tools for Java programmers to run and store Java applets (programs) and settings.

KeyChain Access

This utility is for storing the passwords and usernames you create on file servers and certain Web sites. It also stores any user names and passwords you use in your email programs like Mail or Microsoft Entourage.

NetInfo Manager

NetInfo Manager is the database where information about network-related items, such as access privileges, printers, user accounts, and passwords, are stored. You don't need to open this utility unless you're a network administrator.

Network Utility

This utility is used to find information about Web sites and your network. For example, the Info tab tells you your Mac's IP address and the speed of your network connection (Link Speed). You can use the Whois tab to find out who owns a Web site, and you can use the Traceroute tab to see how many routers you have to pass through to communicate with a specific server.

ODBC Administrator

This utility administrates Open Database Connectivity access requests. Unless you work with ODBC databases (and you would know it if you did), you don't need to use this at all.

Printer Setup Utility

This utility manages print jobs between your Mac and any printers connected to your Mac or over your network. See Chapter 6, "*Printing, Fonts, and Faxing*" for information on Printer Setup Utility.

StuffIt Expander

A program for decompressing stuffed, zipped, or otherwise compressed files. See Chapter 7, "*Installing Applications*," for information on using StuffIt Expander.

Terminal

Terminal is your entry point into the Unix part of OS X. Opening this application gives you a command-line interface. Unless you know Unix, there's very little you can do in here.

B.

Online Resources

H•O•T

Mac OS X Panther

This appendix provides a categorical list of Apple-related sites that offer you access to multiple aspects of the Macintosh world. These sites will not only allow you to keep up on the latest news and rumors, but they'll also teach you a few tricks to increase your Mac proficiency. I also strongly encourage you to explore some of the Web forums listed here. If you've never participated in a Web forum before, you may be amazed at the number of people who are willing to help you with your Mac issues and answer your questions. Somewhere out there, someone has run into the same problem you're having and may have already discovered a creative solution.

Finally, be sure to visit this book's companion Web site at **www.lynda.com/books/HOT/OSX103** for updates and corrections.

Apple News

These sites deal mostly with factually confirmed Apple-related news.

Mac Surfer's Headline News
`www.macsurfer.com`
Updated several times each day, this site tracks and links to Apple-related articles all over the Web.

Mac Minute
`www.macminute.com`
Updated several times each day, this site publishes press releases and information concerning Mac- and Apple-related news.

Insanely Great Mac
`www.insanely-great.com`
News and events related to Apple as well as general computing and Internet news. Each article includes editorial comments and observations.

The Mac Observer
`www.macobserver.com`
In addition to Apple-related news, this site also contains tips, reviews, and user forums.

MacCentral Online
`maccentral.macworld.com`
This site is updated daily with Apple- and Mac-related articles.

PowerBook Central
`powerbookcentral.com`
A news site with an emphasis on PowerBook-related news. Also includes a PowerBook price tracker to help you find the lowest prices.

O'Grady's PowerPage
`www.powerpage.org`
This site features news, reviews, and opinions of software and hardware with a wireless and Mac-related slant.

Apple Rumors

Reports at Apple rumor sites should usually be taken with large grains of salt.

Think Secret
`www.thinksecret.com`
Arguably the most popular and reliable source of unofficial Apple-related news.

Spy Mac

www.spymac.com

In addition to posting rumors (some of them pretty wild), this site also features user forums and image galleries.

Mac Rumors

www.macrumors.com

This site collects and links to Apple rumors from around the Web.

Mac Tips and Tutorials

These sites provide useful tidbits and lessons on using Mac OS X.

Mac OS X Hints

www.macosxhints.com

A vast library of reader-submitted tips related to Mac OS X. Updated nearly every day.

OS X FAQ

www.osxfaq.com

Bob "Dr. Mac" LeVitus' site for OS X news and support. Features a daily tip, tutorials, and user forums.

OS X Guide

www.osxguide.com

In their own words, "How to do stuff on Mac OS X."

Apple Troubleshooting and User Forums

These troubleshooting Web sites are dedicating to tracking problems users may run into using Apple products. User forums are the best place to get answers to your troubleshooting and technical questions–there's almost always someone willing to respond to your inquiry.

Apple Discussions

discussions.info.apple.com

Apple's forum for discussing hardware, software, and networking-related issues.

Mac Fixit and Mac Fixit Forums

www.macfixit.com and www.macfixitforums.com

Mac Fixit provides daily updates on troubleshooting tips, both hardware- and software-related; Mac Fixit Forums is a vast resource of discussions and solutions for common troubleshooting issues.

Accelerate Your Mac

www.xlr8yourmac.com

This site tracks hardware and software problems based on user reports, with an emphasis on upgrading your Mac. It also provides hardware reviews and, of course, a user forum for feedback.

Mac OS X.com

`www.macosx.com/forums`

A large online community of Mac users discussing all sorts of Apple-related topics.

Apple Software

Version Tracker

`www.versiontracker.com`

If you're not sure if you have the most current version of a software program, check Version Tracker. You'll not only find links to the most current versions, but also user reviews of applications and links to the software manufacturers themselves. This site tracks software for Mac OS X and below, Windows, and Palm OS.

Mac Update

`www.macupdate.com`

A site similar to Version Tracker, but dedicated exclusively to tracking Mac software.

Third-Party Add-Ons

These applications and sites feature software applications and plug-ins designed to enhance Mac OS X and its applications.

TinkerTool

`http://www.bresink.de/osx/TinkerTool.html`

TinkerTool is an additional control pane for Systems Preferences that allows you to access more system settings than are regularly available. It's extremely useful for further controlling Dock behavior, changing aspects of OS X's appearance, and viewing invisible files.

Cocktail

`www.macosxcocktail.com`

Cocktail is a free utility for users who don't want to venture into OS X's UNIX world. Cocktail handles several routine maintenance tasks such as deleting locked files, removing various system caches, and viewing system log files.

Virtix

`www.virtix.com`

Virtix provides inexpensive filters, effects, and themes for iMovie and iDVD. If you're a frequent iMovie user, you'll probably find many of their products extremely useful for enhancing your video projects.

iDVD Theme PAK Central

`www.idvdthemepak.com`

If iDVD's preinstalled themes just aren't enough for you, check out this site for a diverse collection of themes to add to your collection.

C.
Troubleshooting Guide

H•O•T

Mac OS X Panther

This appendix is the first place to check if you're having a problem with any of the exercises in this book. You should also check the book's Web site at **www.lynda.com/books/HOT/OSX103** to see if any errata have been posted. Also keep in mind the numerous online resources available to you (listed in Appendix B, "*Online Resources*") as well as Apple's online Knowledge Base, which can be accessed through their Web site or through Sherlock.

If you're still having problems, drop us an email at **osxfaq@lynda.com**. Due to the high volume of email we receive, we can't help you with OS X issues not related to the exercises in this book. Please allow 72 hours for us to respond to your message (longer over holidays or weekends).

What can I do if I forgot my user password?

If you've forgotten the password you created for your user account, have your Mac's administrator log in, open **System Preferences**, click **Users**, and edit your account to re-create your password. If you are the administrator, you'll need to restart your Mac using the OS X installation CD and reset your password. Insert the CD and restart your Mac while holding the **C** key until the **Installer** screen appears. When it does, choose **Installer > Reset Password**. Select the drive on which OS X is installed and choose your account from the first pop-up menu. Create a new password, click **Save**, close the window, and restart your Mac.

I'm not seeing a drive or a network folder in the Places sidebar.

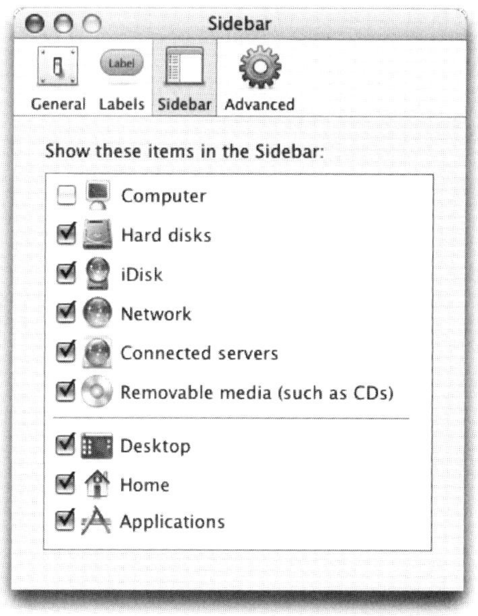

If the icon for a hard drive or server is missing, choose **Finder > Preferences** and click the **Sidebar** button. Make sure a check appears next to the item you want to see. While you have the **Preferences** window open, you might also want to click the **General** button to select which items you want to appear on the **Desktop**.

When I double-click a folder, it opens up in a new window. How do I get it to open in the same window it came from?

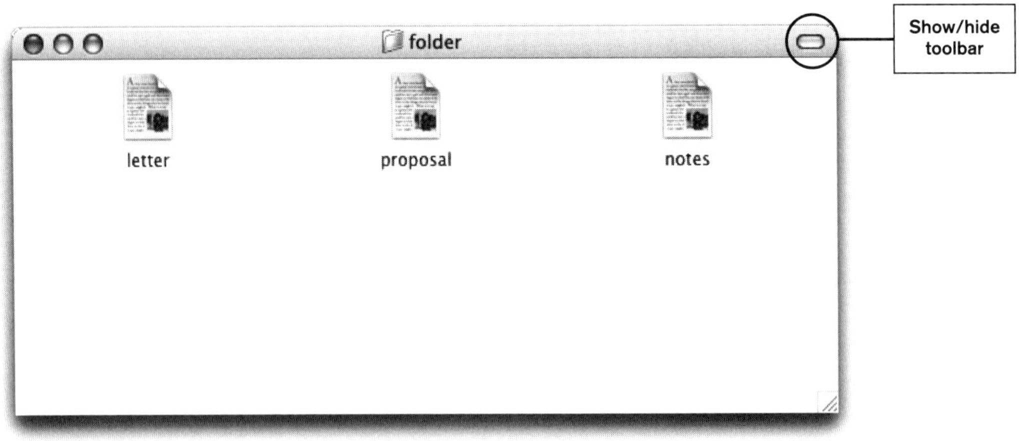

To open a folder in the same window, the window's toolbar must be visible when you double-click the folder. Click the **Show/hide toolbar** button in the upper-right corner of the window to see the toolbar.

I'm trying to drag a file to a folder's icon in the Dock, but the icon keeps moving out of the way. How can I keep it from moving?

Hold the **Cmd** key when you drag the item to the **Dock**. The folder and all the other icons will remain where they are, making it much easier to drag the item where you want it.

Why do my documents open in the wrong application?

Some documents and files can be opened by multiple applications. For instance, image files can be opened in Preview or Adobe Photoshop, and text documents can be opened in TextEdit or Microsoft Word. If double-clicking a file opens it in the wrong application (or an application other than the one you prefer), you have a few options. You can drag the file to the preferred application's icon in the **Dock** or in your **Applications** folder to open it manually. This works, but it doesn't solve the double-clicking problem. To make a file open in your preferred application by default, click the file and then choose **File > Get Info** (**Cmd+I**).

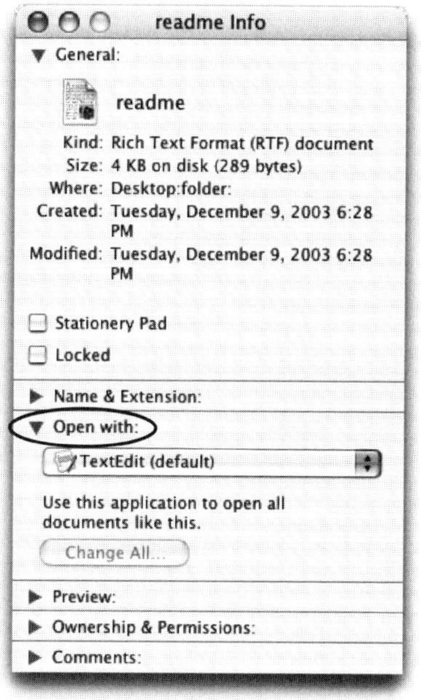

Click the toggle arrow next to **Open with** and then choose the application from the pop-up menu there. If you want this application to open all files of this type (for instance, if you want Preview to open all PDF files), click **Change All**. Then close the **Get Info** window and double-click your file.

I'm sick of my Mac constantly checking for software updates. How do I tell it to leave the checking to me?

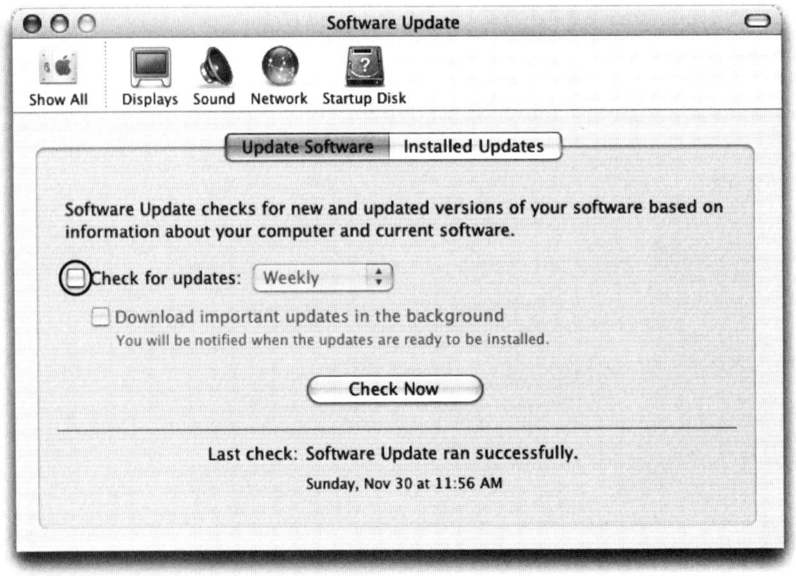

Open **System Preferences** and click the **Update Software** button. Uncheck **Check for updates**. From this point on, you'll have to click **Check Now** to manually search for updates.

I want to use Photoshop (or some other image-editing program) to edit the pictures in my iPhoto library. What's the easiest way to do this?

There are a few ways to edit your iPhoto library with an image-editing program. If you only want to edit pictures in Photoshop occasionally, place Photoshop's icon in the **Dock** (or just have Photoshop running), and then drag the picture's thumbnail from your iPhoto library to the **Photoshop** icon in the **Dock**. If you want to use Photoshop to edit all your images, choose **iPhoto > Preferences**.

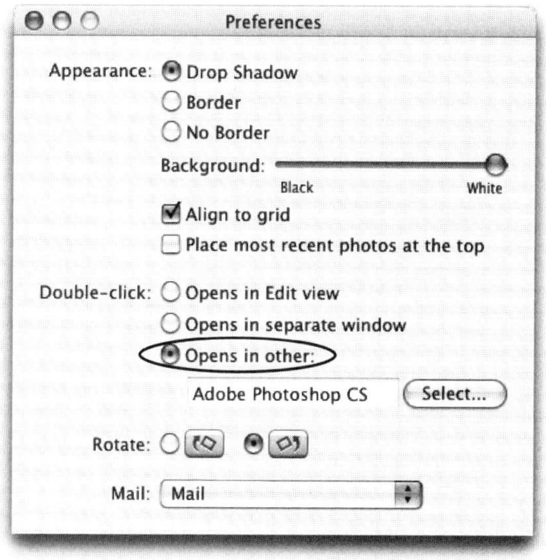

In the **Preferences** window, select **Opens in other**. Select **Photoshop** from your **Applications** folder. Now, anytime you double-click a thumbnail in iPhoto, it will open in Photoshop.

Why can't iTunes find a song in my library?

If you use the Finder to move or rename a song file that's part of your iTunes library, iTunes won't be able to find the track the next time you try to play it.

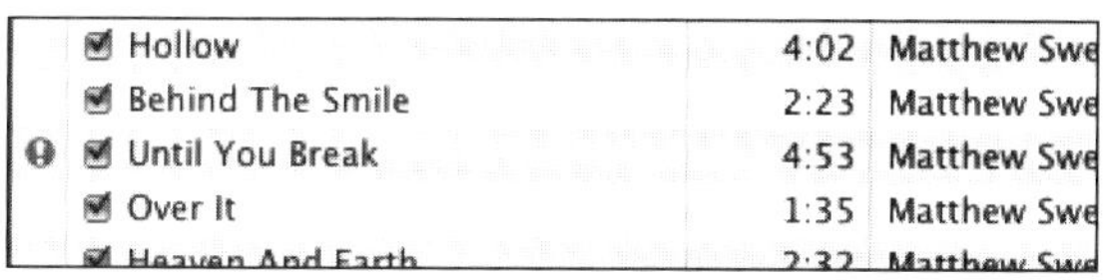

An exclamation point icon will instead appear next to the song. If you know that the song file still exists on your Mac, double-click the song in your library. You'll be asked if you want to manually locate the file; click **Yes**. Navigate to the song on your hard drive and click **Choose**.

Index

H•O•T

Mac OS X Panther

A

B

C

D

E

F

G-H

I

J-K

L

M

N

O

P

Q-R

S

T

U

V

W-Z

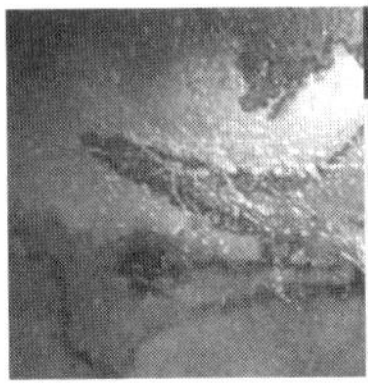

CD-ROM LICENSE AGREEMENT

THIS SOFTWARE LICENSE AGREEMENT CONSTITUTES AN AGREEMENT BETWEEN YOU AND LYNDA.COM, INC. YOU SHOULD CAREFULLY READ THE FOLLOWING TERMS AND CONDITIONS BEFORE OPENING THIS ENVELOPE. COPYING THIS SOFTWARE TO YOUR MACHINE, BREAKING THE SEAL, OR OTHERWISE REMOVING OR USING THE SOFTWARE INDICATES YOUR ACCEPTANCE OF THESE TERMS AND CONDITIONS. IF YOU DO NOT AGREE TO BE BOUND BY THE PROVISIONS OF THIS LICENSE AGREEMENT, YOU SHOULD PROMPTLY DELETE THE SOFTWARE FROM YOUR MACHINE.

TERMS AND CONDITIONS:

1. GRANT OF LICENSE. In consideration of payment of the License Fee, which was a part of the price you paid for this product, LICENSOR grants to you (the "Licensee") a non-exclusive right to use and display this copy of a Software program, along with any updates or upgrade releases of the Software for which you have paid (all parts and elements of the Software as well as the Software as a whole are hereinafter referred to as the "Software") on a single computer only (i.e., with a single CPU) at a single location, all as more particularly set forth and limited below. LICENSOR reserves all rights not expressly granted to you as Licensee in this License Agreement.

2. OWNERSHIP OF SOFTWARE. The license granted herein is not a sale of the original Software or of any copy of the Software. As Licensee, you own only the rights to use the Software as described herein and the magnetic or other physical media on which the Software is originally or subsequently recorded or fixed. LICENSOR retains title and ownership of the Software recorded on the original disk(s), as well as title and ownership of any subsequent copies of the Software irrespective of the form of media on or in which the Software is recorded or fixed. This license does not grant you any intellectual or other proprietary or other rights of any nature whatsoever in the Software.

3. USE RESTRICTIONS. As Licensee, you may use the Software only as expressly authorized in this License Agreement under the terms of paragraph 4. You may physically transfer the Software from one computer to another provided that the Software is used on only a single computer at any one time. You may not: (i) electronically transfer the Software from one computer to another over a network; (ii) make the Software available through a time-sharing service, network of computers, or other multiple user arrangement; (iii) distribute copies of the Software or related written materials to any third party, whether for sale or otherwise; (iv) modify, adapt, translate, reverse engineer, decompile, disassemble, or prepare any derivative work based on the Software or any element thereof; (v) make or distribute, whether for sale or otherwise, any hard copy or printed version of any of the Software nor any portion thereof nor any work of yours containing the Software or any component thereof; (vi) use any of the Software or any of its components in any other work.

4. THIS IS WHAT YOU CAN AND CANNOT DO WITH THE SOFTWARE. Even though in the preceding paragraph and elsewhere, LICENSOR has restricted your use of the Software, the following is the only thing you can do with the Software and the various elements of the Software: THE ARTWORK AND DATA CONTAINED ON THIS CD-ROM MAY NOT BE USED IN ANY MANNER WHATSOEVER OTHER THAN TO VIEW THE SAME ON YOUR COMPUTER, OR POST TO YOUR PERSONAL, NON-COMMERCIAL WEB SITE FOR EDUCATIONAL PURPOSES ONLY. THIS MATERIAL IS SUBJECT TO ALL OF THE RESTRICTION PROVISIONS OF THIS SOFTWARE LICENSE. SPECIFICALLY BUT NOT IN LIMITATION OF THESE RESTRICTIONS, YOU MAY NOT DISTRIBUTE, RESELL, OR TRANSFER THIS PART OF THE SOFTWARE DESIGNATED AS "CLUTS," NOR ANY OF YOUR DESIGN OR OTHER WORK CONTAINING ANY OF THE SOFTWARE OR DATA ON THIS CD-ROM, NOR ANY OF YOUR DESIGN OR OTHER WORK CONTAINING ANY DATA FROM THIS CD-ROM, ALL AS MORE PARTICULARLY RESTRICTED IN THE WITHIN SOFTWARE LICENSE.

5. COPY RESTRICTIONS. The Software and accompanying written materials are protected under United States copyright laws. Unauthorized copying and/or distribution of the Software and/or the related written materials are expressly forbidden. You may be held legally responsible for any copyright infringement that is caused, directly or indirectly, by your failure to abide by the terms of this License Agreement. Subject to the terms of this License Agreement and if the software is not otherwise copy protected, you may make one copy of the Software for backup purposes only. The copyright notice and any other proprietary notices which were included in the original Software must be reproduced and included on any such backup copy.

6. TRANSFER RESTRICTIONS. The license herein granted is personal to you, the Licensee. You may not transfer the Software nor any of its components or elements to anyone else, nor may you sell, lease, loan, sublicense, assign, or otherwise dispose of the Software nor any of its components or elements without the express written consent of LICENSOR, which consent may be granted or withheld at Licensor's sole discretion.

7. TERMINATION. The license herein granted hereby will remain in effect until terminated. This license will terminate automatically without further notice from LICENSOR in the event of the violation of any of the provisions hereof. As Licensee, you agree that upon such termination, you will promptly destroy any and all copies of the Software that remain in your possession and, upon request, will certify to such destruction in writing to LICENSOR.

8. LIMITATION AND DISCLAIMER OF WARRANTIES. a) THE SOFTWARE AND RELATED WRITTEN MATERIALS, INCLUDING ANY INSTRUCTIONS FOR USE, ARE PROVIDED ON AN "AS IS" BASIS, WITHOUT WARRANTY OF ANY KIND, EXPRESS OR IMPLIED. THIS DISCLAIMER OF WARRANTY EXPRESSLY INCLUDES, BUT IS NOT LIMITED TO, ANY IMPLIED WARRANTIES OF MERCHANTABILITY AND/OR OF FITNESS FOR A PARTICULAR PURPOSE. NO WARRANTY OF ANY KIND IS MADE AS TO WHETHER OR NOT THIS SOFTWARE INFRINGES UPON ANY RIGHTS OF ANY OTHER THIRD PARTIES. NO ORAL OR WRITTEN INFORMATION GIVEN BY LICENSOR, ITS SUPPLIERS, DISTRIBUTORS, DEALERS, EMPLOYEES, OR AGENTS, SHALL CREATE OR OTHERWISE ENLARGE THE SCOPE OF ANY WARRANTY HEREUNDER. LICENSEE ASSUMES THE ENTIRE RISK AS TO THE QUALITY AND THE PERFORMANCE OF SUCH SOFTWARE. SHOULD THE SOFTWARE PROVE DEFECTIVE, YOU, AS LICENSEE (AND NOT LICENSOR, ITS SUPPLIERS, DISTRIBUTORS, DEALERS, OR AGENTS), ASSUME THE ENTIRE COST OF ALL NECESSARY CORRECTION, SERVICING, OR REPAIR. b) LICENSOR warrants the disk(s) on which this copy of the Software is recorded or fixed to be free from defects in materials and workmanship, under normal use and service, for a period of ninety (90) days from the date of delivery, as evidenced by a copy of the applicable receipt. LICENSOR hereby limits the duration of any implied warranties with respect to the disk(s) to the duration of the express warranty. This limited warranty shall not apply if the disk(s) have been damaged by unreasonable use, accident, negligence, or by any other causes unrelated to defective materials or workmanship. c) LICENSOR does not warrant that the functions contained in the Software will be uninterrupted or error free and Licensee is encouraged to test the Software for Licensee's intended use prior to placing any reliance thereon. All risk of the use of the Software will be on you, as Licensee. d) THE LIMITED WARRANTY SET FORTH ABOVE GIVES YOU SPECIFIC LEGAL RIGHTS, AND YOU MAY ALSO HAVE OTHER RIGHTS, WHICH VARY FROM STATE TO STATE. SOME STATES DO NOT ALLOW THE LIMITATION OR EXCLUSION OF IMPLIED WARRANTIES OR OF INCIDENTAL OR CONSEQUENTIAL DAMAGES, SO THE LIMITATIONS AND EXCLUSIONS CONCERNING THE SOFTWARE AND RELATED WRITTEN MATERIALS SET FORTH ABOVE MAY NOT APPLY TO YOU.

9. LIMITATION OF REMEDIES. Licensor's entire liability and Licensee's exclusive remedy shall be the replacement of any disk(s) not meeting the limited warranty set forth in Section 8 above, which is returned to LICENSOR with a copy of the applicable receipt within the warranty period. Any replacement disk(s)will be warranted for the remainder of the original warranty period or thirty (30) days, whichever is longer.

10. LIMITATION OF LIABILITY. IN NO EVENT WILL LICENSOR OR ANYONE ELSE INVOLVED IN THE CREATION, PRODUCTION, AND/OR DELIVERY OF THIS SOFTWARE PRODUCT BE LIABLE TO LICENSEE OR ANY OTHER PERSON OR ENTITY FOR ANY DIRECT, INDIRECT, OR OTHER DAMAGES, INCLUDING, WITHOUT LIMITATION, ANY INTERRUPTION OF SERVICES, LOST PROFITS, LOST SAVINGS, LOSS OF DATA, OR ANY OTHER CONSEQUENTIAL, INCIDENTAL, SPECIAL, OR PUNITIVE DAMAGES ARISING OUT OF THE PURCHASE, USE, INABILITY TO USE, OR OPERATION OF THE SOFTWARE, EVEN IF LICENSOR OR ANY AUTHORIZED LICENSOR DEALER HAS BEEN ADVISED OF THE POSSIBILITY OF SUCH DAMAGES. BY YOUR USE OF THE SOFTWARE, YOU ACKNOWLEDGE THAT THE LIMITATION OF LIABILITY SET FORTH IN THIS LICENSE WAS THE BASIS UPON WHICH THE SOFTWARE WAS OFFERED BY LICENSOR, AND YOU ACKNOWLEDGE THAT THE PRICE OF THE SOFTWARE LICENSE WOULD BE HIGHER IN THE ABSENCE OF SUCH LIMITATION. SOME STATES DO NOT ALLOW THE LIMITATION OR EXCLUSION OF LIABILITY FOR INCIDENTAL OR CONSEQUENTIAL DAMAGES, SO THE ABOVE LIMITATIONS AND EXCLUSIONS MAY NOT APPLY TO YOU.

11. UPDATES. LICENSOR, at its sole discretion, may periodically issue updates of the Software, which you may receive upon request and payment of the applicable update fee in effect from time to time and in such event, all of the provisions of the within License Agreement shall apply to such updates.

12. EXPORT RESTRICTIONS. Licensee agrees not to export or re-export the Software and accompanying documentation (or any copies thereof) in violation of any applicable U.S. laws or regulations.

13. ENTIRE AGREEMENT. YOU, AS LICENSEE, ACKNOWLEDGE THAT: (i) YOU HAVE READ THIS ENTIRE AGREEMENT AND AGREE TO BE BOUND BY ITS TERMS AND CONDITIONS; (ii) THIS AGREEMENT IS THE COMPLETE AND EXCLUSIVE STATEMENT OF THE UNDERSTANDING BETWEEN THE PARTIES AND SUPERSEDES ANY AND ALL PRIOR ORAL OR WRITTEN COMMUNICATIONS RELATING TO THE SUBJECT MATTER HEREOF; AND (iii) THIS AGREEMENT MAY NOT BE MODIFIED, AMENDED, OR IN ANY WAY ALTERED EXCEPT BY A WRITING SIGNED BY BOTH YOURSELF AND AN OFFICER OR AUTHORIZED REPRESENTATIVE OF LICENSOR.

14. SEVERABILITY. In the event that any provision of this License Agreement is held to be illegal or otherwise unenforceable, such provision shall be deemed to have been deleted from this License Agreement while the remaining provisions of this License Agreement shall be unaffected and shall continue in full force and effect.

15. GOVERNING LAW. This License Agreement shall be governed by the laws of the State of California applicable to agreements wholly to be performed therein and of the United States of America, excluding that body of the law related to conflicts of law. This License Agreement shall not be governed by the United Nations Convention on Contracts for the International Sale of Goods, the application of which is expressly excluded. No waiver of any breach of the provisions of this License Agreement shall be deemed a waiver of any other breach of this License Agreement.

16. RESTRICTED RIGHTS LEGEND. Use, duplication, or disclosure by the Government is subject to restrictions as set forth in subparagraph (c)(1)(ii) of the Rights in Technical Data and Computer Software clause at 48 CFR § 252.227-7013 and DFARS § 252.227-7013 or subparagraphs (c) (1) and (c)(2) of the Commercial Computer Software-Restricted Rights at 48 CFR § 52.227.19, as applicable. Contractor/manufacturer: LICENSOR: LYNDA.COM, INC, c/o PEACHPIT PRESS, 1249 Eighth Street, Berkeley, CA 94710.